# TOYOTA PREVIA
## 1991-97 REPAIR MANUAL

# CHILTON'S

Covers all U.S. and Canadian models of
Toyota Previa

by Dawn M. Hoch, S.A.E.

**CHILTON** Automotive Books

PUBLISHED BY HAYNES NORTH AMERICA, Inc.

Haynes

APAA
AUTOMOTIVE
PARTS &
ACCESSORIES
ASSOCIATION MEMBER

Manufactured in USA
© 1998 Haynes North America, Inc.
ISBN 0-8019-9091-2
Library of Congress Catalog Card No. 98-71360
2345678901  9876543210

**Haynes Publishing Group**
Sparkford Nr Yeovil
Somerset BA22 7JJ England

**Haynes North America, Inc**
861 Lawrence Drive
Newbury Park
California 91320 USA

ABCDE
FGHIJ
KLMN

Chilton is a registered trademark of W.G. Nichols, Inc., and has been licensed to Haynes North America, Inc.

# Contents

## 1 GENERAL INFORMATION AND MAINTENANCE

- 1-2 HOW TO USE THIS BOOK
- 1-3 TOOLS AND EQUIPMENT
- 1-7 SERVICING YOUR VEHICLE SAFELY
- 1-9 FASTENERS, MEASUREMENTS AND CONVERSIONS
- 1-14 SERIAL NUMBER IDENTIFICATION
- 1-17 ROUTINE MAINTENANCE AND TUNE-UP
- 1-50 FLUIDS AND LUBRICANTS
- 1-70 TRAILER TOWING
- 1-71 TOWING THE VEHICLE
- 1-72 JUMP STARTING A DEAD BATTERY
- 1-72 JACKING

## 2 ENGINE ELECTRICAL

- 2-2 ELECTRONIC SPARK ADVANCE SYSTEM
- 2-8 FIRING ORDERS
- 2-9 CHARGING SYSTEM
- 2-12 STARTING SYSTEM
- 2-16 SENDING UNITS AND SENSORS

## 3 ENGINE AND ENGINE OVERHAUL

- 3-2 ENGINE MECHANICAL
- 3-49 EXHAUST SYSTEM
- 3-52 ENGINE RECONDITIONING

## 4 DRIVEABILITY AND EMISSIONS CONTROLS

- 4-2 AIR POLLUTION
- 4-3 AUTOMOTIVE EMISSIONS
- 4-5 EMISSION CONTROLS
- 4-17 ELECTRONIC ENGINE CONTROLS
- 4-30 COMPONENT LOCATIONS
- 4-31 TROUBLE CODES
- 4-39 VACUUM DIAGRAMS

## 5 FUEL SYSTEM

- 5-2 BASIC FUEL SYSTEM DIAGNOSIS
- 5-2 FUEL LINES AND FITTINGS
- 5-2 FUEL INJECTION SYSTEM
- 5-13 FUEL TANK

## 6 CHASSIS ELECTRICAL

- 6-2 UNDERSTANDING AND TROUBLESHOOTING ELECTRICAL SYSTEMS
- 6-9 BATTERY CABLES
- 6-9 AIR BAG (SUPPLEMENTAL RESTRAINT SYSTEM)
- 6-12 HEATING AND AIR CONDITIONING
- 6-20 CRUISE CONTROL
- 6-21 ENTERTAINMENT SYSTEMS
- 6-23 WINDSHIELD WIPERS AND WASHERS
- 6-27 INSTRUMENTS AND SWITCHES
- 6-29 LIGHTING
- 6-36 TRAILER WIRING
- 6-37 CIRCUIT PROTECTION
- 6-41 WIRING DIAGRAMS

# Contents

| | | | | |
|---|---|---|---|---|
| **7-2** | MANUAL TRANSMISSION | **7-21** | DRIVELINE | |
| **7-8** | CLUTCH | **7-28** | FRONT DRIVE AXLE | **DRIVE TRAIN — 7** |
| **7-13** | AUTOMATIC TRANSMISSION | **7-32** | REAR AXLE | |
| **7-20** | TRANSFER CASE | | | |

| | | | | |
|---|---|---|---|---|
| **8-2** | WHEELS | **8-17** | REAR SUSPENSION | **SUSPENSION AND STEERING — 8** |
| **8-4** | FRONT SUSPENSION | **8-21** | STEERING | |

| | | | | |
|---|---|---|---|---|
| **9-2** | BRAKE OPERATING SYSTEM | **9-28** | PARKING BRAKE | |
| **9-13** | DISC BRAKES | **9-33** | ANTI-LOCK BRAKE SYSTEM | **BRAKES — 9** |
| **9-22** | DRUM BRAKES | | | |

| | | | | |
|---|---|---|---|---|
| **10-2** | EXTERIOR | **10-13** | INTERIOR | **BODY AND TRIM — 10** |

**10-29** GLOSSARY

**GLOSSARY**

**10-33** MASTER INDEX

**MASTER INDEX**

## SAFETY NOTICE

Proper service and repair procedures are vital to the safe, reliable operation of all motor vehicles, as well as the personal safety of those performing repairs. This manual outlines procedures for servicing and repairing vehicles using safe, effective methods. The procedures contain many NOTES, CAUTIONS and WARNINGS which should be followed, along with standard procedures to eliminate the possibility of personal injury or improper service which could damage the vehicle or compromise its safety.

It is important to note that repair procedures and techniques, tools and parts for servicing motor vehicles, as well as the skill and experience of the individual performing the work vary widely. It is not possible to anticipate all of the conceivable ways or conditions under which vehicles may be serviced, or to provide cautions as to all possible hazards that may result. Standard and accepted safety precautions and equipment should be used when handling toxic or flammable fluids, and safety goggles or other protection should be used during cutting, grinding, chiseling, prying, or any other process that can cause material removal or projectiles.

Some procedures require the use of tools specially designed for a specific purpose. Before substituting another tool or procedure, you must be completely satisfied that neither your personal safety, nor the performance of the vehicle will be endangered.

Although information in this manual is based on industry sources and is complete as possible at the time of publication, the possibility exists that some car manufacturers made later changes which could not be included here. While striving for total accuracy, the authors or publishers cannot assume responsibility for any errors, changes or omissions that may occur in the compilation of this data.

## PART NUMBERS

Part numbers listed in this reference are not recommendations by Haynes North America, Inc. for any product brand name. They are references that can be used with interchange manuals and aftermarket supplier catalogs to locate each brand supplier's discrete part number.

## SPECIAL TOOLS

Special tools are recommended by the vehicle manufacturer to perform their specific job. Use has been kept to a minimum, but where absolutely necessary, they are referred to in the text by the part number of the tool manufacturer. These tools can be purchased, under the appropriate part number, from your local dealer or regional distributor, or an equivalent tool can be purchased locally from a tool supplier or parts outlet. Before substituting any tool for the one recommended, read the SAFETY NOTICE at the top of this page.

## ACKNOWLEDGMENTS

The publisher expresses appreciation to Toyota Motor Co. for their generous assistance.

---

All rights reserved. No part of this book may be reproduced or transmitted in any form or by any means, electronic or mechanical, including photocopying, recording or by any information storage or retrieval system, without permission in writing from the copyright holder.

While every attempt is made to ensure that the information in this manual is correct, no liability can be accepted by the authors or publishers for loss, damage or injury caused by any errors in, or omissions from, the information given.

**HOW TO USE THIS BOOK 1-2**
WHERE TO BEGIN 1-2
AVOIDING TROUBLE 1-2
MAINTENANCE OR REPAIR? 1-2
AVOIDING THE MOST COMMON MISTAKES 1-2
**TOOLS AND EQUIPMENT 1-3**
SPECIAL TOOLS 1-7
**SERVICING YOUR VEHICLE SAFELY 1-7**
DO'S 1-7
DON'TS 1-8
**FASTENERS, MEASUREMENTS AND CONVERSIONS 1-9**
BOLTS, NUTS AND OTHER THREADED RETAINERS 1-9
TORQUE 1-10
  TORQUE WRENCHES 1-10
  TORQUE ANGLE METERS 1-12
STANDARD AND METRIC MEASUREMENTS 1-13
**SERIAL NUMBER IDENTIFICATION 1-14**
VEHICLE 1-14
MODEL IDENTIFICATION 1-14
ENGINE 1-14
TRANSMISSION 1-16
**ROUTINE MAINTENANCE AND TUNE-UP 1-17**
AIR CLEANER (ELEMENT) 1-19
  REMOVAL & INSTALLATION 1-19
FUEL FILTER 1-19
  REMOVAL & INSTALLATION 1-19
PCV VALVE 1-21
  REMOVAL & INSTALLATION 1-21
EVAPORATIVE CANISTER (CHARCOAL CANISTER) 1-23
  SERVICING 1-23
BATTERY 1-23
  PRECAUTIONS 1-23
  GENERAL MAINTENANCE 1-24
  BATTERY FLUID 1-24
  CABLES 1-25
  CHARGING 1-26
  REPLACEMENT 1-26
BELTS 1-26
  INSPECTION 1-26
  REMOVAL, INSTALLATION & ADJUSTMENT 1-28
HOSES 1-28
  INSPECTION 1-28
  REMOVAL & INSTALLATION 1-29
CV-BOOTS 1-30
  INSPECTION 1-30
SPARK PLUGS 1-30
  SPARK PLUG HEAT RANGE 1-31
  REMOVAL & INSTALLATION 1-31
  INSPECTION & GAPPING 1-33
SPARK PLUG WIRES 1-34
  TESTING 1-34
DISTRIBUTOR CAP AND ROTOR 1-34
  REMOVAL & INSTALLATION 1-34
  INSPECTION 1-35
IGNITION TIMING 1-35
  GENERAL INFORMATION 1-35
  INSPECTION & ADJUSTMENT 1-36
VALVE LASH 1-38
  ADJUSTMENT 1-38
IDLE SPEED AND MIXTURE ADJUSTMENTS 1-42
AIR CONDITIONING SYSTEM 1-42
  SYSTEM SERVICE & REPAIR 1-42
  PREVENTIVE MAINTENANCE 1-43
  SYSTEM INSPECTION 1-43
WINDSHIELD WIPERS 1-44
  ELEMENT (REFILL) CARE & REPLACEMENT 1-44
TIRES AND WHEELS 1-46
  TIRE ROTATION 1-46
  TIRE DESIGN 1-47
  TIRE STORAGE 1-47
  INFLATION & INSPECTION 1-48
  CARE OF SPECIAL WHEELS 1-50
MAINTENANCE LIGHTS 1-50
  RESETTING 1-50
**FLUIDS AND LUBRICANTS 1-50**

FLUID DISPOSAL 1-50
FUEL AND ENGINE OIL RECOMMENDATIONS 1-50
  OIL 1-50
  FUEL 1-51
  OPERATION IN FOREIGN COUNTRIES 1-52
ENGINE 1-52
  OIL LEVEL CHECK 1-52
  OIL & FILTER CHANGE 1-53
MANUAL TRANSMISSION 1-55
  FLUID RECOMMENDATIONS 1-55
  LEVEL CHECK 1-55
  DRAIN & REFILL 1-55
AUTOMATIC TRANSMISSION 1-56
  FLUID RECOMMENDATIONS 1-56
  LEVEL CHECK 1-56
  DRAIN & REFILL 1-57
  PAN & FILTER SERVICE 1-58
TRANSFER CASE 1-61
  FLUID RECOMMENDATIONS 1-61
  LEVEL CHECK 1-61
  DRAIN & REFILL 1-61
DRIVE AXLE 1-63
  FLUID RECOMMENDATIONS 1-63
  LEVEL CHECK 1-63
  DRAIN & REFILL 1-63
SUPERCHARGER 1-65
  FLUID RECOMMENDATIONS 1-65
  LEVEL CHECK 1-65
  DRAIN & REFILL 1-65
COOLING SYSTEM 1-65
  FLUID RECOMMENDATIONS 1-65
  LEVEL CHECK 1-65
  DRAIN & REFILL 1-66
  FLUSHING & CLEANING THE SYSTEM 1-67
BRAKE MASTER CYLINDER 1-67
  FLUID RECOMMENDATIONS 1-67
  LEVEL CHECK 1-67
CLUTCH MASTER CYLINDER 1-68
  FLUID RECOMMENDATIONS 1-68
  LEVEL CHECK 1-68
POWER STEERING PUMP 1-68
  FLUID RECOMMENDATIONS 1-68
  LEVEL CHECK 1-68
CHASSIS GREASING 1-69
BODY LUBRICATION AND MAINTENANCE 1-69
  LOCK CYLINDERS 1-69
  DOOR HINGES & HINGE CHECKS 1-69
  TAILGATE 1-59
  BODY DRAIN HOLES 1-69
WHEEL BEARINGS 1-69
**TRAILER TOWING 1-70**
GENERAL RECOMMENDATIONS 1-70
TRAILER WEIGHT 1-70
HITCH (TONGUE) WEIGHT 1-70
ENGINE 1-70
TRANSMISSION 1-70
HANDLING A TRAILER 1-70
**TOWING THE VEHICLE 1-71**
**JUMP STARTING A DEAD BATTERY 1-72**
JUMP STARTING PRECAUTIONS 1-72
JUMP STARTING PROCEDURE 1-72
**JACKING 1-72**
JACKING PRECAUTIONS 1-73
**COMPONENT LOCATIONS**
UNDERHOOD MAINTENANCE COMPONENT LOCATIONS 1-17
UNDERVEHICLE MAINTENANCE COMPONENT LOCATIONS 1-18
**SPECIFICATIONS CHARTS**
VEHICLE IDENTIFICATION CHART 1-14
ENGINE IDENTIFICATION 1-16
GENERAL ENGINE SPECIFICATIONS 1-16
GASOLINE ENGINE TUNE-UP SPECIFICATIONS 1-42
RECOMMENDED MAINTENANCE INTERVALS 1-74
CAPACITIES 1-77

# 1

# GENERAL INFORMATION AND MAINTENANCE

HOW TO USE THIS BOOK 1-2
TOOLS AND EQUIPMENT 1-3
SERVICING YOUR VEHICLE SAFELY 1-7
FASTENERS, MEASUREMENTS AND CONVERSIONS 1-9
SERIAL NUMBER IDENTIFICATION 1-14
ROUTINE MAINTENANCE AND TUNE-UP 1-17
FLUIDS AND LUBRICANTS 1-50
TRAILER TOWING 1-70
TOWING THE VEHICLE 1-71
JUMP STARTING A DEAD BATTERY 1-72
JACKING 1-72

# 1-2 GENERAL INFORMATION AND MAINTENANCE

## HOW TO USE THIS BOOK

Chilton's Total Car Care manual for the Toyota Previa is intended to help you learn more about the inner workings of your vehicle while saving you money on its upkeep and operation.

The beginning of the book will likely be referred to the most, since that is where you will find information for maintenance and tune-up. The other sections deal with the more complex systems of your vehicle. Operating systems from engine through brakes are covered to the extent that the average do-it-yourselfer becomes mechanically involved. This book will not explain such things as rebuilding a differential for the simple reason that the expertise required and the investment in special tools make this task uneconomical. It will, however, give you detailed instructions to help you change your own brake pads and shoes, replace spark plugs, and perform many more jobs that can save you money, give you personal satisfaction and help you avoid expensive problems.

A secondary purpose of this book is a reference for owners who want to understand their vehicle and/or their mechanics better. In this case, no tools at all are required.

## Where to Begin

Before removing any bolts, read through the entire procedure. This will give you the overall view of what tools and supplies will be required. There is nothing more frustrating than having to walk to the bus stop on Monday morning because you were short one bolt on Sunday afternoon. So read ahead and plan ahead. Each operation should be approached logically and all procedures thoroughly understood before attempting any work.

All sections contain adjustments, maintenance, removal and installation procedures, and in some cases, repair or overhaul procedures. When repair is not considered practical, we tell you how to remove the part and then how to install the new or rebuilt replacement. In this way, you at least save the labor costs. Backyard repair of some components is just not practical.

## Avoiding Trouble

Many procedures in this book require you to "label and disconnect . . ." a group of lines, hoses or wires. Don't be lulled into thinking you can remember where everything goes—you won't. If you hook up vacuum or fuel lines incorrectly, the vehicle will run poorly, if at all. If you hook up electrical wiring incorrectly, you may instantly learn a very expensive lesson.

You don't need to know the official or engineering name for each hose or line. A piece of masking tape on the hose and a piece on its fitting will allow you to assign your own label such as the letter A or a short name. As long as you remember your own code, the lines can be reconnected by matching similar letters or names. Do remember that tape will dissolve in gasoline or other fluids; if a component is to be washed or cleaned, use another method of identification. A permanent felt-tipped marker can be very handy for marking metal parts. Remove any tape or paper labels after assembly.

## Maintenance or Repair?

It's necessary to mention the difference between maintenance and repair. Maintenance includes routine inspections, adjustments, and replacement of parts which show signs of normal wear. Maintenance compensates for wear or deterioration. Repair implies that something has broken or is not working. A need for repair is often caused by lack of maintenance. Example: draining and refilling the automatic transmission fluid is maintenance recommended by the manufacturer at specific mileage intervals. Failure to do this can ruin the transmission, requiring very expensive repairs. While no maintenance program can prevent items from breaking or wearing out, a general rule can be stated: MAINTENANCE IS CHEAPER THAN REPAIR.

Two basic mechanic's rules should be mentioned here. First, whenever the left side of the vehicle or engine is referred to, it is meant to specify the driver's side. Conversely, the right side of the vehicle means the passenger's side. Second, most screws and bolts are removed by turning counterclockwise, and tightened by turning clockwise.

Safety is always the most important rule. Constantly be aware of the dangers involved in working on an automobile and take the proper precautions. See the information in this section regarding SERVICING YOUR VEHICLE SAFELY and the SAFETY NOTICE on the acknowledgment page.

## Avoiding the Most Common Mistakes

Pay attention to the instructions provided. There are 3 common mistakes in mechanical work:

1. Incorrect order of assembly, disassembly or adjustment. When taking something apart or putting it together, performing steps in the wrong order usually just costs you extra time; however, it CAN break something. Read the entire procedure before beginning disassembly. Perform everything in the order in which the instructions say you should, even if you can't immediately see a reason for it. When you're taking apart something that is very intricate, you might want to draw a picture of how it looks when assembled at one point in order to make sure you get everything back in its proper position. We will supply exploded views whenever possible. When making adjustments, perform them in the proper order; often, one adjustment affects another, and you cannot expect even satisfactory results unless each adjustment is made only when it cannot be changed by any other.

2. Overtorquing (or undertorquing). While it is more common for overtorquing to cause damage, undertorquing may allow a fastener to vibrate loose causing serious damage. Especially when dealing with aluminum parts, pay attention to torque specifications and utilize a torque wrench in assembly. If a torque figure is not available, remember that if you are using the right tool to perform the job, you will probably not have to strain yourself to get a fastener tight enough. The pitch of most threads is so slight that the tension you put on the wrench will be multiplied many times in actual force on what you are tightening. A good example of how critical torque is can be seen in the case of spark plug installation, especially where you are putting the plug into an aluminum cylinder head. Too little torque can fail to crush the gasket, causing leakage of combustion gases and consequent overheating of the plug and engine parts. Too much torque can damage the threads or distort the plug, changing the spark gap.

There are many commercial products available for ensuring that fasteners won't come loose, even if they are not torqued just right (a very common brand is Loctite®). If you're worried about getting something together tight enough to hold, but loose enough to avoid mechanical damage during assembly, one of these products might offer substantial insurance. Before choosing a threadlocking compound, read the label on the package and make sure the product is compatible with the materials, fluids, etc. involved.

3. Crossthreading. This occurs when a part such as a bolt is screwed into a nut or casting at the wrong angle and forced. Crossthreading is more likely to occur if access is difficult. It helps to clean and lubricate fasteners, then to start threading with the part to be installed positioned straight in. Then, start the bolt, spark plug, etc. with your fingers. If you encounter resistance, unscrew the part and start over again at a different angle until it can be inserted and turned several times without much effort. Keep in mind that many parts, especially spark plugs, have tapered threads, so that gentle turning will automatically bring the part you're threading to the proper angle, but only if you don't force it or resist a change in angle. Don't put a wrench on the part until it's been tightened a couple of turns by hand. If you suddenly encounter resistance, and the part has not seated fully, don't force it. Pull it back out to make sure it's clean and threading properly.

Always take your time and be patient; once you have some experience, working on your vehicle may well become an enjoyable hobby.

# GENERAL INFORMATION AND MAINTENANCE  1-3

## TOOLS AND EQUIPMENT

▶ See Figures 1 thru 15

Naturally, without the proper tools and equipment it is impossible to properly service your vehicle. It would also be virtually impossible to catalog every tool that you would need to perform all of the operations in this book. Of course, It would be unwise for the amateur to rush out and buy an expensive set of tools on the theory that he/she may need one or more of them at some time.

The best approach is to proceed slowly, gathering a good quality set of those tools that are used most frequently. Don't be misled by the low cost of bargain tools. It is far better to spend a little more for better quality. Forged wrenches, 6 or 12-point sockets and fine tooth ratchets are by far preferable to their less expensive counterparts. As any good mechanic can tell you, there are few worse experiences than trying to work on a vehicle with bad tools. Your monetary savings will be far outweighed by frustration and mangled knuckles.

Begin accumulating those tools that are used most frequently: those associated with routine maintenance and tune-up. In addition to the normal assortment of screwdrivers and pliers, you should have the following tools:

- Wrenches/sockets and combination open end/box end wrenches in sizes from 1/8–3/4 in. or 3mm–19mm (depending on whether your vehicle uses standard or metric fasteners) and a 13/16 in. or 5/8 in. spark plug socket (depending on plug type).

➡ If possible, buy various length socket drive extensions. Universal-joint and wobble extensions can be extremely useful, but be careful when using them, as they can change the amount of torque applied to the socket.

- Jackstands for support.
- Oil filter wrench.
- Spout or funnel for pouring fluids.
- Grease gun for chassis lubrication (unless your vehicle is not equipped with any grease fittings—for details, please refer to information on Fluids and Lubricants, later in this section).
- Hydrometer for checking the battery (unless equipped with a sealed, maintenance-free battery).
- A container for draining oil and other fluids.
- Rags for wiping up the inevitable mess.

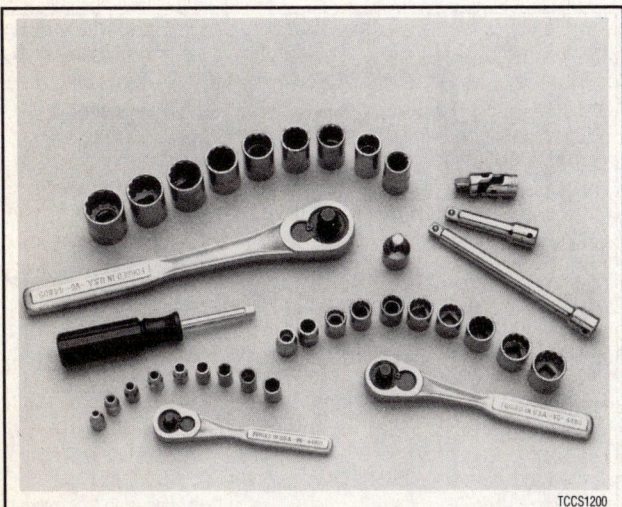

Fig. 1 All but the most basic procedures will require an assortment of ratchets and sockets

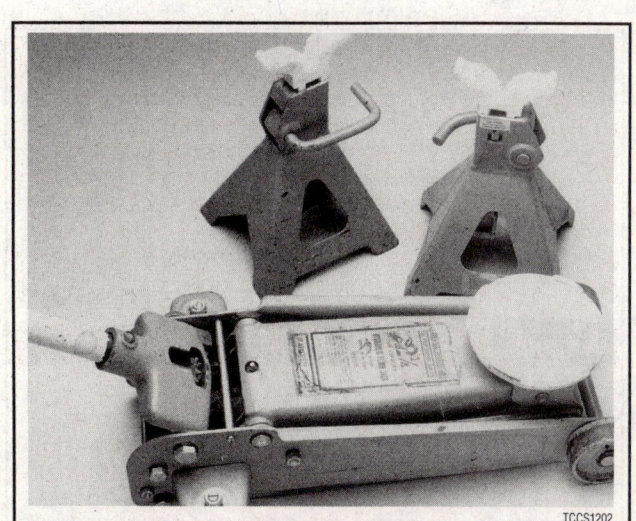

Fig. 3 A hydraulic floor jack and a set of jackstands are essential for lifting and supporting the vehicle

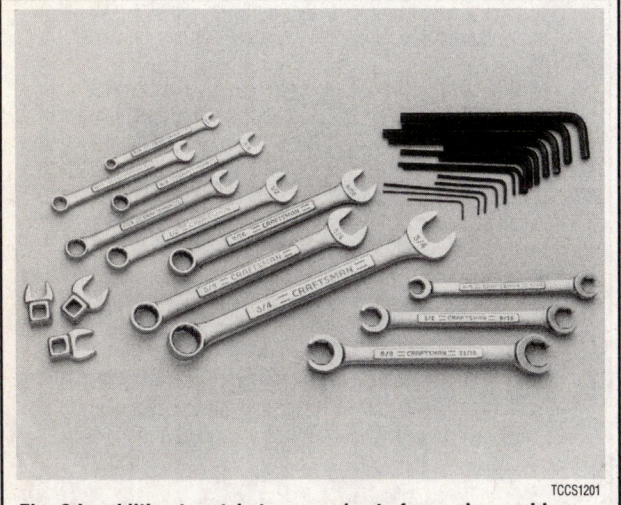

Fig. 2 In addition to ratchets, a good set of wrenches and hex keys will be necessary

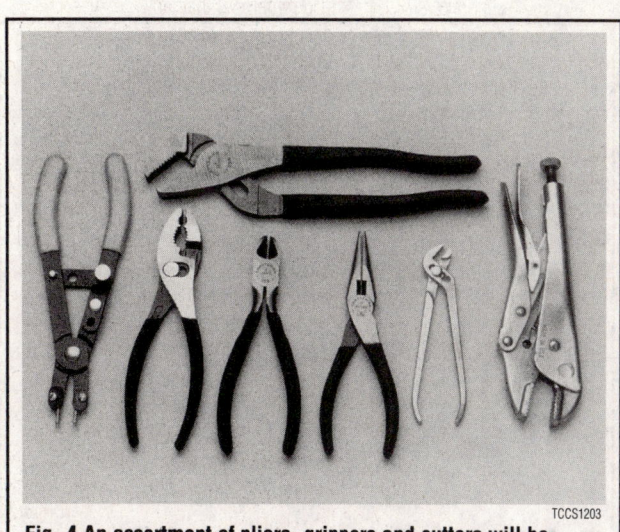

Fig. 4 An assortment of pliers, grippers and cutters will be handy for old rusted parts and stripped bolt heads

# 1-4  GENERAL INFORMATION AND MAINTENANCE

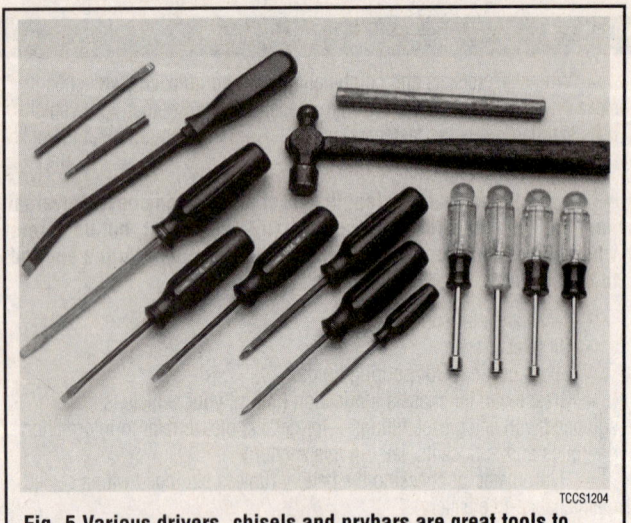

Fig. 5 Various drivers, chisels and prybars are great tools to have in your toolbox

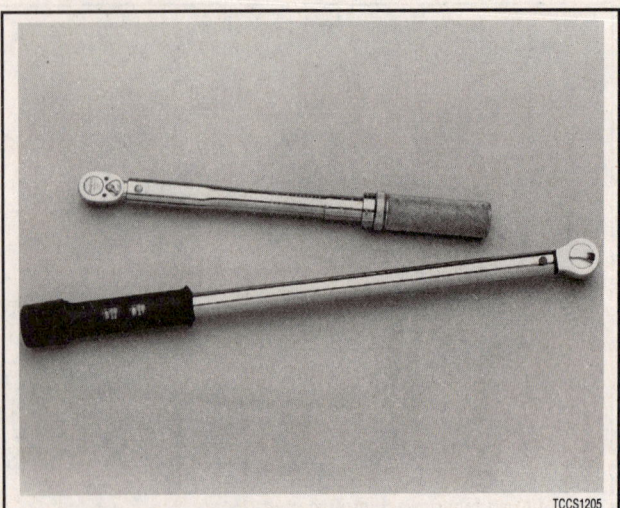

Fig. 6 Many repairs will require the use of a torque wrench to assure the components are properly fastened

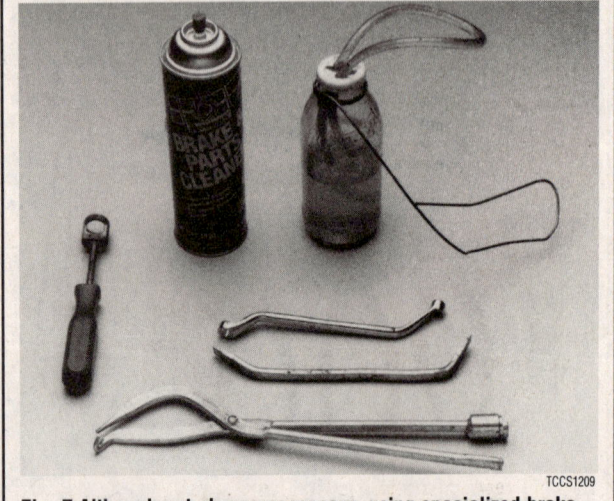

Fig. 7 Although not always necessary, using specialized brake tools will save time

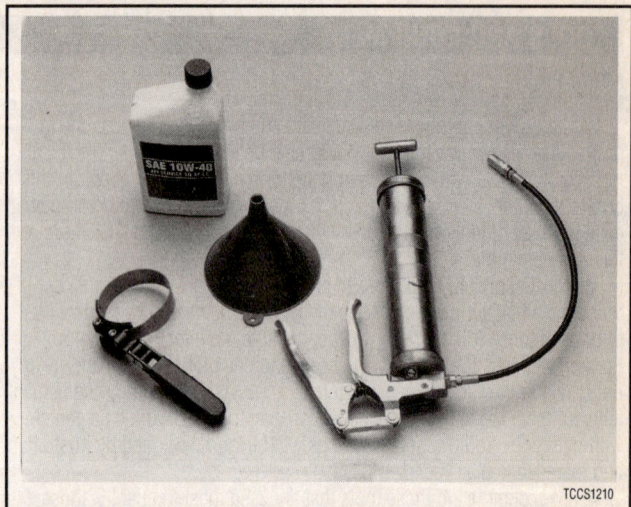

Fig. 8 A few inexpensive lubrication tools will make maintenance easier

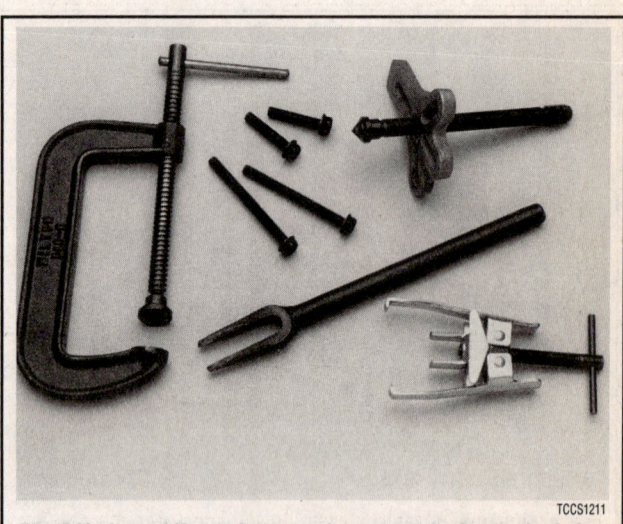

Fig. 9 Various pullers, clamps and separator tools are needed for many larger, more complicated repairs

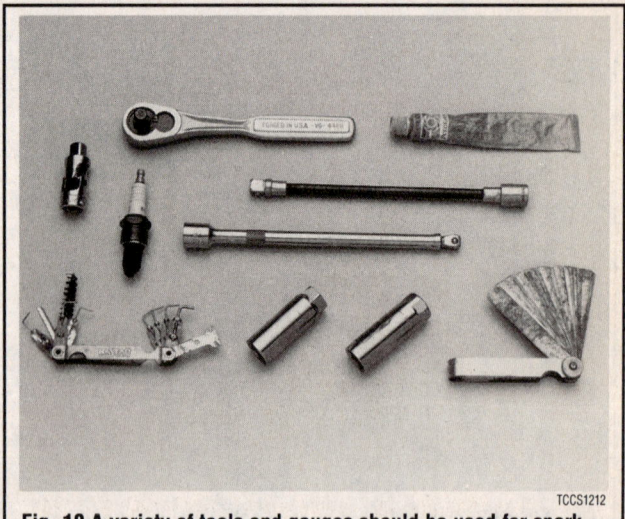

Fig. 10 A variety of tools and gauges should be used for spark plug gapping and installation

# GENERAL INFORMATION AND MAINTENANCE  1-5

In addition to the above items there are several others that are not absolutely necessary, but handy to have around. These include Oil Dry® (or an equivalent oil absorbent gravel—such as cat litter) and the usual supply of lubricants, antifreeze and fluids, although these can be purchased as needed. This is a basic list for routine maintenance, but only your personal needs and desire can accurately determine your list of tools.

After performing a few projects on the vehicle, you'll be amazed at the other tools and non-tools on your workbench. Some useful household items are: a large turkey baster or siphon, empty coffee cans and ice trays (to store parts), ball of twine, electrical tape for wiring, small rolls of colored tape for tagging lines or hoses, markers and pens, a note pad, golf

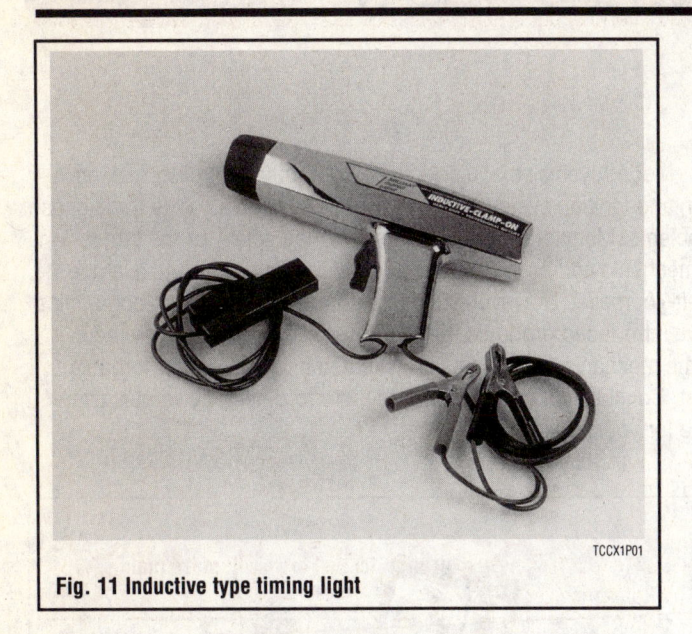

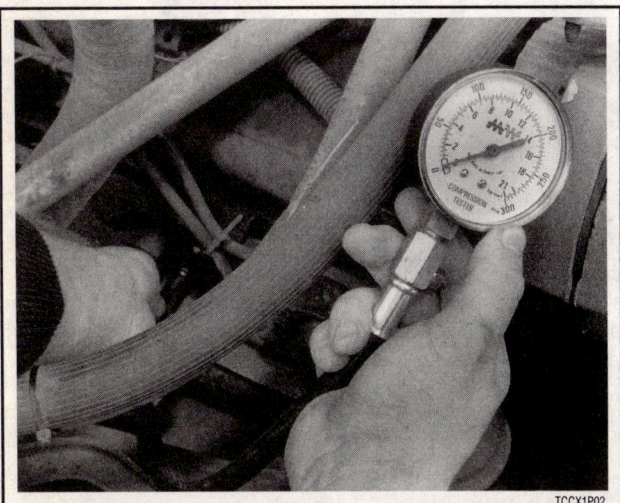

Fig. 11 Inductive type timing light

Fig. 12 A screw-in type compression gauge is recommended for compression testing

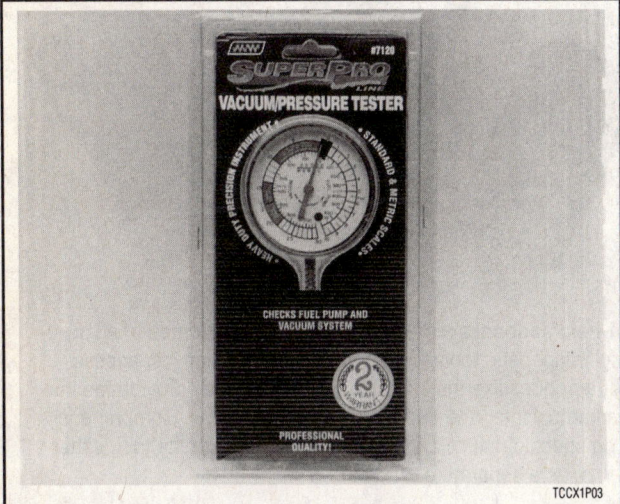

Fig. 13 A vacuum/pressure tester is necessary for many testing procedures

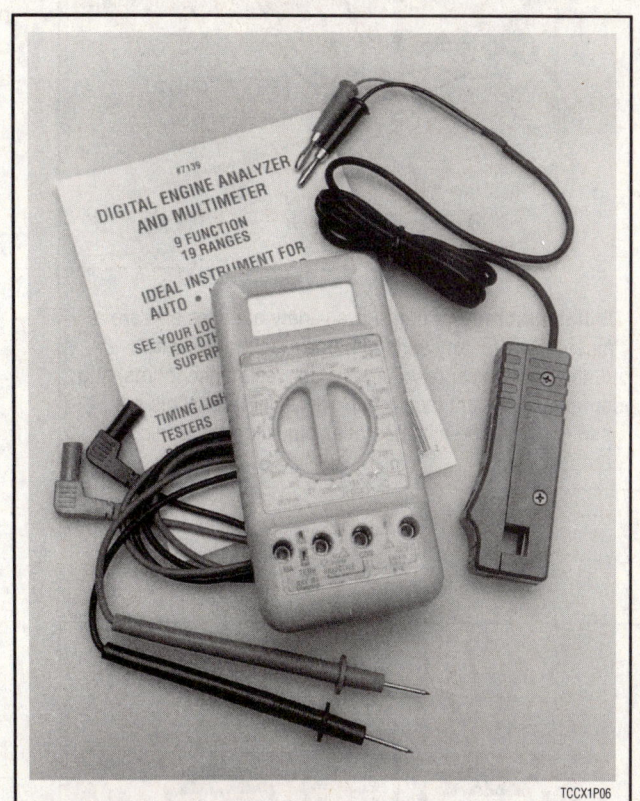

Fig. 14 Most modern automotive multimeters incorporate many helpful features

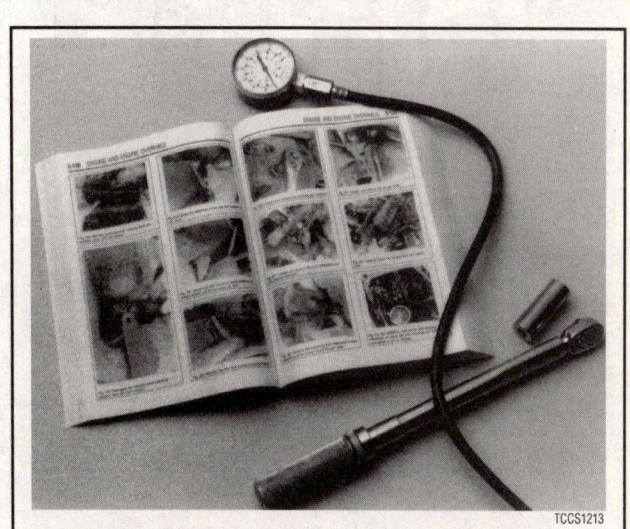

Fig. 15 Proper information is vital, so always have a Chilton Total Car Care manual handy

# DIAGNOSTIC TEST EQUIPMENT

Modern vehicles equipped with computer-controlled fuel, emission and ignition systems require modern electronic tools to diagnose problems. Many of these tools are designed solely for the professional mechanic and are too costly and difficult to use for the average do-it-yourselfer. However, various automotive aftermarket companies have introduced products that address the needs of the average home mechanic, providing sophisticated information at affordable cost. Consult your local auto parts store to determine what is available for your vehicle.

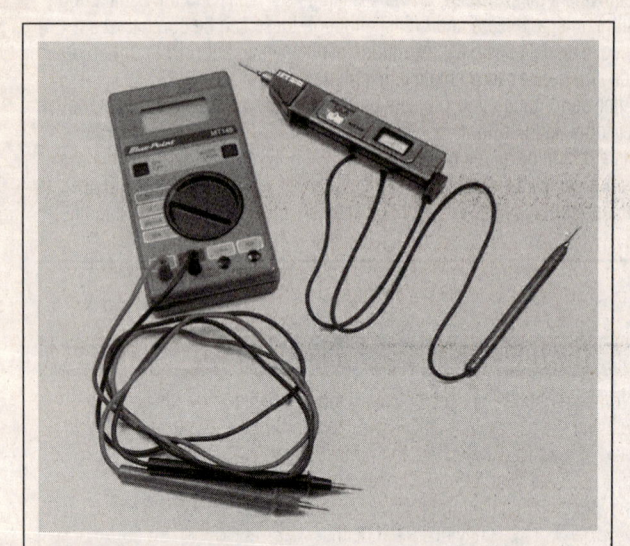

**Digital multimeters** come in a variety of styles and are a "must-have" for any serious home mechanic. Digital multimeters measure voltage (volts), resistance (ohms) and sometimes current (amperes). These versatile tools are used for checking all types of electrical or electronic components

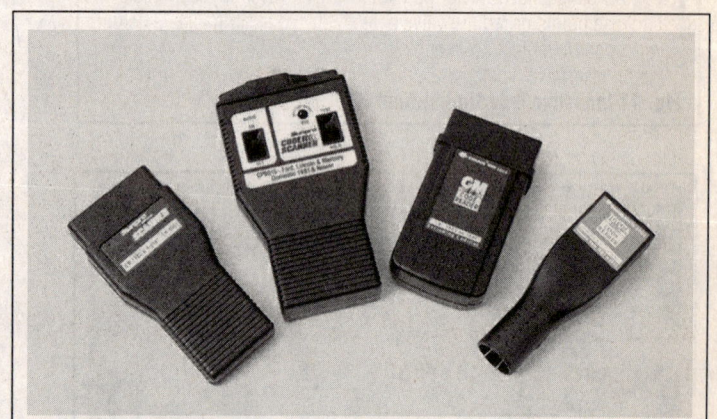

**Trouble code tools** allow the home mechanic to extract the "fault code" number from an on-board computer that has sensed a problem (usually indicated by a Check Engine light). Armed with this code, the home mechanic can focus attention on a suspect system or component

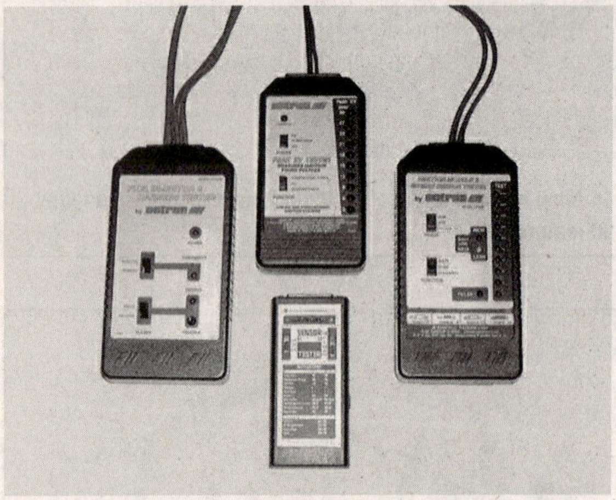

**Sensor testers** perform specific checks on many of the sensors and actuators used on today's computer-controlled vehicles. These testers can check sensors both on or off the vehicle, as well as test the accompanying electrical circuits

**Hand-held scanners** represent the most sophisticated of all do-it-yourself diagnostic tools. These tools do more than just access computer codes like the code readers above; they provide the user with an actual interface into the vehicle's computer. Comprehensive data on specific makes and models will come with the tool, either built-in or as a separate cartridge

# GENERAL INFORMATION AND MAINTENANCE  1-7

tees (for plugging vacuum lines), metal coat hangers or a roll of mechanics's wire (to hold things out of the way), dental pick or similar long, pointed probe, a strong magnet, and a small mirror (to see into recesses and under manifolds).

A more advanced set of tools, suitable for tune-up work, can be drawn up easily. While the tools are slightly more sophisticated, they need not be outrageously expensive. There are several inexpensive tach/dwell meters on the market that are every bit as good for the average mechanic as a professional model. Just be sure that it goes to a least 1200–1500 rpm on the tach scale and that it works on 4, 6 and 8-cylinder engines. (If you have one or more vehicles with a diesel engine, a special tachometer is required since diesels don't use spark plug ignition systems). The key to these purchases is to make them with an eye towards adaptability and wide range. A basic list of tune-up tools could include:

- Tach/dwell meter.
- Spark plug wrench and gapping tool.
- Feeler gauges for valve or point adjustment. (Even if your vehicle does not use points or require valve adjustments, a feeler gauge is helpful for many repair/overhaul procedures).

A tachometer/dwell meter will ensure accurate tune-up work on vehicles without electronic ignition. The choice of a timing light should be made carefully. A light which works on the DC current supplied by the vehicle's battery is the best choice; it should have a xenon tube for brightness. On any vehicle with an electronic ignition system, a timing light with an inductive pickup that clamps around the No. 1 spark plug cable is preferred.

In addition to these basic tools, there are several other tools and gauges you may find useful. These include:

- Compression gauge. The screw-in type is slower to use, but eliminates the possibility of a faulty reading due to escaping pressure.
- Manifold vacuum gauge.
- 12V test light.
- A combination volt/ohmmeter
- Induction Ammeter. This is used for determining whether or not there is current in a wire. These are handy for use if a wire is broken somewhere in a wiring harness.

As a final note, you will probably find a torque wrench necessary for all but the most basic work. The beam type models are perfectly adequate, although the newer click types (breakaway) are easier to use. The click type torque wrenches tend to be more expensive. Also keep in mind that all types of torque wrenches should be periodically checked and/or recalibrated. You will have to decide for yourself which better fits your purpose.

## Special Tools

Normally, the use of special factory tools is avoided for repair procedures, since these are not readily available for the do-it-yourself mechanic. When it is possible to perform the job with more commonly available tools, it will be pointed out, but occasionally, a special tool was designed to perform a specific function and should be used. Before substituting another tool, you should be convinced that neither your safety nor the performance of the vehicle will be compromised.

Special tools can usually be purchased from an automotive parts store or from your dealer. In some cases special tools may be available directly from the tool manufacturer.

## SERVICING YOUR VEHICLE SAFELY

▶ See Figures 16, 17, 18 and 19

It is virtually impossible to anticipate all of the hazards involved with automotive maintenance and service, but care and common sense will prevent most accidents.

The rules of safety for mechanics range from "don't smoke around gasoline," to "use the proper tool(s) for the job." The trick to avoiding injuries is to develop safe work habits and to take every possible precaution.

### Do's

- Do keep a fire extinguisher and first aid kit handy.
- Do wear safety glasses or goggles when cutting, drilling, grinding or prying, even if you have 20–20 vision. If you wear glasses for the sake of vision, wear safety goggles over your regular glasses.
- Do shield your eyes whenever you work around the battery. Batteries contain sulfuric acid. In case of contact with the eyes or skin, flush the area with water or a mixture of water and baking soda, then seek immediate medical attention.
- Do use safety stands (jackstands) for any undervehicle service. Jacks are for raising vehicles; jackstands are for making sure the vehicle stays raised until you want it to come down. Whenever the vehicle is raised, block the wheels remaining on the ground and set the parking brake.
- Do use adequate ventilation when working with any chemicals or hazardous materials. Like carbon monoxide, the asbestos dust resulting from some brake lining wear can be hazardous in sufficient quantities.
- Do disconnect the negative battery cable when working on the electrical system. The secondary ignition system contains EXTREMELY HIGH VOLTAGE. In some cases it can even exceed 50,000 volts.

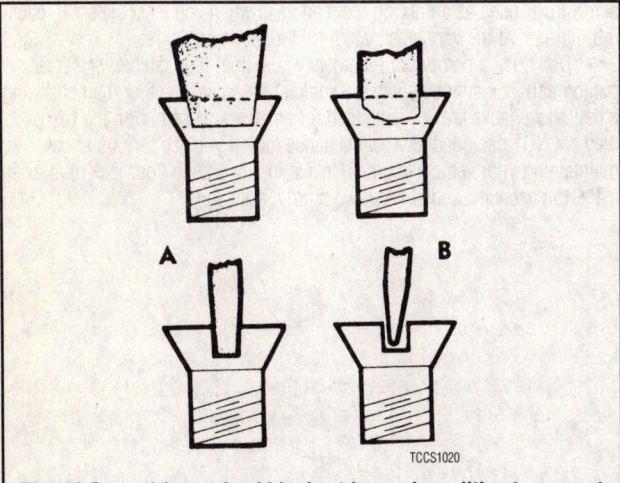

Fig. 16 Screwdrivers should be kept in good condition to prevent injury or damage which could result if the blade slips from the screw

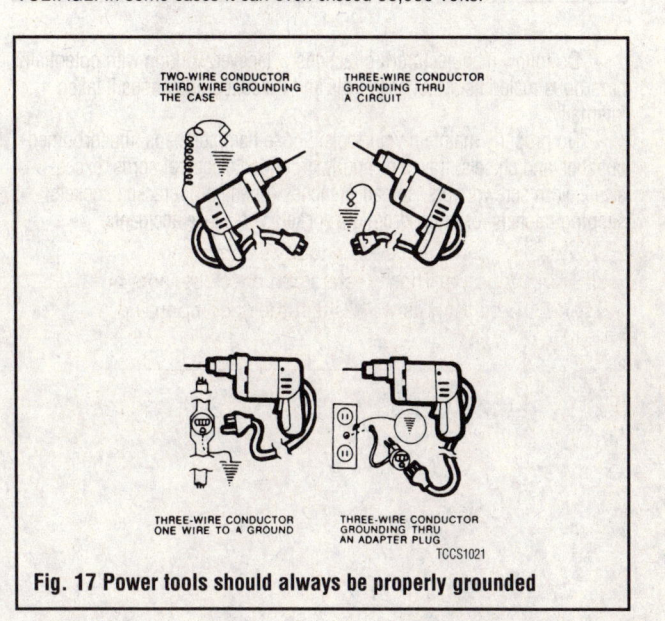

Fig. 17 Power tools should always be properly grounded

# 1-8 GENERAL INFORMATION AND MAINTENANCE

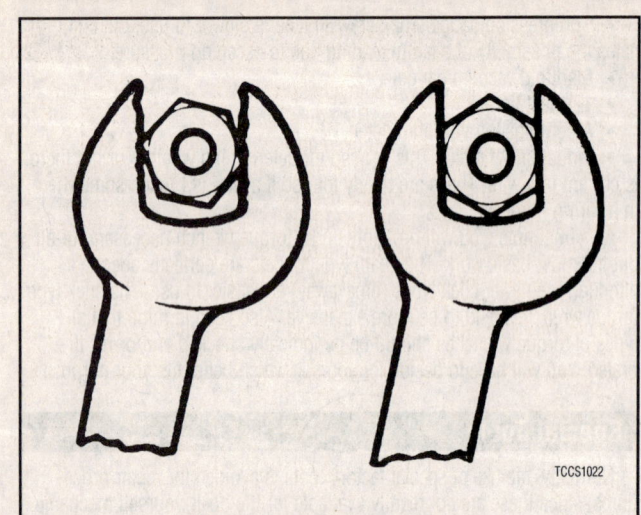

Fig. 18 Using the correct size wrench will help prevent the possibility of rounding off a nut

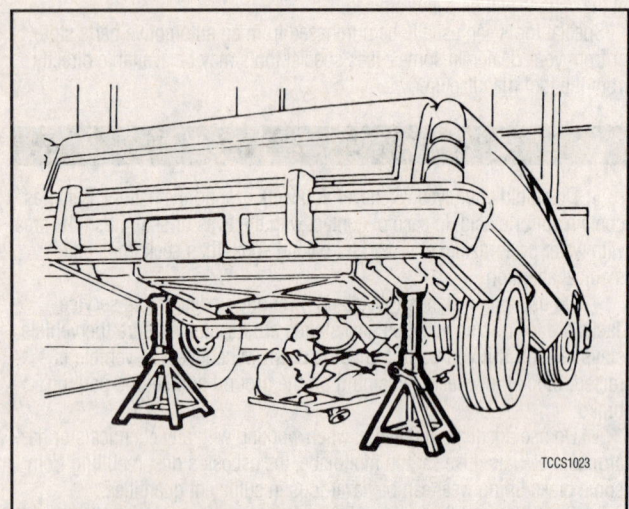

Fig. 19 NEVER work under a vehicle unless it is supported using safety stands (jackstands)

- Likewise, keep your tools clean; a greasy wrench can slip off a bolt head, ruining the bolt and often harming your knuckles in the process.
- Do use the proper size and type of tool for the job at hand. Do select a wrench or socket that fits the nut or bolt. The wrench or socket should sit straight, not cocked.
- Do, when possible, pull on a wrench handle rather than push on it, and adjust your stance to prevent a fall.
- Do be sure that adjustable wrenches are tightly closed on the nut or bolt and pulled so that the force is on the side of the fixed jaw.
- Do strike squarely with a hammer; avoid glancing blows.
- Do set the parking brake and block the drive wheels if the work requires a running engine.

## Don'ts

- Don't run the engine in a garage or anywhere else without proper ventilation—EVER! Carbon monoxide is poisonous; it takes a long time to leave the human body and you can build up a deadly supply of it in your system by simply breathing in a little every day. You may not realize you are slowly poisoning yourself. Always use power vents, windows, fans and/or open the garage door.
- Don't work around moving parts while wearing loose clothing. Short sleeves are much safer than long, loose sleeves. Hard-toed shoes with neoprene soles protect your toes and give a better grip on slippery surfaces. Jewelry such as watches, fancy belt buckles, beads or body adornment of any kind is not safe working around a vehicle. Long hair should be tied back under a hat or cap.
- Don't use pockets for toolboxes. A fall or bump can drive a screwdriver deep into your body. Even a rag hanging from your back pocket can wrap around a spinning shaft or fan.
- Don't smoke when working around gasoline, cleaning solvent or other flammable material.
- Don't smoke when working around the battery. When the battery is being charged, it gives off explosive hydrogen gas.
- Don't use gasoline to wash your hands; there are excellent soaps available. Gasoline contains dangerous additives which can enter the body through a cut or through your pores. Gasoline also removes all the natural oils from the skin so that bone dry hands will suck up oil and grease.
- Don't service the air conditioning system unless you are equipped with the necessary tools and training. When liquid or compressed gas refrigerant is released to atmospheric pressure it will absorb heat from whatever it contacts. This will chill or freeze anything it touches. Although refrigerant is normally non-toxic, R-12 becomes a deadly poisonous gas in the presence of an open flame. One good whiff of the vapors from burning refrigerant can be fatal.
- Don't use screwdrivers for anything other than driving screws! A screwdriver used as an prying tool can snap when you least expect it, causing injuries. At the very least, you'll ruin a good screwdriver.
- Don't use a bumper or emergency jack (that little ratchet, scissors, or pantograph jack supplied with the vehicle) for anything other than changing a flat! These jacks are only intended for emergency use out on the road; they are NOT designed as a maintenance tool. If you are serious about maintaining your vehicle yourself, invest in a hydraulic floor jack of at least a 1½ ton capacity, and at least two sturdy jackstands.

- Do follow manufacturer's directions whenever working with potentially hazardous materials. Most chemicals and fluids are poisonous if taken internally.
- Do properly maintain your tools. Loose hammerheads, mushroomed punches and chisels, frayed or poorly grounded electrical cords, excessively worn screwdrivers, spread wrenches (open end), cracked sockets, slipping ratchets, or faulty droplight sockets can cause accidents.

# GENERAL INFORMATION AND MAINTENANCE  1-9

## FASTENERS, MEASUREMENTS AND CONVERSIONS

### Bolts, Nuts and Other Threaded Retainers

▶ See Figures 20, 21, 22 and 23

Although there are a great variety of fasteners found in the modern car or truck, the most commonly used retainer is the threaded fastener (nuts, bolts, screws, studs, etc). Most threaded retainers may be reused, provided that they are not damaged in use or during the repair. Some retainers (such as stretch bolts or torque prevailing nuts) are designed to deform when tightened or in use and should not be reinstalled.

Whenever possible, we will note any special retainers which should be replaced during a procedure. But you should always inspect the condition of a retainer when it is removed and replace any that show signs of damage. Check all threads for rust or corrosion which can increase the torque necessary to achieve the desired clamp load for which that fastener was originally selected. Additionally, be sure that the driver surface of the fastener has not been compromised by rounding or other damage. In some cases a driver surface may become only partially rounded, allowing the driver to catch in only one direction. In many of these occurrences, a fastener may be installed and tightened, but the dri-

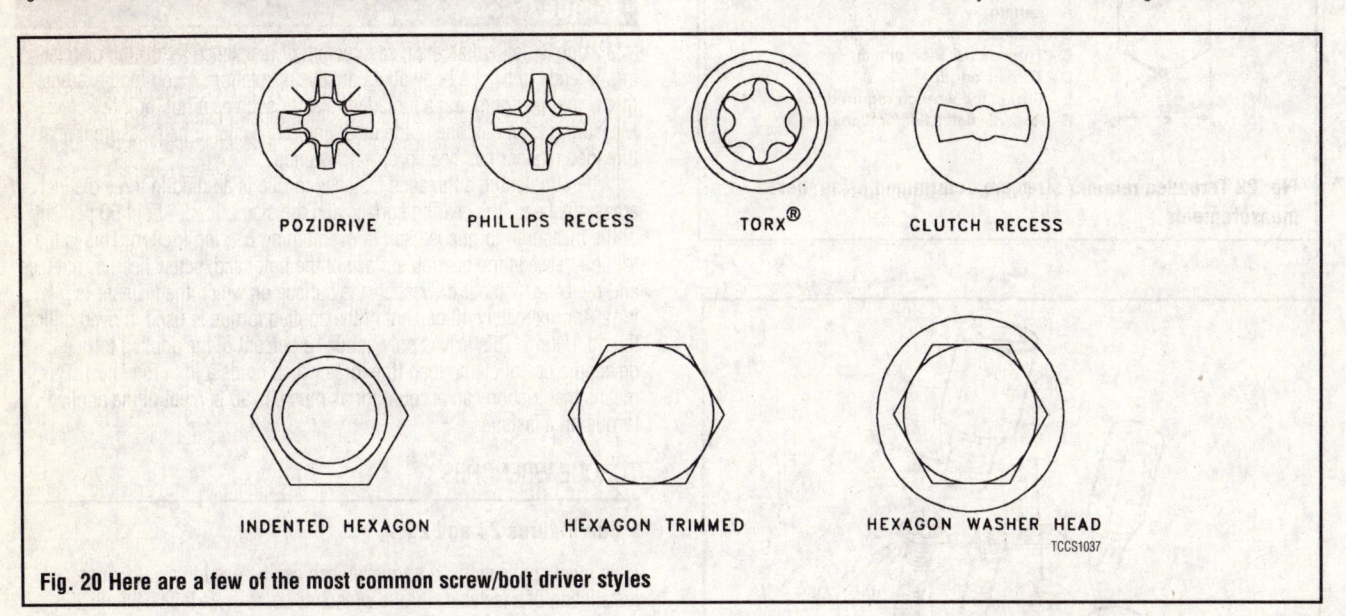

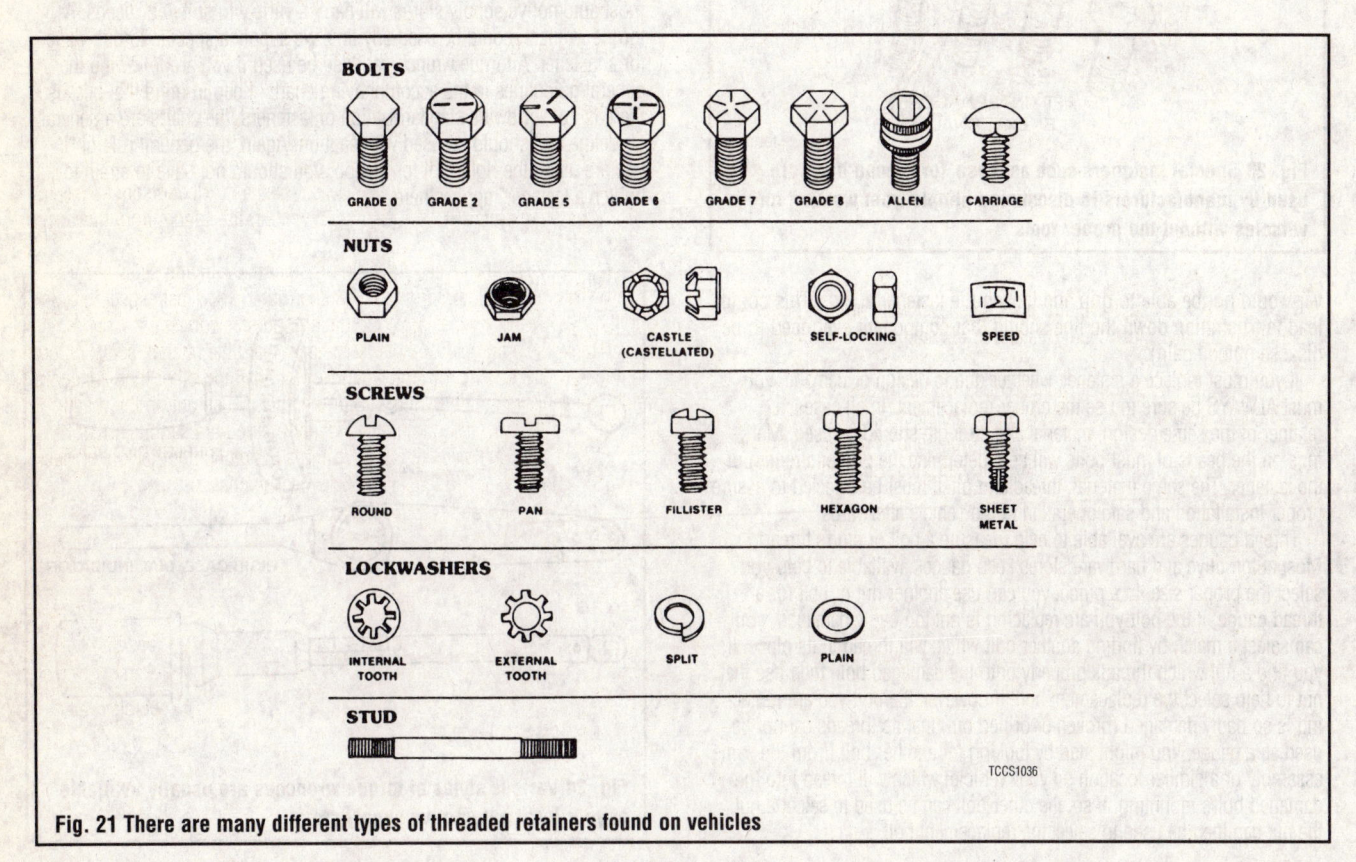

Fig. 20 Here are a few of the most common screw/bolt driver styles

Fig. 21 There are many different types of threaded retainers found on vehicles

# 1-10 GENERAL INFORMATION AND MAINTENANCE

**Fig. 22 Threaded retainer sizes are determined using these measurements**

A - Length
B - Diameter (major diameter)
C - Threads per inch or mm
D - Thread length
E - Size of the wrench required
F - Root diameter (minor diameter)

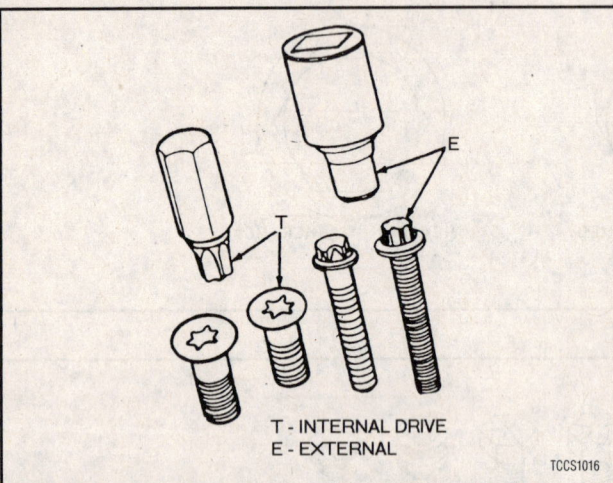

**Fig. 23 Special fasteners such as these Torx® head bolts are used by manufacturers to discourage people from working on vehicles without the proper tools**

T - INTERNAL DRIVE
E - EXTERNAL

ver would not be able to grip and loosen the fastener again. (This could lead to frustration down the line should that component ever need to be disassembled again).

If you must replace a fastener, whether due to design or damage, you must ALWAYS be sure to use the proper replacement. In all cases, a retainer of the same design, material and strength should be used. Markings on the heads of most bolts will help determine the proper strength of the fastener. The same material, thread and pitch must be selected to assure proper installation and safe operation of the vehicle afterwards.

Thread gauges are available to help measure a bolt or stud's thread. Most automotive and hardware stores keep gauges available to help you select the proper size. In a pinch, you can use another nut or bolt for a thread gauge. If the bolt you are replacing is not too badly damaged, you can select a match by finding another bolt which will thread in its place. If you find a nut which threads properly onto the damaged bolt, then use that nut to help select the replacement bolt. If however, the bolt you are replacing is so badly damaged (broken or drilled out) that its threads cannot be used as a gauge, you might start by looking for another bolt (from the same assembly or a similar location on your vehicle) which will thread into the damaged bolt's mounting. If so, the other bolt can be used to select a nut; the nut can then be used to select the replacement bolt.

In all cases, be absolutely sure you have selected the proper replacement. Don't be shy, you can always ask the store clerk for help.

### ✷✷ WARNING

**Be aware that when you find a bolt with damaged threads, you may also find the nut or drilled hole it was threaded into has also been damaged. If this is the case, you may have to drill and tap the hole, replace the nut or otherwise repair the threads. NEVER try to force a replacement bolt to fit into the damaged threads.**

## Torque

Torque is defined as the measurement of resistance to turning or rotating. It tends to twist a body about an axis of rotation. A common example of this would be tightening a threaded retainer such as a nut, bolt or screw. Measuring torque is one of the most common ways to help assure that a threaded retainer has been properly fastened.

When tightening a threaded fastener, torque is applied in three distinct areas, the head, the bearing surface and the clamp load. About 50 percent of the measured torque is used in overcoming bearing friction. This is the friction between the bearing surface of the bolt head, screw head or nut face and the base material or washer (the surface on which the fastener is rotating). Approximately 40 percent of the applied torque is used in overcoming thread friction. This leaves only about 10 percent of the applied torque to develop a useful clamp load (the force which holds a joint together). This means that friction can account for as much as 90 percent of the applied torque on a fastener.

### TORQUE WRENCHES

▶ See Figures 24 and 25

In most applications, a torque wrench can be used to assure proper installation of a fastener. Torque wrenches come in various designs and most automotive supply stores will carry a variety to suit your needs. A torque wrench should be used any time we supply a specific torque value for a fastener. A torque wrench can also be used if you are following the general guidelines in the accompanying charts. Keep in mind that because there is no worldwide standardization of fasteners, the charts are a general guideline and should be used with caution. Again, the general rule of "if you are using the right tool for the job, you should not have to strain to tighten a fastener" applies here.

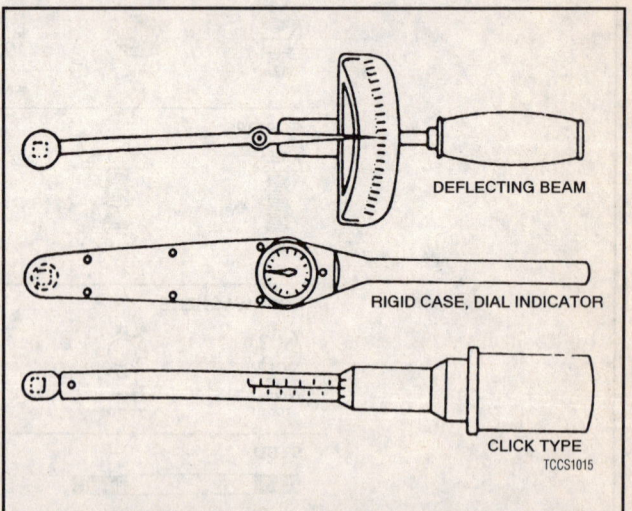

**Fig. 24 Various styles of torque wrenches are usually available at your local automotive supply store**

DEFLECTING BEAM
RIGID CASE, DIAL INDICATOR
CLICK TYPE

# GENERAL INFORMATION AND MAINTENANCE 1-11

## Standard Torque Specifications and Fastener Markings

In the absence of specific torques, the following chart can be used as a guide to the maximum safe torque of a particular size/grade of fastener.
- There is no torque difference for fine or coarse threads.
- Torque values are based on clean, dry threads. Reduce the value by 10% if threads are oiled prior to assembly.
- The torque required for aluminum components or fasteners is considerably less.

### U.S. Bolts

| SAE Grade Number | 1 or 2 | | | 5 | | | 6 or 7 | | |
|---|---|---|---|---|---|---|---|---|---|
| Bolt Size (Inches)—(Thread) | Ft./Lbs. | Kgm | Nm | Ft./Lbs. | Kgm | Nm | Ft./Lbs. | Kgm | Nm |
| ¼ — 20 | 5 | 0.7 | 6.8 | 8 | 1.1 | 10.8 | 10 | 1.4 | 13.5 |
| — 28 | 6 | 0.8 | 8.1 | 10 | 1.4 | 13.6 | | | |
| ⁵⁄₁₆ — 18 | 11 | 1.5 | 14.9 | 17 | 2.3 | 23.0 | 19 | 2.6 | 25.8 |
| — 24 | 13 | 1.8 | 17.6 | 19 | 2.6 | 25.7 | | | |
| ⅜ — 16 | 18 | 2.5 | 24.4 | 31 | 4.3 | 42.0 | 34 | 4.7 | 46.0 |
| — 24 | 20 | 2.75 | 27.1 | 35 | 4.8 | 47.5 | | | |
| ⁷⁄₁₆ — 14 | 28 | 3.8 | 37.0 | 49 | 6.8 | 66.4 | 55 | 7.6 | 74.5 |
| — 20 | 30 | 4.2 | 40.7 | 55 | 7.6 | 74.5 | | | |
| ½ — 13 | 39 | 5.4 | 52.8 | 75 | 10.4 | 101.7 | 85 | 11.75 | 115.2 |
| — 20 | 41 | 5.7 | 55.6 | 85 | 11.7 | 115.2 | | | |
| ⁹⁄₁₆ — 12 | 51 | 7.0 | 69.2 | 110 | 15.2 | 149.1 | 120 | 16.6 | 162.7 |
| — 18 | 55 | 7.6 | 74.5 | 120 | 16.6 | 162.7 | | | |
| ⅝ — 11 | 83 | 11.5 | 112.5 | 150 | 20.7 | 203.3 | 167 | 23.0 | 226.5 |
| — 18 | 95 | 13.1 | 128.8 | 170 | 23.5 | 230.5 | | | |
| ¾ — 10 | 105 | 14.5 | 142.3 | 270 | 37.3 | 366.0 | 280 | 38.7 | 379.6 |
| — 16 | 115 | 15.9 | 155.9 | 295 | 40.8 | 400.0 | | | |
| ⅞ — 9 | 160 | 22.1 | 216.9 | 395 | 54.6 | 535.5 | 440 | 60.9 | 596.5 |
| — 14 | 175 | 24.2 | 237.2 | 435 | 60.1 | 589.7 | | | |
| 1 — 8 | 236 | 32.5 | 318.6 | 590 | 81.6 | 799.9 | 660 | 91.3 | 894.8 |
| — 14 | 250 | 34.6 | 338.9 | 660 | 91.3 | 849.8 | | | |

### Metric Bolts

| Relative Strength Marking | 4.6, 4.8 | | | 8.8 | | |
|---|---|---|---|---|---|---|
| Bolt Size Thread Size x Pitch (mm) | Ft./Lbs. | Kgm | Nm | Ft./Lbs. | Kgm | Nm |
| 6 x 1.0 | 2–3 | .2–.4 | 3–4 | 3–6 | 4–.8 | 5–8 |
| 8 x 1.25 | 6–8 | .8–1 | 8–12 | 9–14 | 1.2–1.9 | 13–19 |
| 10 x 1.25 | 12–17 | 1.5–2.3 | 16–23 | 20–29 | 2.7–4.0 | 27–39 |
| 12 x 1.25 | 21–32 | 2.9–4.4 | 29–43 | 35–53 | 4.8–7.3 | 47–72 |
| 14 x 1.5 | 35–52 | 4.8–7.1 | 48–70 | 57–85 | 7.8–11.7 | 77–110 |
| 16 x 1.5 | 51–77 | 7.0–10.6 | 67–100 | 90–120 | 12.4–16.5 | 130–160 |
| 18 x 1.5 | 74–110 | 10.2–15.1 | 100–150 | 130–170 | 17.9–23.4 | 180–230 |
| 20 x 1.5 | 110–140 | 15.1–19.3 | 150–190 | 190–240 | 26.2–46.9 | 160–320 |
| 22 x 1.5 | 150–190 | 22.0–26.2 | 200–260 | 250–320 | 34.5–44.1 | 340–430 |
| 24 x 1.5 | 190–240 | 26.2–46.9 | 260–320 | 310–410 | 42.7–56.5 | 420–550 |

Fig. 25 Standard and metric bolt torque specifications based on bolt strengths—WARNING: use only as a guide

## Beam Type
▶ See Figure 26

The beam type torque wrench is one of the most popular types. It consists of a pointer attached to the head that runs the length of the flexible beam (shaft) to a scale located near the handle. As the wrench is pulled, the beam bends and the pointer indicates the torque using the scale.

## Click (Breakaway) Type
▶ See Figure 27

Another popular design of torque wrench is the click type. To use the click type wrench you pre-adjust it to a torque setting. Once the torque is reached, the wrench has a reflex signaling feature that causes a momentary breakaway of the torque wrench body, sending an impulse to the operator's hand.

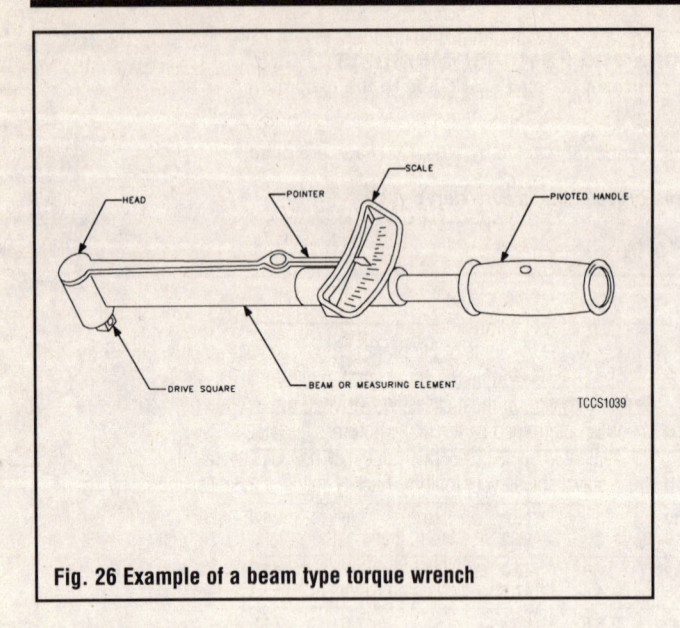

# 1-12 GENERAL INFORMATION AND MAINTENANCE

Fig. 26 Example of a beam type torque wrench

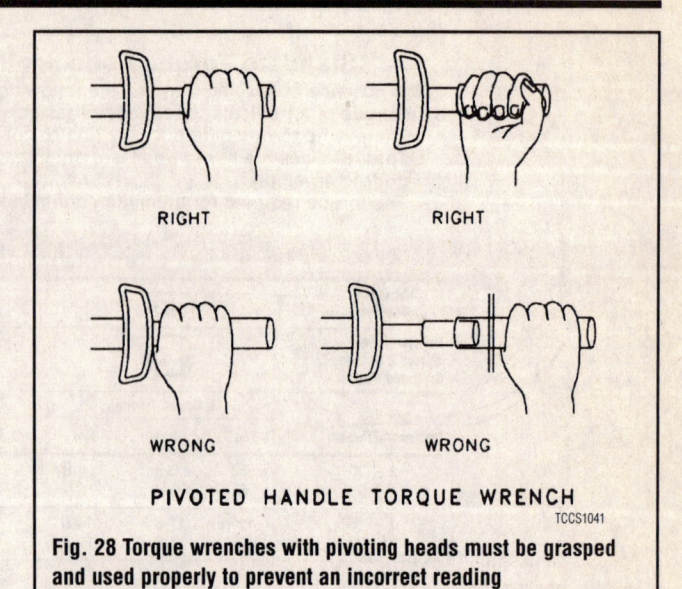

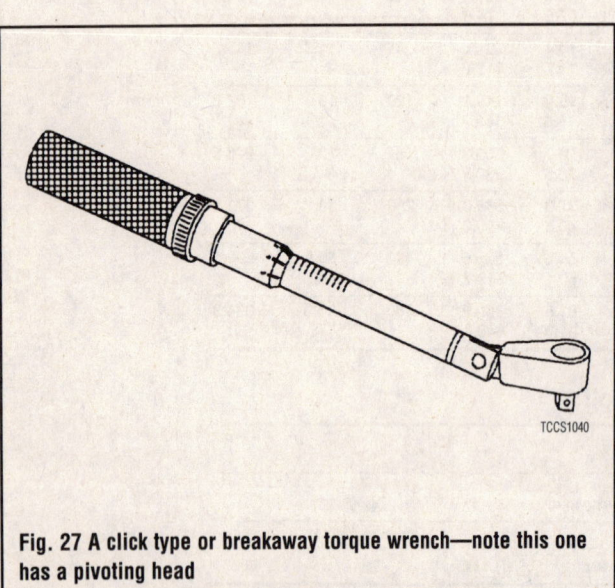

Fig. 27 A click type or breakaway torque wrench—note this one has a pivoting head

Fig. 28 Torque wrenches with pivoting heads must be grasped and used properly to prevent an incorrect reading

## Rigid Case (Direct Reading)

♦ See Figure 29

A rigid case or direct reading torque wrench is equipped with a dial indicator to show torque values. One advantage of these wrenches is that they can be held at any position on the wrench without affecting accuracy. These wrenches are often preferred because they tend to be compact, easy to read and have a great degree of accuracy.

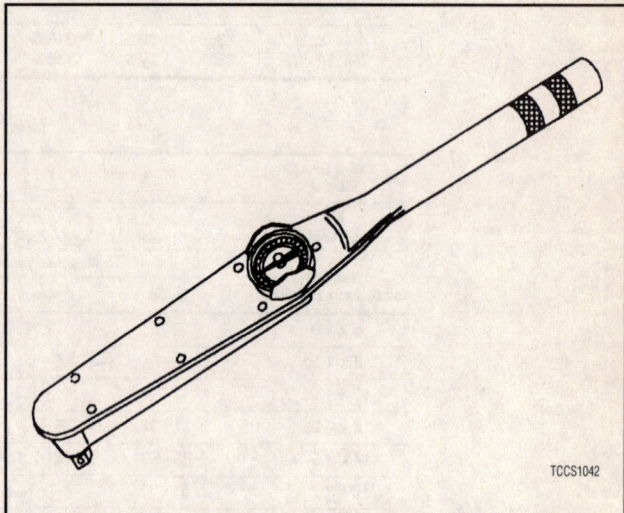

Fig. 29 The rigid case (direct reading) torque wrench uses a dial indicator to show torque

## Pivot Head Type

♦ See Figures 27 and 28

Some torque wrenches (usually of the click type) may be equipped with a pivot head which can allow it to be used in areas of limited access. BUT, it must be used properly. To hold a pivot head wrench, grasp the handle lightly, and as you pull on the handle, it should be floated on the pivot point. If the handle comes in contact with the yoke extension during the process of pulling, there is a very good chance the torque readings will be inaccurate because this could alter the wrench loading point. The design of the handle is usually such as to make it inconvenient to deliberately misuse the wrench.

➡ It should be mentioned that the use of any U-joint, wobble or extension will have an effect on the torque readings, no matter what type of wrench you are using. For the most accurate readings, install the socket directly on the wrench driver. If necessary, straight extensions (which hold a socket directly under the wrench driver) will have the least effect on the torque reading. Avoid any extension that alters the length of the wrench from the handle to the head/driving point (such as a crow's foot). U-joint or wobble extensions can greatly affect the readings; avoid their use at all times.

## TORQUE ANGLE METERS

♦ See Figure 30

Because the frictional characteristics of each fastener or threaded hole will vary, clamp loads which are based strictly on torque will vary as well. In most applications, this variance is not significant enough to cause worry. But, in certain applications, a manufacturer's engineers may determine that more precise clamp loads are necessary (such is the case with many aluminum cylinder heads). In these cases, a torque angle method of installation would be specified. When installing fasteners which are torque angle

# GENERAL INFORMATION AND MAINTENANCE　1-13

tightened, a predetermined seating torque and standard torque wrench are usually used first to remove any compliance from the joint. The fastener is then tightened the specified additional portion of a turn measured in degrees. A torque angle gauge (mechanical protractor) is used for these applications.

## Standard and Metric Measurements

♦ See Figure 31

Throughout this manual, specifications are given to help you determine the condition of various components on your vehicle, or to assist you in their installation. Some of the most common measurements include length (in. or cm/mm), torque (ft. lbs, inch lbs. or Nm) and pressure (psi, in. Hg, kPa or mm Hg). In most cases, we strive to provide the proper measurement as determined by the manufacturer's engineers.

Though, in some cases, that value may not be conveniently measured with what is available in your toolbox. Luckily, many of the measuring devices which are available today will have two scales so the Standard or Metric measurements may easily be taken. If any of the various measuring tools which are available to you do not contain the same scale as listed in the specifications, use the accompanying conversion factors to determine the proper value.

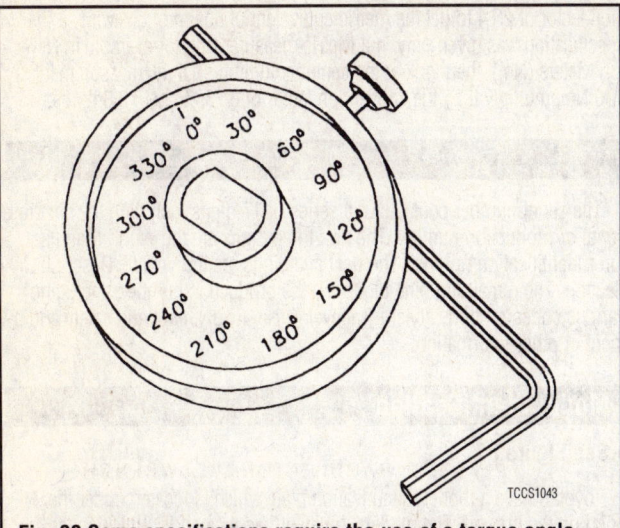

Fig. 30 Some specifications require the use of a torque angle meter (mechanical protractor)

## CONVERSION FACTORS

**LENGTH–DISTANCE**

| | | | | |
|---|---|---|---|---|
| Inches (in.) | x 25.4 | = Millimeters (mm) | x .0394 | = Inches |
| Feet (ft.) | x .305 | = Meters (m) | x 3.281 | = Feet |
| Miles | x 1.609 | = Kilometers (km) | x .0621 | = Miles |

**VOLUME**

| | | | | |
|---|---|---|---|---|
| Cubic Inches (in3) | x 16.387 | = Cubic Centimeters | x .061 | = in3 |
| IMP Pints (IMP pt.) | x .568 | = Liters (L) | x 1.76 | = IMP pt. |
| IMP Quarts (IMP qt.) | x 1.137 | = Liters (L) | x .88 | = IMP qt. |
| IMP Gallons (IMP gal.) | x 4.546 | = Liters (L) | x .22 | = IMP gal. |
| IMP Quarts (IMP qt.) | x 1.201 | = US Quarts (US qt.) | x .833 | = IMP qt. |
| IMP Gallons (IMP gal.) | x 1.201 | = US Gallons (US gal.) | x .833 | = IMP gal. |
| Fl. Ounces | x 29.573 | = Milliliters | x .034 | = Ounces |
| US Pints (US pt.) | x .473 | = Liters (L) | x 2.113 | = Pints |
| US Quarts (US qt.) | x .946 | = Liters (L) | x 1.057 | = Quarts |
| US Gallons (US gal.) | x 3.785 | = Liters (L) | x .264 | = Gallons |

**MASS–WEIGHT**

| | | | | |
|---|---|---|---|---|
| Ounces (oz.) | x 28.35 | = Grams (g) | x .035 | = Ounces |
| Pounds (lb.) | x .454 | = Kilograms (kg) | x 2.205 | = Pounds |

**PRESSURE**

| | | | | |
|---|---|---|---|---|
| Pounds Per Sq. In. (psi) | x 6.895 | = Kilopascals (kPa) | x .145 | = psi |
| Inches of Mercury (Hg) | x .4912 | = psi | x 2.036 | = Hg |
| Inches of Mercury (Hg) | x 3.377 | = Kilopascals (kPa) | x .2961 | = Hg |
| Inches of Water (H$_2$O) | x .07355 | = Inches of Mercury | x 13.783 | = H$_2$O |
| Inches of Water (H$_2$O) | x .03613 | = psi | x 27.684 | = H$_2$O |
| Inches of Water (H$_2$O) | x .248 | = Kilopascals (kPa) | x 4.026 | = H$_2$O |

**TORQUE**

| | | | | |
|---|---|---|---|---|
| Pounds–Force Inches (in–lb) | x .113 | = Newton Meters (N·m) | x 8.85 | = in–lb |
| Pounds–Force Feet (ft–lb) | x 1.356 | = Newton Meters (N·m) | x .738 | = ft–lb |

**VELOCITY**

| | | | | |
|---|---|---|---|---|
| Miles Per Hour (MPH) | x 1.609 | = Kilometers Per Hour (KPH) | x .621 | = MPH |

**POWER**

| | | | | |
|---|---|---|---|---|
| Horsepower (Hp) | x .745 | = Kilowatts | x 1.34 | = Horsepower |

**FUEL CONSUMPTION***

| | | | | |
|---|---|---|---|---|
| Miles Per Gallon IMP (MPG) | x .354 | = Kilometers Per Liter (Km/L) | | |
| Kilometers Per Liter (Km/L) | x 2.352 | = IMP MPG | | |
| Miles Per Gallon US (MPG) | x .425 | = Kilometers Per Liter (Km/L) | | |
| Kilometers Per Liter (Km/L) | x 2.352 | = US MPG | | |

*It is common to covert from miles per gallon (mpg) to liters/100 kilometers (l/100 km), where mpg (IMP) x l/100 km = 282 and mpg (US) x l/100 km = 235.

**TEMPERATURE**

Degree Fahrenheit (°F) = (°C x 1.8) + 32
Degree Celsius (°C) = (°F − 32) x .56

Fig. 31 Standard and metric conversion factors chart

# 1-14  GENERAL INFORMATION AND MAINTENANCE

The conversion factor chart is used by taking the given specification and multiplying it by the necessary conversion factor. For instance, looking at the first line, if you have a measurement in inches such as "free-play should be 2 in." but your ruler reads only in millimeters, multiply 2 in. by the conversion factor of 25.4 to get the metric equivalent of 50.8mm. Likewise, if the specification was given only in a Metric measurement, for example in Newton Meters (Nm), then look at the center column first. If the measurement is 100 Nm, multiply it by the conversion factor of 0.738 to get 73.8 ft. lbs.

## SERIAL NUMBER IDENTIFICATION

### Vehicle

▶ See Figure 32

All models have the Vehicle Identification Number (VIN) stamped on a plate attached to the left side of the instrument panel. The plate is visible by looking through the windshield from the outside.

Some Previa's also have the VIN stamped into the metal of the cowl panel on the right side of the vehicle. The number also appears on the Certification Label attached to the left door pillar.

The serial number consists of a series of 17 digits including the six digit serial or production number. The first three digits are the World Manufacturer Identification number. The next five digits are the Vehicle Description Section. The remaining nine digits are the production numbers including various codes on body style, trim level (base, luxury, etc.) and safety equipment or other information.

### Model Identification

▶ See Figure 33

Toyota's have a model identification plate which is located under the hood on the firewall. The models are identified by a code. These codes explain exactly what your van is and has. For example; model number TCR20L–RFSGVA is a 1997 Previa 4WD, 4 speed automatic transmission, 4 door wagon LE, DOHC supercharged 4 cylinder. When you walk into a dealer or your local parts store to purchase a part for your van, and are not sure exactly the type of vehicle you drive, the model number and vehicle identification numbers are the key.

### Engine

▶ See Figure 34

Each engine is referred to by both its family designation, such as 2TZ-FE, and its production or serial number. The serial number can be important when ordering parts. Certain changes may have been made during production of the engine; different parts will be required if the engine was assembled before or after the change date. Generally, parts stores and dealers list this data in their catalogs, so have the engine number handy when you go.

It's a good idea to record the engine number while the vehicle is new. Jotting it inside the cover of the owner's manual or similar easy-to-find

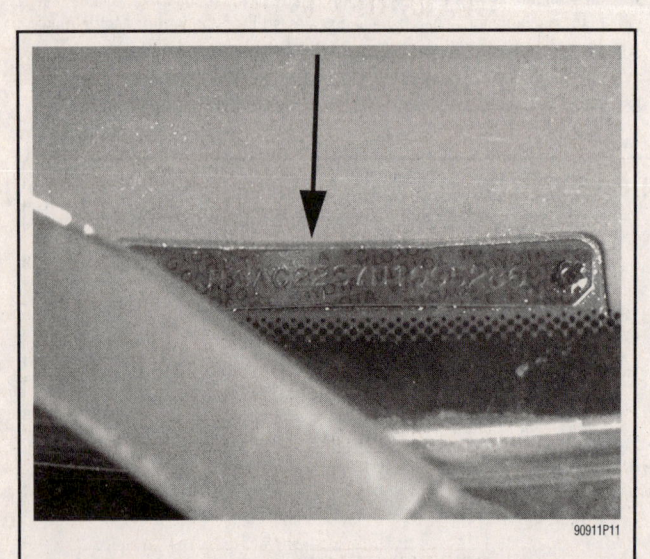

Fig. 32 The VIN plate is visible through the windshield

### VEHICLE IDENTIFICATION CHART

| Engine Code | | | | | | Model Year | |
|---|---|---|---|---|---|---|---|
| Engine Series (ID/VIN) | Engine Displacement Liters (cc) | Cubic Inches | No. of Cylinders | Fuel System | Eng. Mfg. | Code | Year |
| 2TZ-FE | 2.4 (2438) | 148 | 4 | EFI | Toyota | M | 91 |
| 2TZ-FZE | 2.4 (2438) | 148 | 4 | EFI | Toyota | N | 92 |
| | | | | | | P | 93 |
| | | | | | | R | 94 |
| | | | | | | S | 95 |
| | | | | | | T | 96 |
| | | | | | | V | 97 |

# GENERAL INFORMATION AND MAINTENANCE  1-15

## MODEL CODE

### TCR20 L – R F S G V A
###     1      2     3  4  5  6  7  8

**1 BASIC MODEL CODE**

| CODE | DRIVE TYPE | ENGINE | REAR SUSPENSION | BODY TYPE |
|---|---|---|---|---|
| TCR10 | 2WD | 2TZ-FZE | 4-Link Coil Spring | Wagon |
| TCR20 | All-Trac / 4WD | | | |

**2 STEERING WHEEL POSITION**
L : Left-Hand Drive

**3 BODY TYPE**
R : Standard Roof, 4-Door Wagon

**4 SEATING CAPACITY**
E : 7 (5 for models prior to '94 model)
F : 7

**5 GEARSHIFT TYPE**
S : 4-Speed Automatic, Column

**6 GRADE**
D : DLX
G : LE

**7 ENGINE SPECIFICATION**
V : DOHC with Supercharger and MFI

**8 DESTINATION**
A : U.S.A.
K : Canada

## MODEL LINE-UP

| DESTINATION | DRIVE TYPE | ENGINE TYPE | BODY TYPE | SEATING CAPACITY | GRADE | A340E | A340F |
|---|---|---|---|---|---|---|---|
| U.S.A. | 2WD | 2TZ-FZE | Wagon | 7 | DLX | TCR10L-RESDVA | |
| | | | | | LE | TCR10L-RFSGVA | |
| | All-Trac | | | | DLX | | TCR20L-RESDVA |
| | | | | | LE | | TCR20L-RFSGVA |
| Canada | 2WD | | | | DLX | TCR10L-RESDVK | |
| | | | | | LE | TCR10L-RFSGVK | |
| | 4WD | | | | LE | | TCR20L-RFSGVK |

Transmission: 4-Speed Automatic, Column

Fig. 33 The model code is helpful for obtaining the correct part

# 1-16 GENERAL INFORMATION AND MAINTENANCE

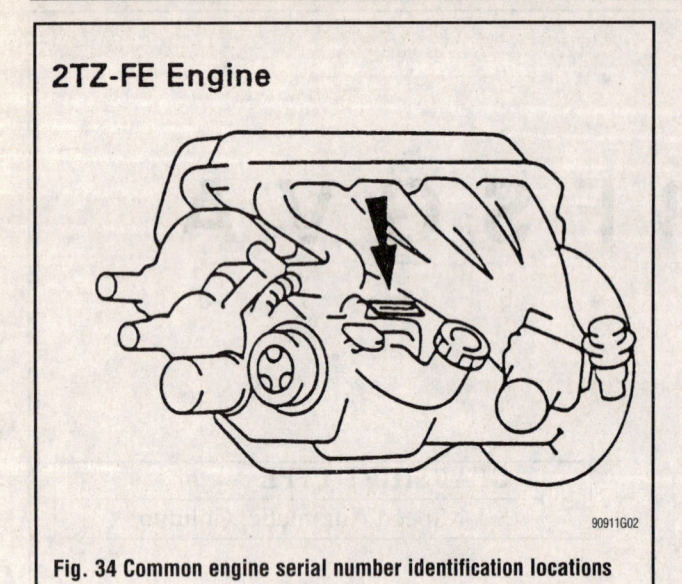

**2TZ-FE Engine**

Fig. 34 Common engine serial number identification locations

location will prevent having to scrape many years of grime off the engine when the number is finally needed.

The engine serial number consists of an engine series identification number, followed by a 6–digit production number.

## Transmission

The manual and automatic transmission identification number is stamped on the assembly housing. The following transmissions are offered in the Previa van:

- 1991–93 2WD—G59 5 speed manual
- 1991–93 4WD—G57 5 speed manual
- 1991–93 2WD—A46DE automatic
- 1991–93 4WD—A46DF automatic
- 1994–95 2TZ-FE 2WD—A46DE automatic
- 1994–95 2TZ-FE 4WD—A46DF automatic
- 1994–97 2TZ-FZE 2WD—A340E automatic
- 1994–97 2TZ-FZE 4WD—A340F automatic

## ENGINE IDENTIFICATION

| Year | Model | Engine Displacement Liters (cc) | Engine Series (ID/VIN) | Fuel System | No. of Cylinders | Engine Type |
|---|---|---|---|---|---|---|
| 1991 | Previa | 2.4 (2438) | 2TZ-FE | EFI | 4 | DOHC |
| 1992 | Previa | 2.4 (2438) | 2TZ-FE | EFI | 4 | DOHC |
| 1993 | Previa | 2.4 (2438) | 2TZ-FE | EFI | 4 | DOHC |
| 1994 | Previa | 2.4 (2438) | 2TZ-FE | EFI | 4 | DOHC |
|  | Previa | 2.4 (2438) | 2TZ-FZE | EFI | 4 | SC/DOHC |
| 1995 | Previa | 2.4 (2438) | 2TZ-FE | EFI | 4 | DOHC |
|  | Previa | 2.4 (2438) | 2TZ-FZE | EFI | 4 | SC/DOHC |
| 1996 | Previa | 2.4 (2438) | 2TZ-FZE | EFI | 4 | SC/DOHC |
| 1997 | Previa | 2.4 (2438) | 2TZ-FZE | EFI | 4 | SC/DOHC |

SC Supercharged

## GENERAL ENGINE SPECIFICATIONS

| Year | Engine ID/VIN | Engine Displacement Liters (cc) | Fuel System Type | Net Horsepower @ rpm | Net Torque @ rpm (ft. lbs.) | Bore x Stroke (in.) | Compression Ratio | Oil Pressure @ rpm |
|---|---|---|---|---|---|---|---|---|
| 1991 | 2TZ-FE | 2.4 (2438) | EFI | 138 @ 5000 | 154 @ 4000 | 3.74 x 3.39 | 9.3:1 | 36 @ 3000 |
| 1992 | 2TZ-FE | 2.4 (2438) | EFI | 138 @ 5000 | 154 @ 4000 | 3.74 x 3.39 | 9.3:1 | 36 @ 3000 |
| 1993 | 2TZ-FE | 2.4 (2438) | EFI | 138 @ 5000 | 154 @ 4000 | 3.74 x 3.39 | 9.3:1 | 36 @ 3000 |
| 1994 | 2TZ-FE | 2.4 (2438) | EFI | 138 @ 5000 | 154 @ 4000 | 3.74 x 3.39 | 9.3:1 | 36 @ 3000 |
|  | 2TZ-FZE | 2.4 (2438) | EFI | 161 @ 5000 | 201 @ 3600 | 3.74 x 3.39 | 8.9:1 | 36 @ 3000 |
| 1995 | 2TZ-FE | 2.4 (2438) | EFI | 138 @ 5000 | 154 @ 4000 | 3.74 x 3.39 | 9.3:1 | 36 @ 3000 |
|  | 2TZ-FZE | 2.4 (2438) | EFI | 161 @ 5000 | 201 @ 3600 | 3.74 x 3.39 | 8.9:1 | 36 @ 3000 |
| 1996 | 2TZ-FZE | 2.4 (2438) | EFI | 161 @ 5000 | 201 @ 3600 | 3.74 x 3.39 | 8.9:1 | 36 @ 3000 |
| 1997 | 2TZ-FZE | 2.4 (2438) | EFI | 161 @ 5000 | 201 @ 3600 | 3.74 x 3.39 | 8.9:1 | 36 @ 3000 |

# GENERAL INFORMATION AND MAINTENANCE 1-17

## ROUTINE MAINTENANCE AND TUNE-UP

**UNDERHOOD MAINTENANCE COMPONENT LOCATIONS**

1. Air cleaner assembly
2. Battery
3. Brake master cylinder reservoir
4. Power steering reservoir
5. Engine coolant reservoir
6. Engine oil tank reservoir
7. Windshield washer reservoir

# 1-18 GENERAL INFORMATION AND MAINTENANCE

**UNDERVEHICLE MAINTENANCE COMPONENT LOCATIONS**

1. Oil filter
2. Thermostat
3. Fuel filter
4. Carbon canister
5. Starter
6. Automatic transmission pan
7. Engine oil pan

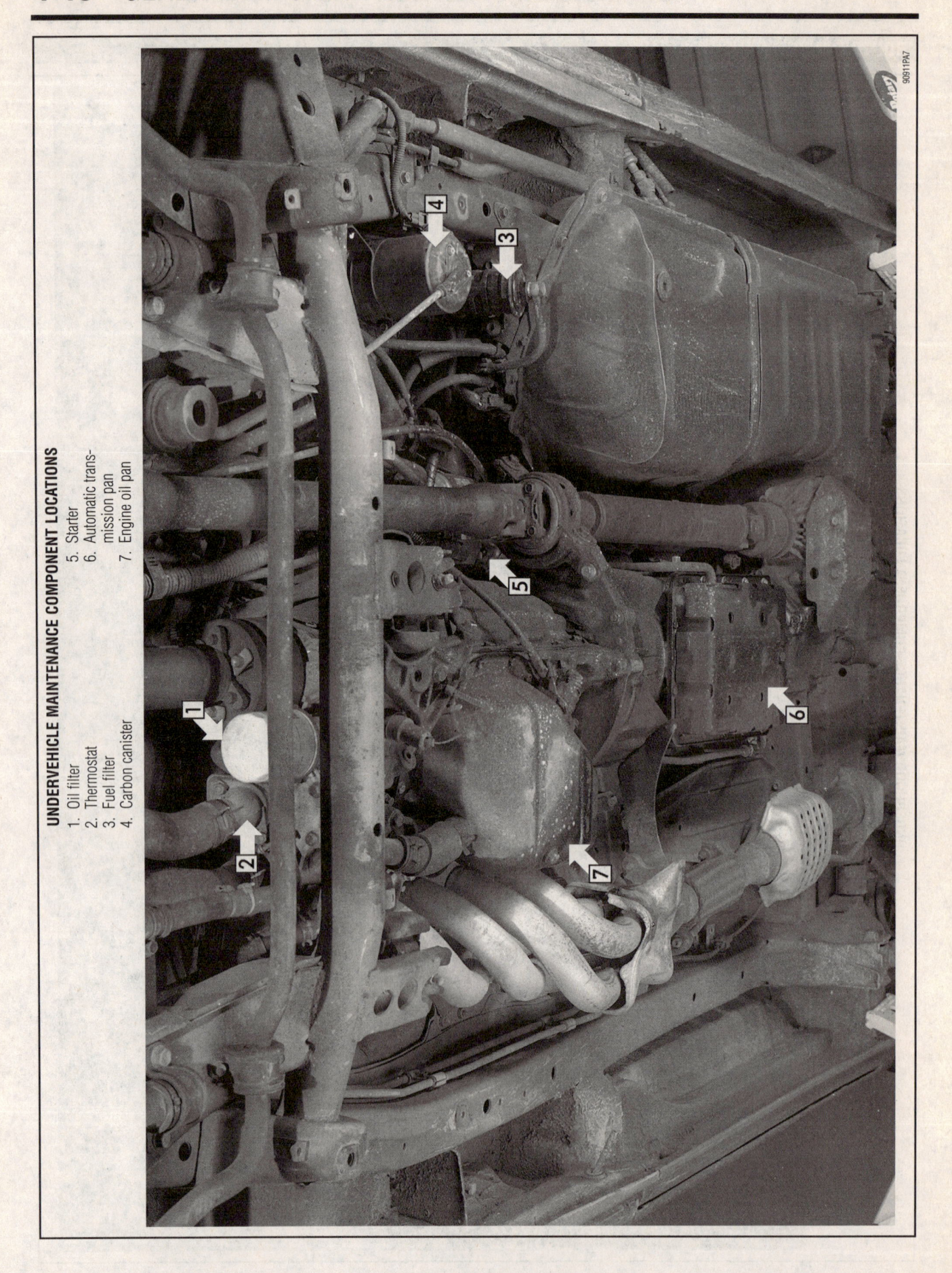

## GENERAL INFORMATION AND MAINTENANCE　1-19

Proper maintenance and tune-up is the key to long and trouble-free vehicle life, and the work can yield its own rewards. Studies have shown that a properly tuned and maintained vehicle can achieve better gas mileage than an out-of-tune vehicle. As a conscientious owner and driver, set aside a Saturday morning, say once a month, to check or replace items which could cause major problems later. Keep your own personal log to jot down which services you performed, how much the parts cost you, the date, and the exact odometer reading at the time. Keep all receipts for such items as engine oil and filters, so that they may be referred to in case of related problems or to determine operating expenses. As a do-it-yourselfer, these receipts are the only proof you have that the required maintenance was performed. In the event of a warranty problem, these receipts will be invaluable.

The literature provided with your vehicle when it was originally delivered includes the factory recommended maintenance schedule. If you no longer have this literature, replacement copies are usually available from the dealer. A maintenance schedule is provided later in this section, in case you do not

### Air Cleaner (Element)

REMOVAL & INSTALLATION

▶ See Figures 35, 36 and 37

1. Disconnect the Mass Air Flow (MAF) meter wiring.
2. Disconnect the A/C idle-up valve wiring.
3. Disconnect the 2 air hoses from the A/C idle-up valve.
4. Loosen the air cleaner hose clamp.
5. Unclasp the 4 clips, and remove the air cleaner cap and MAF meter assembly.
6. Lift the air cleaner element out of the housing, clean and replace as necessary.

**To install:**
7. Insert a new air cleaner element into the housing.
8. Place the air cleaner lid with MAF meter assembly into position and secure with the clips.
9. Attach all wiring to the air cleaner assembly.

Fig. 35 Unclasp the housing clips

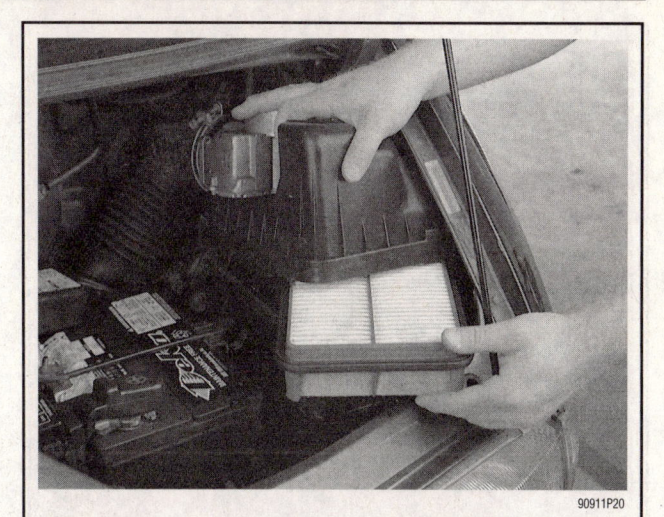

Fig. 36 Lift the air cleaner lid and extract the filter from the housing

Fig. 37 Inspect the air filter for dirt and damage

### Fuel Filter

REMOVAL & INSTALLATION

▶ See Figures 38 thru 44

➡ The fuel filter is located under the vehicle on the drivers side near the charcoal canister. Access is much easier from under the vehicle.

**※※ CAUTION**

Never smoke when working around or near gasoline. Make sure that there are no active ignition sources (heaters, electric motors or fans, welders, anything with sparks or open flame.) in the area. Have a fire extinguisher within arm's reach at all times.

# 1-20 GENERAL INFORMATION AND MAINTENANCE

Fig. 38 The fuel filter is mounted on the drivers side under the vehicle with two bolts

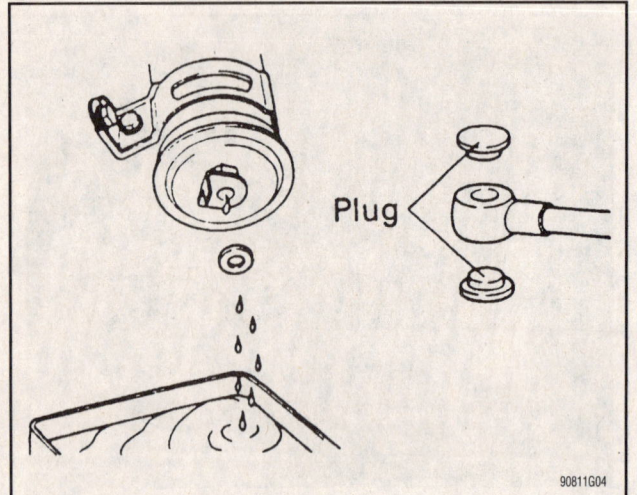

Fig. 39 Place a pan under the delivery pipe to catch the dripping fuel

Fig. 40 Use two wrenches to remove the fuel lines from the filter

Fig. 41 Lift the union and pipe

Fig. 42 Replace the sealing washers when installing the filter

Fig. 43 Unbolt the filter . . .

# GENERAL INFORMATION AND MAINTENANCE  1-21

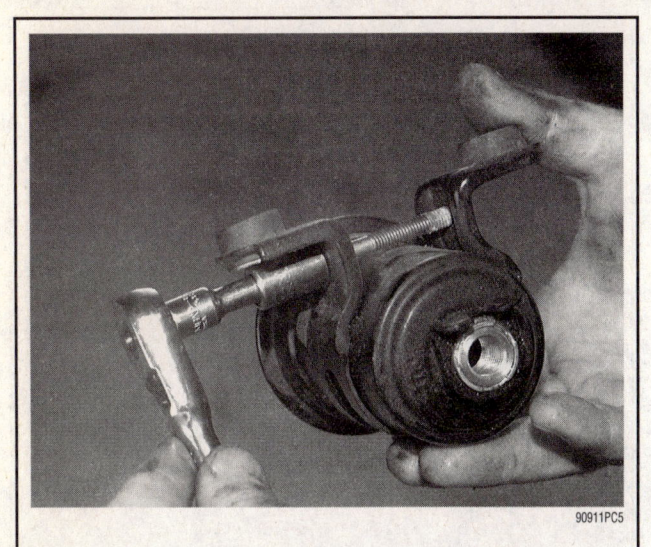

Fig. 44 If necessary, remove the bracket from the old filter

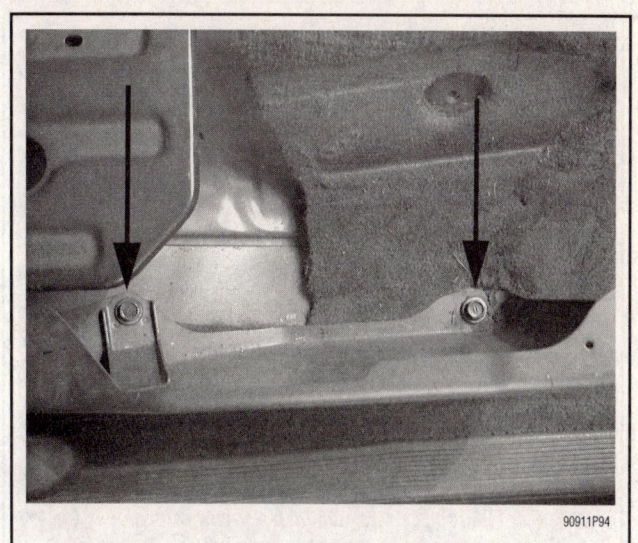

Fig. 45 Remove these two bolts for the seat leg

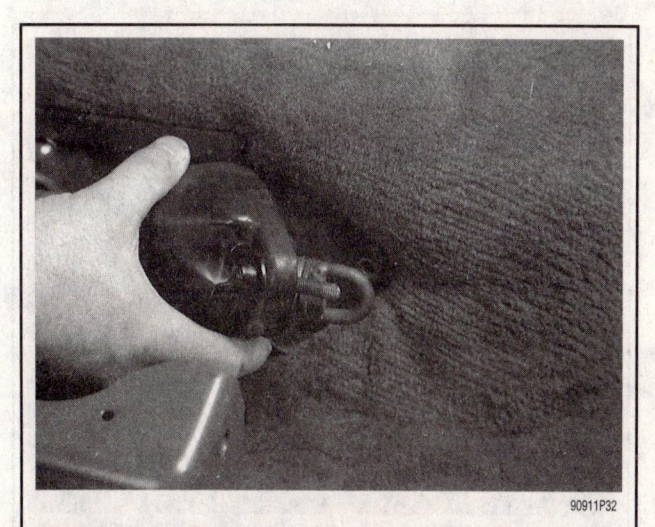

Fig. 46 Remove the bracket retaining the jack from the side of the seat . . .

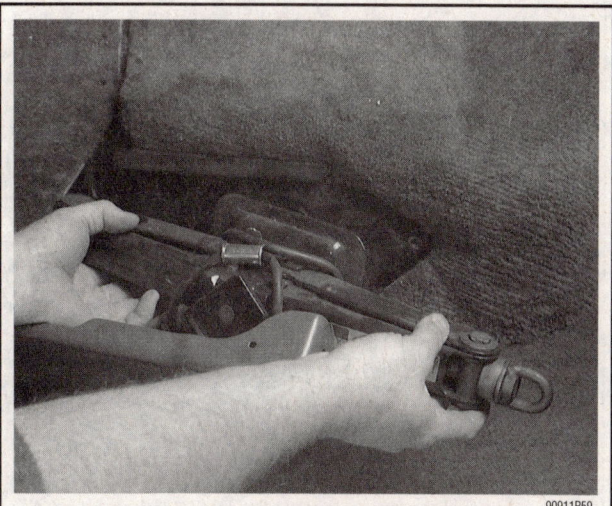

Fig. 47 . . . then lift out the jack

1. Unbolt the retaining screws and remove the protective shield from the fuel filter if equipped.
2. Place a pan under the delivery pipe to catch the dripping fuel and SLOWLY loosen the union bolt to bleed off the fuel pressure. The fuel system is under pressure. Release pressure slowly and contain spillage. Observe "no smoking/no open flame precautions".
3. Remove the union bolt and drain the remaining fuel.
4. Disconnect and plug the inlet line.
5. Unbolt and remove the fuel filter.

To install:

➡ When tightening the fuel line bolts to the fuel filter, you must use a torque wrench. The tightening torque is very important, as under or over tightening may cause fuel leakage. Insure that there is no fuel line interference and that there is sufficient space between the fuel lines and other components.

6. Coat the flare unit, union nut and all bolt threads with engine oil.
7. Hand-tighten the inlet line to the fuel filter.
8. Install the fuel filter and then tighten the inlet line nut to 22 ft. lbs. (29 Nm).
9. Reconnect the delivery pipe using new gaskets and then tighten the union bolt to 22 ft. lbs. (29 Nm).
10. Run the engine for a short period and check for any fuel leaks.
11. Install the protective shield if equipped.

## PCV Valve

The PCV valve regulates crankcase ventilation during various engine operating conditions. At high vacuum (idle speed and partial load range) it will open slightly and at low vacuum (full throttle) it will open fully. This causes vapor to be removed from the crankcase by the engine vacuum and then sucked into the combustion chamber where it is burned along with the fuel.

➡ The PCV system will not function properly unless the oil filler cap is tightly sealed. Check the gasket on the cap and be certain it is not leaking. Replace the cap or gasket or both if necessary to ensure proper sealing.

### REMOVAL & INSTALLATION

▶ See Figures 45 thru 55

1. Remove the right side engine cover to access the PCV valve as follows:
   a. Remove the 3 screws and scuff plate.
   b. Unbolt and disconnect the right side seat belt from the front floor panel.

## 1-22 GENERAL INFORMATION AND MAINTENANCE

Fig. 48 Remove the two bolts retaining the jack bracket

Fig. 49 Lift out the jack bracket and set it aside

Fig. 50 Lift up the carpet and expose the right side engine cover

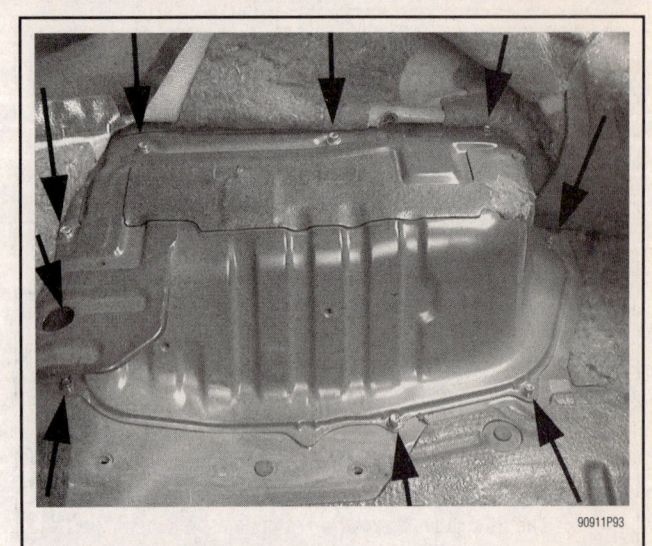

Fig. 51 Remove these 9 bolts . . .

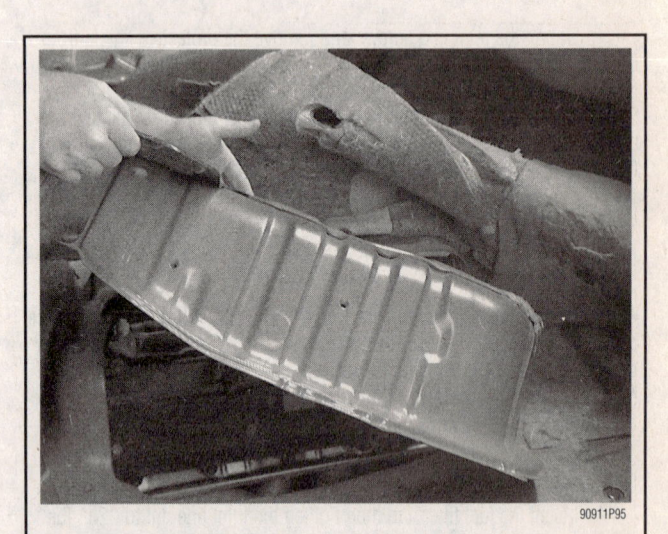

Fig. 52 . . . then lift the right engine cover and remove it from the vehicle

Fig. 53 Remove the hose clamp from the PCV valve

# GENERAL INFORMATION AND MAINTENANCE 1-23

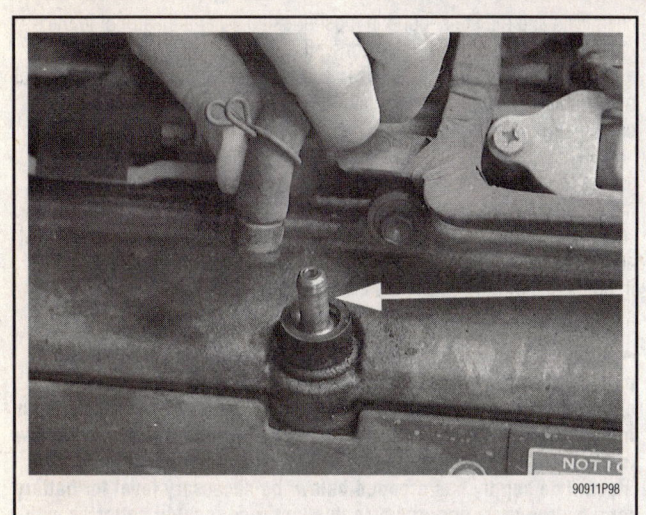

Fig. 54 The PCV valve is recessed in the grommet on the valve cover

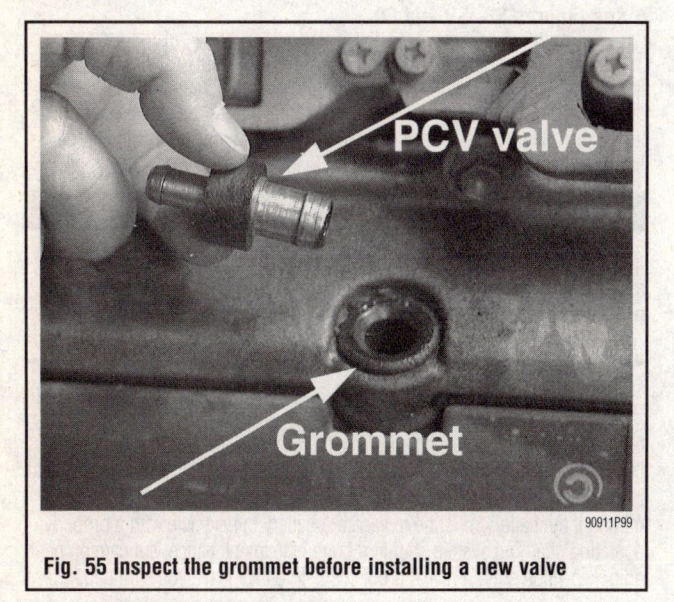

Fig. 55 Inspect the grommet before installing a new valve

  c. Remove the 4 bolts and right front seat.
  d. Remove the 2 bolts retaining the right front seat leg.
  e. Remove the jack and tool bag.
  f. Unbolt and extract jack holder.
  g. Remove the 9 bolts and right engine service cover.
2. Locate the PCV valve in the No. 2 cylinder head cover and remove it by pulling it upward.
3. Pull the PCV valve off the hose. If applicable, slide the clamp up the hose first.

**To install:**
4. Slip the hose back onto the proper end of the PCV valve. Secure the clamp if equipped.
5. Press the valve into the retaining grommet in the cylinder head cover.
6. Install the right side engine hole cover:
  a. Attach the cover and tighten the bolts to 10 ft lbs. (14 Nm).
  b. Install and tighten the jack holder bolts to 10 ft. lbs. (14 Nm). Install the tool bag and jack.
  c. Position and secure the right seat leg to 29 ft. lbs. (39 Nm).
  d. Position the seat assembly into the vehicle and secure with the mounting bolts. Tighten the bolts to 29 ft. lbs. (39 Nm).
  e. Attach the seat belt to the front floor panel and tighten to 31 ft. lbs. (42 Nm).
  f. Install the scuff plate and secure.

## Evaporative Canister (Charcoal Canister)

### SERVICING

▶ See Figure 56

The canister recycles the fuel vapor from the fuel tank. The activated charcoal element within the canister acts as a storage device for the fuel vapors at times when the engine operating conditions do not allow efficient burning of the vapors.

The only required service for the canister is inspection at the intervals specified in the Maintenance Chart at the end of this section. If the charcoal element is saturated, the entire canister will require replacement. Additional testing of the evaporative emission system can be found in Section 4.
1. Label and remove the vacuum lines leading to the canister.
2. Unfasten the retaining bolts from the canister.
3. Pull the lower hose off the tube attached to the lower portion of the canister.
4. Inspect the case for any cracking or damage.

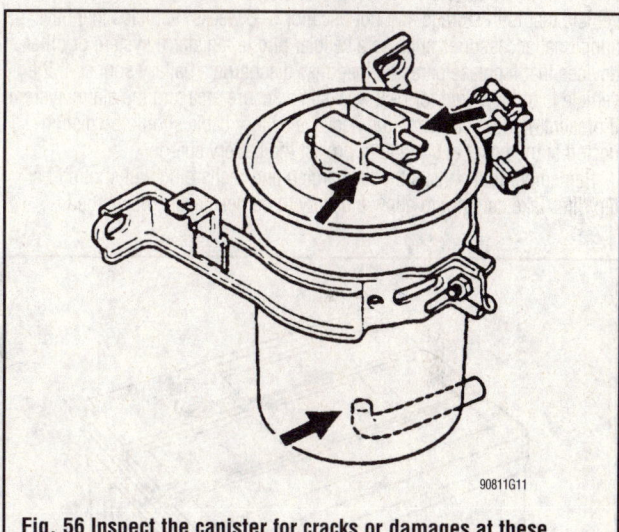

Fig. 56 Inspect the canister for cracks or damages at these points

## Battery

### PRECAUTIONS

Always use caution when working on or near the battery. Never allow a tool to bridge the gap between the negative and positive battery terminals. Also, be careful not to allow a tool to provide a ground between the positive cable/terminal and any metal component on the vehicle. Either of these conditions will cause a short circuit, leading to sparks and possible personal injury.

Do not smoke, have an open flame or create sparks near a battery; the gases contained in the battery are very explosive and, if ignited, could cause severe injury or death.

All batteries, regardless of type, should be carefully secured by a battery hold-down device. If this is not done, the battery terminals or casing may crack from stress applied to the battery during vehicle operation. A battery which is not secured may allow acid to leak out, making it discharge faster; such leaking corrosive acid can also eat away at components under the hood.

# 1-24  GENERAL INFORMATION AND MAINTENANCE

Always visually inspect the battery case for cracks, leakage and corrosion. A white corrosive substance on the battery case or on nearby components would indicate a leaking or cracked battery. If the battery is cracked, it should be replaced immediately.

## GENERAL MAINTENANCE

♦ See Figure 57

A battery that is not sealed must be checked periodically for electrolyte level. You cannot add water to a sealed maintenance-free battery (though not all maintenance-free batteries are sealed); however, a sealed battery must also be checked for proper electrolyte level, as indicated by the color of the built-in hydrometer "eye."

Always keep the battery cables and terminals free of corrosion. Check these components about once a year. Refer to the removal, installation and cleaning procedures outlined in this section.

Keep the top of the battery clean, as a film of dirt can help completely discharge a battery that is not used for long periods. A solution of baking soda and water may be used for cleaning, but be careful to flush this off with clear water. DO NOT let any of the solution into the filler holes. Baking soda neutralizes battery acid and will de-activate a battery cell.

Batteries in vehicles which are not operated on a regular basis can fall victim to parasitic loads (small current drains which are constantly drawing current from the battery). Normal parasitic loads may drain a battery on a vehicle that is in storage and not used for 6–8 weeks. Vehicles that have additional accessories such as a cellular phone, an alarm system or other devices that increase parasitic load may discharge a battery sooner. If the vehicle is to be stored for 6–8 weeks in a secure area and the alarm system, if present, is not necessary, the negative battery cable should be disconnected at the onset of storage to protect the battery charge.

Remember that constantly discharging and recharging will shorten battery life. Take care not to allow a battery to be needlessly discharged.

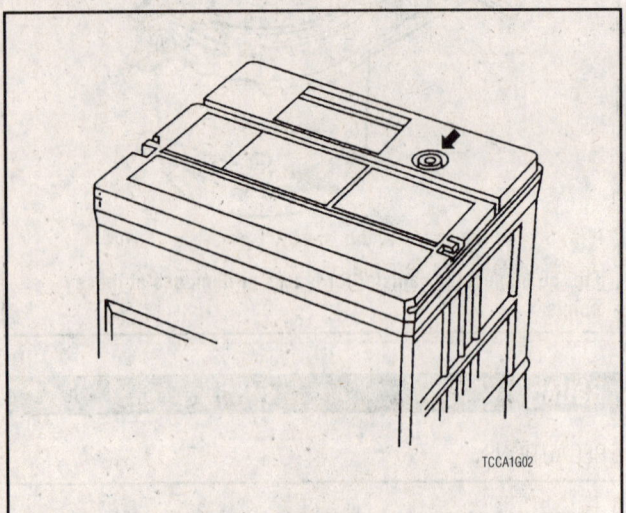

Fig. 57 A typical location for the built-in hydrometer on maintenance-free batteries

## BATTERY FLUID

Check the battery electrolyte level at least once a month, or more often in hot weather or during periods of extended vehicle operation. On non-sealed batteries, the level can be checked either through the case on translucent batteries or by removing the cell caps on opaque-cased types. The electrolyte level in each cell should be kept filled to the split ring inside each cell, or the line marked on the outside of the case.

If the level is low, add only distilled water through the opening until the level is correct. Each cell is separate from the others, so each must be checked and filled individually. Distilled water should be used, because the chemicals and minerals found in most drinking water are harmful to the battery and could significantly shorten its life.

If water is added in freezing weather, the vehicle should be driven several miles to allow the water to mix with the electrolyte. Otherwise, the battery could freeze.

Although some maintenance-free batteries have removable cell caps for access to the electrolyte, the electrolyte condition and level on all sealed maintenance-free batteries must be checked using the built-in hydrometer "eye." The exact type of eye varies between battery manufacturers, but most apply a sticker to the battery itself explaining the possible readings. When in doubt, refer to the battery manufacturer's instructions to interpret battery condition using the built-in hydrometer.

➡ Although the readings from built-in hydrometers found in sealed batteries may vary, a green eye usually indicates a properly charged battery with sufficient fluid level. A dark eye is normally an indicator of a battery with sufficient fluid, but one which may be low in charge. And a light or yellow eye is usually an indication that electrolyte supply has dropped below the necessary level for battery (and hydrometer) operation. In this last case, sealed batteries with an insufficient electrolyte level must usually be discarded.

### Checking the Specific Gravity

♦ See Figures 58, 59 and 60

A hydrometer is required to check the specific gravity on all batteries that are not maintenance-free. On batteries that are maintenance-free, the specific gravity is checked by observing the built-in hydrometer "eye" on the top of the battery case. Check with your battery's manufacturer for proper interpretation of its built-in hydrometer readings.

**※※ CAUTION**

**Battery electrolyte contains sulfuric acid. If you should splash any on your skin or in your eyes, flush the affected area with plenty of clear water. If it lands in your eyes, get medical help immediately.**

The fluid (sulfuric acid solution) contained in the battery cells will tell you many things about the condition of the battery. Because the cell plates must be kept submerged below the fluid level in order to operate, maintaining the fluid level is extremely important. And, because the specific gravity of the acid is an indication of electrical charge, testing the fluid can be an aid in determining if the battery must be replaced. A battery in a vehicle with a properly operating charging system should require little maintenance, but careful, periodic inspection should reveal problems before they leave you stranded.

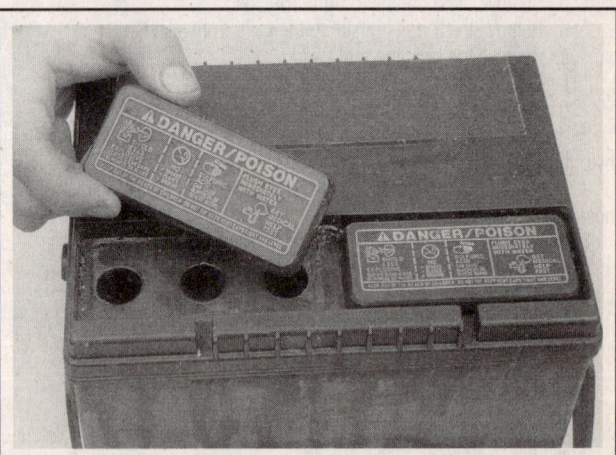

Fig. 58 On non-maintenance-free batteries, the fluid level can be checked through the case on translucent models; the cell caps must be removed on other models

# GENERAL INFORMATION AND MAINTENANCE 1-25

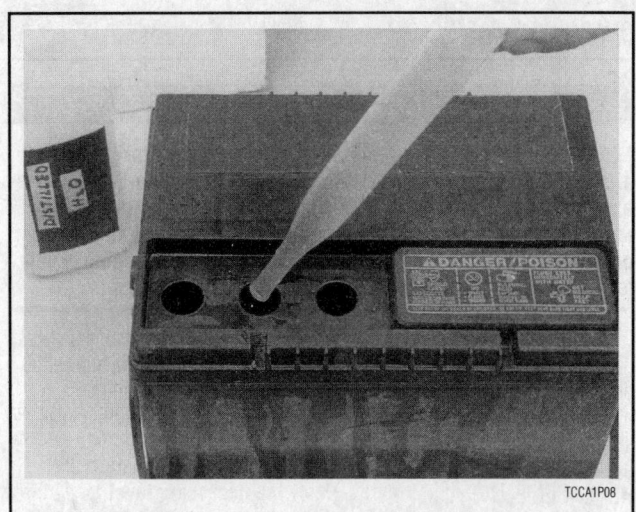

Fig. 59 If the fluid level is low, add only distilled water through the opening until the level is correct

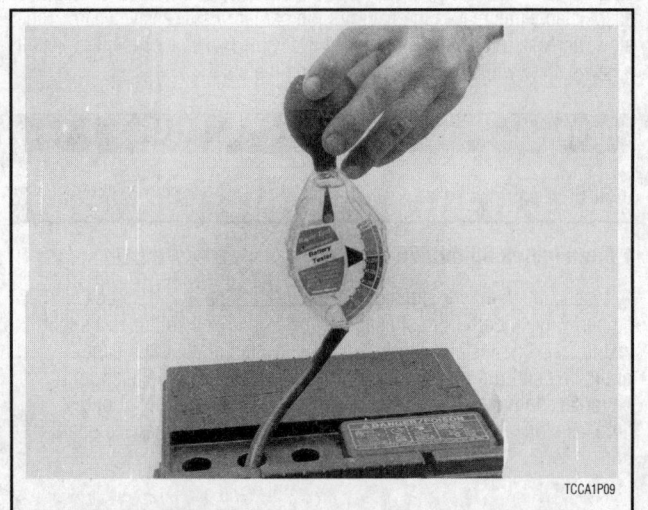

Fig. 60 Check the specific gravity of the battery's electrolyte with a hydrometer

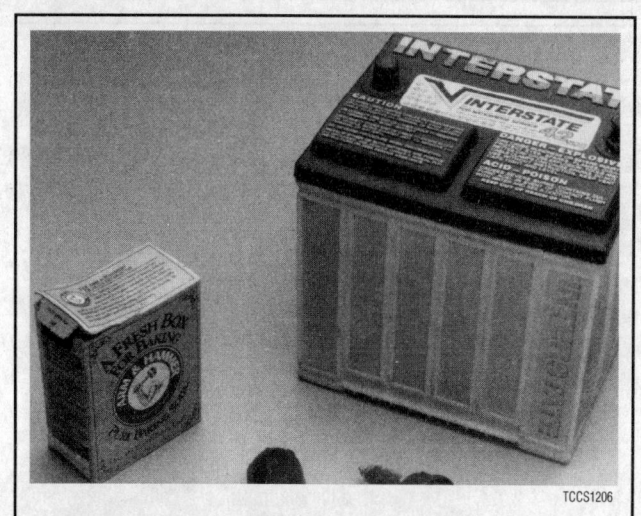

Fig. 61 Maintenance is performed with household items and with special tools like this post cleaner

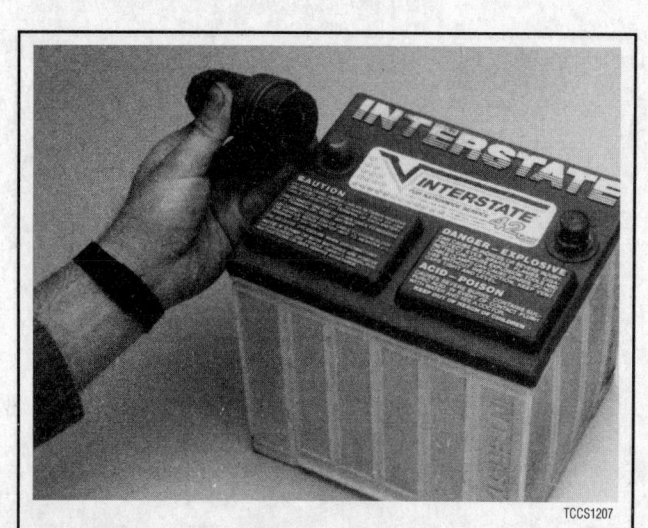

Fig. 62 The underside of this special battery tool has a wire brush to clean post terminals

Fig. 63 Place the tool over the battery posts and twist to clean until the metal is shiny

As stated earlier, the specific gravity of a battery's electrolyte level can be used as an indication of battery charge. At least once a year, check the specific gravity of the battery. It should be between 1.20 and 1.26 on the gravity scale. Most auto supply stores carry a variety of inexpensive battery testing hydrometers. These can be used on any non-sealed battery to test the specific gravity in each cell.

The battery testing hydrometer has a squeeze bulb at one end and a nozzle at the other. Battery electrolyte is sucked into the hydrometer until the float is lifted from its seat. The specific gravity is then read by noting the position of the float. If gravity is low in one or more cells, the battery should be slowly charged and checked again to see if the gravity has come up. Generally, if after charging, the specific gravity between any two cells varies more than 50 points (0.50), the battery should be replaced, as it can no longer produce sufficient voltage to guarantee proper operation.

## CABLES

▶ See Figures 61, 62, 63, 64 and 65

Once a year (or as necessary), the battery terminals and the cable clamps should be cleaned. Loosen the clamps and remove the cables, negative cable first. On batteries with posts on top, the use of a puller specially made for this

# 1-26 GENERAL INFORMATION AND MAINTENANCE

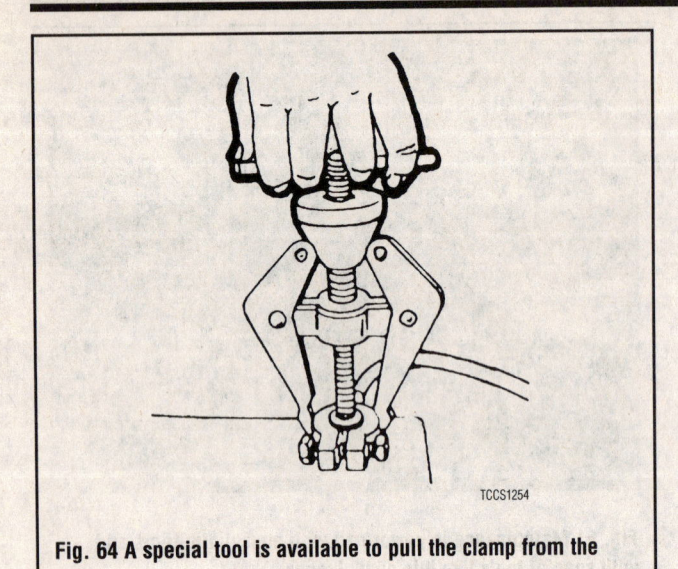

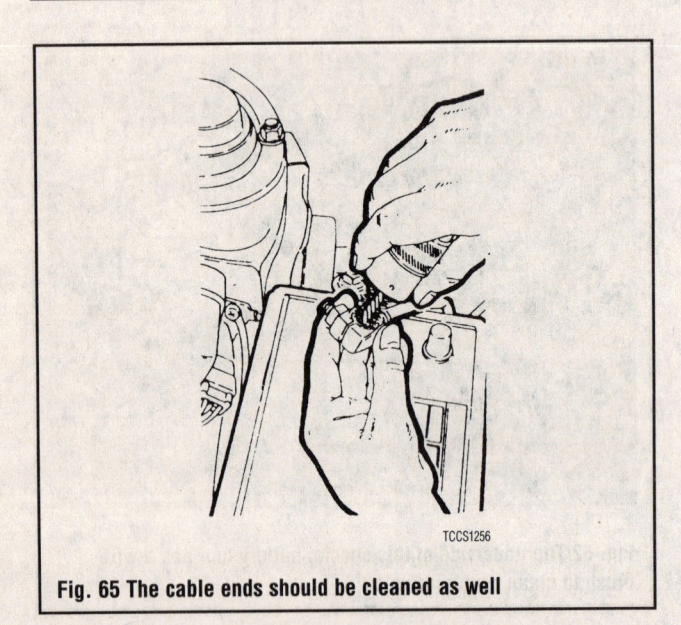

**Fig. 64 A special tool is available to pull the clamp from the post**

**Fig. 65 The cable ends should be cleaned as well**

purpose is recommended. These are inexpensive and available in most auto parts stores. Side terminal battery cables are secured with a small bolt.

Clean the cable clamps and the battery terminal with a wire brush, until all corrosion, grease, etc., is removed and the metal is shiny. It is especially important to clean the inside of the clamp thoroughly (an old knife is useful here), since a small deposit of foreign material or oxidation there will prevent a sound electrical connection and inhibit either starting or charging. Special tools are available for cleaning these parts, one type for conventional top post batteries and another type for side terminal batteries. It is also a good idea to apply some dielectric grease to the terminal, as this will aid in the prevention of corrosion.

After the clamps and terminals are clean, reinstall the cables, negative cable last; DO NOT hammer the clamps onto battery posts. Tighten the clamps securely, but do not distort them. Give the clamps and terminals a thin external coating of grease after installation, to retard corrosion.

Check the cables at the same time that the terminals are cleaned. If the cable insulation is cracked or broken, or if the ends are frayed, the cable should be replaced with a new cable of the same length and gauge.

## CHARGING

> ※※ **CAUTION**
>
> The chemical reaction which takes place in all batteries generates explosive hydrogen gas. A spark can cause the battery to explode and splash acid. To avoid serious personal injury, be sure there is proper ventilation and take appropriate fire safety precautions when connecting, disconnecting, or charging a battery and when using jumper cables.

A battery should be charged at a slow rate to keep the plates inside from getting too hot. However, if some maintenance-free batteries are allowed to discharge until they are almost "dead," they may have to be charged at a high rate to bring them back to "life." Always follow the charger manufacturer's instructions on charging the battery.

## REPLACEMENT

When it becomes necessary to replace the battery, select one with an amperage rating equal to or greater than the battery originally installed. Deterioration and just plain aging of the battery cables, starter motor, and associated wires makes the battery's job harder in successive years. The slow increase in electrical resistance over time makes it prudent to install a new battery with a greater capacity than the old.

## Belts

### INSPECTION

♦ See Figures 66 thru 75

Inspect the belts for signs of glazing or cracking. A glazed belt will be perfectly smooth from slippage, while a good belt will have a slight texture of fabric visible. Cracks will usually start at the inner edge of the belt and run outward. All worn or damaged drive belts should be replaced immediately. It is best to replace all drive belts at one time, as a preventive maintenance measure, during this service operation.

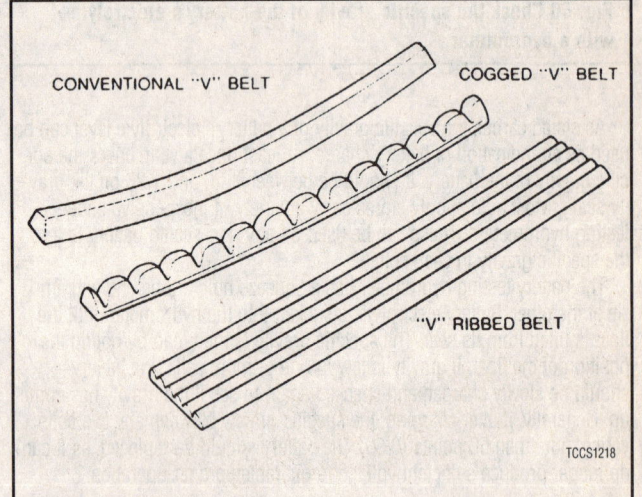

**Fig. 66 There are typically 3 types of accessory drive belts found on vehicles today**

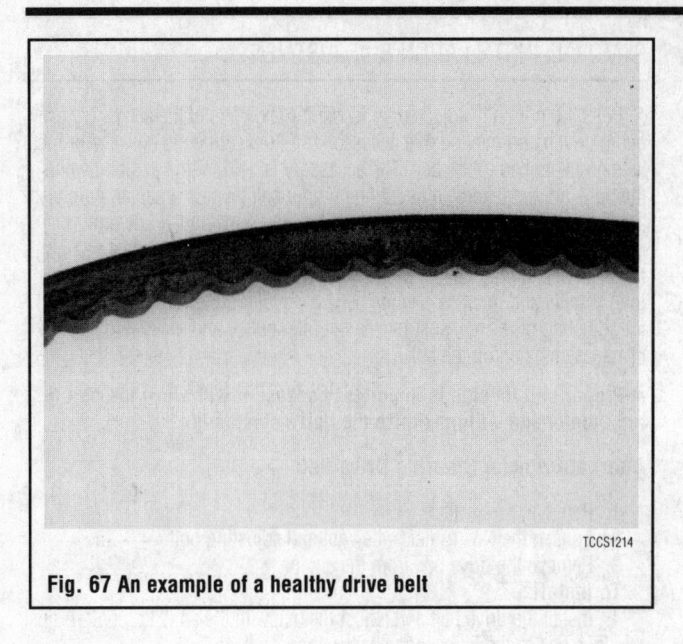

# GENERAL INFORMATION AND MAINTENANCE  1-27

Fig. 67 An example of a healthy drive belt

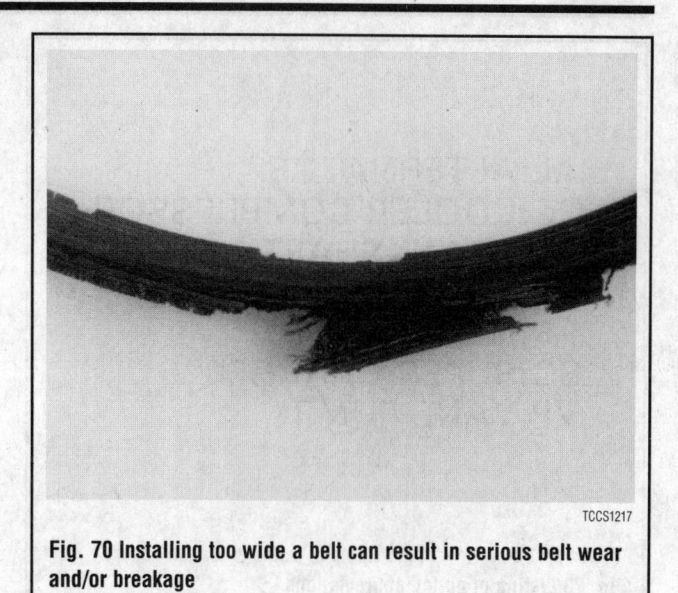

Fig. 68 Deep cracks in this belt will cause flex, building up heat that will eventually lead to belt failure

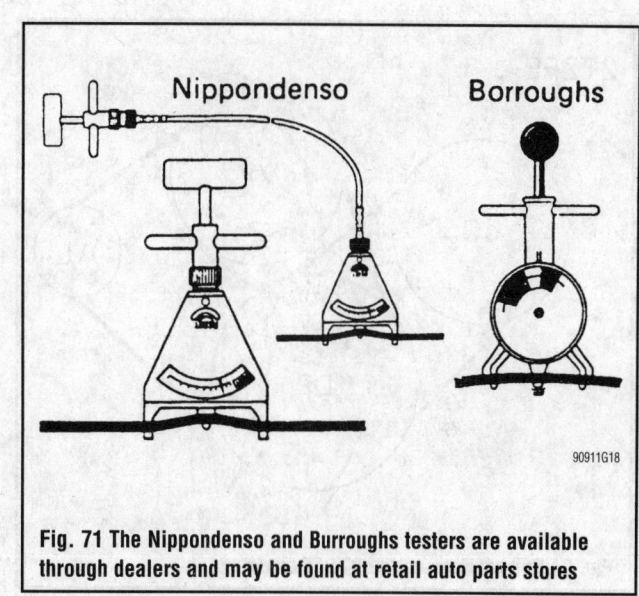

Fig. 69 The cover of this belt is worn, exposing the critical reinforcing cords to excessive wear

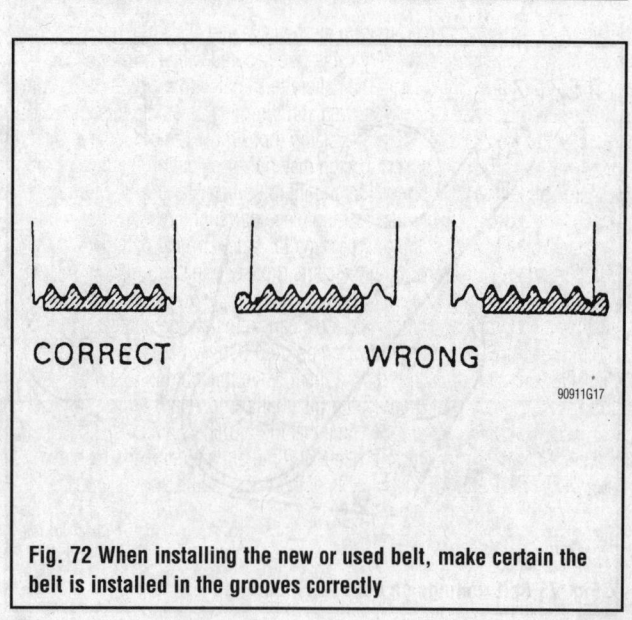

Fig. 70 Installing too wide a belt can result in serious belt wear and/or breakage

Fig. 71 The Nippondenso and Burroughs testers are available through dealers and may be found at retail auto parts stores

Fig. 72 When installing the new or used belt, make certain the belt is installed in the grooves correctly

# 1-28  GENERAL INFORMATION AND MAINTENANCE

```
AL: ALTERNATOR
CC: COOLER COMPRESSOR
CK: CRANKSHAFT
DP: DRIVE PULLEY
IP: IDLE PULLEY
SC: SUPER CHARGER
VP: VANE PUMP
```

Fig. 73 Listing of pulley abbreviations

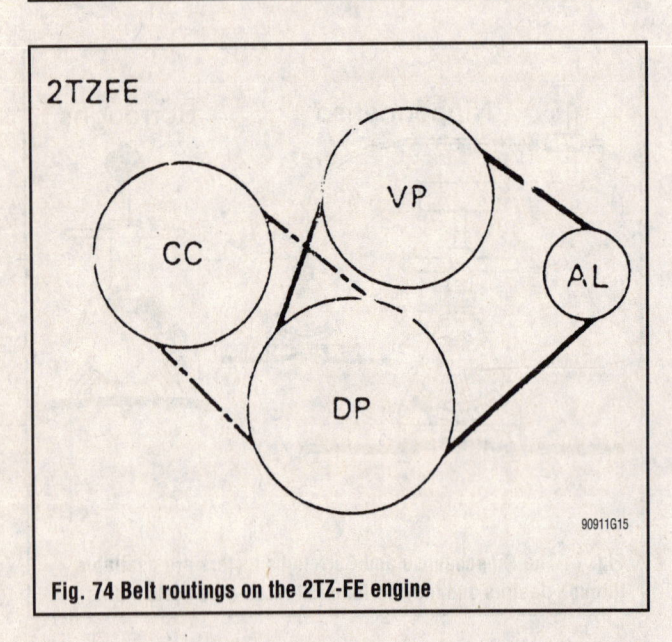

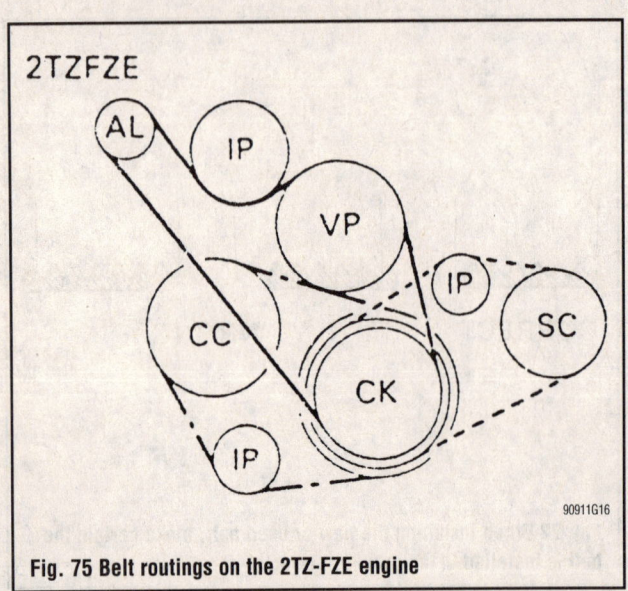

Fig. 74 Belt routings on the 2TZ-FE engine

Fig. 75 Belt routings on the 2TZ-FZE engine

## REMOVAL, INSTALLATION & ADJUSTMENT

Belts are normally adjusted by loosening the bolts of the accessory being driven and moving that accessory on its pivot points until the proper tension is applied to the belt. The accessory is held in this position while the bolts are tightened. To determine proper belt tension, you can purchase a belt tension gauge or simply use the deflection method. To determine deflection, press inward on the belt at the mid-point of its longest straight run. The belt should deflect (move inward) ⅜–½ in. (10–13mm). Some long V-belts and most serpentine belts have idler pulleys which are used for adjusting purposes. Just loosen the idler pulley and move it to take up or release tension on the belt.

➡ Proper belt tension is important because it will allow the belt to run quietly and will maximize the belt's service life.

### Alternator/Power Steering Drive Belt

1. Remove the air duct.
2. Loosen the No. 1 idler pulley nut and adjusting bolt.
3. Remove the drive belt from the engine.

**To install:**

4. Install the drive belt and adjust the belt with the adjusting bolt. Adjust the drive belt to the following specifications:
   - New belt—160–180 ft. lbs.
   - Used belt—115–135 ft. lbs.
5. Tighten the No. 1 idler pulley nut.
6. Install the air duct.

### Supercharger Drive Belt

1. Remove the alternator/power steering drive belt from the engine.
2. Loosen the No. 2 idler pulley nut and adjusting bolt.
3. Remove the drive belt from the supercharger.

**To install:**

4. Install the drive belt to the supercharger.
5. Tighten the adjusting bolt and adjust the drive belt to the following specifications:
   - New belt—160–180 ft. lbs.
   - Used belt—115–135 ft. lbs.
6. Install the alternator/power steering drive belt to the engine.

### A/C Compressor Drive Belt

1. Remove the alternator/power steering drive belt.
2. Remove the supercharger drive belt.
3. Raise and safely support the vehicle.
4. Loosen the idler pulley lock nut.
5. Loosen the adjusting bolt to the idler pulley and remove the compressor drive belt.

**To install:**

6. Install the compressor drive belt to the engine and tighten the adjusting bolt to the idler pulley. Drive belt tension is as follows:
   - New belt—145–185 lbs.
   - Used belt—110–150 lbs.
7. Tighten the idler pulley lock nut to 29 ft. lbs. (39 Nm).
8. Install the supercharger drive belt.
9. Install the alternator/power steering drive belt.
10. Recheck belt tension.

## Hoses

### INSPECTION

♦ See Figures 76, 77, 78 and 79

Upper and lower radiator hoses along with the heater hoses should be checked for deterioration, leaks and loose hose clamps at least every 15,000 miles (24,000 km). It is also wise to check the hoses periodically in early

# GENERAL INFORMATION AND MAINTENANCE 1-29

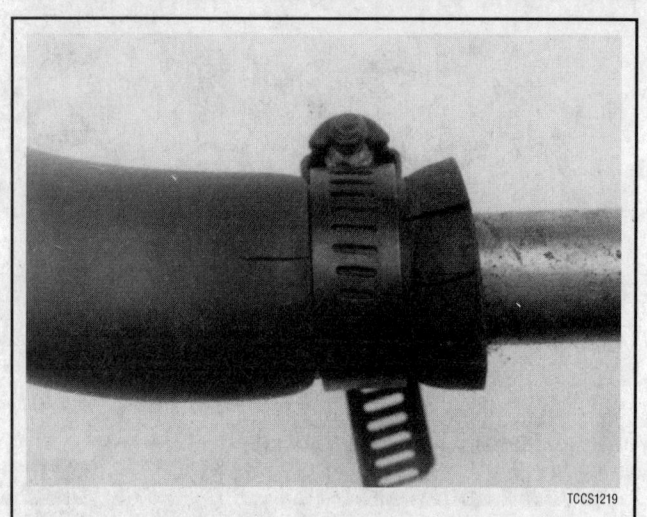

Fig. 76 The cracks developing along this hose are a result of age-related hardening

Fig. 77 A hose clamp that is too tight can cause older hoses to separate and tear on either side of the clamp

Fig. 78 A soft spongy hose (identifiable by the swollen section) will eventually burst and should be replaced

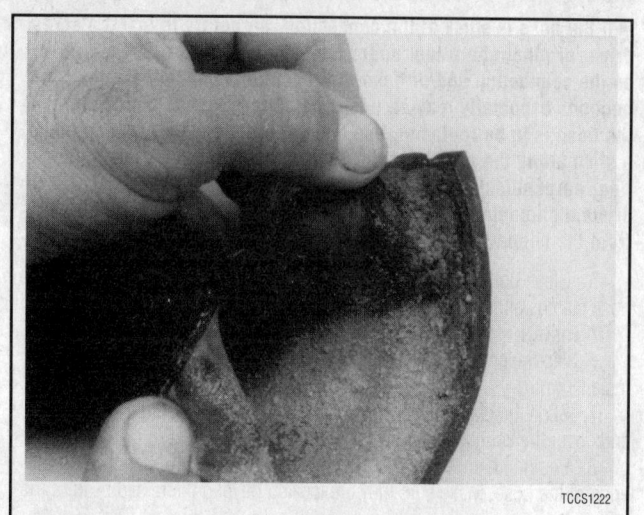

Fig. 79 Hoses are likely to deteriorate from the inside if the cooling system is not periodically flushed

spring and at the beginning of the fall or winter when you are performing other maintenance. A quick visual inspection could discover a weakened hose which might have left you stranded if it had remained unrepaired.

Whenever you are checking the hoses, make sure the engine and cooling system are cold. Visually inspect for cracking, rotting or collapsed hoses, and replace as necessary. Run your hand along the length of the hose. If a weak or swollen spot is noted when squeezing the hose wall, the hose should be replaced.

### REMOVAL & INSTALLATION

1. Remove the radiator pressure cap.

> **※ CAUTION**
>
> Never remove the pressure cap while the engine is running, or personal injury from scalding hot coolant or steam may result. If possible, wait until the engine has cooled to remove the pressure cap. If this is not possible, wrap a thick cloth around the pressure cap and turn it slowly to the stop. Step back while the pressure is released from the cooling system. When you are sure all the pressure has been released, use the cloth to turn and remove the cap.

2. Position a clean container under the radiator and/or engine draincock or plug, then open the drain and allow the cooling system to drain to an appropriate level. For some upper hoses, only a little coolant must be drained. To remove hoses positioned lower on the engine, such as a lower radiator hose, the entire cooling system must be emptied.

> **※ CAUTION**
>
> When draining coolant, keep in mind that cats and dogs are attracted by ethylene glycol antifreeze, and are quite likely to drink any that is left in an uncovered container or in puddles on the ground. This will prove fatal in sufficient quantity. Always drain coolant into a sealable container. Coolant may be reused unless it is contaminated or several years old.

3. Loosen the hose clamps at each end of the hose requiring replacement. Clamps are usually either of the spring tension type (which require pliers to squeeze the tabs and loosen) or of the screw tension type (which require screw or hex drivers to loosen). Pull the clamps back on the hose away from the connection.

4. Twist, pull and slide the hose off the fitting, taking care not to damage the neck of the component from which the hose is being removed.

# 1-30 GENERAL INFORMATION AND MAINTENANCE

➥ If the hose is stuck at the connection, do not try to insert a screwdriver or other sharp tool under the hose end in an effort to free it, as the connection and/or hose may become damaged. Heater connections especially may be easily damaged by such a procedure. If the hose is to be replaced, use a single-edged razor blade to make a slice along the portion of the hose which is stuck on the connection, perpendicular to the end of the hose. Do not cut deep so as to prevent damaging the connection. The hose can then be peeled from the connection and discarded.

5. Clean both hose mounting connections. Inspect the condition of the hose clamps and replace them, if necessary.

To install:

6. Dip the ends of the new hose into clean engine coolant to ease installation.

7. Slide the clamps over the replacement hose, then slide the hose ends over the connections into position.

8. Position and secure the clamps at least ¼ inch (6.35mm) from the ends of the hose. Make sure they are located beyond the raised bead of the connector.

9. Close the radiator or engine drains and properly refill the cooling system with the clean drained engine coolant or a suitable mixture of ethylene glycol coolant and water.

10. If available, install a pressure tester and check for leaks. If a pressure tester is not available, run the engine until normal operating temperature is reached (allowing the system to naturally pressurize), then check for leaks.

**✱✱ CAUTION**

If you are checking for leaks with the system at normal operating temperature, BE EXTREMELY CAREFUL not to touch any moving or hot engine parts. Once temperature has been reached, shut the engine OFF, and check for leaks around the hose fittings and connections which were removed earlier.

## CV-Boots

### INSPECTION

▶ See Figures 80 and 81

The CV (Constant Velocity) boots should be checked for damage each time the oil is changed and any other time the vehicle is raised for service. Toyota recommends this every 3750 miles (6000 km). These boots keep water, grime, dirt and other damaging matter from entering the CV-joints.

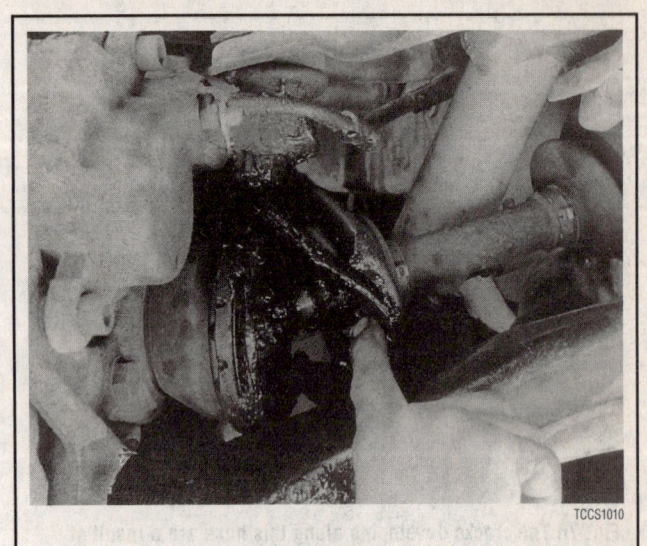

Fig. 81 A torn boot should be replaced immediately

Any of these could cause early CV-joint failure which can be expensive to repair. Heavy grease thrown around the inside of the front wheel(s) and on the brake caliper/drum can be an indication of a torn boot. Thoroughly check the boots for missing clamps and tears. If the boot is damaged, it should be replaced immediately. Please refer to Section 7 for procedures.

## Spark Plugs

▶ See Figure 82

All Toyota Previas are equipped from the factory with platinum tipped plugs. Platinum tipped plugs should always be used on your vehicle, never be gapped or cleaned and always replaced at 60,000 mile (96,000km) intervals.

A typical spark plug consists of a metal shell surrounding a ceramic insulator. A metal electrode extends downward through the center of the insulator and protrudes a small distance. Located at the end of the plug and attached to the side of the outer metal shell is the side electrode. The side electrode bends in at a 90⁻ angle so that its tip is just past and parallel to the tip of the center electrode. The distance between these two electrodes (measured in thousandths of an inch or hundredths of a millimeter) is called the spark plug gap.

The spark plug does not produce a spark but instead provides a gap

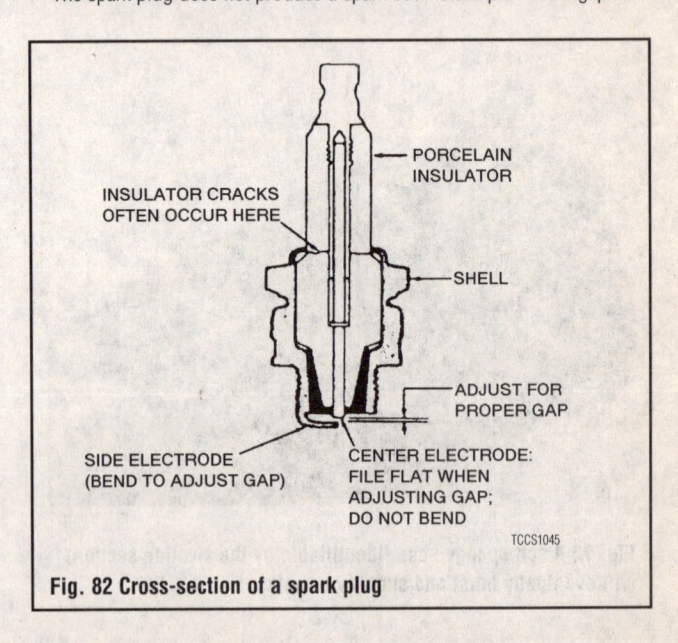

Fig. 80 CV-boots must be inspected periodically for damage

Fig. 82 Cross-section of a spark plug

# GENERAL INFORMATION AND MAINTENANCE  1-31

across which the current can arc. The coil produces anywhere from 20,000 to 50,000 volts (depending on the type and application) which travels through the wires to the spark plugs. The current passes along the center electrode and jumps the gap to the side electrode, and in doing so, ignites the air/fuel mixture in the combustion chamber.

## SPARK PLUG HEAT RANGE

▶ See Figure 83

Spark plug heat range is the ability of the plug to dissipate heat. The longer the insulator (or the farther it extends into the engine), the hotter the plug will operate; the shorter the insulator (the closer the electrode is to the block's cooling passages) the cooler it will operate. A plug that absorbs little heat and remains too cool will quickly accumulate deposits of oil and carbon since it is not hot enough to burn them off. This leads to plug fouling and consequently to misfiring. A plug that absorbs too much heat will have no deposits but, due to the excessive heat, the electrodes will burn away quickly and might possibly lead to preignition or other ignition problems. Preignition takes place when plug tips get so hot that they glow sufficiently to ignite the air/fuel mixture before the actual spark occurs. This early ignition will usually cause a pinging during low speeds and heavy loads.

The general rule of thumb for choosing the correct heat range when picking a spark plug is: if most of your driving is long distance, high speed travel, use a colder plug; if most of your driving is stop and go, use a hotter plug. Original equipment plugs are generally a good compromise between the 2 styles and most people never have the need to change their plugs from the factory-recommended heat range.

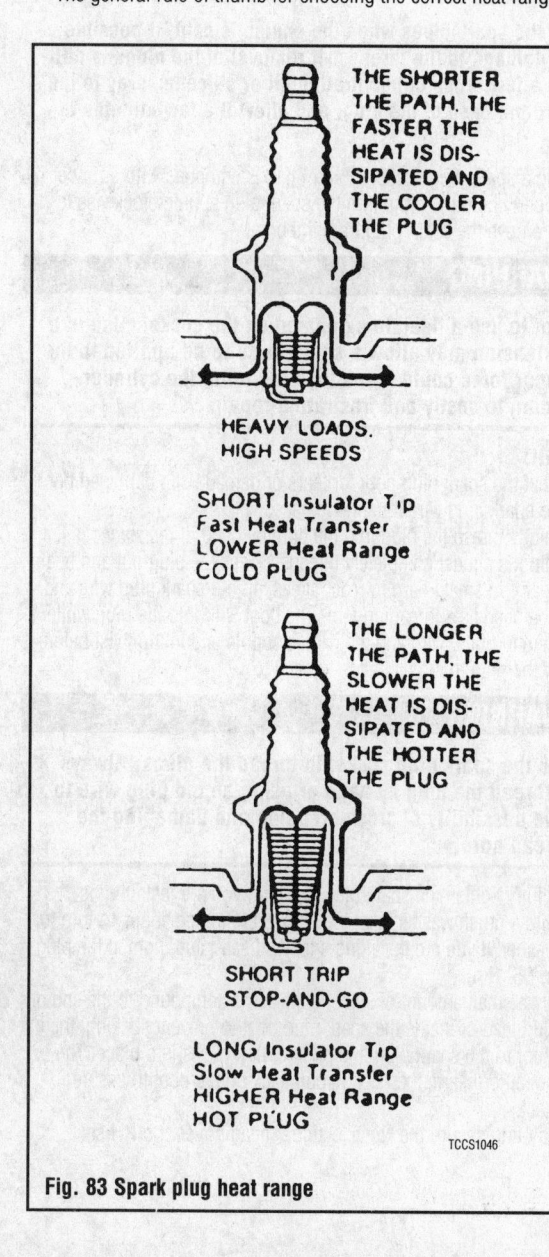

## REMOVAL & INSTALLATION

▶ See Figures 84, 85, 86, 87 and 88

A set of spark plugs on these models requires replacement at 100,000 miles (160,000 km). In normal operation plug gap increases about 0.001 in. (0.025mm) for every 2500 miles (4000 km). As the gap increases, the plug's voltage requirement also increases. It requires a greater voltage to jump the wider gap and about two to three times as much voltage to fire the plug at high speeds than at idle. The improved air/fuel ratio control of modern fuel injection combined with the higher voltage output of modern ignition systems will often allow an engine to run significantly longer on a set of standard spark plugs, but keep in mind that efficiency will drop as the gap widens (along with fuel economy and power).

When you're removing spark plugs, work on one at a time. Don't start by removing the plug wires all at once, because, unless you number them,

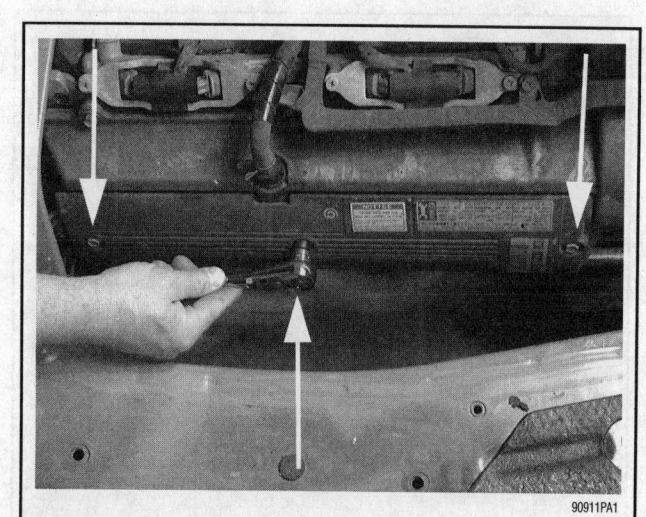

Fig. 83 Spark plug heat range

Fig. 84 Remove the 3 bolts retaining the No. 2 cylinder head cover

Fig. 85 Pull the cover off and set aside

# 1-32 GENERAL INFORMATION AND MAINTENANCE

**Fig. 86 Carefully twist and remove the spark plug wires**

**Fig. 87 A deep socket is required to access these plugs**

**Fig. 88 Check the condition of the spark plug. Replace as necessary**

they may become mixed up. Take a minute before you begin and number the wires with tape.

1. If the vehicle has been run recently, allow the engine to thoroughly cool.
2. Remove the RH seat and No. 2 cylinder head cover to access the spark plugs. To remove the seat perform the following:
   a. Remove the 3 screws and scuff plate.
   b. Remove the bolt and disconnect the RH seat belt from the front floor panel.
   c. Remove the 4 bolts and the RH front seat.
   d. Remove the 2 bolts and the RH front seat leg.
   e. Remove the 2 bolts and the jack holder.
   f. Remove the 9 bolts and the RH engine service cover.
3. Carefully twist the spark plug wire boot to loosen it, then pull upward and remove the boot from the plug. Be sure to pull on the boot and not on the wire, otherwise the connector located inside the boot may become separated.
4. Using compressed air, blow any water or debris from the spark plug well to assure that no harmful contaminants are allowed to enter the combustion chamber when the spark plug is removed. If compressed air is not available, use a rag or a brush to clean the area.

➡ Remove the spark plugs when the engine is cold, if possible, to prevent damage to the threads. If removal of the plugs is difficult, apply a few drops of penetrating oil or silicone spray to the area around the base of the plug, and allow it a few minutes to work.

5. Using a spark plug socket (16mm) that is equipped with a rubber insert to properly hold the plug, turn the spark plug counterclockwise to loosen and remove the spark plug from the bore.

**✳✳ WARNING**

**Be sure not to use a flexible extension on the socket. Use of a flexible extension may allow a shear force to be applied to the plug. A shear force could break the plug off in the cylinder head, leading to costly and frustrating repairs.**

To install:

6. Inspect the spark plug boot for tears or damage. If a damaged boot is found, the spark plug wire must be replaced.
7. Carefully thread the plug into the bore by hand. If resistance is felt before the plug is almost completely threaded, back the plug out and begin threading again. In small, hard to reach areas, an old spark plug wire and boot could be used as a threading tool. The boot will hold the plug while you twist the end of the wire and the wire is supple enough to twist before it would allow the plug to crossthread.

**✳✳ WARNING**

**Do not use the spark plug socket to thread the plugs. Always carefully thread the plug by hand or using an old plug wire to prevent the possibility of crossthreading and damaging the cylinder head bore.**

8. Carefully tighten the spark plug. the plug you are installing is equipped with a crush washer, seat the plug, then tighten about ¼ turn to crush the washer. If you are installing a tapered seat plug, tighten the plug to 14 ft. lbs. (20 Nm).
9. Apply a small amount of silicone dielectric compound to the end of the spark plug lead or inside the spark plug boot to prevent sticking, then install the boot to the spark plug and push until it clicks into place. The click may be felt or heard, then gently pull back on the boot to assure proper contact.
10. Install and secure the No. 2 cylinder head cover and RH seat.

# GENERAL INFORMATION AND MAINTENANCE 1-33

a. Tighten the bolts to the following specifications:
- Service hole cover bolts—10 ft. lbs. (14 Nm)
- Jack holder—10 ft. lbs. (14 Nm)
- RH seat leg—29 ft. lbs. (39 Nm)
- RH seat—29 ft. lbs. (39 Nm)
- RH seat belt-to-floor pan—31 ft. lbs. (42 Nm)

## INSPECTION & GAPPING

▶ See Figure 89

All Toyota Previas are equipped from the factory with platinum tipped plugs. Platinum tipped plugs should always be used on your vehicle and

**A normally worn** spark plug should have light tan or gray deposits on the firing tip.

**A carbon fouled** plug, identified by soft, sooty, black deposits, may indicate an improperly tuned vehicle. Check the air cleaner, ignition components and engine control system.

This spark plug has been **left in the engine too long,** as evidenced by the extreme gap- Plugs with such an extreme gap can cause misfiring and stumbling accompanied by a noticeable lack of power.

**An oil fouled** spark plug indicates an engine with worn poston rings and/or bad valve seals allowing excessive oil to enter the chamber.

**A physically damaged** spark plug may be evidence of severe detonation in that cylinder. Watch that cylinder carefully between services, as a continued detonation will not only damage the plug, but could also damage the engine.

**A bridged or almost bridged** spark plug, identified by a build-up between the electrodes caused by excessive carbon or oil build-up on the plug.

Fig. 89 Inspect the spark plugs to determine engine running conditions

# 1-34 GENERAL INFORMATION AND MAINTENANCE

never be gapped or cleaned. Inspect the plugs for damage and deposits. It can give you a good idea as to how well your engine is running.

## Spark Plug Wires

### TESTING

♦ See Figure 90

At every tune-up/inspection, visually check the spark plug cables for burns cuts, or breaks in the insulation. Check the boots and the nipples on the distributor cap and/or coil. Replace any damaged wiring.

Every 50,000 miles (80,000 Km) or 60 months, the resistance of the wires should be checked with an ohmmeter. Wires with excessive resistance will cause misfiring, and may make the engine difficult to start in damp weather.

Using an ohmmeter, measure the resistance of the plug wire. Place the negative terminal of the ohmmeter on the cap end of the wire and the positive terminal end on the plug end. Maximum resistance should be 25 kilometer per wire. If the resistance is not within specifications, it is advisable to replace all the plug wires as a set.

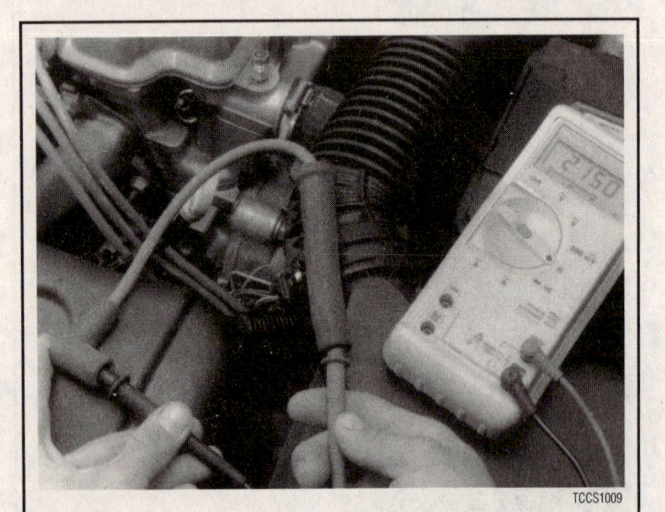

Fig. 90 Checking individual plug wire resistance with a digital ohmmeter

## Distributor Cap and Rotor

### REMOVAL & INSTALLATION

♦ See Figures 91, 92, 93, 94 and 95

1. Remove the RH seat and No. 2 cylinder head cover.
   a. Remove the 3 screws and scuff plate.
   b. Remove the bolt and disconnect the RH seat belt from the front floor panel.
   c. Remove the 4 bolts and the RH front seat.
   d. Remove the 2 bolts and the RH front seat leg.
   e. Remove the 2 bolts and the jack holder.
   f. Remove the 9 bolts and the RH engine service cover.
2. Label and disconnect the spark plug wires from the distributor cap.
3. Unscrew the retainers and remove the cap from the distributor.
4. Remove the screw from the rotor and pull it off.

**To install:**

5. Position the rotor on the distributor, and tighten the retaining screws.
6. Place the cap into position and secure with the retaining screws.

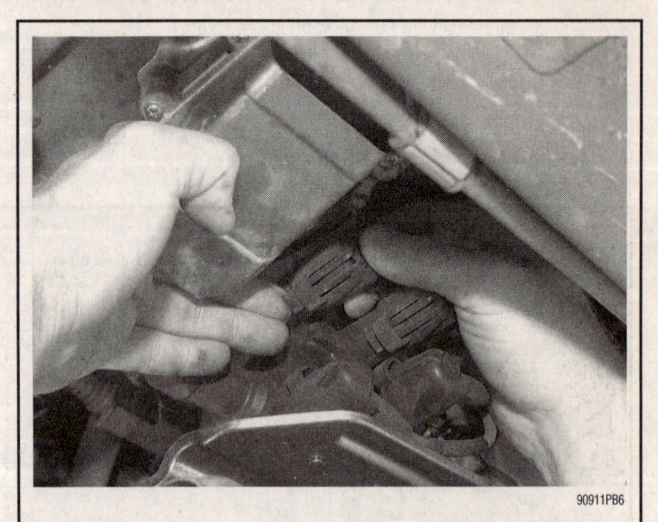

Fig. 91 Release the clip on each wire to remove them from the cap

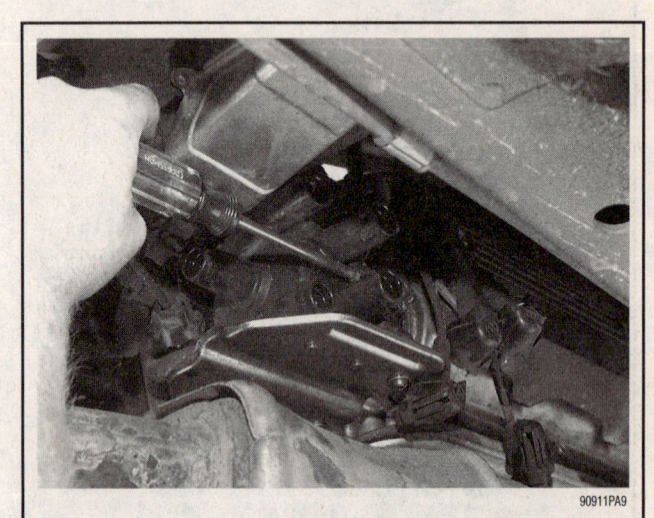

Fig. 92 Unscrew the retainers and remove the cap from the distributor

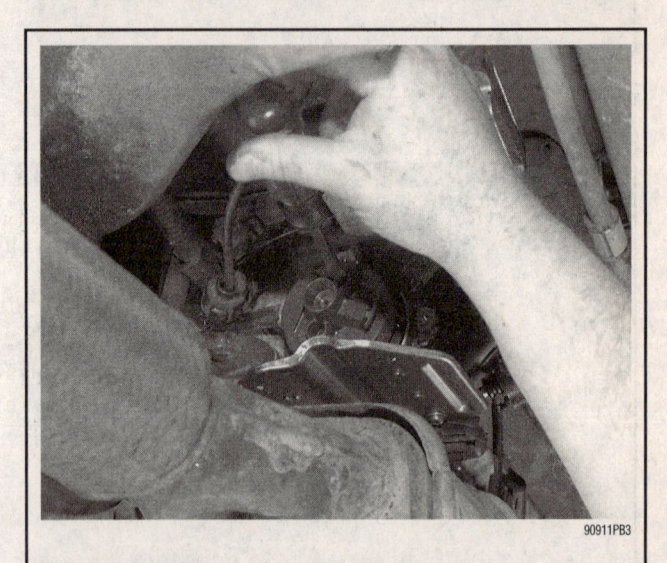

Fig. 93 Remove the screw and remove the rotor

# GENERAL INFORMATION AND MAINTENANCE   1-35

Fig. 94 Be sure to place the wires in the correct locations

Fig. 96 Check the inside of the cap for cracks, burns or wear

Fig. 95 Insert the coil wire last and make sure it is secure

Fig. 97 Inspect the rotor tip for burning

7. Connect the spark plug wires in their correct locations.
8. Install and secure the No. 2 cylinder head cover and RH seat.
   a. Tighten the bolts to the following specifications:
- Service hole cover bolts—10 ft. lbs. (14 Nm)
- Jack holder—10 ft. lbs. (14 Nm)
- RH seat leg—29 ft. lbs. (39 Nm)
- RH seat—29 ft. lbs. (39 Nm)
- RH seat belt-to-floor pan—31 ft. lbs. (42 Nm)
9. Start the vehicle and check for proper operation.

## INSPECTION

▶ See Figures 96 and 97

When inspecting a cap and rotor, look for signs of cracks, carbon tracking, burns and wear. The inside of the cap may be burnt or have wear on the carbon ends. On the rotor, look at the tip for burning and excessive wear.

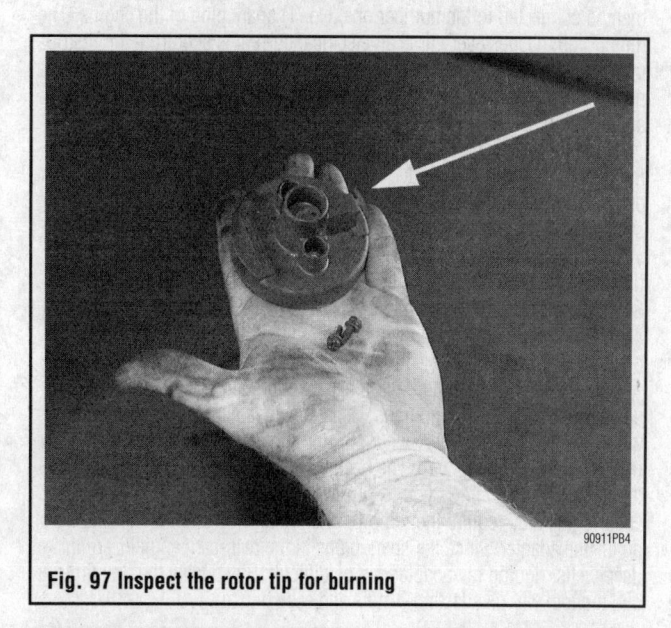

### Ignition Timing

## GENERAL INFORMATION

Ignition timing is the measurement (in degrees) of crankshaft position at the instant the spark plug fires. Ignition timing is adjusted by loosening the distributor locking device and turning the distributor in the engine.

It takes a fraction of a second for the spark from the plug to completely ignite the mixture in the cylinder. Because of this, the spark plug must fire before the piston reaches TDC (top dead center, the highest point in its travel), if the mixture is to be completely ignited as the piston passes TDC. This measurement is given in degrees (of crankshaft rotation) before the piston reaches top dead center (BTDC). If the ignition timing setting for your engine is 10° BTDC, this means that the spark plug must fire at a time when the piston for that cylinder is 10° before top dead center of its compression stroke. However, this only holds true while your engine is at idle speed.

# 1-36 GENERAL INFORMATION AND MAINTENANCE

As you accelerate from idle, the speed of your engine (rpm) increases. The increase in rpm means that the pistons are now traveling up and down much faster. Because of this, the spark plugs will have to fire even sooner if the mixture is to be completely ignited as the piston passes TDC. To accomplish this, the distributor incorporates means to advance the timing of the spark as the engine speed increases.

On fuel injected vehicles there is no centrifugal advance or vacuum unit to advance the timing. All engine timing changes are controlled electronically by the ECU. This solid state "brain" ECU receives data from many sensors and commands changes in spark timing based on immediate driving conditions. This instant response allows the engine to be kept at peak performance and economy throughout the driving cycle. Basic timing and idle speed can still be checked and adjusted on these engines.

If the ignition timing is set too far advanced (BTDC), the ignition and expansion of the air/fuel mixture in the cylinder will try to force the piston down while it is still traveling upward. This causes engine ping, a sound which resembles marbles being dropped into an empty tin can. If the ignition timing is too far retarded (after, or ATDC), the piston will have already started down on the power stroke when the air/fuel mixture ignites and expands. This will cause the piston to be forced down only a portion of its travel. This results in poor engine performance and lack of power.

Ignition timing adjustment is checked with a timing light. This instrument is connected to the number one (No. 1) spark plug of the engine. The timing light flashes every time an electrical current is sent from the distributor through the No. 1 spark plug wire to the spark plug. The crankshaft pulley and the front cover of the engine are marked with a timing pointer and a timing scale.

When the timing pointer is aligned with the 0 mark on the timing scale, the piston in the No. 1 cylinder is at TDC of it compression stroke. With the engine running, and the timing light aimed at the timing pointer and timing scale, the stroboscopic (periodic) flashes from the timing light will allow you to check the ignition timing setting of the engine. The timing light flashes every time the spark plug in the No. 1 cylinder of the engine fires. Since the flash from the timing light makes the crankshaft pulley seem to stand still for a moment, you will be able to read the exact position of the piston in the No. 1 cylinder on the timing scale on the front of the engine.

If you're buying a timing light, make sure the unit you select is rated for electronic or solid-state ignitions. Generally, these lights have two wires which connect to the battery with alligator clips and a third wire which connects to the No. 1 plug wire. The best lights have an inductive pick-up on the third wire; this allows you to simply clip the small box over the wire. Older lights may require the removal of the plug wire and the installation of an in-line adapter. Since the spark plugs in the twin-cam engines are in deep wells, rigging the adapter can be difficult. Buy quality the first time and the tool will give lasting results and ease of use.

## INSPECTION & ADJUSTMENT

### 2TZ-FE and 1991–95 Models

♦ See Figures 98 thru 103

This service procedure is for setting base ignition timing. Refer to underhood emission sticker for any additional service procedure steps and/or specifications.

These engines require a tachometer hook-up to the check connector—see illustrations. NEVER allow the tachometer terminal to become grounded; severe and expensive damage can occur to the coil and/or igniter.

Some tachometers are not compatible with this ignition system, confirm the compatibility of your unit before using.

1. Warm the engine to normal operating temperature. Turn off all electrical accessories. Do not attempt to check timing specification or idle speed on a cold engine.

2. Connect a tachometer (connect the tachometer (+) terminal to the terminal IG- of the check connector) and check the engine idle speed to be sure it is within the specification given in the Tune-Up Specifications chart or underhood emission sticker.

3. Remove the cap on the diagnostic check connector. Using a small jumper wire or Special Service Tool SST 09843-18020, short terminals TE1 (test terminal No. 1) and E1 (earth-ground) together.

4. If the timing marks are difficult to see, shut the engine **OFF** and use a dab of paint or chalk to make them more visible.

5. Connect the timing light power source terminal to terminal 30 of the starter and test probe to the No. 1 spark plug wire (light blue).

6. Start the engine and use the timing light to observe the timing marks. With the jumper wire in the check connector the timing should be 5° BTDC (refer to underhood emission sticker as necessary) with the engine fully warmed up (at correct idle speed) and the transmission in correct position. If the timing is not correct, loosen the bolts at the distributor just enough so that the distributor can be turned. Turn the distributor to

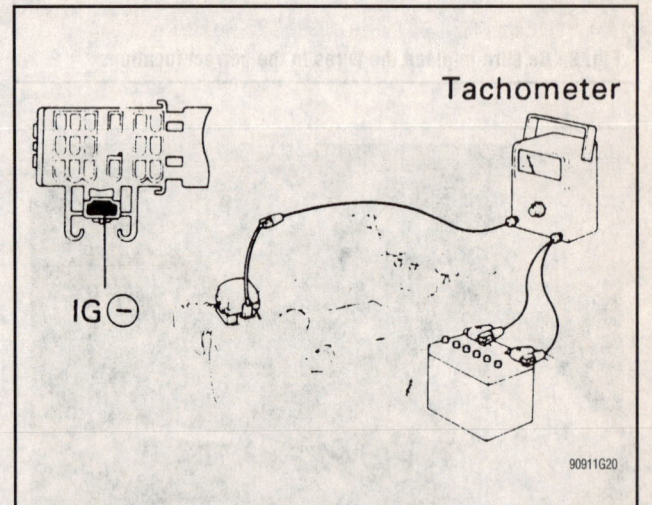

Fig. 98 Attach the tachometer to the battery and check connector terminal IG—1991–93 models

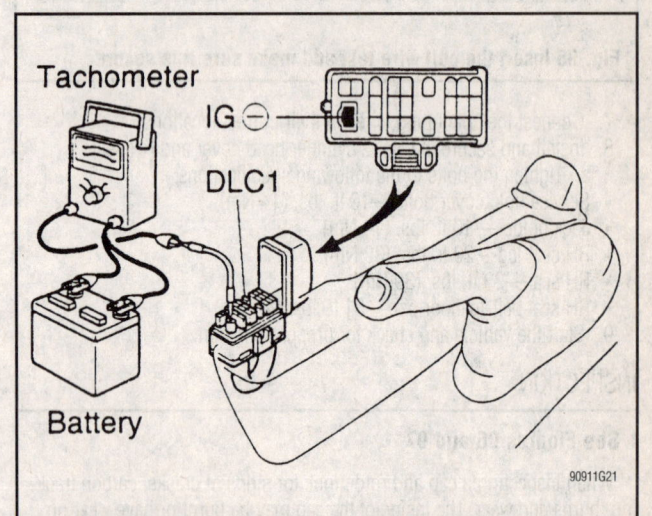

Fig. 99 Attach the tachometer to the battery and check connector terminal IG—1994–95 models

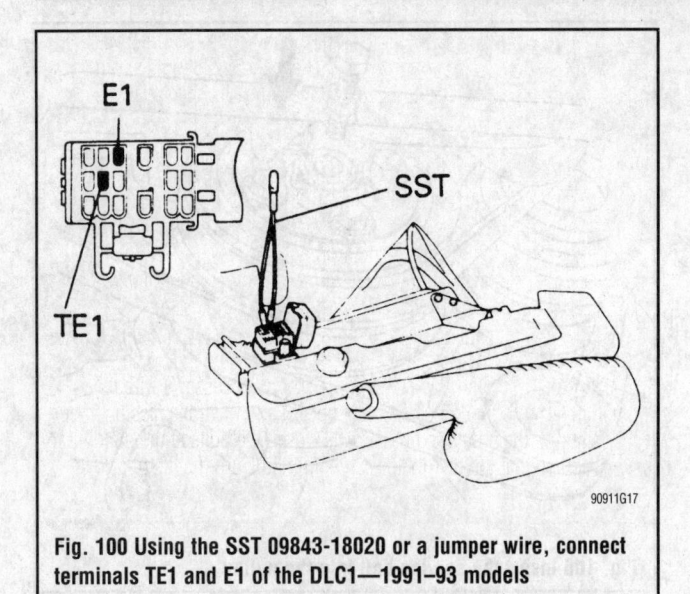

# GENERAL INFORMATION AND MAINTENANCE 1-37

Fig. 100 Using the SST 09843-18020 or a jumper wire, connect terminals TE1 and E1 of the DLC1—1991–93 models

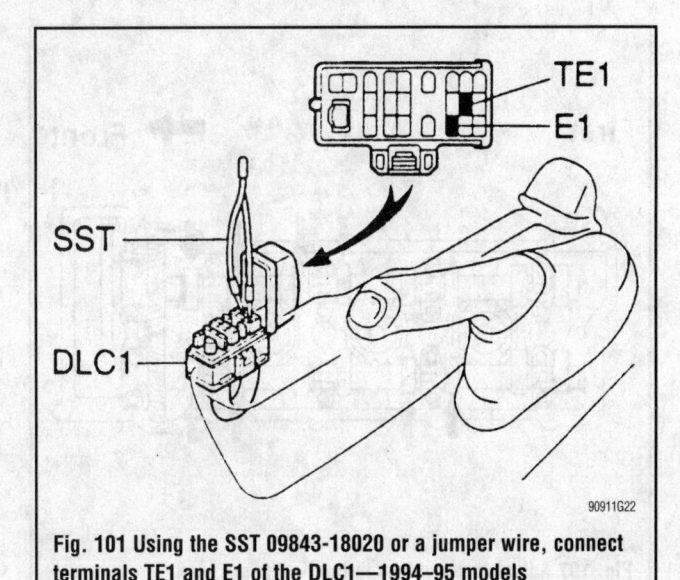

Fig. 101 Using the SST 09843-18020 or a jumper wire, connect terminals TE1 and E1 of the DLC1—1994–95 models

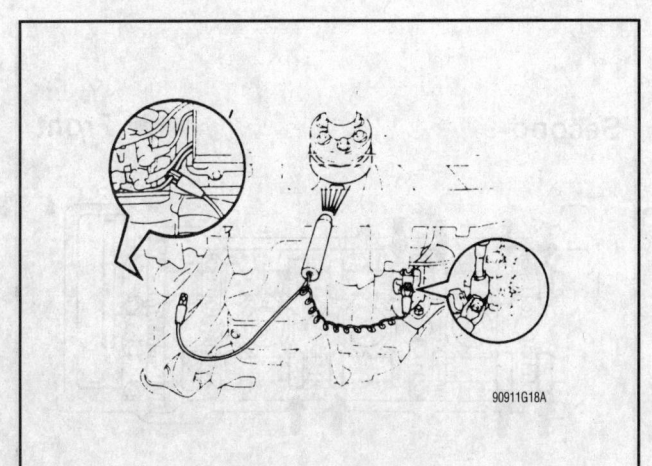

Fig. 102 Connect the timing light power source terminal to terminal 30 of the starter and test probe to the No. 1 spark plug wire (light blue)

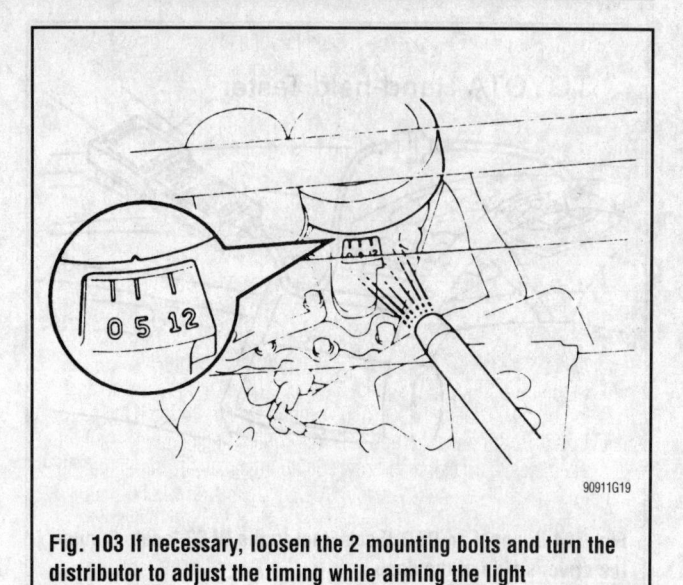

Fig. 103 If necessary, loosen the 2 mounting bolts and turn the distributor to adjust the timing while aiming the light

advance or retard the timing as required. Once the proper marks are seen to align with the timing light, timing is correct.

7. Without changing the position of the distributor, tighten the distributor bolts and double check the timing with the light (check idle speed as necessary).
8. Disconnect the jumper wire or Special Service Tool (SST) at the diagnostic check connector.

➥This jumper will be used repeatedly during diagnostics in later sections. Take the time to make a proper jumper with correct terminals or probes. It's a valuable special tool for very low cost.

9. Refer to the underhood emission sticker for timing specification and any additional service procedure steps. If necessary, repeat the timing adjustment procedure.
10. Shut the engine **OFF** and disconnect all test equipment. Roadtest the vehicle for proper operation.

### 2TZ-FZE and 1996–97 Models

◆ See Figure 104

➥Toyota's hand-held tester or an equivalent OBD-II scan tool must be used for this procedure.

1. Warm the engine to normal operating temperature.
2. Connect an OBD-II compliant scan tool to the DLC3 located under the dash on the driver's side. Refer to Section 4 for more information.
3. Connect the timing light power source terminal to terminal 30 of the starter and test probe to the No. 1 spark plug wire (light blue).
4. Using SST 09843–18020 or its equivalent jumper wire, connect terminals TE1 and E1 of the DLC1 under the hood.
5. After the engine speed is kept at about 2500 rpm for 5 seconds, check that it returns to idle speed.
6. Check the ignition timing, the reading should be 10° BTDC at idle.
7. If adjustment is necessary, loosen the 2 hold-down bolts, and adjust by turning the IIA. Tighten the hold-down bolts to 14 ft. lbs. (20 Nm), and recheck the ignition timing.
8. Remove the jumper wire from the DLC1.
9. Recheck the timing, the mark ranges:
   - 2TZ-FE—5° BTDC at idle
   - 2TZ-FZE—7°–17° BTDC at idle
10. Disconnect the scan tool.
11. Disconnect the timing light.

# 1-38 GENERAL INFORMATION AND MAINTENANCE

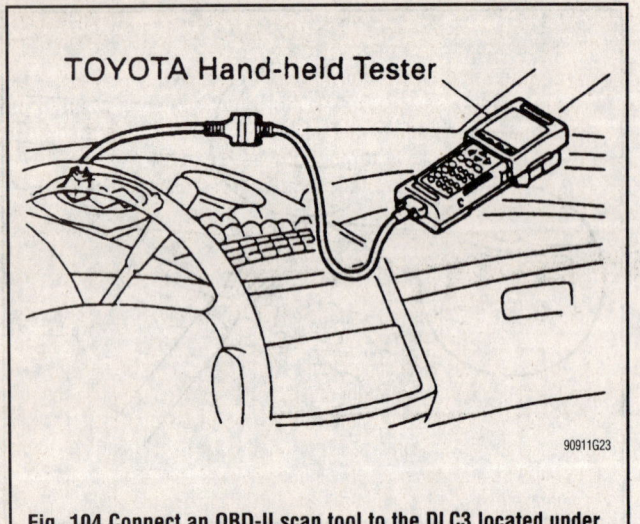

Fig. 104 Connect an OBD-II scan tool to the DLC3 located under the driver's side of the dash

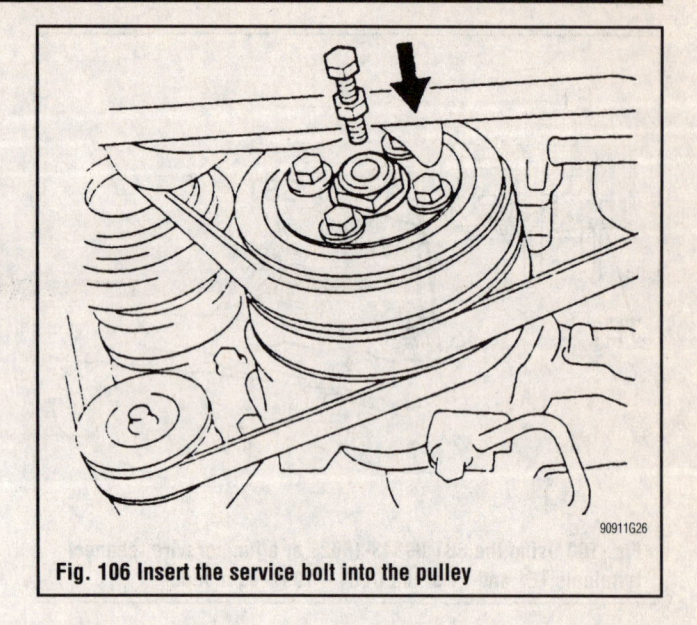

Fig. 106 Insert the service bolt into the pulley

## Valve Lash

### ADJUSTMENT

▶ See Figures 105 thru 113

1. Disconnect the negative battery cable.
2. Remove the right side seat and engine service hole cover as follows:
   a. Remove the three screws and the scuff plate.
   b. Unbolt and disconnect the right seat belt from the front floor panel.
   c. Remove the four bolts holding the right front seat.
   d. Remove the two bolts and the right front seat leg.
   e. Remove the jack, the jack stand and the tool bag.
   f. Remove the engine service hole cover.
3. Remove the No. 2 cylinder head cover with the gasket.
4. Remove the PCV hose and disconnect the four spark plug wires from the spark plugs.
5. Remove the No. 2 cord clamp support plate.
6. Remove the No. 1 cylinder head cover and the gasket.
7. Install a bolt 12mm x 1.25mm and nut to the equipment drive shaft.

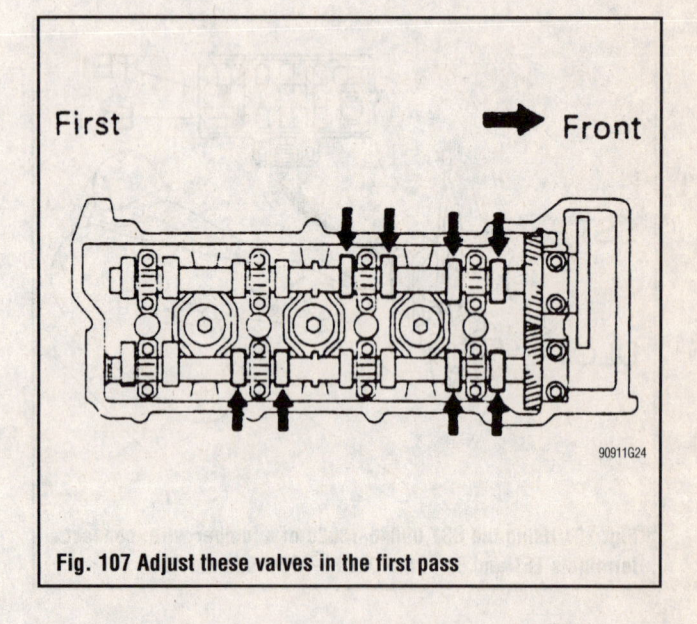

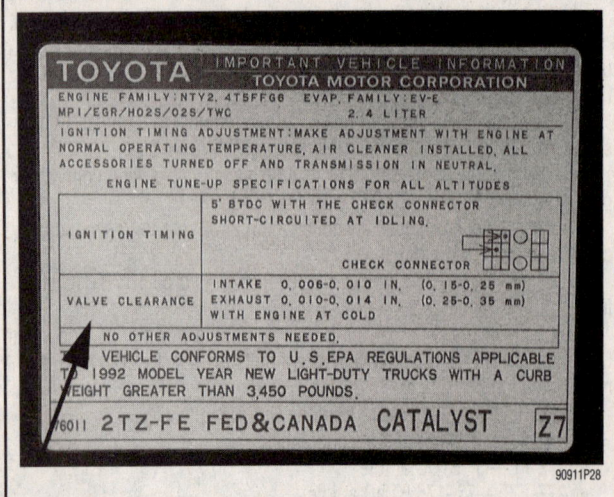

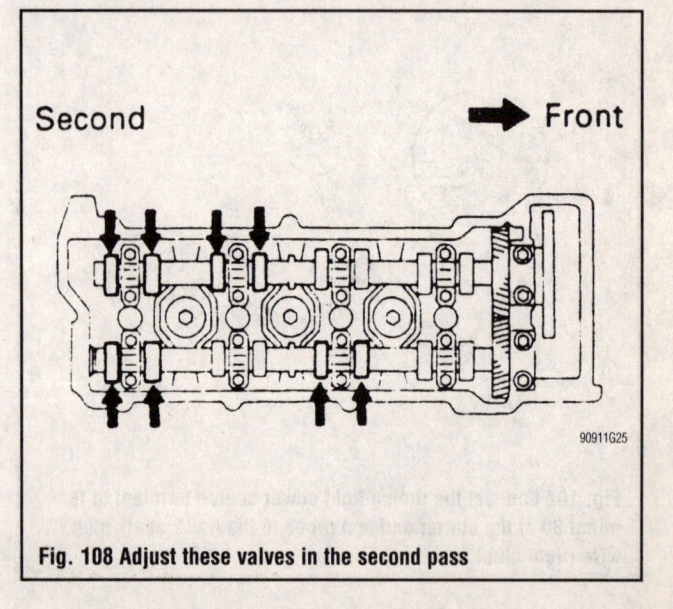

Fig. 107 Adjust these valves in the first pass

Fig. 105 The valve lash clearance is marked on a label under the hood

Fig. 108 Adjust these valves in the second pass

## GENERAL INFORMATION AND MAINTENANCE                                1-39

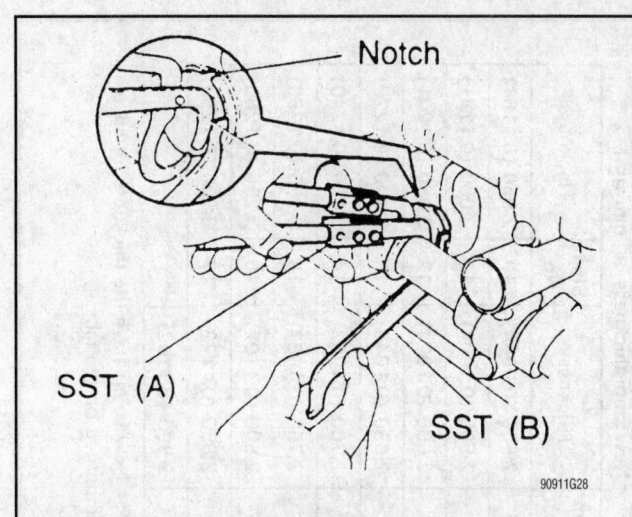

Fig. 109 Using tool (A), press down the valve lifter, then place tool (B) between the camshaft and the valve lifter

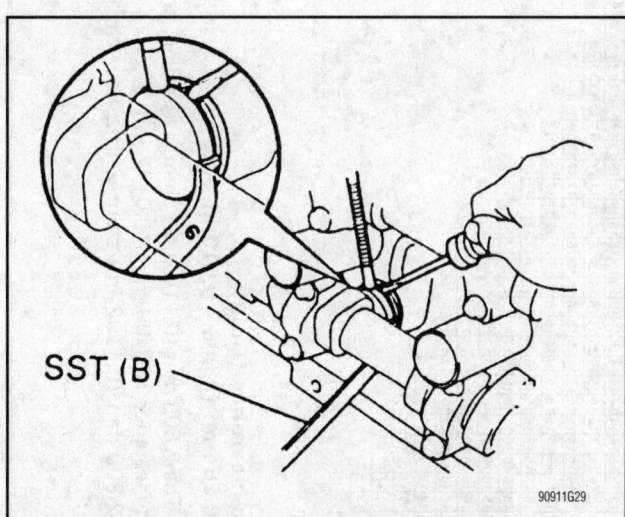

Fig. 110 With the aid of a magnet and small flatbladed tool, remove the shim

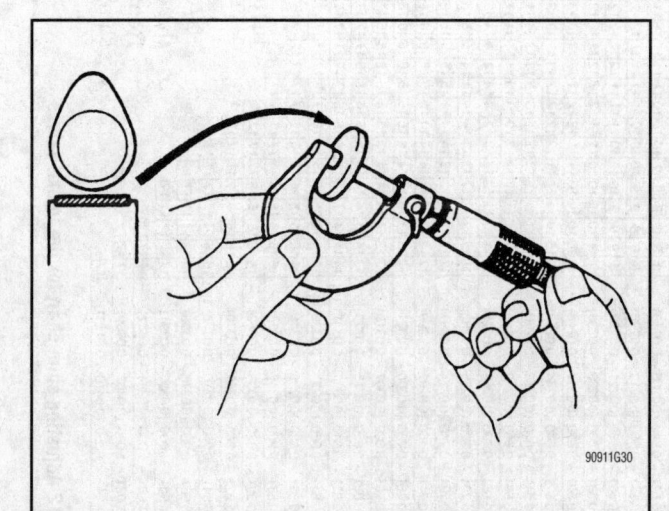

Fig. 111 A micrometer is used to measure the thickness of shims

### ** WARNING

**When rotating the driveshaft or engine by hand, this can be done by inserting a service bolt 12mm x 1.25mm with a nut into the screw hole at the end of the drive shaft. After doing the operation, do not forget to remove the service bolt and nut. If the service bolt is left installed, the bolt head may be hit and damage the cooling fan.**

8. Set the No. 1 cylinder to TDC in the compression stroke.
   a. Turn the equipment drive shaft with a wrench to align the timing marks at TDC. Set the groove on the crankshaft pulley to the **0** position.
   b. Check that the valve lifters on the No. 1 cylinder are loose and the valve lifters on the No. 4 are tight. If not, turn the equipment drive shaft one complete revolution and align the marks as above.
9. Inspect the valve clearance.
   a. Measure the clearance between the valve lifter and the camshaft. Measure the first and second intake and the first and third exhaust valves.
   b. Turn the equipment drive shaft one revolution (360°) and align the marks as above. Measure the third and fourth intake and the second and fourth exhaust valves.
10. Valve clearance cold should be:
- Intake: 0.006–0.010 inch (0.15–0.25mm)
- Exhaust: 0.010–0.014 inch (0.25–0.35mm)
11. Adjust the valve clearance by using adjusting shims.
    a. Turn the equipment drive shaft so that the cam lobe for the valve to be adjusted faces up.
    b. Using retaining tool (SST 09248–05410) or equivalent, press down the valve lifter and place SST 09248–05420 or equivalent, between the camshaft and the valve lifter. Remove SST 09248–55040.
    c. Remove the adjusting shim with a small flat prying tool and a magnetic finger.
    d. Determine the replacement adjusting shim size according to the following formula, or use the adjusting shim charts.
    e. Using a micrometer, measure the thickness of the removed shim. Calculate the thickness of a new shim so that the valve clearance comes within the specified value.
- T: Thickness of the removed shim
- A: Measured valve clearance
- N: Thickness of the new shim
    f. Intake: N=T+ (A—0.008 inch (0.20mm)
    g. Exhaust: N=T+ (A—0.012 inch (0.30mm)
    h. Install a new adjusting shim. Place it on the valve lifter. Using the SST 09248–05410, press down the valve lifter and remove SST 09248–05420.
    i. Recheck the valve clearance.
12. After adjustments have been made, remove the equipment drive shaft bolt and nut. If not removed, the bolt head will hit and damage the cooling fan.
13. Install the No. 1 cylinder head cover bolts in the sequence. Torque to 6 ft. lbs. (8 Nm).
14. Install the No. 2 cord clamp support plate and tighten the bolt to 3.7 ft. lbs. (5 Nm).
15. Connect the spark plug wires. Install the PCV hose.
16. Install the No. 2 cylinder head cover and tighten the bolts to 10 ft. lbs. (14 Nm).
    a. Install the right engine service hole cover and tighten the bolts to 10 ft. lbs. (14 Nm).
    b. Install the jack holder, the jack and the tool bag.
    c. Install the bolts holding the right front seat leg and tighten to 29 ft. lbs. (39 Nm).
    d. Install the right front seat and tighten the bolts to 29 ft. lbs. (39 Nm).
    e. Install the bolt holding the seat belt to the front floor panel and tighten to 31 ft. lbs. (42 Nm).
    f. Install the scuff plate.

# 1-40 GENERAL INFORMATION AND MAINTENANCE

**Fig. 112 Adjusting shim chart for the intake valves**

## New shim thickness mm (in.)

| Shim No. | Thickness | Shim No. | Thickness |
|---|---|---|---|
| 1 | 2.500 (0.0984) | 10 | 2.950 (0.1161) |
| 2 | 2.550 (0.1004) | 11 | 3.000 (0.1181) |
| 3 | 2.600 (0.1024) | 12 | 3.050 (0.1201) |
| 4 | 2.650 (0.1043) | 13 | 3.100 (0.1220) |
| 5 | 2.700 (0.1063) | 14 | 3.150 (0.1240) |
| 6 | 2.750 (0.1083) | 15 | 3.200 (0.1260) |
| 7 | 2.800 (0.1102) | 16 | 3.250 (0.1280) |
| 8 | 2.850 (0.1122) | 17 | 3.300 (0.1299) |
| 9 | 2.900 (0.1142) | | |

HINT: New shims have the thickness in millimeters imprinted on the face.

**Intake valve clearance (Cold):**
0.15 – 0.25 mm (0.006 – 0.010 in.)

EXAMPLE: The 2.800 mm (0.1102 in.) shim is installed, and the measured clearance is 0.450 mm (0.0177 in.).
Replace the 2.800 mm (0.1102 in.) shim with a new No.12 shim.

# GENERAL INFORMATION AND MAINTENANCE 1-41

**Adjusting Shim Selection Chart (Exhaust)**

**Exhaust valve clearance (Cold):**
0.25 – 0.35 mm (0.010 – 0.014 in.)

EXAMPLE: The 2.800 mm (0.1102 in.) shim is installed, and the measured clearance is 0.450 mm (0.0177 in.). Replace the 2.800 mm (0.1102 in.) shim with a new No.10 shim.

### New shim thickness mm (in.)

| Shim No. | Thickness | Shim No. | Thickness |
|---|---|---|---|
| 1 | 2.500 (0.0984) | 10 | 2.950 (0.1161) |
| 2 | 2.550 (0.1004) | 11 | 3.000 (0.1181) |
| 3 | 2.600 (0.1024) | 12 | 3.050 (0.1201) |
| 4 | 2.650 (0.1043) | 13 | 3.100 (0.1220) |
| 5 | 2.700 (0.1063) | 14 | 3.150 (0.1240) |
| 6 | 2.750 (0.1083) | 15 | 3.200 (0.1260) |
| 7 | 2.800 (0.1102) | 16 | 3.250 (0.1280) |
| 8 | 2.850 (0.1122) | 17 | 3.300 (0.1299) |
| 9 | 2.900 (0.1142) | | |

HINT: New shims have the thickness in millimeters imprinted on the face.

Fig. 113 Adjusting shim chart for the exhaust valves

# 1-42 GENERAL INFORMATION AND MAINTENANCE

## GASOLINE ENGINE TUNE-UP SPECIFICATIONS

| Year | Engine ID/VIN | Engine Displacement Liters (cc) | Spark Plugs Gap (in.) | Ignition Timing (deg.) MT | Ignition Timing (deg.) AT | Fuel Pump (psi) | Idle Speed (rpm) MT | Idle Speed (rpm) AT | Valve Clearance In. | Valve Clearance Ex. |
|---|---|---|---|---|---|---|---|---|---|---|
| 1991 | 2TZ-FE | 2.4 (2438) | 0.43 | 5 BTDC | 5 BTDC | 38-44 | 700 | 750 | 0.006-0.010 | 0.010-0.014 |
| 1992 | 2TZ-FE | 2.4 (2438) | 0.43 | 5 BTDC | 5 BTDC | 38-44 | 700 | 750 | 0.006-0.010 | 0.010-0.014 |
| 1993 | 2TZ-FE | 2.4 (2438) | 0.43 | 5 BTDC | 5 BTDC | 38-44 | 700 | 750 | 0.006-0.010 | 0.010-0.014 |
| 1994 | 2TZ-FE | 2.4 (2438) | 0.43 | 5 BTDC | 5 BTDC | 38-44 | 700 | 750 | 0.006-0.010 | 0.010-0.014 |
|  | 2TZ-FZE | 2.4 (2438) | 0.43 | 5 BTDC | 5 BTDC | 33-40 | - | 750 | 0.006-0.010 | 0.010-0.014 |
| 1995 | 2TZ-FE | 2.4 (2438) | 0.43 | 5 BTDC | 5 BTDC | 38-44 | - | 750 | 0.006-0.010 | 0.010-0.014 |
|  | 2TZ-FZE | 2.4 (2438) | 0.43 | 5 BTDC | 5 BTDC | 33-40 | - | 750 | 0.006-0.010 | 0.010-0.014 |
| 1996 | 2TZ-FZE | 2.4 (2438) | 0.43 | 5 BTDC | 5 BTDC | 33-40 | - | 750 | 0.006-0.010 | 0.010-0.014 |
| 1997 | 2TZ-FZE | 2.4 (2438) | 0.43 | 5 BTDC | 5 BTDC | 33-40 | - | 750 | 0.006-0.010 | 0.010-0.014 |

90911C03

## Idle Speed and Mixture Adjustments

There are no provisions for adjustment of the idle speed and mixture on the Previa models.

## Air Conditioning System

### SYSTEM SERVICE & REPAIR

▶ See Figure 114

➡ It is recommended that the A/C system be serviced by an EPA Section 609 certified automotive technician utilizing a refrigerant recovery/recycling machine.

The do-it-yourselfer should not service his/her own vehicle's A/C system for many reasons, including legal concerns, personal injury, environmental damage and cost. The following are some of the reasons why you may decide not to service your own vehicle's A/C system.

According to the US Clean Air Act, it is a federal crime to service or repair (involving the refrigerant) a Motor Vehicle Air Conditioning (MVAC) system for money without being EPA certified. It is also illegal to vent R-12 and R-134a refrigerants into the atmosphere. Selling or distributing A/C system refrigerant (in a container which contains less than 20 pounds of refrigerant) to any person who is not EPA 609 certified is also not allowed by law.

State and/or local laws may be more strict than the federal regulations, so be sure to check with your state and/or local authorities for further information. For further federal information on the legality of servicing your A/C system, call the EPA Stratospheric Ozone Hotline.

➡ Federal law dictates that a fine of up to $25,000 may be levied on people convicted of venting refrigerant into the atmosphere. Additionally, the EPA may pay up to $10,000 for information or services leading to a criminal conviction of the violation of these laws.

When servicing an A/C system you run the risk of handling or coming in contact with refrigerant, which may result in skin or eye irritation or frostbite. Although low in toxicity (due to chemical stability), inhalation of concentrated refrigerant fumes is dangerous and can result in death; cases of fatal cardiac arrhythmia have been reported in people accidentally subjected to high levels of refrigerant. Some early symptoms include loss of concentration and drowsiness.

➡ Generally, the limit for exposure is lower for R-134a than it is for R-12. Exceptional care must be practiced when handling R-134a.

Also, refrigerants can decompose at high temperatures (near gas heaters or open flame), which may result in hydrofluoric acid, hydrochloric acid and phosgene (a fatal nerve gas).

R-12 refrigerant can damage the environment because it is a Chlorofluorocarbon (CFC), which has been proven to add to ozone layer depletion, leading to increasing levels of UV radiation. UV radiation has been linked with an increase in skin cancer, suppression of the human immune system, an increase in cataracts, damage to crops, damage to aquatic organisms, an increase in ground-level ozone, and increased global warming.

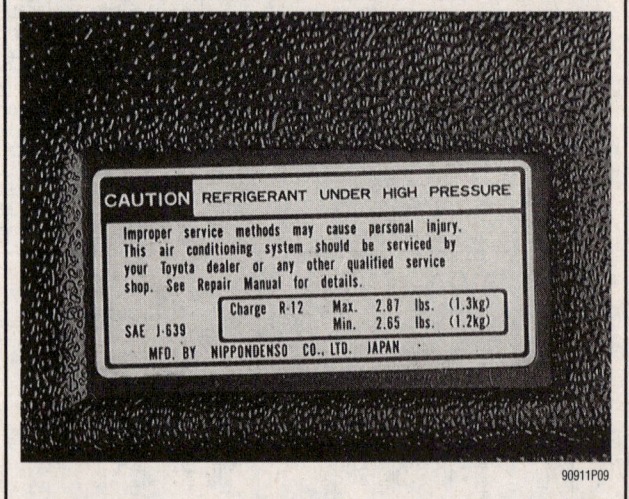

Fig. 114 Look for a label specifying the type of refrigerant that is in your vehicle

# GENERAL INFORMATION AND MAINTENANCE    1-43

R-134a refrigerant is a greenhouse gas which, if allowed to vent into the atmosphere, will contribute to global warming (the Greenhouse Effect).

It is usually more economically feasible to have a certified MVAC automotive technician perform A/C system service on your vehicle. Some possible reasons for this are as follows:

• While it is illegal to service an A/C system without the proper equipment, the home mechanic would have to purchase an expensive refrigerant recovery/recycling machine to service his/her own vehicle.

• Since only a certified person may purchase refrigerant—according to the Clean Air Act, there are specific restrictions on selling or distributing A/C system refrigerant—it is legally impossible (unless certified) for the home mechanic to service his/her own vehicle. Procuring refrigerant in an illegal fashion exposes one to the risk of paying a $25,000 fine to the EPA.

### R-12 Refrigerant Conversion

If your vehicle still uses R-12 refrigerant, one way to save A/C system costs down the road is to investigate the possibility of having your system converted to R-134a. The older R-12 systems can be easily converted to R-134a refrigerant by a certified automotive technician by installing a few new components and changing the system oil.

The cost of R-12 is steadily rising and will continue to increase, because it is no longer imported or manufactured in the United States. Therefore, it is often possible to have an R-12 system converted to R-134a and recharged for less than it would cost to just charge the system with R-12.

If you are interested in having your system converted, contact local automotive service stations for more details and information.

## PREVENTIVE MAINTENANCE

▶ See Figures 115 and 116

Although the A/C system should not be serviced by the do-it-yourselfer, preventive maintenance can be practiced and A/C system inspections can be performed to help maintain the efficiency of the vehicle's A/C system. For preventive maintenance, perform the following:

• The easiest and most important preventive maintenance for your A/C system is to be sure that it is used on a regular basis. Running the system for five minutes each month (no matter what the season) will help ensure that the seals and all internal components remain lubricated.

➡ Some newer vehicles automatically operate the A/C system compressor whenever the windshield defroster is activated. When running, the compressor lubricates the A/C system components; therefore, the A/C system would not need to be operated each month.

Fig. 115 A coolant tester can be used to determine the freezing and boiling levels of the coolant in your vehicle

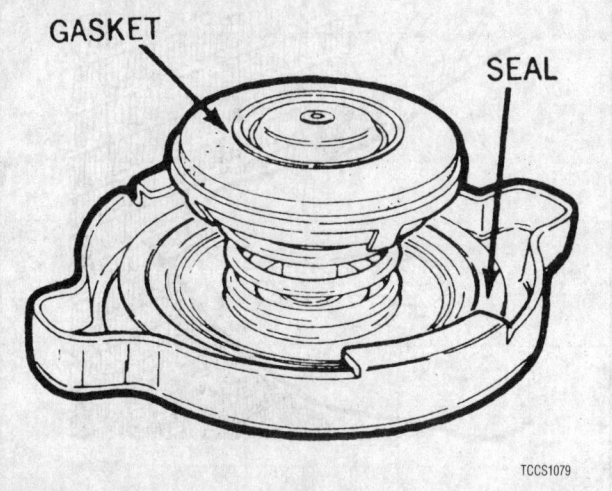

Fig. 116 To ensure efficient cooling system operation, inspect the radiator cap gasket and seal

• In order to prevent heater core freeze-up during A/C operation, it is necessary to maintain proper antifreeze protection. Use a hand-held coolant tester (hydrometer) to periodically check the condition of the antifreeze in your engine's cooling system.

➡ Antifreeze should not be used longer than the manufacturer specifies.

• For efficient operation of an air conditioned vehicle's cooling system, the radiator cap should have a holding pressure which meets manufacturer's specifications. A cap which fails to hold these pressures should be replaced.

• Any obstruction of or damage to the condenser configuration will restrict air flow which is essential to its efficient operation. It is, therefore, a good rule to keep this unit clean and in proper physical shape.

➡ Bug screens which are mounted in front of the condenser (unless they are original equipment) are regarded as obstructions.

• The condensation drain tube expels any water which accumulates on the bottom of the evaporator housing into the engine compartment. If this tube is obstructed, the air conditioning performance can be restricted and condensation buildup can spill over onto the vehicle's floor.

## SYSTEM INSPECTION

▶ See Figure 117

Although the A/C system should not be serviced by the do-it-yourselfer, preventive maintenance can be practiced and A/C system inspections can be performed to help maintain the efficiency of the vehicle's A/C system. For A/C system inspection, perform the following:

The easiest and often most important check for the air conditioning system consists of a visual inspection of the system components. Visually inspect the air conditioning system for refrigerant leaks, damaged compressor clutch, abnormal compressor drive belt tension and/or condition, plugged evaporator drain tube, blocked condenser fins, disconnected or broken wires, blown fuses, corroded connections and poor insulation.

A refrigerant leak will usually appear as an oily residue at the leakage point in the system. The oily residue soon picks up dust or dirt particles from the surrounding air and appears greasy. Through time, this will build up and appear to be a heavy dirt impregnated grease.

For a thorough visual and operational inspection, check the following:

• Check the surface of the radiator and condenser for dirt, leaves or other material which might block air flow.

• Check for kinks in hoses and lines. Check the system for leaks.

• Make sure the drive belt is properly tensioned. When the air conditioning is operating, make sure the drive belt is free of noise or slippage.

• Make sure the blower motor operates at all appropriate positions, then

# 1-44 GENERAL INFORMATION AND MAINTENANCE

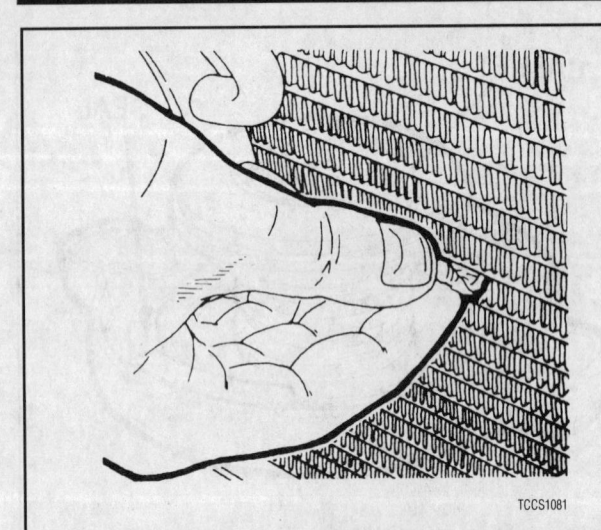

Fig. 117 Periodically remove any debris from the condenser and radiator fins

Fig. 118 Bosch® wiper blade and fit kit

Fig. 119 Lexor® wiper blade and fit kit

Fig. 120 Pylon® wiper blade and adapter

check for distribution of the air from all outlets with the blower on **HIGH** or **MAX**.

➡ Keep in mind that under conditions of high humidity, air discharged from the A/C vents may not feel as cold as expected, even if the system is working properly. This is because vaporized moisture in humid air retains heat more effectively than dry air, thereby making humid air more difficult to cool.

- Make sure the air passage selection lever is operating correctly. Start the engine and warm it to normal operating temperature, then make sure the temperature selection lever is operating correctly.

## Windshield Wipers

### ELEMENT (REFILL) CARE & REPLACEMENT

♦ See Figures 118 thru 127

For maximum effectiveness and longest element life, the windshield and wiper blades should be kept clean. Dirt, tree sap, road tar and so on will cause streaking, smearing and blade deterioration if left on the glass. It is advisable to wash the windshield carefully with a commercial glass cleaner at least once a month. Wipe off the rubber blades with the wet rag afterwards. Do not attempt to move wipers across the windshield by hand; damage to the motor and drive mechanism will result.

To inspect and/or replace the wiper blade elements, place the wiper switch in the **LOW** speed position and the ignition switch in the **ACC** position. When the wiper blades are approximately vertical on the windshield, turn the ignition switch to **OFF**.

Examine the wiper blade elements. If they are found to be cracked, broken or torn, they should be replaced immediately. Replacement intervals will vary with usage, although ozone deterioration usually limits element life to about one year. If the wiper pattern is smeared or streaked, or if the blade chatters across the glass, the elements should be replaced. It is easiest and most sensible to replace the elements in pairs.

If your vehicle is equipped with aftermarket blades, there are several different types of refills and your vehicle might have any kind. Aftermarket blades and arms rarely use the exact same type blade or refill as the original equipment. Here are some typical aftermarket blades; not all may be available for your vehicle:

The Anco® type uses a release button that is pushed down to allow the refill to slide out of the yoke jaws. The new refill slides back into the frame and locks in place.

Some Trico® refills are removed by locating where the metal backing strip or the refill is wider. Insert a small screwdriver blade between the

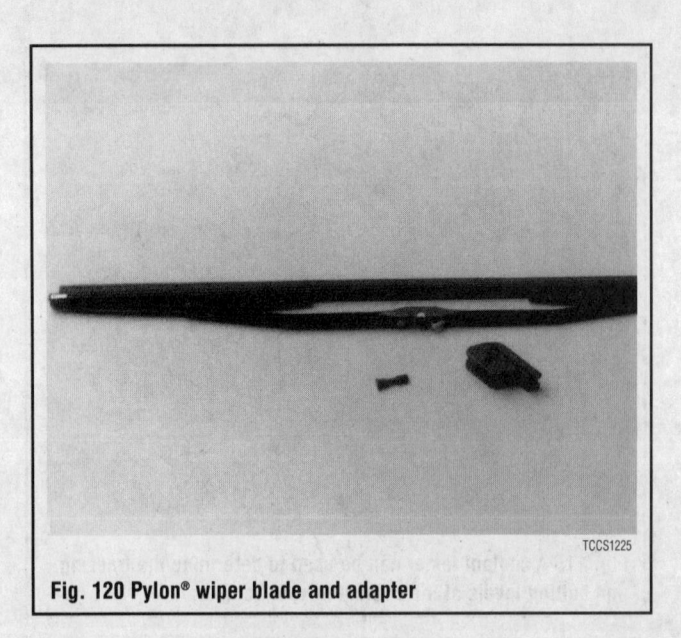

# GENERAL INFORMATION AND MAINTENANCE     1-45

Fig. 121 Trico® wiper blade and fit kit

Fig. 122 Tripledge® wiper blade and fit kit

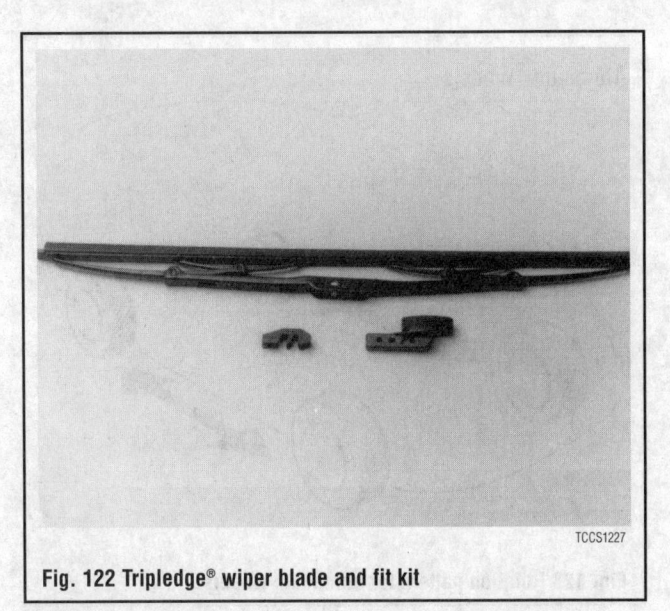

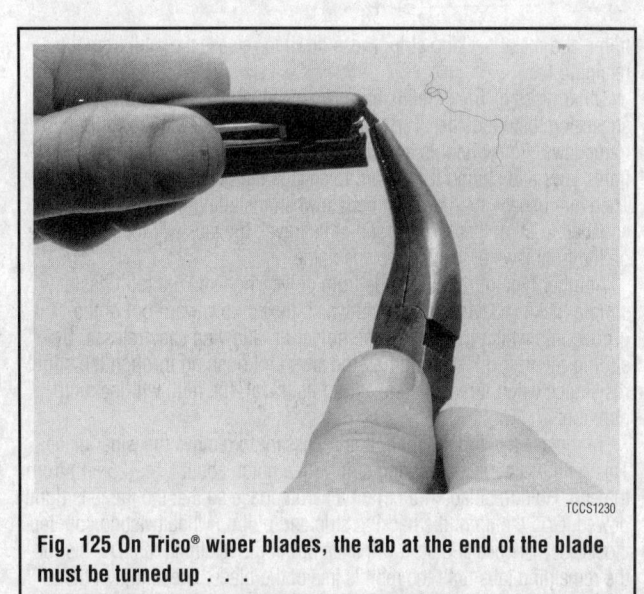

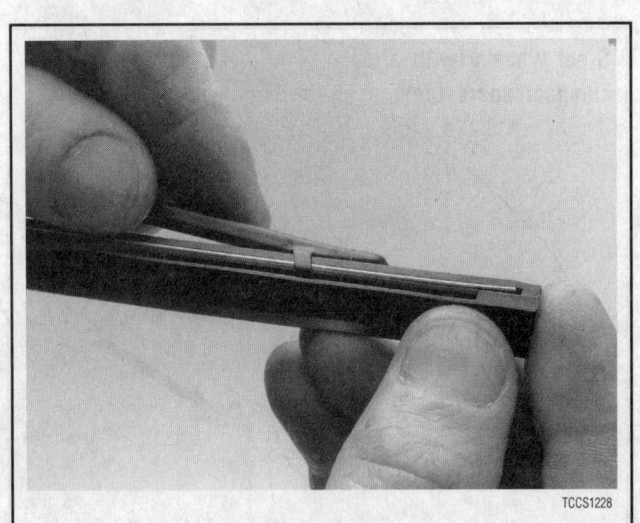

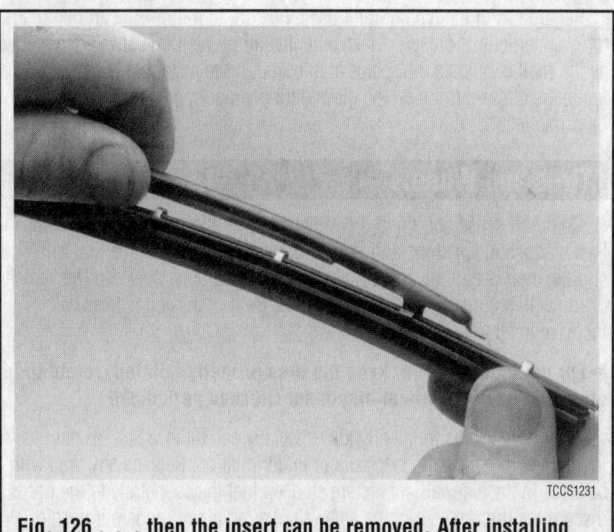

Fig. 123 To remove and install a Lexor® wiper blade refill, slip out the old insert and slide in a new one

Fig. 124 On Pylon® inserts, the clip at the end has to be removed prior to sliding the insert off

Fig. 125 On Trico® wiper blades, the tab at the end of the blade must be turned up . . .

Fig. 126 . . . then the insert can be removed. After installing the replacement insert, bend the tab back

# 1-46 GENERAL INFORMATION AND MAINTENANCE

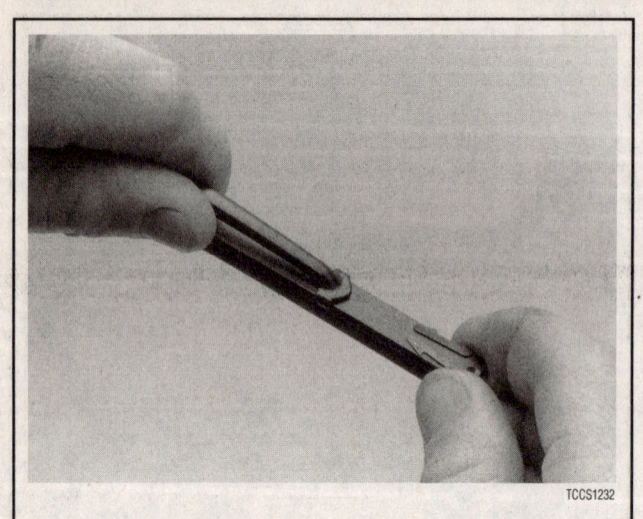

**Fig. 127 The Tripledge® wiper blade insert is removed and installed using a securing clip**

frame and metal backing strip. Press down to release the refill from the retaining tab.

Other types of Trico® refills have two metal tabs which are unlocked by squeezing them together. The rubber filler can then be withdrawn from the frame jaws. A new refill is installed by inserting the refill into the front frame jaws and sliding it rearward to engage the remaining frame jaws. There are usually four jaws; be certain when installing that the refill is engaged in all of them. At the end of its travel, the tabs will lock into place on the front jaws of the wiper blade frame.

Another type of refill is made from polycarbonate. The refill has a simple locking device at one end which flexes downward out of the groove into which the jaws of the holder fit, allowing easy release. By sliding the new refill through all the jaws and pushing through the slight resistance when it reaches the end of its travel, the refill will lock into position.

To replace the Tridon® refill, it is necessary to remove the wiper blade. This refill has a plastic backing strip with a notch about 1 in. (25mm) from the end. Hold the blade (frame) on a hard surface so that the frame is tightly bowed. Grip the tip of the backing strip and pull up while twisting counterclockwise. The backing strip will snap out of the retaining tab. Do this for the remaining tabs until the refill is free of the blade. The length of these refills is molded into the end and they should be replaced with identical types.

Regardless of the type of refill used, be sure to follow the part manufacturer's instructions closely. Make sure that all of the frame jaws are engaged as the refill is pushed into place and locked. If the metal blade holder and frame are allowed to touch the glass during wiper operation, the glass will be scratched.

## Tires and Wheels

Common sense and good driving habits will afford maximum tire life. Fast starts, sudden stops and hard cornering are hard on tires and will shorten their useful life span. Make sure that you don't overload the vehicle or run with incorrect pressure in the tires. Both of these practices will increase tread wear.

➡ For optimum tire life, keep the tires properly inflated, rotate them often and have the wheel alignment checked periodically.

Inspect your tires frequently. Be especially careful to watch for bubbles in the tread or sidewall, deep cuts or underinflation. Replace any tires with bubbles in the sidewall. If cuts are so deep that they penetrate to the cords, discard the tire. Any cut in the sidewall of a radial tire renders it unsafe. Also look for uneven tread wear patterns that may indicate the front end is out of alignment or that the tires are out of balance.

### TIRE ROTATION

◆ See Figures 128, 129, 130 and 131

Tires must be rotated periodically to equalize wear patterns that vary with a tire's position on the vehicle. Tires will also wear in an uneven way as the front steering/suspension system wears to the point where the alignment should be reset.

Rotating the tires will ensure maximum life for the tires as a set, so you will not have to discard a tire early due to wear on only part of the tread. Regular rotation is required to equalize wear.

When rotating "unidirectional tires," make sure that they always roll in the same direction. This means that a tire used on the left side of the vehicle must not be switched to the right side and vice-versa. Such tires should only be rotated front-to-rear or rear-to-front, while always remaining on the same side of the vehicle. These tires are marked on the sidewall as to the direction of rotation; observe the marks when reinstalling the tire(s).

Some styled or "mag" wheels may have different offsets front to rear. In these cases, the rear wheels must not be used up front and vice-versa. Furthermore, if these wheels are equipped with unidirectional tires, they cannot be rotated unless the tire is remounted for the proper direction of rotation.

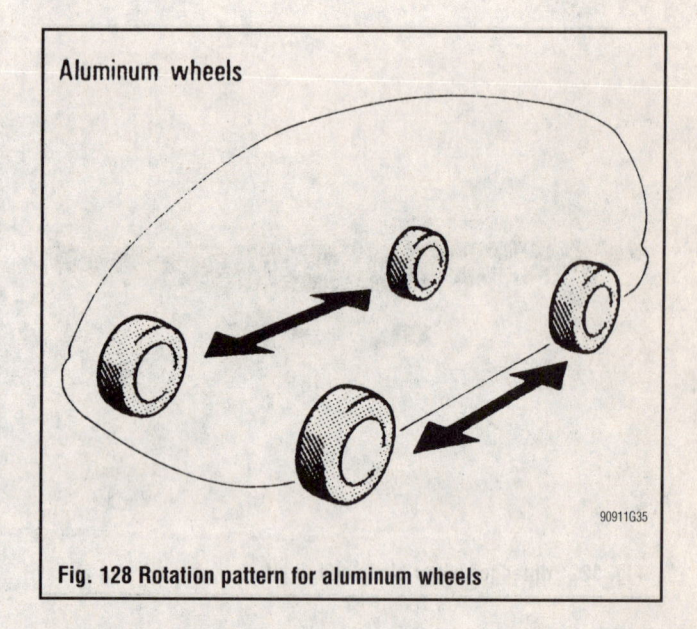

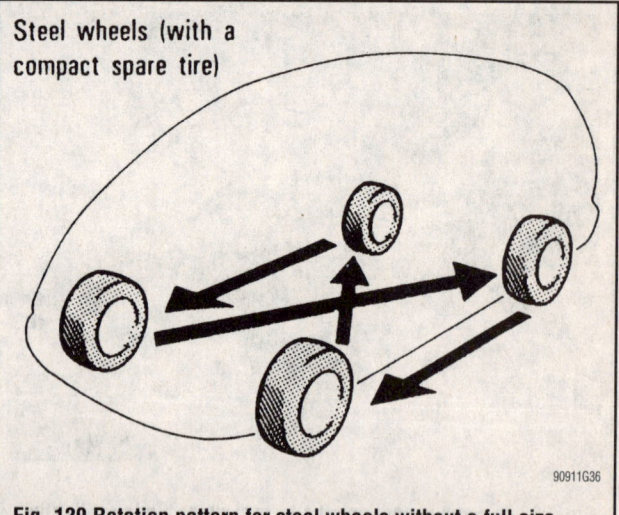

**Fig. 128 Rotation pattern for aluminum wheels**

**Fig. 129 Rotation pattern for steel wheels without a full size spare**

# GENERAL INFORMATION AND MAINTENANCE  1-47

Fig. 130 Rotation pattern for steel wheels with a full sized spare

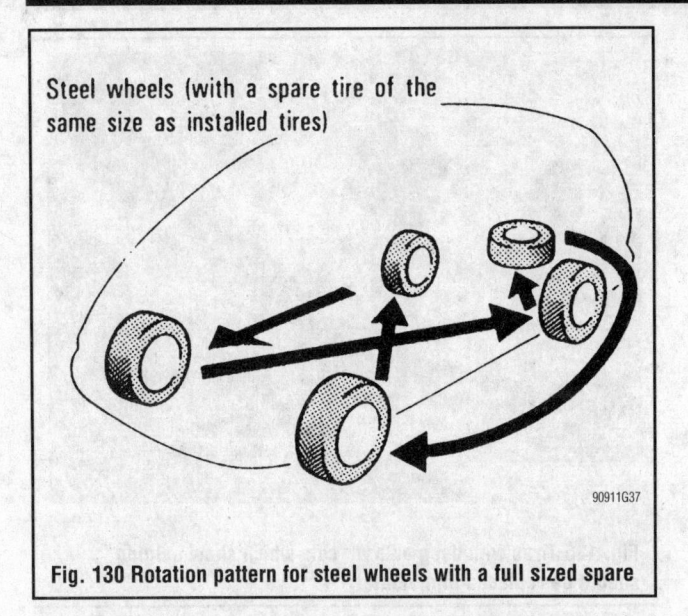

Fig. 132 P-Metric tire coding

Fig. 131 Unidirectional tires are identifiable by sidewall arrows and/or the word "rotation"

➡The compact or space-saver spare is strictly for emergency use. It must never be included in the tire rotation or placed on the vehicle for everyday use.

## TIRE DESIGN

♦ See Figure 132

For maximum satisfaction, tires should be used in sets of four. Mixing of different types (radial, bias-belted, fiberglass belted) must be avoided. In most cases, the vehicle manufacturer has designated a type of tire on which the vehicle will perform best. Your first choice when replacing tires should be to use the same type of tire that the manufacturer recommends.

When radial tires are used, tire sizes and wheel diameters should be selected to maintain ground clearance and tire load capacity equivalent to the original specified tire. Radial tires should always be used in sets of four.

### ✱✱ CAUTION

**Radial tires should never be used on only the front axle.**

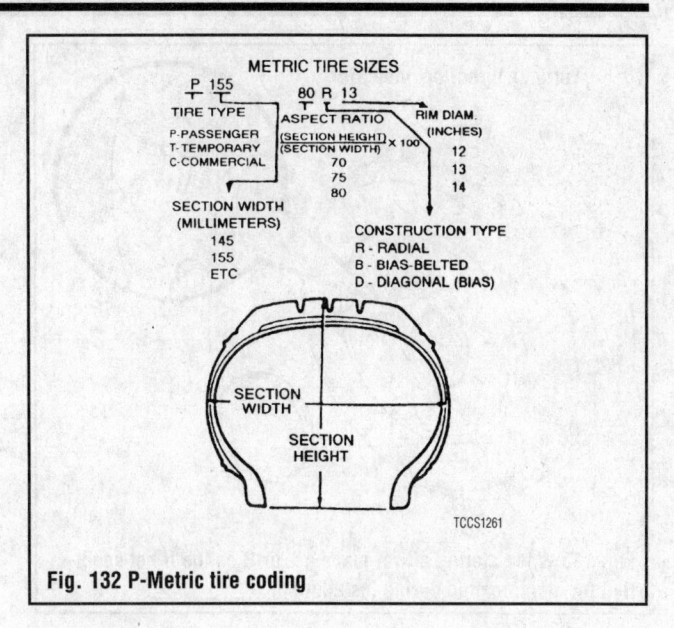

When selecting tires, pay attention to the original size as marked on the tire. Most tires are described using an industry size code sometimes referred to as P-Metric. This allows the exact identification of the tire specifications, regardless of the manufacturer. If selecting a different tire size or brand, remember to check the installed tire for any sign of interference with the body or suspension while the vehicle is stopping, turning sharply or heavily loaded.

### Snow Tires

Good radial tires can produce a big advantage in slippery weather, but in snow, a street radial tire does not have sufficient tread to provide traction and control. The small grooves of a street tire quickly pack with snow and the tire behaves like a billiard ball on a marble floor. The more open, chunky tread of a snow tire will self-clean as the tire turns, providing much better grip on snowy surfaces.

To satisfy municipalities requiring snow tires during weather emergencies, most snow tires carry either an M + S designation after the tire size stamped on the sidewall, or the designation "all-season." In general, no change in tire size is necessary when buying snow tires.

Most manufacturers strongly recommend the use of 4 snow tires on their vehicles for reasons of stability. If snow tires are fitted only to the drive wheels, the opposite end of the vehicle may become very unstable when braking or turning on slippery surfaces. This instability can lead to unpleasant endings if the driver can't counteract the slide in time.

Note that snow tires, whether 2 or 4, will affect vehicle handling in all non-snow situations. The stiffer, heavier snow tires will noticeably change the turning and braking characteristics of the vehicle. Once the snow tires are installed, you must re-learn the behavior of the vehicle and drive accordingly.

➡**Consider buying extra wheels on which to mount the snow tires. Once done, the "snow wheels" can be installed and removed as needed. This eliminates the potential damage to tires or wheels from seasonal removal and installation. Even if your vehicle has styled wheels, see if inexpensive steel wheels are available. Although the look of the vehicle will change, the expensive wheels will be protected from salt, curb hits and pothole damage.**

## TIRE STORAGE

♦ See Figure 133

If they are mounted on wheels, store the tires at proper inflation pressure. All tires should be kept in a cool, dry place. If they are stored in the garage or basement, do not let them stand on a concrete floor; set them on

# 1-48 GENERAL INFORMATION AND MAINTENANCE

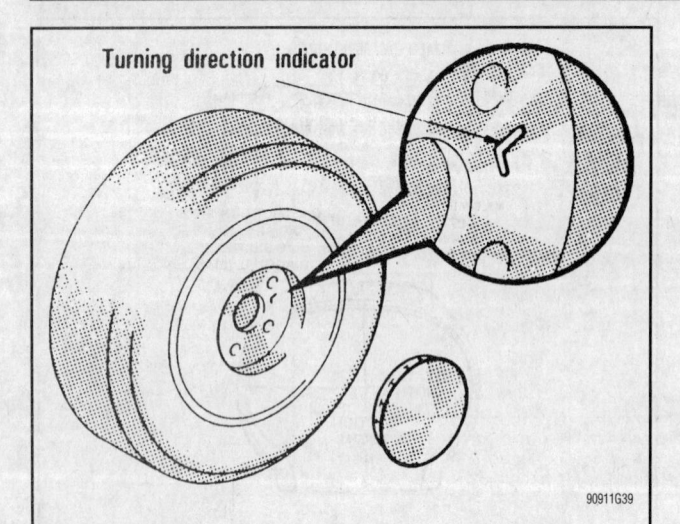

Fig. 133 When storing a tire, place a L or R on the if not specified for identification during installation

Fig. 135 Tires with deep cuts, or cuts which show bulging, should be replaced immediately

strips of wood, a mat or a large stack of newspaper. Keeping them away from direct moisture is of paramount importance. Tires should not be stored upright, but in a flat position.

## INFLATION & INSPECTION

▶ See Figures 134 thru 141

The importance of proper tire inflation cannot be overemphasized. A tire employs air as part of its structure. It is designed around the supporting strength of the air at a specified pressure. For this reason, improper inflation drastically reduces the tire's ability to perform as intended. A tire will lose some air in day-to-day use; having to add a few pounds of air periodically is not necessarily a sign of a leaking tire.

Two items should be a permanent fixture in every glove compartment: an accurate tire pressure gauge and a tread depth gauge. Check the tire pressure (including the spare) regularly with a pocket type gauge. Too often, the gauge on the end of the air hose at your corner garage is not accurate because it suffers too much abuse. Always check tire pressure when the tires are cold, as pressure increases with temperature. If you must move the vehicle to check the tire inflation, do not drive more than a mile before checking. A cold tire is generally one that has not been driven for more than three hours.

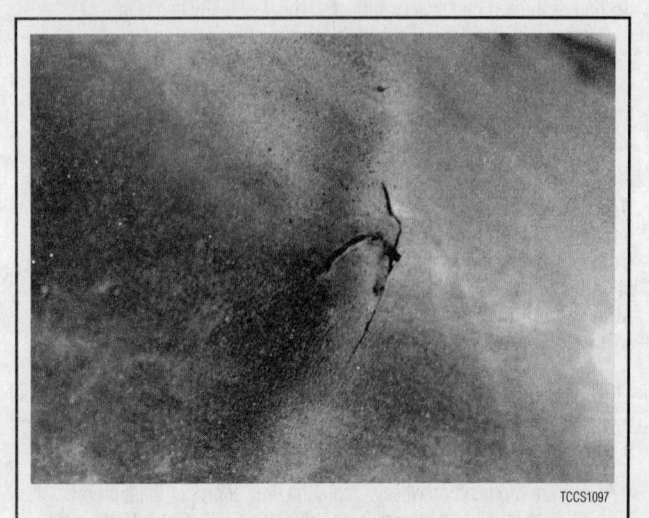

Fig. 136 Examples of inflation-related tire wear patterns

- DRIVE WHEEL HEAVY ACCELERATION
- OVERINFLATION

- HARD CORNERING
- UNDERINFLATION
- LACK OF ROTATION

Fig. 134 Tires should be checked frequently for any sign of puncture or damage

PROPERLY INFLATED    IMPROPERLY INFLATED

RADIAL TIRE

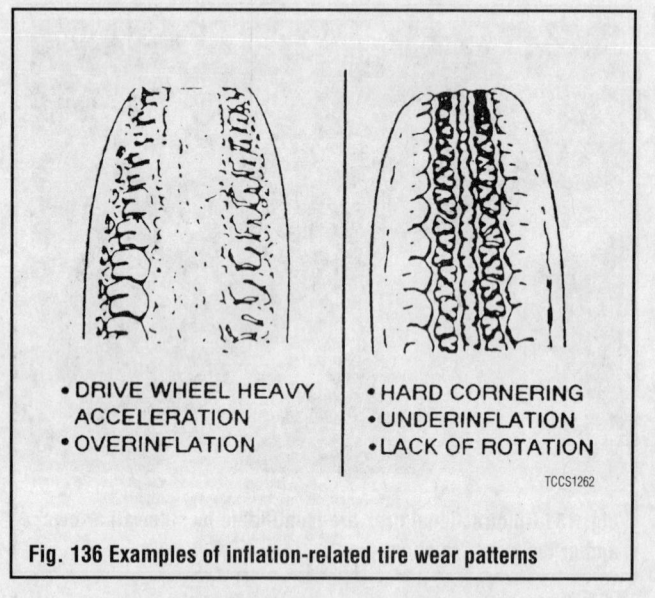

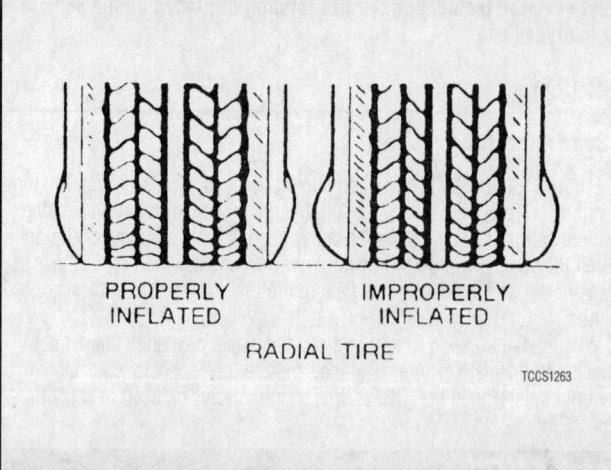

Fig. 137 Radial tires have a characteristic sidewall bulge; don't try to measure pressure by looking at the tire. Use a quality air pressure gauge

# GENERAL INFORMATION AND MAINTENANCE 1-49

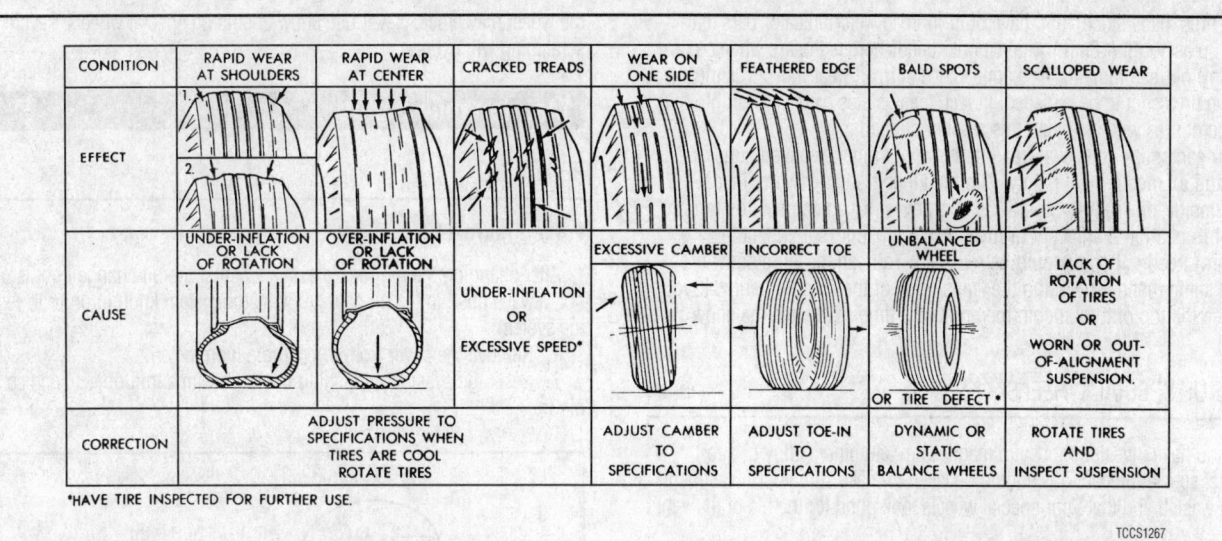

| CONDITION | RAPID WEAR AT SHOULDERS | RAPID WEAR AT CENTER | CRACKED TREADS | WEAR ON ONE SIDE | FEATHERED EDGE | BALD SPOTS | SCALLOPED WEAR |
|---|---|---|---|---|---|---|---|
| EFFECT | | | | | | | |
| CAUSE | UNDER-INFLATION OR LACK OF ROTATION | OVER-INFLATION OR LACK OF ROTATION | UNDER-INFLATION OR EXCESSIVE SPEED* | EXCESSIVE CAMBER | INCORRECT TOE | UNBALANCED WHEEL OR TIRE DEFECT* | LACK OF ROTATION OF TIRES OR WORN OR OUT-OF-ALIGNMENT SUSPENSION. |
| CORRECTION | ADJUST PRESSURE TO SPECIFICATIONS WHEN TIRES ARE COOL ROTATE TIRES | | | ADJUST CAMBER TO SPECIFICATIONS | ADJUST TOE-IN TO SPECIFICATIONS | DYNAMIC OR STATIC BALANCE WHEELS | ROTATE TIRES AND INSPECT SUSPENSION |

*HAVE TIRE INSPECTED FOR FURTHER USE.

Fig. 138 Common tire wear patterns and causes

Fig. 139 Tread wear indicators will appear when the tire is worn

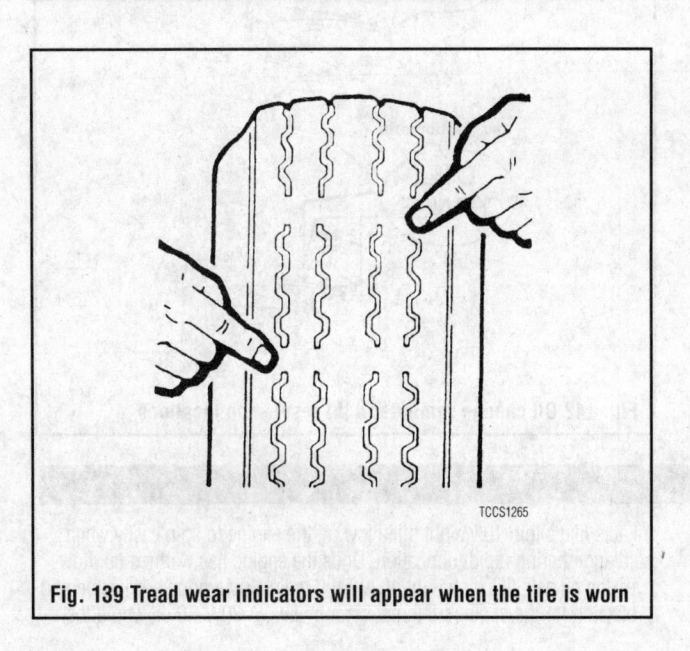

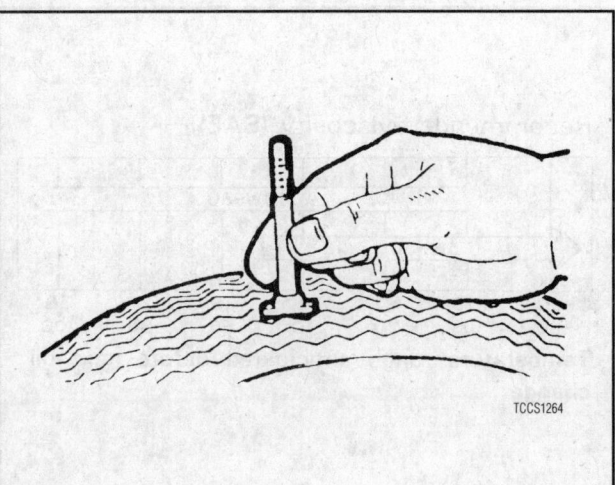

Fig. 141 A penny works well for a quick check of tread depth

Fig. 140 Accurate tread depth indicators are inexpensive and handy

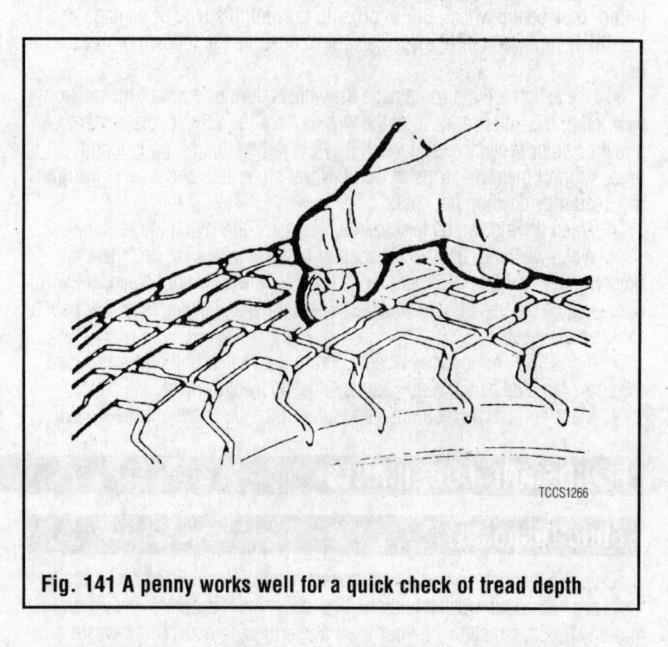

A plate or sticker is normally provided somewhere in the vehicle (door post, hood, tailgate or trunk lid) which shows the proper pressure for the tires. Never counteract excessive pressure build-up by bleeding off air pressure (letting some air out). This will cause the tire to run hotter and wear quicker.

## ✼✼ CAUTION

**Never exceed the maximum tire pressure embossed on the tire! This is the pressure to be used when the tire is at maximum loading, but it is rarely the correct pressure for everyday driving. Consult the owner's manual or the tire pressure sticker for the correct tire pressure.**

Once you've maintained the correct tire pressures for several weeks, you'll be familiar with the vehicle's braking and handling personality. Slight adjustments in tire pressures can fine-tune these characteristics, but never change the cold pressure specification by more than 2 psi. A slightly softer tire pressure will give a softer ride but also yield lower fuel mileage. A slightly harder tire will give crisper dry road handling but can cause skidding on wet surfaces. Unless you're fully attuned to the vehicle, stick to the recommended inflation pressures.

# 1-50 GENERAL INFORMATION AND MAINTENANCE

All tires made since 1968 have built-in tread wear indicator bars that show up as ½ in. (13mm) wide smooth bands across the tire when 1/16 in. (1.5mm) of tread remains. The appearance of tread wear indicators means that the tires should be replaced. In fact, many states have laws prohibiting the use of tires with less than this amount of tread.

You can check your own tread depth with an inexpensive gauge or by using a Lincoln head penny. Slip the Lincoln penny (with Lincoln's head upside-down) into several tread grooves. If you can see the top of Lincoln's head in 2 adjacent grooves, the tire has less than 1/16 in. (1.5mm) tread left and should be replaced. You can measure snow tires in the same manner by using the "tails" side of the Lincoln penny. If you can see the top of the Lincoln memorial, it's time to replace the snow tire(s).

## CARE OF SPECIAL WHEELS

If you have invested money in magnesium, aluminum alloy or sport wheels, special precautions should be taken to make sure your investment is not wasted and that your special wheels look good for the life of the vehicle.

Special wheels are easily damaged and/or scratched. Occasionally check the rims for cracking, impact damage or air leaks. If any of these are found, replace the wheel. But in order to prevent this type of damage and the costly replacement of a special wheel, observe the following precautions:

- Use extra care not to damage the wheels during removal, installation, balancing, etc. After removal of the wheels from the vehicle, place them on a mat or other protective surface. If they are to be stored for any length of time, support them on strips of wood. Never store tires and wheels upright; the tread may develop flat spots.
- When driving, watch for hazards; it doesn't take much to crack a wheel.
- When washing, use a mild soap or non-abrasive dish detergent (keeping in mind that detergent tends to remove wax). Avoid cleansers with abrasives or the use of hard brushes. There are many cleaners and polishes for special wheels.
- If possible, remove the wheels during the winter. Salt and sand used for snow removal can severely damage the finish of a wheel.
- Make certain the recommended lug nut torque is never exceeded or the wheel may crack. Never use snow chains on special wheels; severe scratching will occur.

## Maintenance Lights

### RESETTING

◆ See Figure 142

After changing the oil, regardless of whether the oil change light is on or not, always push in the oil change indicator system knob in order to reset the system.
1. Remove the cover from the combination meter.
2. Reset the system by pushing the knob with a thin object such as a pin tip.

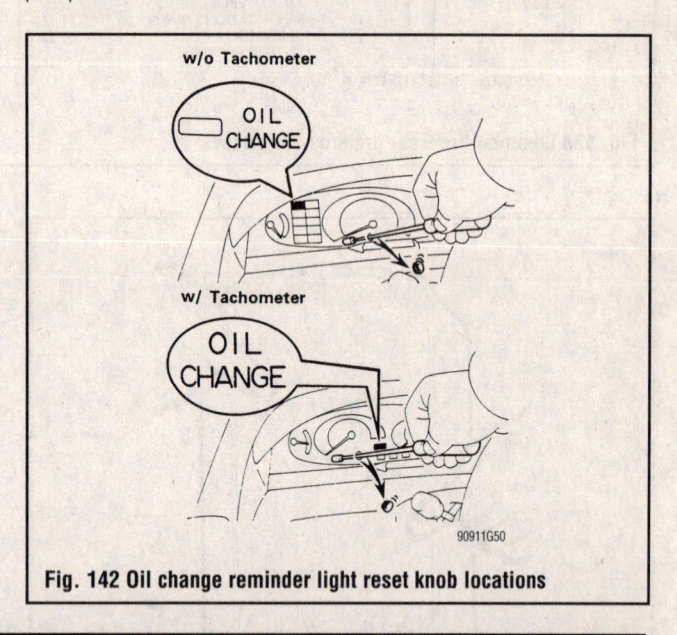

Fig. 142 Oil change reminder light reset knob locations

## FLUIDS AND LUBRICANTS

### Fluid Disposal

Used fluids such as engine oil, transmission fluid, antifreeze and brake fluid are hazardous wastes and must be disposed of properly. Before draining any fluids, consult with your local authorities; in many areas waste oil, etc. is being accepted as a part of recycling programs. A number of service stations and auto parts stores are also accepting waste fluids for recycling.

Be sure of the recycling center's policies before draining any fluids, as many will not accept different fluids that have been mixed together.

### Fuel and Engine Oil Recommendations

◆ See Figures 143, 144 and 145

OIL

The SAE (Society of Automotive Engineers) grade number indicates the viscosity of the engine oil; its resistance to flow at a given temperature. The lower the SAE grade number, the lighter the oil. For example, the monograde oils begin with SAE 5 weight, which is a thin light oil, and continue in viscosity up to SAE 80 or 90 weight, which are heavy gear lubricants. These oils are also known as "straight weight", meaning they are of a single viscosity, and do not vary with engine temperature.

Multi-viscosity oils offer the important advantage of being adaptable to temperature extremes. These oils have designations such as 10W-40, 20W-50, etc. The "10W-40" means that in winter (the "W" in the designation) the oil acts like a thin 10 weight oil, allowing the engine to spin easily when cold and offering rapid lubrication. Once the engine has warmed up, however, the oil acts like a straight 40 weight, maintaining good lubrication and protection for the engine's internal components. A 20W-50 oil would there-

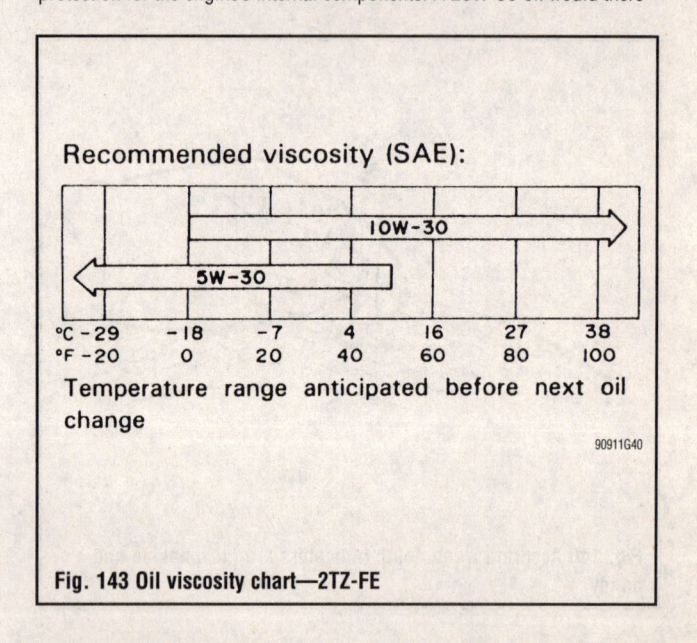

Fig. 143 Oil viscosity chart—2TZ-FE

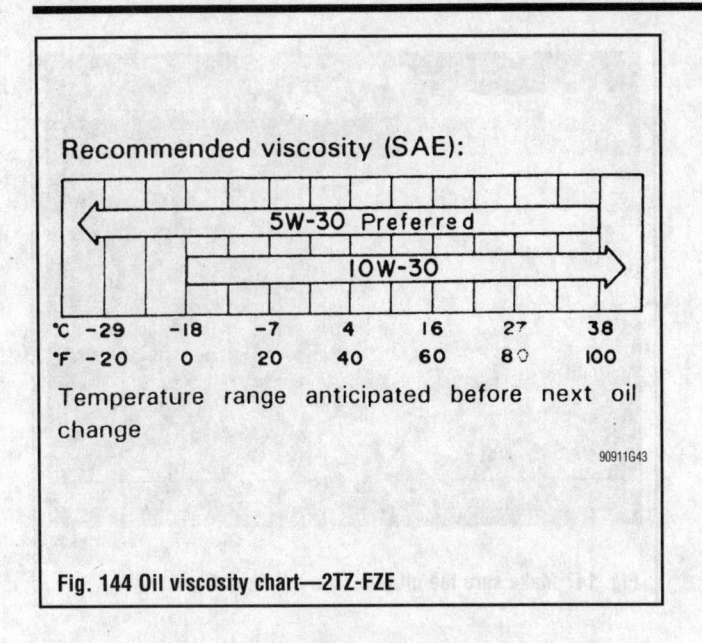

# GENERAL INFORMATION AND MAINTENANCE 1-51

**Fig. 144 Oil viscosity chart—2TZ-FZE**

**Fig. 145 Look for the API oil identification label when choosing your engine oil**

fore be slightly heavier than and not as ideal in cold weather as the 10W-40, but would offer better protection at higher rpm and temperatures because when warm it acts like a 50 weight oil. Whichever oil viscosity you choose when changing the oil, make sure you are anticipating the temperatures your engine will be operating in until the oil is changed again. Refer to the oil viscosity chart for oil recommendations according to temperature.

The API (American Petroleum Institute) designation indicates the classification of engine oil used under certain given operating conditions. Only oils designated for use "Service SH" (or its superseding type) should be used. Oils of the SH type perform a variety of functions inside the engine in addition to the basic function as a lubricant. Through a balanced system of metallic detergents and polymeric dispersants, the oil prevents the formation of high and low temperature deposits and also keeps sludge and particles of dirt in suspension. Acids, particularly sulfuric acid, as well as other by-products of combustion, are neutralized. Both the SAE grade number and the APE designation can be found on top of the oil can.

Diesel engines also require SH engine oil. In addition, the oil must qualify for a CC rating. The API has a number of different diesel engine ratings, including CB, CC, and CD. Any of these other oils are fine as long as the designation CC appears on the can along with them. Do not use oil labeled only SH or only CC. Both designations must always appear together.

For recommended oil viscosity's, refer to the chart. Note that 10W-30 and 10W-40 grade oils are not recommended for sustained high speed driving when the temperature rises above the indicated limit.

### Synthetic Oil

There are many excellent synthetic and fuel-efficient oils currently available that can provide better gas mileage, longer service life, and in some cases better engine protection. These benefits do not come without a few hitches, however, the main one being the price of synthetic oils, which is three or four times the price per quart of conventional oil.

Synthetic oil is not for every car and every type of driving, so you should consider your engine's condition and your type of driving. Also, check your car's warranty conditions regarding the use of synthetic oils.

Both brand new engines and older, high mileage engines are the wrong candidates for synthetic oil. The synthetic oils are so slippery that they can prevent the proper break-in of new engines; most manufacturer's recommend that you wait until the engine is properly broken in 5,000 miles (8,046km) before using synthetic oil.

Consider your type of driving. If most of your accumulated mileage is high speed, highway type driving, the more expensive synthetic oils may be of benefit. Extended highway driving gives the engine a chance to warm up, accumulating less acids in the oil and putting less stress on the engine over the long run. Under these conditions, the oil change interval can be extended (as long as your oil filter can last the extended life of the oil) up to the advertised mileage claims of the synthetics. Cars with synthetic oils may show increased fuel economy in highway driving, due to less internal friction. However, many automotive experts agree that 50,000 miles (80,465km) is too long to keep any oil in your engine.

Cars used under harder circumstances, such as stop-and-go, city type driving, short trips, or extended idling, should be serviced more frequently. For the engines in these cars, the much greater cost of synthetic or fuel-efficient oils may not be worth the investment. Internal wear increases much quicker on these cars, causing greater oil consumption and leakage.

## FUEL

It is important to use fuel of the proper octane rating in your car. Octane rating is based on the quantity of anti-knock compounds added to the fuel and it determines the speed at which the gas will burn. The lower the octane rating, the faster it burns. The higher the octane, the slower the fuel will burn and a greater percentage of compounds in the fuel prevent spark ping (knock), detonation and preignition (dieseling).

As the temperature of the engine increases, the air/fuel mixture exhibits a tendency to ignite before the spark plug is fired. If fuel of an octane rating too low for the engine is used, this will allow combustion to occur before the piston has completed its compression stroke, thereby creating a very high pressure very rapidly.

Fuel of the proper octane rating, for the compression ratio and ignition timing of your car, will slow the combustion process sufficiently to allow the spark plug enough time to ignite the mixture completely and smoothly. Many non-catalyst models are designed to run on regular fuel. The use of some super-premium fuel is no substitution for a properly tuned and maintained engine. Chances are that if your engine exhibits any signs of spark ping, detonation or pre-ignition when using regular fuel, the ignition timing should be checked against specifications or the cylinder head should be removed for decarbonizing.

Vehicles equipped with catalytic converters must use UNLEADED GASOLINE ONLY. Use of unleaded fuel shortened the life of spark plugs, exhaust systems and EGR valves and can damage the catalytic converter. Most converter equipped models are designed to operate using unleaded gasoline with a minimum rating of 87 octane. Use of unleaded gas with octane ratings lower than 87 can cause persistent spark knock which could lead to engine damage.

Light spark knock may be noticed when accelerating or driving up hills. The slight knocking may be considered normal (with 87 octane) because the maximum fuel economy is obtained under condition of occasional light spark knock. Gasoline with an octane rating higher than 87 may be used, but Toyota recommends a 91 octane rating for proper operation.

# 1-52 GENERAL INFORMATION AND MAINTENANCE

➡Your engine's fuel requirement can change with time, mainly due to carbon buildup, which changes the compression ratio. If your engine pings, knocks or runs on, switch to a higher grade of fuel. Sometimes just changing brands will cure the problem. If it becomes necessary to retard the timing from specifications, don't change it more than a few degrees. Retarded timing will reduce power output and fuel mileage and will increase the engine temperature.

OPERATION IN FOREIGN COUNTRIES

If you plan to drive your car outside the United States or Canada, there is a possibility that fuels will be too low in anti-knock quality and could produce engine damage. It is wise to consult with local authorities upon arrival in a foreign country to determine the best fuels available.

## Engine

### ✱✱ CAUTION

**Prolonged and repeated skin contact with used engine oil, with no effort to remove the oil, may be harmful. Always follow these simple precautions when handling used motor oil:**

- Avoid prolonged skin contact with used motor oil.
- Remove oil from skin by washing thoroughly with soap and water or waterless hand cleaner. Do not use gasoline, thinners or other solvents.
- Avoid prolonged skin contact with oil-soaked clothing.

The engine oil auto feeder system replaces the normal amount of oil consumed and does not lengthen the period of time between oil changes, so carry out the engine oil changes at the times prescribed.

If oil is poured only into the tank after the oil has been removed from the engine side, large quantities of oil are not immediately supplied to the engine, so always pour oil into the engine side.

The engine warning level light operates in response to the oil level sensor installed in the oil pan, so when the oil level warning light is lit up, it will not go off, even if oil is added to the oil tank.

OIL LEVEL CHECK

▸ See Figures 146 thru 151

Every time you stop for fuel, check the engine oil as follows:
1. Park the vehicle on level ground.
2. When checking the oil level it is best for the engine to be at operating temperature, although checking the oil immediately after a stopping will

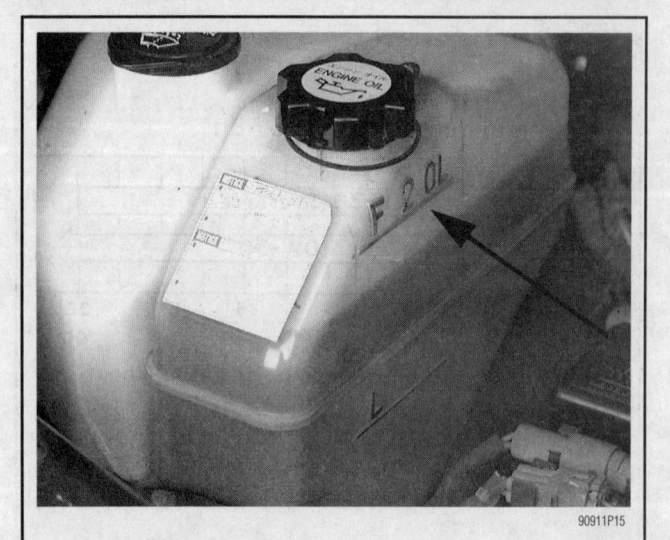

Fig. 147 Make sure the oil tank is to the F mark

Fig. 148 The oil dipstick is located under the driver's side engine access hole cover

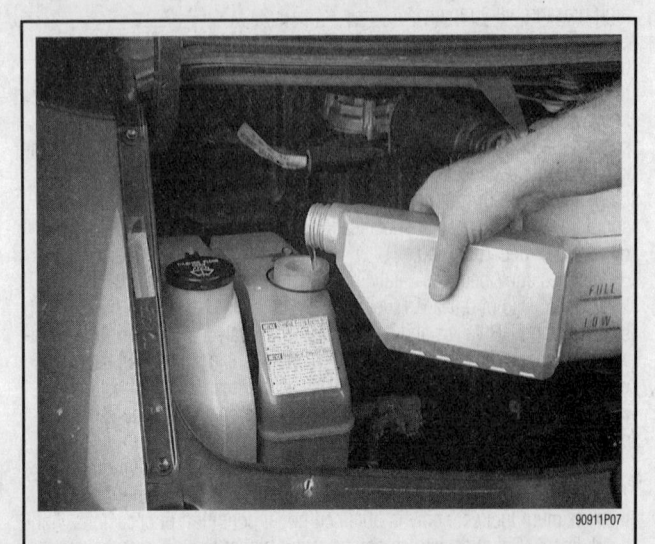

Fig. 146 Fill the engine oil tank located under the hood first

Fig. 149 Place your finger through the hole and pull straight up to remove

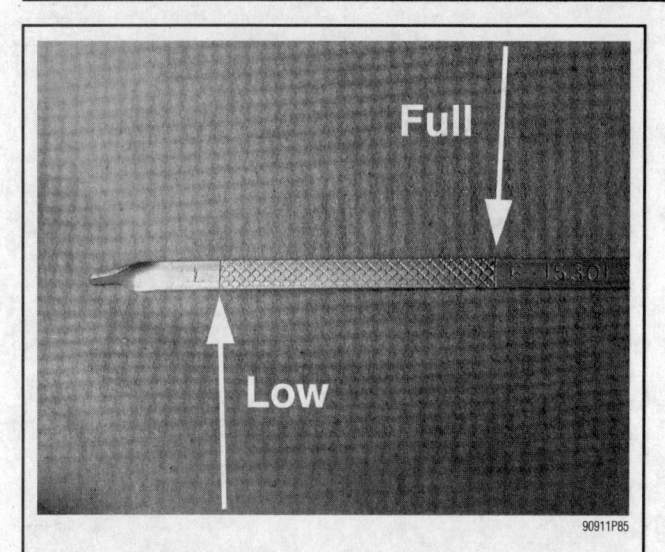

# GENERAL INFORMATION AND MAINTENANCE  1-53

Fig. 150 The oil dipstick has two markings for level check

Fig. 152 Remove the engine oil pan drain plug

Fig. 151 To fill the crankcase, remove the engine oil filler cap

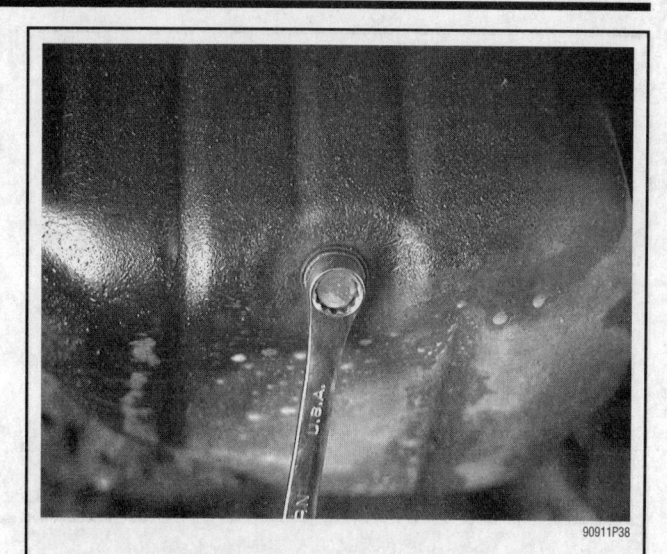

Fig. 153 Step back and allow the old oil to flow from the engine

Fig. 154 Remove the engine cover directly below the oil filter

lead to a false reading. Wait a few minutes after turning off the engine to allow the oil to drain back into the crankcase.

3. Open the hood and inspect the level of the engine oil tank. The fluid level on the tank should read between FULL or F and LOW or L.
4. If the level is below the LOW or L line, remove the cap and add enough engine oil to reach the FULL or F line.
5. Install the oil cap and hand tighten.
6. After filling the oil tank, remove the engine access hole cover on the drivers side.
7. Remove the engine oil dipstick and wipe it clean.
8. Reinsert the dipstick, push it in as far as it will go, the pull it out and look at the level on the end.
9. If necessary, insert more oil through the oil filler cap next to the dipstick, this will completely top off the system.

## OIL & FILTER CHANGE

▶ See Figures 152 thru 158

The oil should be changed every 7500 miles (12,000 km) (refer to the maintenance interval charts at the end of this section). Toyota recommends changing the oil filter with every other oil change; we suggest that the filter be changed with every oil change. There is approximately 1 quart of dirty

## 1-54  GENERAL INFORMATION AND MAINTENANCE

Fig. 155 Use a filter wrench to remove the oil filter

Fig. 156 Remember, some fluid will drain from the filter too

Fig. 157 Before installing a new oil filter, lightly coat the rubber gasket with clean oil

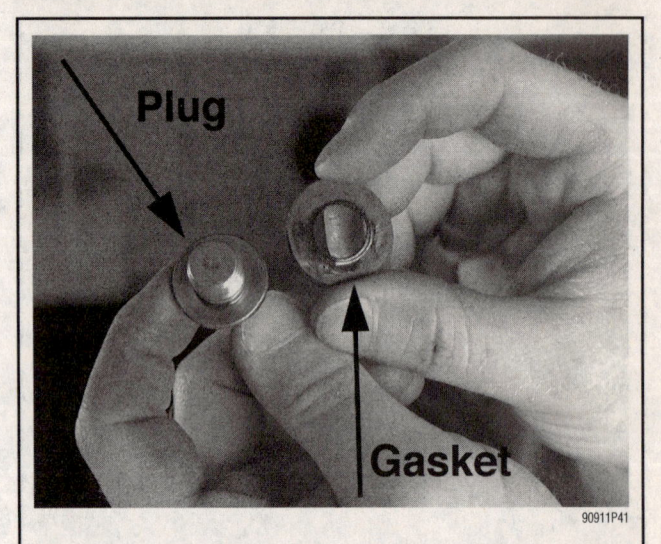

Fig. 158 Inspect the plug threads and always replace the gasket

oil left remaining in the old oil filter if it is not changed! A few dollars more every year seems a small price to pay for extended engine life so change the filter every time you change the oil!

### ✲✲ CAUTION

**Prolonged and repeated skin contact with used engine oil, with no effort to remove the oil, may be harmful. Always follow these simple precautions when handling used motor oil.**

- Avoid prolonged skin contract with used motor oil.
- Remove oil from skin by washing thoroughly with soap and water or waterless hand cleaner. Do not use gasoline, thinners or other solvents.
- Avoid prolonged skin contact with oil-soaked clothing.

If your car is being used under dusty, polluted or off-road conditions, change the oil and filter more frequently than specified. The same goes for cars driven in stop-and-go traffic or only for short distances. Always drain the oil after the engine has been running long enough to bring it to normal operating temperature. Hot oil will flow easier and more contaminants will be removed along with the oil than if it were drained cold. To change the oil and filter:

1. Warm the oil by running the engine for a short period of time or at least until the needle on the temperature gauge rises above the **C** mark. This will make the oil flow more freely from the oil pan.
2. Park on a level surface, apply the parking brake and block the wheels. Stop the engine. Raise the hood and remove the oil filler cap from the top of the valve cover. Also remove the oil filler cap on the oil tank located under the hood. This allows the air to enter the engine as the oil drains. Remove the dipstick, wipe it off and set it aside.
3. Position a suitable oil drain pan under the drain plug.

➥All engines hold approximately 6 quarts of oil, so choose a drain pan that exceeds this amount to allow for movement of the oil when the pan is pulled from under the vehicle. This will prevent time lost to the cleaning up of messy oil spills.

4. With the proper size metric socket or closed end wrench (DO NOT use pliers or vise grips), loosen the drain plug. Back out the drain plug while maintaining a slight upward force on it to keep the oil from running out around it (and your hand). Allow the oil to drain into the drain pan. It is recommended to discard the old gasket and replace with a new one each oil change.

### ✲✲ CAUTION

**The engine oil will be hot. Keep your arms, face and hands away from the oil as it is draining**

# GENERAL INFORMATION AND MAINTENANCE 1-55

5. Remove the drain pan and wipe any excess oil from the area around the hole using a clean rag. Clean the threads of the drain plug and the drain plug gasket to remove any sludge deposits that may have accumulated.
6. To keep from engine oil spilling onto the engine cover, it may be necessary to remove it prior to the filter.
7. With a filter wrench, loosen the oil filter counterclockwise and back the filter off the filter post the rest of the way by hand. Keep the filter end up so that the oil does not spill out. Tilt the filter into the drain pan to drain the oil.
8. Remove the drain pan from under the vehicle and position it off to the side.
9. With a clean rag, wipe off the filter seating surface to ensure a proper seal. Make sure that the old gasket is not stuck to the seating surface. If it is, remove it and thoroughly clean the seating surface of the old gasket material.
10. Open a container of new oil and smear some of this oil onto the rubber gasket of the new oil filter. Get a feel for where the filter post is and start the filter by hand until the gasket contacts the seat. Using the filter wrench, turn the filter an additional ¾ turn.
11. Install the drain plug and metal gasket. Be sure that the plug is tight enough that the oil does not leak out, but not tight enough to strip the threads. Over time you will develop a sense of what the proper tightness of the drain plug is. If a torque wrench is available, tighten the plug to 27 ft. lbs. (37 Nm).

➡ **Replace the drain plug gasket every time you change the oil to prevent leakage.**

12. Through a suitable plastic or metal funnel, add clean new oil of the proper grade and viscosity through the oil filler on the top of the valve cover. Be sure that the oil level registers near the **F** (full) mark on the dipstick.
13. Install and tighten the oil filler cap.
14. Open the hood and fill the engine oil tank. The fluid level on the tank should read FULL or F.
15. Start the engine and allow it to run for several minutes. Check for leaks at the filter and drain plug. Sometimes leaks will not be revealed until the engine reaches normal operating temperature.
16. Stop the engine and recheck the oil level. Add oil as necessary.

## Manual Transmission

### FLUID RECOMMENDATIONS

All Previa van manual transmissions use Grade GL-4 or GL-5 with the viscosity of SAE75W-90 gear oil.

### LEVEL CHECK

▶ See Figure 159

The oil in the manual transmission should be checked at least every 15,000 miles (24,000 km) and replaced every 25,000–30,000 miles (40,000–48,000 km), even more frequently if driven in deep water.
1. With the vehicle parked on a level surface, remove the filler plug from the transmission housing.
2. If the lubricant begins to trickle out of the hole, there is enough. Otherwise, carefully insert your finger (watch out for sharp threads!) and check to see if the oil is up to the edge of the hole.
3. If not, add oil through the hole until the level is at the edge of the hole. Most gear lubricants come in a plastic squeeze bottle with a nozzle; making additions simple.
4. Replace the filler plug and tighten it to 27 ft. lbs. (37 Nm). Run the engine and check for leaks.

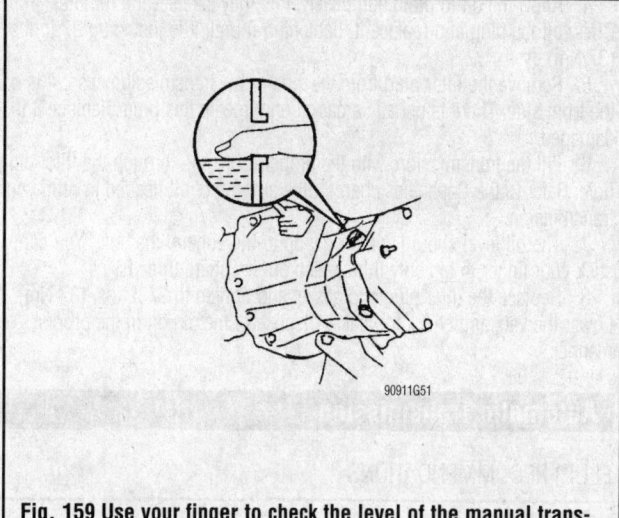

Fig. 159 Use your finger to check the level of the manual transmission fluid

### DRAIN & REFILL

▶ See Figure 160

1. The transmission oil should be hot before it is drained. If the engine is at normal operating temperature, the transmission oil should be hot enough.
2. Raise the car and support it properly on jackstands so that you can safely work underneath. You will probably not have enough room to work if the van is not raised.
3. The drain plug is located on the bottom of the transmission. Place a pan under the drain plug and remove it. Keep a slight upward pressure on the plug while unscrewing it, this will keep the oil from pouring out until the plug is removed.

**✲✲ CAUTION**

The oil will be HOT! Be careful when you remove the plug so that you don't take a bath in hot gear oil.

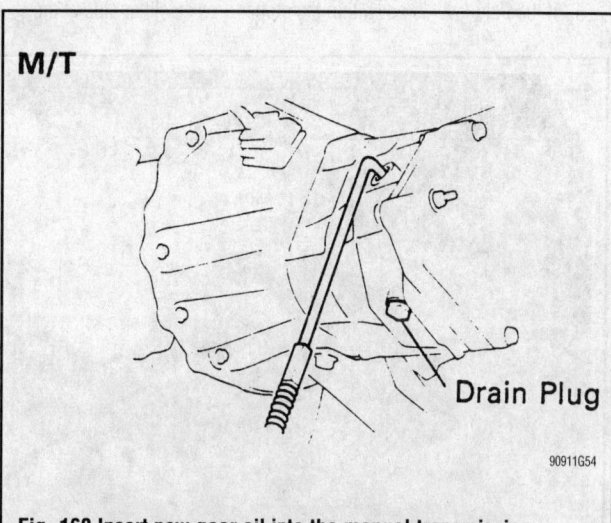

Fig. 160 Insert new gear oil into the manual transmission through the fill plug hole

# 1-56 GENERAL INFORMATION AND MAINTENANCE

4. Allow the oil to drain completely, this may take several minutes. Clean off the plug and replace it, tightening it until it is just snug 27 ft. lbs. (37 Nm).

5. Remove the filler plug from the side of the transmission case. It is on the front side. There is usually a gasket underneath this plug. Replace it if damaged.

6. Fill the transmission, with the proper lubricant, through the filler plug hole. Refer to the Capacities chart for the amount of oil needed to refill your transmission.

7. The oil level should come right up to the edge of the hole. You can stick your finger in to verify this. Watch out for sharp threads!

8. Replace the filler plug and gasket and tighten to 27 ft. lbs. (37 Nm). Lower the van, and check for leaks. Dispose of the old oil in the proper manner.

## Automatic Transmission

### FLUID RECOMMENDATIONS

All Toyota Previa automatic transmissions use ATF Dexron® II or Dexron® III fluid.

### LEVEL CHECK

▶ See Figures 161, 162 and 163

Check the automatic transmission fluid level at least every 15,000 miles (24,000 km). The dipstick is located in the under engine access hole cover compartment. The fluid level should be checked only when the transmission is hot (normal operating temperature). The transmission is considered hot after about 20 miles of highway driving.

1. Park the van on a level surface with the engine idling. Shift the transmission into **P** and set the parking brake.

2. Remove the dipstick, wipe it clean and reinsert if firmly. Be sure that it has been pushed all the way in. Remove the dipstick and check the fluid level while holding it horizontally. All models have a HOT and a COLD side to the dipstick.

- **COLD**—The fluid level should fall in this range when the engine has been running for only a short time.
- **HOT**—The fluid level should fall in this range when the engine has reached normal running temperatures.

3. If the fluid level is not within the proper area on either side of the dipstick, pour ATF into the dipstick tube. This is easily done with the aid of a funnel. Check the level often as you are filling the transmission. Be extremely careful not to overfill it. Overfilling will cause slippage, seal damage and overheating. Approximately one pint of ATF will raise the level from one notch to the other.

➡ **Always use the proper transmission fluid when filling your car's transmission. All Previa models use Dexron® II or Dexron® III. Always check with the owner's manual to be sure. NEVER use Type F or Type T in a transmission requiring Dexron® II/Dexron® III or vice versa, as severe damage will result.**

### ※※ CAUTION

**The fluid on the dipstick should always be a bright red color. It if is discolored (brown or black), or smells burnt, serious transmission troubles, probably due to overheating, should be suspected. The transmission should be inspected by a qualified service technician to locate the cause of the burnt fluid.**

Fig. 162 While the engine is idling, pull out the dipstick and check the fluid level

Fig. 161 Push back the lever on the automatic transmission dipstick

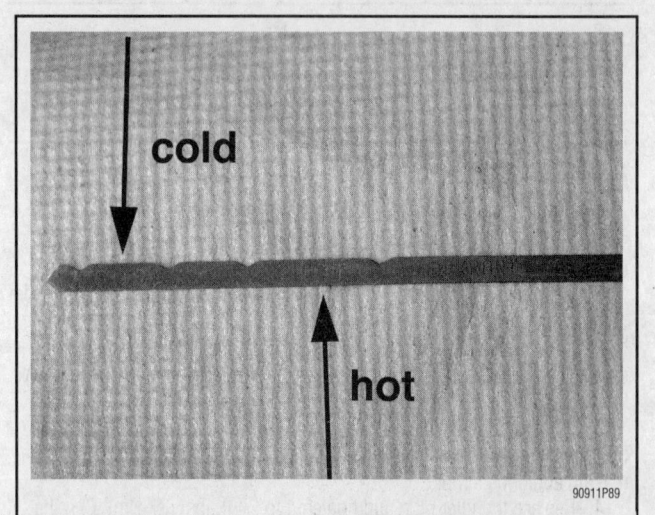

Fig. 163 Level indicators are marked on the dipstick for the transmission

# GENERAL INFORMATION AND MAINTENANCE  1-57

## DRAIN & REFILL

▶ See Figures 164, 165, 166, 167 and 168

The automatic transmission fluid should be changed at least every 25,000–30,000 miles (40,000–48,000 km). If the van is normally used in severe service, such as stop-and-go driving, trailer towing or the like, the interval should be halved. The fluid should be hot before it is drained; a 20 minute drive will accomplish this.

1. Remove the dipstick from the filler tube and install a funnel in the opening.
2. Position a suitable drain pan under the drain plug. Loosen the drain plug and allow the fluid to drain.
3. Install and tighten the drain plug to 15 ft. lbs. (20 Nm).
4. Through the filler tube opening, add the proper amount of transmission fluid as specified in the Capacities Chart.
5. Start the engine and shift the selector into all positions from P through L, the shift into P.
6. Check the fluid level and add as required.

### ❈❈ WARNING

**Do not overfill the transmission.**

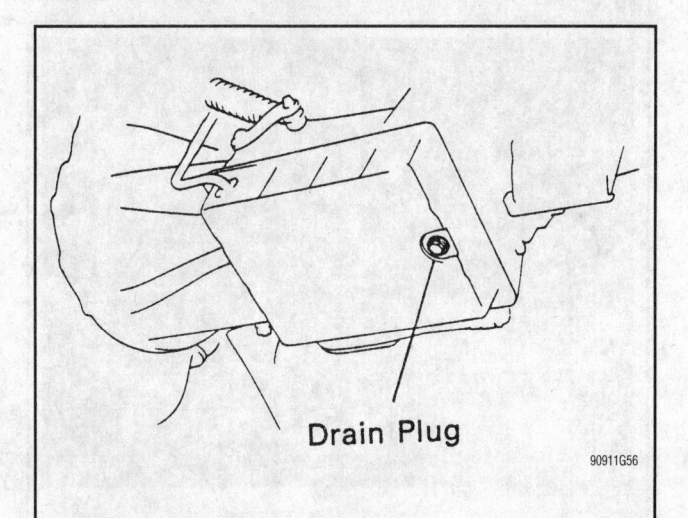

Fig. 164 The automatic transmission drain plug is located at the bottom of the pan

Fig. 165 Loosen and remove the drain plug on the automatic transmission

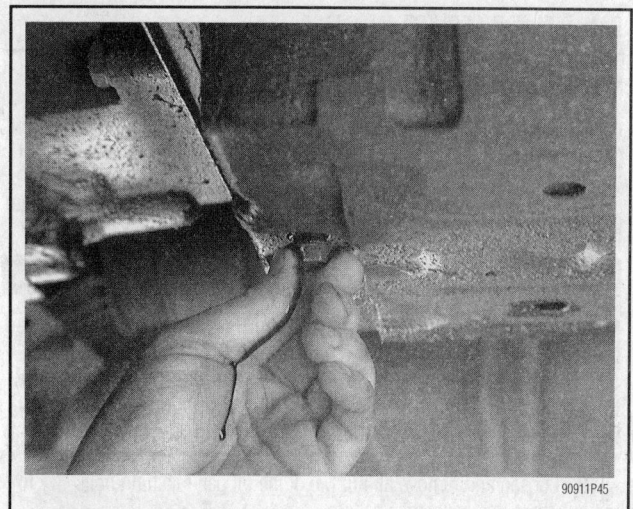

Fig. 166 Some fluid may drip onto your hand as you remove the plug

Fig. 167 Allow all the fluid to flow from the pan into a suitable container

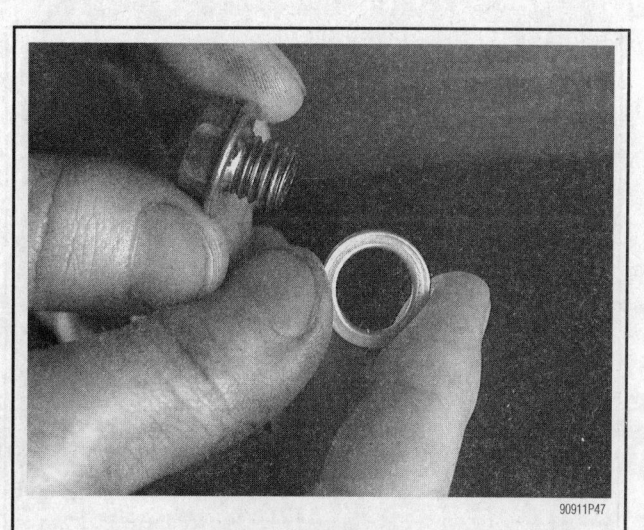

Fig. 168 Before installing, inspect the plug and gasket for damaged threads and deterioration

## 1-58 GENERAL INFORMATION AND MAINTENANCE

PAN & FILTER SERVICE

▶ See Figures 169 thru 183

1. To avoid contamination of the transmission, thoroughly clean the exterior of the oil pan and surrounding area to remove any deposits of dirt and grease.
2. Position a suitable drain pan under the oil pan and remove the drain plug. Allow the oil to drain from the pan. Set the drain plug aside.

**✳✳ CAUTION**

Check the fluid in the drain pan, it should always be a bright red color. It if is discolored (brown or black), or smells burnt, serious transmission troubles, probably due to overheating, should be suspected. The transmission should be inspected by a qualified service technician to locate the cause of the burnt fluid.

3. Loosen and remove all but two of the oil pan retaining bolts. Try to remove them in a crisscross pattern.
4. Support the pan by hand and slowly remove the remaining two bolts.

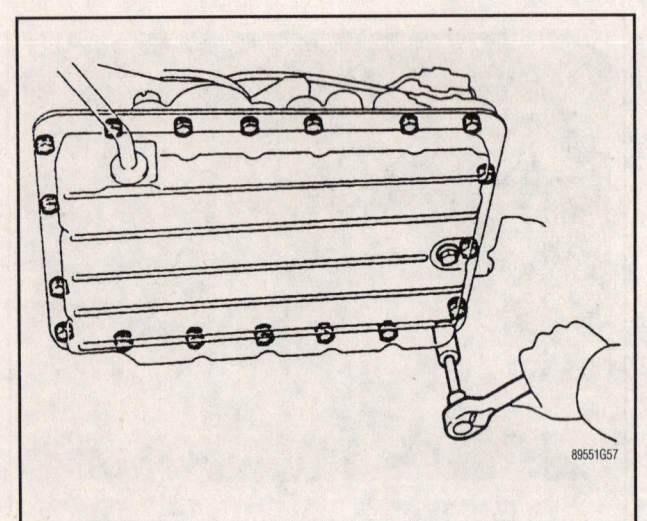

Fig. 169 Remove the transmission pan retaining bolts in a crisscross pattern

Fig. 170 Remove all of these bolts when lowering the automatic drain pan

Fig. 171 Always use two hands to lower the pan

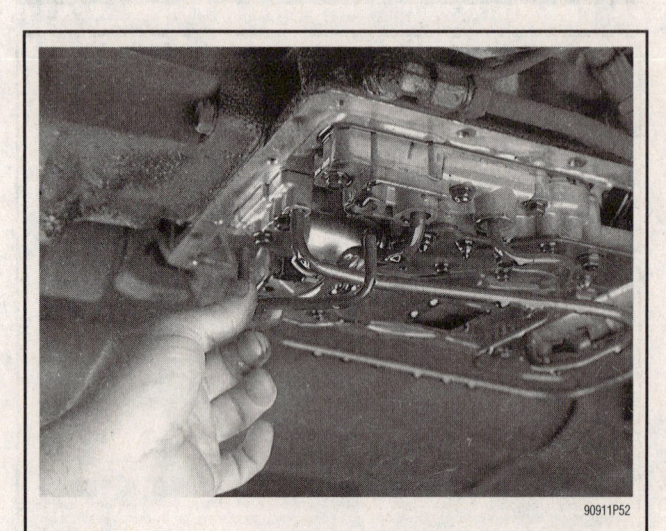

Fig. 172 On some models, the transmission tubes will need to be removed

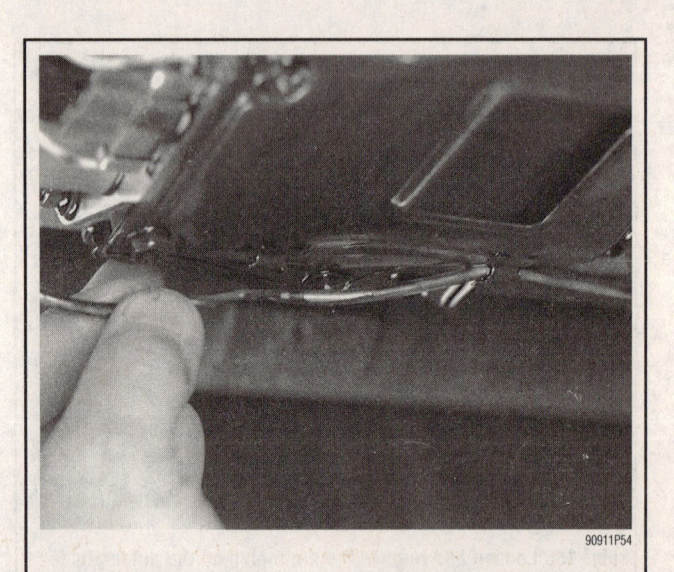

Fig. 173 Disengage the wiring for the solenoids if present

# GENERAL INFORMATION AND MAINTENANCE 1-59

Fig. 174 Remove the oil strainer retaining bolts . . .

Fig. 175 . . . then lower the strainer

Fig. 176 Scrape any old gasket material from around the mating area

Fig. 177 Clean and inspect the magnets in the bottom of the transmission pan

Fig. 178 Clean all the mating areas around the transmission

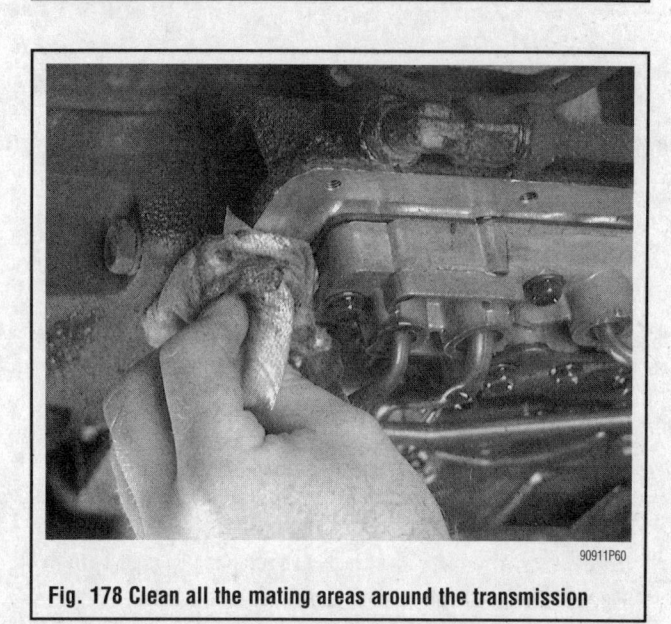

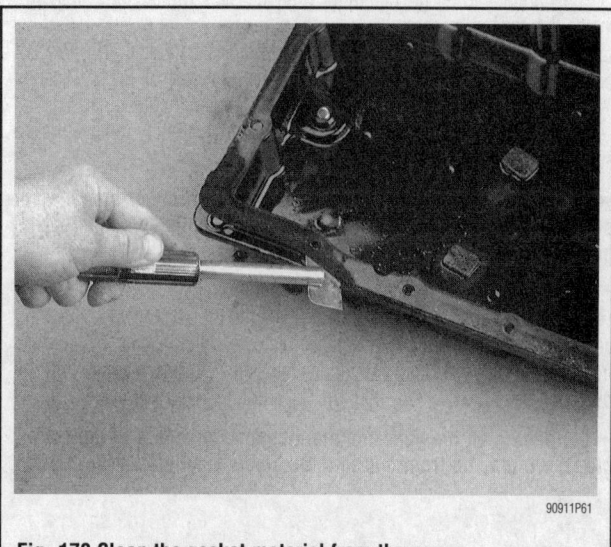

Fig. 179 Clean the gasket material from the pan

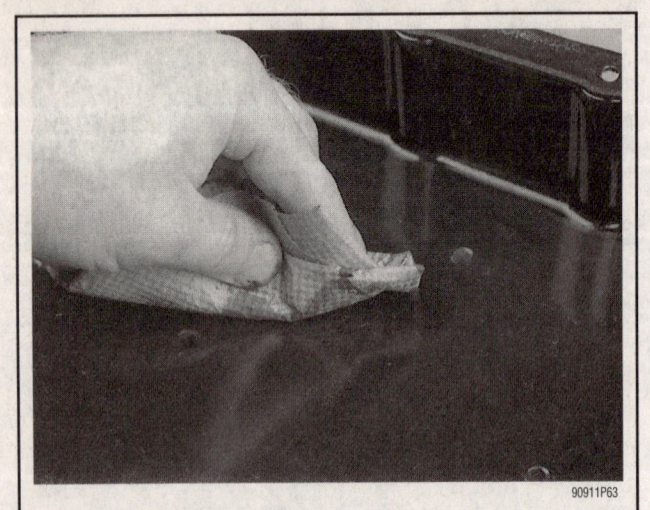

# 1-60 GENERAL INFORMATION AND MAINTENANCE

Fig. 180 A rag can be used to thoroughly clean the inside of the pan

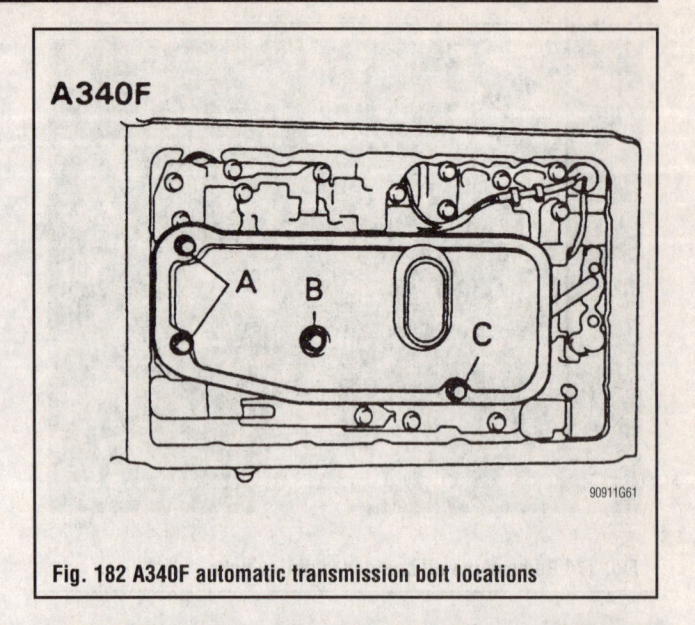

Fig. 182 A340F automatic transmission bolt locations

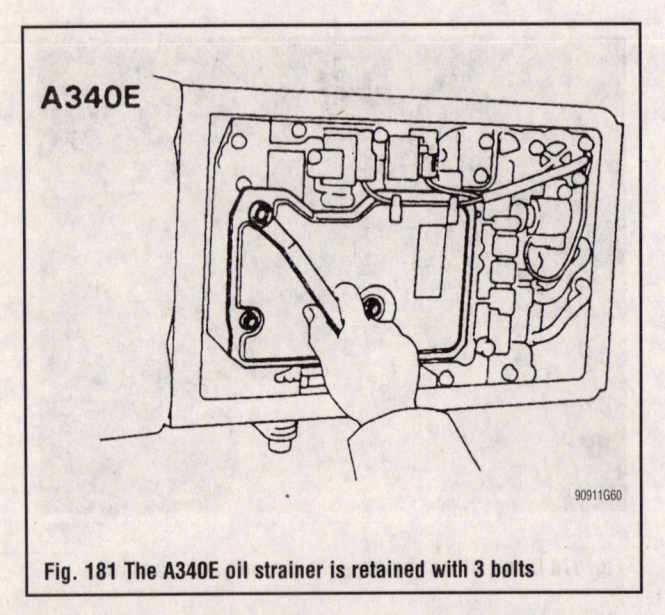

Fig. 181 The A340E oil strainer is retained with 3 bolts

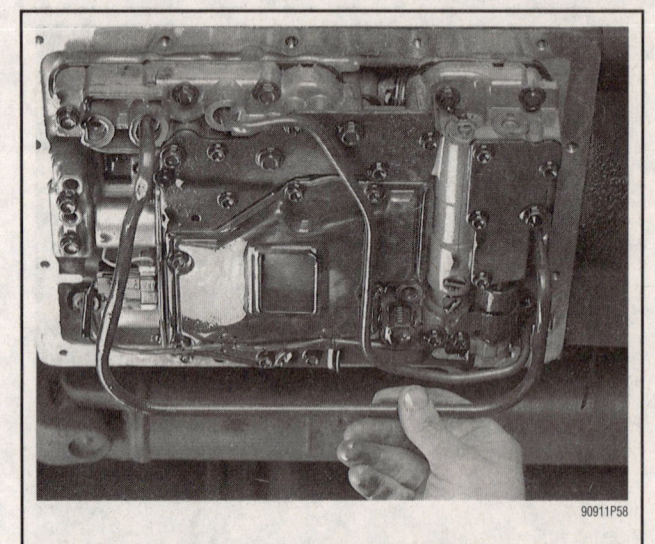

Fig. 183 Install the oil tubes on models equipped

5. Carefully lower the pan to the ground. There will be some fluid still inside the pan, so be careful.
6. On the A46DE and A46DF, oil tubes cover the strainer area. Pry up both oil tube ends with a large tool and remove the four oil tubes. Disconnect the wiring from the No. 1 and No. 2 and the No. 3 solenoids.
7. Remove the oil strainer attaching bolts and carefully remove the strainer. The strainer will also contain some fluid.

➡ Some of the oil strainer bolts may be slightly longer than the others. Make a mental note of where the longer bolts go so that it may be reinstalled in the original position.

8. Remove the oil strainer and discard the old gaskets.
9. Drain the remainder of the fluid from the oil pan and wipe the pan clean with a rag. With a gasket scraper, remove any old gasket material from the flanges of the pan and the transmission. All van automatic transmissions use FIPG (08826–00090), Three bond 1281 or equivalent.

➡ Depending on the year and maintenance schedule of the vehicle, there may be from one to three small magnets on the bottom of the pan. These magnets were installed by the manufacturer at the time the transmission was assembled. The magnets function to collect metal chips and filings from clutch plates, bushings and bearings that accumulate during the normal break-in process that a new transmission experiences. So, don't be alarmed if such accumulations are present. Clean the magnets and reinstall them. They are useful tools for determining transmission component wear.

To install:
10. Install the new oil strainer with new gaskets. Tighten the retaining bolts in their proper locations.
11. Tighten the oil strainer bolts to the following:
- A46DE and A46DF—48 inch lbs. (5 Nm)
- A340E and A340F—7 ft. lbs. (10 Nm)
12. When installing the bolts on the A340F, insert as specified:
- A—0.63 inch (16mm)
- B—0.79 inch (20mm)
- C—1.10 inch (28mm)

# GENERAL INFORMATION AND MAINTENANCE  1-61

13. Install any components such as the oil tubes.
14. Install the new sealant onto the oil pan. Position the magnets so that they will not interfere with the oil tubes.
15. Raise the pan and gasket into position on the transmission and install the retaining bolts. Tighten the retaining bolts in a crisscross pattern to:
   - A340E and A340F—65 inch lbs. (7 Nm)
   - A46DE and A46DF—39 inch lbs. (4 Nm)
16. Install and tighten the drain plug to 15 ft. lbs. (20 Nm).
17. Fluid is added only through the dipstick tube. Use only the proper automatic transmission fluid; do not overfill.
18. Replace the dipstick after filling. Start the engine and allow it to idle. DO NOT race the engine!
19. After the engine has idled for a few minutes, shift the transmission slowly through the gears and then return it to **P**. With the engine still idling, check the fluid level on the dipstick. If necessary, add more fluid to raise the level to where it is supposed to be.

## Transfer Case

### FLUID RECOMMENDATIONS

All Previa van transfer cases use Grade GL-4 or GL-5 with the viscosity of SAE75W-90 gear oil.

### LEVEL CHECK

▶ See Figures 184, 185 and 186

The oil in the transfer case should be checked at least every 15,000 miles (24,000 km) and replaced every 25,000–30,000 miles (40,000–48,000 km), even more frequently if driven in deep water.

1. With the van parked on a level surface, remove the filler plug from the transfer case housing. the filler plug is the higher of the two plugs on the unit.
2. If the lubricant begins to trickle out of the hole, there is enough. Otherwise, carefully insert your finger (watch out for sharp threads!) and check to see if the oil is up to the edge of the hole.
3. If not, add oil through the hole until the level is at the edge of the hole. Most gear lubricants come in a plastic squeeze bottle with a nozzle; making additions simple.
4. Replace the filler plug and tighten it to 29 ft. lbs. (39 Nm). Run the engine and check for leaks.

### DRAIN & REFILL

▶ See Figures 187 thru 192

Once every 30,000 miles (48,000 km), the oil in the transfer case should be changed.

1. The transfer case oil should be hot before it is drained. If the engine is at normal operating temperature, the oil should be hot enough.
2. Raise the van and support it properly on jackstands so that you can safely work underneath. You will probably not have enough room to work if the van is not raised.
3. Remove the filler plug from the side of the case. There will be a gasket underneath this plug. Replace it if damaged.

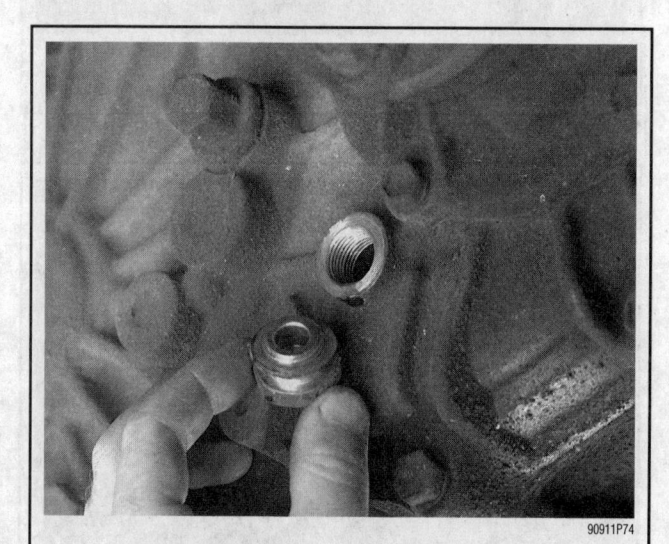

Fig. 184 Remove the filler plug with gasket . . .

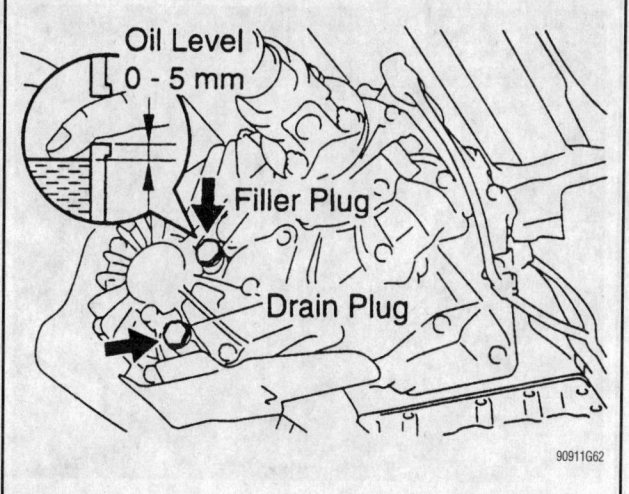

Fig. 185 . . . then use your finger to check the level of the transfer case fluid

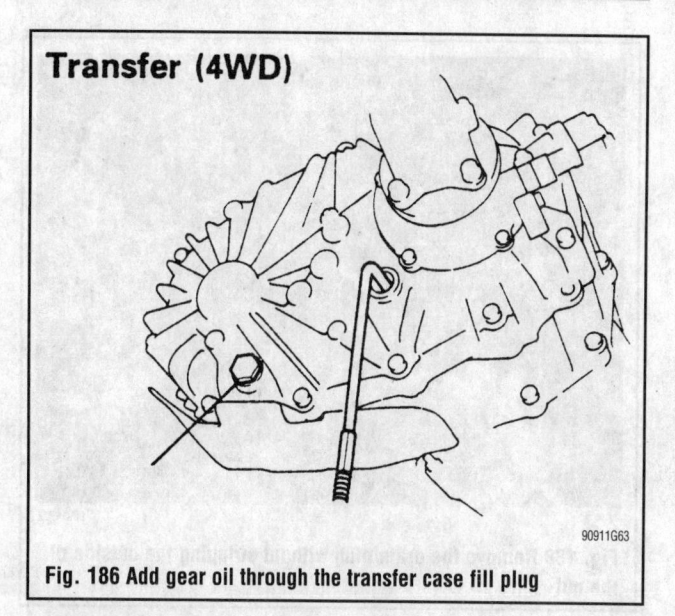

Fig. 186 Add gear oil through the transfer case fill plug

## 1-62 GENERAL INFORMATION AND MAINTENANCE

Fig. 187 Loosen and remove the filler plug before the drain plug

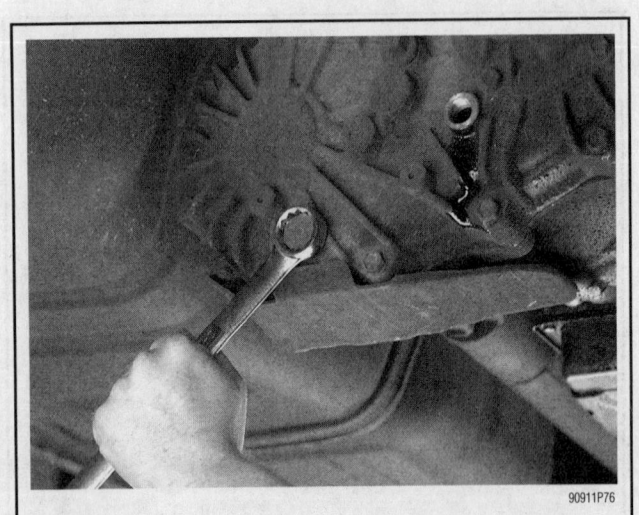

Fig. 188 Remove the drain plug without stripping the outside of the nut

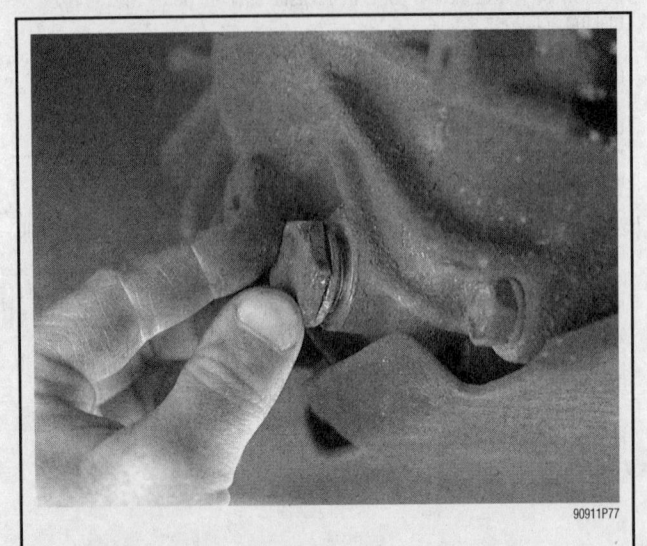

Fig. 189 Be careful when you remove the plug . . .

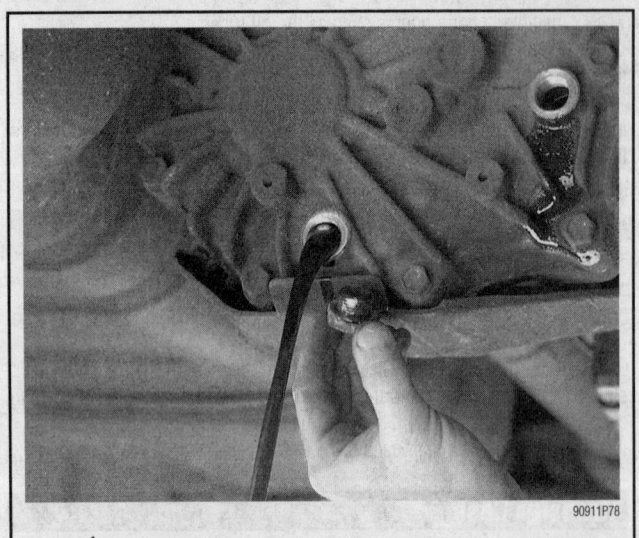

Fig. 190 . . . the fluid will come out very quickly

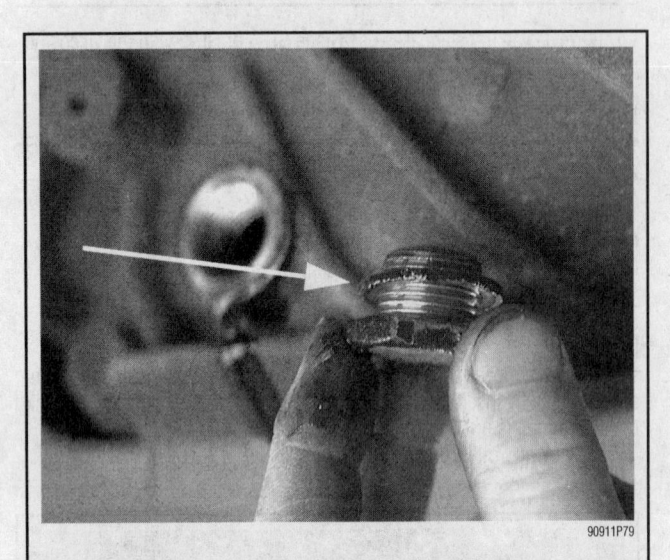

Fig. 191 Inspect and discard the gasket if deteriorated

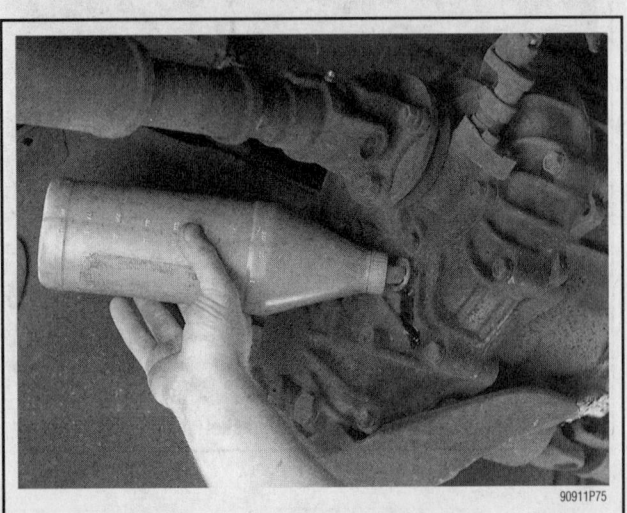

Fig. 192 Fill the transfer case through the filler hole until fluid starts to flow out

# GENERAL INFORMATION AND MAINTENANCE 1-63

4. The drain plug is located on the bottom of the transfer case. Place a pan under the drain plug and remove it. Keep a slight inward pressure on the plug while unscrewing it, this will keep the oil from pouring out until the plug is removed.

### ※※ CAUTION

The oil will be HOT. Be careful when you remove the plug so that you don't take a bath in hot gear oil.

5. Allow the oil to drain completely. Clean off the plug and replace it, tightening it until it is just snug 29 ft. lbs. (39 Nm).
6. Fill the transfer case with gear oil through the filler plug hole as detailed previously. Refer to the Capacities chart for the amount of oil needed to refill your transfer case.
7. The oil level should come right up to the edge of the hole. You can stick your finger in to verify this. Watch out for sharp threads.
8. Replace the filler plug and gasket, tighten to 29 ft. lbs. (39 Nm), lower the van, and check for leaks. Dispose of the old oil in the proper manner.

## Drive Axle

### FLUID RECOMMENDATIONS

All Previa van drive axles (front and rear) use Grade GL-4 or GL-5 with the viscosity of SAE75W-90 gear oil.

### LEVEL CHECK

▶ See Figures 193, 194 and 195

1. Raise and safely support the vehicle.
2. Visually check the area around the fill and drain plugs of the axle.
3. Clean the areas, the remove the fill plug.

➡It is always a good idea to remove the fill plug before the drain plug. In case the plug is stripped or stuck and you are left with an empty axle and no way to install fresh fluid.

4. If the lubricant begins to trickle out of the hole, there is enough. Otherwise, carefully insert your finger (watch out for sharp threads!) and check to see if the oil is up to the edge of the hole.
5. If not, add oil through the hole until the level is at the edge of the

Fig. 193 Loosen and remove the fill plug on the drive axle

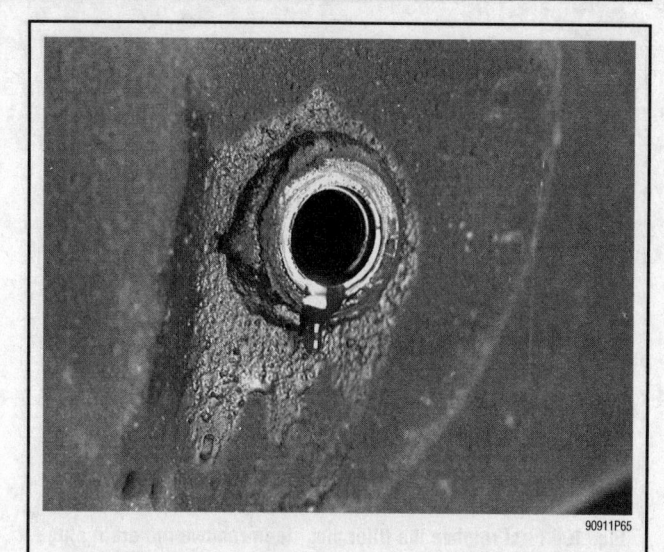

Fig. 194 Check for fluid trickling out of the fill plug hole

Fig. 195 Use a squeeze bottle to top off or fill the drive axle with gear oil

hole. Most gear lubricants come in a plastic squeeze bottle with a nozzle; making additions simple.

6. Install the filler plug and tighten it to 29 ft. lbs. (39 Nm) on the front and 36 ft. lbs. (49 Nm) for the rear axle. Check for leaks.

### DRAIN & REFILL

▶ See Figures 196 thru 201

1. The axle oil should be hot before it is drained. If the engine is at normal operating temperature, the oil should be hot enough.
2. Raise the van and support it properly on jackstands so that you can safely work underneath. You will probably not have enough room to work if the van is not raised.
3. Remove the filler plug from the back of the gear housing. There will be a gasket underneath this plug. Replace it if damaged.
4. The drain plug is located on the bottom of the gear case. Place a pan under the drain plug and remove it. Keep a slight inward pressure on the plug while unscrewing it, this will keep the oil from pouring out until the plug is removed.

# 1-64 GENERAL INFORMATION AND MAINTENANCE

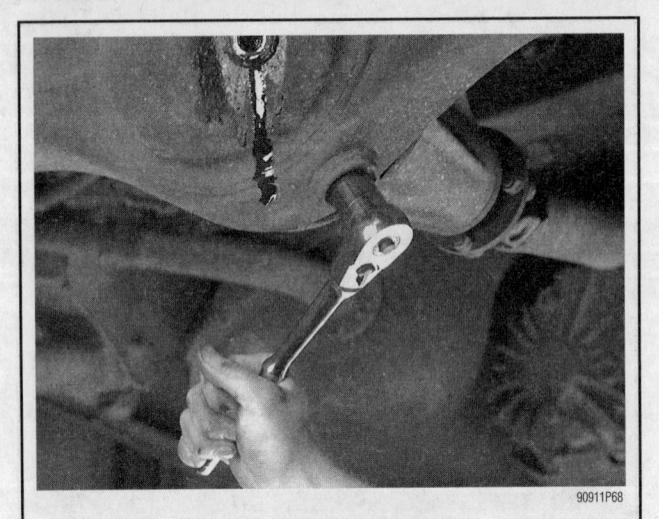

Fig. 196 First remove the filler plug, then remove the drain plug located in the bottom of the axle

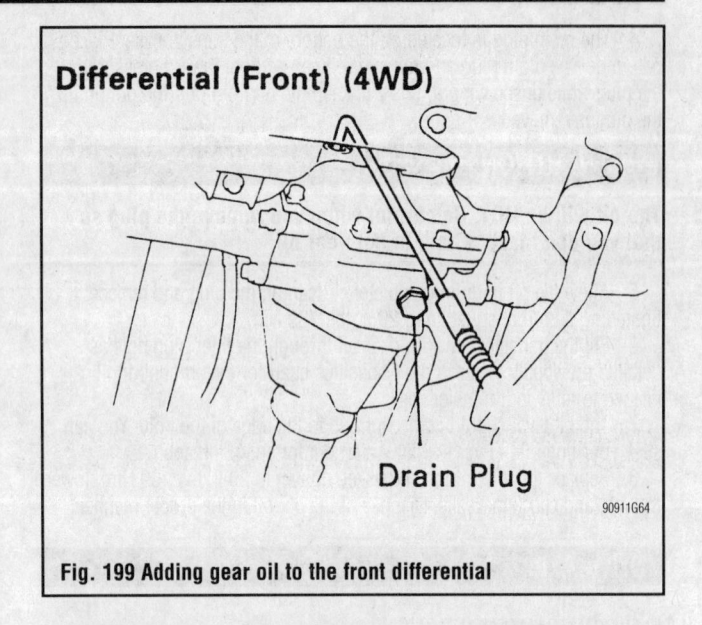

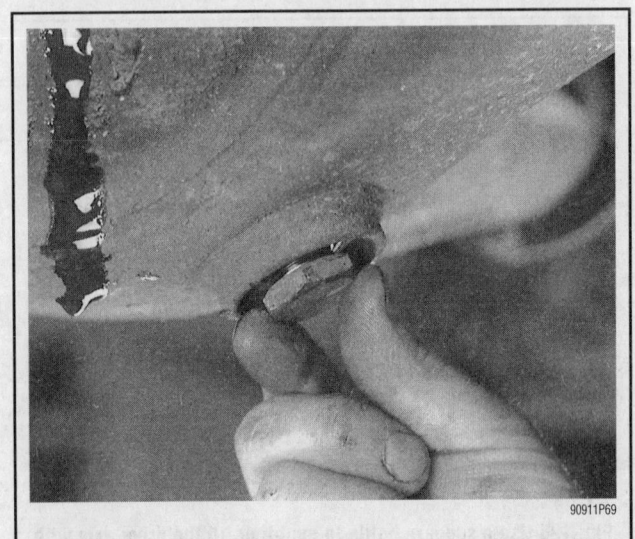

Fig. 197 Keep inward pressure on the plug . . .

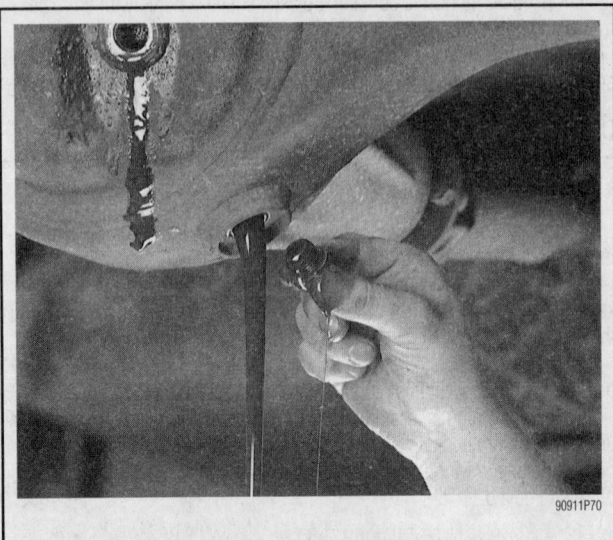

Fig. 198 . . . then quickly pull the plug away from the axle

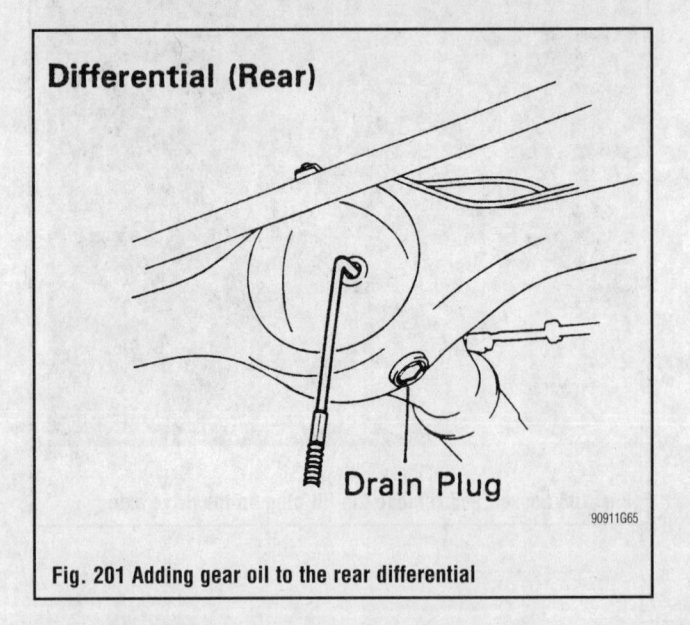

## Differential (Front) (4WD)

Fig. 199 Adding gear oil to the front differential

Fig. 200 If necessary, use a hose extension to add fluid

## Differential (Rear)

Fig. 201 Adding gear oil to the rear differential

# GENERAL INFORMATION AND MAINTENANCE 1-65

## ✻✻ CAUTION

The oil will be hot. Be careful when you remove the plug so that you don't take a bath in hot gear oil.

5. Allow the oil to drain completely. Clean off the plug and replace it, tightening it to 36 ft. lbs. (49 Nm).
6. Fill the gear housing with gear oil through the filler plug hole as detailed previously.
7. The oil level should come right up to the edge of the hole. You can stick your finger in to verify this. Watch out for sharp threads.
8. Install the filler plug and gasket, tighten to 29 ft. lbs. (39 Nm) on front housings and 36 ft. lbs. (49 Nm) on rears. Lower the van, and check for leaks. Dispose of the old oil in the proper manner.

## Supercharger

### FLUID RECOMMENDATIONS

All Previa superchargers use a special supercharger oil (08885–80108) or equivalent.

### LEVEL CHECK

♦ See Figures 202 and 203

➥When the engine is cold, check the level of the supercharger dipstick. Inspect the supercharger oil every 30,000 miles (48,000 km).

1. Park the vehicle on a level spot and turn the engine off.
2. On the 4WD models, remove the left front suspension support member and the shift cable stay.
3. Turn the yellow headed supercharger oil level dipstick counterclockwise and pull it out.
4. Wipe the dipstick with a clean rag.
5. Reinsert the dipstick, turn it fully clockwise or the reading will not be correct.
6. Remove the dipstick again and look at the oil level on the end.
7. The oil level should be between the **L** and **F** marks on the dipstick.
8. If the level is low, check for leakage and Air Control Valve (ACV), and add oil up to the **F** mark.
9. Add supercharger oil through the dipstick tube using a vinyl tube and syringe. Recheck the oil level.

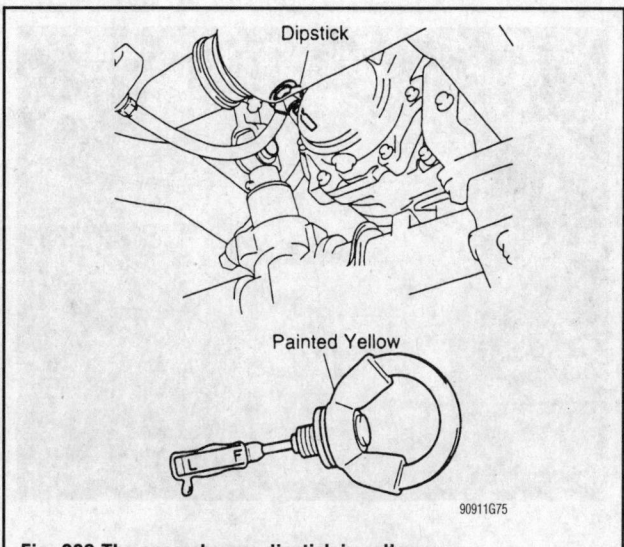

Fig. 202 The supercharger dipstick is yellow

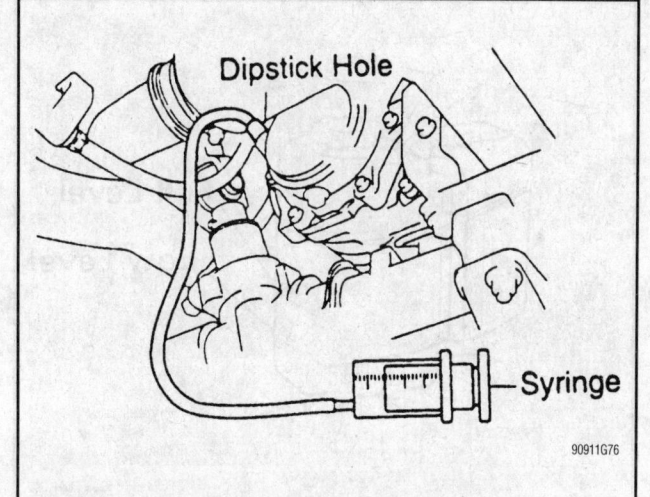

Fig. 203 Using a syringe and vinyl tube, insert the supercharger oil into the dipstick tube

➥The supercharger could be damaged if it is overfilled or the oil level is low.

10. On the 4WD models, reinstall the left front suspension support member and shift cable assembly.

### DRAIN & REFILL

➥Inspect the supercharger oil every 30,000 miles (48,000 km). Toyota does not have an interval to drain and refill the system. If necessary, remove the magnetic plug under the rear cover and drain the oil. Insert the plug with gasket and using a syringe and vinyl tube, fill the system with supercharger oil.

## Cooling System

### FLUID RECOMMENDATIONS

The correct coolant is any permanent, high quality ethylene glycol antifreeze mixed in a 50/50 concentration with water. This mixture gives the best combination of antifreeze and anti-boil characteristics within the engine.

### LEVEL CHECK

♦ See Figure 204

### ✻✻ CAUTION

Always allow the van to sit and cool for an hour or so (longer is better) before removing the reservoir tank cap. To avoid injury when working on a warm engine, cover the reservoir tank cap with a thick cloth and turn it slowly counterclockwise until the pressure begins to escape. After the pressure is completely removed, remove the cap. Never remove the cap until the pressure is gone. There should be no excessive rust deposits around the cap or tank filler hole. The coolant should be free from any oil. On a COLD engine, place your finger in the coolant and check for oil or rust deposits.

It's best to check the coolant level when the engine is COLD. The radiator coolant level should be between the LOW and the FULL lines on the reservoir tank when the engine is cold. If low, check for leakage and add coolant up to the FULL line but do not overfill.

➥Check the freeze protection rating of the antifreeze at least once a year or as necessary with a suitable antifreeze tester.

## 1-66 GENERAL INFORMATION AND MAINTENANCE

Fig. 204 Check the levels on the reservoir tank for fluid capacity

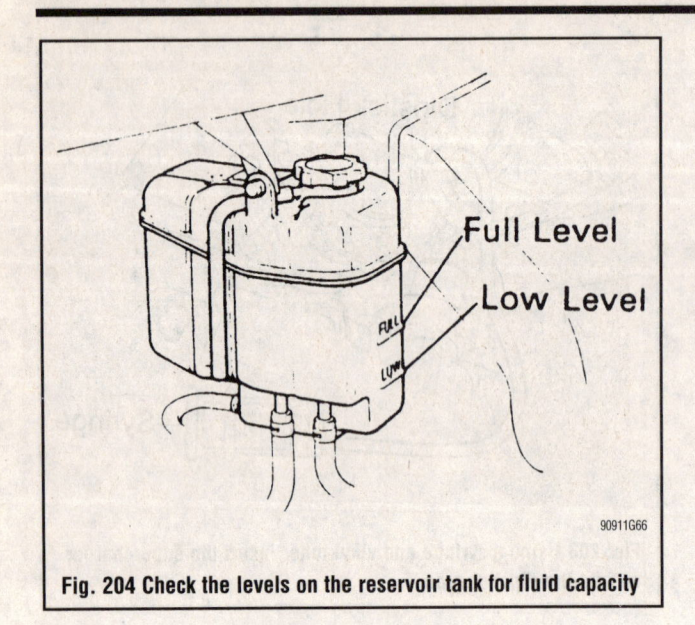

Fig. 206 Always turn the draincock counterclockwise when loosening it

### DRAIN & REFILL

▶ See Figures 205, 206, 207, 208 and 209

1. Draining the cooling system is always done with the engine **COLD**.
2. Remove the reservoir tank cap.
3. Position the drain pan under the draincock on the bottom of the radiator. Additionally, some engines have a draincock on the side of the engine block, near the oil filter. This should be opened to aid in draining the cooling system completely. If for some reason the radiator draincock can't be used, you can loosen and remove the lower radiator hose at its joint to the radiator.

**※ CAUTION**

When draining the coolant, keep in mind that cats and dogs are attracted by the ethylene glycol antifreeze, and are quite likely to drink any that is left in an uncovered container or in puddles on the ground. This will prove fatal in sufficient quantity. Always drain the coolant into a sealable container. Coolant should be reused unless it is contaminated or several years old.

Fig. 207 Use a socket and extension to loosen the draincock in the engine block

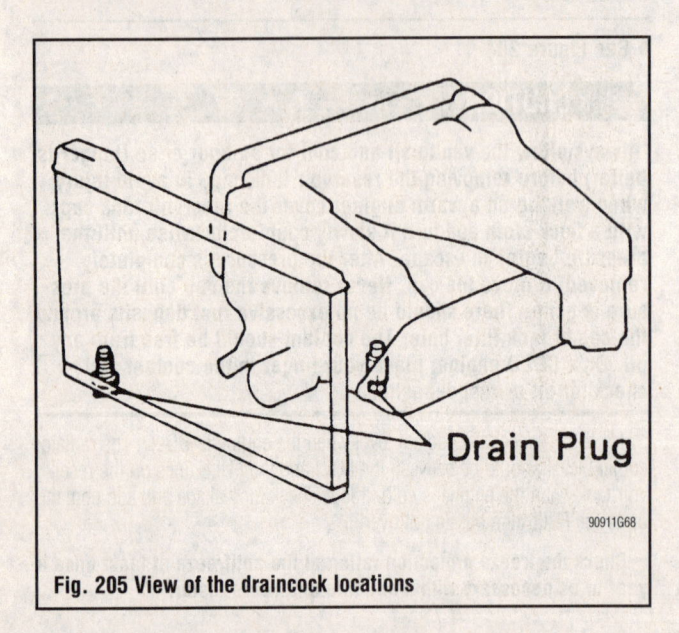

Fig. 205 View of the draincock locations

Fig. 208 Check the level in the reservoir

# GENERAL INFORMATION AND MAINTENANCE 1-67

Fig. 209 Use a funnel to fill the coolant reservoir

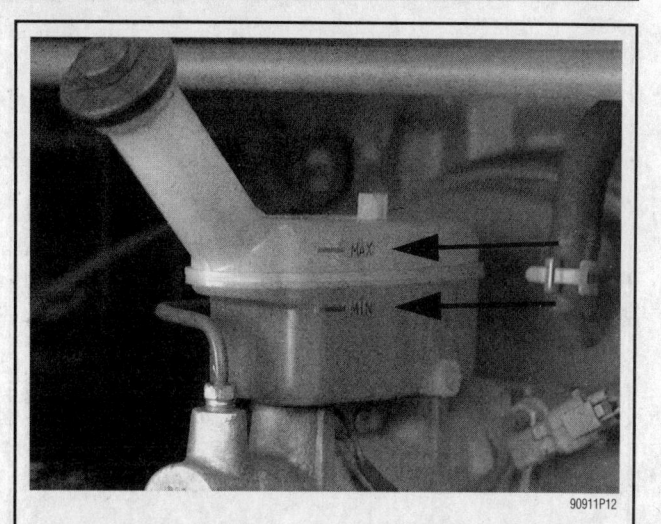

Fig. 210 The brake master cylinder has fluid level markings on the side of the reservoir

4. When the system stops draining, close both draincocks as necessary.
5. Using a funnel if necessary, fill the reservoir tank with a 50/50 solution of antifreeze and water. Allow time for the fluid to run through the hoses and into the engine.
6. Start the engine and let it idle about 10 minuets; add the coolant/water mixture up to the FULL level.
7. Tighten the cap.
8. Race the engine 2000–3000 rpms for about 5 minutes, then stop the engine.
9. After the coolant drops, remove the cap and add coolant to the FULL level again.
10. Securely tighten the cap again, then start the engine and check the level.

## FLUSHING & CLEANING THE SYSTEM

Proceed with draining the system as outlined above. When the system has drained, reconnect any hoses close to the radiator draincock. Move the temperature control for the heater to its hottest position; this allows the heater core to be flushed as well. Using a garden hose or bucket, fill the reservoir and allow the water to run out the engine drain cock. Continue until the water runs clear. Be sure to clean the expansion tank as well.

If the system is badly contaminated with rust or scale, you can use a commercial flushing solution to clean it out. Follow the manufacturer's instructions. Some causes of rust are air in the system, failure to change the coolant regularly, use of excessively hard or soft water, and/or failure to use the correct mix of antifreeze and water.

After the system has been flushed, continue with the refill procedures outlined above. Check the condition of the radiator cap and its gasket, replacing the radiator cap as necessary.

## Brake Master Cylinder

### FLUID RECOMMENDATIONS

All Previas use DOT 3 or SAE J1703 brake fluid.

### LEVEL CHECK

▶ See Figures 210, 211, 212, 213 and 214

The brake master cylinder is located under the hood, in the left rear side of the compartment. It is made of translucent plastic so that the levels may be checked without removing the top. The fluid level in the reservoir should

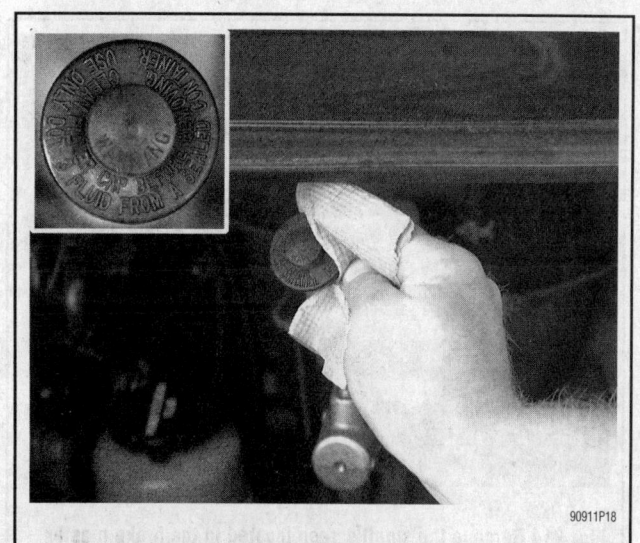

Fig. 211 Clean the cap prior to removal

Fig. 212 Notice the label on the cap

# 1-68 GENERAL INFORMATION AND MAINTENANCE

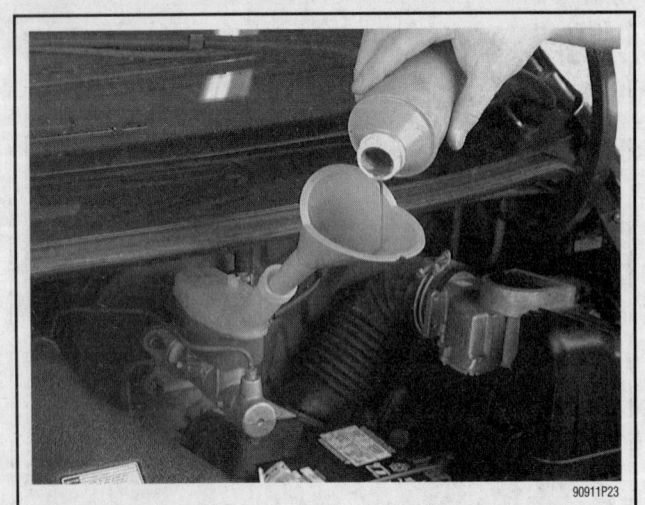

Fig. 213 Use a funnel to add fluid to the master cylinder reservoir

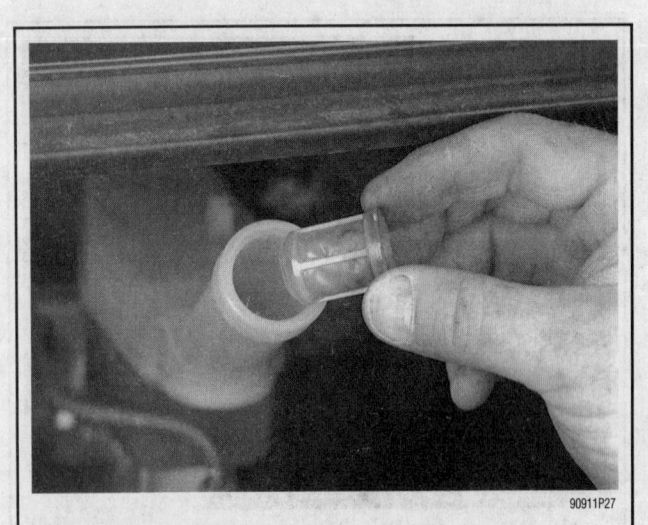

Fig. 214 Remove the small screen located in the brake master reservoir and inspect for tears and dirt deposits

be checked at least every 15,000 miles (24,000km) or 1 year. The fluid level should be maintained at the uppermost mark on the side of the reservoir. Any sudden decrease in the level indicates a possible leak in the system and should be checked out immediately.

When adding fluid, use only fresh, uncontaminated brake fluid meeting or exceeding DOT 3 standards. Be careful not to spill any brake fluid on painted surfaces, as it eats the paint. Do not allow the brake fluid container or the master cylinder reservoir to remain open any longer than necessary; brake fluid absorbs moisture from the air, reducing its effectiveness and causing corrosion in the lines.

A filter is located inside the reservoir. Remove it when checking the levels and inspect for a damaged screen or dirt.

## Clutch Master Cylinder

### FLUID RECOMMENDATIONS

All vehicles use DOT 3 or SAE J1703 brake fluid.

### LEVEL CHECK

The clutch master cylinder is located under the hood, in the left rear section of the engine compartment near the brake master. The clutch master reservoir is made of a translucent plastic so that the levels may be checked without removing the top. The fluid level in the reservoir should be checked at least every 15,000 miles (24,000 km) or 1 year. The fluid level should be maintained at the uppermost mark on the side of the reservoir. Any sudden decrease in the level indicates a possible leak in the system and should be checked out immediately.

When adding fluid, use only fresh, uncontaminated brake fluid meeting or exceeding DOT 3 standards. Be careful not to spill any brake fluid on painted surfaces, as it eats the paint. Do not allow the brake fluid container or the master cylinder reservoir to remain open any longer than necessary; brake fluid absorbs moisture from the air, reducing its effectiveness and causing corrosion in the lines.

## Power Steering Pump

### FLUID RECOMMENDATIONS

All vehicles use Dexron®II or III type automatic transmission fluid in the power steering system.

### LEVEL CHECK

▶ See Figures 215, 216 and 217

Check the power steering fluid level every 6 months or 6000 miles (9600 km).

1. Make sure that the vehicle is level. If the reservoir is dirty, wipe it off.
2. Start the engine and allow it to idle.
3. With the engine at idle, move the steering wheel from LOCK to LOCK several times to raise the temperature of the fluid.
4. The power steering pump reservoir is translucent, so the fluid level may be checked without removing the cap. Look through the reservoir and check for foaming or emulsification.

➡Foaming or emulsification indicates the either there is air in the system or the fluid level is low.

Fig. 215 The level indicators are located on the side of the reservoir tank

# GENERAL INFORMATION AND MAINTENANCE   1-69

Fig. 216 Check the reservoir for foaming or emulsification

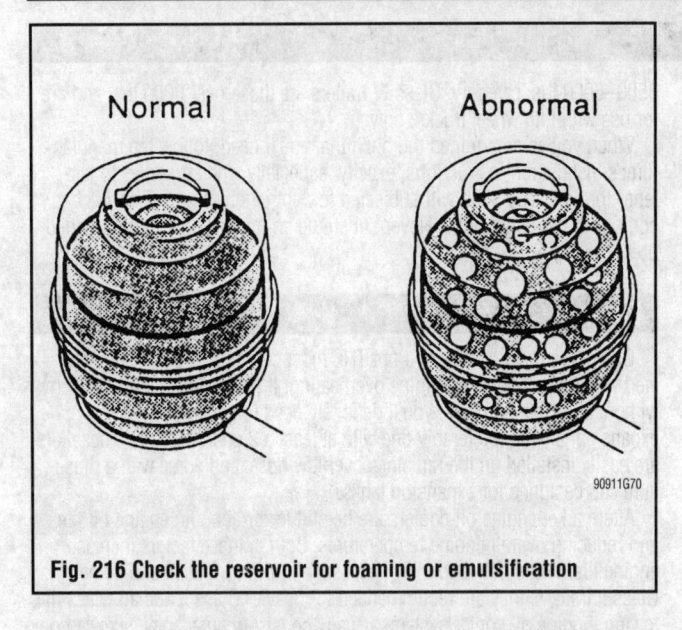

Fig. 217 Add fluid to the power steering reservoir until it reaches the MAX level indicator

5. Check the fluid level in the reservoir. The fluid should be within the **HOT LEVEL** of the reservoir. If the fluid is checked when cold, the level should be within the **COLD LEVEL** of the reservoir.
6. Add fluid as required until the proper level is reached. To add fluid, remove the filler cap by turning it counterclockwise and lifting up. After the proper amount of fluid is added, replace the cap making sure that the arrows on the cap are properly aligned with the arrows on the tank.
7. This is also a good time to check the steering box case, vane pump and hose connections for leaks and damage. Simple preventative maintenance checks like these can identify minor problems before turn into major problems and also increase your familiarity with the locations of steering system components.

## Chassis Greasing

▶ See Figure 218

The Toyota Previa only requires the lubrication of the propeller shaft. Repack the sleeve yoke with grease (NLGI No. 2). Before pumping the grease, wipe off any mud or dust on the fitting.

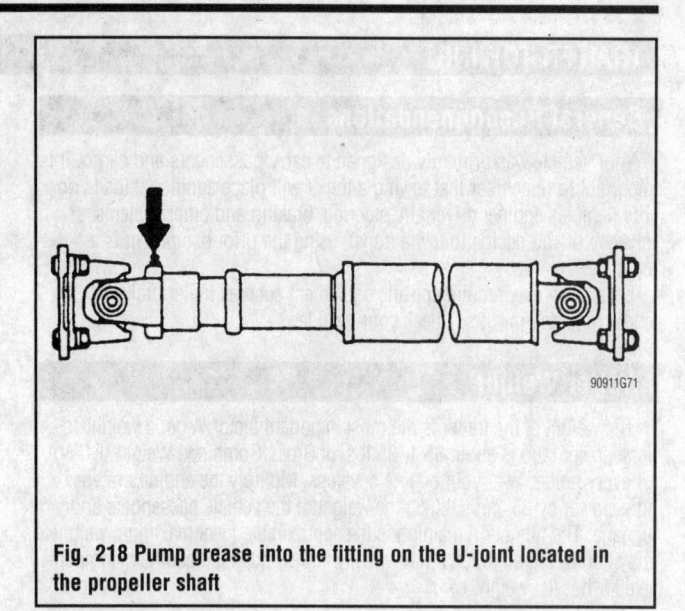

Fig. 218 Pump grease into the fitting on the U-joint located in the propeller shaft

## Body Lubrication and Maintenance

There is no set period recommended by Toyota for body lubrication. However, it is a good idea to lubricate the following body points at least once a year, especially in the fall before cold weather.

### LOCK CYLINDERS

Apply graphite lubricant sparingly thought the key slot. Insert the key and operate the lock several times to be sure that the lubricant is worked into the lock cylinder.

### DOOR HINGES & HINGE CHECKS

Spray a silicone lubricant or apply white lithium grease on the hinge pivot points to eliminate any binding conditions. Open and close the door several times to be sure that the lubricant is evenly and thoroughly distributed. When applying grease, the use of a small acid brush is very helpful in getting the grease to those hard to reach areas.

### TAILGATE

Spray a silicone lubricant on all of the pivot and friction surfaces to eliminate any squeaks or binds. Work the tailgate to distribute the lubricant

### BODY DRAIN HOLES

Be sure that the drain holes in the doors and rocker panels are cleared of obstruction. A small screwdriver can be used to clear them of any debris.

## Wheel Bearings

The Toyota Previa models are equipped with sealed bearing assemblies. The bearing assemblies are nonserviceable. If the assembly is damaged, the complete unit must be replaced. Refer to Section 8 for the bearing removal and installation procedure.

## TRAILER TOWING

### General Recommendations

Your vehicle was primarily designed to carry passengers and cargo. It is important to remember that towing a trailer will place additional loads on your vehicles engine, drivetrain, steering, braking and other systems. However, if you decide to tow a trailer, using the prior equipment is a must.

Local laws may require specific equipment such as trailer brakes or fender mounted mirrors. Check your local laws.

### Trailer Weight

The weight of the trailer is the most important factor. A good weight-to-horsepower ratio is about 35:1, 35 lbs. of Gross Combined Weight (GCW) for every horsepower your engine develops. Multiply the engine's rated horsepower by 35 and subtract the weight of the vehicle passengers and luggage. The number remaining is the approximate ideal maximum weight you should tow, although a numerically higher axle ratio can help compensate for heavier weight.

### Hitch (Tongue) Weight

♦ See Figure 219

Calculate the hitch weight in order to select a proper hitch. The weight of the hitch is usually 9–11% of the trailer gross weight and should be measured with the trailer loaded. Hitches fall into various categories: those that mount on the frame and rear bumper, the bolt-on type, or the weld-on distribution type used for larger trailers. Axle mounted or clamp-on bumper hitches should never be used.

Check the gross weight rating of your trailer. Tongue weight is usually figured as 10% of gross trailer weight. Therefore, a trailer with a maximum gross weight of 2000 lbs. will have a maximum tongue weight of 200 lbs. Class I trailers fall into this category. Class II trailers are those with a gross weight rating of 2000–3000 lbs., while Class III trailers fall into the 3500–6000 lbs. category. Class IV trailers are those over 6000 lbs. and are for use with fifth wheel trucks, only.

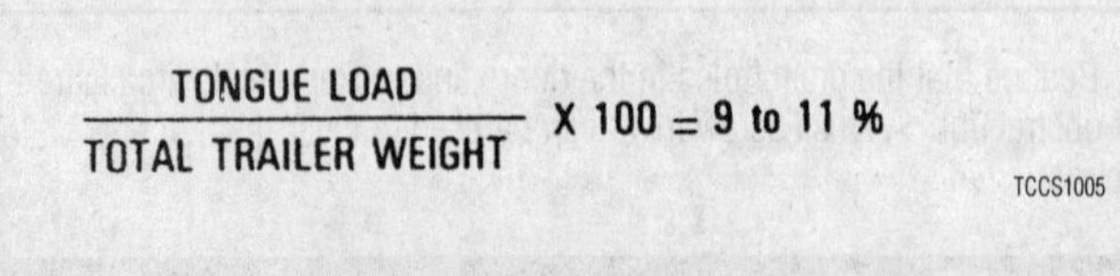

When you've determined the hitch that you'll need, follow the manufacturer's installation instructions, exactly, especially when it comes to fastener torques. The hitch will subjected to a lot of stress and good hitches come with hardened bolts. Never substitute an inferior bolt for a hardened bolt.

### Engine

One of the most common, if not THE most common, problems associated with trailer towing is engine overheating. If you have a cooling system without an expansion tank, you'll definitely need to get an aftermarket expansion tank kit, preferably one with at least a 2 quart capacity. These kits are easily installed on the radiator's overflow hose, and come with a pressure cap designed for expansion tanks.

Aftermarket engine oil coolers are helpful for prolonging engine oil life and reducing overall engine temperatures. Both of these factors increase engine life. While not absolutely necessary in towing Class I and some Class II trailers, they are recommended for heavier Class II and all Class III towing. Engine oil cooler systems usually consist of an adapter, screwed on in place of the oil filter, a remote filter mounting and a multi-tube, finned heat exchanger, which is mounted in front of the radiator or air conditioning condenser.

### Transmission

An automatic transmission is usually recommended for trailer towing. Modern automatics have proven reliable and, of course, easy to operate, in trailer towing. The increased load of a trailer, however, causes an increase in the temperature of the automatic transmission fluid. Heat is the worst enemy of an automatic transmission. As the temperature of the fluid increases, the life of the fluid decreases.

It is essential, therefore, that you install an automatic transmission cooler. The cooler, which consists of a multi-tube, finned heat exchanger, is usually installed in front of the radiator or air conditioning compressor, and hooked in-line with the transmission cooler tank inlet line. Follow the cooler manufacturer's installation instructions.

Select a cooler of at least adequate capacity, based upon the combined gross weights of the vehicle and trailer.

Cooler manufacturers recommend that you use an aftermarket cooler in addition to, and not instead of, the present cooling tank in your radiator. If you do want to use it in place of the radiator cooling tank, get a cooler at least two sizes larger than normally necessary.

➡**A transmission cooler can, sometimes, cause slow or harsh shifting in the transmission during cold weather, until the fluid has a chance to come up to normal operating temperature. Some coolers can be purchased with or retrofitted with a temperature bypass valve which will allow fluid flow through the cooler only when the fluid has reached above a certain operating temperature.**

### Handling A Trailer

Towing a trailer with ease and safety requires a certain amount of experience. It's a good idea to learn the feel of a trailer by practicing turning, stopping and backing in an open area such as an empty parking lot.

Fig. 219 Calculating proper tongue weight for your trailer

$$\frac{\text{TONGUE LOAD}}{\text{TOTAL TRAILER WEIGHT}} \times 100 = 9 \text{ to } 11\%$$

# GENERAL INFORMATION AND MAINTENANCE        1-71

## TOWING THE VEHICLE

▶ See Figure 220

The absolute best way to have the vehicle towed or transported is on a flat-bed or rollback transporter. These units are becoming more common and are very useful for moving disabled vehicles quickly. Most vehicles have lower bodywork and undertrays which can be easily damaged by the sling of a conventional tow truck; an operator unfamiliar with your particular model can cause severe damage to the suspension or drive line by hooking up chains and J-hooks incorrectly.

If a flatbed is not available (you should specifically request one), the vehicle may be towed by a hoist or conventional tow vehicle. Vehicles with automatic transmissions must be towed with the drive wheels off the ground. Manual transmissions can be towed with either end up in the air or with all four wheels on the ground. You need only remember that the transmission must be in neutral, the parking brake must be off and the ignition switch must be in the **ACC** position. The steering column lock is not strong enough to hold the front wheels straight under towing.

The 4WD vehicle presents its own towing problems. Since the front and rear wheels are connected through the drive system, all four wheels must be considered in the towing arrangement. A flatbed should be used (refer to the illustration).

Most vehicles have conveniently located tie-down hooks at the front of the vehicle. These make ideal locations to secure a rope or chain for towing the vehicle or extracting it from an off-road excursion. The vehicle may only be towed on hard surfaced roads and only in a normal or forward direction.

---

### WHEN TOWING ALL−TRAC/4WD VEHICLES

1. Use one of the methods shown below to tow the vehicle.
2. When there is trouble with the chassis and drive train, use method ① (flat bed truck)
3. Recommended Method: No. ①
   Emergency Method: No. ②

| Towing Method / Conditions | Parking Brake | Transmission Shift Lever Position |
|---|---|---|
| ① Flat Bed Truck | Applied | Any Position |
| ② Towing with a Rope | Released | Neutral (N range) |

**NOTICE : Do not use any towing method other than those shown above.**
Fox example, the towing methods shown below are dangerous or will damage the vehicle, so do not use them.

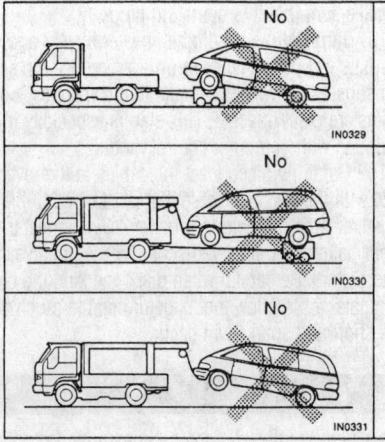

| | |
|---|---|
| No | • During towing with this towing method, there is a danger of the drivetrain heating up and causing breakdown, or of the front wheels flying off the dolly.<br>• Never perform towing using a method where the lifted-up wheel cannot rotate. |
| No | • Do not perform sling type towing as this method causes damage to the bumper, engine undercover, suspension lower arm bushing and the air conditioning condensor during towing. |
| No | |

Fig. 220 Previa 4WD towing precautions

# 1-72 GENERAL INFORMATION AND MAINTENANCE

## JUMP STARTING A DEAD BATTERY

♦ See Figure 221

Whenever a vehicle is jump started, precautions must be followed in order to prevent the possibility of personal injury. Remember that batteries contain a small amount of explosive hydrogen gas which is a by-product of battery charging. Sparks should always be avoided when working around batteries, especially when attaching jumper cables. To minimize the possibility of accidental sparks, follow the procedure carefully.

**✲✲ CAUTION**

**NEVER hook the batteries up in a series circuit or the entire electrical system will go up in smoke, including the starter!**

Vehicles equipped with a diesel engine may utilize two 12 volt batteries. If so, the batteries are connected in a parallel circuit (positive terminal to positive terminal, negative terminal to negative terminal). Hooking the batteries up in parallel circuit increases battery cranking power without increasing total battery voltage output. Output remains at 12 volts. On the other hand, hooking two 12 volt batteries up in a series circuit (positive terminal to negative terminal, positive terminal to negative terminal) increases total battery output to 24 volts (12 volts plus 12 volts).

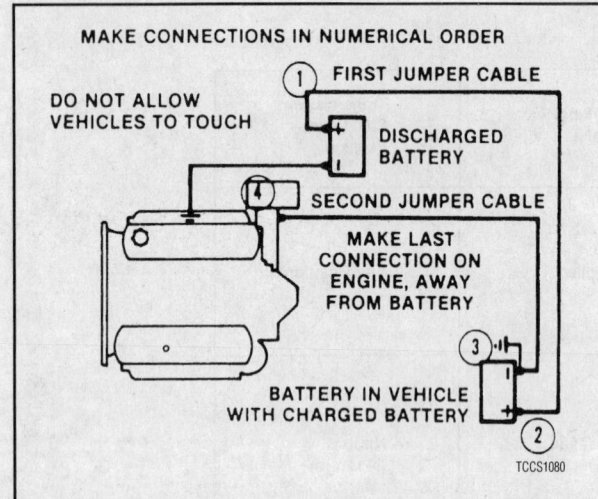

Fig. 221 Connect the jumper cables to the batteries and engine in the order shown

### Jump Starting Precautions

- Be sure that both batteries are of the same voltage. Vehicles covered by this manual and most vehicles on the road today utilize a 12 volt charging system.
- Be sure that both batteries are of the same polarity (have the same terminal, in most cases NEGATIVE grounded).
- Be sure that the vehicles are not touching or a short could occur.
- On serviceable batteries, be sure the vent cap holes are not obstructed.
- Do not smoke or allow sparks anywhere near the batteries.
- In cold weather, make sure the battery electrolyte is not frozen. This can occur more readily in a battery that has been in a state of discharge.
- Do not allow electrolyte to contact your skin or clothing.

## JACKING

♦ See Figures 222, 223, 224 and 225

Your vehicle was supplied with a jack for emergency road repairs. This jack is fine for changing a flat tire or other short term procedures not requiring you to go beneath the vehicle. If it is used in an emergency situa-

### Jump Starting Procedure

1. Make sure that the voltages of the 2 batteries are the same. Most batteries and charging systems are of the 12 volt variety.
2. Pull the jumping vehicle (with the good battery) into a position so the jumper cables can reach the dead battery and that vehicle's engine. Make sure that the vehicles do NOT touch.
3. Place the transmissions of both vehicles in **Neutral** (MT) or **P** (AT), as applicable, then firmly set their parking brakes.

➡If necessary for safety reasons, the hazard lights on both vehicles may be operated throughout the entire procedure without significantly increasing the difficulty of jumping the dead battery.

4. Turn all lights and accessories OFF on both vehicles. Make sure the ignition switches on both vehicles are turned to the **OFF** position.
5. Cover the battery cell caps with a rag, but do not cover the terminals.
6. Make sure the terminals on both batteries are clean and free of corrosion or proper electrical connection will be impeded. If necessary, clean the battery terminals before proceeding.
7. Identify the positive (+) and negative (-) terminals on both batteries.
8. Connect the first jumper cable to the positive (+) terminal of the dead battery, then connect the other end of that cable to the positive (+) terminal of the booster (good) battery.
9. Connect one end of the other jumper cable to the negative (-) terminal on the booster battery and the final cable clamp to an engine bolt head, alternator bracket or other solid, metallic point on the engine with the dead battery. Try to pick a ground on the engine that is positioned away from the battery in order to minimize the possibility of the 2 clamps touching should one loosen during the procedure. DO NOT connect this clamp to the negative (-) terminal of the bad battery.

**✲✲ CAUTION**

**Be very careful to keep the jumper cables away from moving parts (cooling fan, belts, etc.) on both engines.**

10. Check to make sure that the cables are routed away from any moving parts, then start the donor vehicle's engine. Run the engine at moderate speed for several minutes to allow the dead battery a chance to receive some initial charge.
11. With the donor vehicle's engine still running slightly above idle, try to start the vehicle with the dead battery. Crank the engine for no more than 10 seconds at a time and let the starter cool for at least 20 seconds between tries. If the vehicle does not start in 3 tries, it is likely that something else is also wrong or that the battery needs additional time to charge.
12. Once the vehicle is started, allow it to run at idle for a few seconds to make sure that it is operating properly.
13. Turn ON the headlights, heater blower and, if equipped, the rear defroster of both vehicles in order to reduce the severity of voltage spikes and subsequent risk of damage to the vehicles' electrical systems when the cables are disconnected. This step is especially important to any vehicle equipped with computer control modules.
14. Carefully disconnect the cables in the reverse order of connection. Start with the negative cable that is attached to the engine ground, then the negative cable on the donor battery. Disconnect the positive cable from the donor battery and finally, disconnect the positive cable from the formerly dead battery. Be careful when disconnecting the cables from the positive terminals not to allow the alligator clips to touch any metal on either vehicle or a short and sparks will occur.

tion, carefully follow the instructions provided either with the jack or in your owner's manual. Do not attempt to use the jack on any portions of the vehicle other than specified by the vehicle manufacturer. Always block the diagonally opposite wheel when using a jack.

# GENERAL INFORMATION AND MAINTENANCE  1-73

Fig. 222 In the front of the vehicle, place the jack under the center crossmember

Fig. 224 In the rear of the vehicle, place the jack under the axle

Fig. 223 Always place two jackstands under the vehicle to support the vehicle when raising the front end

Fig. 225 Place jackstands under the frame rails on each side of the body to support the vehicle

A more convenient way of jacking is the use of a garage or floor jack. You may use the floor jack to raise and support the vehicle more safely. Place the floor jack in an appropriate position and carefully raise the vehicle. Be sure to block the wheels and use stands for added support.

Never place the jack under the radiator, engine or transmission components. Severe and expensive damage will result when the jack is raised. Additionally, never jack under the floorpan or bodywork; the metal will deform.

Whenever you plan to work under the vehicle, you must support it on jackstands or ramps. Never use cinder blocks or stacks of wood to support the vehicle, even if you're only going to be under it for a few minutes. Never crawl under the vehicle when it is supported only by the tire-changing jack or other floor jack.

➡Always position a block of wood or small rubber pad on top of the jack or jackstand to protect the lifting point's finish when lifting or supporting the vehicle.

Small hydraulic, screw, or scissors jacks are satisfactory for raising the vehicle. Drive-on trestles or ramps are also a handy and safe way to both raise and support the vehicle. Be careful though, some ramps may be too steep to drive your vehicle onto without scraping the front bottom panels. Never support the vehicle on any suspension member (unless specifically instructed to do so by a repair manual) or by an underbody panel.

## Jacking Precautions

The following safety points cannot be overemphasized:
- Always block the opposite wheel or wheels to keep the vehicle from rolling off the jack.
- When raising the front of the vehicle, firmly apply the parking brake.
- When the drive wheels are to remain on the ground, leave the vehicle in gear to help prevent it from rolling.
- Always use jackstands to support the vehicle when you are working underneath. Place the stands beneath the vehicle's jacking brackets. Before climbing underneath, rock the vehicle a bit to make sure it is firmly supported.

## NORMAL RECOMMENDED MAINTENANCE INTERVALS (1996-97)

### VEHICLE MAINTENANCE INTERVAL

| km (x1000) | 6 | 12 | 18 | 24 | 30 | 36 | 42 | 48 | 54 | 60 | 66 | 72 | 78 | 84 | 90 | 96 | Months |
|---|---|---|---|---|---|---|---|---|---|---|---|---|---|---|---|---|---|
| Miles (x1000) | 3.75 | 7.5 | 11.25 | 15 | 18.75 | 22.5 | 26.25 | 30 | 33.75 | 37.5 | 41.25 | 45 | 48.75 | 52.5 | 56.25 | 60 | |
| **Component** | | | | | | | | | | | | | | | | | |
| Engine oil and filter | R | R | R | R | R | R | R | R | R | R | R | R | R | R | R | R | I: Every 4 |
| Valve clearance | | | | | | | | | | A | | | | | | A | R: Every 48 |
| Drive belts | | | | | | | | I | | A | | | | | | I | |
| Engine coolant | | | | I | | | | R | | | | I | | | | R | |
| Exhaust pipes | | | | | | | | I | | | | I | | | | I | I: Every 24 |
| Air cleaner filter | | I | | I | | I | | R | | I | | I | | I | | R | I: Every 6 |
| Fuel lines and connections | | | | | | | | I | | | | | | | | I | I: Every 24 |
| Fuel tank cap gasket | | | | | | | | | | | | | | | | R | R: Every 72 |
| Spark plugs- platinum | | | | | | | | | | | | | | | | R | R: Every 72 |
| Charcoal canister | | | | | | | | | | | | | | | | I | I: Every 48 |
| Brake linings and drums | | I | | I | | I | | I | | I | | I | | I | | I | I: Every 12 |
| Brake pads and discs | | I | | I | | I | | I | | I | | I | | I | | I | I: Every 12 |
| Brake line hose and connections | | | | I | | | | I | | | | I | | | | I | I: Every 24 |
| Steering linkage | | I | | I | | I | | I | | I | | I | | I | | I | I: Every 12 |
| SRS air bags | | | | | | | | | | | | | | | | | I: Every 12 |
| Ball joints and dust covers | | I | | I | | I | | I | | I | | I | | I | | I | I: Every 12 |
| Drive shaft boots | | I | | I | | I | | I | | I | | I | | I | | I | I: Every 12 |
| Transfer | | R | | R | | R | | R | | R | | R | | R | | R | R: Every 12 |
| Propeller shaft- grease | | R | | R | | R | | R | | R | | R | | R | | R | R: Every 12 |
| Transmission/ Differential | | | | R | | | | R | | | | R | | | | R | R: Every 24 |
| Steering gear box | | | | I | | | | I | | | | I | | | | I | I: Every 24 |
| Bolts and nuts on chassis and body | | I | | I | | I | | I | | I | | I | | I | | I | I: Every 24 |

I: Inspect
R: Replace
A: Adjust

# GENERAL INFORMATION AND MAINTENANCE 1-75

## SEVERE RECOMMENDED MAINTENANCE INTERVALS (1996-97)

| Component | km (x1000) | 6 | 12 | 18 | 24 | 30 | 36 | 42 | 48 | 54 | 60 | 66 | 72 | 78 | 84 | 90 | 96 | Months |
|---|---|---|---|---|---|---|---|---|---|---|---|---|---|---|---|---|---|---|
| | Miles (x1000) | 3.75 | 7.5 | 11.25 | 15 | 18.75 | 22.5 | 26.25 | 30 | 33.75 | 37.5 | 41.25 | 45 | 48.75 | 52.5 | 56.25 | 60 | |
| Engine oil and filter | | R | R | R | R | R | R | R | R | R | R | R | R | R | R | R | R | I: Every 4 |
| Timing Belt | | | | | | | | | | | | | | | | | R | |
| Valve clearance | | | | | | | | | | | A | | | | | | A | R: Every 48 |
| Drive belts | | | | | | | | | I | | A | | | | | | I | |
| Engine coolant | | | | | I | | | | R | | | | I | | | | R | |
| Exhaust pipes | | | | | | | | | I | | | | I | | | | I | I: Every 24 |
| Air cleaner filter | | | I | | I | | I | | R | | I | | I | | I | | R | I: Every 6 |
| Fuel lines and connections | | | | | | | | | I | | | | | | | | I | I: Every 24 |
| Fuel tank cap gasket | | | | | | | | | | | | | | | | | R | R: Every 72 |
| Spark plugs-platinum | | | | | | | | | | | | | | | | | R | R: Every 72 |
| Charcoal canister | | | | | | | | | | | | | | | | | I | I: Every 48 |
| Brake linings and drums | | | I | | I | | I | | I | | I | | I | | I | | I | I: Every 12 |
| Brake pads and discs | | | I | | I | | I | | I | | I | | I | | I | | I | I: Every 12 |
| Brake line hose and connections | | | | | I | | | | I | | | | I | | | | I | I: Every 24 |
| Steering linkage | | | I | | I | | I | | I | | I | | I | | I | | I | I: Every 12 |
| SRS air bags | | | | | | | | | | | | | | | | | | I: Every 12 |
| Ball joints and dust covers | | | I | | I | | I | | I | | I | | I | | I | | I | I: Every 12 |
| Drive shaft boots | | | I | | I | | I | | I | | I | | I | | I | | I | I: Every 12 |
| Transmissin/Differential | | | | | R | | | | R | | | | R | | | | R | R: Every 24 |
| Transfer | | | | | I | | | | I | | | | I | | | | I | I: Every 24 |
| Propeller shaft-grease | | | | | R | | | | R | | | | R | | | | R | R: Every 24 |
| Steering gear box | | | | | I | | | | I | | | | I | | | | I | I: Every 24 |
| Bolts and nuts on chassis and body | | | I | | I | | I | | I | | I | | I | | I | | I | I: Every 24 |

I: Inspect
R: Replace
A: Adjust

90911C5A

# 1-76 GENERAL INFORMATION AND MAINTENANCE

## NORMAL RECOMMENDED MAINTENANCE INTERVALS (1991-95)

### VEHICLE MAINTENANCE INTERVAL

| Component | km (x1000): 6 | 12 | 18 | 24 | 30 | 36 | 42 | 48 | 54 | 60 | 66 | 72 | 78 | 84 | 90 | 96 | Months |
| --- | --- | --- | --- | --- | --- | --- | --- | --- | --- | --- | --- | --- | --- | --- | --- | --- | --- |
|  | Miles (x1000): 3.75 | 7.5 | 11.25 | 15 | 18.75 | 22.5 | 26.25 | 30 | 33.75 | 37.5 | 41.25 | 45 | 48.75 | 52.5 | 56.25 | 60 |  |
| Engine oil and filter | R | R | R | R | R | R | R | R | R | R | R | R | R | R | R | R | I: Every 6 |
| Valve clearance |  |  |  |  |  |  |  |  |  | A |  |  |  |  |  | A | R: Every 72 |
| Drive belts |  |  |  |  |  |  |  |  |  |  |  |  |  |  |  | I | I: Every 12 |
| Engine coolant |  |  |  |  | I |  |  | R |  |  |  | I |  |  |  | R |  |
| Exhaust pipes |  |  |  |  |  |  |  | I |  |  |  | I |  |  |  | I | I: Every 24 |
| Air cleaner filter |  |  |  |  |  |  |  | R |  |  |  |  |  |  |  | R | I: Every 6 |
| Fuel lines and connections |  |  |  |  |  | I |  |  |  |  |  |  |  |  |  | I | I: Every 36 |
| Fuel tank cap gasket |  |  |  |  |  |  |  |  |  |  |  |  |  |  |  | R | R: Every 72 |
| Spark plugs-platinum |  |  |  |  |  |  |  |  |  |  |  |  |  |  |  | R | R: Every 72 |
| Charcoal canister |  |  |  |  |  |  |  |  |  |  |  |  |  |  |  | I | I: Every 72 |
| Brake linings and drums |  | I |  | I |  | I |  | I |  | I |  | I |  | I |  | I | I: Every 12 |
| Brake pads and discs |  | I |  | I |  | I |  | I |  | I |  | I |  | I |  | I | I: Every 12 |
| Brake line hose and connections |  |  |  | I |  |  |  | I |  |  |  | I |  |  |  | I | I: Every 24 |
| Steering linkage |  | I |  | I |  | I |  | I |  | I |  | I |  | I |  | I | I: Every 12 |
| SRS air bags |  |  |  |  |  |  |  |  |  |  |  |  |  |  |  |  | I: Every 12 |
| Ball joints and dust covers |  | I |  | I |  | I |  | I |  | I |  | I |  | I |  | I | I: Every 12 |
| Drive shaft boots |  | I |  | I |  | I |  | I |  | I |  | I |  | I |  | I | I: Every 12 |
| Transmission/Differential |  |  |  | R |  |  |  | R |  |  |  | R |  |  |  | R | R: Every 24 |
| Transfer |  | R |  | R |  | R |  | R |  | R |  | R |  | R |  | R | R: Every 12 |
| Propeller shaft-grease |  | R |  | R |  | R |  | R |  | R |  | R |  | R |  | R | R: Every 12 |
| Steering gear box |  |  |  | I |  |  |  | I |  |  |  | I |  |  |  | I | I: Every 24 |
| Bolts and nuts on chassis and body |  | I |  | I |  | I |  | I |  | I |  | I |  | I |  | I | I: Every 24 |

I: Inspect
R: Replace
A: Adjust

90911C06

# GENERAL INFORMATION AND MAINTENANCE 1-77

## SEVERE RECOMMENDED MAINTENANCE INTERVALS (1991-95)

| Component | km (x1000): 6 | 12 | 18 | 24 | 30 | 36 | 42 | 48 | 54 | 60 | 66 | 72 | 78 | 84 | 90 | 96 | Months |
|---|---|---|---|---|---|---|---|---|---|---|---|---|---|---|---|---|---|
| Miles (x1000): | 3.75 | 7.5 | 11.25 | 15 | 18.75 | 22.5 | 26.25 | 30 | 33.75 | 37.5 | 41.25 | 45 | 48.75 | 52.5 | 56.25 | 60 | |
| Engine oil and filter | R | R | R | R | R | R | R | R | R | R | R | R | R | R | R | R | I: Every 6 |
| Valve clearance | | | | | | | | | | A | | | | | | A | R: Every 72 |
| Drive belts | | | | | | | | I | | A | | | | | | I | I: Every 72 |
| Engine coolant | | | | I | | | | R | | | | I | | | | R | R: Every 24 |
| Exhaust pipes | | | | | | | | I | | | | I | | | | I | I: Every 24 |
| Air cleaner filter | | | | | | | | R | | | | | | | | R | I: Every 6 |
| Fuel lines and connections | | | | | | | | I | | | | | | | | I | I: Every 36 |
| Fuel tank cap gasket | | | | | | | | | | | | | | | | R | R: Every 72 |
| Spark plugs-platinum | | | | | | | | | | | | | | | | R | R: Every 72 |
| Charcoal canister | | | | | | | | | | | | | | | | I | I: Every 72 |
| Brake linings and drums | | I | | I | | I | | I | | I | | I | | I | | I | I: Every 12 |
| Brake pads and discs | | I | | I | | I | | I | | I | | I | | I | | I | I: Every 12 |
| Brake line hose and connections | | | | | | | | I | | | | I | | | | I | I: Every 24 |
| Steering linkage | | I | | I | | I | | I | | I | | I | | I | | I | I: Every 12 |
| SRS air bags | | | | | | | | | | | | | | | | | I: Every 12 |
| Ball joints and dust covers | | I | | I | | I | | I | | I | | I | | I | | I | I: Every 12 |
| Drive shaft boots | | I | | I | | I | | I | | I | | I | | I | | I | I: Every 12 |
| Transmission/Differential | | | | R | | | | R | | | | R | | | | R | R: Every 24 |
| Transfer | | | | I | | | | I | | | | I | | | | I | I: Every 24 |
| Propeller shaft-grease | | | | R | | | | R | | | | R | | | | R | R: Every 24 |
| Steering gear box | | | | I | | | | I | | | | I | | | | I | I: Every 24 |
| Bolts and nuts on chassis and body | | I | | I | | I | | I | | I | | I | | I | | I | I: Every 24 |

I: Inspect
R: Replace
A: Adjust

90911C6A

## CAPACITIES

| Year | Model | Engine ID/VIN | Engine Displacement Liters (cc) | Engine Oil with Filter | Transmission (pts.) 4-Spd | 5-Spd | Auto. | Transfer Case (qts.) | Drive Axle Front (pts.) | Rear (pts.) | Fuel Tank (gal.) | Cooling System (qts.) |
|---|---|---|---|---|---|---|---|---|---|---|---|---|
| 1991 | Previa | 2TZ-FE | 2.4 (2438) | 6.1 | - | ① | 2.5 | 1.1 | - | - | 19.8 | ② |
| 1992 | Previa | 2TZ-FE | 2.4 (2438) | 6.1 | - | ① | 2.5 | 1.1 | - | - | 19.8 | ② |
| 1993 | Previa | 2TZ-FE | 2.4 (2438) | 6.1 | - | ① | 2.5 | 1.1 | - | - | 19.8 | 13.0 |
| 1994 | Previa | 2TZ-FE | 2.4 (2438) | 6.1 | - | - | 2.5 | 1.1 | - | - | 19.8 | 13.0 |
| | Previa | 2TZ-FZE | 2.4 (2438) | 6.1 | - | - | 1.7 | 1.1 | - | - | 19.8 | 12.4 |
| 1995 | Previa | 2TZ-FE | 2.4 (2438) | 6.1 | - | - | 2.5 | 1.1 | - | - | 19.8 | 13.0 |
| | Previa | 2TZ-FZE | 2.4 (2438) | 6.1 | - | - | 1.7 | 1.1 | - | - | 19.8 | 12.4 |
| 1996 | Previa | 2TZ-FZE | 2.4 (2438) | 6.1 | - | - | 1.7 | 1.1 | - | - | 19.8 | 12.4 |
| 1997 | Previa | 2TZ-FZE | 2.4 (2438) | 6.1 | - | - | 1.7 | 1.1 | - | - | 19.8 | 12.4 |

① 2WD: 4.7
   4WD: 5.5

② Without towing pkg. 12.3
   With towing pkg. 13.0

90911C04

## ENGLISH TO METRIC CONVERSION: MASS (WEIGHT)

Current mass measurement is expressed in pounds and ounces (lbs. & ozs.). The metric unit of mass (or weight) is the kilogram (kg). Even although this table does not show conversion of masses (weights) larger than 15 lbs, it is easy to calculate larger units by following the data immediately below.

To convert ounces (oz.) to grams (g): multiply th number of ozs. by 28
To convert grams (g) to ounces (oz.): multiply the number of grams by .035

To convert pounds (lbs.) to kilograms (kg): multiply the number of lbs. by .45
To convert kilograms (kg) to pounds (lbs.): multiply the number of kilograms by 2.2

| lbs | kg | lbs | kg | oz | kg | oz | kg |
|---|---|---|---|---|---|---|---|
| 0.1 | 0.04 | 0.9 | 0.41 | 0.1 | 0.003 | 0.9 | 0.024 |
| 0.2 | 0.09 | 1 | 0.4 | 0.2 | 0.005 | 1 | 0.03 |
| 0.3 | 0.14 | 2 | 0.9 | 0.3 | 0.008 | 2 | 0.06 |
| 0.4 | 0.18 | 3 | 1.4 | 0.4 | 0.011 | 3 | 0.08 |
| 0.5 | 0.23 | 4 | 1.8 | 0.5 | 0.014 | 4 | 0.11 |
| 0.6 | 0.27 | 5 | 2.3 | 0.6 | 0.017 | 5 | 0.14 |
| 0.7 | 0.32 | 10 | 4.5 | 0.7 | 0.020 | 10 | 0.28 |
| 0.8 | 0.36 | 15 | 6.8 | 0.8 | 0.023 | 15 | 0.42 |

## ENGLISH TO METRIC CONVERSION: TEMPERATURE

To convert Fahrenheit (°F) to Celsius (°C): take number of °F and subtract 32; multiply result by 5; divide result by 9
To convert Celsius (°C) to Fahrenheit (°F): take number of °C and multiply by 9; divide result by 5; add 32 to total

| Fahrenheit (F) | | Celsius (C) | | Fahrenheit (F) | | Celsius (C) | | Fahrenheit (F) | | Celsius (C) | |
|---|---|---|---|---|---|---|---|---|---|---|---|
| °F | °C | °C | °F | °F | °C | °C | °F | °F | °C | °C | °F |
| −40 | −40 | −38 | −36.4 | 80 | 26.7 | 18 | 64.4 | 215 | 101.7 | 80 | 176 |
| −35 | −37.2 | −36 | −32.8 | 85 | 29.4 | 20 | 68 | 220 | 104.4 | 85 | 185 |
| −30 | −34.4 | −34 | −29.2 | 90 | 32.2 | 22 | 71.6 | 225 | 107.2 | 90 | 194 |
| −25 | −31.7 | −32 | −25.6 | 95 | 35.0 | 24 | 75.2 | 230 | 110.0 | 95 | 202 |
| −20 | −28.9 | −30 | −22 | 100 | 37.8 | 26 | 78.8 | 235 | 112.8 | 100 | 212 |
| −15 | −26.1 | −28 | −18.4 | 105 | 40.6 | 28 | 82.4 | 240 | 115.6 | 105 | 221 |
| −10 | −23.3 | −26 | −14.8 | 110 | 43.3 | 30 | 86 | 245 | 118.3 | 110 | 230 |
| −5 | −20.6 | −24 | −11.2 | 115 | 46.1 | 32 | 89.6 | 250 | 121.1 | 115 | 239 |
| 0 | −17.8 | −22 | −7.6 | 120 | 48.9 | 34 | 93.2 | 255 | 123.9 | 120 | 248 |
| 1 | −17.2 | −20 | −4 | 125 | 51.7 | 36 | 96.8 | 260 | 126.6 | 125 | 257 |
| 2 | −16.7 | −18 | −0.4 | 130 | 54.4 | 38 | 100.4 | 265 | 129.4 | 130 | 266 |
| 3 | −16.1 | −16 | 3.2 | 135 | 57.2 | 40 | 104 | 270 | 132.2 | 135 | 275 |
| 4 | −15.6 | −14 | 6.8 | 140 | 60.0 | 42 | 107.6 | 275 | 135.0 | 140 | 284 |
| 5 | −15.0 | −12 | 10.4 | 145 | 62.8 | 44 | 112.2 | 280 | 137.8 | 145 | 293 |
| 10 | −12.2 | −10 | 14 | 150 | 65.6 | 46 | 114.8 | 285 | 140.6 | 150 | 302 |
| 15 | −9.4 | −8 | 17.6 | 155 | 68.3 | 48 | 118.4 | 290 | 143.3 | 155 | 311 |
| 20 | −6.7 | −6 | 21.2 | 160 | 71.1 | 50 | 122 | 295 | 146.1 | 160 | 320 |
| 25 | −3.9 | −4 | 24.8 | 165 | 73.9 | 52 | 125.6 | 300 | 148.9 | 165 | 329 |
| 30 | −1.1 | −2 | 28.4 | 170 | 76.7 | 54 | 129.2 | 305 | 151.7 | 170 | 338 |
| 35 | 1.7 | 0 | 32 | 175 | 79.4 | 56 | 132.8 | 310 | 154.4 | 175 | 347 |
| 40 | 4.4 | 2 | 35.6 | 180 | 82.2 | 58 | 136.4 | 315 | 157.2 | 180 | 356 |
| 45 | 7.2 | 4 | 39.2 | 185 | 85.0 | 60 | 140 | 320 | 160.0 | 185 | 365 |
| 50 | 10.0 | 6 | 42.8 | 190 | 87.8 | 62 | 143.6 | 325 | 162.8 | 190 | 374 |
| 55 | 12.8 | 8 | 46.4 | 195 | 90.6 | 64 | 147.2 | 330 | 165.6 | 195 | 383 |
| 60 | 15.6 | 10 | 50 | 200 | 93.3 | 66 | 150.8 | 335 | 168.3 | 200 | 392 |
| 65 | 18.3 | 12 | 53.6 | 205 | 96.1 | 68 | 154.4 | 340 | 171.1 | 205 | 401 |
| 70 | 21.1 | 14 | 57.2 | 210 | 98.9 | 70 | 158 | 345 | 173.9 | 210 | 410 |
| 75 | 23.9 | 16 | 60.8 | 212 | 100.0 | 75 | 167 | 350 | 176.7 | 215 | 414 |

# GENERAL INFORMATION AND MAINTENANCE

## ENGLISH TO METRIC CONVERSION: LENGTH

To convert inches (ins.) to millimeters (mm): multiply number of inches by 25.4
To convert millimeters (mm) to inches (ins.): multiply number of millimeters by .04

| Inches | Decimals | Milli-meters | Inches to millimeters inches | mm | Inches | Decimals | Milli-meters | Inches to millimeters inches | mm |
|---|---|---|---|---|---|---|---|---|---|
| | 1/64 0.051625 | 0.3969 | 0.0001 | 0.00254 | | 33/64 0.515625 | 13.0969 | 0.6 | 15.24 |
| 1/32 | 0.03125 | 0.7937 | 0.0002 | 0.00508 | 17/32 | 0.53125 | 13.4937 | 0.7 | 17.78 |
| | 3/64 0.046875 | 1.1906 | 0.0003 | 0.00762 | | 35/64 0.546875 | 13.8906 | 0.8 | 20.32 |
| 1/16 | 0.0625 | 1.5875 | 0.0004 | 0.01016 | 9/16 | 0.5625 | 14.2875 | 0.9 | 22.86 |
| | 5/64 0.078125 | 1.9844 | 0.0005 | 0.01270 | | 37/64 0.578125 | 14.6844 | 1 | 25.4 |
| 3/32 | 0.09375 | 2.3812 | 0.0006 | 0.01524 | 19/32 | 0.59375 | 15.0812 | 2 | 50.8 |
| | 7/64 0.109375 | 2.7781 | 0.0007 | 0.01778 | | 39/64 0.609375 | 15.4781 | 3 | 76.2 |
| 1/8 | 0.125 | 3.1750 | 0.0008 | 0.02032 | 5/8 | 0.625 | 15.8750 | 4 | 101.6 |
| | 9/64 0.140625 | 3.5719 | 0.0009 | 0.02286 | | 41/64 0.640625 | 16.2719 | 5 | 127.0 |
| 5/32 | 0.15625 | 3.9687 | 0.001 | 0.0254 | 21/32 | 0.65625 | 16.6687 | 6 | 152.4 |
| | 11/64 0.171875 | 4.3656 | 0.002 | 0.0508 | | 43/64 0.671875 | 17.0656 | 7 | 177.8 |
| 3/16 | 0.1875 | 4.7625 | 0.003 | 0.0762 | 11/16 | 0.6875 | 17.4625 | 8 | 203.2 |
| | 13/64 0.203125 | 5.1594 | 0.004 | 0.1016 | | 45/64 0.703125 | 17.8594 | 9 | 228.6 |
| 7/32 | 0.21875 | 5.5562 | 0.005 | 0.1270 | 23/32 | 0.71875 | 18.2562 | 10 | 254.0 |
| | 15/64 0.234375 | 5.9531 | 0.006 | 0.1524 | | 47/64 0.734375 | 18.6531 | 11 | 279.4 |
| 1/4 | 0.25 | 6.3500 | 0.007 | 0.1778 | 3/4 | 0.75 | 19.0500 | 12 | 304.8 |
| | 17/64 0.265625 | 6.7469 | 0.008 | 0.2032 | | 49/64 0.765625 | 19.4469 | 13 | 330.2 |
| 9/32 | 0.28125 | 7.1437 | 0.009 | 0.2286 | 25/32 | 0.78125 | 19.8437 | 14 | 355.6 |
| | 19/64 0.296875 | 7.5406 | 0.01 | 0.254 | | 51/64 0.796875 | 20.2406 | 15 | 381.0 |
| 5/16 | 0.3125 | 7.9375 | 0.02 | 0.508 | 13/16 | 0.8125 | 20.6375 | 16 | 406.4 |
| | 21/64 0.328125 | 8.3344 | 0.03 | 0.762 | | 53/64 0.828125 | 21.0344 | 17 | 431.8 |
| 11/32 | 0.34375 | 8.7312 | 0.04 | 1.016 | 27/32 | 0.84375 | 21.4312 | 18 | 457.2 |
| | 23/64 0.359375 | 9.1281 | 0.05 | 1.270 | | 55/64 0.859375 | 21.8281 | 19 | 482.6 |
| 3/8 | 0.375 | 9.5250 | 0.06 | 1.524 | 7/8 | 0.875 | 22.2250 | 20 | 508.0 |
| | 25/64 0.390625 | 9.9219 | 0.07 | 1.778 | | 57/64 0.890625 | 22.6219 | 21 | 533.4 |
| 13/32 | 0.40625 | 10.3187 | 0.08 | 2.032 | 29/32 | 0.90625 | 23.0187 | 22 | 558.8 |
| | 27/64 0.421875 | 10.7156 | 0.09 | 2.286 | | 59/64 0.921875 | 23.4156 | 23 | 584.2 |
| 7/16 | 0.4375 | 11.1125 | 0.1 | 2.54 | 15/16 | 0.9375 | 23.8125 | 24 | 609.6 |
| | 29/64 0.453125 | 11.5094 | 0.2 | 5.08 | | 61/64 0.953125 | 24.2094 | 25 | 635.0 |
| 15/32 | 0.46875 | 11.9062 | 0.3 | 7.62 | 31/32 | 0.96875 | 24.6062 | 26 | 660.4 |
| | 31/64 0.484375 | 12.3031 | 0.4 | 10.16 | | 63/64 0.984375 | 25.0031 | 27 | 690.6 |
| 1/2 | 0.5 | 12.7000 | 0.5 | 12.70 | | | | | |

## ENGLISH TO METRIC CONVERSION: TORQUE

To convert foot-pounds (ft. lbs.) to Newton-meters: multiply the number of ft. lbs. by 1.3
To convert inch-pounds (in. lbs.) to Newton-meters: multiply the number of in. lbs. by .11

| in lbs | N-m | in lbs | N-m | in lbs | N-m | in lbs | N-m | in lbs | N-m |
|---|---|---|---|---|---|---|---|---|---|
| 0.1 | 0.01 | 1 | 0.11 | 10 | 1.13 | 19 | 2.15 | 28 | 3.16 |
| 0.2 | 0.02 | 2 | 0.23 | 11 | 1.24 | 20 | 2.26 | 29 | 3.28 |
| 0.3 | 0.03 | 3 | 0.34 | 12 | 1.36 | 21 | 2.37 | 30 | 3.39 |
| 0.4 | 0.04 | 4 | 0.45 | 13 | 1.47 | 22 | 2.49 | 31 | 3.50 |
| 0.5 | 0.06 | 5 | 0.56 | 14 | 1.58 | 23 | 2.60 | 32 | 3.62 |
| 0.6 | 0.07 | 6 | 0.68 | 15 | 1.70 | 24 | 2.71 | 33 | 3.73 |
| 0.7 | 0.08 | 7 | 0.78 | 16 | 1.81 | 25 | 2.82 | 34 | 3.84 |
| 0.8 | 0.09 | 8 | 0.90 | 17 | 1.92 | 26 | 2.94 | 35 | 3.95 |
| 0.9 | 0.10 | 9 | 1.02 | 18 | 2.03 | 27 | 3.05 | 36 | 4.0 |

## 1-80 GENERAL INFORMATION AND MAINTENANCE

### ENGLISH TO METRIC CONVERSION: TORQUE

Torque is now expressed as either foot-pounds (ft./lbs.) or inch-pounds (in./lbs.). The metric measurement unit for torque is the Newton-meter (Nm). This unit—the Nm—will be used for all SI metric torque references, both the present ft./lbs. and in./lbs.

| ft lbs | N-m | ft lbs | N-m | ft lbs | N-m | ft lbs | N-m |
|---|---|---|---|---|---|---|---|
| 0.1 | 0.1 | 33 | 44.7 | 74 | 100.3 | 115 | 155.9 |
| 0.2 | 0.3 | 34 | 46.1 | 75 | 101.7 | 116 | 157.3 |
| 0.3 | 0.4 | 35 | 47.4 | 76 | 103.0 | 117 | 158.6 |
| 0.4 | 0.5 | 36 | 48.8 | 77 | 104.4 | 118 | 160.0 |
| 0.5 | 0.7 | 37 | 50.7 | 78 | 105.8 | 119 | 161.3 |
| 0.6 | 0.8 | 38 | 51.5 | 79 | 107.1 | 120 | 162.7 |
| 0.7 | 1.0 | 39 | 52.9 | 80 | 108.5 | 121 | 164.0 |
| 0.8 | 1.1 | 40 | 54.2 | 81 | 109.8 | 122 | 165.4 |
| 0.9 | 1.2 | 41 | 55.6 | 82 | 111.2 | 123 | 166.8 |
| 1 | 1.3 | 42 | 56.9 | 83 | 112.5 | 124 | 168.1 |
| 2 | 2.7 | 43 | 58.3 | 84 | 113.9 | 125 | 169.5 |
| 3 | 4.1 | 44 | 59.7 | 85 | 115.2 | 126 | 170.8 |
| 4 | 5.4 | 45 | 61.0 | 86 | 116.6 | 127 | 172.2 |
| 5 | 6.8 | 46 | 62.4 | 87 | 118.0 | 128 | 173.5 |
| 6 | 8.1 | 47 | 63.7 | 88 | 119.3 | 129 | 174.9 |
| 7 | 9.5 | 48 | 65.1 | 89 | 120.7 | 130 | 176.2 |
| 8 | 10.8 | 49 | 66.4 | 90 | 122.0 | 131 | 177.6 |
| 9 | 12.2 | 50 | 67.8 | 91 | 123.4 | 132 | 179.0 |
| 10 | 13.6 | 51 | 69.2 | 92 | 124.7 | 133 | 180.3 |
| 11 | 14.9 | 52 | 70.5 | 93 | 126.1 | 134 | 181.7 |
| 12 | 16.3 | 53 | 71.9 | 94 | 127.4 | 135 | 183.0 |
| 13 | 17.6 | 54 | 73.2 | 95 | 128.8 | 136 | 184.4 |
| 14 | 18.9 | 55 | 74.6 | 96 | 130.2 | 137 | 185.7 |
| 15 | 20.3 | 56 | 75.9 | 97 | 131.5 | 138 | 187.1 |
| 16 | 21.7 | 57 | 77.3 | 98 | 132.9 | 139 | 188.5 |
| 17 | 23.0 | 58 | 78.6 | 99 | 134.2 | 140 | 189.8 |
| 18 | 24.4 | 59 | 80.0 | 100 | 135.6 | 141 | 191.2 |
| 19 | 25.8 | 60 | 81.4 | 101 | 136.9 | 142 | 192.5 |
| 20 | 27.1 | 61 | 82.7 | 102 | 138.3 | 143 | 193.9 |
| 21 | 28.5 | 62 | 84.1 | 103 | 139.6 | 144 | 195.2 |
| 22 | 29.8 | 63 | 85.4 | 104 | 141.0 | 145 | 196.6 |
| 23 | 31.2 | 64 | 86.8 | 105 | 142.4 | 146 | 198.0 |
| 24 | 32.5 | 65 | 88.1 | 106 | 143.7 | 147 | 199.3 |
| 25 | 33.9 | 66 | 89.5 | 107 | 145.1 | 148 | 200.7 |
| 26 | 35.2 | 67 | 90.8 | 108 | 146.4 | 149 | 202.0 |
| 27 | 36.6 | 68 | 92.2 | 109 | 147.8 | 150 | 203.4 |
| 28 | 38.0 | 69 | 93.6 | 110 | 149.1 | 151 | 204.7 |
| 29 | 39.3 | 70 | 94.9 | 111 | 150.5 | 152 | 206.1 |
| 30 | 40.7 | 71 | 96.3 | 112 | 151.8 | 153 | 207.4 |
| 31 | 42.0 | 72 | 97.6 | 113 | 153.2 | 154 | 208.8 |
| 32 | 43.4 | 73 | 99.0 | 114 | 154.6 | 155 | 210.2 |

TCCS1C03

# GENERAL INFORMATION AND MAINTENANCE　1-81

## ENGLISH TO METRIC CONVERSION: FORCE

Force is presently measured in pounds (lbs.). This type of measurement is used to measure spring pressure, specifically how many pounds it takes to compress a spring. Our present force unit (the pound) will be replaced in SI metric measurements by the Newton (N). This term will eventually see use in specifications for electric motor brush spring pressures, valve spring pressures, etc.

To convert pounds (lbs.) to Newton (N): multiply the number of lbs. by 4.45

| lbs | N | lbs | N | lbs | N | oz | N |
|---|---|---|---|---|---|---|---|
| 0.01 | 0.04 | 21 | 93.4 | 59 | 262.4 | 1 | 0.3 |
| 0.02 | 0.09 | 22 | 97.9 | 60 | 266.9 | 2 | 0.6 |
| 0.03 | 0.13 | 23 | 102.3 | 61 | 271.3 | 3 | 0.8 |
| 0.04 | 0.18 | 24 | 106.8 | 62 | 275.8 | 4 | 1.1 |
| 0.05 | 0.22 | 25 | 111.2 | 63 | 280.2 | 5 | 1.4 |
| 0.06 | 0.27 | 26 | 115.6 | 64 | 284.6 | 6 | 1.7 |
| 0.07 | 0.31 | 27 | 120.1 | 65 | 289.1 | 7 | 2.0 |
| 0.08 | 0.36 | 28 | 124.6 | 66 | 293.6 | 8 | 2.2 |
| 0.09 | 0.40 | 29 | 129.0 | 67 | 298.0 | 9 | 2.5 |
| 0.1 | 0.4 | 30 | 133.4 | 68 | 302.5 | 10 | 2.8 |
| 0.2 | 0.9 | 31 | 137.9 | 69 | 306.9 | 11 | 3.1 |
| 0.3 | 1.3 | 32 | 142.3 | 70 | 311.4 | 12 | 3.3 |
| 0.4 | 1.8 | 33 | 146.8 | 71 | 315.8 | 13 | 3.6 |
| 0.5 | 2.2 | 34 | 151.2 | 72 | 320.3 | 14 | 3.9 |
| 0.6 | 2.7 | 35 | 155.7 | 73 | 324.7 | 15 | 4.2 |
| 0.7 | 3.1 | 36 | 160.1 | 74 | 329.2 | 16 | 4.4 |
| 0.8 | 3.6 | 37 | 164.6 | 75 | 333.6 | 17 | 4.7 |
| 0.9 | 4.0 | 38 | 169.0 | 76 | 338.1 | 18 | 5.0 |
| 1 | 4.4 | 39 | 173.5 | 77 | 342.5 | 19 | 5.3 |
| 2 | 8.9 | 40 | 177.9 | 78 | 347.0 | 20 | 5.6 |
| 3 | 13.4 | 41 | 182.4 | 79 | 351.4 | 21 | 5.8 |
| 4 | 17.8 | 42 | 186.8 | 80 | 355.9 | 22 | 6.1 |
| 5 | 22.2 | 43 | 191.3 | 81 | 360.3 | 23 | 6.4 |
| 6 | 26.7 | 44 | 195.7 | 82 | 364.8 | 24 | 6.7 |
| 7 | 31.1 | 45 | 200.2 | 83 | 369.2 | 25 | 7.0 |
| 8 | 35.6 | 46 | 204.6 | 84 | 373.6 | 26 | 7.2 |
| 9 | 40.0 | 47 | 209.1 | 85 | 378.1 | 27 | 7.5 |
| 10 | 44.5 | 48 | 213.5 | 86 | 382.6 | 28 | 7.8 |
| 11 | 48.9 | 49 | 218.0 | 87 | 387.0 | 29 | 8.1 |
| 12 | 53.4 | 50 | 224.4 | 88 | 391.4 | 30 | 8.3 |
| 13 | 57.8 | 51 | 226.9 | 89 | 395.9 | 31 | 8.6 |
| 14 | 62.3 | 52 | 231.3 | 90 | 400.3 | 32 | 8.9 |
| 15 | 66.7 | 53 | 235.8 | 91 | 404.8 | 33 | 9.2 |
| 16 | 71.2 | 54 | 240.2 | 92 | 409.2 | 34 | 9.4 |
| 17 | 75.6 | 55 | 244.6 | 93 | 413.7 | 35 | 9.7 |
| 18 | 80.1 | 56 | 249.1 | 94 | 418.1 | 36 | 10.0 |
| 19 | 84.5 | 57 | 253.6 | 95 | 422.6 | 37 | 10.3 |
| 20 | 89.0 | 58 | 258.0 | 96 | 427.0 | 38 | 10.6 |

TCCS1C04

## GENERAL INFORMATION AND MAINTENANCE

### ENGLISH TO METRIC CONVERSION: LIQUID CAPACITY

Liquid or fluid capacity is presently expressed as pints, quarts or gallons, or a combination of all of these. In the metric system the liter (l) will become the basic unit. Fractions of a liter would be expressed as deciliters, centiliters, or most frequently (and commonly) as milliliters.

To convert pints (pts.) to liters (l): multiply the number of pints by .47
To convert liters (l) to pints (pts.): multiply the number of liters by 2.1
To convert quarts (qts.) to liters (l): multiply the number of quarts by .95

To convert liters (l) to quarts (qts.): multiply the number of liters by 1.06
To convert gallons (gals.) to liters (l): multiply the number of gallons by 3.8
To convert liters (l) to gallons (gals.): multiply the number of liters by .26

| gals | liters | qts | liters | pts | liters |
|---|---|---|---|---|---|
| 0.1 | 0.38 | 0.1 | 0.10 | 0.1 | 0.05 |
| 0.2 | 0.76 | 0.2 | 0.19 | 0.2 | 0.10 |
| 0.3 | 1.1 | 0.3 | 0.28 | 0.3 | 0.14 |
| 0.4 | 1.5 | 0.4 | 0.38 | 0.4 | 0.19 |
| 0.5 | 1.9 | 0.5 | 0.47 | 0.5 | 0.24 |
| 0.6 | 2.3 | 0.6 | 0.57 | 0.6 | 0.28 |
| 0.7 | 2.6 | 0.7 | 0.66 | 0.7 | 0.33 |
| 0.8 | 3.0 | 0.8 | 0.76 | 0.8 | 0.38 |
| 0.9 | 3.4 | 0.9 | 0.85 | 0.9 | 0.43 |
| 1 | 3.8 | 1 | 1.0 | 1 | 0.5 |
| 2 | 7.6 | 2 | 1.9 | 2 | 1.0 |
| 3 | 11.4 | 3 | 2.8 | 3 | 1.4 |
| 4 | 15.1 | 4 | 3.8 | 4 | 1.9 |
| 5 | 18.9 | 5 | 4.7 | 5 | 2.4 |
| 6 | 22.7 | 6 | 5.7 | 6 | 2.8 |
| 7 | 26.5 | 7 | 6.6 | 7 | 3.3 |
| 8 | 30.3 | 8 | 7.6 | 8 | 3.8 |
| 9 | 34.1 | 9 | 8.5 | 9 | 4.3 |
| 10 | 37.8 | 10 | 9.5 | 10 | 4.7 |
| 11 | 41.6 | 11 | 10.4 | 11 | 5.2 |
| 12 | 45.4 | 12 | 11.4 | 12 | 5.7 |
| 13 | 49.2 | 13 | 12.3 | 13 | 6.2 |
| 14 | 53.0 | 14 | 13.2 | 14 | 6.6 |
| 15 | 56.8 | 15 | 14.2 | 15 | 7.1 |
| 16 | 60.6 | 16 | 15.1 | 16 | 7.6 |
| 17 | 64.3 | 17 | 16.1 | 17 | 8.0 |
| 18 | 68.1 | 18 | 17.0 | 18 | 8.5 |
| 19 | 71.9 | 19 | 18.0 | 19 | 9.0 |
| 20 | 75.7 | 20 | 18.9 | 20 | 9.5 |
| 21 | 79.5 | 21 | 19.9 | 21 | 9.9 |
| 22 | 83.2 | 22 | 20.8 | 22 | 10.4 |
| 23 | 87.0 | 23 | 21.8 | 23 | 10.9 |
| 24 | 90.8 | 24 | 22.7 | 24 | 11.4 |
| 25 | 94.6 | 25 | 23.6 | 25 | 11.8 |
| 26 | 98.4 | 26 | 24.6 | 26 | 12.3 |
| 27 | 102.2 | 27 | 25.5 | 27 | 12.8 |
| 28 | 106.0 | 28 | 26.5 | 28 | 13.2 |
| 29 | 110.0 | 29 | 27.4 | 29 | 13.7 |
| 30 | 113.5 | 30 | 28.4 | 30 | 14.2 |

# GENERAL INFORMATION AND MAINTENANCE

## ENGLISH TO METRIC CONVERSION: PRESSURE

The basic unit of pressure measurement used today is expressed as pounds per square inch (psi). The metric unit for psi will be the kilopascal (kPa). This will apply to either fluid pressure or air pressure, and will be frequently seen in tire pressure readings, oil pressure specifications, fuel pump pressure, etc.

To convert pounds per square inch (psi) to kilopascals (kPa): multiply the number of psi by 6.89

| Psi | kPa | Psi | kPa | Psi | kPa | Psi | kPa |
|---|---|---|---|---|---|---|---|
| 0.1 | 0.7 | 37 | 255.1 | 82 | 565.4 | 127 | 875.6 |
| 0.2 | 1.4 | 38 | 262.0 | 83 | 572.3 | 128 | 882.5 |
| 0.3 | 2.1 | 39 | 268.9 | 84 | 579.2 | 129 | 889.4 |
| 0.4 | 2.8 | 40 | 275.8 | 85 | 586.0 | 130 | 896.3 |
| 0.5 | 3.4 | 41 | 282.7 | 86 | 592.9 | 131 | 903.2 |
| 0.6 | 4.1 | 42 | 289.6 | 87 | 599.8 | 132 | 910.1 |
| 0.7 | 4.8 | 43 | 296.5 | 88 | 606.7 | 133 | 917.0 |
| 0.8 | 5.5 | 44 | 303.4 | 89 | 613.6 | 134 | 923.9 |
| 0.9 | 6.2 | 45 | 310.3 | 90 | 620.5 | 135 | 930.8 |
| 1 | 6.9 | 46 | 317.2 | 91 | 627.4 | 136 | 937.7 |
| 2 | 13.8 | 47 | 324.0 | 92 | 634.3 | 137 | 944.6 |
| 3 | 20.7 | 48 | 331.0 | 93 | 641.2 | 138 | 951.5 |
| 4 | 27.6 | 49 | 337.8 | 94 | 648.1 | 139 | 958.4 |
| 5 | 34.5 | 50 | 344.7 | 95 | 655.0 | 140 | 965.2 |
| 6 | 41.4 | 51 | 351.6 | 96 | 661.9 | 141 | 972.2 |
| 7 | 48.3 | 52 | 358.5 | 97 | 668.8 | 142 | 979.0 |
| 8 | 55.2 | 53 | 365.4 | 98 | 675.7 | 143 | 985.9 |
| 9 | 62.1 | 54 | 372.3 | 99 | 682.6 | 144 | 992.8 |
| 10 | 69.0 | 55 | 379.2 | 100 | 689.5 | 145 | 999.7 |
| 11 | 75.8 | 56 | 386.1 | 101 | 696.4 | 146 | 1006.6 |
| 12 | 82.7 | 57 | 393.0 | 102 | 703.3 | 147 | 1013.5 |
| 13 | 89.6 | 58 | 399.9 | 103 | 710.2 | 148 | 1020.4 |
| 14 | 96.5 | 59 | 406.8 | 104 | 717.0 | 149 | 1027.3 |
| 15 | 103.4 | 60 | 413.7 | 105 | 723.9 | 150 | 1034.2 |
| 16 | 110.3 | 61 | 420.6 | 106 | 730.8 | 151 | 1041.1 |
| 17 | 117.2 | 62 | 427.5 | 107 | 737.7 | 152 | 1048.0 |
| 18 | 124.1 | 63 | 434.4 | 108 | 744.6 | 153 | 1054.9 |
| 19 | 131.0 | 64 | 441.3 | 109 | 751.5 | 154 | 1061.8 |
| 20 | 137.9 | 65 | 448.2 | 110 | 758.4 | 155 | 1068.7 |
| 21 | 144.8 | 66 | 455.0 | 111 | 765.3 | 156 | 1075.6 |
| 22 | 151.7 | 67 | 461.9 | 112 | 772.2 | 157 | 1082.5 |
| 23 | 158.6 | 68 | 468.8 | 113 | 779.1 | 158 | 1089.4 |
| 24 | 165.5 | 69 | 475.7 | 114 | 786.0 | 159 | 1096.3 |
| 25 | 172.4 | 70 | 482.6 | 115 | 792.9 | 160 | 1103.2 |
| 26 | 179.3 | 71 | 489.5 | 116 | 799.8 | 161 | 1110.0 |
| 27 | 186.2 | 72 | 496.4 | 117 | 806.7 | 162 | 1116.9 |
| 28 | 193.0 | 73 | 503.3 | 118 | 813.6 | 163 | 1123.8 |
| 29 | 200.0 | 74 | 510.2 | 119 | 820.5 | 164 | 1130.7 |
| 30 | 206.8 | 75 | 517.1 | 120 | 827.4 | 165 | 1137.6 |
| 31 | 213.7 | 76 | 524.0 | 121 | 834.3 | 166 | 1144.5 |
| 32 | 220.6 | 77 | 530.9 | 122 | 841.2 | 167 | 1151.4 |
| 33 | 227.5 | 78 | 537.8 | 123 | 848.0 | 168 | 1158.3 |
| 34 | 234.4 | 79 | 544.7 | 124 | 854.9 | 169 | 1165.2 |
| 35 | 241.3 | 80 | 551.6 | 125 | 861.8 | 170 | 1172.1 |
| 36 | 248.2 | 81 | 558.5 | 126 | 868.7 | 171 | 1179.0 |

TCCS1C06

# 1-84 GENERAL INFORMATION AND MAINTENANCE

## ENGLISH TO METRIC CONVERSION: PRESSURE

The basic unit of pressure measurement used today is expressed as pounds per square inch (psi). The metric unit for psi will be the kilopascal (kPa). This will apply to either fluid pressure or air pressure, and will be frequently seen in tire pressure readings, oil pressure specifications, fuel pump pressure, etc.

To convert pounds per square inch (psi) to kilopascals (kPa): multiply the number of psi by 6.89

| Psi | kPa | Psi | kPa | Psi | kPa | Psi | kPa |
|-----|------|-----|------|-----|------|-----|------|
| 172 | 1185.9 | 216 | 1489.3 | 260 | 1792.6 | 304 | 2096.0 |
| 173 | 1192.8 | 217 | 1496.2 | 261 | 1799.5 | 305 | 2102.9 |
| 174 | 1199.7 | 218 | 1503.1 | 262 | 1806.4 | 306 | 2109.8 |
| 175 | 1206.6 | 219 | 1510.0 | 263 | 1813.3 | 307 | 2116.7 |
| 176 | 1213.5 | 220 | 1516.8 | 264 | 1820.2 | 308 | 2123.6 |
| 177 | 1220.4 | 221 | 1523.7 | 265 | 1827.1 | 309 | 2130.5 |
| 178 | 1227.3 | 222 | 1530.6 | 266 | 1834.0 | 310 | 2137.4 |
| 179 | 1234.2 | 223 | 1537.5 | 267 | 1840.9 | 311 | 2144.3 |
| 180 | 1241.0 | 224 | 1544.4 | 268 | 1847.8 | 312 | 2151.2 |
| 181 | 1247.9 | 225 | 1551.3 | 269 | 1854.7 | 313 | 2158.1 |
| 182 | 1254.8 | 226 | 1558.2 | 270 | 1861.6 | 314 | 2164.9 |
| 183 | 1261.7 | 227 | 1565.1 | 271 | 1868.5 | 315 | 2171.8 |
| 184 | 1268.6 | 228 | 1572.0 | 272 | 1875.4 | 316 | 2178.7 |
| 185 | 1275.5 | 229 | 1578.9 | 273 | 1882.3 | 317 | 2185.6 |
| 186 | 1282.4 | 230 | 1585.8 | 274 | 1889.2 | 318 | 2192.5 |
| 187 | 1289.3 | 231 | 1592.7 | 275 | 1896.1 | 319 | 2199.4 |
| 188 | 1296.2 | 232 | 1599.6 | 276 | 1903.0 | 320 | 2206.3 |
| 189 | 1303.1 | 233 | 1606.5 | 277 | 1909.8 | 321 | 2213.2 |
| 190 | 1310.0 | 234 | 1613.4 | 278 | 1916.7 | 322 | 2220.1 |
| 191 | 1316.9 | 235 | 1620.3 | 279 | 1923.6 | 323 | 2227.0 |
| 192 | 1323.8 | 236 | 1627.2 | 280 | 1930.5 | 324 | 2233.9 |
| 193 | 1330.7 | 237 | 1634.1 | 281 | 1937.4 | 325 | 2240.8 |
| 194 | 1337.6 | 238 | 1641.0 | 282 | 1944.3 | 326 | 2247.7 |
| 195 | 1344.5 | 239 | 1647.8 | 283 | 1951.2 | 327 | 2254.6 |
| 196 | 1351.4 | 240 | 1654.7 | 284 | 1958.1 | 328 | 2261.5 |
| 197 | 1358.3 | 241 | 1661.6 | 285 | 1965.0 | 329 | 2268.4 |
| 198 | 1365.2 | 242 | 1668.5 | 286 | 1971.9 | 330 | 2275.3 |
| 199 | 1372.0 | 243 | 1675.4 | 287 | 1978.8 | 331 | 2282.2 |
| 200 | 1378.9 | 244 | 1682.3 | 288 | 1985.7 | 332 | 2289.1 |
| 201 | 1385.8 | 245 | 1689.2 | 289 | 1992.6 | 333 | 2295.9 |
| 202 | 1392.7 | 246 | 1696.1 | 290 | 1999.5 | 334 | 2302.8 |
| 203 | 1399.6 | 247 | 1703.0 | 291 | 2006.4 | 335 | 2309.7 |
| 204 | 1406.5 | 248 | 1709.9 | 292 | 2013.3 | 336 | 2316.6 |
| 205 | 1413.4 | 249 | 1716.8 | 293 | 2020.2 | 337 | 2323.5 |
| 206 | 1420.3 | 250 | 1723.7 | 294 | 2027.1 | 338 | 2330.4 |
| 207 | 1427.2 | 251 | 1730.6 | 295 | 2034.0 | 339 | 2337.3 |
| 208 | 1434.1 | 252 | 1737.5 | 296 | 2040.8 | 240 | 2344.2 |
| 209 | 1441.0 | 253 | 1744.4 | 297 | 2047.7 | 341 | 2351.1 |
| 210 | 1447.9 | 254 | 1751.3 | 298 | 2054.6 | 342 | 2358.0 |
| 211 | 1454.8 | 255 | 1758.2 | 299 | 2061.5 | 343 | 2364.9 |
| 212 | 1461.7 | 256 | 1765.1 | 300 | 2068.4 | 344 | 2371.8 |
| 213 | 1468.7 | 257 | 1772.0 | 301 | 2075.3 | 345 | 2378.7 |
| 214 | 1475.5 | 258 | 1778.8 | 302 | 2082.2 | 346 | 2385.6 |
| 215 | 1482.4 | 259 | 1785.7 | 303 | 2089.1 | 347 | 2392.5 |

**ELECTRONIC SPARK ADVANCE
SYSTEM 2-2**
GENERAL INFORMATION 2-2
DIAGNOSIS AND TESTING 2-2
  NO START TEST 2-2
  SIGNAL GENERATOR AIR GAP
    INSPECTION 2-3
IGNITION COIL 2-4
  TESTING 2-4
  REMOVAL & INSTALLATION 2-4
IGNITER 2-5
  REMOVAL & INSTALLATION 2-5
DISTRIBUTOR 2-5
  REMOVAL & INSTALLATION 2-5
CRANKSHAFT POSITION (CKP)
  SENSOR 2-8
**FIRING ORDERS 2-8**
**CHARGING SYSTEM 2-9**
GENERAL INFORMATION 2-9
ALTERNATOR PRECAUTIONS 2-9
ALTERNATOR 2-9
  TESTING 2-9
  REMOVAL & INSTALLATION 2-10
**STARTING SYSTEM 2-12**
GENERAL INFORMATION 2-12
STARTER 2-12
  TESTING 2-12
  REMOVAL & INSTALLATION 2-13
  SOLENOID REPLACEMENT 2-15
  RELAY REPLACEMENT 2-15
**SENDING UNITS AND SENSORS 2-16**
GENERAL INFORMATION 2-16
COOLANT TEMPERATURE SENSOR 2-16
  TESTING 2-16
  REMOVAL & INSTALLATION 2-16
OIL PRESSURE SENSOR 2-16
  TESTING 2-16
  REMOVAL & INSTALLATION 2-17
**TROUBLESHOOTING CHARTS**
  BASIC STARTING SYSTEM
    PROBLEMS 2-17
  BASIC CHARGING SYSTEM
    PROBLEMS 2-18

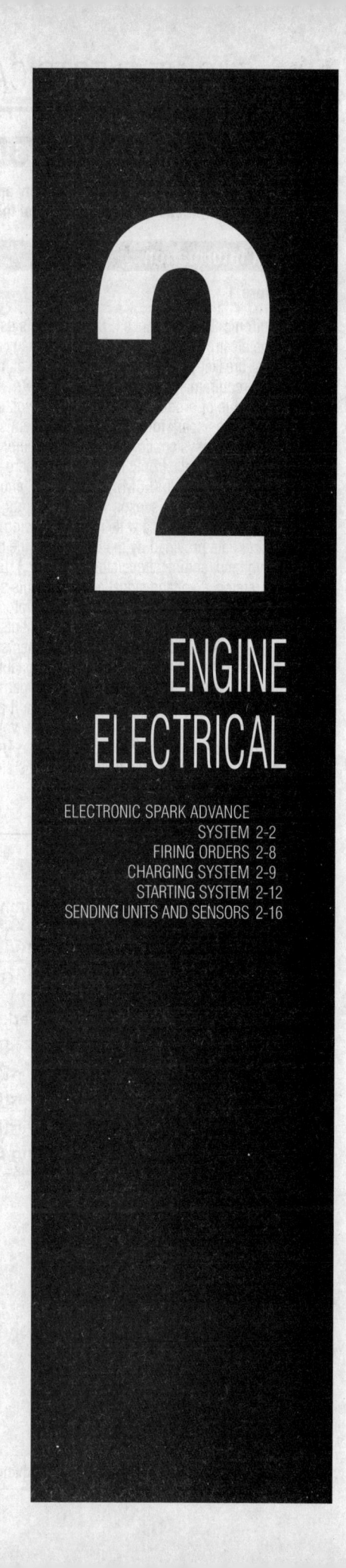

# 2

# ENGINE ELECTRICAL

ELECTRONIC SPARK ADVANCE
SYSTEM 2-2
FIRING ORDERS 2-8
CHARGING SYSTEM 2-9
STARTING SYSTEM 2-12
SENDING UNITS AND SENSORS 2-16

## 2-2  ENGINE ELECTRICAL

### ELECTRONIC SPARK ADVANCE SYSTEM

➡ For information on understanding electricity and troubleshooting electrical circuits, please refer to Section 6 of this manual.

### General Information

▶ See Figure 1

The Electronic Spark Advance (ESA) system is used on all Toyota Previas. The electronic ignition system offers many advantages over the conventional breaker points ignition system. By eliminating the points, maintenance requirements are greatly reduced. An electronic ignition system is capable of producing a much higher voltage which in turn aide in starting, reduces spark fouling and provides emission control.

The ESA ignition system consists of a distributor with a signal generator, ignition coil (s), electronic igniter and a micro-computer called an Electronic Control Module (ECM). The 2TZ-FZE engine also uses a Crankshaft Position (CKP) sensor. The ECM is programmed with data for optimum ignition timing for a wide range of driving and operating conditions. Using data provided by the various engine mounting sensors (intake air volume, engine temperature, rpm, etc.), the ECM converts the data into a reference voltage signal and sends this signal to the igniter mounted inside the distributor. The signal generator receives a reference voltage from the ECM and activates the components of the igniter. The signal generator consists of three main components: the signal rotor, pick-up coil and the permanent magnet. The signal rotor revolves with the distributor shaft, while the pick-up coil and permanent magnet are stationary. as the signal; rotor spins the teeth on it pass a projection leading from the pick-up coil. When this occurs, voltage is allowed to flow through the system and fire the spark plugs. This process happens without physical contact or electrical arching; therefore, there is no need to replace burnt or worn parts.

### Diagnosis and Testing

NO START TEST

▶ See Figures 2, 3, 4, 5 and 6

1. First, conduct a spark test as follows.
2. On the 2TZ-FZE engines, remove the exhaust pipe heat insulator.

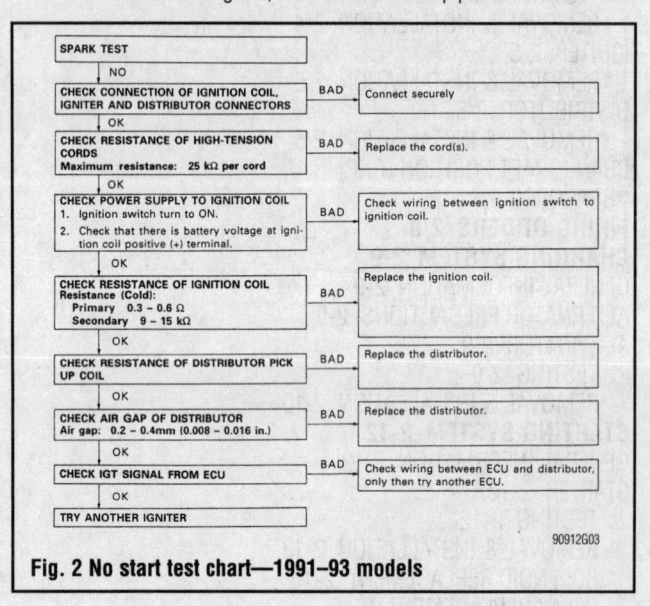

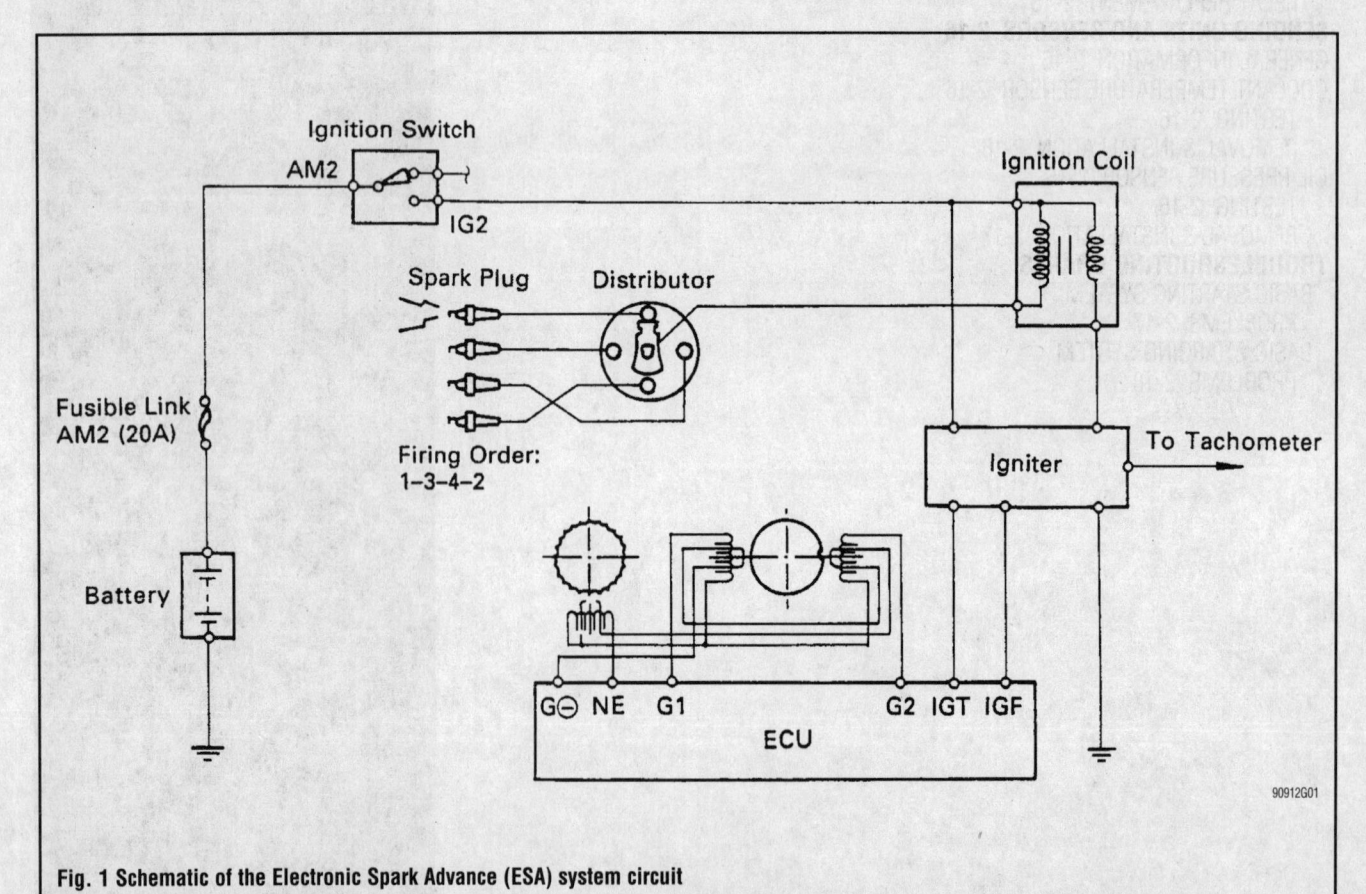

Fig. 2 No start test chart—1991–93 models

Fig. 1 Schematic of the Electronic Spark Advance (ESA) system circuit

# ENGINE ELECTRICAL  2-3

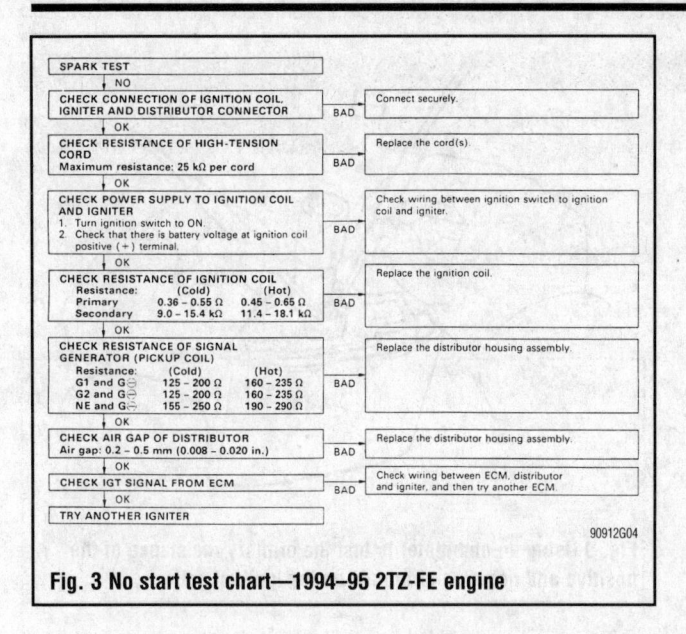

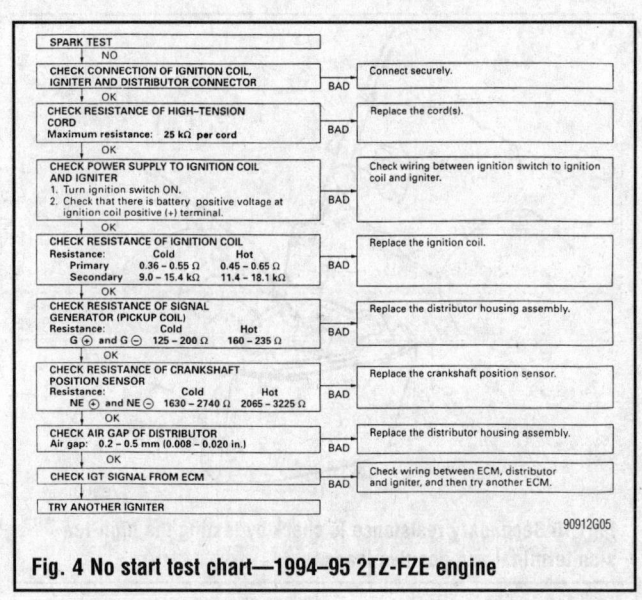

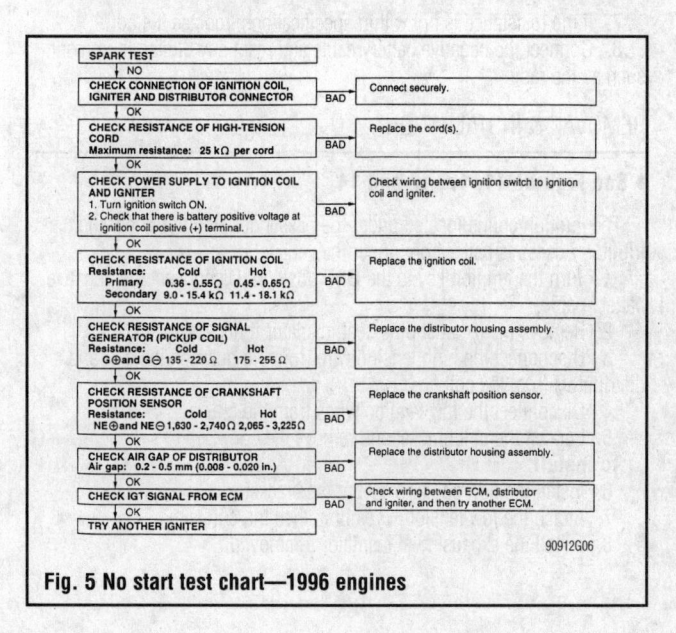

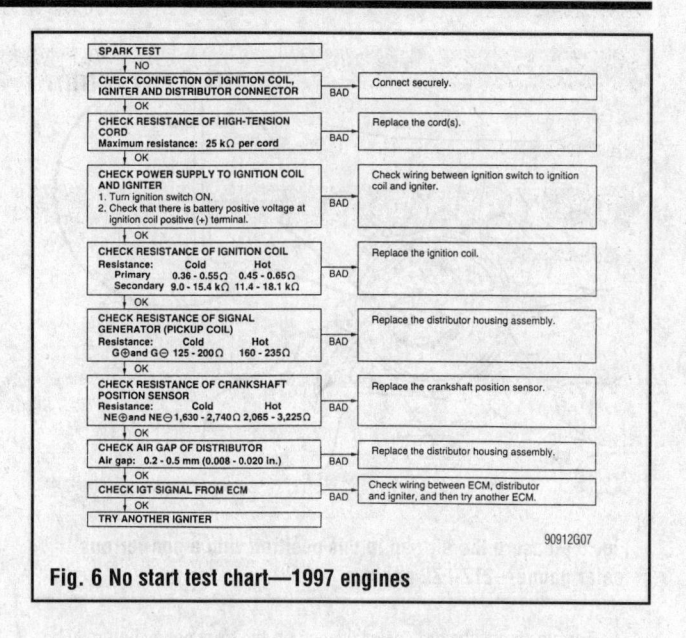

Fig. 3 No start test chart—1994–95 2TZ-FE engine

Fig. 4 No start test chart—1994–95 2TZ-FZE engine

Fig. 5 No start test chart—1996 engines

Fig. 6 No start test chart—1997 engines

3. Disconnect the coil wire from distributor. Hold the coil wire end about ½ inch (12.5mm) from a good body ground; check if spark occurs while engine is being cranked.

➡ **Crank the engine for no more than 2 seconds at a time to prevent flooding the engine with gasoline.**

4. If good spark does not occur (should be bright blue), follow the correct diagnostic flow chart (engine and year) and necessary service procedures. If good spark does occur, the ignition system is probably not at fault.

## SIGNAL GENERATOR AIR GAP INSPECTION

◆ See Figures 7 and 8

➡ The air gap in the distributor should be check periodically. Distributor air gap may only be checked and can only be adjusted by component replacement.

1. Remove the hold-down bolts from the top of the distributor cap.
2. Remove the distributor cap from the housing without disconnecting the ignition wires.
3. Pull the ignition rotor (not the signal rotor) straight up and remove it. If the contacts are worn, pitted or burnt, replace it. Do not file the contacts.

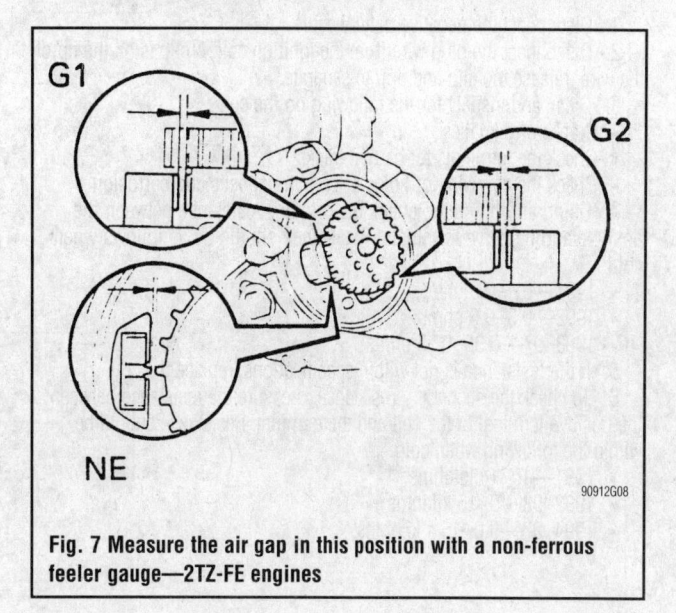

Fig. 7 Measure the air gap in this position with a non-ferrous feeler gauge—2TZ-FE engines

# 2-4 ENGINE ELECTRICAL

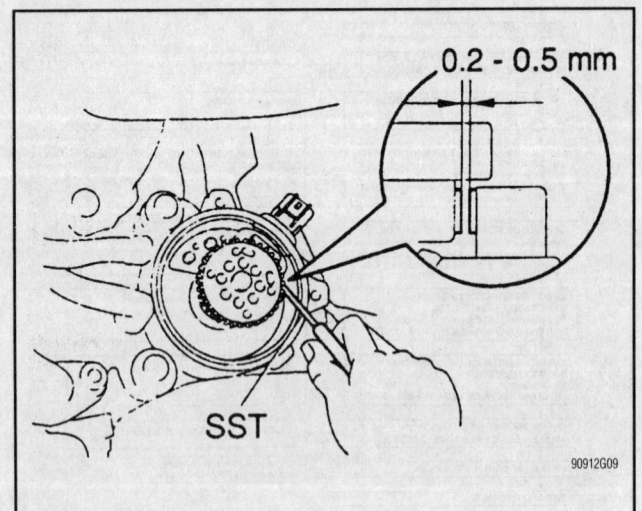

Fig. 8 Measure the air gap in this position with a non-ferrous feeler gauge—2TZ-FZE engines

4. Turn the crankshaft (a socket wrench on the front pulley bolt may be used to do this) until a tooth on the signal rotor aligns with the projection of the pick-up coil.
5. Using a non-ferrous feeler gauge (brass, copper or plastic) measure the gap between the signal rotor and the pick-up coil projection. DO NOT USE AND ORDINARY METAL FEELER GAUGE! The gauge should just touch either side of the gap (snug fit). The acceptable range for the air gap is as follows:
- 1991–92 models—0.008–0.016 inch (0.20–0.40mm)
- 1993–97 models—0.008–0.020 inch (0.20–0.50mm)
6. If the air gap is not within specifications, replace the IIA distributor housing.
7. Check to make sure the housing gasket is in position on the housing.
8. Install the rotor.
9. Install the distributor cap with attached wiring. Attach the cap to the housing and tighten the hold-down bolts.

## Ignition Coil

### TESTING

▶ See Figures 9 and 10

1. Disconnect the negative battery cable.
2. Disconnect the plug wire from the ignition coil. A clip is on the tip of the wire, release the clip and pull to separate.
3. Clean and inspect for the following on the coil:
- Cracks or damages
- Check the terminals for carbon tracks
- Check the coil wire for holes or carbon deposits and corrosion
4. Using an ohmmeter, check the primary resistance between the positive and negative terminals. Resistance should be as follows when cold:
- 1991—0.4–0.5 ohms.
- 1992—0.3–0.6 ohms
- 1993–97—0.36–0.55 ohms
5. If the resistance is not within specifications, replace the coil.
6. To check the secondary resistance, measure the resistance between the positive terminal of the coil and the terminal. Resistance should be within the following when cold:
- 1991—10–14 kilohms.
- 1992–93—9–15 kilohms
- 1994–97—9.0–15.4 kilohms

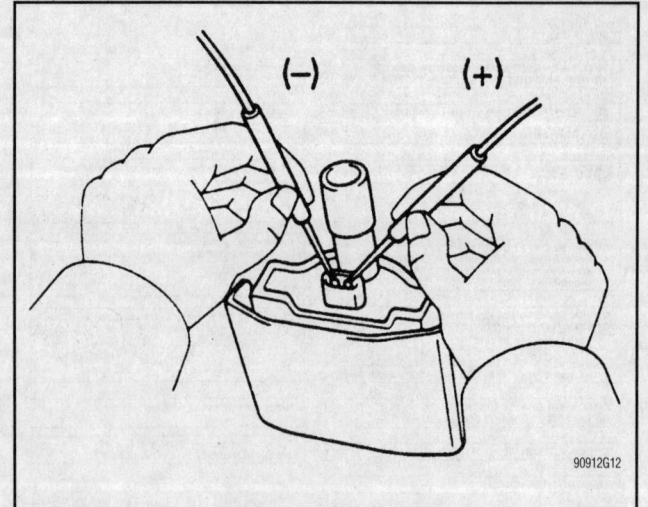

Fig. 9 Using an ohmmeter to test the primary resistance of the positive and negative terminals on the ignition coil

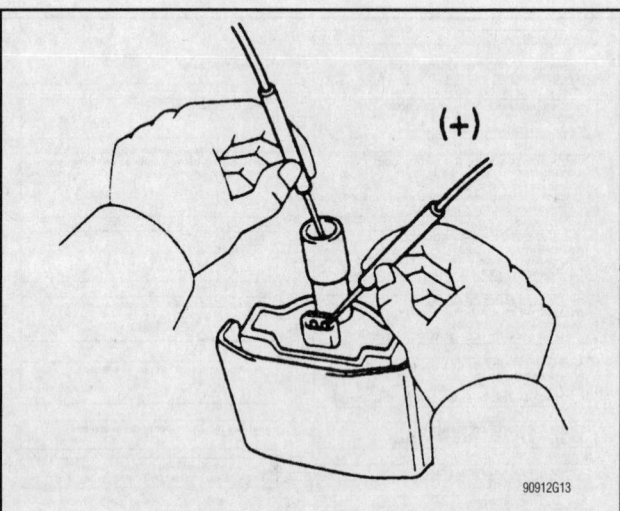

Fig. 10 Secondary resistance is check by testing the high-tension terminal and positive leads

7. If the resistance is not within specifications, replace the coil.
8. Connect the negative battery cable and reset any digital equipment such as the radio.

### REMOVAL & INSTALLATION

▶ See Figures 11, 12, 13 and 14

The ignition coil is located under the passenger side floor near the distributor. Access is better from under the vehicle.

1. Turn the ignition key to the **OFF** position. Disconnect the negative battery cable.
2. Remove the exhaust pipe heat insulator if necessary.
3. Disconnect the high tension wire (running between the coil and the distributor) from the coil.
4. Disconnect the low tension wires from the coil.
5. Loosen the coil bracket and remove the coil.

**To install:**

6. Install the new coil and secure the bracket.
7. Attach the low tension wires first, then the coil wire.
8. Install the exhaust heat insulator if removed.

# ENGINE ELECTRICAL  2-5

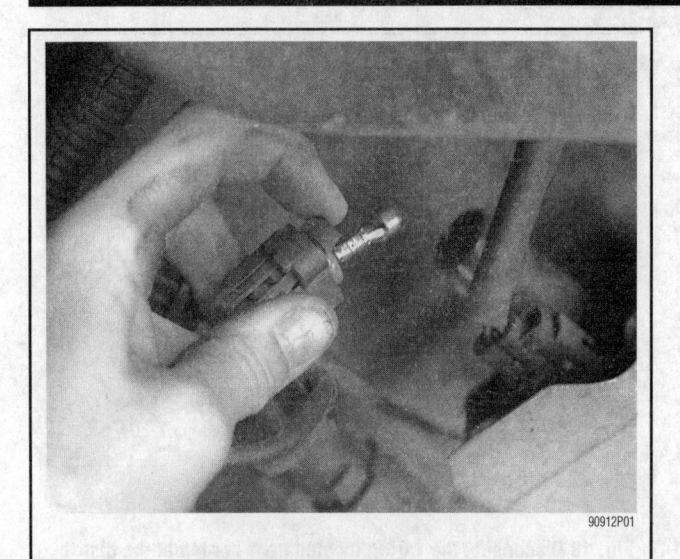

Fig. 11 Release the clip on the tip of the coil wire

Fig. 12 Disconnect the low tension wiring from the coil

Fig. 13 Remove these two mounting bolts

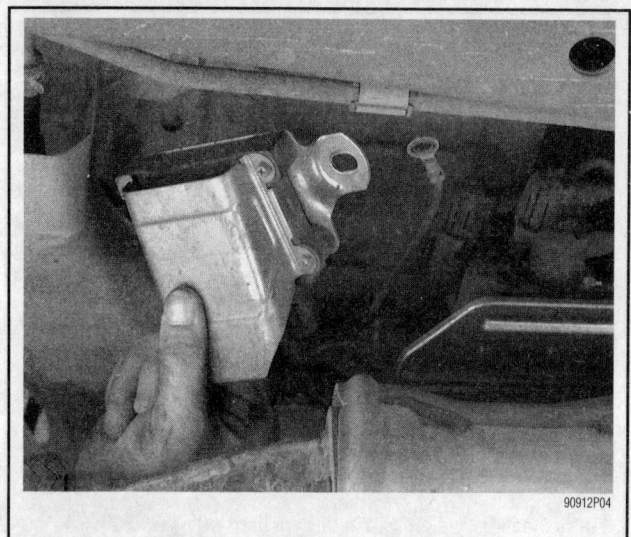

Fig. 14 Extract the coil with bracket from the floor

9. Reconnect the negative battery cable.
10. Reset any various digital equipment such as radio memory and the clock if necessary.

## Igniter

### REMOVAL & INSTALLATION

1. Turn the ignition key to the **OFF** position. Disconnect the negative battery cable.
2. Separate the wiring harness connections.
3. Unbolt the igniter.
4. Loosen the nut holding the wire lead onto the coil.
5. Tag and disconnect the wire lead.
6. Lift the igniter off its mount.

**To install:**

7. Mount the igniter to the bracket.
8. Attach the wire lead to the coil.
9. Connect the harness.
10. Connect the negative battery cable. Reset any digital equipment such as radio memory and the clock if necessary.

## Distributor

### REMOVAL & INSTALLATION

▶ See Figures 15 thru 24

1. Raise and support the vehicle. the distributor is located on the passenger side of the vehicle.
2. On the 2TZ-FZE engine, remove the exhaust pipe heat insulator.
3. Disconnect the negative battery cable.
4. Label and disconnect the spark plug wires. Each wire has a clip to be depressed for release.
5. Remove the cap and packing.
6. Disconnect the distributor wiring and ventilation hoses.
7. Set the No. 1 cylinder to TDC of the compression stroke. Install the service bolt and nut into the equipment driveshaft to turn the crankshaft pulley until the timing mark is aligned with the 0 mark on the timing chain cover.
8. Turn the crankshaft one turn if the rotor is not facing No. 1 spark plug wire.

➡Check that the rotor direction is as shown, if not, turn the drive pulley one complete revolution.

## 2-6 ENGINE ELECTRICAL

Fig. 15 Exploded view of the distributor assembly

Fig. 16 The distributor is located under the vehicle in the side of the engine on the passengers side

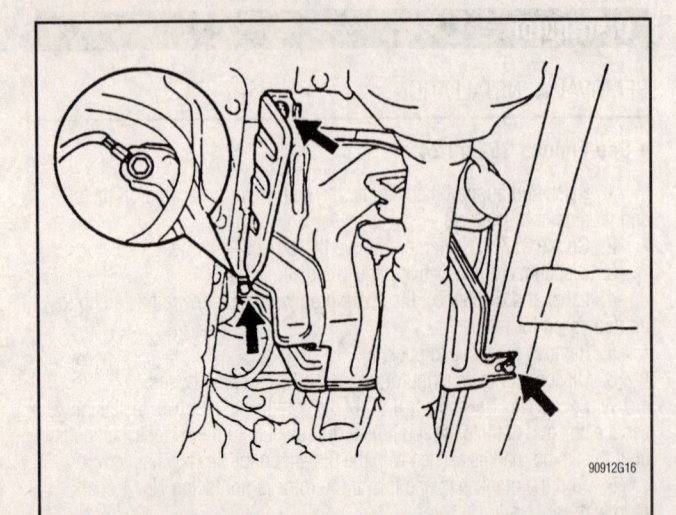

Fig. 17 Remove the 3 retaining bolts and extract the exhaust pipe heat insulator on the 2TZ-FZE engine

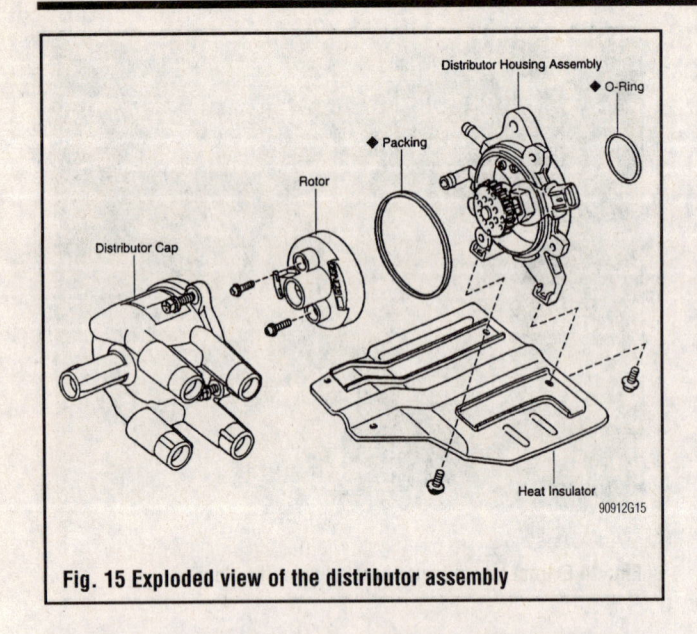

Fig. 18 Disconnect the wiring located near the top of the distributor

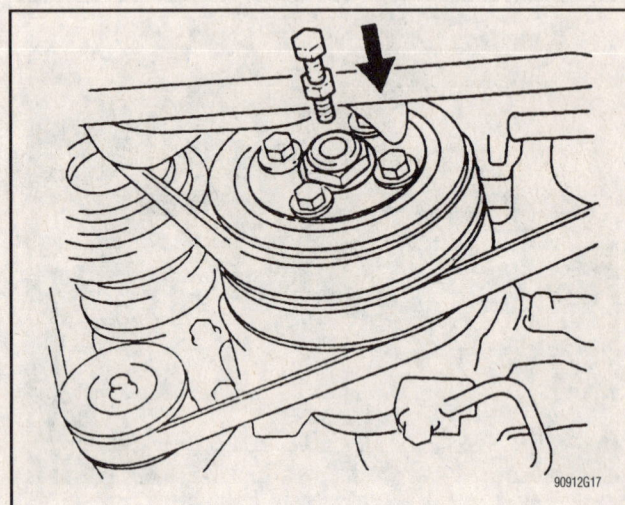

Fig. 19 Place a service bolt with nut into the equipment drive pulley

Fig. 20 Turn the drive pulley until the timing mark is aligned with the 0 mark on the chain case

# ENGINE ELECTRICAL 2-7

**Fig. 21 Place matchmarks on the housing and rotor positions**

**Fig. 22 Remove the hoses attached to the distributor; be sure to label them if there is more than one**

**Fig. 23 Remove the two hold-down bolts . . .**

**Fig. 24 . . . and pull out the distributor assembly from the cylinder head**

9. Place markings on the distributor housing, and rotor positions. Remove the two hold-down bolts and pull the distributor out of the engine.
10. Disconnect and label any hoses attached to the distributor assembly.

**To install:**

**Engine Not Rotated**

▶ See Figure 25

1. Install a new O-ring to the distributor and lubricate with engine oil if it has not recently been replaced.
2. Insert the distributor, aligning the center of the distributor housing flange with the bolt hole on the cylinder head.
3. Engage the distributor drive with the oil pump drive shaft.
4. Install the distributor hold-down clamp, the cap, the high tension wire, the primary wire or the electrical connector and the vacuum line(s).
5. Install the spark plug cables.
6. Connect the negative battery cable.
7. Reset all digital components such as the radio.

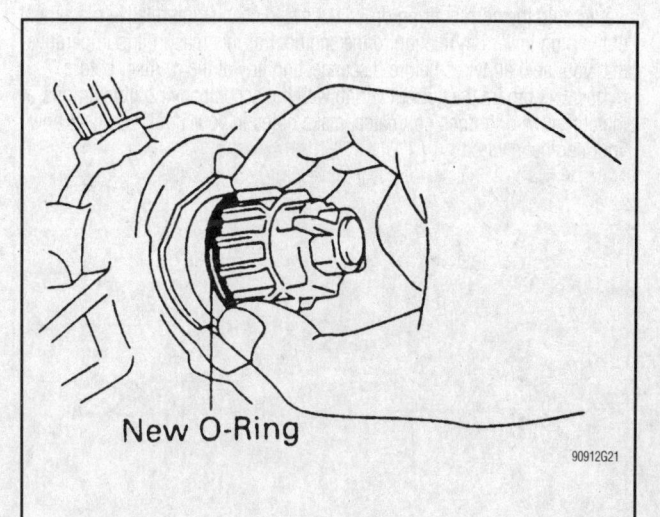

**Fig. 25 Lubricate and install a new O-ring to the end of the distributor**

## 2-8 ENGINE ELECTRICAL

**Engine Rotated**

▶ See Figures 25, 26 and 27

1. If the engine was disturbed while the distributor was removed, continue as follows:
2. Turn the drive pulley clockwise, and position the slit of the exhaust camshaft as shown in the illustration.

→Make sure the slit in the exhaust camshaft is in the proper position.

3. Remove the service bolt and nut.
4. Align the cut out portion of the coupling with the groove on the housing.

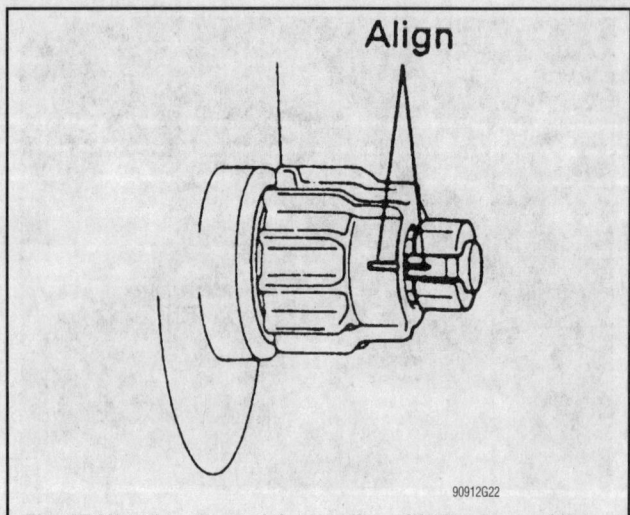

Fig. 27 Align the cut out of the coupling with the groove of the distributor housing

5. Install the distributor and align the center of the flange with the bolt hole on the cylinder head.
6. Install the hold-down bolt loosely.
7. Install the seal packing, distributor cap, air hoses and connect the wiring.
8. Adjust the timing to specifications and tighten the hold-down bolt to 14 ft. lbs. (19 Nm).

### Crankshaft Position (CKP) Sensor

Refer to Electronic Engine Controls in Section 4 for information on servicing the crankshaft position sensor.

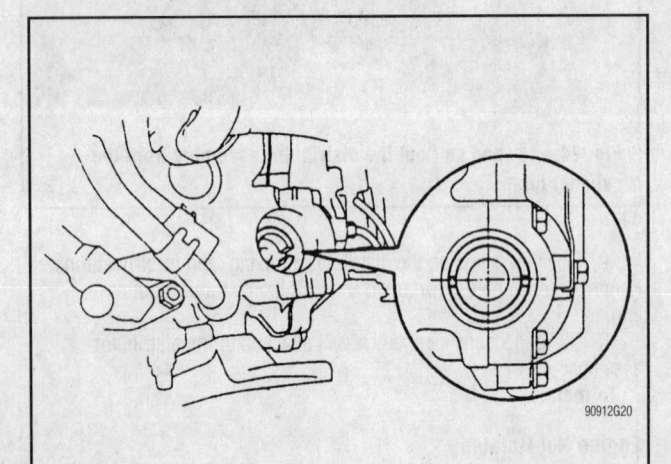

Fig. 26 Turn the drive pulley clockwise and position the slit of the exhaust camshaft

## FIRING ORDERS

▶ See Figure 28

→To avoid confusion, remove and tag the spark plug wires one at a time, for replacement.

If a distributor is not keyed for installation with only one orientation, it could have been removed previously and rewired. The resultant wiring would hold the correct firing order, but could change the relative placement of the plug towers in relation to the engine. For this reason it is imperative that you label all wires before disconnecting any of them. Also, before removal, compare the current wiring with the accompanying illustrations. If the current wiring does not match, make notes in your book to reflect how your engine is wired.

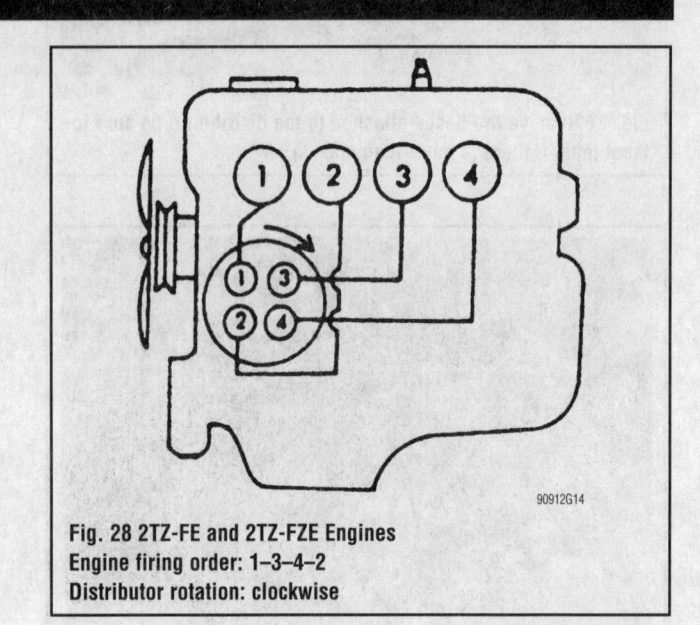

Fig. 28 2TZ-FE and 2TZ-FZE Engines
Engine firing order: 1–3–4–2
Distributor rotation: clockwise

# ENGINE ELECTRICAL 2-9

## CHARGING SYSTEM

### General Information

The charging system is a negative (−) ground system which consists of an alternator, a regulator, a charge indicator lamp, a storage battery, circuit protection and wiring connecting the components.

The alternator is belt-driven from the engine. Energy is supplied from the alternator (with integral regulator) to the rotating field through brushes to slip-rings. The slip-rings are mounted on the rotor shaft and are connected to the field coil. This energy supplied to the rotating field from the battery is called excitation current and is used to initially energize the field to begin the generation of electricity. Once the alternator starts to generate electricity, the excitation current comes from its own output rather than the battery.

The alternator produces power in the form of alternating current. The alternating current is rectified by diodes into direct current. The direct current is used to charge the battery and power the rest of the electrical system. When the ignition key is turned on, current flows from the battery, through the charging system indicator light on the instrument panel, to the voltage regulator, and to the alternator. Since the alternator is not producing any current, the alternator warning light comes on. When the engine is started, the alternator begins to produce current and turns the alternator light off.

As the alternator turns and produces current, the current is divided in two ways: charging the battery and powering the electrical components of the vehicle. Part of the current is returned to the alternator to enable it to increase its output. In this situation, the alternator is receiving current from the battery and from itself. A voltage regulator is wired into the current supply to the alternator to prevent it from receiving too much current, which would cause it to overproduce current. Conversely, if the voltage regulator does not allow the alternator to receive enough current, the battery will not be fully charged and will eventually go dead.

The battery is connected to the alternator at all times, whether the ignition key is turned on or off. If the battery were shorted to ground, the alternator would also be shorted. This would damage the alternator. To prevent this, circuit protection (usually in the form of a fuse link) is installed in the wiring between the battery and the alternator. If the battery is shorted, the circuit protection will protect the alternator.

### Alternator Precautions

To prevent damage to the alternator and regulator, the following precautionary measures must be taken when working with the electrical system.

1. Never reverse the battery connections. Always check the battery polarity visually. This is to be done before any connections are made to ensure that all of the connections correspond to the battery ground polarity of the car.
2. Booster batteries must be connected properly. Make sure the positive cable of the booster battery is connected to the positive terminal of the battery which is getting the boost.
3. Disconnect the battery cables before using a fast charger; the charger has a tendency to force current through the diodes in the opposite direction for which they were designed.
4. Never use a fast charger as a booster for starting the car.
5. Never disconnect the voltage regulator while the engine is running, unless as noted for testing purposes.
6. Do not ground the alternator output terminal.
7. Do not operate the alternator on an open circuit with the field energized.
8. Do not attempt to polarize the alternator.
9. Disconnect the battery cables and remove the alternator before using an electric arc welder on the car.
10. Protect the alternator from excessive moisture. If the engine is to be steam cleaned, cover or remove the alternator.

### Alternator

TESTING

♦ See Figure 29

A voltmeter and ammeter are necessary for testing.

1. Make sure the battery terminals are not loose or corroded. Check the fusible link for continuity.
2. Inspect the drive belt for excessive wear. Check the drive belt tension. If necessary adjust the drive belt.

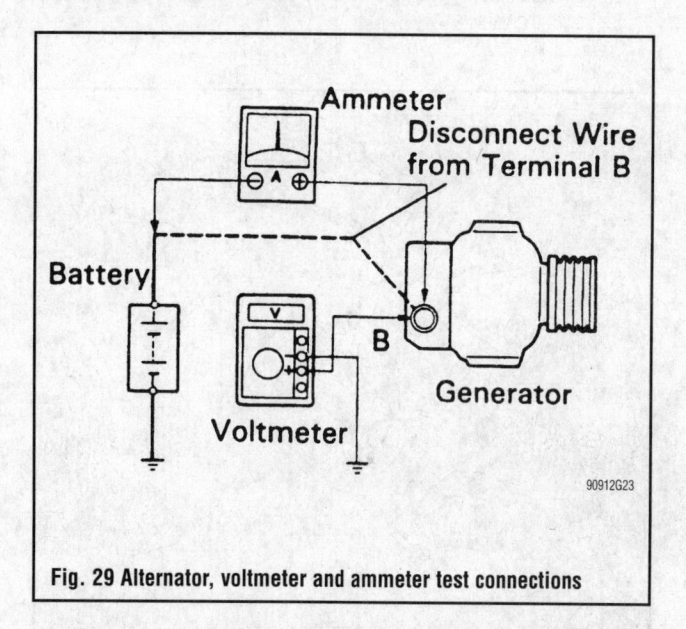

Fig. 29 Alternator, voltmeter and ammeter test connections

3. Check the following fuses for continuity: ENGINE, CHARGE, IGN fuses.
4. Visually check alternator wiring and listen for abnormal noises.
5. Check that the discharge warning light comes ON when the ignition switch is turned **ON**. Start the engine. Check that the warning light goes out.
6. Check the charging circuit WITHOUT A LOAD.
   a. Disconnect the wire from terminal B of the alternator and attach it to the negative lead of the ammeter.
   b. Connect the positive lead of the ammeter to terminal B of the alternator.
   c. Connect the positive lead of the voltmeter to terminal B of the alternator.
   d. Ground the negative lead of the voltmeter.
   e. To check the charging circuit, run the engine from idle to 2000 rpms and check the reading on the ammeter and voltmeter. Standard amperage is 10 amps or less. Standard voltage is as follows:
   - 77°F (25°C)—14.0–15.0 volts
   - 239°F (115°C)—13.5–14.3 volts

## 2-10 ENGINE ELECTRICAL

f. If the voltmeter reading is more than standard voltage, replace the voltage regulator. If the voltmeter reading is less than standard, check the alternator.
7. Check the charging circuit WITH A LOAD.
   a. With the engine running at 2000 rpm, turn on high beams and heater fan to HI.
   b. Check the standard amperage, it should be 30 amps or more. If the ammeter is less than standard, replace the alternator.
8. Replace the necessary parts. Recheck the charging system.

➡If a battery is fully charged, sometimes the indication will be less than 30 amps.

### REMOVAL & INSTALLATION

#### 2TZ-FE Engine

▶ See Figures 30 thru 36

1. Raise and safely support the vehicle.
2. Remove the No. 1 engine undercover.
3. Lower the vehicle.

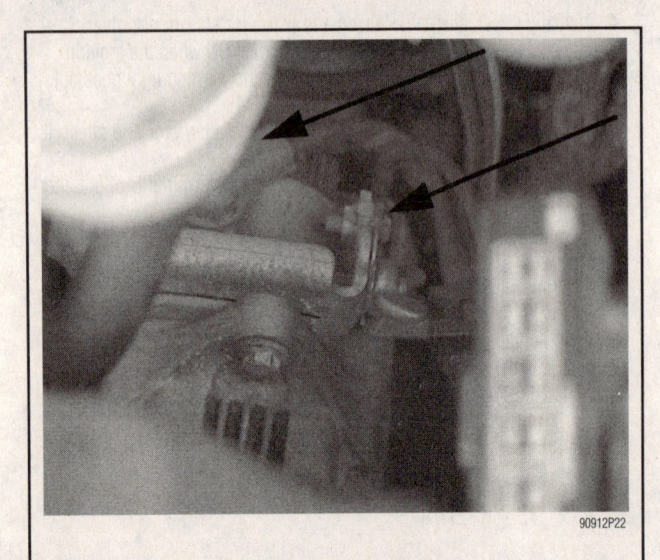

Fig. 30 Alternator mounting—2TZ-FE engine

Fig. 31 Some of the wiring is hard to access

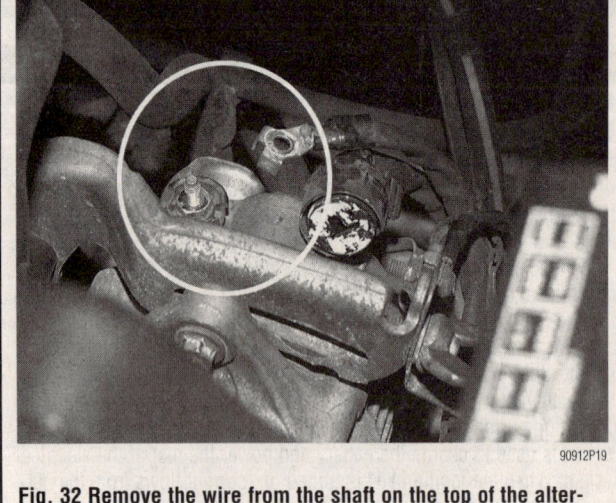

Fig. 32 Remove the wire from the shaft on the top of the alternator

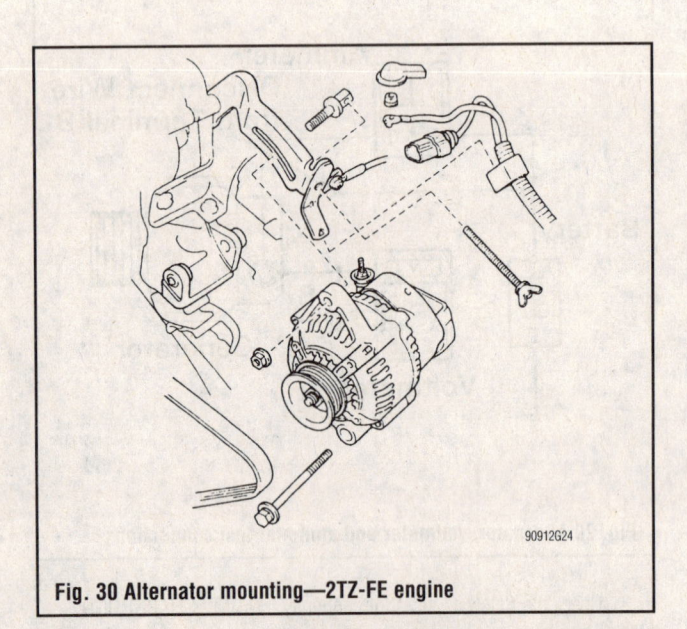

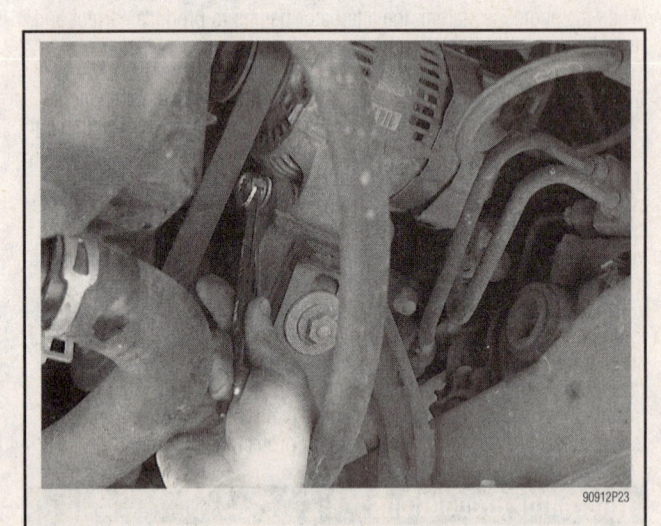

Fig. 33 Loosen the bolts on the alternator to remove the drive belt

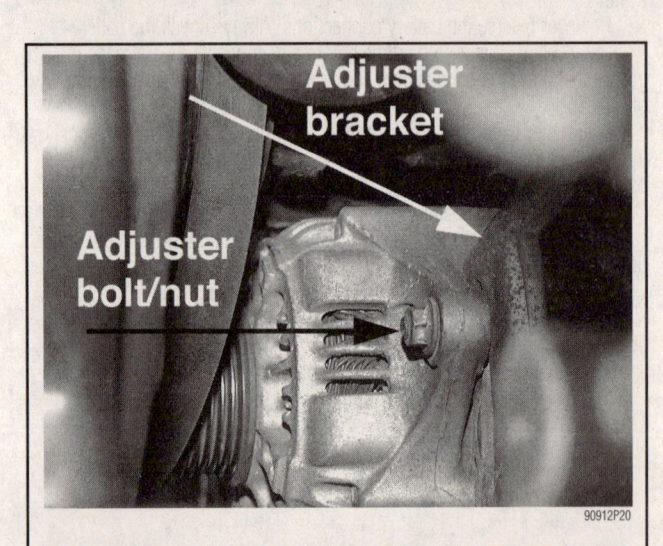

Fig. 34 The adjuster bracket and bolt are located on the side of the alternator

# ENGINE ELECTRICAL  2-11

Fig. 35 Pull the lock bolt from the lower portion of the alternator

Fig. 36 Extract the alternator from the bottom of the vehicle

4. Disconnect the alternator wire from the adjusting bar.
5. Detach the alternator connector.
6. Remove the nut, and disconnect the alternator wire.
7. Loosen the lock bolt, adjusting bolt and pivot bolt then remove the drive belt.
8. Remove the pivot bolt and lock bolt.
9. Hold the alternator and extract it from the vehicle.

**To install:**
Mount the alternator on the bracket with the pivot bolt and lock bolt. Do not tighten them yet.
10. Install and adjust the drive belt with the adjusting bolt. Tighten the lock bolt to 13 ft. lbs. (18 Nm) and the pivot bolt to 37 ft. lbs. (50 Nm).
11. Attach the alternator connector.
12. Connect the alternator wire with the nut.
13. Connect the alternator wore to the adjusting bar with the bolt.

14. Raise and support the vehicle and install the No. 1 engine undercover.
15. Perform the on vehicle testing inspection.

### 2TZ-FZE Engine

▶ See Figures 37, 38 and 39

1. Remove the air duct.
2. Remove the engine coolant reservoir.
3. Remove the battery. Be sure to disconnect the negative battery cable first.
4. Loosen the No. 1 idler pulley nut and adjusting bolt, then extract the drive belt.
5. Disconnect the alternator wires and connector from the unit and stay.
6. Remove the 3 bolts and extract the alternator. One bolt is strictly for the alternator, the other two retain the stay to the alternator.

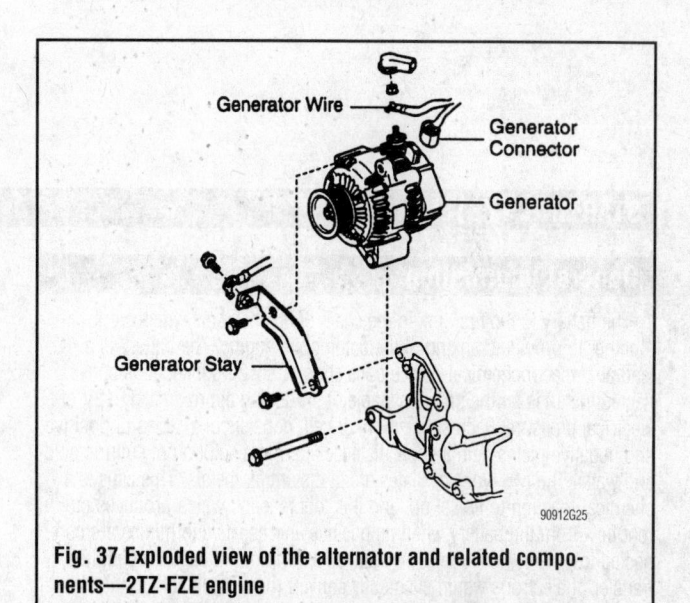

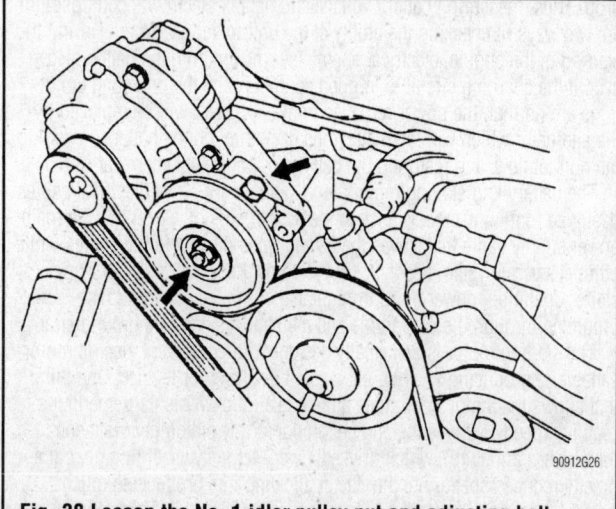

Fig. 37 Exploded view of the alternator and related components—2TZ-FZE engine

Fig. 38 Loosen the No. 1 idler pulley nut and adjusting bolt—2TZ-FZE engine

## 2-12 ENGINE ELECTRICAL

**To install:**
Position the alternator with the 3 bolts and tighten the alternator bolt to 37 ft. lbs. (50 Nm). Tighten the stay bolts to 20 ft. lbs. (26 Nm).

7. Attach the alternator wires and connector to the unit and stay.
8. Install and adjust the drive belt with the adjusting bolt and No. 1 idler pulley nut.
9. Install the battery.
10. Install the engine coolant reservoir and air duct.
11. Perform the on vehicle testing inspection.

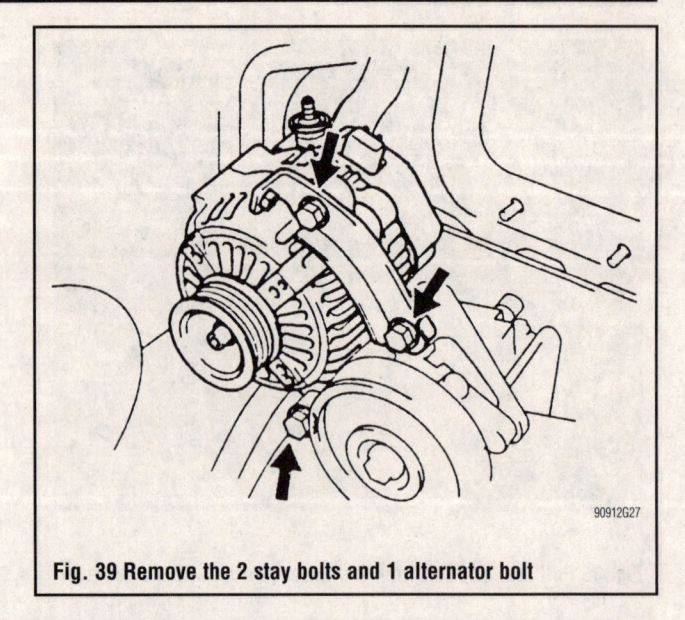

Fig. 39 Remove the 2 stay bolts and 1 alternator bolt

## STARTING SYSTEM

### General Information

The battery is the first link in the chain of mechanisms which work together to provide cranking of the automobile engine. The battery is a lead/acid electrochemical device consisting of six 2V subsections connected in series so the unit is capable of producing approximately 12V of electrical pressure. Each subsection, or cell, consists of a series of positive and negative plates held a short distance apart in a solution of sulfuric acid and water. The two types of plates are of dissimilar metals. This causes a chemical reaction to be set up, and it is this reaction which produces current flow from the battery when its positive and negative terminals are connected to an electrical appliance such as a lamp or motor. The continued transfer of electrons would eventually convert the sulfuric acid in the electrolyte to water, and make the two plates identical in chemical composition. As electrical energy is removed from the battery, its voltage output tends to drop. Thus, measuring battery voltage and battery electrolyte composition are two ways of checking the ability of the unit to supply power. During the starting of the engine, electrical energy is removed from the battery. However, if the charging circuit is in good condition and the operating conditions are normal, the power removed from the battery will be replaced by the alternator which will force electrons back through the battery, reversing the normal flow, and restoring the battery to its original chemical state.

The battery and starting motor are linked by very heavy electrical cables designed to minimize resistance to the flow of current. Generally, the major power supply cable that leaves the battery goes directly to the starter, while other electrical system needs are supplied by a smaller cable. During starter operation, power flows from the battery to the starter and is grounded through the car's frame and the battery's negative ground strap.

The starting motor is a specially designed, direct current electric motor capable of producing a very great amount of power for its size. One thing that allows the motor to produce a great deal of power is its tremendous rotating speed. It drives the engine through a tiny pinion gear (attached to the starter's armature), which drives the very large flywheel ring gear at a greatly reduced speed. Another factor allowing it to produce so much power is that only intermittent operation is required of it. This, little allowance for air circulation is required, and the windings can be built into a very small space.

A magnetic switch mounted on the starter housing, is supplied by current from the starting switch circuit of the ignition switch. This magnetic action of the switch mechanically engages the starter clutch assembly and electrically closes the heavy switch which connects it to the battery. The starting switch circuit consists of the starting switch contained within the ignition switch, a transmission neutral safety switch or clutch pedal switch, and the wiring necessary to connect these in series with the starter solenoid or relay.

A pinion, which is a small gear, is mounted to a one-way drive clutch. This clutch is splined to the starter armature shaft. When the ignition switch is moved to the **START** position, the solenoid plunger slides the pinion toward the flywheel ring gear via a collar and spring. If the teeth on the pinion and flywheel match properly, the pinion will engage the flywheel immediately. If the gear teeth butt one another, the spring will be compressed and will force the gears to mesh as soon as the starter turns far enough to allow them to do so. As the solenoid plunger reaches the end of its travel, it closes the contacts that connect the battery and starter and then the engine is cranked.

As soon as the engine starts, the flywheel gear begins turning fast enough to drive the pinion at an extremely high rate of speed. At this point, the one-way clutch begins allowing the pinion to spin faster than the starter shaft so that the starter will not operate at excessive speed. When the ignition switch is released from the starter position, the solenoid is de-energized, and a spring contained within the solenoid assembly pulls the gear out of mesh and interrupts the current flow to the starter.

The starter uses a separate relay, mounted on the left hand cowl, to switch the motor and magnetic switch current on and off. The relay is used to reduce the amount of current the starting switch must carry.

### Starter

TESTING

#### ✱✱ WARNING

**This tests must be performed within 3 to 5 seconds to avoid burning out the coil.**

**Pull-In**

▶ See Figure 40

Disconnect the field coil lead from the terminal C. Connect the battery to the solenoid switch as shown. See if the clutch pinion gear movement is outward. If the gear does not move perform the hold-in test.

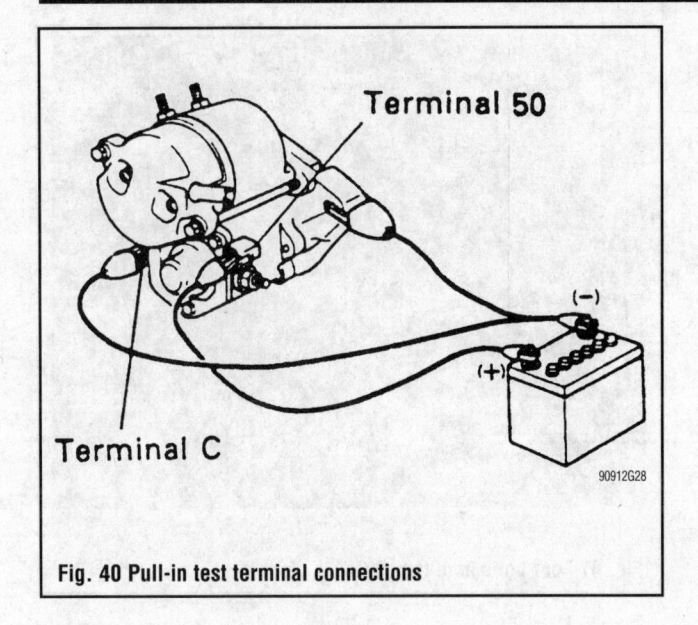

ENGINE ELECTRICAL    **2-13**

Fig. 40 Pull-in test terminal connections

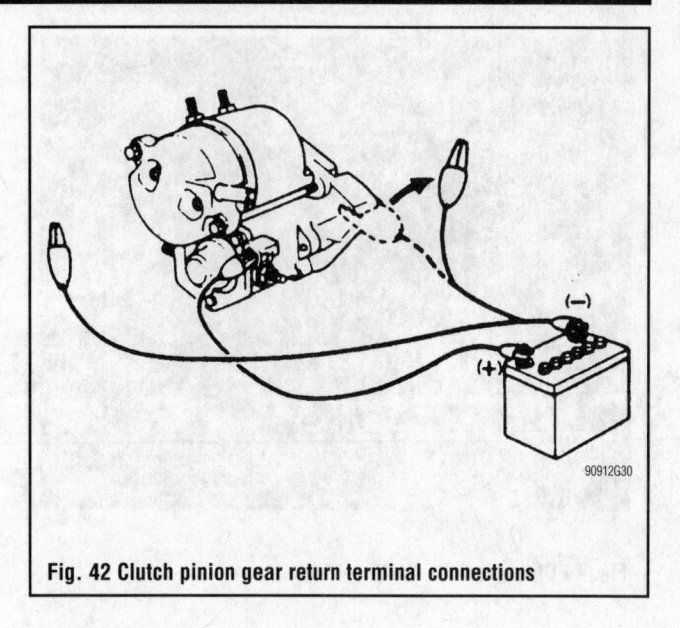

Fig. 42 Clutch pinion gear return terminal connections

### Hold-In

▶ See Figure 41

Attach the battery to the starter as shown and with the clutch pinion gear out, disconnect the negative lead from terminal C. Check to make sure the pinion gear stays in the outward position. If the clutch gear returns inward, perform the clutch pinion gear return test.

### No-Load

▶ See Figure 43

Attach a battery and ammeter to the starter. Check that the starter rotates smoothly and steadily with the pinion gear moving out. Check the ammeter shows the correct current. 90 amps or less at 11.5 volts on gasoline engines and 180 amps or less at 11.0 volts on diesel engines. If not replace the starter.

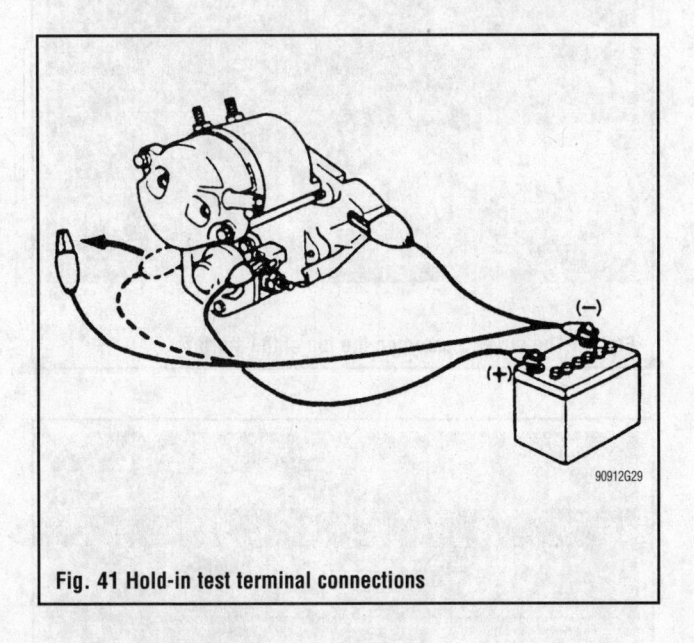

Fig. 41 Hold-in test terminal connections

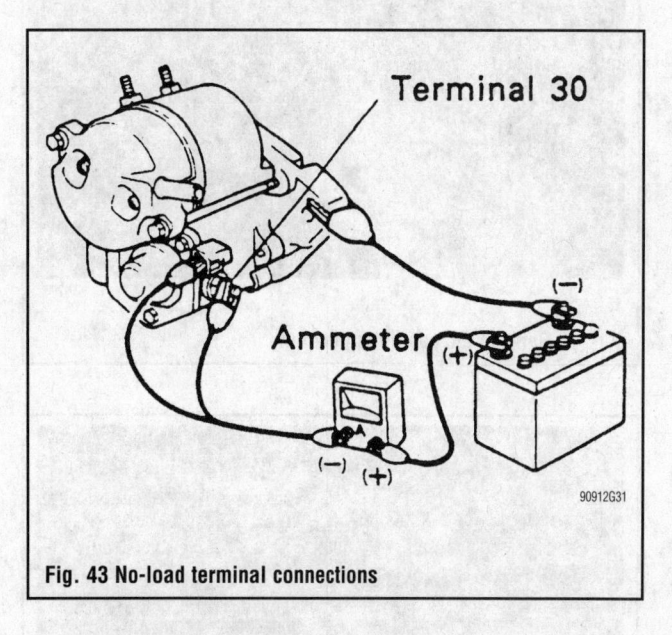

Fig. 43 No-load terminal connections

### Clutch Pinion Gear Return

▶ See Figure 42

Disconnect the negative lead from the solenoid body. Check the clutch pinion gear returns inward. If not perform the no-load test.

## REMOVAL & INSTALLATION

▶ See Figures 44 thru 51

1. Disconnect the negative battery cable from the battery.
2. Raise and safely support the vehicle.
3. If equipped with 4WD, remove the front driveshaft.

## 2-14 ENGINE ELECTRICAL

Fig. 44 Disengage the starter wiring

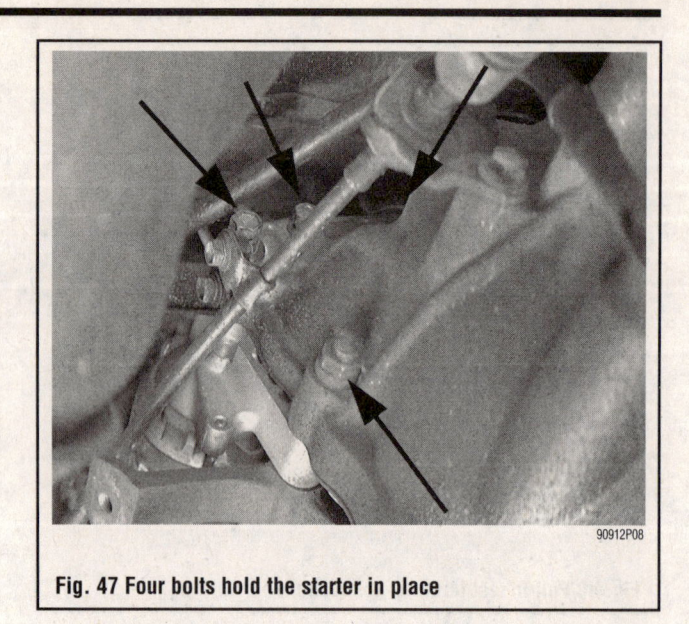

Fig. 45 Remove the cap hiding the nut

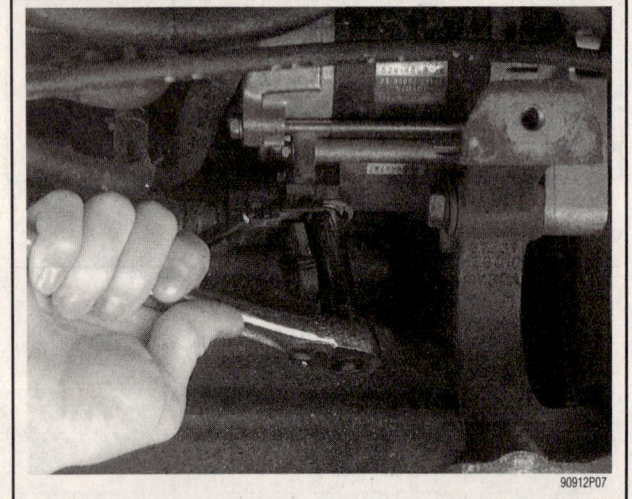

Fig. 46 It will be necessary to use an extension to remove the nut

Fig. 47 Four bolts hold the starter in place

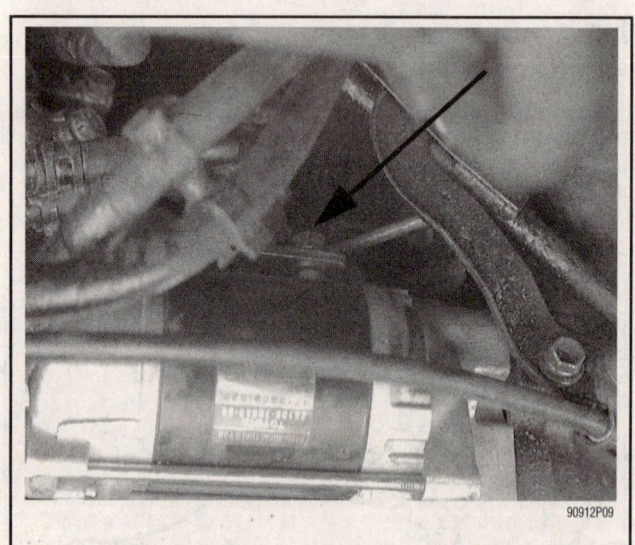

Fig. 48 The nut is located on the top of the starter

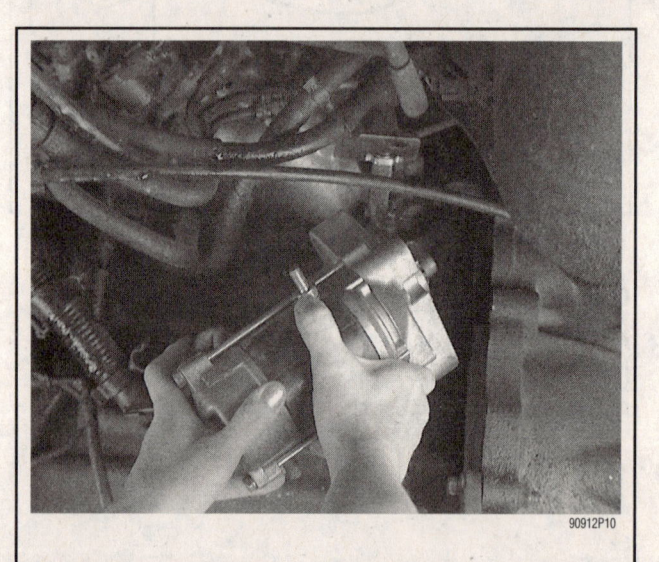

Fig. 49 Extract the starter from the engine

## ENGINE ELECTRICAL 2-15

Fig. 50 Bolt locations on the 2WD models

Fig. 51 Bolt locations on the 4WD models

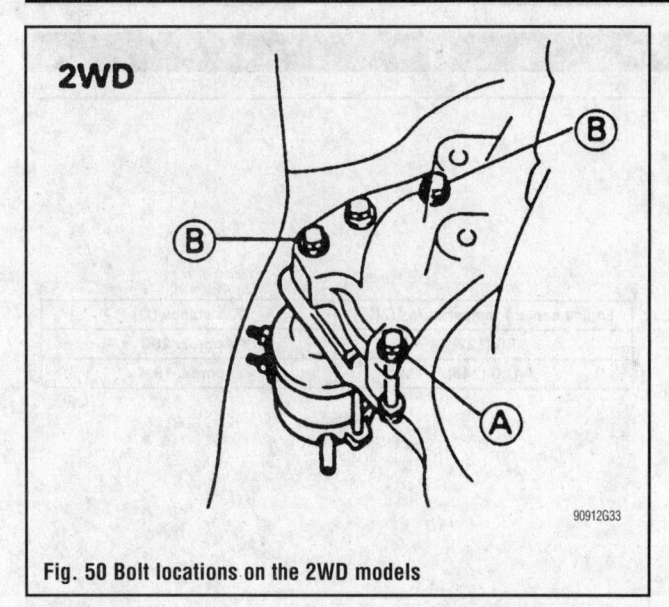

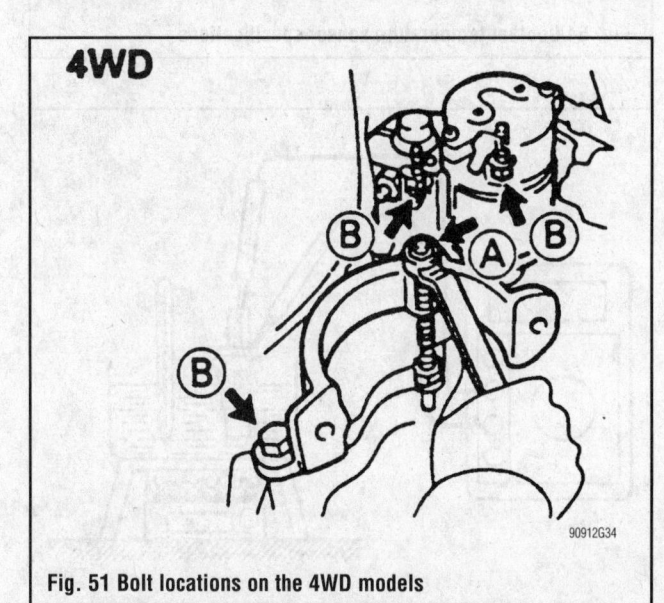

4. Remove the nut and disconnect the starter wire.
5. Disconnect the starter connector.
6. Remove the bolt holding the starter stay to the upper stiffener plate.
7. If equipped with 2WD, remove the starter by removing the nut and three bolts.
8. If equipped with 4WD, remove the starter by removing the nut, four bolts, and the center bracket.

**To install:**
9. If equipped with 4WD, install the starter, the center support bracket, nut, and the four bolts. Tighten the bolts as follows:
 • Bolt A to 41 ft. lbs. (56 Nm)
 • Bolt B to 30 ft. lbs. (41 Nm)
10. If equipped with 2WD, install the starter, nut and three bolts. Tighten the bolts as follows:
 • Bolt A to 41 ft. lbs. (56 Nm)
 • Bolt B to 30 ft. lbs. (41 Nm)
11. Install the bolt to hold the starter stay to the upper stiffener plate. Tighten the bolt to 43 inch lbs. (5 Nm).
12. Install the starter connector.
13. Connect the starter wire with the nut. Tighten the nut to 78 inch lbs. (9 Nm).
14. If equipped with 4WD, install the front driveshaft.
15. Connect the negative battery cable.

### SOLENOID REPLACEMENT

The starter solenoid (magnetic switch) is an integral part of the starter assembly.
1. Remove the starter from the van. Remove the heat insulator from the starter assembly, if equipped.
2. Disconnect the wire lead from the magnetic switch terminal.
3. Remove the two long, through bolts holding the field frame to the magnetic switch. Pull out the field frame with the armature from the magnetic switch.
4. To separate the starter housing from the magnetic switch assembly, remove the two screws and the starter housing with the pinion gear (1.6 kW), idler and clutch assembly.

**To install:**
5. If necessary, install the gears and clutch assembly to the starter housing. Apply grease to the gear and clutch assemblies and place the clutch assembly, idler gear, bearing and pinion gear (1.6 kW) in the starter housing.
6. Insert the spring into the clutch shaft hole and place the starter housing onto the magnetic switch. Install the two screws.
7. Install the field frame with the armature onto the magnetic switch assembly and install the two through bolts. Tighten the bolts on the 1.4 kW to 52 inch lbs. (6 Nm) and on the 1.6 kW to 82 inch lbs. (9 Nm).

➡ There is a protrusion or tab on each part; make sure you line them up correctly during assembly.

8. Connect the wire to the terminal on the magnetic switch and tighten the nut to 52 inch lbs. (6 Nm). Install the heat insulator, if equipped.
9. Reinstall the starter on the vehicle. Check starter system for proper operation.

### RELAY REPLACEMENT

▶ See Figure 52

The starter relay is located up under the dash on the driver side of the vehicle behind the cruise control actuator. Remove the actuator and extract the relay from the fuse block. Simply pull the relay out of the block.

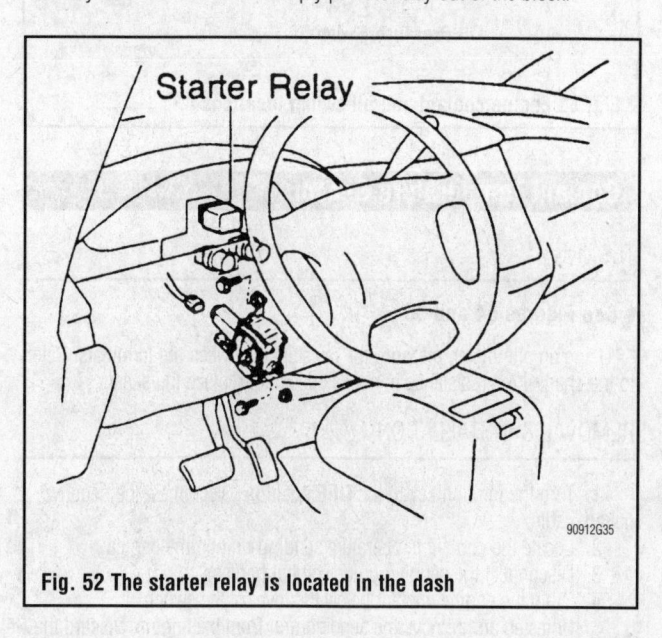

Fig. 52 The starter relay is located in the dash

## 2-16 ENGINE ELECTRICAL

### SENDING UNITS AND SENSORS

#### General Information

♦ See Figure 53

→This section describes the operating principles of sending units, warning lights and gauges. Sensors which provide information to the Electronic Control Module (ECM) are covered in Section 4 of this manual.

Instrument panels contain a number of indicating devices (gauges and warning lights). These devices are composed of two separate components. One is the sending unit, mounted on the engine or other remote part of the vehicle, and the other is the actual gauge or light in the instrument panel.

Several types of sending units exist, however most can be characterized as being either a pressure type or a resistance type. Pressure type sending units convert liquid pressure into an electrical signal which is sent to the gauge. Resistance type sending units are most often used to measure temperature and use variable resistance to control the current flow back to the indicating device. Both types of sending units are connected in series by a wire to the battery (through the ignition switch). When the ignition is turned **ON**, current flows from the battery through the indicating device and on to the sending unit.

| Engine coolant temperature °C (°F) | Resistance (Ω) |
|---|---|
| 50 (122) | Approx. 200 |
| 120 (248) | Approx. 19.4 |

Fig. 54 Coolant temperature sensor specifications

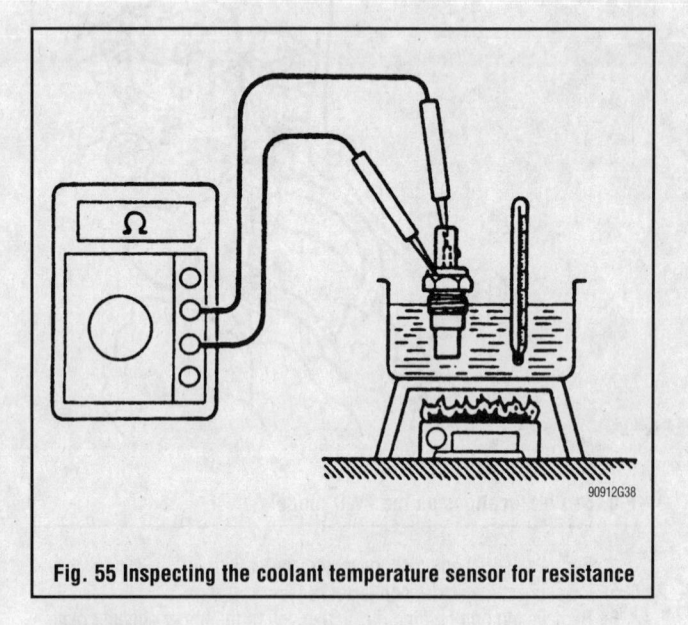

Fig. 53 Engine coolant and oil switch locations

Fig. 55 Inspecting the coolant temperature sensor for resistance

#### Coolant Temperature Sensor

TESTING

♦ See Figures 54 and 55

Using an ohmmeter, measure the resistance between the terminals. Refer to the chart, if the resistance is not as specified, replace the sensor.

REMOVAL & INSTALLATION

1. Turn the ignition key to the **OFF** position. Disconnect the negative battery cable.
2. Locate the coolant temperature sending unit on the engine.
3. Disconnect the sending unit electrical harness.
4. Drain the engine coolant below the level of the switch.
5. Unfasten and remove the sending unit from the engine. Discard the old gasket if equipped.

To install:
6. Coat the new sending unit with Teflon® tape or electrically conductive sealer. Place a new gasket on the sender.
7. Install the sending unit and tighten to 18 ft. lbs. (24 Nm).
8. Attach the sending unit's electrical connector.
9. Fill the engine with coolant.
10. Start the engine, allow it to reach operating temperature and check for leaks.
11. Check for proper sending unit operation.

#### Oil Pressure Sensor

TESTING

A quick way to determine if the gauge (idiot light) or sending unit is faulty is to disconnect the sending unit electrical harness and ground it (if two terminal, jumper between the terminals). If the gauge responds, the sending unit may be faulty. Proceed with the sending unit test.

# ENGINE ELECTRICAL 2-17

1. Disconnect the sending unit electrical harness.
2. Using an ohmmeter, check continuity of the sending unit terminals (sending unit terminal and ground).
3. With the engine stopped, continuity should exist.
4. With the engine running, continuity should not exist.
5. If continuity does not exist as stated, the sending unit is faulty.

## REMOVAL & INSTALLATION

1. Turn the ignition key to the **OFF** position. Disconnect the negative battery cable.
2. Locate the oil pressure sending unit on the engine.
3. Disconnect the sending unit electrical harness.
4. Unfasten and remove the sending unit from the engine.

**To install:**

5. Coat the new sending unit with Teflon® tape or electrically conductive sealer.
6. Install the sending unit and tighten to 11 ft. lbs. (15 Nm).
7. Attach the sending unit's electrical connector.
8. Start the engine, allow it to reach operating temperature and check for leaks.
9. Check for proper sending unit operation.

## Troubleshooting Basic Starting System Problems

| Problem | Cause | Solution |
|---|---|---|
| Starter motor rotates engine slowly | • Battery charge low or battery defective<br>• Defective circuit between battery and starter motor<br>• Low load current<br><br>• High load current | • Charge or replace battery<br>• Clean and tighten, or replace cables<br>• Bench-test starter motor. Inspect for worn brushes and weak brush springs.<br>• Bench-test starter motor. Check engine for friction, drag or coolant in cylinders. Check ring gear-to-pinion gear clearance. |
| Starter motor will not rotate engine | • Battery charge low or battery defective<br>• Faulty solenoid<br><br>• Damaged drive pinion gear or ring gear<br>• Starter motor engagement weak<br>• Starter motor rotates slowly with high load current<br><br>• Engine seized | • Charge or replace battery<br><br>• Check solenoid ground. Repair or replace as necessary.<br>• Replace damaged gear(s)<br><br>• Bench-test starter motor<br>• Inspect drive yoke pull-down and point gap, check for worn end bushings, check ring gear clearance<br>• Repair engine |
| Starter motor drive will not engage (solenoid known to be good) | • Defective contact point assembly<br>• Inadequate contact point assembly ground<br>• Defective hold-in coil | • Repair or replace contact point assembly<br>• Repair connection at ground screw<br>• Replace field winding assembly |
| Starter motor drive will not disengage | • Starter motor loose on flywheel housing<br>• Worn drive end busing<br>• Damaged ring gear teeth<br>• Drive yoke return spring broken or missing | • Tighten mounting bolts<br><br>• Replace bushing<br>• Replace ring gear or driveplate<br>• Replace spring |
| Starter motor drive disengages prematurely | • Weak drive assembly thrust spring<br>• Hold-in coil defective | • Replace drive mechanism<br>• Replace field winding assembly |
| Low load current | • Worn brushes<br>• Weak brush springs | • Replace brushes<br>• Replace springs |

TCCS2C01

## Troubleshooting Basic Charging System Problems

| Problem | Cause | Solution |
| --- | --- | --- |
| Noisy alternator | • Loose mountings<br>• Loose drive pulley<br>• Worn bearings<br>• Brush noise<br>• Internal circuits shorted (High pitched whine) | • Tighten mounting bolts<br>• Tighten pulley<br>• Replace alternator<br>• Replace alternator<br>• Replace alternator |
| Squeal when starting engine or accelerating | • Glazed or loose belt | • Replace or adjust belt |
| Indicator light remains on or ammeter indicates discharge (engine running) | • Broken belt<br>• Broken or disconnected wires<br>• Internal alternator problems<br>• Defective voltage regulator | • Install belt<br>• Repair or connect wiring<br>• Replace alternator<br>• Replace voltage regulator/alternator |
| Car light bulbs continually burn out—battery needs water continually | • Alternator/regulator overcharging | • Replace voltage regulator/alternator |
| Car lights flare on acceleration | • Battery low<br>• Internal alternator/regulator problems | • Charge or replace battery<br>• Replace alternator/regulator |
| Low voltage output (alternator light flickers continually or ammeter needle wanders) | • Loose or worn belt<br>• Dirty or corroded connections<br>• Internal alternator/regulator problems | • Replace or adjust belt<br>• Clean or replace connections<br>• Replace alternator/regulator |

TCCS2C02

**ENGINE MECHANICAL 3-2**
ENGINE 3-6
   REMOVAL & INSTALLATION 3-6
ROCKER ARM (VALVE) COVER 3-7
   REMOVAL & INSTALLATION 3-7
THERMOSTAT 3-8
   REMOVAL & INSTALLATION 3-8
INTAKE MANIFOLD 3-10
   REMOVAL & INSTALLATION 3-10
EXHAUST MANIFOLD 3-10
   REMOVAL & INSTALLATION 3-10
SUPERCHARGER 3-11
   REMOVAL & INSTALLATION 3-11
SUPERCHARGER BY-PASS (SCB)
  VALVE 3-13
   REMOVAL & INSTALLATION 3-13
CHARGE AIR COOLER (CAC) 3-14
   REMOVAL & INSTALLATION 3-14
RADIATOR 3-14
   REMOVAL & INSTALLATION 3-14
ENGINE FAN 3-17
   REMOVAL & INSTALLATION 3-17
WATER PUMP 3-17
   REMOVAL & INSTALLATION 3-17
EQUIPMENT DRIVESHAFT 3-19
   PRECAUTIONS 3-19
   REMOVAL & INSTALLATION 3-20
EQUIPMENT DRIVE HOUSING 3-25
   REMOVAL & INSTALLATION 3-25
CYLINDER HEAD 3-26
   REMOVAL & INSTALLATION 3-26
OIL PAN 3-31
   REMOVAL & INSTALLATION 3-31
OIL PUMP 3-32
   REMOVAL & INSTALLATION 3-32
TIMING CHAIN COVER AND SEAL 3-33
   REMOVAL & INSTALLATION 3-33
   SEAL REPLACEMENT 3-34
TIMING CHAIN AND GEARS 3-34
   REMOVAL & INSTALLATION 3-34
CAMSHAFT, BEARINGS AND
  LIFTERS 3-38
   REMOVAL & INSTALLATION 3-38
   INSPECTION 3-45
REAR MAIN SEAL 3-48
   REMOVAL & INSTALLATION 3-48
FLYWHEEL/FLEXPLATE 3-49
   REMOVAL & INSTALLATION 3-49
**EXHAUST SYSTEM 3-49**
INSPECTION 3-49
   REPLACEMENT 3-51
**ENGINE RECONDITIONING 3-52**
DETERMINING ENGINE CONDITION 3-52
   COMPRESSION TEST 3-53
   OIL PRESSURE TEST 3-53
BUY OR REBUILD? 3-53
ENGINE OVERHAUL TIPS 3-54
   TOOLS 3-54
   OVERHAUL TIPS 3-54
   CLEANING 3-54
   REPAIRING DAMAGED
     THREADS 3-55
ENGINE PREPARATION 3-56
CYLINDER HEAD 3-57
   DISASSEMBLY 3-57
   INSPECTION 3-60
   REFINISHING & REPAIRING 3-62
   ASSEMBLY 3-63
ENGINE BLOCK 3-64
   GENERAL INFORMATION 3-64
   DISASSEMBLY 3-64
   INSPECTION 3-65
   REFINISHING 3-67
   ASSEMBLY 3-68
ENGINE START-UP AND BREAK-IN 3-71
   STARTING THE ENGINE 3-71
   BREAKING IT IN 3-71
   KEEP IT MAINTAINED 3-71
**SPECIFICATIONS CHARTS**
  ENGINE MECHANICAL
    SPECIFICATIONS 3-2
  TORQUE SPECIFICATIONS 3-72

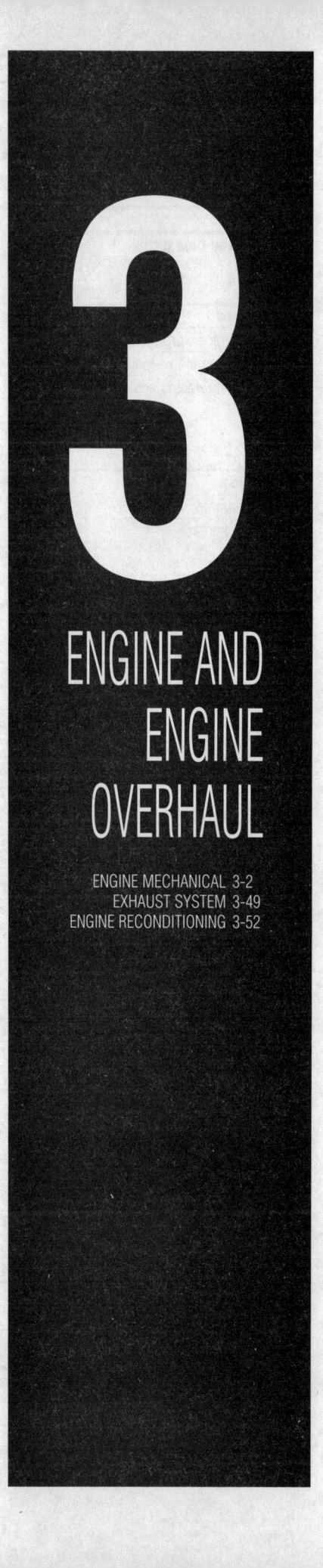

# 3

# ENGINE AND ENGINE OVERHAUL

ENGINE MECHANICAL 3-2
EXHAUST SYSTEM 3-49
ENGINE RECONDITIONING 3-52

# 3-2 ENGINE AND ENGINE OVERHAUL

## ENGINE MECHANICAL

### ENGINE MECHANICAL SPECIFICATIONS

| Description | | | English Specifications | Metric Specifications |
|---|---|---|---|---|
| **Compression pressure** | | | | |
| | STD | | 178 psi | 1226 kPa |
| | Limit | | 128 psi | 883 kPa |
| **Cylinder head** | | | | |
| Head surface warpage | | | 0.0059 inch | 0.15mm |
| Manifold surface warpage | | | 0.0079 inch | 0.20mm |
| Valve seat refacing angle | | | | |
| | intake | 1991-93 | 30, 45, 60 degrees | 30, 45, 60 degrees |
| | exhaust | 1991-93 | 15, 45, 60 degrees | 15, 45, 60 degrees |
| | | 1994-97 | 30, 45, 75 degrees | 30, 45, 75 degrees |
| **Valve guide** | | | | |
| Inner diameter | | | 0.2366-0.2374 inch | 6.01-6.03mm |
| Outer diameter | | | | |
| | STD | 1991-93 | 0.4344-0.4348 inch | 11.033-11.044mm |
| | O/S 0.5 | 1991-93 | 0.4363-0.4368 inch | 11.083-11.094mm |
| | STD | 1994-97 | 0.4331-0.4341 inch | 11.000-11.027mm |
| | O/S 0.5 | 1994-97 | 0.4350-0.4361 inch | 11.050-11.077mm |
| Replacing temperature cylinder head side | | | 194 F | 90 C |
| **Valve** | | | | |
| Overall length | | | | |
| STD | intake | 1991-93 | 4.0728 inch | 103.45mm |
| | | 1994-97 | 4.0728 inch | 103.45mm |
| | exhaust | 1991-93 | 4.0787 inch | 103.60mm |
| | | 1994-97 | 4.0905 inch | 103.90mm |
| limit | exhaust | 1991-93 | 4.0590 inch | 103.10mm |
| | | 1994-97 | 4.0709 inch | 103.40mm |
| | intake | 1991-93 | 4.0531 inch | 102.95mm |
| | | 1994-97 | 4.0531 inch | 102.95mm |
| Face angle | | | 44.5 degrees | 44.5 degrees |
| Stem diameter | intake | | 0.2350-0.2356 inch | 5.970-5.985mm |
| | exhaust | | 0.2348-0.2354 inch | 5.965-5.980mm |
| Stem oil clearance | | | | |
| STD | intake | 1991-97 | 0.0010-0.0024 inch | 0.025-0.060mm |
| | exhaust | 1991-97 | 0.0012-0.0026 inch | 0.030-0.065mm |
| limit | intake | 1994-97 | 0.0031 inch | 0.08mm |
| | exhaust | 1994-97 | 0.0039 inch | 0.10mm |
| Margin thickness | | | 0.020 inch | 0.50mm |
| **Valve Spring** | | | | |
| Free length | | | 1.6425 inch | 41.72mm |
| Installed tension | | | | |
| STD | | 1991-93 | 63.1 lbf | 280 N |
| | | 1994-97 | 42.8 lbf | 190 N |
| minimum | | 1991-93 | 56.8 lbf | 252 N |
| | | 1994-94 | 38.7 lbf | 172 N |
| **Camshaft** | | | | |
| Thrust clearance | | | | |
| | STD | | 0.0016-0.0037 inch | 0.40-0.095mm |
| | limit | | 0.0047 inch | 0.12mm |
| Journal oil clearance | | | | |
| | STD | | 0.0010-0.0024 inch | 0.025-0.062mm |
| | limit | | 0.0031 inch | 0.08mm |

# ENGINE AND ENGINE OVERHAUL 3-3

## ENGINE MECHANICAL SPECIFICATIONS

| Description | | | English Specifications | Metric Specifications |
|---|---|---|---|---|
| **Camshaft continued:** | | | | |
| Journal diameter | | | 1.0614-1.0620 inch | 26.959-26.975mm |
| Circle runout | | | 0.0024 inch | 0.06mm |
| Cam lobe height | | | | |
|     intake | | | 1.7839-1.787 inch | 45.31-45.41mm |
|     exhaust | | | 1.7740-1.7779 inch | 45.06-45.16mm |
| Camshaft gear backlash | | | | |
|     STD | | | 0.0008-0.0079 inch | 0.020-0.200mm |
|     limit | | | 0.0188 inch | 0.30mm |
| Camshaft gear spring end free distance | | | 0.886-0.902 inch | 22.5-22.9mm |
| **Valve lifter** | | | | |
| Lifter diameter | | | 1.2191-1.2195 inch | 30.966-30.976mm |
| Lifter bore diameter | | | 1.2205-1.2211 inch | 31.000-31.016mm |
| Oil clearance | | | | |
|     STD | | | 0.0009-0.0020 inch | 0.24-0.50mm |
|     limit | | | 0.0028 inch | 0.07mm |
| **Exhaust and intake manifolds** | | | | |
| Surface limit | | | 0.016 inch | 0.4mm |
| **Chain and sprocket** | | | | |
| Elongation | | | | |
|     limit | No. 1 chain 16 links | | 5.772 inch | 146.0mm |
| | No. 2 chain 18 links | | 5.531 inch | 140.5mm |
| Crankshaft sprocket wear | | | | |
|     limit | No. 1 chain 16 links | | 2.339 inch | 59.4mm |
| | No. 2 chain 18 links | | 2.752 inch | 69.9mm |
| Camshaft sprocket wear | | | 4.480 inch | 113.8mm |
| Idle gear sprocket wear | | | 2.244 inch | 57.0mm |
| **Chain damper and slipper** | | | 0.039 inch | 1.0mm |
| **Cylinder block** | | | | |
| Head surface warpage | | | 0.0020 inch | 0.05mm |
| Cylinder bore | | | | |
| | | 1991-93 | 3.7398-3.7402 inch | 94.99-95.00mm |
| | | 1994-97 | 3.7398-3.7403 inch | 94.990-95.003mm |
| Bore wear | | | | |
|     STD | | | 3.745 inch | 95.06mm |
|     OS 0.50 | | | 3.7622 inch | 95.56mm |
| Taper | | | 0.0004 inch | 0.01mm |
| Out-of-round | | | 0.0008 inch | 0.02mm |
| Block main journal bore | | | | |
|     STD | No. 1 | 1991-93 | 2.5198-2.5201 inch | 64.004-64.010mm |
| | No. 2 | 1991-93 | 2.5201-2.5203 inch | 64.011-64.016mm |
| | No. 3 | 1991-93 | 2.5203-2.5205 inch | 64.017-64.022mm |
|     U/S | 0.25 | 1991-93 | 2.5197-2.5206 inch | 64.000-64.024mm |
| Main bearing bolt outside diameter | | | | |
|     STD | | 1994-97 | 0.4236-0.4319 inch | 10.76-10.97mm |
|     maximum | | 1994-97 | 0.4094 inch | 10.40mm |
| **Piston and Rings** | | | | |
| Piston diameter | | | | |
|     STD | | | 3.7382-3.7386 inch | 94.95-94.96mm |
|     O/S 0.50 | | | 3.7579-3.7583 inch | 95.45-95.46mm |
| Piston-to-cylinder clearance | | | 0.0012-0.0020 inch | 0.03-0.05mm |

## 3-4 ENGINE AND ENGINE OVERHAUL

### ENGINE MECHANICAL SPECIFICATIONS

| Description | | | English Specifications | Metric Specifications |
|---|---|---|---|---|
| **Piston and Rings continued:** | | | | |
| Piston ring end gap | | | | |
| STD | No. 1 | | 0.0118-0.0169 inch | 0.30-0.43mm |
| | No. 2 | | 0.0177-0.0236 inch | 0.45-0.60mm |
| | oil | | 0.0051-0.0150 inch | 0.13-0.38mm |
| limit | No. 1 | | 0.0406 inch | 1.03mm |
| | No. 2 | | 0.0472 inch | 1.20mm |
| | oil | | 0.0386 inch | 0.98mm |
| Ring-to-ring groove clearance (new rings) | | | | |
| STD | No. 1 | | 0.0008-0.0028 inch | 0.02-0.07mm |
| | No. 2 | | 0.0012-0.0028 inch | 0.03-0.07mm |
| limit | | | 0.008 inch | 0.02mm |
| **Connecting Rod and Bearing** | | | | |
| Thrust clearance | | | | |
| STD | | | 0.0063-0.0123 inch | 0.160-0.312mm |
| maximum | | | 0.0138 inch | 0.35mm |
| Big end inner diameter | | | | |
| STD | No. 1 | | 2.2047-2.2050 inch | 56.000-56.008mm |
| | No. 2 | | 2.2051-2.2053 inch | 56.009-56.016mm |
| | No. 3 | | 2.2054-2.2057 inch | 56.017-56.024mm |
| Big end inner diameter - continued | | | | |
| U/S | 0.25 | | 2.2047-2.2057 inch | 56.000-56.024mm |
| Rod bearing center wall thickness | | | | |
| STD | No. 1 | | 0.0583-0.0585 inch | 1.482-1.485mm |
| | No. 2 | | 0.0585-0.0586 inch | 1.485-1.488mm |
| | No. 3 | 1991-93 | 0.0587-0.0588 inch | 1.490-1.493mm |
| | No. 3 | 1994-97 | 0.0586-0.0587 inch | 1.488-1.491mm |
| U/S | 0.25 | | 0.0630-0.0633 inch | 1.601-1.607mm |
| Bearing oil clearance | | | | |
| STD | | 1991-93 | 0.0012-0.0023 inch | 0.030-0.059mm |
| limit | | 1991-93 | 0.004 inch | 0.1mm |
| Rod oil clearance | | | | |
| STD | STD | 1994-97 | 0.0012-0.0022 inch | 0.030-0.055mm |
| | U/S 0.25 | 1994-97 | 0.0012-0.0028 inch | 0.031-0.071mm |
| maximum | | 1994-97 | 0.0039 inch | 0.10mm |
| Pin-to-busing oil clearance | | | | |
| STD | | | 0.0002-0.0004 inch | 0.005-0.011mm |
| limit | | | 0.0006 inch | 0.015mm |
| Piston pin diameter | | | 0.9449-0.9452 inch | 24.000-24.009mm |
| Bushing inside diameter | | | 0.9452-0.9455 inch | 24.008-24.017mm |
| **Crankshaft** | | | | |
| Thrust clearance | | | | |
| STD | | | 0.0008-0.0087 inch | 0.020-0.220mm |
| maximum | | | 0.0012 inch | 0.3mm |
| Thrust washer thickness | | | 0.0961-0.0980 inch | 2.440-2.490mm |

90913C03

# ENGINE AND ENGINE OVERHAUL 3-5

## ENGINE MECHANICAL SPECIFICATIONS

| Description | | | English Specifications | Metric Specifications |
|---|---|---|---|---|
| **Crankshaft continued:** | | | | |
| Main journal oil clearance | | | | |
| STD | STD | 1991-93 | 0.0009-0.0019 inch | 0.024-0.049mm |
| No. 1, 2, 4, 5 | STD | 1994-97 | 0.0009-0.0019 inch | 0.024-0.049mm |
| No. 3 | STD | 1994-97 | 0.0012-0.0022 inch | 0.030-0.055mm |
| STD | U/S 0.25 | 1994-97 | 0.0010-0.0026 inch | 0.025-0.065mm |
| Main journal oil clearance continued: | | | | |
| STD | U/S 0.25 | 1994-97 | 0.0012-0.0028 inch | 0.030-0.070mm |
| limit | | 1991-97 | 0.004 inch | 0.1mm |
| Main journal diameter | | | | |
| STD | STD | 1991-93 | 2.3617-2.3622 inch | 59.987-60.000mm |
| No. 1, 2, 4, 5 | STD | 1994-97 | 2.3617-2.3622 inch | 59.987-60.000mm |
| No. 3 | STD | 1994-97 | 2.3615-2.3620 inch | 59.981-59.994mm |
| STD | U/S 0.25 | 1991-93 | 2.3522-2.3526 inch | 59.745-59.755mm |
| No. 1, 2, 4, 5 | U/S 0.25 | 1994-97 | 2.3522-2.3526 inch | 59.745-59.755mm |
| No. 3 | U/S 0.25 | 1994-97 | 2.3520-2.3524 inch | 59.740-59.750mm |
| Main journal wall thickness | | | | |
| Mark 1 | STD | | 0.0782-0.0783 inch | 1.987-1.990mm |
| Mark 2 | STD | | 0.0784-0.0785 inch | 1.991-1.993mm |
| Mark 3 | STD | | 0.0785-0.0786 inch | 1.994-1.996mm |
| | U/S 0.25 | | 0.0829-0.0831 inch | 2.106-2.112mm |
| Crank pin diameter | | | | |
| STD | | | 2.0861-2.0866 inch | 52.987-53.000mm |
| U/S 0.25 | | | 2.0766-2.0770 inch | 52.745-52.755mm |
| Circle run-out | | | 0.0012 inch | 0.03mm |

# 3-6 ENGINE AND ENGINE OVERHAUL

## Engine

### REMOVAL & INSTALLATION

In the process of removing the engine, you will come across a number of steps which call for the removal of a separate component or system, such as "disconnect the exhaust system" or "remove the radiator." In most instances, a detailed removal procedure can be found elsewhere in this manual.

It is virtually impossible to list each individual wire and hose which must be disconnected, simply because so many different model and engine combinations have been manufactured. Careful observation and common sense are the best possible approaches to any repair procedure.

Removal and installation of the engine can be made easier if you follow these basic points:

- If you have to drain any of the fluids, use a suitable container.
- Always tag any wires or hoses and, if possible, the components they came from before disconnecting them.
- Because there are so many bolts and fasteners involved, store and label the retainers from components separately in muffin pans, jars or coffee cans. This will prevent confusion during installation.
- After unbolting the transmission, always make sure it is properly supported.
- If it is necessary to disconnect the air conditioning system, have this service performed by a qualified technician using a recovery/recycling station. If the system does not have to be disconnected, unbolt the compressor and set it aside.
- When unbolting the engine mounts, always make sure the engine is properly supported. When removing the engine, make sure that any lifting devices are properly attached to the engine. It is recommended that if your engine is supplied with lifting hooks, your lifting apparatus be attached to them.
- Lift the engine from its compartment slowly, checking that no hoses, wires or other components are still connected.
- After the engine is clear of the compartment, place it on an engine stand or workbench.
- After the engine has been removed, you can perform a partial or full teardown of the engine using the procedures outlined in this manual.

**※※ CAUTION**

**Fuel injection systems remain under pressure after the engine has been turned OFF. Properly relieve fuel pressure before disconnecting any fuel lines. Failure to do so may result in fire or personal injury.**

1. Disconnect the negative battery cable. Wait at least 90 seconds to proceed working on the vehicle if equipped with an airbag.

**※※ CAUTION**

**Some models covered by this manual may be equipped with a Supplemental Restraint System (SRS), which uses an air bag. Whenever working near any of the SRS components, such as the impact sensors, the air bag module, steering column and instrument panel, disable the SRS, as described in Section 6.**

2. Drain the engine coolant and oil.
3. Relieve the fuel system pressure.
4. Raise the vehicle and support safely. Remove the engine under covers.
5. Drain the engine oil and cooling system.
6. On 4WD vehicles, disconnect the front driveshaft.
7. Remove the rear driveshaft.
8. Remove the air duct.
9. Matchmark and disconnect the equipment (separated accessory drive system) driveshaft from the crankshaft pulley.
10. Disconnect the A/T shift cable.
11. Remove the air intake duct.
12. Disconnect the ground strap from the left hand front engine mounting.
13. Disconnect the starter wire.
14. Disconnect the following hoses:
    - No. 4 radiator hose from the water inlet
    - No. 1 radiator hose from the water inlet
    - Heater hose from the water pump
    - Oil auto feeder hose from the No. 1 oil return pipe
    - Disconnect the A/C idle up air hose from the union under the intake manifold
    - Disconnect the power steering idle up air hose from the union under the intake manifold
    - Disconnect the water bypass hose from the floor pipe
    - Disconnect the brake booster hose from the floor pipe
    - Disconnect the two vacuum hoses for the fuel pressure control Vacuum Switching Valve (VSV) from the engine wire and vacuum transmitting pipe on the throttle body
    - Air hose for the distributor ventilation from the water bypass pipe under the intake manifold
    - Disconnect the vacuum hose for the EVAP from the charcoal canister
15. If equipped with automatic transmission, disconnect the shift cable.
16. Remove the intake pipe hose.
17. Disconnect the accelerator cable from the throttle body.
18. Disengage the Vacuum Switching Valve (VSV) connector for the fuel pressure control.
19. Disconnect the engine wire from the engine left side as follows:
    a. Disengage the igniter connector.
    b. Disconnect the two Electronic Control Module (ECM) harnesses.
    c. Disconnect the four harnesses from the cowl wire on the front floor panel.
    d. Separate the engine wire from the front floor panel by removing the bolt and detaching the three clamps.
    e. Pull out the engine wire from the front floor panel hose.
20. Remove the A/T oil dipstick.
21. Disconnect the fuel inlet and return hoses.
22. Remove the front exhaust pipe.
23. Remove the exhaust pipe heat insulator and ground strap by removing the four bolts.
24. Disconnect the two A/T oil cooler hoses.
25. Remove the ignition coil and disconnect the ground strap for the engine.
26. Disconnect the condenser wiring.
27. Disconnect the four clamps and engine wire.
28. Disconnect the A/T and park/neutral position switch wiring.
29. Remove the engine with the transmission as follows:
    a. Support the engine and transmission with a supporting device.
    b. Lower the vehicle while supporting the engine and transmission with the engine lifter.
    c. Remove the two bolts, two nuts and two plate washers holding the right and left engine mountings to the engine front support member.
    d. Remove the four through bolts, four plate washers and four nuts holding the rear mounting to the No. 2 rear engine mounting bracket.
    e. Make sure the engine and transmission are clear of all wiring, hoses and cables.
    f. Lower the engine and transmission to the floor.
30. Install the engine in the reverse order of removal while paying close attention to the following.
31. Raise the engine and install the two bolts, two plate washers and two nuts to hold the right and left engine front mountings to the engine front support member. Tighten the bolts and nuts to 27 ft. lbs. (37 Nm).
32. Install the two through bolts, four washers and four nuts to hold the engine rear mounting to the No. 2 rear engine mounting bracket. Tighten the bolts and nuts to 31 ft. lbs. (42 Nm).
33. Install the rear driveshaft. If equipped with 4WD, install the front driveshaft. Install a new oil filter and fill the engine with oil. Fill the engine with engine coolant. Install the engine undercovers. Start the engine and check for leaks.

# ENGINE AND ENGINE OVERHAUL    3-7

## Rocker Arm (Valve) Cover

### REMOVAL & INSTALLATION

▶ See Figures 1 thru 9

1. Remove the right side engine service hole cover.
   a. Remove the three screws and the scuff plate.
   b. Unbolt and disconnect the right seat belt from the front floor panel.
   c. Remove the four bolts holding the right front seat.
   d. Remove the two bolts and the right front seat leg.
   e. Remove the jack, the jack stand and the tool bag.
   f. Remove the engine service hole cover.
2. Remove the No. 2 cylinder head cover with the gasket.
3. Remove the PCV hose and disconnect the four spark plug wires from the spark plugs.
4. Remove the No. 2 cord clamp support plate.
5. Remove the No. 1 cylinder head cover and the gasket.

**To install:**

6. Clean the valve cover and mating surfaces of any gasket or packing materials with a scraper.

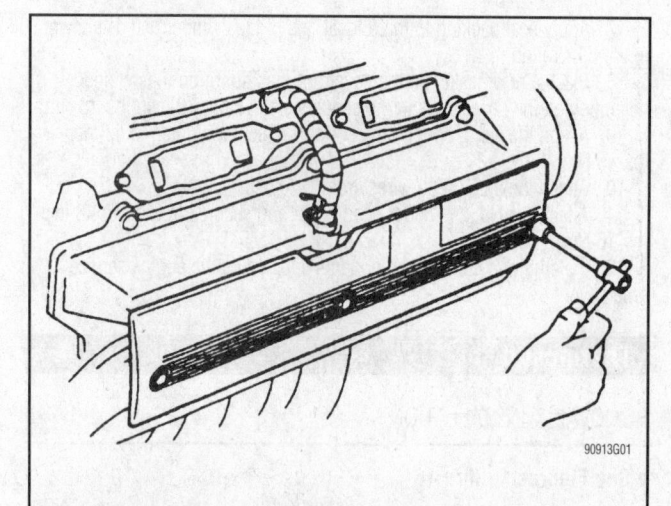

Fig. 1 Remove the 3 bolts retaining the No. 2 cylinder head cover to extract it from the engine

Fig. 2 Remove the four spark plug wires and PCV hose, then . . .

Fig. 3 . . . remove the valve cover retaining bolts

Fig. 4 Pull the cover off and . . .

Fig. 5 . . . remember the gasket on the cylinder head

## 3-8 ENGINE AND ENGINE OVERHAUL

Fig. 6 Sometimes it may be stuck to the valve cover

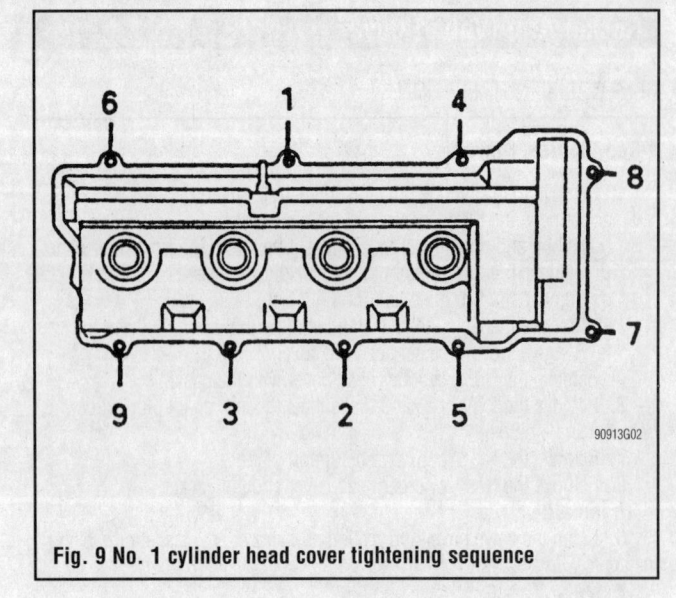

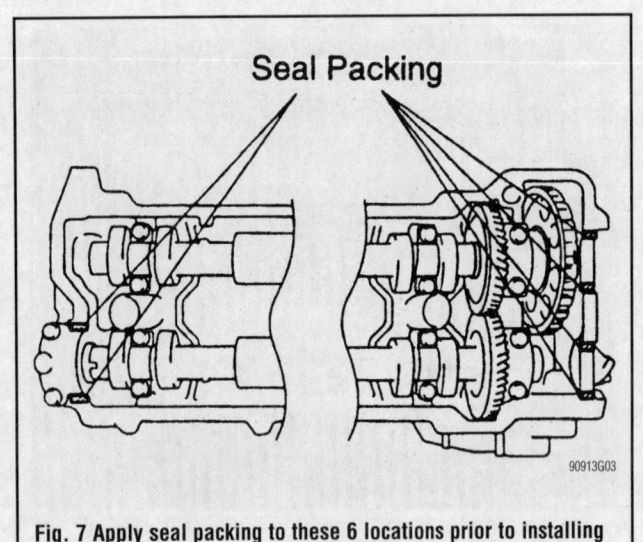

Fig. 7 Apply seal packing to these 6 locations prior to installing the valve cover

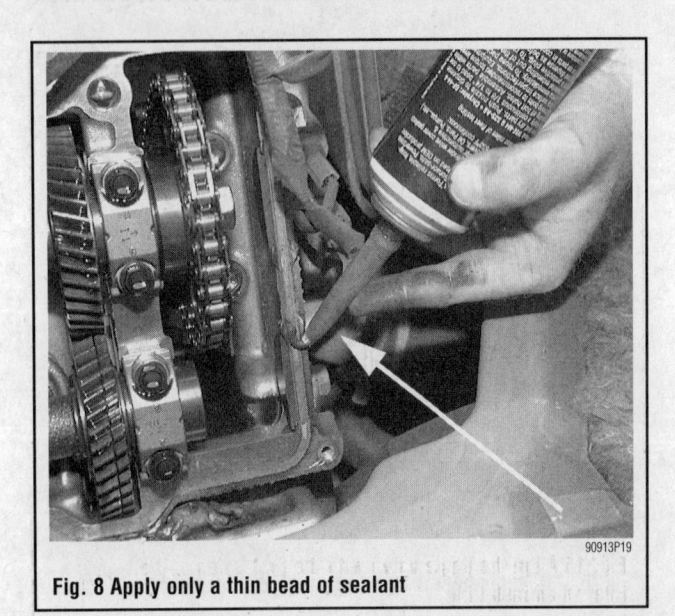

Fig. 8 Apply only a thin bead of sealant

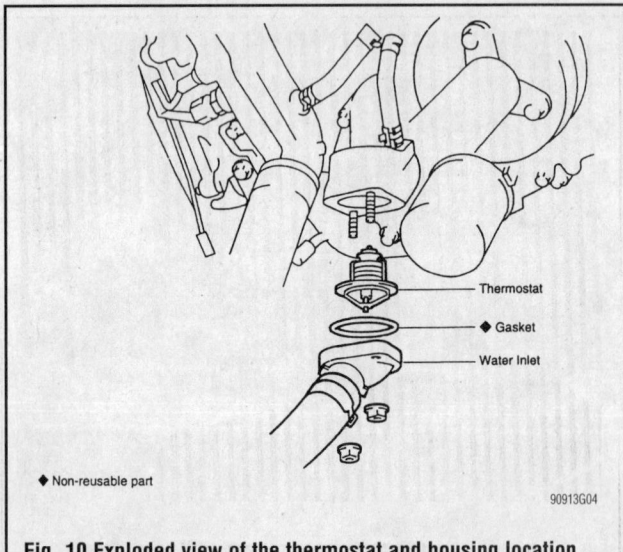

Fig. 9 No. 1 cylinder head cover tightening sequence

7. Apply seal packing to the 6 locations of the cylinder had as shown in the illustration.
8. Place a new gasket on the cover and position it on the cylinder head. tighten the cover bolts in the sequence shown to 69 inch lbs. (8 Nm).
9. Attach the No. 2 cord clamp support plate and tighten to 43 inch lbs. (5 Nm).
10. Attach the spark plug wires and PCV hose.
11. Attach the No. 2 cylinder head cover and secure the bolts to 48 inch lbs. (6 Nm).
12. Install the remaining components and secure the engine service hole cover.

### Thermostat

REMOVAL & INSTALLATION

♦ See Figures 10 thru 15

1. Drain the engine coolant into a suitable container.

➡ The thermostat housing is located next to the oil filter

Fig. 10 Exploded view of the thermostat and housing location

# ENGINE AND ENGINE OVERHAUL    3-9

2. If necessary, disconnect the lower radiator hose from the water inlet housing.

➡ It is not necessary to remove the radiator hose from the housing to replace the thermostat.

3. Remove the two water inlet nuts and remove the water inlet from the water pump cover.

➡ Fluid will drain from the housing, have a pan ready.

4. Remove the thermostat and gasket.

**To install:**

5. Install a new gasket to the thermostat.
6. Align the jiggle valve with the protrusion and insert the thermostat to the water inlet.
7. Install the water inlet to the water pump cover and tighten the two nuts to 14 ft. lbs. (19 Nm) engine.
8. Fill the engine with coolant.
9. Check the oil level.
10. Start the engine, bleed the cooling system, check for leaks, and verify proper operation of the thermostat.

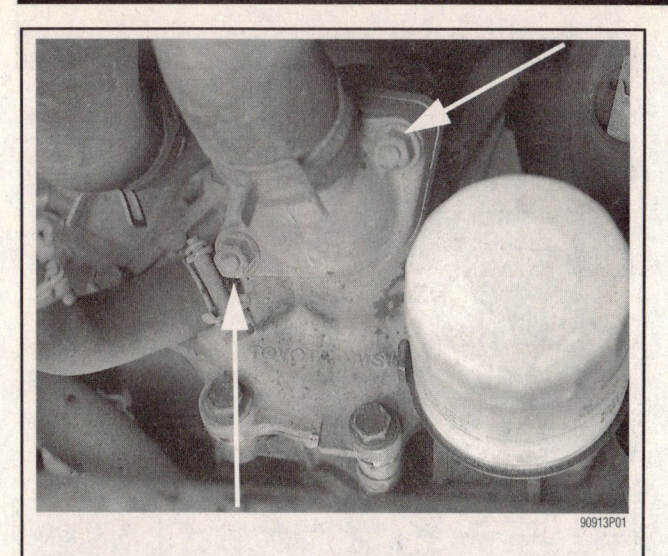

Fig. 11 Remove these two nuts to access the thermostat

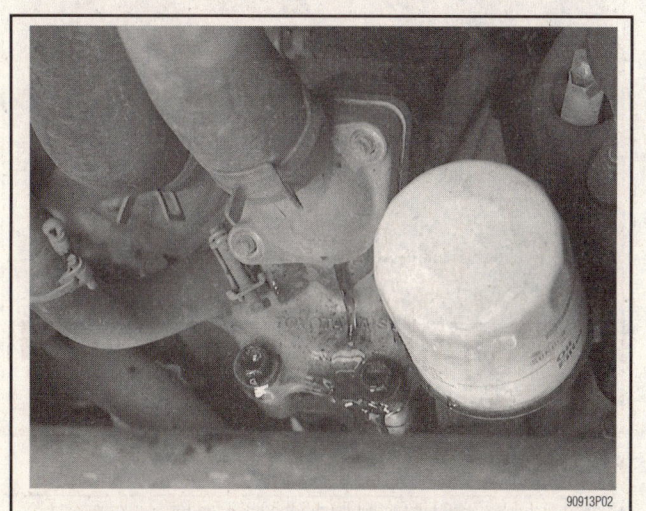

Fig. 12 Fluid will flow from the thermostat housing once the nuts are removed

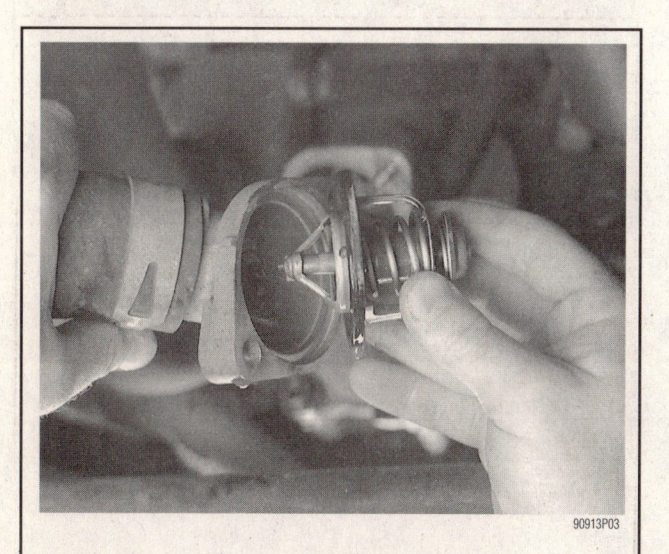

Fig. 13 Pull the housing off and extract the thermostat

Fig. 14 When installing the thermostat, align these components

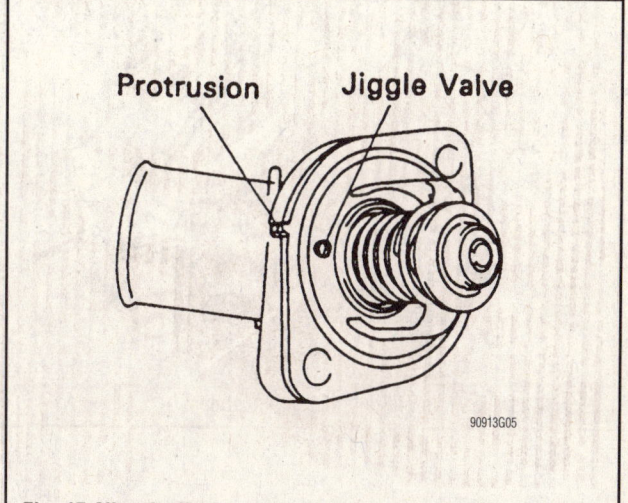

Fig. 15 Align the jiggle valve with the protrusion of the water inlet when installing

# 3-10 ENGINE AND ENGINE OVERHAUL

## Intake Manifold

### REMOVAL & INSTALLATION

▶ See Figure 16

1. Remove the air intake connector.
2. Disconnect and tag all wires, harnesses, coolant and vacuum hoses from the intake manifold.
3. Disconnect the shift and accelerator cables.
4. Remove the fuel pipes.
5. Remove the distributor and EGR valve.
6. Remove the PCV hose.
7. Remove the water outlet, by-pass pipe and gasket from the manifold.
8. Disconnect the water hose form the water pump and remove the bolt holding the water by-pass pipe and timing chain case.
9. Remove the intake manifold stays.
10. Remove the 2 nuts and 4 bolts and extract the intake manifold with gasket. Remove the cylinder block insulators.

**To install:**

11. Position the cylinder block insulator on the cylinder head.
12. Position a new gasket on the cylinder head and install the intake manifold with the 2 nuts and 4 bolts. Tighten the fasteners to 15 ft. lbs. (21 Nm). Use a crisscross pattern starting from the center and work outward.
13. Install the intake manifold stays and secure to 27 ft. lbs. (37 Nm) to the block and 13 ft. lbs. (18 Nm) to the intake manifold.
14. Install the bolt holding the water by-pass pipe and timing chain case and tighten to 13 ft. lbs. (18 Nm). Connect the water hose to the water pump.
15. Install the delivery pipe, water outlet and EGR valve.
16. Install the distributor.
17. Connect all wires, connectors, coolant and vacuum hoses from the intake manifold.
18. Connect the shift and accelerator cables.
19. Install the air intake connector.
20. Fill and bleed the cooling system.
21. Start the engine and check for leaks.

Fig. 16 Intake manifold bolt and nut locations

## Exhaust Manifold

### REMOVAL & INSTALLATION

▶ See Figures 17 thru 22

1. Raise and safely support the vehicle.
2. Disconnect the front exhaust pipe from the exhaust manifold by removing the three nuts.
3. Remove the 5 nuts and remove the exhaust manifold and gasket.

**To install:**

4. Install the exhaust manifold with a new gasket. Install and tighten the exhaust manifold nuts to 36 Nm (41 Nm). Use a crisscross pattern starting from the center and work outward.
5. Connect the front exhaust pipe to the manifold by installing new gaskets and three nuts. Tighten the nuts to 46 ft. lbs. (62 Nm).

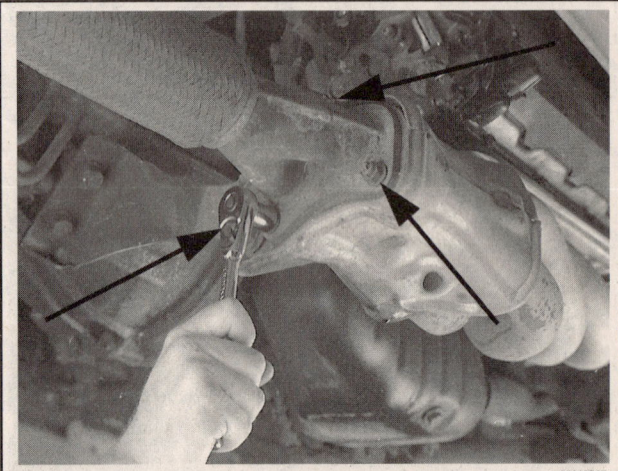

Fig. 17 Remove the header pipe attached to the exhaust manifold retaining nuts

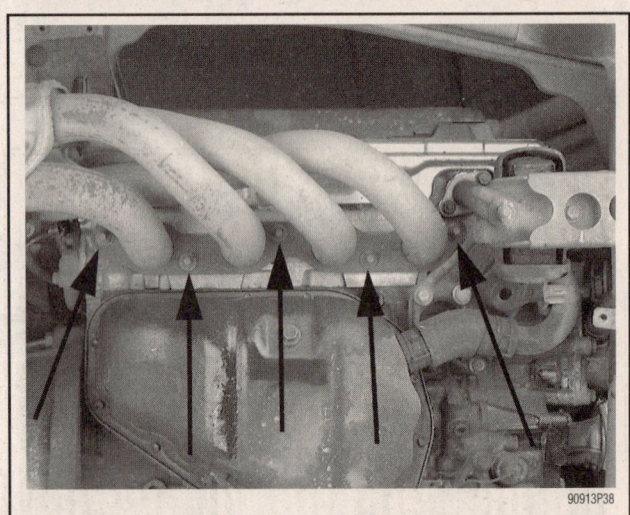

Fig. 18 Remove these nuts retaining the exhaust manifold to the engine

# ENGINE AND ENGINE OVERHAUL  3-11

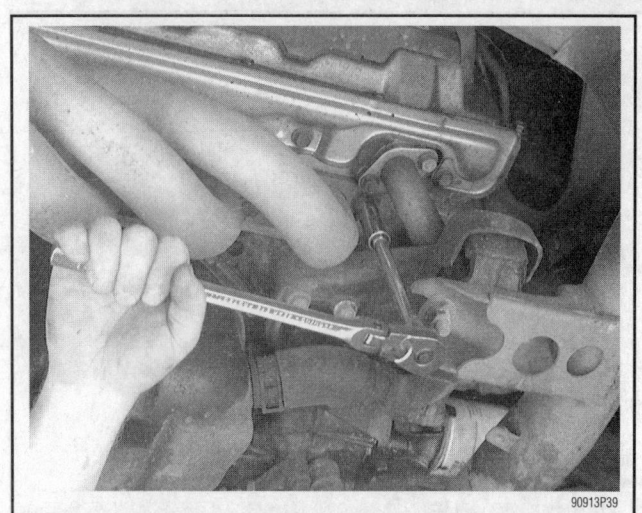

Fig. 19 An extension is necessary to access these nuts on the manifold

Fig. 20 Scrape any gasket residue from the mating areas with a razor tipped tool

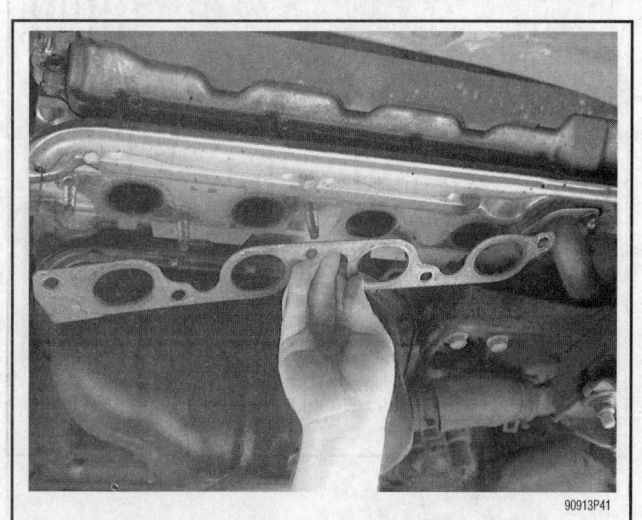

Fig. 21 Position a gasket over the studs before the exhaust manifold

Fig. 22 When installing, place the manifold over the studs

6. Lower the vehicle.
7. Start the engine and check for leaks.

## Supercharger

### REMOVAL & INSTALLATION

◆ See Figures 23 and 24

1. Drain the engine coolant from the radiator.
2. Remove the air duct.
3. Remove the engine coolant reservoir tank and bracket.
4. Remove the air damper case.
5. Remove the supercharger blower.
6. Disconnect the power steering reservoir.
7. Remove the radiator.
8. Remove the throttle body.
9. Remove the alternator/power steering drive belt.
10. Remove the power steering pump.
11. Remove the drive belt for the supercharger.
12. Remove the No. 2 idler pulley by extracting the nut, plate, and the spacer.
13. Remove the No. 1 air inlet duct with the supercharger bypass valve as follows:
    a. Disconnect the supercharger bypass valve harness.
    b. Disconnect the brake booster hose.
    c. Disconnect the A/C idle up air hose.
    d. Disengage the supercharger magnetic clutch connector.
    e. Disengage the supercharger magnetic clutch connector from the No.1 hose support bracket.
    f. Remove the air hoses and three way.
    g. Remove the two bolts and two nuts holding the supercharger bypass valve to the No. 1 air outlet duct.
    h. Remove the five nuts and the No. 1 air inlet duct with the supercharger bypass valve.
    i. Remove the supercharger bypass valve and No. 1 air inlet duct gaskets.
14. Pull off the No. 1 idle up pipe by removing the bolt and air hose.
15. Disconnect the No. 1 air tube.
16. Remove the No. 1 intake air connector bracket by removing the two bolts.
17. Remove the supercharger as follows:
    a. Remove the two bolts and two nuts holding the supercharger to the equipment drive housing.

## 3-12 ENGINE AND ENGINE OVERHAUL

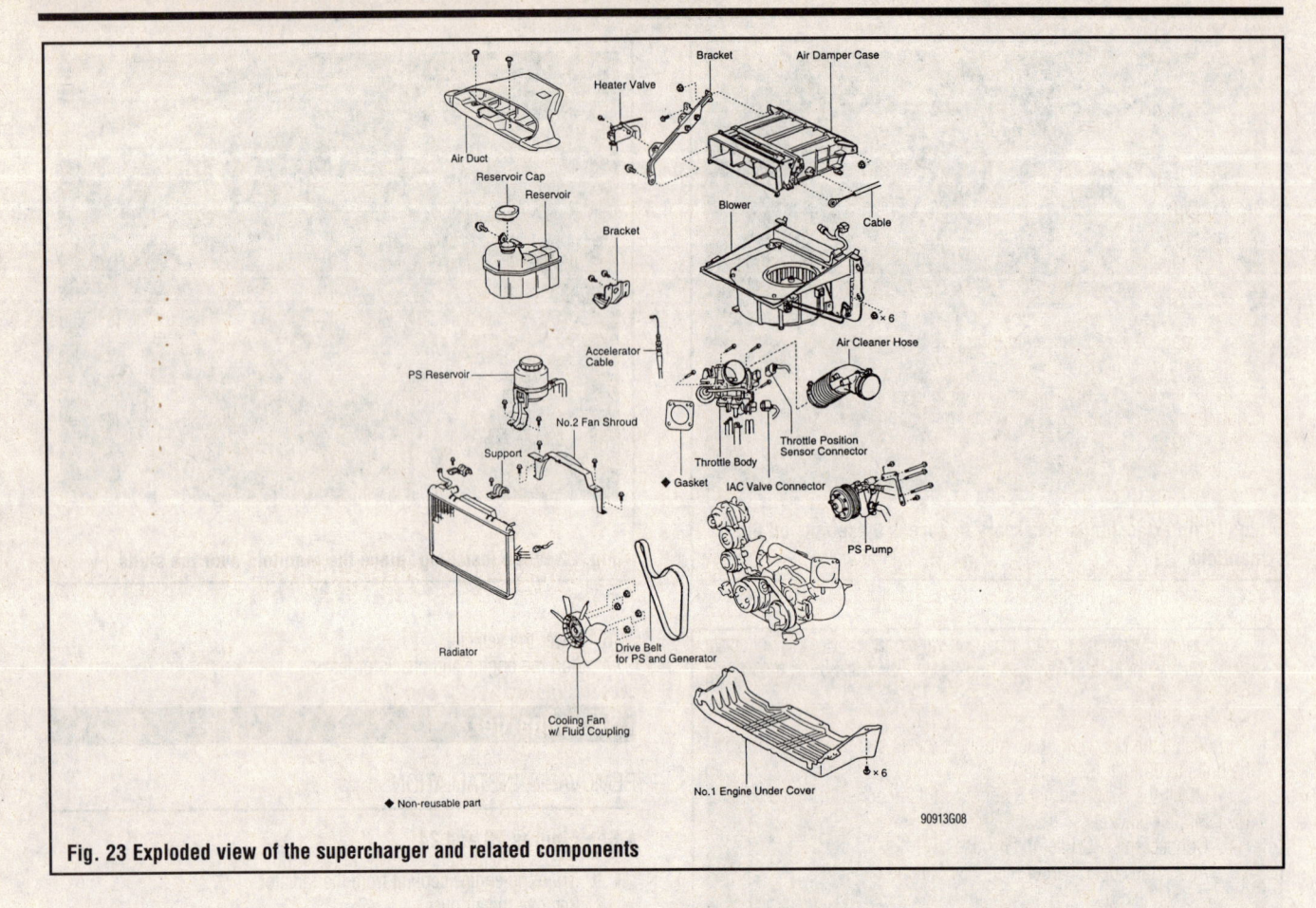

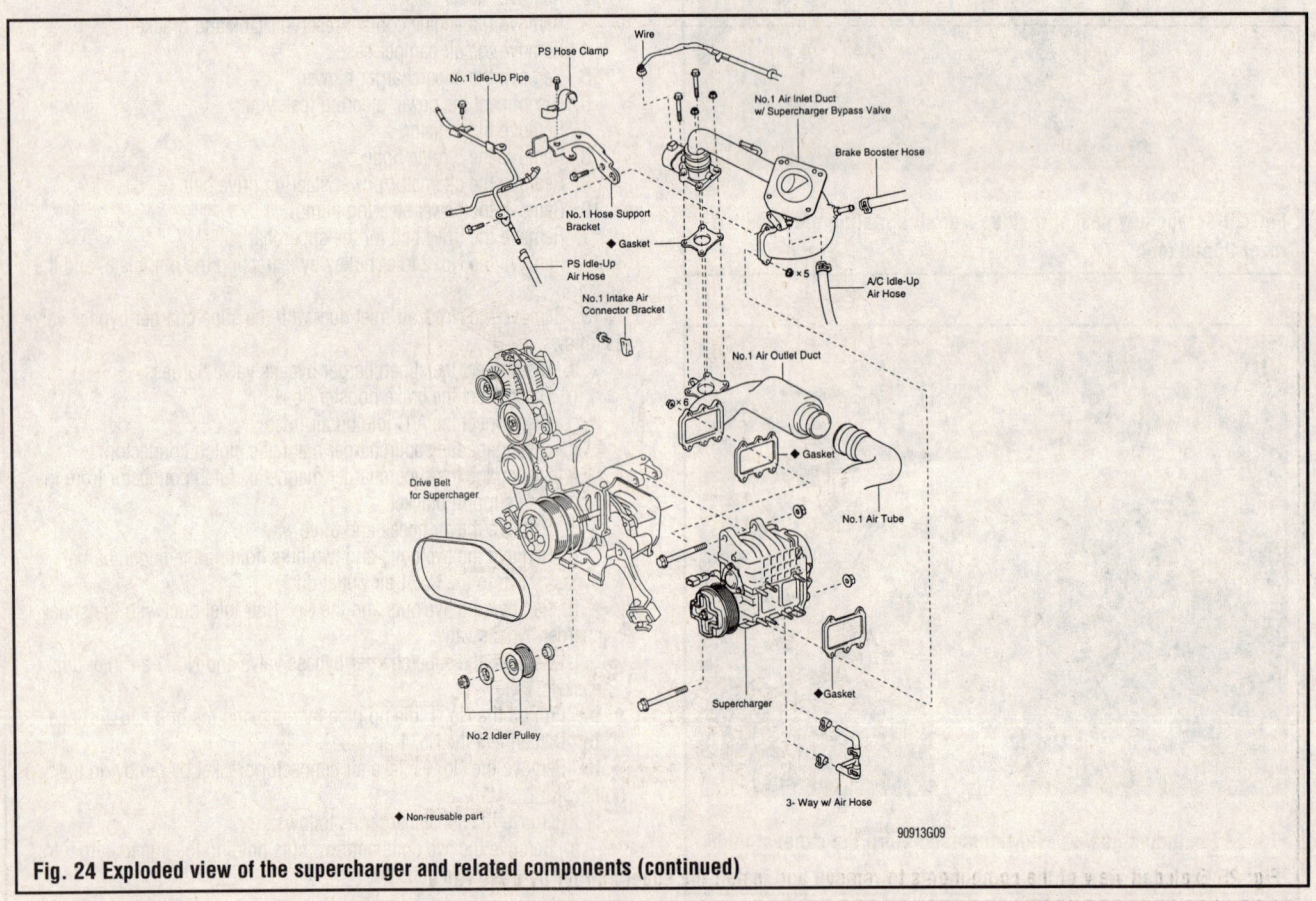

Fig. 23 Exploded view of the supercharger and related components

Fig. 24 Exploded view of the supercharger and related components (continued)

## ENGINE AND ENGINE OVERHAUL  3-13

   b. Remove the six nuts holding the supercharger to the No. 1 air outlet duct.
   c. Separate the supercharger and No. 1 air outlet duct and remove the gasket.
   d. Remove the supercharger and No. 1 air outlet duct from the vehicle.

**To install:**

18. Install the supercharger as follows:
   a. Install the supercharger and No. 1 air outlet duct to the vehicle.
   b. Connect the supercharger and No. 1 air outlet duct with a new gasket.
   c. Install the six nuts to hold the supercharger to the No. 1 air outlet duct. Tighten the nuts to 82 inch lbs. (9 Nm).
   d. Install the two bolts and two nuts to hold the supercharger to the equipment drive housing. Tighten the bolts and nuts to 27 ft. lbs. (37 Nm).
19. Install the No. 1 intake air connector bracket with the two bolts. Tighten the bolts to 13 ft. lbs. (18 Nm).
20. Connect the No.1 air tube.
21. Install the No. 1 idle up pipe by connecting the air hose and installing the bolt. Tighten the bolts to 69 inch lbs. (7.5 Nm).
22. Install the No. 1 air inlet duct with the supercharger bypass valve as follows:
   a. Connect the supercharger bypass valve to the No. 1 air outlet duct. Install the two bolts and two nuts and tighten the bolts and nuts to 48 inch lbs. (5 Nm).
   b. Install the air hoses and three way valve.
   c. Install the No. 1 air hose support bracket and two bolts. Tighten the bolts to 69 inch lbs. (8 Nm).
   d. attach the supercharger magnetic clutch connector to the No. 1 hose support bracket.
   e. Connect the A/C idle up air hose.
   f. Attach the supercharger magnetic clutch connector.
   g. Connect the brake booster hose.
   h. Attach the supercharger bypass valve connector.
23. Install the No. 2 idler pulley with the spacer, plate, and the nut.
24. Install and adjust the drive belt for the supercharger.
25. Position the power steering pump. Tighten the long bolts to 35 ft. lbs. (48 Nm) and the short bolts to 27 ft. lbs. (36 Nm).
26. Install and adjust the alternator/power steering drive belts.
27. Install the throttle body.
28. Install the radiator. Tighten the radiator bolts to 13 ft. lbs. (18 Nm). Attach all connectors, hoses and shrouds.
29. Connect the power steering reservoir with the two bolts. Tighten the bolts to 9 ft. lbs. (13 Nm).
30. Install the supercharger blower.
31. Attach the air damper case.
32. Install the engine coolant reservoir and bracket.
33. Install the air duct.
34. Fill the radiator with engine coolant.
35. Reset any electronic components such as the radio.
36. Check all fluids.

### Supercharger By-Pass (SCB) Valve

REMOVAL & INSTALLATION

♦ See Figures 25, 26 and 27

1. Drain the engine coolant.
2. Remove the air duct.
3. Remove the engine coolant reservoir and bracket.
4. Remove the air damper case.
5. Remove the blower.
6. Disconnect the power steering reservoir.
7. Remove the throttle body.

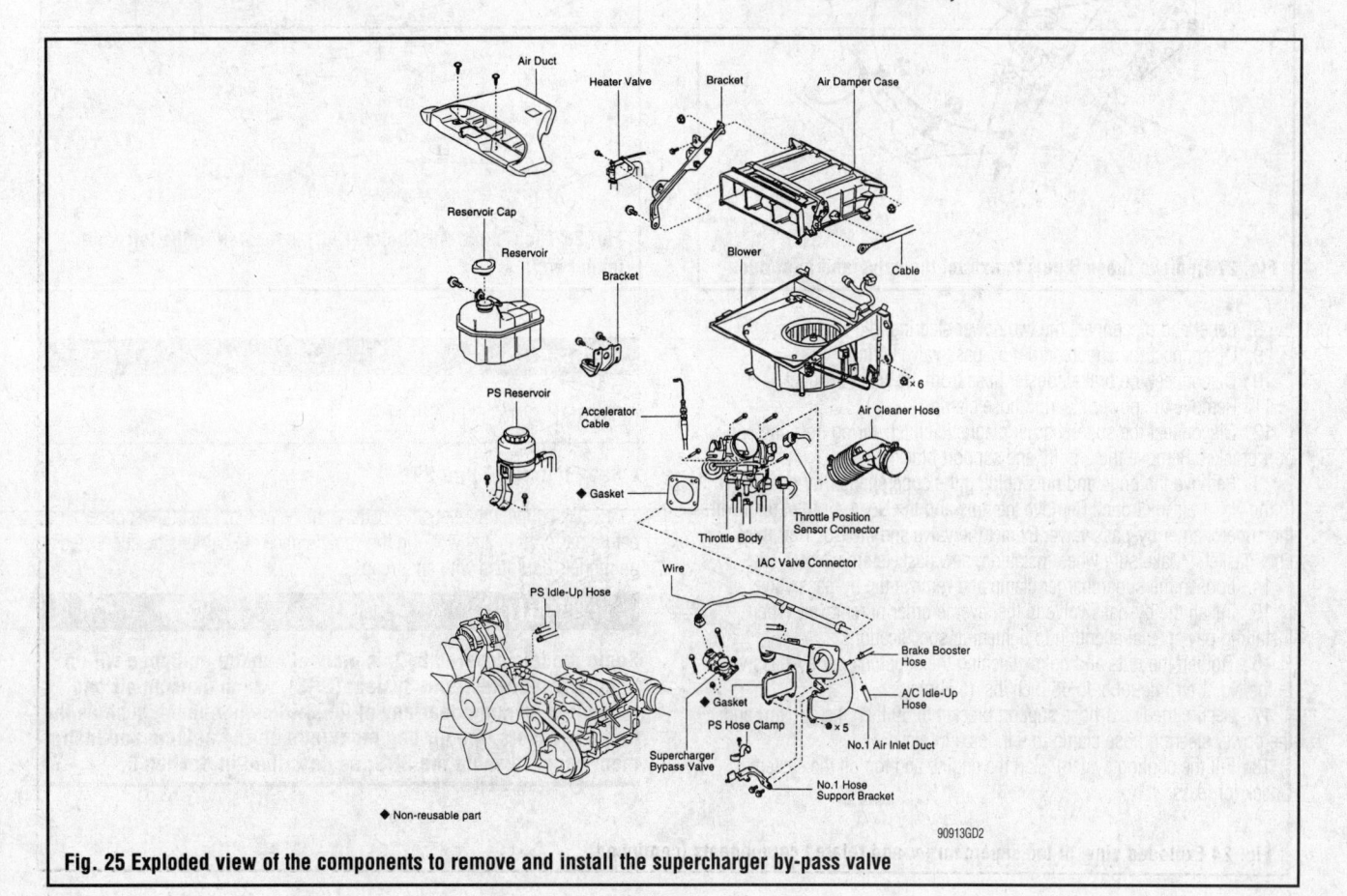

Fig. 25 Exploded view of the components to remove and install the supercharger by-pass valve

# 3-14 ENGINE AND ENGINE OVERHAUL

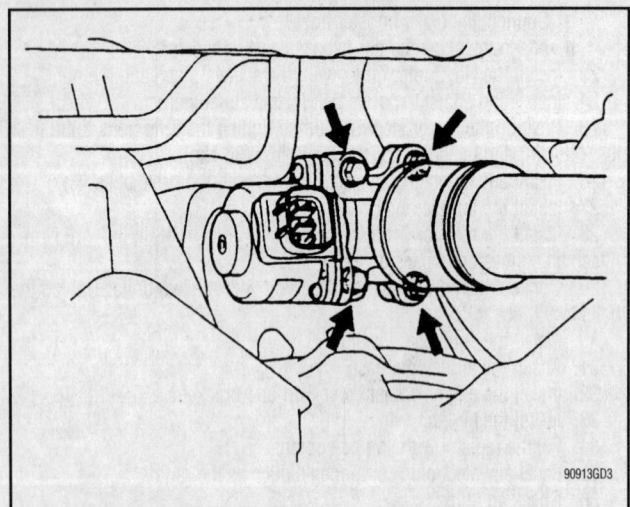

**Fig. 26 Remove the 2 nuts and 2 bolts holding the by-pass valve to the No. 1 air inlet duct**

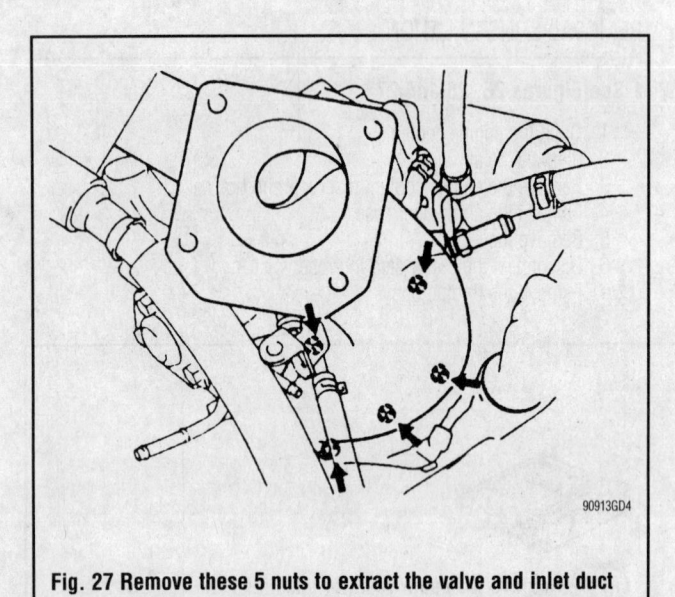

**Fig. 27 Remove these 5 nuts to extract the valve and inlet duct**

8. Label and disconnect the two power steering idle-up hoses.
9. Disconnect the supercharger by-pass valve wiring.
10. Disconnect the brake booster hose from the No. 1 air duct.
11. Remove the power steering hose clamp.
12. Disconnect the supercharger magnetic clutch wiring from the support bracket. Remove the 2 bolts and support bracket.
13. Remove the bolts and nuts holding the supercharger by-pass valve to the No. 1 air inlet duct. Remove the nuts and the No. 1 air inlet duct with the supercharger by-pass valve. Extract the valve and the No. 1 air inlet duct gaskets. Make sure when installing, new gaskets are used.
14. Loosen the supercharger clamp and remove the by-pass valve.
15. Install the by-pass valve in the reverse order of removal. When installing pay special attention to tightening specifications.
16. Tighten the nuts and bolts attaching the supercharger by-pass valve to the No. 1 air inlet duct to 48 inch lbs. (5 Nm).
17. Secure the No. 1 hose support bracket to 69 inch lbs. (7 Nm) and the power steering hose clamp to 9 ft. lbs. (11 Nm).
18. Fill the cooling system, start the engine and top off the system. Check for leaks.

## Charge Air Cooler (CAC)

### REMOVAL & INSTALLATION

▶ See Figure 28

1. Disconnect the No. 1 air tube from the charge air cooler.
2. Remove the left fender splash shield.
3. Disconnect the No. 2 air tube from the CAC.
4. Remove the bolt holding the CAC to the wheel extension. Remove the bolts holding the CAC to the left side member. Separate the CAC and duct assembly.
5. Unbolt the CAC from the duct.

**To install:**

6. Attach the CAC to the duct and tighten the bolts to 43 inch lbs. (5 Nm).
7. Position the CAC with attached duct to the vehicle and attach the left side member. tighten the member bolts to 9 ft. lbs. (12 Nm). Attach the CAC to the wheel housing and tighten to 9 ft. lbs. (12 Nm).
8. Attach the No. 2 air tube to the CAC and tighten the clamp.
9. install and secure the left fender splash shield.
10. Attach the No. 1 air tube to the CAC.

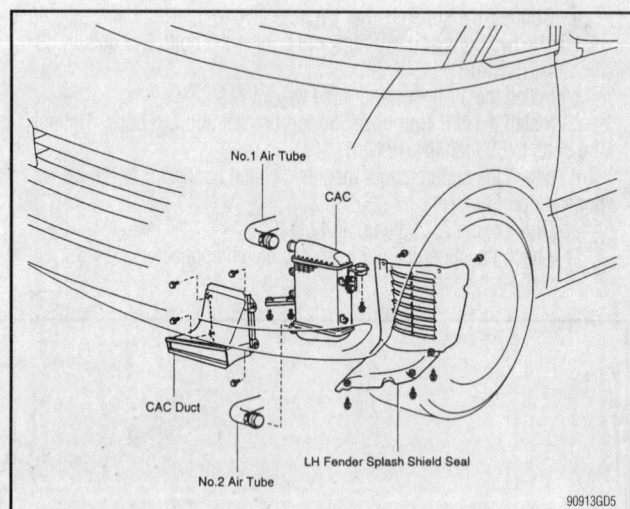

**Fig. 28 The Charge Air Cooler (CAC) is located in the left front fender well**

## Radiator

### REMOVAL & INSTALLATION

▶ See Figures 29 thru 39

1. Disconnect the negative battery cable. Wait at least 90 seconds before performing any work on the vehicle once the cable is disconnected on models equipped with an airbag.

### ✽✽ CAUTION

Some models covered by this manual may be equipped with a Supplemental Restraint System (SRS), which uses an air bag. Whenever working near any of the SRS components, such as the impact sensors, the air bag module, steering column and instrument panel, disable the SRS, as described in Section 6.

# ENGINE AND ENGINE OVERHAUL  3-15

2. Raise and safely support the vehicle.
3. Remove the air intake duct.
4. Remove the No. 1 engine under cover.
5. Drain the cooling system.
6. Disconnect the radiator hoses and coolant reservoir hose from the radiator.
7. On 1995–97 vehicles, disconnect the power steering reservoir by removing the two bolts.
8. On 1995–97 vehicles, disconnect the water bypass hose for the throttle body.
9. If equipped with an automatic transmission, disconnect the transmission cooling lines.
10. Extract the upper fan shrouds by removing the bolts.
11. Remove the lower fan shroud bolts but leave the shroud in the vehicle.

➡ It may be necessary to positive battery cable to make clearance for the radiator shroud.

12. Remove the radiator supports by removing the two bolts.
13. Remove the radiator from the vehicle.

**To install:**

14. Install the radiator into the vehicle. Tighten the support bolts to 13 ft. lbs. (18 Nm).
15. Install the fan shrouds and bolts.

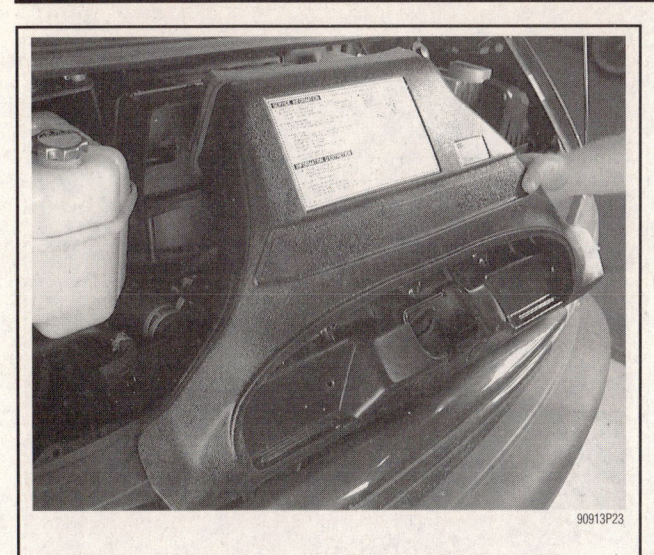

Fig. 29 Unbolt and remove the air inlet duct under the hood

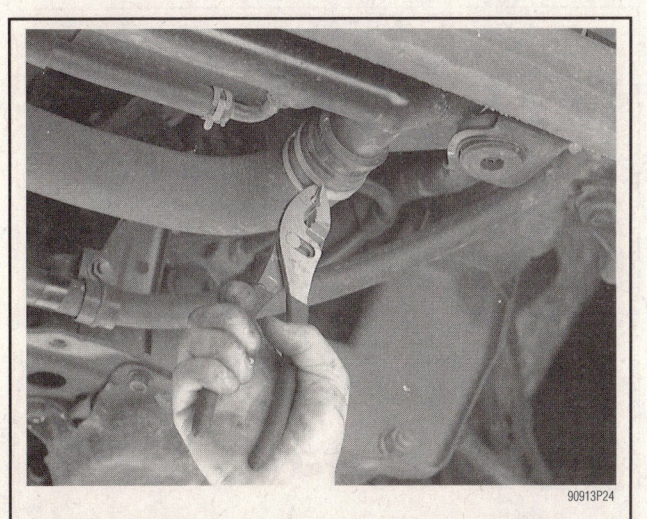

Fig. 30 Remove the lower radiator hose clamp, and slide it towards the back . . .

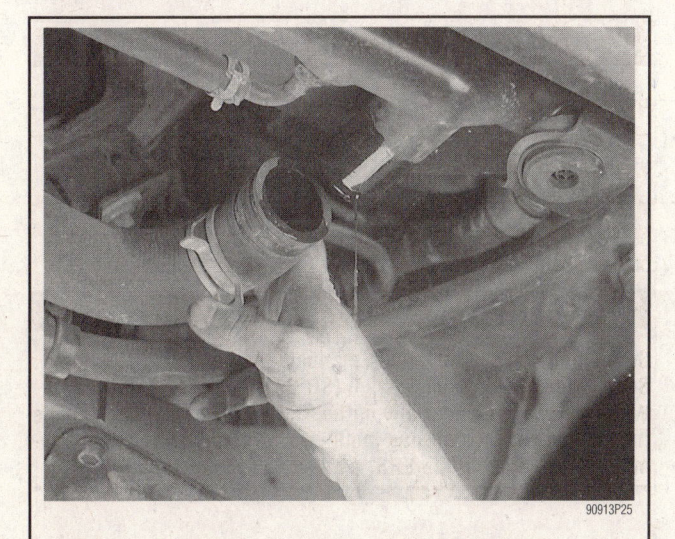

Fig. 31 . . . pull the hose off of the radiator outlet

Fig. 32 Remove the upper radiator hose also

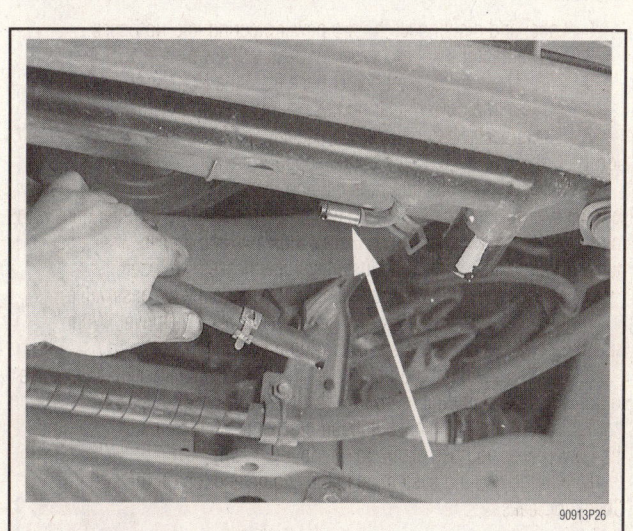

Fig. 33 On automatic transmissions, separate the oil cooler line from the radiator

## 3-16 ENGINE AND ENGINE OVERHAUL

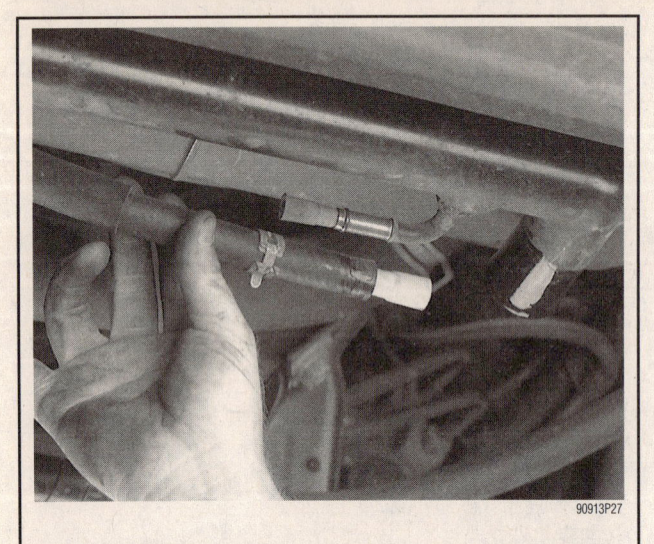

Fig. 34 It is always a good idea to plug the line once removed

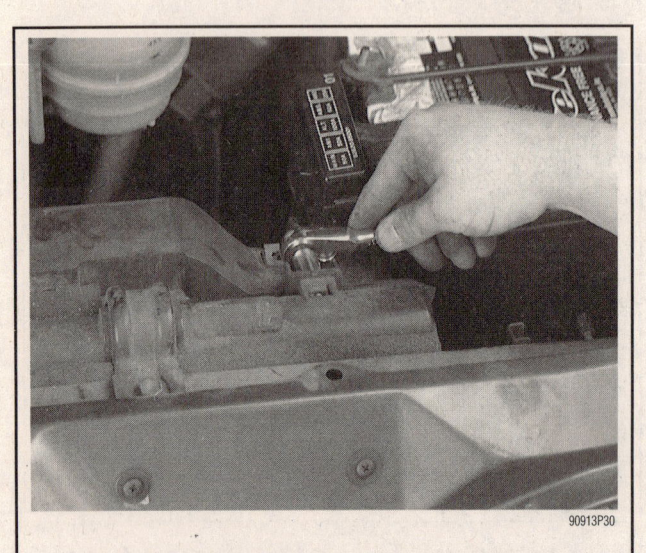

Fig. 35 Remove the upper shroud retaining bolts

Fig. 36 Then extract it from the vehicle

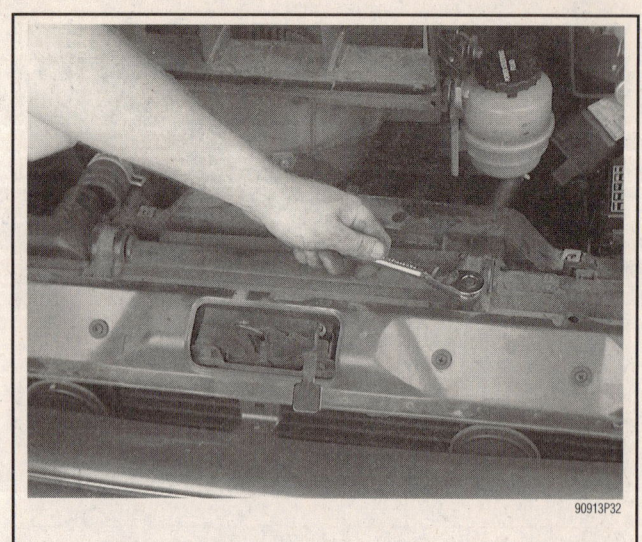

Fig. 37 Unbolt the upper radiator supports . . .

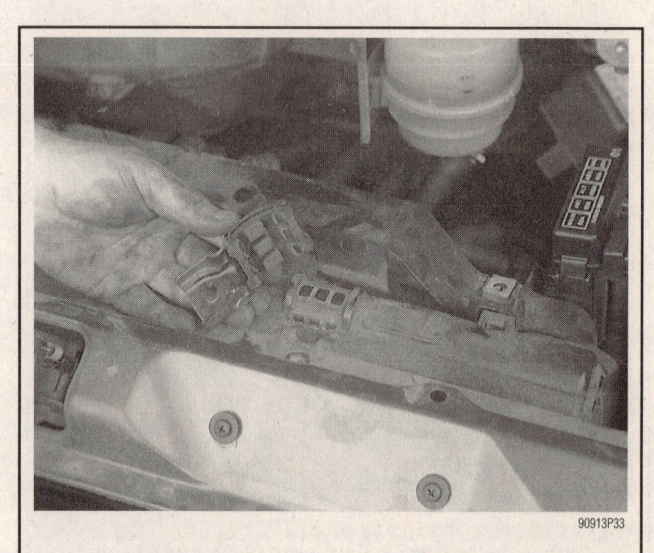

Fig. 38 . . . and remove them on each side of the radiator

Fig. 39 Extract the radiator from the vehicle

# ENGINE AND ENGINE OVERHAUL   3-17

16. Connect the radiator hoses.
17. On 1995–97 vehicles, connect the water bypass hose from the throttle body.
18. If equipped with an automatic transmission, connect the transmission cooler lines.
19. On 1995–97 vehicles, install the power steering reservoir and tighten the bolts to 9 ft. lbs. (13 Nm).
20. Install the engine under cover.
21. Install the air intake duct.
22. Lower the vehicle.
23. Connect the negative battery cable. Reset any electronic components such as the radio.
24. Refill the cooling system. Start the engine, bleed the cooling system, and check for leaks.

## Engine Fan

### REMOVAL & INSTALLATION

▶ See Figures 40 and 41

1. Remove the air duct.
2. Remove the No. 2 fan shroud.

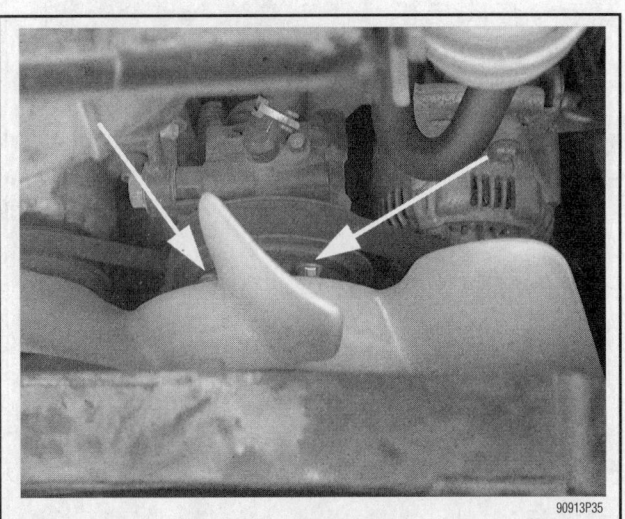

Fig. 40 The fan blade is attached to the clutch with nuts, not all shown

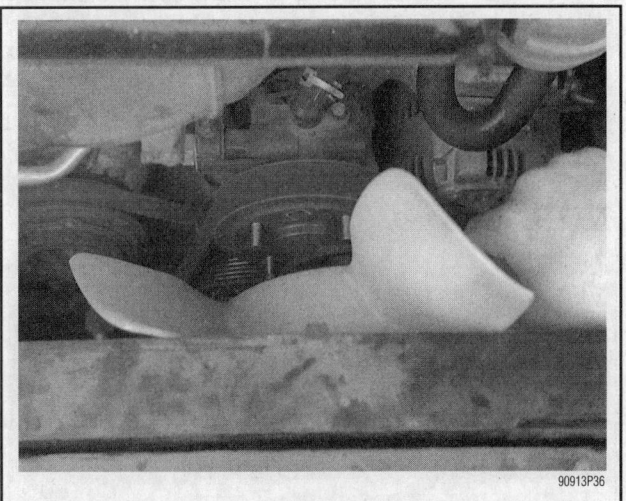

Fig. 41 Once the nuts are removed, the blade comes off easily from the studs

3. Stretch the drive belt down and loosen the four nuts for the fan and clutch.
4. Remove the nuts and the fan clutch with the cooling fan.

**To install:**
5. Install the fan clutch with the fan to the engine.
6. Install the fan nuts.
7. While retaining the drive belt, tighten the nuts to 10 ft. lbs. (13 Nm).
8. Install the No. 2 fan shroud.
9. Install the air duct.

## Water Pump

### REMOVAL & INSTALLATION

▶ See Figures 42 thru 51

1. Raise the vehicle and support safely.
2. Remove the engine under covers.
3. Drain the engine coolant.
4. Drain the engine oil.
5. Disconnect the heater hose and radiator outlet hoses.
6. Remove the oil filter bracket.

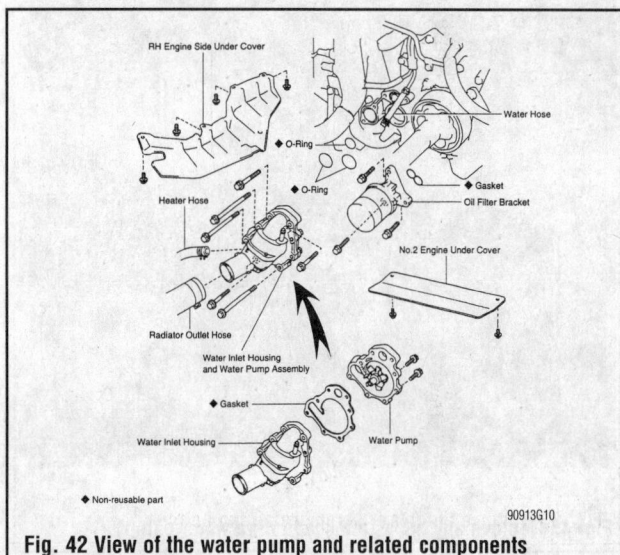

Fig. 42 View of the water pump and related components

Fig. 43 Unbolt and remove the oil filter bracket

## 3-18 ENGINE AND ENGINE OVERHAUL

Fig. 44 Remember to discard the old gasket for the bracket

Fig. 45 Remove any hoses attached to the water pump

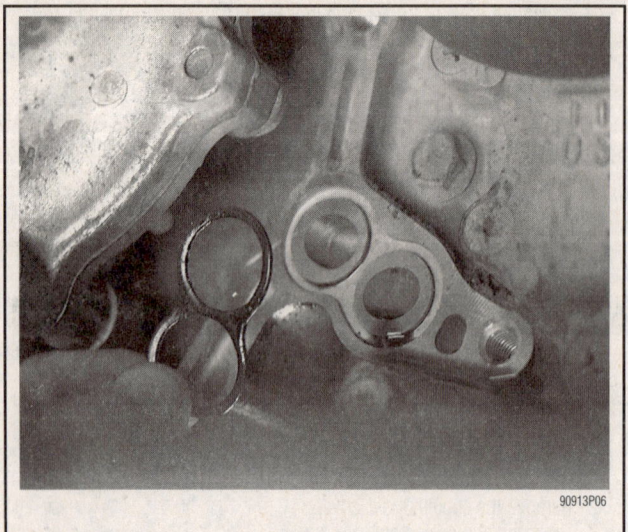

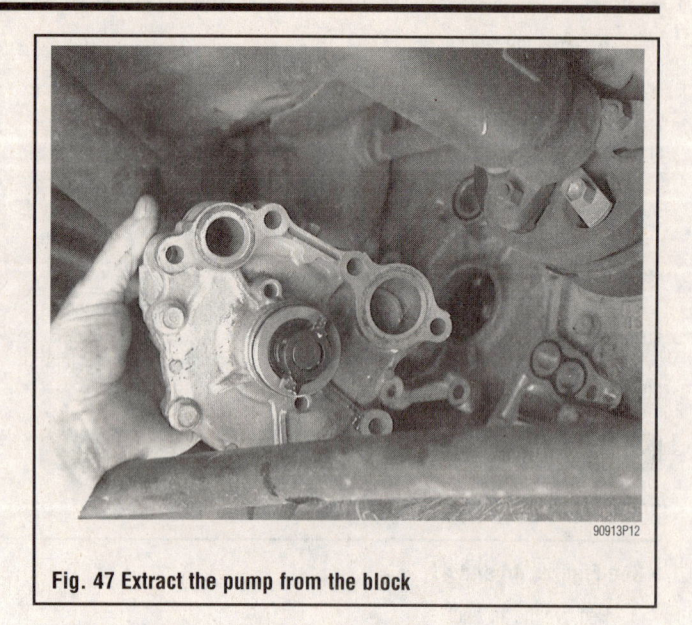

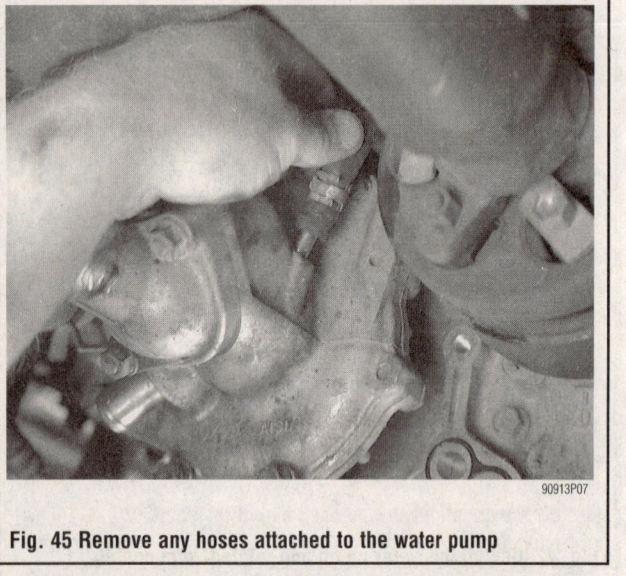

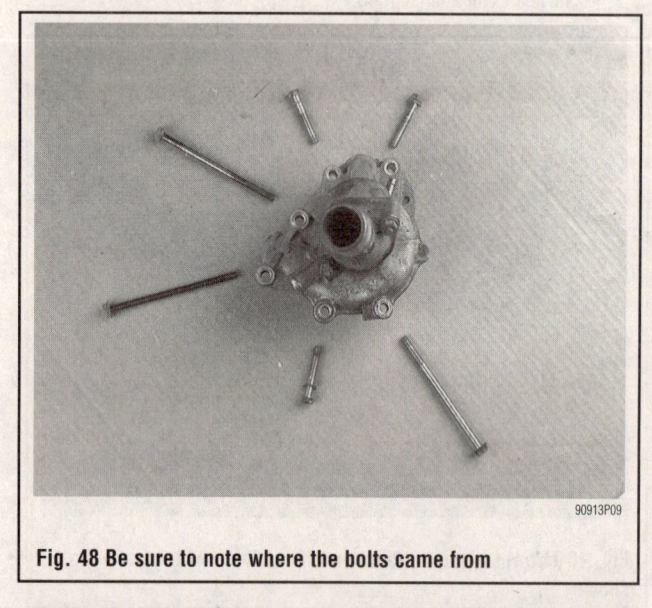

Fig. 46 Remove any bolts attaching the water pump to the engine

Fig. 47 Extract the pump from the block

Fig. 48 Be sure to note where the bolts came from

Fig. 49 Remove all the o-rings from the water pump area

# ENGINE AND ENGINE OVERHAUL 3-19

Fig. 50 View of the water pump gasket mating area

Fig. 51 Waterpump bolt identification

7. Disconnect the water hose from the water pump.
8. Remove the water pump retaining bolts and pump from the timing cover.
9. Remove the O-ring from the water pump.
10. Remove the water pump from the housing by removing the two bolts.

**To install:**
11. Install the water pump with a new gasket and tighten the bolts to 14 ft. lbs. (20 Nm).
12. Install the water pump to the timing cover and install the bolts. Tighten the bolts for the water pump as follows:
- Bolt A: 14 ft. lbs. (20 Nm)
- Bolt B: 21 ft. lbs. (28 Nm)
13. Connect the water hose to the water pump.
14. Install the oil filter bracket to the engine using a new O-ring.
15. Connect the heater hose and radiator outlet hose.
16. Fill the engine with oil.
17. Fill the engine and radiator with coolant.
18. Start the engine and check for leaks.

## Equipment Driveshaft

### PRECAUTIONS

▶ See Figures 52 thru 58

1. The flexible coupling is not to be disassembled. Do not re-use a flexible coupling which has been disassembled.
2. The driveshaft must be installed in a straight line without forcing it. The coupling is made out of rubber, so it can easily bend out of shape. When performing service related to the driveshaft, observe the following:
- Do not disconnect the rear end of the driveshaft from the engine and the leave the shaft resting at an angle for a long period. When leaving the driveshaft disconnected for long periods, support it with a sling so that it is horizontal, in a straight line with the engine.
- Store the driveshaft in a straight line without bending it.
- When installing the driveshaft, visually check that the flexible coupling is not twisted or squeezed out of shape. If the coupling is out of shape, disconnect it and install it again.
- When installing the equipment driveshaft and drive housing, measure the installation angle of the driveshaft in front of and behind the flexible

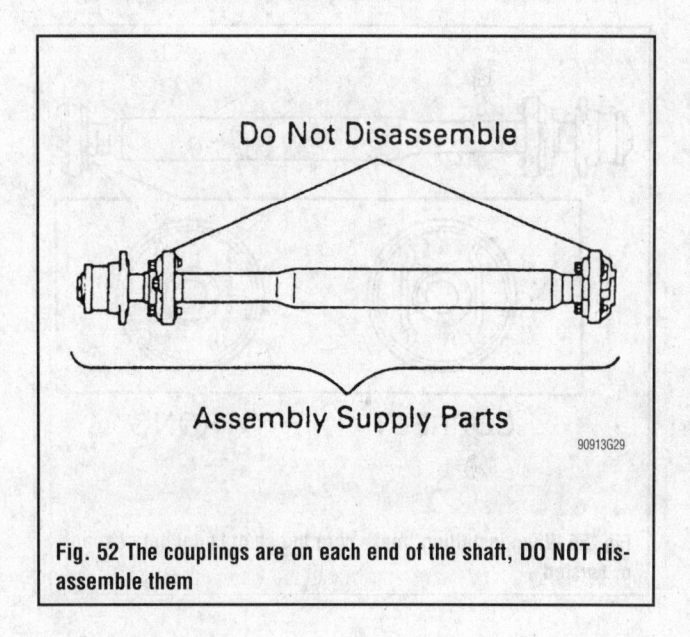

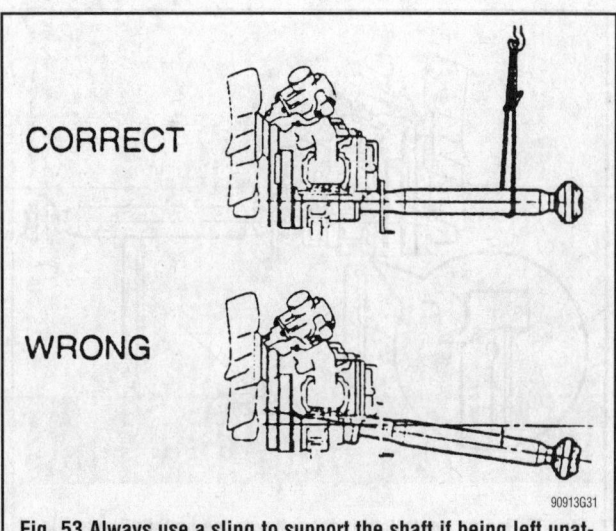

Fig. 52 The couplings are on each end of the shaft, DO NOT disassemble them

Fig. 53 Always use a sling to support the shaft if being left unattached for long periods of time

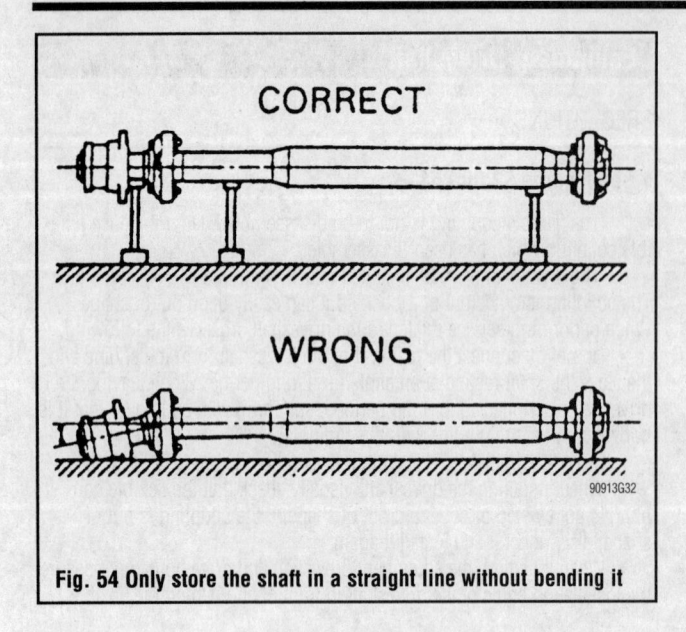

# 3-20  ENGINE AND ENGINE OVERHAUL

Fig. 54 Only store the shaft in a straight line without bending it

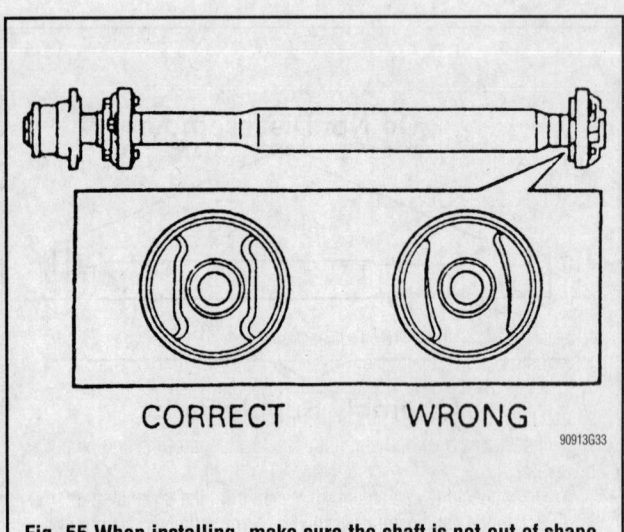

Fig. 55 When installing, make sure the shaft is not out of shape or twisted

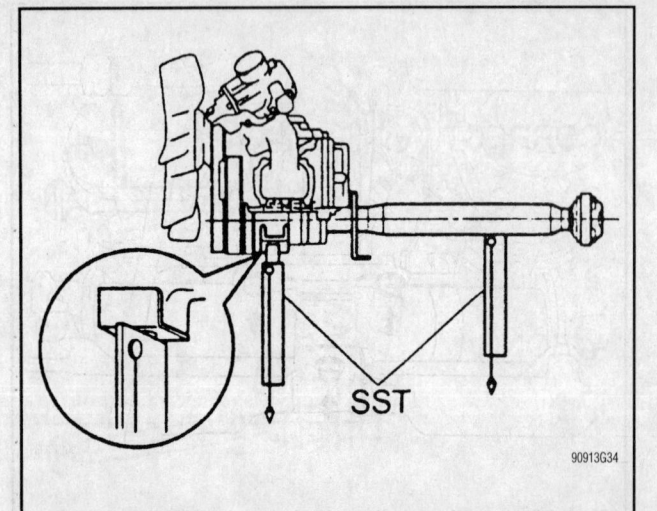

Fig. 56 Use an angle gauge to measure the installation angle of the driveshaft in the front and behind the coupling

Fig. 57 Check all ground straps to see if they are all secure

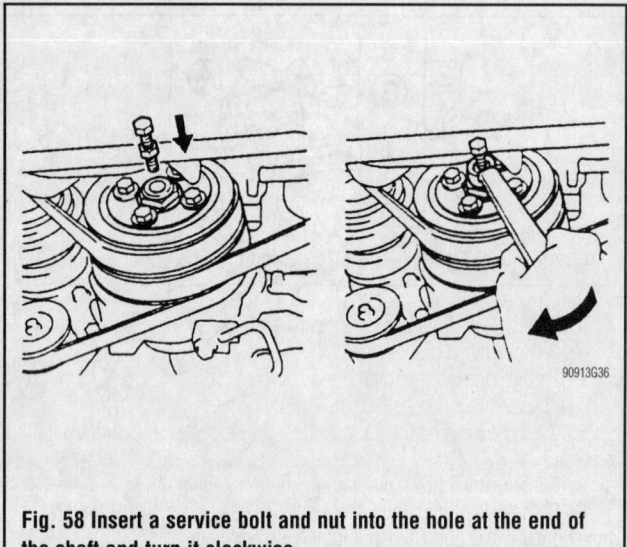

Fig. 58 Insert a service bolt and nut into the hole at the end of the shaft and turn it clockwise

coupling. If the difference in the angle between each section is 2° or more, correct the installation angle by adjusting the position of the No. 3 equipment drive housing stay and No. 2 equipment drive housing insulator. The angle gauge is 09370–50010 or equivalent.
- For vehicle which have been in a serious accident, also check the body dimensions.

3. There are ground straps between the equipment drive housing and body, and between the alternator and negative battery terminal. After completing the operation, always check that the ground straps are firmly attached.

4. When rotating the driveshaft or engine by hand, this can be done by inserting a service bolt 12mm damper and 1.25mm pitch with a nut into the screw hole at the end of the driveshaft. After doing the operation, do forget to remove the service bolt and nut. If the service bolt is left installed, the bolt head may be hit and damage the cooling fan.

## REMOVAL & INSTALLATION

▶ See Figures 59 thru 79

1. Remove the air duct.
2. Remove the No. 2 fan shroud.
3. Remove the fluid coupling with cooling fan.

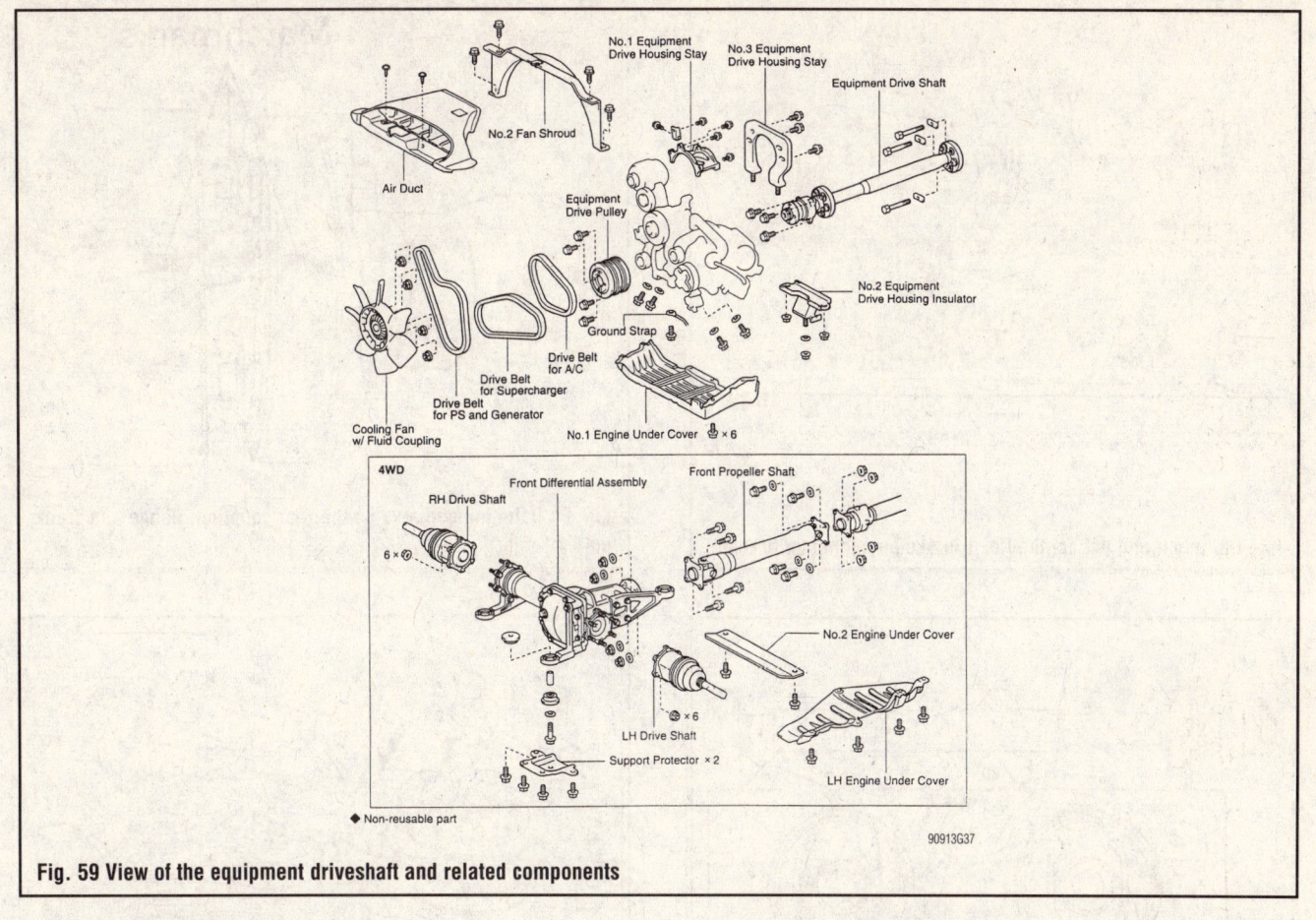

## ENGINE AND ENGINE OVERHAUL  3-21

Fig. 59 View of the equipment driveshaft and related components

4. Remove the drive belt for the alternator and power steering pump.
5. Remove the supercharger belt.
6. Remove the engine under cover.
7. Remove the drive belt for the A/C compressor.
8. On the 4WD models, remove the front propeller shaft and front differential.
9. Remove the 4 bolts and equipment drive pulley.
10. Remove the three bolts, three nuts, plate washer, No. 3 equipment drive housing stay and No. 2 equipment drive insulator.
11. Remove the No. 1 intake air connector bracket.
12. Unbolt and extract the No. 1 equipment drive housing stay.
13. To remove the equipment driveshaft perform the following:
   a. Paint matchmarks on the rear flexible coupling, flange and crankshaft pulley. Do not place marks using punch etc.
   b. Install a service bolt and nut to the front end of the equipment driveshaft.
   c. Disconnect the equipment driveshaft from the ground strap.
   d. Rotate the equipment driveshaft by turning the service nut to a position where the bolts are easy to remove, then remove the 3 bolts (A) and 3 washers.

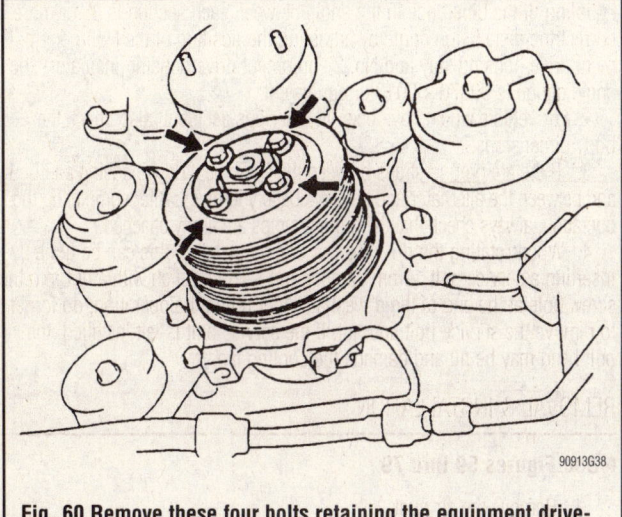

Fig. 60 Remove these four bolts retaining the equipment driveshaft pulley

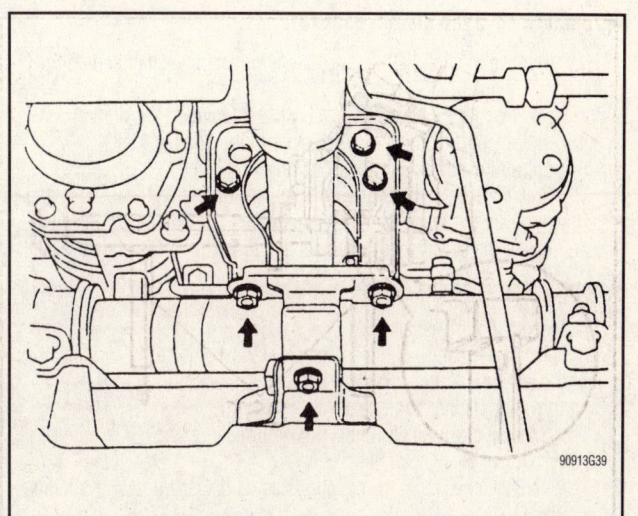

Fig. 61 Remove these bolts and nuts to extract the No. 2 equipment drive housing insulator and No. 3 housing stay

## 3-22　ENGINE AND ENGINE OVERHAUL

Fig. 62 Unbolt and extract the No. 1 intake air connector bracket

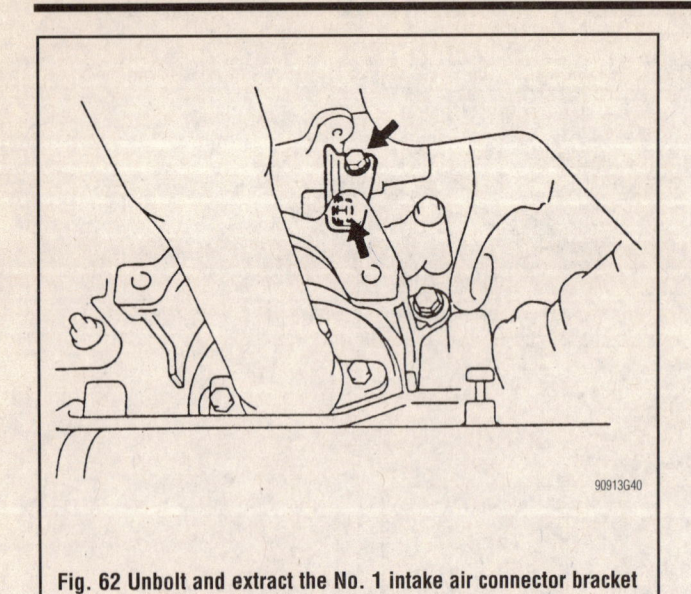

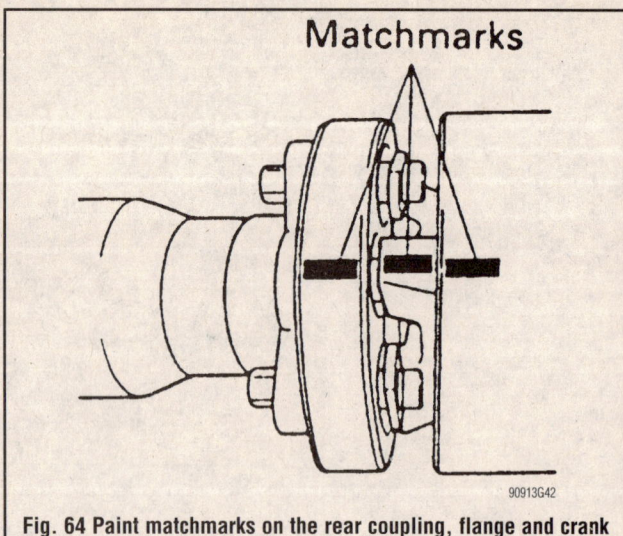

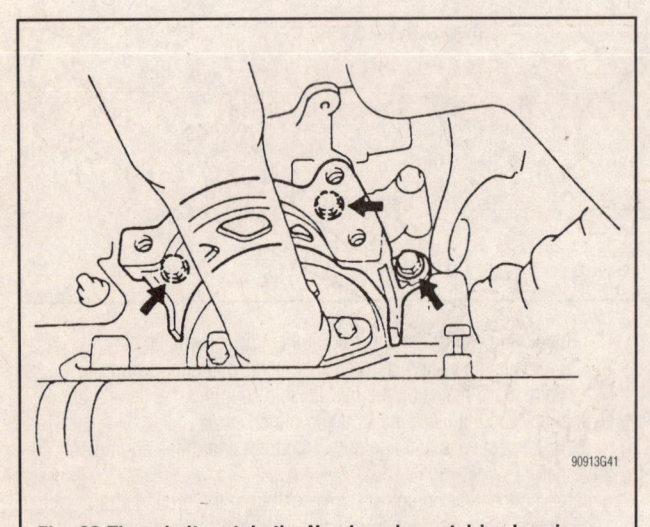

Fig. 63 Three bolts retain the No. 1 equipment drive housing stay

Fig. 64 Paint matchmarks on the rear coupling, flange and crank pulley

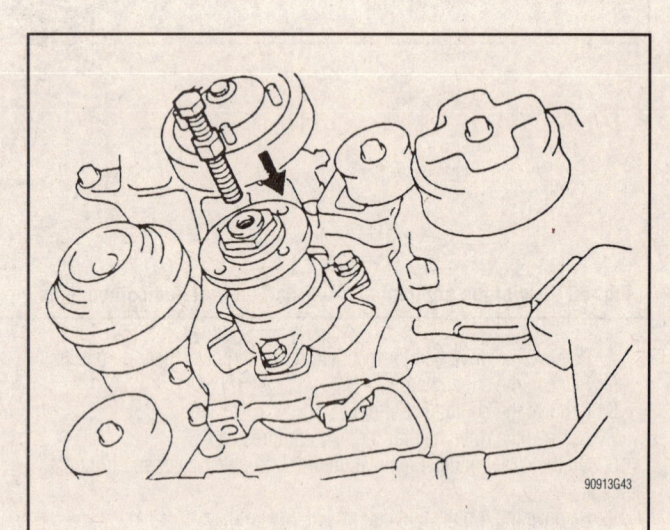

Fig. 65 Install a special service bolt and nut to the front of the driveshaft

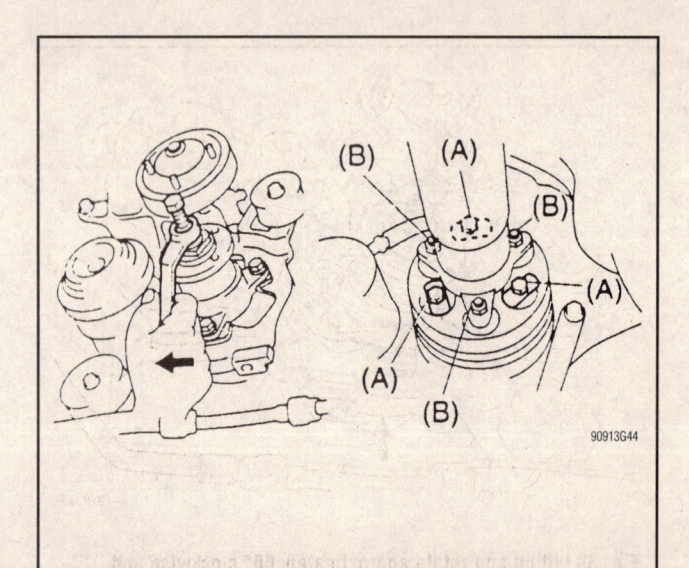

Fig. 66 Rotate the shaft and remove ONLY bolts A and washers

➡ **Do not remove the other 3 bolts (B).**

　e. Remove the 3 bolts holding the equipment driveshaft and equipment drive housing.
　f. Remove the 4 bolts and 4 plate washers holding the right and left hand equipment drive housing insulators to the body bracket.
　g. Lift up the equipment drive housing.
　h. Rotate the equipment driveshaft approximately 60° clockwise and remove it from the rear end of the equipment drive housing.
　i. Lower the equipment drive housing and set it in the body bracket.

➡ **Refer to the cautions earlier in this section.**

14. Inspect the driveshaft.
　a. Rotate the flange of the equipment driveshaft bearing and check that the equipment driveshaft bearing rotates smoothly and without any strange noise.
　b. Check the driveshaft runout, maximum should be 0.031 inch (0.8mm).
　c. Visually check that the coupling has no damage, leaks or silicone oil leakage.

# ENGINE AND ENGINE OVERHAUL  3-23

**Fig. 67 Unbolt the equipment driveshaft and drive housing**

**Fig. 68 Unbolt and extract the right and left drive housing insulators**

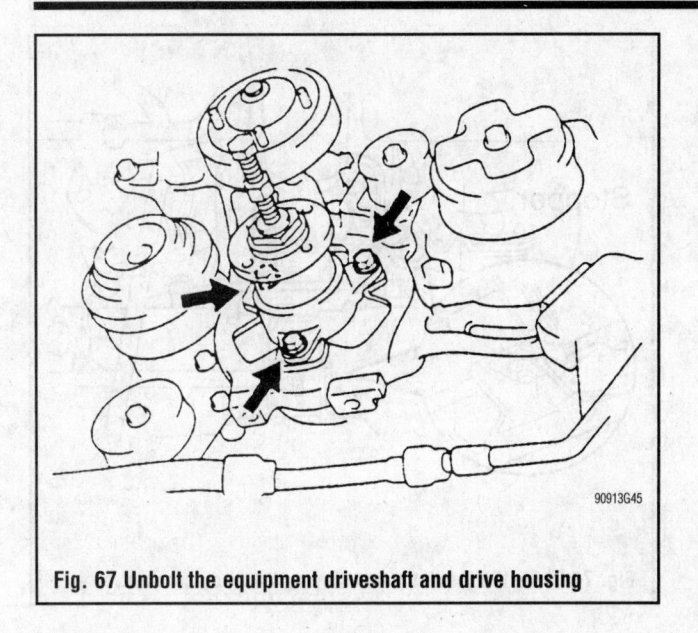

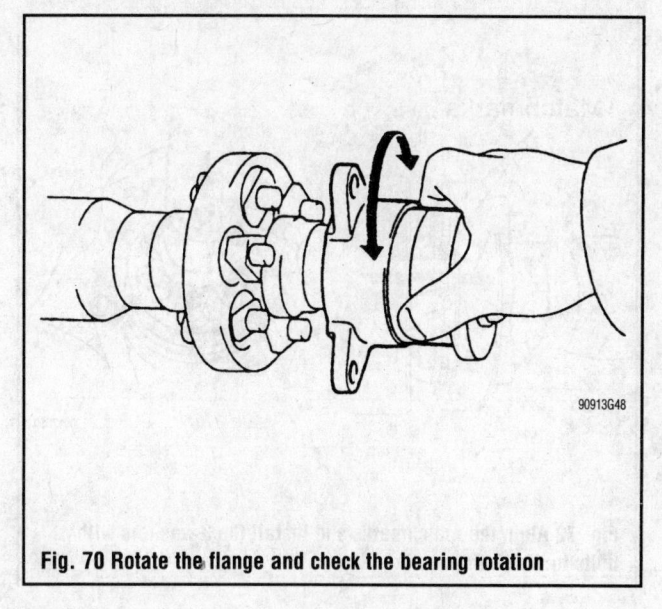

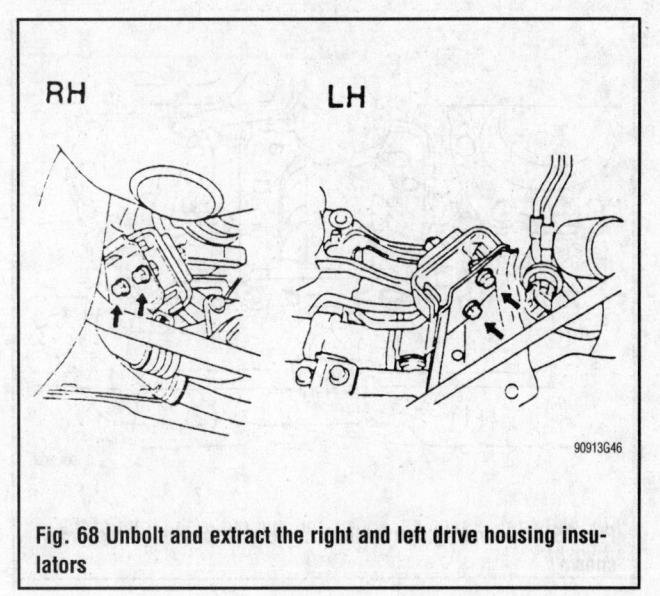

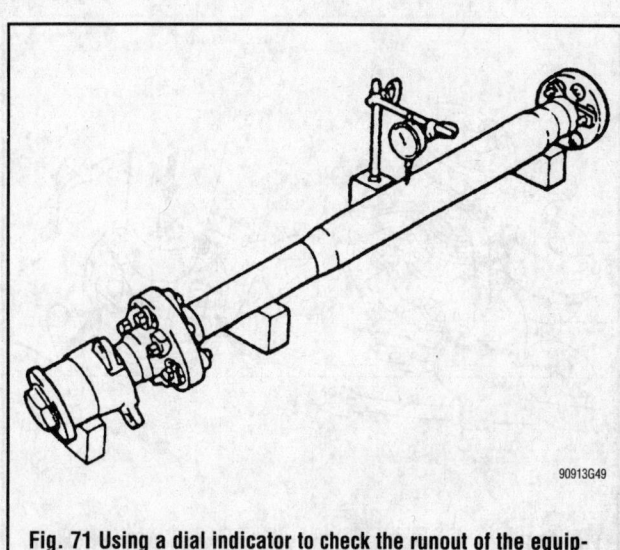

**Fig. 69 Lift up and rotate approximately 60° clockwise and remove the housing**

**Fig. 70 Rotate the flange and check the bearing rotation**

**Fig. 71 Using a dial indicator to check the runout of the equipment driveshaft**

**To install:**
15. Lift up the equipment drive housing. Insert the driveshaft through the hole at the rear of the equipment drive housing and set it to the crankshaft pulley and equipment drive housing.

   a. Align the matchmarks of the coupling and crankshaft pulley which were placed at removal. Lower the driveshaft housing. Temporarily install the 3 washers and bolts.

   b. Install and tighten the 3 bolts holding the driveshaft to the housing to 38 ft. lbs. (51 Nm).

   c. Rotate the driveshaft to the position where it is easy to tighten the 3 washers and 3 bolts on the rear side. Tighten the 3 bolts to 25 ft. lbs. (33 Nm).

   d. Remove the service bolt and nut installed on the front end of the driveshaft.

   e. Install the 4 plate washers and 4 bolts holding the right and left side No. 1 equipment drive housing insulators to the body bracket to 13 ft. lbs. (18 Nm).

   f. Connect the ground strap to the housing and tighten to 24 ft. lbs. (33 Nm).

16. Install the plate washer and nut holding the body bracket to the insulator. Tighten to 18 ft. lbs. (25 Nm).

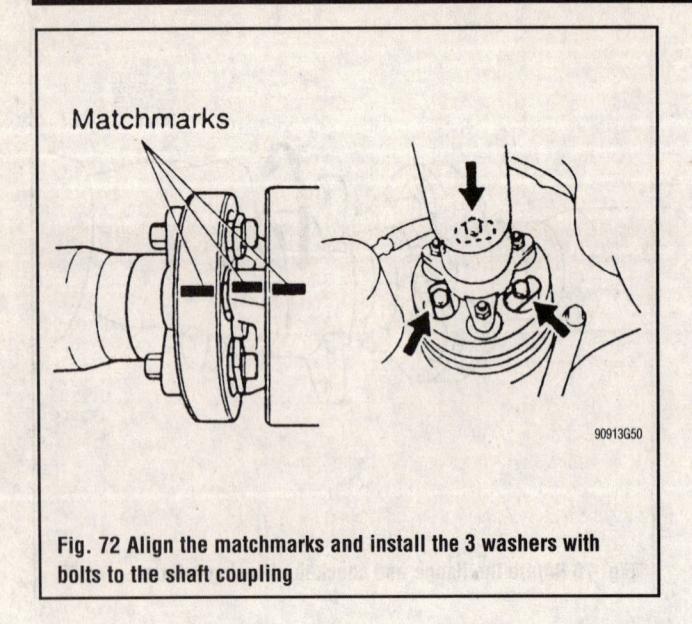

# 3-24  ENGINE AND ENGINE OVERHAUL

Fig. 72 Align the matchmarks and install the 3 washers with bolts to the shaft coupling

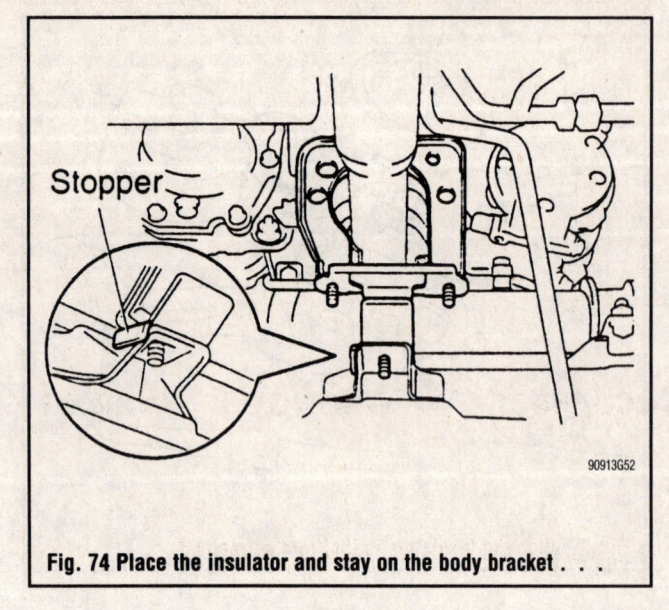

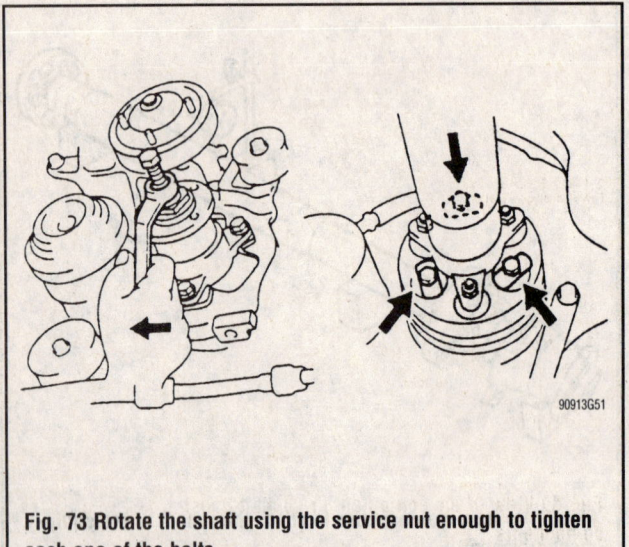

Fig. 73 Rotate the shaft using the service nut enough to tighten each one of the bolts

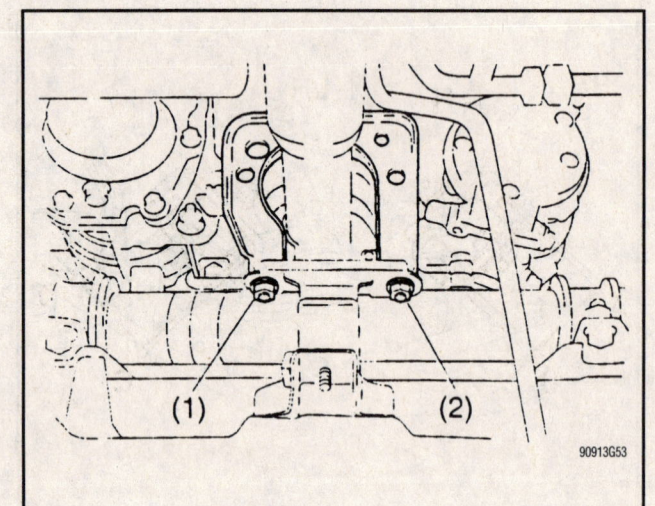

Fig. 74 Place the insulator and stay on the body bracket . . .

Fig. 75 . . . and tighten the nuts in several passes in the order shown

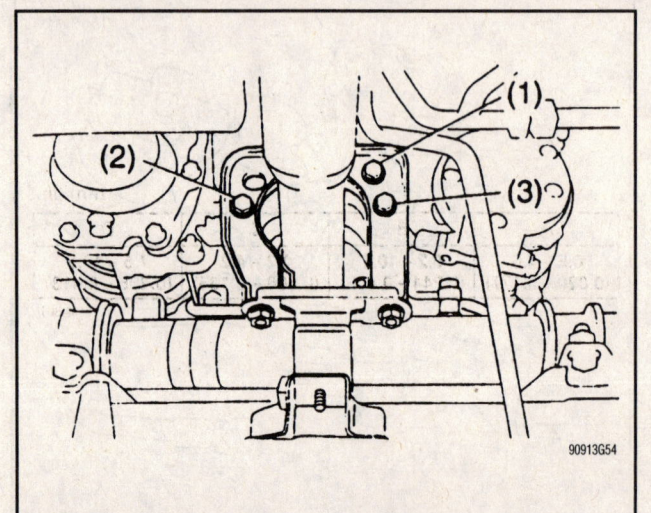

Fig. 76 Attach the No. 3 housing stay to the No. 1 housing stay and tighten in several passes in the order shown

➡ The stopper must be secured against the body bracket. The equipment driveshaft must not be twisted.

17. Check the alignment and gap of the insulators as follows:
    a. Check the insulators are correctly aligned at the front. If they are not correctly aligned, adjust the position of the insulators.
    b. Check that gaps A, B, C and D shown of the No. 1 equipment drive housing insulator are as specified.
- A—0.020–0.177 inch (0.5–4.5mm)
- B—0.0244–0.402 inch (6.2–10.2mm)
- C—0.008–0.165 inch (0.2–4.2mm)
- D—0.295–0.413 inch (7.5–10.5mm)

   c. If the gaps are not as specified, adjust the position of the insulator.
18. Check the installation angle of the driveshaft. Refer to the precautions earlier in this section.
19. Install the equipment drive pulley and tighten the bolts to 21 ft. lbs. (39 Nm).
20. On the 4WD models, install the front differential and front propeller shaft.
21. Install and adjust the A/C, supercharger, alternator/power steering pump belts.

# ENGINE AND ENGINE OVERHAUL  3-25

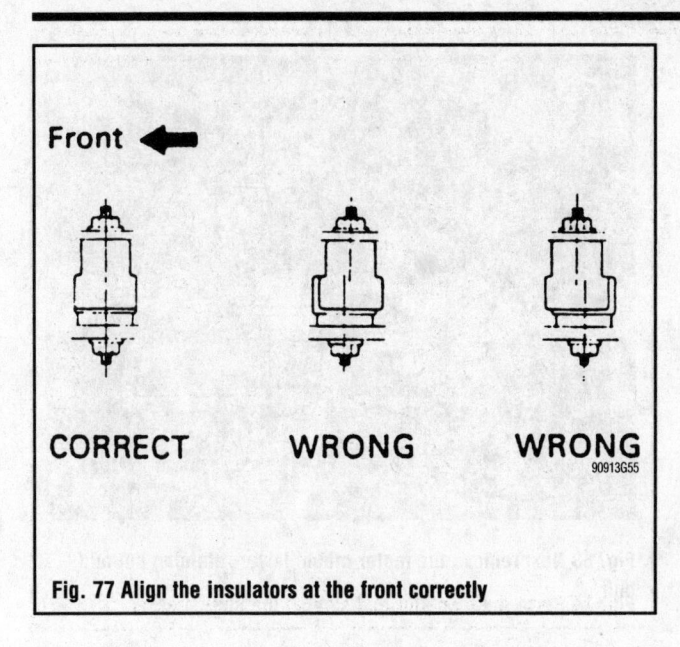

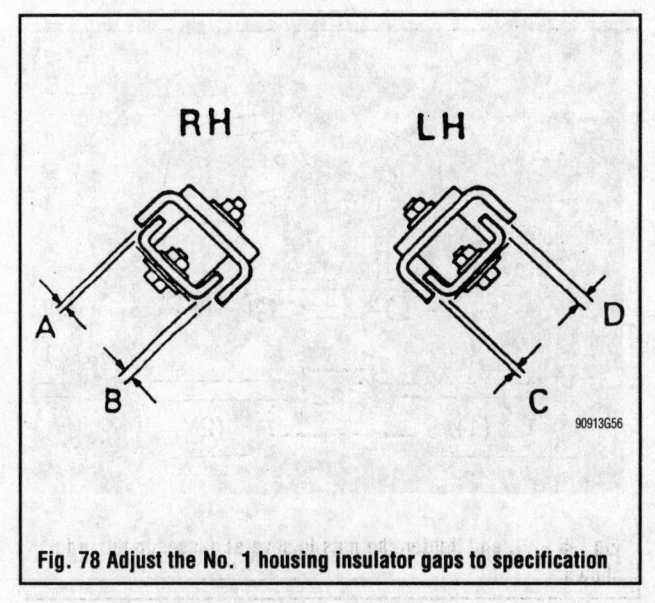

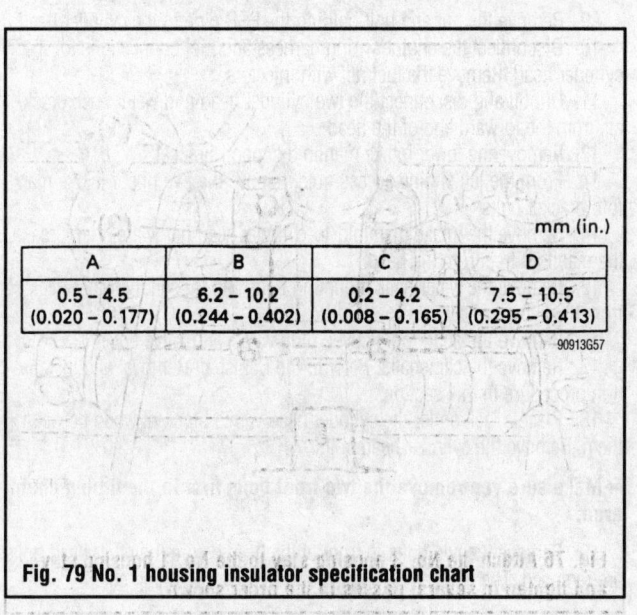

22. Install the fluid coupling with cooling fan and tighten the nuts to 10 ft. lbs. (13.5 Nm).
23. Install the No. 2 fan shroud.
24. Install the air duct.
25. Check the installation of the negative battery cable.
26. Install the No. 1 engine under cover.
27. Start the engine and check for abnormal noises or vibrations.

## Equipment Drive Housing

### REMOVAL & INSTALLATION

♦ See Figures 80 and 81

1. Remove the supercharger.
2. Remove the alternator.
3. Unbolt and extract the No. 1 idler pulley.
4. Loosen the A/C idler pulley nut and adjusting bolt, and remove the A/C drive belt. Remove the A/C idler pulley.
5. Unbolt the A/C compressor and set aside. Keep the hoses attached. Do NOT disconnect the hose.

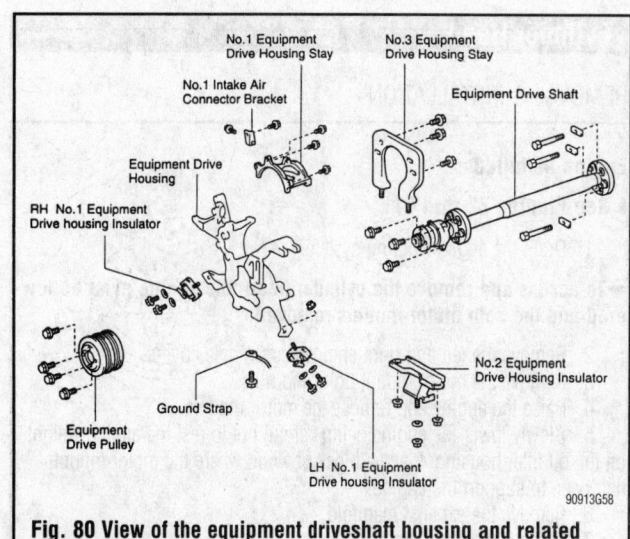

Fig. 77 Align the insulators at the front correctly

Fig. 78 Adjust the No. 1 housing insulator gaps to specification

Fig. 80 View of the equipment driveshaft housing and related components

6. On 4WD models, remove the front propeller shaft and front differential.
7. Remove the equipment driveshaft.
8. Unbolt and remove the equipment drive housing.
9. Remove the No. 1 equipment drive housing insulators.

**To install:**

10. Align the hole and knock pin when installing the drive housing insulators and secure to 18 ft. lbs. (25 Nm).
11. Install the equipment drive housing and driveshaft.
12. On the 4WD models install the front differential and front propeller shaft.
13. Position the A/C compressor and tighten the mounting bolts to 18 ft. lbs. (25 Nm).
14. Attach the A/C idler pulley and tighten the 3 bolts to 18 ft. lbs. (25 Nm).
15. Install the A/C belt and tighten the idler pulley nut to 31 ft. lbs. (43 Nm) and the adjusting bolt to 43 inch lbs. (5 Nm).
16. Attach the No. 1 idler pulley and tighten the bolts to 13 ft. lbs. 918 Nm).
17. Install and secure the alternator. Tighten the alternator bolt to 37 ft. lbs. (50 Nm) and the stay to 20 ft. lbs. (26 Nm).
18. Install the supercharger.

mm (in.)

| A | B | C | D |
| --- | --- | --- | --- |
| 0.5 – 4.5 (0.020 – 0.177) | 6.2 – 10.2 (0.244 – 0.402) | 0.2 – 4.2 (0.008 – 0.165) | 7.5 – 10.5 (0.295 – 0.413) |

Fig. 79 No. 1 housing insulator specification chart

# 3-26 ENGINE AND ENGINE OVERHAUL

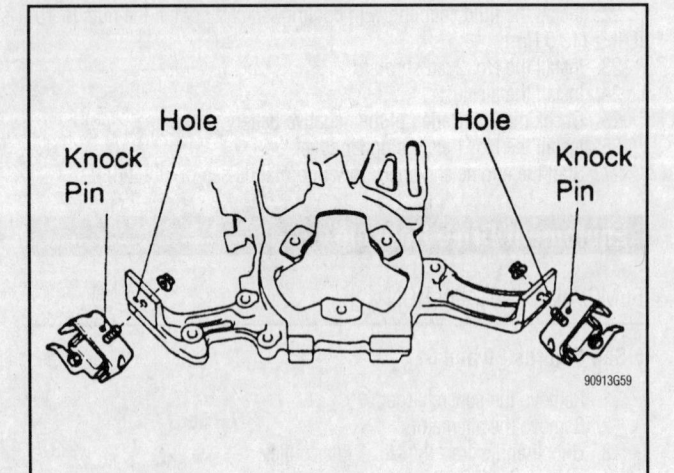

Fig. 81 Aligning the hole with the knock pin when installing the insulators

Fig. 83 Next remove the motor mount lower retaining nut and bolt

## Cylinder Head

### REMOVAL & INSTALLATION

**Engine Installed**

♦ See Figures 82 thru 91

1. Drain the engine cooling system.

→To access and remove the cylinder head, the engine must be lowered and the both motor mounts removed.

2. Remove the left and right engine access hole covers.
3. Remove the motor mount bolts and nuts.
4. Raise the engine and remove the motor mounts.
5. Slowly lower the engine being careful not to rest the engine weight on the oil filter housing. Place a block of wood where the motor mounts had been to support the engine.
6. Remove the exhaust manifold.
7. Remove the distributor.
8. Disconnect the EGR pipe bracket-to-intake manifold bolt. This bolt can be reached from the right hand access hole. Follow the EGR pipe from the cylinder head back until you find the bracket and bolt.

Fig. 82 Loosen and remove the upper mount nut

Fig. 84 Slide the mount out from between the members

9. Remove the nut and bolt holding the EGR pipe to the cylinder head.
10. Disconnect the engine wiring harness and fuel connections for the cylinder head. Remove the fuel rail with injectors.
11. Unbolt and disconnect the two cylinder head and water neck brackets from the forward end of the head.
12. Remove the lower intake manifold support bracket.
13. From the left engine access hole, remove the two upper intake manifold bracket bolts.
14. Remove the intake manifold-to-cylinder head hardware, then break the manifold free from the head.
15. Remove the water neck mounting bolts and loosen the water neck from the cylinder head.
16. Remove the spark plug cover, plug wires, and valve cover.
17. Remove the camshafts. Refer to the Camshaft Removal and Installation procedure in this section.
18. Place a jack under the cylinder head with a block of wood between them. Remove the cylinder head bolts.

→Make sure you remove the two front bolts first in the timing chain area.

19. Remove the two bolts in front of the head before the other head bolts are removed. The two bolts are located in front of the timing chain.

# ENGINE AND ENGINE OVERHAUL 3-27

20. Uniformly remove the head bolts following the sequence.

➡ The cylinder head is positioned on the engine sideways and is very heavy. Be careful not to drop the head during removal. It is advised to have an assistant ready to help.

21. Pull the cylinder head from the dowels on the cylinder block.
22. Remove the cylinder head gasket.

**To install:**

➡ Always clean and inspect the cylinder head and mating surface for cracks and flatness when removed.

23. Clean the gasket mating surfaces and check for warpage.
24. Apply seal packing to two locations on the cylinder block as shown.
25. Install the head gasket and cylinder head.
26. If the camshaft timing gear was removed, align the matchmarks placed on the timing gear and chain during removal.
27. Place the cylinder head in position on the gasket.
28. Oil the bolts and using the proper sequence, tighten the bolts in 3 steps.
    a. Uniformly tighten the head bolts to 29 ft. lbs. (39 Nm).
    b. Mark the front of the cylinder head bolt with paint.

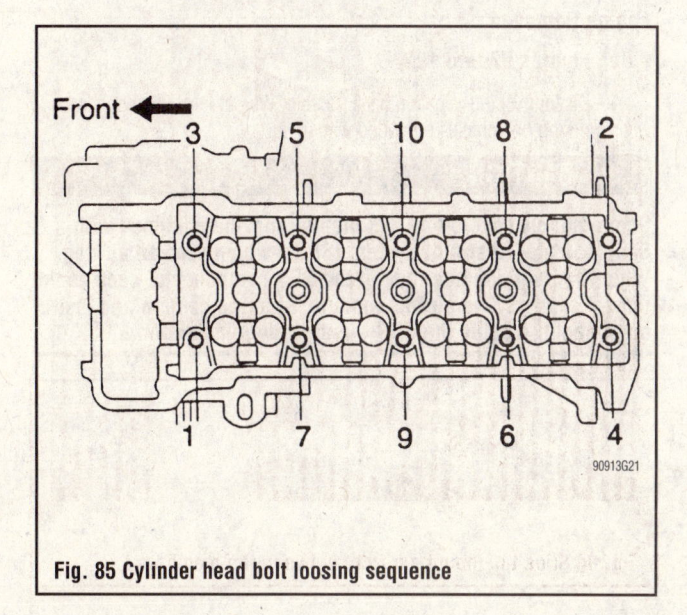

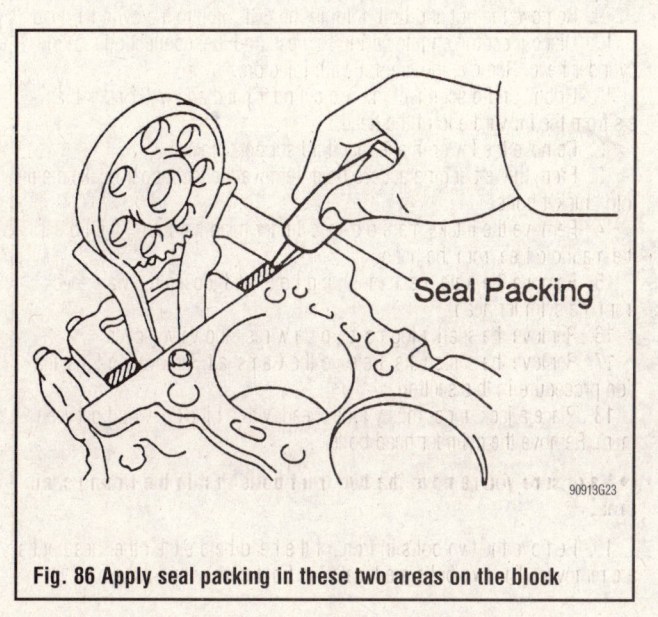

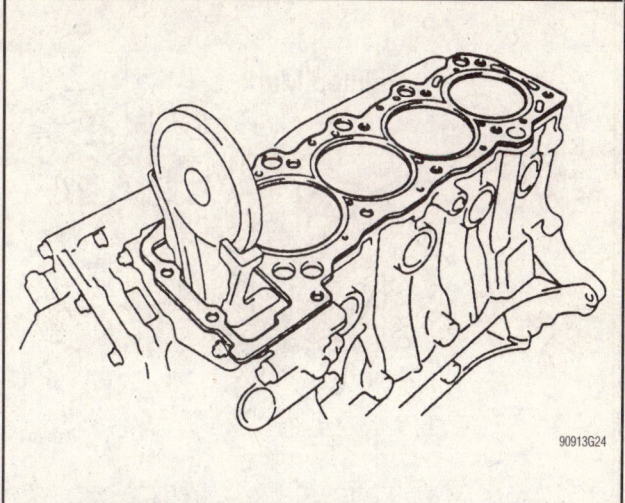

Fig. 87 Place the head gasket in the correct position on the block

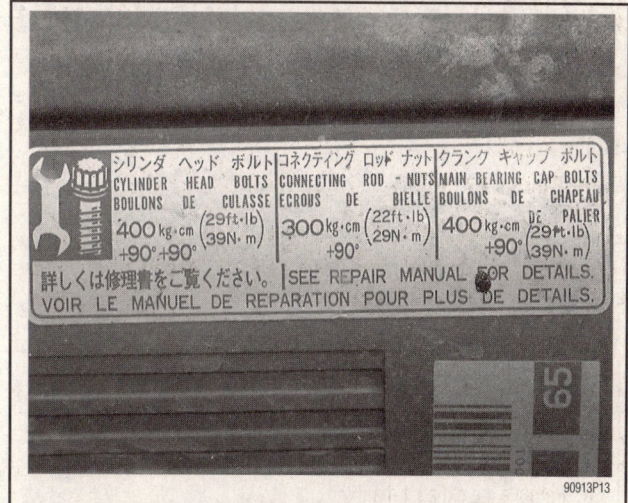

Fig. 85 Cylinder head bolt loosing sequence

Fig. 88 Tightening specifications can be found on a label located on the No. 2 cylinder head cover

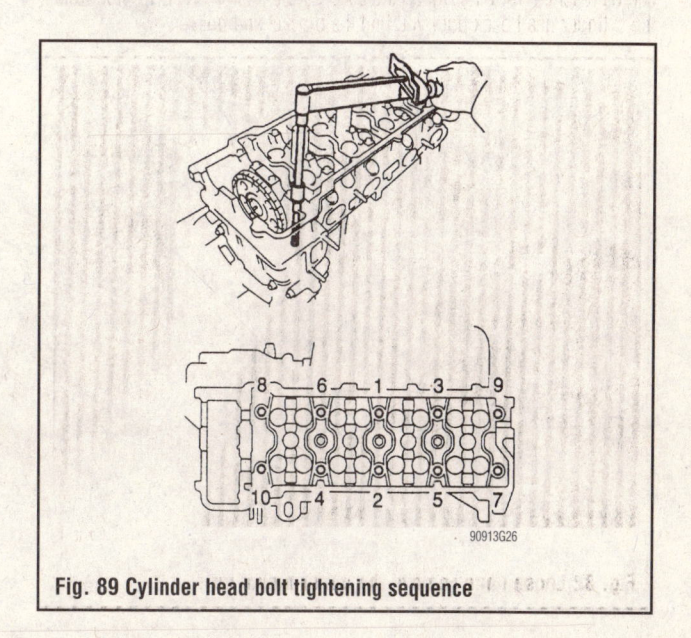

Fig. 86 Apply seal packing in these two areas on the block

Fig. 89 Cylinder head bolt tightening sequence

# 3-28 ENGINE AND ENGINE OVERHAUL

**Fig. 90 Mark the front of the head bolt with paint**

**Fig. 91 Retighten the head bolts 90° in the order shown**

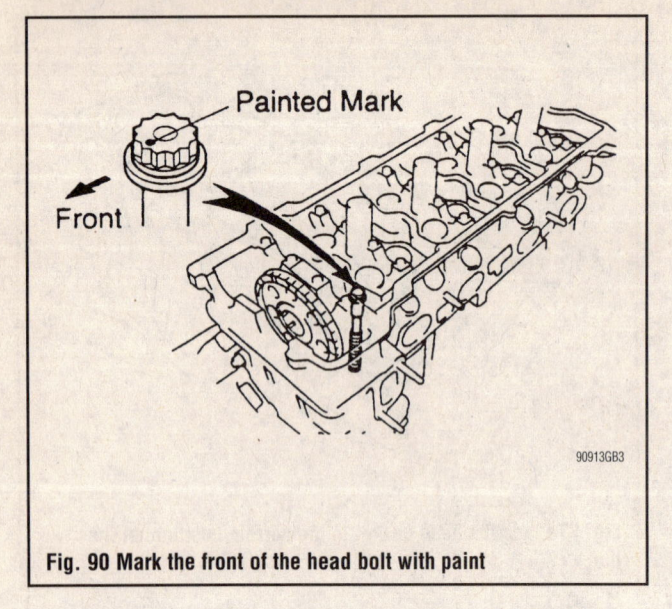

    c. Retighten the cylinder head bolts 90° in the numerical order as shown.
    d. Check that the painted mark is now facing sideward.
    e. Retighten the cylinder head bolts an additional 90°.
    f. Check that the painted mark is now facing rearward.
29. Install and tighten the 2 front mounting bolts to 15 ft. lbs. (21 Nm).
30. Install the camshafts.
31. Install all remaining components.
32. Fill the cooling system and fill the engine with oil.
33. Connect the battery cable, start the engine, and check for leaks.
34. Road test the vehicle for proper operation and recheck all fluid levels.

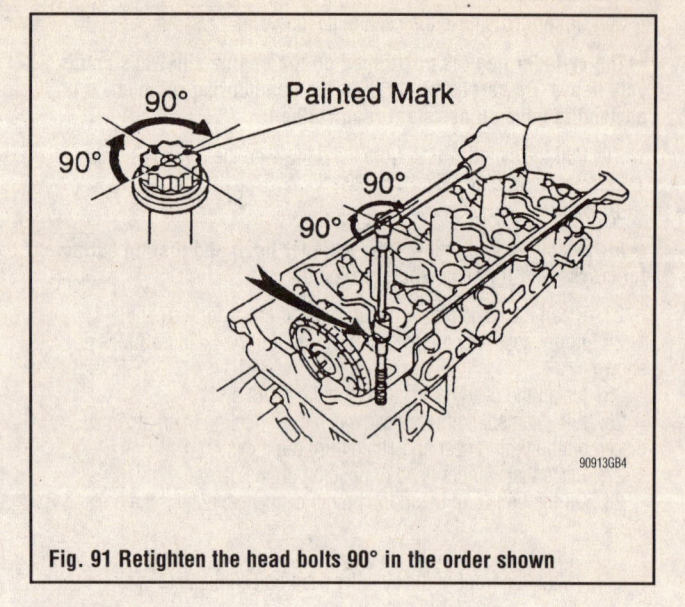

### Engine Removed

♦ See Figures 92 thru 102

1. Disconnect the negative battery cable. Wait at least 90 seconds when working on vehicles equipped with an airbag.

### ❊❊ CAUTION

**Some models covered by this manual may be equipped with a Supplemental Restraint System (SRS), which uses an air bag. Whenever working near any of the SRS components, such as the impact sensors, the air bag module, steering column and instrument panel, disable the SRS, as described in Section 6.**

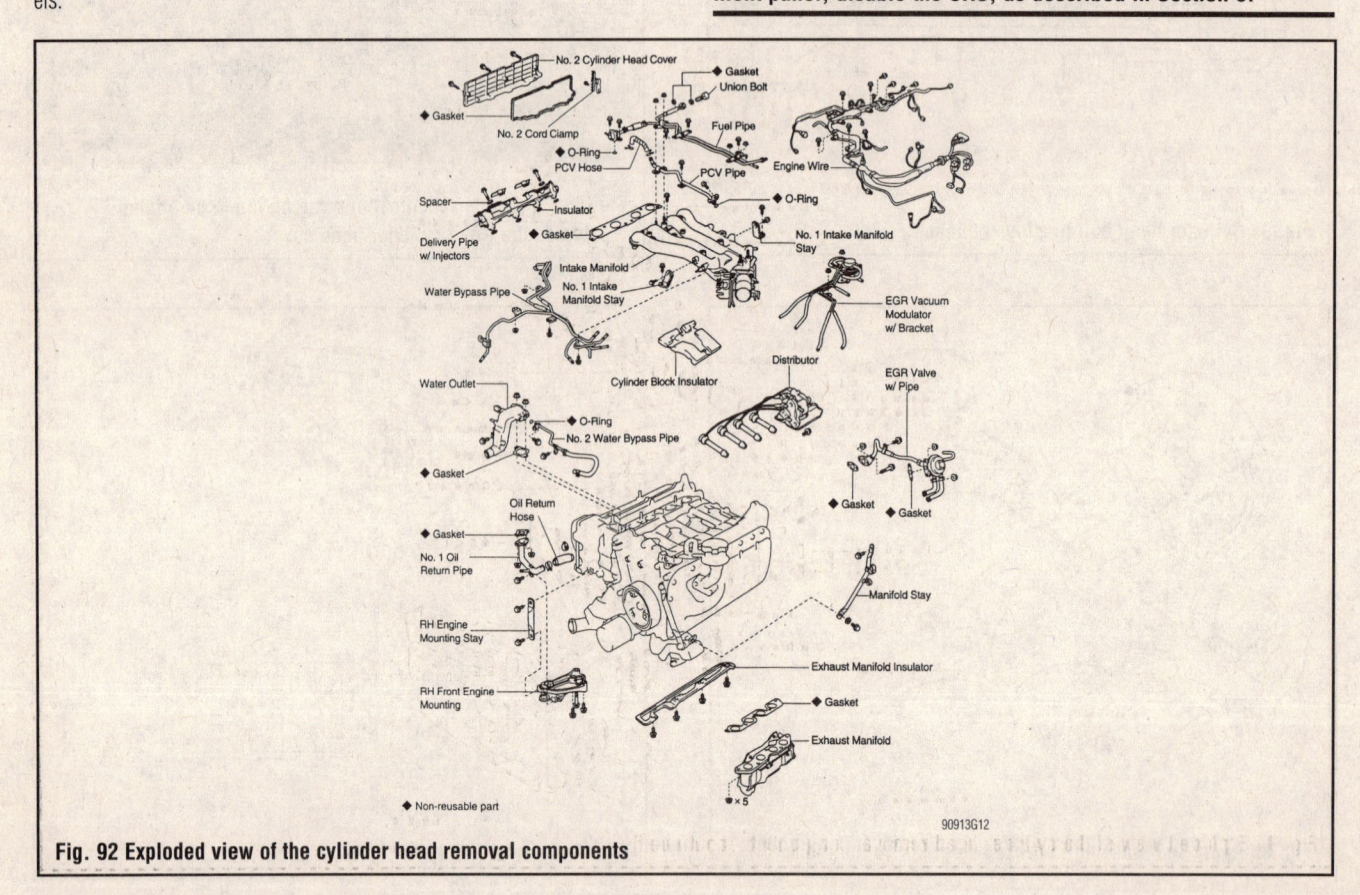

**Fig. 92 Exploded view of the cylinder head removal components**

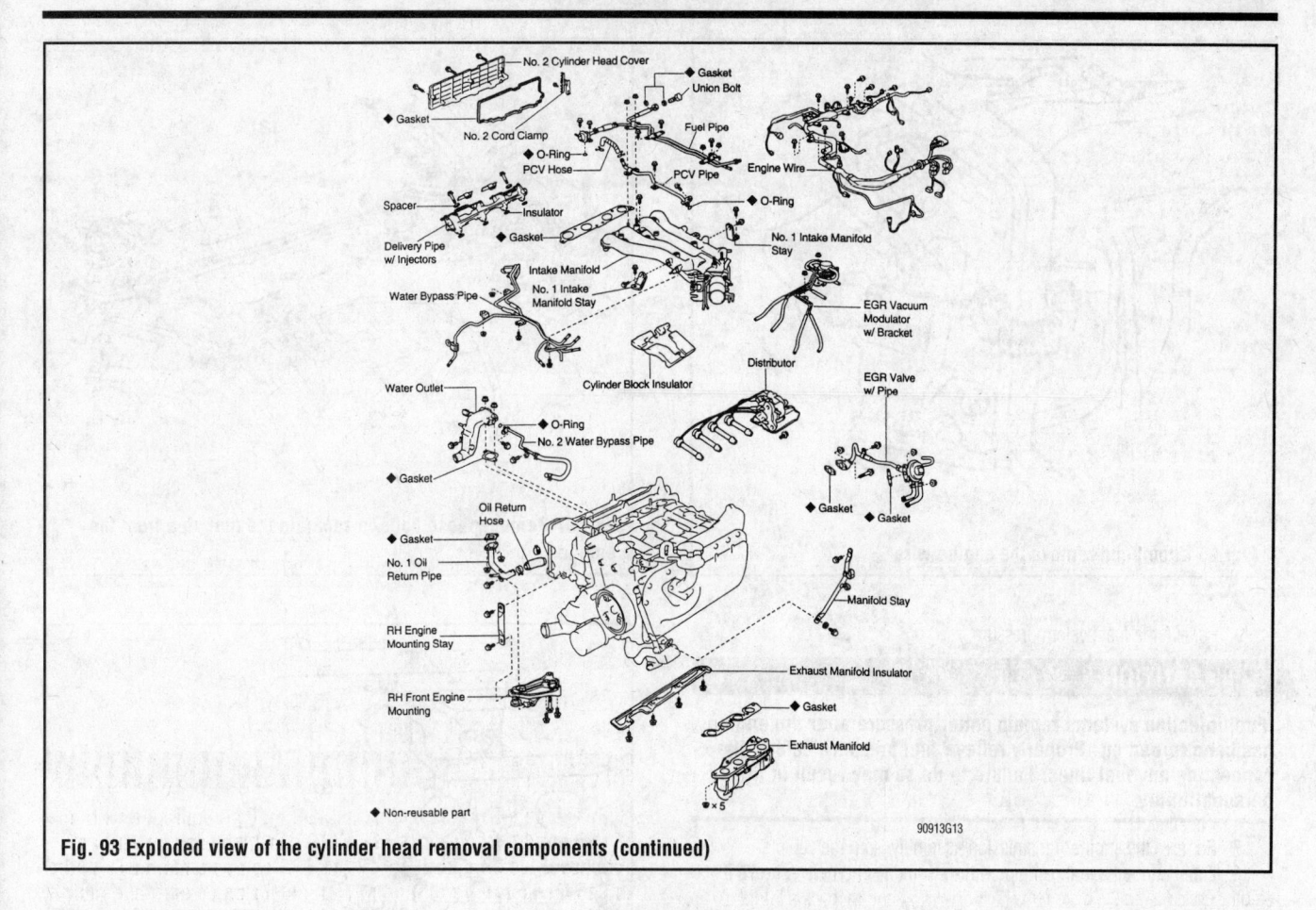

# ENGINE AND ENGINE OVERHAUL    3-29

Fig. 93 Exploded view of the cylinder head removal components (continued)

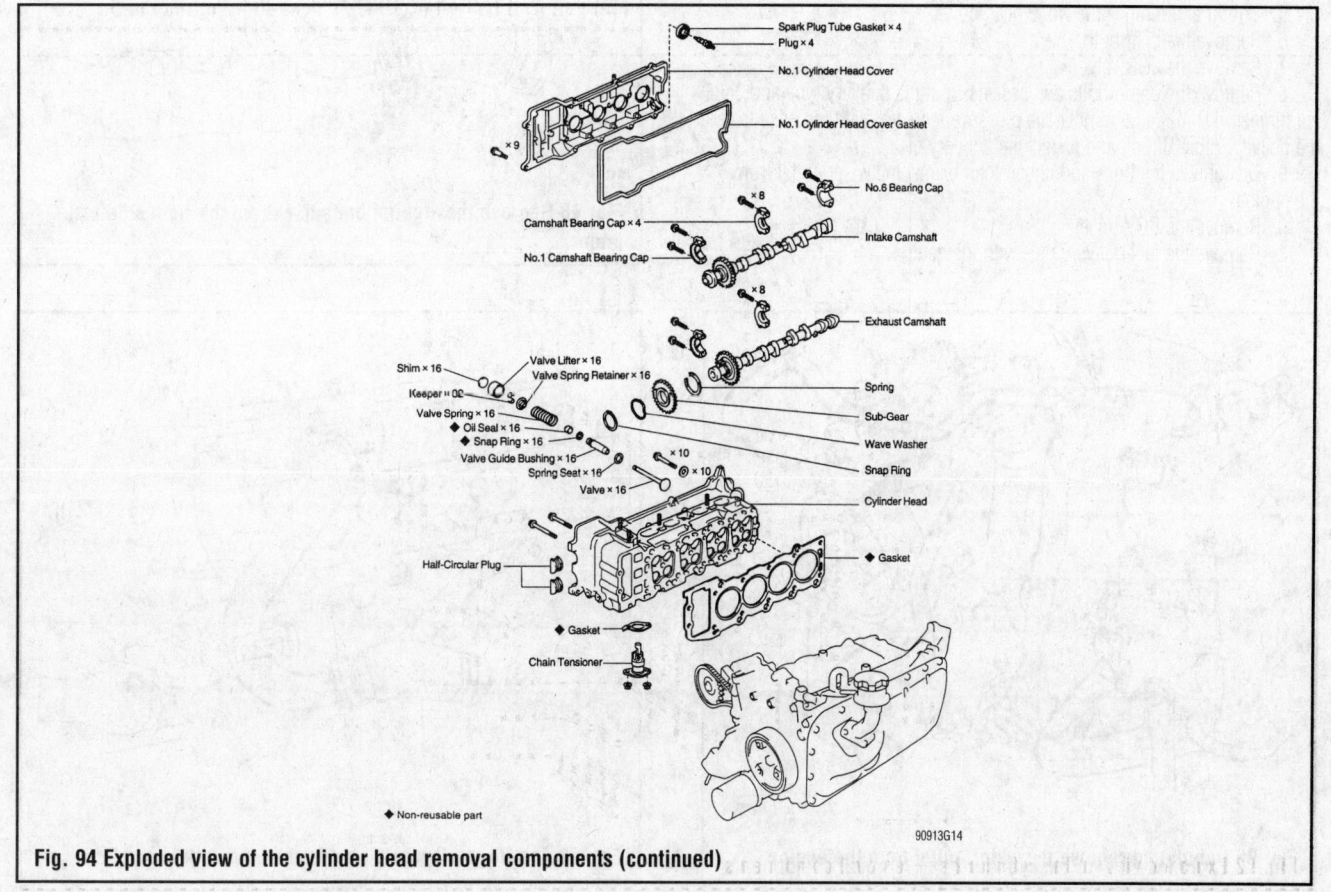

Fig. 94 Exploded view of the cylinder head removal components (continued)

## 3-30 ENGINE AND ENGINE OVERHAUL

**Fig. 95 Unbolt and remove the engine wire**

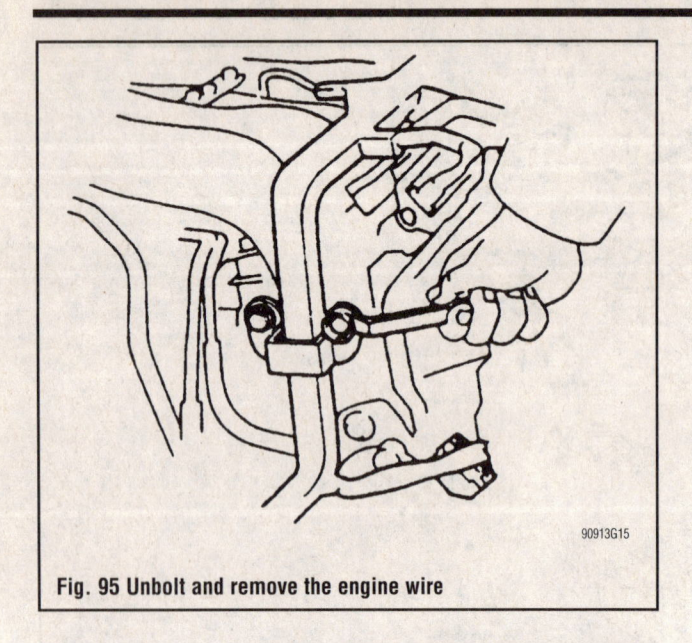

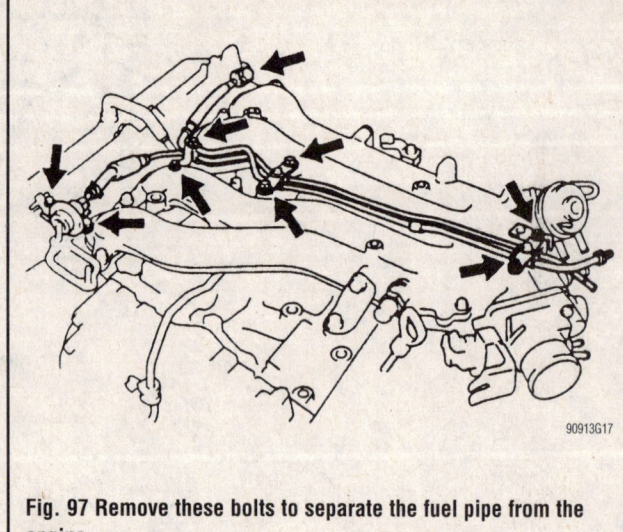

2. Relieve the fuel system pressure.

> ※※ **CAUTION**
>
> Fuel injection systems remain under pressure after the engine has been turned off. Properly relieve fuel pressure before disconnecting any fuel lines. Failure to do so may result in fire or personal injury.

3. Remove the engine/transmission assembly from the vehicle.
4. Label and remove the engine wiring from the engine and move it aside.
5. Unbolt and remove the No. 2 head cover.
6. Remove the distributor.
7. Remove the EGR valve.
8. Remove the union bolts and gaskets from the delivery pipe and cold start injector. Unbolt and remove the pressure regulator with the hose from the delivery pipe. Unbolt and extract the delivery pipe.
9. Disconnect the hose and unbolt then extract the water outlet from the engine.
10. Remove the PCV hose.
11. Remove the fuel delivery pipe with insulators.

**Fig. 96 Unbolt and remove the water outlet from the engine**

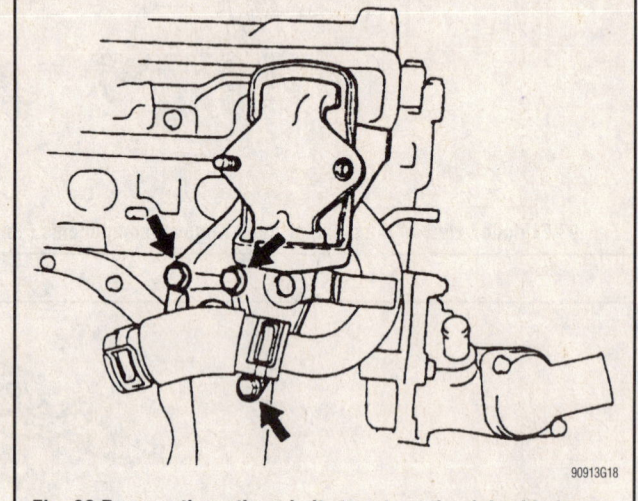

**Fig. 97 Remove these bolts to separate the fuel pipe from the engine**

**Fig. 98 Remove these three bolts to extract the right side insulator**

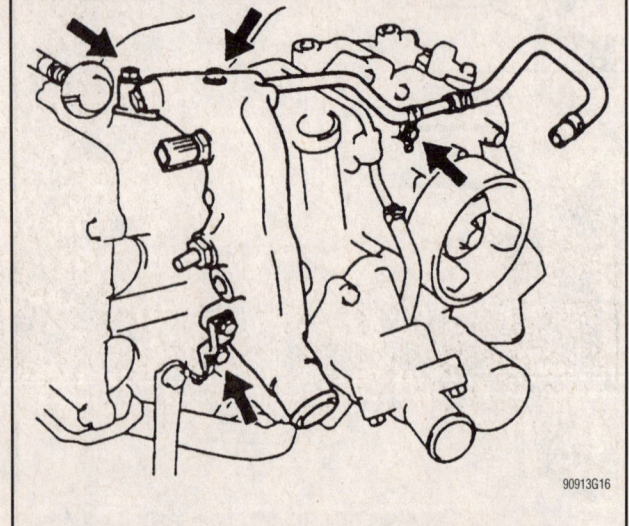

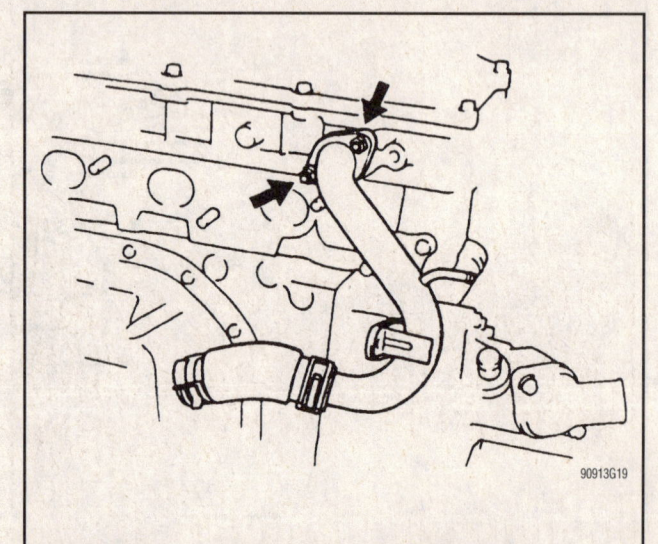

**Fig. 99 The No. 1 oil return pipe is retained with two bolts**

# ENGINE AND ENGINE OVERHAUL 3-31

12. Remove the intake manifold.
13. Remove the right side engine mounting.
14. Remove the exhaust manifold and heat insulator.
15. Remove the No. 1 oil return pipe.
16. Remove the No. 1 cylinder head cover and half moons.
17. See the procedure under Camshaft Removal and Installation and remove the camshafts.
18. Remove the 2 bolts in front of the head before the other head bolts are removed.
19. Using a 12 sided socket wrench, remove the 10 cylinder head retaining bolts in the proper sequence.
20. Remove the cylinder head from the block as follows:
    a. Remove the two bolts in front of the head before the other head bolts are removed. The two bolts are located in front of the timing chain.
    b. Uniformly remove the 10 head bolts in the reverse of the torque sequence.
    c. Pull the cylinder head from the dowels on the cylinder block.
    d. If the head is difficult to remove, pry with a suitable tool between the head and block surfaces
    e. Remove the cylinder head gasket.

To install:

→Always clean and inspect the cylinder head and mating surface for cracks and flatness when removed.

21. Clean the gasket mating surfaces and check for warpage.
22. Apply seal packing to two locations on the cylinder block as shown.
23. Install the head gasket and cylinder head.
24. If the camshaft timing gear was removed, align the matchmarks placed on the timing gear and chain during removal.
25. Place the cylinder head in position on the gasket.
26. Oil the bolts and using the proper sequence, tighten the bolts in 3 steps.
    a. Uniformly tighten the head bolts to 29 ft. lbs. (39 Nm).
    b. Mark the front of the cylinder head bolt with paint.
    c. Retighten the cylinder head bolts 90° in the numerical order as shown.
    d. Check that the painted mark is now facing sideward.
    e. Retighten the cylinder head bolts an additional 90°.
    f. Check that the painted mark is now facing rearward.
27. Install and tighten the 2 front mounting bolts to 15 ft. lbs. (21 Nm).
28. See the procedure under Camshaft Removal and Installation and install the camshafts.

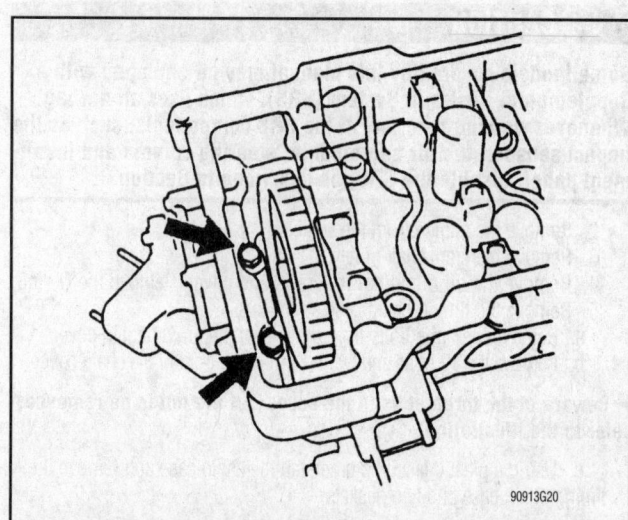

Fig. 100 Remove these two bolts in the front of the head before the others

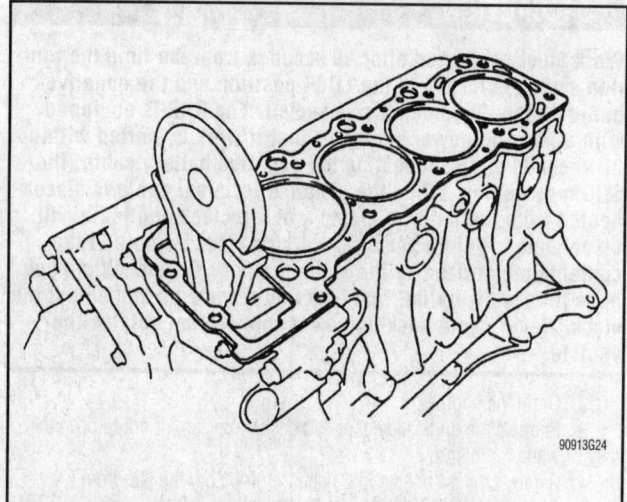

Fig. 102 Place the head gasket in the correct position on the block

29. Install all remaining components.
30. Install the engine/transmission assembly into the vehicle.
31. Fill the cooling system and fill the engine with oil.
32. Connect the battery cable, start the engine, and check for leaks.
33. Road test the vehicle for proper operation and recheck all fluid levels.

## Oil Pan

### REMOVAL & INSTALLATION

▶ See Figure 103

→This engine has 2 oil pans. If the crankshaft is going to be serviced, the side crankcase pan has to be removed. If the oil pump sump is going to be serviced, the bottom oil pan has to be removed.

1. Disconnect the negative battery cable. Wait at least 90 seconds after the negative battery cable is disconnected before performing work on models equipped with an airbag.

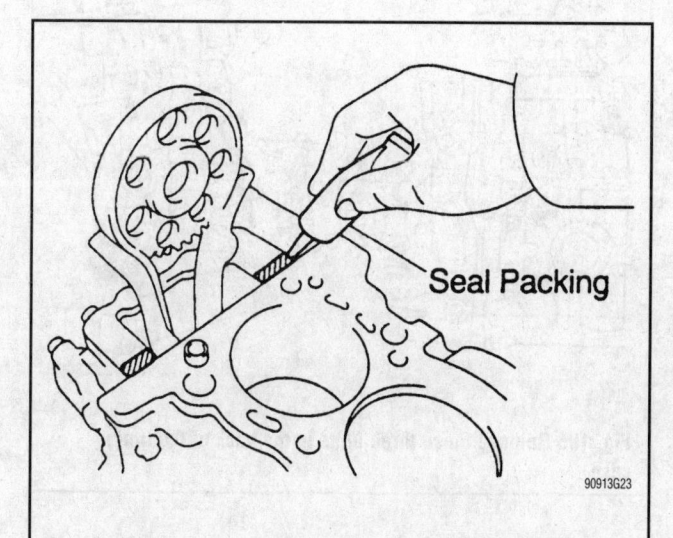

Fig. 101 Apply seal packing in these two areas on the block

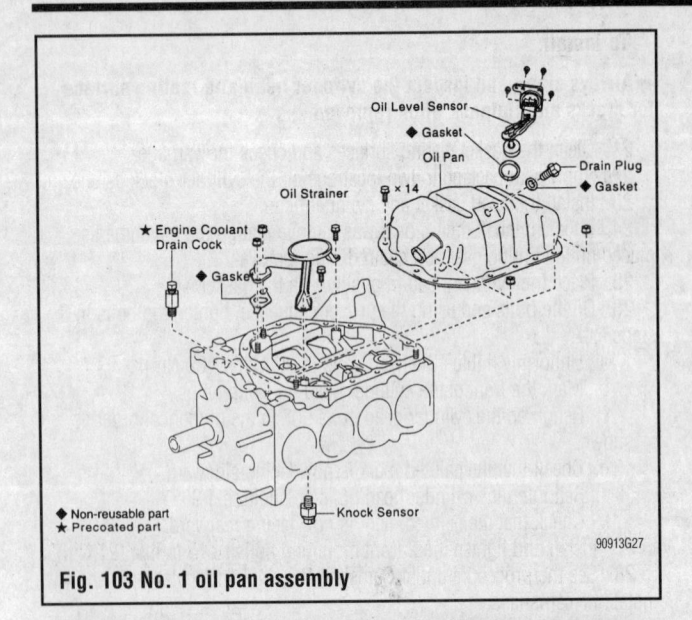

# 3-32 ENGINE AND ENGINE OVERHAUL

Fig. 103 No. 1 oil pan assembly

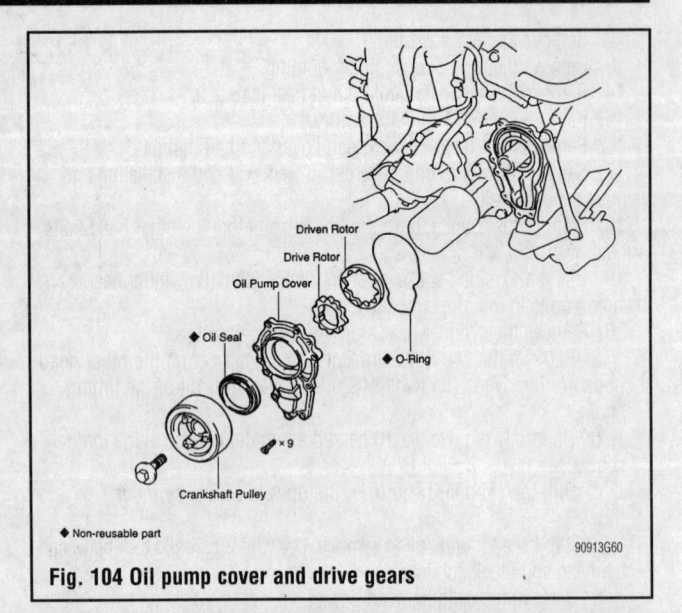

Fig. 104 Oil pump cover and drive gears

### ✱✱ CAUTION

Work must be started after 90 seconds from the time the ignition switch is turned to the LOCK position and the negative battery cable has been disconnected. The SRS is equipped with a back-up power source so that if work is started within 90 seconds of disconnecting the negative battery cable, the SRS may deploy. When the negative terminal cable is disconnected from the battery, memory of the clock and radio will be canceled. Before you start working, make a note of the contents memorized by the audio memory system. When you have finished working, reset the audio systems and adjust the clock. Never use a back-up power supply from outside the vehicle.

  2. Drain the engine oil.
  3. Remove the oil level sensor and gasket. Be careful not to drop the sensor when removing.
  4. Remove the 14 bolts and 2 nuts. Carefully pry the pan from the engine, being careful not to damage the flange.

**To install:**
  5. Before installing, thoroughly clean the gasket mating surfaces. Apply gasket sealer 08826-00080 or equivalent, to the pan and assembly within 5 minutes.
  6. Install the pan and tighten the bolts and nuts to 48 inch lbs. (5 Nm).
  7. Install the gasket, oil sensor and tighten to 9 ft. lbs. (13 Nm).
  8. Install the remaining components.
  9. Refill the engine with oil.
  10. Connect the negative battery cable. Start the engine and check for leaks.

## Oil Pump

### REMOVAL & INSTALLATION

♦ See Figures 104, 105, 106, 107 and 108

  1. Disconnect the negative battery cable. Wait at least 90 seconds after the negative battery cable is disconnected before performing work on models equipped with an airbag.

### ✱✱ CAUTION

Some models covered by this manual may be equipped with a Supplemental Restraint System (SRS), which uses an air bag. Whenever working near any of the SRS components, such as the impact sensors, the air bag module, steering column and instrument panel, disable the SRS, as described in Section 6.

  2. Remove the engine from the vehicle.
  3. Remove the crankshaft pulley.
  4. Remove the oil pump cover screws and cover. Remove the O-ring.
  5. Remove the timing chain case as follows:
    a. Remove the three bolts from the rear of the timing chain cover.
    b. Remove the 12 bolts and two nuts from the front of the chain cover.

➡ Beware of the three bolts in the cover that are not to be removed, refer to the illustration.

    c. Using a plastic faced hammer, tap the chain case and remove the timing chain case and two gaskets.

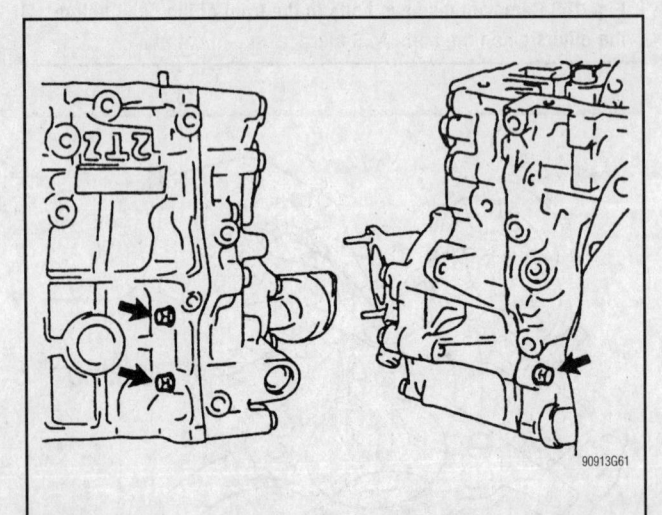

Fig. 105 Remove these three bolts in the back of the timing case

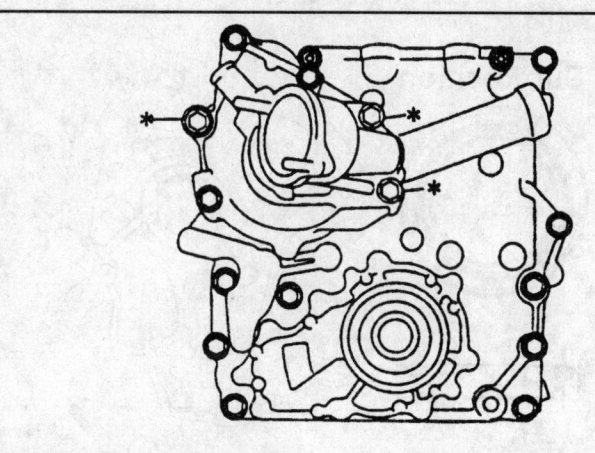

# ENGINE AND ENGINE OVERHAUL  3-33

**Fig. 106 Remove only these twelve bolts not the other three shown**

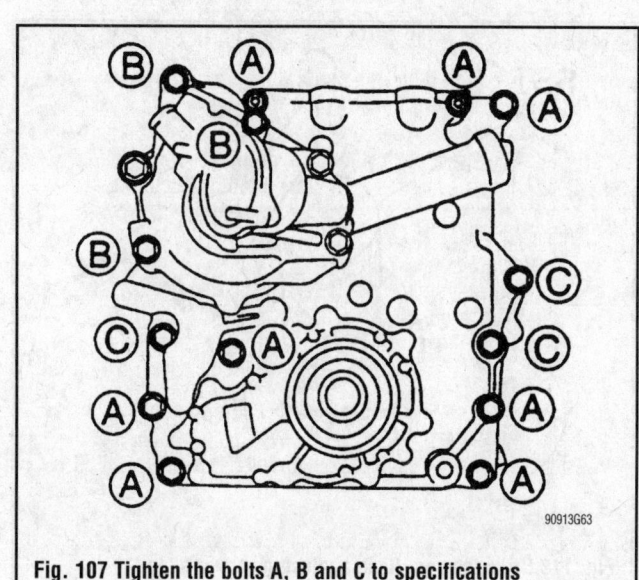

\* Do Not Remove

**Fig. 107 Tighten the bolts A, B and C to specifications**

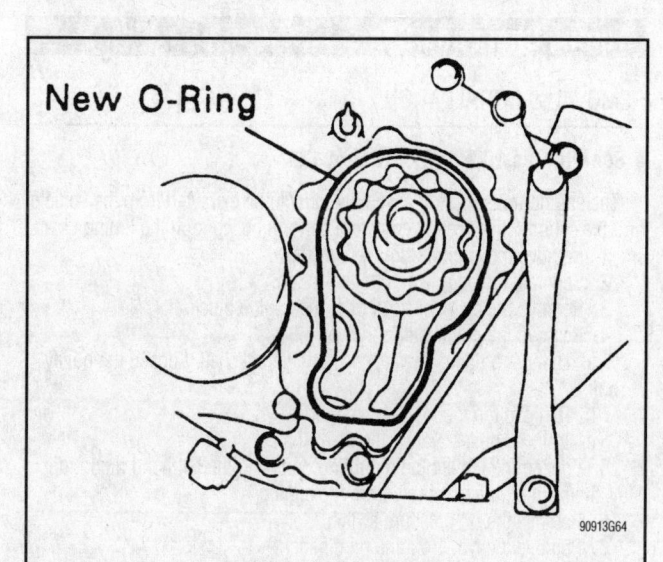

**Fig. 108 Replace the old O-ring if it has not been done before**

New O-Ring

**To install:**
6. Install the timing chain case as follows:
   a. Clean the gasket surface for the timing chain case.
   b. Install two new gaskets over the dowels.
   c. Slide on the chain case over the dowels.
   d. Install the bolts and nuts and tighten the bolts as follows:
   • A to 14 ft. lbs. (20 Nm)
   • B to 21 ft. lbs. (28 Nm)
   • C to 32 ft. lbs. (44 Nm)
   e. Install and tighten the three chain case bolts (rear) to 13 ft. lbs. (18 Nm).
7. Place a new O-ring into the groove of the timing chain case.
8. Install the oil pump cover. Tighten the screws to 8 ft. lbs. (10 Nm).
9. Install the crankshaft pulley.
10. Install the engine.
11. Connect the negative battery cable. Road test the vehicle for proper operation.

## Timing Chain Cover and Seal

### REMOVAL & INSTALLATION

1. Disconnect the negative battery cable. Wait at least 90 seconds after the negative battery cable is disconnected before performing work on models equipped with an airbag.

**✲✲ CAUTION**

**Some models covered by this manual may be equipped with a Supplemental Restraint System (SRS), which uses an air bag. Whenever working near any of the SRS components, such as the impact sensors, the air bag module, steering column and instrument panel, disable the SRS, as described in Section 6.**

2. Remove the engine from the vehicle.
3. Remove the cylinder head from the engine.
4. Remove the crankshaft pulley and damper.
5. Unbolt and remove the left engine mounting.
6. Remove the oil pressure switch and engine ventilation case.
7. Extract the engine oil dipstick. Remove the No. 2 engine hanger.
8. If equipped, remove the crankshaft position sensor.
9. Remove the 16 bolts and 2 nuts retaining the oil pan. To separate, insert a pry tool and carefully tap it with a brass bar.
10. Remove the No. 2 oil dipstick guide and oil baffle plate.
11. Remove the 3 bolts and oil filter bracket from the timing cover.
12. Remove the 12 bolts, 2 nuts and timing cover.

➡ There are 3 bolts located in back of the cover. Be careful not to damage the mating surfaces during removal.

**To install:**
13. Before installing, clean all gasket surfaces and check for warpage.
14. Install the timing chain cover using a new gasket. Tighten the following bolts:
   • A—14 ft. lbs. (21 Nm)
   • B—21 ft. lbs. (28 Nm)
   • C—32 ft. lbs. (43 Nm)
15. Install the oil filter bracket and tighten to 14 ft. lbs. (21 Nm).
16. Install the crankcase baffle plate, oil pan, No. 1 dipstick tube guide and ventilation case. Tighten the baffle plate to 43 inch lbs. (5 Nm), oil pan bolts to 9 ft. lbs. (13 Nm), ventilation case to 69 inch lbs. (8 Nm) and the No. 1 dipstick tube guide to 22 ft. lbs. (29 Nm).
17. Attach the No. 2 engine hanger to the block and tighten to 27 ft. lbs. (37 Nm).
18. Install the engine oil dipstick and secure.

## 3-34 ENGINE AND ENGINE OVERHAUL

19. Install the oil pressure switch, left engine mount and stay. Tighten the left engine mount bolts to 30 ft. lbs. (41 Nm) and stay bolts to 27 ft. lbs. (37 Nm).
20. Install the crankshaft pulley and tighten the bolt to 192 ft. lbs. (260 Nm).
21. Install the cylinder head and engine assembly into the vehicle.
22. Install the remaining components and check for leaks.

### SEAL REPLACEMENT

◆ See Figures 109, 110, 111 and 112

There are two methods of replacing the oil seal depending on weather the oil pump cover is assembled to the engine or not.

If the oil pump is not installed to the timing chain case, use a flatbladed tool and rag to pry the old seal out. Apply multipurpose grease to the new oil seal lip. Using a seal installer, tap the seal into place.

If the oil pump is installed on the timing chain case, use a knife to cut off the lip of the seal and pry it out. Check the oil seal lip contact surface of the crankshaft for cracks or damage. Apply multi-purpose grease to the new oil seal lip. Using a seal installer, drive the new seal flush against the cover edge.

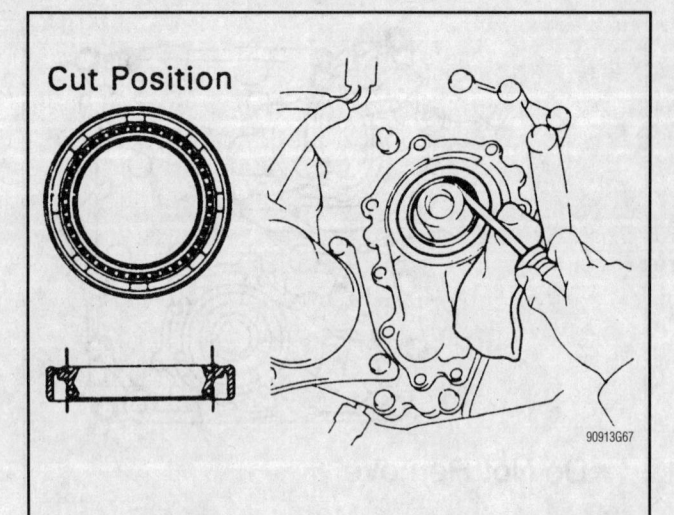

Fig. 111 Carefully cut off the oil seal lip, then pry the seal from the cover

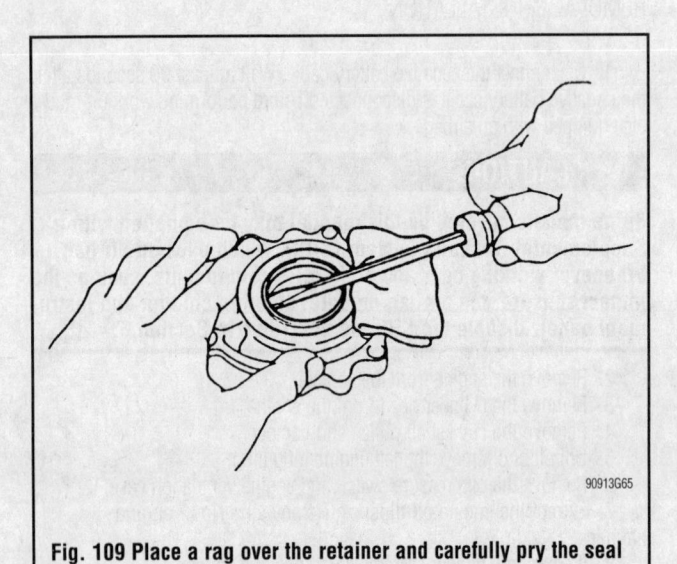

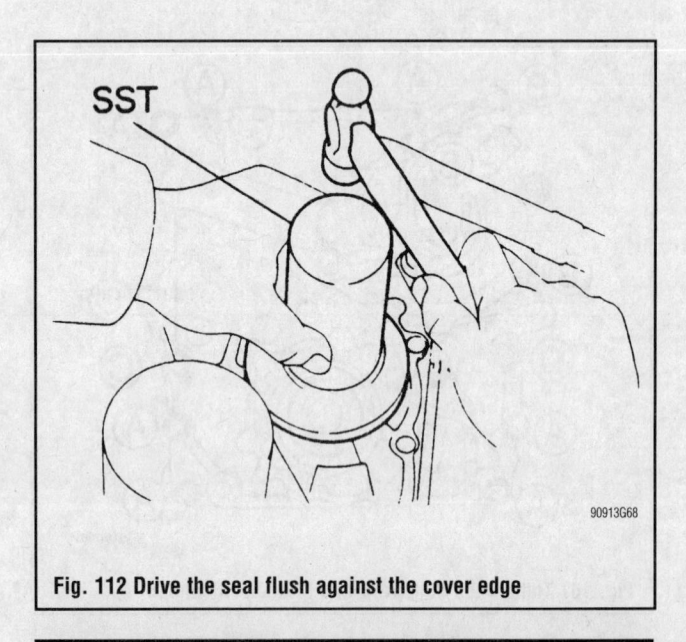

Fig. 109 Place a rag over the retainer and carefully pry the seal out

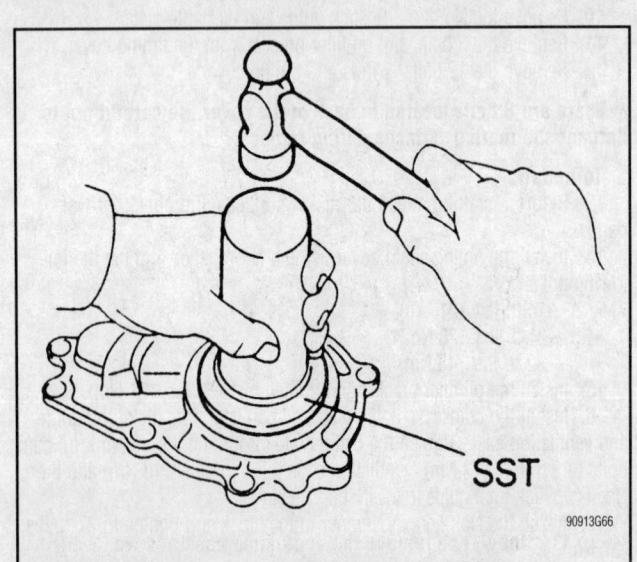

Fig. 112 Drive the seal flush against the cover edge

Fig. 110 Install the seal using the proper sized driver

### Timing Chain and Gears

#### REMOVAL & INSTALLATION

◆ See Figures 105, 106, 113 thru 129

The engine/transmission assembly must to be extracted from the vehicle and the cylinder head removed before performing work on the timing chain.

1. Remove the engine from the vehicle.
2. Separate the engine and transmission.
3. Remove the cylinder head from the engine block.
4. Remove the crankshaft pulley as follows:
   a. Using a holding device, secure the crankshaft. Loosen the pulley bolt.
   b. Remove the tool and pulley bolt.
   c. Using a puller, extract the crankshaft pulley.
5. Loosen the left engine mounting bolts and the left hand mounting stay, then extract the assembly from the engine.
6. Remove the oil pressure switch.
7. Remove the No. 1 engine oil dipstick.
8. Unbolt and remove the No. 2 engine hanger.

# ENGINE AND ENGINE OVERHAUL 3-35

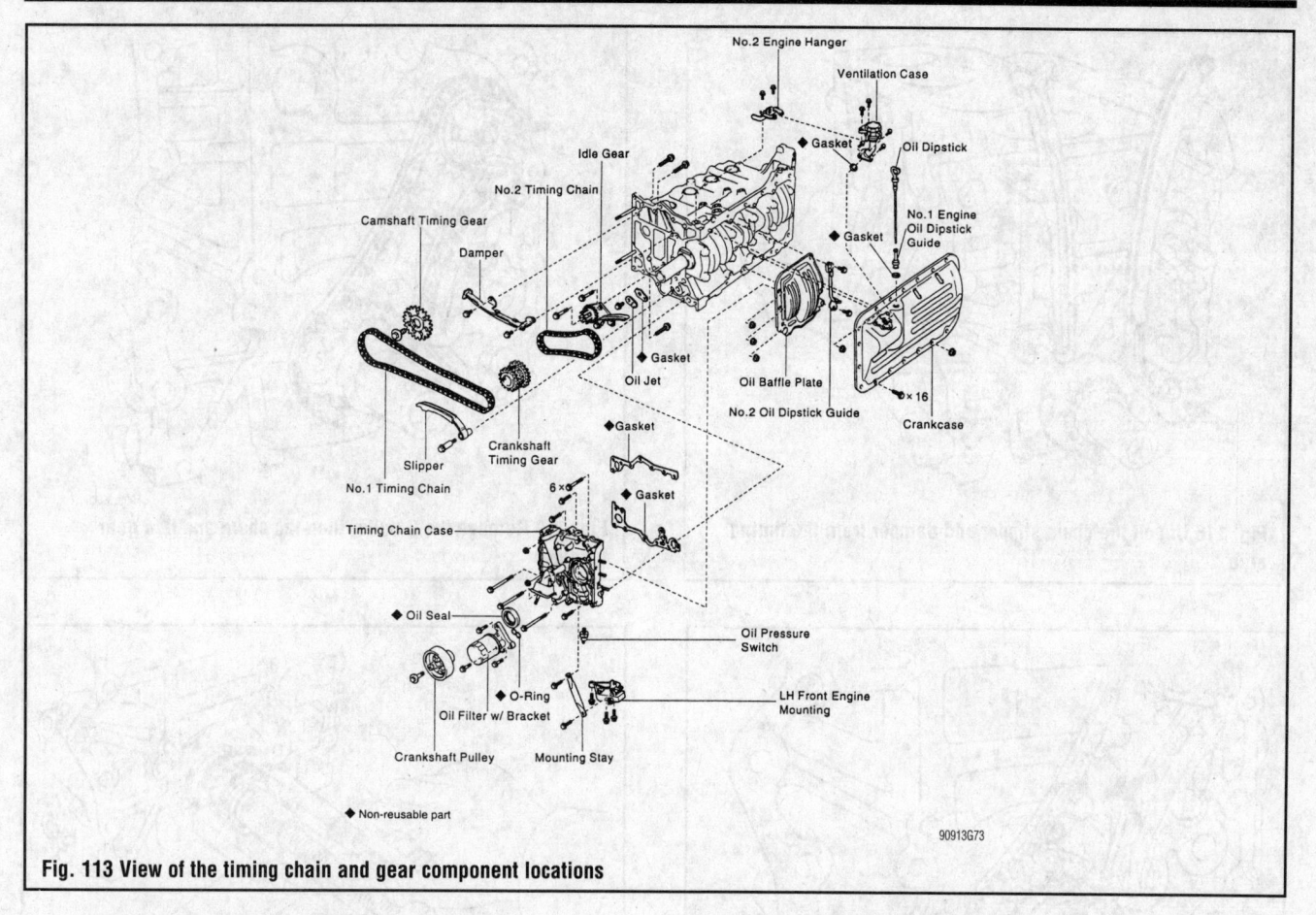

**Fig. 113 View of the timing chain and gear component locations**

9. Unbolt and extract the ventilation case, discard the gasket.
10. Remove the No. 1 oil dipstick guide and gasket.
11. Remove the crankshaft position sensor if equipped.
12. Remove the crankcase as follows:
    a. Remove the 16 bolts and 2 nuts on the case.
    b. Using a pry tool (09032–00100), and a brass bar, separate the crankcase from the cylinder block.
13. Remove the No. 2 oil dipstick guide and oil baffle plate by removing the two bolts and three nuts.
14. Unbolt and remove the oil filter bracket with the oil filter. Remove the O-ring from the timing chain case.
15. Remove the timing chain case as follows:
    a. Remove the three bolts from the rear of the timing chain cover.
    b. Remove the 12 bolts and two nuts from the front of the chain cover.
    c. Using a plastic faced hammer, tap the chain case and remove the timing chain case and two gaskets.
16. Remove the No. 1 timing chain and camshaft timing gear.
17. Unbolt and remove the chain slipper and damper.
18. Remove the oil jet by removing the bolt.
19. Remove the No. 2 timing chain and idle gear as follows:
    a. Loosen the two bolts to the idle gear chain guide.

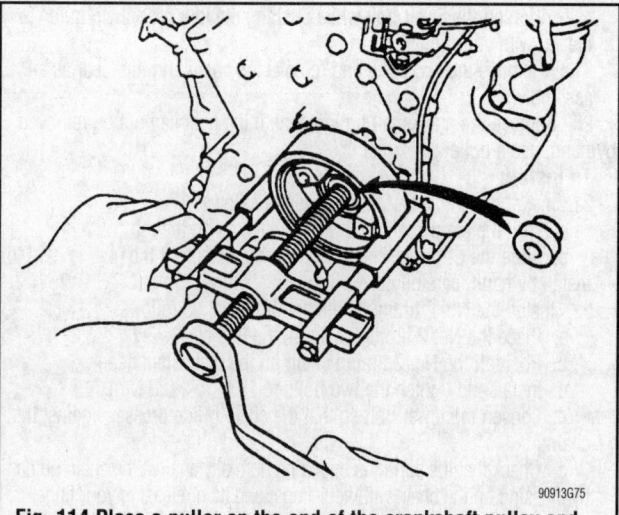

**Fig. 114 Place a puller on the end of the crankshaft pulley and remove it**

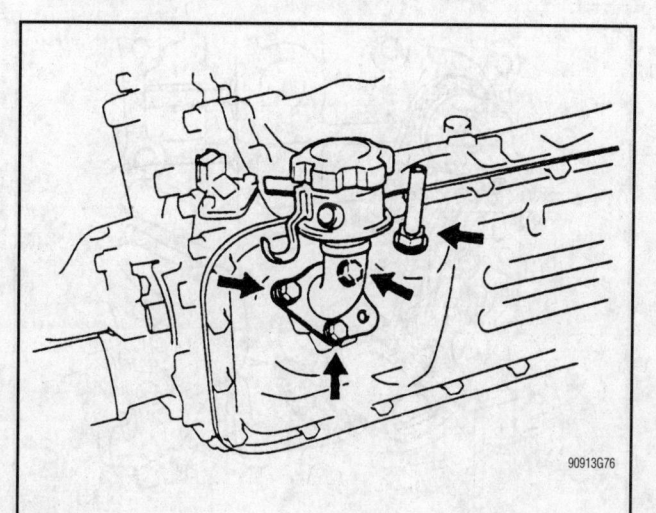

**Fig. 115 Unbolt and remove the ventilation case and No. 1 oil dipstick guide**

## ENGINE AND ENGINE OVERHAUL

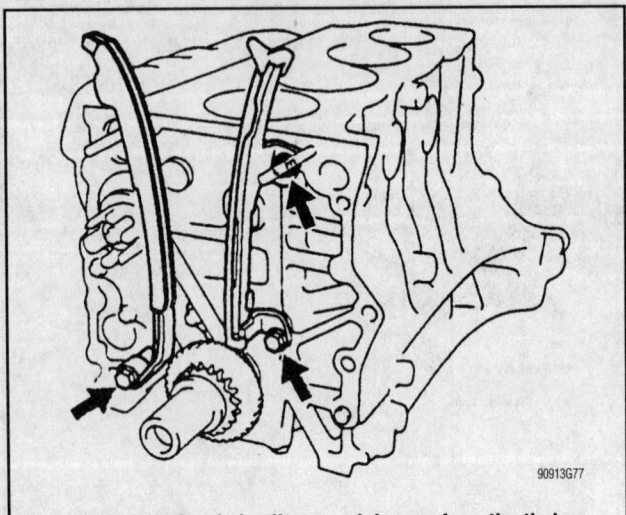

**Fig. 116** Unbolt the chain slipper and damper from the timing area

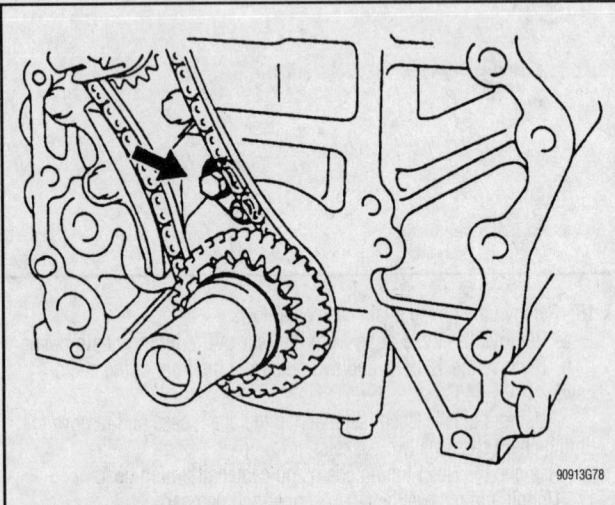

**Fig. 117** The oil jet is retained with one bolt in the center of the No. 2 timing chain

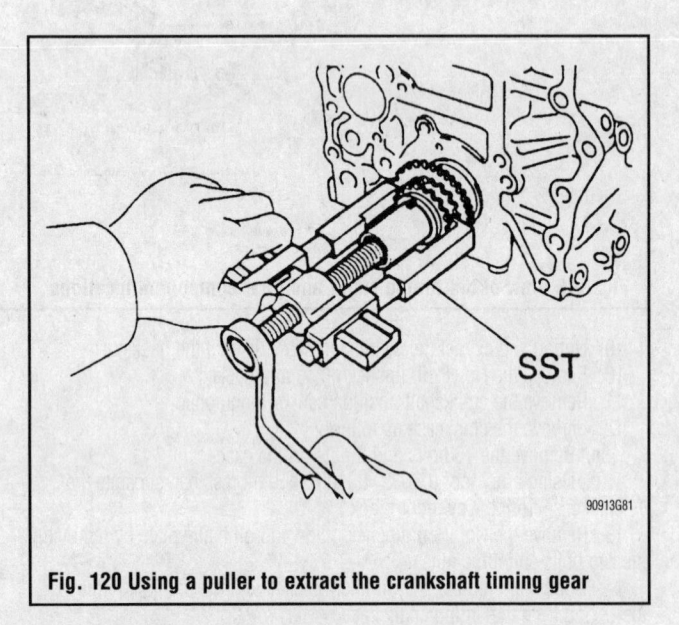

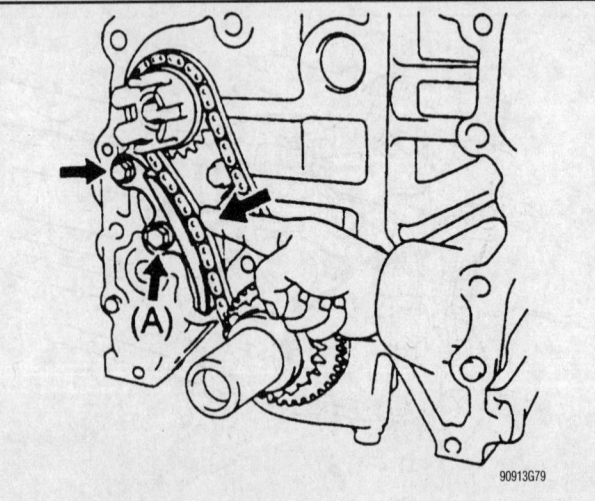

**Fig. 118** Tighten bolt A while pushing the chain guide to the left with your finger

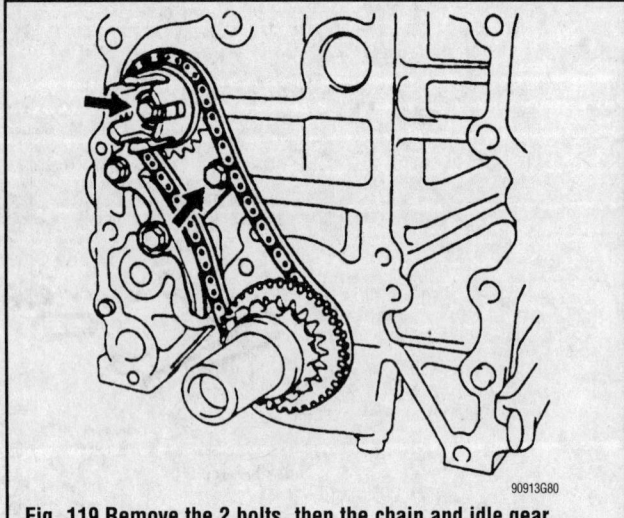

**Fig. 119** Remove the 2 bolts, then the chain and idle gear together

**Fig. 120** Using a puller to extract the crankshaft timing gear

   b. Tighten the lower bolt while pushing the idle gear chain guide to the left with your finger.
   c. Remove the two bolts and remove the chain and idle gear as an assembly.
20. Remove the crankshaft timing gear. If the gear can not be removed by hand, use a puller to extract it.

**To install:**
21. Install the crankshaft timing gear as follows:
   a. Turn the crankshaft until the shaft key is on the top.
   b. Slide the gear over the key on the crankshaft. If the gear is hard to install by hand, carefully drive it in.
22. Install the No. 2 timing chain and idle gear as follows:
   a. Place the No. 2 timing chain on the idle gear.
   b. Position the No. 2 timing chain on the crankshaft gear.
   c. Install and tighten the two bolts to 14 ft. lbs. (20 Nm).
   d. Loosen the lower bolt so that the chain guide presses against the chain.
   e. Check that the spring is operating normally against the chain guide by pressing on the chain with your finger and then releasing your finger.
   f. With the chain guide pressing against the chain, tighten the bolts to hold the chain guide in place. Tighten the bolts to 14 ft. lbs. (20 Nm).

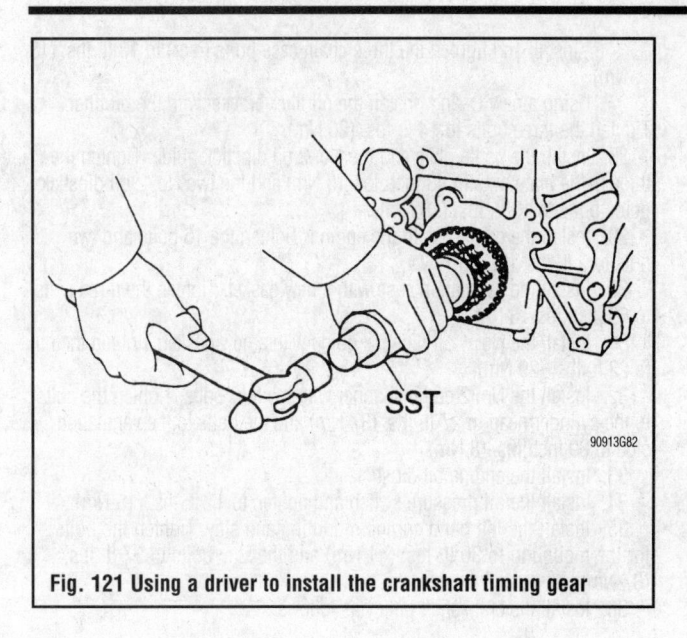

# ENGINE AND ENGINE OVERHAUL  3-37

**Fig. 121 Using a driver to install the crankshaft timing gear**

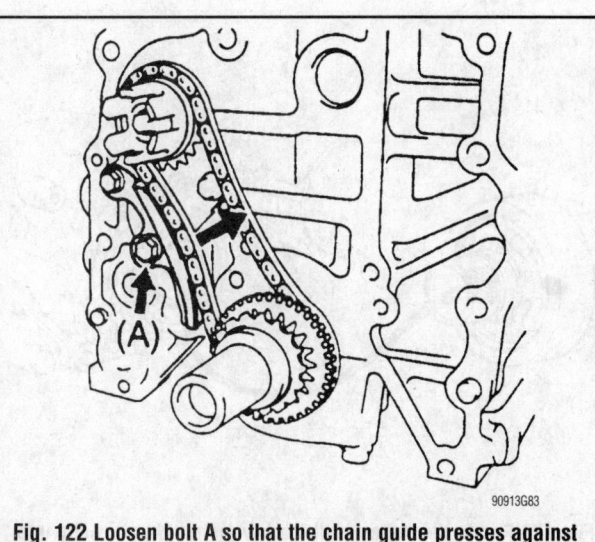

**Fig. 122 Loosen bolt A so that the chain guide presses against the chain**

**Fig. 123 Press your finger against the chain to test the tension . . .**

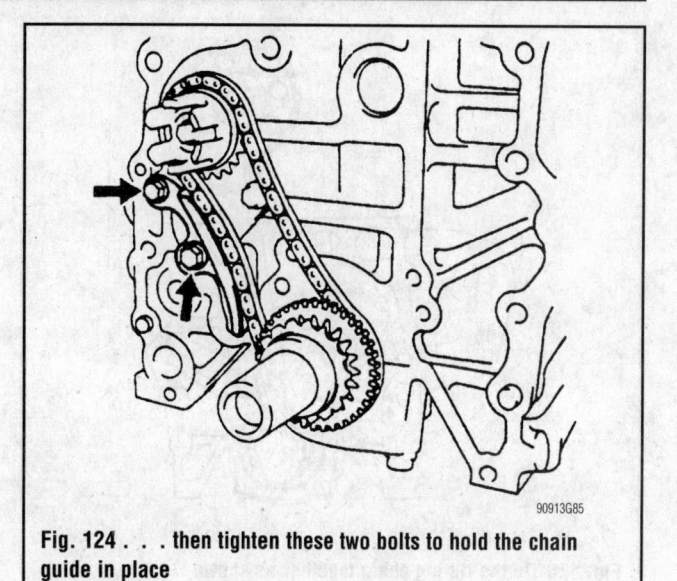

**Fig. 124 . . . then tighten these two bolts to hold the chain guide in place**

23. Install the oil jet with a new gasket. Tighten the bolt to 13 ft. lbs. (18 Nm).
24. Install the chain damper and slipper by installing the three bolts. Tighten the chain damper bolts to 13 ft. lbs. (18 Nm) and the chain slipper bolt to 20 ft. lbs. (27 Nm).
25. Place the No. 1 timing chain and camshaft timing gear as follows:
    a. Place the timing chain on the camshaft timing gear so that the timing mark is between the two bright chain links.
    b. Position the timing chain on the crankshaft timing gear with the single bright link aligned with the timing mark on the crankshaft timing gear.
    c. Make sure the timing chain is positioned between the damper and slipper.
    d. Turn the camshaft timing gear counterclockwise to take the slack out of the chain.
    e. Tie the timing chain with a cord and make sure it doesn't come loose.
26. Install the timing chain case as follows:
    a. Clean the gasket surface for the timing chain case.
    b. Install two new gaskets over the dowels.
    c. Slide on the chain case over the dowels.
    d. Install the bolts and nuts and tighten the bolts as follows:
- A to 14 ft. lbs. (20 Nm)
- B to 21 ft. lbs. (28 Nm)
- C to 32 ft. lbs. (44 Nm)

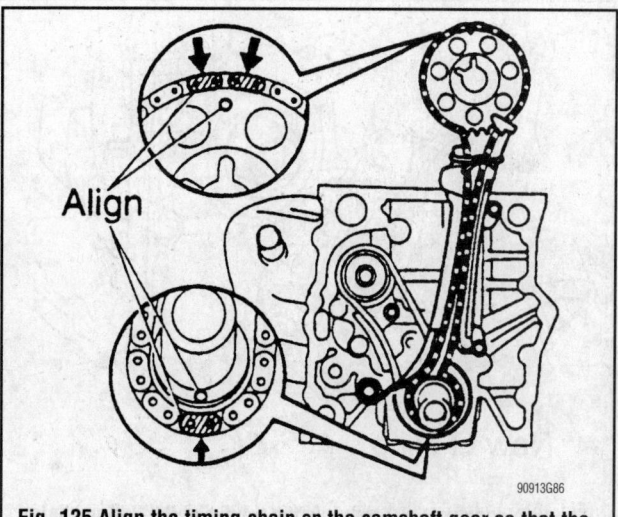

**Fig. 125 Align the timing chain on the camshaft gear so that the timing mark is between the two bright links**

## 3-38 ENGINE AND ENGINE OVERHAUL

Fig. 126 Tie the timing chain together as shown

Fig. 127 Timing chain cover bolt locations

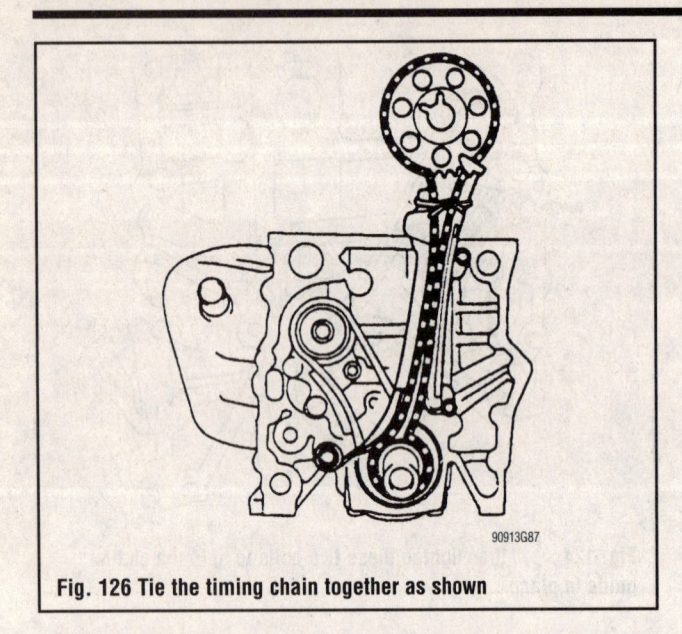

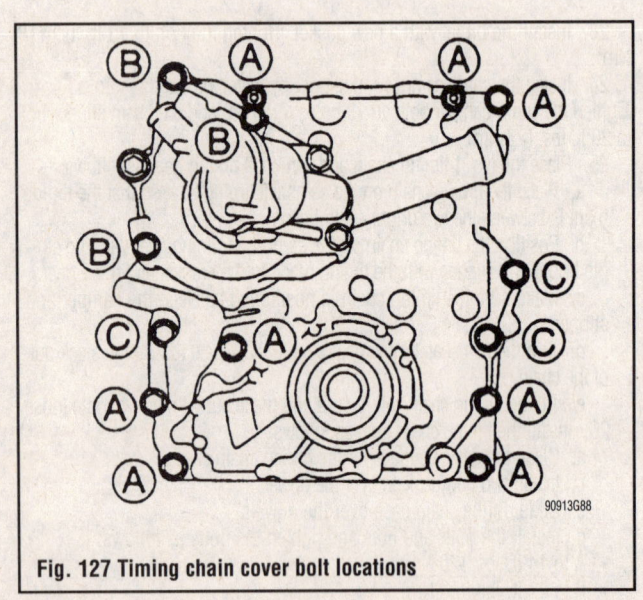

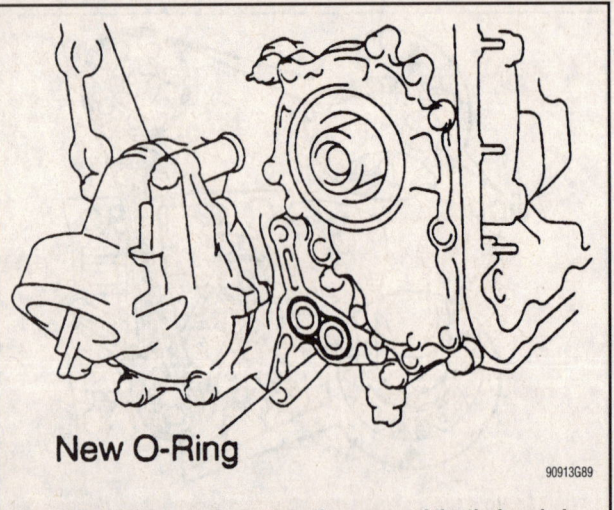

Fig. 128 Place new a O-ring into the groove of the timing chain case when necessary

e. Install and tighten the three chain case bolts (rear) to 13 ft. lbs. (18 Nm).
27. Using a new O-ring, Install the oil filter bracket with the oil filter. Tighten the three bolts to 14 ft. lbs. (20 Nm).
28. Install the baffle plate and the No. 2 oil dipstick guide. Tighten the three baffle plate nuts to 43 inch lbs. (5 Nm) and the two No. 2 oil dipstick guide bolts to 13 ft. lbs. (18 Nm).
29. Install the crankcase to the engine. Tighten the 16 bolts and two nuts to 9 ft. lbs. (12 Nm).
30. Install the ventilation case with a new gasket. Tighten the three bolts to 69 inch lbs. (8 Nm).
31. Install the No. 1 oil dipstick guide with a new gasket. Tighten the nut to 22 ft. lbs. (29 Nm).
32. Install the No. 2 engine hanger with the four bolts. Tighten the bolts to the cylinder head to 27 ft. lbs. (37 Nm) and the bolts to the ventilation side to 69 inch lbs. (8 Nm).
33. Install the engine oil dipstick.
34. Install the oil pressure switch and tighten to 11 ft. lbs. (15 Nm).
35. Install the left hand engine mounting and stay. Tighten the bolts for the mounting to 30 ft. lbs. (41 Nm) and the stay bolts to 27 ft. lbs. (37 Nm).
36. Install the crankshaft pulley as follows:

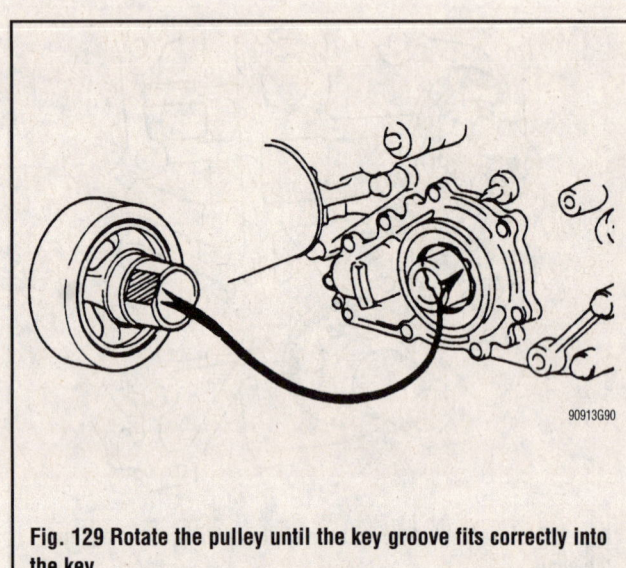

Fig. 129 Rotate the pulley until the key groove fits correctly into the key

a. Install the crankshaft pulley to the crankshaft with the spline teeth of the crankshaft pulley engaged with the large teeth of the oil pump.
b. Rotate the crankshaft pulley to the left and right and check that the key groove of the crankshaft pulley correctly fits the crankshaft key.
c. Install the crankshaft pulley bolt.
d. Using the holding device, 09213–58012 and 09330–00021, or equivalent, tighten the bolt to 192 ft. lbs. (260 Nm).
37. Remove the cord from the timing chain.
38. Install the cylinder head.
39. Connect the engine and transmission.
40. Install the engine and transmission to the vehicle.
41. Top off all fluid levels. Test drive the vehicle.

### Camshaft, Bearings and Lifters

#### REMOVAL & INSTALLATION

♦ See Figures 130 thru 163

1. Disconnect the negative battery cable. Wait at least 90 seconds before performing any work after the cable has been disconnected on models with an airbag.

# ENGINE AND ENGINE OVERHAUL  3-39

**✸✸ CAUTION**

Some models covered by this manual may be equipped with a Supplemental Restraint System (SRS), which uses an air bag. Whenever working near any of the SRS components, such as the impact sensors, the air bag module, steering column and instrument panel, disable the SRS, as described in Section 6.

2. Relieve the fuel system pressure.

**✸✸ CAUTION**

Fuel injection systems remain under pressure after the engine has been turned OFF. Properly relieve fuel pressure before disconnecting any fuel lines. Failure to do so may result in fire or personal injury.

3. Remove the engine wiring from the engine and move it aside.
4. Remove the No. 2 valve cover.
5. Mark the spark plug wires and disconnect. Matchmark the distributor, rotor and cylinder head. Remove the distributor and disconnect the wiring.
6. Remove the PCV hose.

Fig. 130 Remove the half circular plugs (half-moons) from the side of the head

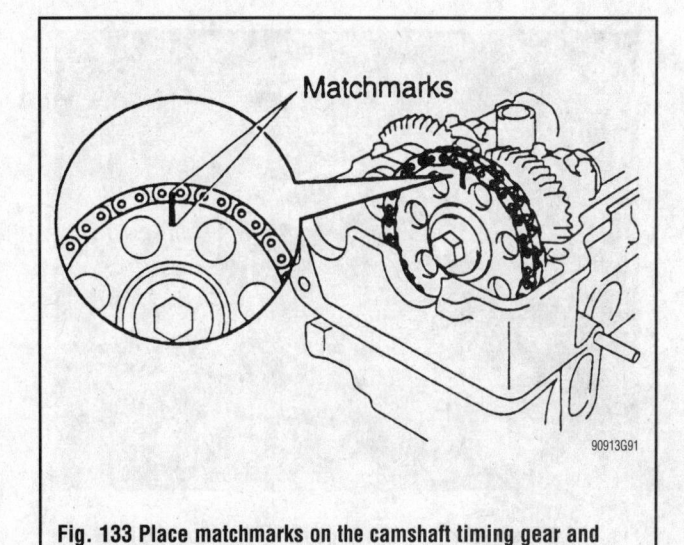

Fig. 131 Remove these bolts to access the tensioner

Fig. 132 Pull the tensioner out of the engine in the upright position, do not turn it upside down

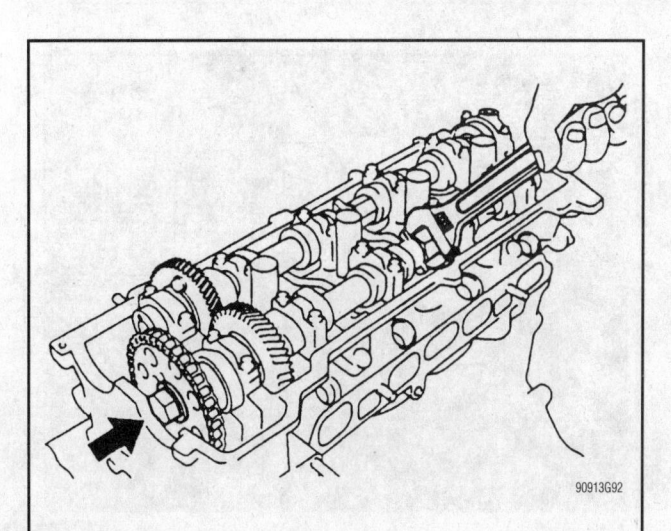

Fig. 133 Place matchmarks on the camshaft timing gear and chain before removal

Fig. 134 Hold the intake camshaft with a wrench and remove the bolt

# 3-40 ENGINE AND ENGINE OVERHAUL

Fig. 135 Be sure to place the wrench on a portion of the camshaft where it will not be damaged

Fig. 136 The sprocket bolt is a large headed bolt on the front of the cam

Fig. 137 Place a tie rap around the cam sprocket and chain to secure them

Fig. 138 Remove the cam sprocket and chain as an assembly

7. Remove the No. 1 valve cover and two half circular plugs.
8. Remove the chain tensioner and gasket.
9. Place matchmarks on the timing sprocket and chain. Hold the intake camshaft with a wrench and remove the sprocket bolt.

➡ It is a good idea to tie the chain and sprocket together with a tie rap.

10. Remove the cam sprocket and chain from the camshaft and leave on the slipper and damper.

➡ Be sure not to remove the slipper and damper. Since the thrust clearance of the camshaft is small, the camshaft must be kept level while it is being removed. If the camshaft is not kept level, the portion of the cylinder head receiving the shaft thrust may crack or be damaged, causing the camshaft to seize or break. To avoid this, follow the steps carefully.

11. To remove exhaust camshaft:
    a. Set the knock pin hole of the exhaust camshaft at the 5–30 degree BTDC of camshaft angle.

➡ The above angle helps to lift the exhaust camshaft level and evenly by pushing No. 2 and No. 4 cylinder cam lobes of the exhaust camshaft to their valve lifters.

    b. Secure the exhaust camshaft sub-gear to main gear with a service bolt. The recommended size bolt is 0.63–0.79 inch (16–20mm) bolt length, 6mm thread diameter and 1.0mm thread pitch.

➡ When removing the camshaft, make sure that the torsional spring force of the sub-gear has been eliminated by the previous step.

    c. Uniformly loosen the 8 bolts on the No. 1, No. 2, No. 3 and No. 5 bearing caps in several passes in the proper sequence.

➡ Do not remove No. 4 bearing cap bolt at this stage.

    d. Remove the No. 1, No. 2, No. 3 and No. 5 bearing caps.
    e. Alternately loosen No. 4 bearing cap. As No. 4 bearing cap bolts are loosened, check that the camshaft is being lifted out straight and level.

➡ If the camshaft is not being lifted out straight and level, retighten the 2 No. 4 bearing cap bolts. Repeat steps, in order, (e) to (a) and reset the knock pin hole of the exhaust camshaft at 5–30°BTDC, then repeat steps (b) to (e) again. Do not pry or attempt to force the camshaft with a tool or another object.

    f. Remove the No. 4 bearing cap and exhaust camshaft.

# ENGINE AND ENGINE OVERHAUL    3-41

Fig. 139 Set knock pin hole of exhaust camshaft at 5–30 degrees BTDC of camshaft angle

Fig. 140 Secure exhaust camshaft sub-gear to main gear with service bolt

Fig. 141 A service bolt should be the correct size to fit in the hole of the gear

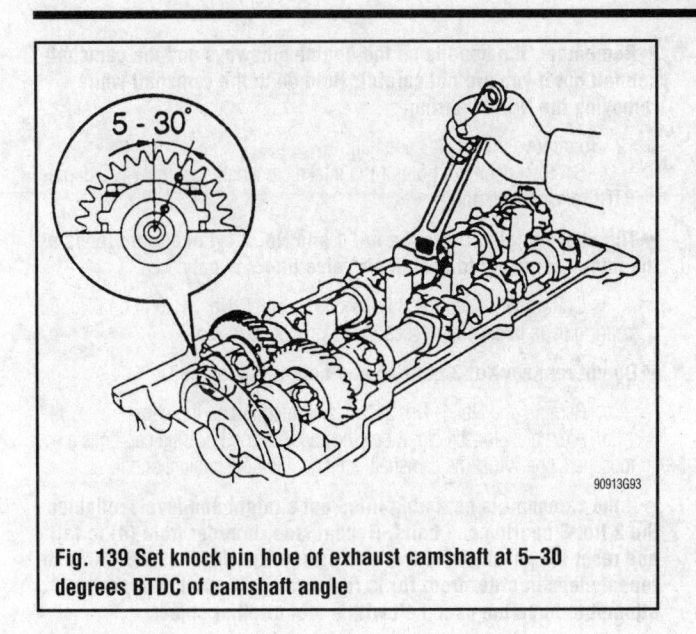

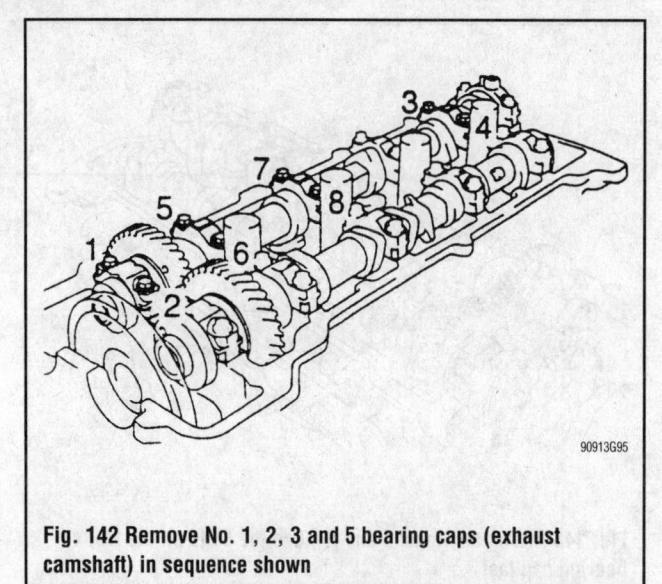

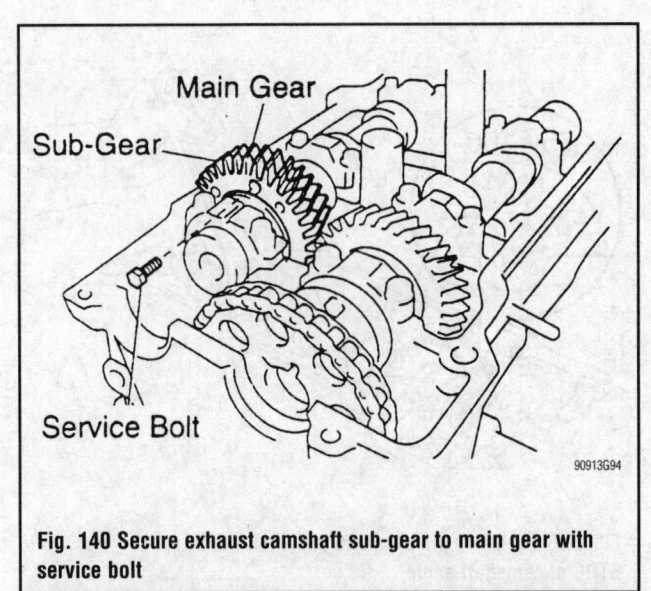

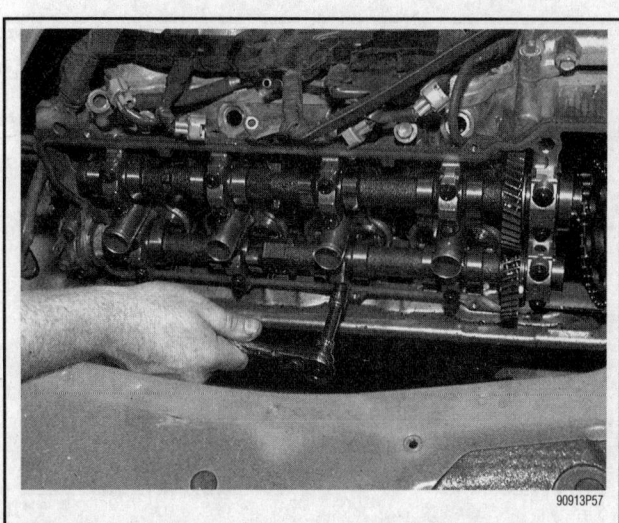

Fig. 142 Remove No. 1, 2, 3 and 5 bearing caps (exhaust camshaft) in sequence shown

Fig. 143 Loosening the No. 3 exhaust camshaft bearing cap bolts

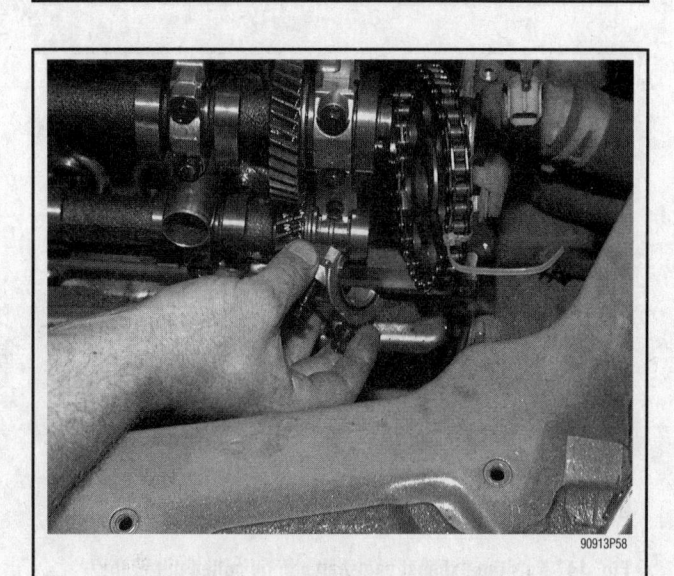

Fig. 144 Removing the No. 1 exhaust camshaft bearing

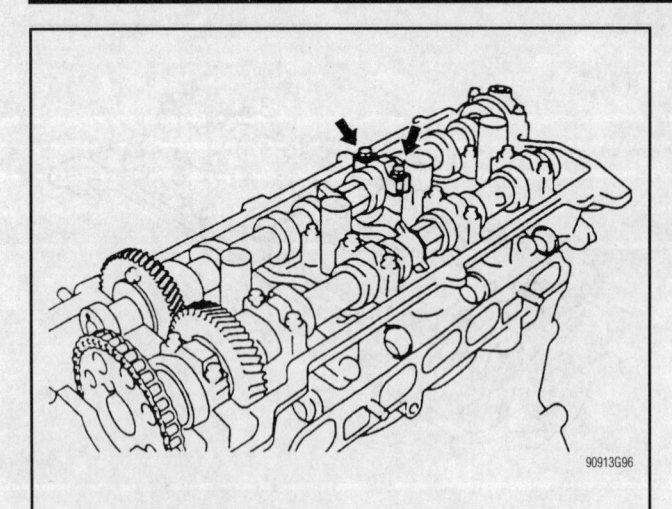

## 3-42  ENGINE AND ENGINE OVERHAUL

➡ Remember, the head is on the engine sideways and the camshaft can fall out if you are not careful. Hold on to the camshaft while removing the No. 4 bearing.

12. To remove the intake camshaft:

a. Set the knock pin hole of the intake camshaft at the 75–100 degree BTDC of camshaft angle.

➡ The above angle allows the no. 1 and No. 3 cylinder cam lobes of the intake camshaft to push their valve lifters evenly.

b. Uniformly loosen the 8 bolts on the No. 1, No. 2, No. 4 and No. 5 bearing caps in several passes in the proper sequence.

➡ Do not remove No. 3 bearing cap bolt at this stage.

c. Remove the No. 1, No. 2, No. 4 and No. 5 bearing caps.

d. Alternately loosen No. 3 bearing cap. As No. 3 bearing cap bolts are loosened, check that the camshaft is being lifted out straight and level.

➡ If the camshaft is not being lifted out straight and level, retighten the 2 No. 3 bearing cap bolts. Repeat step, in order from (d) to (a) and reset the knock pin of the intake camshaft at 75–100°BTDC, and repeat steps in order from (b) to (d) once again. Do not pry or attempt to force the camshaft with a tool or other object.

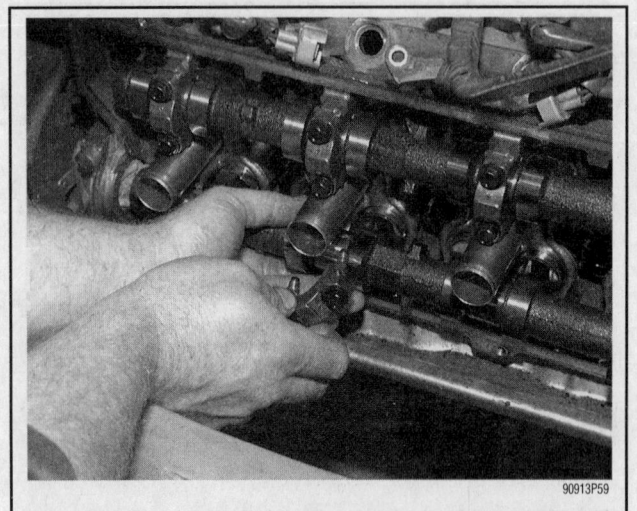

Fig. 145 Alternately loosen and remove the bolts on the No. 4 bearing cap last

Fig. 146 The No. 4 exhaust camshaft bearing is always removed last

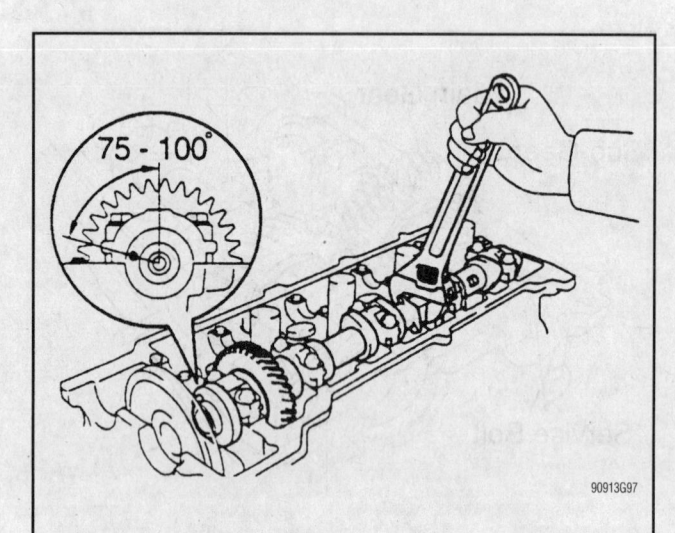

Fig. 147 Now the exhaust camshaft can be pulled out of the head

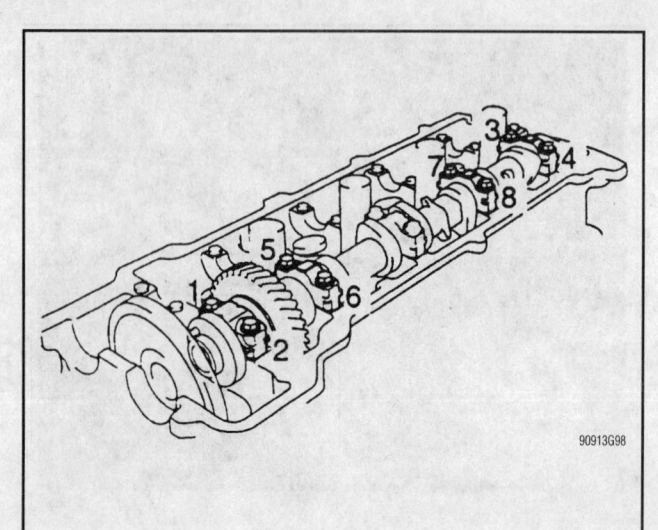

Fig. 148 Set knock pin of intake camshaft at 75–100 degrees BTDC of camshaft angle

Fig. 149 Remove No. 1, 2, 4 and 5 bearing caps (intake camshaft) in sequence shown

# ENGINE AND ENGINE OVERHAUL     3-43

Fig. 150 Uniformly loosen and remove the intake camshaft bearing cap bolts

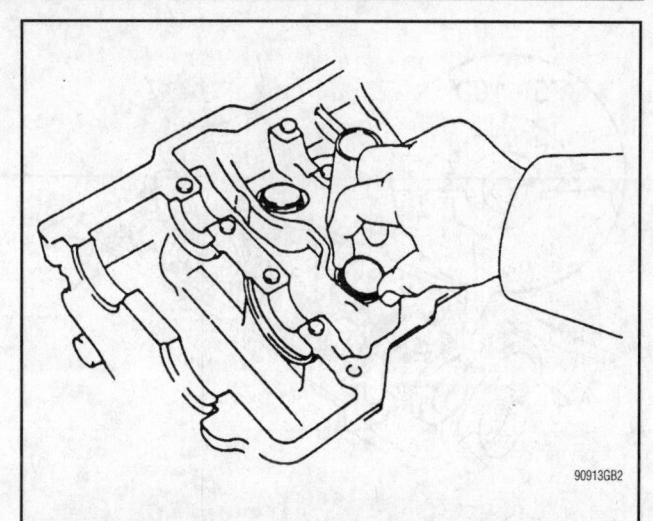

Fig. 153 Remove the lifters and shims together from the cylinder head

Fig. 151 Remove the No. 3 intake camshaft bearing cap last

Fig. 154 The shims and lifters are located in the head

Fig. 152 The intake camshaft can fall out if not grabbed quickly

    e. Remove the No. 3 bearing cap and the intake camshaft.

13. Remove the valve lifters from the engine. Keep the shims and the lifters together. The lifters and the shims must be reinstalled in their original location.

**To install:**

➡ If any of the bolts break, deform or do not meet the tighten specification replace them.

14. Install the valve lifters and shims.
15. Install the intake camshaft:
    a. Apply MP grease to the thrust portion of the intake camshaft.
    b. Place the intake camshaft at 75–100 degrees BTDC. Install the bearing caps with the marking arrows facing forward. Uniformly tighten the bearing cap bolts in several passes in the proper sequence to 12 ft. lbs. (16 Nm).
16. Install the exhaust camshaft:
    a. Set the knock pin of the intake camshaft at 5–30 degrees BTDC of camshaft angle.
    b. Apply MP grease to the thrust portion of the exhaust camshaft.
    c. Engage the exhaust camshaft gear to the intake camshaft gear by matching the installation marks (timing marks).

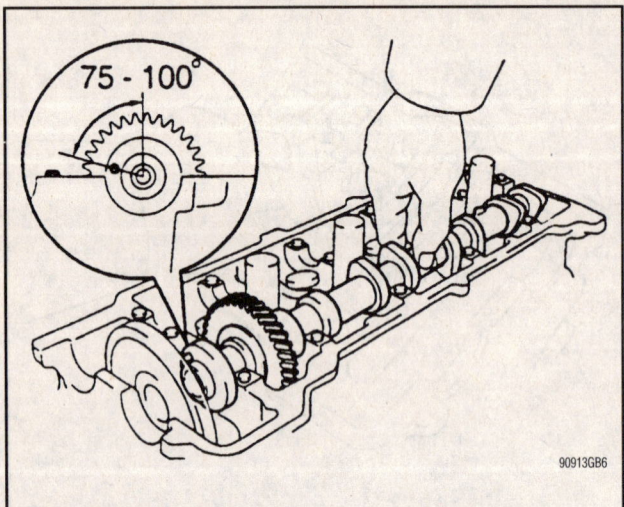

# 3-44 ENGINE AND ENGINE OVERHAUL

Fig. 155 Place the intake camshaft at 75–100°BTDC of the camshaft angle on the head

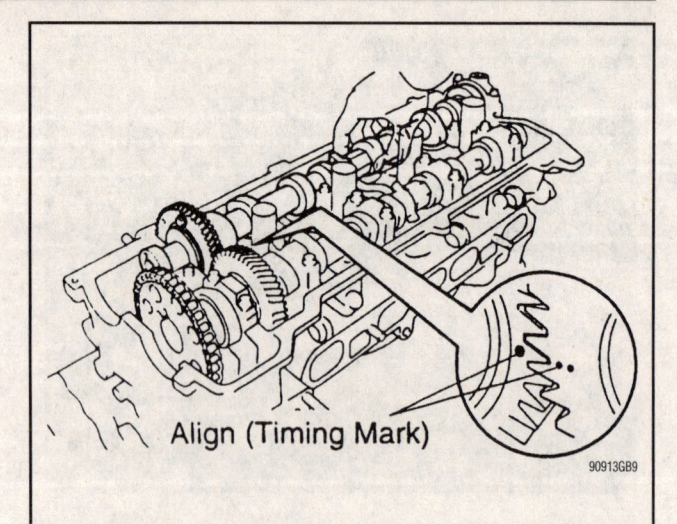

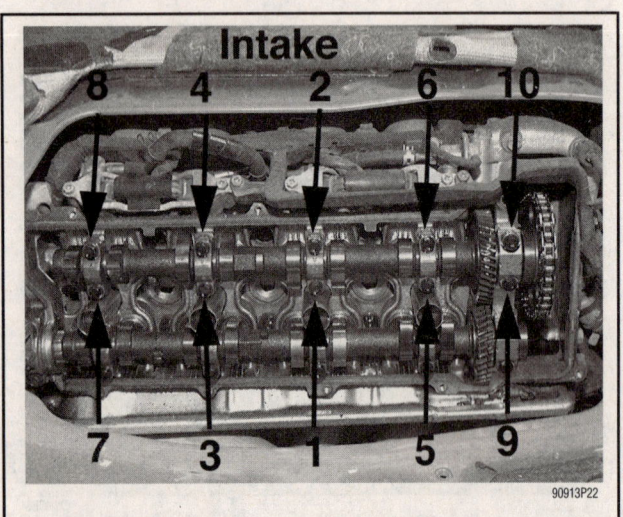

Fig. 156 Camshaft bearing cap bolts tightening sequence; intake and exhaust are the same

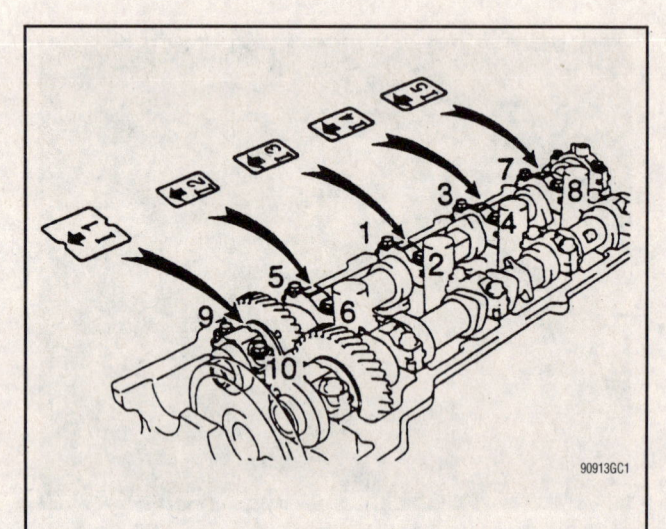

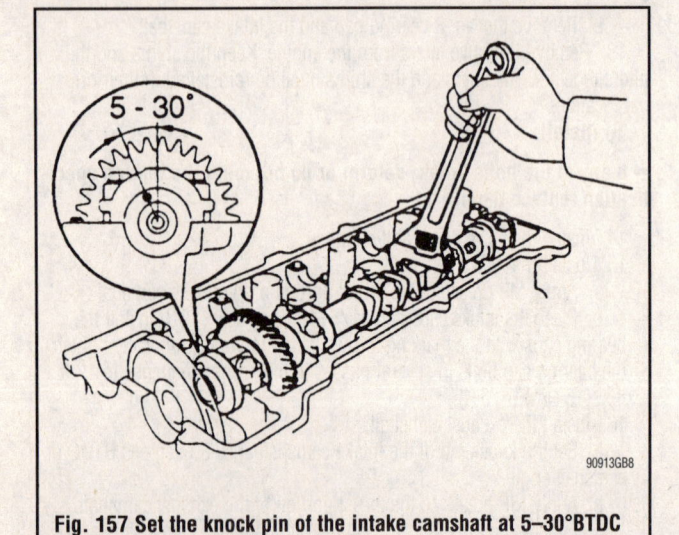

Fig. 157 Set the knock pin of the intake camshaft at 5–30°BTDC of the camshaft angle

Fig. 158 Engage the exhaust and intake camshafts by matching the timing marks to each gear

Fig. 159 Install and uniformly tighten the 10 bearing cap bolts in several passes in this sequence

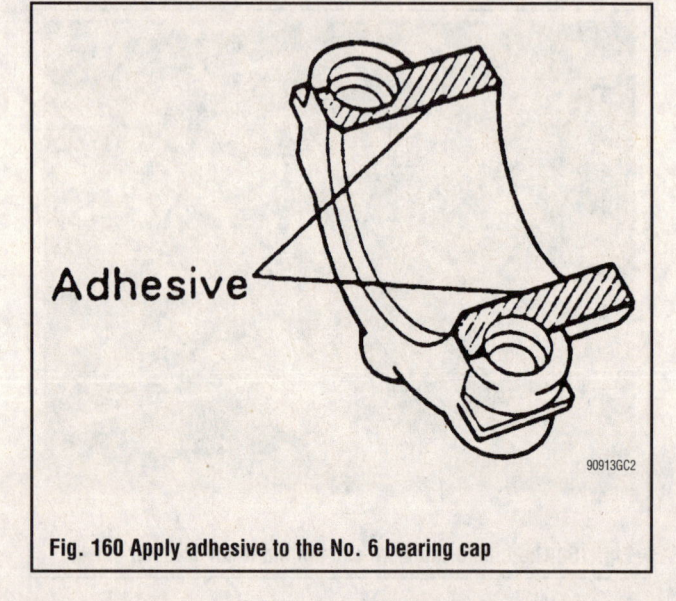

Fig. 160 Apply adhesive to the No. 6 bearing cap

# ENGINE AND ENGINE OVERHAUL  3-45

**Fig. 161 Retain the camshaft and tighten the bolt**

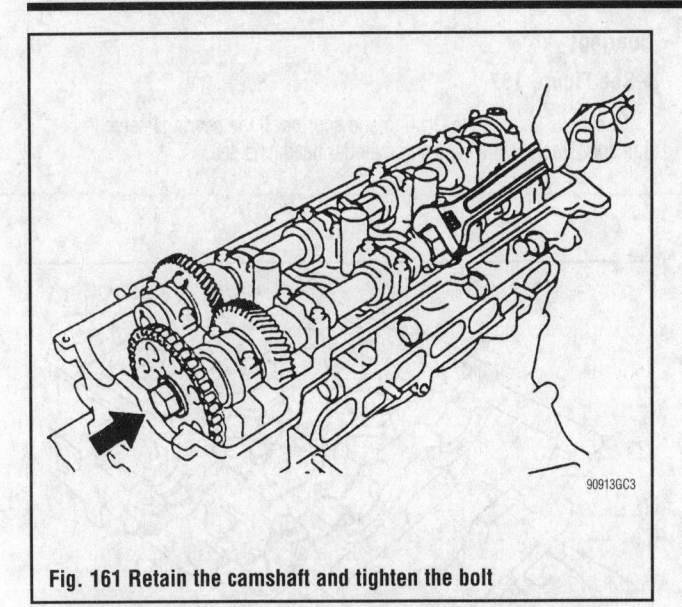

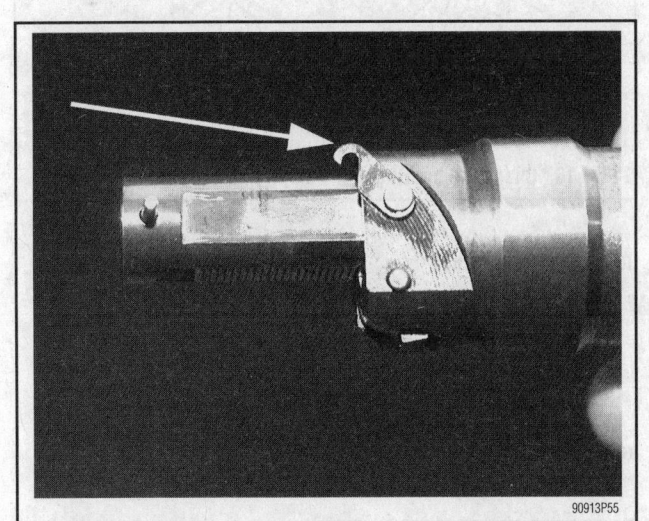

**Fig. 162 The tensioner has a hook to hold the plunger in the down position**

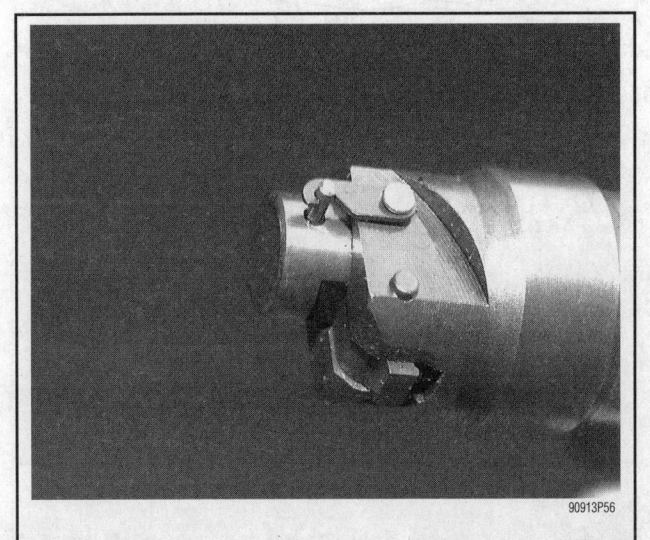

**Fig. 163 Push the plunger in and position the hook over the pin**

d. Roll down the exhaust camshaft onto the bearing journals while engaging the gears with each other. Make sure the exhaust and intake camshaft gear alignment marks are facing each other. The one gear has 2 dots and the other has 1 dot.

e. Install the bearing caps with the marking arrows facing forward.

f. Uniformly tighten the bearing cap bolts in several passes in the proper sequence to 12 ft. lbs. (16 Nm).

17. Apply sealer to the bottom of No. 6 bearing cap and install. Tighten the cap to 12 ft. lbs. (16 Nm).

18. Install the camshaft sprocket and chain. Hold the camshaft with a wrench and tighten the bolt to 54 ft. lbs. (74 Nm).

19. Release the chain tensioner ratchet pawl. Fully push in the plunger and apply the hook to the pin so the plunger can not spring out and install the tensioner. Tighten the bolts to 15 ft. lbs. (21 Nm).

20. Set the tensioner: Turn the crankshaft to the left so the hook of the tensioner is released from the pin. If it does not spring out, press the slipper into the tensioner to release the hook.

21. Adjust the valve clearance.

22. Apply sealant 08826–00080 or equivalent to the cylinder head. Install the 2 half-circular plugs to the cylinder head and install the valve cover. Tighten the bolts to 69 inch lbs. (8 Nm).

23. Install the PCV hose.
24. Install the distributor.
25. Install the No. 2 cylinder head cover.
26. Install the engine wire and connect all connectors.
27. Install the engine/transmission assembly into the vehicle.
28. Fill the cooling system. Fill the engine with oil.
29. Connect the battery cable. Start the engine and check for leaks.
30. Road test the vehicle for proper operation. Recheck all fluid levels.

### INSPECTION

**Runout**

▶ See Figure 164

1. Place the camshaft on V-blocks.
2. Using a dial indicator, measure the circle runout at the center journal. Maximum circle runout is 0.0024 inch (0.06mm). If the runout is greater than maximum, replace the camshaft.

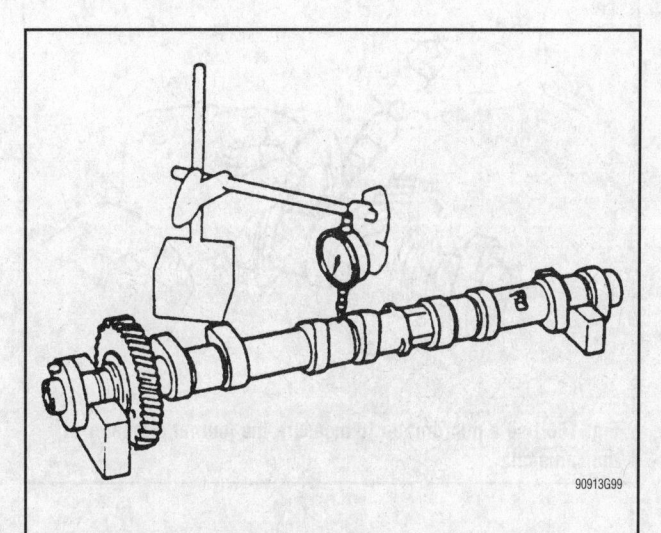

**Fig. 164 Use a dial indicator to measure circle runout of the camshaft**

# ENGINE AND ENGINE OVERHAUL

## Lobe Height

▶ See Figure 165

1. Using a micrometer, measure the cam lobe height. Standard cam lobe height:
   - 2TZ-FE Intake—1.7839–1.7878 inch (45.31–45.41mm)
   - 2TZ-FZE Intake—1.7720–1.7760 inch (45.01–45.11mm)

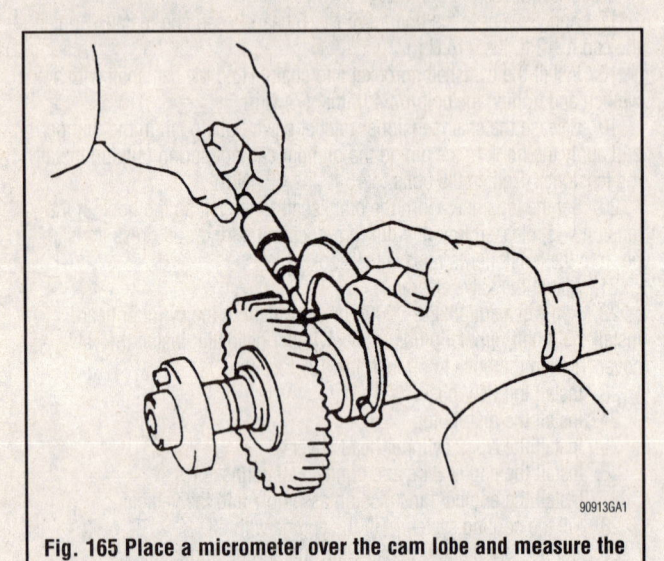

Fig. 165 Place a micrometer over the cam lobe and measure the height, if less than minimum, replace the camshaft

   - Exhaust—1.7740–1.7779 inch (45.06–45.16mm)
2. If the cam lobe height is less than minimum, replace the camshaft.

## Journals

▶ See Figure 166

1. Using a micrometer, measure the journal diameter. Standard diameter is 1.0614–1.0620 inch (26.959–26.975mm). If the diameter is not as specified, check the oil clearance.

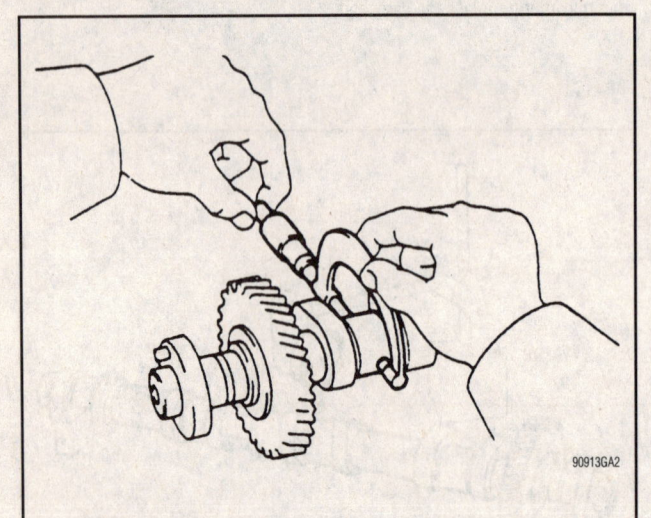

Fig. 166 Use a micrometer to measure the journal diameter of the camshaft

## Bearings

▶ See Figure 167

Check the bearings for flaking and scoring. If the bearings seem to be damaged, replace the caps and cylinder head as a set.

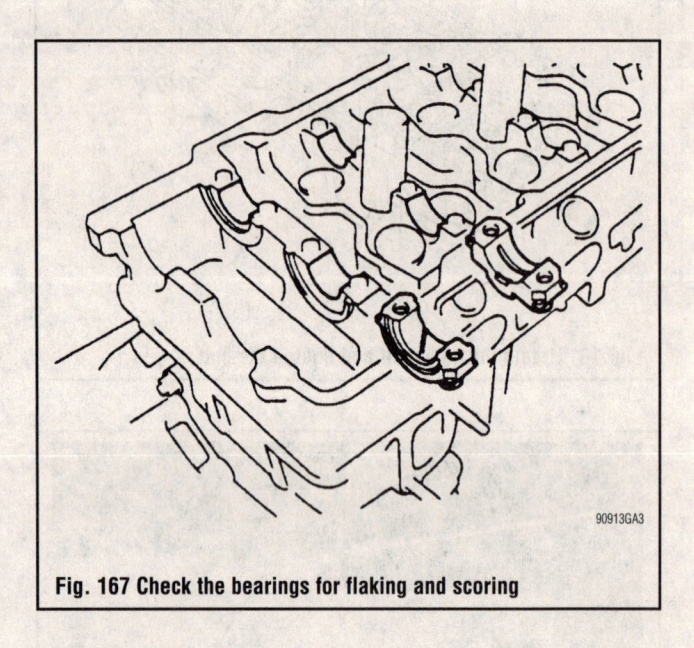

Fig. 167 Check the bearings for flaking and scoring

## Journal Oil Clearance

▶ See Figures 168 and 169

1. Clean the bearing caps and camshaft journals.
2. Place the camshafts on the cylinder head.
3. Lay a strip of Plastigage® across each camshaft journal.
4. Install the bearing caps and tighten to 12 ft. lbs. (15 Nm). Do not turn the camshaft.
5. Remove the bearing caps.

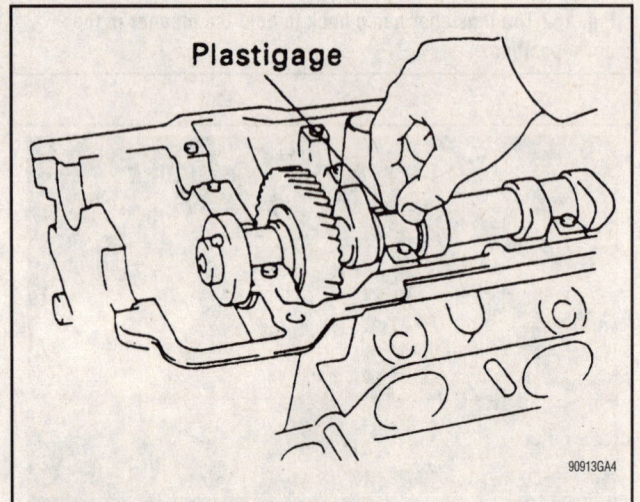

Fig. 168 Place the gauging material across the camshaft journals . . .

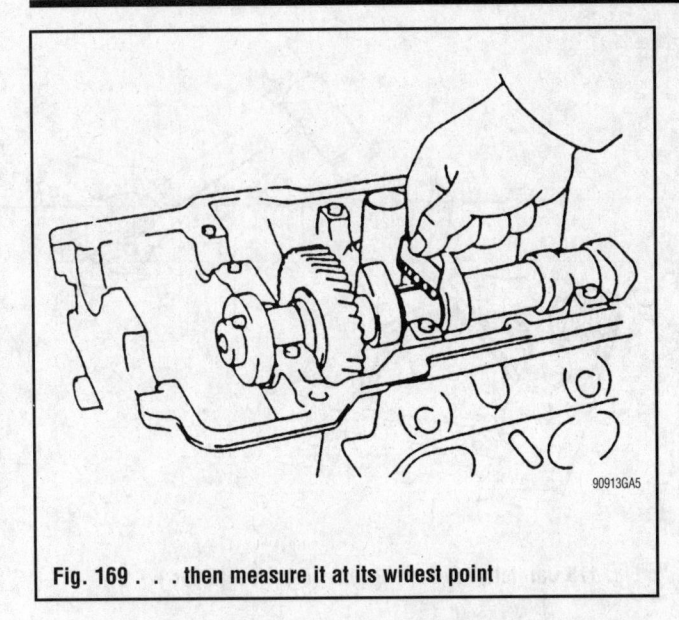

# ENGINE AND ENGINE OVERHAUL

**Fig. 169 . . . then measure it at its widest point**

6. Measure the Plastigage® at its widest point. Standard oil clearance is 0.0010–0.0024 inch (0.025–0.062mm). Maximum oil clearance is 0.0031 inch (0.08mm). If the oil clearance is greater than maximum, replace the camshaft. If necessary, replace the bearing caps and cylinder head as a set.
7. Completely remove the gauge material.

### Thrust Clearance

▶ See Figure 170

1. install the camshaft.
2. Using a dial indicator, measure the thrust clearance while moving the camshaft back and forth.

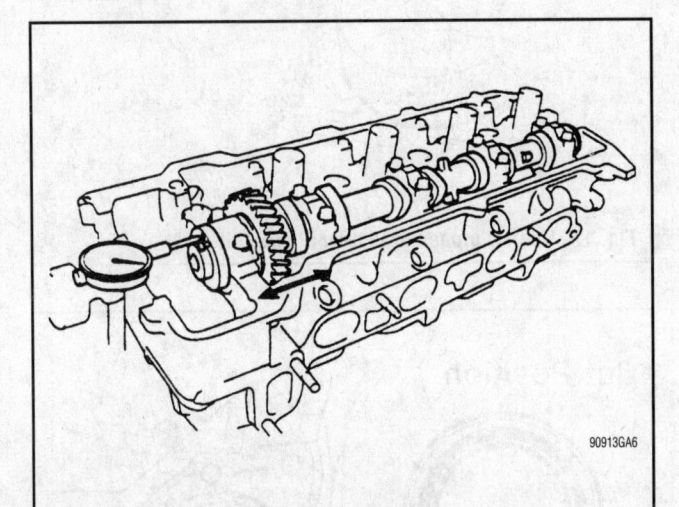

**Fig. 170 Place a dial indicator at the end of the camshaft as shown and measure the thrust clearance**

- Standard thrust clearance—0.0016–0.0037 inch
- Maximum thrust clearance—0.0047 inch (0.12mm)

3. If the thrust clearance is greater than maximum, replace the camshaft. If necessary, replace the bearing caps and cylinder head as a set.

### Camshaft Gear Backlash

▶ See Figure 171

1. Install the camshafts without installing the exhaust cam subgear.
2. Using a dial indicator, measure the gear backlash.

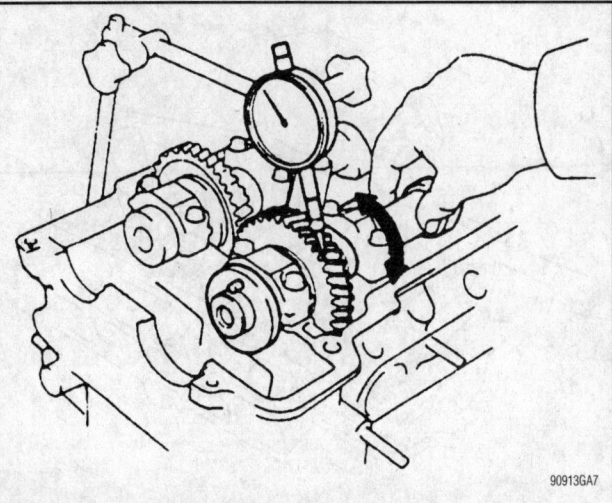

**Fig. 171 Place a dial indicator on the camshaft gear and measure the gear backlash**

- Standard backlash—0.0008–0.0079 inch (0.020–0.200mm)
- Maximum backlash—0.0118 inch (0.30mm)

3. If the backlash is greater than maximum, replace the camshafts.

### Camshaft Gear Spring

▶ See Figure 172

Using a venire caliper, measure the free distance between the spring ends. The distance should be between 0.886–0.902 inch (22.5–22.9mm). If the free distance is not as specified, replace the gear spring.

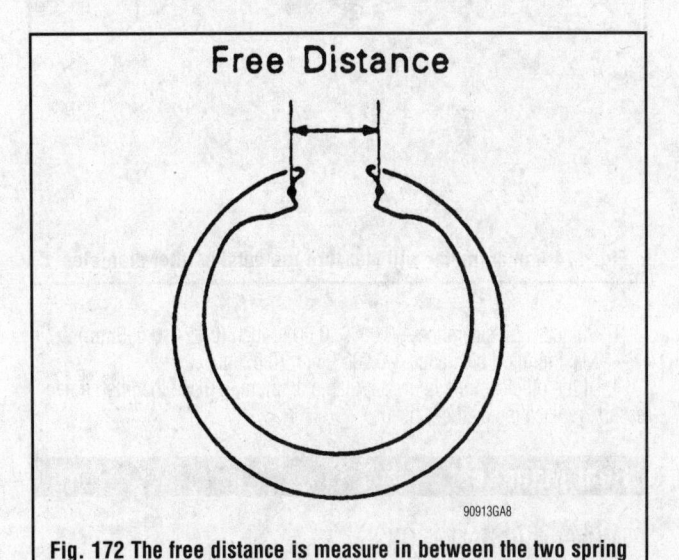

**Fig. 172 The free distance is measure in between the two spring ends**

### Valve Lifters and Lifter Bores

▶ See Figures 173 and 174

1. Using a caliper gage, measure the lifter bore diameter of the cylinder head. Standard lifter bore diameter is 1.2205–1.2211 inch (31.000–31.016mm).
2. Using a micrometer, measure the lifter diameter. Standard diameter is 1.2191–1.2195 inch 930.966–30.976mm).
3. Subtract the lifter diameter measurement from the lifter bore diameter measurement.

# 3-48 ENGINE AND ENGINE OVERHAUL

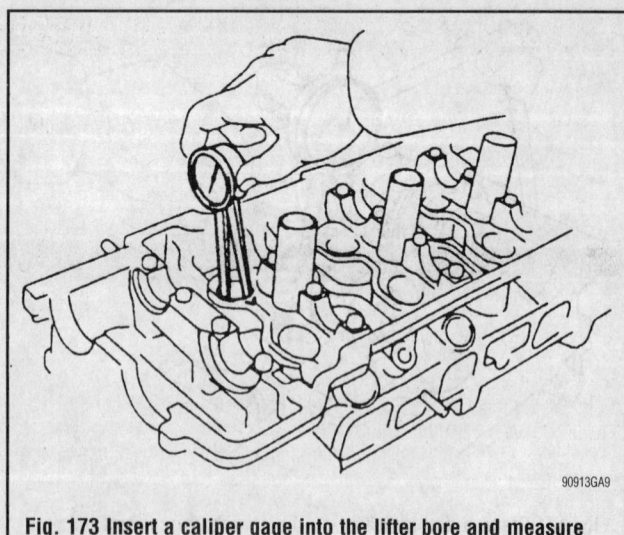

Fig. 173 Insert a caliper gage into the lifter bore and measure the diameter

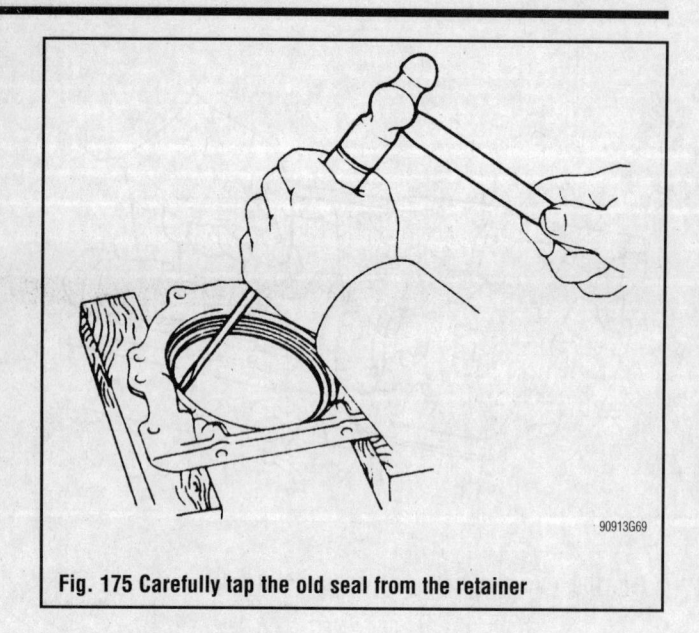

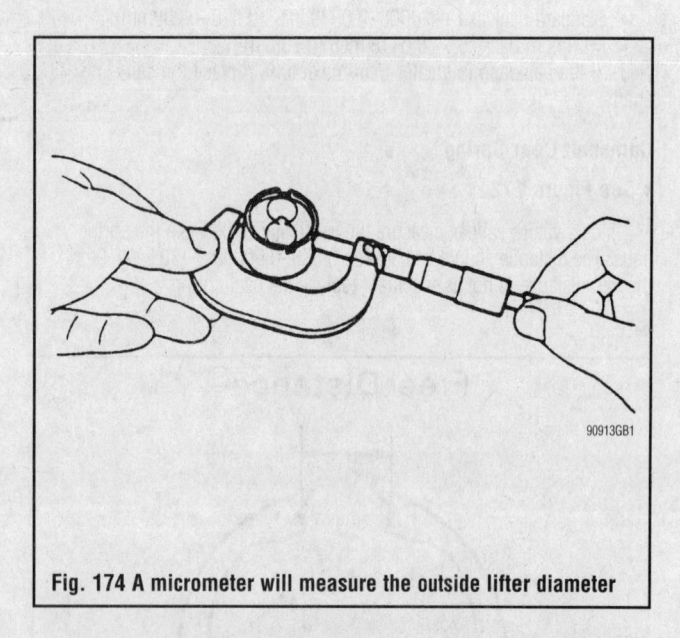

Fig. 174 A micrometer will measure the outside lifter diameter

- Standard oil clearance—0.0009–0.0020 inch (0.024–0.050mm)
- Maximum oil clearance—0.0028 inch (0.07mm)

4. If the oil clearance is greater than maximum, replace the lifter. If necessary, replace the cylinder head.

## Rear Main Seal

### REMOVAL & INSTALLATION

▶ See Figures 175, 176, 177 and 178

If the rear oil seal retainer is not installed to the block, use a taped ended screwdriver and hammer to remove the oil seal. Apply multipurpose grease to the new oil seal lip. Using a seal driver, tap the seal into place. Be careful not to install it slantwise.

If the rear oil seal retainer is installed on the cylinder block, using a knife, cut off the lip of the seal. Using a taped ended pry tool, pry the old seal out of the retainer. inspect the oil seal lip contacting surface of the crankshaft for cracks or damage. Apply multipurpose grease to the new oil seal, then tap the seal in place with a seal installer. Be careful not to install the seal slantwise.

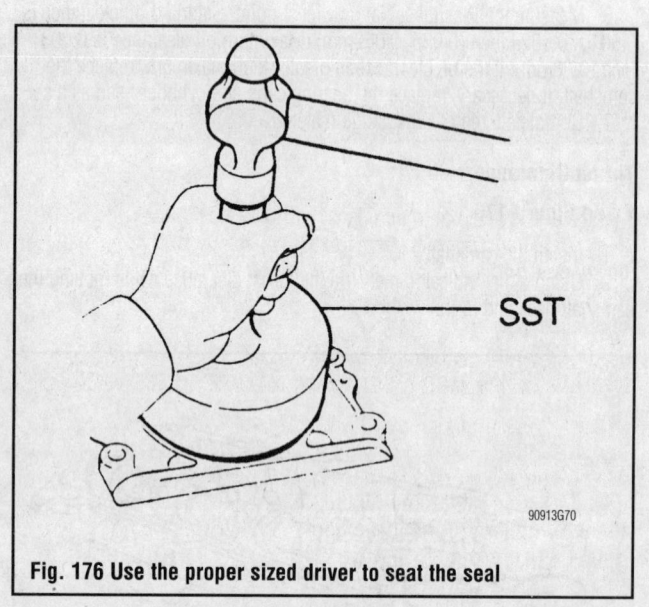

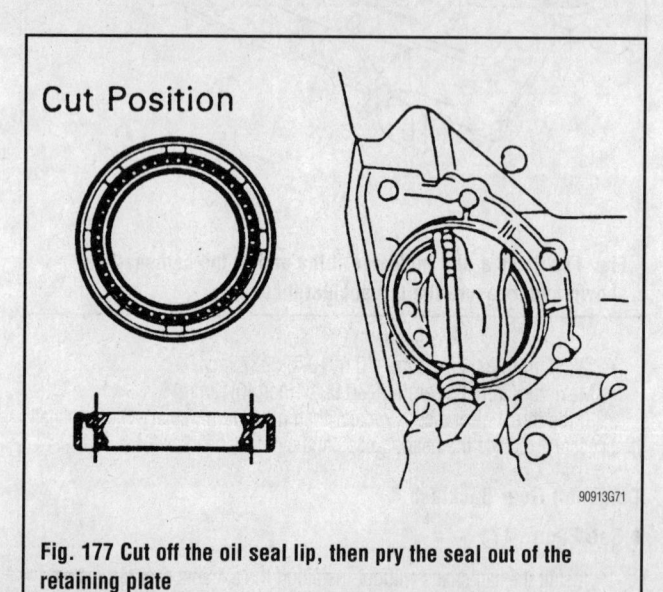

Fig. 175 Carefully tap the old seal from the retainer

Fig. 176 Use the proper sized driver to seat the seal

Fig. 177 Cut off the oil seal lip, then pry the seal out of the retaining plate

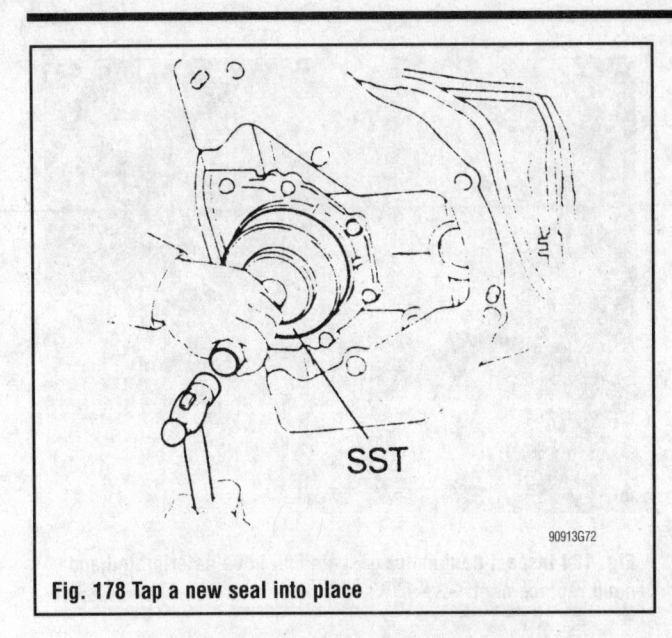

# ENGINE AND ENGINE OVERHAUL 3-49

Fig. 178 Tap a new seal into place

## Flywheel/Flexplate

### REMOVAL & INSTALLATION

1. Remove the transmission.
2. Remove the clutch assembly, on manual transmissions and the torque converter on automatics.
3. Place matchmarks on the flywheel and crankshaft end. Loosen the bolts holding the flywheel or driveplate a little at a time in a criss-cross pattern. Remove the flywheel. Protect the flywheel/flexplate from damage or impact.

➡ Keep your feet clear of accidental dropping.

### To install:

4. Thoroughly clean the flywheel/flexplate bolts. coat the first 3 or 4 threads of each bolt with sealant.
5. Install the flywheel/flexplate, aligning the previously made marks. Install the bolts finger-tight.
6. Tighten the bolts in a criss-cross pattern in several passes to:
- Manual—65 ft. lbs. (88 Nm)
- Automatic—54 ft. lbs. (74 Nm)
7. Install the remaining components.

## EXHAUST SYSTEM

### Inspection

▶ See Figures 179 thru 185

➡ Safety glasses should be worn at all times when working on or near the exhaust system. Older exhaust systems will almost always be covered with loose rust particles which will shower you when disturbed. These particles are more than a nuisance and could injure your eye.

### ✳✳ CAUTION

DO NOT perform exhaust repairs or inspection with the engine or exhaust hot. Allow the system to cool completely before attempting any work. Exhaust systems are noted for sharp edges, flaking metal and rusted bolts. Gloves and eye protection are required. A healthy supply of penetrating oil and rags is highly recommended.

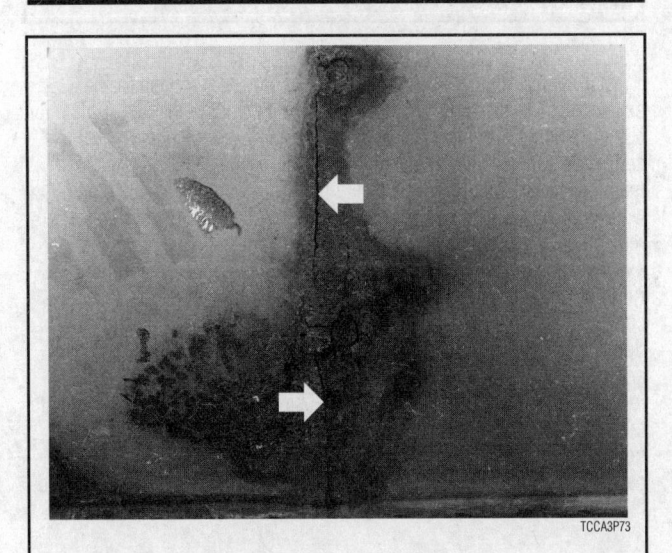

Fig. 179 Cracks in the muffler are a guaranteed leak

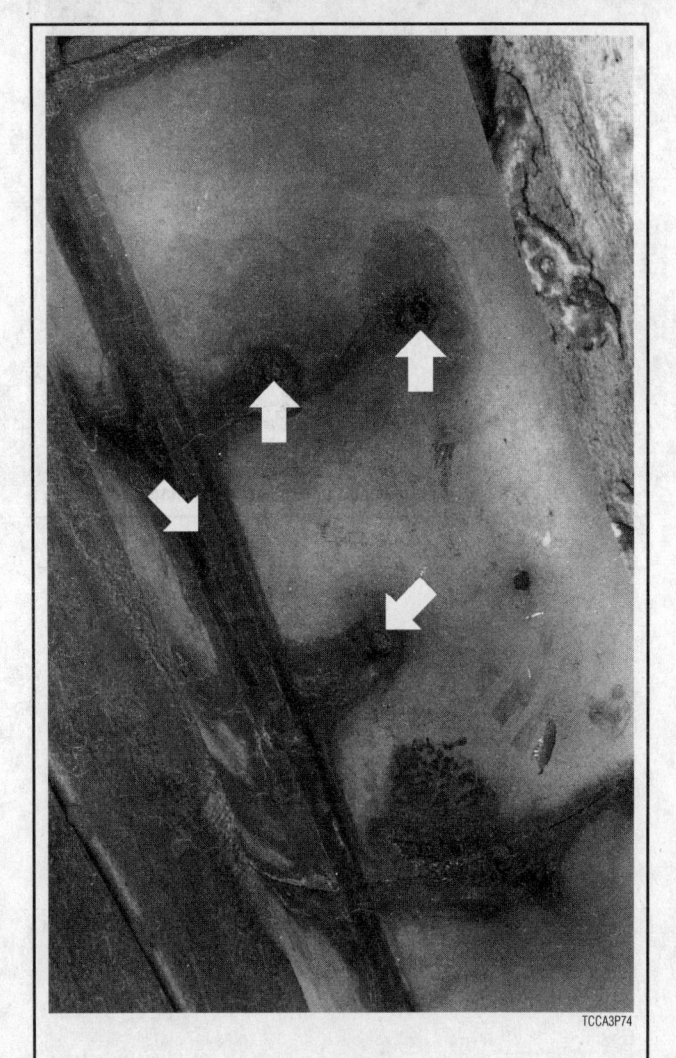

Fig. 180 Check the muffler for rotted spot welds and seams

## 3-50 ENGINE AND ENGINE OVERHAUL

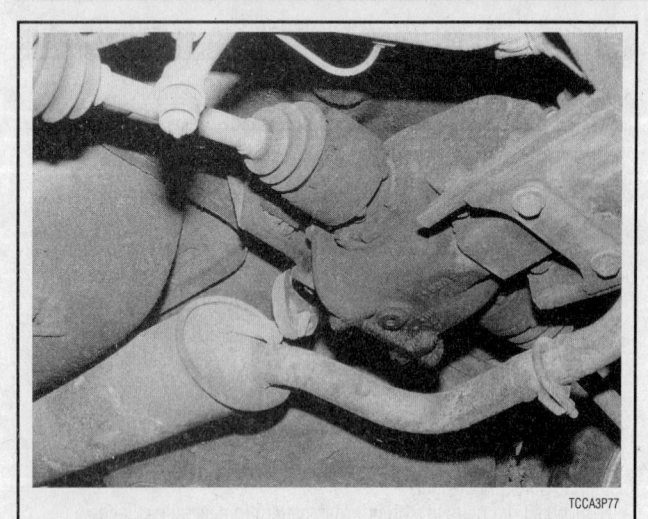

Fig. 181 Make sure the exhaust components are not contacting the body or suspension

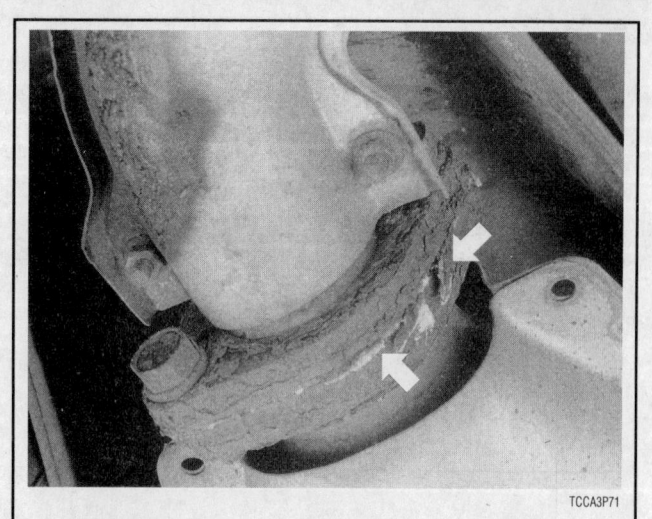

Fig. 184 Inspect flanges for gaskets that have deteriorated and need replacement

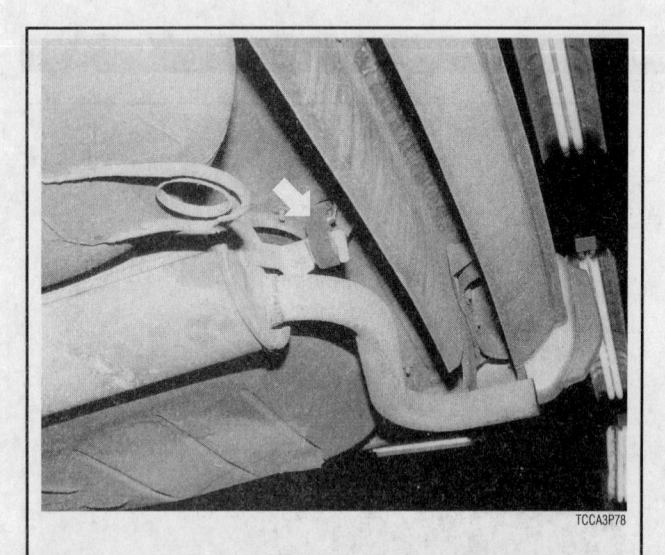

Fig. 182 Check for overstretched or torn exhaust hangers

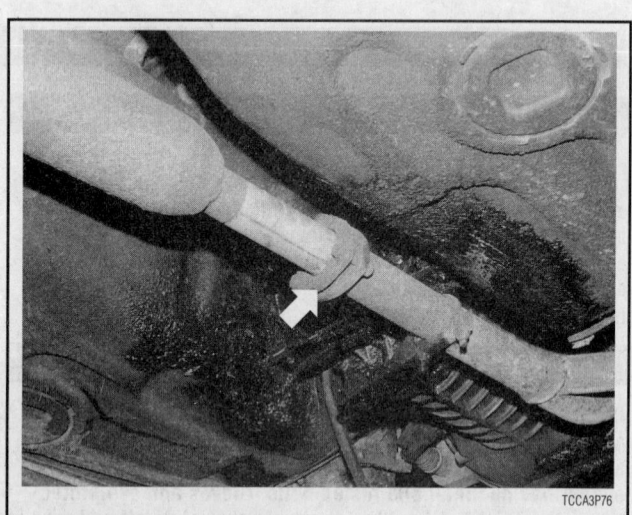

Fig. 185 Some systems, like this one, use large O-rings (donuts) in between the flanges

Fig. 183 Example of a badly deteriorated exhaust pipe

Your vehicle must be raised and supported safely to inspect the exhaust system properly. By placing 4 safety stands under the vehicle for support should provide enough room for you to slide under the vehicle and inspect the system completely. Start the inspection at the exhaust manifold or turbocharger pipe where the header pipe is attached and work your way to the back of the vehicle. On dual exhaust systems, remember to inspect both sides of the vehicle. Check the complete exhaust system for open seams, holes loose connections, or other deterioration which could permit exhaust fumes to seep into the passenger compartment. Inspect all mounting brackets and hangers for deterioration, some models may have rubber O-rings that can be overstretched and non-supportive. These components will need to be replaced if found. It has always been a practice to use a pointed tool to poke up into the exhaust system where the deterioration spots are to see whether or not they crumble. Some models may have heat shield covering certain parts of the exhaust system , it will be necessary to remove these shields to have the exhaust visible for inspection also.

# ENGINE AND ENGINE OVERHAUL 3-51

## REPLACEMENT

▶ See Figures 186, 187 and 188

There are basically two types of exhaust systems. One is the flange type where the component ends are attached with bolts and a gasket in-between. The other exhaust system is the slip joint type. These components slip into one another using clamps to retain them together.

### ✱✱ CAUTION

Allow the exhaust system to cool sufficiently before spraying a solvent exhaust fasteners. Some solvents are highly flammable and could ignite when sprayed on hot exhaust components.

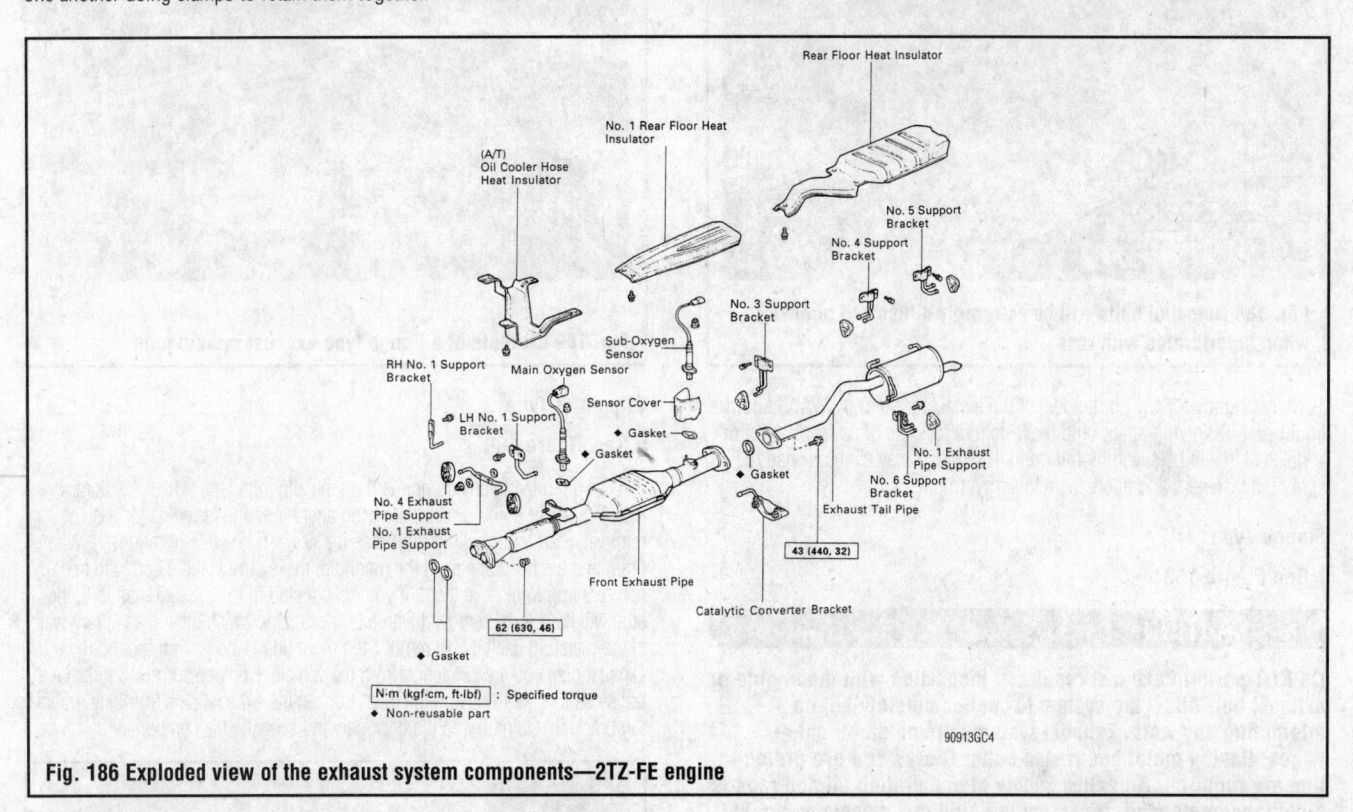

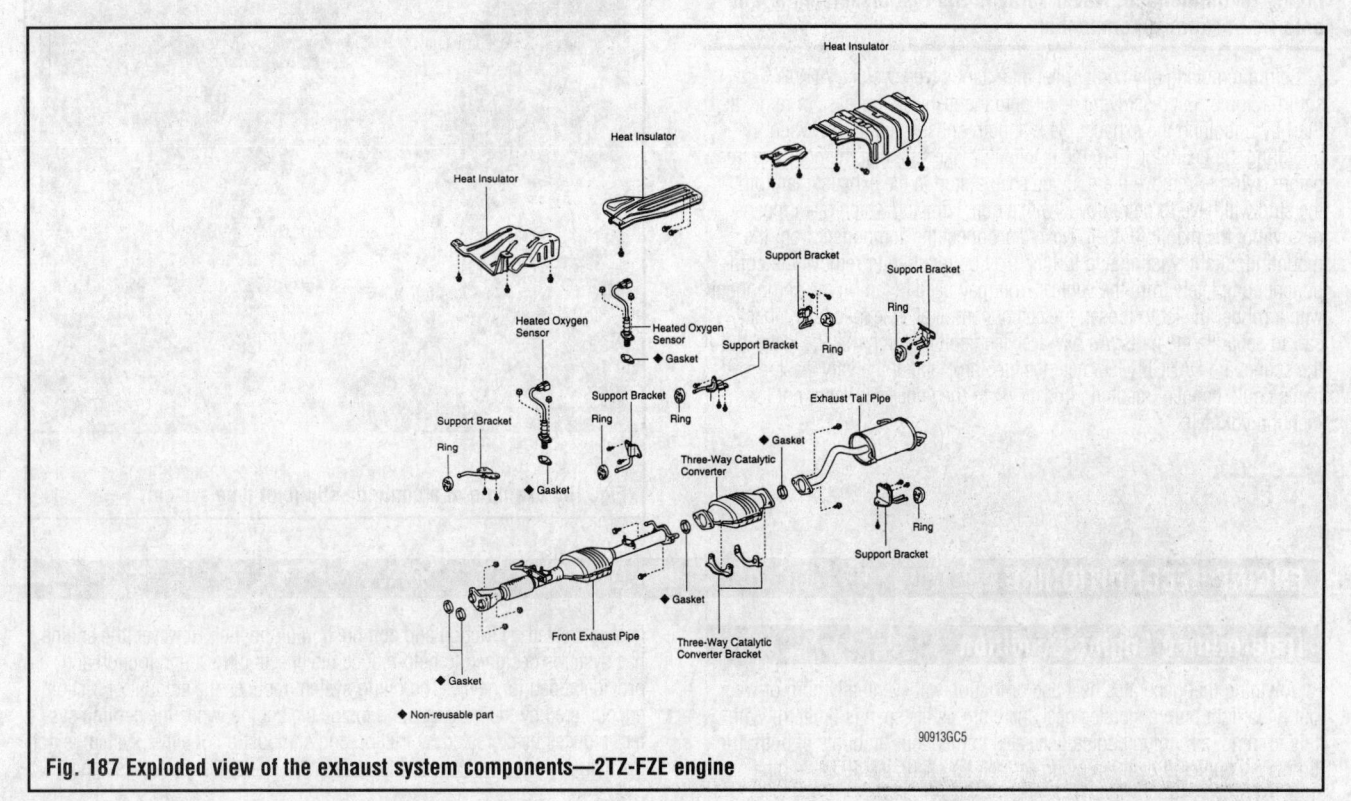

Fig. 186 Exploded view of the exhaust system components—2TZ-FE engine

Fig. 187 Exploded view of the exhaust system components—2TZ-FZE engine

# 3-52 ENGINE AND ENGINE OVERHAUL

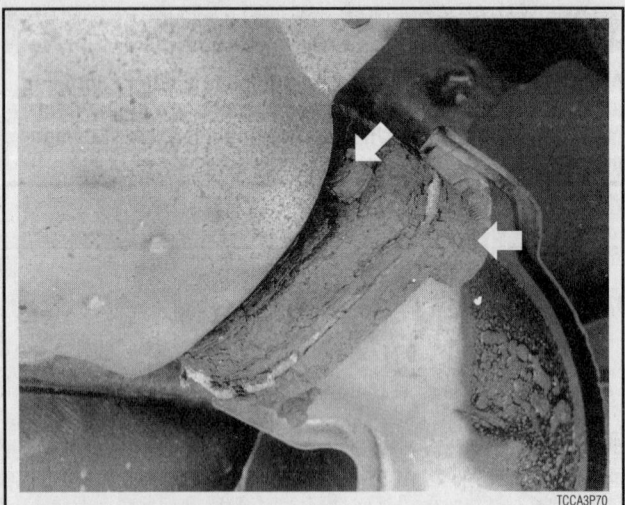

**Fig. 188 Nuts and bolts will be extremely difficult to remove when deteriorated with rust**

**Fig. 189 Example of a flange type exhaust system joint**

Before removing any component of the exhaust system, ALWAYS squirt a liquid rust dissolving agent onto the fasteners for ease of removal. A lot of knuckle skin will be saved by following this rule. It may even be wise to spray the fasteners and allow them to sit overnight.

### Flange Type
▶ See Figure 189

> **⁂⁂ CAUTION**
>
> Do NOT perform exhaust repairs or inspection with the engine or exhaust hot. Allow the system to cool completely before attempting any work. Exhaust systems are noted for sharp edges, flaking metal and rusted bolts. Gloves and eye protection are required. A healthy supply of penetrating oil and rags is highly recommended. Never spray liquid rust dissolving agent onto a hot exhaust component.

Before removing any component on a flange type system, ALWAYS squirt a liquid rust dissolving agent onto the fasteners for ease of removal. Start by unbolting the exhaust piece at both ends (if required). When unbolting the headpipe from the manifold, make sure that the bolts are free before trying to remove them. if you snap a stud in the exhaust manifold, the stud will have to be removed with a bolt extractor, which often means removal of the manifold itself. Next, disconnect the component from the mounting; slight twisting and turning may be required to remove the component completely from the vehicle. You may need to tap on the component with a rubber mallet to loosen the component. If all else fails, use a hacksaw to separate the parts. An oxy-acetylene cutting torch may be faster but the sparks are DANGEROUS near the fuel tank, and at the very least, accidents could happen, resulting in damage to the under-car parts, not to mention yourself.

### Slip Joint Type
▶ See Figure 190

Before removing any component on the slip joint type exhaust system, ALWAYS squirt a liquid rust dissolving agent onto the fasteners for ease of removal. Start by unbolting the exhaust piece at both ends (if required). When unbolting the headpipe from the manifold, make sure that the bolts are free before trying to remove them. if you snap a stud in the exhaust manifold, the stud will have to be removed with a bolt extractor, which often means removal of the manifold itself. Next, remove the mounting U-bolts from around the exhaust pipe you are extracting from the vehicle. Don't be surprised if the U-bolts break while removing the nuts. Loosen the exhaust pipe from any mounting brackets retaining it to the floor pan and separate the components.

**Fig. 190 Example of a common slip joint type system**

## ENGINE RECONDITIONING

### Determining Engine Condition

Anything that generates heat and/or friction will eventually burn or wear out (ie. a light bulb generates heat, therefore its life span is limited). With this in mind, a running engine generates tremendous amounts of both; friction is encountered by the moving and rotating parts inside the engine and heat is created by friction and combustion of the fuel. However, the engine has systems designed to help reduce the effects of heat and friction and provide added longevity. The oiling system reduces the amount of friction encountered by the moving parts inside the engine, while the cooling system reduces heat created by friction and combustion. If either system is not maintained, a break-down will be inevitable. Therefore, you can see how

# ENGINE AND ENGINE OVERHAUL  3-53

regular maintenance can affect the service life of your vehicle. If you do not drain, flush and refill your cooling system at the proper intervals, deposits will begin to accumulate in the radiator, thereby reducing the amount of heat it can extract from the coolant. The same applies to your oil and filter; if it is not changed often enough it becomes laden with contaminates and is unable to properly lubricate the engine. This increases friction and wear.

There are a number of methods for evaluating the condition of your engine. A compression test can reveal the condition of your pistons, piston rings, cylinder bores, head gasket(s), valves and valve seats. An oil pressure test can warn you of possible engine bearing, or oil pump failures. Excessive oil consumption, evidence of oil in the engine air intake area and/or bluish smoke from the tail pipe may indicate worn piston rings, worn valve guides and/or valve seals. As a general rule, an engine that uses no more than one quart of oil every 1000 miles is in good condition. Engines that use one quart of oil or more in less than 1000 miles should first be checked for oil leaks. If any oil leaks are present, have them fixed before determining how much oil is consumed by the engine, especially if blue smoke is not visible at the tail pipe.

## COMPRESSION TEST

▶ See Figure 191

A noticeable lack of engine power, excessive oil consumption and/or poor fuel mileage measured over an extended period are all indicators of internal engine wear. Worn piston rings, scored or worn cylinder bores, blown head gaskets, sticking or burnt valves, and worn valve seats are all possible culprits. A check of each cylinder's compression will help locate the problem.

➡ **A screw-in type compression gauge is more accurate than the type you simply hold against the spark plug hole. Although it takes slightly longer to use, it's worth the effort to obtain a more accurate reading.**

1. Make sure that the proper amount and viscosity of engine oil is in the crankcase, then ensure the battery is fully charged.
2. Warm-up the engine to normal operating temperature, then shut the engine **OFF**.
3. Disable the ignition system.
4. Label and disconnect all of the spark plug wires from the plugs.
5. Thoroughly clean the cylinder head area around the spark plug ports, then remove the spark plugs.
6. Set the throttle plate to the fully open (wide-open throttle) position. You can block the accelerator linkage open for this, or you can have an assistant fully depress the accelerator pedal.
7. Install a screw-in type compression gauge into the No. 1 spark plug hole until the fitting is snug.

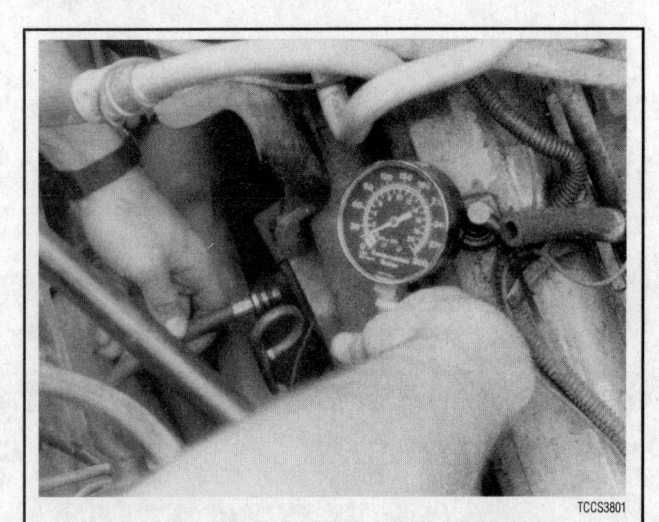

Fig. 191 A screw-in type compression gauge is more accurate and easier to use without an assistant

### ✽✽ WARNING

**Be careful not to crossthread the spark plug hole.**

8. According to the tool manufacturer's instructions, connect a remote starting switch to the starting circuit.
9. With the ignition switch in the **OFF** position, use the remote starting switch to crank the engine through at least five compression strokes (approximately 5 seconds of cranking) and record the highest reading on the gauge.
10. Repeat the test on each cylinder, cranking the engine approximately the same number of compression strokes and/or time as the first.
11. Compare the highest readings from each cylinder to that of the others. The indicated compression pressures are considered within specifications if the lowest reading cylinder is within 75 percent of the pressure recorded for the highest reading cylinder. For example, if your highest reading cylinder pressure was 150 psi (1034 kPa), then 75 percent of that would be 113 psi (779 kPa). So the lowest reading cylinder should be no less than 113 psi (779 kPa).
12. If a cylinder exhibits an unusually low compression reading, pour a tablespoon of clean engine oil into the cylinder through the spark plug hole and repeat the compression test. If the compression rises after adding oil, it means that the cylinder's piston rings and/or cylinder bore are damaged or worn. If the pressure remains low, the valves may not be seating properly (a valve job is needed), or the head gasket may be blown near that cylinder. If compression in any two adjacent cylinders is low, and if the addition of oil doesn't help raise compression, there is leakage past the head gasket. Oil and coolant in the combustion chamber, combined with blue or constant white smoke from the tail pipe, are symptoms of this problem. However, don't be alarmed by the normal white smoke emitted from the tail pipe during engine warm-up or from cold weather driving. There may be evidence of water droplets on the engine dipstick and/or oil droplets in the cooling system if a head gasket is blown.

## OIL PRESSURE TEST

Check for proper oil pressure at the sending unit passage with an externally mounted mechanical oil pressure gauge (as opposed to relying on a factory installed dash-mounted gauge). A tachometer may also be needed, as some specifications may require running the engine at a specific rpm.

1. With the engine cold, locate and remove the oil pressure sending unit.
2. Following the manufacturer's instructions, connect a mechanical oil pressure gauge and, if necessary, a tachometer to the engine.
3. Start the engine and allow it to idle.
4. Check the oil pressure reading when cold and record the number. You may need to run the engine at a specified rpm, so check the specifications chart located earlier in this section.
5. Run the engine until normal operating temperature is reached (upper radiator hose will feel warm).
6. Check the oil pressure reading again with the engine hot and record the number. Turn the engine **OFF**.
7. Compare your hot oil pressure reading to that given in the chart. If the reading is low, check the cold pressure reading against the chart. If the cold pressure is well above the specification, and the hot reading was lower than the specification, you may have the wrong viscosity oil in the engine. Change the oil, making sure to use the proper grade and quantity, then repeat the test.

Low oil pressure readings could be attributed to internal component wear, pump related problems, a low oil level, or oil viscosity that is too low. High oil pressure readings could be caused by an overfilled crankcase, too high of an oil viscosity or a faulty pressure relief valve.

### Buy or Rebuild?

Now that you have determined that your engine is worn out, you must make some decisions. The question of whether or not an engine is worth rebuilding is largely a subjective matter and one of personal worth. Is the

# 3-54 ENGINE AND ENGINE OVERHAUL

engine a popular one, or is it an obsolete model? Are parts available? Will it get acceptable gas mileage once it is rebuilt? Is the car it's being put into worth keeping? Would it be less expensive to buy a new engine, have your engine rebuilt by a pro, rebuild it yourself or buy a used engine from a salvage yard? Or would it be simpler and less expensive to buy another car? If you have considered all these matters and more, and have still decided to rebuild the engine, then it is time to decide how you will rebuild it.

➡ The editors at Chilton feel that most engine machining should be performed by a professional machine shop. Don't think of it as wasting money, rather, as an assurance that the job has been done right the first time. There are many expensive and specialized tools required to perform such tasks as boring and honing an engine block or having a valve job done on a cylinder head. Even inspecting the parts requires expensive micrometers and gauges to properly measure wear and clearances. Also, a machine shop can deliver to you clean, and ready to assemble parts, saving you time and aggravation. Your maximum savings will come from performing the removal, disassembly, assembly and installation of the engine and purchasing or renting only the tools required to perform the above tasks. Depending on the particular circumstances, you may save 40 to 60 percent of the cost doing these yourself.

A complete rebuild or overhaul of an engine involves replacing all of the moving parts (pistons, rods, crankshaft, camshaft, etc.) with new ones and machining the non-moving wearing surfaces of the block and heads. Unfortunately, this may not be cost effective. For instance, your crankshaft may have been damaged or worn, but it can be machined undersize for a minimal fee.

So, as you can see, you can replace everything inside the engine, but, it is wiser to replace only those parts which are really needed, and, if possible, repair the more expensive ones. Later in this section, we will break the engine down into its two main components: the cylinder head and the engine block. We will discuss each component, and the recommended parts to replace during a rebuild on each.

## Engine Overhaul Tips

Most engine overhaul procedures are fairly standard. In addition to specific parts replacement procedures and specifications for your individual engine, this section is also a guide to acceptable rebuilding procedures. Examples of standard rebuilding practice are given and should be used along with specific details concerning your particular engine.

Competent and accurate machine shop services will ensure maximum performance, reliability and engine life. In most instances it is more profitable for the do-it-yourself mechanic to remove, clean and inspect the component, buy the necessary parts and deliver these to a shop for actual machine work.

Much of the assembly work (crankshaft, bearings, piston rods, and other components) is well within the scope of the do-it-yourself mechanic's tools and abilities. You will have to decide for yourself the depth of involvement you desire in an engine repair or rebuild.

### TOOLS

The tools required for an engine overhaul or parts replacement will depend on the depth of your involvement. With a few exceptions, they will be the tools found in a mechanic's tool kit (see Section 1 of this manual). More in-depth work will require some or all of the following:

- A dial indicator (reading in thousandths) mounted on a universal base
- Micrometers and telescope gauges
- Jaw and screw-type pullers
- Scraper
- Valve spring compressor
- Ring groove cleaner
- Piston ring expander and compressor
- Ridge reamer
- Cylinder hone or glaze breaker
- Plastigage®
- Engine stand

The use of most of these tools is illustrated in this section. Many can be rented for a one-time use from a local parts jobber or tool supply house specializing in automotive work.

Occasionally, the use of special tools is called for. See the information on Special Tools and the Safety Notice in the front of this book before substituting another tool.

### OVERHAUL TIPS

Aluminum has become extremely popular for use in engines, due to its low weight. Observe the following precautions when handling aluminum parts:

- Never hot tank aluminum parts (the caustic hot tank solution will eat the aluminum.
- Remove all aluminum parts (identification tag, etc.) from engine parts prior to the tanking.
- Always coat threads lightly with engine oil or anti-seize compounds before installation, to prevent seizure.
- Never overtighten bolts or spark plugs especially in aluminum threads.

When assembling the engine, any parts that will be exposed to frictional contact must be prelubed to provide lubrication at initial start-up. Any product specifically formulated for this purpose can be used, but engine oil is not recommended as a prelube in most cases.

When semi-permanent (locked, but removable) installation of bolts or nuts is desired, threads should be cleaned and coated with Loctite® or another similar, commercial non-hardening sealant.

### CLEANING

▶ See Figures 192, 193, 194 and 195

Before the engine and its components are inspected, they must be thoroughly cleaned. You will need to remove any engine varnish, oil sludge and/or carbon deposits from all of the components to insure an accurate inspection. A crack in the engine block or cylinder head can easily become overlooked if hidden by a layer of sludge or carbon.

Most of the cleaning process can be carried out with common hand tools and readily available solvents or solutions. Carbon deposits can be chipped away using a hammer and a hard wooden chisel. Old gasket material and varnish or sludge can usually be removed using a scraper and/or cleaning solvent. Extremely stubborn deposits may require the use of a power drill with a wire brush. If using a wire brush, use extreme care around any critical machined surfaces (such as the gasket surfaces, bearing saddles, cylinder bores, etc.). USE OF A WIRE BRUSH IS NOT RECOM-

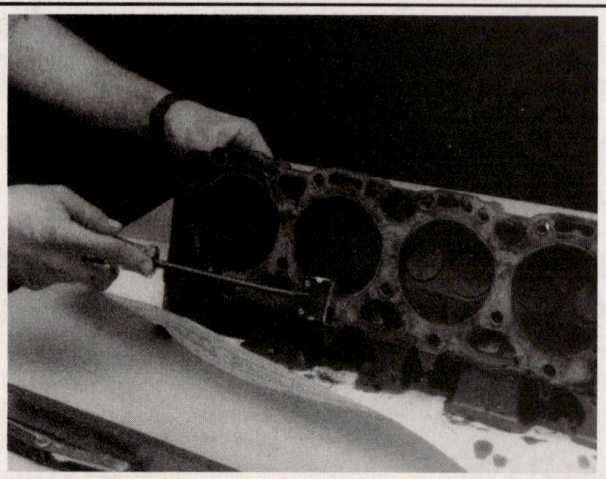

Fig. 192 Use a gasket scraper to remove the old gasket material from the mating surfaces

# ENGINE AND ENGINE OVERHAUL  3-55

**Fig. 193 Use a ring expander tool to remove the piston rings**

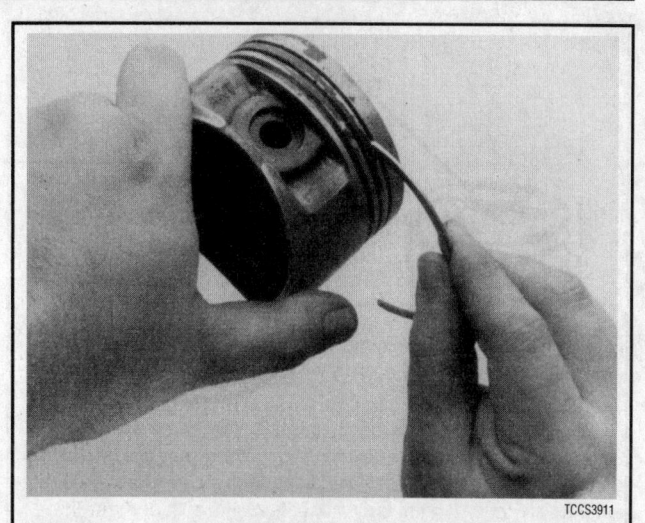

**Fig. 195 . . . use a piece of an old ring to clean the grooves. Be careful, the ring can be quite sharp**

MENDED ON ANY ALUMINUM COMPONENTS. Always follow any safety recommendations given by the manufacturer of the tool and/or solvent. You should always wear eye protection during any cleaning process involving scraping, chipping or spraying of solvents.

An alternative to the mess and hassle of cleaning the parts yourself is to drop them off at a local garage or machine shop. They will, more than likely, have the necessary equipment to properly clean all of the parts for a nominal fee.

### ✲✲ CAUTION

**Always wear eye protection during any cleaning process involving scraping, chipping or spraying of solvents.**

Remove any oil galley plugs, freeze plugs and/or pressed-in bearings and carefully wash and degrease all of the engine components including the fasteners and bolts. Small parts such as the valves, springs, etc., should be placed in a metal basket and allowed to soak. Use pipe cleaner type brushes, and clean all passageways in the components. Use a ring expander and remove the rings from the pistons. Clean the piston ring grooves with a special tool or a piece of broken ring. Scrape the carbon off of the top of the piston. You should never use a wire brush on the pistons. After preparing all of the piston assemblies in this manner, wash and degrease them again.

### ✲✲ WARNING

**Use extreme care when cleaning around the cylinder head valve seats. A mistake or slip may cost you a new seat.**

When cleaning the cylinder head, remove carbon from the combustion chamber with the valves installed. This will avoid damaging the valve seats.

### REPAIRING DAMAGED THREADS

▶ See Figures 196, 197, 198, 199 and 200

Several methods of repairing damaged threads are available. Heli-Coil® (shown here), Keenserts® and Microdot® are among the most widely used. All involve basically the same principle—drilling out stripped threads, tapping the hole and installing a prewound insert—making welding, plugging and oversize fasteners unnecessary.

Two types of thread repair inserts are usually supplied: a standard type for most inch coarse, inch fine, metric course and metric fine thread sizes and a spark lug type to fit most spark plug port sizes. Consult the individual tool manufacturer's catalog to determine exact applications. Typical thread repair kits will contain a selection of prewound threaded inserts, a tap (corresponding to the outside diameter threads of the insert) and an

**Fig. 194 Clean the piston ring grooves using a ring groove cleaner tool, or . . .**

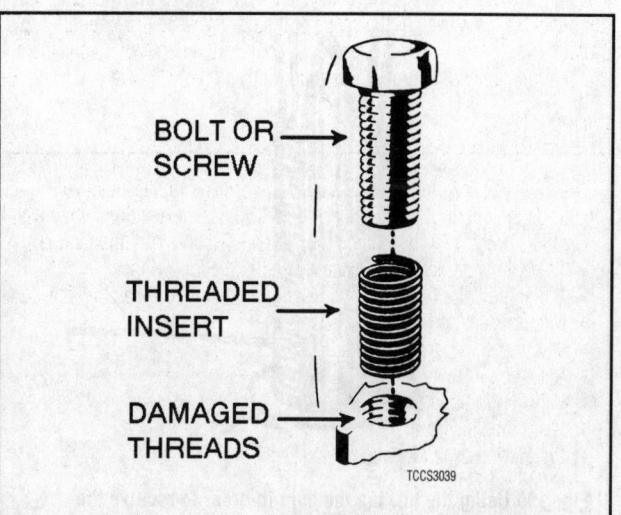

**Fig. 196 Damaged bolt hole threads can be replaced with thread repair inserts**

# ENGINE AND ENGINE OVERHAUL

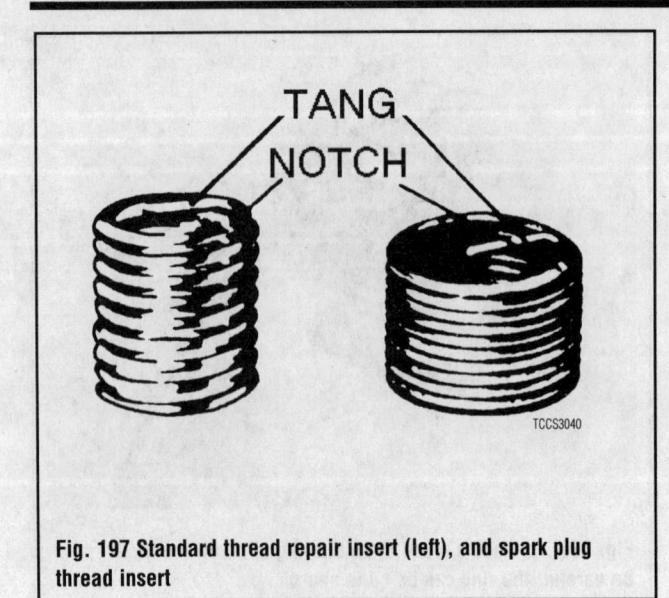

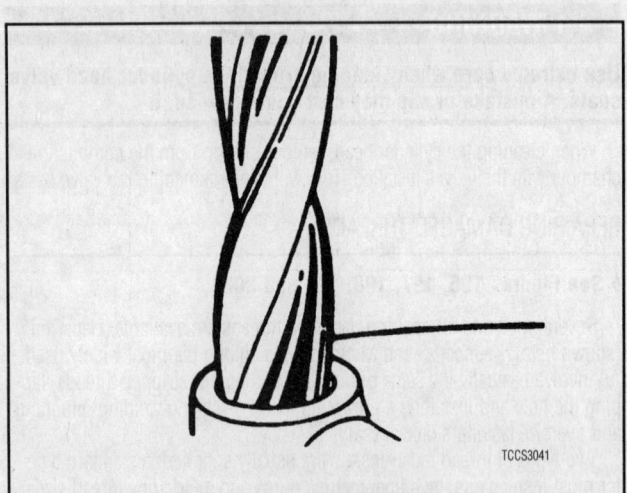

Fig. 197 Standard thread repair insert (left), and spark plug thread insert

Fig. 198 Drill out the damaged threads with the specified size bit. Be sure to drill completely through the hole or to the bottom of a blind hole

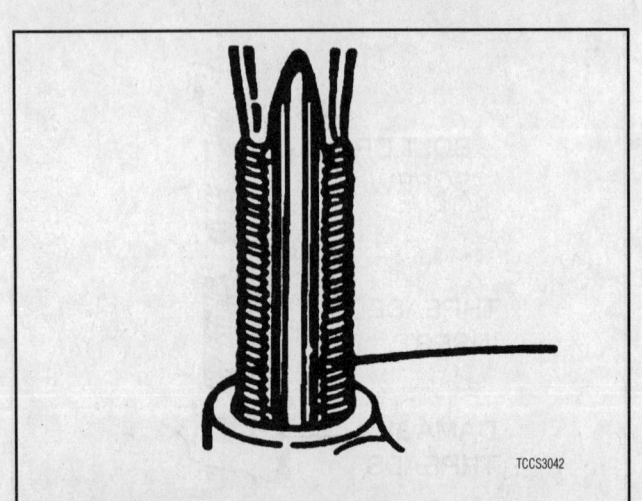

Fig. 199 Using the kit, tap the hole in order to receive the thread insert. Keep the tap well oiled and back it out frequently to avoid clogging the threads

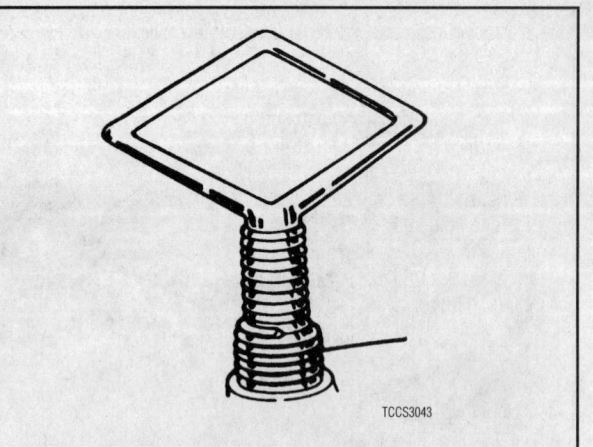

Fig. 200 Screw the insert onto the installer tool until the tang engages the slot. Thread the insert into the hole until it is ¼–½ turn below the top surface, then remove the tool and break off the tang using a punch

installation tool. Spark plug inserts usually differ because they require a tap equipped with pilot threads and a combined reamer/tap section. Most manufacturers also supply blister-packed thread repair inserts separately in addition to a master kit containing a variety of taps and inserts plus installation tools.

Before attempting to repair a threaded hole, remove any snapped, broken or damaged bolts or studs. Penetrating oil can be used to free frozen threads. The offending item can usually be removed with locking pliers or using a screw/stud extractor. After the hole is clear, the thread can be repaired, as shown in the series of accompanying illustrations and in the kit manufacturer's instructions.

## Engine Preparation

To properly rebuild an engine, you must first remove it from the vehicle, then disassemble and diagnose it. Ideally you should place your engine on an engine stand. This affords you the best access to the engine components. Follow the manufacturer's directions for using the stand with your particular engine. Remove the flywheel or flexplate before installing the engine to the stand.

Now that you have the engine on a stand, and assuming that you have drained the oil and coolant from the engine, it's time to strip it of all but the necessary components. Before you start disassembling the engine, you may want to take a moment to draw some pictures, or fabricate some labels or containers to mark the locations of various components and the bolts and/or studs which fasten them. Modern day engines use a lot of little brackets and clips which hold wiring harnesses and such, and these holders are often mounted on studs and/or bolts that can be easily mixed up. The manufacturer spent a lot of time and money designing your vehicle, and they wouldn't have wasted any of it by haphazardly placing brackets, clips or fasteners on the vehicle. If it's present when you disassemble it, put it back when you assemble, you will regret not remembering that little bracket which holds a wire harness out of the path of a rotating part.

You should begin by unbolting any accessories still attached to the engine, such as the water pump, power steering pump, alternator, etc. Then, unfasten any manifolds (intake or exhaust) which were not removed during the engine removal procedure. Finally, remove any covers remaining on the engine such as the rocker arm, front or timing cover and oil pan. Some front covers may require the vibration damper and/or crank pulley to be removed beforehand. The idea is to reduce the engine to the bare necessities (cylinder head(s), valve train, engine block, crankshaft, pistons and connecting rods), plus any other 'in block' components such as oil pumps, balance shafts and auxiliary shafts.

Finally, remove the cylinder head(s) from the engine block and carefully place on a bench. Disassembly instructions for each component follow later in this section.

# ENGINE AND ENGINE OVERHAUL  3-57

## Cylinder Head

There are two basic types of cylinder heads used on today's automobiles: the Overhead Valve (OHV) and the Overhead Camshaft (OHC). The latter can also be broken down into two subgroups: the Single Overhead Camshaft (SOHC) and the Dual Overhead Camshaft (DOHC). Generally, if there is only a single camshaft on a head, it is just referred to as an OHC head. Also, an engine with an OHV cylinder head is also known as a pushrod engine.

Most cylinder heads these days are made of an aluminum alloy due to its light weight, durability and heat transfer qualities. However, cast iron was the material of choice in the past, and is still used on many vehicles today. Whether made from aluminum or iron, all cylinder heads have valves and seats. Some use two valves per cylinder, while the more hi-tech engines will utilize a multi-valve configuration using 3, 4 and even 5 valves per cylinder. When the valve contacts the seat, it does so on precision machined surfaces, which seals the combustion chamber. All cylinder heads have a valve guide for each valve. The guide centers the valve to the seat and allows it to move up and down within it. The clearance between the valve and guide can be critical. Too much clearance and the engine may consume oil, lose vacuum and/or damage the seat. Too little, and the valve can stick in the guide causing the engine to run poorly if at all, and possibly causing severe damage. The last component all cylinder heads have are valve springs. The spring holds the valve against its seat. It also returns the valve to this position when the valve has been opened by the valve train or camshaft. The spring is fastened to the valve by a retainer and valve locks (sometimes called keepers). Aluminum heads will also have a valve spring shim to keep the spring from wearing away the aluminum.

An ideal method of rebuilding the cylinder head would involve replacing all of the valves, guides, seats, springs, etc. with new ones. However, depending on how the engine was maintained, often this is not necessary. A major cause of valve, guide and seat wear is an improperly tuned engine. An engine that is running too rich, will often wash the lubricating oil out of the guide with gasoline, causing it to wear rapidly. Conversely, an engine which is running too lean will place higher combustion temperatures on the valves and seats allowing them to wear or even burn. Springs fall victim to the driving habits of the individual. A driver who often runs the engine rpm to the redline will wear out or break the springs faster then one that stays well below it. Unfortunately, mileage takes it toll on all of the parts. Generally, the valves, guides, springs and seats in a cylinder head can be machined and re-used, saving you money. However, if a valve is burnt, it may be wise to replace all of the valves, since they were all operating in the same environment. The same goes for any other component on the cylinder head. Think of it as an insurance policy against future problems related to that component.

Unfortunately, the only way to find out which components need replacing, is to disassemble and carefully check each piece. After the cylinder head(s) are disassembled, thoroughly clean all of the components.

### DISASSEMBLY

▶ See Figures 201 and 202

Whether it is a single or dual overhead camshaft cylinder head, the disassembly procedure is relatively unchanged. One aspect to pay attention to is careful labeling of the parts on the dual camshaft cylinder head. There will be an intake camshaft and followers as well as an exhaust camshaft and followers and they must be labeled as such. In some cases, the components are identical and could easily be installed incorrectly. DO NOT MIX THEM UP! Determining which is which is very simple; the intake camshaft and components are on the same side of the head as was the intake manifold. Conversely, the exhaust camshaft and components are on the same side of the head as was the exhaust manifold.

Fig. 201 Exploded view of a valve, seal, spring, retainer and locks from an OHC cylinder head

Fig. 202 Example of a multi-valve cylinder head. Note how it has 2 intake and 2 exhaust valve ports

## 3-58 ENGINE AND ENGINE OVERHAUL

### CUP TYPE CAMSHAFT FOLLOWERS

▶ See Figures 203, 204 and 205

Most cylinder heads with cup type camshaft followers will have the valve spring, retainer and locks recessed within the follower's bore. You will need a C-clamp style valve spring compressor tool, an OHC spring removal tool (or equivalent) and a small magnet to disassemble the head.

1. If not already removed, remove the camshaft(s) and/or followers. Mark their positions for assembly.
2. Position the cylinder head to allow use of a C-clamp style valve spring compressor tool.

➡It is preferred to position the cylinder head gasket surface facing you with the valve springs facing the opposite direction and the head laying horizontal.

Fig. 203 C-clamp type spring compressor and an OHC spring removal tool (center) for cup type followers

3. With the OHC spring removal adapter tool positioned inside of the follower bore, compress the valve spring using the C-clamp style valve spring compressor.
4. Remove the valve locks. A small magnetic tool or screwdriver will aid in removal.

Fig. 204 Most cup type follower cylinder heads retain the camshaft using bolt-on bearing caps

Fig. 205 Position the OHC spring tool in the follower bore, then compress the spring with a C-clamp type tool

5. Release the compressor tool and remove the spring assembly.
6. Withdraw the valve from the cylinder head.
7. If equipped, remove the valve seal.

➡Special valve seal removal tools are available. Regular or needlenose type pliers, if used with care, will work just as well. If using ordinary pliers, be sure not to damage the follower bore. The follower and its bore are machined to close tolerances and any damage to the bore will effect this relationship.

8. If equipped, remove the valve spring shim. A small magnetic tool or screwdriver will aid in removal.
9. Repeat Steps 3 through 8 until all of the valves have been removed.

### ROCKER ARM TYPE CAMSHAFT FOLLOWERS

▶ See Figures 206 thru 214

Most cylinder heads with rocker arm-type camshaft followers are easily disassembled using a standard valve spring compressor. However, certain models may not have enough open space around the spring for the standard tool and may require you to use a C-clamp style compressor tool instead.

1. If not already removed, remove the rocker arms and/or shafts and the camshaft. If applicable, also remove the hydraulic lash adjusters. Mark their positions for assembly.
2. Position the cylinder head to allow access to the valve spring.
3. Use a valve spring compressor tool to relieve the spring tension from the retainer.

# ENGINE AND ENGINE OVERHAUL  3-59

Fig. 206 Example of the shaft mounted rocker arms on some OHC heads

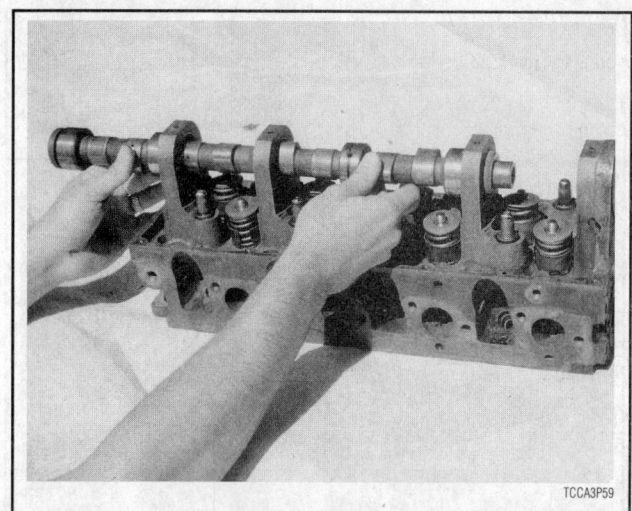

Fig. 209 . . . then the camshaft can be removed by sliding it out (shown), or unbolting a bearing cap (not shown)

Fig. 207 Another example of the rocker arm type OHC head. This model uses a follower under the camshaft

Fig. 210 Compress the valve spring . . .

Fig. 208 Before the camshaft can be removed, all of the followers must first be removed . . .

Fig. 211 . . . then remove the valve locks from the valve stem and spring retainer

# 3-60 ENGINE AND ENGINE OVERHAUL

➡ Due to engine varnish, the retainer may stick to the valve locks. A gentle tap with a hammer may help to break it loose.

4. Remove the valve locks from the valve tip and/or retainer. A small magnet may help in removing the small locks.
5. Lift the valve spring, tool and all, off of the valve stem.
6. If equipped, remove the valve seal. If the seal is difficult to remove with the valve in place, try removing the valve first, then the seal. Follow the steps below for valve removal.
7. Position the head to allow access for withdrawing the valve.

➡ Cylinder heads that have seen a lot of miles and/or abuse may have mushroomed the valve lock grove and/or tip, causing difficulty in removal of the valve. If this has happened, use a metal file to carefully remove the high spots around the lock grooves and/or tip. Only file it enough to allow removal.

8. Remove the valve from the cylinder head.
9. If equipped, remove the valve spring shim. A small magnetic tool or screwdriver will aid in removal.
10. Repeat Steps 3 though 9 until all of the valves have been removed.

### INSPECTION

Now that all of the cylinder head components are clean, it's time to inspect them for wear and/or damage. To accurately inspect them, you will need some specialized tools:
- A 0–1 inch micrometer for the valves
- A dial indicator or inside diameter gauge for the valve guides
- A spring pressure test gauge

If you do not have access to the proper tools, you may want to bring the components to a shop that does.

**Valves**

▶ See Figures 215 and 216

The first thing to inspect are the valve heads. Look closely at the head, margin and face for any cracks, excessive wear or burning. The margin is the best place to look for burning. It should have a squared edge with an even width all around the diameter. When a valve burns, the margin will look melted and the edges rounded. Also inspect the valve head for any signs of tulipping. This will show as a lifting of the edges or dishing in the center of the head and will usually not occur to all of the valves. All of the heads should look the same, any that seem dished more than others are probably bad. Next, inspect the valve lock grooves and valve tips. Check for any burrs around the lock grooves, especially if you had to file them to

Fig. 212 Remove the valve spring and retainer from the cylinder head

Fig. 213 Remove the valve seal from the guide. Some gentle prying or pliers may help to remove stubborn ones

Fig. 214 All aluminum and some cast iron heads will have these valve spring shims. Remove all of them as well

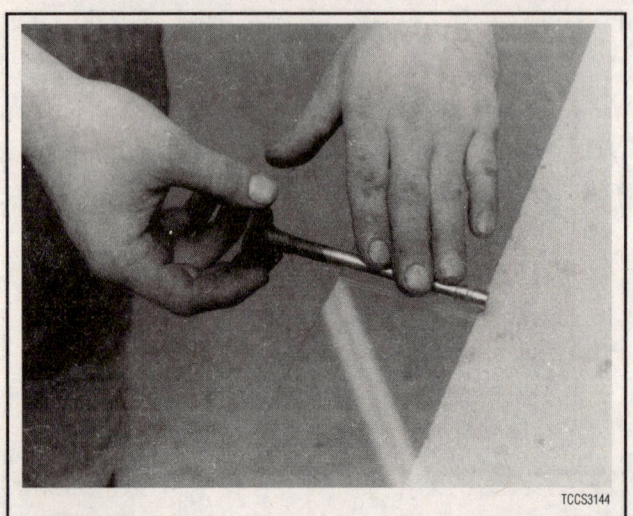

Fig. 215 Valve stems may be rolled on a flat surface to check for bends

# ENGINE AND ENGINE OVERHAUL  3-61

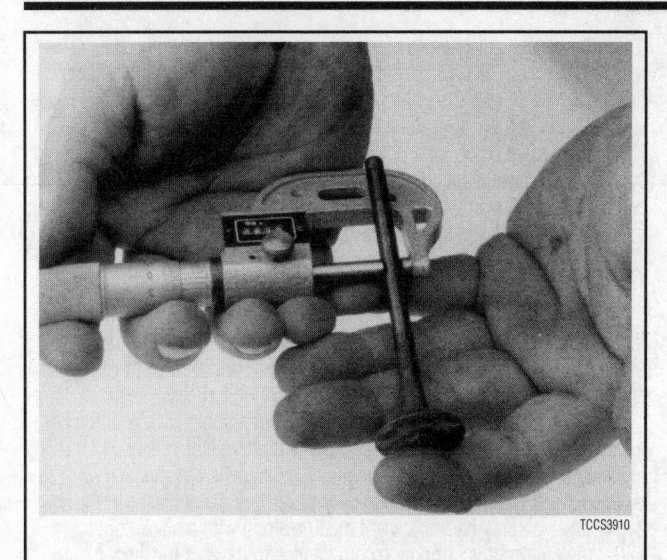

Fig. 216 Use a micrometer to check the valve stem diameter

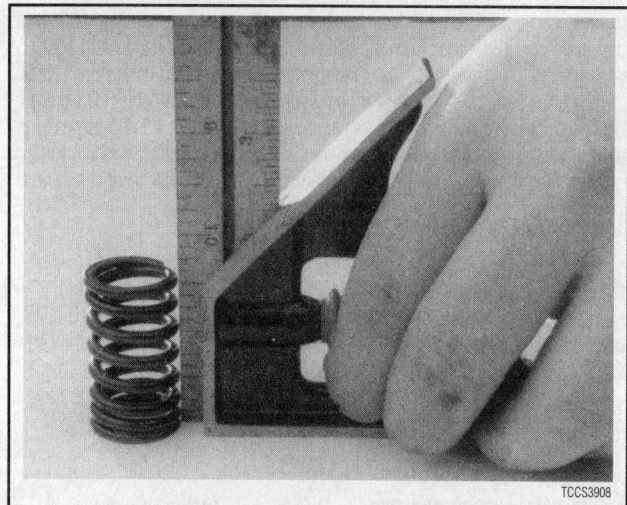

Fig. 218 Check the valve spring for squareness on a flat surface; a carpenter's square can be used

remove the valve. Valve tips should appear flat, although slight rounding with high mileage engines is normal. Slightly worn valve tips will need to be machined flat. Last, measure the valve stem diameter with the micrometer. Measure the area that rides within the guide, especially towards the tip where most of the wear occurs. Take several measurements along its length and compare them to each other. Wear should be even along the length with little to no taper. If no minimum diameter is given in the specifications, then the stem should not read more than 0.001 inch (0.025mm) below the specification. Any valves that fail these inspections should be replaced.

### Springs, Retainers and Valve Locks
▶ See Figures 217 and 218

The first thing to check is the most obvious, broken springs. Next check the free length and squareness of each spring. If applicable, insure to distinguish between intake and exhaust springs. Use a ruler and/or carpenters square to measure the length. A carpenters square should be used to check the springs for squareness. If a spring pressure test gauge is available, check each springs rating and compare to the specifications chart. Check the readings against the specifications given. Any springs that fail these inspections should be replaced.

The spring retainers rarely need replacing, however they should still be checked as a precaution. Inspect the spring mating surface and the valve lock retention area for any signs of excessive wear. Also check for any signs of cracking. Replace any retainers that are questionable.

Valve locks should be inspected for excessive wear on the outside contact area as well as on the inner notched surface. Any locks which appear worn or broken and its respective valve should be replaced.

### Cylinder Head

There are several things to check on the cylinder head: valve guides, seats, cylinder head surface flatness, cracks and physical damage.

#### VALVE GUIDES
▶ See Figure 219

Now that you know the valves are good, you can use them to check the guides, although a new valve, if available, is preferred. Before you measure anything, look at the guides carefully and inspect them for any cracks, chips or breakage. Also if the guide is a removable style (as in most aluminum heads), check them for any looseness or evidence of movement. All of the guides should appear to be at the same height from the spring seat. If any seem lower (or higher) from another, the guide has moved. Mount a dial indicator onto the spring side of the cylinder head. Lightly oil the valve stem and insert it into the cylinder head. Position the dial indicator against the valve stem near the tip and zero the gauge. Grasp the valve stem and wiggle

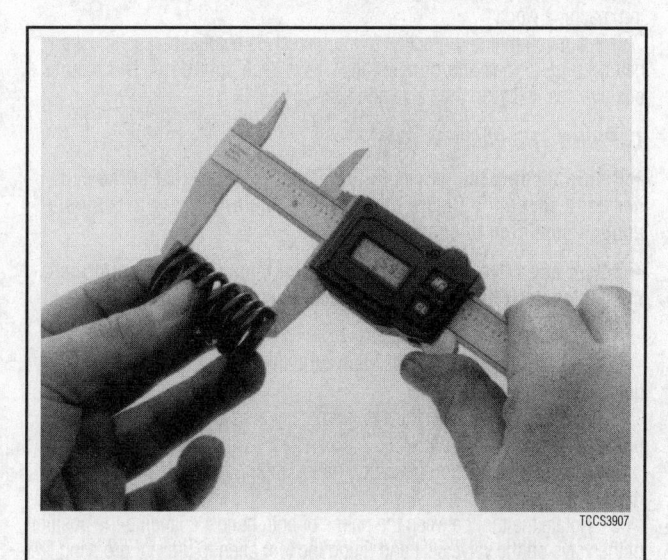

Fig. 217 Use a caliper to check the valve spring free-length

Fig. 219 A dial gauge may be used to check valve stem-to-guide clearance; read the gauge while moving the valve stem

# ENGINE AND ENGINE OVERHAUL

towards and away from the dial indicator and observe the readings. Mount the dial indicator 90 degrees from the initial point and zero the gauge and again take a reading. Compare the two readings for a out of round condition. Check the readings against the specifications given. An Inside Diameter (I.D.) gauge designed for valve guides will give you an accurate valve guide bore measurement. If the I.D. gauge is used, compare the readings with the specifications given. Any guides that fail these inspections should be replaced or machined.

### VALVE SEATS

A visual inspection of the valve seats should show a slightly worn and pitted surface where the valve face contacts the seat. Inspect the seat carefully for severe pitting or cracks. Also, a seat that is badly worn will be recessed into the cylinder head. A severely worn or recessed seat may need to be replaced. All cracked seats must be replaced. A seat concentricity gauge, if available, should be used to check the seat run-out. If run-out exceeds specifications the seat must be machined (if no specification is given use 0.002 inch (0.051mm).

### CYLINDER HEAD SURFACE FLATNESS

▸ See Figures 220 and 221

After you have cleaned the gasket surface of the cylinder head of any old gasket material, check the head for flatness.

Place a straightedge across the gasket surface. Using feeler gauges, determine the clearance at the center of the straightedge and across the cylinder head at several points. Check along the centerline and diagonally on the head surface. If the warpage exceeds 0.003 inch (0.076mm) within a 6.0 inch (15.2cm) span, or 0.006 inch (0.152mm) over the total length of the head, the cylinder head must be resurfaced. After resurfacing the heads of a V-type engine, the intake manifold flange surface should be checked, and if necessary, milled proportionally to allow for the change in its mounting position.

### CRACKS AND PHYSICAL DAMAGE

Generally, cracks are limited to the combustion chamber, however, it is not uncommon for the head to crack in a spark plug hole, port, outside of the head or in the valve spring/rocker arm area. The first area to inspect is always the hottest: the exhaust seat/port area.

A visual inspection should be performed, but just because you don't see a crack does not mean it is not there. Some more reliable methods for inspecting for cracks include Magnaflux®, a magnetic process or Zyglo®, a dye penetrant. Magnaflux® is used only on ferrous metal (cast iron) heads. Zyglo® uses a spray on fluorescent mixture along with a black light to reveal the cracks. It is strongly recommended to have your cylinder head checked professionally for cracks, especially if the engine was known to have overheated and/or leaked or consumed coolant. Contact a local shop for availability and pricing of these services.

Physical damage is usually very evident. For example, a broken mounting ear from dropping the head or a bent or broken stud and/or bolt. All of these defects should be fixed or, if unrepairable, the head should be replaced.

#### Camshaft and Followers

Inspect the camshaft(s) and followers as described earlier in this section.

### REFINISHING & REPAIRING

Many of the procedures given for refinishing and repairing the cylinder head components must be performed by a machine shop. Certain steps, if the inspected part is not worn, can be performed yourself inexpensively. However, you spent a lot of time and effort so far, why risk trying to save a couple bucks if you might have to do it all over again?

#### Valves

Any valves that were not replaced should be refaced and the tips ground flat. Unless you have access to a valve grinding machine, this should be done by a machine shop. If the valves are in extremely good condition, as well as the valve seats and guides, they may be lapped in without performing machine work.

It is a recommended practice to lap the valves even after machine work has been performed and/or new valves have been purchased. This insures a positive seal between the valve and seat.

### LAPPING THE VALVES

➡ Before lapping the valves to the seats, read the rest of the cylinder head section to insure that any related parts are in acceptable enough condition to continue.

➡ Before any valve seat machining and/or lapping can be performed, the guides must be within factory recommended specifications.

1. Invert the cylinder head.
2. Lightly lubricate the valve stems and insert them into the cylinder head in their numbered order.
3. Raise the valve from the seat and apply a small amount of fine lapping compound to the seat.
4. Moisten the suction head of a hand-lapping tool and attach it to the head of the valve.
5. Rotate the tool between the palms of both hands, changing the position of the valve on the valve seat and lifting the tool often to prevent grooving.

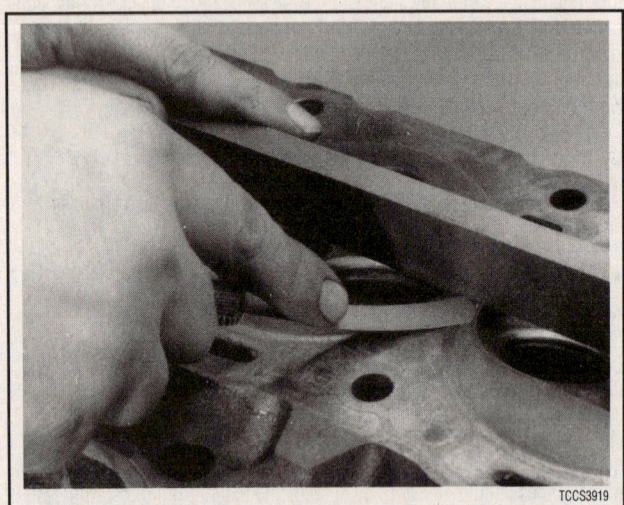

Fig. 220 Check the head for flatness across the center of the head surface using a straightedge and feeler gauge

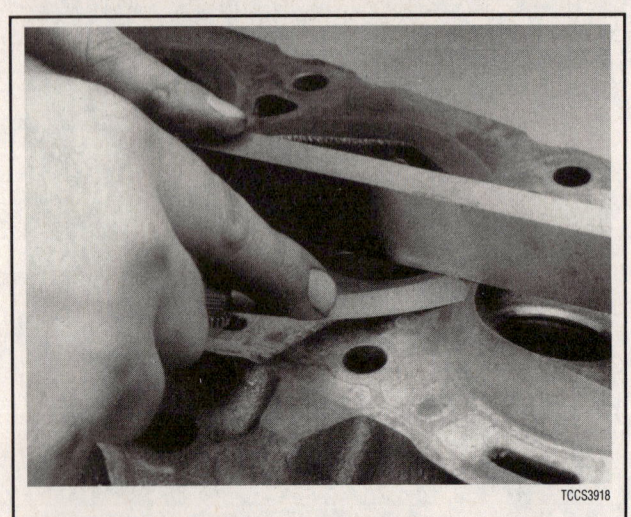

Fig. 221 Checks should also be made along both diagonals of the head surface

## ENGINE AND ENGINE OVERHAUL    3-63

6. Lap the valve until a smooth, polished circle is evident on the valve and seat.
7. Remove the tool and the valve. Wipe away all traces of the grinding compound and store the valve to maintain its lapped location.

### ✱✱ WARNING

**Do not get the valves out of order after they have been lapped. They must be put back with the same valve seat with which they were lapped.**

#### Springs, Retainers and Valve Locks

There is no repair or refinishing possible with the springs, retainers and valve locks. If they are found to be worn or defective, they must be replaced with new (or known good) parts.

#### Cylinder Head

Most refinishing procedures dealing with the cylinder head must be performed by a machine shop. Read the sections below and review your inspection data to determine whether or not machining is necessary.

##### *VALVE GUIDE*

➡ **If any machining or replacements are made to the valve guides, the seats must be machined.**

Unless the valve guides need machining or replacing, the only service to perform is to thoroughly clean them of any dirt or oil residue.

There are only two types of valve guides used on automobile engines: the replaceable-type (all aluminum heads) and the cast-in integral-type (most cast iron heads). There are four recommended methods for repairing worn guides.
- Knurling
- Inserts
- Reaming oversize
- Replacing

Knurling is a process in which metal is displaced and raised, thereby reducing clearance, giving a true center, and providing oil control. It is the least expensive way of repairing the valve guides. However, it is not necessarily the best, and in some cases, a knurled valve guide will not stand up for more than a short time. It requires a special knurlizer and precision reaming tools to obtain proper clearances. It would not be cost effective to purchase these tools, unless you plan on rebuilding several of the same cylinder head.

Installing a guide insert involves machining the guide to accept a bronze insert. One style is the coil-type which is installed into a threaded guide. Another is the thin-walled insert where the guide is reamed oversize to accept a split-sleeve insert. After the insert is installed, a special tool is then run through the guide to expand the insert, locking it to the guide. The insert is then reamed to the standard size for proper valve clearance.

Reaming for oversize valves restores normal clearances and provides a true valve seat. Most cast-in type guides can be reamed to accept an valve with an oversize stem. The cost factor for this can become quite high as you will need to purchase the reamer and new, oversize stem valves for all guides which were reamed. Oversizes are generally 0.003 to 0.030 inch (0.076 to 0.762mm), with 0.015 inch (0.381mm) being the most common.

To replace cast-in type valve guides, they must be drilled out, then reamed to accept replacement guides. This must be done on a fixture which will allow centering and leveling off of the original valve seat or guide, otherwise a serious guide-to-seat misalignment may occur making it impossible to properly machine the seat.

Replaceable-type guides are pressed into the cylinder head. A hammer and a stepped drift or punch may be used to install and remove the guides. Before removing the guides, measure the protrusion on the spring side of the head and record it for installation. Use the stepped drift to hammer out the old guide from the combustion chamber side of the head. When installing, determine whether or not the guide also seals a water jacket in the head, and if it does, use the recommended sealing agent. If there is no water jacket, grease the valve guide and its bore. Use the stepped drift, and hammer the new guide into the cylinder head from the spring side of the cylinder head. A stack of washers the same thickness as the measured protrusion may help the installation process.

##### *VALVE SEATS*

➡ **Before any valve seat machining can be performed, the guides must be within factory recommended specifications.**

➡ **If any machining or replacements were made to the valve guides, the seats must be machined.**

If the seats are in good condition, the valves can be lapped to the seats, and the cylinder head assembled. See the valves section for instructions on lapping.

If the valve seats are worn, cracked or damaged, they must be serviced by a machine shop. The valve seat must be perfectly centered to the valve guide, which requires very accurate machining.

##### *CYLINDER HEAD SURFACE*

If the cylinder head is warped, it must be machined flat. If the warpage is extremely severe, the head may need to be replaced. In some instances, it may be possible to straighten a warped head enough to allow machining. In either case, contact a professional machine shop for service.

➡ **Any OHC cylinder head that shows excessive warpage should have the camshaft bearing journals align bored after the cylinder head has been resurfaced.**

### ✱✱ WARNING

**Failure to align bore the camshaft bearing journals could result in severe engine damage including but not limited to: valve and piston damage, connecting rod damage, camshaft and/or crankshaft breakage.**

##### *CRACKS AND PHYSICAL DAMAGE*

Certain cracks can be repaired in both cast iron and aluminum heads. For cast iron, a tapered threaded insert is installed along the length of the crack. Aluminum can also use the tapered inserts, however welding is the preferred method. Some physical damage can be repaired through brazing or welding. Contact a machine shop to get expert advice for your particular dilemma.

### ASSEMBLY

The first step for any assembly job is to have a clean area in which to work. Next, thoroughly clean all of the parts and components that are to be assembled. Finally, place all of the components onto a suitable work space and, if necessary, arrange the parts to their respective positions.

◆ See Figure 222

#### Cup Type Camshaft Followers

To install the springs, retainers and valve locks on heads which have these components recessed into the camshaft follower's bore, you will need a small screwdriver-type tool, some clean white grease and a lot of patience. You will also need the C-clamp style spring compressor and the OHC tool used to disassemble the head.

1. Lightly lubricate the valve stems and insert all of the valves into the cylinder head. If possible, maintain their original locations.
2. If equipped, install any valve spring shims which were removed.
3. If equipped, install the new valve seals, keeping the following in mind:

- If the valve seal presses over the guide, lightly lubricate the outer guide surfaces.
- If the seal is an O-ring type, it is installed just after compressing the spring but before the valve locks.

## 3-64 ENGINE AND ENGINE OVERHAUL

4. Place the valve spring and retainer over the stem.
5. Position the spring compressor and the OHC tool, then compress the spring.
6. Using a small screwdriver as a spatula, fill the valve stem side of the lock with white grease. Use the excess grease on the screwdriver to fasten the lock to the driver.
7. Carefully install the valve lock, which is stuck to the end of the screwdriver, to the valve stem then press on it with the screwdriver until the grease squeezes out. The valve lock should now be stuck to the stem.
8. Repeat Steps 6 and 7 for the remaining valve lock.
9. Relieve the spring pressure slowly and insure that neither valve lock becomes dislodged by the retainer.
10. Remove the spring compressor tool.
11. Repeat Steps 2 through 10 until all of the springs have been installed.
12. Install the followers, camshaft(s) and any other components that were removed for disassembly.

Fig. 222 Once assembled, check the valve clearance and correct as needed

### Rocker Arm Type Camshaft Followers

1. Lightly lubricate the valve stems and insert all of the valves into the cylinder head. If possible, maintain their original locations.
2. If equipped, install any valve spring shims which were removed.
3. If equipped, install the new valve seals, keeping the following in mind:
   - If the valve seal presses over the guide, lightly lubricate the outer guide surfaces.
   - If the seal is an O-ring type, it is installed just after compressing the spring but before the valve locks.
4. Place the valve spring and retainer over the stem.
5. Position the spring compressor tool and compress the spring.
6. Assemble the valve locks to the stem.
7. Relieve the spring pressure slowly and insure that neither valve lock becomes dislodged by the retainer.
8. Remove the spring compressor tool.
9. Repeat Steps 2 through 8 until all of the springs have been installed.
10. Install the camshaft(s), rockers, shafts and any other components that were removed for disassembly.

## Engine Block

### GENERAL INFORMATION

A thorough overhaul or rebuild of an engine block would include replacing the pistons, rings, bearings, timing chain assembly and oil pump. For OHV engines also include a new camshaft and lifters. The block would then have the cylinders bored and honed oversize (or if using removable cylinder sleeves, new sleeves installed) and the crankshaft would be cut undersize to provide new wearing surfaces and perfect clearances. However, your particular engine may not have everything worn out. What if only the piston rings have worn out and the clearances on everything else are still within factory specifications? Well, you could just replace the rings and put it back together, but this would be a very rare example. Chances are, if one component in your engine is worn, other components are sure to follow, and soon. At the very least, you should always replace the rings, bearings and oil pump. This is what is commonly called a "freshen up".

### Cylinder Ridge Removal

Because the top piston ring does not travel to the very top of the cylinder, a ridge is built up between the end of the travel and the top of the cylinder bore.

Pushing the piston and connecting rod assembly past the ridge can be difficult, and damage to the piston ring lands could occur. If the ridge is not removed before installing a new piston or not removed at all, piston ring breakage and piston damage may occur.

➡ It is always recommended that you remove any cylinder ridges before removing the piston and connecting rod assemblies. If you know that new pistons are going to be installed and the engine block will be bored oversize, you may be able to forego this step. However, some ridges may actually prevent the assemblies from being removed, necessitating its removal.

There are several different types of ridge reamers on the market, none of which are inexpensive. Unless a great deal of engine rebuilding is anticipated, borrow or rent a reamer.

1. Turn the crankshaft until the piston is at the bottom of its travel.
2. Cover the head of the piston with a rag.
3. Follow the tool manufacturers instructions and cut away the ridge, exercising extreme care to avoid cutting too deeply.
4. Remove the ridge reamer, the rag and as many of the cuttings as possible. Continue until all of the cylinder ridges have been removed.

### DISASSEMBLY

▶ See Figures 223 and 224

The engine disassembly instructions following assume that you have the engine mounted on an engine stand. If not, it is easiest to disassemble the engine on a bench or the floor with it resting on the bellhousing or transmission mounting surface. You must be able to access the connecting rod fasteners and turn the crankshaft during disassembly. Also, all engine covers (timing, front, side, oil pan, whatever) should have already been removed. Engines which are seized or locked up may not be able to be completely disassembled, and a core (salvage yard) engine should be purchased.

If not done during the cylinder head removal, remove the timing chain/belt and/or gear/sprocket assembly. Remove the oil pick-up and pump assembly and, if necessary, the pump drive. If equipped, remove any balance or auxiliary shafts. If necessary, remove the cylinder ridge from the top of the bore. See the cylinder ridge removal procedure earlier in this section.

# ENGINE AND ENGINE OVERHAUL    3-65

Fig. 223 Place rubber hose over the connecting rod studs to protect the crankshaft and cylinder bores from damage

Rotate the engine over so that the crankshaft is exposed. Use a number punch or scribe and mark each connecting rod with its respective cylinder number. The cylinder closest to the front of the engine is always number 1. However, depending on the engine placement, the front of the engine could either be the flywheel or damper/pulley end. Generally the front of the engine faces the front of the vehicle. Use a number punch or scribe and also mark the main bearing caps from front to rear with the front most cap being number 1 (if there are five caps, mark them 1 through 5, front to rear).

### ✱✱ WARNING

**Take special care when pushing the connecting rod up from the crankshaft because the sharp threads of the rod bolts/studs will score the crankshaft journal. Insure that special plastic caps are installed over them, or cut two pieces of rubber hose to do the same.**

Again, rotate the engine, this time to position the number one cylinder bore (head surface) up. Turn the crankshaft until the number one piston is at the bottom of its travel, this should allow the maximum access to its connecting rod. Remove the number one connecting rods fasteners and cap and place two lengths of rubber hose over the rod bolts/studs to protect the crankshaft from damage. Using a sturdy wooden dowel and a hammer, push the connecting rod up about 1 inch (25mm) from the crankshaft and remove the upper bearing insert. Continue pushing or tapping the connecting rod up until the piston rings are out of the cylinder bore. Remove the piston and rod by hand, put the upper half of the bearing insert back into the rod, install the cap with its bearing insert installed, and hand-tighten the cap fasteners. If the parts are kept in order in this manner, they will not get lost and you will be able to tell which bearings came form what cylinder if any problems are discovered and diagnosis is necessary. Remove all the other piston assemblies in the same manner. On V-style engines, remove all of the pistons from one bank, then reposition the engine with the other cylinder bank head surface up, and remove that banks piston assemblies.

The only remaining component in the engine block should now be the crankshaft. Loosen the main bearing caps evenly until the fasteners can be turned by hand, then remove them and the caps. Remove the crankshaft from the engine block. Thoroughly clean all of the components.

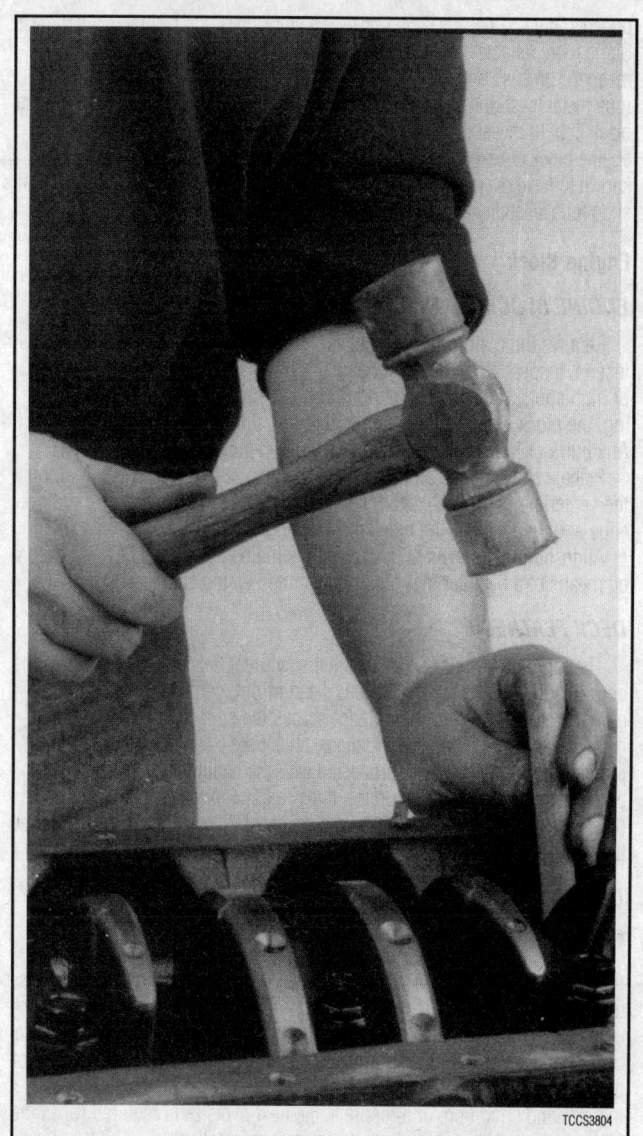

Fig. 224 Carefully tap the piston out of the bore using a wooden dowel

### INSPECTION

Now that the engine block and all of its components are clean, it's time to inspect them for wear and/or damage. To accurately inspect them, you will need some specialized tools:
- Two or three separate micrometers to measure the pistons and crankshaft journals
- A dial indicator
- Telescoping gauges for the cylinder bores
- A rod alignment fixture to check for bent connecting rods

If you do not have access to the proper tools, you may want to bring the components to a shop that does.

Generally, you shouldn't expect cracks in the engine block or its components unless it was known to leak, consume or mix engine fluids, it was severely overheated, or there was evidence of bad bearings and/or crankshaft damage. A visual inspection should be performed on all of the components, but just because you don't see a crack does not mean it is not there. Some more reliable methods for inspecting for cracks include Magnaflux®, a magnetic process or Zyglo®, a dye penetrant. Magnaflux® is used only on ferrous metal (cast iron). Zyglo® uses a spray on fluorescent mixture along with a black light to reveal the cracks. It is strongly recommended to have your engine block checked professionally for cracks, especially if the engine was known to have overheated and/or leaked or consumed coolant. Contact a local shop for availability and pricing of these services.

## Engine Block

### ENGINE BLOCK BEARING ALIGNMENT

Remove the main bearing caps and, if still installed, the main bearing inserts. Inspect all of the main bearing saddles and caps for damage, burrs or high spots. If damage is found, and it is caused from a spun main bearing, the block will need to be align-bored or, if severe enough, replacement. Any burrs or high spots should be carefully removed with a metal file.

Place a straightedge on the bearing saddles, in the engine block, along the centerline of the crankshaft. If any clearance exists between the straightedge and the saddles, the block must be align-bored.

Align-boring consists of machining the main bearing saddles and caps by means of a flycutter that runs through the bearing saddles.

### DECK FLATNESS

The top of the engine block where the cylinder head mounts is called the deck. Insure that the deck surface is clean of dirt, carbon deposits and old gasket material. Place a straightedge across the surface of the deck along its centerline and, using feeler gauges, check the clearance along several points. Repeat the checking procedure with the straightedge placed along both diagonals of the deck surface. If the reading exceeds 0.003 inch (0.076mm) within a 6.0 inch (15.2cm) span, or 0.006 inch (0.152mm) over the total length of the deck, it must be machined.

### CYLINDER BORES

▶ See Figure 225

The cylinder bores house the pistons and are slightly larger than the pistons themselves. A common piston-to-bore clearance is 0.0015–0.0025 inch (0.0381mm–0.0635mm). Inspect and measure the cylinder bores. The bore should be checked for out-of-roundness, taper and size. The results of this inspection will determine whether the cylinder can be used in its existing size and condition, or a rebore to the next oversize is required (or in the case of removable sleeves, have replacements installed).

The amount of cylinder wall wear is always greater at the top of the cylinder than at the bottom. This wear is known as taper. Any cylinder that has a taper of 0.0012 inch (0.305mm) or more, must be rebored. Measurements are taken at a number of positions in each cylinder: at the top, middle and bottom and at two points at each position; that is, at a point 90 degrees from the crankshaft centerline, as well as a point parallel to the crankshaft centerline. The measurements are made with either a special dial indicator or a telescopic gauge and micrometer. If the necessary precision tools to check the bore are not available, take the block to a machine shop and have them mike it. Also if you don't have the tools to check the cylinder bores, chances are you will not have the necessary devices to check the pistons, connecting rods and crankshaft. Take these components with you and save yourself an extra trip.

For our procedures, we will use a telescopic gauge and a micrometer. You will need one of each, with a measuring range which covers your cylinder bore size.

1. Position the telescopic gauge in the cylinder bore, loosen the gauges lock and allow it to expand.

➡ **Your first two readings will be at the top of the cylinder bore, then proceed to the middle and finally the bottom, making a total of six measurements.**

2. Hold the gauge square in the bore, 90 degrees from the crankshaft centerline, and gently tighten the lock. Tilt the gauge back to remove it from the bore.
3. Measure the gauge with the micrometer and record the reading.
4. Again, hold the gauge square in the bore, this time parallel to the crankshaft centerline, and gently tighten the lock. Again, you will tilt the gauge back to remove it from the bore.
5. Measure the gauge with the micrometer and record this reading. The difference between these two readings is the out-of-round measurement of the cylinder.
6. Repeat steps 1 through 5, each time going to the next lower position, until you reach the bottom of the cylinder. Then go to the next cylinder, and continue until all of the cylinders have been measured.

The difference between these measurements will tell you all about the wear in your cylinders. The measurements which were taken 90 degrees from the crankshaft centerline will always reflect the most wear. That is because at this position is where the engine power presses the piston against the cylinder bore the hardest. This is known as thrust wear. Take your top, 90 degree measurement and compare it to your bottom, 90 degree measurement. The difference between them is the taper. When you measure your pistons, you will compare these readings to your piston sizes and determine piston-to-wall clearance.

## Crankshaft

Inspect the crankshaft for visible signs of wear or damage. All of the journals should be perfectly round and smooth. Slight scores are normal for a used crankshaft, but you should hardly feel them with your fingernail. When measuring the crankshaft with a micrometer, you will take readings at the front and rear of each journal, then turn the micrometer 90 degrees and take two more readings, front and rear. The difference between the front-to-rear readings is the journal taper and the first-to-90 degree reading is the out-of-round measurement. Generally, there should be no taper or out-of-roundness found, however, up to 0.0005 inch (0.0127mm) for either can be overlooked. Also, the readings should fall within the factory specifications for journal diameters.

If the crankshaft journals fall within specifications, it is recommended that it be polished before being returned to service. Polishing the crankshaft insures that any minor burrs or high spots are smoothed, thereby reducing the chance of scoring the new bearings.

## Pistons and Connecting Rods

### PISTONS

▶ See Figure 226

The piston should be visually inspected for any signs of cracking or burning (caused by hot spots or detonation), and scuffing or excessive wear on the skirts. The wristpin attaches the piston to the connecting rod.

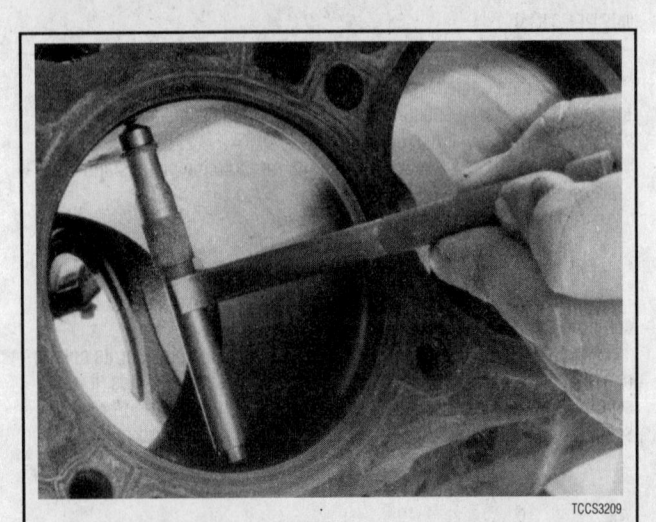

Fig. 225 Use a telescoping gauge to measure the cylinder bore diameter—take several readings within the same bore

# ENGINE AND ENGINE OVERHAUL  3-67

**Fig. 226 Measure the piston's outer diameter, perpendicular to the wrist pin, with a micrometer**

The piston should move freely on the wrist pin, both sliding and pivoting. Grasp the connecting rod securely, or mount it in a vise, and try to rock the piston back and forth along the centerline of the wristpin. There should not be any excessive play evident between the piston and the pin. If there are C-clips retaining the pin in the piston then you have wrist pin bushings in the rods. There should not be any excessive play between the wrist pin and the rod bushing. Normal clearance for the wrist pin is approx. 0.001–0.002 inch (0.025mm–0.051mm).

Use a micrometer and measure the diameter of the piston, perpendicular to the wrist pin, on the skirt. Compare the reading to its original cylinder measurement obtained earlier. The difference between the two readings is the piston-to-wall clearance. If the clearance is within specifications, the piston may be used as is. If the piston is out of specification, but the bore is not, you will need a new piston. If both are out of specification, you will need the cylinder rebored and oversize pistons installed. Generally if two or more pistons/bores are out of specification, it is best to rebore the entire block and purchase a complete set of oversize pistons.

### CONNECTING ROD

You should have the connecting rod checked for straightness at a machine shop. If the connecting rod is bent, it will unevenly wear the bearing and piston, as well as place greater stress on these components. Any bent or twisted connecting rods must be replaced. If the rods are straight and the wrist pin clearance is within specifications, then only the bearing end of the rod need be checked. Place the connecting rod into a vice, with the bearing inserts in place, install the cap to the rod and tighten the fasteners to specifications. Use a telescoping gauge and carefully measure the inside diameter of the bearings. Compare this reading to the rods original crankshaft journal diameter measurement. The difference is the oil clearance. If the oil clearance is not within specifications, install new bearings in the rod and take another measurement. If the clearance is still out of specifications, and the crankshaft is not, the rod will need to be reconditioned by a machine shop.

➡You can also use Plastigage® to check the bearing clearances. The assembling section has complete instructions on its use.

### Camshaft

Inspect the camshaft and lifters/followers as described earlier in this section.

### Bearings

All of the engine bearings should be visually inspected for wear and/or damage. The bearing should look evenly worn all around with no deep scores or pits. If the bearing is severely worn, scored, pitted or heat blued, then the bearing, and the components that use it, should be brought to a machine shop for inspection. Full-circle bearings (used on most camshafts, auxiliary shafts, balance shafts, etc.) require specialized tools for removal and installation, and should be brought to a machine shop for service.

### Oil Pump

➡The oil pump is responsible for providing constant lubrication to the whole engine and so it is recommended that a new oil pump be installed when rebuilding the engine.

Completely disassemble the oil pump and thoroughly clean all of the components. Inspect the oil pump gears and housing for wear and/or damage. Insure that the pressure relief valve operates properly and there is no binding or sticking due to varnish or debris. If all of the parts are in proper working condition, lubricate the gears and relief valve, and assemble the pump.

## REFINISHING

▶ See Figure 227

Almost all engine block refinishing must be performed by a machine shop. If the cylinders are not to be rebored, then the cylinder glaze can be removed with a ball hone. When removing cylinder glaze with a ball hone, use a light or penetrating type oil to lubricate the hone. Do not allow the hone to run dry as this may cause excessive scoring of the cylinder bores and wear on the hone. If new pistons are required, they will need to be installed to the connecting rods. This should be performed by a machine shop as the pistons must be installed in the correct relationship to the rod or engine damage can occur.

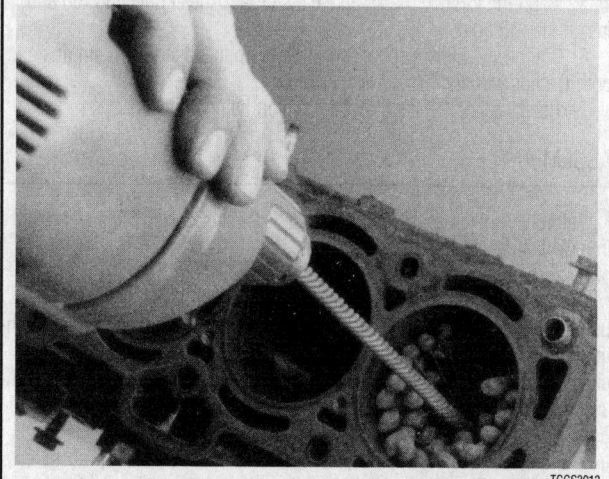

**Fig. 227 Use a ball type cylinder hone to remove any glaze and provide a new surface for seating the piston rings**

### Pistons and Connecting Rods

▶ See Figure 228

Only pistons with the wrist pin retained by C-clips are serviceable by the home-mechanic. Press fit pistons require special presses and/or heaters to remove/install the connecting rod and should only be performed by a machine shop.

All pistons will have a mark indicating the direction to the front of the engine and the must be installed into the engine in that manner. Usually it is a notch or arrow on the top of the piston, or it may be the letter F cast or stamped into the piston.

1. Note the location of the forward mark on the piston and mark the connecting rod in relation.
2. Remove the C-clips from the piston and withdraw the wrist pin.

## 3-68 ENGINE AND ENGINE OVERHAUL

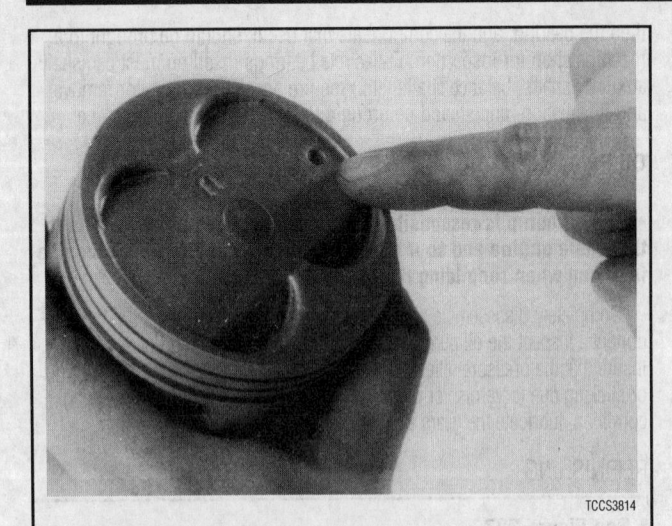

**Fig. 228 Most pistons are marked to indicate positioning in the engine (usually a mark means the side facing the front)**

➡ Varnish build-up or C-clip groove burrs may increase the difficulty of removing the wrist pin. If necessary, use a punch or drift to carefully tap the wrist pin out.

3. Insure that the wrist pin bushing in the connecting rod is usable, and lubricate it with assembly lube.
4. Remove the wrist pin from the new piston and lubricate the pin bores on the piston.
5. Align the forward marks on the piston and the connecting rod and install the wrist pin.
6. The new C-clips will have a flat and a rounded side to them. Install both C-clips with the flat side facing out.
7. Repeat all of the steps for each piston being replaced.

### ASSEMBLY

Before you begin assembling the engine, first give yourself a clean, dirt free work area. Next, clean every engine component again. The key to a good assembly is cleanliness.

Mount the engine block into the engine stand and wash it one last time using water and detergent (dishwashing detergent works well). While washing it, scrub the cylinder bores with a soft bristle brush and thoroughly clean all of the oil passages. Completely dry the engine and spray the entire assembly down with an anti-rust solution such as WD-40® or similar product. Take a clean lint-free rag and wipe up any excess anti-rust solution from the bores, bearing saddles, etc. Repeat the final cleaning process on the crankshaft. Replace any freeze or oil galley plugs which were removed during disassembly.

### Crankshaft

▶ See Figures 229, 230, 231 and 232

1. Remove the main bearing inserts from the block and bearing caps.
2. If the crankshaft main bearing journals have been refinished to a definite undersize, install the correct undersize bearing. Be sure that the bearing inserts and bearing bores are clean. Foreign material under inserts will distort bearing and cause failure.
3. Place the upper main bearing inserts in bores with tang in slot.

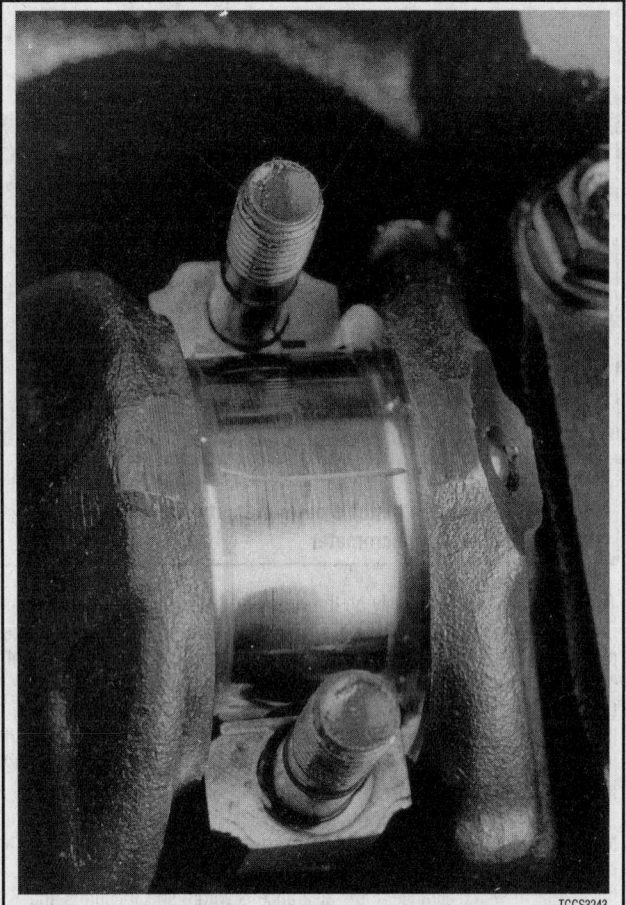

**Fig. 229 Apply a strip of gauging material to the bearing journal, then install and tighten the cap**

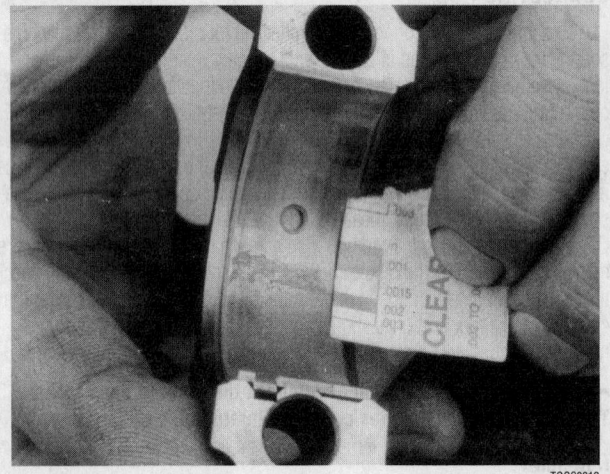

**Fig. 230 After the cap is removed again, use the scale supplied with the gauging material to check the clearance**

# ENGINE AND ENGINE OVERHAUL 3-69

**Fig. 231 A dial gauge may be used to check crankshaft end-play**

**Fig. 232 Carefully pry the crankshaft back and forth while reading the dial gauge for end-play**

➡ The oil holes in the bearing inserts must be aligned with the oil holes in the cylinder block.

 4. Install the lower main bearing inserts in bearing caps.
 5. Clean the mating surfaces of block and rear main bearing cap.
 6. Carefully lower the crankshaft into place. Be careful not to damage bearing surfaces.
 7. Check the clearance of each main bearing by using the following procedure:
　a. Place a piece of Plastigage® or its equivalent, on bearing surface across full width of bearing cap and about ¼ inch off center.
　b. Install cap and tighten bolts to specifications. Do not turn crankshaft while Plastigage® is in place.
　c. Remove the cap. Using the supplied Plastigage® scale, check width of Plastigage® at widest point to get maximum clearance. Difference between readings is taper of journal.
　d. If clearance exceeds specified limits, try a 0.001 inch or 0.002 inch undersize bearing in combination with the standard bearing. Bearing clearance must be within specified limits. If standard and 0.002 inch undersize bearing does not bring clearance within desired limits, refinish crankshaft journal, then install undersize bearings.
 8. After the bearings have been fitted, apply a light coat of engine oil to the journals and bearings. Install the rear main bearing cap. Install all bearing caps except the thrust bearing cap. Be sure that main bearing caps are installed in original locations. Tighten the bearing cap bolts to specifications.
 9. Install the thrust bearing cap with bolts finger-tight.
 10. Pry the crankshaft forward against the thrust surface of upper half of bearing.
 11. Hold the crankshaft forward and pry the thrust bearing cap to the rear. This aligns the thrust surfaces of both halves of the bearing.
 12. Retain the forward pressure on the crankshaft. Tighten the cap bolts to specifications.
 13. Measure the crankshaft end-play as follows:
　a. Mount a dial gauge to the engine block and position the tip of the gauge to read from the crankshaft end.
　b. Carefully pry the crankshaft toward the rear of the engine and hold it there while you zero the gauge.
　c. Carefully pry the crankshaft toward the front of the engine and read the gauge.
　d. Confirm that the reading is within specifications. If not, install a new thrust bearing and repeat the procedure. If the reading is still out of specifications with a new bearing, have a machine shop inspect the thrust surfaces of the crankshaft, and if possible, repair it.
 14. Rotate the crankshaft so as to position the first rod journal to the bottom of its stroke.
 15. Install the rear main seal.

## Pistons and Connecting Rods

▶ See Figures 233, 234, 235 and 236

 1. Before installing the piston/connecting rod assembly, oil the pistons, piston rings and the cylinder walls with light engine oil. Install connecting rod bolt protectors or rubber hose onto the connecting rod bolts/studs. Also perform the following:
　a. Select the proper ring set for the size cylinder bore.
　b. Position the ring in the bore in which it is going to be used.
　c. Push the ring down into the bore area where normal ring wear is not encountered.
　d. Use the head of the piston to position the ring in the bore so that the ring is square with the cylinder wall. Use caution to avoid damage to the ring or cylinder bore.
　e. Measure the gap between the ends of the ring with a feeler gauge. Ring gap in a worn cylinder is normally greater than specification. If the ring gap is greater than the specified limits, try an oversize ring set.
　f. Check the ring side clearance of the compression rings with a feeler gauge inserted between the ring and its lower land according to specification. The gauge should slide freely around the entire ring circumference without binding. Any wear that occurs will form a step at the inner portion of the lower land. If the lower lands have high steps, the piston should be replaced.
 2. Unless new pistons are installed, be sure to install the pistons in the cylinders from which they were removed. The numbers on the connecting rod and bearing cap must be on the same side when installed in the cylinder bore. If a connecting rod is ever transposed from one engine or cylinder to another, new bearings should be fitted and the connecting rod should be numbered to correspond with the new cylinder number. The notch on the piston head goes toward the front of the engine.

# 3-70 ENGINE AND ENGINE OVERHAUL

Fig. 233 Checking the piston ring-to-ring groove side clearance using the ring and a feeler gauge

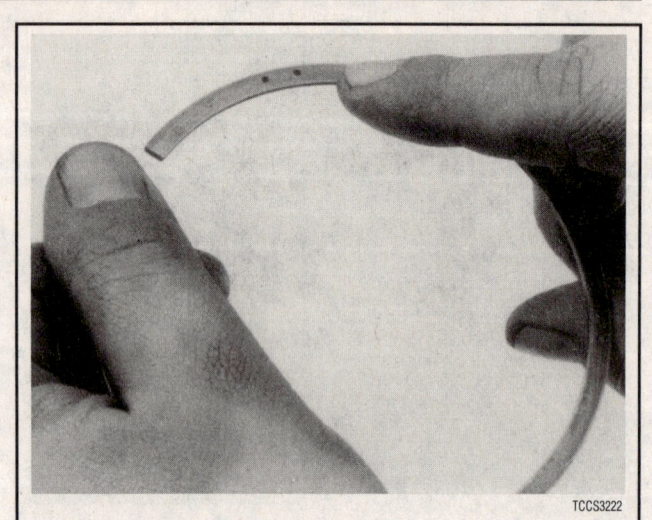

Fig. 235 Most rings are marked to show which side of the ring should face up when installed to the piston

3. Install all of the rod bearing inserts into the rods and caps.
4. Install the rings to the pistons. Install the oil control ring first, then the second compression ring and finally the top compression ring. Use a piston ring expander tool to aid in installation and to help reduce the chance of breakage.
5. Make sure the ring gaps are properly spaced around the circumference of the piston. Fit a piston ring compressor around the piston and slide the piston and connecting rod assembly down into the cylinder bore, pushing it in with the wooden hammer handle. Push the piston down until it is only slightly below the top of the cylinder bore. Guide the connecting rod onto the crankshaft bearing journal carefully, to avoid damaging the crankshaft.
6. Check the bearing clearance of all the rod bearings, fitting them to the crankshaft bearing journals. Follow the procedure in the crankshaft installation above.
7. After the bearings have been fitted, apply a light coating of assembly oil to the journals and bearings.

Fig. 234 The notch on the side of the bearing cap matches the tang on the bearing insert

Fig. 236 Install the piston and rod assembly into the block using a ring compressor and the handle of a hammer

# ENGINE AND ENGINE OVERHAUL 3-71

8. Turn the crankshaft until the appropriate bearing journal is at the bottom of its stroke, then push the piston assembly all the way down until the connecting rod bearing seats on the crankshaft journal. Be careful not to allow the bearing cap screws to strike the crankshaft bearing journals and damage them.

9. After the piston and connecting rod assemblies have been installed, check the connecting rod side clearance on each crankshaft journal.

10. Prime and install the oil pump and the oil pump intake tube.
11. Install the auxiliary/balance shaft(s)/assembly(ies).
12. Install the cylinder head(s) using new gaskets.
13. Install the timing sprockets/gears and the belt/chain assemblies.

## Engine Covers and Components

Install the timing cover(s) and oil pan. Refer to your notes and drawings made prior to disassembly and install all of the components that were removed. Install the engine into the vehicle.

## Engine Start-up and Break-in

### STARTING THE ENGINE

Now that the engine is installed and every wire and hose is properly connected, go back and double check that all coolant and vacuum hoses are connected. Check that you oil drain plug is installed and properly tightened. If not already done, install a new oil filter onto the engine. Fill the crankcase with the proper amount and grade of engine oil. Fill the cooling system with a 50/50 mixture of coolant/water.

1. Connect the vehicle battery.
2. Start the engine. Keep your eye on your oil pressure indicator; if it does not indicate oil pressure within 10 seconds of starting, turn the vehicle off.

### ✱✱ WARNING

Damage to the engine can result if it is allowed to run with no oil pressure. Check the engine oil level to make sure that it is full. Check for any leaks and if found, repair the leaks before continuing. If there is still no indication of oil pressure, you may need to prime the system.

3. Confirm that there are no fluid leaks (oil or other).
4. Allow the engine to reach normal operating temperature (the upper radiator hose will be hot to the touch).
5. If necessary, set the ignition timing.
6. Install any remaining components such as the air cleaner (if removed for ignition timing) or body panels which were removed.

### BREAKING IT IN

Make the first miles on the new engine, easy ones. Vary the speed but do not accelerate hard. Most importantly, do not lug the engine, and avoid sustained high speeds until at least 100 miles. Check the engine oil and coolant levels frequently. Expect the engine to use a little oil until the rings seat. Change the oil and filter at 500 miles, 1500 miles, then every 3000 miles past that.

### KEEP IT MAINTAINED

Now that you have just gone through all of that hard work, keep yourself from doing it all over again by thoroughly maintaining it. Not that you may not have maintained it before, heck you could have had one to two hundred thousand miles on it before doing this. However, you may have bought the vehicle used, and the previous owner did not keep up on maintenance. Which is why you just went through all of that hard work. See?

# ENGINE AND ENGINE OVERHAUL

## TORQUE SPECIFICATIONS

| Components | English Specifications | Metric Specifications |
|---|---|---|
| Cylinder head-to-camshaft bearing cap | 12 ft. lbs. | 16 Nm |
| Cylinder head-to-EGR pipe | 13 ft. lbs. | 18 Nm |
| Cylinder head-to-spark plug | 14 ft. lbs. | 20 Nm |
| Cylinder head-to-No. 1 head cover | 69 inch lbs. | 8 Nm |
| Cylinder head-to-tensioner | 15 ft. lbs. | 21 Nm |
| Cylinder head-to-exhaust manifold | 36 ft. lbs. | 49 Nm |
| Cylinder head-to-exhaust heat insulator | 13 ft. lbs. | 18 Nm |
| Cylinder head-to-oil return pipe | 15 ft. lbs. | 21 Nm |
| Cylinder head-to-intake manifold | 15 ft. lbs. | 21 Nm |
| Cylinder head-to-water outlet | 15 ft. lbs. | 21 Nm |
| Cylinder head-to-outlet stay | 13 ft. lbs. | 18 Nm |
| Cylinder head-to-distributor | 14 ft. lbs. | 19 Nm |
| Water outlet-to-union bolt | 9 ft. lbs. | 12 Nm |
| Water outlet-to-outlet stay | 13 ft. lbs. | 18 Nm |
| Water outlet-to-No. 2 water bypass | 43 inch lbs. | 5 Nm |
| No. 2 head cover-to-No. 1 head cover | 48 inch lbs. | 5 Nm |
| PCV pipe-to-intake manifold | 43 inch lbs. | 5 Nm |
| Engine mounting-to-insulator 1991-93 | 33 ft. lbs. | 45 Nm |
| RH engine mounting-to-cylinder block | 30 ft. lbs. | 42 Nm |
| Engine mounting stay-to-LH mounting | 27 ft. lbs. | 37 Nm |
| Engine mounting stay-to-RH mounting | 27 ft. lbs. | 37 Nm |
| No. 1 camshaft-to-camshaft timing gear | 54 ft. lbs. | 74 Nm |
| Engine rear mounting-to-No. 2 rear engine bracket (2TZ-FZE) | 50 ft. lbs. | 67 Nm |
| EGR valve-to-intake manifold | 13 ft. lbs. | 18 Nm |
| EGR valve-to-head | 13 ft. lbs. | 18 Nm |
| EGR pipe-to-intake manifold | 13 ft. lbs. | 18 Nm |
| EGR valve-to-EGR pipe | 58 ft. lbs. | 78 Nm |
| Timing chain case-to-oil filter bracket (2TZ-FE) | 14 ft. lbs. | 20 Nm |
| Timing chain case-to-oil baffle plate (2TZ-FE) | 43 inch lbs. | 5 Nm |
| Timing chain case-to-water inlet (2TZ-FE) | 14 ft. lbs. | 20 Nm |
| Crankshaft pulley-to-crankshaft | 192 ft. lbs. | 260 Nm |
| Ventilation case-to-crankcase | 69 inch lbs. | 8 Nm |
| No. 1 oil dipstick guide-to-crankcase | 22 ft. lbs. | 29 Nm |
| No. 2 engine hanger-to-ventilation case | 74 inch lbs. | 8 Nm |
| Cylinder block-to-oil knozzle | 13 ft. lbs. | 18 Nm |
| Cylinder block-to-slipper | 20 ft. lbs. | 26 Nm |
| Cylinder block-to-damper | 13 ft. lbs. | 20 Nm |
| Cylinder block-to-idle sprocket | 14 ft. lbs. | 20 Nm |
| Cylinder block-to-engine mounting bracket | 30 ft. lbs. | 41 Nm |
| Cylinder block-to-oil pan | 48 inch lbs. | 5 Nm |
| Cylinder block-to-oil strainer | 13 ft. lbs. | 18 Nm |
| Cylinder block-to-coolant drain cock | 18 ft. lbs. | 25 Nm |
| Cylinder block-to-No. 2 engine hanger | 27 ft. lbs. | 37 Nm |
| Cylinder block-to-rear oil seal retainer | 10 ft. lbs. | 13 Nm |
| Cylinder block-to-crankcase | 9 ft. lbs. | 13 Nm |
| Cylinder block-to-oil dipstick guide | 13 ft. lbs. | 18 Nm |
| Oil pan drain plug | 27 ft. lbs. | 37 Nm |
| Cylinder block-to-head | | |
|     1st | 29 ft. lbs. | 39 ft. lbs. |
|     2nd | 90 degree turn | 90 degree turn |
|     3rd | 90 degree turn | 90 degree turn |

# ENGINE AND ENGINE OVERHAUL 3-73

## TORQUE SPECIFICATIONS

| Components | English Specifications | Metric Specifications |
|---|---|---|
| Cylinder head-to-camshaft bearing cap | 12 ft. lbs. | 16 Nm |
| Cylinder block-to-crankshaft bearing cap | | |
|   1st | 29 ft. lbs. | 39 ft. lbs. |
|   2nd | 90 degree turn | 90 degree turn |
| Connecting rod-to-rod cap | | |
|   1st | 22 ft. lbs. | 29 Nm |
|   2nd | 90 degree turn | 90 degree turn |
| Crankshaft-to-flywheel MT | 65 ft. lbs. | 88 Nm |
| Crankshaft-to-flexplate AT | 54 ft. lbs. | 74 Nm |
| RH engine service hole cover | 10 ft. lbs. | 14 Nm |
| Jack holder | 10 ft. lbs. | 14 Nm |
| Front seat leg-to-seat | 29 ft. lbs. | 39 Nm |
| Front seat-to-body | 29 ft. lbs. | 39 Nm |
| Water pump-to-timing chain case short bolt | 14 ft. lbs. | 20 Nm |
| Water pump-to-timing chain case long bolt | 21 ft. lbs. | 28 Nm |
| Water inlet housing-to-water pump | 14 ft. lbs. | 20 Nm |
| Water inlet-to-inlet housing | 14 ft. lbs. | 20 Nm |
| Radiator support-to-body | 11 ft. lbs. | 18 Nm |
| Equipment driveshaft-to-drive housing | 328 ft. lbs. | 51 Nm |
| Radiator lower tank-to-nut for oil cooler | 74 inch lbs. | 8 Nm |
| Radiator lower tank-to-pipe- for oil cooler | 11 ft. lbs. | 15 Nm |
| Equipment driveshaft-to-crankshaft pulley | 25 ft lbs. | 33 Nm |
| No. 1 equipment drive housing insulator-to-body bracket | 24 ft. lbs. | 32 Nm |
| Ground strap-to-Equipment drive housing | 24 ft. lbs. | 25 Nm |
| No. 3 equipment drive housing stay-to-No. 2 housing insulator | 18 ft. lbs. | 25 Nm |
| No. 3 equipment drive housing stay-to-No. 1 housing stay | 13 ft. lbs. | 18 Nm |
| No. 3 equipment drive housing stay-to-No. 2 housing stay | 13 ft. lbs. | 18 Nm |
| No. 2 equipment drive housing insulator-to-body bracket | 18 ft. lbs. | 25 Nm |
| Equipment drive pulley-to-equipment drive shaft | 21 ft. lbs. | 25 Nm |
| No. 1 equipment drive housing stay-to-equipment drive housing | 13 ft. lbs. | 18 Nm |
| No. 2 equipment drive housing stay-to-equipment drive housing | 13 ft. lbs. | 18 Nm |
| No. 1 equipment drive housing insulator-to-drive housing | 18 ft. lbs. | 25 Nm |
| No. 4 equipment drive housing stay-to-No. 1 drive housing stay | 13 ft. lbs. | 18 Nm |
| No. 5 equipment drive housing stay-to-No. 2 drive housing stay | 13 ft. lbs. | 18 Nm |
| Idle gear-to-cylinder block (2TZ-FZE) | 14 ft. lbs. | 20 Nm |
| Crankshaft position sensor-to-timing chain case | 74 inch lbs. | 8 Nm |
| Timing chain case-to-cylinder block (2TZ-FZE) | | |
|   Bolt A | 14 ft. lbs. | 20 Nm |
|   Nut A | 14 ft. lbs. | 20 Nm |
|   Bolt B | 21 ft. lbs. | 28 Nm |
|   Bolt C | 32 ft. lbs. | 44 Nm |
| Oil level sensor-to-oil pan | 9 ft. lbs. | 13 Nm |
| Oil pan-to-block | 48 inch lbs. | 5 Nm |
| Supercharger rear plate-to-housing bolt | 43 inch lbs. | 5 Nm |
| Supercharger rear plate-to-housing nut | 36 ft.. lbs. | 49 Nm |
| Supercharger rear cover-to-rear plate | 52 inch lbs. | 6 Nm |
| Supercharger front cover-to-housing | 52 inch lbs. | 6 Nm |
| Supercharger clutch pulley-to-flange | 18 ft. lbs. | 24 Nm |
| Supercharger clutch hub-to-rear plate | 23 ft. lbs. | 31 Nm |
| No. 1 idle-up pipe-to-supercharger | 74 inch lbs. | 8 Nm |
| Fluid coupling-to-power steering pump | 10 ft. lbs. | 13 Nm |

90913C07

# 3-74 ENGINE AND ENGINE OVERHAUL

## USING A VACUUM GAUGE

*White needle = steady needle    Dark needle = drifting needle*

The vacuum gauge is one of the most useful and easy-to-use diagnostic tools. It is inexpensive, easy to hook up, and provides valuable information about the condition of your engine.

**Indication:** Normal engine in good condition

Gauge reading: Steady, from 17–22 in./Hg.

**Indication:** Sticking valve or ignition miss

Gauge reading: Needle fluctuates from 15–20 in./Hg. at idle

**Indication:** Late ignition or valve timing, low compression, stuck throttle valve, leaking carburetor or manifold gasket.

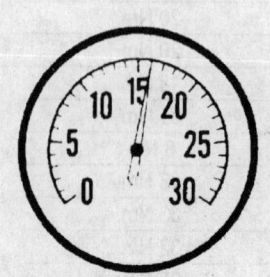

Gauge reading: Low (15–20 in./Hg.) but steady

**Indication:** Improper carburetor adjustment, or minor intake leak at carburetor or manifold

*NOTE: Bad fuel injector O-rings may also cause this reading.*

Gauge reading: Drifting needle

**Indication:** Weak valve springs, worn valve stem guides, or leaky cylinder head gasket (vibrating excessively at all speeds).

*NOTE: A plugged catalytic converter may also cause this reading.*

Gauge reading: Needle fluctuates as engine speed increases

**Indication:** Burnt valve or improper valve clearance. The needle will drop when the defective valve operates.

Gauge reading: Steady needle, but drops regularly

**Indication:** Choked muffler or obstruction in system. Speed up the engine. Choked muffler will exhibit a slow drop of vacuum to zero.

Gauge reading: Gradual drop in reading at idle

**Indication:** Worn valve guides

Gauge reading: Needle vibrates excessively at idle, but steadies as engine speed increases

TCCS3C01

# ENGINE AND ENGINE OVERHAUL 3-75

## Troubleshooting Engine Mechanical Problems

| Problem | Cause | Solution |
|---|---|---|
| External oil leaks | • Cylinder head cover RTV sealant broken or improperly seated | • Replace sealant; inspect cylinder head cover sealant flange and cylinder head sealant surface for distortion and cracks |
| | • Oil filler cap leaking or missing | • Replace cap |
| | • Oil filter gasket broken or improperly seated | • Replace oil filter |
| | • Oil pan side gasket broken, improperly seated or opening in RTV sealant | • Replace gasket or repair opening in sealant; inspect oil pan gasket flange for distortion |
| | • Oil pan front oil seal broken or improperly seated | • Replace seal; inspect timing case cover and oil pan seal flange for distortion |
| | • Oil pan rear oil seal broken or improperly seated | • Replace seal; inspect oil pan rear oil seal flange; inspect rear main bearing cap for cracks, plugged oil return channels, or distortion in seal groove |
| | • Timing case cover oil seal broken or improperly seated | • Replace seal |
| | • Excess oil pressure because of restricted PCV valve | • Replace PCV valve |
| | • Oil pan drain plug loose or has stripped threads | • Repair as necessary and tighten |
| | • Rear oil gallery plug loose | • Use appropriate sealant on gallery plug and tighten |
| | • Rear camshaft plug loose or improperly seated | • Seat camshaft plug or replace and seal, as necessary |
| Excessive oil consumption | • Oil level too high | • Drain oil to specified level |
| | • Oil with wrong viscosity being used | • Replace with specified oil |
| | • PCV valve stuck closed | • Replace PCV valve |
| | • Valve stem oil deflectors (or seals) are damaged, missing, or incorrect type | • Replace valve stem oil deflectors |
| | • Valve stems or valve guides worn | • Measure stem-to-guide clearance and repair as necessary |
| | • Poorly fitted or missing valve cover baffles | • Replace valve cover |
| | • Piston rings broken or missing | • Replace broken or missing rings |
| | • Scuffed piston | • Replace piston |
| | • Incorrect piston ring gap | • Measure ring gap, repair as necessary |
| | • Piston rings sticking or excessively loose in grooves | • Measure ring side clearance, repair as necessary |
| | • Compression rings installed upside down | • Repair as necessary |
| | • Cylinder walls worn, scored, or glazed | • Repair as necessary |

TCCS3C02

# 3-76 ENGINE AND ENGINE OVERHAUL

## Troubleshooting Engine Mechanical Problems

| Problem | Cause | Solution |
|---|---|---|
| Excessive oil consumption (cont.) | • Piston ring gaps not properly staggered<br>• Excessive main or connecting rod bearing clearance | • Repair as necessary<br>• Measure bearing clearance, repair as necessary |
| No oil pressure | • Low oil level<br>• Oil pressure gauge, warning lamp or sending unit inaccurate<br>• Oil pump malfunction<br>• Oil pressure relief valve sticking<br>• Oil passages on pressure side of pump obstructed<br>• Oil pickup screen or tube obstructed<br>• Loose oil inlet tube | • Add oil to correct level<br>• Replace oil pressure gauge or warning lamp<br>• Replace oil pump<br>• Remove and inspect oil pressure relief valve assembly<br>• Inspect oil passages for obstruction<br>• Inspect oil pickup for obstruction<br>• Tighten or seal inlet tube |
| Low oil pressure | • Low oil level<br>• Inaccurate gauge, warning lamp or sending unit<br>• Oil excessively thin because of dilution, poor quality, or improper grade<br>• Excessive oil temperature<br>• Oil pressure relief spring weak or sticking<br>• Oil inlet tube and screen assembly has restriction or air leak<br>• Excessive oil pump clearance<br>• Excessive main, rod, or camshaft bearing clearance | • Add oil to correct level<br>• Replace oil pressure gauge or warning lamp<br>• Drain and refill crankcase with recommended oil<br>• Correct cause of overheating engine<br>• Remove and inspect oil pressure relief valve assembly<br>• Remove and inspect oil inlet tube and screen assembly. (Fill inlet tube with lacquer thinner to locate leaks.)<br>• Measure clearances<br>• Measure bearing clearances, repair as necessary |
| High oil pressure | • Improper oil viscosity<br>• Oil pressure gauge or sending unit inaccurate<br>• Oil pressure relief valve sticking closed | • Drain and refill crankcase with correct viscosity oil<br>• Replace oil pressure gauge<br>• Remove and inspect oil pressure relief valve assembly |
| Main bearing noise | • Insufficient oil supply<br>• Main bearing clearance excessive<br>• Bearing insert missing<br>• Crankshaft end-play excessive<br>• Improperly tightened main bearing cap bolts<br>• Loose flywheel or drive plate<br>• Loose or damaged vibration damper | • Inspect for low oil level and low oil pressure<br>• Measure main bearing clearance, repair as necessary<br>• Replace missing insert<br>• Measure end-play, repair as necessary<br>• Tighten bolts with specified torque<br>• Tighten flywheel or drive plate attaching bolts<br>• Repair as necessary |

TCCS3C03

# ENGINE AND ENGINE OVERHAUL

## Troubleshooting Engine Mechanical Problems

| Problem | Cause | Solution |
|---|---|---|
| Connecting rod bearing noise | • Insufficient oil supply | • Inspect for low oil level and low oil pressure |
| | • Carbon build-up on piston | • Remove carbon from piston crown |
| | • Bearing clearance excessive or bearing missing | • Measure clearance, repair as necessary |
| | • Crankshaft connecting rod journal out-of-round | • Measure journal dimensions, repair or replace as necessary |
| | • Misaligned connecting rod or cap | • Repair as necessary |
| | • Connecting rod bolts tightened improperly | • Tighten bolts with specified torque |
| Piston noise | • Piston-to-cylinder wall clearance excessive (scuffed piston) | • Measure clearance and examine piston |
| | • Cylinder walls excessively tapered or out-of-round | • Measure cylinder wall dimensions, rebore cylinder |
| | • Piston ring broken | • Replace all rings on piston |
| | • Loose or seized piston pin | • Measure piston-to-pin clearance, repair as necessary |
| | • Connecting rods misaligned | • Measure rod alignment, straighten or replace |
| | • Piston ring side clearance excessively loose or tight | • Measure ring side clearance, repair as necessary |
| | • Carbon build-up on piston is excessive | • Remove carbon from piston |
| Valve actuating component noise | • Insufficient oil supply | • Check for:<br>(a) Low oil level<br>(b) Low oil pressure<br>(c) Wrong hydraulic tappets<br>(d) Restricted oil gallery<br>(e) Excessive tappet to bore clearance |
| | • Rocker arms or pivots worn | • Replace worn rocker arms or pivots |
| | • Foreign objects or chips in hydraulic tappets | • Clean tappets |
| | • Excessive tappet leak-down | • Replace valve tappet |
| | • Tappet face worn | • Replace tappet; inspect corresponding cam lobe for wear |
| | • Broken or cocked valve springs | • Properly seat cocked springs; replace broken springs |
| | • Stem-to-guide clearance excessive | • Measure stem-to-guide clearance, repair as required |
| | • Valve bent | • Replace valve |
| | • Loose rocker arms | • Check and repair as necessary |
| | • Valve seat runout excessive | • Regrind valve seat/valves |
| | • Missing valve lock | • Install valve lock |
| | • Excessive engine oil | • Correct oil level |

TCCS3C04

# ENGINE AND ENGINE OVERHAUL

## Troubleshooting Engine Performance

| Problem | Cause | Solution |
|---|---|---|
| Hard starting (engine cranks normally) | • Faulty engine control system component<br>• Faulty fuel pump<br>• Faulty fuel system component<br>• Faulty ignition coil<br>• Improper spark plug gap<br>• Incorrect ignition timing<br>• Incorrect valve timing | • Repair or replace as necessary<br>• Replace fuel pump<br>• Repair or replace as necessary<br>• Test and replace as necessary<br>• Adjust gap<br>• Adjust timing<br>• Check valve timing; repair as necessary |
| Rough idle or stalling | • Incorrect curb or fast idle speed<br>• Incorrect ignition timing<br>• Improper feedback system operation<br>• Faulty EGR valve operation<br>• Faulty PCV valve air flow<br>• Faulty TAC vacuum motor or valve<br>• Air leak into manifold vacuum<br>• Faulty distributor rotor or cap<br>• Improperly seated valves<br>• Incorrect ignition wiring<br>• Faulty ignition coil<br>• Restricted air vent or idle passages<br>• Restricted air cleaner | • Adjust curb or fast idle speed (If possible)<br>• Adjust timing to specification<br>• Refer to Chapter 4<br>• Test EGR system and replace as necessary<br>• Test PCV valve and replace as necessary<br>• Repair as necessary<br>• Inspect manifold vacuum connections and repair as necessary<br>• Replace rotor or cap (Distributor systems only)<br>• Test cylinder compression, repair as necessary<br>• Inspect wiring and correct as necessary<br>• Test coil and replace as necessary<br>• Clean passages<br>• Clean or replace air cleaner filter element |
| Faulty low-speed operation | • Restricted idle air vents and passages<br>• Restricted air cleaner<br>• Faulty spark plugs<br>• Dirty, corroded, or loose ignition secondary circuit wire connections<br>• Improper feedback system operation<br>• Faulty ignition coil high voltage wire<br>• Faulty distributor cap | • Clean air vents and passages<br>• Clean or replace air cleaner filter element<br>• Clean or replace spark plugs<br>• Clean or tighten secondary circuit wire connections<br>• Refer to Chapter 4<br>• Replace ignition coil high voltage wire (Distributor systems only)<br>• Replace cap (Distributor systems only) |
| Faulty acceleration | • Incorrect ignition timing<br>• Faulty fuel system component<br>• Faulty spark plug(s)<br>• Improperly seated valves<br>• Faulty ignition coil | • Adjust timing<br>• Repair or replace as necessary<br>• Clean or replace spark plug(s)<br>• Test cylinder compression, repair as necessary<br>• Test coil and replace as necessary |

# ENGINE AND ENGINE OVERHAUL 3-79

## Troubleshooting Engine Performance

| Problem | Cause | Solution |
|---|---|---|
| Faulty acceleration (cont.) | • Improper feedback system operation | • Refer to Chapter 4 |
| Faulty high speed operation | • Incorrect ignition timing<br>• Faulty advance mechanism | • Adjust timing (if possible)<br>• Check advance mechanism and repair as necessary (Distributor systems only) |
|  | • Low fuel pump volume<br>• Wrong spark plug air gap or wrong plug | • Replace fuel pump<br>• Adjust air gap or install correct plug |
|  | • Partially restricted exhaust manifold, exhaust pipe, catalytic converter, muffler, or tailpipe | • Eliminate restriction |
|  | • Restricted vacuum passages<br>• Restricted air cleaner | • Clean passages<br>• Cleaner or replace filter element as necessary |
|  | • Faulty distributor rotor or cap | • Replace rotor or cap (Distributor systems only) |
|  | • Faulty ignition coil<br>• Improperly seated valve(s) | • Test coil and replace as necessary<br>• Test cylinder compression, repair as necessary |
|  | • Faulty valve spring(s) | • Inspect and test valve spring tension, replace as necessary |
|  | • Incorrect valve timing | • Check valve timing and repair as necessary |
|  | • Intake manifold restricted | • Remove restriction or replace manifold |
|  | • Worn distributor shaft | • Replace shaft (Distributor systems only) |
|  | • Improper feedback system operation | • Refer to Chapter 4 |
| Misfire at all speeds | • Faulty spark plug(s)<br>• Faulty spark plug wire(s)<br>• Faulty distributor cap or rotor | • Clean or relace spark plug(s)<br>• Replace as necessary<br>• Replace cap or rotor (Distributor systems only) |
|  | • Faulty ignition coil<br>• Primary ignition circuit shorted or open intermittently<br>• Improperly seated valve(s) | • Test coil and replace as necessary<br>• Troubleshoot primary circuit and repair as necessary<br>• Test cylinder compression, repair as necessary |
|  | • Faulty hydraulic tappet(s)<br>• Improper feedback system operation<br>• Faulty valve spring(s) | • Clean or replace tappet(s)<br>• Refer to Chapter 4<br>• Inspect and test valve spring tension, repair as necessary |
|  | • Worn camshaft lobes<br>• Air leak into manifold | • Replace camshaft<br>• Check manifold vacuum and repair as necessary |
|  | • Fuel pump volume or pressure low<br>• Blown cylinder head gasket<br>• Intake or exhaust manifold passage(s) restricted | • Replace fuel pump<br>• Replace gasket<br>• Pass chain through passage(s) and repair as necessary |
| Power not up to normal | • Incorrect ignition timing<br>• Faulty distributor rotor | • Adjust timing<br>• Replace rotor (Distributor systems only) |

TCCS3C06

# ENGINE AND ENGINE OVERHAUL

## Troubleshooting Engine Performance

| Problem | Cause | Solution |
| --- | --- | --- |
| Power not up to normal (cont.) | • Incorrect spark plug gap<br>• Faulty fuel pump<br>• Faulty fuel pump<br>• Incorrect valve timing<br>• Faulty ignition coil<br>• Faulty ignition wires<br>• Improperly seated valves<br>• Blown cylinder head gasket<br>• Leaking piston rings<br>• Improper feedback system operation | • Adjust gap<br>• Replace fuel pump<br>• Replace fuel pump<br>• Check valve timing and repair as necessary<br>• Test coil and replace as necessary<br>• Test wires and replace as necessary<br>• Test cylinder compression and repair as necessary<br>• Replace gasket<br>• Test compression and repair as necessary<br>• Refer to Chapter 4 |
| Intake backfire | • Improper ignition timing<br>• Defective EGR component<br>• Defective TAC vacuum motor or valve | • Adjust timing<br>• Repair as necessary<br>• Repair as necessary |
| Exhaust backfire | • Air leak into manifold vacuum<br>• Faulty air injection diverter valve<br>• Exhaust leak | • Check manifold vacuum and repair as necessary<br>• Test diverter valve and replace as necessary<br>• Locate and eliminate leak |
| Ping or spark knock | • Incorrect ignition timing<br>• Distributor advance malfunction<br>• Excessive combustion chamber deposits<br>• Air leak into manifold vacuum<br>• Excessively high compression<br>• Fuel octane rating excessively low<br>• Sharp edges in combustion chamber<br>• EGR valve not functioning properly | • Adjust timing<br>• Inspect advance mechanism and repair as necessary (Distributor systems only)<br>• Remove with combustion chamber cleaner<br>• Check manifold vacuum and repair as necessary<br>• Test compression and repair as necessary<br>• Try alternate fuel source<br>• Grind smooth<br>• Test EGR system and replace as necessary |
| Surging (at cruising to top speeds) | • Low fuel pump pressure or volume<br>• Improper PCV valve air flow<br>• Air leak into manifold vacuum<br>• Incorrect spark advance<br>• Restricted fuel filter<br>• Restricted air cleaner<br>• EGR valve not functioning properly<br>• Improper feedback system operation | • Replace fuel pump<br>• Test PCV valve and replace as necessary<br>• Check manifold vacuum and repair as necessary<br>• Test and replace as necessary<br>• Replace fuel filter<br>• Clean or replace air cleaner filter element<br>• Test EGR system and replace as necessary<br>• Refer to Chapter 4 |

# ENGINE AND ENGINE OVERHAUL 3-81

## Troubleshooting the Serpentine Drive Belt

| Problem | Cause | Solution |
| --- | --- | --- |
| Tension sheeting fabric failure (woven fabric on outside circumference of belt has cracked or separated from body of belt) | • Grooved or backside idler pulley diameters are less than minimum recommended<br>• Tension sheeting contacting (rubbing) stationary object<br>• Excessive heat causing woven fabric to age<br>• Tension sheeting splice has fractured | • Replace pulley(s) not conforming to specification<br>• Correct rubbing condition<br>• Replace belt<br>• Replace belt |
| Noise (objectional squeal, squeak, or rumble is heard or felt while drive belt is in operation) | • Belt slippage<br>• Bearing noise<br>• Belt misalignment<br>• Belt-to-pulley mismatch<br>• Driven component inducing vibration<br>• System resonant frequency inducing vibration | • Adjust belt<br>• Locate and repair<br>• Align belt/pulley(s)<br>• Install correct belt<br>• Locate defective driven component and repair<br>• Vary belt tension within specifications. Replace belt. |
| Rib chunking (one or more ribs has separated from belt body) | • Foreign objects imbedded in pulley grooves<br>• Installation damage<br>• Drive loads in excess of design specifications<br>• Insufficient internal belt adhesion | • Remove foreign objects from pulley grooves<br>• Replace belt<br>• Adjust belt tension<br>• Replace belt |
| Rib or belt wear (belt ribs contact bottom of pulley grooves) | • Pulley(s) misaligned<br>• Mismatch of belt and pulley groove widths<br>• Abrasive environment<br>• Rusted pulley(s)<br>• Sharp or jagged pulley groove tips<br>• Rubber deteriorated | • Align pulley(s)<br>• Replace belt<br>• Replace belt<br>• Clean rust from pulley(s)<br>• Replace pulley<br>• Replace belt |
| Longitudinal belt cracking (cracks between two ribs) | • Belt has mistracked from pulley groove<br>• Pulley groove tip has worn away rubber-to-tensile member | • Replace belt<br>• Replace belt |
| Belt slips | • Belt slipping because of insufficient tension<br>• Belt or pulley subjected to substance (belt dressing, oil, ethylene glycol) that has reduced friction<br>• Driven component bearing failure<br>• Belt glazed and hardened from heat and excessive slippage | • Adjust tension<br>• Replace belt and clean pulleys<br>• Replace faulty component bearing<br>• Replace belt |
| "Groove jumping" (belt does not maintain correct position on pulley, or turns over and/or runs off pulleys) | • Insufficient belt tension<br>• Pulley(s) not within design tolerance<br>• Foreign object(s) in grooves | • Adjust belt tension<br>• Replace pulley(s)<br>• Remove foreign objects from grooves |

TCCS3C09

## ENGINE AND ENGINE OVERHAUL

### Troubleshooting the Serpentine Drive Belt

| Problem | Cause | Solution |
|---|---|---|
| "Groove jumping" (belt does not maintain correct position on pulley, or turns over and/or runs off pulleys) | • Excessive belt speed<br>• Pulley misalignment<br>• Belt-to-pulley profile mismatched<br>• Belt cordline is distorted | • Avoid excessive engine acceleration<br>• Align pulley(s)<br>• Install correct belt<br>• Replace belt |
| Belt broken (Note: identify and correct problem before replacement belt is installed) | • Excessive tension<br>• Tensile members damaged during belt installation<br>• Belt turnover<br>• Severe pulley misalignment<br>• Bracket, pulley, or bearing failure | • Replace belt and adjust tension to specification<br>• Replace belt<br>• Replace belt<br>• Align pulley(s)<br>• Replace defective component and belt |
| Cord edge failure (tensile member exposed at edges of belt or separated from belt body) | • Excessive tension<br>• Drive pulley misalignment<br>• Belt contacting stationary object<br>• Pulley irregularities<br>• Improper pulley construction<br>• Insufficient adhesion between tensile member and rubber matrix | • Adjust belt tension<br>• Align pulley<br>• Correct as necessary<br>• Replace pulley<br>• Replace pulley<br>• Replace belt and adjust tension to specifications |
| Sporadic rib cracking (multiple cracks in belt ribs at random intervals) | • Ribbed pulley(s) diameter less than minimum specification<br>• Backside bend flat pulley(s) diameter less than minimum<br>• Excessive heat condition causing rubber to harden<br>• Excessive belt thickness<br>• Belt overcured<br>• Excessive tension | • Replace pulley(s)<br>• Replace pulley(s)<br>• Correct heat condition as necessary<br>• Replace belt<br>• Replace belt<br>• Adjust belt tension |

TCCS3C10

# ENGINE AND ENGINE OVERHAUL 3-83

## Troubleshooting the Cooling System

| Problem | Cause | Solution |
|---|---|---|
| High temperature gauge indication—overheating | • Coolant level low<br>• Improper fan operation<br>• Radiator hose(s) collapsed<br>• Radiator airflow blocked<br><br>• Faulty pressure cap<br>• Ignition timing incorrect<br>• Air trapped in cooling system<br>• Heavy traffic driving<br><br><br>• Incorrect cooling system component(s) installed<br>• Faulty thermostat<br>• Water pump shaft broken or impeller loose<br>• Radiator tubes clogged<br>• Cooling system clogged<br>• Casting flash in cooling passages<br><br><br><br>• Brakes dragging<br>• Excessive engine friction<br>• Antifreeze concentration over 68%<br><br>• Missing air seals<br>• Faulty gauge or sending unit<br><br>• Loss of coolant flow caused by leakage or foaming<br>• Viscous fan drive failed | • Replenish coolant<br>• Repair or replace as necessary<br>• Replace hose(s)<br>• Remove restriction (bug screen, fog lamps, etc.)<br>• Replace pressure cap<br>• Adjust ignition timing<br>• Purge air<br>• Operate at fast idle in neutral intermittently to cool engine<br>• Install proper component(s)<br><br>• Replace thermostat<br>• Replace water pump<br><br>• Flush radiator<br>• Flush system<br>• Repair or replace as necessary. Flash may be visible by removing cooling system components or removing core plugs.<br>• Repair brakes<br>• Repair engine<br>• Lower antifreeze concentration percentage<br>• Replace air seals<br>• Repair or replace faulty component<br>• Repair or replace leaking component, replace coolant<br>• Replace unit |
| Low temperature indication—undercooling | • Thermostat stuck open<br>• Faulty gauge or sending unit | • Replace thermostat<br>• Repair or replace faulty component |
| Coolant loss—boilover | • Overfilled cooling system<br><br>• Quick shutdown after hard (hot) run<br>• Air in system resulting in occasional "burping" of coolant<br>• Insufficient antifreeze allowing coolant boiling point to be too low<br>• Antifreeze deteriorated because of age or contamination<br>• Leaks due to loose hose clamps, loose nuts, bolts, drain plugs, faulty hoses, or defective radiator | • Reduce coolant level to proper specification<br>• Allow engine to run at fast idle prior to shutdown<br>• Purge system<br><br>• Add antifreeze to raise boiling point<br><br>• Replace coolant<br><br>• Pressure test system to locate source of leak(s) then repair as necessary |

TCCS3C11

# ENGINE AND ENGINE OVERHAUL

## Troubleshooting the Cooling System

| Problem | Cause | Solution |
|---|---|---|
| Coolant loss—boilover | • Faulty head gasket<br>• Cracked head, manifold, or block<br>• Faulty radiator cap | • Replace head gasket<br>• Replace as necessary<br>• Replace cap |
| Coolant entry into crankcase or cylinder(s) | • Faulty head gasket<br>• Crack in head, manifold or block | • Replace head gasket<br>• Replace as necessary |
| Coolant recovery system inoperative | • Coolant level low<br>• Leak in system<br>• Pressure cap not tight or seal missing, or leaking<br>• Pressure cap defective<br>• Overflow tube clogged or leaking<br>• Recovery bottle vent restricted | • Replenish coolant to FULL mark<br>• Pressure test to isolate leak and repair as necessary<br>• Repair as necessary<br>• Replace cap<br>• Repair as necessary<br>• Remove restriction |
| Noise | • Fan contacting shroud<br><br>• Loose water pump impeller<br>• Glazed fan belt<br>• Loose fan belt<br>• Rough surface on drive pulley<br>• Water pump bearing worn<br><br>• Belt alignment | • Reposition shroud and inspect engine mounts (on electric fans inspect assembly)<br>• Replace pump<br>• Apply silicone or replace belt<br>• Adjust fan belt tension<br>• Replace pulley<br>• Remove belt to isolate. Replace pump.<br>• Check pulley alignment. Repair as necessary. |
| No coolant flow through heater core | • Restricted return inlet in water pump<br>• Heater hose collapsed or restricted<br>• Restricted heater core<br>• Restricted outlet in thermostat housing<br>• Intake manifold bypass hole in cylinder head restricted<br>• Faulty heater control valve<br>• Intake manifold coolant passage restricted | • Remove restriction<br><br>• Remove restriction or replace hose<br>• Remove restriction or replace core<br>• Remove flash or restriction<br><br>• Remove restriction<br><br>• Replace valve<br>• Remove restriction or replace intake manifold |

**NOTE:** *Immediately after shutdown, the engine enters a condition known as heat soak. This is caused by the cooling system being inoperative while engine temperature is still high. If coolant temperature rises above boiling point, expansion and pressure may push some coolant out of the radiator overflow tube. If this does not occur frequently it is considered normal.*

# 4 DRIVEABILITY AND EMISSIONS CONTROLS

**AIR POLLUTION 4-2**
NATURAL POLLUTANTS 4-2
INDUSTRIAL POLLUTANTS 4-2
AUTOMOTIVE POLLUTANTS 4-2
   TEMPERATURE INVERSION 4-2
   HEAT TRANSFER 4-2
**AUTOMOTIVE EMISSIONS 4-3**
EXHAUST GASES 4-3
   HYDROCARBONS 4-3
   CARBON MONOXIDE 4-3
   NITROGEN 4-3
   OXIDES OF SULFUR 4-4
   PARTICULATE MATTER 4-4
CRANKCASE EMISSIONS 4-4
EVAPORATIVE EMISSIONS 4-4
**EMISSION CONTROLS 4-5**
POSITIVE CRANKCASE VENTILATION
  (PCV) SYSTEM 4-5
   OPERATION 4-5
   TESTING 4-5
   REMOVAL & INSTALLATION 4-6
EVAPORATIVE EMISSION CONTROLS 4-6
   OPERATION 4-6
   COMPONENT TESTING 4-6
   REMOVAL & INSTALLATION 4-9
EXHAUST GAS RECIRCULATION
  SYSTEM 4-9
   OPERATION 4-9
   COMPONENT TESTING 4-10
   REMOVAL & INSTALLATION 4-15
**ELECTRONIC ENGINE
  CONTROLS 4-17**
GENERAL INFORMATION 4-17
ENGINE CONTROL MODULE (ECM) 4-17
   OPERATION 4-17
   PRECAUTIONS 4-17
   REMOVAL & INSTALLATION 4-17
OXYGEN SENSOR 4-18
   OPERATION 4-18
   TESTING 4-18
   REMOVAL & INSTALLATION 4-19
KNOCK SENSOR 4-20
   OPERATION 4-20
   TESTING 4-20
   REMOVAL & INSTALLATION 4-20
IDLE AIR CONTROL (IAC) VALVE 4-20
   OPERATION 4-20
   TESTING 4-21
   REMOVAL & INSTALLATION 4-22
COOLANT TEMPERATURE SENSOR 4-22
   OPERATION 4-22
   TESTING 4-22
   REMOVAL & INSTALLATION 4-23
INTAKE AIR TEMPERATURE (IAT)
  SENSOR 4-23
   OPERATION 4-23
VOLUME AIRFLOW METER 4-23
   OPERATION 4-23
   TESTING 4-23

   REMOVAL & INSTALLATION 4-24
MASS AIRFLOW METER (MAF) 4-24
   OPERATION 4-24
   TESTING 4-25
   REMOVAL & INSTALLATION 4-25
THROTTLE POSITION SENSOR 4-26
   OPERATION 4-26
   TESTING 4-26
   REMOVAL & INSTALLATION 4-27
   ADJUSTMENT 4-28
CAMSHAFT POSITION SENSOR 4-28
   OPERATION 4-28
   TESTING 4-29
   REMOVAL & INSTALLATION 4-29
CRANKSHAFT POSITION SENSOR 4-29
   OPERATION 4-29
   TESTING 4-29
   REMOVAL & INSTALLATION 4-29
**COMPONENT LOCATIONS 4-30**
**TROUBLE CODES 4-31**
GENERAL INFORMATION 4-31
DATA LINK CONNECTOR (DLC) 4-31
READING CODES 4-32
   2TZ-FE ENGINE 4-32
   2TZ-FZE ENGINE 4-33
CLEARING CODES 4-33
   2TZ-FE ENGINE 4-33
   2TZ-FZE ENGINE 4-34
**VACUUM DIAGRAMS 4-39**

AIR POLLUTION 4-2
AUTOMOTIVE EMISSIONS 4-3
EMISSION CONTROLS 4-5
ELECTRONIC ENGINE CONTROLS 4-17
COMPONENT LOCATIONS 4-30
TROUBLE CODES 4-31
VACUUM DIAGRAMS 4-39

# 4-2 DRIVEABILITY AND EMISSIONS CONTROLS

## AIR POLLUTION

The earth's atmosphere, at or near sea level, consists approximately of 78 percent nitrogen, 21 percent oxygen and 1 percent other gases. If it were possible to remain in this state, 100 percent clean air would result. However, many varied sources allow other gases and particulates to mix with the clean air, causing our atmosphere to become unclean or polluted.

Some of these pollutants are visible while others are invisible, with each having the capability of causing distress to the eyes, ears, throat, skin and respiratory system. Should these pollutants become concentrated in a specific area and under certain conditions, death could result due to the displacement or chemical change of the oxygen content in the air. These pollutants can also cause great damage to the environment and to the many man made objects that are exposed to the elements.

To better understand the causes of air pollution, the pollutants can be categorized into 3 separate types, natural, industrial and automotive.

### Natural Pollutants

Natural pollution has been present on earth since before man appeared and continues to be a factor when discussing air pollution, although it causes only a small percentage of the overall pollution problem. It is the direct result of decaying organic matter, wind born smoke and particulates from such natural events as plain and forest fires (ignited by heat or lightning), volcanic ash, sand and dust which can spread over a large area of the countryside.

Such a phenomenon of natural pollution has been seen in the form of volcanic eruptions, with the resulting plume of smoke, steam and volcanic ash blotting out the sun's rays as it spreads and rises higher into the atmosphere. As it travels into the atmosphere the upper air currents catch and carry the smoke and ash, while condensing the steam back into water vapor. As the water vapor, smoke and ash travel on their journey, the smoke dissipates into the atmosphere while the ash and moisture settle back to earth in a trail hundreds of miles long. In some cases, lives are lost and millions of dollars of property damage result.

### Industrial Pollutants

Industrial pollution is caused primarily by industrial processes, the burning of coal, oil and natural gas, which in turn produce smoke and fumes. Because the burning fuels contain large amounts of sulfur, the principal ingredients of smoke and fumes are sulfur dioxide and particulate matter. This type of pollutant occurs most severely during still, damp and cool weather, such as at night. Even in its less severe form, this pollutant is not confined to just cities. Because of air movements, the pollutants move for miles over the surrounding countryside, leaving in its path a barren and unhealthy environment for all living things.

Working with Federal, State and Local mandated regulations and by carefully monitoring emissions, big business has greatly reduced the amount of pollutant introduced from its industrial sources, striving to obtain an acceptable level. Because of the mandated industrial emission clean up, many land areas and streams in and around the cities that were formerly barren of vegetation and life, have now begun to move back in the direction of nature's intended balance.

### Automotive Pollutants

The third major source of air pollution is automotive emissions. The emissions from the internal combustion engines were not an appreciable problem years ago because of the small number of registered vehicles and the nation's small highway system. However, during the early 1950's, the trend of the American people was to move from the cities to the surrounding suburbs. This caused an immediate problem in transportation because the majority of suburbs were not afforded mass transit conveniences. This lack of transportation created an attractive market for the automobile manufacturers, which resulted in a dramatic increase in the number of vehicles produced and sold, along with a marked increase in highway construction between cities and the suburbs. Multi-vehicle families emerged with a growing emphasis placed on an individual vehicle per family member. As the increase in vehicle ownership and usage occurred, so did pollutant levels in and around the cities, as suburbanites drove daily to their businesses and employment, returning at the end of the day to their homes in the suburbs.

It was noted that a smoke and fog type haze was being formed and at times, remained in suspension over the cities, taking time to dissipate. At first this "smog," derived from the words "smoke" and "fog," was thought to result from industrial pollution but it was determined that automobile emissions shared the blame. It was discovered that when normal automobile emissions were exposed to sunlight for a period of time, complex chemical reactions would take place.

It is now known that smog is a photo chemical layer which develops when certain oxides of nitrogen (NOx) and unburned hydrocarbons (HC) from automobile emissions are exposed to sunlight. Pollution was more severe when smog would become stagnant over an area in which a warm layer of air settled over the top of the cooler air mass, trapping and holding the cooler mass at ground level. The trapped cooler air would keep the emissions from being dispersed and diluted through normal air flows. This type of air stagnation was given the name "Temperature Inversion."

## TEMPERATURE INVERSION

In normal weather situations, surface air is warmed by heat radiating from the earth's surface and the sun's rays. This causes it to rise upward, into the atmosphere. Upon rising it will cool through a convection type heat exchange with the cooler upper air. As warm air rises, the surface pollutants are carried upward and dissipated into the atmosphere.

When a temperature inversion occurs, we find the higher air is no longer cooler, but is warmer than the surface air, causing the cooler surface air to become trapped. This warm air blanket can extend from above ground level to a few hundred or even a few thousand feet into the air. As the surface air is trapped, so are the pollutants, causing a severe smog condition. Should this stagnant air mass extend to a few thousand feet high, enough air movement with the inversion takes place to allow the smog layer to rise above ground level but the pollutants still cannot dissipate. This inversion can remain for days over an area, with the smog level only rising or lowering from ground level to a few hundred feet high. Meanwhile, the pollutant levels increase, causing eye irritation, respiratory problems, reduced visibility, plant damage and in some cases, even disease.

This inversion phenomenon was first noted in the Los Angeles, California area. The city lies in terrain resembling a basin and with certain weather conditions, a cold air mass is held in the basin while a warmer air mass covers it like a lid.

Because this type of condition was first documented as prevalent in the Los Angeles area, this type of trapped pollution was named Los Angeles Smog, although it occurs in other areas where a large concentration of automobiles are used and the air remains stagnant for any length of time.

## HEAT TRANSFER

Consider the internal combustion engine as a machine in which raw materials must be placed so a finished product comes out. As in any machine operation, a certain amount of wasted material is formed. When we relate this to the internal combustion engine, we find that through the input of air and fuel, we obtain power during the combustion process to drive the vehicle. The by-product or waste of this power is, in part, heat and exhaust gases with which we must dispose.

The heat from the combustion process can rise to over 4000°F (2204°C). The dissipation of this heat is controlled by a ram air effect, the use of cooling fans to cause air flow and a liquid coolant solution surrounding the combustion area to transfer the heat of combustion through the cylinder walls and into the coolant. The coolant is then directed to a thin-finned, multi-tubed radiator, from which the excess heat is transferred

# DRIVEABILITY AND EMISSIONS CONTROLS

to the atmosphere by 1 of the 3 heat transfer methods, conduction, convection or radiation.

The cooling of the combustion area is an important part in the control of exhaust emissions. To understand the behavior of the combustion and transfer of its heat, consider the air/fuel charge. It is ignited and the flame front burns progressively across the combustion chamber until the burning charge reaches the cylinder walls. Some of the fuel in contact with the walls is not hot enough to burn, thereby snuffing out or quenching the combustion process. This leaves unburned fuel in the combustion chamber. This unburned fuel is then forced out of the cylinder and into the exhaust system, along with the exhaust gases.

Many attempts have been made to minimize the amount of unburned fuel in the combustion chambers due to quenching, by increasing the coolant temperature and lessening the contact area of the coolant around the combustion area. However, design limitations within the combustion chambers prevent the complete burning of the air/fuel charge, so a certain amount of the unburned fuel is still expelled into the exhaust system, regardless of modifications to the engine.

## AUTOMOTIVE EMISSIONS

Before emission controls were mandated on internal combustion engines, other sources of engine pollutants were discovered along with the exhaust emissions. It was determined that engine combustion exhaust produced approximately 60 percent of the total emission pollutants, fuel evaporation from the fuel tank and carburetor vents produced 20 percent, with the final 20 percent being produced through the crankcase as a by-product of the combustion process.

### Exhaust Gases

The exhaust gases emitted into the atmosphere are a combination of burned and unburned fuel. To understand the exhaust emission and its composition, we must review some basic chemistry.

When the air/fuel mixture is introduced into the engine, we are mixing air, composed of nitrogen (78 percent), oxygen (21 percent) and other gases (1 percent) with the fuel, which is 100 percent hydrocarbons (HC), in a semi-controlled ratio. As the combustion process is accomplished, power is produced to move the vehicle while the heat of combustion is transferred to the cooling system. The exhaust gases are then composed of nitrogen, a diatomic gas ($N_2$), the same as was introduced in the engine, carbon dioxide ($CO_2$), the same gas that is used in beverage carbonation, and water vapor ($H_2O$). The nitrogen ($N_2$), for the most part, passes through the engine unchanged, while the oxygen ($O_2$) reacts (burns) with the hydrocarbons (HC) and produces the carbon dioxide ($CO_2$) and the water vapors ($H_2O$). If this chemical process would be the only process to take place, the exhaust emissions would be harmless. However, during the combustion process, other compounds are formed which are considered dangerous. These pollutants are hydrocarbons (HC), carbon monoxide (CO), oxides of nitrogen (NOx) oxides of sulfur (SOx) and engine particulates.

### HYDROCARBONS

Hydrocarbons (HC) are essentially fuel which was not burned during the combustion process or which has escaped into the atmosphere through fuel evaporation. The main sources of incomplete combustion are rich air/fuel mixtures, low engine temperatures and improper spark timing. The main sources of hydrocarbon emission through fuel evaporation on most vehicles used to be the vehicle's fuel tank and carburetor float bowl.

To reduce combustion hydrocarbon emission, engine modifications were made to minimize dead space and surface area in the combustion chamber. In addition, the air/fuel mixture was made more lean through the improved control which feedback carburetion and fuel injection offers and by the addition of external controls to aid in further combustion of the hydrocarbons outside the engine. Two such methods were the addition of air injection systems, to inject fresh air into the exhaust manifolds and the installation of catalytic converters, units that are able to burn traces of hydrocarbons without affecting the internal combustion process or fuel economy.

To control hydrocarbon emissions through fuel evaporation, modifications were made to the fuel tank to allow storage of the fuel vapors during periods of engine shut-down. Modifications were also made to the air intake system so that at specific times during engine operation, these vapors may be purged and burned by blending them with the air/fuel mixture.

### CARBON MONOXIDE

Carbon monoxide is formed when not enough oxygen is present during the combustion process to convert carbon (C) to carbon dioxide ($CO_2$). An increase in the carbon monoxide (CO) emission is normally accompanied by an increase in the hydrocarbon (HC) emission because of the lack of oxygen to completely burn all of the fuel mixture.

Carbon monoxide (CO) also increases the rate at which the photo chemical smog is formed by speeding up the conversion of nitric oxide (NO) to nitrogen dioxide ($NO_2$). To accomplish this, carbon monoxide (CO) combines with oxygen ($O_2$) and nitric oxide (NO) to produce carbon dioxide ($CO_2$) and nitrogen dioxide ($NO_2$). ($CO + O_2 + NO = CO_2 + NO_2$).

The dangers of carbon monoxide, which is an odorless and colorless toxic gas are many. When carbon monoxide is inhaled into the lungs and passed into the blood stream, oxygen is replaced by the carbon monoxide in the red blood cells, causing a reduction in the amount of oxygen supplied to the many parts of the body. This lack of oxygen causes headaches, lack of coordination, reduced mental alertness and, should the carbon monoxide concentration be high enough, death could result.

### NITROGEN

Normally, nitrogen is an inert gas. When heated to approximately 2500°F (1371°C) through the combustion process, this gas becomes active and causes an increase in the nitric oxide (NO) emission.

Oxides of nitrogen (NOx) are composed of approximately 97–98 percent nitric oxide (NO). Nitric oxide is a colorless gas but when it is passed into the atmosphere, it combines with oxygen and forms nitrogen dioxide ($NO_2$). The nitrogen dioxide then combines with chemically active hydrocarbons (HC) and when in the presence of sunlight, causes the formation of photochemical smog.

#### Ozone

To further complicate matters, some of the nitrogen dioxide ($NO_2$) is broken apart by the sunlight to form nitric oxide and oxygen. ($NO_2$ + sunlight = NO + O). This single atom of oxygen then combines with diatomic (meaning 2 atoms) oxygen ($O_2$) to form ozone ($O_3$). Ozone is one of the smells associated with smog. It has a pungent and offensive odor, irritates the eyes and lung tissues, affects the growth of plant life and causes rapid deterioration of rubber products. Ozone can be formed by sunlight as well as electrical discharge into the air.

The most common discharge area on the automobile engine is the secondary ignition electrical system, especially when inferior quality spark plug cables are used. As the surge of high voltage is routed through the secondary cable, the circuit builds up an electrical field around the wire, which acts upon the oxygen in the surrounding air to form the ozone. The faint glow along the cable with the engine running that may be visible on a dark night, is called the "corona discharge." It is the result of the electrical field passing from a high along the cable, to a low in the surrounding air, which forms the ozone gas. The combination of corona and ozone has been a major cause of cable deterioration. Recently, different and better quality insulating materials have lengthened the life of the electrical cables.

# 4-4 DRIVEABILITY AND EMISSIONS CONTROLS

Although ozone at ground level can be harmful, ozone is beneficial to the earth's inhabitants. By having a concentrated ozone layer called the "ozonosphere," between 10 and 20 miles (16–32 km) up in the atmosphere, much of the ultra violet radiation from the sun's rays are absorbed and screened. If this ozone layer were not present, much of the earth's surface would be burned, dried and unfit for human life.

## OXIDES OF SULFUR

Oxides of sulfur (SOx) were initially ignored in the exhaust system emissions, since the sulfur content of gasoline as a fuel is less than 1/10 of 1 percent. Because of this small amount, it was felt that it contributed very little to the overall pollution problem. However, because of the difficulty in solving the sulfur emissions in industrial pollutions and the introduction of catalytic converter to the automobile exhaust systems, a change was mandated. The automobile exhaust system, when equipped with a catalytic converter, changes the sulfur dioxide ($SO_2$) into sulfur trioxide ($SO_3$).

When this combines with water vapors ($H_2O$), a sulfuric acid mist ($H_2SO_4$) is formed and is a very difficult pollutant to handle since it is extremely corrosive. This sulfuric acid mist that is formed, is the same mist that rises from the vents of an automobile battery when an active chemical reaction takes place within the battery cells.

When a large concentration of vehicles equipped with catalytic converters are operating in an area, this acid mist may rise and be distributed over a large ground area causing land, plant, crop, paint and building damage.

## PARTICULATE MATTER

A certain amount of particulate matter is present in the burning of any fuel, with carbon constituting the largest percentage of the particulates. In gasoline, the remaining particulates are the burned remains of the various other compounds used in its manufacture. When a gasoline engine is in good internal condition, the particulate emissions are low but as the engine wears internally, the particulate emissions increase. By visually inspecting the tail pipe emissions, a determination can be made as to where an engine defect may exist. An engine with light gray or blue smoke emitting from the tail pipe normally indicates an increase in the oil consumption through burning due to internal engine wear. Black smoke would indicate a defective fuel delivery system, causing the engine to operate in a rich mode. Regardless of the color of the smoke, the internal part of the engine or the fuel delivery system should be repaired to prevent excess particulate emissions.

Diesel and turbine engines emit a darkened plume of smoke from the exhaust system because of the type of fuel used. Emission control regulations are mandated for this type of emission and more stringent measures are being used to prevent excess emission of the particulate matter. Electronic components are being introduced to control the injection of the fuel at precisely the proper time of piston travel, to achieve the optimum in fuel ignition and fuel usage. Other particulate after-burning components are being tested to achieve a cleaner emission.

Good grades of engine lubricating oils should be used, which meet the manufacturers specification. Cut-rate oils can contribute to the particulate emission problem because of their low flash or ignition temperature point. Such oils burn prematurely during the combustion process causing emission of particulate matter.

The cooling system is an important factor in the reduction of particulate matter. The optimum combustion will occur, with the cooling system operating at a temperature specified by the manufacturer. The cooling system must be maintained in the same manner as the engine oiling system, as each system is required to perform properly in order for the engine to operate efficiently for a long time.

## Crankcase Emissions

Crankcase emissions are made up of water, acids, unburned fuel, oil fumes and particulates. These emissions are classified as hydrocarbons (HC) and are formed by the small amount of unburned, compressed air/fuel mixture entering the crankcase from the combustion area (between the cylinder walls and piston rings) during the compression and power strokes. The head of the compression and combustion help to form the remaining crankcase emissions.

Since the first engines, crankcase emissions were allowed into the atmosphere through a road draft tube, mounted on the lower side of the engine block. Fresh air came in through an open oil filler cap or breather. The air passed through the crankcase mixing with blow-by gases. The motion of the vehicle and the air blowing past the open end of the road draft tube caused a low pressure area (vacuum) at the end of the tube. Crankcase emissions were simply drawn out of the road draft tube into the air.

To control the crankcase emission, the road draft tube was deleted. A hose and/or tubing was routed from the crankcase to the intake manifold so the blow-by emission could be burned with the air/fuel mixture. However, it was found that intake manifold vacuum, used to draw the crankcase emissions into the manifold, would vary in strength at the wrong time and not allow the proper emission flow. A regulating valve was needed to control the flow of air through the crankcase.

Testing, showed the removal of the blow-by gases from the crankcase as quickly as possible, was most important to the longevity of the engine. Should large accumulations of blow-by gases remain and condense, dilution of the engine oil would occur to form water, soot, resins, acids and lead salts, resulting in the formation of sludge and varnishes. This condensation of the blow-by gases occurs more frequently on vehicles used in numerous starting and stopping conditions, excessive idling and when the engine is not allowed to attain normal operating temperature through short runs.

## Evaporative Emissions

Gasoline fuel is a major source of pollution, before and after it is burned in the automobile engine. From the time the fuel is refined, stored, pumped and transported, again stored until it is pumped into the fuel tank of the vehicle, the gasoline gives off unburned hydrocarbons (HC) into the atmosphere. Through the redesign of storage areas and venting systems, the pollution factor was diminished, but not eliminated, from the refinery standpoint. However, the automobile still remained the primary source of vaporized, unburned hydrocarbon (HC) emissions.

Fuel pumped from an underground storage tank is cool but when exposed to a warmer ambient temperature, will expand. Before controls were mandated, an owner might fill the fuel tank with fuel from an underground storage tank and park the vehicle for some time in warm area, such as a parking lot. As the fuel would warm, it would expand and should no provisions or area be provided for the expansion, the fuel would spill out of the filler neck and onto the ground, causing hydrocarbon (HC) pollution and creating a severe fire hazard. To correct this condition, the vehicle manufacturers added overflow plumbing and/or gasoline tanks with built in expansion areas or domes.

However, this did not control the fuel vapor emission from the fuel tank. It was determined that most of the fuel evaporation occurred when the vehicle was stationary and the engine not operating. Most vehicles carry 5–25 gallons (19–95 liters) of gasoline. Should a large concentration of vehicles be parked in one area, such as a large parking lot, excessive fuel vapor emissions would take place, increasing as the temperature increases.

To prevent the vapor emission from escaping into the atmosphere, the fuel systems were designed to trap the vapors while the vehicle is stationary, by sealing the system from the atmosphere. A storage system is used to collect and hold the fuel vapors from the carburetor (if equipped) and the fuel tank when the engine is not operating. When the engine is started, the storage system is then purged of the fuel vapors, which are drawn into the engine and burned with the air/fuel mixture.

# DRIVEABILITY AND EMISSIONS CONTROLS 4-5

## EMISSION CONTROLS

### ♦ See Figure 1

Due to varying state, federal, and provincial regulations, specific emission control equipment may vary by area of sale. The US emission equipment is divided into two categories: California and 49 State (or Federal). In this section, the term "California" applies only to cars originally built to be sold in California. Some California emissions equipment is not shared with equipment installed on cars built to be sold in the other 49 states. Models built to be sold in Canada also have specific emissions equipment, although in many cases the 49 State and Canadian equipment is the same.

Fig. 1 Example of an emission control system information label

## Positive Crankcase Ventilation (PCV) System

### OPERATION

### ♦ See Figures 2 and 3

Exhaust blow-by gasses are routed from the crankcase to the intake manifold, where they are combined with the fuel/air mixture and burned during combustion. This reduces the amount of hydrocarbons emitted by the exhaust.

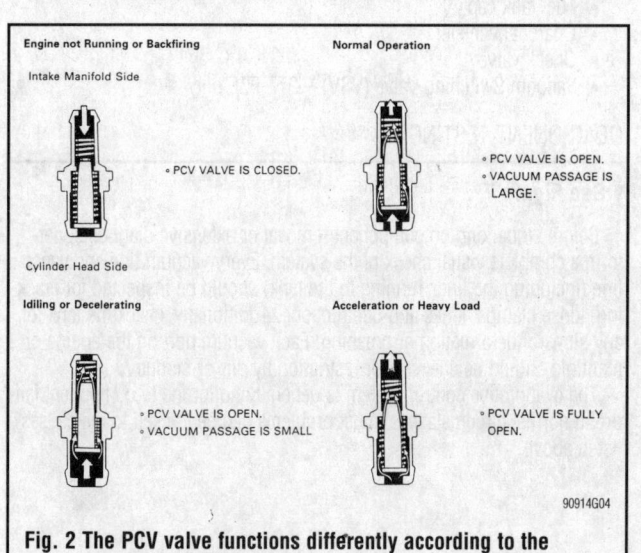

A PCV valve is used in the line to prevent the gases in the crankcase from being ignited in case of a backfire. The amount of blow-by gasses entering the mixture is also regulated by the PCV valve, which is spring loaded and has a variable orifice.

The important components of the PCV system are the following:
- PCV valve
- Valve cover
- Air intake chamber
- Ventilation case
- Hoses, connections and gaskets

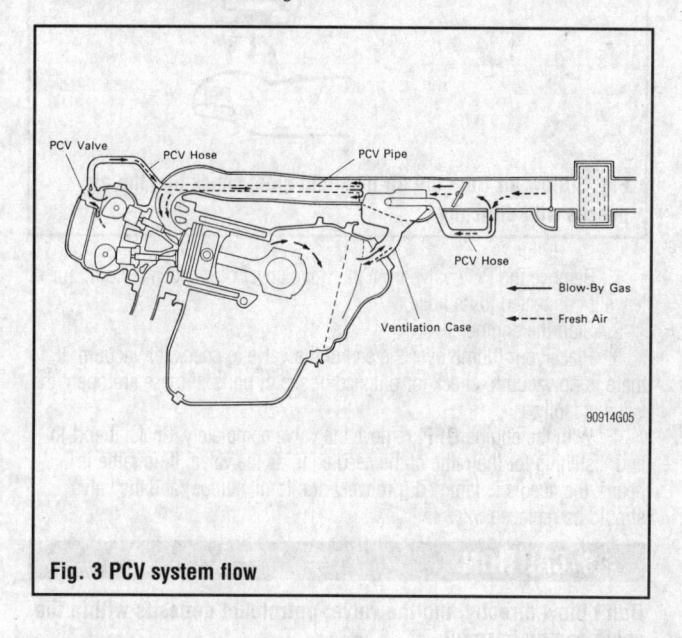

Fig. 3 PCV system flow

### TESTING

### ♦ See Figures 4, 5 and 6

Inspect the PCV system hoses and connections at each tune-up and replace any deteriorated hoses. Check the PCV valve at every tune-up and replace it at 30,000 mile (48,000 km) intervals.

The PCV valve is easily checked with the engine running at normal idle speed (warmed up).

Fig. 2 The PCV valve functions differently according to the engine operating conditions

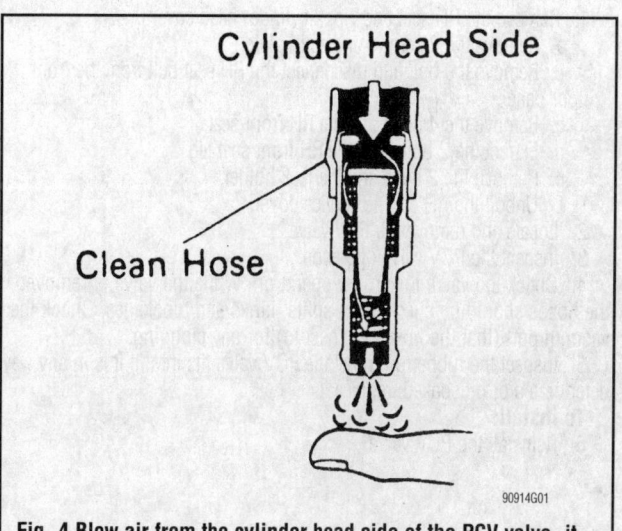

Fig. 4 Blow air from the cylinder head side of the PCV valve, it should flow easily

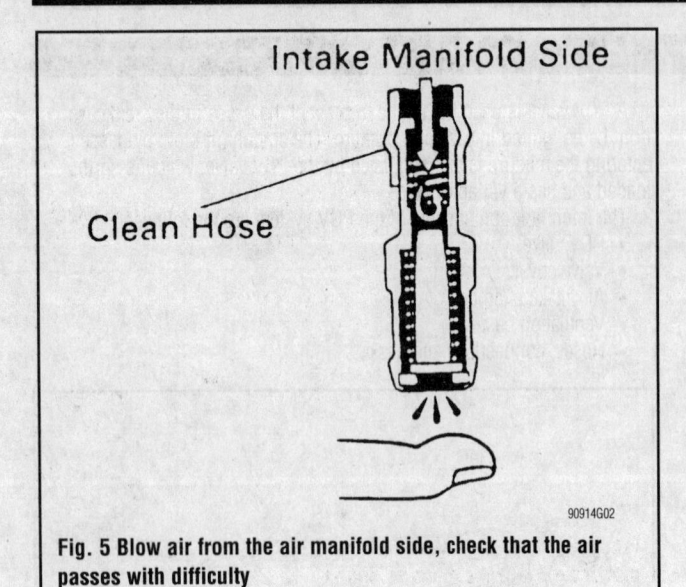

# 4-6 DRIVEABILITY AND EMISSIONS CONTROLS

**Fig. 5 Blow air from the air manifold side, check that the air passes with difficulty**

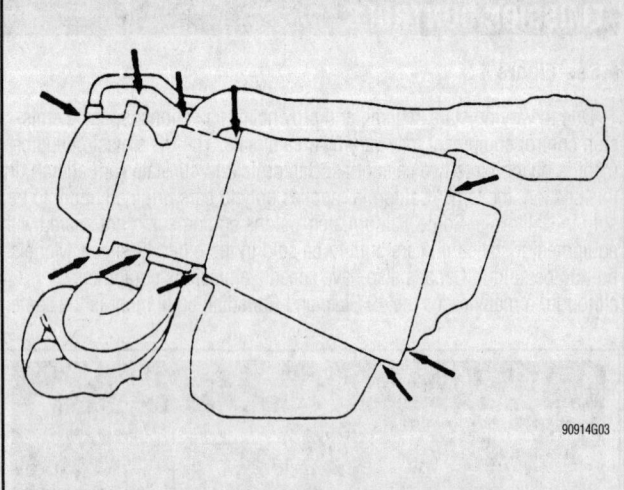

**Fig. 6 Leaks from any of these areas can cause the PCV system to malfunction**

1. Remove the PCV valve from the valve cover or intake manifold, but leave it connected to its hose.
2. Start the engine.
3. Place your thumb over the end of the valve to check for vacuum. If there is no vacuum, check for plugged hoses or ports. If these are open, the valve is faulty.
4. With the engine **OFF**, remove the valve completely. Shake it end-to-end, listening for the rattle of the needle inside the valve. If no rattle is heard, the needle is jammed (probably due to oil sludge) and the valve should be replaced.

### ※※ CAUTION

**Don't blow directly into the valve; petroleum deposits within the valve can be harmful.**

An engine without crankcase ventilation is quickly damaged. It is important to check the PCV at regular intervals. When replacing a PCV valve you must use the correct one for the engine. Many valves look alike on the outside, but have different mechanical values. Putting the incorrect valve on a vehicle can cause a great deal of driveability problems.

### REMOVAL & INSTALLATION

1. Remove the RH seat and No. 2 cylinder head cover.
   a. Remove the 3 screws and scuff plate.
   b. Remove the bolt and disconnect the RH seat belt from the front floor panel.
   c. Remove the 4 bolts and the RH front seat.
   d. Extract the 2 bolts and the RH front seat leg.
   e. Remove the 2 bolts and the jack holder.
   f. Unbolt the RH engine service cover.
2. Locate and remove the PCV valve.
3. Inspect the PCV valve operation.
4. Check the valve for proper operation. While the valve is removed, the hoses should be checked for splits, kinks and blockages. Check the vacuum port (that the hoses connect to) for any clogging.
5. Inspect the rubber grommet the PCV valve fits into. If it is in any way deteriorated or oil soaked, replace it.

**To install:**

6. Reinstall the PCV valve.
7. Attach the RH engine hole cover.
8. Install and secure the No. 2 cylinder head cover and RH seat.
   a. Tighten the bolts to the following specifications:
- Service hole cover bolts—10 ft. lbs. (14 Nm)
- Jack holder—10 ft. lbs. (14 Nm)
- RH seat leg—29 ft. lbs. (39 Nm)
- RH seat—29 ft. lbs. (39 Nm)
- RH seat belt-to-floor pan—31 ft. lbs. (42 Nm)

## Evaporative Emission Controls

### OPERATION

The Evaporative Emission Control (EVAP) system is designed to prevent fuel tank vapors from being emitted into the atmosphere. When the engine is not running, gasoline vapors from the tank are stored in a charcoal canister. The charcoal canister absorbs the gasoline vapors and stores them until certain engine conditions are met and the vapors can be purged and burned by the engine. In some vehicles, any liquid fuel entering the canister goes into a reservoir in the bottom of the canister to protect the integrity of the carbon element in the canister above. These systems employ the following components:
- Fuel tank cap
- Charcoal canister
- Check valve
- Vacuum Switching Valve (VSV)—2TZ-FZE only

### COMPONENT TESTING

♦ See Figure 7

Before embarking on component removal or extensive diagnosis, perform a complete visual check of the system. Every vacuum line and vapor line (including the lines running to the tank) should be inspected for cracking, loose clamps, kinks and obstructions. Additionally, check the tank for any signs of deformation or crushing. Each vacuum port on the engine or manifold should be checked for restriction by dirt or sludge.

The evaporative control system is generally not prone to component failure in normal circumstances; most problems can be tracked to the causes listed above.

## DRIVEABILITY AND EMISSIONS CONTROLS   4-7

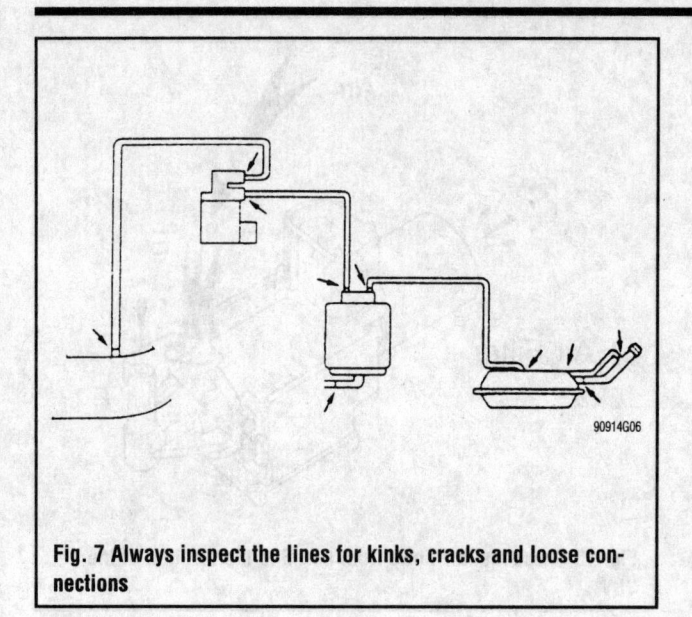

Fig. 7 Always inspect the lines for kinks, cracks and loose connections

### Fuel Filler Cap
▶ See Figure 8

Check that the filler cap seals effectively. Replace the filler cap if the seal is defective.

### Charcoal Canister
▶ See Figures 9 and 10

1. Remove the charcoal canister from the vehicle.
2. Remove the cap from the canister.
3. Visually check the charcoal canister for cracks or damage.
4. Check for a clogged filter and stuck check valve. Using low pressure compressed air (0.68 psi. or 4 kPa), blow into the tank pipe and check that the air flows without resistance from the other pipes. If this does not test positive replace the canister.
5. Next blow air into the purge pipe and check that air does not flow from the other pipes.
6. Clean the filter in the canister by blowing no more than 43 psi (294 kPa) of compressed air into the purge pipe to the outer vent control valve while holding the purge pipe closed.

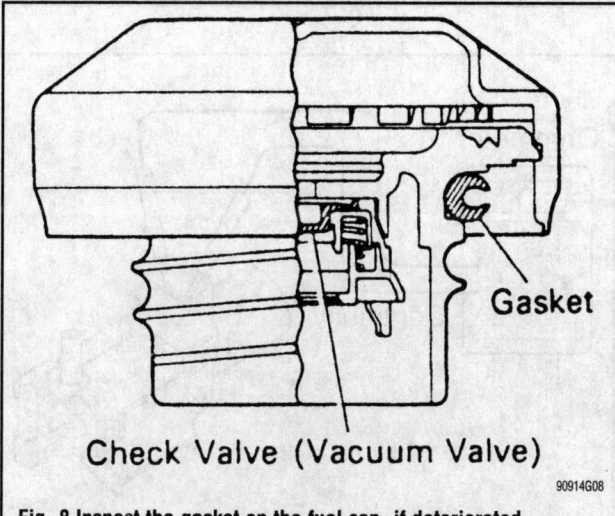

Fig. 8 Inspect the gasket on the fuel cap, if deteriorated, replace the gasket or cap as necessary

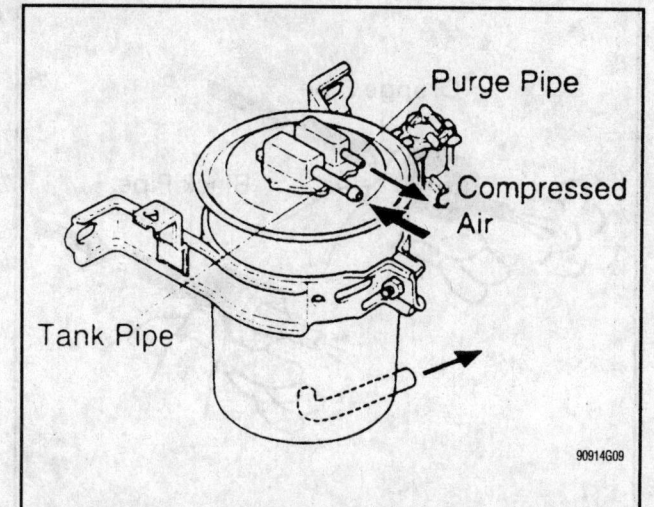

Fig. 9 To check for a clogged filter or check valve, blow compressed air into the pipes as shown

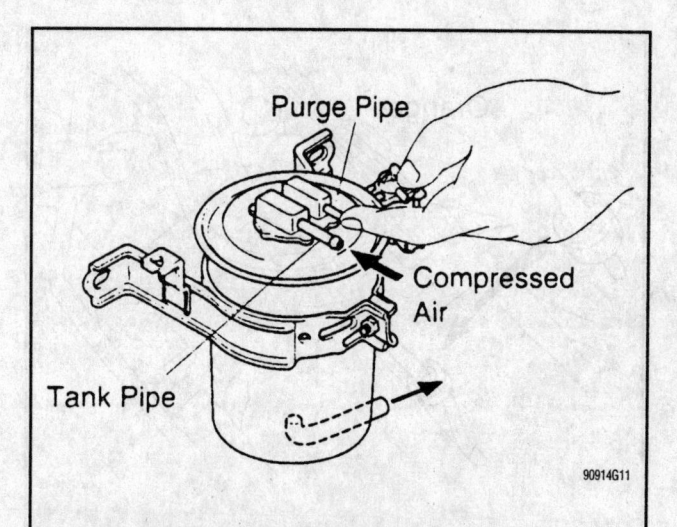

Fig. 10 To clean the filter blow compressed air into the tank pipe while holding the purge pipe closed

➡ Do not attempt to wash the charcoal canister. Also be sure that no activated carbon comes out of the canister during the cleaning process.

7. Replace or reinstall the canister as needed.

### Check Valve
▶ See Figures 11 and 12

1. Remove the check valve from the engine.
2. Blow air into the orange side of the pipe and check for air flow from the orange side.
3. Blow air into the orange side of the pipe and check that no air flows from the black side.
4. If the testing is not as specified, replace the check valve.
5. Reinstall the check valve with the orange side facing the No. 2 air inlet duct side.

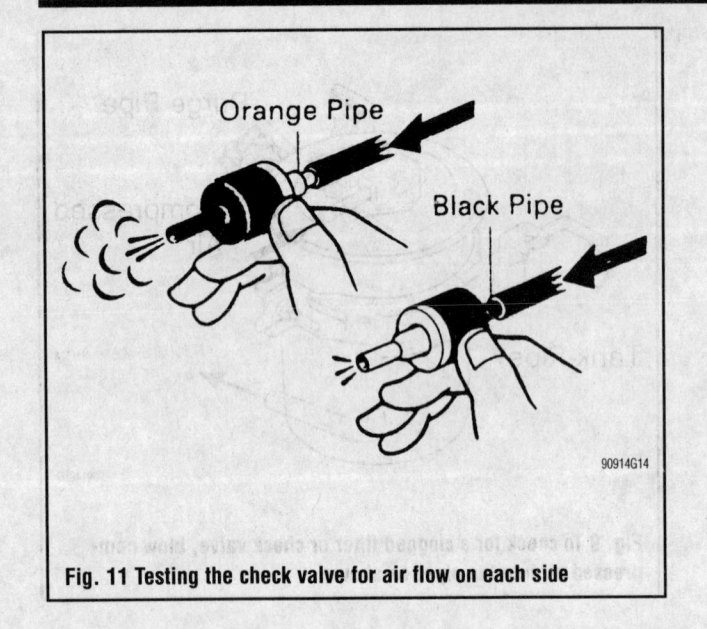

## 4-8 DRIVEABILITY AND EMISSIONS CONTROLS

**Fig. 11 Testing the check valve for air flow on each side**

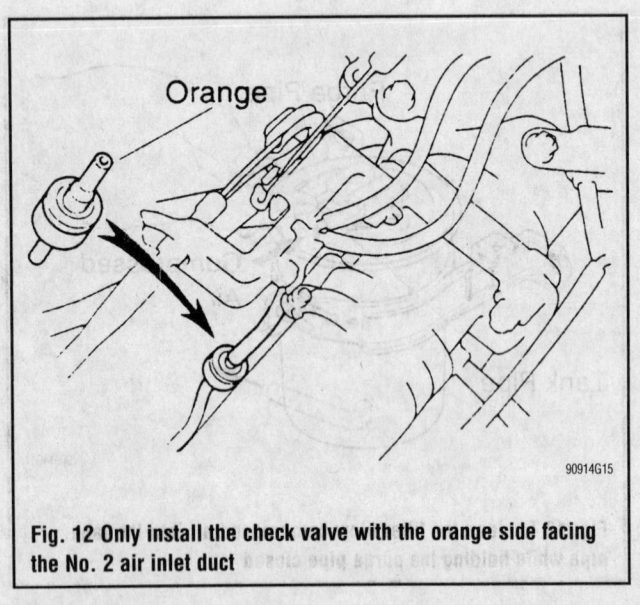

**Fig. 12 Only install the check valve with the orange side facing the No. 2 air inlet duct**

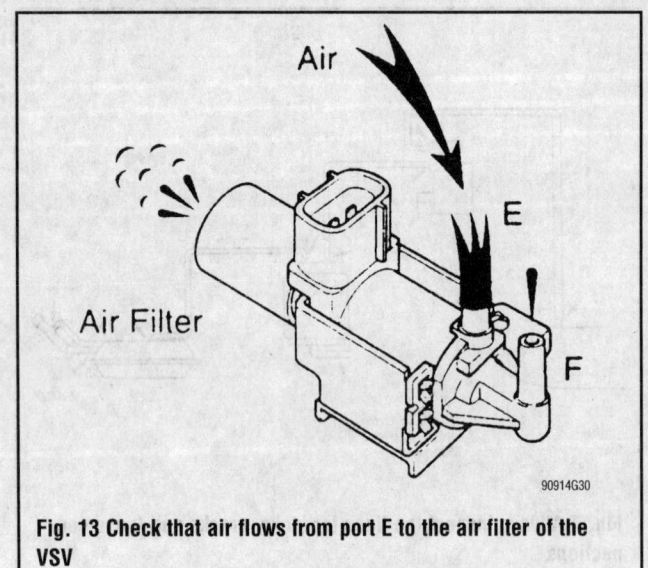

**Fig. 13 Check that air flows from port E to the air filter of the VSV**

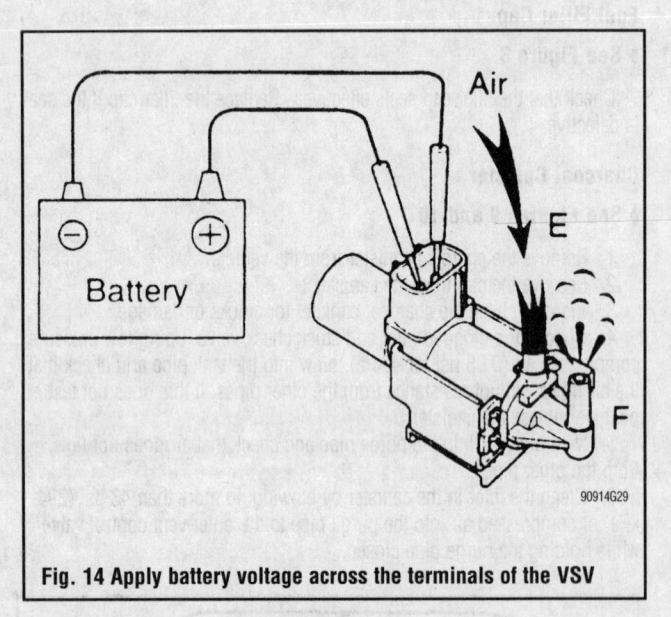

**Fig. 14 Apply battery voltage across the terminals of the VSV**

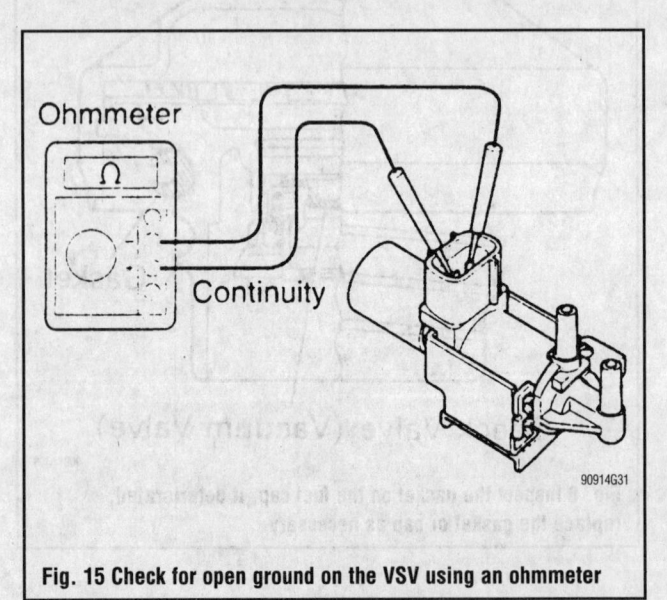

**Fig. 15 Check for open ground on the VSV using an ohmmeter**

### Vacuum Switching Valve (VSV)

#### FILTERED TYPE

♦ See Figures 13, 14, 15 and 16

The VSV is attached to the No. 2 air inlet duct. Some VSV models are equipped with an air filter at the end.

1. Check that air flows from port **E** to the air filter.
2. Connect the vacuum switching valve terminals to the battery.
3. Check that air flows from port **E** to port **F**.
4. If the VSV fails this test replace it. Any doubts perform the following test.
5. Remove the VSV.
6. Check for an open circuit. Using an ohmmeter, measure the resistance (ohms) between the two terminals of the valve. The resistance (cold) should be 30–34 ohms. If the resistance is not within specifications, replace the VSV.
7. Check for a short circuit within the valve. Using an ohmmeter, check that there is no continuity between the terminals and the VSV body. If there is continuity, replace the VSV.

## DRIVEABILITY AND EMISSIONS CONTROLS 4-9

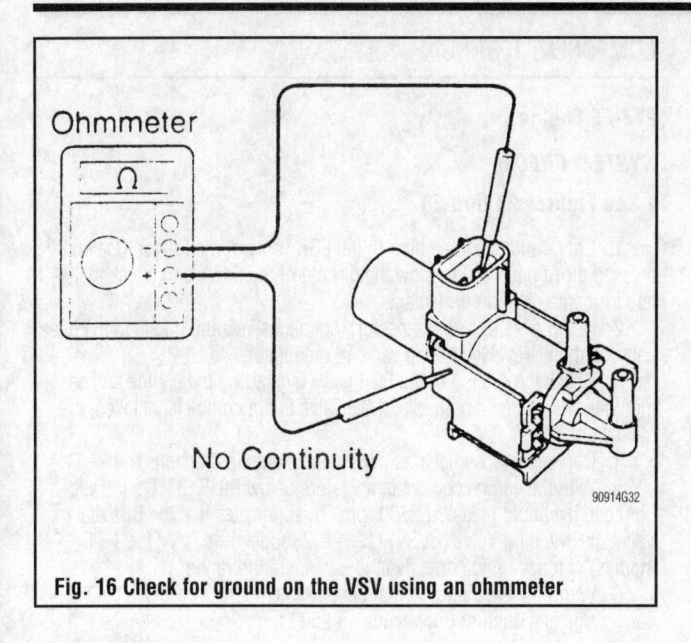

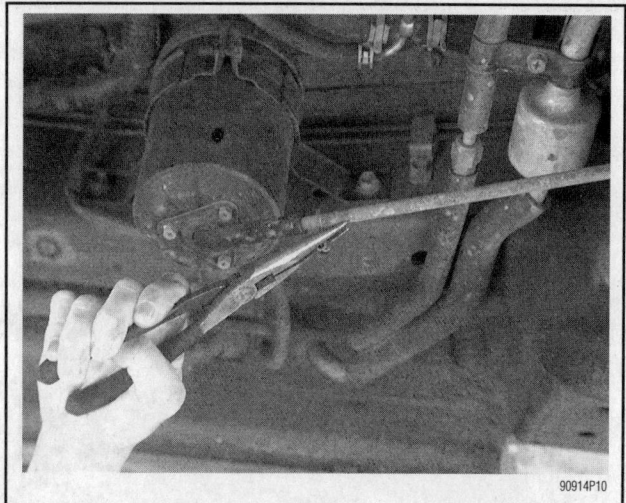

Fig. 16 Check for ground on the VSV using an ohmmeter

Fig. 17 Remove the hose clamp for the lower tube on the charcoal canister

### NON-FILTERED TYPE

1. Check that air does not flow from port **E** to port **F**.
2. Connect the vacuum switching valve terminals to the battery.
3. Check that air flows from port **E** to port **F**.
4. If the VSV fails this test replace it. Any doubts perform the following test.
5. Remove the VSV.
6. Check for an open circuit. Using an ohmmeter, measure the resistance (ohms) between the two terminals of the valve. The resistance (cold) should be 30–34 ohms. If the resistance is not within specifications, replace the VSV.
7. Check for a short circuit within the valve. Using an ohmmeter, check that there is no continuity between the terminals and the VSV body. If there is continuity, replace the VSV.

### REMOVAL & INSTALLATION

➡ When replacing any EVAP system hoses, always use hoses that are fuel-resistant or are marked EVAP. Use of hose which is not fuel-resistant will lead to premature hose failure.

#### Charcoal Canister

♦ See Figures 17, 18, 19, 20 and 21

Label and disconnect the lines running to the canister. Make sure to plug the lines with a bolt or like. Disconnect the wiring harness. Unbolt and remove the charcoal canister from the vehicle. Do not attempt to wash the charcoal canister. Also be sure that no activated carbon comes out of the canister during the cleaning process. Attach the charcoal canister to its mounting bracket and secure. Connect the vacuum hoses in their proper locations.

#### Vacuum Switching Valve (VSV)

♦ See Figure 22

Disconnect the wiring from the VSV. Label and removed the vacuum hoses from the valve. Loosen the nut and extract the VSV from the No. 2 air inlet duct.

## Exhaust Gas Recirculation System

### OPERATION

The EGR system reduces oxides of nitrogen. This is accomplished by recirculating some of the exhaust gases through the EGR valve to the intake manifold, lowering peak combustion temperatures.

Fig. 18 Disconnect the wiring harness leading to the canister

Fig. 19 Remove the two canister mounting bolts

# 4-10  DRIVEABILITY AND EMISSIONS CONTROLS

## COMPONENT TESTING

### 2TZ-FE Engine

#### SYSTEM CHECK

▶ See Figures 23 thru 28

1. Check and clean the filter in the EGR vacuum modulator. Use compressed air (if possible) to blow the dirt out of the filters and check the filters for contamination or damage.
2. Using a tee (3-way connector), connect a vacuum gauge to the hose between the EGR valve and the vacuum modulator.
3. Check the seating of the EGR valve by starting the engine and seeing that it runs at a smooth idle. If the valve is not completely closed, the idle will be rough.
4. Connect a tachometer as per manufactures instructions.
5. With the engine coolant temperature below 99°F (37°C), the vacuum gauge should read 0 at 2500 rpm. This indicates that the Bi-metal Vacuum Switching Valve (BVSV) (1991–92 models) or TVV (1993–95 models) is functioning correctly at this temperature range.
6. Warm the engine to normal operating temperature. Check the vacuum gauge and confirm low vacuum at 2500 rpm.

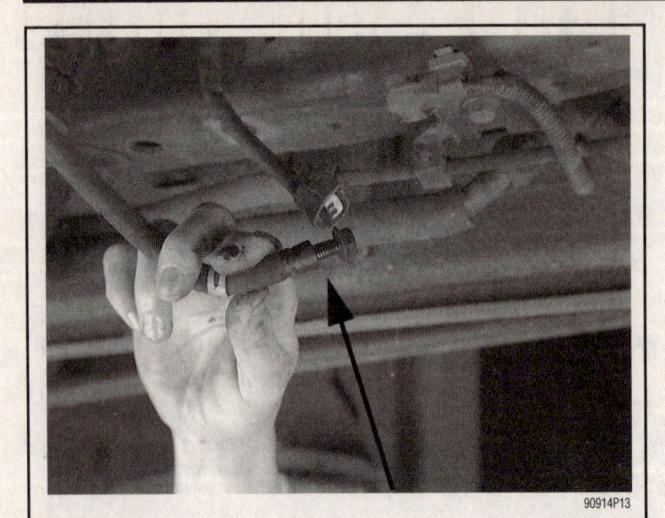

Fig. 20 Always plug the hoses to prevent gas vapors from escaping

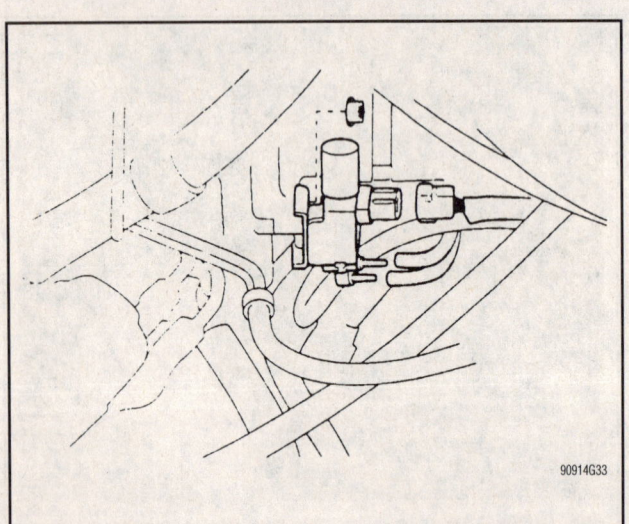

Fig. 21 View of the common charcoal canister

Fig. 22 The Vacuum Switching Valve is attached to the No. 2 air inlet duct

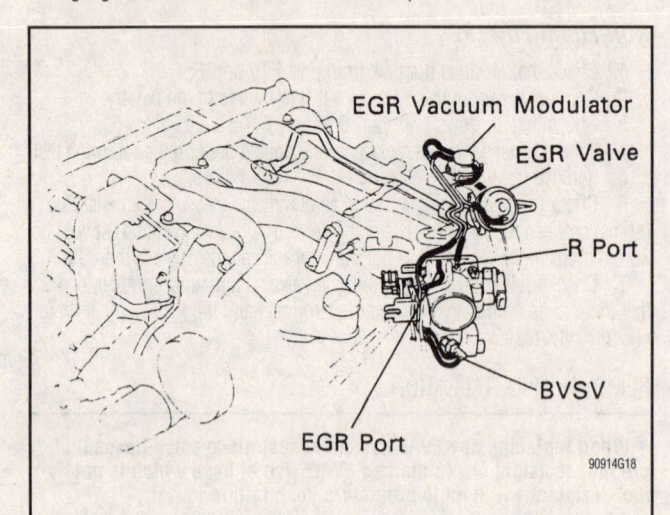

Fig. 23 Exhaust Gas Recirculation (EGR) system components—1991–92 2TZ-FE engine

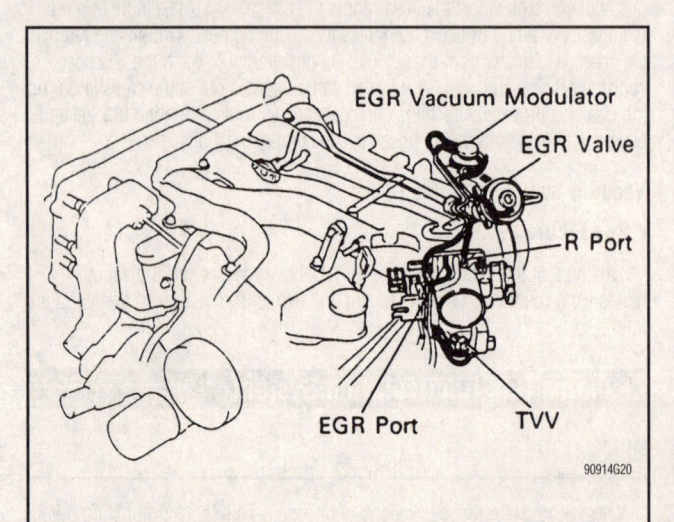

Fig. 24 Exhaust Gas Recirculation (EGR) system components—1993–95 2TZ-FE engine

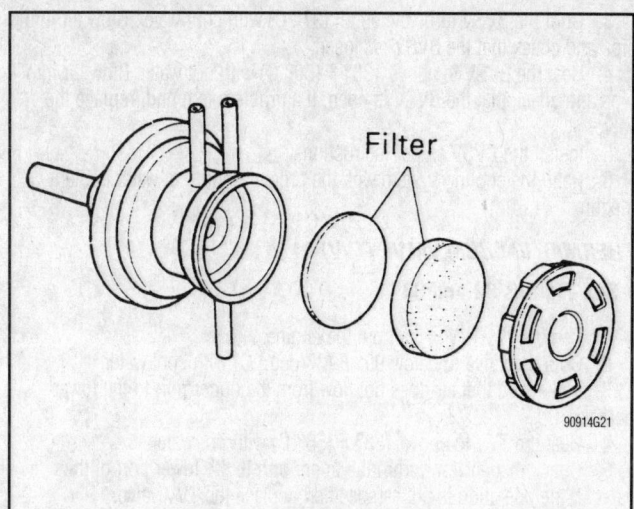

# DRIVEABILITY AND EMISSIONS CONTROLS  4-11

Fig. 25 Check the filter of the EGR modulator for contamination or damage

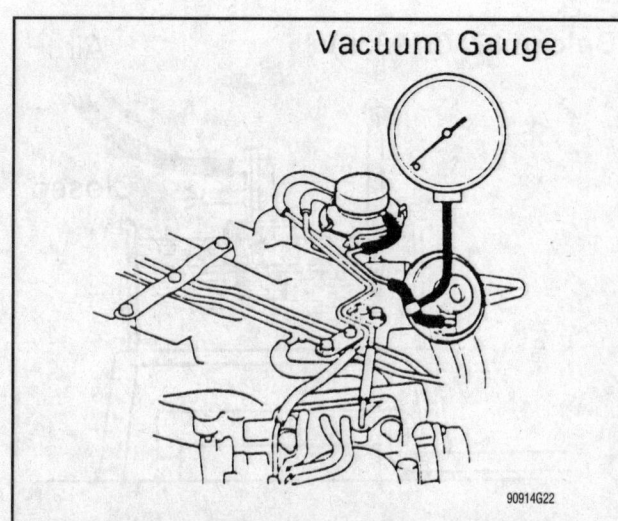

Fig. 26 Place a 3-way union on the EGR valve hose, then connect a vacuum gauge to it

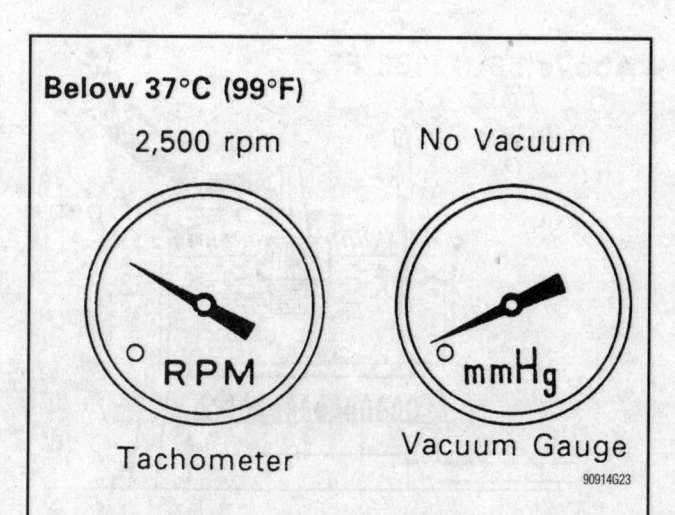

Fig. 27 With the coolant level cold, inspect the vacuum gauge reading

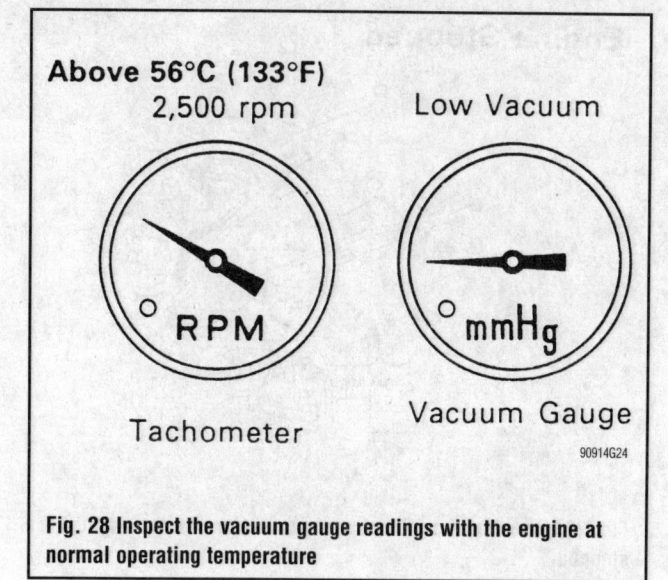

Fig. 28 Inspect the vacuum gauge readings with the engine at normal operating temperature

7. Disconnect the vacuum hose from the **R** port on the EGR vacuum modulator and, using another piece of hose, connect the **R** port directly to the intake manifold. Check that the vacuum gauge indicates high vacuum at 3500 rpm.

➡ Port R is the lower of the two ports. As a large amount of exhaust gas enters, the engine will misfire slightly at this time.

8. Remove the tachometer.
9. Disconnect the vacuum gauge and reconnect the vacuum hoses to their proper locations.
10. Check the EGR valve by applying vacuum directly to the valve with the engine at idle. (This may be accomplished either by bridging vacuum directly from the intake manifold or by using a hand-held vacuum pump.) The engine should falter and die as the full load of recalculated gasses enters the engine.
11. If no problem is found with this inspection, the system is OK; otherwise inspect each part.

### EGR VALVE

1. Remove the EGR valve.
2. Check the valve for sticking and heavy carbon deposits. If a problem is found, replace the valve.
3. Reinstall the EGR valve with a new gasket.

### EGR VACUUM MODULATOR

♦ See Figures 29, 30 and 31

1. Label and disconnect the vacuum hoses from ports **P**, **Q**, and **R** of the EGR vacuum modulator.
2. Plug the **P** and **R** ports with your fingers.
3. Blow air into port **Q**. Check that the air passes freely through the sides of the air filter.

➡ Port Q is the single port on the one side of the modulator.

4. Start the engine and maintain 2500 rpm.
5. Repeat the test above. Check that there is a strong resistance to air flow.
6. Reconnect the vacuum hoses to the proper locations.
7. If the operation is not as specified, replace the EGR vacuum modulator.

### BIMETAL VACUUM SWITCHING VALVE (BVSV)

1. Drain and recycle the engine coolant.
2. Remove the BVSV.

# 4-12 DRIVEABILITY AND EMISSIONS CONTROLS

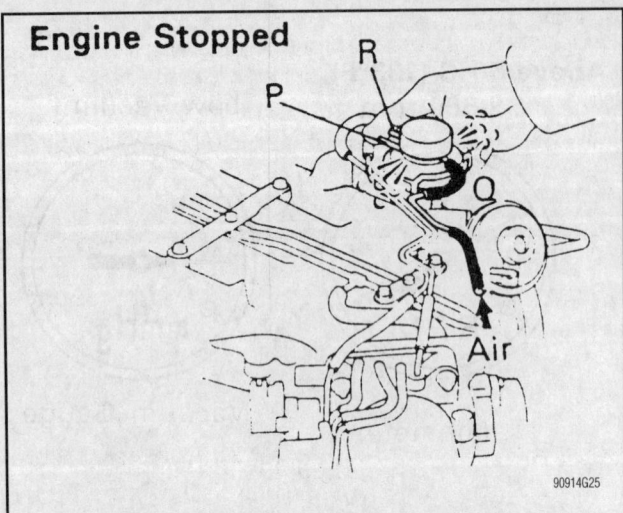

Fig. 29 Inspecting the EGR vacuum modulator with the engine stopped

3. Cool the BVSV to below 99° F (37° C) with cool water. Blow air into pipe and check that the BVSV is closed.
4. Heat the BVSV to above 133° F (56° C) with hot water. Blow air into pipe and check that the BVSV is open. If a problem is found, replace the valve.
5. Install the BVSV as per instructions.
6. Refill the cooling system with the proper amount of water coolant mixture.

### THERMAL VACUUM VALVE (TVV)

▶ See Figures 32 and 33

1. Remove the TVV valve from the engine.
2. Cool the valve to below 99° F (37(deg.) C) with cool water.
3. Make sure that air does not flow from the upper port to the lower port.
4. Heat the TVV to above 133° F (56° C) with hot water.
5. Check that air flows from the upper port to the lower port of the valve. If the operation is not as specified, replace the TVV valve.
6. Reinstall the TVV valve.

Fig. 30 The EGR vacuum modulator has labeled ports

Fig. 31 Inspecting the EGR vacuum modulator with the engine at 2500 rpms

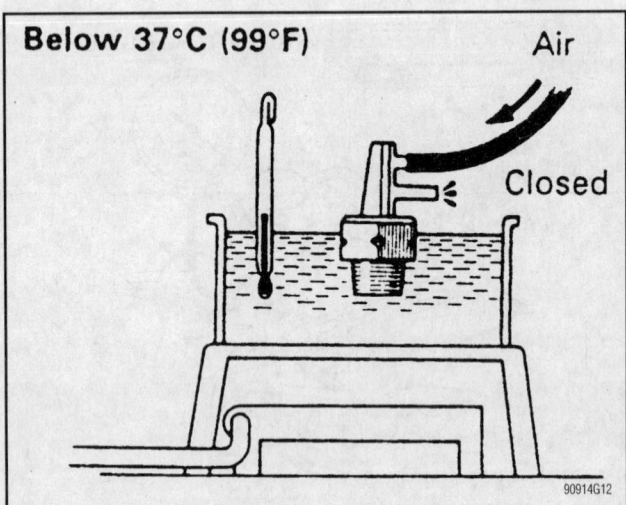

Fig. 32 Place the Thermal Vacuum Valve (TVV) into cool water while blowing air into the top port

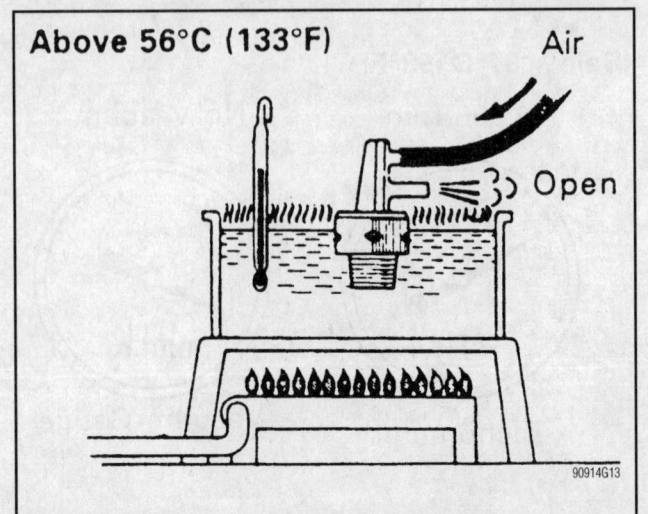

Fig. 33 Next place the TVV in hot water and apply air to the top port

# DRIVEABILITY AND EMISSIONS CONTROLS 4-13

## EGR GAS TEMPERATURE SENSOR

▶ See Figure 34

1. Remove the EGR gas temperature sensor.
2. Place the sensor in a container of oil.
3. Using an ohmmeter, measure the resistance between terminals.
- 69–89 kilohms @ 112°F (50°C)

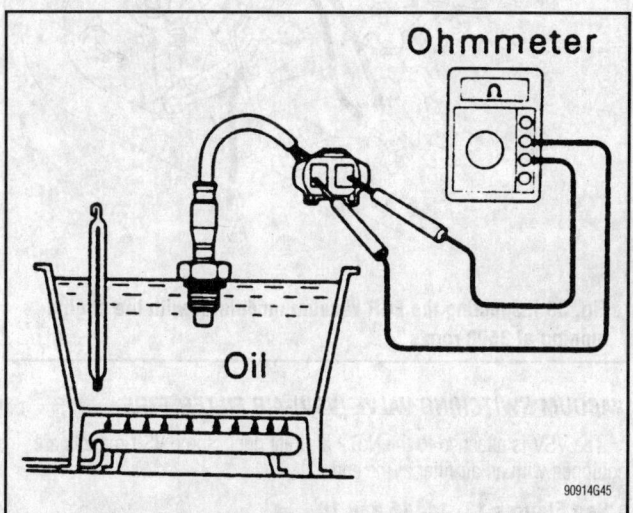

Fig. 34 Place the EGR gas temperature sensor in a container of oil and measure the resistance

- 11–15 kilohms @ 212°F (100°C)
- 2–4 kilohms @ 302°F (150°C)

4. If the resistance is not within the specifications, replace the sensor.
5. Install and secure the sensor.

### 2TZ-FZE Engine

#### SYSTEM CHECK

▶ See Figures 35 and 36

1. Check and clean the filter in the EGR vacuum modulator. Remove the cap and filter, then using compressed air (if possible) to blow the dirt out of the filter and check for contamination or damage. Reinstall the filter and cap.

➡ Install the filter with the coarse side facing outward.

2. Using a tee (3-way connector), connect a vacuum gauge to the hose between the EGR valve and the VSV.
3. Check the seating of the EGR valve by starting the engine and seeing that it runs at a smooth idle. Check that the EGR valve is fully seated.
4. Connect a Toyota hand-held tester or OBDII scan tool. Refer to the manufactures instructions.
5. Inspect the Vacuum Switching Valve (VSV) with the engine coolant temperature below 113°F (45°C), the vacuum gauge should read 0 at 3500 rpm.
6. Warm the engine to normal operating temperature. Check the vacuum gauge and confirm zero vacuum at 4500 rpm.
7. Lightly race the engine and check that the vacuum gauge reads a vacuum and then returns to zero vacuum immediately.
8. Check the vacuum hose between the EGR valve and the EGR vacuum modulator. Warm the engine to above 122°F (50°C). Check that the vacuum gauge indicates low vacuum at 3500 rpm.

9. Disconnect the vacuum hose from the **R** port on the EGR vacuum modulator and, using another piece of hose, connect the **R** port directly to the intake manifold. Check that the vacuum gauge indicates high vacuum at 3500 rpm.

➡ As a large amount of exhaust gas enters, the engine will misfire slightly at this time.

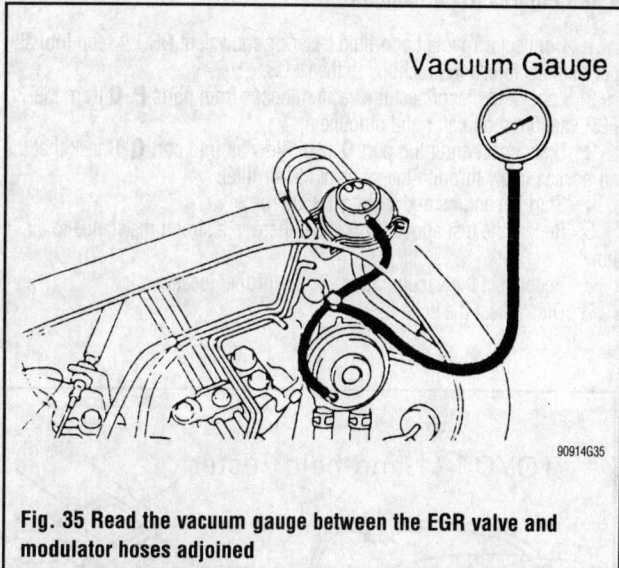

Fig. 35 Read the vacuum gauge between the EGR valve and modulator hoses adjoined

10. Disconnect the scan tool and vacuum gauge, then reconnect the hoses to their proper locations.
11. Check the EGR valve by applying vacuum directly to the valve with the engine at idle. (This may be accomplished either by bridging vacuum directly from the intake manifold or by using a hand-held vacuum pump.) The engine should falter and die as the full load of recalculated gasses enters the engine.
12. If no problem is found with this inspection, the system is OK; otherwise inspect each part.

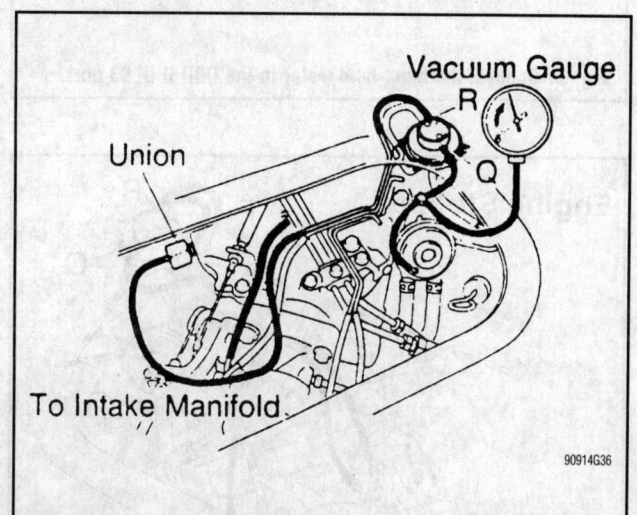

Fig. 36 Locations of port R and Q of the vacuum modulator during testing

# 4-14 DRIVEABILITY AND EMISSIONS CONTROLS

## EGR VALVE

1. Remove the EGR valve.
2. Check the valve for sticking and heavy carbon deposits. If a problem is found, replace the valve.
3. Reinstall the EGR valve with a new gasket.

## EGR VACUUM MODULATOR

▶ See Figures 37, 38 and 39

1. Connect a Toyota hand-held tester or equivalent OBD II scan tool as per manufacturer's instructions to the DLC3.
2. Label and disconnect the vacuum hoses from ports **P**, **Q** from the EGR vacuum modulator and plug them.
3. Disconnect and plug port **Q** also. Blow air into port **Q**. Check that the air passes freely through the sides of the air filter.
4. Start the engine and maintain 3500 rpms.
5. Repeat the test above. Check that there is a strong resistance to air flow.
6. Reconnect the vacuum hoses to the proper locations.
7. Disconnect the scan tool.

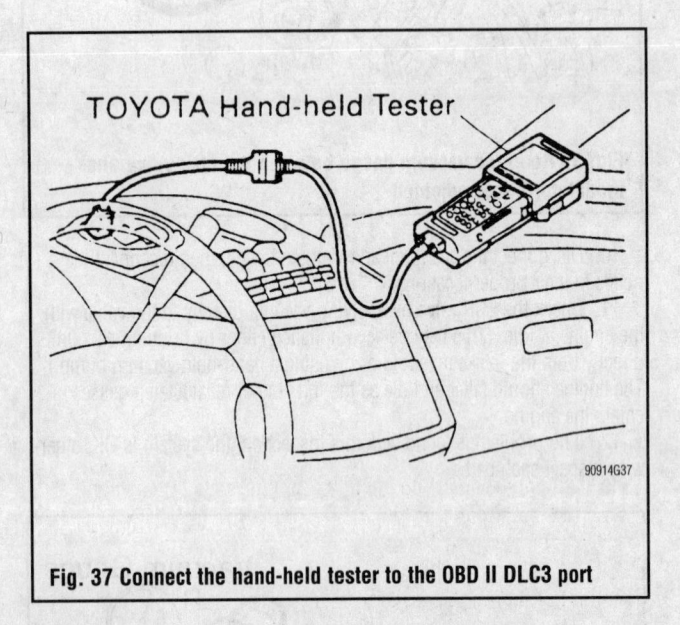

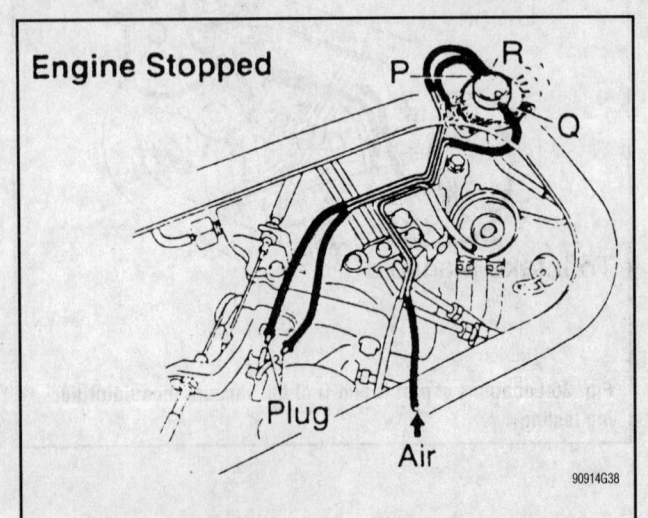

Fig. 37 Connect the hand-held tester to the OBD II DLC3 port

Fig. 38 Inspecting the EGR vacuum modulator with the engine stopped

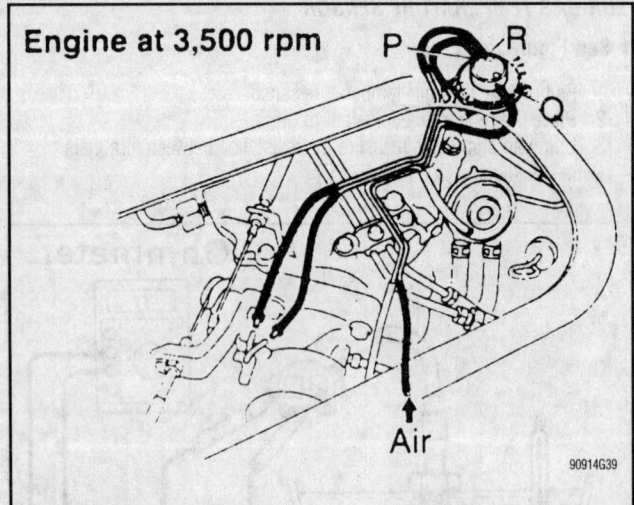

Fig. 39 Inspecting the EGR vacuum modulator with the engine running at 3500 rpm's

## VACUUM SWITCHING VALVE (VSV)-AIR FILTER TYPE

The VSV is attached to the No. 2 air inlet duct. Some VSV models are equipped with an air filter at the end.

▶ See Figures 13, 14, 15 and 16

1. Check that air flows from port **E** to the air filter.
2. Connect the vacuum switching valve terminals to the battery.
3. Check that air flows from port **E** to port **F**.
4. If the VSV fails this test replace it. Any doubts perform the following test.
5. Remove the VSV.
6. Check for an open circuit. Using an ohmmeter, measure the resistance (ohms) between the two terminals of the valve. The resistance (cold) should be 37–44 ohms. If the resistance is not within specifications, replace the VSV.
7. Check for a short circuit within the valve. Using an ohmmeter, check that there is no continuity between the terminals and the VSV body. If there is continuity, replace the VSV.

## VACUUM SWITCHING VALVE (VSV)-NON-AIR FILTER TYPE

1. Check that air does not flow from port **E** to port **F**.
2. Connect the vacuum switching valve terminals to the battery.
3. Check that air flows from port **E** to port **F**.
4. If the VSV fails this test replace it. Any doubts perform the following test.
5. Remove the VSV.
6. Check for an open circuit. Using an ohmmeter, measure the resistance (ohms) between the two terminals of the valve. The resistance (cold) should be 37–44 ohms. If the resistance is not within specifications, replace the VSV.
7. Check for a short circuit within the valve. Using an ohmmeter, check that there is no continuity between the terminals and the VSV body. If there is continuity, replace the VSV.

## EGR GAS TEMPERATURE SENSOR

▶ See Figure 34

1. Remove the EGR gas temperature sensor.
2. Place the sensor in a container of oil.
3. Using an ohmmeter, measure the resistance between terminals.
   - 64–97 kilohms @ 112°F (50°C)
   - 11–16 kilohms @ 212°F (100°C)
   - 2–4 kilohms @ 302°F (150°C)
4. If the resistance is not within the specifications, replace the sensor.
5. Install and secure the sensor.

# DRIVEABILITY AND EMISSIONS CONTROLS  4-15

## REMOVAL & INSTALLATION

### Bimetal Vacuum Switching Valve (BVSV)

▶ See Figures 40 and 41

The Bimetal Vacuum Switching Valve (BVSV) is threaded into the Idle Speed Control (ISC) valve bolted to the throttle body.
1. Drain the coolant from the system into a suitable container.
2. Unscrew the BVSV from the Idle Speed Control (ISC) valve.

**To install:**

3. Apply liquid sealer to the first 2–3 threads of the BVSV. Carefully thread the valve into the ISC and first tighten the valve to 9 ft. lbs. (12), then tighten the valve until it reached this position. Maximum torque of the valve is 25 ft. lbs. (34 Nm).

➡ Do not rotate the valve counter-clockwise in order to align the port as shown.

4. Fill the cooling system. Start the engine, check and top off the fluid level.

Fig. 40 The BVSV is threaded into the IAC bolted to the throttle body

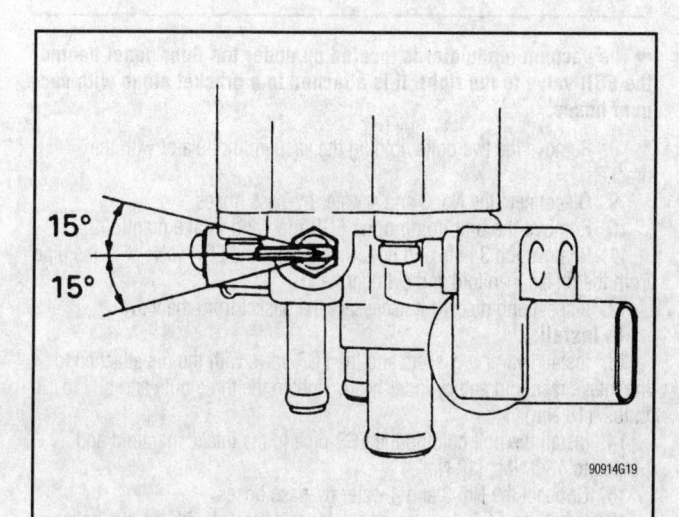

Fig. 41 On the second pass of tightening the BVSV, ensure the valve faces between this angle

### Thermal Vacuum Valve (TVV)

▶ See Figure 42

The Thermal Vacuum Valve (TVV) is threaded into the IAC valve bolted to the throttle body. Note the position of the valve prior to removal, it must be facing the same direction on installation.
1. Drain the coolant the from the engine.
2. Disconnect the vacuum hoses from the charcoal canister and throttle body.
3. Remove the TVV from the Intake Air Control (IAC).

**To install:**

4. Apply adhesive to 2 or 3 of the threads of the TVV, first tighten the valve to 9 ft. lbs. (12 Nm), then tighten it to 25 ft. lbs. (34 Nm) in the position it was removed from.
5. Reattach the vacuum hoses.
6. Refill the cooling system. Start the engine, check and top off the fluid level.

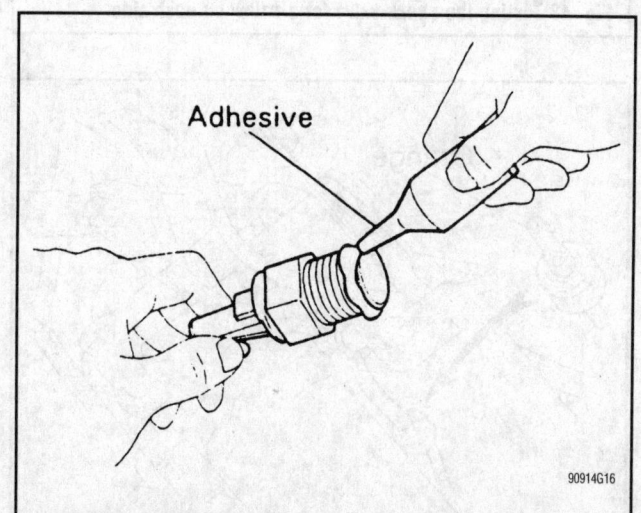

Fig. 42 Apply adhesive to the first 2 or 3 threads of the valve prior to installation

### Vacuum Switching Valve (VSV)

▶ See Figure 22

Disconnect the wiring from the VSV. Label and removed the vacuum hoses from the valve. Loosen the nut and extract the VSV from the No. 2 air inlet duct.

### EGR Gas Temperature Sensor

The EGR gas temperature sensor is located near the EGR valve usually threaded into the intake manifold.
1. Remove the engine access hole cover.
2. Located the EGR gas temperature sensor and unscrew it from the engine. If the old gasket is unreusable, discard it
3. Install a new gasket if necessary. place the sensor into position and tighten to 14 ft. lbs. (20 Nm).
4. Install the remaining components.

### Check Valve

▶ See Figures 43 and 44

1. Remove the check valve from the engine.
2. Blow air into the orange side of the pipe and check for air flow from the orange side.

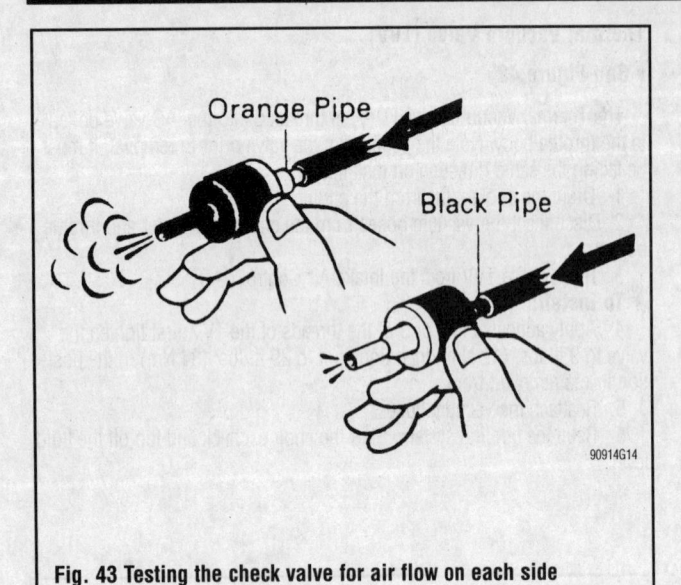

## 4-16 DRIVEABILITY AND EMISSIONS CONTROLS

Fig. 43 Testing the check valve for air flow on each side

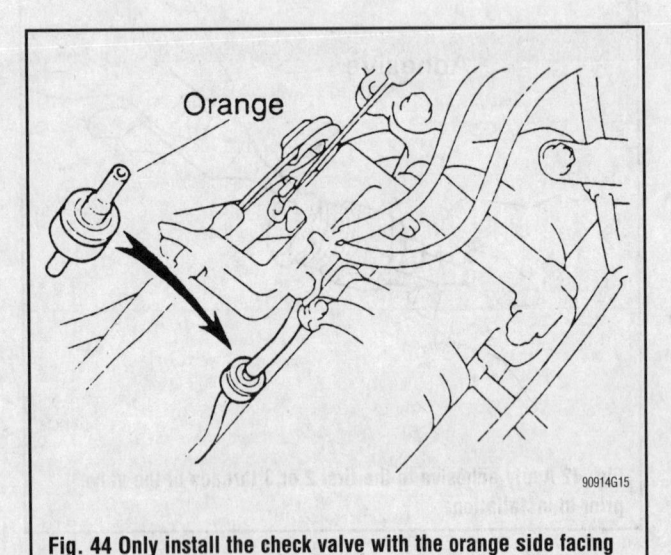

Fig. 44 Only install the check valve with the orange side facing the No. 2 air inlet duct

Fig. 45 EGR vacuum modulator (1), EGR valve (2) and bracket retaining bolts are circled

Fig. 46 Remove the union nut, EGR nuts (1) and by-pass hoses (2)

3. Blow air into the orange side of the pipe and check that no air flows from the black side.
4. If the testing is not as specified, replace the check valve.
5. Reinstall the check valve with the orange side facing the No. 2 air inlet duct side.

### EGR Valve

▶ See Figures 45 and 46

➡ To access and remove the EGR valve the engine must be lowered and the both motor mounts removed.

1. Drain the coolant from the engine.
2. Remove the left engine access hole cover.
3. Remove the motor mount bolts and nuts.
4. Jack up the engine and remove the motor mounts.
5. Slowly lower the engine being careful not to rest the engine weight on the oil filter housing. Place a block of wood where the motor mounts had been to support the engine.
6. Label and disconnect the vacuum hoses from the throttle body to the EGR valve.
7. Label and disconnect the vacuum modulator hose.

➡ The vacuum modulator is located up under the floor panel behind the EGR valve to the right. It is attached to a bracket along with vacuum hoses.

8. Remove the two bolts holding the vacuum modulator with the bracket.
9. Disconnect the No. 3 and 4 water by-pass hoses.
10. Remove the bolt holding the EGR pipe and intake manifold.
11. Remove the 3 nuts and bolt, then extract the EGR valve with the pipe from the intake manifold and cylinder head.
12. Inspect and discard if necessary the gasket from the valve.

**To install:**

13. Install two new gaskets and the EGR valve with the pie attached to the intake manifold and cylinder head. Tighten the three nuts and bolt to 13 ft. lbs. (18 Nm).
14. Install the bolt holding the EGR pipe to the intake manifold and tighten to 13 ft. lbs. (18 Nm).
15. Connect the No. 3 and 4 water by-pass hoses.
16. Install the EGR vacuum modulator and bracket with the two bolts and tighten to 9 ft. lbs. (12 Nm).
17. Attach the vacuum modulator hose. connect the three vacuum hoses to the No. 1 vacuum pipe.

# DRIVEABILITY AND EMISSIONS CONTROLS  4-17

**EGR Vacuum Modulator**

▶ See Figure 47

1. Unbolt the vacuum modulator bracket and extract.
2. Label and disconnect the hoses attached to the modulator.
3. Pull the clips apart and remove the modulator.

**To install:**

4. Insert the modulator into the bracket clips.
5. Attach the hoses in their proper positions.
6. Position the bracket/modulator assembly on the engine and secure the mounting bolts to 9 ft. lbs. (12 Nm).

Fig. 47 The throttle body ports are marked for the proper hoses

## ELECTRONIC ENGINE CONTROLS

### General Information

The Electronic Fuel Injection (EFI) system precisely controls fuel injection to match engine requirements. This in turn reduces emissions and increases driveability. The ECM receives input from various sensors to determine engine operating conditions. These sensors provide the input to the control unit which determines the amount of fuel to be injected as well as other variables such as idle speed. These inputs and their corresponding sensors include:

- Intake air temperature—Intake Air Temperature Sensor
- Coolant temperature—Water Temperature Sensor
- Engine speed—Pulse signal from the distributor
- Throttle valve opening—Throttle Position Sensor
- Exhaust oxygen content—Oxygen Sensor

### Engine Control Module (ECM)

OPERATION

The ECM receives signals from various sensors on the engine. It will then process this information and calculate the correct air/fuel mixture under all operating conditions. The ECM is a very fragile and expensive component. Always follow the precautions when servicing the electronic control system.

PRECAUTIONS

※※ **CAUTION**

**Some models covered by this manual may be equipped with a Supplemental Restraint System (SRS), which uses an air bag. Whenever working near any of the SRS components, such as the impact sensors, the air bag module, steering column and instrument panel, disable the SRS, as described in Section 6.**

- Do not permit parts to receive a severe impact during removal or installation. Always handle all fuel injection parts with care, especially the ECM. DO NOT open the ECM cover!
- Before removing the fuel injected wiring connectors, terminals, etc., first disconnect the power by either disconnecting the negative battery cable or turning the ignition switch **OFF**.
- Always check the diagnostic trouble code before disconnecting the terminal cable from the battery.

- Do not be careless during troubleshooting as there are numerous amounts of transistor circuits; even a slight terminal contact can induce troubles.
- When inspecting during rainy days, take extra caution not to allow entry of water in or on the unit. When washing the engine compartment, prevent water from getting on the fuel injection parts and wiring connectors.

REMOVAL & INSTALLATION

▶ See Figure 48

The ECM is located on the drivers side of the vehicle bolted to the front seat leg. Refer to the Precautions prior to removal of the ECM. Checking for trouble codes before removal is recommended.

1. Check for any trouble codes. Refer to the procedure later in this section.
2. Note any electronic device settings such as the radio stations, clock etc. These will no longer be set once the battery cable is disconnected.
3. Disconnect the negative battery cable. Wait at least 90 seconds before proceeding on models equipped with an air bag.

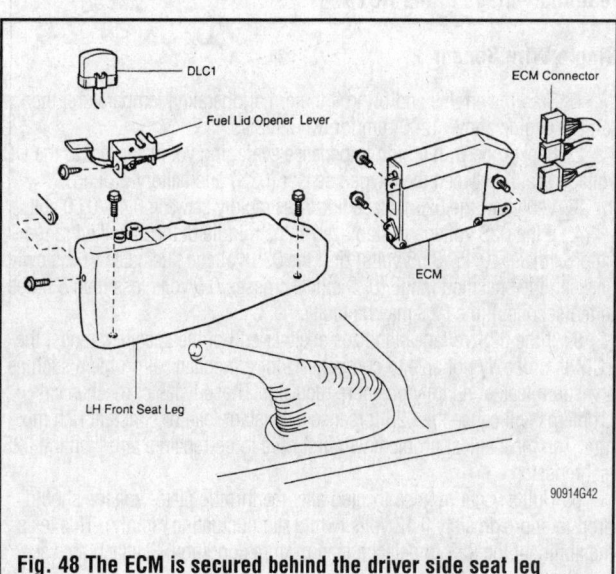

Fig. 48 The ECM is secured behind the driver side seat leg

# 4-18 DRIVEABILITY AND EMISSIONS CONTROLS

4. From under the drivers seat, unbolt the ECM from the leg.
5. Carefully disengage the 3 harnesses form the ECM.

**To install:**

6. Attach the harnesses to the ECM. Secure to the seat leg with the mounting bolts.
7. Connect the negative battery cable. Reset any electronic devises such as the radio, clock, etc.

## Oxygen Sensor

### OPERATION

The exhaust oxygen sensor or O2S, is mounted in the exhaust stream where it monitors oxygen content in the exhaust gas. The oxygen content in the exhaust is a measure of the air/fuel mixture going into the engine. The oxygen in the exhaust reacts with the oxygen sensor to produce a voltage which is read by the ECM.

There are two types of oxygen sensors used in these vehicles. They are the single wire oxygen sensor (O2S) and the heated oxygen sensor (HO2S). The oxygen sensor is a spark plug shaped device that is screwed into the exhaust pipes. It monitors the oxygen content of the exhaust gases and sends a voltage signal to the Electronic Control Module (ECM). The ECM monitors this voltage and, depending on the value of the received signal, issues a command to the mixture control solenoid on the carburetor to adjust for rich or lean conditions.

The heated oxygen sensor has a heating element incorporated into the sensor to aid in the warm up to the proper operating temperature and to maintain that temperature.

The proper operation of the oxygen sensor depends upon four basic conditions:

• Good electrical connections. Since the sensor generates low currents, good clean electrical connections at the sensor are a must.
• Outside air supply. Air must circulate to the internal portion of the sensor. When servicing the sensor, do not restrict the air passages.
• Proper operating temperatures. The ECM will not recognize the sensor's signals until the sensor reaches approximately 600°F (316°C).
• Non-leaded fuel. The use of leaded gasoline will damage the sensor very quickly.

### TESTING

**※※ WARNING**

**Do not pierce the wires when testing this sensor; this can lead to wiring harness damage. Backprobe the connector to properly read the voltage of the HO2S.**

#### Single Wire Sensor

1. Start the engine and bring it to normal operating temperature, then run the engine above 1200 rpm for two minutes.
2. Backprobe with a high impedance averaging voltmeter (set to the DC voltage scale) between the oxygen sensor (O2S) and battery ground.
3. Verify that the O2S voltage fluctuates rapidly between 0.40–0.60 volts.
4. If the O2S voltage is stabilized at the middle of the specified range (approximately 0.45–0.55 volts) or if the O2S voltage fluctuates very slowly between the specified range (O2S signal crosses 0.5 volts less than 5 times in ten seconds), the O2S may be faulty.
5. If the O2S voltage stabilizes at either end of the specified range, the ECM is probably not able to compensate for a mechanical problem such as a vacuum leak or a faulty pressure regulator. These types of mechanical problems will cause the O2S to sense a constant lean or constant rich mixture. The mechanical problem will first have to be repaired and then the O2S test repeated.
6. Pull a vacuum hose located after the throttle plate. Voltage should drop to approximately 0.12 volts (while still fluctuating rapidly). This tests the ability of the O2S to detect a lean mixture condition. Reattach the vacuum hose.

7. Richen the mixture using a propane enrichment tool. Voltage should rise to approximately 0.90 volts (while still fluctuating rapidly). This tests the ability of the O2S to detect a rich mixture condition.
8. If the O2S voltage is above or below the specified range, the O2S and/or the O2S wiring may be faulty. Check the wiring for any breaks, repair as necessary and repeat the test.

#### Heated Oxygen Sensor

▶ See Figure 49

1. Start the engine and bring it to normal operating temperature, then run the engine above 1200 rpm for two minutes.
2. Turn the ignition **OFF** disengage the HO2S harness connector.
3. Connect a test light between harness terminals +B and HT. With the ignition switch **ON** and the engine off, verify that the test light is lit. If the test light is not lit, either the supply voltage to the HO2S heater or the ground circuit of the HO2S heater is faulty. Check the HO2S wiring and the fuse.
4. Next, connect a high impedance ohmmeter between the HO2S terminals of the heating element and verify that the resistance is 11.0–16.0 ohms at 68° F (20° C).
5. If the HO2S heater resistance is not as specified, the HO2S may be faulty.
6. Start the engine and bring it to normal operating temperature, then run the engine above 1200 rpm for two minutes.
7. Backprobe with a high impedance averaging voltmeter (set to the DC voltage scale) between the oxygen sensor (O2S) signal wire and battery ground.
8. Verify that the O2S voltage fluctuates rapidly between 0.40–0.60 volts.
9. If the O2S voltage is stabilized at the middle of the specified range (approximately 0.45–0.55 volts) or if the O2S voltage fluctuates very slowly between the specified range (O2S signal crosses 0.5 volts less than 5 times in ten seconds), the O2S may be faulty.
10. If the O2S voltage stabilizes at either end of the specified range, the ECM is probably not able to compensate for a mechanical problem such as a vacuum leak or a faulty fuel pressure regulator. These types of mechanical problems will cause the O2S to sense a constant lean or constant rich mixture. The mechanical problem will first have to be repaired and then the O2S test repeated.
11. Pull a vacuum hose located after the throttle plate. Voltage should drop to approximately 0.12 volts (while still fluctuating rapidly). This tests the ability of the O2S to detect a lean mixture condition. Reattach the vacuum hose.
12. Richen the mixture using a propane enrichment tool. Voltage should rise to approximately 0.90 volts (while still fluctuating rapidly). This tests the ability of the O2S to detect a rich mixture condition.
13. If the O2S voltage is above or below the specified range, the O2S and/or the O2S wiring may be faulty. Check the wiring for any breaks, repair as necessary and repeat the test.

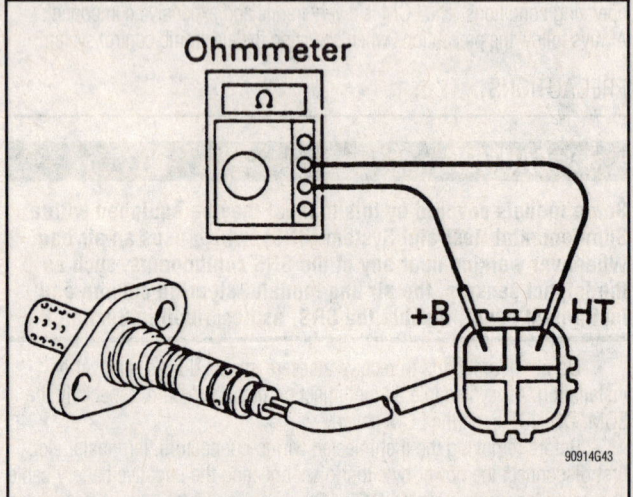

Fig. 49 Using an ohmmeter, measure the resistance between the terminals of the oxygen sensor

# DRIVEABILITY AND EMISSIONS CONTROLS 4-19

REMOVAL & INSTALLATION

▶ See Figures 50 thru 55

The oxygen sensor can be located in the front pipe/catalytic converter. On some models, there are two sensors in the pipe, the rear one is always the sub-sensor. The vehicle must be raised and supported in the air in most situations to remove the sensor(s).

### ※※ WARNING

**Care should be used during the removal of the oxygen sensor. Both the sensor and its wire can be easily damaged.**

1. The best condition in which to remove the sensor is when the engine is moderately warm. This is generally achieved after two to five minutes (depending on outside temperature) of running after a cold start. Wearing heat resistant gloves is highly recommended during this repair.
2. With the ignition **OFF**, unplug the connector for the sensor.
3. Remove the two sensor attaching nuts.
4. Remove the oxygen sensor from its mount and discard the gasket.

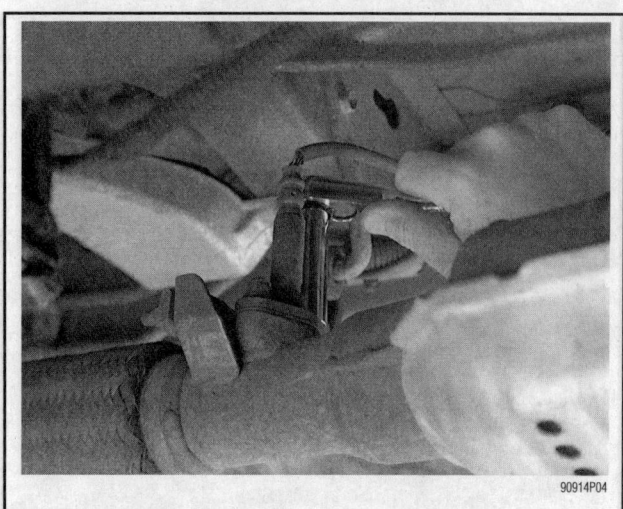

Fig. 52 Sometimes it may be hard to access the retaining nuts securing the sensors

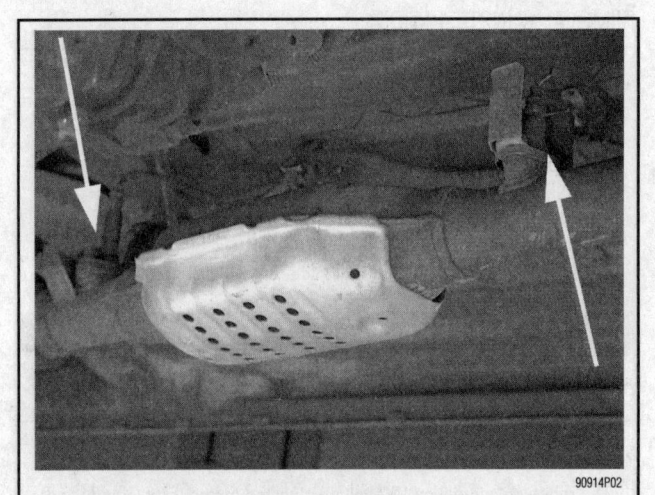

Fig. 50 On some models, there are two oxygen sensors located on either side of the catalytic converter

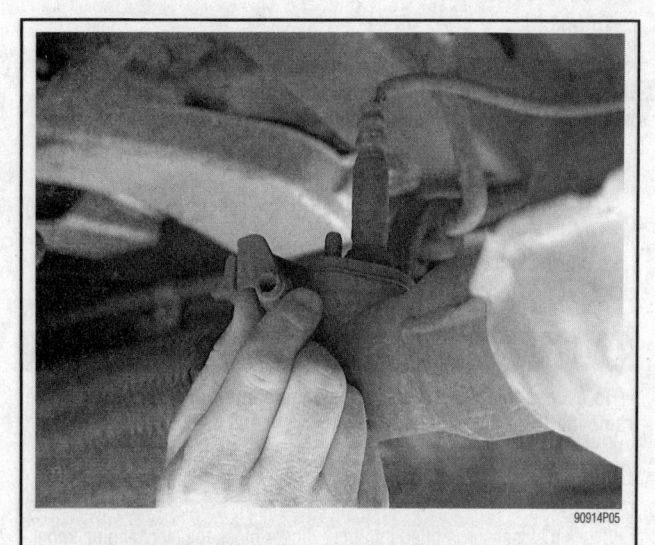

Fig. 53 Inspect the old nuts, and replace them if necessary

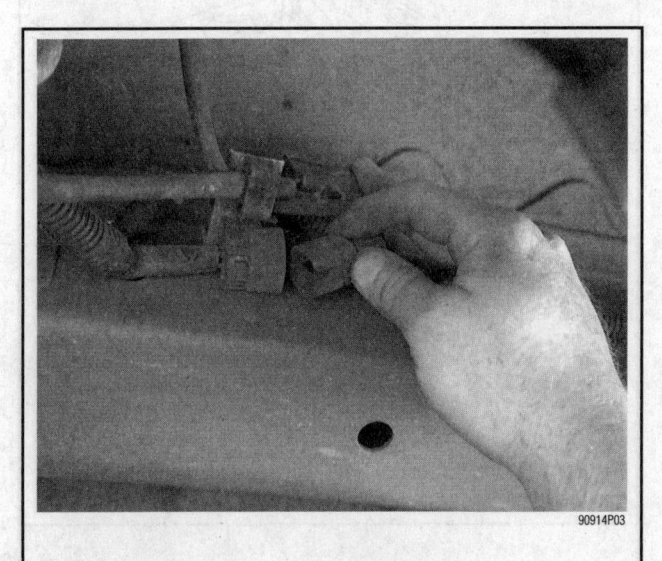

Fig. 51 Disconnecting the sensor wiring harness

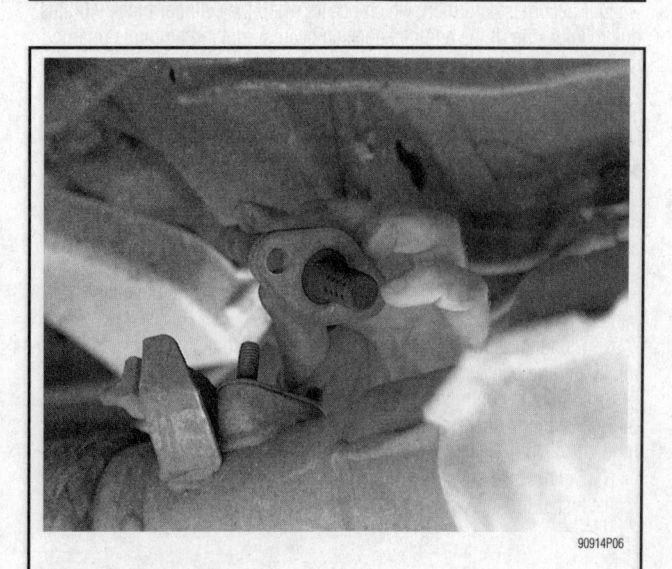

Fig. 54 Remove the sensor . . .

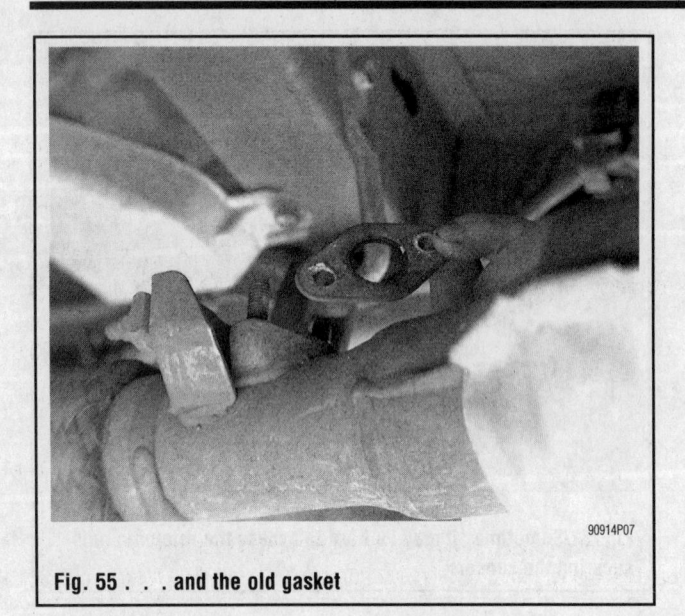

# 4-20 DRIVEABILITY AND EMISSIONS CONTROLS

Fig. 55 . . . and the old gasket

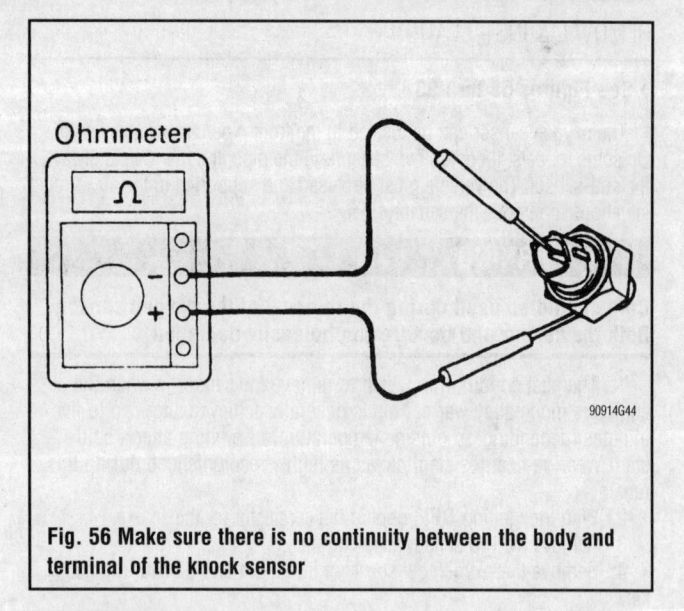

Fig. 56 Make sure there is no continuity between the body and terminal of the knock sensor

To install:

➡During and after the removal, use great care to protect the tip of the sensor if it is to be reused. Do not allow it to come in contact with fluids or dirt. Do not attempt to clean it or wash it.

5. Apply a coat of anti-seize compound to the bolt threads but DO NOT allow any to get on the tip of the sensor.
6. Position a new gasket, install and secure the sensor to 14 ft. lbs. (20 Nm).
7. Reattach the electrical wiring and insure a clean, tight connection.

## Knock Sensor

➡To access the knock sensor, the engine and transmission must be removed from the vehicle.

### OPERATION

The knock sensor is fitted into the cylinder block to detect engine knocking. This sensor contains a piezoelectric element which generates a voltage when it becomes deformed, which occurs when the cylinder block vibrates due to knocking. If the engine knocking occurs, ignition timing is retarded to suppress it.

### TESTING

♦ See Figure 56

1. Remove the engine and transmission assembly from the vehicle
2. Remove the intake manifold.
3. Disconnect the wiring from the knock sensor.
4. Using tool 09816–30010 or an equivalent socket, remove the knock sensor from the vehicle.
5. Using an ohmmeter, check that there is no continuity between the terminal and the body.
6. If there is continuity, replace the sensor.
7. Install the knock sensor with the special tool, tighten securely to 33 ft. lbs. (44 Nm).
8. Connect the sensor wiring.
9. Install the intake manifold. Reinstall the engine in the vehicle.

### REMOVAL & INSTALLATION

1. Remove the engine from the vehicle.
2. Remove the intake manifold.
3. Remove the knock sensor from the engine.
4. Inspect the vacuum hose over its entire length for any signs of cracking or splitting. The slightest leak can cause improper operation.

To install:
5. Install the knock sensor; tighten securely to 34 ft. lbs. (45 Nm).
6. Reinstall the intake manifold. Install the engine.

## Idle Air Control (IAC) Valve

### OPERATION

♦ See Figure 57

The rotary solenoid type IAC valve is located on the throttle body and intake air bypassing the throttle valve is directed to the IAC valve through a

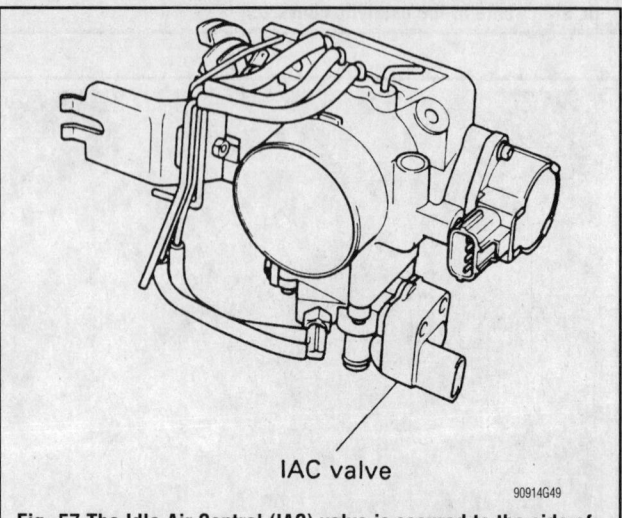

Fig. 57 The Idle Air Control (IAC) valve is secured to the side of the throttle body

# DRIVEABILITY AND EMISSIONS CONTROLS 4-21

hose. In this way the intake air volume bypassing the throttle valve is regulated, controlling the engine speed. The ECM operates only the IAC valve to perform idle-up and provide feedback for the target idling speed and a Vacuum Switching Valve (VSV) for idle-up control is also added for models with air conditioning.

## TESTING

### 2TZ-FE Engine

♦ See Figures 58, 59, 60 and 61

1. Disconnect the IAC valve wiring.
2. Using an ohmmeter, measure the resistance between terminals +B and the other terminals (ISC1 and ISC2 or ISCC and ISSC, depending on the year of the van).
3. Resistance should be between 18.8–22.8 ohms.
4. If the resistance is not within specifications, replace the IAC valve.
5. To check the operation of the IAC valve, the engine should be at normal operating temperature and the transmission in Neutral.
6. Using a jumper wire, connect terminals TE1 and E1 of the DLC1.

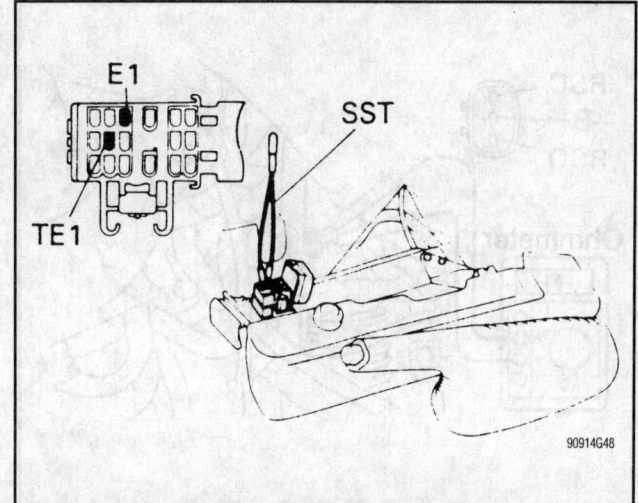

Fig. 60 A jumper wire is placed on these two terminals of the DLC1 to test the IAC valve operation—ISC1 and ISC2 type

Fig. 58 Use an ohmmeter to measure the resistance between the terminals of the IAC valve—ISC1 and ISC2 type

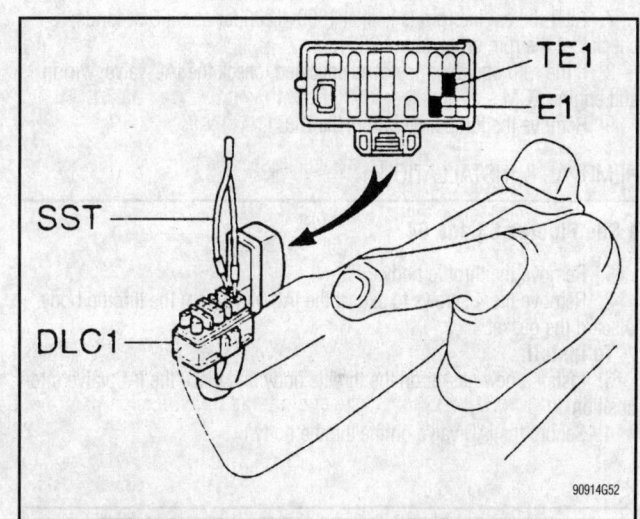

Fig. 61 A jumper wire is placed on these two terminals of the DLC1 to test the IAC valve operation—ISCC and ISSC type

7. After the engine rpm is kept at 1000–1200 for about 5 seconds, check that the rpm drops about 200 rpm.
8. If the rpm operation is not as specified, check the IAC valve, wiring and engine ECM.
9. Remove the jumper wire form the DLC1.

### 2TZ-FZE Engine

♦ See Figures 61 and 62

1. Disconnect the IAC valve wiring.
2. Using an ohmmeter, measure the resistance between terminals +B and the other terminals RSC and RSO.
3. Resistance should be between 17.0–24.5 ohms cold and 21.5–28.5 ohms hot.
4. If the resistance is not within specifications, replace the IAC valve.
5. To check the operation of the IAC valve, the engine should be at normal operating temperature and the transmission in Neutral.
6. Using a jumper wire, connect terminals TE1 and E1 of the DLC1.

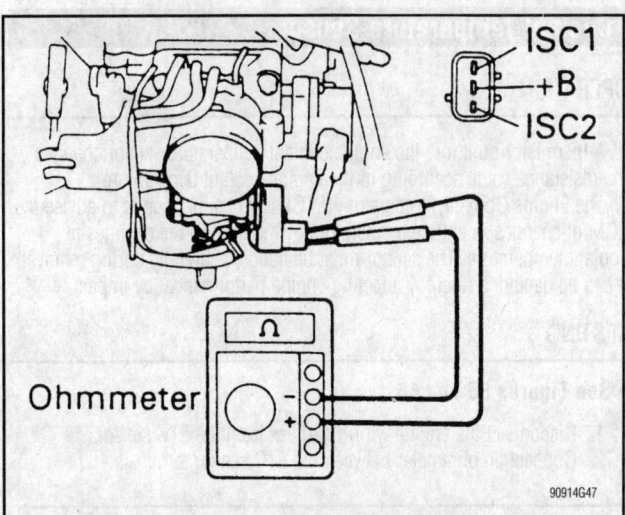

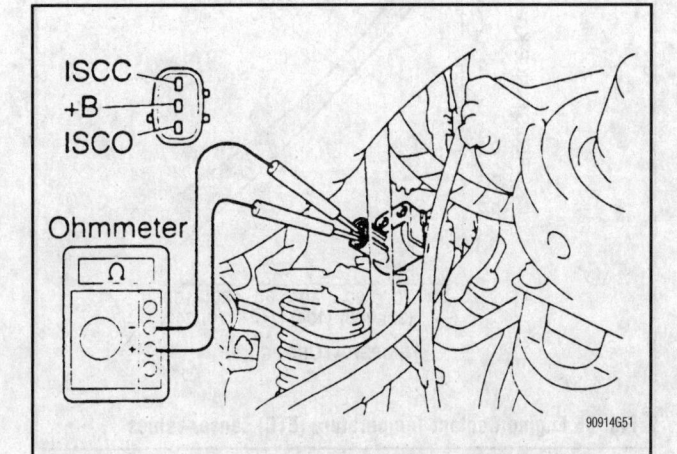

Fig. 59 Use an ohmmeter to measure the resistance between the terminals of the IAC valve—2TZ-FE engine—ISCC and ISSC type

# 4-22 DRIVEABILITY AND EMISSIONS CONTROLS

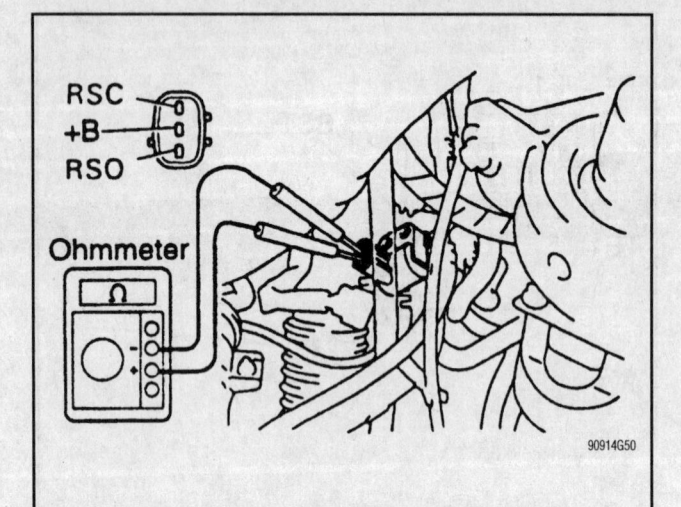

Fig. 62 Use an ohmmeter to measure the resistance between the terminals of the IAC valve—2TZ-FZE engine

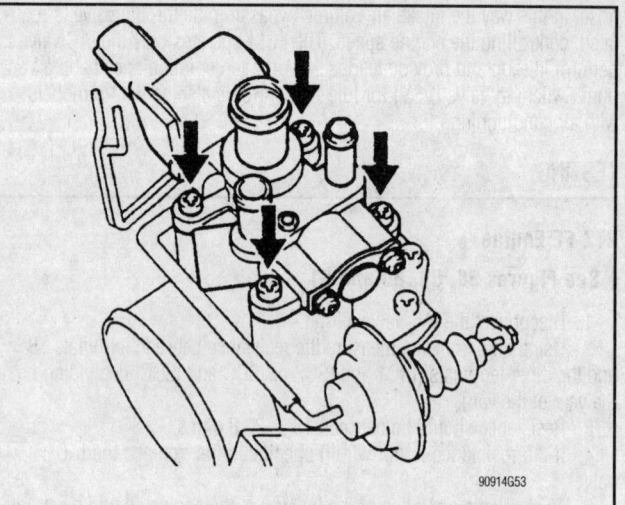

Fig. 64 Remove these four bolts to extract the IAC valve from the throttle body

7. After the engine rpm is kept at 1000–1200 for about 5 seconds, check that the rpm drops about 200 rpm.
8. If the rpm operation is not as specified, check the IAC valve, wiring and engine ECM.
9. Remove the jumper wire from the DLC1.

## REMOVAL & INSTALLATION

▶ See Figures 63 and 64

1. Remove the throttle body.
2. Remove the 4 screws to extract the IAC valve from the throttle body. Discard the gasket.

**To install:**

3. Install a new gasket on the throttle body and place the IAC valve into position.
4. Secure the IAC valve on the throttle body.

## Coolant Temperature Sensor

### OPERATION

A thermistor built into the engine coolant temperature sensor changes the resistance value according to the engine coolant temperature.

The Engine Coolant Temperature (ETC) sensor's function is to advise the ECM of changes in engine temperature by monitoring the changes in coolant temperature. The sensor must be handled carefully during removal. It can be damaged (thereby affecting engine performance) by impact.

### TESTING

▶ See Figures 65 and 66

1. Disconnect the engine wiring harness from the ETC sensor.
2. Connect an ohmmeter between the ETC sensor terminals.

Fig. 63 The IAC valve is attached to the throttle body

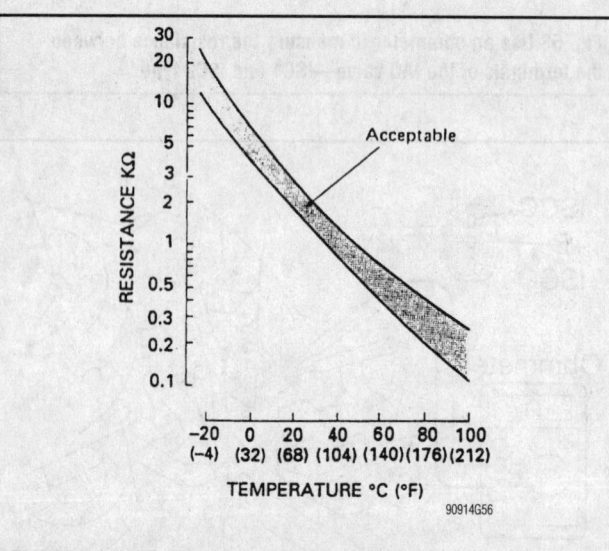

Fig. 65 Engine Coolant Temperature (ETC) sensor values

# DRIVEABILITY AND EMISSIONS CONTROLS 4-23

**Fig. 66 Test both terminals of the coolant temperature sensor using an ohmmeter**

3. With the engine cold and the ignition switch in the **OFF** position, measure and note the ETC sensor resistance.
4. Connect the engine wiring harness to the sensor.
5. Start the engine and allow the engine to reach normal operating temperature.
6. Once the engine has reached normal operating temperature, turn the engine **OFF**.
7. Once again, disconnect the engine wiring harness from the ETC sensor.
8. Measure and note the ETC sensor resistance with the engine hot.
9. Compare the cold and hot ETC sensor resistance measurements with the accompanying chart.
10. If readings do not approximate those in the chart, the sensor may be faulty.

## REMOVAL & INSTALLATION

▶ See Figure 67

1. Drain the engine coolant.
2. Remove the RH seat and engine service hole cover.
3. Disconnect the ETC sensor wiring.
4. Remove the sensor and gasket.

**Fig. 67 Remove the wiring from the coolant temperature sensor, then unthread it**

**To install:**
5. Install the new sensor with gasket. Tighten the sensor to 17 ft. lbs. (25 Nm).
6. Connect the wiring to the sensor.
7. Reinstall RH seat and engine service hole cover.
8. Refill the engine with coolant and water mixture.

## Intake Air Temperature (IAT) Sensor

### OPERATION

The Intake Air Temperature sensor is built into the mass air flow meter and senses the intake air temperature. A thermistor built into the sensor changes the resistance value according to the intake air temperature. The lower the intake air temperature, the greater the thermistor resistance value, and the higher the intake air temperature, the lower the thermistor resistance value. The intake air temperature is connected to the ECM. If the IAT sensor is faulty it cannot be replaced separately. The MAF meter must be replaced as an assembly. Refer to the air flow meter procedures.

## Volume Airflow Meter

### OPERATION

The 2TZ-FE engine utilizes a Volume Air Flow Meter (VAF) contains a spring-loaded measuring plate. The plate is connected to a potentiometer which controls the signal to the ECM. In this way, the control unit is advised of intake air volume and can control injector duration and ignition advance accordingly.

### TESTING

▶ See Figures 68, 69, 70 and 71

1. To test the VAF meter on the vehicle, disconnect the meter wiring.
   a. Using an ohmmeter, measure the resistance between each terminal.
   b. If the resistance is not within specifications, replace the VAF meter.
   c. Reconnect the harness to the VAF meter.
2. Testing the meter off the vehicle perform the following:
   a. Using an ohmmeter, measure the resistance between each terminal by moving the measuring plate.
   b. The resistance between terminals E2 and VS will change in a wave pattern as the measuring plate slowly opens.
   c. If the resistance is not as specified, replace the VAF meter.

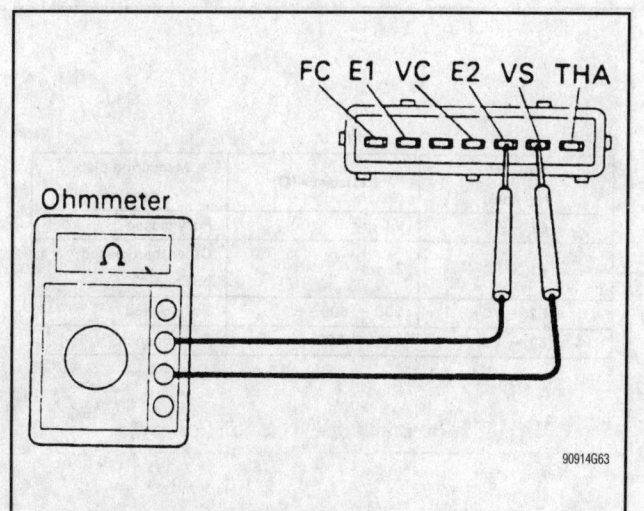

**Fig. 68 Use the ohmmeter to test between each of the terminals on the VAF meter—2TZ-FE engine**

# 4-24 DRIVEABILITY AND EMISSIONS CONTROLS

| Between terminals | Resistance | Temperature |
|---|---|---|
| VS – E2 | 200 – 600 Ω | — |
| VC – E2 | 200 – 400 Ω | — |
| THA – E2 | 10 – 20 kΩ | –20°C (4°F) |
| THA – E2 | 4 – 7 kΩ | 0°C (32°F) |
| THA – E2 | 2 – 3 kΩ | 20°C (68°F) |
| THA – E2 | 0.9 – 1.3 kΩ | 40°C (104°F) |
| THA – E2 | 0.4 – 0.7 kΩ | 60°C (140°F) |
| THA – E2 | 0.2 – 0.4 kΩ | 80°C (176°F) |
| FC – E1 | Infinity | — |

Fig. 69 On-vehicle VAF meter resistance values—2TZ-FE engine

Fig. 70 Measure the resistance between each terminal by moving the measuring plate of the VAF meter

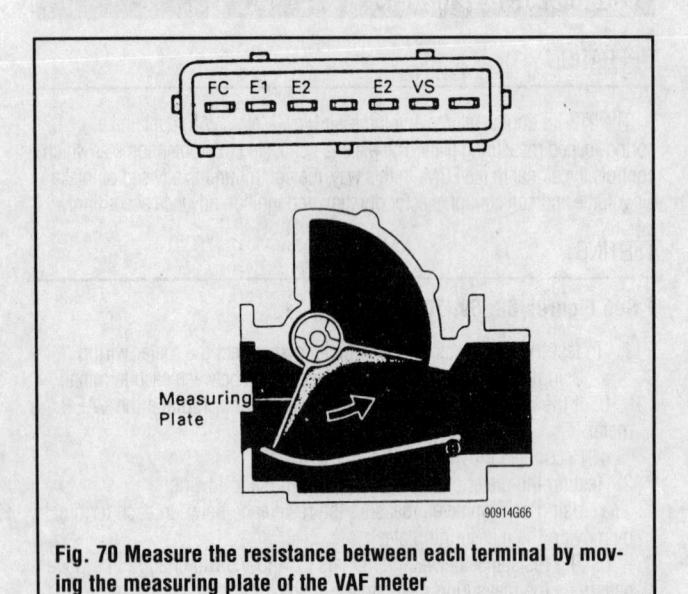

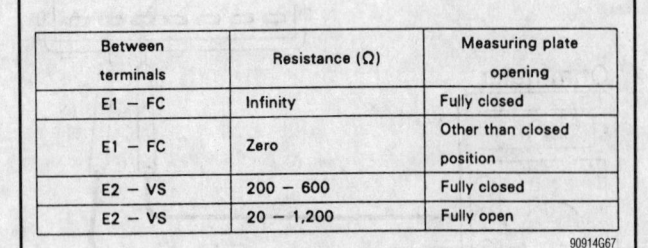

| Between terminals | Resistance (Ω) | Measuring plate opening |
|---|---|---|
| E1 – FC | Infinity | Fully closed |
| E1 – FC | Zero | Other than closed position |
| E2 – VS | 200 – 600 | Fully closed |
| E2 – VS | 20 – 1,200 | Fully open |

Fig. 71 Off-vehicle VAF meter resistance values—2TZ-FE engine

## REMOVAL & INSTALLATION

♦ See Figures 72 and 73

1. Disconnect the VAF meter wiring.
2. Disconnect the air intake temperature sensor wiring.
3. Remove the air cleaner cap and VAF meter as an assembly.
4. To separate the two components, pry off the lock plate, remove the 4 nuts and washers, lock plate, VAF meter and gasket.
5. Installation is the reverse of removal.

## Mass Airflow Meter (MAF)

### OPERATION

♦ See Figure 74

The Mass Airflow Meter (MAF) is only applicable to the 2TZ-FZE engines. The MAF uses a platinum hot wire. The hot wire air flow meter consists of a platinum hot wire, thermistor and control circuit installed in a plastic housing. The hot wire air flow meter works on the principle that the

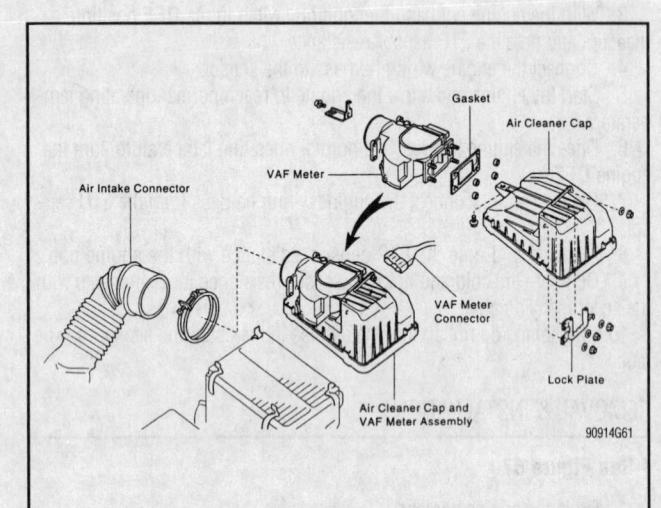

Fig. 72 The Volume Airflow Meter is attached to the air cleaner cap—2TZ-FE engine

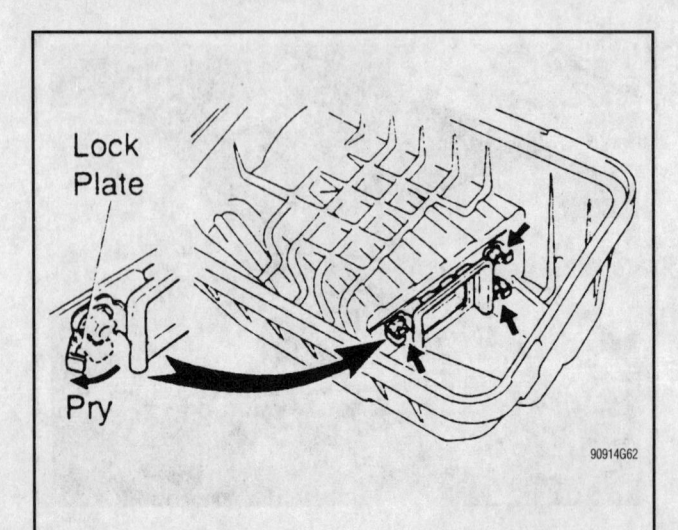

Fig. 73 Pry off the lock plate on the VAF meter first when separating the two components

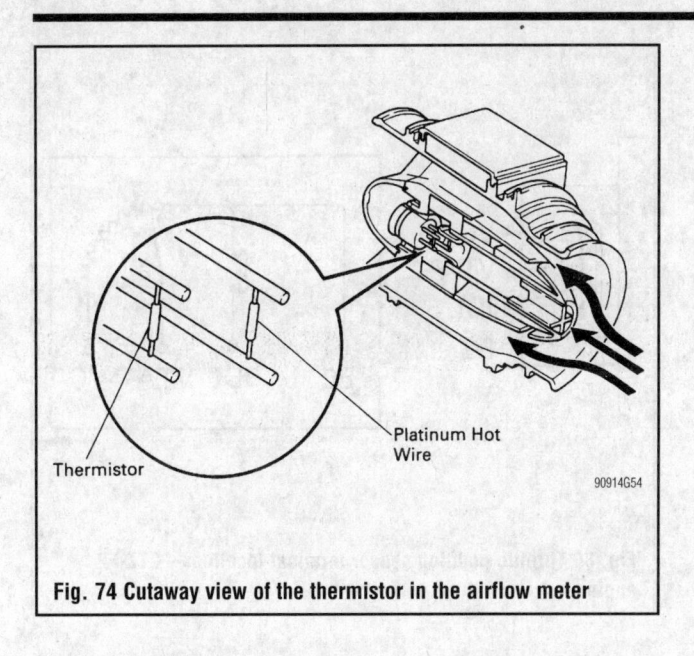

## DRIVEABILITY AND EMISSIONS CONTROLS 4-25

**Fig. 74 Cutaway view of the thermistor in the airflow meter**

| Between terminals | Resistance | Temperature |
|---|---|---|
| THA – E2 | 10 – 20 kΩ | −20°C (−4°F) |
| THA – E2 | 4 – 7 kΩ | 0°C (32°F) |
| THA – E2 | 2 – 3 kΩ | 20°C (68°F) |
| THA – E2 | 0.9 – 1.3 kΩ | 40°C (104°F) |
| THA – E2 | 0.4 – 0.7 kΩ | 60°C (140°F) |
| THA – E2 | 0.2 – 0.4 kΩ | 80°C (176°F) |

**Fig. 76 Mass Airflow Meter resistance values—2TZ-FZE engine**

hot wire and thermistor are located in the intake air bypass of the housing detect any changes in the intake air temperature.

The hot wire is maintained at the set temperature controlling by the current flow though the hot wire. This current flow is then measured as the output voltage of the air flow meter.

### TESTING

♦ See Figures 75, 76 and 77

Testing can be done without removing the MAF meter from the vehicle.
1. If necessary, remove the MAF meter from the vehicle.
2. Disconnect the wiring from the airflow meter.
3. Using an ohmmeter, measure the resistance between each terminal (THA and E2) as shown in the charts.
4. If the resistance is not as specified, replace the air flow meter.
5. Inspect the meter operation. Connect the MAF meter wiring.
6. Connect a voltmeter to the positive (+) test probe to the VG and the negative (−) test probe to terminal E3.
7. Blow air into the meter and check that the voltage fluctuates.
8. If the operation is not as specified, replace the MAF meter.

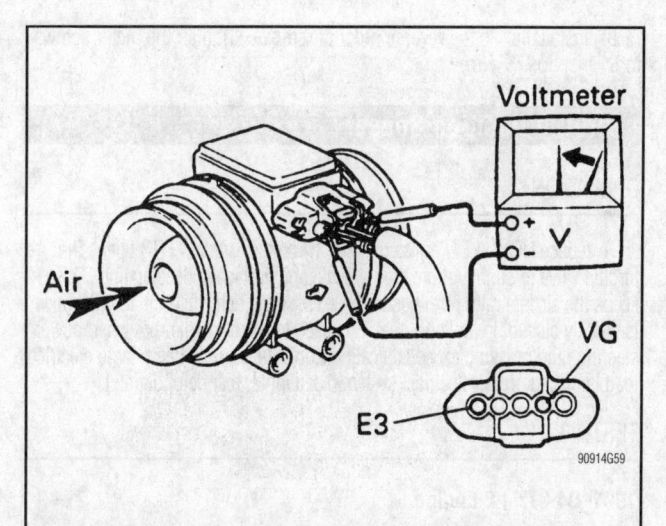

**Fig. 77 Attach the test probe terminals to the E3 (first pin) and VG (fourth pin) from the left of the MAF meter—2TZ-FZE engine**

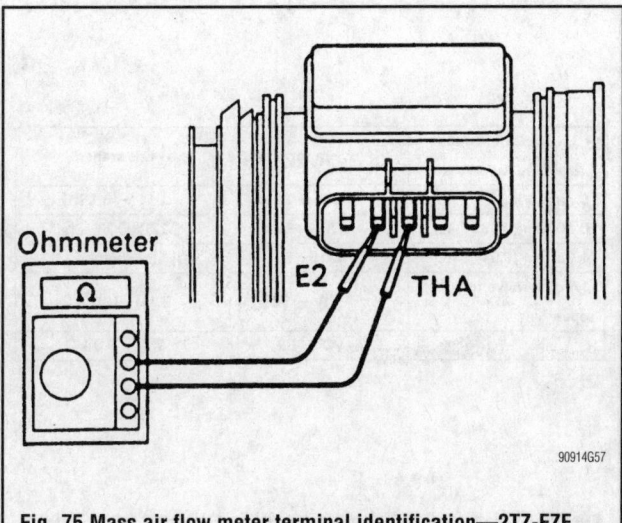

### REMOVAL & INSTALLATION

♦ See Figure 78

1. Disconnect the negative battery cable. Wait at least 90 seconds before proceeding on models with an airbag.

**※※ CAUTION**

Some models covered by this manual may be equipped with a Supplemental Restraint System (SRS), which uses an air bag. Whenever working near any of the SRS components, such as the impact sensors, the air bag module, steering column and instrument panel, disable the SRS, as described in Section 6.

2. Disconnect the air flow meter wiring harness from the unit.
3. Disconnect the A/C idle-up valve wiring.
4. Separate the A/C idle-up air hoses form the valve.
5. Loosen the air cleaner hose clamp.
6. Loosen the 4 clips, and remove the air cleaner cap with MAF meter as an assembly off the engine.
7. Remove the MAF meter retaining bolts.

**Fig. 75 Mass air flow meter terminal identification—2TZ-FZE engine**

# 4-26 DRIVEABILITY AND EMISSIONS CONTROLS

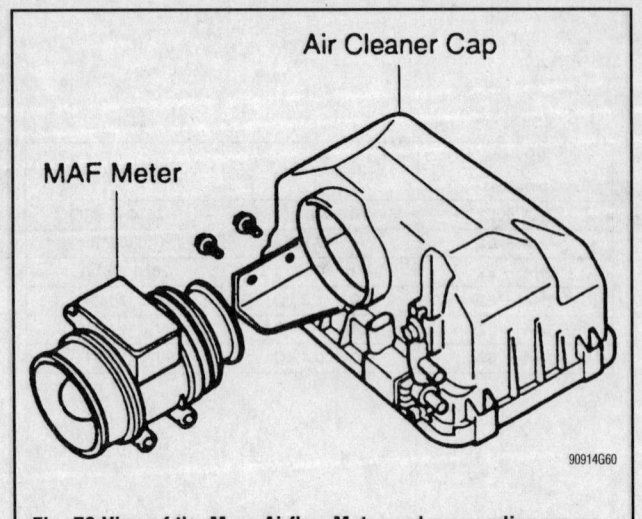

Fig. 78 View of the Mass Airflow Meter and surrounding components—2TZ-FZE engine

8. Installation is the reverse order of removal. Tighten the meter screws to 61 inch lbs. (7 Nm).

## Throttle Position Sensor

### OPERATION

To reduce HC and CO emissions, the Throttle Positioner (TP) opens the throttle valve to slightly more than the idle position when decelerating. This keeps the air/fuel ratio from becoming excessively rich when the throttle valve is quickly closed. In addition, the TP is used to increase idle rpm when power steering fluid pressure exceeds a calibrated value and/or when a large electrical load is placed on the electrical system (headlights, rear defogger etc).

### TESTING

**1991–94 2TZ-FE Engine**

♦ See Figures 79, 80, 81 and 82

1. To check the resistance between the terminals of the throttle position sensor, unplug the wiring from the unit.

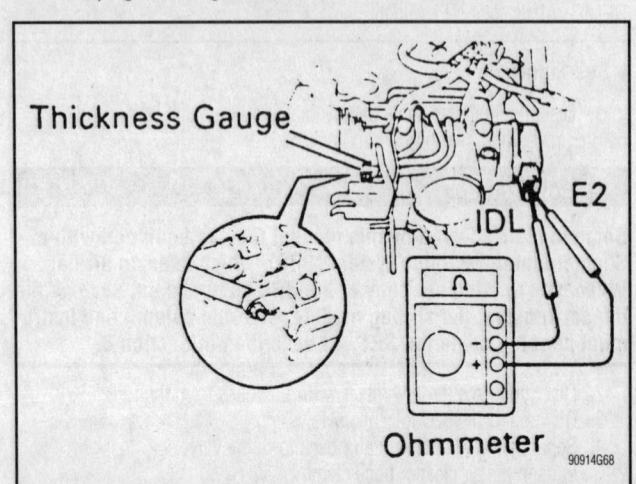

Fig. 79 Insert a thickness gauge between the throttle stop screw and stop lever to check the throttle position sensor—2TZ-FE engine

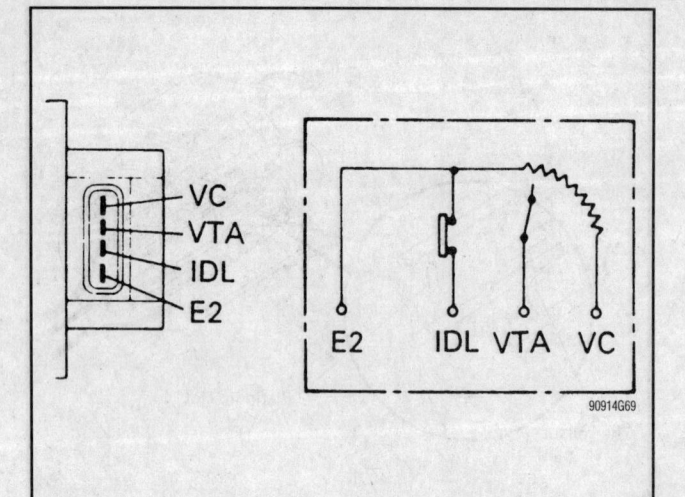

Fig. 80 Throttle position sensor terminal locations—2TZ-FE engine

| Clearance between lever and stop screw | Between terminals | Resistance |
|---|---|---|
| 0 mm (0 in) | VTA – E2 | 0.3 – 6.3 kΩ |
| 0.60 mm (0.0398 in.) | IDL – E2 | 2.3 kΩ or less |
| 1.05 mm (0.0413 in.) | IDL – E2 | infinity |
| Throttle valve fully opened | VTA – E2 | 3.5 – 10.3 kΩ |
| – | VC – E2 | 4.25 – 8.25 kΩ |

Fig. 81 Throttle position sensor resistance values—1991–93 models

| Clearance between lever and stop screw | Between terminals | Resistance |
|---|---|---|
| 0 mm (0 in.) | VTA – E2 | 0.47 – 6.1 kΩ |
| 0.60 mm (0.0398 in.) | IDL – E2 | 2.3 kΩ or less |
| 1.05 mm (0.0413 in.) | IDL – E2 | Infinity |
| Throttle valve fully open | VTA – E2 | 3.1 – 12.1 kΩ |
| – | VC – E2 | 3.9 – 9.0 kΩ |

Fig. 82 Throttle position sensor resistance values—1994 models

# DRIVEABILITY AND EMISSIONS CONTROLS  4-27

2. Insert a thickness gauge between the throttle stop screw and lever.
3. Using an ohmmeter, check the resistance between each terminal.
4. If the testing is not up to specifications replace the sensor.
5. Reattach the sensor connector.

### 1995–97 2TZ-FE and 2TZ-FZE Engines

▶ See Figures 83, 84, 85 and 86

1. To check the resistance between the terminals of the throttle position sensor, unplug the wiring from the unit.
2. Disconnect the vacuum hose from the throttle opener.
3. Apply vacuum to the feeler gage between the throttle stop screw and stop lever.
4. Using an ohmmeter, measure the resistance between each terminal.
5. Reattach the throttle position sensor wiring.
6. Reconnect the vacuum hose to the throttle opener.

### REMOVAL & INSTALLATION

▶ See Figure 87

1. Remove the mounting screws and extract the sensor.

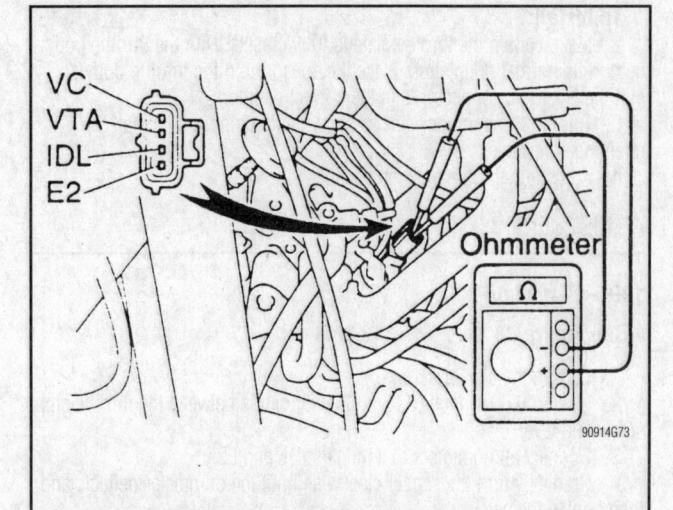

Fig. 85 Place the ohmmeter probes on each terminal of the throttle position sensor to measure the resistance

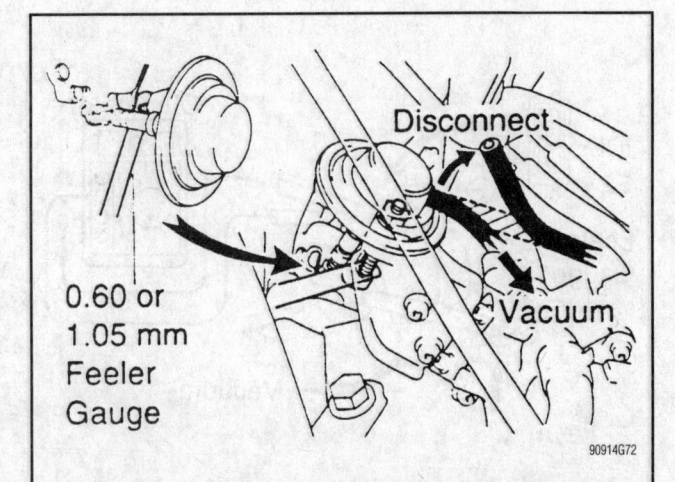

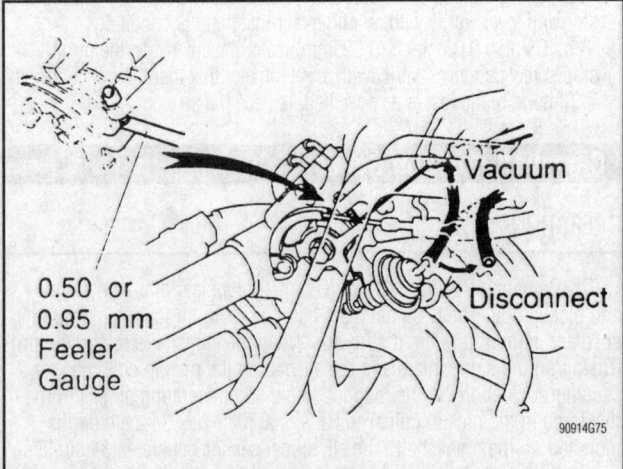

Fig. 83 Disconnect the vacuum hose from the throttle opener and insert a feeler gauge to test the throttle position sensor—1995 models

| Clearance between lever and stop screw | Between terminals | Resistance |
|---|---|---|
| 0 mm (0 in.) | VTA – E2 | 0.2 – 5.7 kΩ |
| 0.60 mm (0.023 in.) | IDL – E2 | 2.3 kΩ or less |
| 1.05 mm (0.041 in.) | IDL – E2 | Infinity |
| Throttle valve fully open | VTA – E2 | 2.0 – 10.2 kΩ |
| — | VC – E2 | 2.5 – 5.9 kΩ |

Fig. 86 Throttle position sensor resistance values—1995–97 2TZ-FE and 2TZ-FZE engines

Fig. 84 Disconnect the vacuum hose from the throttle opener and insert a feeler gauge to test the throttle position sensor—1996–97 2TZ-FZE engine

Fig. 87 The throttle position sensor is located on the side of the throttle body

# 4-28 DRIVEABILITY AND EMISSIONS CONTROLS

**To install:**

2. Make certain the throttle plate is fully closed. With the throttle body held in its normal orientation, place the sensor onto the throttle body so that the electrical connector is in the correct position.
3. Turn the sensor clockwise as shown and temporarily install the retaining screws.
4. Adjust the throttle position sensor.

## ADJUSTMENT

### 1991–94 Models

▶ See Figure 88

1. Loosen the sensor screws.
2. Insert a 0.0325 inch (0.83mm) feeler gauge between the throttle stop screw and lever.
3. Connect an ohmmeter to terminals IDL and E2.
4. Gradually turn the sensor clockwise until the ohmmeter deflects and then tighten the screws.
5. Using a 0.398 inch (0.60mm) feeler gauge between the throttle stop and lever, verify with an ohmmeter that there is continuity.

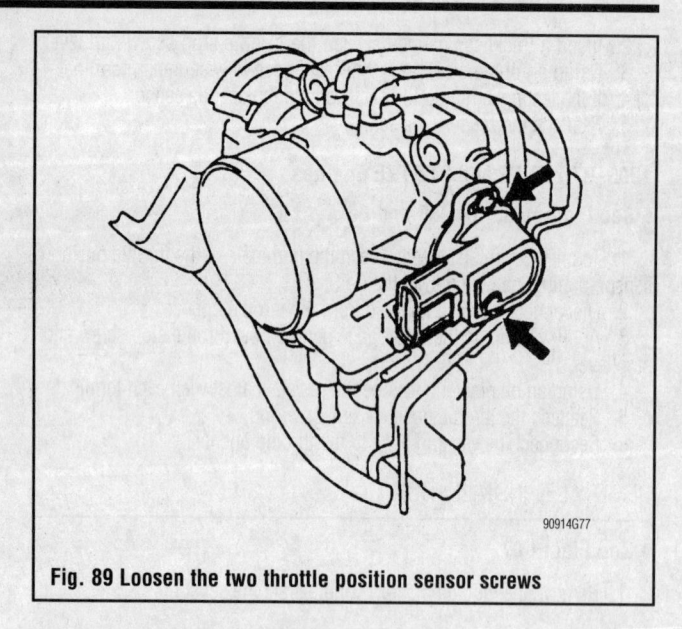

Fig. 89 Loosen the two throttle position sensor screws

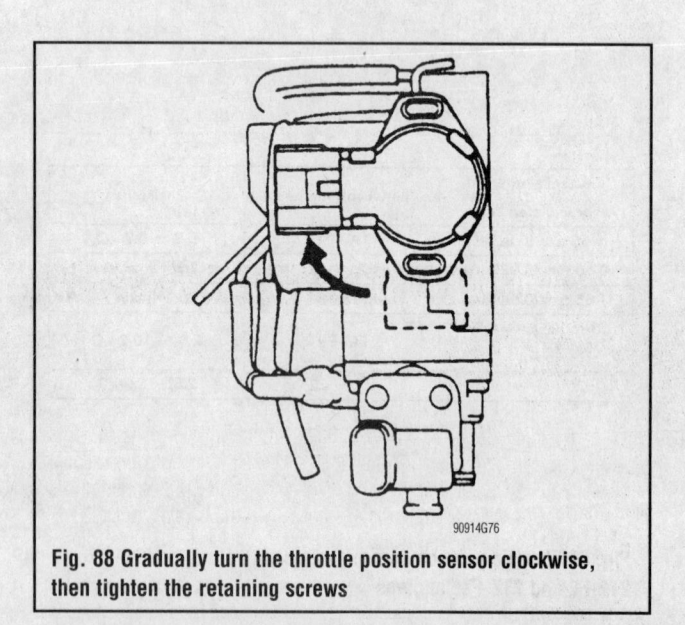

Fig. 88 Gradually turn the throttle position sensor clockwise, then tighten the retaining screws

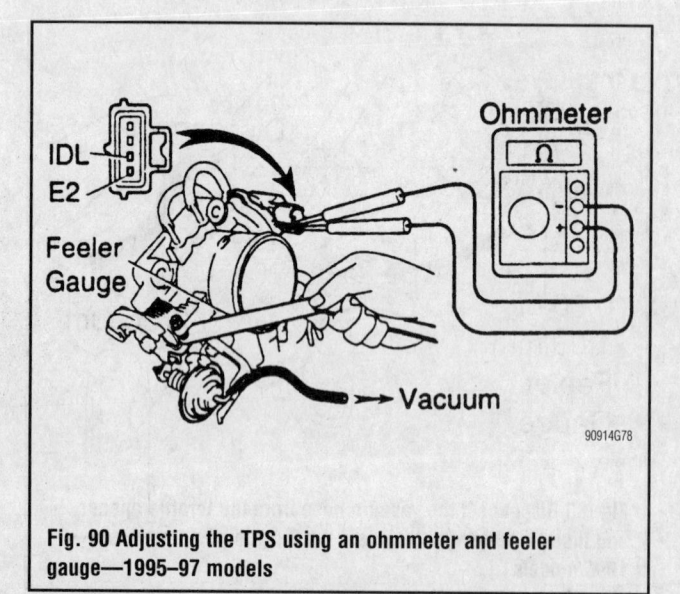

6. Using a 0.413 inch (1.05mm) feeler gage between the throttle stop screw and lever, verify with an ohmmeter that there is not continuity.
7. If none of the test is as specified, replace the sensor.

### 1995–97 Models

▶ See Figures 89 and 90

1. Loosen the sensor screws. Apply vacuum to the throttle opener, if equipped.
2. Insert a 0.029 inch (0.073mm) feeler gauge between the throttle stop screw and lever.
3. Connect an ohmmeter to terminals IDL and E2 of the sensor.
4. Gradually turn the sensor clockwise until the ohmmeter deflects and then tighten the screws.
5. On the 1995 models:
   a. Using a 0.024 inch (0.060mm) feeler gauge between the throttle stop and lever, verify with an ohmmeter that there is continuity.
   b. Using a 0.041 inch (1.05mm) feeler gage between the throttle stop screw and lever, verify with an ohmmeter that there is not continuity.
6. On the 1996–97 models:

   a. Using a 0.020 inch (0.050mm) feeler gauge between the throttle stop and lever, verify with an ohmmeter that there is continuity.
   b. Using a 0.037 inch (0.095mm) feeler gage between the throttle stop screw and lever, verify with an ohmmeter that there is not continuity.
7. If none of the test is as specified, replace the sensor.

Fig. 90 Adjusting the TPS using an ohmmeter and feeler gauge—1995–97 models

## Camshaft Position Sensor

### OPERATION

The Camshaft Position sensor (G signal) consists of a signal plate and pickup coil. The G signal plate has one tooth on its outer circumference and is built into the distributor. When the camshafts rotate, the protrusion on the signal plate and the air gap on the pickup coil change, causing fluctuations in the magnetic field and generating an electromotive force in the pickup coil. The NE signal plate has 34 teeth and is mounted on the crankshaft. The NE signal sensor generates 34 signals every engine revolution. The ECM detects the standard crankshaft angle based on the G signals and the actual crankshaft angle and the engine speed by the NE signals.

# DRIVEABILITY AND EMISSIONS CONTROLS  4-29

## TESTING

### 1991 Models

▶ See Figure 91

1. Using a suitable ohmmeter, check the resistance cold between the terminals of the signal generator.
2. The signal generator (pick-up coil) resistance cold should be as follows:
   - NE–G- —180–220 ohms
   - G1–G- —140–180 ohms
   - G2–G- —140–180 ohms
3. If the resistance is not correct, replace the distributor housing assembly.

### 1992 Models

1. Using a suitable ohmmeter, check the resistance cold between the terminals of the signal generator.
2. The signal generator (pick-up coil) resistance cold should be as follows:
   - NE–G- —155–240 ohms
   - G1–G- —125–190 ohms
   - G2–G- —125–190 ohms
3. If the resistance is not correct, replace the distributor housing assembly.

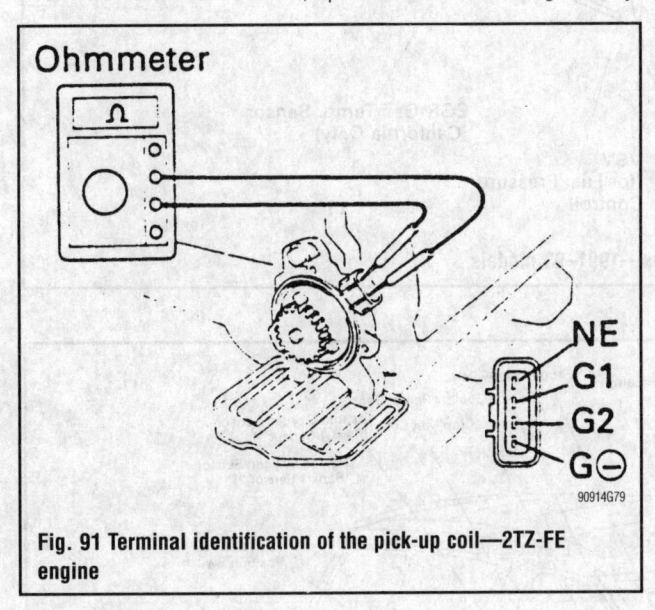

Fig. 91 Terminal identification of the pick-up coil—2TZ-FE engine

### 1993–95 2TZ-FE Engines

1. Using a suitable ohmmeter, check the resistance cold between the terminals of the signal generator.
2. The signal generator (pick-up coil) resistance cold should be as follows:
   - NE–G- —155–250 ohms
   - G1–G- —125–200 ohms
   - G2–G- —125–200 ohms
3. If the resistance is not correct, replace the distributor housing assembly.

### 1995–97 2TZ-FZE Engines

▶ See Figure 92

1. Using a suitable ohmmeter, check the resistance of the signal generator.
2. Pick up coil resistance should be as follows:
   - 1995 Cold—125–200 ohms
   - 1995 Hot—160–235 ohms
   - 1996 Cold—135–220 ohms
   - 1996 Hot—175–255 ohms
   - 1997 Cold—125–200 ohms
   - 1997 Hot—160–235 ohms

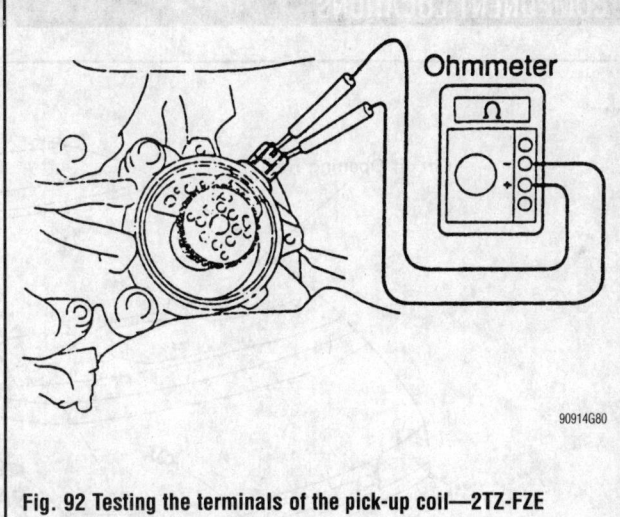

Fig. 92 Testing the terminals of the pick-up coil—2TZ-FZE engine

3. If the resistance is not correct, replace the distributor housing assembly.

## REMOVAL & INSTALLATION

The camshaft position sensor is integrated with the distributor assembly. If the camshaft position sensor is found to be faulty, the distributor assembly must be replaced.

## Crankshaft Position Sensor

### OPERATION

The Crankshaft Position Sensor is only on the 2TZ-FZE engines. The sensor (NE signal) consists of a signal plate and pickup coil. The NE signal plate has 34 teeth and is mounted on the crankshaft. The NE signal sensor generates 34 signals for every engine revolution. The ECM detects the standard crankshaft angle based on the G signals, and the actual crankshaft angle and the engine speed by the NE signals.

### TESTING

➡ The testing of this sensor is done with the engine hot and cold. Cold is from 14–122°F (-10–50°C), hot is from 122–212°F (50–100°C).

1. Disconnect the crankshaft position sensor wiring.
2. Using an ohmmeter, measure the resistance between terminals.
   - Cold—1630–2740 ohms
   - Hot—2065–3225 ohms
3. If the resistance is not as specified, replace the crankshaft position sensor.
4. Reattach the sensor wiring.

### REMOVAL & INSTALLATION

1. Remove the No. 2 engine hanger.
2. Disconnect the crankshaft position sensor wiring.
3. Remove the 2 bolts and the crankshaft position sensor.

**To install:**

4. Place the sensor into position and secure with the screws to 74 inch lbs. (9 Nm).
5. Attach the sensor wiring.
6. Install and secure the No. 2 engine hanger.

# 4-30 DRIVEABILITY AND EMISSIONS CONTROLS

## COMPONENT LOCATIONS

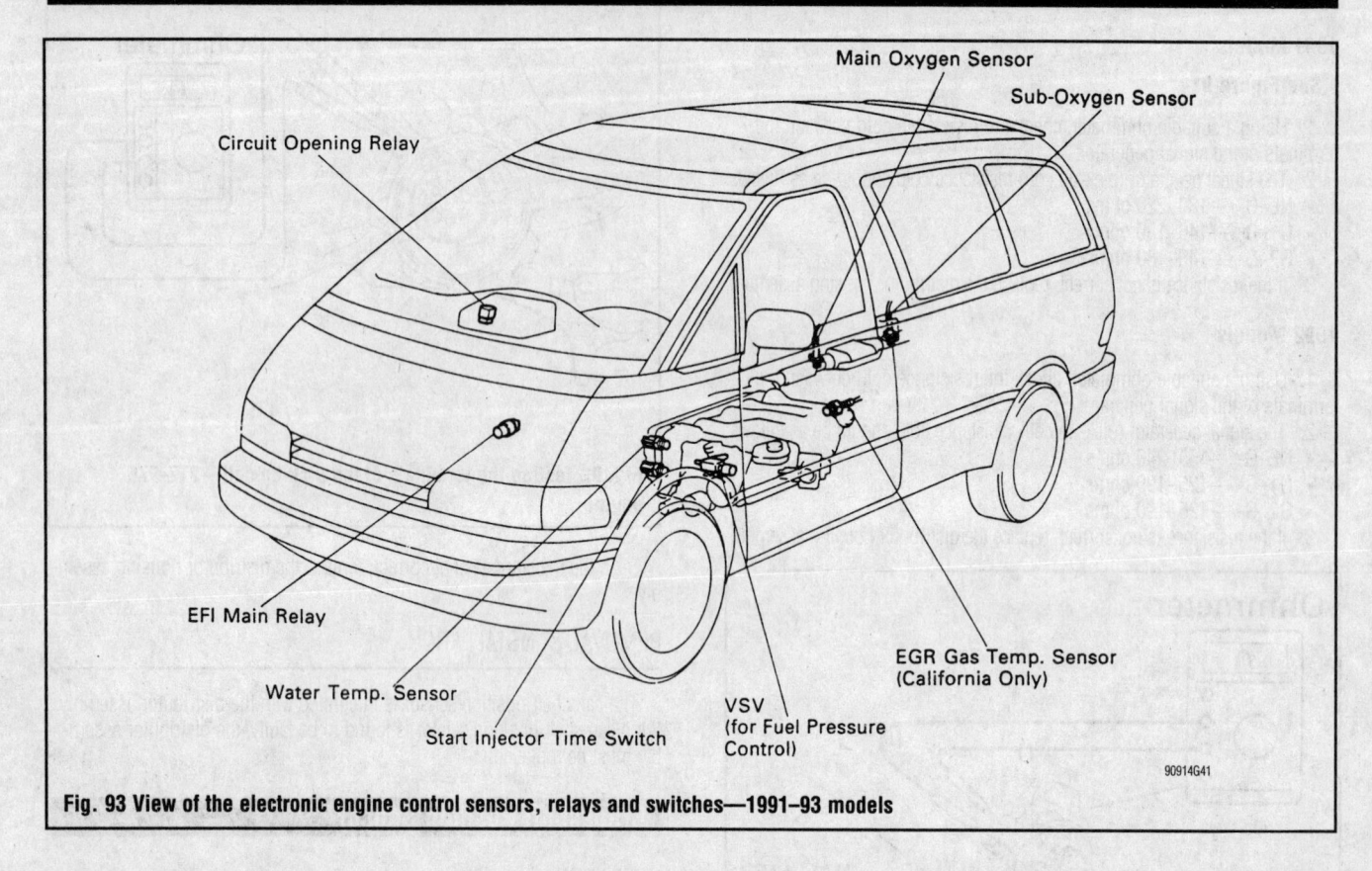

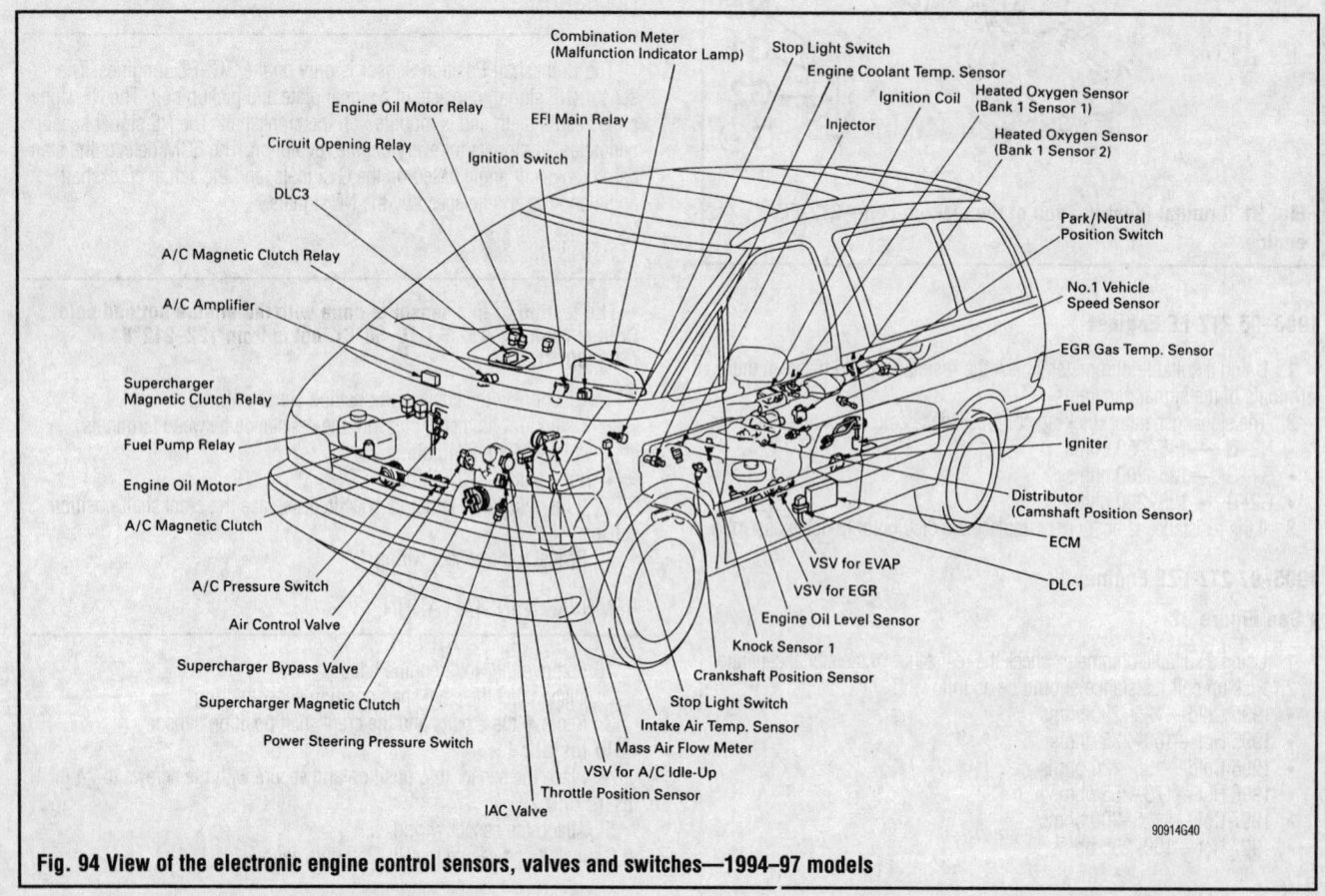

Fig. 93 View of the electronic engine control sensors, relays and switches—1991–93 models

Fig. 94 View of the electronic engine control sensors, valves and switches—1994–97 models

# DRIVEABILITY AND EMISSIONS CONTROLS   4-31

## TROUBLE CODES

### General Information

► See Figure 95

The ECM contains a built-in, self-diagnosis system which detects troubles within the engine signal network. Once a malfunction is detected, the Malfunction Indicator Lamp (MIL), located on the instrument panel, will light.

By analyzing various signals, the ECM detects system malfunctions related to the operating sensors. The ECM stores the failure code associated with the detected failure until the diagnosis system is cleared.

The MIL on the instrument panel informs the driver that a malfunction has been detected. The light will go out automatically once the malfunction has been cleared.

### Data Link Connector (DLC)

► See Figures 96, 97, 98, 99 and 100

The DLC1 is located under the drivers seat. The DLC3 is located in the fuse box at the center of the upper driver's side dash.

Fig. 97 Open the DLC1 cap and read the terminal locations

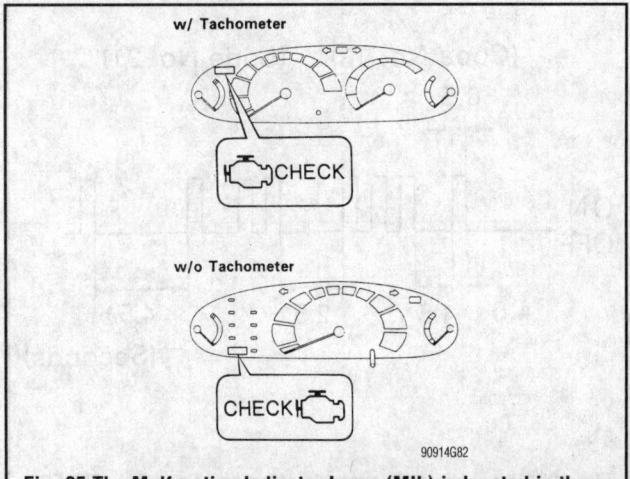

Fig. 95 The Malfunction Indicator Lamp (MIL) is located in the instrument panel and illuminates each time the vehicle is started

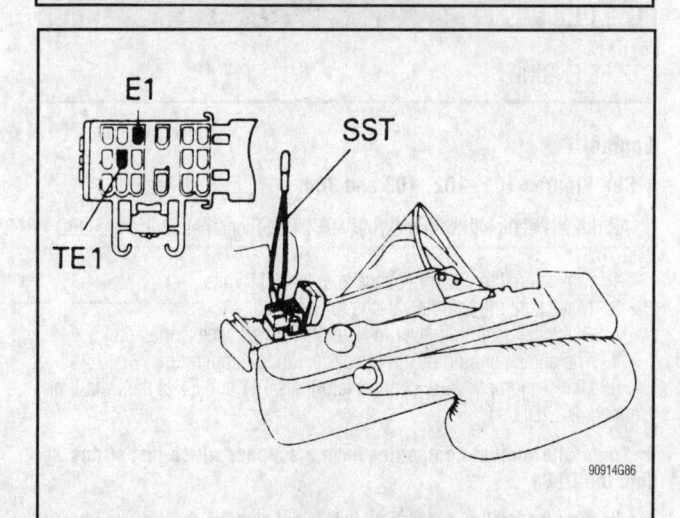

Fig. 98 The Data Link Connector 1 (DLC1) terminal identification—1991–94 models

Fig. 96 Pull this lever to lift up the drivers seat in order to access the engine compartment

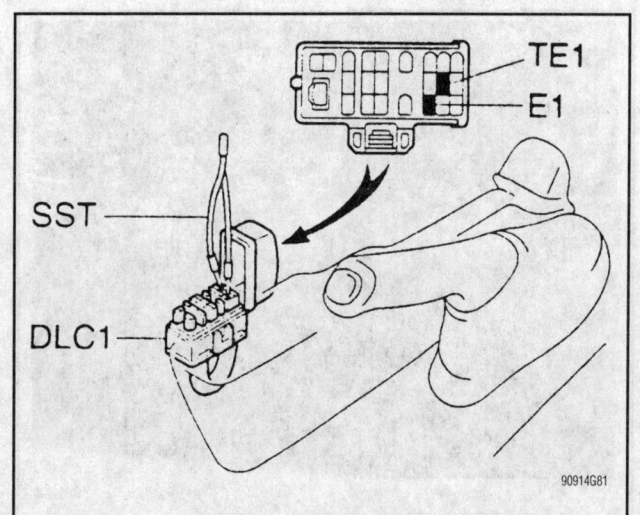

Fig. 99 Data Link Connector 1 (DLC1) terminal identification—1995 models

# 4-32 DRIVEABILITY AND EMISSIONS CONTROLS

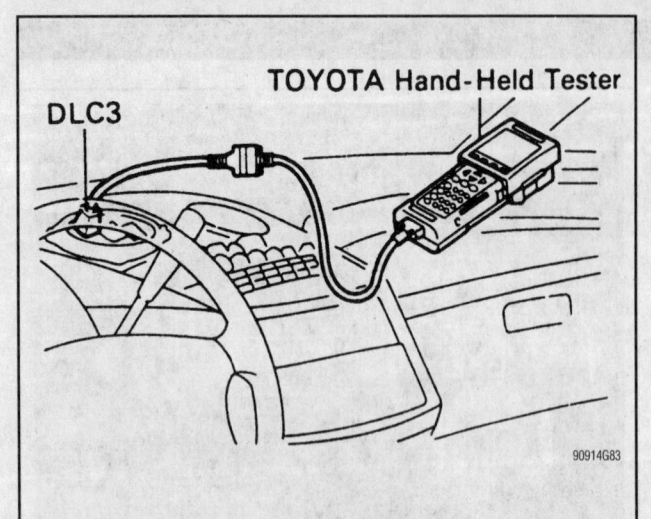

Fig. 100 The DLC3 is located in the fuse box at the center upper portion of the instrument panel

Fig. 102 A normal system operation will illuminate the light every ¼ second

## Reading Codes

### 2TZ-FE ENGINE

**Engine**

▶ See Figures 101, 102, 103 and 104

All models equipped with the 1991–95 2TZ-FE engines utilize the OBD I system.
1. Make sure the battery voltage is at least 11 volts.
2. Make sure the throttle valve is fully closed.
3. Place the gear shift lever in Neutral. Turn all accessories off.
4. The engine should be at normal operating temperature.
5. Using a jumper wire, connect terminals TE1 and E1 of the Data Link Connector 1 (DLC1).

➥Some aftermarket companies have a scanner which just slides into the DLC1

6. Turn the ignition switch **ON**, but do not start the engine. Read the diagnostic code by the counting the number of flashes of the malfunction indicator lamp.

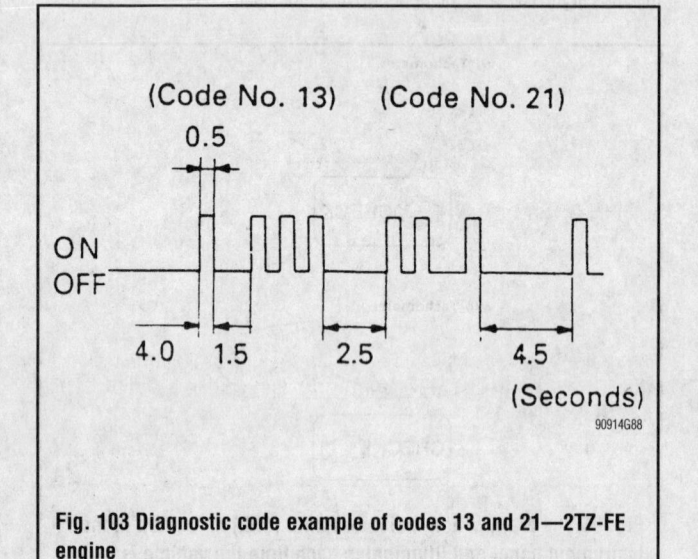

Fig. 103 Diagnostic code example of codes 13 and 21—2TZ-FE engine

Fig. 101 Count the number of flashes on the CHECK ENGINE light

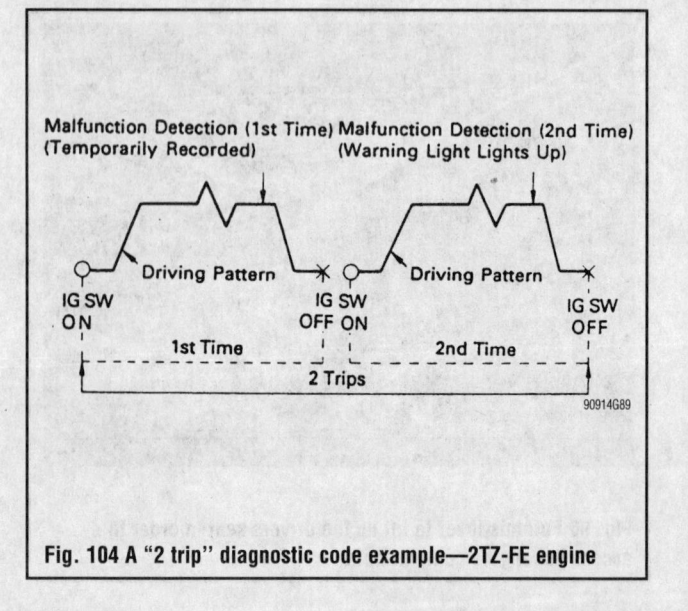

Fig. 104 A "2 trip" diagnostic code example—2TZ-FE engine

# DRIVEABILITY AND EMISSIONS CONTROLS  4-33

➡ The check connector is located under the drivers seat.

7. Codes will flash in numerical order. If no faults are stored, the lamp flashes continuously every ¼ second. This is sometimes called the Normal or System Clear signal.

8. The light will blink a number of time equal to the malfunction code indication as follows:
   a. Between the first and second digit, 1.5 seconds.
   b. Between codes, 2.5 seconds.
   c. Between sets of codes 4.5 seconds.

9. The code series will be repeated as long as the check connector terminals TE1 and E1 are connected. In the event that there many be more than one trouble code, indication will begin from the small value and continue to the larger in order.

10. After the diagnosis check, turn the ignition OFF and remove the jumper wire.
   a. Diagnostic codes 25, 26, 27 and 71 use 2 trip detection logic. With this logic, when a malfunction is first detected, it is temporarily stored in the ECM memory. If the same symptom is detected again during the second drive test, it causes the CHECK warning light to illuminate. The 2 trip repeats the same mode a 2nd time.

➡ The ignition switch must be turned OFF between the 1st and 2nd time. In the test mode, the CHECK engine light illuminates the 1st time a malfunction is detected.

11. Compare the codes found to the applicable diagnostic code chart. If necessary, refer to the individual component tests in this section. If the component tests are OK, test the wire harness and connectors for shorts, opens and poor connections.

12. After diagnosis is complete, remove the jumper wire.

### Automatic Transmission

▸ See Figure 105

1. Turn the ignition switch and Over Drive (O/D) switch to the ON position, but do not start the engine.

➡ Warning and diagnostic codes can be read only when the O/D switch is on. If it is off, the overdrive off light will be lit continuously and not blink.

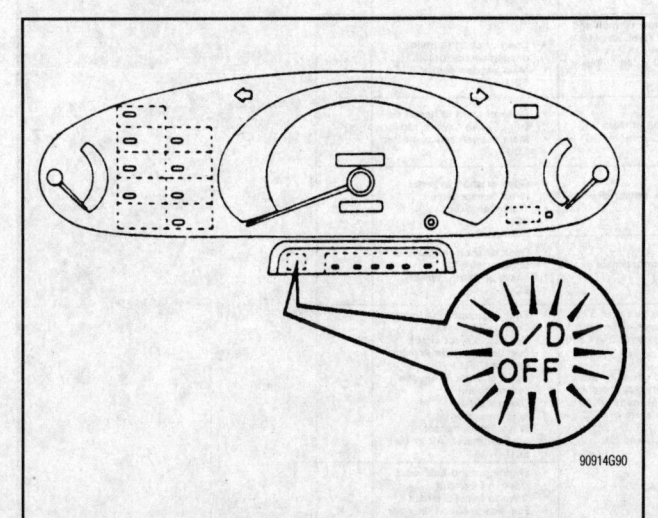

Fig. 105 Read the number of times the O/D light flashes to determine the codes

2. Using a jumper wire, connect terminals TE1 and E1 of the DLC1.
3. Read the diagnostic code as indicated by the number of times the O/D off light flashes
4. If the system is operating normally, the light will flash 2 times per second.
5. In the even that there is a malfunction, the light will flash 1.5 times per second. The number of blinks will equal the first number then, after 1.5 seconds the second number will flash a code. If there are more than two or more codes, there will be 2.5 seconds between each code.

➡ In the event of several trouble codes occurring simultaneously, indication will begin from the smaller value and continue to the larger.

6. Remove the jumper wire.

## 2TZ-FZE ENGINE

### Engine and Automatic Transmission

▸ See Figure 100

All 1994–97 2TZ-FZE engines are equipped with OBD II.

➡ These models require the use of the Toyota's hand held scan tool or an equivalent OBD II compliant scan tool.

1. Prepare the scan tool according to the manufacturers instructions.
2. Connect the OBD II scan tool, to the DLC3 in the fuse box located in the center upper portion of the instrument panel.

➡ When the diagnosis system is switched from the normal mode to the check mode, it erases all Diagnostic Trouble Codes (DTC) and freeze frame data recorded. Before switching modes, always check the DTC and freeze frame data and write them down.

3. Turn the ignition switch to the ON and switch the OBD II scan tool switch on.
4. Use the OBD II scan tool to check the DTC and freeze frame data. Write them down.
5. Compare the codes found to the applicable diagnostic code chart. If necessary, refer to the individual component tests in this section. If the component tests are OK, test the wire harness and connectors for shorts, opens and poor connections.

## Clearing Codes

### 2TZ-FE ENGINE

### Engine and Automatic Transmission

▸ See Figure 106

After repair of the circuit, the diagnostic code(s) must be removed from the ECM memory. With the ignition turned OFF, remove the 15 amp EFI fuse for 30 seconds or more. Once the time period has been observed, reinstall the fuse and check for normal code output.

If the diagnostic code is not erased, it will be retained by the ECM and appear along with a new code in event of future trouble.

Cancellation of the trouble code can also be accomplished by disconnecting the negative battery cable. However, disconnecting the battery cable will erase the other memory systems including the clock and radio settings. If this method is used, always reset these components once the trouble code has been erased.

## 4-34 DRIVEABILITY AND EMISSIONS CONTROLS

### 2TZ-FZE ENGINE

**Engine and Automatic Transmission**

▶ See Figure 106

The OBDII scan tool can clear DTC's, refer to the owners manual, or refer to the next few steps.

After repair of the circuit, the diagnostic code(s) must be removed from the ECM memory. With the ignition turned **OFF**, remove the 15 amp EFI fuse for 30 seconds or more. Once the time period has been observed, reinstall the fuse and check for normal code output.

If the diagnostic code is not erased, it will be retained by the ECM and appear along with a new code in event of future trouble.

Cancellation of the trouble code can also be accomplished by disconnecting the negative battery cable. However, disconnecting the battery cable will erase the other memory systems including the clock and radio settings. If this method is used, always reset these components once the trouble code has been erased.

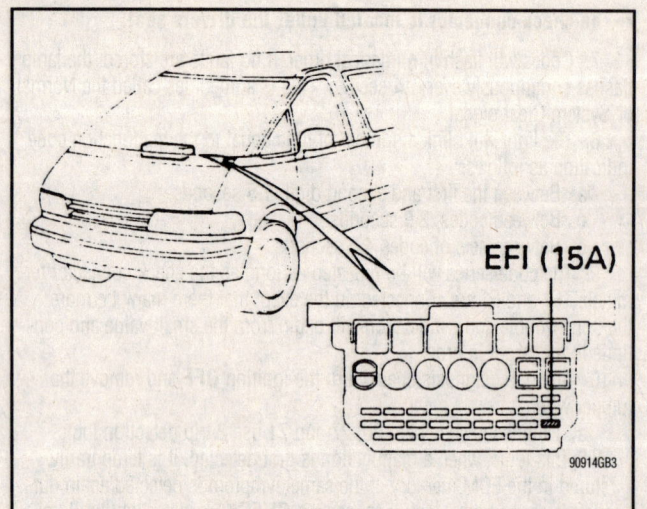

Fig. 106 The EFI fuse is located in the fuse box in the dash, check your owners manual for exact position

### DIAGNOSTIC CODES

HINT:
- If a malfunction is detected during the diagnostic code check, refer to the circuit indicated in the table, and turn to the corresponding page.
- Your readings may vary from the parameters listed in the chart depending on the instruments used.

| Code No. | Number of blinks "CHECK" engine warning light | System | *1 "CHECK" Engine Warning Light | Diagnosis | Trouble Area | *2 Memory |
|---|---|---|---|---|---|---|
| — | (continuous) | Normal | — | Output when no other code is recorded. | — | — |
| 12 | | RPM Signal | ON | No "NE" or "G" signal is input to the ECU for 2 secs. or more after STA turns ON. | • Open or short in NE circuit<br>• Distributor<br>• Igniter circuit<br>• Igniter<br>• Open or short in STA circuit<br>• ECU | ○ |
| 13 | | RPM Signal | ON | NE signal is not input to ECU for 0.3 sec. or more when engine speed is 1,000 rpm or more. | • Open or short in NE circuit<br>• Distributor<br>• ECU | ○ |
| 14 | | Ignition Signal | ON | IGF signal from igniter is not input to ECU for 8 – 9 consecutive ignitions. | • Open or short in IGF or IGT circuit from igniter to ECU<br>• Igniter<br>• ECU | ○ |
| 21 | | Main Oxygen Sensor Signal | ON | At normal driving speed (below 60 mph and engine speed is above 1,700 rpm), amplitude of main oxygen sensor signal (OX1) is reduced to between 0.35 – 0.70 V continuously for 60 secs. or more.<br>*6 (2 trip detection logic) (2) | • Open or short in main oxygen sensor circuit<br>• Main oxygen sensor<br>• ECU | ○ |
| | | Main Oxygen Sensor Heater | ON | Open or short in heater circuit of main oxygen sensor for 500 msec. or more. (HT) | • Open or short in heater circuit of main oxygen sensor<br>• Main oxygen sensor heater<br>• ECU | |
| 22 | | Water Temp. Sensor Signal | ON | Open or short in water temp. sensor circuit for 500 msec. or more. (THW) | • Open or short in water temp. sensor circuit<br>• Water temp. sensor<br>• ECU | ○ |
| 24 | | Intake Air Temp. Sensor Signal | *3 ON | Open or short in intake air temp. sensor circuit for 500 msec. or more. (THA) | • Open or short in intake air temp. circuit<br>• Intake air temp. sensor<br>• ECU | ○ |
| 25 | | Air-Fuel Ratio Lean Malfunction | ON | (1) Oxygen sensor output is less than 0.45 V for at least 90 secs. when oxygen sensor is warmed up. (Only for code 25 in Calif. spec.)<br>*4<br>(2) When the engine speed varies by more than 40 rpm over the preceding crank angle period within 50 seconds at idle with the coolant temperature of 60°C (140°F) or above.<br>*6 (2 trip detection logic) (1) and (2) | • Engine ground bolt loose<br>• Open in E1 circuit<br>• Open in injector circuit<br>• Fuel line pressure (Injector blockage, etc.)<br>• Open or short in oxygen sensor circuit<br>• Oxygen sensor<br>• Ignition system<br>• Water temp. sensor<br>• Air flow meter (Air intake)<br>• ECU | ○ |
| *5 26 | | Air-Fuel Ratio Rich Malfunction | ON | | • Engine ground bolt loose<br>• Open in E1 circuit<br>• Open in injector circuit<br>• Fuel line pressure (Injector leakage, etc.)<br>• Open or short in cold start injector circuit<br>• Cold start injector<br>• Open or short in oxygen sensor circuit<br>• Oxygen sensor<br>• Water temp. sensor<br>• Air flow meter<br>• Compression pressure<br>• ECU | ○ |

Fig. 107 Engine diagnostic codes—2TZ-FE engine

# DRIVEABILITY AND EMISSIONS CONTROLS 4-35

## DIAGNOSTIC CODES

| Code No. | Light Pattern | Diagnosis System Normal |
|---|---|---|
| — | | |
| 42 | | Defective No. 1 speed sensor (in combination meter) – severed wire harness or short circuit |
| 61 | | Defective No. 2 speed sensor (in ATM) – severed wire harness or short circuit |
| 62 | | Severed No. 1 solenoid or short circuit – severed wire harness or short circuit |
| 63 | | Severed No. 2 solenoid or short circuit – severed wire harness or short circuit |
| 64 | | Severed lock-up solenoid or short circuit – severed wire harness or short circuit |

HINT: If codes 62, 63 or 64 appear, there is an electrical malfunction in the solenoid. Causes due to mechanical failure, such as a stuck valve, will not appear.

Fig. 109 Automatic transmission diagnostic codes—2TZ-FE engine

## DIAGNOSTIC CODES (Cont'd)

| Code No. | Number of blinks "CHECK" engine warning light | System | "CHECK" Engine Warning Light *1 | Diagnosis | Trouble Area | Memory *2 |
|---|---|---|---|---|---|---|
| *5 27 | | Sub-Oxygen Sensor Signal | ON | (1) When sub-oxygen sensor is warmed up and full acceleration continued for 2 seconds, output of main oxygen sensor is 0.45 V or more (rich) and output of sub-oxygen sensor is 0.45 V or less (2) Open or short detected continuously for 0.5 sec. or more in sub-oxygen sensor heater circuit *6 (2 trip detection logic) (1) and (2) | Short or open in sub-oxygen sensor circuit Sub-oxygen sensor Open or short in sub-oxygen sensor heater ECU | O |
| 31 | | Air Flow Meter Signal | ON | At idling, open or short detected continuously for 0.5 sec. or more in air flow meter circuit. • Open — VC • Short — VC – E2 | Open or short in air flow meter circuit Air flow meter ECU | O |
| 32 | | Air Flow Meter Signal | ON | Open or short detected continuously for 0.5 sec. or more in air flow meter circuit. • Open — E2 • Short — VS – VC | | O |
| 41 | | Throttle Position Sensor Signal | *3 ON | Open or short detected in throttle position sensor signal (VTA) for 0.5 sec. or more. | Open or short in throttle position sensor circuit Throttle position sensor ECU | O |
| 42 | | Vehicle Speed Sensor Signal | OFF | SPD signal is not input to the ECU for at least 8 seconds during high load driving with engine speed between 2,000 rpm and 5,000 rpm. | Open or short in vehicle speed sensor circuit Vehicle speed sensor ECU | O |
| 43 | | Starter Signal | OFF | Starter signal (STA) is not input to ECU even once until engine reaches 800 rpm or more when cranking. | Open or short in starter signal circuit Open or short in IG SW or main relay circuit ECU | O |
| 52 | | Knock Sensor Signal | ON | With engine speed between 1,600 rpm and 5,200 rpm, knock signal from knock sensor is not input to ECU for 2 crank revolution. (KNK) | Open or short in knock sensor circuit Knock sensor (looseness, etc.) ECU | O |
| 53 | | Knock Control Signal | ON | With engine speed between 650 rpm and 5,600 rpm, the engine control computer (for knock control) malfunction is detected. | ECU | X |
| *5 71 | | EGR System Malfunction | ON | With the coolant temp. at 65°C (149°F) or more, 50 secs. from start of EGR operation. The EGR gas temp. is less than 70°C (158°F) and the EGR gas temp. has risen less than 3°C (5°F) during the 50 secs. *6 (2 trip detection logic) | Open in EGR gas temp. sensor circuit EGR gas temp. sensor Open in VSV circuit for EGR EGR vacuum hose disconnected, valve stuck Clogged EGR gas passage ECU | O |
| 51 | | Switch Condition Signal | OFF | Displayed when IDL contact OFF or shift position in "R", "2", or "L" ranges with the check terminals E1 and TE1 connected. | Throttle position sensor IDL circuit Neutral start switch circuit Accelerator pedal, cable ECU | X |

REMARKS:
*1: "ON" displayed in the diagnosis mode column indicates that the "CHECK" Engine Warning Light is lighted up when a malfunction is detected. "OFF" indicates that the "CHECK" does not light up during malfunction diagnosis, even if a malfunction is detected.
*2: "O" in the memory column indicates that a diagnostic code is recorded in the ECU memory when a malfunction occurs. "X" indicates that a diagnostic code is not recorded in the ECU memory even if a malfunction occurs. Accordingly, output of diagnostic results is performed with the ignition switch IG SW ON.
*3: The "CHECK" Engine Warning Light comes on if malfunction occurs only for California specifications.
*4: No. (2) in the diagnostic contents of codes No. 25 and 26 apply to California specification vehicles only, while (1) applies to all models.
*5: Code 26, 27, 71 is used only for California specifications.
*6: "2 trip detection logic"

Fig. 108 Engine diagnostic codes—2TZ-FE engine continued

# 4-36 DRIVEABILITY AND EMISSIONS CONTROLS

## DTC CHART (Cont'd)

| DTC No. | Detection Item | Trouble Area | MIL* | Memory |
|---|---|---|---|---|
| P0133 | Heated Oxygen Sensor Circuit Slow Response (Bank 1 Sensor 1) | • Heated oxygen sensor | ○ | ○ |
| P0135 | Heated Oxygen Sensor Heater Circuit Malfunction (Bank 1 Sensor 1) | • Open or short in heater circuit of heated oxygen sensor<br>• Heated oxygen sensor heater<br>• ECM | ○ | ○ |
| P0136 | Heated Oxygen Sensor Circuit Malfunction (Bank 1 Sensor 2) | • Heated oxygen sensor | ○ | ○ |
| P0141 | Heated Oxygen Sensor Heater Circuit Malfunction (Bank 1 Sensor 2) | • Same as DTC No. P0135 | ○ | ○ |
| P0171 | System too Lean (Fuel Trim) | • Air intake (hose loose)<br>• Fuel line pressure<br>• Injector blockage<br>• Heated oxygen sensor malfunction<br>• Mass air flow meter<br>• Engine coolant temp. sensor | ○ | ○ |
| P0172 | System too Rich (Fuel Trim) | • Fuel line pressure<br>• Injector leak, blockage<br>• Heated oxygen sensor malfunction<br>• Mass air flow meter<br>• Engine coolant temp. sensor | ○ | ○ |
| P0300 | Random/Multiple Cylinder Misfire Detected | • Ignition system<br>• Injector<br>• Fuel line pressure<br>• EGR<br>• Compression pressure<br>• Valve clearance not to specification<br>• Valve timing<br>• Mass air flow meter<br>• Engine coolant temp. sensor | ○ | ○ |
| P0301<br>P0302<br>P0303<br>P0304 | Misfire Detected<br>– Cylinder 1<br>– Cylinder 2<br>– Cylinder 3<br>– Cylinder 4 | | ○ | ○ |
| P0325 | Knock Sensor 1 Circuit Malfunction | • Open or short in knock sensor 1 circuit<br>• Knock sensor 1 (looseness)<br>• ECM | ○ | ○ |

*: ○ ...... MIL lights up

Fig. 111 Engine diagnostic codes—2TZ-FZE engine continued

## DTC CHART (SAE Controlled)

HINT: Parameters listed in the chart may not be exactly the same as your reading due to the type of instrument or other factors.
If a malfunction code is displayed during the DTC check in check mode, check the circuit for that code listed in the table below.

| DTC No. | Detection Item | Trouble Area | MIL* | Memory |
|---|---|---|---|---|
| P0100 | Mass Air Flow Circuit Malfunction | • Open or short in mass air flow meter circuit<br>• Mass air flow meter<br>• ECM | ○ | ○ |
| P0101 | Mass Air Flow Circuit Range/Performance Problem | • Mass air flow meter | ○ | ○ |
| P0110 | Intake Air Temp. Circuit Malfunction | • Open or short in intake air temp. sensor circuit<br>• Intake air temp. sensor<br>• ECM | ○ | ○ |
| P0115 | Engine Coolant Temp. Circuit Malfunction | • Open or short in engine coolant temp. sensor circuit<br>• Engine coolant temp. sensor<br>• ECM | ○ | ○ |
| P0116 | Engine Coolant Temp. Circuit Range/Performance Problem | • Engine coolant temp. sensor<br>• Cooling system | ○ | ○ |
| P0120 | Throttle/Pedal Position Sensor/Switch "A" Circuit Malfunction | • Open or short in throttle position sensor circuit<br>• Throttle position sensor<br>• ECM | ○ | ○ |
| P0121 | Throttle/Pedal Position Sensor/Switch "A" Circuit Range/Performance Problem | • Throttle position sensor | ○ | ○ |
| P0125 | Insufficient Coolant Temp. for Closed Loop Fuel Control | • Air intake (hose loose)<br>• Fuel line pressure<br>• Injector blockage<br>• Open or short in heated oxygen sensor circuit<br>• Heated oxygen sensor malfunction<br>• Mass air flow meter<br>• Engine coolant temp. sensor | ○ | ○ |
| P0130 | Heated Oxygen Sensor Circuit Malfunction (Bank 1 Sensor 1) | • Heated oxygen sensor<br>• Fuel trim malfunction | ○ | ○ |

*: ○ ...... MIL lights up

Fig. 110 Engine diagnostic codes—2TZ-FZE engine

# DRIVEABILITY AND EMISSIONS CONTROLS 4-37

## DTC CHART (Cont'd)

| DTC No. | Detection Item | Trouble Area | MIL* | Memory |
|---------|----------------|--------------|------|--------|
| P0335 | Crankshaft Position Sensor "A" Circuit Malfunction | • Open or short in crankshaft position sensor circuit<br>• Crankshaft position sensor<br>• Starter<br>• ECM | ○ | ○ |
| P0340 | Camshaft Position Sensor Circuit Malfunction | • Open or short in camshaft position sensor circuit<br>• Camshaft position sensor<br>• Starter<br>• ECM | ○ | ○ |
| P0401 | Exhaust Gas Recirculation Flow Insufficient Detected | • EGR valve stuck closed<br>• Open in VSV circuit for EGR<br>• Open in EGR gas temp. sensor circuit<br>• EGR hose disconnected<br>• ECM | ○ | ○ |
| P0402 | Exhaust Gas Recirculation Flow Excessive Detected | • EGR valve stuck open<br>• VSV for EGR open malfunction<br>• Short in VSV circuit for EGR<br>• Short in EGR gas temp. sensor circuit<br>• ECM | ○ | ○ |
| P0420 | Catalyst System Efficiency Below Threshold | • Three-way catalytic converter<br>• Open or short in heated oxygen sensor circuit<br>• Heated oxygen sensor | ○ | ○ |
| P0441 | Evaporative Emission Control System Incorrect Purge Flow | • Open or short in VSV circuit for EVAP<br>• VSV for EVAP<br>• ECM<br>• Vacuum hose blocked or disconnected<br>• Charcoal canister | ○ | ○ |
| P0500 | Vehicle Speed Sensor Malfunction | • Open or short in vehicle speed sensor circuit<br>• Vehicle speed sensor<br>• Combination meter<br>• ECM | ○ | ○ |

*: ○ ...... MIL lights up

Fig. 112 Engine diagnostic codes—2TZ-FZE engine continued

## DTC CHART (Cont'd)

| DTC No. | Detection Item | Trouble Area | MIL* | Memory |
|---------|----------------|--------------|------|--------|
| P0505 | Idle Control System Malfunction | • IAC valve is stuck or closed<br>• Open or short in IAC valve circuit<br>• VSV for A/C idle-up<br>• ACV<br>• Air intake (hose loose) | ○ | ○ |
| P0510 | Closed Throttle Position Switch Malfunction | • Open in closed throttle position switch circuit<br>• Closed throttle position switch<br>• ECM | ○ | ○ |

*: ○ ...... MIL lights up

## DTC CHART (Manufacturer Controlled)

| DTC No. | Detection Item | Trouble Area | MIL* | Memory |
|---------|----------------|--------------|------|--------|
| P1300 | Igniter Circuit Malfunction | • Open or short in IGF or IGT circuit from igniter to ECM<br>• Igniter<br>• ECM | ○ | ○ |
| P1335 | Crankshaft Position Sensor Circuit Malfunction (during engine running) | • Open or short in crankshaft position sensor circuit<br>• Crankshaft position sensor<br>• ECM | — | ○ |
| P1500 | Starter Signal Circuit Malfunction | • Open or short in starter signal circuit<br>• Open or short in ignition switch or starter relay circuit<br>• ECM | — | ○ |
| P1510 | Boost Pressure Control Circuit Malfunction | • Open or short in supercharger magnetic clutch relay circuit<br>• Supercharger magnetic clutch relay<br>• Supercharger magnetic clutch<br>• Open or short in supercharger bypass valve circuit<br>• Supercharger bypass valve<br>• ECM<br>• Air intake (hose loose) | — | ○ |
| P1600 | ECM BATT Malfunction | • Open in back up power source circuit<br>• ECM | ○ | ○ |
| P1605 | Knock Control CPU Malfunction | • ECM | ○ | ○ |
| P1780 | Park/Neutral Position Switch Malfunction | • Short in park/neutral position switch circuit<br>• Park/neutral position switch<br>• ECM | ○ | ○ |

*: — ...... MIL does not light up
○ ...... MIL lights up

Fig. 113 Engine diagnostic codes—2TZ-FZE engine continued

## DTC CHART

If a DTC is displayed during the DTC check, check the circuit listed in the table below and proceed to the page given.

| DTC NO. | Detection Item | Trouble Area | MIL* | Memory |
|---------|---------------|--------------|------|--------|
| P0500 | Vehicle Speed Sensor Malfunction | • Open or short in No.1 vehicle speed sensor circuit<br>• No.1 vehicle speed sensor<br>• Combination meter<br>• ECM | ● | ○ |
| P0710 | Transmission Fluid Temperature Sensor Circuit Malfunction (ATF Temperature Sensor) | • Open or short in ATF temperature sensor circuit<br>• ATF Temperature Sensor<br>• ECM | ● | ○ |
| P0750 | Shift Solenoid "A" Malfunction (Shift Solenoid Valve No.1) | • Shift solenoid valve No.1 is stuck open or closed<br>• Valve body is blocked up or stuck | ● | ○ |
| P0753 | Shift Solenoid "A" Electrical Malfunction (Shift Solenoid Valve No.1) | • Open or short in shift solenoid valve No.1 circuit<br>• Shift solenoid valve No.1<br>• ECM | ● | ○ |
| P0755 | Shift Solenoid "B" Malfunction (Shift Solenoid Valve No.2) | • Shift solenoid valve No.2 is stuck open or closed<br>• Valve body is blocked up or stuck | ● | ○ |
| P0758 | Shift Solenoid "B" Electrical Malfunction (Shift Solenoid Valve No.2) | • Open or short in shift solenoid valve No.2 circuit<br>• Shift solenoid valve No.2<br>• ECM | ● | ○ |
| P0770 | Shift Solenoid "E" Malfunction (Shift Solenoid Valve SL) | • Shift solenoid valve SL is stuck open or closed<br>• Valve body is blocked up or stuck<br>• Lock-up clutch | ● | ○ |
| P0773 | Shift Solenoid "E" Electrical Malfunction (Shift Solenoid Valve SL) | • Open or short in shift solenoid valve SL circuit<br>• Shift solenoid valve SL<br>• ECM | ● | ○ |
| P1520 | Stop Light Switch Signal Malfunction | • Open or short in stop light switch circuit<br>• Stop light switch<br>• ECM | ● | ○ |
| P1700 | Speed Sensor No.2 Circuit Malfunction (No.2 Vehicle Speed Sensor) | • Open or short in No.2 vehicle speed sensor circuit<br>• No.2 vehicle speed sensor<br>• ECM | ● | ○ |
| P1780 | Park/Neutral Position Switch Malfunction | • Short in park/neutral position switch circuit<br>• Park/neutral position switch<br>• ECM | ● | ○ |

● ... MIL lights up

Fig. 114 Automatic transmission diagnostic codes—2TZ-FZE engine

# DRIVEABILITY AND EMISSIONS CONTROLS   4-39

## VACUUM DIAGRAMS

Following are vacuum diagrams for most of the engine and emissions package combinations covered by this manual. Because vacuum circuits will vary based on various engine and vehicle options, always refer first to the vehicle emission control information label, if present. Should the label be missing, or should vehicle be equipped with a different engine from the vehicle's original equipment, refer to the diagrams below for the same or similar configuration.

If you wish to obtain a replacement emissions label, most manufacturers make the labels available for purchase. The labels can usually be ordered from a local dealer.

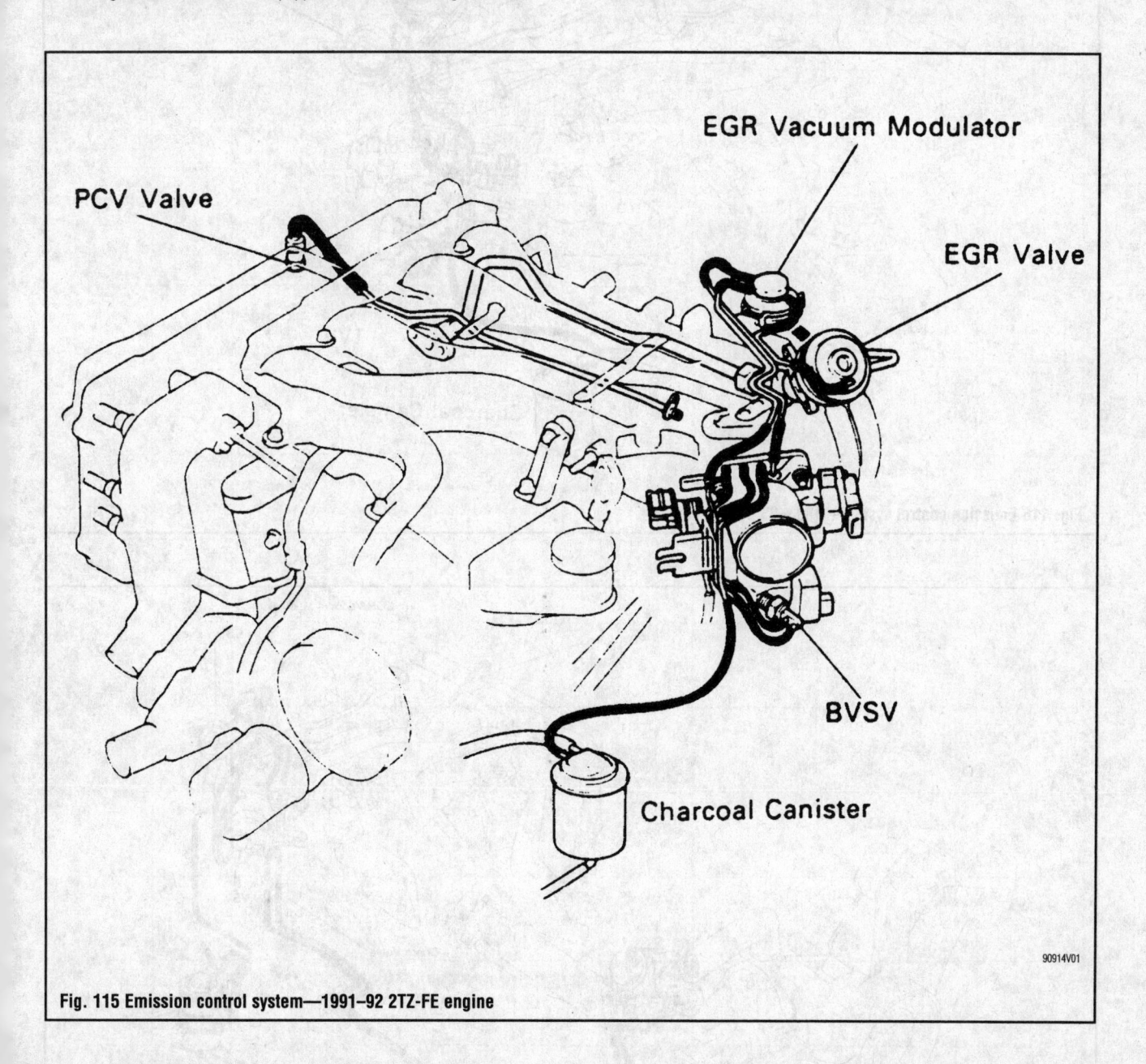

Fig. 115 Emission control system—1991–92 2TZ-FE engine

## 4-40 DRIVEABILITY AND EMISSIONS CONTROLS

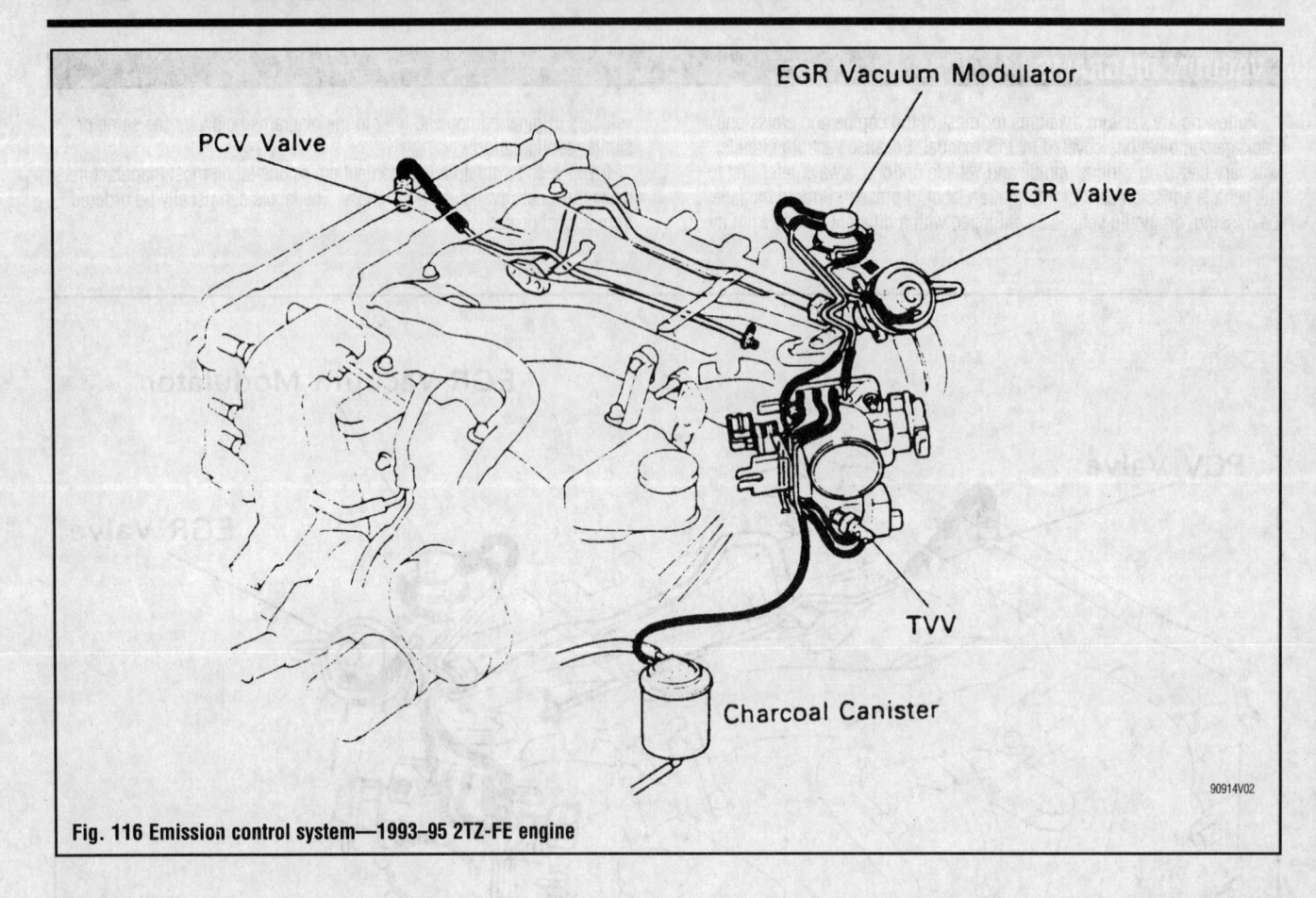

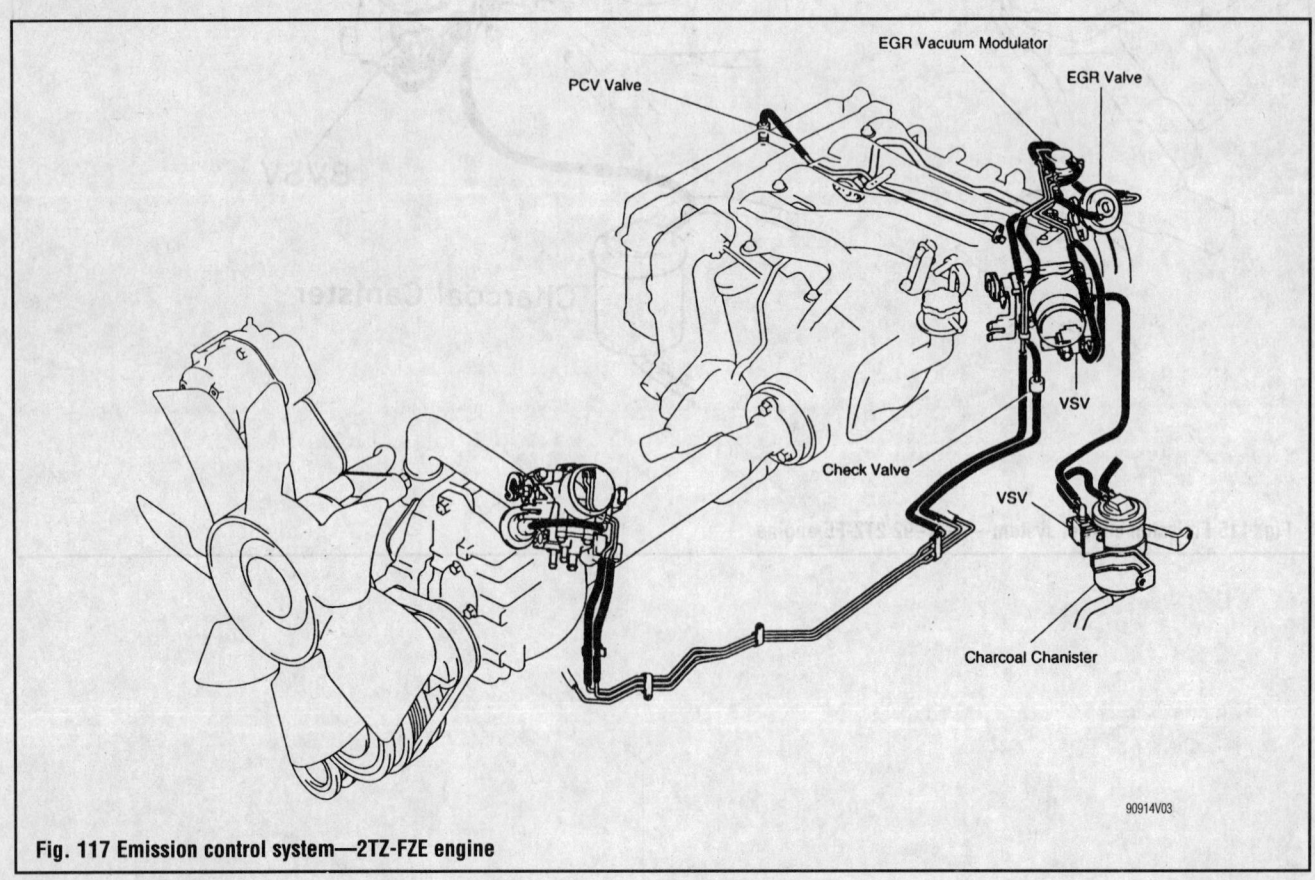

Fig. 116 Emission control system—1993–95 2TZ-FE engine

Fig. 117 Emission control system—2TZ-FZE engine

**BASIC FUEL SYSTEM
  DIAGNOSIS 5-2**
**FUEL LINES AND FITTINGS 5-2**
UNION BOLT TYPE 5-2
FLARE NUT TYPE 5-2
**FUEL INJECTION SYSTEM 5-2**
GENERAL INFORMATION 5-2
RELIEVING FUEL SYSTEM
  PRESSURE 5-2
FUEL PUMP 5-3
  REMOVAL & INSTALLATION 5-3
  TESTING 5-4
THROTTLE BODY 5-4
  REMOVAL & INSTALLATION 5-4
FUEL INJECTORS 5-4
  REMOVAL & INSTALLATION 5-4
  TESTING 5-8
FUEL PRESSURE REGULATOR 5-8
  REMOVAL & INSTALLATION 5-8
COLD START INJECTOR 5-11
  REMOVAL & INSTALLATION 5-11
START INJECTOR TIME SWITCH 5-12
  REMOVAL & INSTALLATION 5-12
  TESTING 5-12
**FUEL TANK 5-13**
TANK ASSEMBLY 5-13
  REMOVAL & INSTALLATION 5-13

# 5

## FUEL SYSTEM

BASIC FUEL SYSTEM DIAGNOSIS 5-2
FUEL LINES AND FITTINGS 5-2
FUEL INJECTION SYSTEM 5-2
FUEL TANK 5-13

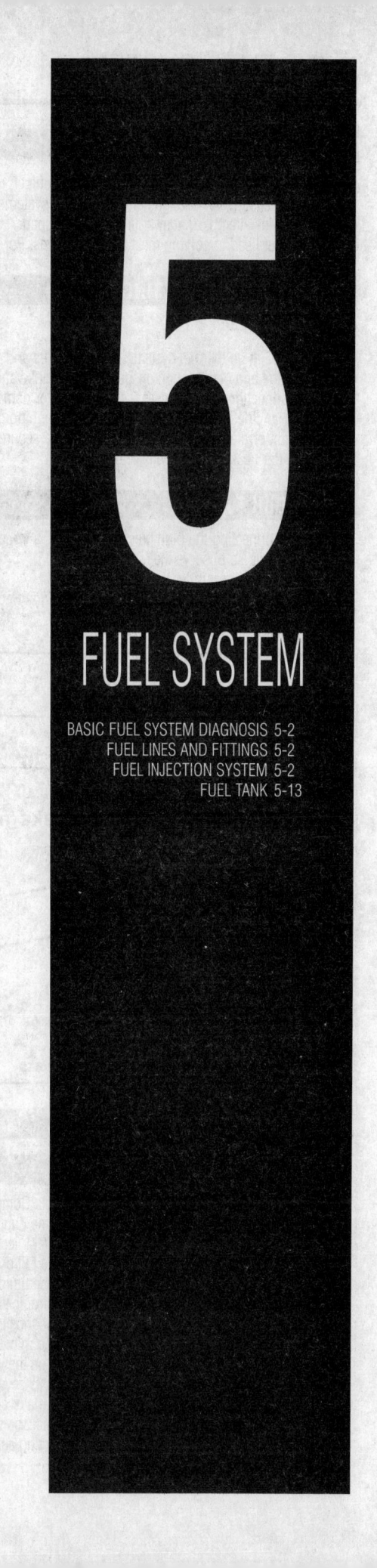

# 5-2 FUEL SYSTEM

## BASIC FUEL SYSTEM DIAGNOSIS

When there is a problem starting or driving a vehicle, two of the most important checks involve the ignition and the fuel systems. The questions most mechanics attempt to answer first, "is there spark?" and "is there fuel?" will often lead to solving most basic problems. For ignition system diagnosis and testing, please refer to the information on engine electrical components and ignition systems found earlier in this manual. If the ignition system checks out (there is spark), then you must determine if the fuel system is operating properly (is there fuel?).

## FUEL LINES AND FITTINGS

♦ See Figures 1 and 2

When working on the fuel system, insect the lines and connections for cracks, leakage and deformation. Inspect the fuel tank vapor vent system hose and connections for looseness, sharp bends or damage. Check the fuel tank for any deformation due to bad driving conditions. Inspect the bands for rust or cracks. The tank bands should be secure and not loose. Check the filler neck for damage or leakage.

### Union Bolt Type

When disconnecting the high pressure fuel line, a large amount of gasoline will spill out, so observe the following.
- Place a container under the connection.
- Slowly loosen the connection. Have a rag handy to clean up any split fuel.
- Separate the connection.
- Plug the connection with a rubber plug.
- When connecting the union bolt on the high pressure line, always use a new gasket.
- Always tighten the union bolt by hand. Tighten the bolt to 22 ft. lbs. (29 Nm).

### Flare Nut Type

Apply a light coat of engine oil to the flare and tighten the flare nut by hand. Using a torque wrench, tighten the flare nut to 23 ft. lbs. (31 Nm).

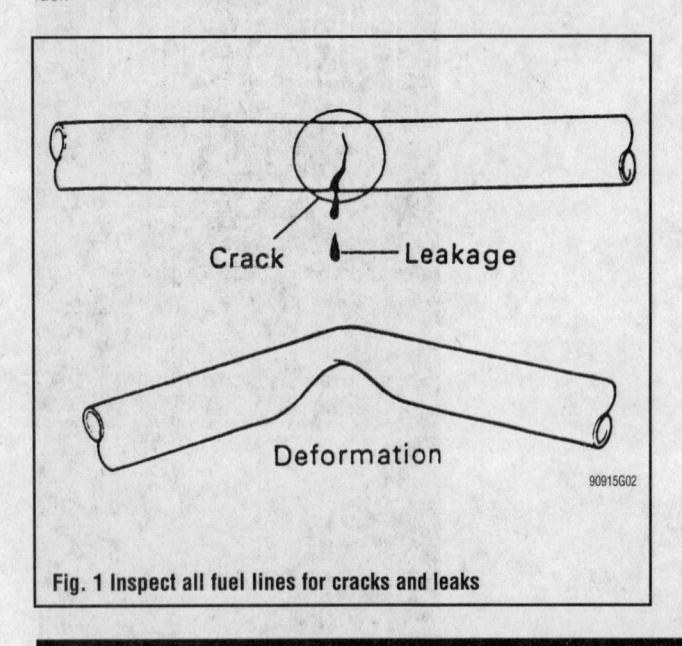

Fig. 1 Inspect all fuel lines for cracks and leaks

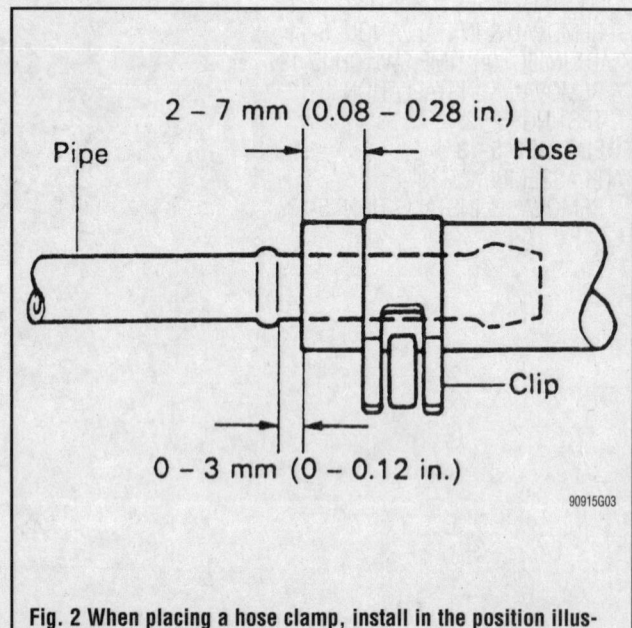

Fig. 2 When placing a hose clamp, install in the position illustrated for a secure hold

## FUEL INJECTION SYSTEM

### General Information

Fuel injected engines are equipped with the Toyota Computer Control System (TCCS). This integrated control system allows the Engine Control Module (ECM) to control other systems as well as the fuel injection. On earlier systems, the fuel management was performed by the EFI computer; in the current system, the control unit also oversees ignition timing and advance, EGR function, idle speed control (ISC system), Electronically Controlled Transmission (ECT) function as well as on-board diagnostics and back-up or fail-safe functions. The control unit is a sophisticated micro-computer, receiving input signals from many sources and locations on the vehicle. It is capable of rapid calculation of many variables and controls several output circuits simultaneously. This system is broken down into 3 major sub-systems: the Fuel System, Air Induction System and the Electronic Control System. Keeping these divisions in mind will shorten troubleshooting and diagnostic time.

An electric fuel pump supplies sufficient fuel, under a constant pressure, to the injectors. These injectors allow a metered quantity of fuel into the intake manifold according to signals from the ECM. The air induction system provides sufficient air for the engine operation. This system includes the throttle body, air intake device and idle control system components.

### Relieving Fuel System Pressure

**✱✱ CAUTION**

**Fuel injection systems remain under pressure after the engine has been turned OFF. Properly relieve fuel pressure before disconnecting any fuel lines. Failure to do so may result in fire or personal injury.**

# FUEL SYSTEM 5-3

1. Disconnect the negative battery terminal.
2. Place a catch-pan under the joint to be disconnected. A large quantity of fuel may be released when the joint is opened.

➡ **Wear eye or full face protection.**

3. Place a shop towel over the area and slowly loosen the joint using a wrench of the correct size. Use a back-up wrench if needed.
4. Allow the fuel left in the line to bleed off slowly before fully disconnecting the joint.
5. Plug the opened lines immediately to prevent fuel spillage or the entry of dirt.
6. Dispose of the released fuel properly.
7. After rejoining the fuel lines, connect the negative battery cable and start the engine.
8. Check for leaks and repair as needed.

## Fuel Pump

### REMOVAL & INSTALLATION

♦ See Figures 3, 4, 5 and 6

**⁂ CAUTION**

**Fuel injection systems remain under pressure after the engine has been turned OFF. Properly relieve fuel pressure before disconnecting any fuel lines. Failure to do so may result in fire or personal injury.**

1. Relieve the fuel pressure.
2. Disconnect the negative battery cable.

Fig. 3 Exploded view of the fuel pump, bracket and related components

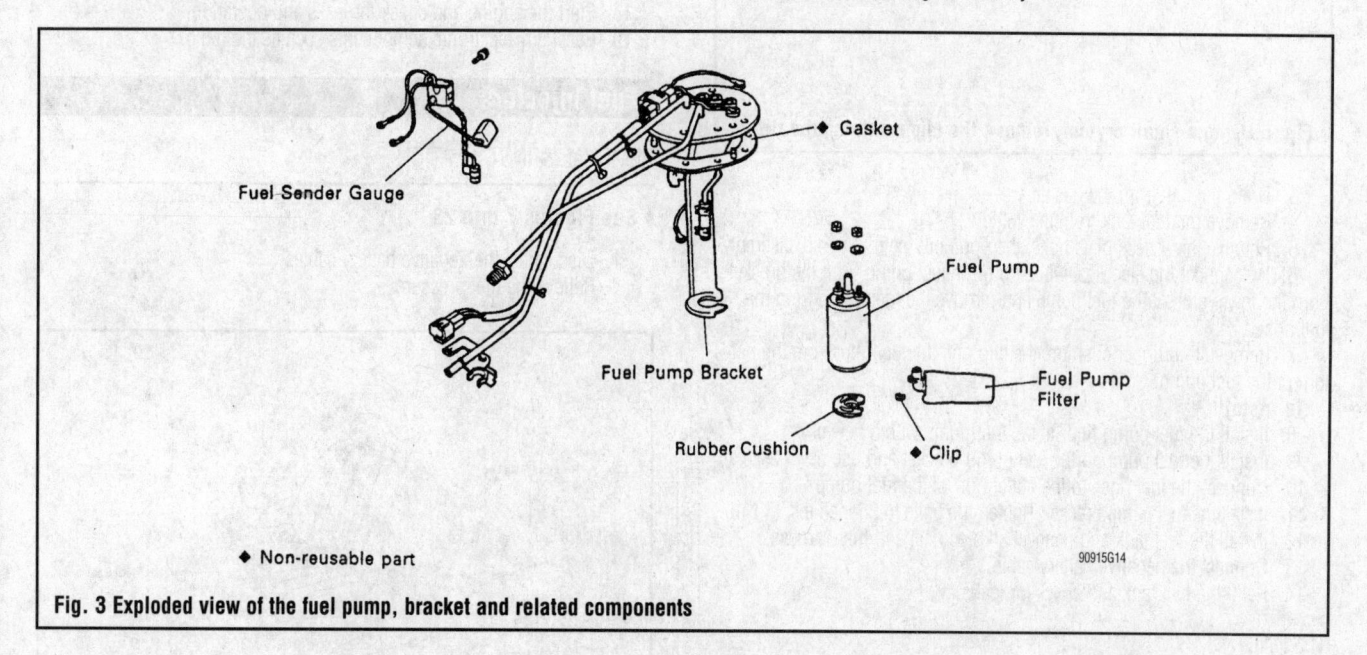

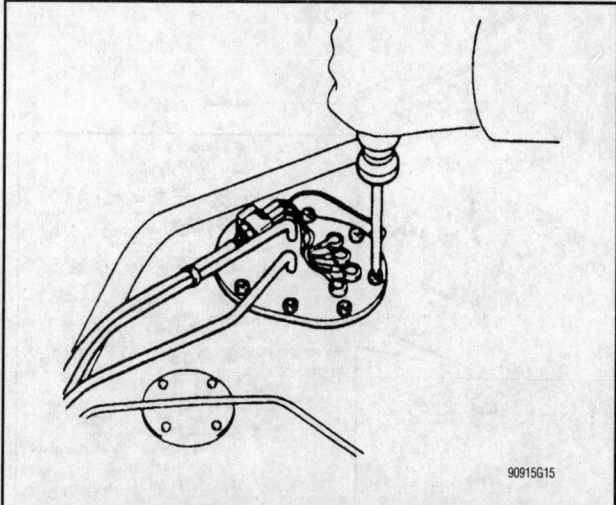

Fig. 4 Remove the fuel pump access bolts; there should be 8 of them

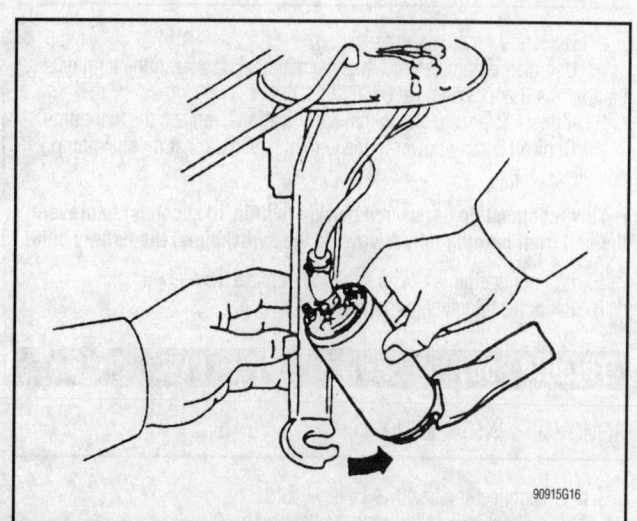

Fig. 5 Remove the pump by sliding out from the bottom as shown

# 5-4 FUEL SYSTEM

Fig. 6 Using a small prytool, remove the clip retaining the filter

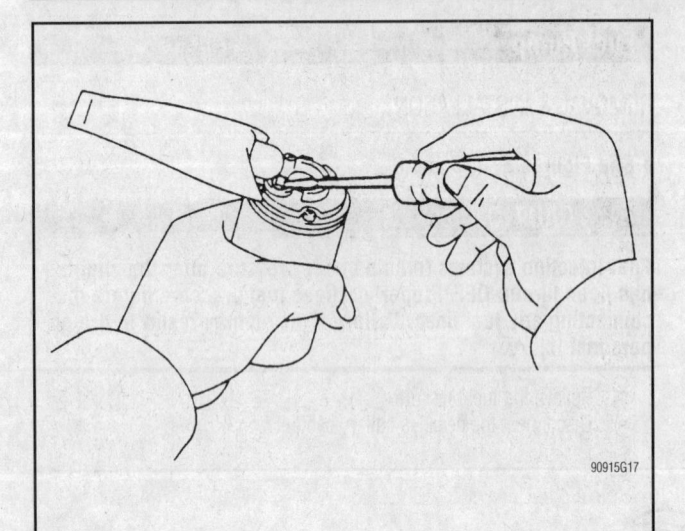

3. Drain the fuel from the gas tank.
4. Remove the fuel tank from the vehicle.
5. Remove the access plate bolts, then pull out the fuel pump assembly.
6. Disconnect the electrical wires from the fuel pump. Pull the bracket from the lower side of the fuel pump and remove the fuel pump from the fuel hose.
7. Remove the rubber cushion, the clip and the fuel filter from the bottom of the fuel pump.

**To install:**
8. Install the fuel pump filter to the fuel pump with a new clip.
9. Install the fuel pump to the fuel pump bracket and use new gaskets.
10. Connect the fuel hose to the outlet port of the fuel pump.
11. Install the fuel pump bracket. Tighten the bolts to 26 inch lbs. (3 Nm).
12. Install the fuel tank and connect all electrical and fuel harness.
13. Connect the negative battery cable.
14. Refill the fuel tank and check for leaks.

## TESTING

1. Disconnect the fuel pump wiring.
2. Using an ohmmeter, measure the resistance between the terminals. Standard is 0.2–0.3 ohms at 68°F (20°C).
3. If the resistance is not within specifications, replace the fuel pump.
4. Connect battery power to the terminals. Check that the fuel pump operates.

➡ This test must be performed quickly (within 10 seconds) to prevent the coil from burning out. Always do the switching at the battery side.

5. If the operation is not as specified, replace the fuel pump.
6. Reconnect the fuel pump wiring.

## Throttle Body

### REMOVAL & INSTALLATION

1. Disconnect the negative battery cable.
2. Drain the coolant from the throttle body.
3. Remove the air intake connector.
4. Disconnect the throttle position sensor and IAC/ISC valve harness.
5. Label and disconnect the vacuum hoses.
6. Label and disconnect the No. 1 and No. 2 water bypass hoses.
7. Separate the throttle, accelerator cable and bracket from the throttle body.
8. Remove the two bolts, nuts and throttle body. Discard the gasket.

**To install:**
9. Clean and inspect the throttle body if reusing the old one. Using a soft brush and carburetor cleaner, clean the cast parts. Using compressed air, clean all the passages and apertures.

➡ Do not clean the throttle position sensor or IAC/ISC valve.

10. Place a new gasket into position and secure the throttle body nuts to 13 ft. lbs. (18 Nm).
11. Attach the accelerator and throttle cables with bracket to the body.
12. Install and secure the water bypass hoses.
13. Connect the vacuum hoses.
14. Connect the throttle position sensor and IAC/ISC harnesses.
15. Install the air intake connector.
16. Refill the engine with the correct amount of anti-freeze and water mixture. Refer to Section 1.
17. Connect the negative battery cable.
18. Start the engine and check for leaks and operation.
19. Reset any electronic components such as the radio.

## Fuel Injectors

### REMOVAL & INSTALLATION

▶ See Figures 7 thru 23

1. Disconnect the negative battery cable.
2. Relieve the fuel pressure.

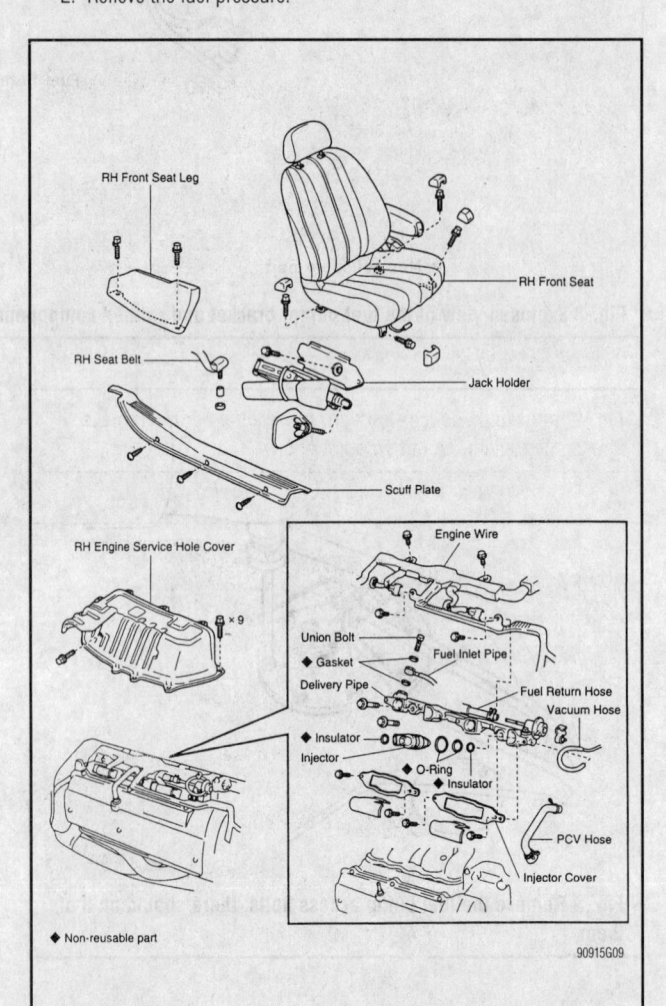

Fig. 7 Exploded view of the fuel injectors and related components necessary for removal

# FUEL SYSTEM  5-5

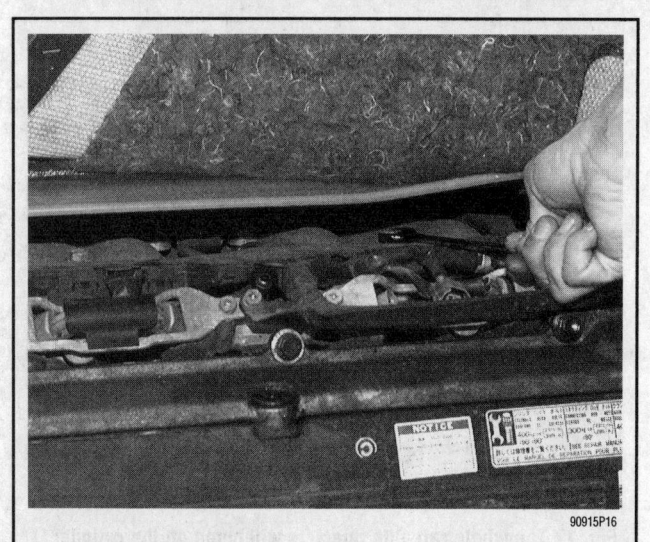

Fig. 8 Remove the PCV hose and valve

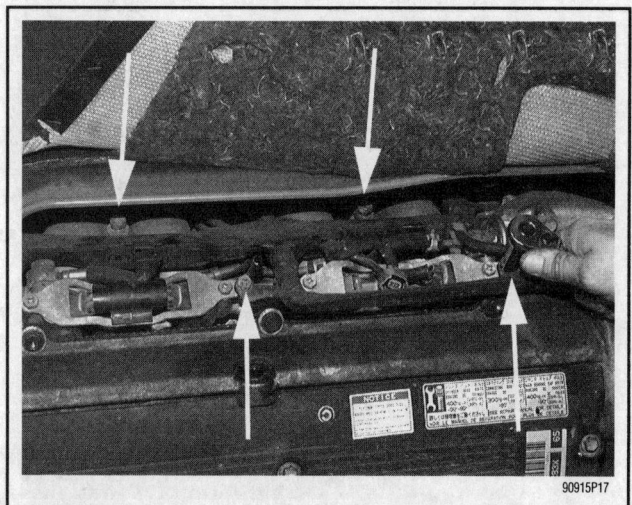

Fig. 9 Remove these four bolts for the engine wiring harness, along with two on the left side not shown

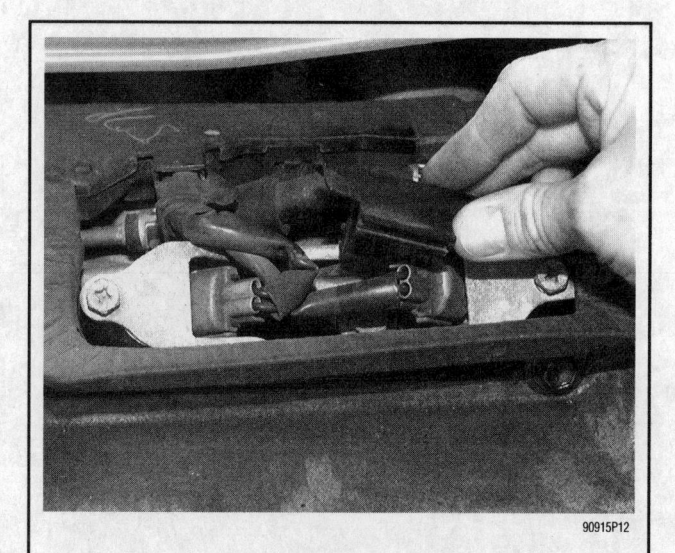

Fig. 10 Remove the injector harness clips

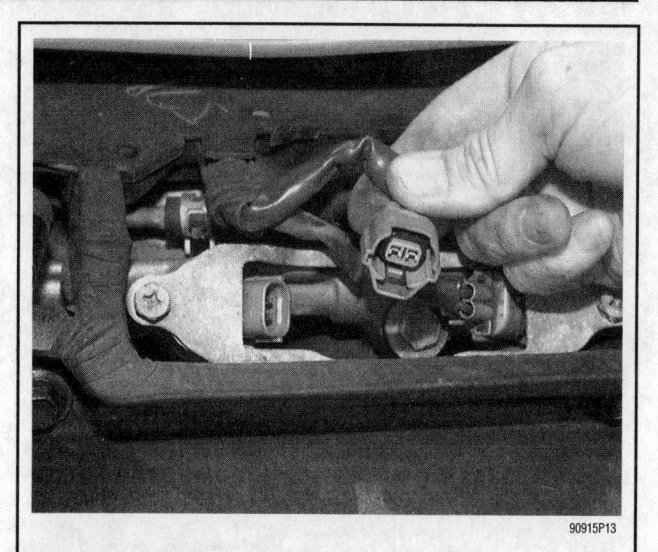

Fig. 11 Remove the harness from the injectors

Fig. 12 Place paper or cloth under the hose fitting before loosening

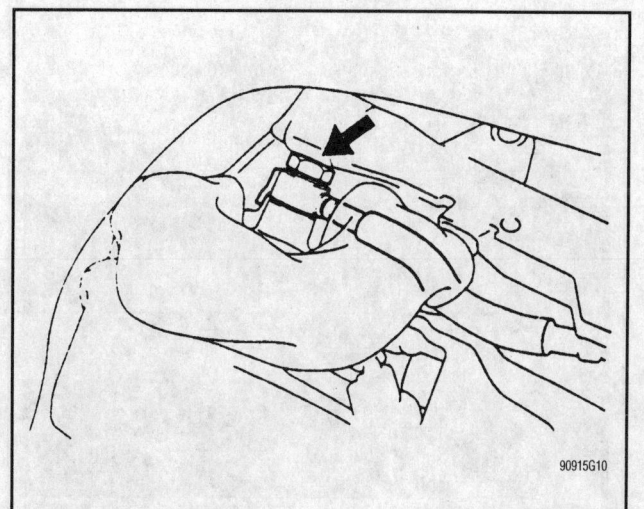

Fig. 13 Remove the union bolt with gaskets to separate the fuel inlet pipe

## 5-6 FUEL SYSTEM

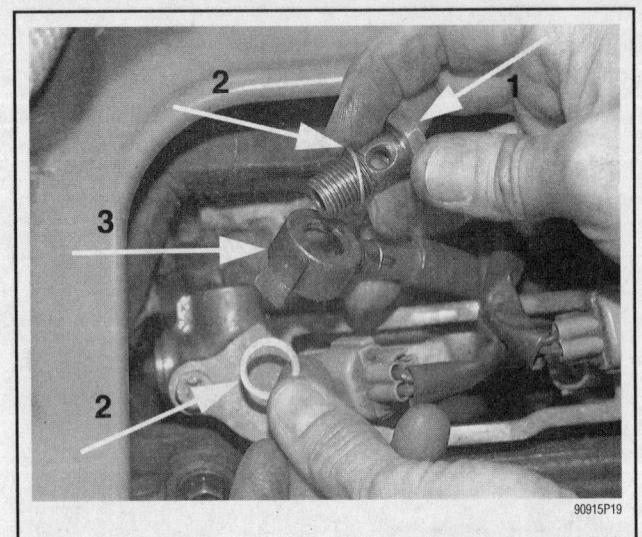

Fig. 14 The union bolt (1), washers (2) and fuel pipe (3)

Fig. 15 Remove these two bolts to extract the delivery pipe . . .

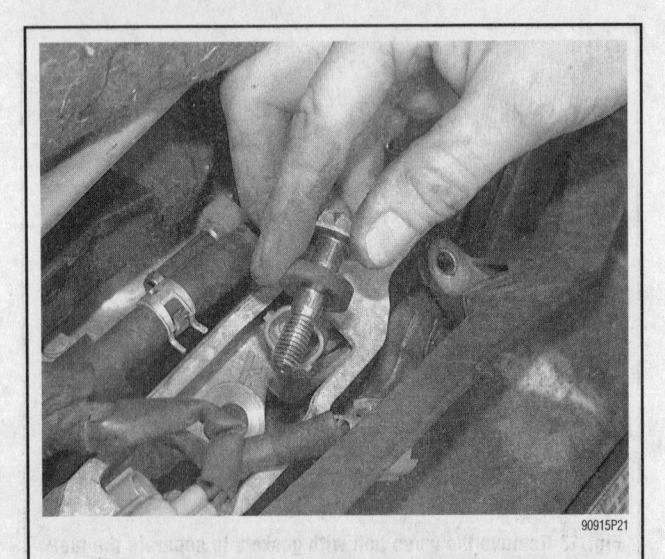

Fig. 16 . . . make sure the spacers are not lost during removal

Fig. 17 The whole rail with injectors will come off the cylinder head

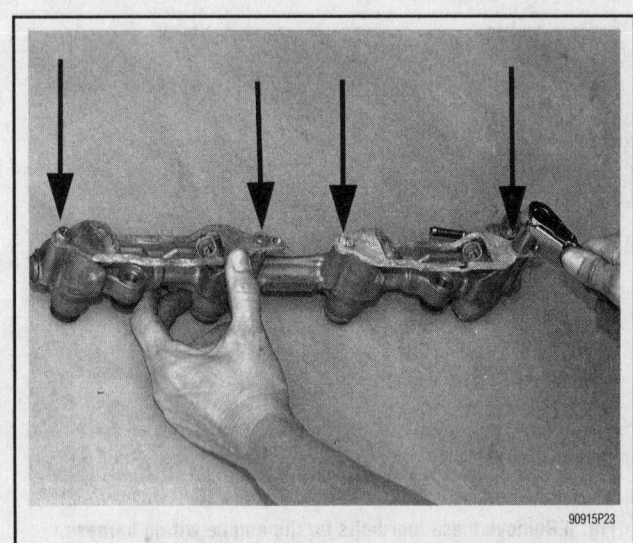

Fig. 18 Remove these four bolts to pull off the injector covers

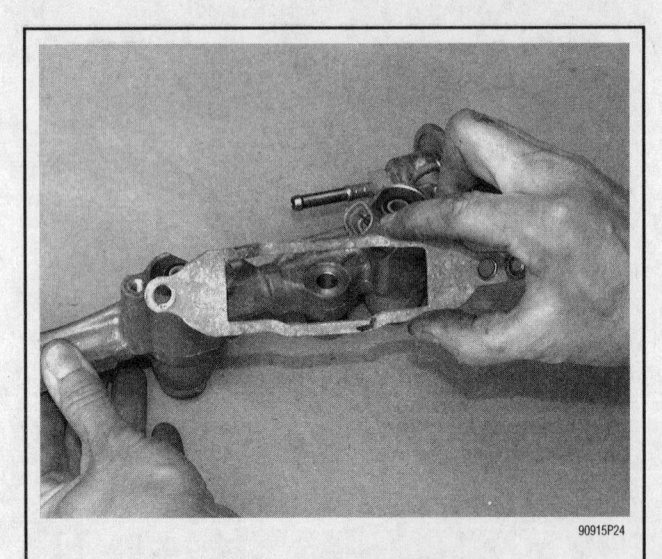

Fig. 19 The covers are simply a small metal plate

# FUEL SYSTEM    5-7

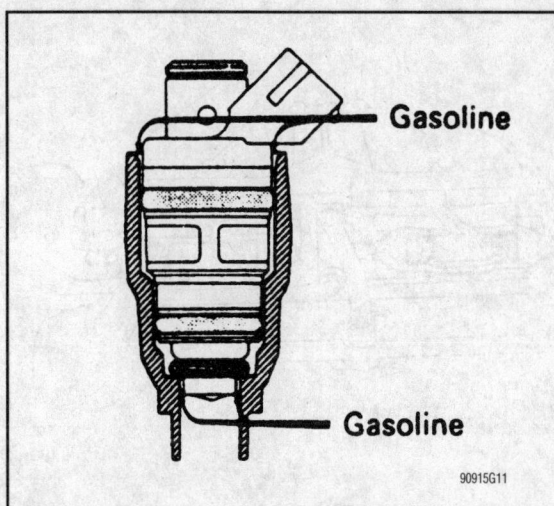

Fig. 20 Apply gasoline between the delivery pipe and injectors before removal

Fig. 21 Remove the four grommets on each end of the delivery pipe where an injector is

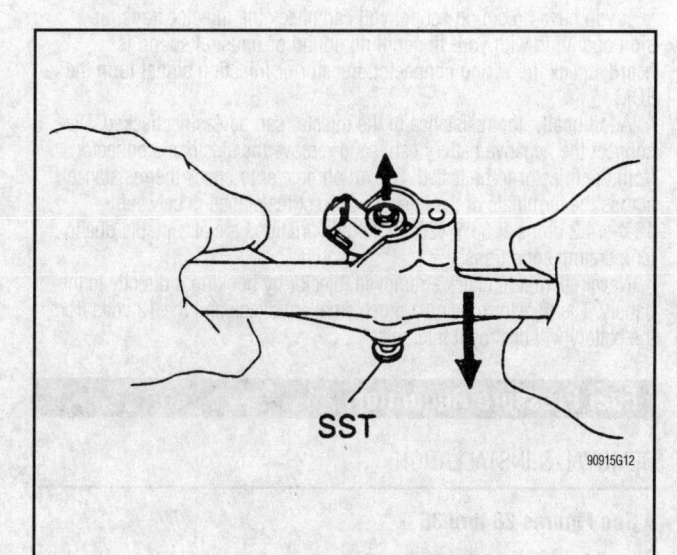

Fig. 22 Press the injector out of the delivery pipe

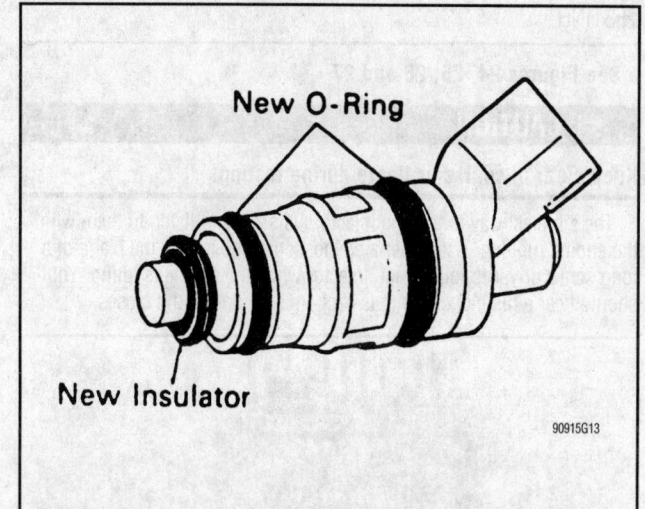

Fig. 23 Apply a light coat of gasoline to O-rings and install them to the injector

**✱✱ CAUTION**

**Fuel injection systems remain under pressure after the engine has been turned OFF. Properly relieve fuel pressure before disconnecting any fuel lines. Failure to do so may result in fire or personal injury.**

3. Remove the right engine service hole cover.
4. Disconnect the PCV hose.
5. Disconnect the vacuum hose and fuel return hose from the pressure regulator.
6. To disconnect the engine wiring harness, separate the harness from the intake manifold and delivery pipe. Disconnect the four injector harnesses. Make sure you label the wiring
7. Disconnect the fuel inlet pipe by removing the union bolt and two gaskets.
8. Unbolt and remove the delivery pipe, injectors and two spacers.
9. Remove the four insulators from the delivery pipe.
10. Remove the injector covers.
11. Remove the delivery pipe with injectors.
12. Remove the four gaskets at the end of the delivery pipe.
13. Apply gasoline between the delivery pipe and injectors.
14. Place SST 09268–74010 or equivalent pin on the injector nozzle and push down on the delivery pipe to press out the injector.
15. Remove the four injectors from the delivery pipe.
16. Remove the insulator and two O-rings from each injector.

**To install:**
17. Apply a light coat of gasoline to two new O-rings.
18. Install the two O-rings and new insulator to each injector.
19. By hand, push in the injector so that the injector connectors are in position.
20. Install the four insulators to the delivery pipe.
21. Install the two spacers, delivery pipe and two bolts. Tighten the bolts to 14 ft. lbs. (20 Nm).
22. Connect the fuel pipe with the gaskets and the union bolt and tighten the bolts to 20 ft. lbs. (29 Nm).
23. Attach the four injector connectors.
24. Secure the engine wire to the intake manifold and delivery pipe.
25. Connect the vacuum hose and fuel return hose to the pressure regulator.
26. Install the PCV hose.
27. Install the right hand engine service hole cover.
28. Connect the negative battery cable.
29. Start the engine and check for leaks.

## 5-8 FUEL SYSTEM

### TESTING

▶ See Figures 24, 25, 26 and 27

**⚠ CAUTION**

**Keep clear of sparks or flame during testing.**

The simplest way to test the injectors is simply to listen to them with the engine running. Use either a stethoscope-type tool or the blade of a long screw driver to touch each injector while the engine is idling. You should hear a distinct clicking as each injector opens and closes.

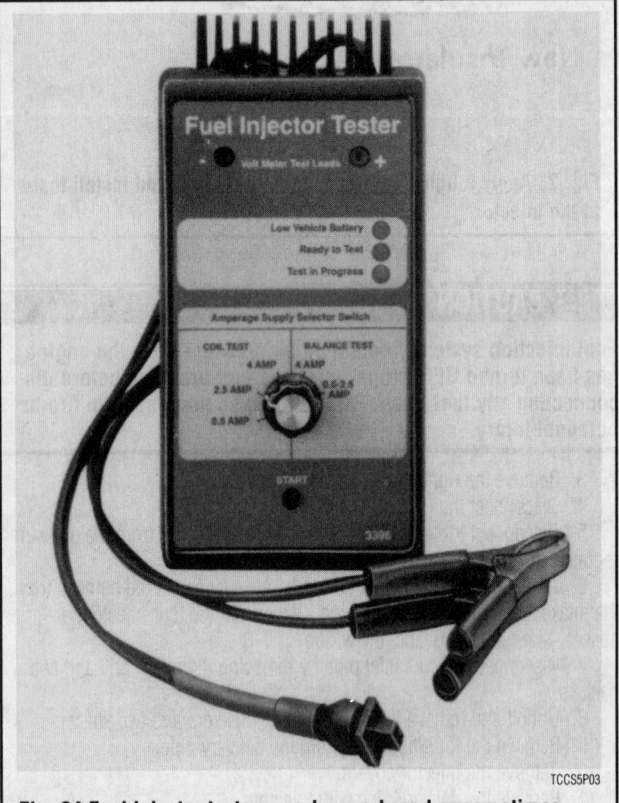

Fig. 24 Fuel injector testers can be purchased or sometimes rented

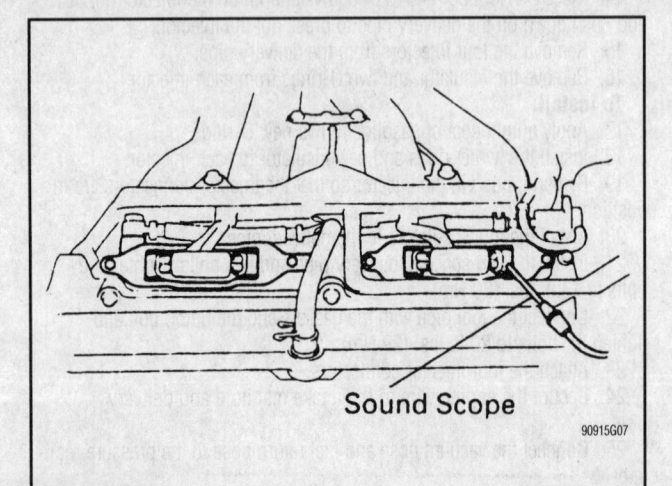

Fig. 25 Place the sound scope on the injector to inspect for normal operation

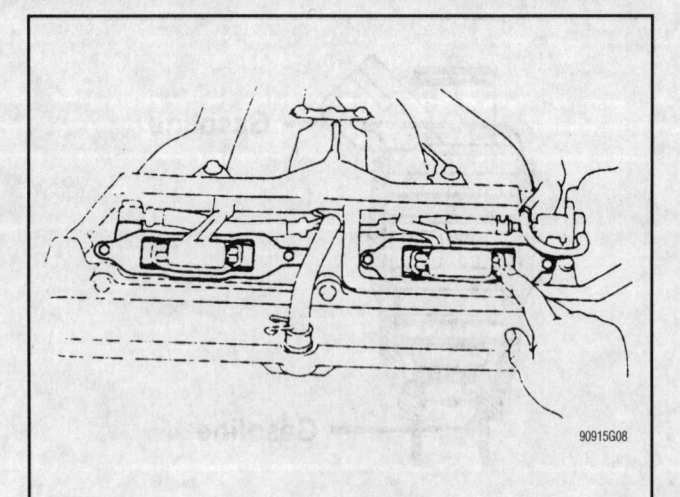

Fig. 26 Place your finger over the injector if a scope is not available

Fig. 27 Testing the fuel injector with an ohmmeter

If you have no sound scope, you can check the injector transmission operation with your finger. If no sound or unusual sound is heard, check the wiring connector, injector or injection signal form the ECM.

Additionally, the resistance of the injector can be easily checked. Disconnect the negative battery cable and remove the electrical connector from the injector to be tested. Use an ohmmeter to check the resistance across the terminals of the injector. Correct resistance is between 13.4–14.2 ohms at 68°F (20°C); slight variations are acceptable due to temperature conditions.

Never attempt to check a removed injector by hooking it directly to the battery. The injector runs on a much smaller voltage and the 12 volts from the battery will destroy it internally.

### Fuel Pressure Regulator

#### REMOVAL & INSTALLATION

▶ See Figures 28 thru 38

1. Remove the RH engine service hole cover.
2. Relieve the fuel pressure.

# FUEL SYSTEM 5-9

◆ Non-reusable part

**Fig. 28 The fuel pressure regulator is located under the passengers seat engine service hole cover**

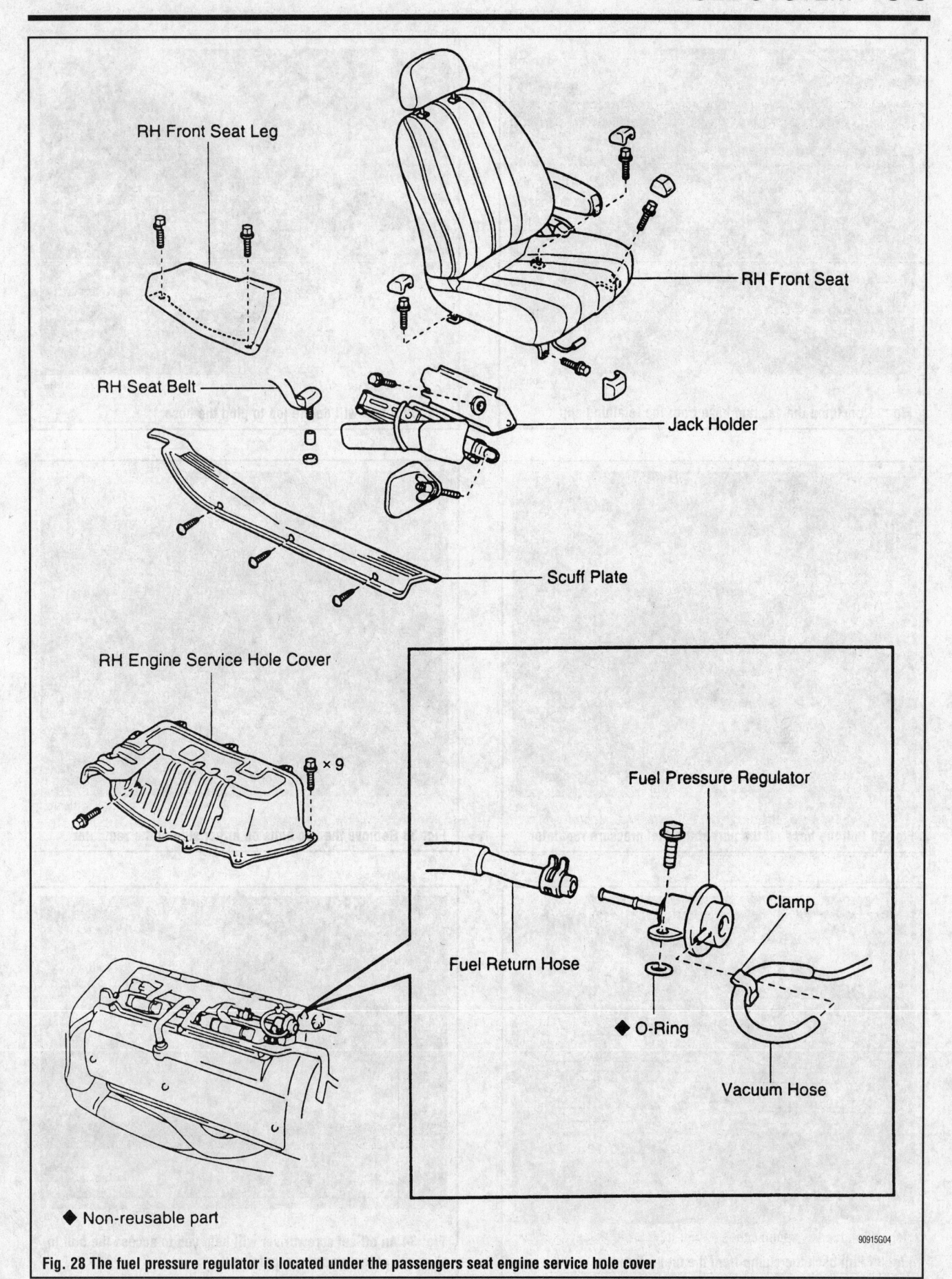

## 5-10 FUEL SYSTEM

Fig. 29 Unclamp the vacuum hose from the retaining clip

Fig. 30 Pull the hose off the port of the fuel pressure regulator

Fig. 31 Pull back the clamp from the fuel return line

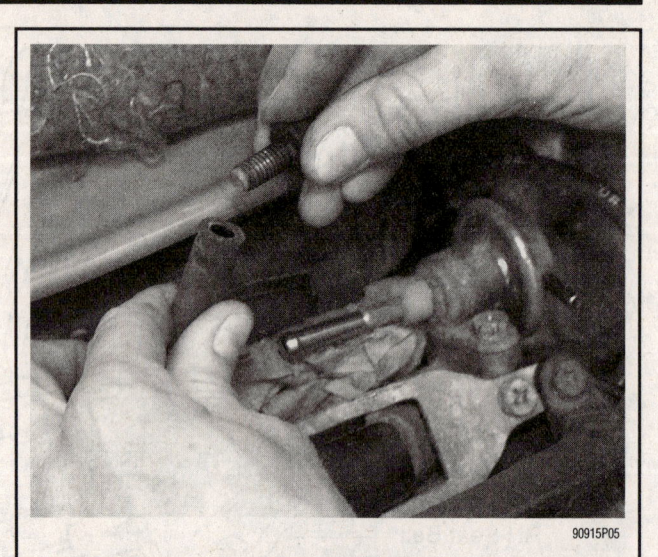

Fig. 32 A bolt will do the job to plug the hose

Fig. 33 Remove the two bolts on either side of the regulator

Fig. 34 An off-set screwdriver will help you to access the bolt in the back of the pressure regulator

# FUEL SYSTEM  5-11

**Fig. 35 Remove the fuel pressure regulator**

**Fig. 36 Place a small piece of cloth or paper in the regulator mating port to prevent dirt from entering**

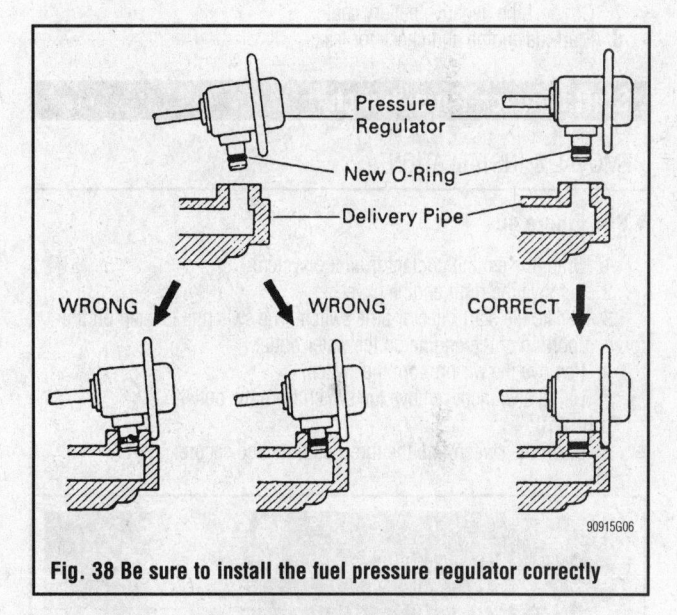

**Fig. 37 Apply a light coat of gasoline on the O-ring prior to installation**

**Fig. 38 Be sure to install the fuel pressure regulator correctly**

3. Disconnect the vacuum hose from the clamp and pull the end of the hose from the port on the valve.
4. Place a suitable container or shop towel under the pressure regulator. Disconnect the fuel return line.
5. Plug the hose with a bolt to keep from excessive fluid loss.
6. Remove the two bolts and extract the regulator from the engine. These bolts have screw heads also.

➡ The rear bolt is hard to get to. An off-set screwdriver can be used to access it.

➡ Place a small piece of cloth or paper in the regulator opening, to keep dirt from entering.

7. Inspect and replace the O-ring if necessary.

**To install:**

8. Apply a light coat of gasoline to the O-ring and install it on the regulator.
9. Attach the pressure regulator to the engine and secure to 48 inch lbs. (5 Nm).
10. Connect the fuel return hose.
11. Attach the vacuum hose and tighten the clamp.
12. Install the RH engine service hole cover.

## Cold Start Injector

### REMOVAL & INSTALLATION

♦ See Figure 39

1. Disconnect the negative battery cable.
2. Disconnect the cold start injector wiring.
3. Place a suitable container or shop towel under the fuel pipe. Slowly remove the union bolt and two gaskets, the disconnect the fuel pipe.
4. Remove the two bolts and extract the cold start injector from the engine

**To install:**

5. Place a new gasket on the cold start injector and secure to the engine with the bolts to 48 inch lbs. (5 Nm).
6. Using new gaskets, connect the fuel tube with the union bolts and secure to 14 ft. lbs. (20 Nm). with gasket.

## 5-12 FUEL SYSTEM

Fig. 39 Remove the wiring from the cold start injector

7. Connect the negative battery cable.
8. Start the engine and check for leaks.

### Start Injector Time Switch

#### REMOVAL & INSTALLATION

▶ See Figure 40

1. Drain the engine coolant from the system.
2. Remove the right engine cover.
3. Locate the start injector time switch. The switch is located on the forward portion of the engine on the water outlet.
4. Remove the wiring from the switch.
5. Using a wrench, remove the switch from the outlet.

**To install:**
6. Insert the switch into the threaded hole and secure.
7. Attach the wiring to the switch.
8. Fill the cooling system, start the engine and check for leaks.
9. Top off the system.
10. Install the right engine cover.

#### TESTING

▶ See Figures 41, 42 and 43

1. Disconnect the crankshaft position sensor wiring.
2. Using an ohmmeter, measure the resistance between the left terminal and ground.
3. Then test the resistance between both terminals.
4. If the resistance is not as specified, replace the start injector time switch.
5. Reattach the sensor wiring.

Fig. 41 Place the negative lead of the meter on ground and the positive on the left terminal

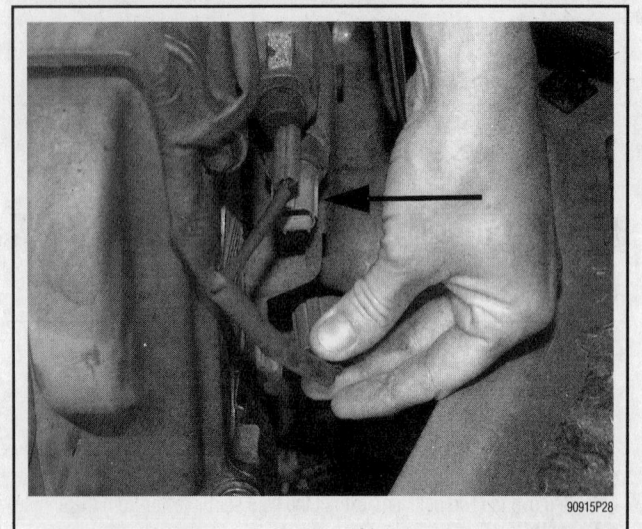

Fig. 40 Disconnect the wiring from the start injector time switch

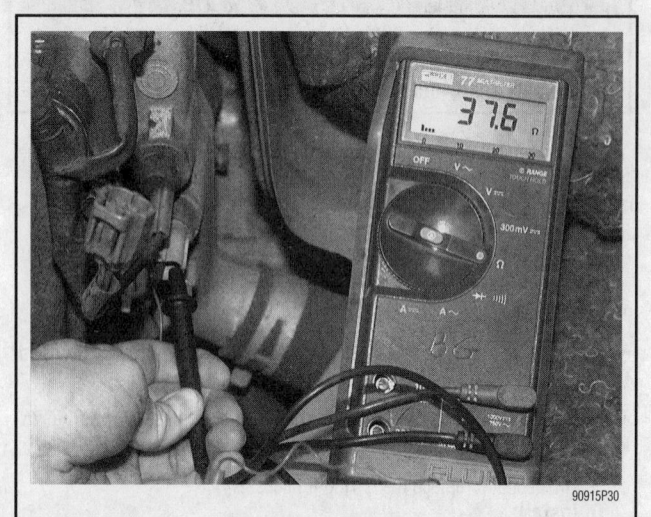

Fig. 42 Test both terminals of the start injector time switch for continuity

# FUEL SYSTEM 5-13

| Between terminals | Resistance (Ω) | Coolant temperature |
|---|---|---|
| STA – STJ | 25 – 45 | below 15°C (59°F) |
| STA – STJ | 65 – 85 | above 30°C (86°F) |
| STA – Ground | 25 – 85 | – |

Fig. 43 Start injector time switch resistance specifications

## FUEL TANK

### Tank Assembly

REMOVAL & INSTALLATION

♦ See Figure 44

→ The fuel tank is mounted drivers on the side of the vehicle. If it is necessary to work on the fuel tank or its components and fittings, the ignition must be switched to the OFF position and the negative battery cable disconnected.

1. Raise and safely support the vehicle. remove all fuel tank safety covers or tank protectors.
2. Before removing the fuel tank, the fuel should be drained out into a suitable gasoline safe container. It should be noted that these models are equipped with a drain plug on the tank.
3. Place a suitable jack under the center of the fuel tank, be sure to use a flat piece of wood between the jack cradle and the tank so as to prevent damaging the tank. Spray the fuel tank retaining strap bolts and nuts with a suitable penetrating fluid.
4. Loosen the fuel tank retraining tank bolts and nuts, but do not remove them yet. Slowly lower the jack so as to take up the slack in the fuel tank retraining straps.
5. If so equipped, remove the trim panel inside the vehicle then reach through the hole and disconnect the fuel evaporative emission control hose and fuel gauge sending unit wiring. If your model is not equipped with this access panel, lower the tank enough to gain access to the wiring and disconnect it.
6. Working from inside the wheel well, disconnect the fuel filler pipe from the fuel tank and the inlet pipe in the body.
7. Relieve the fuel pressure.
8. Disconnect and separate the main and return fuel hoses from the respective tank connecting lines underneath the vehicle.
9. With the tank still supported by the jack, remove the tank strap bolts and slowly but carefully lower the fuel tank. Remove the lines that may still be attached or hindering the removal process in any way.
10. Installation is the reverse of removal.
11. Be sure to always pay attention to the following:
    a. Always use new gaskets when replacing the fuel tank or any tank component.
    b. When reinstalling, be sure to include the rubber protectors on the upper surfaces of the tank and tank band.
    c. Be sure to check all fuel lines and connections for cracks, leakage or connection deformation. Repair as necessary.

## 5-14 FUEL SYSTEM

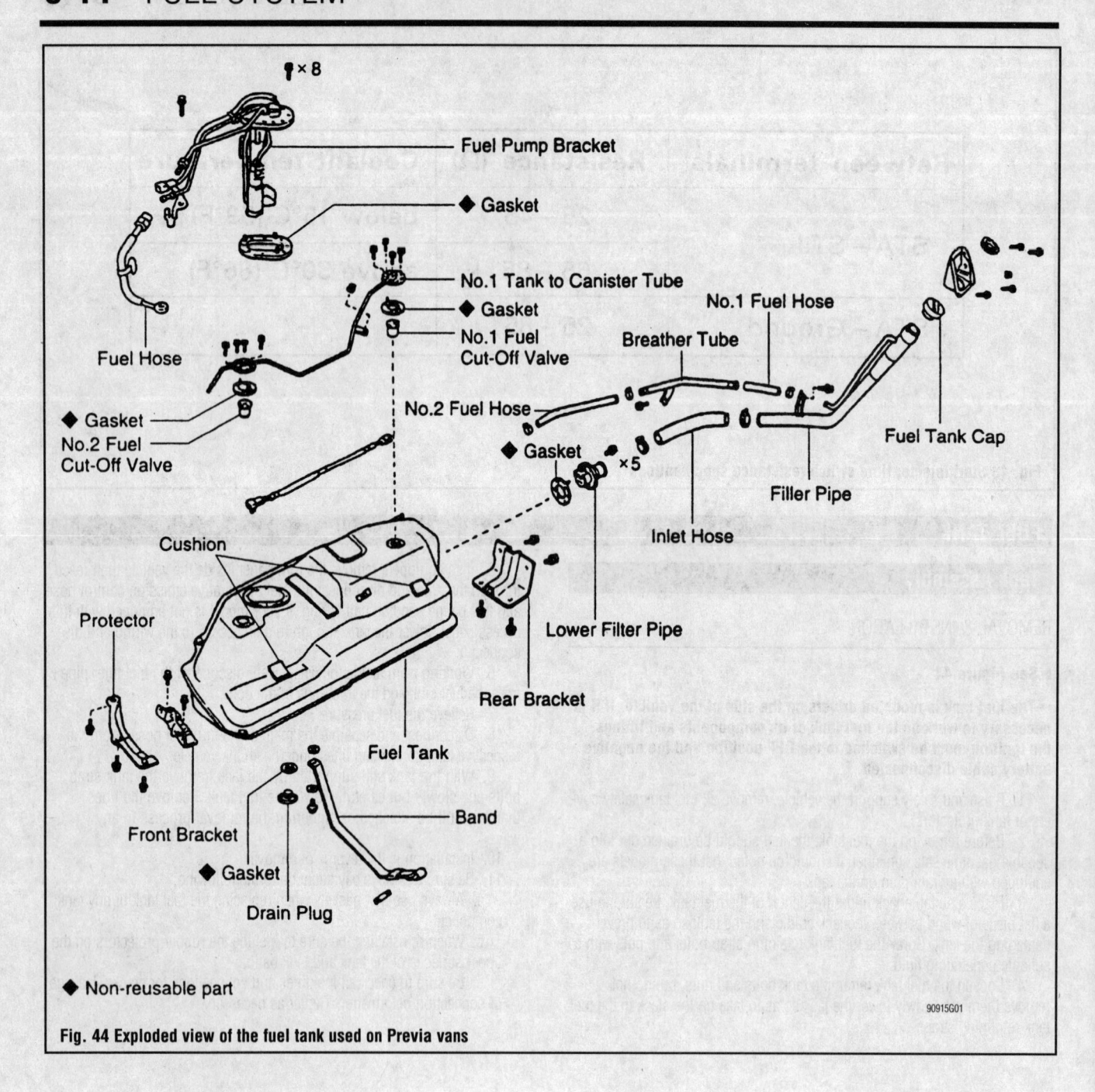

Fig. 44 Exploded view of the fuel tank used on Previa vans

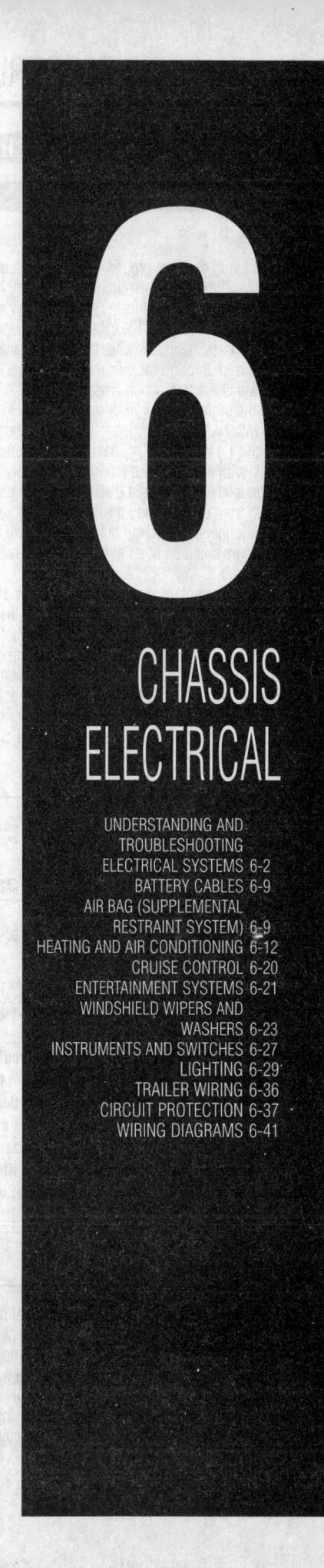

UNDERSTANDING AND
  TROUBLESHOOTING ELECTRICAL
  SYSTEMS 6-2
BASIC ELECTRICAL THEORY 6-2
  THE WATER ANALOGY 6-2
  OHM'S LAW 6-2
ELECTRICAL COMPONENTS 6-2
  POWER SOURCE 6-2
  GROUND 6-3
  PROTECTIVE DEVICES 6-3
  SWITCHES & RELAYS 6-3
  LOAD 6-4
  WIRING & HARNESSES 6-4
  CONNECTORS 6-4
TEST EQUIPMENT 6-5
  JUMPER WIRES 6-5
  TEST LIGHTS 6-5
  MULTIMETERS 6-6
TROUBLESHOOTING ELECTRICAL
  SYSTEMS 6-6
TESTING 6-6
  OPEN CIRCUITS 6-6
  SHORT CIRCUITS 6-7
  VOLTAGE 6-7
  VOLTAGE DROP 6-7
  RESISTANCE 6-8
WIRE AND CONNECTOR REPAIR 6-8
**BATTERY CABLES 6-9**
DISCONNECTING THE CABLES 6-9
**AIR BAG (SUPPLEMENTAL RESTRAINT
  SYSTEM) 6-9**
GENERAL INFORMATION 6-9
  SYSTEM OPERATION 6-9
  SYSTEM COMPONENTS 6-10
  SERVICE PRECAUTIONS 6-11
  DISARMING THE SYSTEM 6-12
  ARMING THE SYSTEM 6-12
**HEATING AND AIR
  CONDITIONING 6-12**
BLOWER MOTOR 6-13
  REMOVAL & INSTALLATION 6-13
BLOWER MOTOR RESISTOR 6-17
  REMOVAL & INSTALLATION 6-17
ICE BOX MOTOR 6-17
  REMOVAL & INSTALLATION 6-17
HEATER WATER CONTROL VALVE 6-17
  REMOVAL & INSTALLATION 6-17
AIR CONDITIONING COMPONENTS 6-17
  REMOVAL & INSTALLATION 6-17
CONTROL CABLES 6-17
  REMOVAL & INSTALLATION 6-17
  ADJUSTMENT 6-17
CONTROL PANEL 6-19
  REMOVAL & INSTALLATION 6-19
**CRUISE CONTROL 6-20**
**ENTERTAINMENT SYSTEMS 6-21**
RADIO RECEIVER/AMPLIFIER/TAPE
  PLAYER/CD PLAYER 6-21
  REMOVAL & INSTALLATION 6-21
SPEAKERS 6-22
  REMOVAL & INSTALLATION 6-22
**WINDSHIELD WIPERS AND
  WASHERS 6-23**
WINDSHIELD WIPER BLADE AND
  ARM 6-23
  REMOVAL & INSTALLATION 6-23
WINDSHIELD WIPER MOTOR 6-25
  REMOVAL & INSTALLATION 6-25
WINDSHIELD WASHER MOTOR 6-26
  REMOVAL & INSTALLATION 6-26
**INSTRUMENTS AND SWITCHES 6-27**
INSTRUMENT CLUSTER 6-27
  REMOVAL & INSTALLATION 6-27
SPEEDOMETER, TACHOMETER, AND
  GAUGES 6-28
  REMOVAL & INSTALLATION 6-28
WINDSHIELD WIPER SWITCH 6-28
  REMOVAL & INSTALLATION 6-28
HEADLIGHT SWITCH 6-28
  REMOVAL & INSTALLATION 6-28
DASH-MOUNTED SWITCHES 6-28
  REMOVAL & INSTALLATION 6-28
CLOCK 6-29
  REMOVAL & INSTALLATION 6-29
HORN 6-29
  REMOVAL & INSTALLATION 6-29
**LIGHTING 6-29**
HEADLIGHTS 6-29
  REMOVAL & INSTALLATION 6-29
  AIMING 6-30
TURN SIGNAL/MARKER LIGHT 6-31
  REMOVAL & INSTALLATION 6-31
TAIL LIGHTS 6-32
  REMOVAL & INSTALLATION 6-32
DOME LIGHT 6-33
  REMOVAL & INSTALLATION 6-33
FOG/DRIVING LIGHTS 6-34
  REMOVAL & INSTALLATION 6-34
THIRD BRAKE LIGHT 6-35
  REMOVAL & INSTALLATION 6-35
LICENSE PLATE LIGHT 6-35
  REMOVAL & INSTALLATION 6-35
REVERSE LIGHTS 6-36
  REMOVAL & INSTALLATION 6-36
**TRAILER WIRING 6-36**
**CIRCUIT PROTECTION 6-37**
FUSES 6-37
  REPLACEMENT 6-37
FUSIBLE LINKS 6-38
  REPLACEMENT 6-38
CIRCUIT BREAKERS 6-38
  REPLACEMENT 6-38
  RESETTING 6-39
RELAYS 6-39
  REPLACEMENT 6-39
**WIRING DIAGRAMS 6-41**
**SPECIFICATIONS CHARTS**
  LIGHT BULB APPLICATIONS 6-36
  FUSE APPLICATIONS—1991–92
    MODELS 6-39
  FUSE APPLICATIONS—1993–97
    MODELS 6-40
**TROUBLESHOOTING CHART**
  CRUISE CONTROL
    TROUBLESHOOTING 6-20

# 6

# CHASSIS ELECTRICAL

UNDERSTANDING AND
TROUBLESHOOTING
ELECTRICAL SYSTEMS 6-2
BATTERY CABLES 6-9
AIR BAG (SUPPLEMENTAL
RESTRAINT SYSTEM) 6-9
HEATING AND AIR CONDITIONING 6-12
CRUISE CONTROL 6-20
ENTERTAINMENT SYSTEMS 6-21
WINDSHIELD WIPERS AND
WASHERS 6-23
INSTRUMENTS AND SWITCHES 6-27
LIGHTING 6-29
TRAILER WIRING 6-36
CIRCUIT PROTECTION 6-37
WIRING DIAGRAMS 6-41

# 6-2 CHASSIS ELECTRICAL

## UNDERSTANDING AND TROUBLESHOOTING ELECTRICAL SYSTEMS

### Basic Electrical Theory

◆ See Figure 1

For any 12 volt, negative ground, electrical system to operate, the electricity must travel in a complete circuit. This simply means that current (power) from the positive terminal (+) of the battery must eventually return to the negative terminal (-) of the battery. Along the way, this current will travel through wires, fuses, switches and components. If, for any reason, the flow of current through the circuit is interrupted, the component fed by that circuit will cease to function properly.

Perhaps the easiest way to visualize a circuit is to think of connecting a light bulb (with two wires attached to it) to the battery—one wire attached to the negative (-) terminal of the battery and the other wire to the positive (+) terminal. With the two wires touching the battery terminals, the circuit would be complete and the light bulb would illuminate. Electricity would follow a path from the battery to the bulb and back to the battery. It's easy to see that with longer wires on our light bulb, it could be mounted anywhere. Further, one wire could be fitted with a switch so that the light could be turned on and off.

The normal automotive circuit differs from this simple example in two ways. First, instead of having a return wire from the bulb to the battery, the current travels through the chassis of the vehicle. Since the negative (-) battery cable is attached to the chassis and the chassis is made of electrically conductive metal, the chassis of the vehicle can serve as a ground wire to complete the circuit. Secondly, most automotive circuits contain multiple components which receive power from a single circuit. This lessens the amount of wire needed to power components on the vehicle.

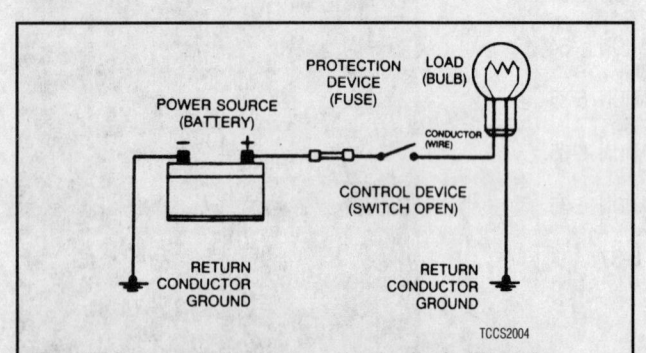

**Fig. 1** This example illustrates a simple circuit. When the switch is closed, power from the positive (+) battery terminal flows through the fuse and the switch, and then to the light bulb. The light illuminates and the circuit is completed through the ground wire back to the negative (-) battery terminal. In reality, the two ground points shown in the illustration are attached to the metal chassis of the vehicle, which completes the circuit back to the battery

### THE WATER ANALOGY

Electricity is the flow of electrons—hypothetical particles thought to constitute the basic "stuff" of electricity. Many people have been taught electrical theory using an analogy with water. In a comparison with water flowing through a pipe, the electrons would be the water.

The flow of electricity can be measured much like the flow of water through a pipe. The unit of measurement used is amperes, frequently abbreviated as amps (a). When connected to a circuit, an ammeter will measure the actual amount of current flowing through the circuit. When relatively few electrons flow through a circuit, the amperage is low. When many electrons flow, the amperage is high.

Just as water pressure is measured in units such as pounds per square inch (psi), electrical pressure is measured in units called volts (v). When a voltmeter is connected to a circuit, it is measuring the electrical pressure. The higher the voltage, the more current will flow through the circuit. The lower the voltage, the less current will flow.

While increasing the voltage in a circuit will increase the flow of current, the actual flow depends not only on voltage, but also on the resistance of the circuit. Resistance is the amount of force necessary to push the current through the circuit. The standard unit for measuring resistance is an ohm (W or omega). Resistance in a circuit varies depending on the amount and type of components used in the circuit. The main factors which determine resistance are:

- Material—some materials have more resistance than others. Those with high resistance are said to be insulators. Rubber is one of the best insulators available, as it allows little current to pass. Low resistance materials are said to be conductors. Copper wire is among the best conductors. Most vehicle wiring is made of copper.
- Size—the larger the wire size being used, the less resistance the wire will have. This is why components which use large amounts of electricity usually have large wires supplying current to them.
- Length—for a given thickness of wire, the longer the wire, the greater the resistance. The shorter the wire, the less the resistance. When determining the proper wire for a circuit, both size and length must be considered to design a circuit that can handle the current needs of the component.
- Temperature—with many materials, the higher the temperature, the greater the resistance. This principle is used in many of the sensors on the engine.

### OHM'S LAW

The preceding definitions may lead the reader into believing that there is no relationship between current, voltage and resistance. Nothing can be further from the truth. The relationship between current, voltage and resistance can be summed up by a statement known as Ohm's law.

Voltage (E) is equal to amperage (I) times resistance (R): $E = I \times R$
Other forms of the formula are $R = E/I$ and $I = E/R$

In each of these formulas, E is the voltage in volts, I is the current in amps and R is the resistance in ohms. The basic point to remember is that as the resistance of a circuit goes up, the amount of current that flows in the circuit will go down, if voltage remains the same.

### Electrical Components

#### POWER SOURCE

The power source for 12 volt automotive electrical systems is the battery. In most modern vehicles, the battery is a lead/acid electrochemical device consisting of six 2 volt subsections (cells) connected in series, so that the unit is capable of producing approximately 12 volts of electrical pressure. Each subsection consists of a series of positive and negative plates held a short distance apart in a solution of sulfuric acid and water.

The two types of plates are of dissimilar metals. This sets up a chemical reaction, and it is this reaction which produces current flow from the battery when its positive and negative terminals are connected to an electrical load. The power removed from the battery is replaced by the alternator, which forces electrons back through the battery, reversing the normal flow, and restoring the battery to its original chemical state.

# CHASSIS ELECTRICAL 6-3

## GROUND

Two types of grounds are used in automotive electric circuits. Direct ground components are grounded through their mounting points. All other components use some sort of ground wire which is attached to the body or chassis of the vehicle. The electrical current runs through the chassis of the vehicle and returns to the battery through the ground (-) cable; if you look, you'll see that the battery ground cable connects between the battery and the body or chassis of the vehicle.

➡ It should be noted that a good percentage of electrical problems can be traced to bad grounds.

## PROTECTIVE DEVICES

♦ See Figure 2

It is possible for large surges of current to pass through the electrical system of your vehicle. If this surge of current were to reach the load in the circuit, it could burn it out or severely damage it. To prevent this, fuses, circuit breakers and/or fusible links are connected into the supply wires of the electrical system. These items are nothing more than a built-in weak spot in the system. When an abnormal amount of current flows through the system, these protective devices work as follows to protect the circuit:

- Fuse—when an excessive electrical current passes through a fuse, the fuse "blows" (the conductor melts) and opens the circuit, preventing the passage of current.
- Circuit Breaker—a circuit breaker is basically a self-repairing fuse. It will open the circuit in the same fashion as a fuse, but when the surge subsides, the circuit breaker can be reset and does not need replacement.
- Fusible Link—a fusible link (fuse link or main link) is a short length of special, Hypalon high temperature insulated wire that acts as a fuse. When an excessive electrical current passes through a fusible link, the thin gauge wire inside the link melts, creating an intentional open to protect the circuit. To repair the circuit, the link must be replaced. Some newer type fusible links are housed in plug-in modules, which are simply replaced like a fuse, while older type fusible links must be cut and spliced if they melt. Since this link is very early in the electrical path, it's the first place to look if nothing on the vehicle works, but the battery seems to be charged and is properly connected.

### ✳✳ CAUTION

**Always replace fuses, circuit breakers and fusible links with identically rated components. Under no circumstances should a component of higher or lower amperage rating be substituted.**

## SWITCHES & RELAYS

♦ See Figures 3 and 4

Switches are used in electrical circuits to control the passage of current. The most common use is to open and close circuits between the battery and the various electric devices in the system. Switches are rated according to the amount of amperage they can handle. If a sufficient amperage rated switch is not used in a circuit, the switch could overload and cause damage.

Some electrical components which require a large amount of current to operate use a special switch called a relay. Since these circuits carry a large amount of current, the thickness of the wire in the circuit is also greater. If this large wire were connected from the load to the control switch on the dashboard, the switch would have to carry the high amperage load and the dash would be twice as large to accommodate the increased size of the wiring harness. To prevent these problems, a relay is used.

Relays are composed of a coil and a switch. These two components are linked together so that when one operates, the other operates at the same time. The large wires in the circuit are connected from the battery to one side of the relay switch and from the opposite side of the relay switch to the load. Most relays are normally open, preventing current from passing through the circuit. Additional, smaller wires are connected from the relay coil to the control switch for the circuit and from the opposite side of the relay coil to ground. When the control switch is turned on, it grounds the smaller wire to the relay coil, causing the coil to operate. The coil pulls the relay switch closed, sending power to the component without routing it through the inside

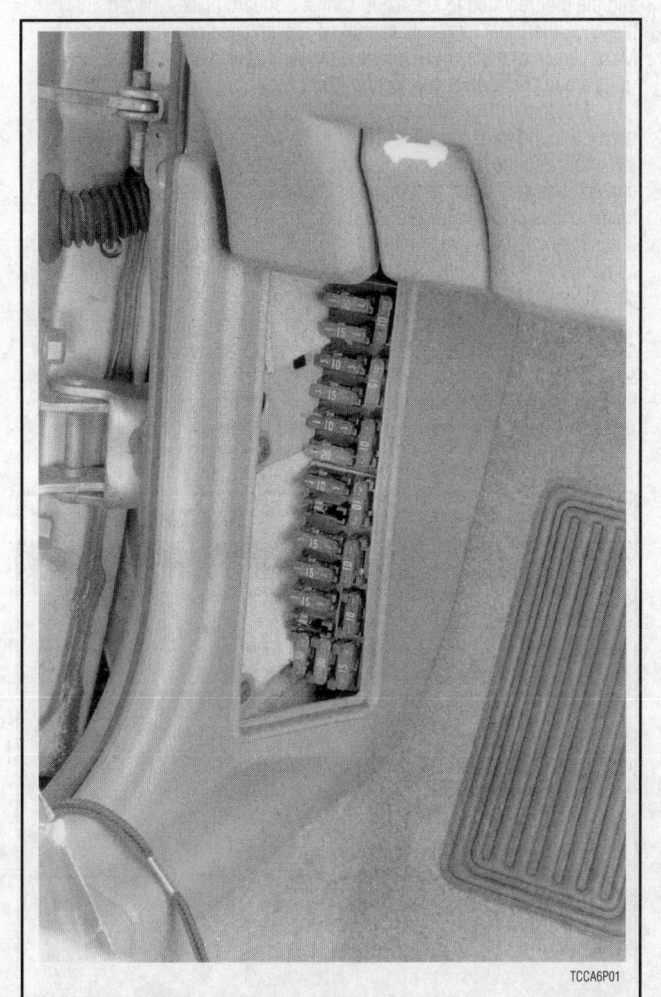

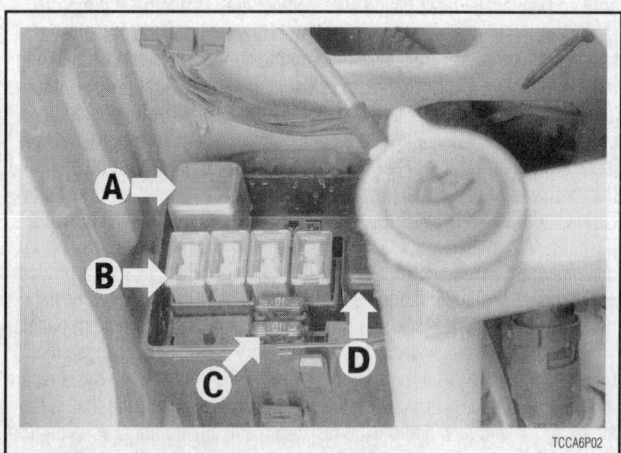

**Fig. 2 Most vehicles use one or more fuse panels. This one is located in the driver's side kick panel**

A. Relay
B. Fusible link
C. Fuse
D. Flasher

**Fig. 3 The underhood fuse and relay panel usually contains fuses, relays, flashers and fusible links**

## 6-4 CHASSIS ELECTRICAL

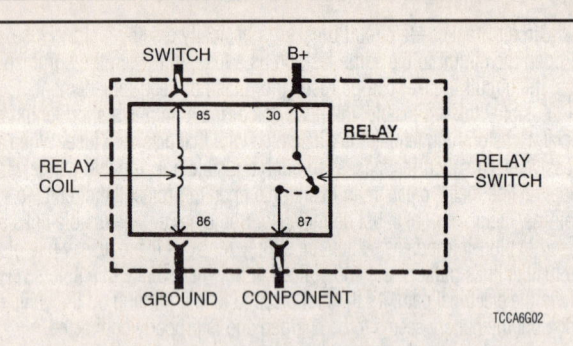

**Fig. 4 Relays are composed of a coil and a switch. These two components are linked together so that when one operates, the other operates at the same time. The large wires in the circuit are connected from the battery to one side of the relay switch (B+) and from the opposite side of the relay switch to the load (component). Smaller wires are connected from the relay coil to the control switch for the circuit and from the opposite side of the relay coil to ground**

of the vehicle. Some common circuits which may use relays are the horn, headlights, starter, electric fuel pump and rear window defogger systems.

### LOAD

Every complete circuit must include a "load" (something to use the electricity coming from the source). Without this load, the battery would attempt to deliver its entire power supply from one pole to another. The electricity would take a short cut to ground and cause a great amount of damage to other components in the circuit by developing a tremendous amount of heat. This condition could develop sufficient heat to melt the insulation on all the surrounding wires and reduce a multiple wire cable to a lump of plastic and copper.

### WIRING & HARNESSES

The average automobile contains about ½ mile of wiring, with hundreds of individual connections. To protect the many wires from damage and to keep them from becoming a confusing tangle, they are organized into bundles, enclosed in plastic or taped together and called wiring harnesses. Different harnesses serve different parts of the vehicle. Individual wires are color coded to help trace them through a harness where sections are hidden from view.

Automotive wiring or circuit conductors can be either single strand wire, multi-strand wire or printed circuitry. Single strand wire has a solid metal core and is usually used inside such components as alternators, motors, relays and other devices. Multi-strand wire has a core made of many small strands of wire twisted together into a single conductor. Most of the wiring in an automotive electrical system is made up of multi-strand wire, either as a single conductor or grouped together in a harness. All wiring is color coded on the insulator, either as a solid color or as a colored wire with an identification stripe. A printed circuit is a thin film of copper or other conductor that is printed on an insulator backing. Occasionally, a printed circuit is sandwiched between two sheets of plastic for more protection and flexibility. A complete printed circuit, consisting of conductors, insulating material and connectors for lamps or other components is called a printed circuit board. Printed circuitry is used in place of individual wires or harnesses in places where space is limited, such as behind instrument panels.

Since automotive electrical systems are very sensitive to changes in resistance, the selection of properly sized wires is critical when systems are repaired. A loose or corroded connection or a replacement wire that is too small for the circuit will add extra resistance and an additional voltage drop to the circuit.

The wire gauge number is an expression of the cross-section area of the conductor. The most common system for expressing wire size is the American Wire Gauge (AWG) system. As gauge number increases, area decreases and the wire becomes smaller. An 18 gauge wire is smaller than a 4 gauge wire. A wire with a higher gauge number will carry less current than a wire with a lower gauge number. Gauge wire size refers to the size of the strands of the conductor, not the size of the complete wire. It is possible, therefore, to have two wires of the same gauge with different diameters because one may have thicker insulation than the other.

12 volt automotive electrical systems generally use 10, 12, 14, 16 and 18 gauge wire. Main power distribution circuits and larger accessories usually use 10 and 12 gauge wire. Battery cables are usually 4 or 6 gauge, although 1 and 2 gauge wires are occasionally used.

It is essential to understand how a circuit works before trying to figure out why it doesn't. An electrical schematic shows the electrical current paths when a circuit is operating properly. Schematics break the entire electrical system down into individual circuits. In a schematic, no attempt is made to represent wiring and components as they physically appear on the vehicle; switches and other components are shown as simply as possible. Face views of harness connectors show the cavity or terminal locations in all multi-pin connectors to help locate test points.

### CONNECTORS

#### ▸ See Figures 5 and 6

Three types of connectors are commonly used in automotive applications—weatherproof, molded and hard shell.

- **Weatherproof**—these connectors are most commonly used in the engine compartment or where the connector is exposed to the elements. Terminals are protected against moisture and dirt by sealing rings which provide a weathertight seal. All repairs require the use of a special terminal and the tool required to service it. Unlike standard blade type terminals, these weatherproof terminals cannot be straightened once they are bent. Make certain that the connectors are properly seated and all of the sealing rings are in place when connecting leads.

- **Molded**—these connectors require complete replacement of the connector if found to be defective. This means splicing a new connector assembly into the harness. All splices should be soldered to insure proper contact. Use care when probing the connections or replacing terminals in them, as it is possible to create a short circuit between opposite terminals. If this happens to the wrong terminal pair, it is possible to damage certain components. Always use jumper wires between connectors for circuit checking and NEVER probe through weatherproof seals.

- **Hard Shell**—unlike molded connectors, the terminal contacts in hard-shell connectors can be replaced. Replacement usually involves the use of a special terminal removal tool that depresses the locking tangs (barbs) on the connector terminal and allows the connector to be removed from the rear of the shell. The connector shell should be replaced if it shows any

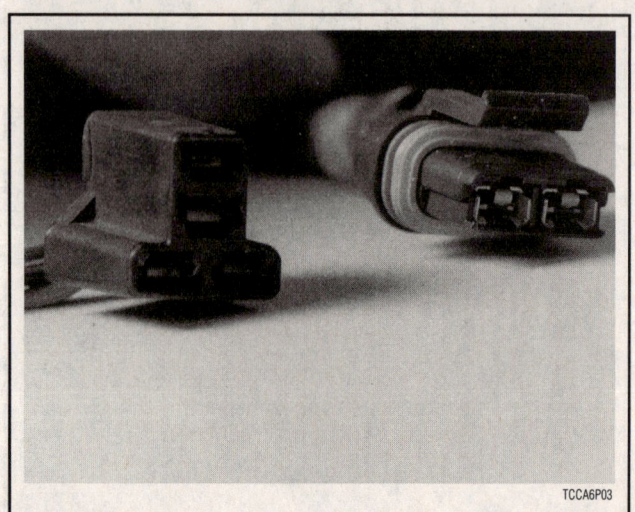

**Fig. 5 Hard shell (left) and weatherproof (right) connectors have replaceable terminals**

# CHASSIS ELECTRICAL  6-5

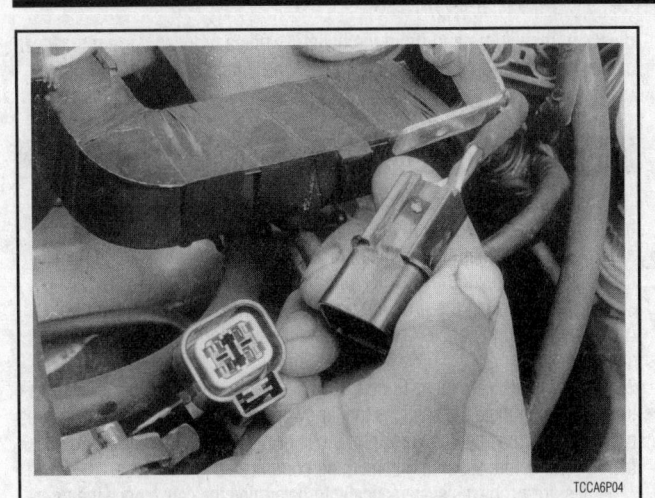

**Fig. 6 Weatherproof connectors are most commonly used in the engine compartment or where the connector is exposed to the elements**

evidence of burning, melting, cracks, or breaks. Replace individual terminals that are burnt, corroded, distorted or loose.

## Test Equipment

Pinpointing the exact cause of trouble in an electrical circuit is most times accomplished by the use of special test equipment. The following describes different types of commonly used test equipment and briefly explains how to use them in diagnosis. In addition to the information covered below, the tool manufacturer's instructions booklet (provided with the tester) should be read and clearly understood before attempting any test procedures.

### JUMPER WIRES

### ✳✳ CAUTION

**Never use jumper wires made from a thinner gauge wire than the circuit being tested. If the jumper wire is of too small a gauge, it may overheat and possibly melt. Never use jumpers to bypass high resistance loads in a circuit. Bypassing resistance's, in effect, creates a short circuit. This may, in turn, cause damage and fire. Jumper wires should only be used to bypass lengths of wire.**

Jumper wires are simple, yet extremely valuable, pieces of test equipment. They are basically test wires which are used to bypass sections of a circuit. Although jumper wires can be purchased, they are usually fabricated from lengths of standard automotive wire and whatever type of connector (alligator clip, spade connector or pin connector) that is required for the particular application being tested. In cramped, hard-to-reach areas, it is advisable to have insulated boots over the jumper wire terminals in order to prevent accidental grounding. It is also advisable to include a standard automotive fuse in any jumper wire. This is commonly referred to as a "fused jumper". By inserting an in-line fuse holder between a set of test leads, a fused jumper wire can be used for bypassing open circuits. Use a 5 amp fuse to provide protection against voltage spikes.

Jumper wires are used primarily to locate open electrical circuits, on either the ground (-) side of the circuit or on the power (+) side. If an electrical component fails to operate, connect the jumper wire between the component and a good ground. If the component operates only with the jumper installed, the ground circuit is open. If the ground circuit is good, but the component does not operate, the circuit between the power feed and component may be open. By moving the jumper wire successively back from the component toward the power source, you can isolate the area of the circuit where the open is located. When the component stops functioning, or the power is cut off, the open is in the segment of wire between the jumper and the point previously tested.

You can sometimes connect the jumper wire directly from the battery to the "hot" terminal of the component, but first make sure the component uses 12 volts in operation. Some electrical components, such as fuel injectors, are designed to operate on about 4 volts, and running 12 volts directly to these components will cause damage.

### TEST LIGHTS

▶ See Figure 7

The test light is used to check circuits and components while electrical current is flowing through them. It is used for voltage and ground tests. To use a 12 volt test light, connect the ground clip to a good ground and probe wherever necessary with the pick. The test light will illuminate when voltage is detected. This does not necessarily mean that 12 volts (or any particular amount of voltage) is present; it only means that some voltage is present. It is advisable before using the test light to touch its ground clip and probe across the battery posts or terminals to make sure the light is operating properly.

### ✳✳ WARNING

**Do not use a test light to probe electronic ignition spark plug or coil wires. Never use a pick-type test light to probe wiring on computer controlled systems unless specifically instructed to do so. Any wire insulation that is pierced by the test light probe should be taped and sealed with silicone after testing.**

Like the jumper wire, the 12 volt test light is used to isolate opens in circuits. But, whereas the jumper wire is used to bypass the open to operate the load, the 12 volt test light is used to locate the presence of voltage in a circuit. If the test light illuminates, there is power up to that point in the circuit; if the test light does not illuminate, there is an open circuit (no power). Move the test light in successive steps back toward the power source until the light in the handle illuminates. The open is between the probe and a point which was previously probed.

The self-powered test light is similar in design to the 12 volt test light, but contains a 1.5 volt penlight battery in the handle. It is most often used in place of a multimeter to check for open or short circuits when power is isolated from the circuit (continuity test).

The battery in a self-powered test light does not provide much current. A weak battery may not provide enough power to illuminate the test light even when a complete circuit is made (especially if there is high resistance in the

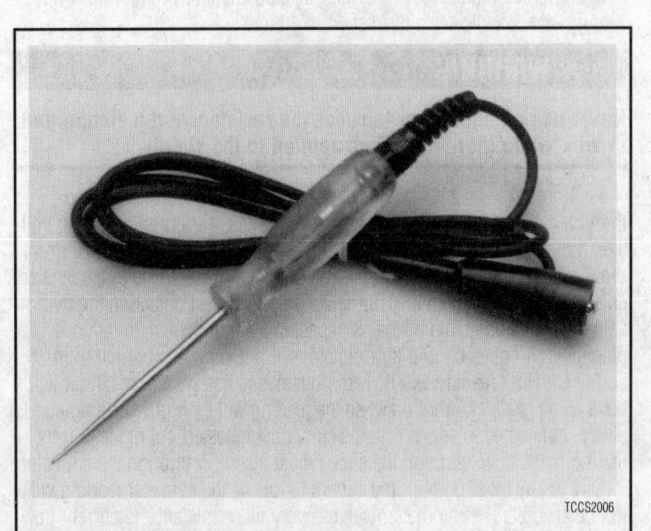

**Fig. 7 A 12 volt test light is used to detect the presence of voltage in a circuit**

## 6-6 CHASSIS ELECTRICAL

circuit). Always make sure that the test battery is strong. To check the battery, briefly touch the ground clip to the probe; if the light glows brightly, the battery is strong enough for testing.

➡ A self-powered test light should not be used on any computer controlled system or component. The small amount of electricity transmitted by the test light is enough to damage many electronic automotive components.

### MULTIMETERS

Multimeters are an extremely useful tool for troubleshooting electrical problems. They can be purchased in either analog or digital form and have a price range to suit any budget. A multimeter is a voltmeter, ammeter and ohmmeter (along with other features) combined into one instrument. It is often used when testing solid state circuits because of its high input impedance (usually 10 megaohms or more). A brief description of the multimeter main test functions follows:

• Voltmeter—the voltmeter is used to measure voltage at any point in a circuit, or to measure the voltage drop across any part of a circuit. Voltmeters usually have various scales and a selector switch to allow the reading of different voltage ranges. The voltmeter has a positive and a negative lead. To avoid damage to the meter, always connect the negative lead to the negative (-) side of the circuit (to ground or nearest the ground side of the circuit) and connect the positive lead to the positive (+) side of the circuit (to the power source or the nearest power source). Note that the negative voltmeter lead will always be black and that the positive voltmeter will always be some color other than black (usually red).

• Ohmmeter—the ohmmeter is designed to read resistance (measured in ohms) in a circuit or component. All ohmmeters will have a selector switch which permits the measurement of different ranges of resistance (usually the selector switch allows the multiplication of the meter reading by 10, 100, 1,000 and 10,000). Since the meters are powered by an internal battery, the ohmmeter can be used as a self-powered test light. When the ohmmeter is connected, current from the ohmmeter flows through the circuit or component being tested. Since the ohmmeter's internal resistance and voltage are known values, the amount of current flow through the meter depends on the resistance of the circuit or component being tested. The ohmmeter can also be used to perform a continuity test for suspected open circuits. In using the meter for making continuity checks, do not be concerned with the actual resistance readings. Zero resistance, or any ohm reading, indicates continuity in the circuit. Infinite resistance indicates an opening in the circuit. A high resistance reading where there should be none indicates a problem in the circuit. Checks for short circuits are made in the same manner as checks for open circuits, except that the circuit must be isolated from both power and normal ground. Infinite resistance indicates no continuity to ground, while zero resistance indicates a dead short to ground.

### ✷✷ WARNING

**Never use an ohmmeter to check the resistance of a component or wire while there is voltage applied to the circuit.**

• Ammeter—an ammeter measures the amount of current flowing through a circuit in units called amperes or amps. At normal operating voltage, most circuits have a characteristic amount of amperes, called "current draw" which can be measured using an ammeter. By referring to a specified current draw rating, then measuring the amperes and comparing the two values, one can determine what is happening within the circuit to aid in diagnosis. An open circuit, for example, will not allow any current to flow, so the ammeter reading will be zero. A damaged component or circuit will have an increased current draw, so the reading will be high. The ammeter is always connected in series with the circuit being tested. All of the current that normally flows through the circuit must also flow through the ammeter; if there is any other path for the current to follow, the ammeter reading will not be accurate. The ammeter itself has very little resistance to current flow and, therefore, will not affect the circuit, but it will measure current draw only when the circuit is closed and electricity is flowing. Excessive current draw can blow fuses and drain the battery, while a reduced current draw can cause motors to run slowly, lights to dim and other components to not operate properly.

### Troubleshooting Electrical Systems

When diagnosing a specific problem, organized troubleshooting is a must. The complexity of a modern automotive vehicle demands that you approach any problem in a logical, organized manner. There are certain troubleshooting techniques which are standard:

• Establish when the problem occurs. Does the problem appear only under certain conditions? Were there any noises, odors or other unusual symptoms?

Isolate the problem area. To do this, make some simple tests and observations, then eliminate the systems that are working properly. Check for obvious problems, such as broken wires and loose or dirty connections. Always check the obvious before assuming something complicated is the cause.

• Test for problems systematically to determine the cause once the problem area is isolated. Are all the components functioning properly? Is there power going to electrical switches and motors. Performing careful, systematic checks will often turn up most causes on the first inspection, without wasting time checking components that have little or no relationship to the problem.

• Test all repairs after the work is done to make sure that the problem is fixed. Some causes can be traced to more than one component, so a careful verification of repair work is important in order to pick up additional malfunctions that may cause a problem to reappear or a different problem to arise. A blown fuse, for example, is a simple problem that may require more than another fuse to repair. If you don't look for a problem that caused a fuse to blow, a shorted wire (for example) may go undetected.

Experience has shown that most problems tend to be the result of a fairly simple and obvious cause, such as loose or corroded connectors, bad grounds or damaged wire insulation which causes a short. This makes careful visual inspection of components during testing essential to quick and accurate troubleshooting.

### Testing

#### OPEN CIRCUITS

▶ See Figure 8

1. Isolate the circuit from power and ground.
2. Connect the self-powered test light or ohmmeter ground clip to a good ground and probe sections of the circuit sequentially.

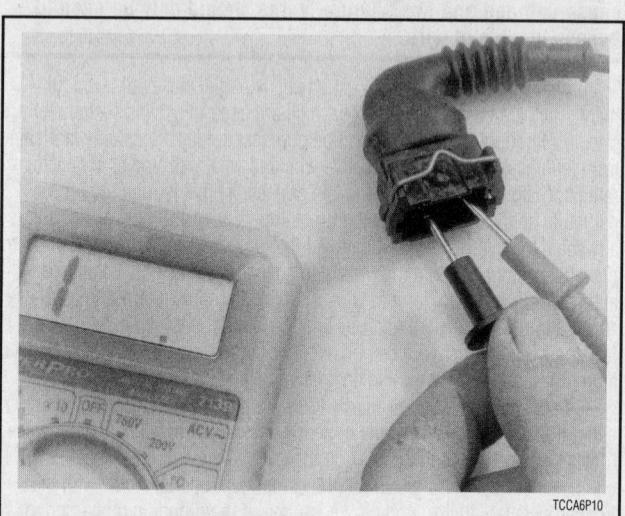

Fig. 8 The infinite reading on this multimeter (1 . ) indicates that the circuit is open

## CHASSIS ELECTRICAL  6-7

3. If the light is out or there is infinite resistance, the open is between the probe and the circuit ground.

4. If the light is on or the meter shows continuity, the open is between the probe and end of the circuit toward the power source.

### SHORT CIRCUITS

➡ **Never use a self-powered test light to perform checks for opens or shorts when power is applied to the electrical system under test. The 12 volt vehicle power will quickly burn out the light bulb in the test light.**

1. Isolate the circuit from power and ground.
2. Connect the self-powered test light or ohmmeter ground clip to a good ground and probe any easy-to-reach test point in the circuit.
3. If the light comes on or there is continuity, there is a short somewhere in the circuit.
4. To isolate the short, probe a test point at either end of the isolated circuit (the light should be on or the meter should indicate continuity).
5. Leave the test light probe engaged and sequentially open connectors or switches, remove parts, etc. until the light goes out or continuity is broken.
6. When the light goes out, the short is between the last two circuit components which were opened.

### VOLTAGE

◆ **See Figures 9 and 10**

This test determines voltage available from the battery and should be the first step in any electrical troubleshooting procedure. Many electrical problems, especially on computer controlled systems, can be caused by a low state of charge in the battery. Excessive corrosion at the battery cable terminals can cause poor contact that will prevent proper charging and full battery current flow.

1. Set the voltmeter selector switch to the 20V position.
2. Connect the multimeter negative lead to the battery's negative (-) post or terminal and the positive lead to the battery's positive (+) post or terminal.

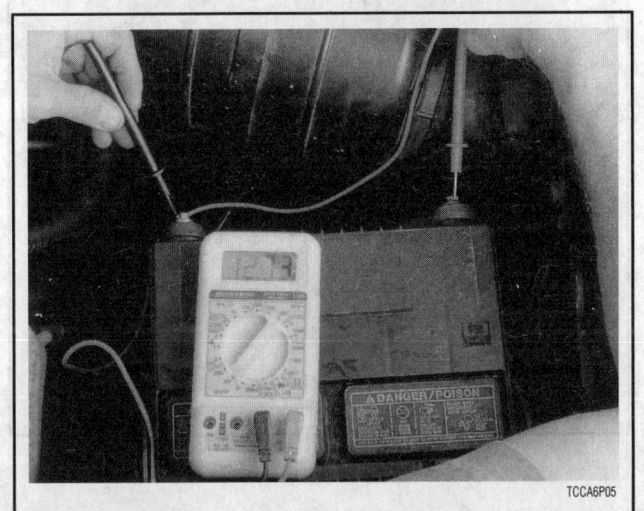

Fig. 9 Using a multimeter to check battery voltage. This battery is fully charged

Fig. 10 Testing voltage output between the alternator's BAT terminal and ground. This voltage reading is normal

3. Turn the ignition switch **ON** to provide a load.
4. A well charged battery should register over 12 volts. If the meter reads below 11.5 volts, the battery power may be insufficient to operate the electrical system properly.

### VOLTAGE DROP

◆ **See Figure 11**

When current flows through a load, the voltage beyond the load drops. This voltage drop is due to the resistance created by the load and also by small resistance's created by corrosion at the connectors and damaged insulation on the wires. The maximum allowable voltage drop under load is critical, especially if there is more than one load in the circuit, since all voltage drops are cumulative.

1. Set the voltmeter selector switch to the 20 volt position.
2. Connect the multimeter negative lead to a good ground.

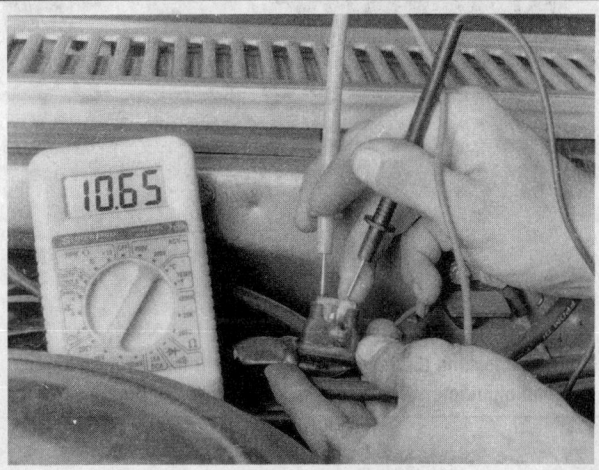

Fig. 11 This voltage drop test revealed high resistance (low voltage) in the circuit

## 6-8 CHASSIS ELECTRICAL

3. Operate the circuit and check the voltage prior to the first component (load).

4. There should be little or no voltage drop in the circuit prior to the first component. If a voltage drop exists, the wire or connectors in the circuit are suspect.

5. While operating the first component in the circuit, probe the ground side of the component with the positive meter lead and observe the voltage readings. A small voltage drop should be noticed. This voltage drop is caused by the resistance of the component.

6. Repeat the test for each component (load) down the circuit.

7. If a large voltage drop is noticed, the preceding component, wire or connector is suspect.

### RESISTANCE

♦ See Figures 12 and 13

**※※ WARNING**

**Never use an ohmmeter with power applied to the circuit. The ohmmeter is designed to operate on its own power supply. The normal 12 volt automotive electrical system current could damage the meter!**

1. Isolate the circuit from the vehicle's power source.
2. Ensure that the ignition key is **OFF** when disconnecting any components or the battery.
3. Where necessary, also isolate at least one side of the circuit to be checked, in order to avoid reading parallel resistance's. Parallel circuit resistance's will always give a lower reading than the actual resistance of either of the branches.
4. Connect the meter leads to both sides of the circuit (wire or component) and read the actual measured ohms on the meter scale. Make sure the selector switch is set to the proper ohm scale for the circuit being tested, to avoid misreading the ohmmeter test value.

Fig. 12 Checking the resistance of a coolant temperature sensor with an ohmmeter. Reading is 1.04 kilohms

### Wire and Connector Repair

Almost anyone can replace damaged wires, as long as the proper tools and parts are available. Automotive wire and terminals are available to fit almost any need. Even the specialized weatherproof, molded and hard shell connectors are now available from aftermarket suppliers.

Be sure the ends of all the wires are fitted with the proper terminal hardware and connectors. Wrapping a wire around a stud is never a permanent solution and will only cause trouble later. Replace wires one at a time to avoid confusion. Always route wires exactly the same as the factory.

➡**If connector repair is necessary, only attempt it if you have the proper tools. Weatherproof and hard shell connectors require special tools to release the pins inside the connector. Attempting to repair these connectors with conventional hand tools will damage them.**

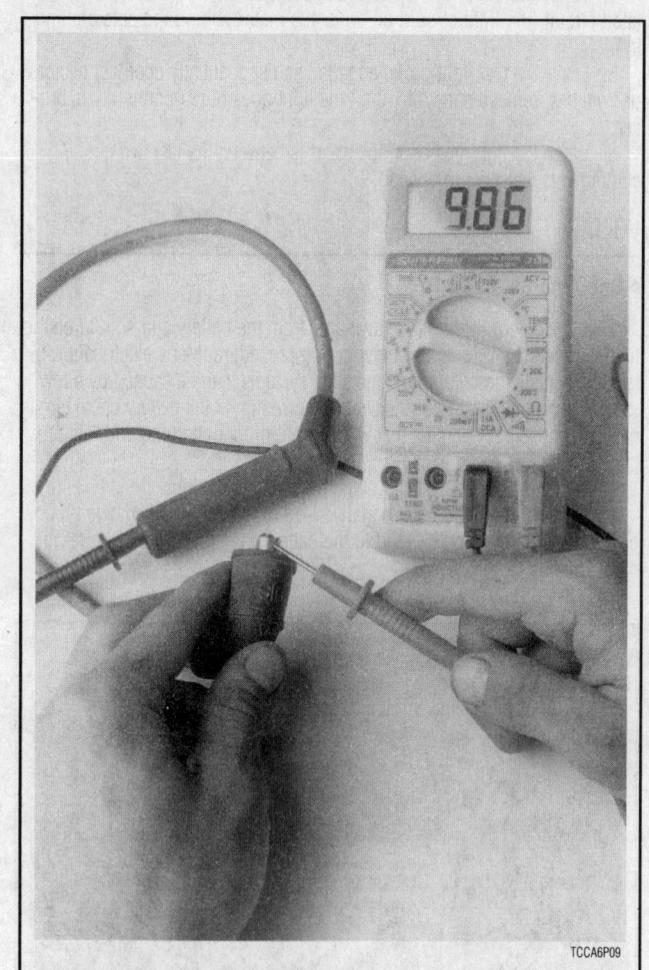

Fig. 13 Spark plug wires can be checked for excessive resistance using an ohmmeter

## CHASSIS ELECTRICAL 6-9

### BATTERY CABLES

#### Disconnecting The Cables

When working on any electrical component on the vehicle, it is always a good idea to disconnect the negative (-) battery cable. This will prevent potential damage to many sensitive electrical components such as the Engine Control Module (ECM), radio, alternator, etc.

➡ Any time you disengage the battery cables, it is recommended that you disconnect the negative (-) battery cable first. This will prevent your accidentally grounding the positive (+) terminal to the body of the vehicle when disconnecting it, thereby preventing damage to the above mentioned components.

Before you disconnect the cable(s), first turn the ignition to the **OFF** position. This will prevent a draw on the battery which could cause arcing (electricity trying to ground itself to the body of a vehicle, just like a spark plug jumping the gap) and, of course, damaging some components such as the alternator diodes.

When the battery cable(s) are reconnected (negative cable last), be sure to check that your lights, windshield wipers and other electrically operated safety components are all working correctly. If your vehicle contains an Electronically Tuned Radio (ETR), don't forget to also reset your radio stations. Ditto for the clock.

### AIR BAG (SUPPLEMENTAL RESTRAINT SYSTEM)

#### General Information

▶ See Figure 14

The air bag system used on Previa vans is referred to as the Supplemental Restraint System (SRS). The SRS provides additional protection for the driver (and front passenger on later models) if a forward collision of sufficient force is encountered. The SRS assists the normal seatbelt restraining system by deploying an air bag, via the steering column.

The center air bag sensor is the heart of the SRS. It consists of safing sensors, ignition control and drive circuit, diagnosis circuit, etc. The center air bag receives signals from the air bag sensors and determines whether the air bag must be activated or not. The center air bag sensor is also used to diagnose system malfunctions.

The air bag warning light circuit is equipped with an electrical connection check mechanism which detects when the connector to the center air bag sensor assembly is not properly connected.

All connectors in the air bag system are colored yellow. These connectors use gold-plated terminals with twin-lock mechanism. This design assures positive locking; there-by, preventing the terminals from coming apart.

#### SYSTEM OPERATION

When the ignition switch is turn to the **ON** or **ACC** position, the air bag warning lamp will turned on for approximately 6 seconds. If no malfunctions are detected in the system, after the 6 second period have elapse, the warning light will go **OFF**.

The safing sensors are designed to trip at a lower deceleration rate than the front or center air bag sensor. When the vehicle is involved in a frontal collision, the shock is great enough to overcome the predetermine level of the front or center air bag sensor. When a safing sensor and a front air bag sensor and/or the center air bag sensor trip simultaneously, it causes the squib of the air bag to ignite and the air bag is deployed automatically. The inflated bag breaks open the steering wheel pad.

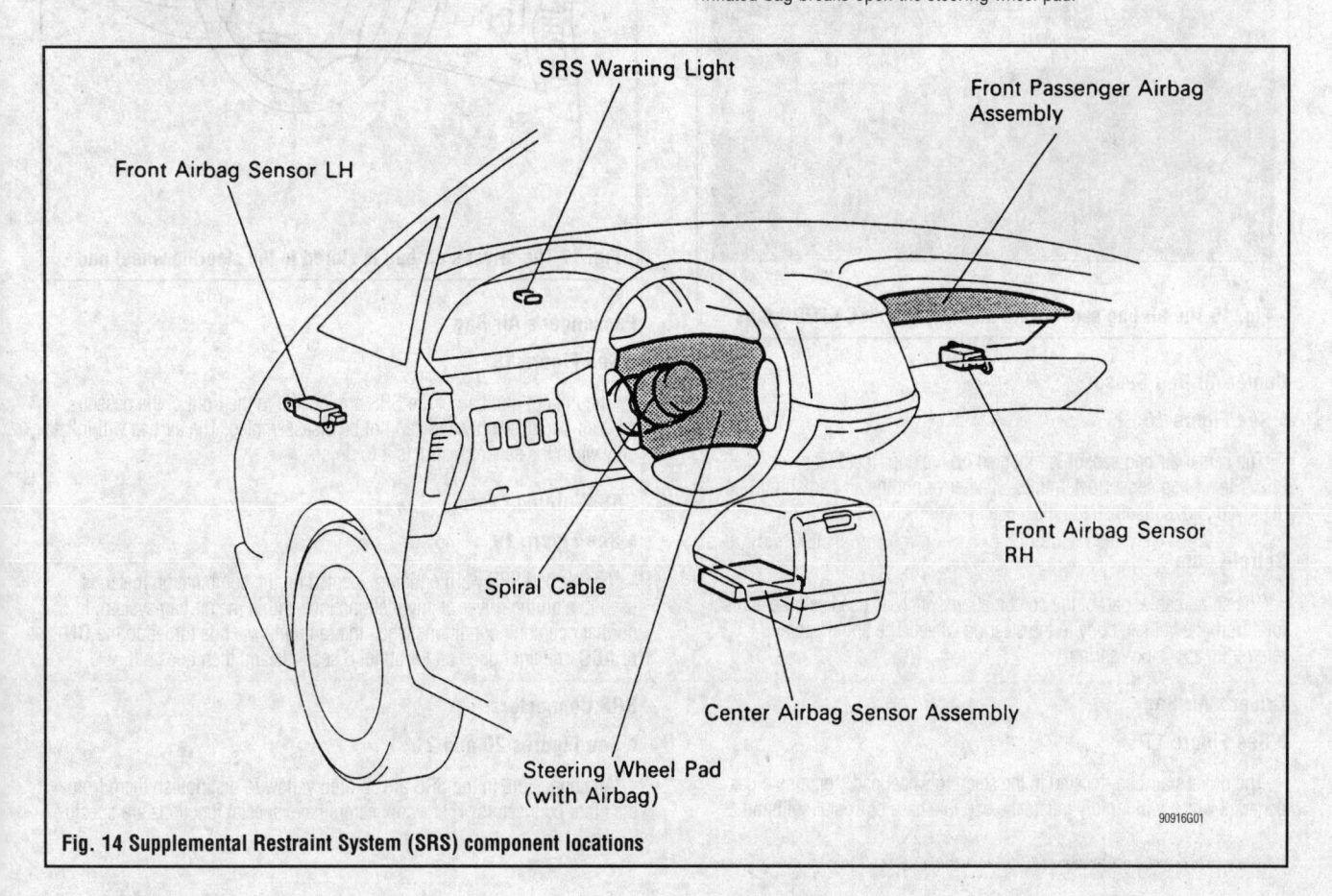

Fig. 14 Supplemental Restraint System (SRS) component locations

# 6-10 CHASSIS ELECTRICAL

After air bag deployment have occurred, the gas is discharged through the discharge holes provided behind the bag. The bag become deflated as a result.

The connector of the air bag contains a short spring plate, which provides an activation prevention mechanism. When the connector is disconnected, the short spring plate automatically connects the power source and grounding terminals of the inflator module (squib).

## SYSTEM COMPONENTS

### Front Air Bag Sensors

♦ See Figure 15

A front air bag sensor is mounted inside each of the front fenders. The sensor unit is basically a mechanical switch. When the sensor detects a deceleration force above a predetermined level in a collision, the contacts in the sensor close, sending a signal to the center air bag sensor assembly. The sensor cannot be disassembled. If the front fenders on the vehicle are damaged in any way, do a visual check of the sensors even if the air bag is not deployed. Inspect for:
- Bracket deformation
- Peeling of paint
- Cracks, dents or chips in the case
- Cracks, chipping or dents in the wiring connector
- Peeling of the label or damage to the series number

Fig. 15 The air bag sensors are all labeled with CAUTION tags

### Center Air Bag Sensor

♦ See Figure 16

The center air bag sensor is mounted on the floor inside the console box. The air bag sensor determines whether or not the air bag should be deployed and is also used to diagnose system malfunction.

### Spiral Cable

The spiral cable, part of the combination switch, is used as an electrical joint from the vehicle body to the steering wheel. The spiral cable is referred to as a clock spring.

### Driver's Air Bag

♦ See Figure 17

The driver's air bag, located in the steering wheel pad, contains a gas generant which will rapidly inflate the bag in a case of frontal collision.

Fig. 16 The center air bag sensor is mounted on the floor inside the console box

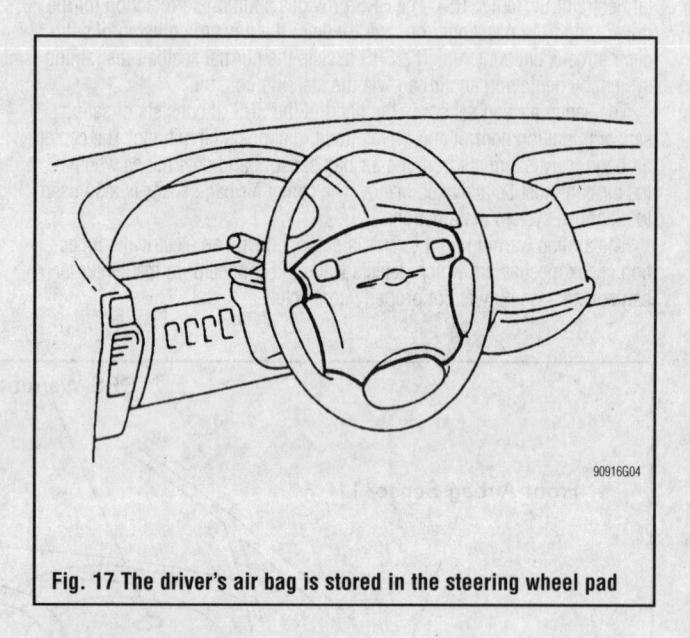

Fig. 17 The driver's air bag is stored in the steering wheel pad

### Passenger's Air Bag

♦ See Figure 18

The inflator and bag of the SRS are located in the front of the passenger's air bag assembly and can not be disassembled. The air bag will inflate only when the sensor instructs it to do so.

### SRS Warning Lamp

♦ See Figure 19

The air bag SRS warning lamp, located on the combination meter, is used to alert the driver of any malfunctions within the air bag system. In normal operating conditions when the ignition switch is turned to the **ON** or **ACC**, the light goes on for about 6 seconds and then goes off.

### SRS Connectors

♦ See Figures 20 and 21

All connectors in the SRS are colored yellow to distinguish them from the other connectors. These connectors have special functions are specifi-

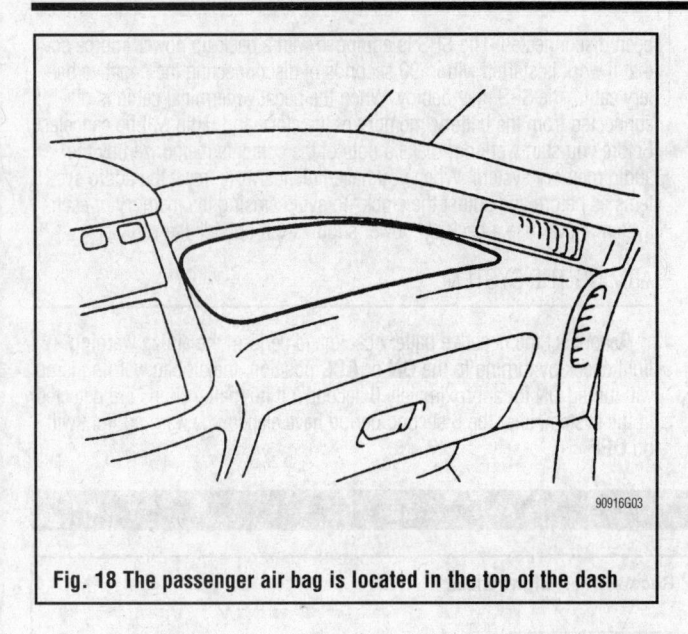

# CHASSIS ELECTRICAL 6-11

Fig. 18 The passenger air bag is located in the top of the dash

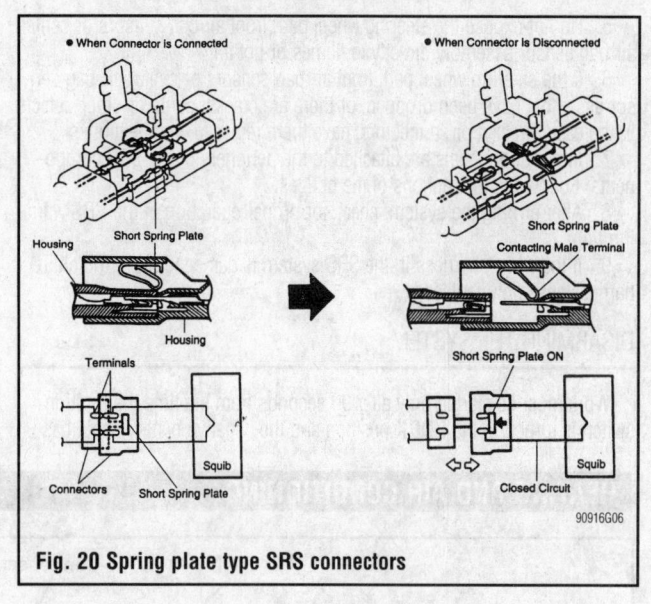

Fig. 20 Spring plate type SRS connectors

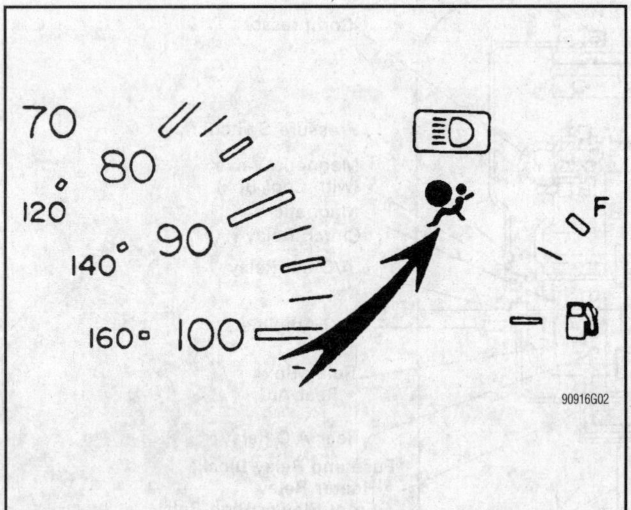

cally designed for the SRS. These connectors use durable gold-plated terminals.

## SERVICE PRECAUTIONS

1. Work must be started after 90 seconds from the time the ignition switch is turned to the **LOCK** position and the negative battery cable has been disconnected. The SRS is equipped with a back-up power source so that if work is started within 90 seconds of disconnecting the negative battery cable, the SRS may deploy. When the negative terminal cable is disconnected from the battery, memory of the clock and radio will be canceled. Before you start working, make a note of the contents memorized by the audio memory system. When you have finished working, reset the audio systems and adjust the clock. Never use a back-up power supply from outside the vehicle.

2. In the event that of a minor frontal collision where the air bag does not deploy, the steering wheel pad, front air bag sensors and center air bag sensor assembly should be inspected.

3. Before repairs, remove the air bag sensors if shocks are likely to be applied to the sensors during repairs.

4. Never disassemble and repair the steering wheel pad, front air bag sensors or center air bag sensors.

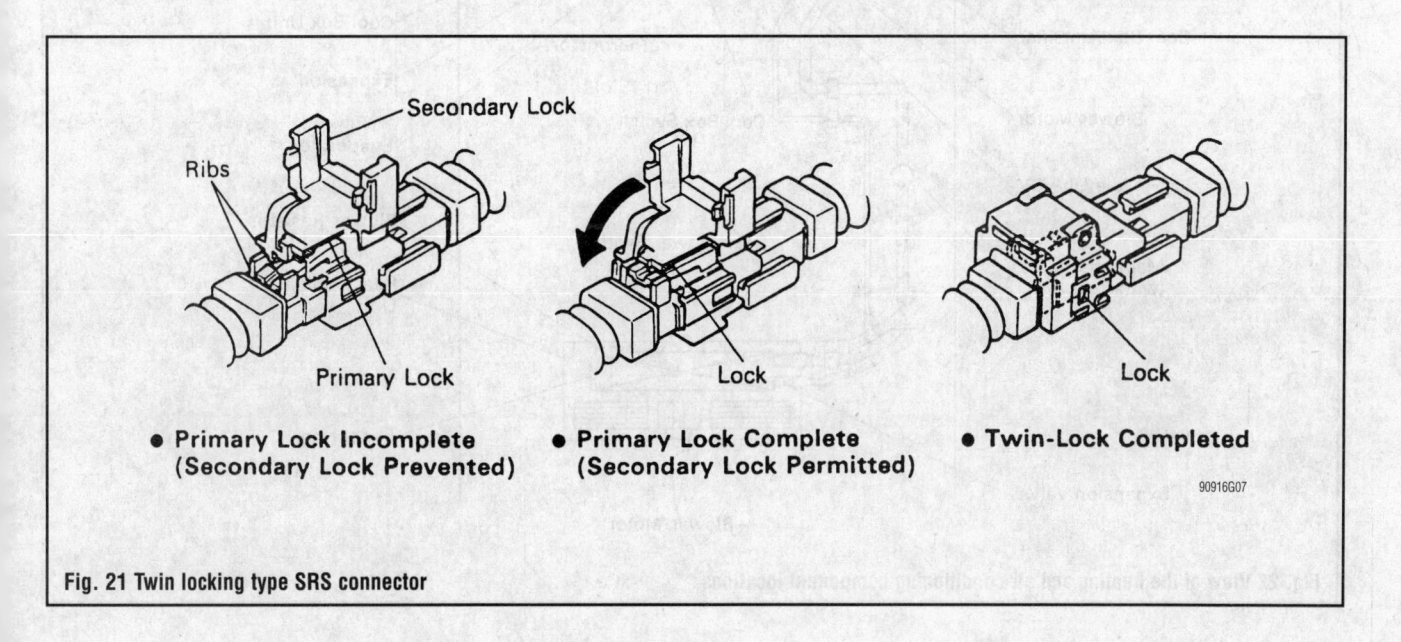

Fig. 19 The air bag warning lamp is located on the combination meter

Fig. 21 Twin locking type SRS connector

## 6-12 CHASSIS ELECTRICAL

5. Do not expose the steering wheel pad, front air bag sensors or center air bag sensor assembly directly to flames or hot air.

6. If the steering wheel pad, front air bag sensors or center air bag sensor assembly have been dropped, or there are cracks, dents or other defects in the case, bracket or connectors, have them replaced with new ones.

7. Information labels are attached to the periphery of the SRS components. Follow the instructions of the notices.

8. After arming the system, check for proper operation of the SRS warning light.

9. If the wiring harness in the SRS system is damaged, have the entire harness assembly replaced.

### DISARMING THE SYSTEM

Work must be started only after 90 seconds from the time the ignition switch is turned to the **LOCK** position and the negative battery cable has been disconnected. The SRS is equipped with a back-up power source so that if work is started within 90 seconds of disconnecting the negative battery cable, the SRS may deploy. When the negative terminal cable is disconnected from the battery, memory of the clock and radio will be canceled. Before you start working, make a note of the contents memorized by the audio memory system. When you have finished work, reset the audio systems as before and adjust the clock. To avoid erasing the memory of each system, never use a back-up power supply from outside the vehicle.

### ARMING THE SYSTEM

Reconnect the negative battery cable and perform the airbag warning light check by turning to the **ON** or **ACC** position, the air bag warning lamp will turned ON for approximately 6 seconds. If no malfunctions are detected in the system, after the 6 second period have elapse, the warning light will go **OFF**.

## HEATING AND AIR CONDITIONING

Fig. 22 View of the heating and air conditioning component locations

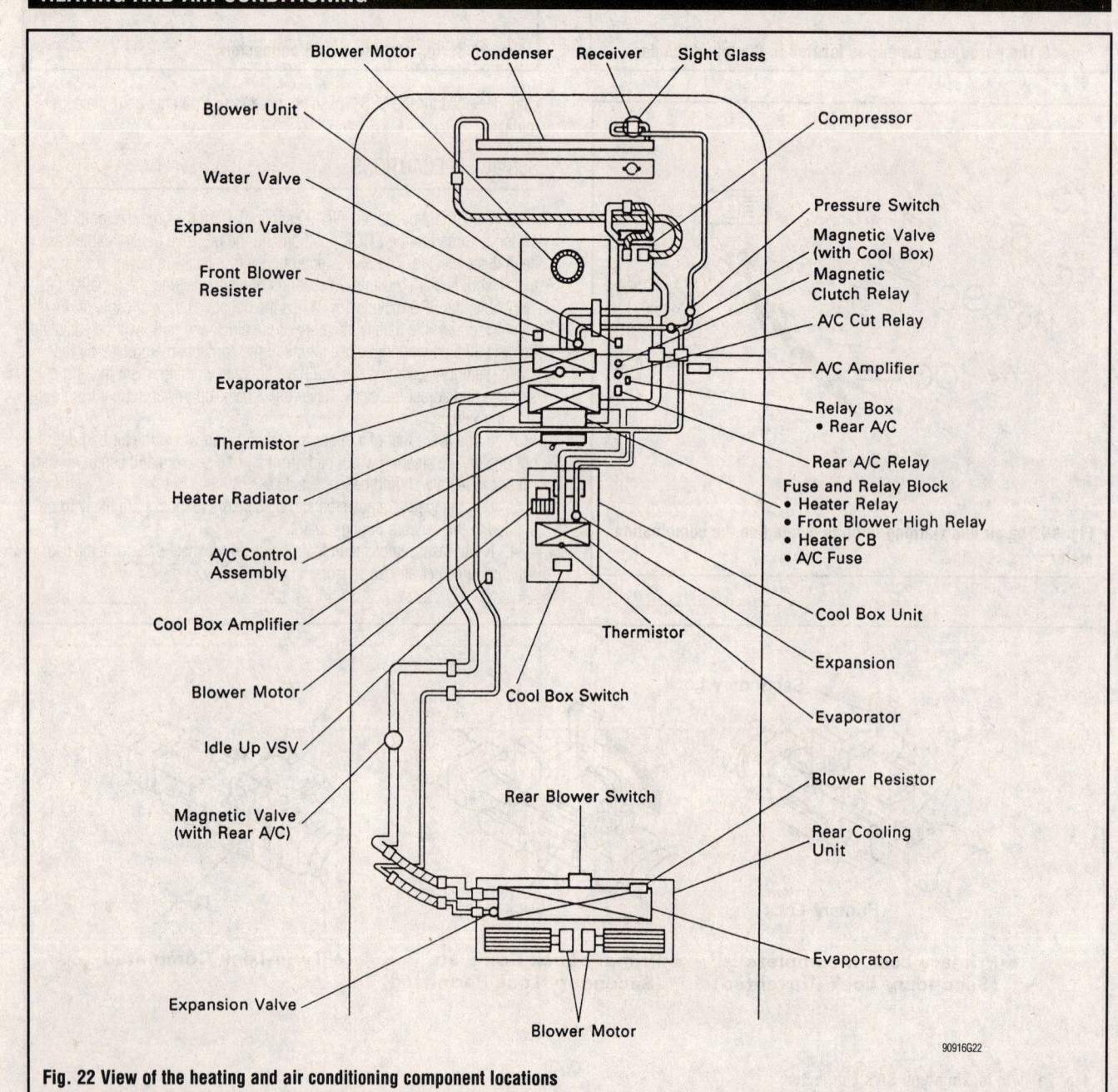

# CHASSIS ELECTRICAL  6-13

## Blower Motor

### REMOVAL & INSTALLATION

**Front**

► See Figures 23 thru 35

→ It may be necessary to remove the upper radiator shroud to perform this procedure.

1. Open and support the hood.
2. Disconnect the negative battery cable and wait at least 90 seconds to proceed working on the vehicle.
3. Disconnect the power steering and coolant reservoirs.
4. Disconnect the coolant reservoir and power steering brackets from the side of the heating unit box.
5. Remove the two bolts that attach the upper and lower portion of the heater box.
6. Disconnect the control cable on the side of the heater unit box.
7. Remove the eight nuts retaining the unit.

Fig. 23 Disconnect the coolant reservoir

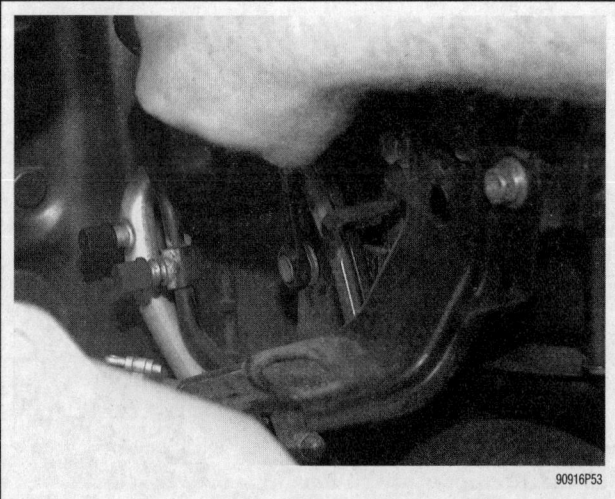

Fig. 24 Remove the coolant reservoir bracket from the side of the heater unit

Fig. 25 Separate the power steering reservoir bracket from the side of the unit also

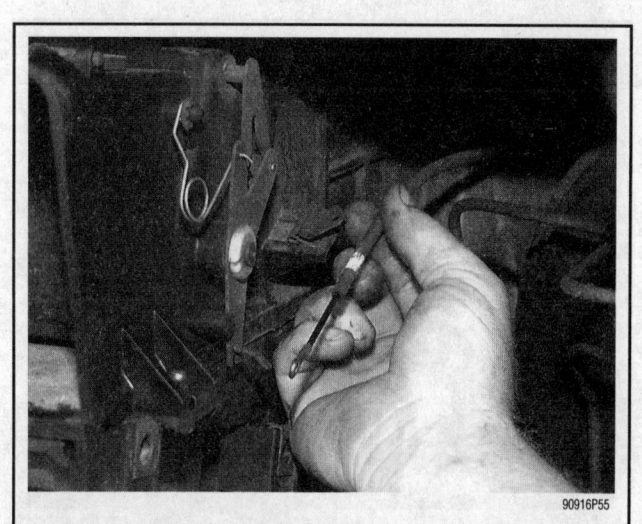

Fig. 26 Disconnect the control cable on the drivers side of the unit

Fig. 27 Remove the nuts (8) from around the heater unit

## 6-14 CHASSIS ELECTRICAL

Fig. 28 There are 4 nuts on each side of the unit

Fig. 29 Separate the upper case from the lower

Fig. 30 Disconnect all wiring leading to the lower heater box

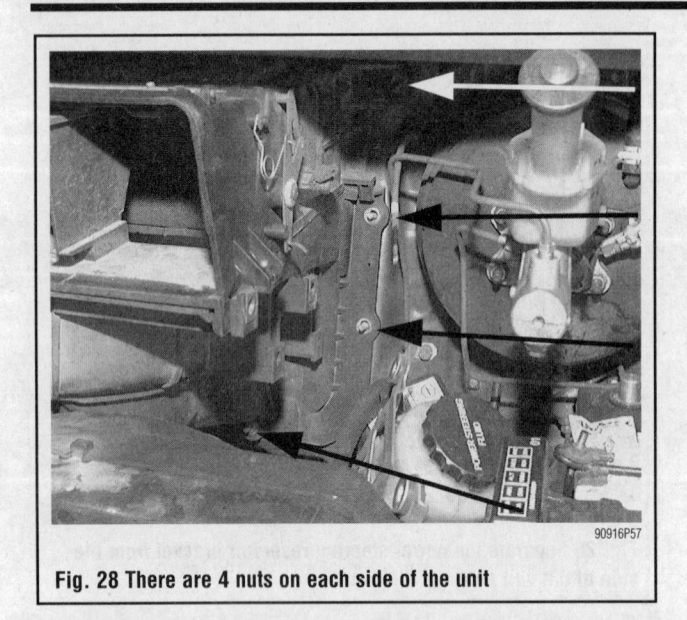

Fig. 31 Extract the lower housing from the vehicle

Fig. 32 Pull the cover off of the bottom of the housing to access the motor

Fig. 33 Pull the blower tube . . .

## CHASSIS ELECTRICAL  6-15

**Fig. 34 . . . and wiring from the motor**

**Fig. 35 Remove the motor with cage out of the lower box**

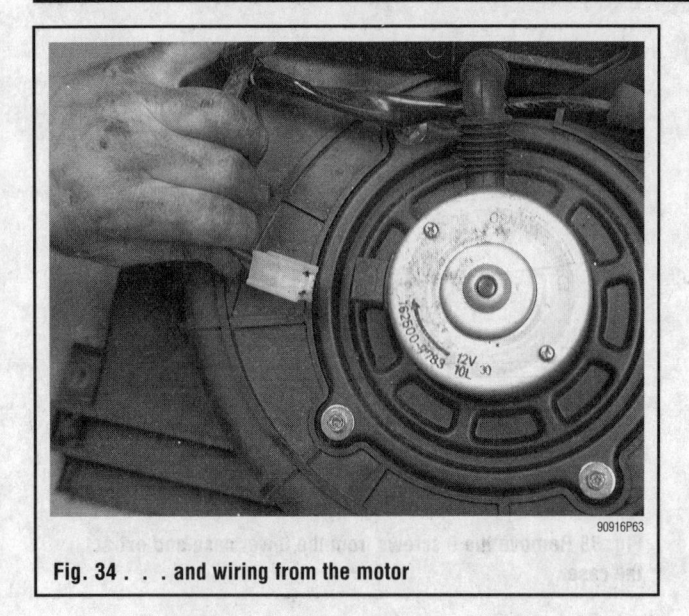

8. Disconnect the heater control valve bracket from the heater box.
9. Separate the top of the control box from the bottom.
10. Label and disconnect all wiring harnesses attached to the lower unit. These are the A/C compressor switch and A/C pressure switch wires along with the two upper white harnesses.
11. Extract the lower housing assembly with the motor and cage from the vehicle.
12. Remove the four lower cover retaining bolts.
13. Disconnect the blower tube, wiring harness and four mounting bolts.

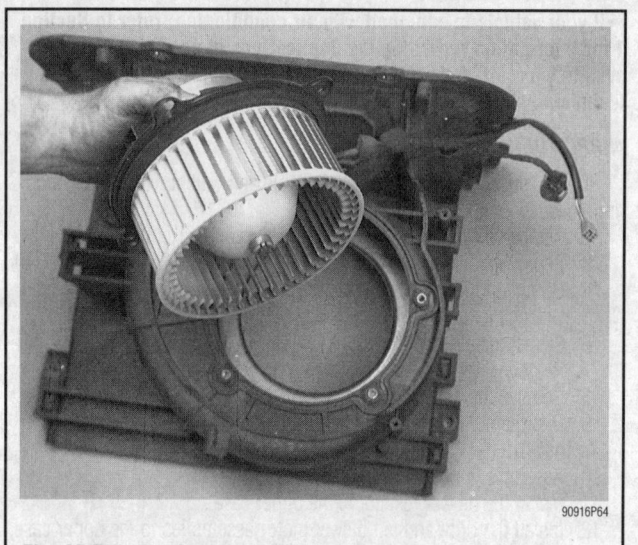

14. Pull the motor with cage from the lower heater housing.
15. Install the blower motor assembly into the housing in the reverse order of removal. Secure all components and wiring harnesses.

### Rear

▶ See Figure 36

It is not necessary to remove the entire rear cooling unit to access the blower motor assemblies.

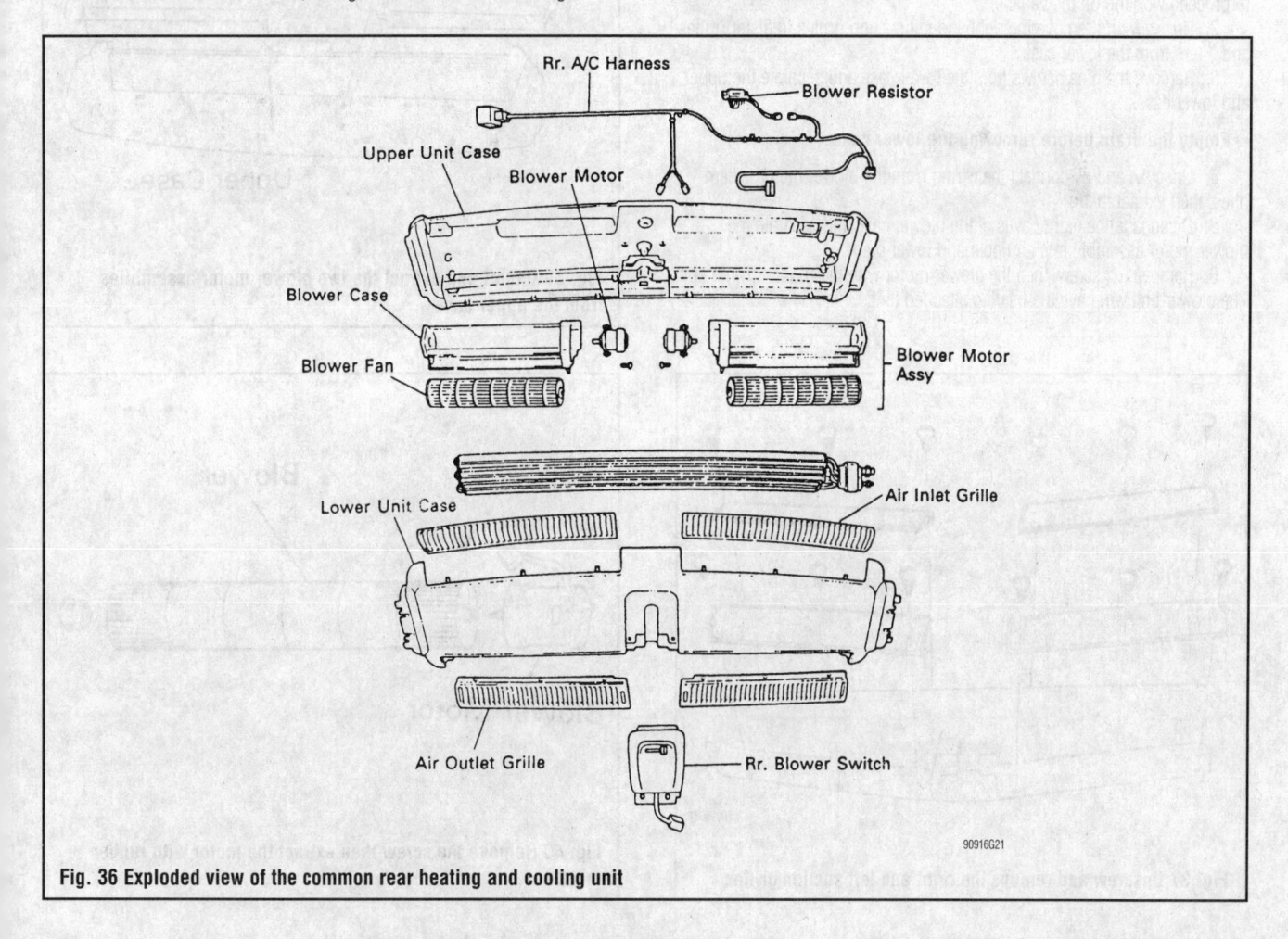

**Fig. 36 Exploded view of the common rear heating and cooling unit**

## 6-16 CHASSIS ELECTRICAL

→If your vehicle is equipped with air conditioning, refer to Section 1 for information regarding the implications of servicing your A/C system yourself. Only a MVAC-trained, EPA-certified, automotive technician should service the A/C system or its components.

### NIPPONDENSO

1. Disconnect the negative battery cable and wait at least 90 seconds to proceed working on the vehicle.
2. Remove the right and left air inlet grilles and air outlet grilles.
3. Remove the filter.
4. Unbolt and remove the lower case.
5. Disengage the rear A/C switch.
6. Extract the evaporator assembly.
7. Remove the right and left blower motor assemblies.
8. Remove the blower resistor.
9. Disassemble the blower motor assemblies to access the motors.

**To install:**
10. Assemble the blower motor assemblies.
11. Install the blower resistor to the upper case.
12. Install the right and left blower motor assemblies to the upper case.
13. Install the evaporator assembly to the upper case.
14. Attach the rear A/C switch to the lower case.
15. Secure the lower case to the upper case.
16. Install the filter.
17. Attach the right and left air inlet grilles and air outlet grilles.
18. Connect the negative battery cable.

### PANASONIC

▶ See Figures 37, 38, 39 and 40

1. Disconnect the negative battery cable and wait at least 90 seconds to proceed working on the vehicle.
2. Unscrew and remove the right and left suction grilles, register grilles and filters from the lower case.
3. Remove the nine screws from the lower case and separate the upper and lower cases.

→Empty the drain before removing the lower case.

4. Unscrew and disconnect the wiring from the blower motor assemblies, then extract them.
5. Disengage the eight pawls of the blower case and separate the blower motor assembly into an upper and lower piece.
6. Remove the screw, then the blower motor with the rubber grommet. The blower unit will have the bearing attached to it.

Fig. 38 Remove the 9 screws from the lower case and extract the case

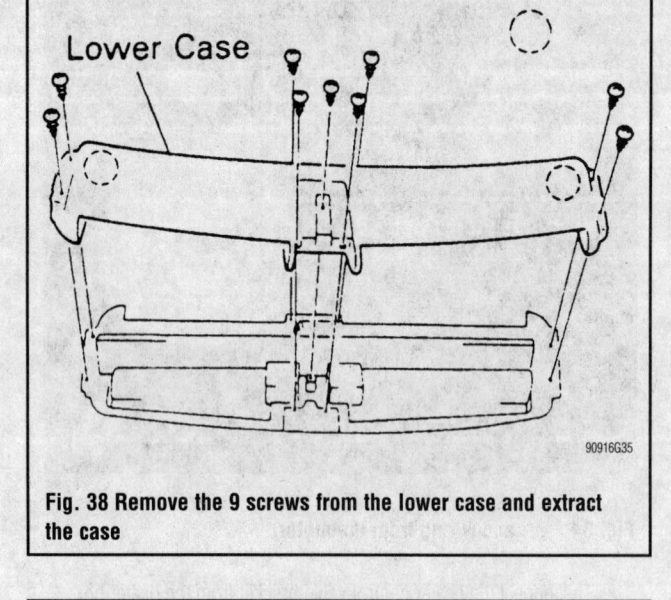

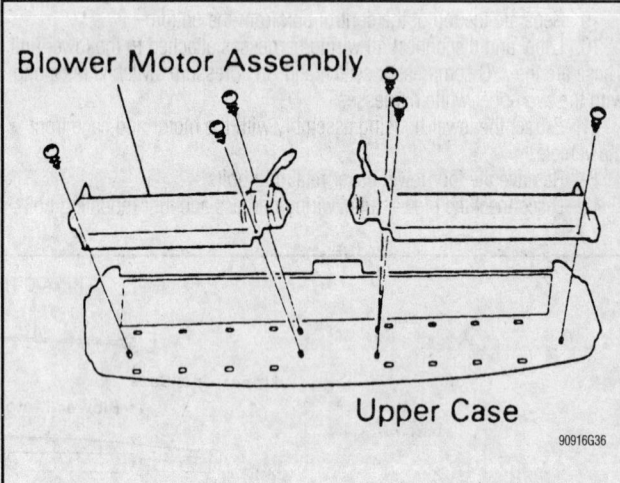

Fig. 39 Unbolt and extract the two blower motor assemblies from the upper case

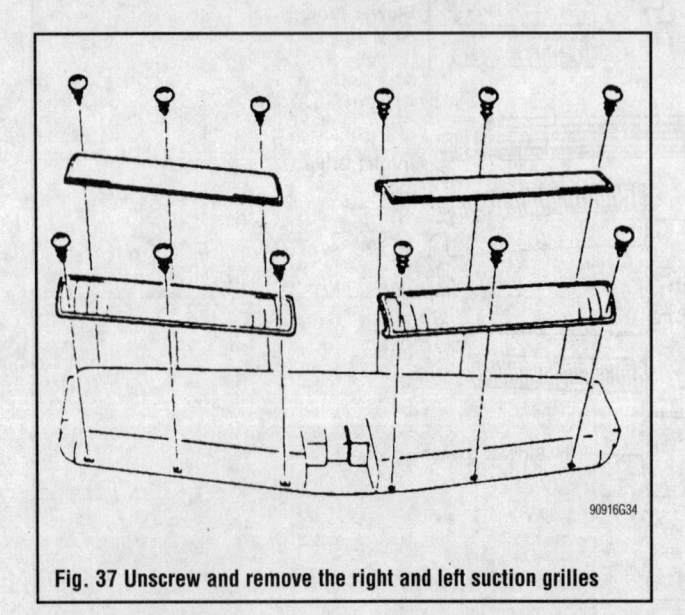

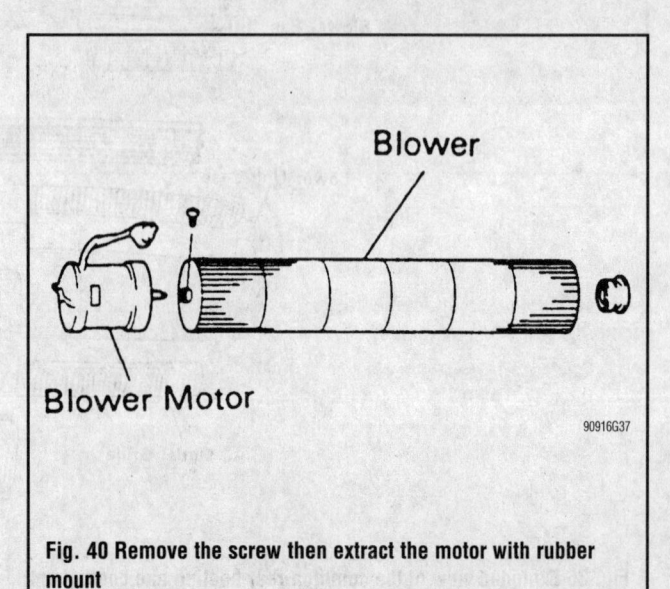

Fig. 37 Unscrew and remove the right and left suction grilles

Fig. 40 Remove the screw then extract the motor with rubber mount

## CHASSIS ELECTRICAL  6-17

➡ You can first remove the blower motor and the blower before separating them.

**To install:**
7. To assemble the motor assembly:
   a. Temporarily secure the blower to the blower motor.
   b. Place the blower motor unit on the blower lower case.
   c. Visually adjust the blower protrusion so that the clearance between the blower and the blower case on the right side is equal to that of the left side.
   d. Tighten the screw and check that the blower rotates smoothly. Assemble the blower upper case to the lower case.
8. Install the blower motor assembly to the upper case.
9. Install the lower case and secure it to the upper case.
10. Install the right and left air filters to the lower case.
11. Install the right and left suction grills, and the register grill to the lower case.
12. Connect the negative battery cable.

### Blower Motor Resistor

#### REMOVAL & INSTALLATION

Remove the front blower motor unit assembly from the vehicle. Remove the two retaining screws and extract the resister from the housing. Insert the resister into the housing and secure with the screws. Install the blower motor housing into the vehicle. Refer to Blower Motor (front) removal and installation in this section.

### Ice Box Motor

#### REMOVAL & INSTALLATION

1. Disconnect the negative battery cable. Wait at least 90 seconds on models equipped with an airbag after disconnection.
2. Remove the cool/ice box amplifier if necessary.
3. Detach the upper case from the ice box assembly.
4. Unbolt and disconnect the wiring from the blower motor, then extract the motor from the lower case.

**To install:**
5. Connect the wiring of the motor to the harness.
6. Attach and secure the blower motor inside the ice box.
7. Attach the upper cover to the lower portion of the box.
8. Install the amplifier if removed.
9. Connect the negative battery cable.

### Heater Water Control Valve

#### REMOVAL & INSTALLATION

1. Partially drain the engine coolant
2. Mark and disconnect the cable from the heater control valve.
3. Disconnect the heater hoses from the heater control valve.

➡ Be careful not to pull on the heater core tubes when removing the heater hoses, since the heater core can be easily damaged.

4. Remove the bolt and the heater control valve.

**To install:**
5. Install the bolt and the heater control valve.
6. Connect the heater hoses to the heater control valve, making sure that the hoses and the clamps are past the outer flaring of the heater control valve tubes. Use new clamps.
7. Install the control cable to its premarked position.
8. Fill the cooling system, then start and warm the engine, making sure it stays full.

9. Stop the engine, pressure test the cooling system and check for leaks. Check for proper heater operation.

### Air Conditioning Components

#### REMOVAL & INSTALLATION

Repair or service of air conditioning components is not covered by this manual, because of the risk of personal injury or death, and because of the legal ramifications of servicing these components without the proper EPA certification and experience. Cost, personal injury or death, environmental damage, and legal considerations (such as the fact that it is a federal crime to vent refrigerant into the atmosphere), dictate that the A/C components on your vehicle should be serviced only by a Motor Vehicle Air Conditioning (MVAC) trained, and EPA certified automotive technician.

➡ If your vehicle's A/C system uses R-12 refrigerant and is in need of recharging, the A/C system can be converted over to R-134a refrigerant (less environmentally harmful and expensive). Refer to Section 1 for additional information on R-12 to R-134a conversions, and for additional considerations dealing with your vehicle's A/C system.

### Control Cables

#### REMOVAL & INSTALLATION

1. Remove the control panel.
2. Disengage the adjusting clip at the heater/cooling unit end of the cable.
3. Disengage the end of the control cable from the control lever.
4. Remove the cable from the vehicle.

**To install:**
5. Attach the cable to the end of the lever on the A/C or heater box.
6. Route the cable through the dash to the control lever and secure to the back of the unit.
7. Adjust the cable.
8. Install the control panel.

#### ADJUSTMENT

**Air Inlet Door**

♦ See Figure 41

1. Disengage the control cable from the lever at the heater/cooling unit end of the cable.

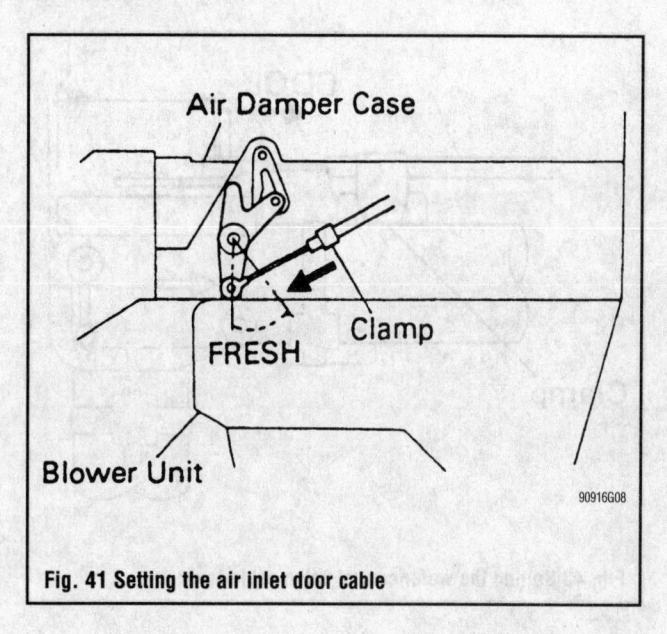

Fig. 41 Setting the air inlet door cable

## 6-18　CHASSIS ELECTRICAL

2. Set both the air inlet door and the control panel to the FRESH position. Then, slide the control cable through the adjusting clip until the eyelet on the cable end can be engaged to the lever. Make sure the cable is secured.

3. Move the control levers left and right and check for stiffness or binding through the full range of the levers. Test control cable operation.

### Air Mix Door
▶ See Figure 42

1. Disengage the control cable from the lever at the heater/cooling unit end of the cable.

2. Set both the air mix door and the control panel to the COOL position. Then, slide the control cable through the adjusting clip until the eyelet on the cable end can be engaged to the lever. Make sure the cable is secured.

3. Move the control levers left and right and check for stiffness or binding through the full range of the levers. Test control cable operation.

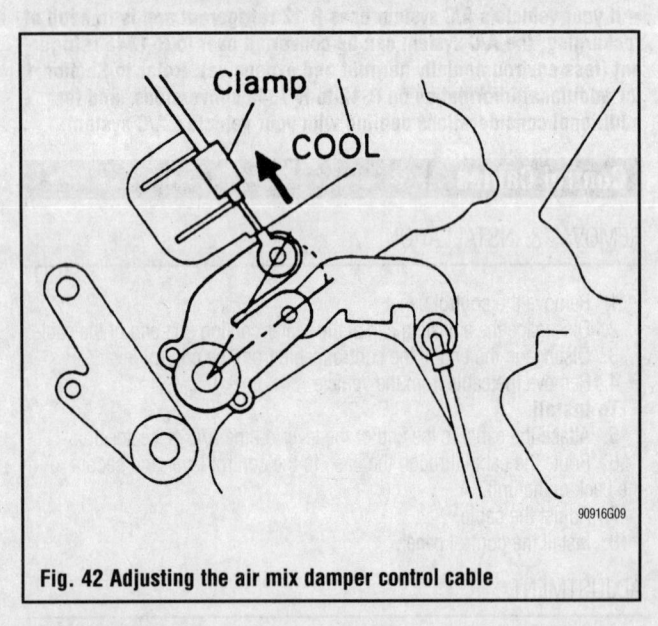

Fig. 42 Adjusting the air mix damper control cable

### Water Control Valve
▶ See Figure 43

1. Disengage the adjusting clip.
2. Place the water valve lever on the COOL position while pushing the outer cable in the COOL direction. Clamp the outer cable to the water valve bracket with the adjusting clip.

3. Move the control levers left and right and check for stiffness or binding through the full range of the levers. Test control cable operation.

### Mode Damper Control
▶ See Figure 44

1. Set the mode damper and the control lever to the VENT position, install the control cable and lock the clamp.

2. Slide the control cable through the adjusting clip until the eyelet on the cable end can be engaged to the lever. Make sure the cable is secured.

3. Move the control levers left and right and check for stiffness or binding through the full range of the levers. Test control cable operation.

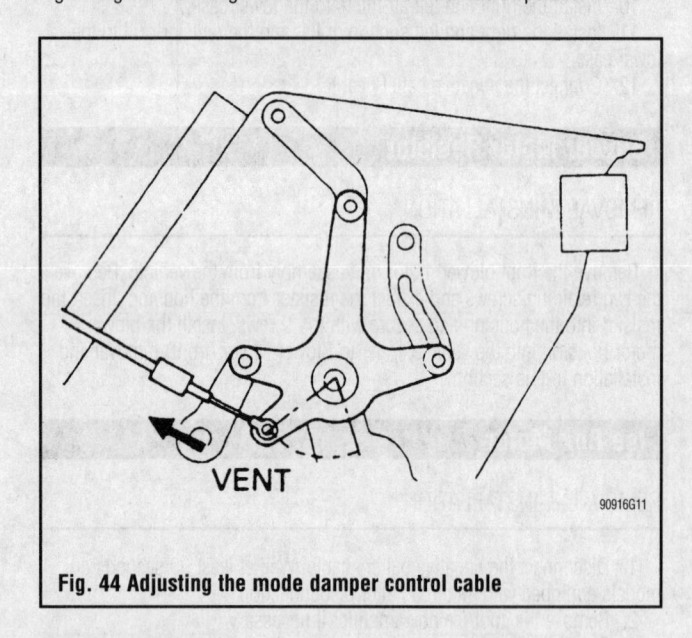

Fig. 44 Adjusting the mode damper control cable

### Rear Heat Damper
▶ See Figure 45

1. Set the rear damper and the control lever to the RR HEAT position, the install the control cable and lock the clamp.

2. Slide the control cable through the adjusting clip until the eyelet on the cable end can be engaged to the lever. Make sure the cable is secured.

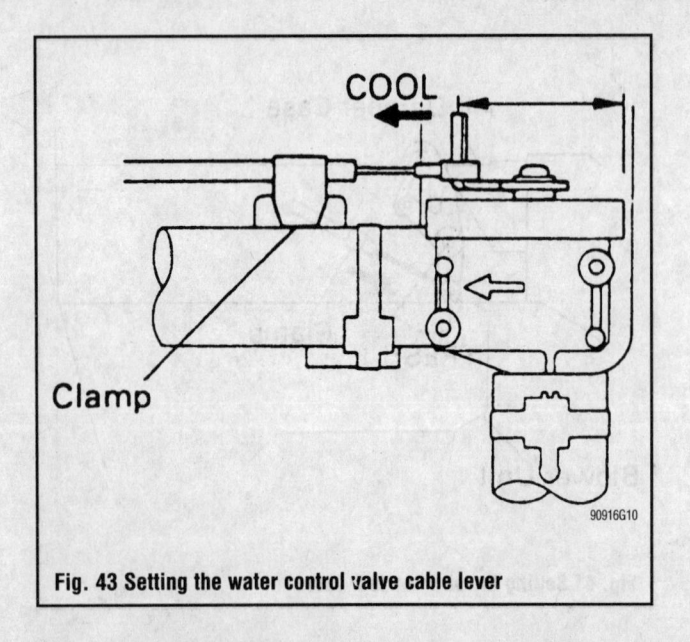

Fig. 43 Setting the water control valve cable lever

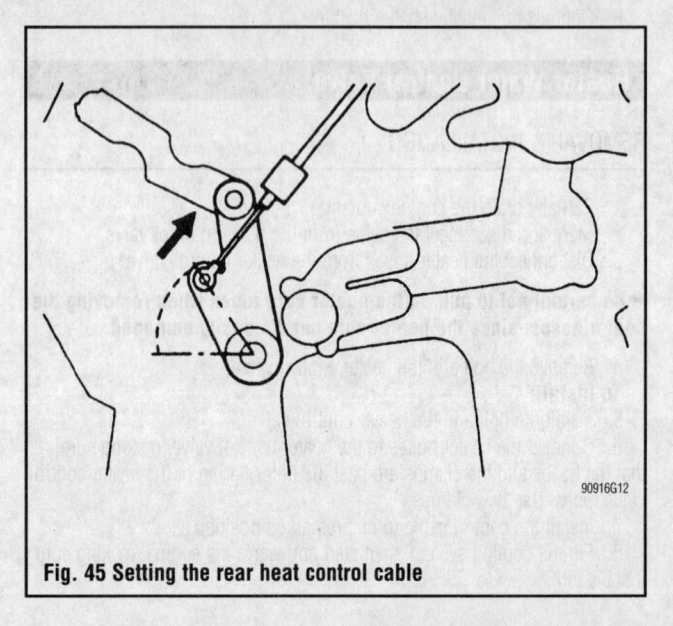

Fig. 45 Setting the rear heat control cable

## CHASSIS ELECTRICAL 6-19

3. Move the control levers left and right and check for stiffness or binding through the full range of the levers. Test control cable operation.

### Side Vent Duct

▶ See Figure 46

1. Set the side vent, duct and the mode control lever to VENT position, then install the control cable and lock the clamp.
2. Then, slide the control cable through the adjusting clip until the eyelet on the cable end can be engaged to the lever. Make sure the cable is secured.
3. Move the control levers left and right and check for stiffness or binding through the full range of the levers. Test control cable operation.

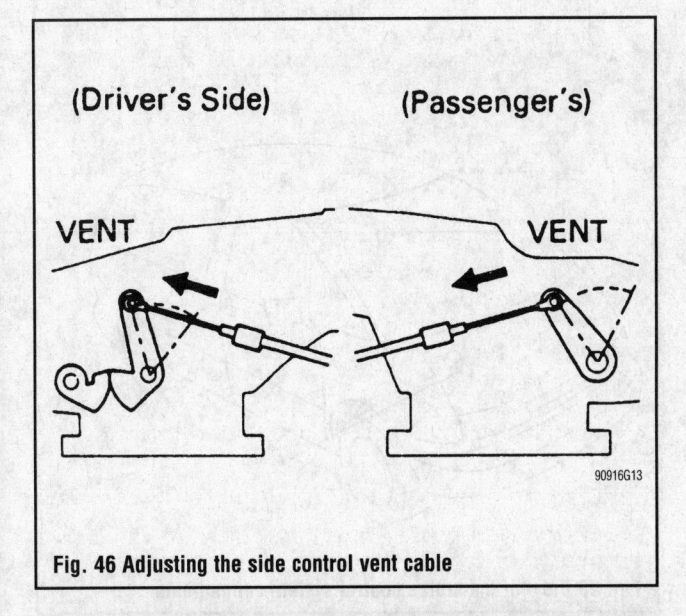

Fig. 46 Adjusting the side control vent cable

### Control Panel

#### REMOVAL & INSTALLATION

▶ See Figures 47, 48 and 49

1. Disconnect the negative battery cable.
2. Remove the console box located below the ashtray.
3. Remove the ashtray retaining screws and disconnect the wiring.
4. Pull off the knobs prior to control panel removal.
5. Carefully pull out the center cluster finish panel.
6. Remove the control panel by removing the 4 screws.

**To install:**

7. Installation is the reverse of removal. Use care when snapping back together plastic components, if so equipped.

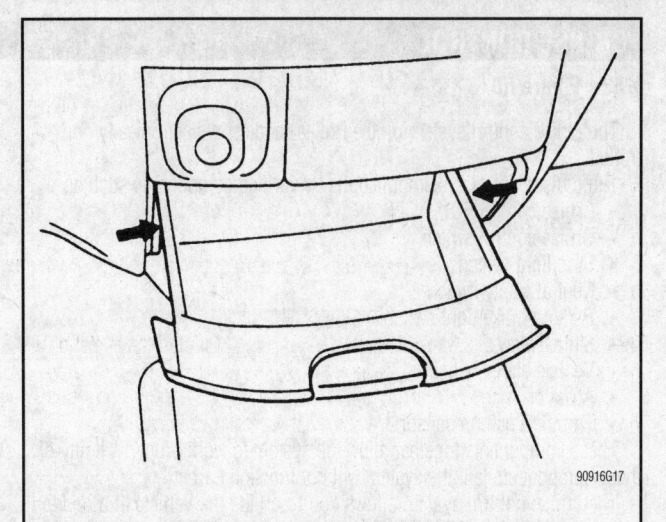

Fig. 47 Press on the sides of the box while pulling outward to extract the console

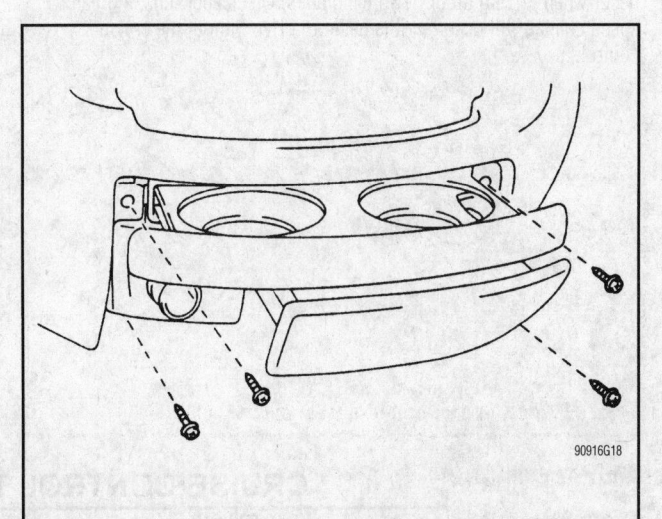

Fig. 48 Remove the four screws and retainer to extract the ash tray

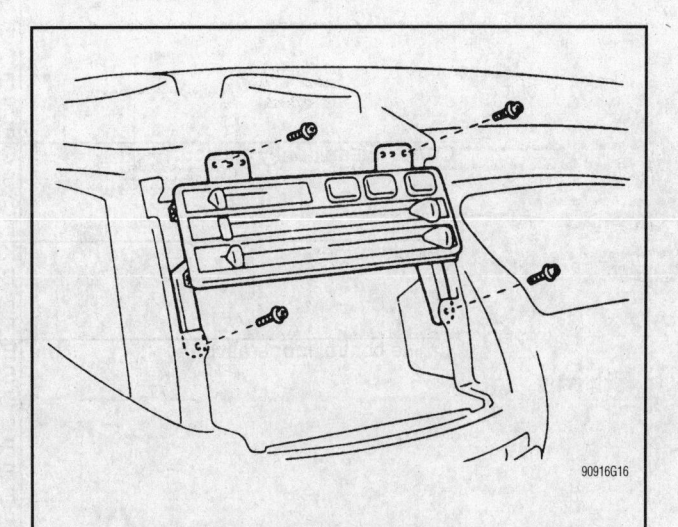

Fig. 49 Remove the four screws surrounding the control assembly and extract the unit from the dash

## CHASSIS ELECTRICAL

### CRUISE CONTROL

▶ See Figure 50

The cruise control system on the Previa models is electronically controlled.

The cruise control system functions by various components such as:
- Cruise control ECU
- Cruise control switch
- Stop light switch
- Neutral safety switch
- Parking brake light switch
- Starter relay
- Vehicle speed sensor
- Actuator
- Throttle Position sensor

These components together allow the system to work properly. If any of these components fail, the system will not function correctly.

The cruise control system allows you to cruise the vehicle at a desired speed over 25 mph (40 km) even when your foot is off the accelerator pedal. The cruising speed is maintained up or down grades within the limits of the engine performance, although a slight speed change may occur when driving up or down the grades. On steeper hills, a greater speed change will occur so it is better to drive without the cruise control.

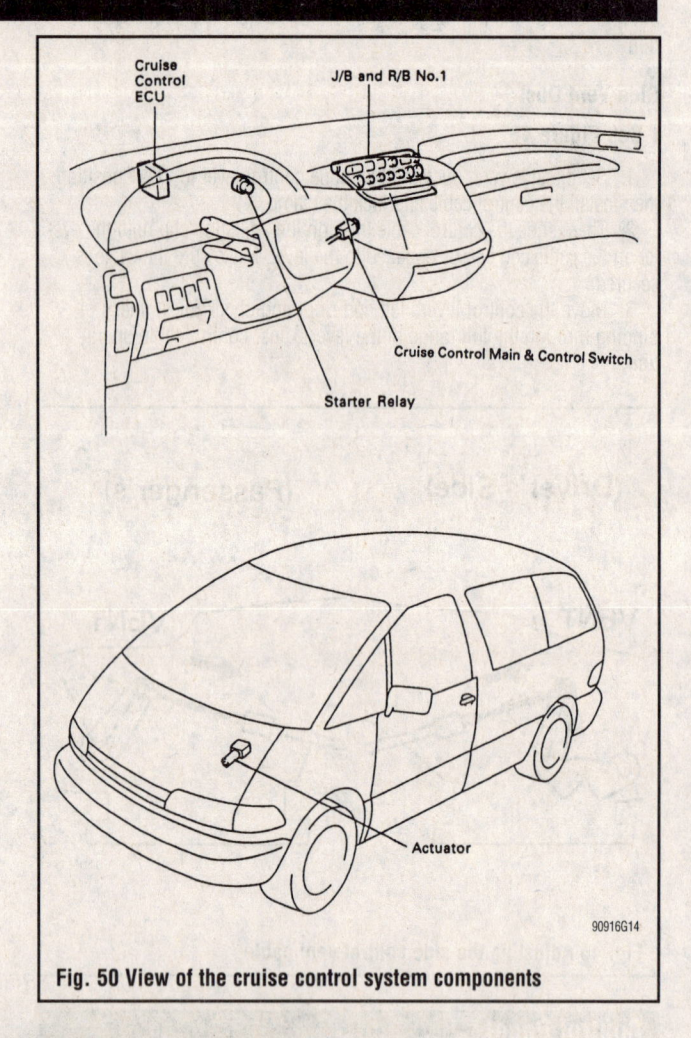

Fig. 50 View of the cruise control system components

### CRUISE CONTROL TROUBLESHOOTING

| Problem | Possible Cause |
|---|---|
| Will not hold proper speed | Incorrect cable adjustment<br>Binding throttle linkage<br>Leaking vacuum servo diaphragm<br>Leaking vacuum tank<br>Faulty vacuum or vent valve<br>Faulty stepper motor<br>Faulty transducer<br>Faulty speed sensor<br>Faulty cruise control module |
| Cruise intermittently cuts out | Clutch or brake switch adjustment too tight<br>Short or open in the cruise control circuit<br>Faulty transducer<br>Faulty cruise control module |
| Vehicle surges | Kinked speedometer cable or casing<br>Binding throttle linkage<br>Faulty speed sensor<br>Faulty cruise control module |
| Cruise control inoperative | Blown fuse<br>Short or open in the cruise control circuit<br>Faulty brake or clutch switch<br>Leaking vacuum circuit<br>Faulty cruise control switch<br>Faulty stepper motor<br>Faulty transducer<br>Faulty speed sensor<br>Faulty cruise control module |

Note: Use this chart as a guide. Not all systems will use the components listed.

tcca6c01

# CHASSIS ELECTRICAL 6-21

## ENTERTAINMENT SYSTEMS

### Radio Receiver/Amplifier/Tape Player/CD Player

REMOVAL & INSTALLATION

▶ See Figures 51, 52 and 53

1. Disconnect the negative battery cable.

**⁂ CAUTION**

On models with an airbag, wait at least 90 seconds from the time that the ignition switch is turned to the LOCK position and the battery is disconnected before performing any further work.

2. Remove the attaching screws from the trim panel.
3. Remove the trim panel, being careful of the concealed spring clips behind the panel.
4. Disconnect the wiring from the switches if so equipped mounted in the trim panel.
5. Remove the mounting screws from the radio.
6. Remove the radio from the dash until the wiring connectors are exposed.
7. Disconnect the electrical harness and the antenna cable from the body of the radio and remove the radio from the vehicle.

**To install:**

8. Reconnect all the wiring and antenna cable first, then place the radio in position within the dash.

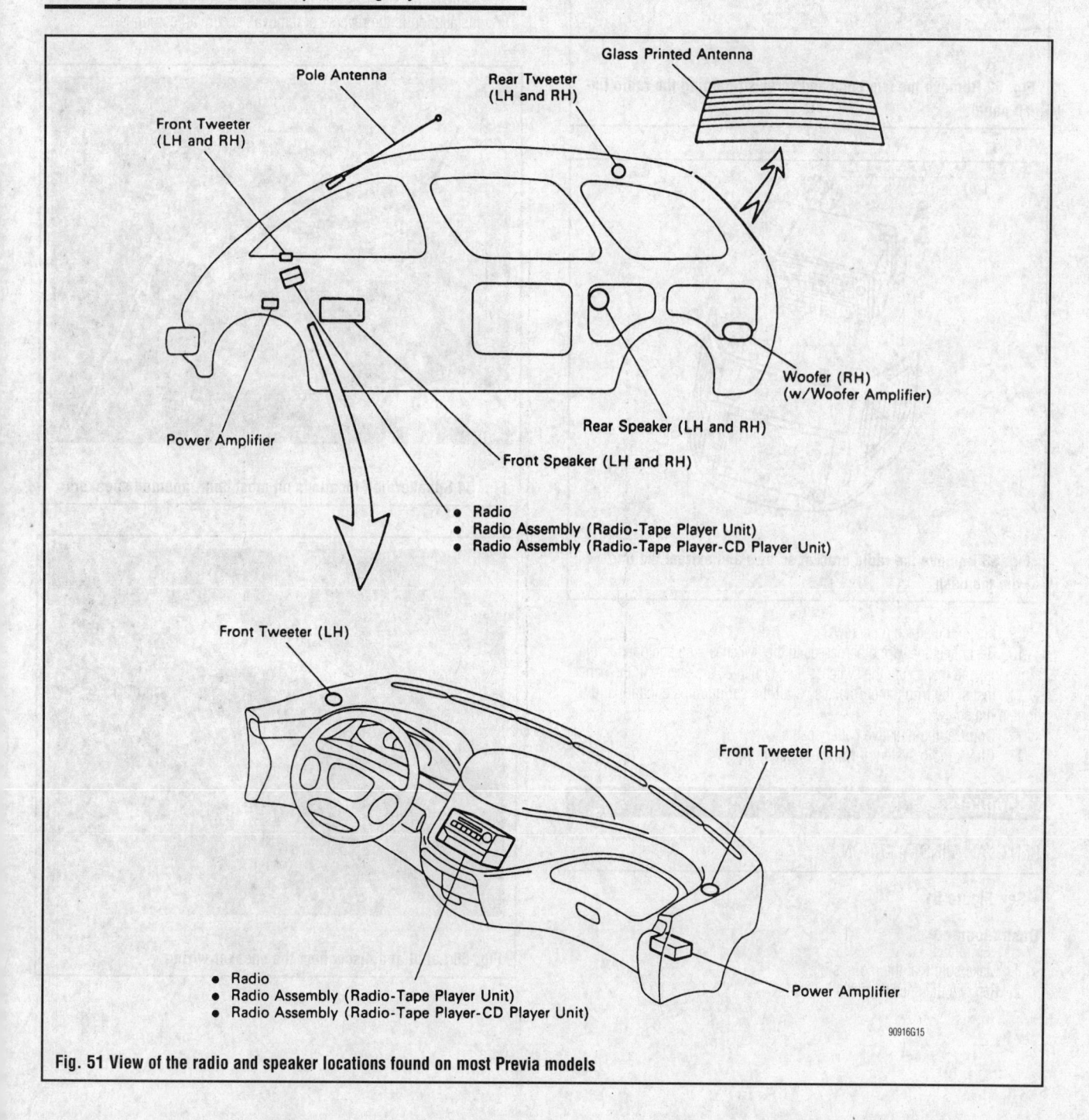

Fig. 51 View of the radio and speaker locations found on most Previa models

# 6-22 CHASSIS ELECTRICAL

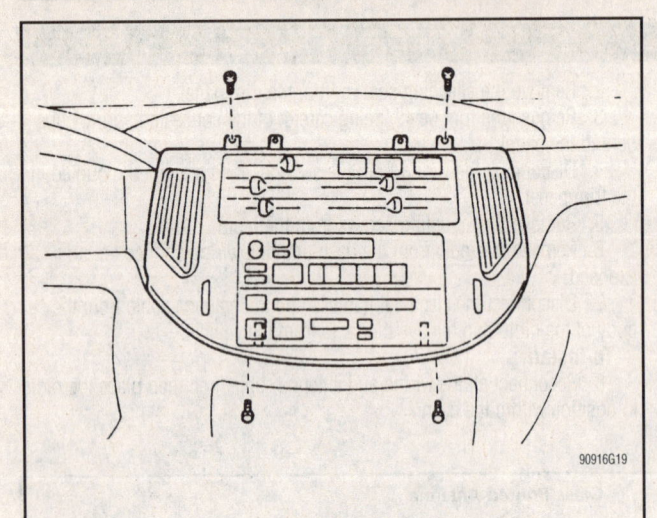

**Fig. 52 Remove the two bolts and screws retaining the radio finish panel**

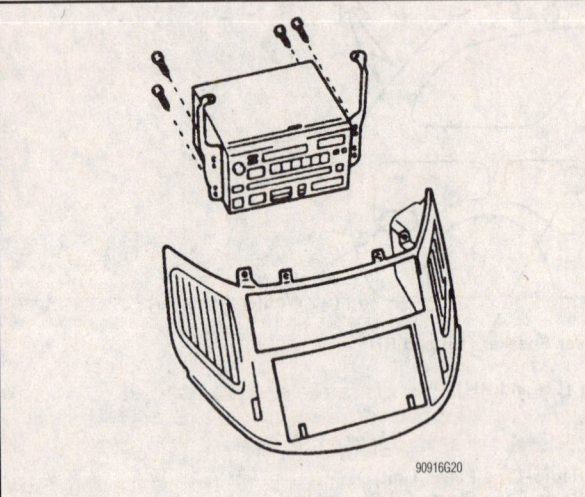

**Fig. 53 Remove the radio bracket screws and extract the unit from the dash**

3. Remove the instrument panel box (some models).
4. Label and disconnect the speaker wires.
5. Remove the screws and extract the speaker.
6. Installation is the reverse of removal be sure to secure all components.

**Door Mounted**

▶ See Figures 54 and 55

1. Make sure that the radio is off.
2. On some models the armrest must be removed.
3. If equipped remove the power window switch or manual window handle.
4. Remove the upper door panel, then the lower door panel.
5. Label and disconnect the speaker wires.
6. Remove the 3 screws and the speaker.
7. Installation is the reverse of removal, secure all components.

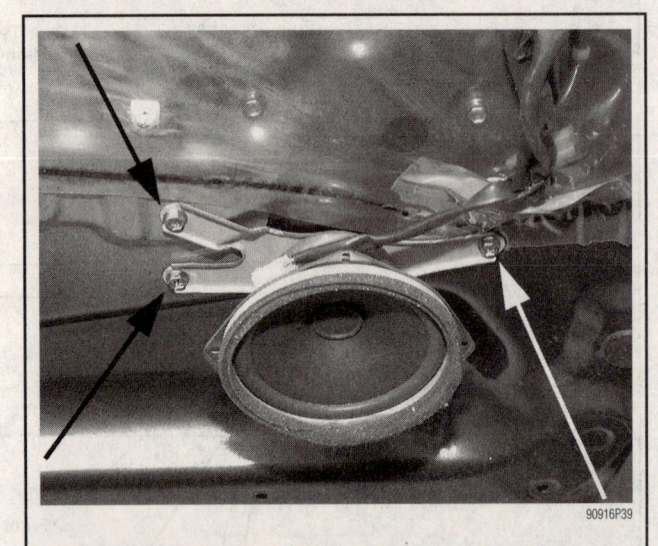

**Fig. 54 Speaker bolt locations on most door mounted speakers**

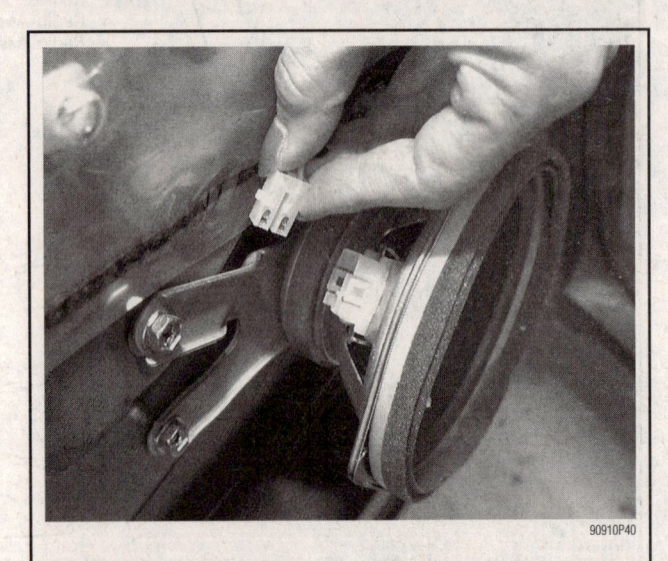

**Fig. 55 Label and disconnect the speaker wiring**

9. Install the attaching screws.
10. Reconnect the wiring harnesses to the switches if so equipped in the trim panel and make sure the switches if so equipped are secure in the panel.
11. Install the trim panel (make sure all the spring clips engage) and tighten the screws.
12. Connect the negative battery cable.
13. Check radio system for proper operation.

## Speakers

### REMOVAL & INSTALLATION

▶ See Figure 51

**Dash Mounted**

1. Make sure that the radio is off.
2. Remove the speaker panel.

# CHASSIS ELECTRICAL  6-23

## WINDSHIELD WIPERS AND WASHERS

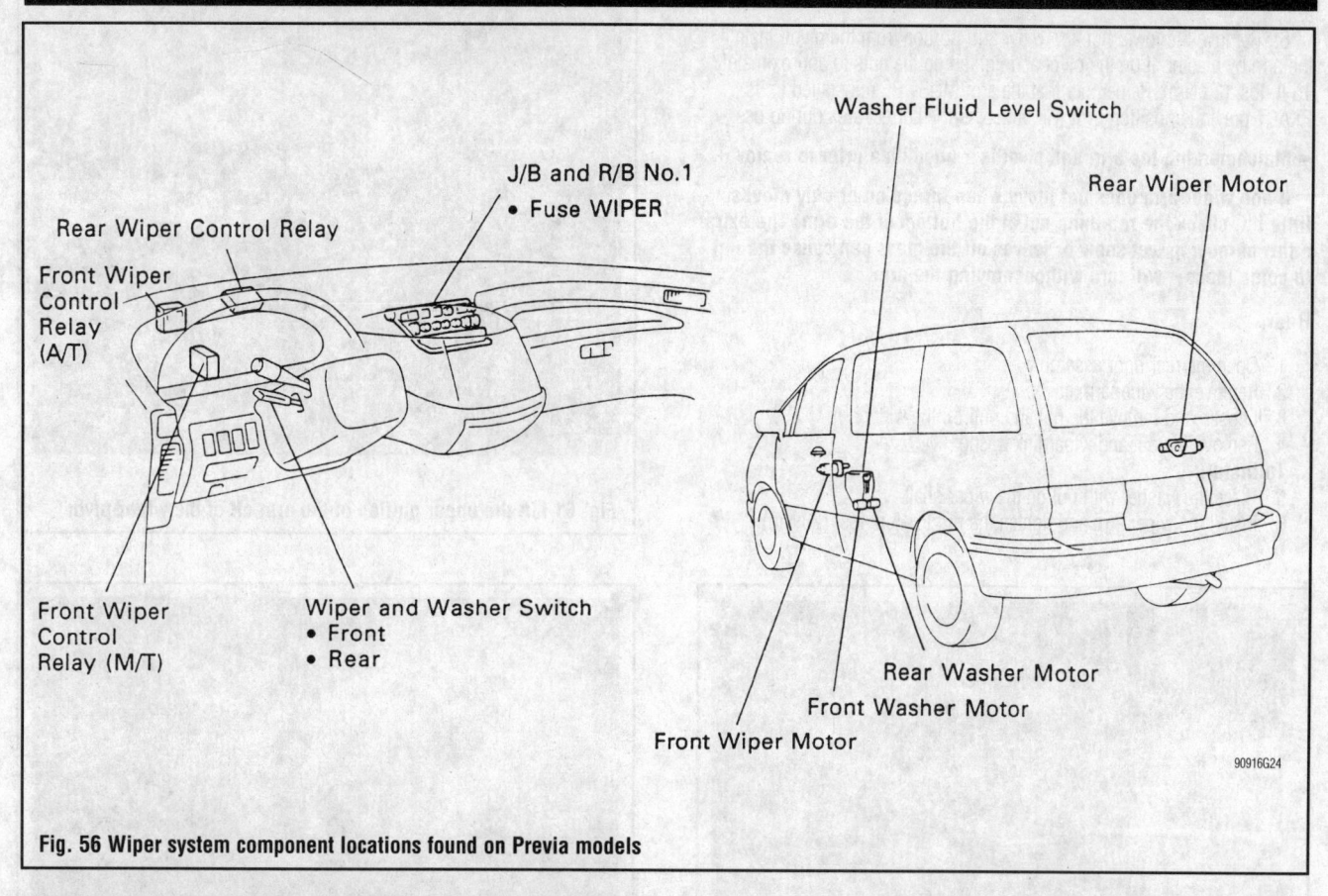

Fig. 56 Wiper system component locations found on Previa models

## Windshield Wiper Blade and Arm

### REMOVAL & INSTALLATION

#### Front

♦ See Figures 57 thru 63

1. To remove the wiper blades, lift up on the spring release tab on the wiper blade-to-wiper arm connector.

2. Pull the blade assembly off the wiper arm.
3. Press the old wiper blade insert down, away from the blade assembly, to free it from the retaining clips on the blade ends. Slide the insert out of the blade. Slide the new insert into the blade assembly and bend the insert upward slightly to engage the retaining clips.

➡Prior to wiper arm removal, it is wise to mark the windshield-to-blade placement with crayon for installation. This will help with blade height.

4. To replace a wiper arm, unscrew the upper acorn nut.

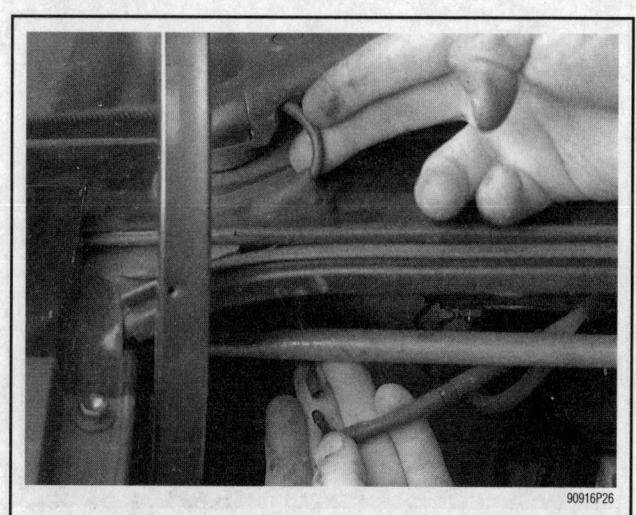

Fig. 57 Always disconnect the hoses leading to the wiper arm prior to replacement

Fig. 58 Lift the cover off the end of the wiper arm to access the nut

## 6-24 CHASSIS ELECTRICAL

5. Lift the upper portion of the wiper arm to access the lower nut and arm.

6. Remove the lower nut and wiper arm portion from the pivot. Install the arm by placing it on the pivot and tightening the nuts to approximately 15 ft. lbs. (20 Nm). Remember that the arm MUST BE reinstalled in its EXACT previous position or it will not cover the correct area during use.

➡ Matchmarking the arm and pivot is a good idea prior to removal.

➡ If one wiper arm does not move when turned on or only moves a little bit, check the retaining nut at the bottom of the arm. The extra effort of moving wet snow or leaves off the glass can cause the nut to come loose—will turn without moving the arm.

### Rear

1. Open the rear door assembly.
2. Remove the wiper arm cover.
3. Loosen and remove the nut and pull off the wiper arm.
4. Remove the nut and wiper link washer.

**To install:**

5. Place the washer with nut on the wiper shaft.
6. Install the wiper arm and tighten the nut to 15 ft. lbs. (20 Nm).

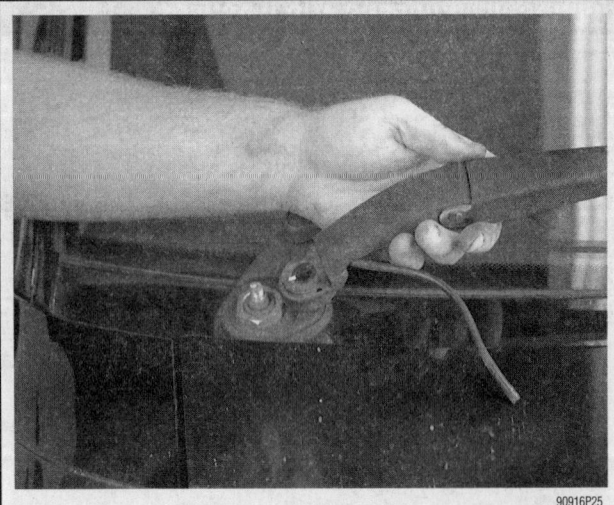

Fig. 61 Lift the upper portion of the arm off of the wiper pivot

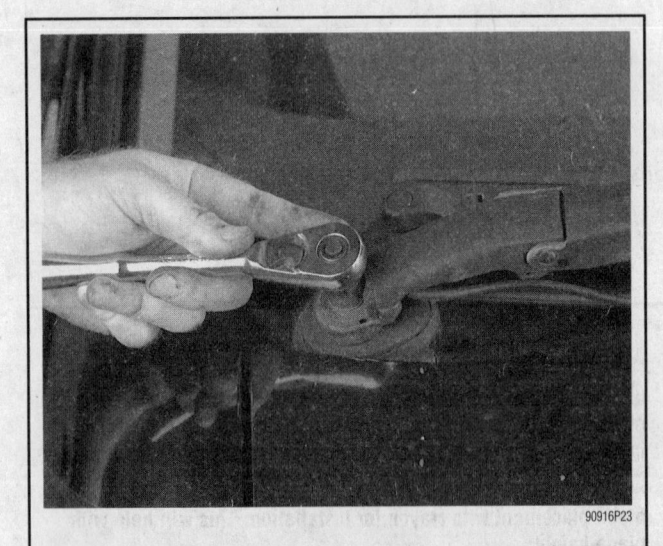

Fig. 59 Use a ratchet to remove the nut

Fig. 62 Remove the lower nut . . .

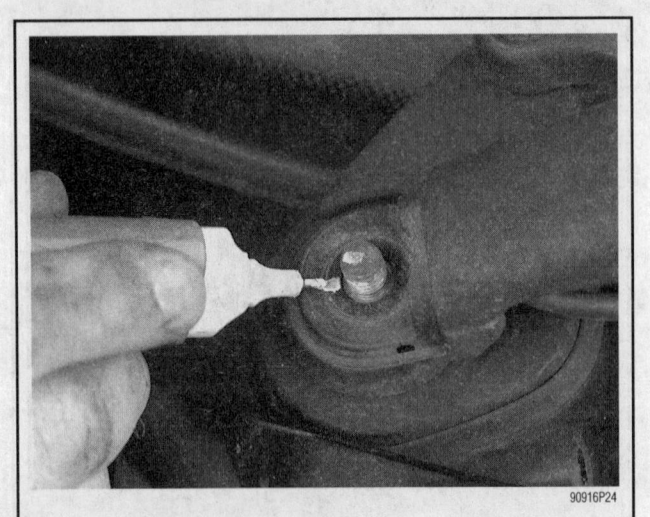

Fig. 60 It is a good idea to matchmark the location of the wiper arm for installation

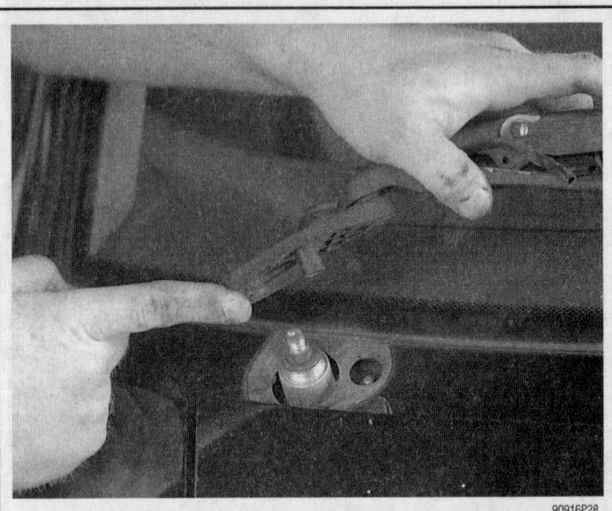

Fig. 63 . . . then lift the entire arm assembly off the pivot

# CHASSIS ELECTRICAL 6-25

## Windshield Wiper Motor

### REMOVAL & INSTALLATION

**Front**

▶ See Figures 64 thru 71

1. Disconnect the negative battery cable. Wait at least 90 seconds to work on vehicles equipped with air bags.

### ✺ CAUTION

Some models covered by this manual may be equipped with a Supplemental Restraint System (SRS), which uses an air bag. Whenever working near any of the SRS components, such as the impact sensors, the air bag module, steering column and instrument panel, disable the SRS, as described in Section 6.

2. Disconnect the wiper motor harness.

Fig. 66 . . .and extract the unit from the vehicle

Fig. 64 Disconnecting the wiper motor wiring harness

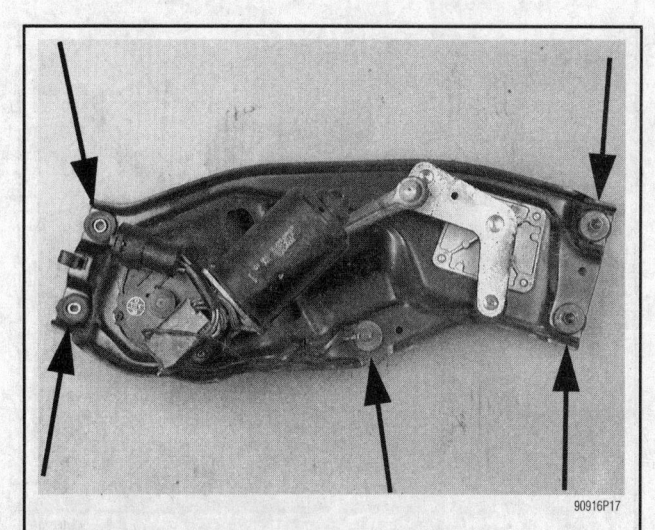

Fig. 67 Remove these two nuts and three bolts from the bracket to extract the wiper assembly

Fig. 65 Unbolt the wiper motor with the bracket . . .

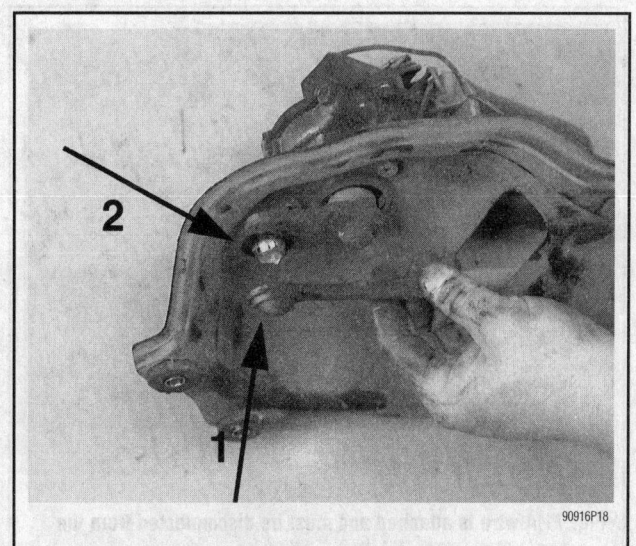

Fig. 68 Detach the linkage (1) from the motor arm (2)

## CHASSIS ELECTRICAL

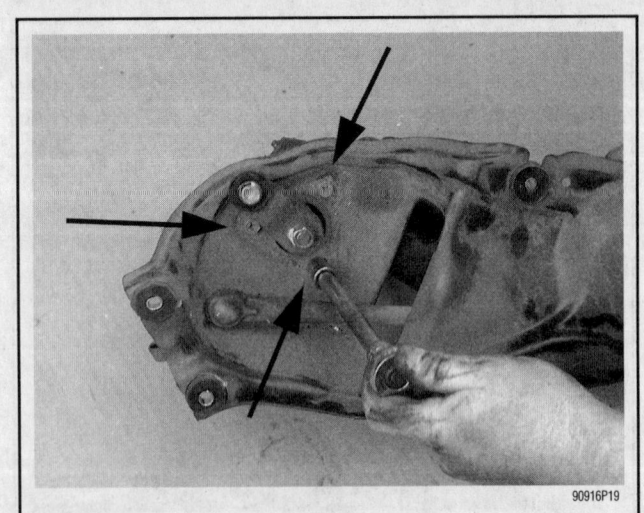

Fig. 69 Remove these 3 screws to separate the arm from the motor

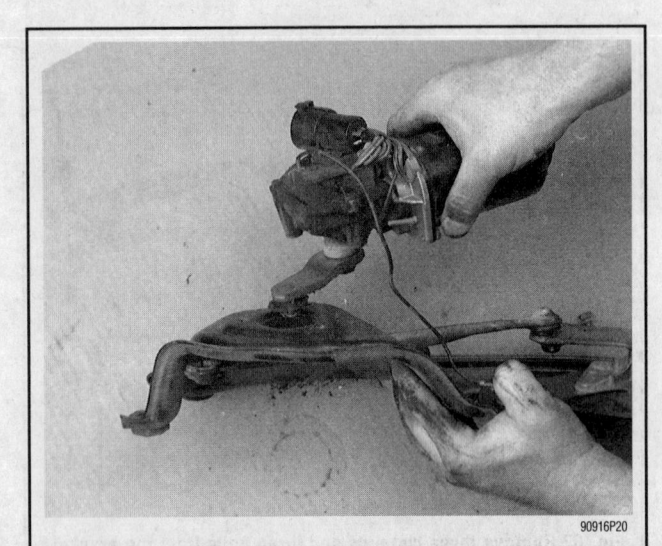

Fig. 70 Pull the motor out from the hole in the bracket

Fig. 71 A wire is attached and must be disconnected from the bracket also

3. Unbolt the wiper motor bracket and extract it slightly from the cowl. There are two nuts and three bolts.
4. Disconnect the wiper linkage from the motor.
5. Remove these three screws to separate the motor arm.
6. Remove the remove the motor from the bracket.
7. Installation is the reverse of removal. Attach all components and secure.

➡Return the motor to the PARK position before installing by cycling the motor on and off once. Do this before connecting the linkage.

### Rear

➡Due to the lack of information available, a general rear wiper motor removal and installation procedure is outlined for the Previa. The removal steps can be altered as required.

1. Disconnect the negative battery cable.

### ✷✷ CAUTION

Some models covered by this manual may be equipped with a Supplemental Restraint System (SRS), which uses an air bag. Whenever working near any of the SRS components, such as the impact sensors, the air bag module, steering column and instrument panel, disable the SRS, as described in Section 6.

2. Remove the wiper arm and rear door trim cover. Disconnect the wiper motor wiring.
3. Remove the motor attaching bolts and withdraw the wiper motor along with the bracket.
4. Remove the mounting bracket from the old motor and transfer it to the new motor.

**To install:**
5. Install the wiper motor with bracket and secure.
6. Attach the wiring and install the rear door trim cover and wiper arm.
7. Connect the negative battery cable and check the motor for proper operation.

## Windshield Washer Motor

### REMOVAL & INSTALLATION

The windshield washer reservoir motor (pump) is located in the washer reservoir. The same pump is used for the front and rear washers.
1. Remove the washer reservoir/motor assembly from the vehicle.
2. Separate the washer fluid motor wiring from the harness.
3. Pull the motor from the rubber grommet retaining it to the washer reservoir.

**To install:**
4. Inspect the rubber grommet for deterioration and replace if necessary.
5. Apply petroleum jelly to the motor before inserting it into the grommet.
6. Attach the harness to the pump.
7. Secure the washer reservoir into the engine compartment.
8. Connect the negative battery cable and test the washer pump for operation.

# CHASSIS ELECTRICAL  6-27

## INSTRUMENTS AND SWITCHES

### Instrument Cluster

➡ When working around a digital or electronic cluster, make sure that the circuitry is not damaged due to static electricity discharge. To lessen the probability of this happening, touch both hands to ground frequently to discharge any static.

REMOVAL & INSTALLATION

▶ See Figures 72 thru 77

1. Disconnect the negative battery cable. Wait at least 90 seconds for models equipped with an air bag.

### ✳✳ CAUTION

Some models covered by this manual may be equipped with a Supplemental Restraint System (SRS), which uses an air bag. Whenever working near any of the SRS components, such as the impact sensors, the air bag module, steering column and instrument panel, disable the SRS, as described in Section 6.

2. Remove the cluster finish center upper panel. Push up the release lock at the center on the lower side of the panel. Pull the panel to extract it from the dash.
3. Unscrew the cluster finish panel retaining screws and carefully pry from the side to remove it from the dash.
4. Unscrew the combination meter. On the automatic models, disconnect the cable from the control lever. Make sure it is in the **P** position. Remove the cable from the roller.
5. Remove the meter, then disconnect the wiring harnesses from the back.

**To install:**

6. On automatic models, connect the cable to the control lever. Install the cable roller.
7. Connect the speedometer cable and harnesses.
8. Position the combination meter and secure into the dash.

Fig. 72 Unscrew and remove the upper cluster finish panel . . .

Fig. 73 . . . then remove these screws for the cluster

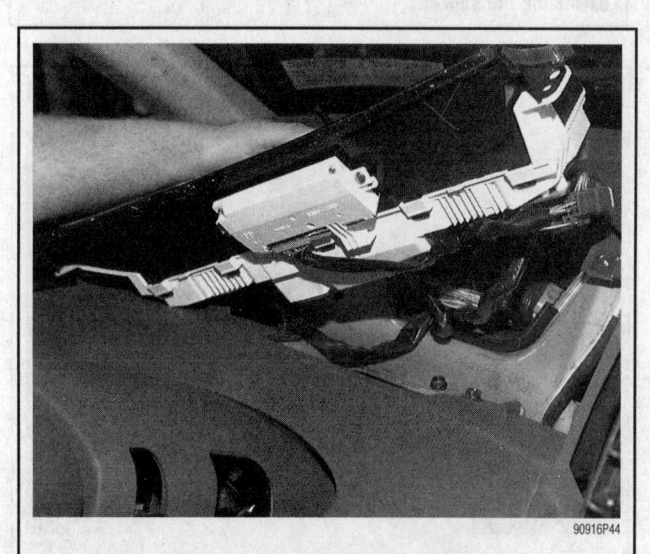

Fig. 74 Extract the meter assembly from the dash

Fig. 75 Disconnect the harnesses attached to the back of the meter

# 6-28 CHASSIS ELECTRICAL

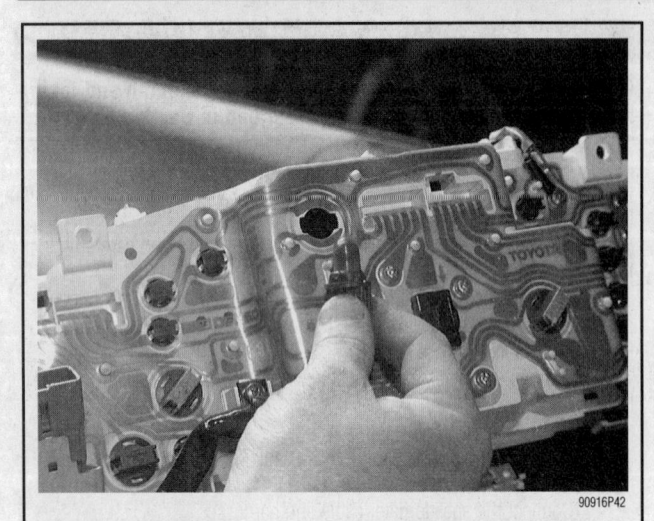

Fig. 76 If necessary, replace any burnt bulbs by twisting and extracting the socket

Fig. 77 A bulb can be simply pulled from the socket for replacement

9. Install the cluster finish panel.
10. Install and attach the cluster finish center upper panel.
11. Connect the negative battery cable.

## Speedometer, Tachometer, and Gauges

### REMOVAL & INSTALLATION

The gauges on all the models covered here can be replaced in the same basic manner. First, remove the instrument cluster and the front lens. Then, remove the gauge's attaching screws on either the front or the back of the cluster.

When replacing a speedometer or odometer assembly, the law requires the odometer reading of the replacement unit to be set to register the same mileage as the prior odometer. If the mileage cannot be set, the law requires that the replacement be set at zero and a proper label be installed on the drivers door frame to show the previous odometer reading and date of replacement.

## Windshield Wiper Switch

### REMOVAL & INSTALLATION

▶ See Figure 78

The windshield wiper/washer switch for the front and rear is part of the Combination Switch Assembly. Refer to Turn Signal/Combination Switch services procedures in Section 8 for additional information.

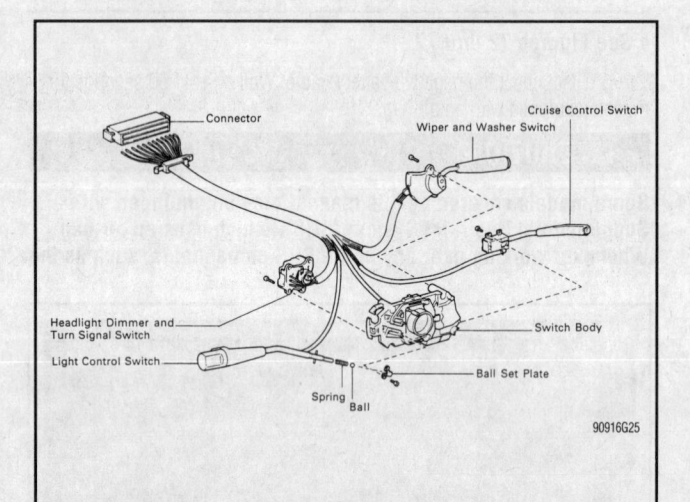

Fig. 78 The wiper and headlight switches are incorporated with the combination switch on all models

## Headlight Switch

### REMOVAL & INSTALLATION

▶ See Figure 78

The headlight switch is part of the Combination Switch Assembly. Refer to Turn Signal/Combination Switch services procedures in Section 8 for additional information.

## Dash-Mounted Switches

### REMOVAL & INSTALLATION

### ✲✲✲ CAUTION

On models equipped with a Supplemental Restraint System (SRS) or "air bag," work must NOT be started until at least 90 seconds have passed from the time that both the ignition switch is turned to the LOCK position and the negative cable is disconnected from the battery.

Most dash-mounted switches can be removed using the same basic procedure. Remove the trim panel which the switch is secured to. Trim panels are usually secured by a series of screws and/or clips. Make sure you remove all attaching screws before attempting to pull on the panel. Do not use excessive force as trim panels are easily damaged. Once the trim panel has been removed, unplug the switch connector, then remove its retaining screws or pry it from the mounting clip. Always disconnect the negative battery cable first.

# CHASSIS ELECTRICAL  6-29

## Clock

### REMOVAL & INSTALLATION

On some models the clock is built into the radio assembly and cannot be removed separately. On all other models proceed with the following.

1. Using a small prytool, pry the clock loose from the dash panel. The clock is usually held in the dash panel or top rear view mirror by 2 small retaining clips.
2. Disconnect the electrical wiring from the rear of the clock and remove the clock.

3. Installation is the reverse of the removal procedure. Check the clock functions for proper operation. Reset the clock.

## Horn

### REMOVAL & INSTALLATION

The horn is located behind the grille. Remove the grille retaining bolts to access. Unbolt the one screw holding the horn assembly to the bracket.

## LIGHTING

### Headlights

### REMOVAL & INSTALLATION

▶ See Figures 79, 80, 81, 82 and 83

➡This procedure only applies to replaceable halogen headlight bulbs (such as Nos. 9004 and 9005); it does not pertain to sealed beam units.

1. Open the vehicle's hood and secure it in an upright position.
2. Unfasten the locking ring which secures the bulb and socket assembly, then withdraw the assembly rearward.
3. To replace the headlight lens:
   a. Remove the aiming nut located in the lower inside corner of the assembly.
   b. Pop off the spring located in the lower inside corner of the lamp.
   c. Loosen and remove the adjuster on the other side of the lens and extract the assembly from the vehicle.

**To install:**
4. Install the new lens and secure.
5. Before installing a light bulb into the socket, ensure that all electrical contact surfaces are free of corrosion or dirt.

6. Line up the replacement headlight bulb with the socket. Firmly push the bulb onto the socket.

Fig. 80 Unclasp the wiring attached to the back of the headlamp bulb

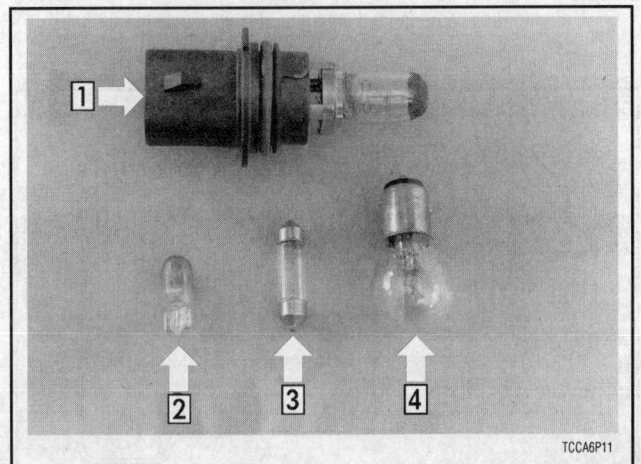

1. Halogen headlight bulb
2. Side marker light bulb
3. Dome light bulb
4. Turn signal/brake light bulb

Fig. 79 Examples of various types of automotive light bulbs

Fig. 81 Twist and remove the bulb with socket from the lens assembly

## 6-30 CHASSIS ELECTRICAL

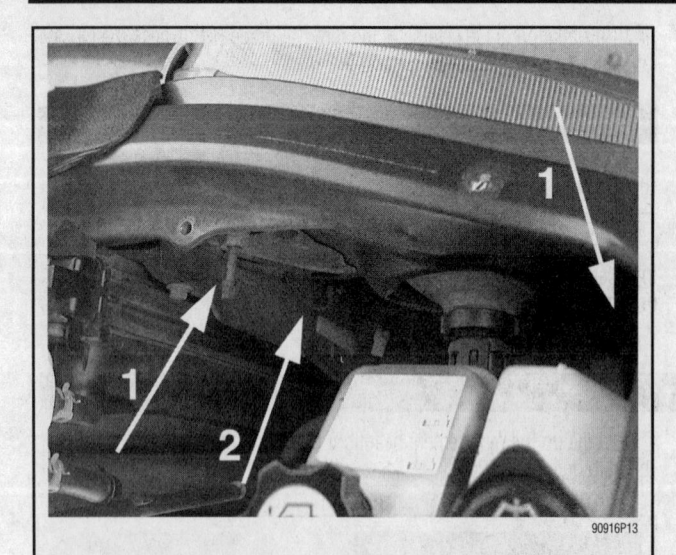

Fig. 82 Unclasp the spring (2) and remove the adjuster nuts (1)

Fig. 83 Pull the lamp assembly out

### ✲✲ WARNING

Do not touch the glass bulb with your fingers. Oil from your fingers can severely shorten the life of the bulb. If necessary, wipe off any dirt or oil from the bulb with rubbing alcohol before completing installation.

7. To ensure that the replacement bulb functions properly, activate the applicable switch to illuminate the bulb which was just replaced. (If this is a combination low and high beam bulb, be sure to check both intensities.) If the replacement light bulb does not illuminate, either it too is faulty or there is a problem in the bulb circuit or switch. Correct if necessary.
8. Position the headlight bulb and secure it with the locking ring.
9. Close the vehicle's hood.

### AIMING

▶ See Figures 84, 85 and 86

The headlights must be properly aimed to provide the best, safest road illumination. The lights should be checked for proper aim and adjusted as necessary. Certain state and local authorities have requirements for headlight aiming; these should be checked before adjustment is made.

### ✲✲ CAUTION

About once a year, when the headlights are replaced or any time front end work is performed on your vehicle, the headlight should be accurately aimed by a reputable repair shop using the proper equipment. Headlights not properly aimed can make it virtually impossible to see and may blind other drivers on the road, possibly causing an accident. Note that the following procedure is a temporary fix, until you can take your vehicle to a repair shop for a proper adjustment.

Headlight adjustment may be temporarily made using a wall, as described below, or on the rear of another vehicle. When adjusted, the lights should not glare in oncoming car or truck windshields, nor should they illuminate the passenger compartment of vehicles driving in front of you. These adjustments are rough and should always be fine-tuned by a repair shop which is equipped with headlight aiming tools. Improper adjustments may be both dangerous and illegal.

For most of the vehicles covered by this manual, horizontal and vertical aiming of each sealed beam unit is provided by two adjusting screws which move the retaining ring and adjusting plate against the tension of a coil spring. There is no adjustment for focus; this is done during headlight manufacturing.

➡Because the composite headlight assembly is bolted into position, no adjustment should be necessary or possible. Some applications, however, may be bolted to an adjuster plate or may be retained by adjusting screws. If so, follow this procedure when adjusting the lights, BUT always have the adjustment checked by a reputable shop.

Before removing the headlight bulb or disturbing the headlamp in any way, note the current settings in order to ease headlight adjustment upon reassembly. If the high or low beam setting of the old lamp still works, this can be done using the wall of a garage or a building:

1. Park the vehicle on a level surface, with the fuel tank about ½ full and with the vehicle empty of all extra cargo (unless normally carried). The vehicle should be facing a wall which is no less than 6 feet (1.8m) high and 12 feet (3.7m) wide. The front of the vehicle should be about 25 feet from the wall.
2. If aiming is to be performed outdoors, it is advisable to wait until

1. Vertical Adjusting Screw
2. Horizontal Adjusting Screw

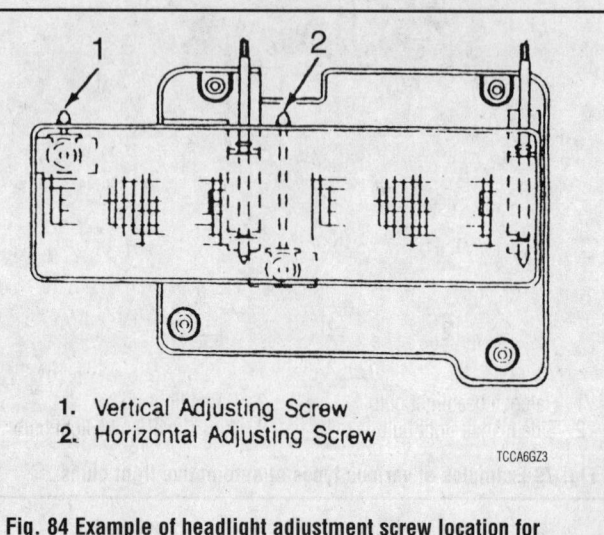

Fig. 84 Example of headlight adjustment screw location for composite headlamps

## CHASSIS ELECTRICAL  6-31

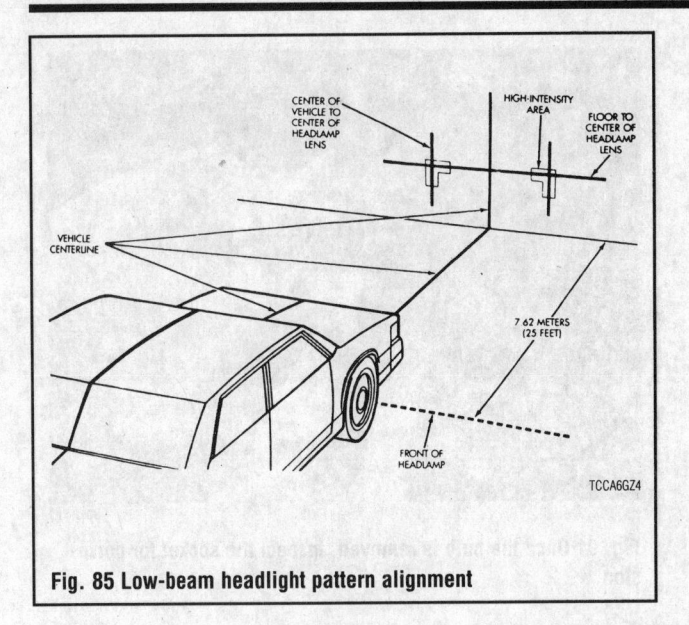

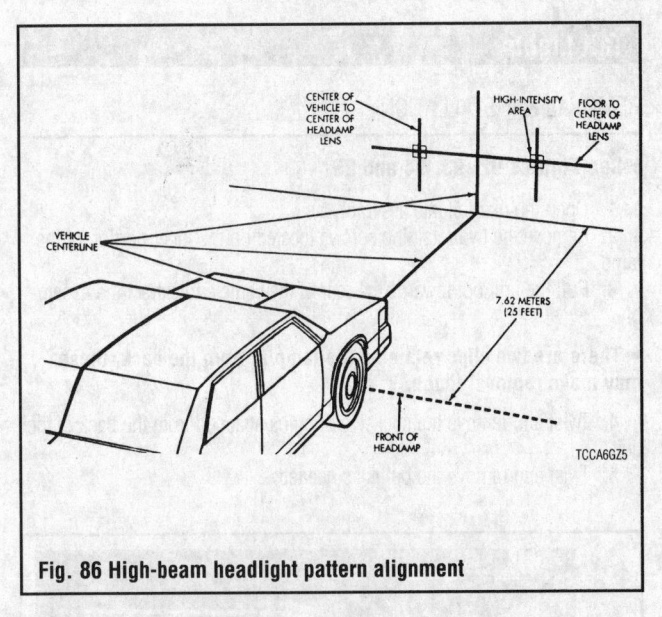

**Fig. 85 Low-beam headlight pattern alignment**

**Fig. 86 High-beam headlight pattern alignment**

dusk in order to properly see the headlight beams on the wall. If done in a garage, darken the area around the wall as much as possible by closing shades or hanging cloth over the windows.

3. Turn the headlights **ON** and mark the wall at the center of each light's low beam, then switch on the brights and mark the center of each light's high beam. A short length of masking tape which is visible from the front of the vehicle may be used. Although marking all four positions is advisable, marking one position from each light should be sufficient.

4. If neither beam on one side is working, and if another like-sized vehicle is available, park the second one in the exact spot where the vehicle was and mark the beams using the same-side light. Then switch the vehicles so the one to be aimed is back in the original spot. It must be parked no closer to or farther away from the wall than the second vehicle.

5. Perform any necessary repairs, but make sure the vehicle is not moved, or is returned to the exact spot from which the lights were marked. Turn the headlights **ON** and adjust the beams to match the marks on the wall.

6. Have the headlight adjustment checked as soon as possible by a reputable repair shop.

### Turn Signal/Marker Light

#### REMOVAL & INSTALLATION

♦ See Figures 87, 88, 89, 90 and 91

1. Remove the one retaining screw from the upper corner of the lens.
2. Tape the end of a pry tool, then carefully extract from the bottom of the lens in a rocking motion till the stud is loosened from the retainer.

➡ Do not pry from the back of the lens, this will crack the lens or damage the paint.

3. Pull the lens assembly straight out from the body towards the front of the vehicle.
4. Twist and remove the wiring from the back of the lens.
5. Twist the bulb and remove it from the socket.

**To install:**

6. Before installing a light bulb into the socket, ensure that all electrical contact surfaces are free of corrosion or dirt.

**Fig. 87 Remove the one screw in the upper corner of the turn signal/marker light lens**

**Fig. 88 Using a taped prytool, carefully extract the lens from the body**

# 6-32　CHASSIS ELECTRICAL

Fig. 89 Twist and remove the socket from the back of the turnsignal/marker lamp

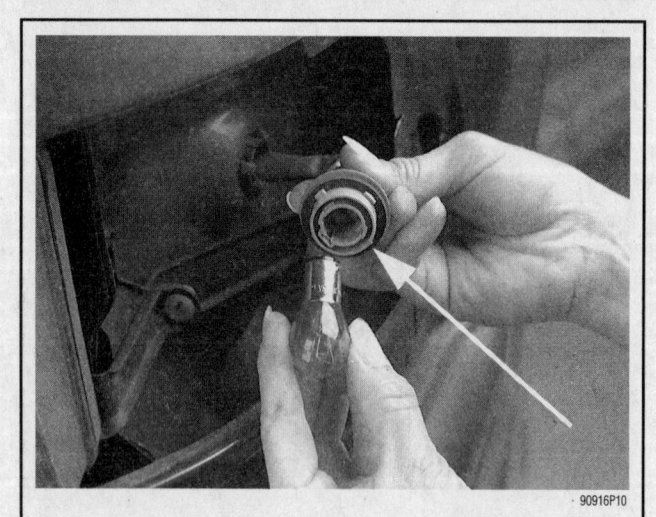

Fig. 91 Once the bulb is removed, inspect the socket for corrosion

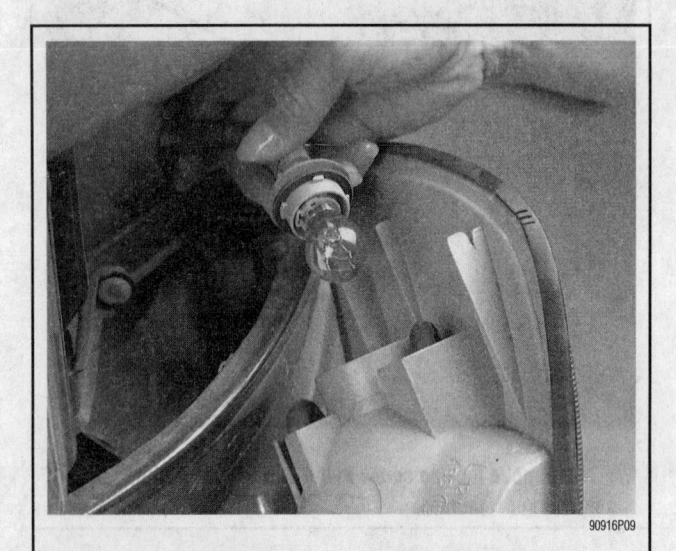

Fig. 90 Inspect the bulb, and replace if necessary

## Tail Lights

### REMOVAL & INSTALLATION

▶ See Figures 92, 93, 94 and 95

1. Open the rear tailgate assembly.
2. Remove the two retaining screws located on the inner portion of the lamp.
3. Pull the unit out towards the rear of the vehicle to extract the assembly.

➥There are two clips retaining the lamp in from the back, these may make removal tough.

4. Twist and remove the socket with bulbs attached from the back of the unit.
5. Twist and remove the bulbs as needed.

➥Before installing the light bulb, note the positions of the two retaining pins on the bulb. They will likely be at different heights on the bulb, to ensure that the bulb is installed correctly. If, when installing the bulb, it does not turn easily, do not force it. Remove the bulb and rotate it 180 degrees from its former position, then reinsert it into the bulb socket.

7. Insert the light bulb into the socket and, while depressing the bulb, twist it 1/8 turn clockwise until the two pins on the light bulb are properly engaged in the socket.
8. To ensure that the replacement bulb functions properly, activate the applicable switch to illuminate the bulb which was just replaced. If the replacement light bulb does not illuminate, either it too is faulty or there is a problem in the bulb circuit or switch. Correct if necessary.
9. Install the socket and bulb assembly into the rear of the lens housing; otherwise, install the lens over the bulb.
10. Insert and secure the lens assembly into the body of the vehicle.

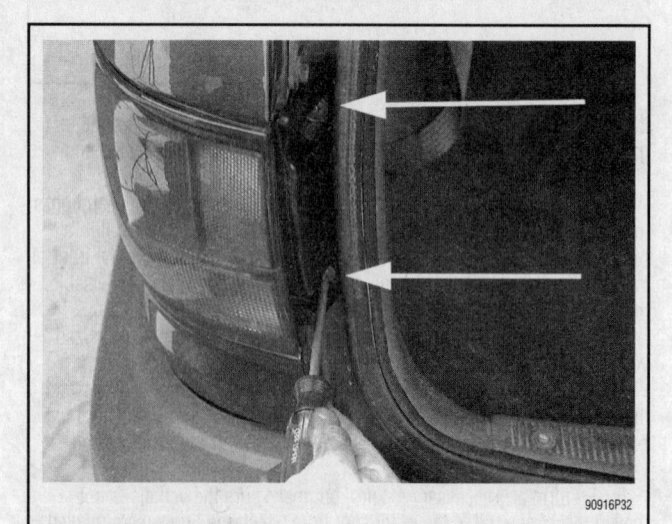

Fig. 92 Remove the two screws on the inside of the trunk area retaining the lamp

## CHASSIS ELECTRICAL  6-33

**To install:**
6. Insert new bulb into the sockets.
7. Position and secure the socket to the back of the assembly.
8. Place the lamp into position and pushing towards the front of the vehicle, secure the clamps.
9. Install and tighten the retaining screws.

### Dome Light

REMOVAL & INSTALLATION

▶ See Figures 96, 97 and 98

1. Using a small prytool, carefully remove the cover lens from the lamp assembly.
2. Remove the bulb from its retaining clip contacts. If the bulb has tapered ends, gently depress the spring clip/metal contact and disengage the light bulb, then pull it free of the two metal contacts.

**To install:**
3. Before installing the light bulb into the metal contacts, ensure that all electrical conducting surfaces are free of corrosion or dirt.

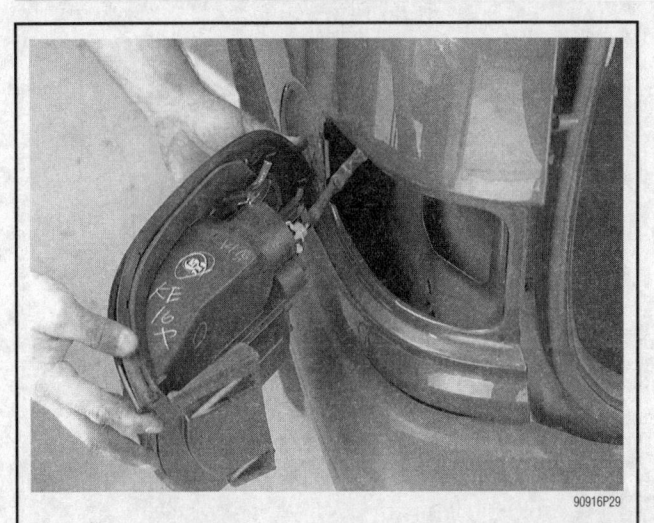

Fig. 93 Slide the tail light unit out towards the rear of the vehicle

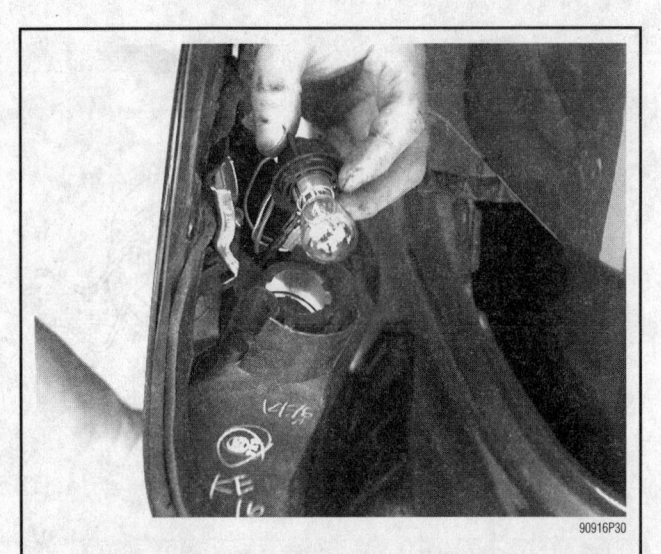

Fig. 94 Twist and remove the socket from the back of the lamp

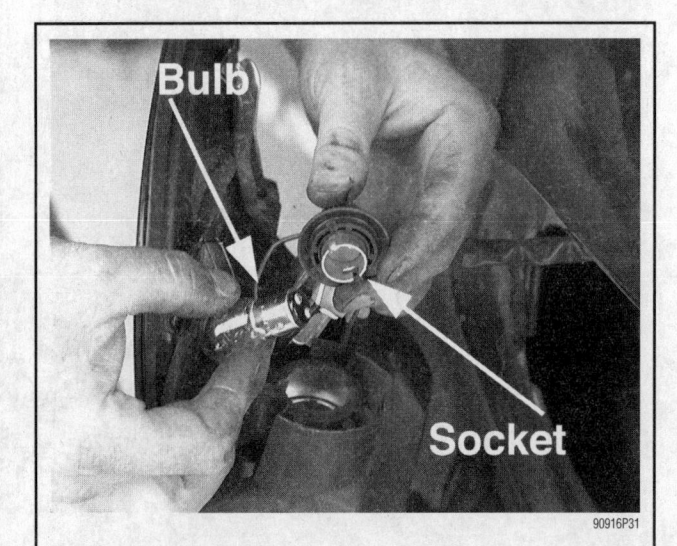

Fig. 95 Twist and pull out the bulb from the socket

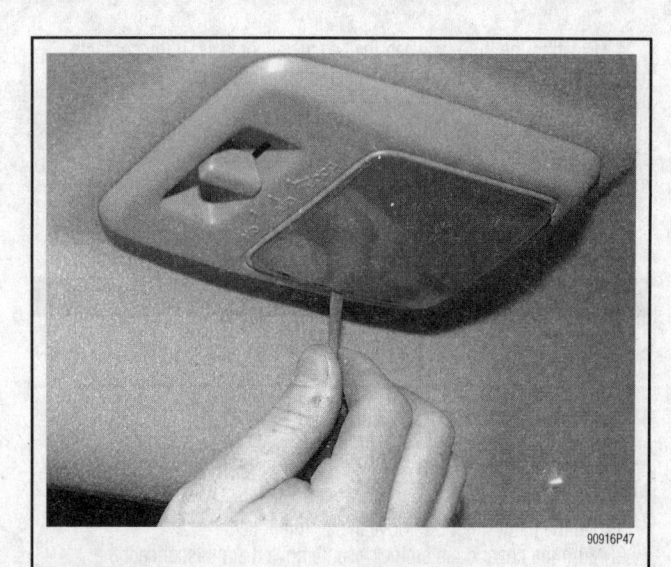

Fig. 96 Carefully pry the lens off the dome lamp

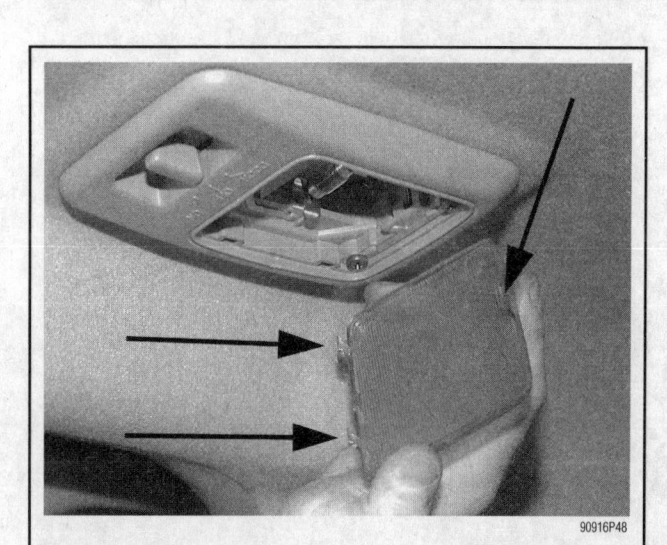

Fig. 97 There are 3 tabs on the lens, be careful not to damage them

## 6-34 CHASSIS ELECTRICAL

Fig. 98 Disengage the spring clip which retains one tapered end of this dome light bulb

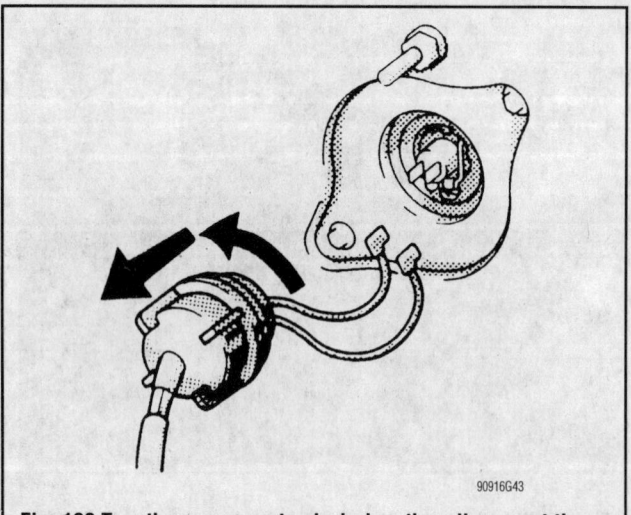

Fig. 100 Turn the cover counterclockwise, then disconnect the wiring

4. Position the bulb between the two metal contacts. If the contacts have small holes, be sure that the tapered ends of the bulb are situated in them.
5. To ensure that the replacement bulb functions properly, activate the applicable switch to illuminate the bulb which was just replaced. If the replacement light bulb does not illuminate, either it is faulty or there is a problem in the bulb circuit or switch. Correct as necessary.
6. Install the cover lens until its retaining tabs are properly engaged.

### Fog/Driving Lights

REMOVAL & INSTALLATION

♦ See Figures 99, 100, 101 and 102

➡Make sure both the fog light switch and headlight switch are off.

1. On the left fog light, remove the air inlet duct.
2. Turn the cover counterclockwise, remove it and disconnect the wiring.

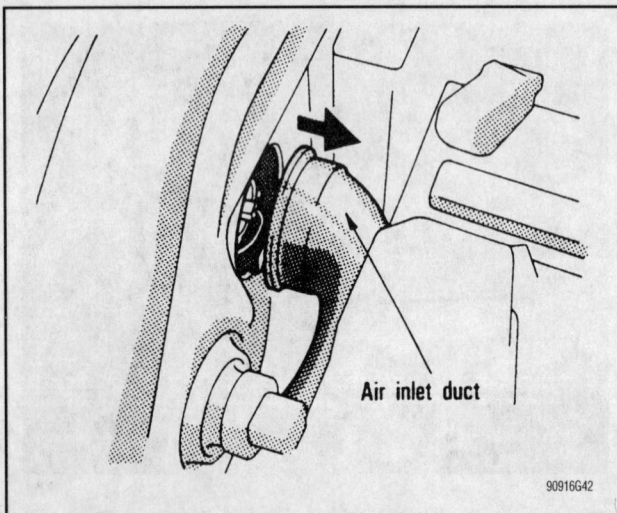

Fig. 101 Release the spring and extract the bulb

Fig. 99 On the left fog light, remove the air inlet duct to access the assembly

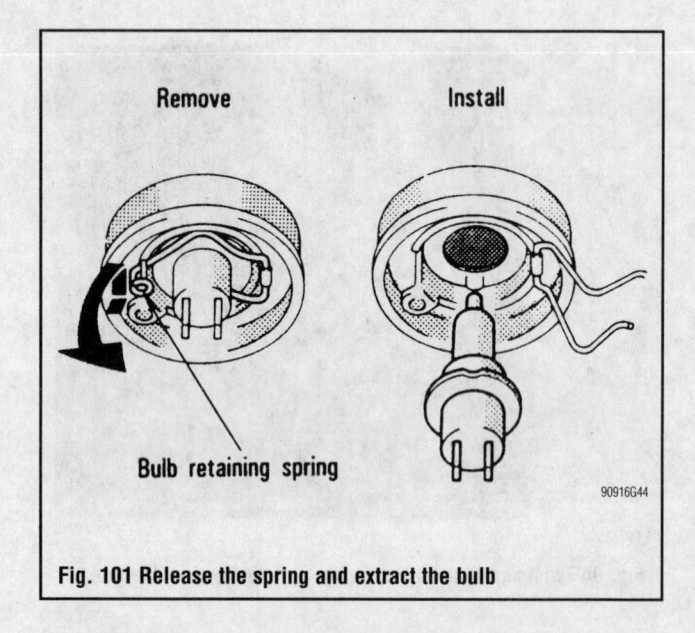

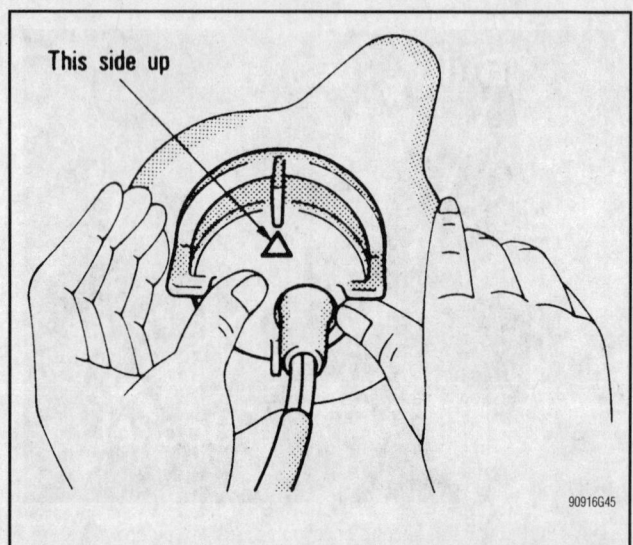

Fig. 102 The triangle must face upwards during installation

## CHASSIS ELECTRICAL  6-35

3. Release the bulb retaining spring and remove the bulb.
4. Install a new bulb and retaining spring. Align the cutouts of the bulb with the protrusions of the mounting hole. Make sure the triangle faces upwards.
5. Connect the cords and install the cover by turning it clockwise.
6. Make sure the cover fits snugly on the mounting body. On the left side, install the air inlet duct.

### Third Brake Light

REMOVAL & INSTALLATION

▶ See Figures 103 and 104

1. Open the trunk to access the third brake light.
2. Push the pin inside the clip using a punch.
3. Pull off the cover and remove the second rear cover. the second cover has the socket assembly integrated.
4. Carefully twist and remove the bulb if necessary.
5. Insert a new bulb.
6. Attach the socket assembly to the body, then install the outer cover.

### License Plate Light

REMOVAL & INSTALLATION

▶ See Figures 105, 106 and 107

1. Unscrew the lens from the tailgate.
2. The lens should pop off the housing quite easily.
3. Pull the bulb from the socket to replace.
4. Installation is the reverse of removal.

### Reverse Lights

REMOVAL & INSTALLATION

▶ See Figure 108

To replace the reverse light bulbs, the rear tail gate trim panel will have to be removed. Reach through the hole in the body panel and detach the socket for the lamp. Replace the bulb and install the socket and trim panel.

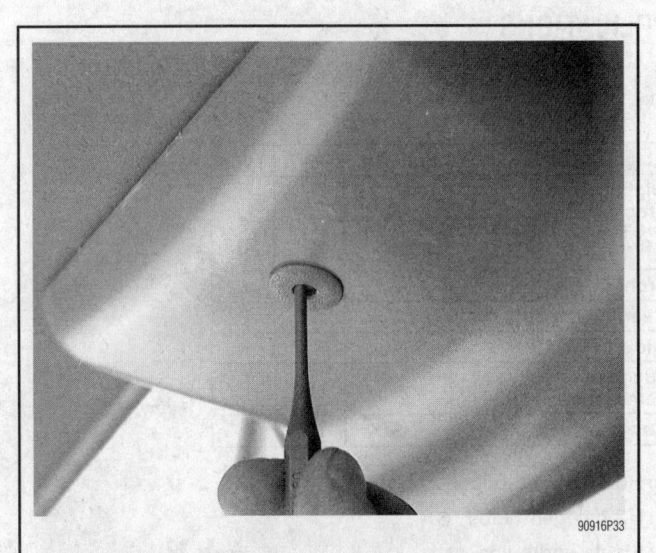

Fig. 103 Using a punch, push in the pin to release the clip

Fig. 105 Remove the lens retaining screws

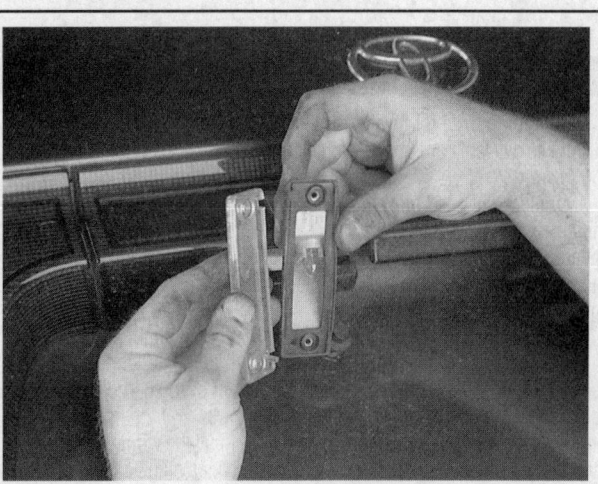

Fig. 104 Pull off the second cover to access the bulb of the third brake light

Fig. 106 The lens is easily separated from the housing of the lamp

# 6-36 CHASSIS ELECTRICAL

Fig. 107 Carefully pull outward to remove the bulb

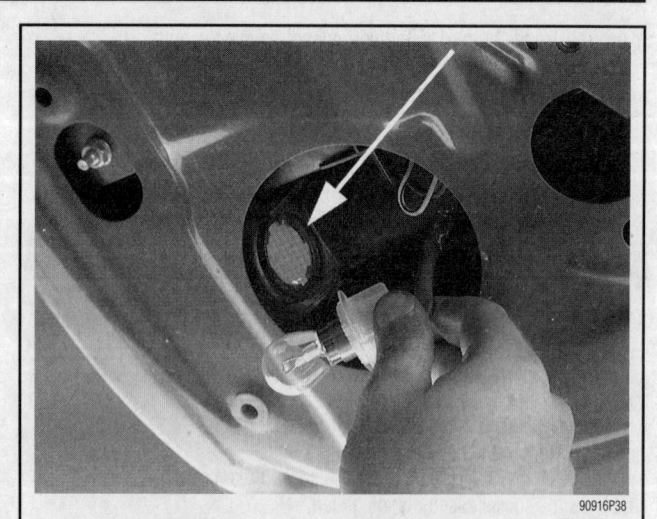

Fig. 108 Twist the socket for the reverse lamp out of the body panel in the tail gate

## LIGHT BULB APPLICATIONS

**NOTICE:**
Only use a bulb of the listed type.

| Light Bulbs | Bulb No. | W | Type |
|---|---|---|---|
| Headlights | HB2 | 60/55 | A |
| Front fog lights | H3 | 55 | B |
| Parking, front side marker and front turn signal lights | 1157NA | 27/8 | C |
| Stop and tail, and rear side marker lights | 1157 | 27/8 | C |
| Rear turn signal lights | 1156 | 27 | C |
| Stop and tail lights | 1157 | 27/8 | C |
| Back-up lights | 1156 | 27 | C |
| License plate lights | 168 | 5 | D |

| Light Bulbs | Bulb No. | W | Type |
|---|---|---|---|
| High mounted stoplights | | | |
| Type A | — | 27 | C |
| Type B | — | 18 | D |
| Front interior light | — | 10 | E |
| Rear interior light | — | 10 | E |
| Glovebox light | — | 1.2 | D |
| Luggage compartment light | — | 5 | E |
| Vanity light | — | 3 | E |

A : HB2 halogen bulbs
B : H3 halogen bulbs
C : Single end bulbs
D : Wedge base bulbs
E : Double end bulbs

## TRAILER WIRING

Wiring the vehicle for towing is fairly easy. There are a number of good wiring kits available and these should be used, rather than trying to design your own.

All trailers will need brake lights and turn signals as well as tail lights and side marker lights. Most areas require extra marker lights for overwide trailers. Also, most areas have recently required back-up lights for trailers, and most trailer manufacturers have been building trailers with back-up lights for several years.

Additionally, some Class I, most Class II and just about all Class III and IV trailers will have electric brakes. Add to this number an accessories wire, to operate trailer internal equipment or to charge the trailer's battery, and you can have as many as seven wires in the harness.

Determine the equipment on your trailer and buy the wiring kit necessary. The kit will contain all the wires needed, plus a plug adapter set which includes the female plug, mounted on the bumper or hitch, and the male plug, wired into, or plugged into the trailer harness.

When installing the kit, follow the manufacturer's instructions. The color coding of the wires is usually standard throughout the industry. One point to note: some domestic vehicles, and most imported vehicles, have separate turn signals. On most domestic vehicles, the brake lights and rear turn signals operate with the same bulb. For those vehicles with separate turn signals, you can purchase an isolation unit so that the brake lights won't blink whenever the turn signals are operated, or, you can go to your local electronics supply house and buy four diodes to wire in series with the brake and turn signal bulbs. Diodes will isolate the brake and turn signals. The choice is yours. The isolation units are simple and quick to install, but far more expensive than the diodes. The diodes, however, require more work to install properly, since they require the cutting of each bulb's wire and soldering in place of the diode.

One, final point, the best kits are those with a spring loaded cover on the vehicle mounted socket. This cover prevents dirt and moisture from corroding the terminals. Never let the vehicle socket hang loosely; always mount it securely to the bumper or hitch.

# CHASSIS ELECTRICAL 6-37

## CIRCUIT PROTECTION

### Fuses

#### REPLACEMENT

▶ See Figures 110 thru 115

There are several fuse blocks. They are located in the engine compartment near the battery and under the center dash instrument panel.

If any light or electrical component in the vehicle does not work, its fuse may be blown. To determine the fuse that is the source of the problem, look on the lid of the fuse box as it will give the name and the circuit serviced by each fuse. To inspect a suspected blown fuse, pull the fuse straight out with the pull-out tool and look at the fuse carefully. If the thin wire that bridges the fuse terminals is broken, the fuse is bad and must be replaced. On a good fuse, the wire will be intact.

Sometimes it is difficult to make an accurate determination. If this is the case, try replacing the fuse with one that you know is good. If the fuse blows repeatedly, then this suggests that a short circuit lies somewhere in the electrical system and you should have the system checked.

### ✲✲ CAUTION

**When making emergency replacements, only use fuses that have an equal or lower amperage rating than the one that is blown, to avoid damage and fire.**

When installing a new fuse, use one with the same amperage rating as the one being replaced. To install the a new fuse, first turn off all the electrical components and the ignition switch. Always use the fuse pull-out tool and install the fuse straight. Twisting of the fuse could cause the terminals to separate too much which may result in a bad connection. It may be a good idea to purchase some extra fuses and put them in the box in case of an emergency.

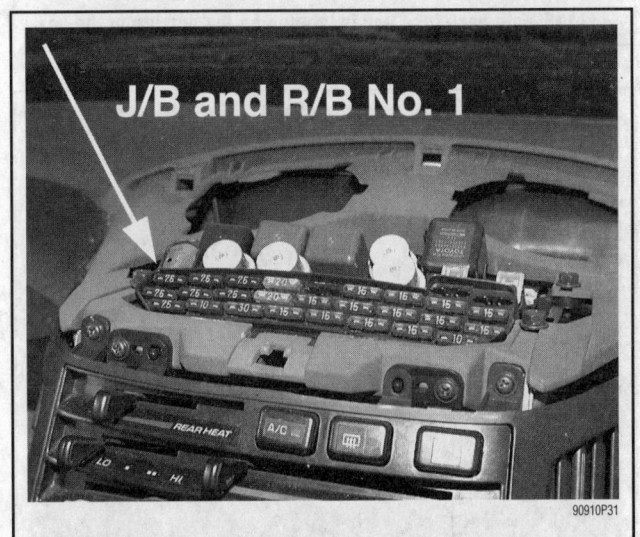

Fig. 110 Lift up the center upper panel to access the fuses

Fig. 111 Fuse, breaker and relay ID is under the center finish panel

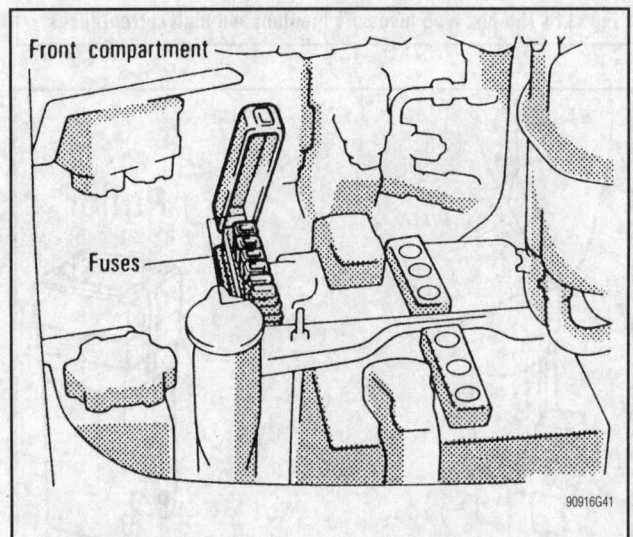

Fig. 112 The other fuse box is located near the battery

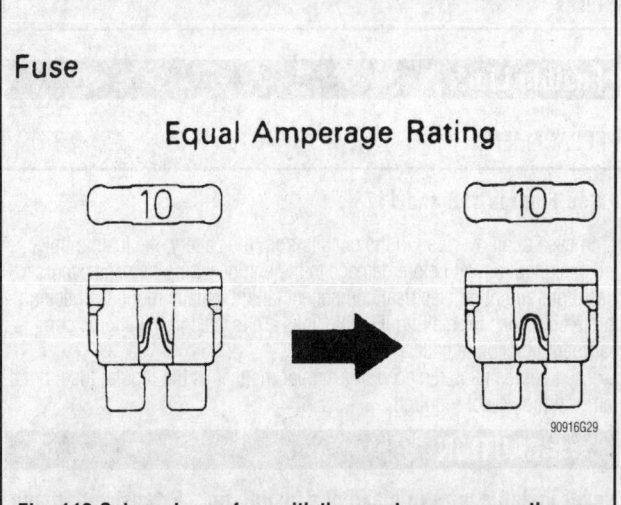

Fig. 113 Only replace a fuse with the exact amperage as the one broken

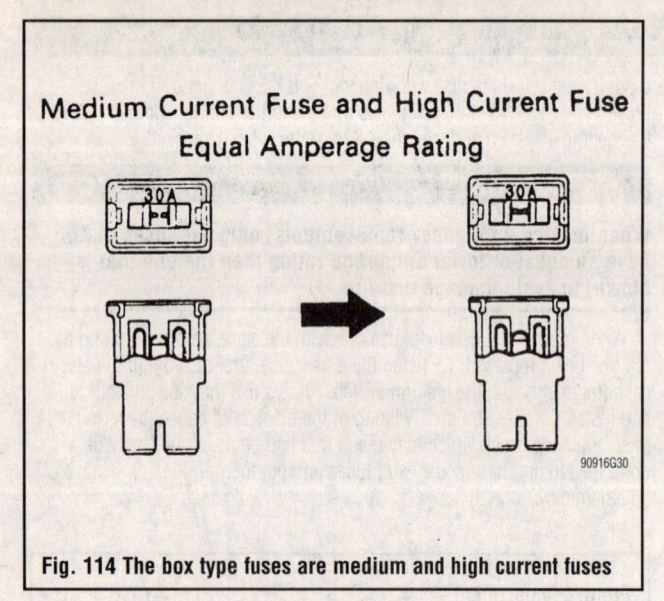

## 6-38 CHASSIS ELECTRICAL

Fig. 114 The box type fuses are medium and high current fuses

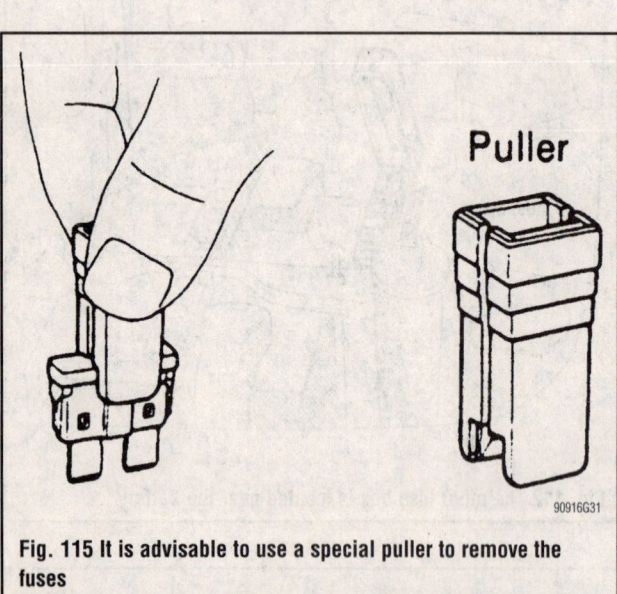

Fig. 115 It is advisable to use a special puller to remove the fuses

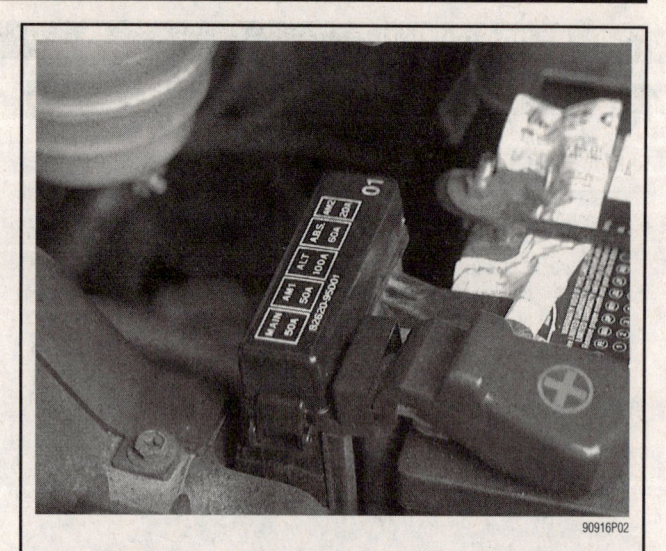

Fig. 116 Note each fuse link is labeled on the outside of the box

Fig. 117 Simply pop the lid, then pull up to extract the fuse

### Fusible Links

#### REPLACEMENT

▶ See Figures 116 and 117

In case of an overload in the circuits from the battery, the fusible links are designed to melt before damage to the engine wiring harness occurs. Headlight and other electrical component failure usually requires checking the fusible links for melting. Fusible links are located in the engine compartment next to the battery.

The fusible link is replaced in a similar manner as the regular fuse, but a removal tool is not required.

### ✷✷ CAUTION

**Never install a wire in place of a fusible link. Extensive damage and fire may occur.**

### Circuit Breakers

In the event the rear window defogger, environmental control system, power windows, power door locks, power tail gate lock, sunroof or automatic shoulder belt does not work, check its circuit breaker. Circuit breakers are located in the passenger's or driver's side kick panel with the fuses.

#### REPLACEMENT

1. Turn the ignition switch to the **OFF** position.
2. Disconnect the negative battery cable. Wait at least 90 seconds before working on models with SRS system.
3. Remove the circuit breaker by unlocking its stopper and pulling it from its socket.

**To install:**

4. Carefully snap the breaker into place and be sure to secure.

# CHASSIS ELECTRICAL  6-39

➡ Always use a new circuit breaker with the same amperage as the old one. If the circuit breaker immediately trips or the component does not operate, the electrical system must be checked.

5. Connect the negative battery cable.

## RESETTING

♦ See Figure 118

1. Insert a thin object into the reset hole and push until a click is heard.
2. Using an ohmmeter, check that there is continuity between both terminals of the circuit breaker. If continuity is not as specified, replace the circuit breaker.

### Relays

## REPLACEMENT

Locate the relay and pull it from its socket. Most should pull directly out, if not check for clips on the side of the unit, release, then pull. Install a new one and check its operation.

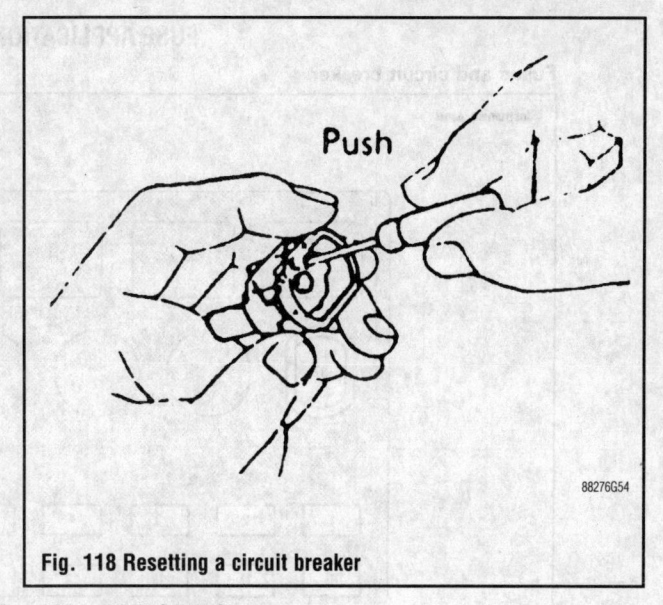

Fig. 118 Resetting a circuit breaker

## FUSE APPLICATIONS—1991–92 MODELS

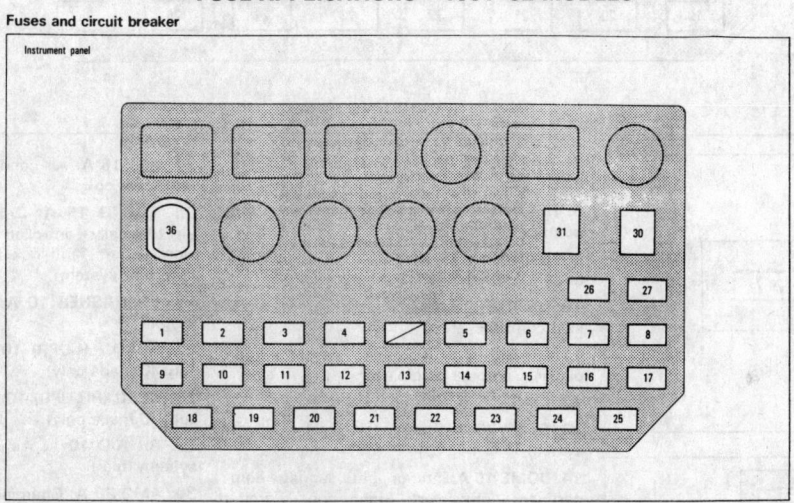

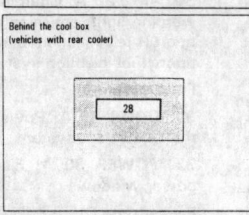

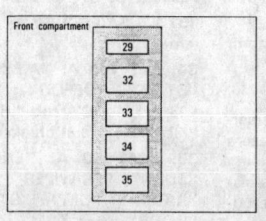

**Fuses (type A)**

1. **ST 7.5 A:** Starter system
2. **IGN 7.5 A:** Charging system, discharge warning light, emission control system, electronic fuel injection system, SRS airbag system
3. **CHARGE 7.5 A:** Charging system, discharge warning light
4. **FOG 20 A:** Front fog lights
5. **TAIL 15 A:** Tail lights, parking lights, side marker lights, license plate lights, instrument panel lights
6. **HAZ-HORN 15 A:** Emergency flashers, horns, turn signal lights
7. **HEAD (LH) 15 A** (U.S.A.)
   **10 A** (Canada)
   : Left-hand headlight
8. **HEAD (RH) 15 A** (U.S.A.)
   **10 A** (Canada)
   : Right-hand headlight
9. **ENGINE 7.5 A:** Charging system, emission control system
10. **RADIO 7.5 A:** Radio, cassette tape player, Compact Disc player
11. **ST-A 7.5 A:** Starter system
12. **STOP 20 A:** Stop lights, anti-lock brake system
13. **DOME 15 A:** Interior lights, luggage compartment light, clock, open door warning light, radio, cassette tape player, Compact Disc player
14. **DEFOG 15 A:** Rear window defogger
15. **ECU-B 15 A:** Anti-lock brake system, electronically controlled automatic transmission system
16. **CIG 15 A:** Cigarette lighter, digital clock display, power rear view mirrors, theft deterrent system, SRS airbag system, automatic transmission shift lock system
17. **EFI 15 A:** Electronic fuel injection system
18. **TURN 7.5 A:** Turn signal lights
19. **GAUGES 10 A:** Gauges and meters, warning lights and buzzers (except discharge and open door warning lights), back-up lights, automatic transmission overdrive system, rear window defogger, electric rear sun roof, power windows, power door lock system
20. **FR-WIPER 30 A:** Windshield wipers and washer
21. **ENGINE OIL 15 A:** Engine oil auto-feed system
22. **RR WIPER 15 A:** Rear window wiper and washer
23. **A/C 15 A:** Air conditioning cooling system, cool box
24. **ECU-IG 15 A:** Cruise control system, electronically controlled automatic transmission system, anti-lock brake system, theft deterrent system
25. **FR-WASHER 10 A:** Windshield washer motor
26. **HEAD (LH-UPR) 10 A** (Canada)
   : Left-hand headlight
27. **HEAD (RH-UPR) 10 A** (Canada)
   : Right-hand headlight
28. **RR A/C 10 A:** Air conditioning cooling system (rear)
29. **AM2 20 A:** Charging system, discharge warning light, emission control system, electronic fuel injection system

**Fuses (type B)**

30. **DOOR 30 A:** Power door lock system, theft deterrent system
31. **POWER 30 A:** Electric rear sun roof, power windows

**Fuses (type C)**

32. **A.B.S. (ESC) 60 A:** Anti-lock brake system
33. **ALT 100 A:** "A.B.S. (ESC)", "AM1", "STOP", "DEFOG", "FOG", "ECU-B", "TAIL", "A.C" and "RR A/C" fuses, and "FR-HTR" circuit breaker
34. **AM1 50 A:** "ENGINE", "GAUGE", "TURN", "FR-WIPER", "ECU-IG", "A.C", "RADIO", "CIG", "ST", "POWER" and "DOOR" fuses
35. **MAIN 50 A:** "HAZ-HORN", "DOME", "HEAD (LH)", "HEAD (RH)" and "EFI" fuses

**Circuit breaker**

36. **FR-HTR 40 A:** Air conditioning control system

## CHASSIS ELECTRICAL

### FUSE APPLICATIONS—1993–97 MODELS

**Fuses and circuit breaker**

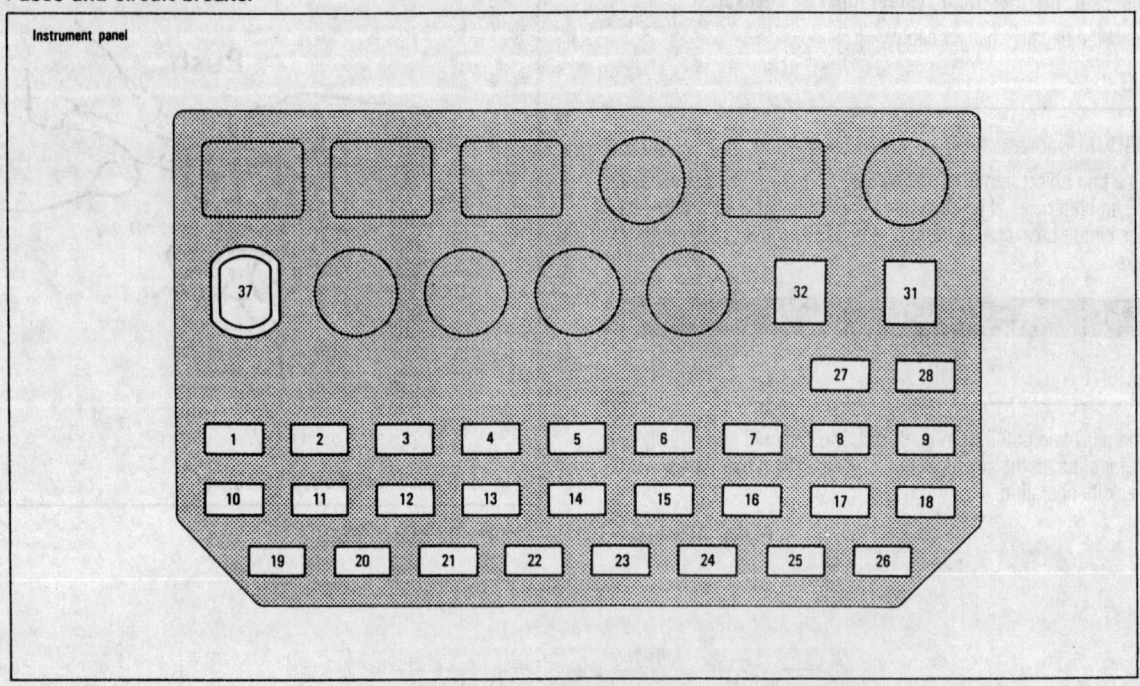

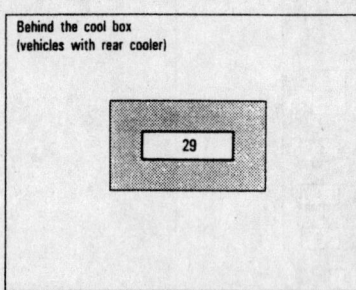

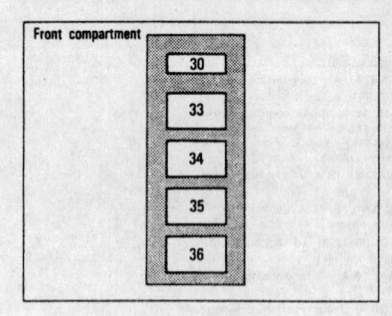

**Fuses (type A)**

1. **ST 7.5 A:** Starter system
2. **IGN 7.5 A:** Charging system, discharge warning light, emission control system, multiport fuel injection system/sequential multiport fuel injection system, SRS airbag system
3. **CHARGE 7.5 A:** Charging system, discharge warning light
4. **FOG 20 A:** Front fog lights
5. **T/M ACC 7.5 A:** Automatic transmission shift indicator
6. **TAIL 15 A:** Tail lights, parking lights, side marker lights, license plate lights, instrument panel lights
7. **HAZ-HORN 15 A:** Emergency flashers, horns, turn signal lights
8. **HEAD (LH) 15 A (U.S.A.) or 10 A (Canada):** Left-hand headlight
9. **HEAD (RH) 15 A (U.S.A.) or 10 A (Canada):** Right-hand headlight
10. **ENGINE 7.5 A:** Charging system, emission control system
11. **RADIO 7.5 A:** Radio, cassette tape player, Compact Disc player
12. **ST-A 7.5 A:** Starter system
13. **STOP 20 A:** Stop lights, anti-lock brake system
14. **DOME 15 A:** Interior lights, luggage compartment light, clock, open door warning light, radio, cassette tape player, Compact Disc player
15. **DEFOG 15 A:** Rear window defogger
16. **ECU-B 15 A:** Anti-lock brake system, electronically controlled automatic transmission system
17. **CIG 15 A:** Cigarette lighter, digital clock display, power rear view mirrors, theft deterrent system, SRS airbag system, automatic transmission shift lock system
18. **EFI 15 A:** Multiport fuel injection system/sequential multiport fuel injection system
19. **TURN 7.5 A:** Turn signal lights
20. **GAUGES 10 A:** Gauges and meters, service reminder indicators and warning buzzers (except discharge and open door warning lights), back-up lights, automatic transmission overdrive system, rear window defogger, electric rear sun roof, power windows, power door lock system
21. **FR-WIPER 30 A:** Windshield wipers and washer
22. **ENGINE OIL 15 A:** Engine oil auto-feed system
23. **RR WIPER 15 A:** Rear window wiper and washer
24. **A/C 15 A:** Air conditioning cooling system, cool box
25. **ECU-IG 15 A:** Cruise control system, electronically controlled automatic transmission system, anti-lock brake system, theft deterrent system
26. **FR-WASHER 10 A:** Windshield washer motor
27. **HEAD (LH-UPR) 10 A:** Left-hand headlight (Canada only)
28. **HEAD (RH-UPR) 10 A:** Right-hand headlight (Canada only)
29. **RR A/C 10 A:** Air conditioning cooling system (rear)
30. **AM2 20 A:** Charging system, discharge warning light, emission control system, multiport fuel injection system/sequential multiport fuel injection system

**Fuses (type B)**

31. **DOOR 30 A:** Power door lock system, theft deterrent system
32. **POWER 30 A:** Electric rear sun roof, power windows

**Fuses (type C)**

33. **A.B.S. (ESC) 60 A:** Anti-lock brake system
34. **ALT 100 A:** "A.B.S. (ESC)", "AM1", "STOP", "DEFOG", "FOG", "ECU-B", "TAIL", "A/C" and "RR A/C" fuses, and "FR-HTR" circuit breaker
35. **AM1 50 A:** "ENGINE", "GAUGE", "TURN", "FR-WIPER", "ECU-IG", "A/C", "RADIO", "CIG", "ST", "POWER" and "DOOR" fuses
36. **MAIN 50 A:** "HAZ-HORN", "DOME", "HEAD (LH)", "HEAD (RH)" and "EFI" fuses

**Circuit breaker**

37. **FR-HTR 40 A:** Air conditioning control system

# CHASSIS ELECTRICAL 6-41

## WIRING DIAGRAMS

# INDEX OF WIRING DIAGRAMS

**DIAGRAM 1**  Sample Diagram: How To Read & Interpret Wiring Diagrams

**DIAGRAM 2**  Wiring Diagram Symbols

**DIAGRAM 3**  1991-93 Previa 2TZ-FE Engine Schematic

**DIAGRAM 4**  1994-95 Previa 2TZ-FE Engine Schematic

**DIAGRAM 5**  1995-97 Previa 2TZ-FZE Engine Schematic

**DIAGRAM 6**  Previa ECM Connector Pin-Out

**DIAGRAM 7**  1991-97 Starting, Charging Chassis Schematics

**DIAGRAM 8**  1991-97 Headlights W/O DRL, Back-up Lights, Stop Lights Chassis Schematics

**DIAGRAM 9**  1991 Headlights W/ DRL, 1991-97 Fuel Pump Chassis Schematics

**DIAGRAM 10**  1992-97 Headlights W/ DRL

**DIAGRAM 11**  1991-97 Parking/ Marker Lights, Turn/ Hazard Lights Chassis Schematics

**DIAGRAM 12**  1991 Power Window Chassis Schematic

**DIAGRAM 13**  1992-97 Power Window Chassis Schematic

**DIAGRAM 14**  1991-97 Front Washer/ Wiper Chassis Schematics

**DIAGRAM 15**  1991-96 Rear Washer/ Wiper Chassis Schematics

**DIAGRAM 16**  1997 Rear Washer/ Wiper, 1991-97 Horn, Remote Mirrors Chassis Schematics

9091W01

## 6-42 CHASSIS ELECTRICAL

### SAMPLE DIAGRAM: HOW TO READ & INTERPRET WIRING DIAGRAMS

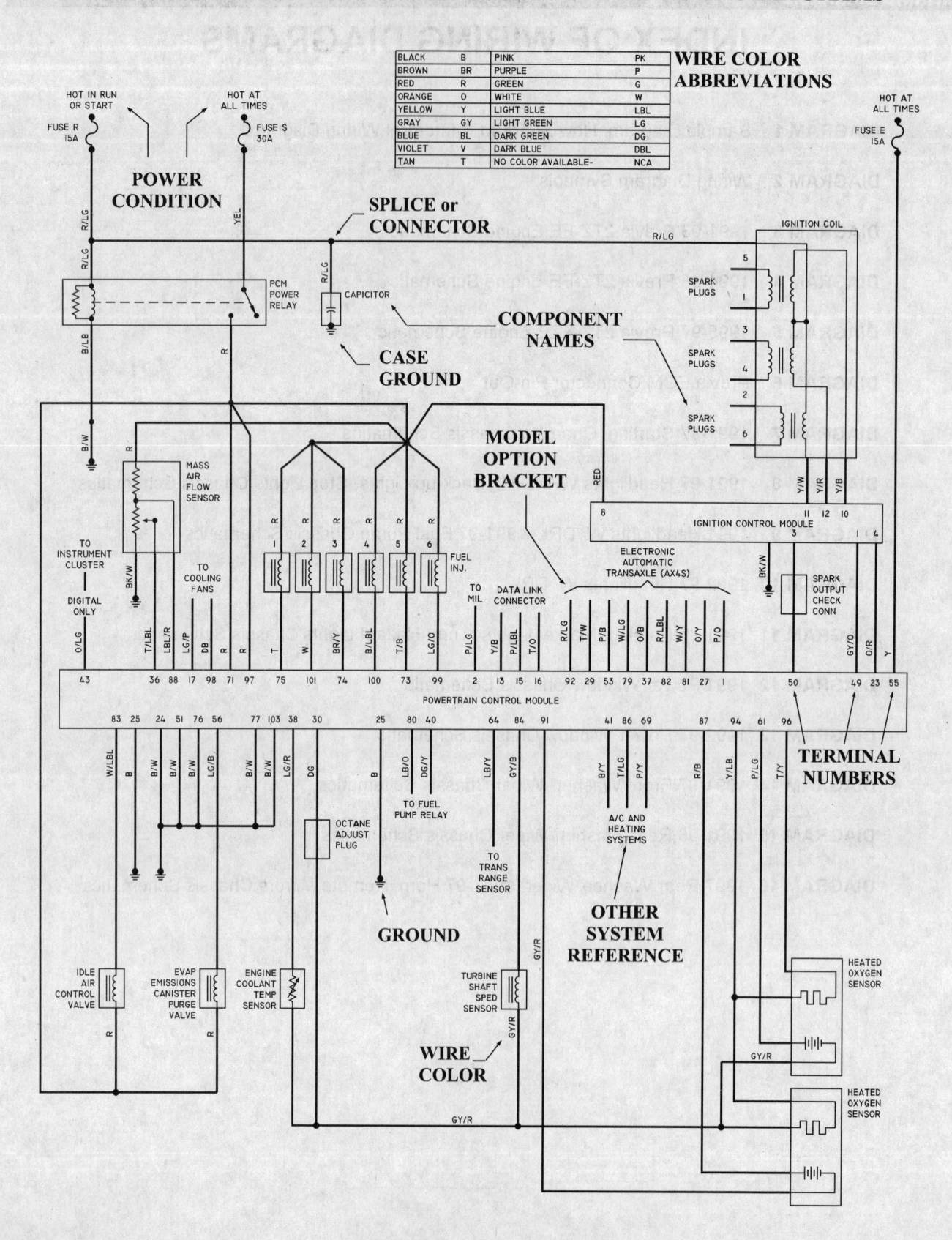

**DIAGRAM 1**

# CHASSIS ELECTRICAL  6-43

## WIRING DIAGRAM SYMBOLS

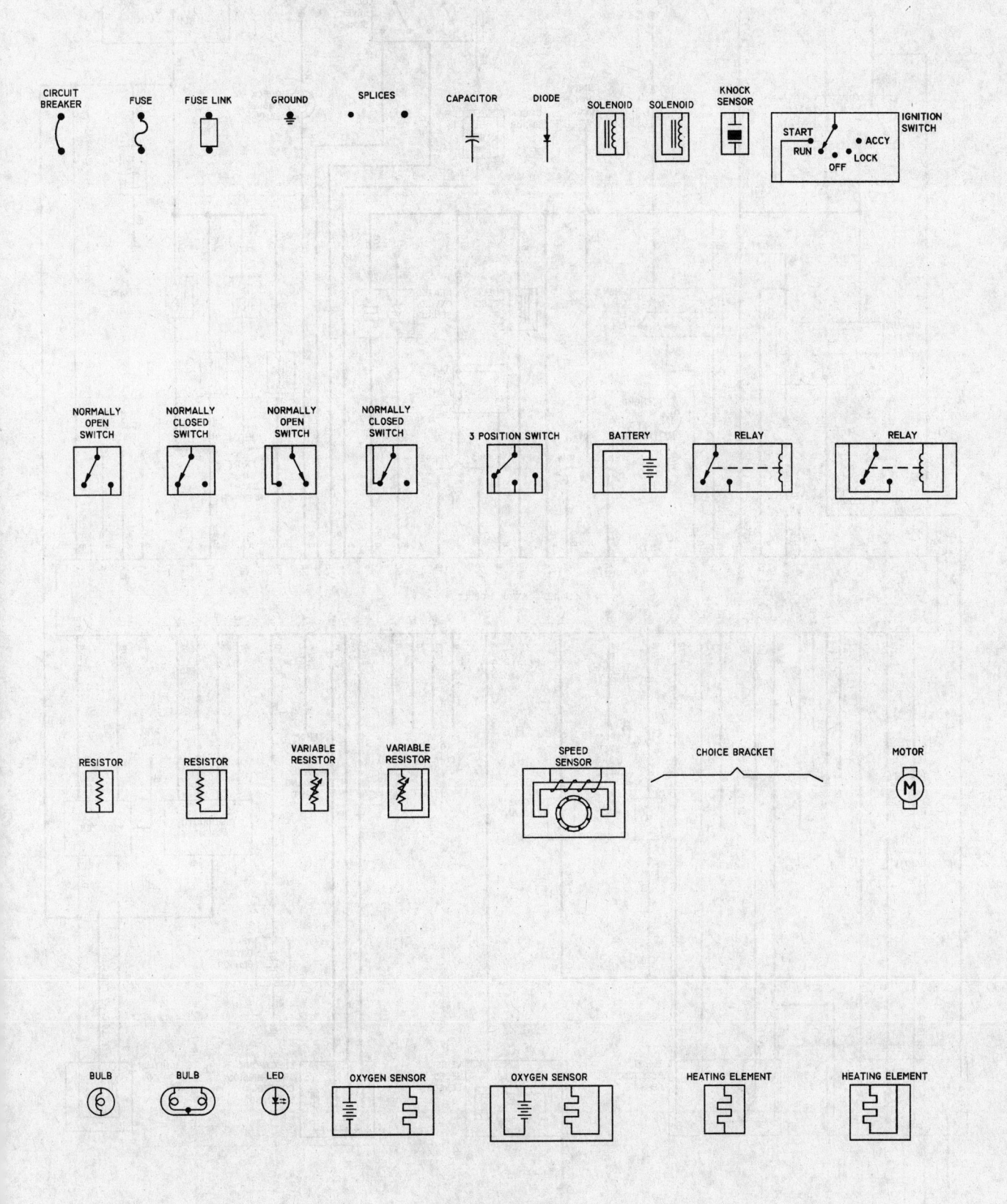

**DIAGRAM 2**

## 6-44 CHASSIS ELECTRICAL

### 1991-93 Previa 2TZ-FE Engine Schematic

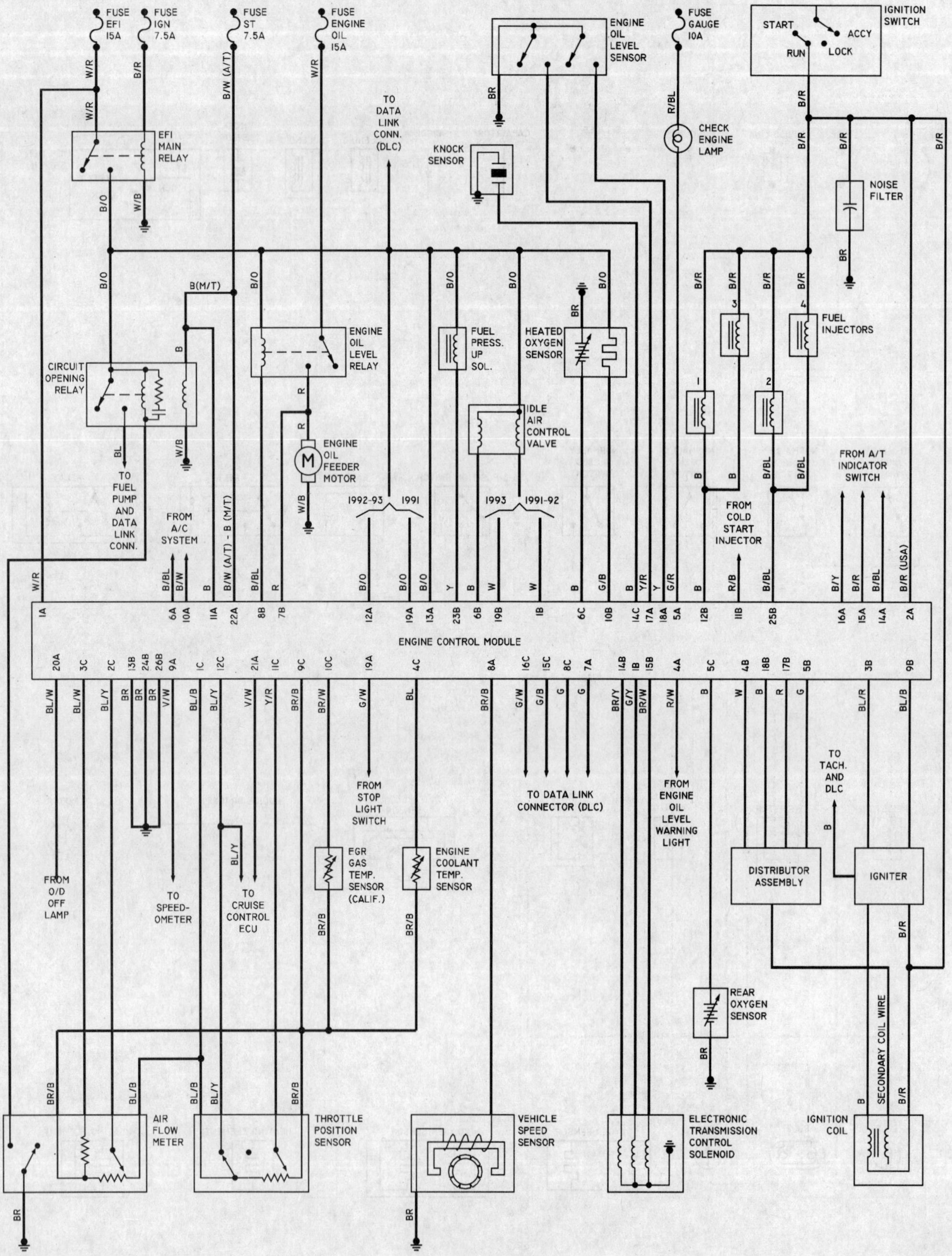

DIAGRAM 3

## CHASSIS ELECTRICAL  6-45

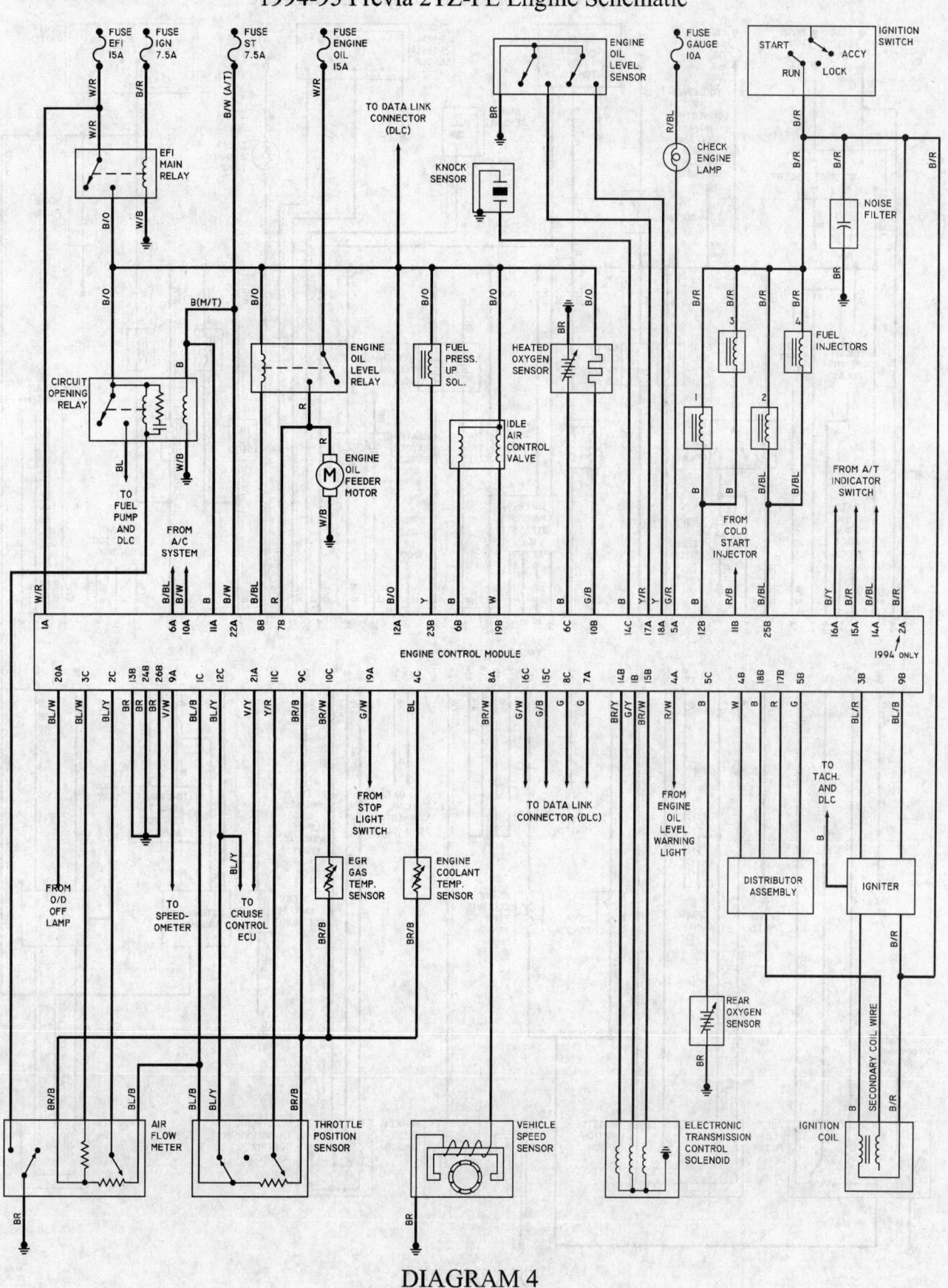

### 1994-95 Previa 2TZ-FE Engine Schematic

DIAGRAM 4

## 6-46  CHASSIS ELECTRICAL

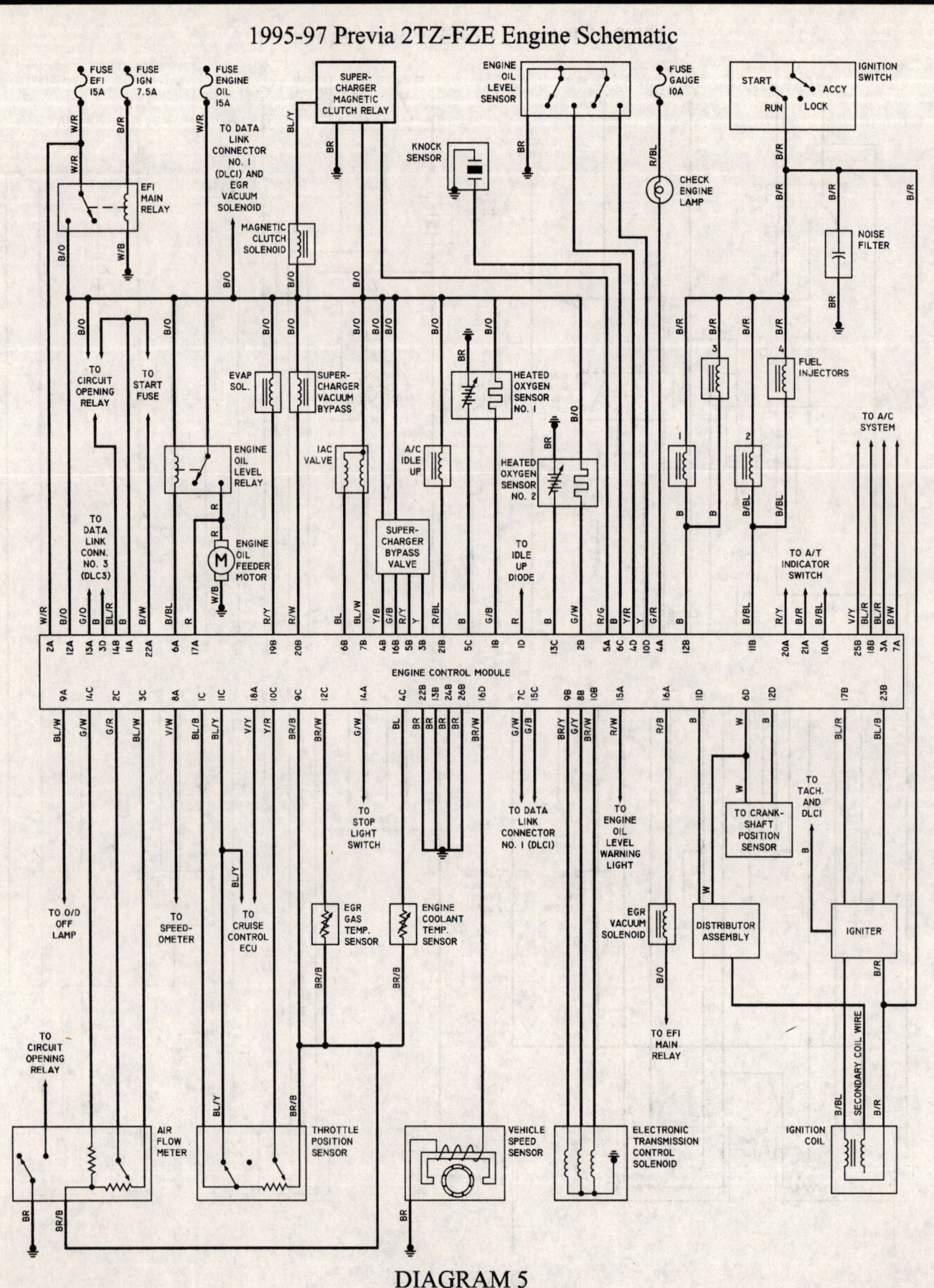

### 1995-97 Previa 2TZ-FZE Engine Schematic

DIAGRAM 5

# CHASSIS ELECTRICAL  6-47

## Toyota Previa ECM Connectors

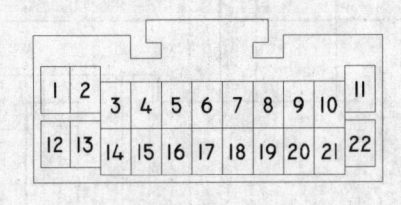

**CONNECTOR A**

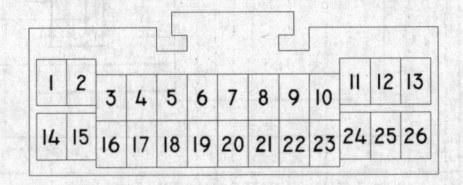

Pins: 1, 2, 3, 4, 5, 6, 7, 8, 9, 10, 11 / 12, 13, 14, 15, 16, 17, 18, 19, 20, 21, 22

**CONNECTOR B**

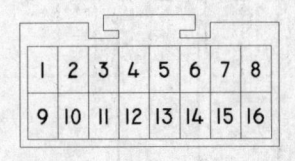

Pins: 1, 2, 3, 4, 5, 6, 7, 8, 9, 10, 11, 12, 13 / 14, 15, 16, 17, 18, 19, 20, 21, 22, 23, 24, 25, 26

**CONNECTOR C**

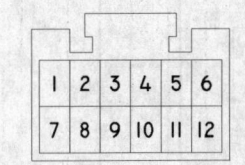

Pins: 1, 2, 3, 4, 5, 6, 7, 8 / 9, 10, 11, 12, 13, 14, 15, 16

**CONNECTOR D**

(1995-97 2TZ-FZE ONLY)

Pins: 1, 2, 3, 4, 5, 6 / 7, 8, 9, 10, 11, 12

VIEW SHOWN IS OF THE WIRE HARNESS CONNECTOR. THE ECM PINS WILL BE THE REVERSE OF THE ABOVE ILLUSTRATIONS.

DIAGRAM 6

90916E04

# 6-48 CHASSIS ELECTRICAL

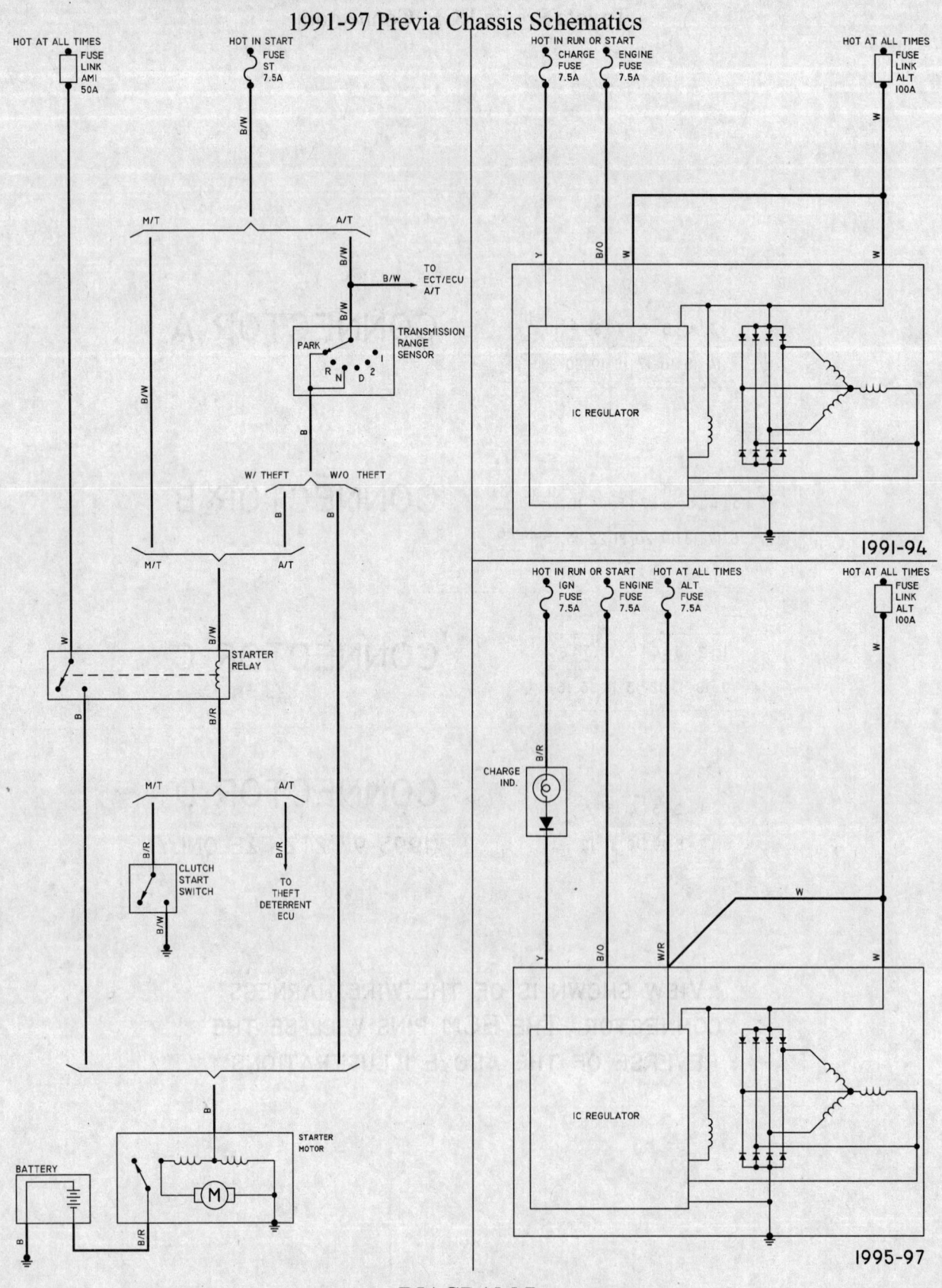

## 1991-97 Previa Chassis Schematics

DIAGRAM 7

# CHASSIS ELECTRICAL 6-49

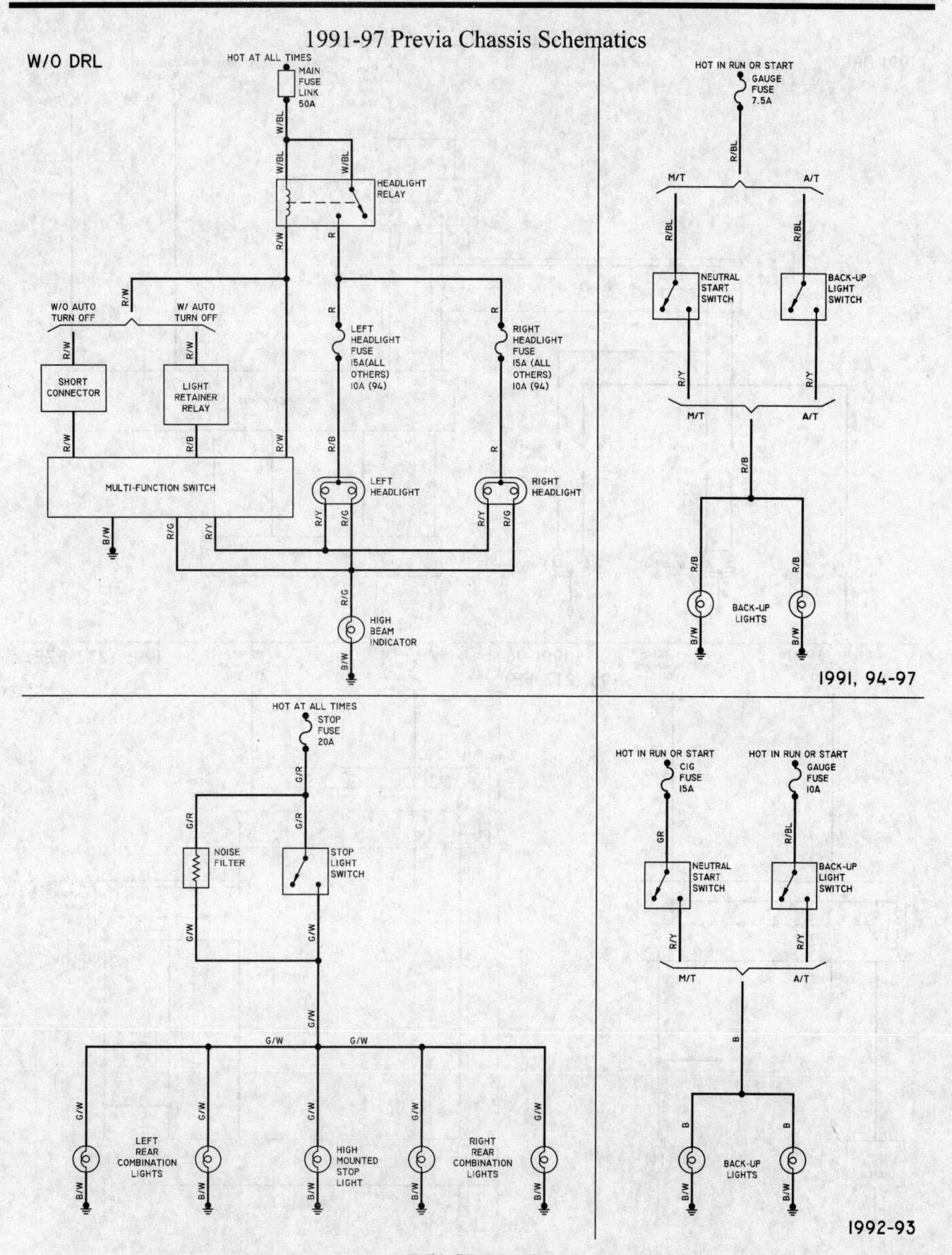

## 1991-97 Previa Chassis Schematics

**DIAGRAM 8**

## 6-50 CHASSIS ELECTRICAL

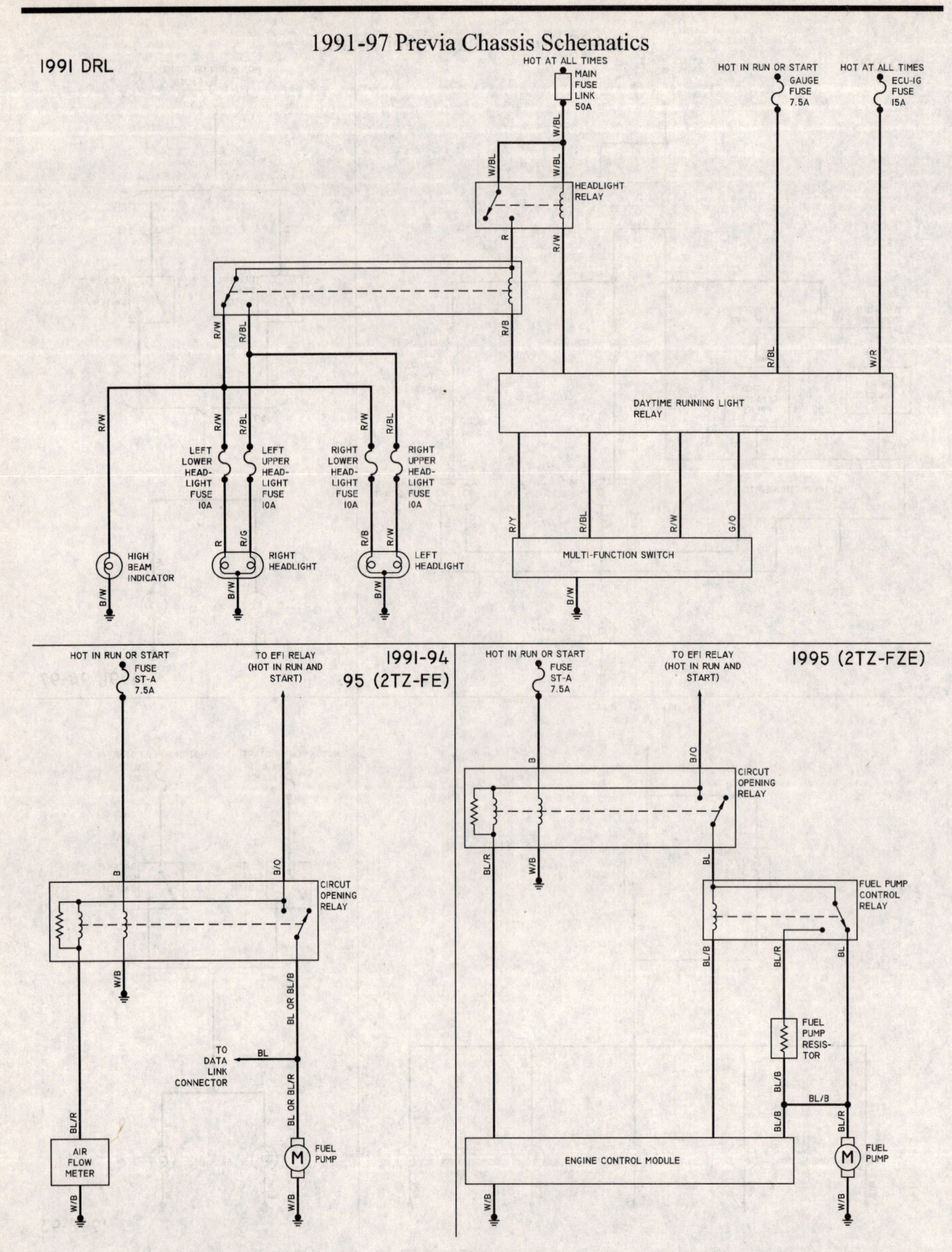

### 1991-97 Previa Chassis Schematics

DIAGRAM 9

## CHASSIS ELECTRICAL 6-51

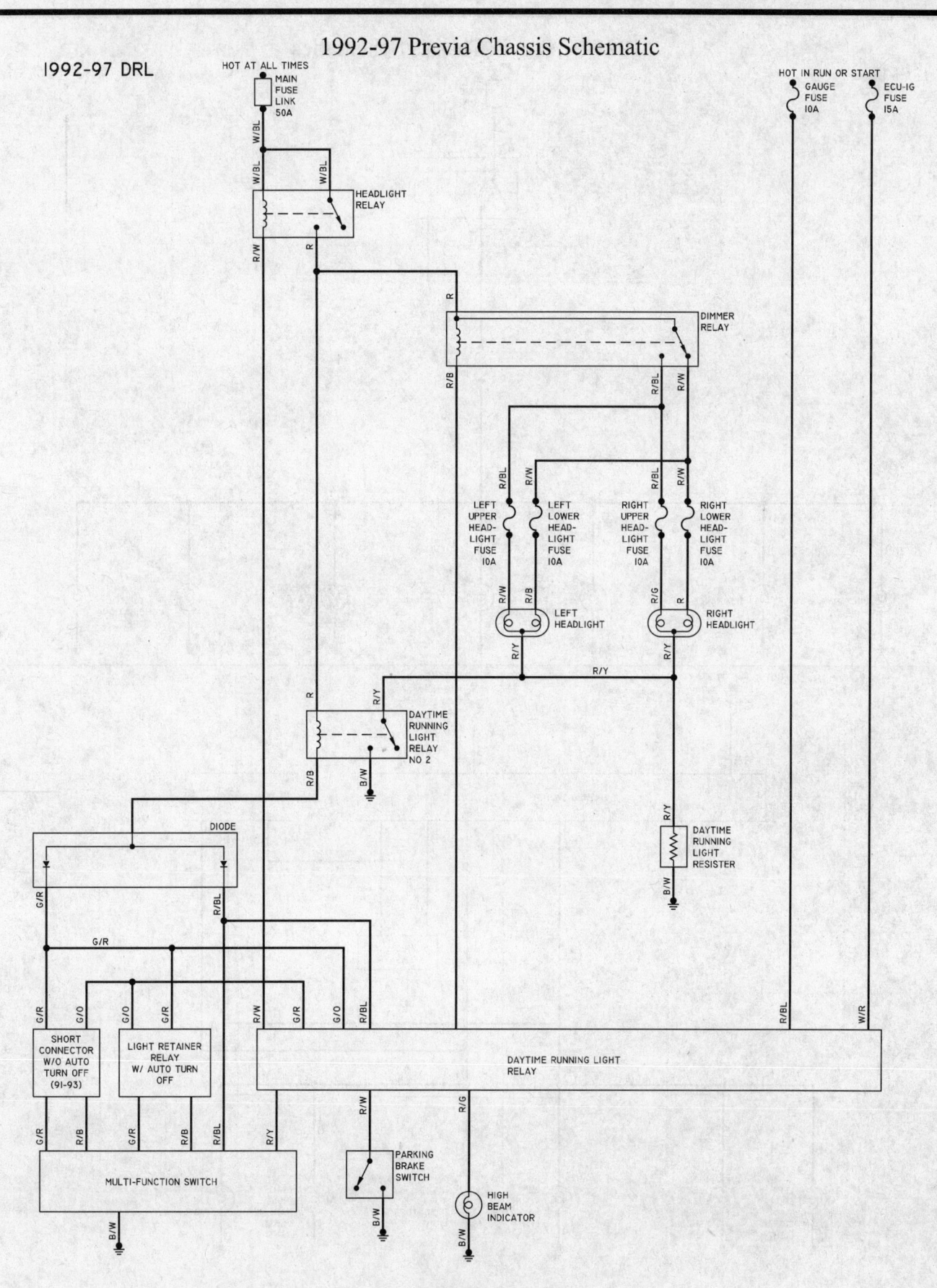

### 1992-97 Previa Chassis Schematic

1992-97 DRL

DIAGRAM 10

## 6-52 CHASSIS ELECTRICAL

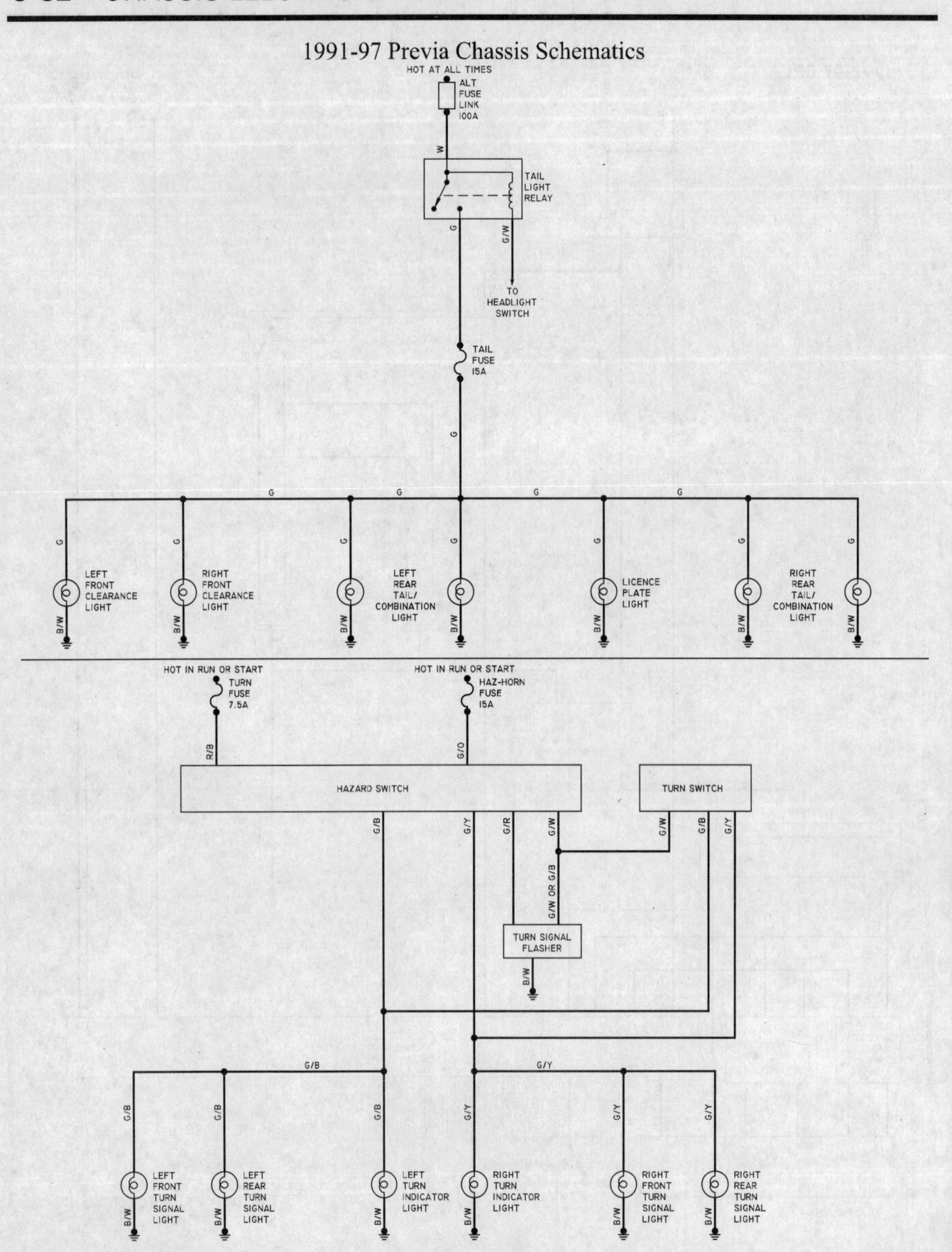

### 1991-97 Previa Chassis Schematics

DIAGRAM 11

## CHASSIS ELECTRICAL 6-53

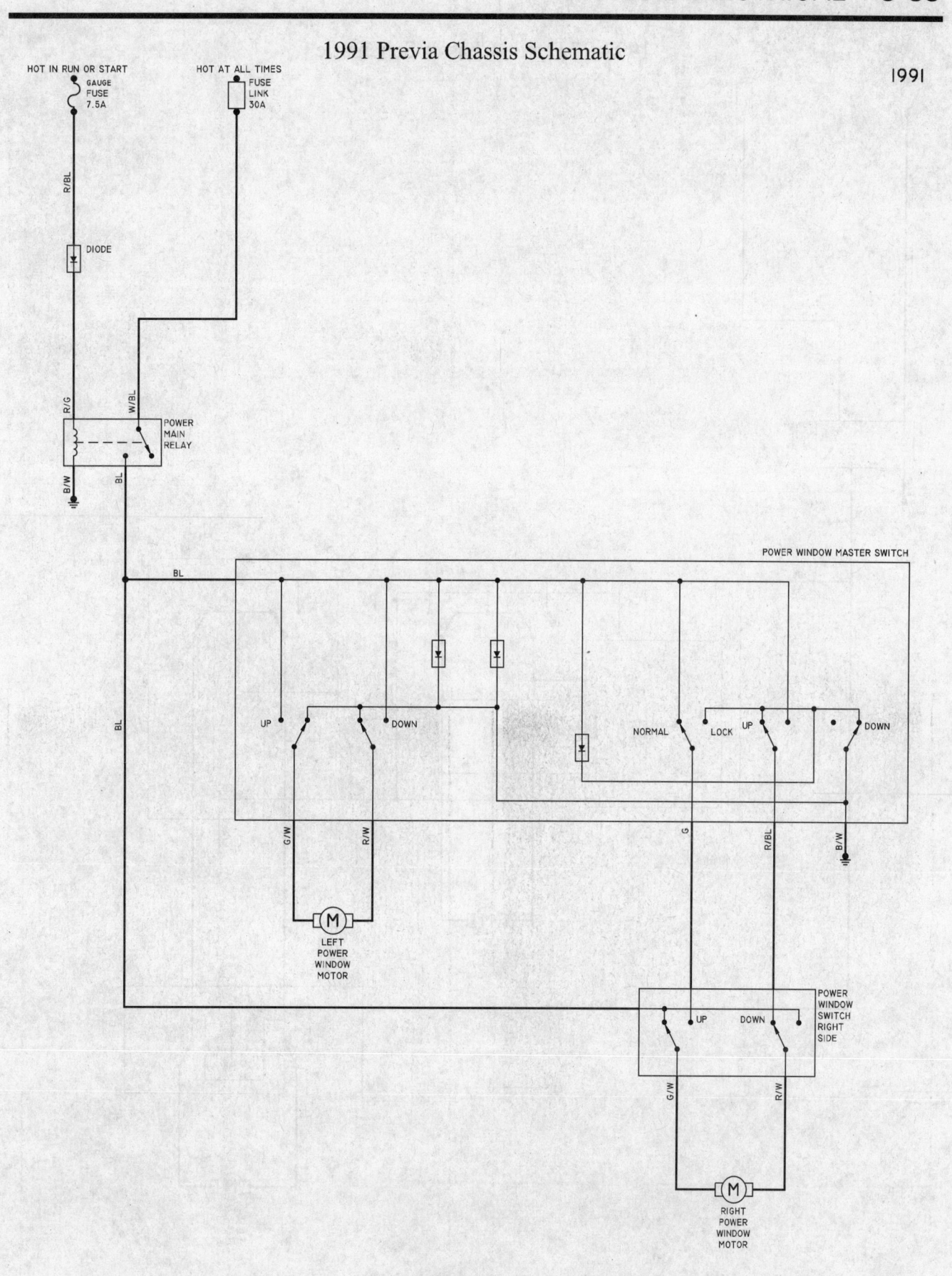

### 1991 Previa Chassis Schematic

1991

DIAGRAM 12

90916B06

## 6-54 CHASSIS ELECTRICAL

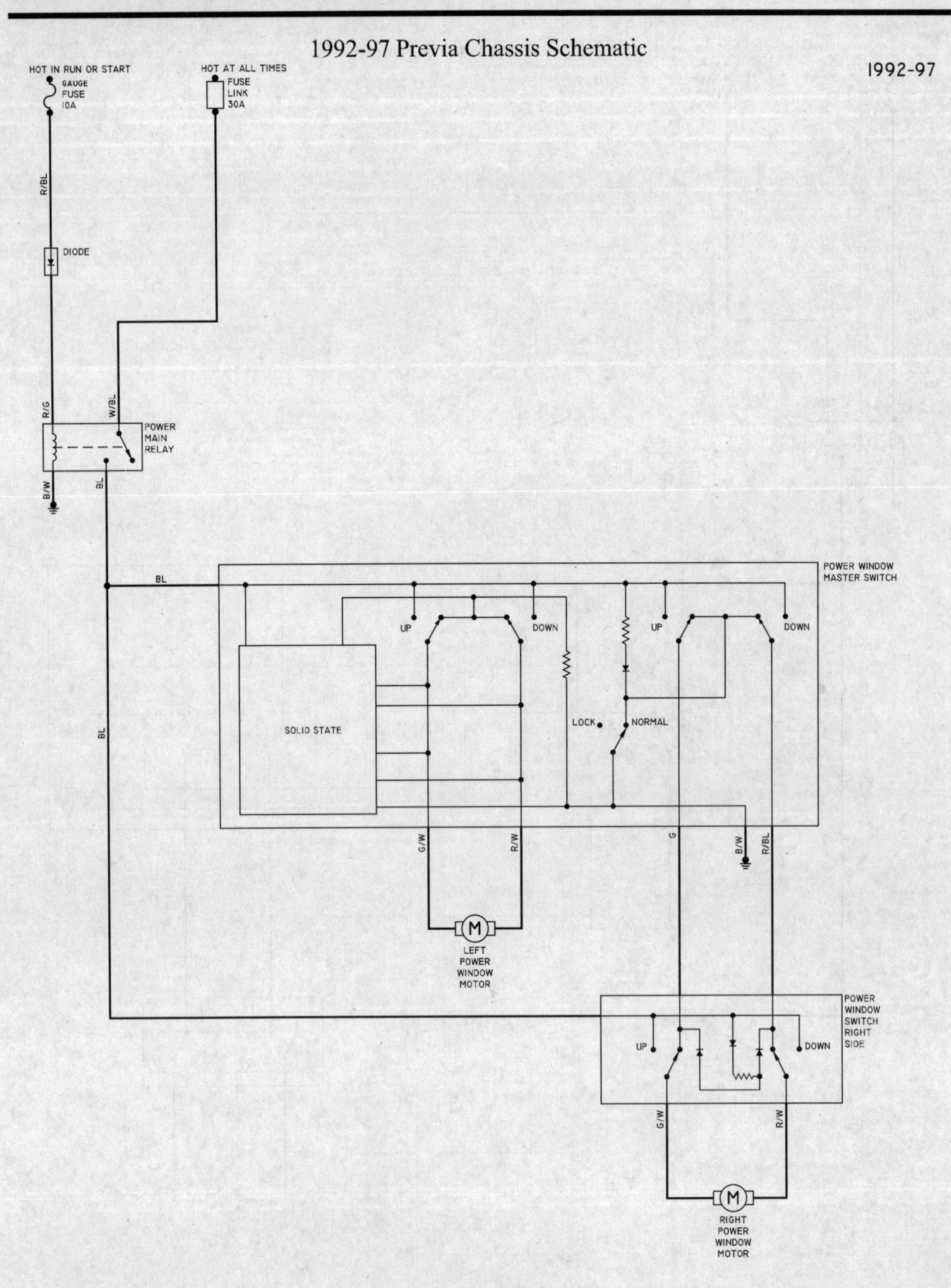

### 1992-97 Previa Chassis Schematic

1992-97

DIAGRAM 13

## CHASSIS ELECTRICAL 6-55

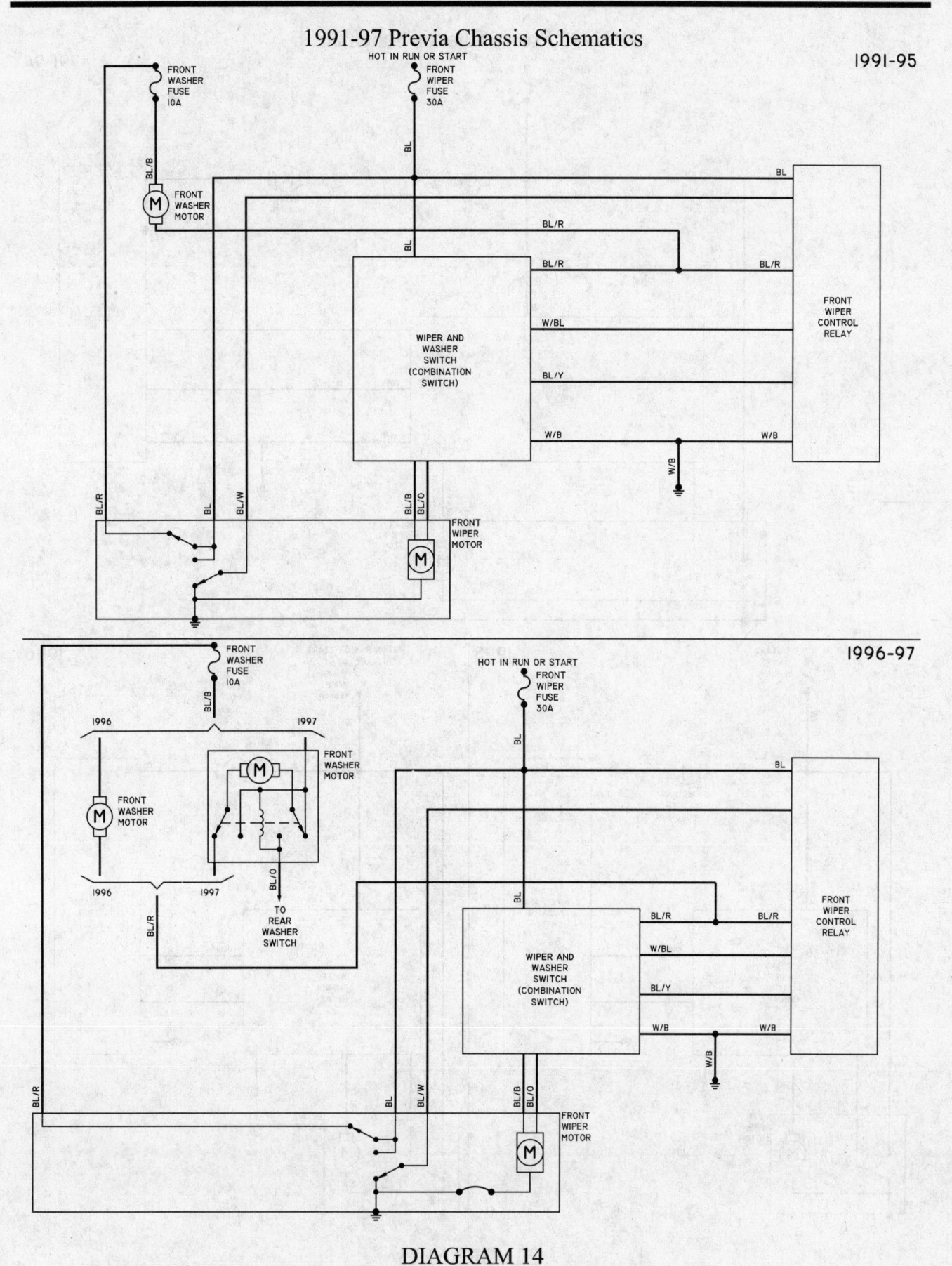

### 1991-97 Previa Chassis Schematics

1991-95

1996-97

DIAGRAM 14

# 6-56 CHASSIS ELECTRICAL

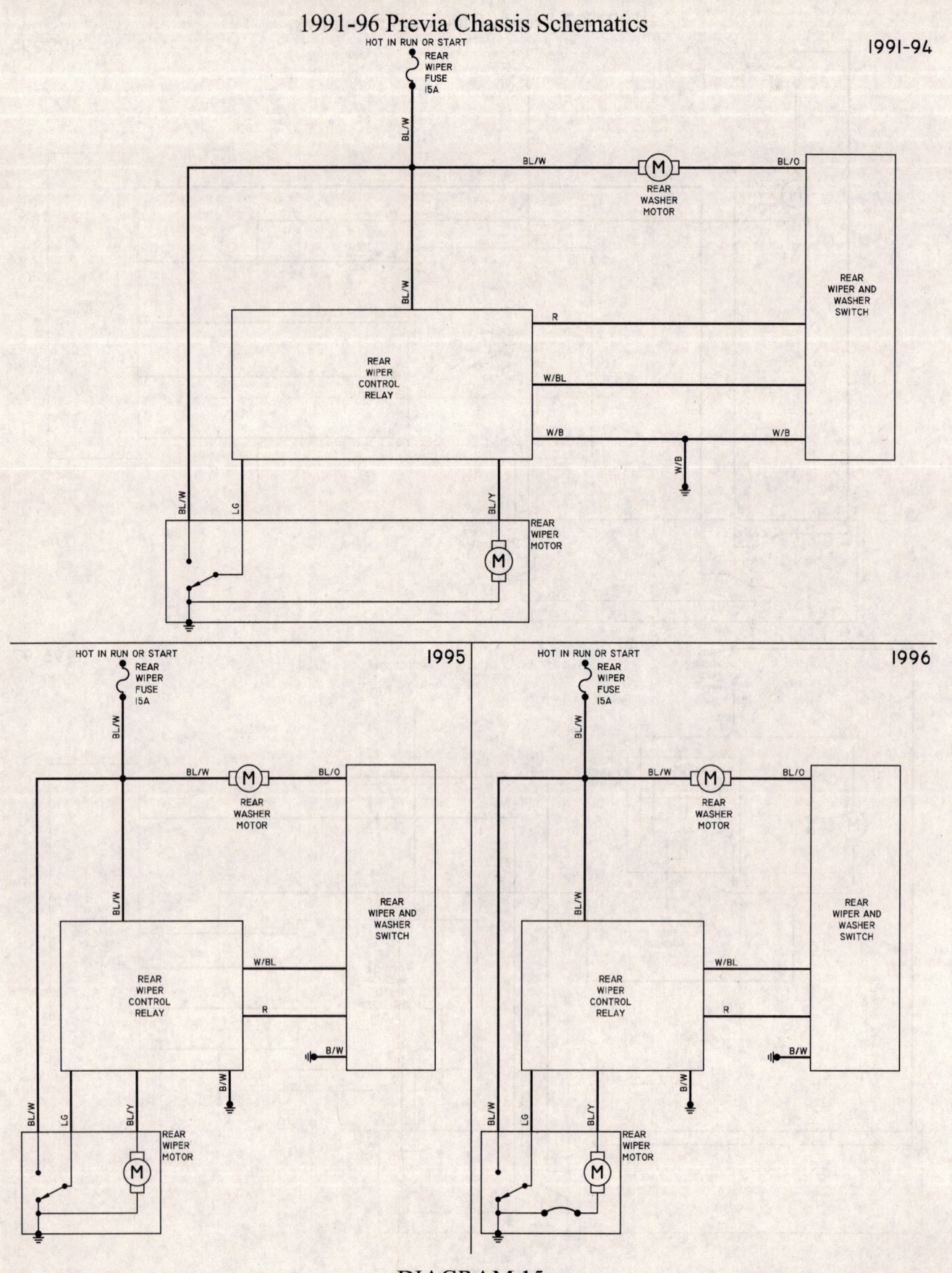

## 1991-96 Previa Chassis Schematics

DIAGRAM 15

# CHASSIS ELECTRICAL 6-57

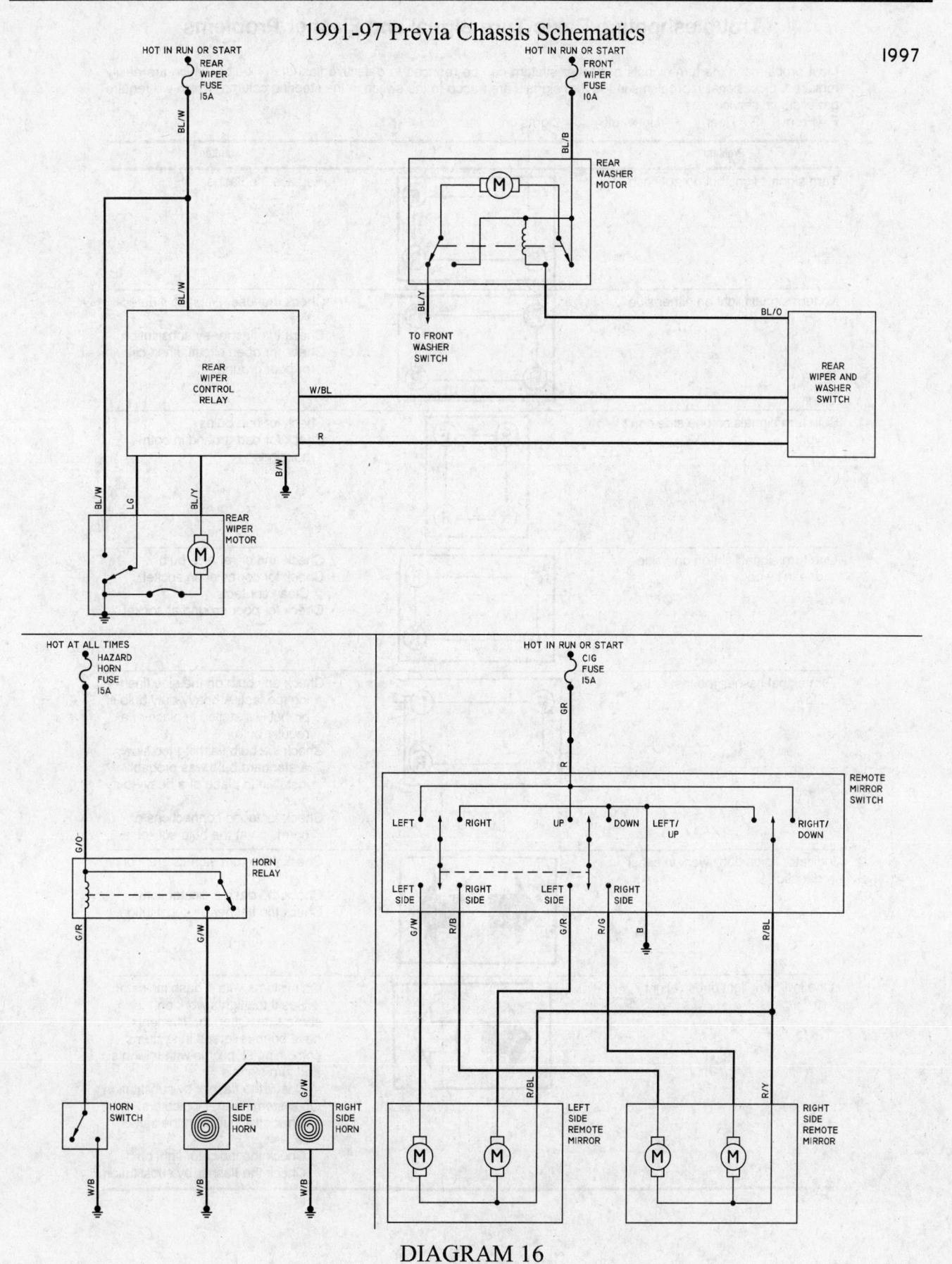

## 1991-97 Previa Chassis Schematics

1997

**DIAGRAM 16**

## CHASSIS ELECTRICAL

### Troubleshooting Basic Turn Signal and Flasher Problems

Most problems in the turn signals or flasher system can be reduced to defective flashers or bulbs, which are easily replaced. Occasionally, problems in the turn signals are traced to the switch in the steering column, which will require professional service.

F = Front   R = Rear   ● = Lights off   ○ = Lights on

| Problem | | Solution |
|---|---|---|
| Turn signals light, but do not flash | | • Replace the flasher |
| No turn signals light on either side | | • Check the fuse. Replace if defective.<br>• Check the flasher by substitution<br>• Check for open circuit, short circuit or poor ground |
| Both turn signals on one side don't work | | • Check for bad bulbs<br>• Check for bad ground in both housings |
| One turn signal light on one side doesn't work | | • Check and/or replace bulb<br>• Check for corrosion in socket. Clean contacts.<br>• Check for poor ground at socket |
| Turn signal flashes too fast or too slow | | • Check any bulb on the side flashing too fast. A heavy-duty bulb is probably installed in place of a regular bulb.<br>• Check the bulb flashing too slow. A standard bulb was probably installed in place of a heavy-duty bulb.<br>• Check for loose connections or corrosion at the bulb socket |
| Indicator lights don't work in either direction | | • Check if the turn signals are working<br>• Check the dash indicator lights<br>• Check the flasher by substitution |
| One indicator light doesn't light | | • On systems with 1 dash indicator: See if the lights work on the same side. Often the filaments have been reversed in systems combining stoplights with taillights and turn signals. Check the flasher by substitution<br>• On systems with 2 indicators: Check the bulbs on the same side. Check the indicator light bulb. Check the flasher by substitution |

TCCA6C02

**MANUAL TRANSMISSION 7-2**
UNDERSTANDING THE MANUAL TRANS-
  MISSION 7-2
BACK-UP LIGHT SWITCH 7-2
  REMOVAL & INSTALLATION 7-2
EXTENSION HOUSING SEAL 7-2
  REMOVAL & INSTALLATION 7-2
MANUAL TRANSMISSION
  ASSEMBLY 7-2
  REMOVAL & INSTALLATION 7-2
HALFSHAFT 7-4
  REMOVAL & INSTALLATION 7-4
  OVERHAUL 7-7
**CLUTCH 7-8**
UNDERSTANDING THE CLUTCH 7-8
DRIVEN DISC AND PRESSURE
  PLATE 7-9
  REMOVAL & INSTALLATION 7-9
  ADJUSTMENTS 7-11
MASTER CYLINDER 7-12
  REMOVAL & INSTALLATION 7-12
SLAVE CYLINDER 7-12
  REMOVAL & INSTALLATION 7-12
CLUTCH ACCUMULATOR 7-12
  REMOVAL & INSTALLATION 7-12
HYDRAULIC SYSTEM BLEEDING 7-13
**AUTOMATIC TRANSMISSION 7-13**
UNDERSTANDING THE AUTOMATIC
  TRANSMISSION 7-13
    TORQUE CONVERTER 7-13
    PLANETARY GEARBOX 7-14
    SERVOS AND ACCUMULATORS 7-15
    HYDRAULIC CONTROL
      SYSTEM 7-15
BACK-UP LIGHT/NEUTRAL SAFETY
  SWITCH 7-15
  REMOVAL & INSTALLATION 7-15
  ADJUSTMENT 7-17
EXTENSION HOUSING SEAL 7-17
  REMOVAL & INSTALLATION 7-17
AUTOMATIC TRANSMISSION
  ASSEMBLY 7-17
  REMOVAL & INSTALLATION 7-17
  ADJUSTMENTS 7-19
**TRANSFER CASE 7-20**
EXTENSION HOUSING SEAL 7-20
  REMOVAL & INSTALLATION 7-20
COMPANION FLANGE SEAL 7-20
  REMOVAL & INSTALLATION 7-20
TRANSFER CASE ASSEMBLY 7-20
  REMOVAL & INSTALLATION 7-20
**DRIVELINE 7-21**
FRONT DRIVESHAFT AND
  U-JOINTS 7-21
  REMOVAL & INSTALLATION 7-21
  U-JOINT REPLACEMENT 7-23
REAR DRIVESHAFT AND U-JOINTS 7-24
  REMOVAL & INSTALLATION 7-24
  U-JOINT REPLACEMENT 7-27

CENTER SUPPORT BEARING 7-27
  REMOVAL & INSTALLATION 7-27
**FRONT DRIVE AXLE 7-28**
AXLE SHAFT, BEARING AND SEAL 7-28
  REMOVAL & INSTALLATION 7-28
PINION SEAL 7-30
  REMOVAL & INSTALLATION 7-30
AXLE HOUSING ASSEMBLY 7-31
  REMOVAL & INSTALLATION 7-31
**REAR AXLE 7-32**
AXLE SHAFT, BEARING AND SEAL 7-32
  REMOVAL & INSTALLATION 7-32
PINION SEAL 7-34
  REMOVAL & INSTALLATION 7-34
DIFFERENTIAL CARRIER 7-35
  REMOVAL & INSTALLATION 7-35
**SPECIFICATIONS CHART**
  TORQUE SPECIFICATIONS 7-36

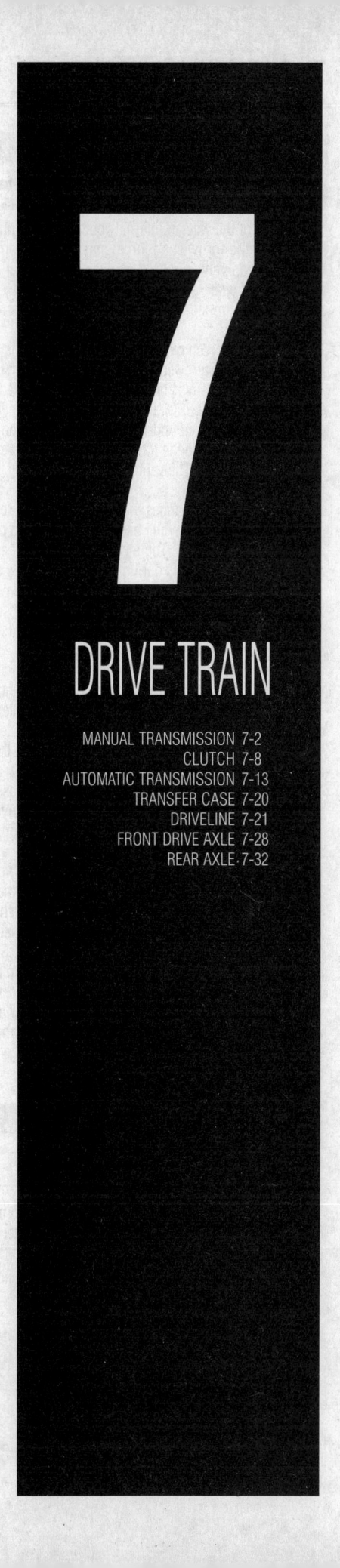

# 7

# DRIVE TRAIN

MANUAL TRANSMISSION 7-2
CLUTCH 7-8
AUTOMATIC TRANSMISSION 7-13
TRANSFER CASE 7-20
DRIVELINE 7-21
FRONT DRIVE AXLE 7-28
REAR AXLE 7-32

# 7-2 DRIVE TRAIN

## MANUAL TRANSMISSION

### Understanding the Manual Transmission

Because of the way an internal combustion engine breathes, it can produce torque (or twisting force) only within a narrow speed range. Most overhead valve pushrod engines must turn at about 2500 rpm to produce their peak torque. Often by 4500 rpm, they are producing so little torque that continued increases in engine speed produce no power increases.

The torque peak on overhead camshaft engines is, generally, much higher, but much narrower.

The manual transmission and clutch are employed to vary the relationship between engine RPM and the speed of the wheels so that adequate power can be produced under all circumstances. The clutch allows engine torque to be applied to the transmission input shaft gradually, due to mechanical slippage. The vehicle can, consequently, be started smoothly from a full stop.

The transmission changes the ratio between the rotating speeds of the engine and the wheels by the use of gears. 4-speed or 5-speed transmissions are most common. The lower gears allow full engine power to be applied to the rear wheels during acceleration at low speeds.

The clutch driveplate is a thin disc, the center of which is splined to the transmission input shaft. Both sides of the disc are covered with a layer of material which is similar to brake lining and which is capable of allowing slippage without roughness or excessive noise.

The clutch cover is bolted to the engine flywheel and incorporates a diaphragm spring which provides the pressure to engage the clutch. The cover also houses the pressure plate. When the clutch pedal is released, the driven disc is sandwiched between the pressure plate and the smooth surface of the flywheel, thus forcing the disc to turn at the same speed as the engine crankshaft.

The transmission contains a mainshaft which passes all the way through the transmission, from the clutch to the driveshaft. This shaft is separated at one point, so that front and rear portions can turn at different speeds.

Power is transmitted by a countershaft in the lower gears and reverse. The gears of the countershaft mesh with gears on the mainshaft, allowing power to be carried from one to the other. Countershaft gears are often integral with that shaft, while several of the mainshaft gears can either rotate independently of the shaft or be locked to it. Shifting from one gear to the next causes one of the gears to be freed from rotating with the shaft and locks another to it. Gears are locked and unlocked by internal dog clutches which slide between the center of the gear and the shaft. The forward gears usually employ synchronizers; friction members which smoothly bring gear and shaft to the same speed before the toothed dog clutches are engaged.

### Back-up Light Switch

#### REMOVAL & INSTALLATION

Locate and unscrew the back-up light switch from the transmission housing. Carefully thread the new switch and tighten to 27 ft. lbs. (37 Nm).

### Extension Housing Seal

#### REMOVAL & INSTALLATION

1. Using a seal puller, remove the oil seal from the extension housing. Lubricate the seal with transmission oil and drive the new oil seal into the housing.

### Manual Transmission Assembly

#### REMOVAL & INSTALLATION

▶ See Figures 1 thru 6

1. Disconnect the negative battery cable. Wait at least 90 seconds to perform any work on models equipped with air bags.

#### ✱✱ CAUTION

**Some models covered by this manual may be equipped with a Supplemental Restraint System (SRS), which uses an air bag. Whenever working near any of the SRS components, such as the impact sensors, the air bag module, steering column and instrument panel, disable the SRS, as described in Section 6.**

2. Drain the transmission fluid.
3. Raise the vehicle and support safely.
4. Remove the starter motor. Matchmark the driveshafts-to-flange and remove the front (4WD) and rear driveshafts.
5. Remove the clutch release cylinder, hose and bracket.
6. Remove the exhaust pipe bracket which is retained by four bolts.
7. Disconnect the control cables/bracket and speed sensor wiring.
8. Remove the engine-to-transmission stiffener plate.
9. Place a suitable transmission jack under the transmission.
10. Remove the engine rear mounting bolts and raise the rear side of the engine.
11. Remove the engine-to-transmission bolts, pull the transmission toward the rear and extract.

**To install:**

12. Align the input shaft with the clutch disc and push the transmission fully into position.
13. Install the transmission bolts and tighten to 53 ft. lbs. (72 Nm).
14. Install the rear engine mounts and stiffener plate. Tighten the bolts to 27 ft. lbs. (37 Nm).
15. Connect the speed sensor and control cables.
16. Install the exhaust pipe bracket and tighten to 37 ft. lbs. (51 Nm).
17. Install the clutch release cylinder, starter and driveshafts. Tighten the starter to 41 ft. lbs. (56 Nm) and driveshaft bolts to 20 ft. lbs. (25 Nm).
18. Lower the vehicle.
19. Connect the battery cable and refill with transmission fluid.

## DRIVE TRAIN 7-3

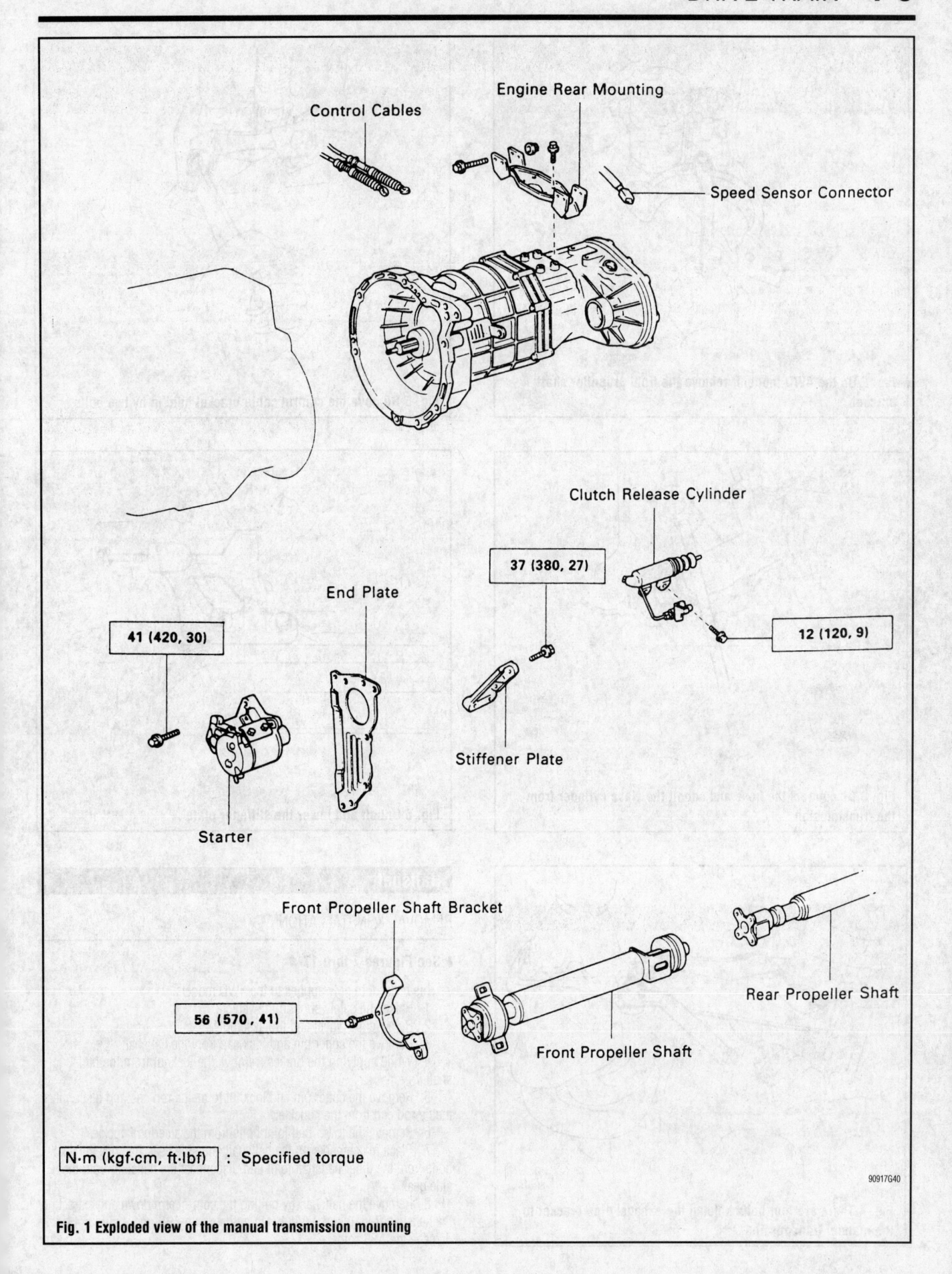

**Fig. 1 Exploded view of the manual transmission mounting**

N·m (kgf·cm, ft·lbf) : Specified torque

Labels: Control Cables, Engine Rear Mounting, Speed Sensor Connector, Clutch Release Cylinder, End Plate, Stiffener Plate, Starter, Front Propeller Shaft Bracket, Front Propeller Shaft, Rear Propeller Shaft

Torque values: 41 (420, 30); 37 (380, 27); 12 (120, 9); 56 (570, 41)

## 7-4 DRIVE TRAIN

Fig. 2 On the 4WD models, remove the front propeller shaft bracket

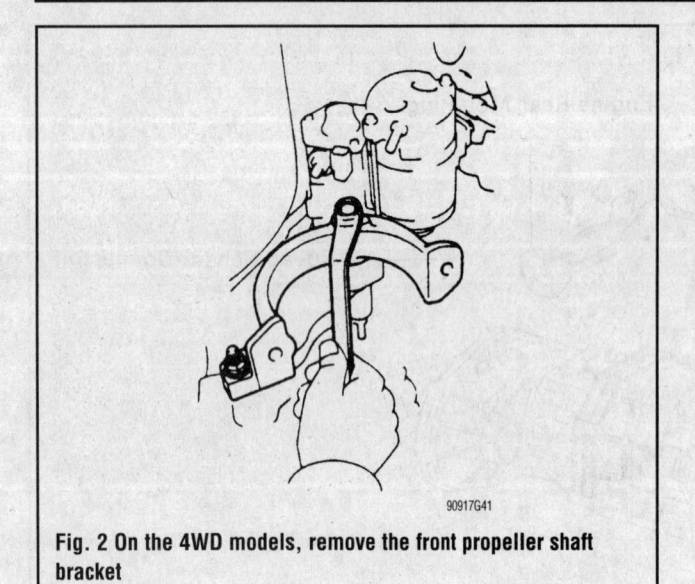

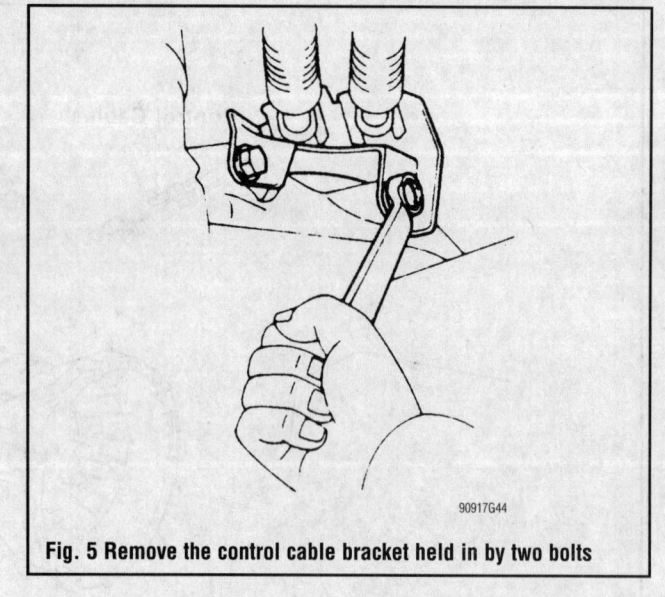

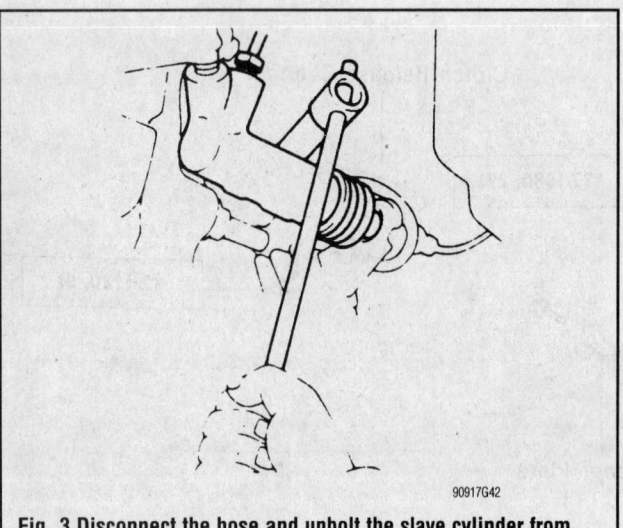

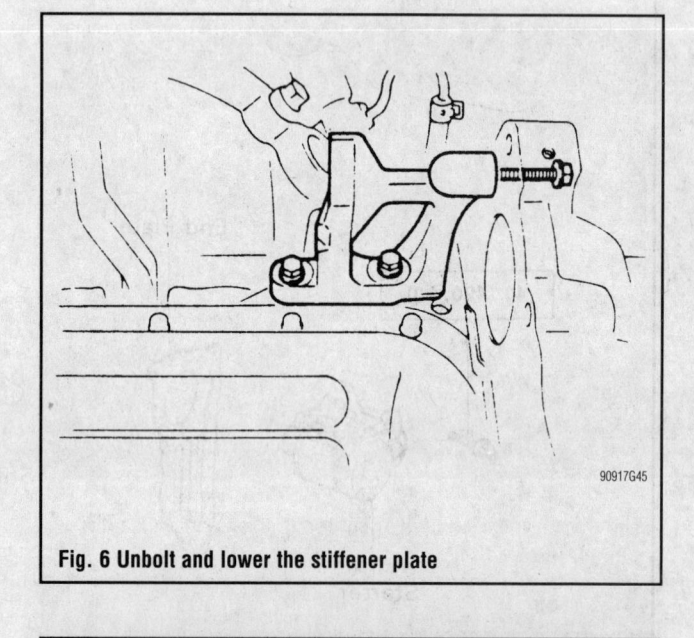

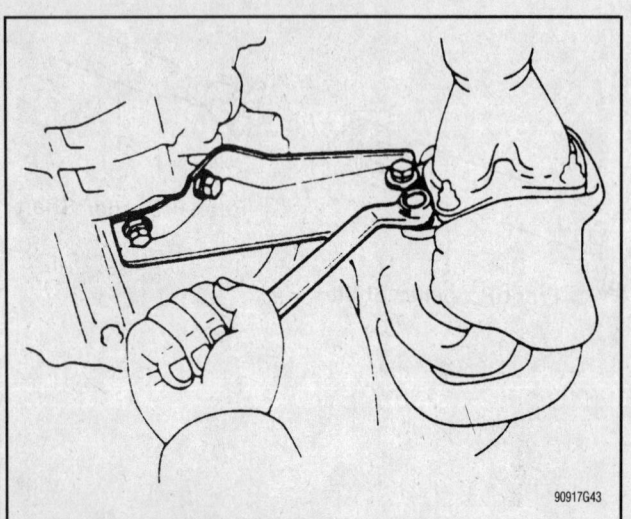

Fig. 3 Disconnect the hose and unbolt the slave cylinder from the transmission

Fig. 4 There are four bolts holding the exhaust pipe bracket to the manual transmission

Fig. 5 Remove the control cable bracket held in by two bolts

Fig. 6 Unbolt and lower the stiffener plate

### Halfshaft

REMOVAL & INSTALLATION

♦ See Figures 7 thru 17

This procedure only applies to the 4WD models.
1. Raise and safely support the vehicle.
2. Remove the wheel and tire assembly.
3. Remove the cotter pin and lock cap from the halfshaft.
4. While applying the brakes, remove the locknut from the halfshaft.
5. Remove the cotter pin and locknut to the tie rod end and disconnect the tie rod end from the knuckle.
6. Remove the lower ball joint bolts from the steering knuckle.
7. Place matchmarks on the halfshaft and side gear. Remove the six bolts from the inner halfshaft joint and disconnect the halfshaft from the side gear.
8. Remove the halfshaft by pulling the control arm down and extracting the halfshaft from the wheel hub. On models with ABS, make sure not to damage the ABS rotor.

## DRIVE TRAIN  7-5

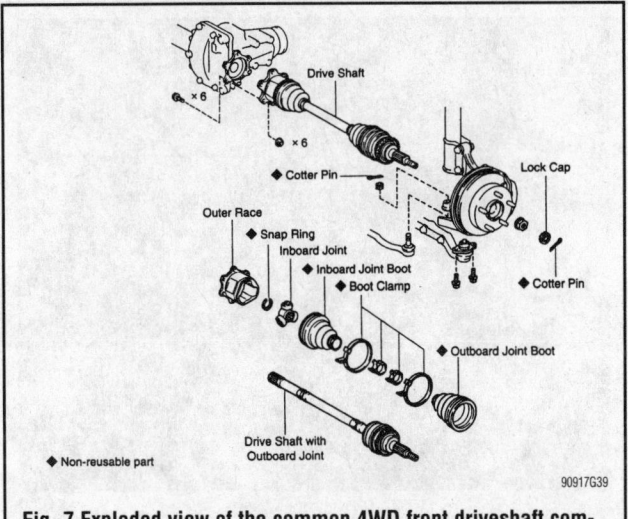

Fig. 7 Exploded view of the common 4WD front driveshaft components

Fig. 8 Remove the cotter pin, discard it, then remove the lockcap

Fig. 9 Retain the rotor to remove the locknut from the halfshaft

Fig. 10 Make sure that there are a few lug nuts on the rotor during the locknut removal

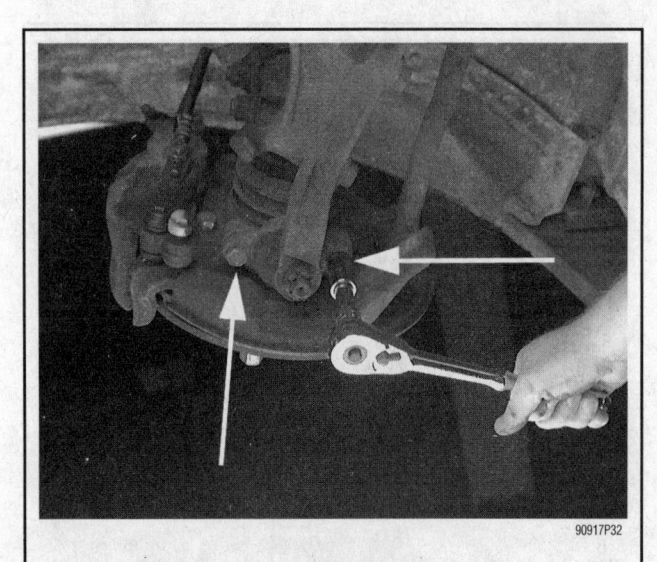

Fig. 11 Remove the lower ball joint bolts . . .

Fig. 12 . . . then pull the arm down slightly

## 7-6 DRIVE TRAIN

Fig. 13 Place matchmarks on the halfshaft and side gear assemblies

Fig. 14 Loosen and remove the bolts on the halfshaft

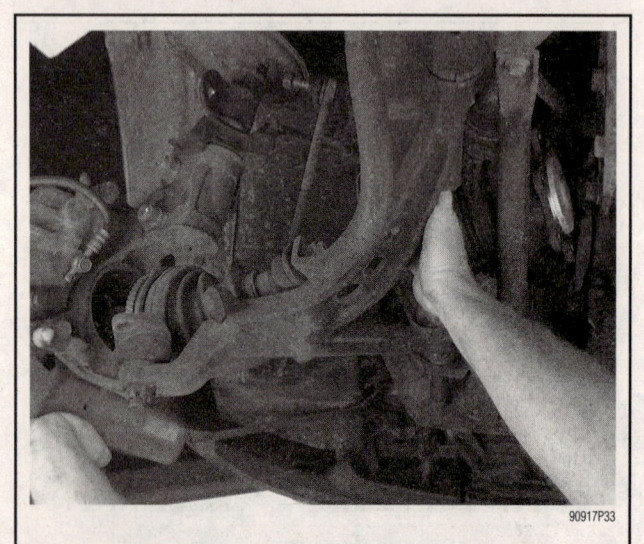

Fig. 15 Pull the control arm down to extract the halfshaft

Fig. 16 Inspect the seal prior to halfshaft installation

Fig. 17 Insert the driveshaft through the hub first

→If the outer shaft will not come out of the hub, soak the splines with penetrating lube, install the nut and tap on the halfshaft with a rubber hammer. Be careful not to damage the shaft threads.

To install:

→Coat the halfshaft splines with anti-seize compound to prevent spline seizure. This will help for future halfshaft removal.

9. Insert the halfshaft into position.
10. Connect the halfshaft to the steering knuckle.
11. Connect the inner halfshaft joint to the side gear and tighten the six bolts to 51 ft. lbs. (61 Nm).
12. Connect the lower ball joint, then tighten the bolts to 94 ft. lbs. (127 Nm).
13. Install the tie rod end, tighten the nut to 36 ft. lbs. (49 Nm) and insert a new cotter pin.
14. Install the halfshaft nut.
15. While a helper is applying the brakes, tighten the drive shaft locknut to:
- 1991—137 ft lbs. (186 Nm)
- 1992–93 models—166 ft. lbs. (226 Nm)
- 1994–97 models—152 ft. lbs. (206 Nm)
   a. Install the lock cap and new cotter pin.

# DRIVE TRAIN  7-7

16. On models with a ABS speed sensor, secure the sensor to 69 inch lbs. (8 Nm).
17. Install the front wheel, hand tighten the lugnuts and lower the vehicle.
18. Tighten the lugnuts to specifications.
19. Check the front end alignment.

## OVERHAUL

▶ See Figures 18 thru 23

1. Remove the halfshaft.
2. Remove the inboard joint boot clamps.
3. Clean the joint before removing the boot.
4. Slide the inboard joint boot toward the outboard joint.
5. Place matchmarks on the inboard joint tulip and the shaft. Remove the inboard joint tulip from the driveshaft.
6. Clamp the driveshaft in a vise. Using a snapring expander, remove the snapring and disassemble the tripod joint.
7. Using a brass bar and hammer, remove the tripod joint from the driveshaft. Do not punch the roller.
8. Remove the inboard joint boot.
9. Remove the outboard joint boot clamps and boot. Do not disassemble the outboard joint.

**To install:**

10. Temporarily install the new boot and new boot clamps to the outboard joint.

➡ Before installing the boot, wrap vinyl tape around the spline of the shaft to prevent damaging the boot.

11. Temporarily install the new boot and the new boot clamps for the inboard joint to the driveshaft.
12. Assemble the tripod joint.
    a. Place the beveled side of the tripod axial spline toward the outboard joint.
    b. Align the matchmarks placed before disassembly.
    c. Using a brass bar and hammer, tap in the tripod joint onto the driveshaft. Do not punch the roller.
13. Using a snap ring expander, install a new snapring.
14. Before assembling the boot to the outboard joint, pack the boot with grease. Usual capacity is 4.2–4.6 oz. (120–130 g).

➡ Keep the grease off the joint connection groove of the boot. Pack in grease all over the ball and contact surface inside the joint.

Fig. 18 Removing the outer band from the CV-boot

Fig. 19 Clean the CV-joint housing prior to removing boot

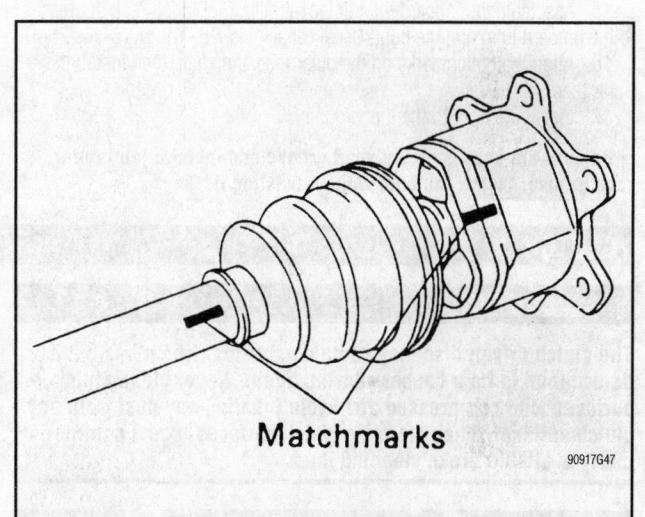

Fig. 20 Place matchmarks on the inboard joint outer race and shaft

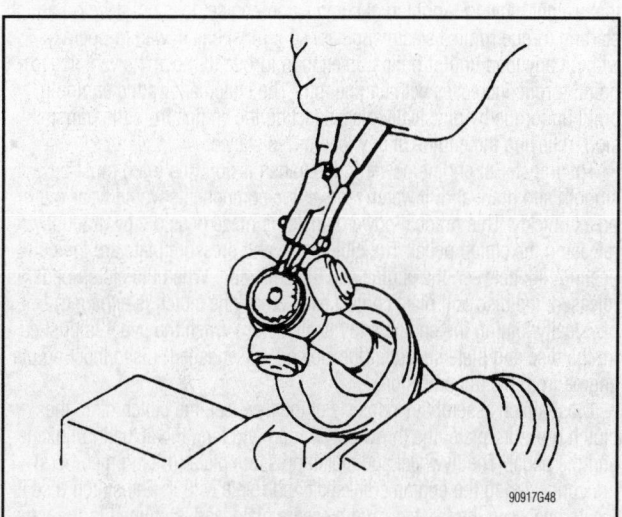

Fig. 21 Use snapring expanders to extract the snapring from the end

# 7-8 DRIVE TRAIN

**Fig. 22 With a brass bar and hammer, tap the joint hard enough to remove**

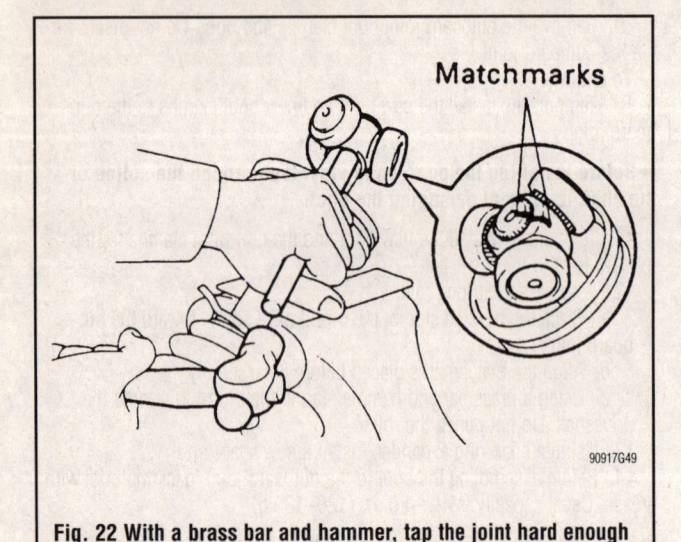

**Fig. 23 Set the length of the driveshaft at the points shown here**

15. Assemble the inboard joint to the inboard joint tulip. Pack in grease to the inboard tulip and the boot. Usual capacity is 7.6–7.9 oz. (215–225 g).
16. Align the matchmarks on the outer race and shaft, then install the outer race.
17. Install the boot to the inboard joint.

➡ Be sure the boot is on the shaft groove and inboard joint outer race groove. Install the boot without twisting it.

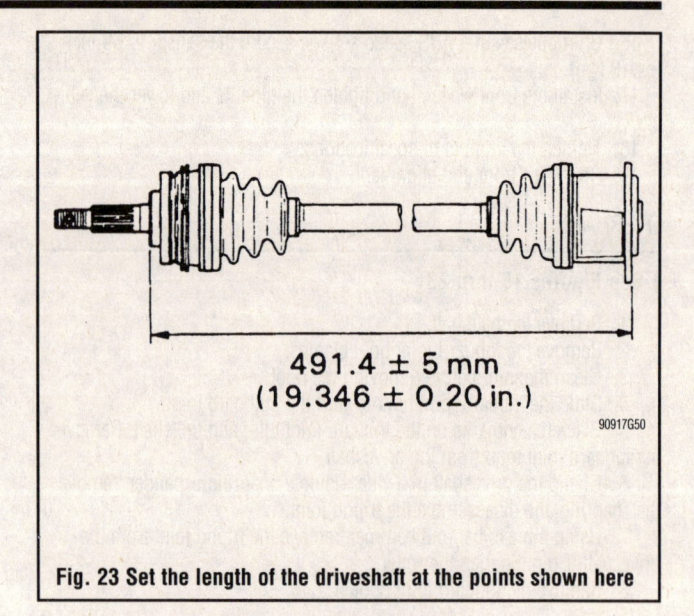

18. Set the length of the shaft to the following:
- 1991 models—19.41–19.81 inch (493–502mm)
- 1992–97 models—19.146–19.546 inch (486.4–496.41mm)

19. Install the two clamps to the inboard joint boot. Bend back the band and lock it.
20. Install the halfshaft.

## CLUTCH

### ✳✳ CAUTION

**The clutch driven disc may contain asbestos, which has been determined to be a cancer causing agent. Never clean clutch surfaces with compressed air! Avoid inhaling any dust from any clutch surface! When cleaning clutch surfaces, use a commercially available brake cleaning fluid.**

### Understanding the Clutch

The purpose of the clutch is to disconnect and connect engine power at the transmission. A vehicle at rest requires a lot of engine torque to get all that weight moving. An internal combustion engine does not develop a high starting torque (unlike steam engines) so it must be allowed to operate without any load until it builds up enough torque to move the vehicle. To a point, torque increases with engine rpm. The clutch allows the engine to build up torque by physically disconnecting the engine from the transmission, relieving the engine of any load or resistance.

The transfer of engine power to the transmission (the load) must be smooth and gradual; if it weren't, drive line components would wear out or break quickly. This gradual power transfer is made possible by gradually releasing the clutch pedal. The clutch disc and pressure plate are the connecting link between the engine and transmission. When the clutch pedal is released, the disc and plate contact each other (the clutch is engaged) physically joining the engine and transmission. When the pedal is pushed in, the disc and plate separate (the clutch is disengaged) disconnecting the engine from the transmission.

Most clutch assemblies consists of the flywheel, the clutch disc, the clutch pressure plate, the throw out bearing and fork, the actuating linkage and the pedal. The flywheel and clutch pressure plate (driving members) are connected to the engine crankshaft and rotate with it. The clutch disc is located between the flywheel and pressure plate, and is splined to the transmission shaft. A driving member is one that is attached to the engine and transfers engine power to a driven member (clutch disc) on the transmission shaft. A driving member (pressure plate) rotates (drives) a driven member (clutch disc) on contact and, in so doing, turns the transmission shaft.

There is a circular diaphragm spring within the pressure plate cover (transmission side). In a relaxed state (when the clutch pedal is fully released) this spring is convex; that is, it is dished outward toward the transmission. Pushing in the clutch pedal actuates the attached linkage. Connected to the other end of this is the throw out fork, which hold the throw out bearing. When the clutch pedal is depressed, the clutch linkage pushes the fork and bearing forward to contact the diaphragm spring of the pressure plate. The outer edges of the spring are secured to the pressure plate and are pivoted on rings so that when the center of the spring is compressed by the throw out bearing, the outer edges bow outward and, by so doing, pull the pressure plate in the same direction—away from the clutch disc. This action separates the disc from the plate, disengaging the clutch and allowing the transmission to be shifted into another gear. A coil type clutch return spring attached to the clutch pedal arm permits full release of the pedal. Releasing the pedal pulls the throw out bearing away from the diaphragm spring resulting in a reversal of spring position. As bearing pressure is gradually released from the spring center, the outer edges of the spring bow outward, pushing the pressure plate into closer contact with the clutch disc. As the disc and plate move closer together, friction between the two increases and slippage is reduced until, when full spring pressure is applied (by fully releasing the pedal) the speed of the disc and plate are the same. This stops all slipping, creating a direct connection between the plate and disc which results in the transfer of power from the engine to the transmission. The clutch disc is now rotating with the pressure plate at engine speed and, because it is splined to the transmission shaft, the shaft now turns at the same engine speed.

The clutch is operating properly if:
1. It will stall the engine when released with the vehicle held stationary.
2. The shift lever can be moved freely between 1st and reverse gears when the vehicle is stationary and the clutch disengaged.

# DRIVE TRAIN  7-9

## Driven Disc and Pressure Plate

### REMOVAL & INSTALLATION

▶ See Figures 24 thru 35

1. Remove the transmission assembly from the vehicle.
2. Machmark the clutch cover to the flywheel.
3. Remove the clutch pressure plate retaining bolts in small amounts and in a crisscross pattern to relieve the clutch disc spring tension.
4. At the clutch cover, loosen each bolt one turn until spring tension is released.
5. Remove the clutch cover-to-flywheel bolts. Remove the clutch cover and the clutch disc.
6. If the clutch release bearing is to be replaced, perform the following:
    a. Remove the bearing retaining clip(s), the bearing and hub.
    b. Remove the release fork and the boot.
    c. The bearing is press fitted to the hub.
    d. Clean all parts and lightly grease the input shaft splines and all of the contact points.

Fig. 26 If necessary, lock the flywheel in place and remove the retaining bolts . . .

Fig. 24 Loosen and remove the clutch and pressure plate bolts evenly, a little at a time . . .

Fig. 27 . . . then remove the flywheel from the crankshaft in order replace it or have it machined

Fig. 25 . . . then remove the clutch and pressure plate assembly

Fig. 28 Upon installation, it is usually a good idea to apply a threadlocking compound to the flywheel bolts

# 7-10 DRIVE TRAIN

Fig. 29 Be sure that the flywheel surface is clean, before installing the clutch

Fig. 30 Check across the flywheel surface, it should be flat

Fig. 31 Install a clutch alignment arbor, to align the clutch assembly during installation

Fig. 32 You may want to use a threadlocking compound on the clutch assembly bolts

Fig. 33 Be sure to use a torque wrench to tighten all bolts

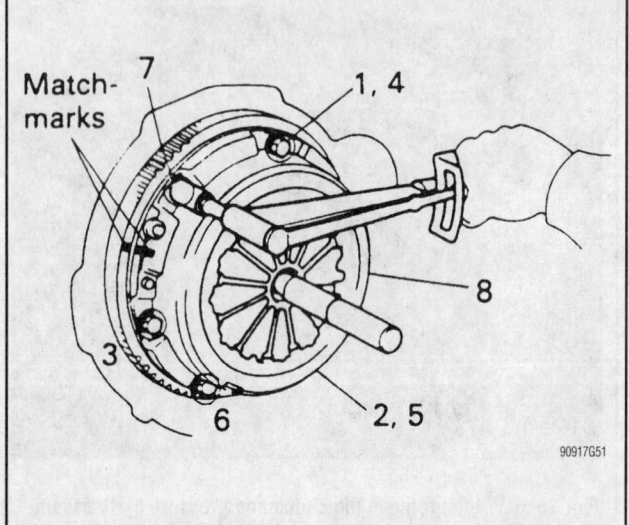

Fig. 34 Tighten the bolts on the clutch cover in this order

# DRIVE TRAIN  7-11

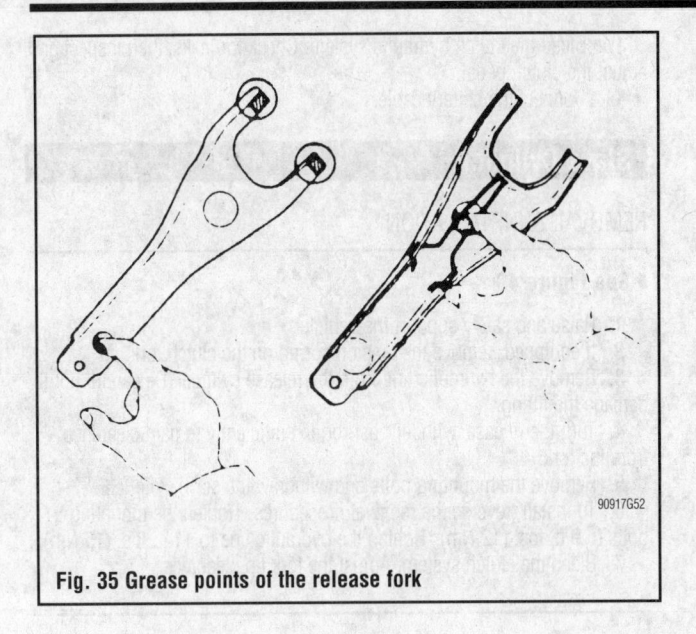

**Fig. 35 Grease points of the release fork**

**Fig. 36 Points for clutch pedal adjustments**

e. Install the bearing/hub assembly, the fork, the boot and the retaining clip(s) in their original locations.

**To install:**

7. Inspect the flywheel surface for cracks, heat scoring (blue marks) and warpage. Replace or resurface the flywheel, if any damage is present.

➡ Before installing any new parts, make sure they are clean. During installation, do not get grease or oil on any of the components, as this will shorten clutch life considerably.

8. Using an clutch alignment tool, position the clutch disc against the flywheel. The raised center section of the disc faces the transmission.
9. Position the clutch cover onto the flywheel and align the matchmarks.
10. Install the clutch cover retaining bolts. Tighten the bolts in a crisscross pattern to 14 ft. lbs. (19 Nm).
11. Lubricate the release fork pivot and contact points, release bearing, bearing hub and input shaft spline surfaces with a suitable molybdenum disulfide lithium based or Multi-purpose grease.
12. Install the boot, release fork, hub, and the bearing assemblies.
13. Install the transmission to the vehicle.
14. Connect the negative battery cable.

## ADJUSTMENTS

### Pedal Height

♦ See Figure 36

1. Check the pedal height from the upper surface of the floor panel. Standard is between 6.10–6.50 inch (155–165mm). Pushrod play at pedal height is 0.04–0.20 inch (1.0–5.0mm).
2. If out of specification, loosen the locknut and turn the stopper bolt until the height is correct. Tighten the locknut.
3. Loosen the locknut and turn the pushrod until the pushrod play is correct. Tighten the locknut.

### Free-Play

♦ See Figure 37

1. Push in the pedal until the beginning of the clutch resistance is felt. Pedal free-play is 0.20–0.59 inch (5.0–15.0mm).
2. To adjust, loosen the locknut and turn the pushrod until the free-play and pushrod play are correct.

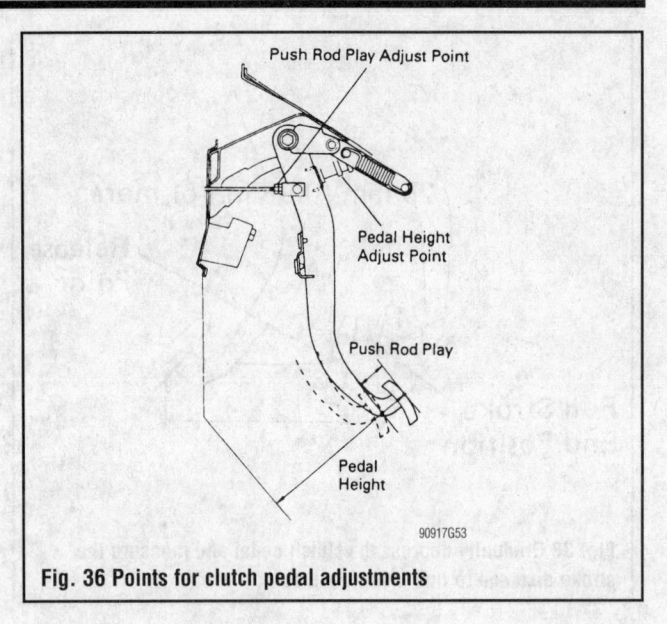

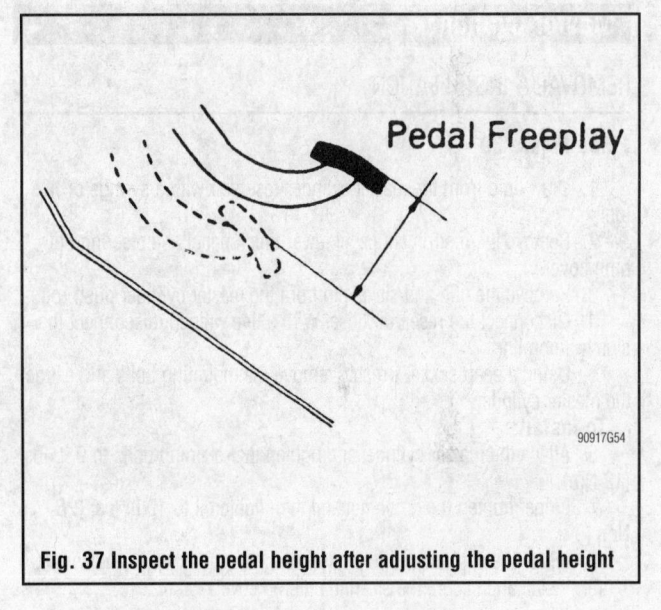

3. Tighten the locknut.
4. After adjusting the pedal free play. Check the pedal height.

### Release Point

♦ See Figure 38

1. Pull the parking brake lever and install a wheel stopper.
2. Start the engine and allow to idle.
3. Without depressing the clutch pedal, slowly shift the shift lever from reverse position until the gears contact.
4. Gradually depress the clutch pedal and measure the stroke distance from the point the gear noise stops (release point) up to the full stroke end position. Standard distance is 0.98 inch (25mm) or more.

➡ From the pedal stroke end position to the release point.

5. If the distance is not as specified, perform the following:
- Inspect the pedal height
- Inspect the pushrod play and pedal free-play
- Bleed the clutch line
- Inspect the clutch cover and disc

**Fig. 37 Inspect the pedal height after adjusting the pedal height**

# 7-12 DRIVE TRAIN

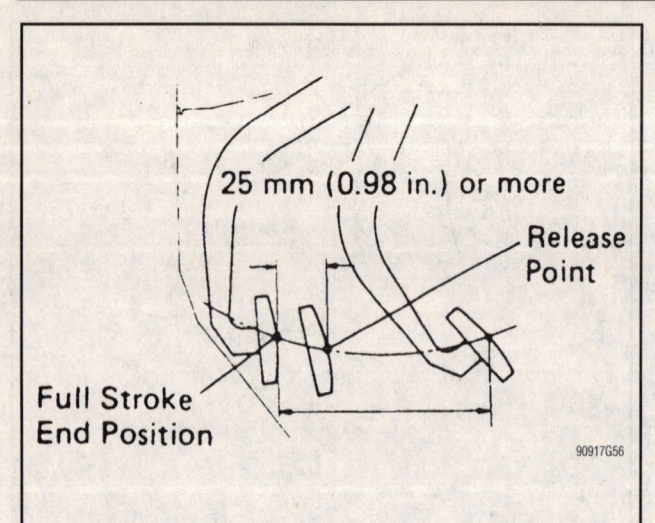

Fig. 38 Gradually depress the clutch pedal and measure the stroke distance to find the release point

10. Bleed the clutch hydraulic system. Check for leaks, then inspect and adjust the clutch pedal.
11. Connect the battery cable.

## Slave Cylinder

### REMOVAL & INSTALLATION

▶ See Figure 40

1. Raise and safely support the vehicle.
2. If equipped, remove the tension spring on the clutch fork.
3. Remove the hydraulic line from the release cylinder. Be careful not to damage the fitting.
4. Turn the release cylinder pushrod in sufficiently to gain clearance from the fork.
5. Remove the mounting bolts and withdraw the slave cylinder.
6. To install, reverse the removal procedures. Tighten the mounting bolts to 9 ft. lbs. (12 Nm). Tighten the hydraulic line to 11 ft. lbs. (15 Nm).
7. Bleed the clutch system. Adjust the fork tip clearance.

## Master Cylinder

### REMOVAL & INSTALLATION

▶ See Figure 39

1. Draw fluid from the master cylinder reservoir with a syringe or like tool.
2. Remove the instrument panel lower finish panel and steering column cover.
3. Remove the clip and clevis pin from the master cylinder push rod.
4. Disconnect the reservoir hose. With a line wrench, disconnect the clutch union line.
5. Using a deep socket wrench, remove the mounting bolts and extract the master cylinder.

**To install:**

6. Attach the master cylinder and tighten the retaining bolts to 9 ft. lbs. (12 Nm).
7. Finger tighten the union nut and then tighten it to 19 ft. lbs. (25 Nm).
8. Install the clip and clevis pin to secure the push rod.
9. Install and secure the steering column cover.

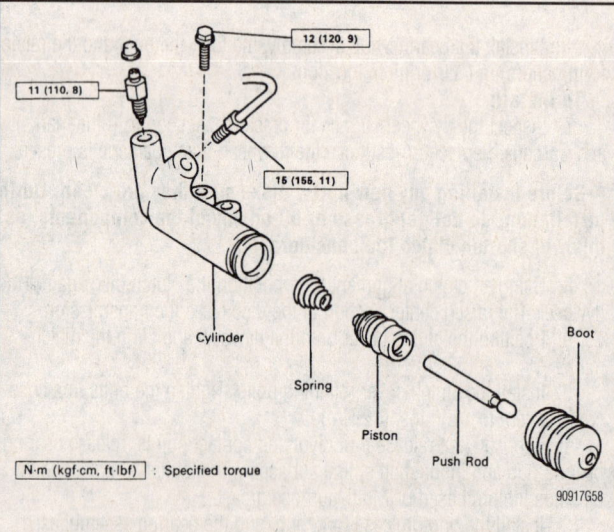

Fig. 40 Exploded view of the clutch slave (release) cylinder

## Clutch Accumulator

### REMOVAL & INSTALLATION

▶ See Figure 41

The clutch accumulator is located under the vehicle near the carbon canister.

1. Raise and safely support the vehicle.
2. Remove the engine under cover.
3. Using a line wrench, disconnect the clutch liner leading to the accumulator.
4. Remove the two bolts holding the accumulator to the body and extract the unit.

**To install:**

5. Position the accumulator to the body of the vehicle and secure the bolts to 9 ft. lbs. (12 Nm).
6. Attach the line to the unit and secure the line union nut to 19 ft. lbs. (25 Nm).
7. Fill the clutch reservoir with brake fluid and bleed the system.
8. Check for leaks.
9. Install the engine under cover.

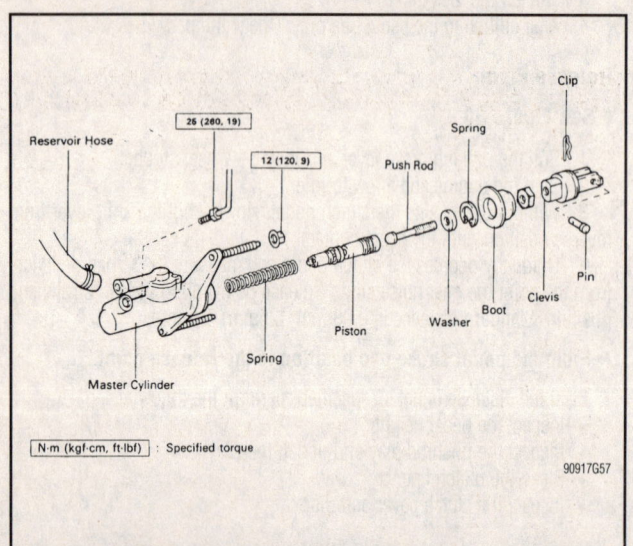

Fig. 39 Exploded view of the clutch master cylinder mounting

# Drive Train  7-13

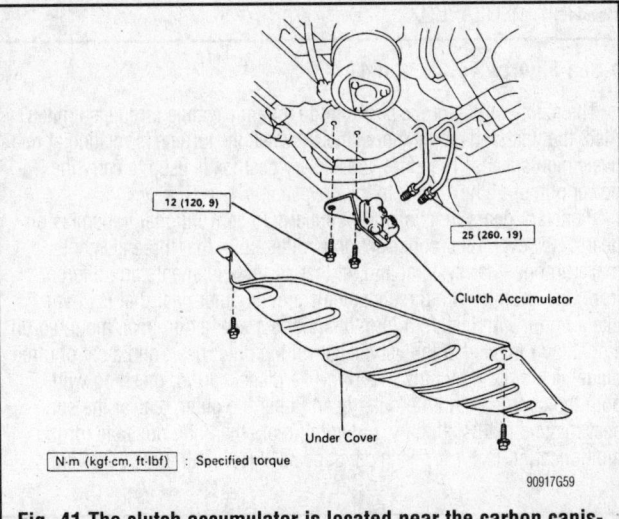

**Fig. 41 The clutch accumulator is located near the carbon canister**

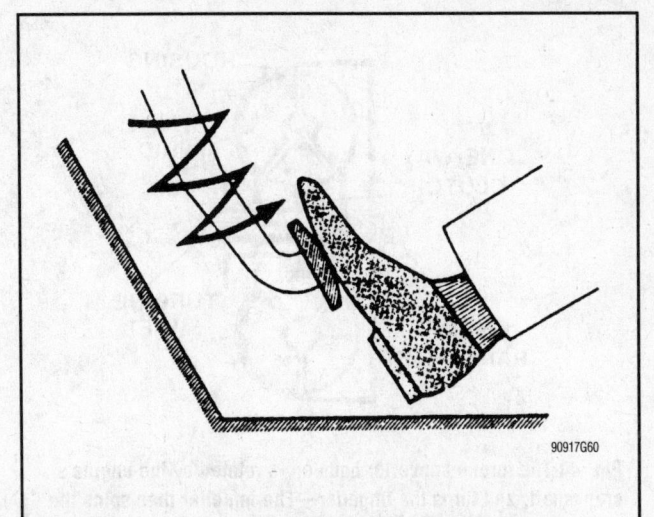

**Fig. 42 Have an assistant pump the clutch pedal several times . . .**

## Hydraulic System Bleeding

▶ See Figures 42 and 43

➡If any maintenance on the clutch system was performed or the system is suspected of containing air, bleed the system. Use care; brake fluid will remove the paint from any surface. If the brake fluid spills onto any painted surface, wash it off immediately with soap and water.

1. Fill the clutch reservoir with brake fluid. Check the reservoir level frequently and add fluid as needed.
2. Connect one end of a vinyl tube to the bleeder plug on the slave cylinder and submerge the other end into a clear container half-filled with brake fluid.
3. Slowly pump the clutch pedal several times.
4. Have an assistant hold the clutch pedal down and loosen the bleeder plug until fluid and/or air starts to run out of the bleeder plug. Close the bleeder plug while the pedal is held to the floor.

➡Do not allow the pedal to rise back up while the bleeder is still open. If this happens, it will allow air to re-enter the slave cylinder and cause the clutch system not to work properly.

5. Repeat Steps 2 and 3 until all the air bubbles are removed from the system.
6. Tighten the bleeder plug when all the air is gone.

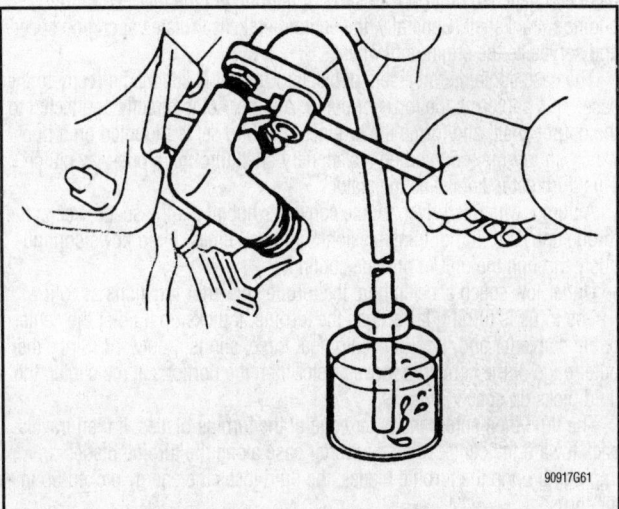

**Fig. 43 . . . while he is holding the pedal down, loosen the bleeder plug until fluid runs out**

7. Refill the master cylinder to the proper level as required.
8. Check the system for leaks.

## AUTOMATIC TRANSMISSION

### Understanding the Automatic Transmission

The automatic transmission allows engine torque and power to be transmitted to the rear wheels within a narrow range of engine operating speeds. It will allow the engine to turn fast enough to produce plenty of power and torque at very low speeds, while keeping it at a sensible rpm at high vehicle speeds (and it does this job without driver assistance). The transmission uses a light fluid as the medium for the transmission of power. This fluid also works in the operation of various hydraulic control circuits and as a lubricant. Because the transmission fluid performs all of these functions, trouble within the unit can easily travel from one part to another. For this reason, and because of the complexity and unusual operating principles of the transmission, a very sound understanding of the basic principles of operation will simplify troubleshooting.

### TORQUE CONVERTER

▶ See Figure 44

The torque converter replaces the conventional clutch. It has three functions:

1. It allows the engine to idle with the vehicle at a standstill, even with the transmission in gear.
2. It allows the transmission to shift from range-to-range smoothly, without requiring that the driver close the throttle during the shift.
3. It multiplies engine torque to an increasing extent as vehicle speed drops and throttle opening is increased. This has the effect of making the transmission more responsive and reduces the amount of shifting required.

The torque converter is a metal case which is shaped like a sphere that

# 7-14 DRIVE TRAIN

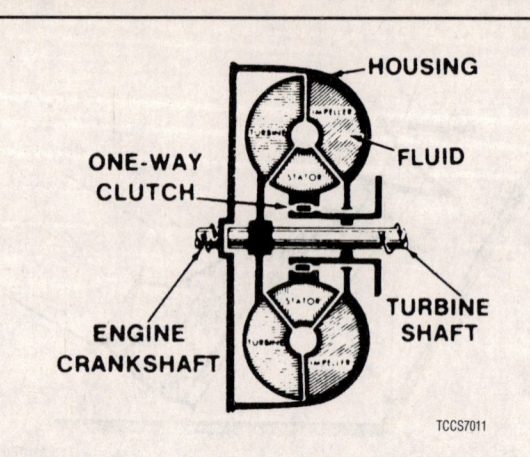

**Fig. 44 The torque converter housing is rotated by the engine's crankshaft, and turns the impeller—The impeller then spins the turbine, which gives motion to the turbine shaft, driving the gears**

has been flattened on opposite sides. It is bolted to the rear end of the engine's crankshaft. Generally, the entire metal case rotates at engine speed and serves as the engine's flywheel.

The case contains three sets of blades. One set is attached directly to the case. This set forms the torus or pump. Another set is directly connected to the output shaft, and forms the turbine. The third set is mounted on a hub which, in turn, is mounted on a stationary shaft through a one-way clutch. This third set is known as the stator.

A pump, which is driven by the converter hub at engine speed, keeps the torque converter full of transmission fluid at all times. Fluid flows continuously through the unit to provide cooling.

Under low speed acceleration, the torque converter functions as follows:

The torus is turning faster than the turbine. It picks up fluid at the center of the converter and, through centrifugal force, slings it outward. Since the outer edge of the converter moves faster than the portions at the center, the fluid picks up speed.

The fluid then enters the outer edge of the turbine blades. It then travels back toward the center of the converter case along the turbine blades. In impinging upon the turbine blades, the fluid loses the energy picked up in the torus.

If the fluid was now returned directly into the torus, both halves of the converter would have to turn at approximately the same speed at all times, and torque input and output would both be the same.

In flowing through the torus and turbine, the fluid picks up two types of flow, or flow in two separate directions. It flows through the turbine blades, and it spins with the engine. The stator, whose blades are stationary when the vehicle is being accelerated at low speeds, converts one type of flow into another. Instead of allowing the fluid to flow straight back into the torus, the stator's curved blades turn the fluid almost 90° toward the direction of rotation of the engine. Thus the fluid does not flow as fast toward the torus, but is already spinning when the torus picks it up. This has the effect of allowing the torus to turn much faster than the turbine. This difference in speed may be compared to the difference in speed between the smaller and larger gears in any gear train. The result is that engine power output is higher, and engine torque is multiplied.

As the speed of the turbine increases, the fluid spins faster and faster in the direction of engine rotation. As a result, the ability of the stator to redirect the fluid flow is reduced. Under cruising conditions, the stator is eventually forced to rotate on its one-way clutch in the direction of engine rotation. Under these conditions, the torque converter begins to behave almost like a solid shaft, with the torus and turbine speeds being almost equal.

## PLANETARY GEARBOX

▶ See Figures 45, 46 and 47

The ability of the torque converter to multiply engine torque is limited. Also, the unit tends to be more efficient when the turbine is rotating at relatively high speeds. Therefore, a planetary gearbox is used to carry the power output of the turbine to the driveshaft.

Planetary gears function very similarly to conventional transmission gears. However, their construction is different in that three elements make up one gear system, and, in that all three elements are different from one another. The three elements are: an outer gear that is shaped like a hoop, with teeth cut into the inner surface; a sun gear, mounted on a shaft and located at the very center of the outer gear; and a set of three planet gears, held by pins in a ring-like planet carrier, meshing with both the sun gear and the outer gear. Either the outer gear or the sun gear may be held stationary, providing more than one possible torque multiplication factor for each set of gears. Also, if all three gears are

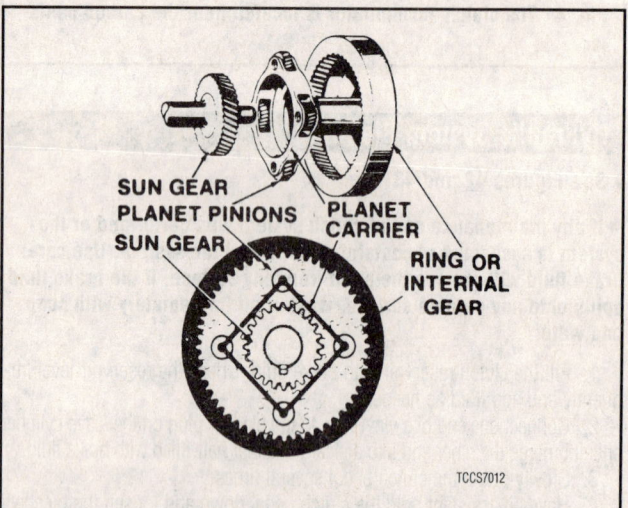

**Fig. 45 Planetary gears work in a similar fashion to manual transmission gears, but are composed of three parts**

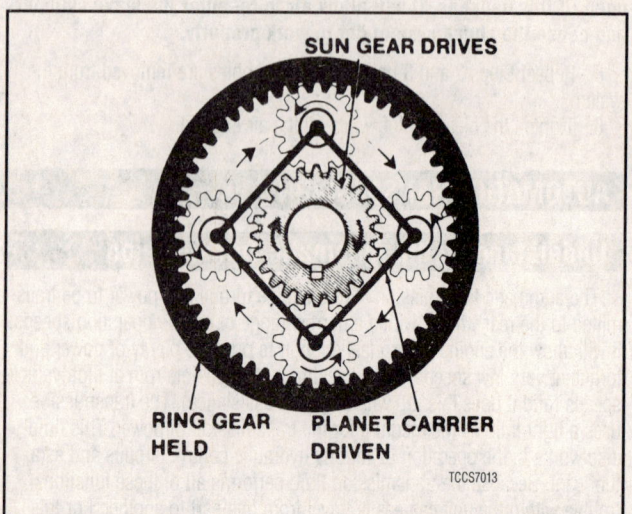

**Fig. 46 Planetary gears in the maximum reduction (low) range. The ring gear is held and a lower gear ratio is obtained**

# DRIVE TRAIN 7-15

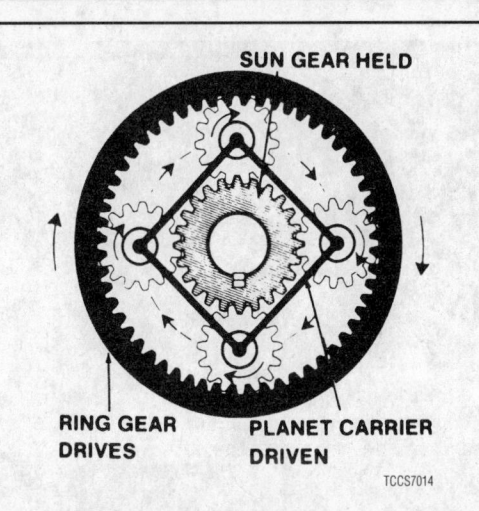

**Fig. 47 Planetary gears in the minimum reduction (drive) range. The ring gear is allowed to revolve, providing a higher gear ratio**

forced to rotate at the same speed, the gearset forms, in effect, a solid shaft.

Most automatics use the planetary gears to provide various reductions ratios. Bands and clutches are used to hold various portions of the gearsets to the transmission case or to the shaft on which they are mounted. Shifting is accomplished, then, by changing the portion of each planetary gearset which is held to the transmission case or to the shaft.

## SERVOS AND ACCUMULATORS

▶ See Figure 48

The servos are hydraulic pistons and cylinders. They resemble the hydraulic actuators used on many other machines, such as bulldozers. Hydraulic fluid enters the cylinder, under pressure, and forces the piston to move to engage the band or clutches.

The accumulators are used to cushion the engagement of the servos. The transmission fluid must pass through the accumulator on the way to the servo. The accumulator housing contains a thin piston which is sprung away from the discharge passage of the accumulator. When fluid passes through the accumulator on the way to the servo, it must move the piston against spring pressure, and this action smoothes out the action of the servo.

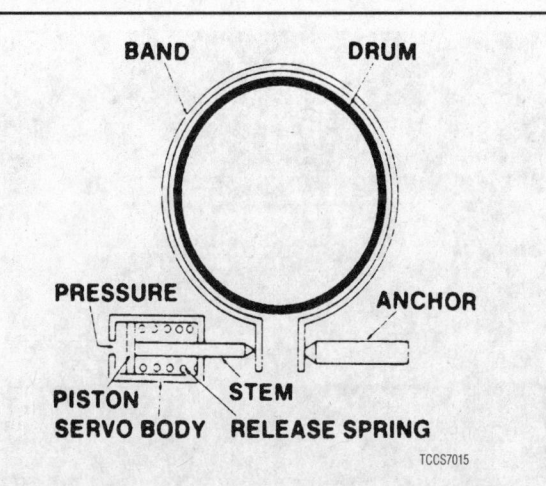

**Fig. 48 Servos, operated by pressure, are used to apply or release the bands, to either hold the ring gear or allow it to rotate**

## HYDRAULIC CONTROL SYSTEM

The hydraulic pressure used to operate the servos comes from the main transmission oil pump. This fluid is channeled to the various servos through the shift valves. There is generally a manual shift valve which is operated by the transmission selector lever and an automatic shift valve for each automatic upshift the transmission provides.

➟**Many new transmissions are electronically controlled. On these models, electrical solenoids are used to better control the hydraulic fluid. Usually, the solenoids are regulated by an electronic control module.**

There are two pressures which affect the operation of these valves. One is the governor pressure which is effected by vehicle speed. The other is the modulator pressure which is effected by intake manifold vacuum or throttle position. Governor pressure rises with an increase in vehicle speed, and modulator pressure rises as the throttle is opened wider. By responding to these two pressures, the shift valves cause the upshift points to be delayed with increased throttle opening to make the best use of the engine's power output.

Most transmissions also make use of an auxiliary circuit for downshifting. This circuit may be actuated by the throttle linkage the vacuum line which actuates the modulator, by a cable or by a solenoid. It applies pressure to a special downshift surface on the shift valve or valves.

The transmission modulator also governs the line pressure, used to actuate the servos. In this way, the clutches and bands will be actuated with a force matching the torque output of the engine.

### Back-up Light/Neutral Safety Switch

The back-up light switch is incorporated with the neutral safety switch.

## REMOVAL & INSTALLATION

### 1991–95 Models

▶ See Figures 49 thru 56

1. Raise and safely support the vehicle.
2. Locate the neutral safety switch on the automatic transmission.
3. Disconnect the wiring harness from the switch.
4. On the 3-speed transmissions, the oil cooler lines may need to be disconnected to access the neutral safety switch. a bracket may need to be detached also on some models.

**Fig. 49 Disconnect the wiring harness from the neutral safety switch**

## 7-16 DRIVE TRAIN

Fig. 50 Disconnect the lines on the oil cooler

Fig. 53 Remove the nut on the neutral safety switch

Fig. 51 Remove the bracket retaining the two pipes

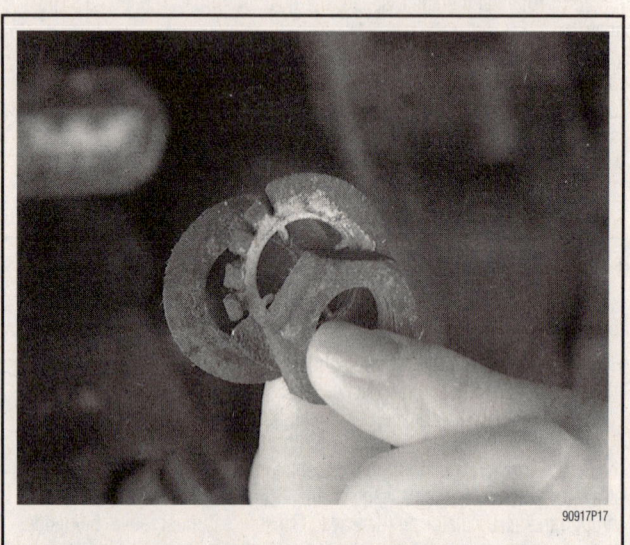

Fig. 54 There will be two washers and one nut

Fig. 52 Inspect the threads of the pipe and replace if damaged

Fig. 55 The bolt is on the side of the switch

# DRIVE TRAIN 7-17

Fig. 56 Extract the switch from the transmission

Fig. 57 Alignment of the groove and the neutral basic line

5. Unstake the lockwasher.
6. Remove the nut and bolt, then extract the neutral safety switch.
7. Remove the lock washer and grommet.

**To install:**

8. Attach the wiring harness to the switch.
9. Insert the neutral safety switch onto the manual valve lever shaft and temporarily tighten the adjusting bolt.
10. Install the grommet and a new lock washer. Install and tighten the nut to 35 inch lbs. (4 Nm).
11. Align the neutral basic line and the switch groove, then tighten the adjusting bolt to 48 inch lbs. (5 Nm).
12. Bend the tabs of the lock washer. Make sure you bend at least two of the tabs.
13. Lower the vehicle. Test the function of the system.

### 1996–97 Models

1. Raise and safely support the vehicle.
2. Locate the neutral safety switch on the side of the automatic transmission.
3. On the 3-speed transmissions, the oil cooler lines may need to be disconnected to access the neutral safety switch.
4. Disconnect the wiring harness from the switch.
5. Pry off the lock washer and remove the nut.
6. Unbolt and separate the switch from the transmission.

**To install:**

7. Attach the wiring harness to the switch.
8. Position the switch on the transmission and tighten the bolt to 9 ft. lbs. (13 Nm).
9. Install a new lock plate and tighten the nut to 35 inch lbs. (4 Nm).
10. Stake the nut with the lock plate. Adjust the neutral safety switch.
11. Lower the vehicle. Test the function of the system.

## ADJUSTMENT

▶ See Figure 57

Check that the engine can be started with the shift lever only in the **N** or **P** position, but not in any other positions. If not, carry out the following adjustment.

1. Loosen the neutral safety switch bolt and set the adjustment shift lever to **N**.
2. Align the groove and neutral basic line.
3. Retain the position and tighten the bolt to 48 inch lbs. (5 Nm) on 1991–95 models and 9 ft. lbs. (13 Nm) on 1996–97 models.

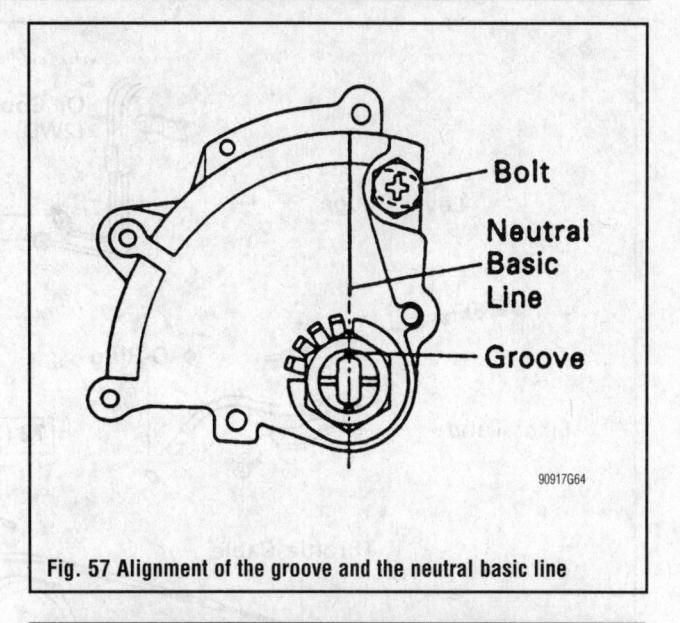

## Extension Housing Seal

### REMOVAL & INSTALLATION

1. Remove the driveshaft.
2. Using a seal puller, extract the seal from the extension housing.
3. Coat the new seal with transmission fluid. Preferable clean fresh fluid.
4. Using a seal driver, tap the seal into position as far as it will go. The lip of the seal should be flush with the extension housing.
5. Install the driveshaft.

## Automatic Transmission Assembly

### REMOVAL & INSTALLATION

▶ See Figure 58

### 4-Speed Transmissions

1. Disconnect the negative battery terminal from the battery. Wait at least 90 seconds after the battery cable is disconnected before working on the vehicle if equipped with air bags.
2. If required, remove the air cleaner assembly.
3. Disconnect the transmission throttle cable from the throttle body.
4. Raise and safely support the vehicle.
5. Drain the transmission fluid.
6. Disconnect the wiring harness for the neutral start switch and the back-up light switch. If equipped, disconnect the solenoid (overdrive) switch wiring at the same location.
7. If equipped, disconnect the oil level gauge.
8. Disconnect the starter wiring at the starter. Remove the mounting bolts and the starter from the engine.
9. Make matchmarks on the rear driveshaft flange and the differential pinion flange. These marks must be aligned during installation.
10. Unbolt the rear driveshaft flange. If the vehicle has a 2 piece driveshaft, remove the center bearing bracket-to-frame bolts. Remove the driveshaft from the vehicle.
11. Disconnect the speedometer cable (tie it aside). Disconnect the shift linkage from the transmission.
12. Disconnect the transmission oil cooler lines at the transmission.
13. Disconnect the exhaust pipe clamp and remove the oil filler tube, as required.

## 7-18 DRIVE TRAIN

Fig. 58 Exploded view of the automatic transmission mounting

N·m (kgf·cm, ft·lbf) : Specified torque
◆ Non-reusable part

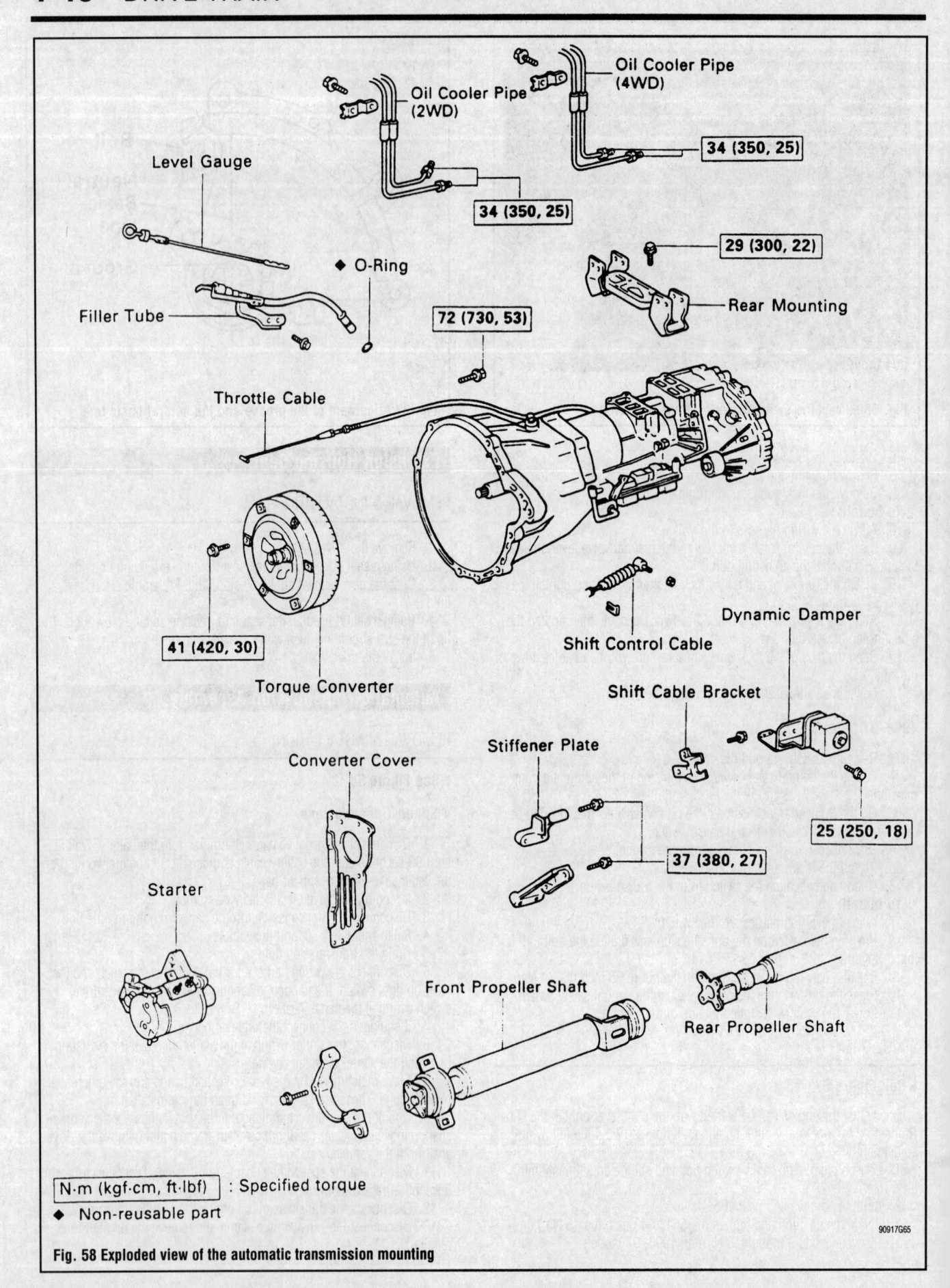

# DRIVE TRAIN  7-19

14. Support the transmission, using a jack with a wooden block placed between the jack and the transmission pan. Raise the transmission, just enough to take the weight off of the rear mount.

15. Remove the rear engine mount with the bracket and the engine under cover, to gain access to the engine crankshaft pulley.

16. Remove the stiffener plates, if equipped.

17. Place a wooden block (or blocks) between the engine oil pan and the front frame crossmember.

18. Slowly, lower the transmission until the engine rests on the wooden block.

19. Remove the rubber plug(s) from the service holes located at the rear of the engine in order to gain access to the torque converter bolts.

20. Rotate the crankshaft (to remove the torque converter bolts) to access the bolts through the service holes.

21. Obtain a bolt of the same dimensions as the torque converter bolts. Cut the head off of the bolt and hacksaw a slot in the bolt opposite the threaded end.

➡This modified bolt is used as a guide pin. Two guides pins are needed to properly install the transmission.

22. Thread the guide pin into one of the torque converter bolt holes. The guide pin will help keep the converter with the transmission.

23. Remove the stiffener plates from the transmission.

24. Remove the transmission-to-engine bolts, then carefully move the transmission rearward by prying on the guide pin through the service hole.

25. Pull the transmission rearward and lower it (front end down) out of the vehicle.

**To install:**

26. Installation is the reverse of removal. Please note the following important steps.

27. Apply a coat of Multi-purpose grease to the torque converter stub shaft and the corresponding pilot hole in the flexplate.

28. Install the torque converter into the front of the transmission. Push inward on the torque converter while rotating it to completely couple the torque converter to the transmission.

29. To make sure the converter is properly installed, measure the distance between the torque converter mounting lugs and the front mounting face of the transmission. The proper distance is 1991–95 models: 1.250 inch (31.75mm) and on 1996–97 models: 0.079 inch (20mm).

30. Install guide pins into 2 opposite mounting lugs of the torque converter.

31. Raise the transmission to the engine, align the transmission with the engine alignment dowels and position the converter guide pins into the mounting holes of the flexplate.

32. Install and tighten the transmission-to-engine mounting bolts. Tighten the bolts to specifications.

33. Remove the converter guide pins and install the converter mounting bolts. Rotate the crankshaft as necessary to gain access to the guide pins and bolts through the service holes. Evenly, tighten the converter mounting bolts to specifications. Install the rubber plugs into the access holes.

34. Install the remaining components by reversing the removal procedure.

35. Adjust the transmission throttle cable.

36. Refill the transmission.

37. Connect the negative battery cable. Start the engine and check for leaks.

38. Road test the vehicle for proper operation.

39. Recheck all fluid levels.

### 3-Speed Transmissions

1. Disconnect the negative battery terminal from the battery. Wait at least 90 seconds after the battery cable is disconnected before working on the vehicle if equipped with air bags.

2. Remove the ATF level gauge.

3. Loosen the nut and disconnect the throttle cable.

4. Remove the equipment driveshaft.

5. Raise and safely support the vehicle.

6. Remove the filler pipe. Remove the driveshaft.

7. Disconnect the control cable.

8. Disconnect the No. 1 and No. 2 vehicle speed sensor harnesses. Disconnect the starter solenoid wiring.

9. Disengage the neutral safety switch harness.

10. Remove the bolt and disconnect the oil pipe clamp. Disconnect the oil cooler pipes. On 4WD disconnect the A/T fluid temperature switch harness.

11. Remove the starter.

12. Using a jack, support the transmission. Remove the stiffener plate.

13. Remove the torque converter clutch cover and turn the crankshaft to gain access and remove the six bolts.

14. Remove the exhaust pipe bracket. Remove the rear mounting bolts.

15. Remove the transmission mounting bolts, then detach the wire harness, and lower the transmission.

16. Installation is the reverse of removal. Please note the following important steps.

17. Connect wire harness and install the transmission. Tighten the bolts to specifications.

18. Install the remaining components and tighten to specifications. Install the equipment driveshaft.

19. Connect the throttle cable and tighten.

20. Install the ATF level gauge.

21. Check the shift lever position.

22. Check the fluid level and fill if necessary.

23. Connect the negative battery cable.

## ADJUSTMENTS

### Throttle Linkage

▶ See Figure 59

1. Depress the accelerator pedal all the way and check that the throttle valve opens fully.

2. If the valve does not open fully, adjust the accelerator cable.

3. Fully depress the accelerator pedal.

4. Measure the distance between the end of the boot and stopper on the cable. Standard distance is 0–0.04 inch (0–1mm).

5. If the distance is not within specifications, adjust the cable by the adjusting nuts.

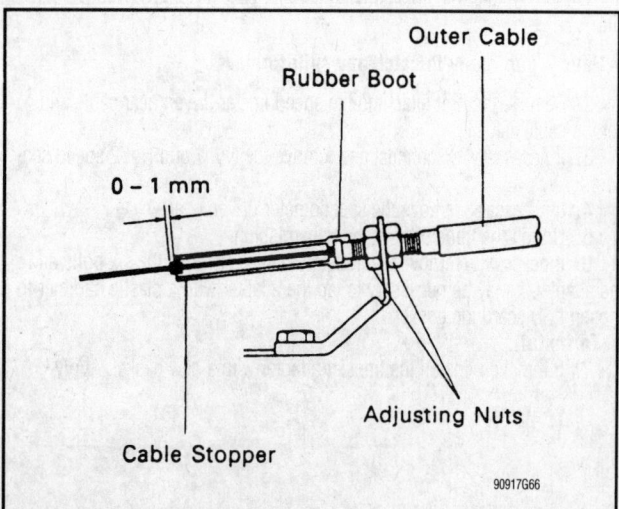

Fig. 59 Measure the distance between the end of the boot and stopper on the throttle cable

# DRIVE TRAIN

## TRANSFER CASE

### Extension Housing Seal

#### REMOVAL & INSTALLATION

1. Using a hammer and chisel, loosen the staked nut part of the nut.
2. With a wrench and retaining tool, hold the flange and remove the flange lock nut.
3. Remove the companion flange.
4. Using a puller, remove the dust deflector from the extension housing.
5. Tape the end of a flat bladed pry tool, then carefully pry the seal from the housing.

**To install:**
6. Coat the lip of the oil seal with Multi-purpose grease.
7. Install a new dust deflector.
8. With a seal installer and hammer, carefully and evenly, drive the new seal into position. Seal drive in depth is 0–0.039 inch (0–1.0mm).
9. Install the companion flange and tighten the lock nut to 90 ft. lbs. (123 Nm).

### Companion Flange Seal

#### REMOVAL & INSTALLATION

1. Remove the companion flange.
2. Drive the old seal from the flange, coat the lip of the new seal with MP grease.
3. Using a 22mm socket wrench, drive in the new oil seal. Make sure the seal if flush.
4. Install the companion flange, tighten the lock nut to 90 ft. lbs. (123 Nm).

### Transfer Case Assembly

#### REMOVAL & INSTALLATION

▶ See Figures 60 and 61

1. Remove the transmission and transfer case assembly from the vehicle.

➡ Have a pan ready to catch any spilt fluid.

2. Remove the bolt attaching the speedometer driven gear cable and set the cable aside.
3. If necessary, disconnect and remove the No. 1 and No. 2 speed sensors.
4. If necessary, remove the speedometer driven gear.
5. Unbolt the transfer from the transmission.
6. If necessary, remove the transfer adapter. Remove the six bolts and the adapter. It may be necessary to tap the adapter with a plastic hammer to loosen it. Discard the gasket.

**To install:**
7. If removed, install the transfer adapter with a new gasket. Apply sealant such as Three bond 1344 or Locktite 242 or equivalent. Tighten the bolts to 25 ft. lbs. (34 Nm).
8. Attach the transfer case to the transmission. Tighten the bolts to 27–37 ft. lbs. (36–50 Nm).
9. Attach the speedometer cable and tighten the bolt to 33 ft. lbs. (45 Nm).
10. If removed, install the speedometer gear and the No. 1 and No. 2 speed sensors.
11. Replace any necessary seals or gaskets. Install the transfer/transmission assembly into the vehicle.

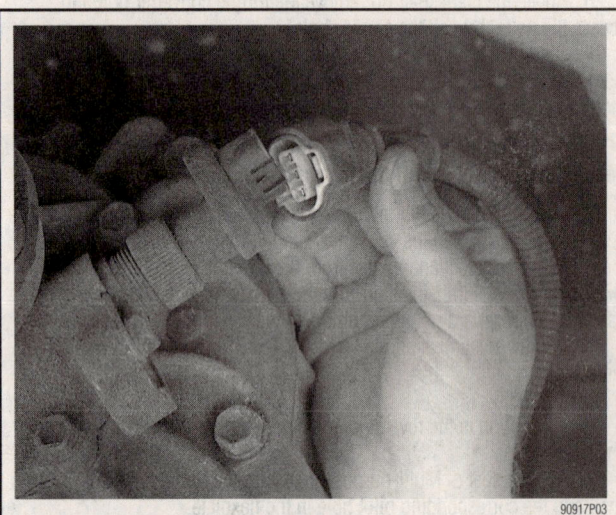

Fig. 60 Disengage the cable from the driven gear

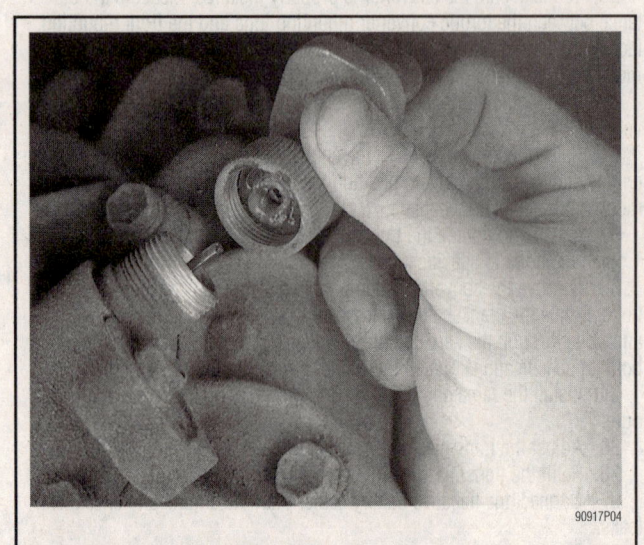

Fig. 61 Remove the driven gear if necessary

# DRIVE TRAIN 7-21

## DRIVELINE

The driveshafts are designed for the 2WD and 4WD use. The 2WD shafts are a 2-joint type. Manual transmission vehicles use a shell type, in which the joints can not be disassembled. Automatic transmission vehicles use a solid type, in which the joints can be disassembled. On the 4WD models, the front and rear driveshafts are a 3-joint type and 2-joint respectively.

### Front Driveshaft and U-Joints

REMOVAL & INSTALLATION

▶ See Figures 62 thru 71

Only 4WD models are equipped with a front driveshaft.
1. Disconnect the negative battery cable from the battery.
2. Raise and safely support the vehicle.
3. Place matchmarks on the flanges of the driveshaft and the differential carrier.
4. Remove the four nuts, bolts and washers and disconnect the front driveshaft from the differential housing.
5. Remove the center support bearing by removing the two bolts.
6. Pull out the driveshaft yoke from the transfer case.
7. Remove the driveshaft from the vehicle.
8. Install a transfer case output shaft plug into the transfer case to prevent fluid loss.

**To install:**
9. Remove the transfer case output shaft plug.
10. Slide the driveshaft into the transfer case.
11. Connect the center support bearing by installing the two bolts. Make sure the bearing is installed with the drain holes facing down. Tighten the bolts to 27 ft. lbs. (36 Nm).
12. Align the matchmarks on the driveshaft and differential flanges.
13. Install the four washers, bolts and nuts to the driveshaft and differential carrier. Tighten the bolts to 31 ft. lbs. (42 Nm).
14. Adjust the center support bearing to keep the intervals, as shown with the vehicle unladen condition. At the same condition, check that the center line of the axle direction. Adjust the bearing if necessary. Tighten the bolts to 27 ft. lbs. (36 Nm).
15. Lower the vehicle and connect the negative battery cable to the battery.

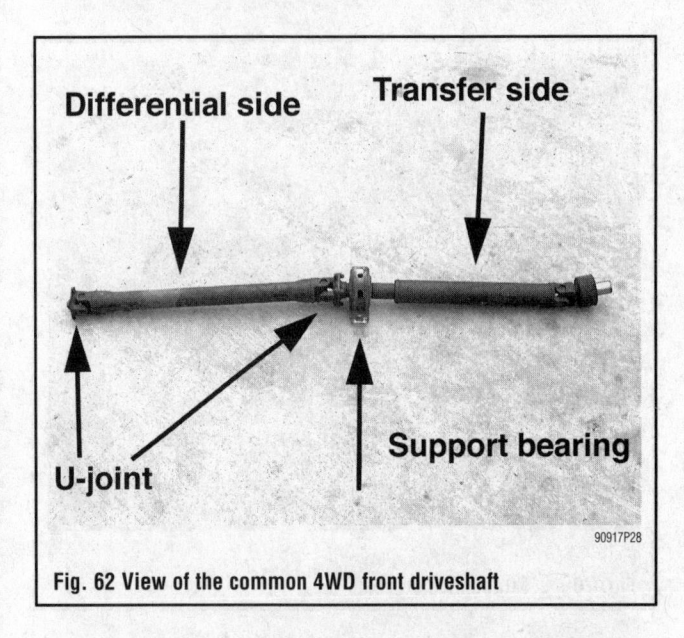

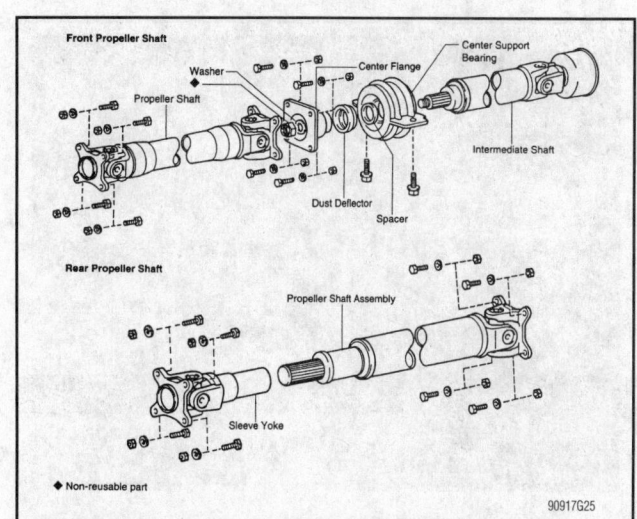

Fig. 62 View of the common 4WD front driveshaft

Fig. 64 Common view of the 4WD front and rear driveshaft assemblies

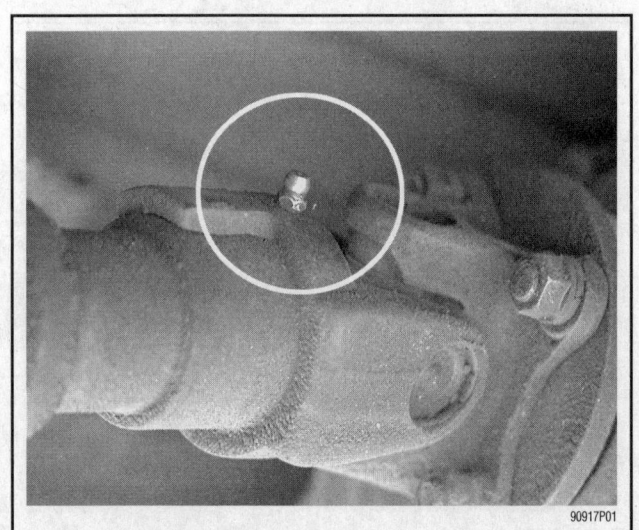

Fig. 63 A grease fitting is used to insert grease into the U-joint

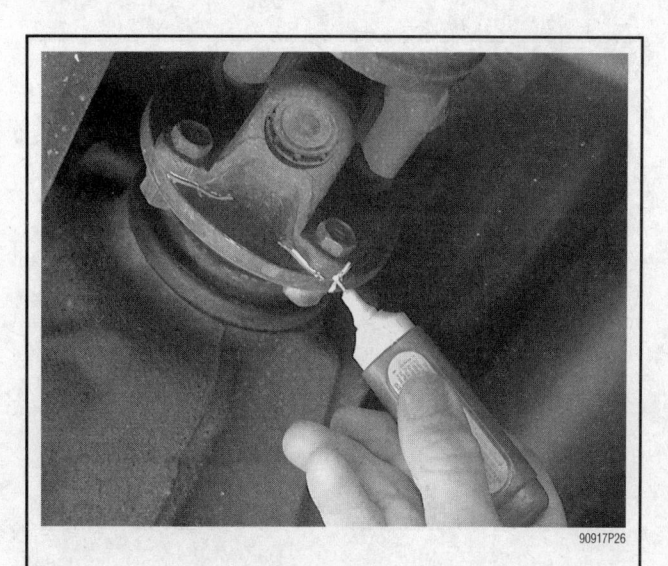

Fig. 65 Place matchmarks on the flange and carrier

## 7-22 DRIVE TRAIN

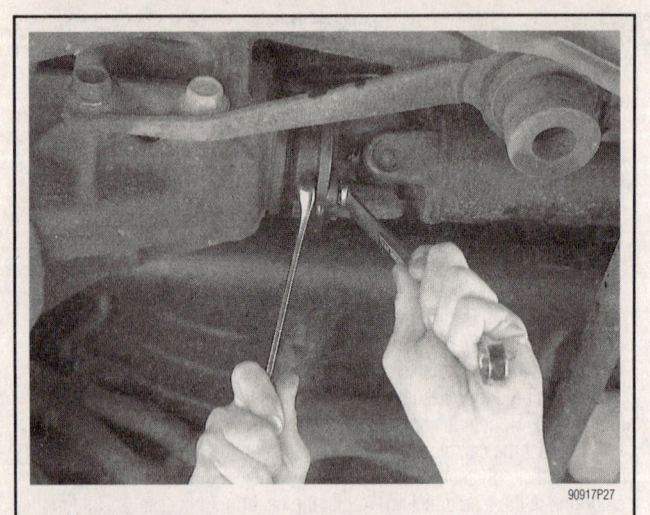

Fig. 66 Two wrenches are needed to remove the four bolts, and sometimes an air wrench

Fig. 69 . . . and using two hands pull the unit up and out of the . . .

Fig. 67 Once the four bolts are removed, pull the front portion of the driveshaft down and allow it to rest

Fig. 70 . . . transmission yoke

Fig. 68 Unbolt the center support bearing . . .

Fig. 71 Align the drive shaft match marks and secure all bolts

# DRIVE TRAIN  7-23

## U-JOINT REPLACEMENT

▶ See Figures 72 thru 80

1. Place matchmarks on the shaft and yoke.
2. Using a brass bar and hammer, slightly tap in the bearing and outer race.
   a. Using 2 screwdrivers, carefully remove the 4 snaprings from the grooves as shown.
3. Using a puller, push out the bearing from the flange. Sufficiently raise the part indicated as **A** so that it does not come into contact with the bearing.
   a. Clamp the bearing outer race in a vise, then tap off the flange with a hammer. Remove the bearing on the opposite side in the same procedure.
   b. Install the 2 removed bearing outer races to the spider. With the special tool, push out the bearing from the yoke.
   c. Clamp the outer bearing race in a vise and tap off the yoke with a hammer. remove the bearing on the opposite side in the same procedure.
4. Select the bearing according to whether or not there is a drill mark in the yoke selection.
   - Yoke with a drill mark—red color bearing
   - Yoke with no drill mark—no color mark bearing

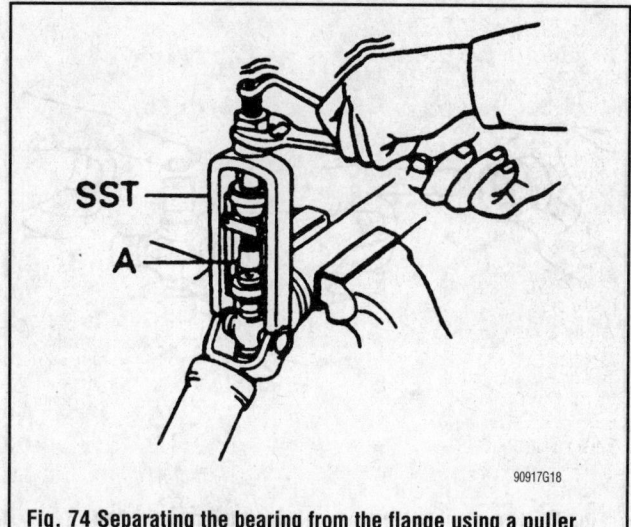

Fig. 74 Separating the bearing from the flange using a puller and vise

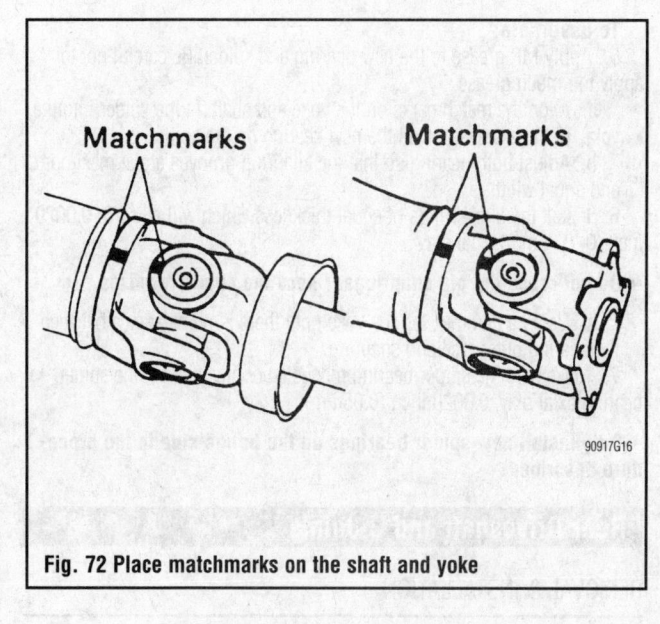

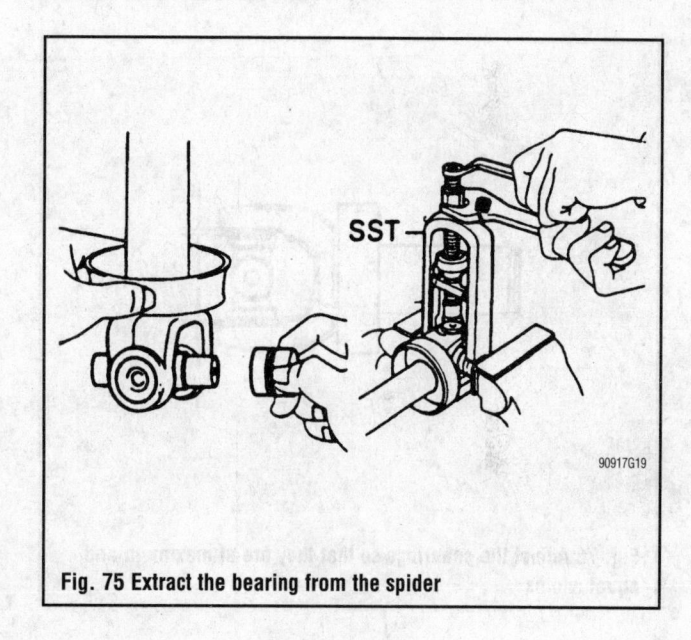

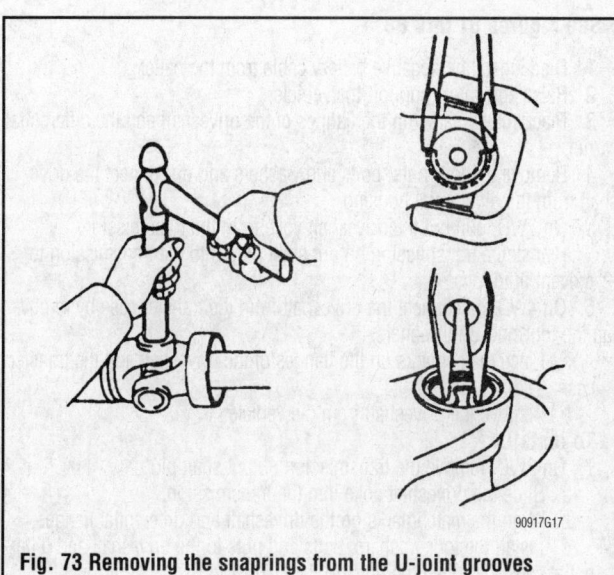

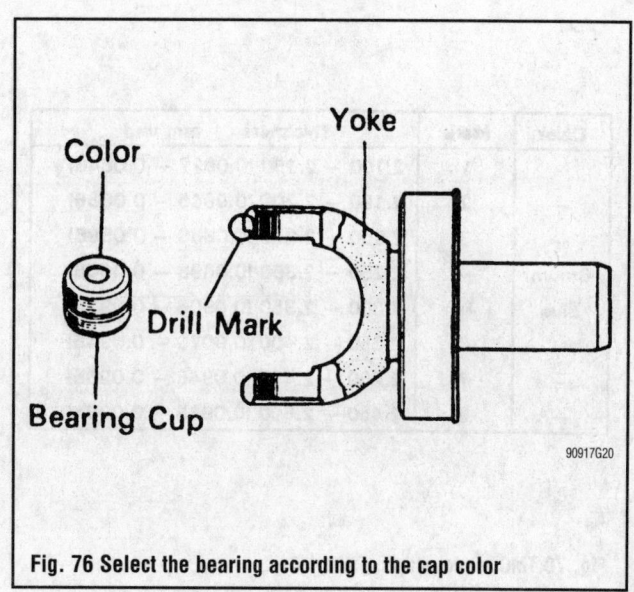

Fig. 72 Place matchmarks on the shaft and yoke

Fig. 75 Extract the bearing from the spider

Fig. 73 Removing the snaprings from the U-joint grooves

Fig. 76 Select the bearing according to the cap color

# 7-24 DRIVE TRAIN

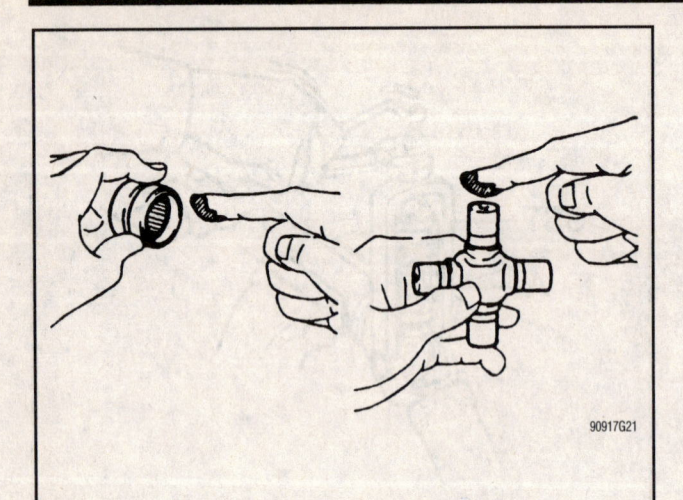

Fig. 77 Always apply MP grease (but not too much) when installing a new bearings to the spider gear

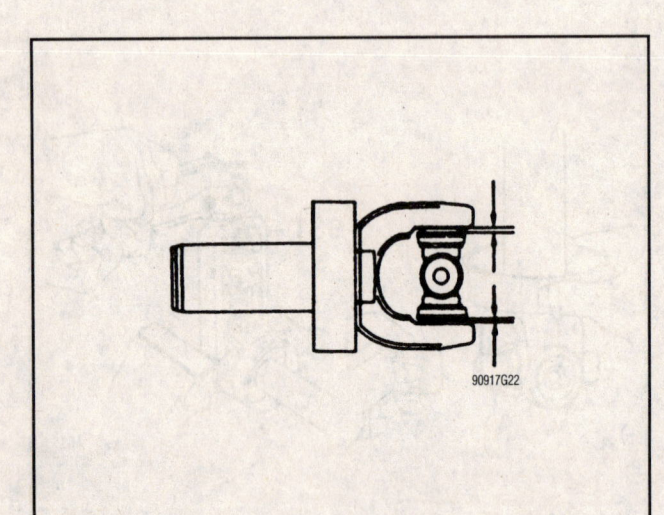

Fig. 78 Adjust the snaprings so that they are at maximum and equal widths

| Color | Mark | Thickness   mm (in.) |
|---|---|---|
| — | 1 | 2.100 – 2.150 (0.0827 – 0.0846) |
| — | 2 | 2.150 – 2.200 (0.0846 – 0.0866) |
| — | 3 | 2.200 – 2.250 (0.0866 – 0.0886) |
| Brown | — | 2.250 – 2.300 (0.0886 – 0.0906) |
| Blue | — | 2.300 – 2.350 (0.0906 – 0.0925) |
| — | 6 | 2.350 – 2.400 (0.0925 – 0.0945) |
| — | 7 | 2.400 – 2.450 (0.0945 – 0.0965) |
| — | 8 | 2.450 – 2.500 (0.0965 – 0.0984) |

Fig. 79 TMC made snapring chart

| Color | Thickness   mm (in.) |
|---|---|
| Green | 1.384 (0.0545) |
| Red | 1.435 (0.0565) |
| Black | 1.486 (0.0585) |
| Copper | 1.511 (0.0595) |
| Silver | 1.537 (0.0605) |
| Yellow | 1.588 (0.0625) |
| Blue | 1.638 (0.0645) |

Fig. 80 DANA made snapring chart

### To assemble:

5. Apply MP grease to the new bearing and spider. Be careful not to apply too much grease.

   a. Align the matchmarks on the yoke and shaft. fit the spider into the yoke. Using a press, install the new bearing on the spider.

   b. Adjust both bearing so that the snapring grooves are at maximum and equal widths.

6. Install the 2 snaprings of equal thickness which will allow 0–0.0020 inch (0–0.05mm) axial play.

➡ Do not reuse the old snaprings. Check the charts for sizes.

   a. Using a hammer, tap the yoke until there is no clearance between the bearing outer race and snapring.

7. Make sure the spider bearing moves smoothly. Inspect the spider bearing axial play, 0.0020 inch (0.05mm).

➡ Only install new spider bearings on the flange side in the procedure described.

## Rear Driveshaft and U-Joints

### REMOVAL & INSTALLATION

▶ See Figures 81 thru 88

1. Disconnect the negative battery cable from the battery.
2. Raise and safely support the vehicle.
3. Place matchmarks on the flanges of the driveshaft and the differential carrier.
4. Remove the four nuts, bolts and washers and disconnect the driveshaft from the differential housing.
5. On 2WD, pull out the driveshaft yoke from the transmission.

   a. Install a transmission output shaft plug into the transmission to prevent fluid loss.

6. On 4WD, disconnect the driveshaft from the transfer case by removing the four nuts and washers.

   a. Place matchmarks on the flanges of the driveshaft and the transfer case.

   b. Remove the driveshaft from the vehicle.

### To install:

7. On 2WD, remove the transmission output shaft plug.

   a. Slide the driveshaft yoke into the transmission.

   b. Align the matchmarks on the driveshaft and differential flanges.

   c. Install the four washers, bolts and nuts to the driveshaft and differential carrier. Tighten the bolts to 54 ft. lbs. (74 Nm).

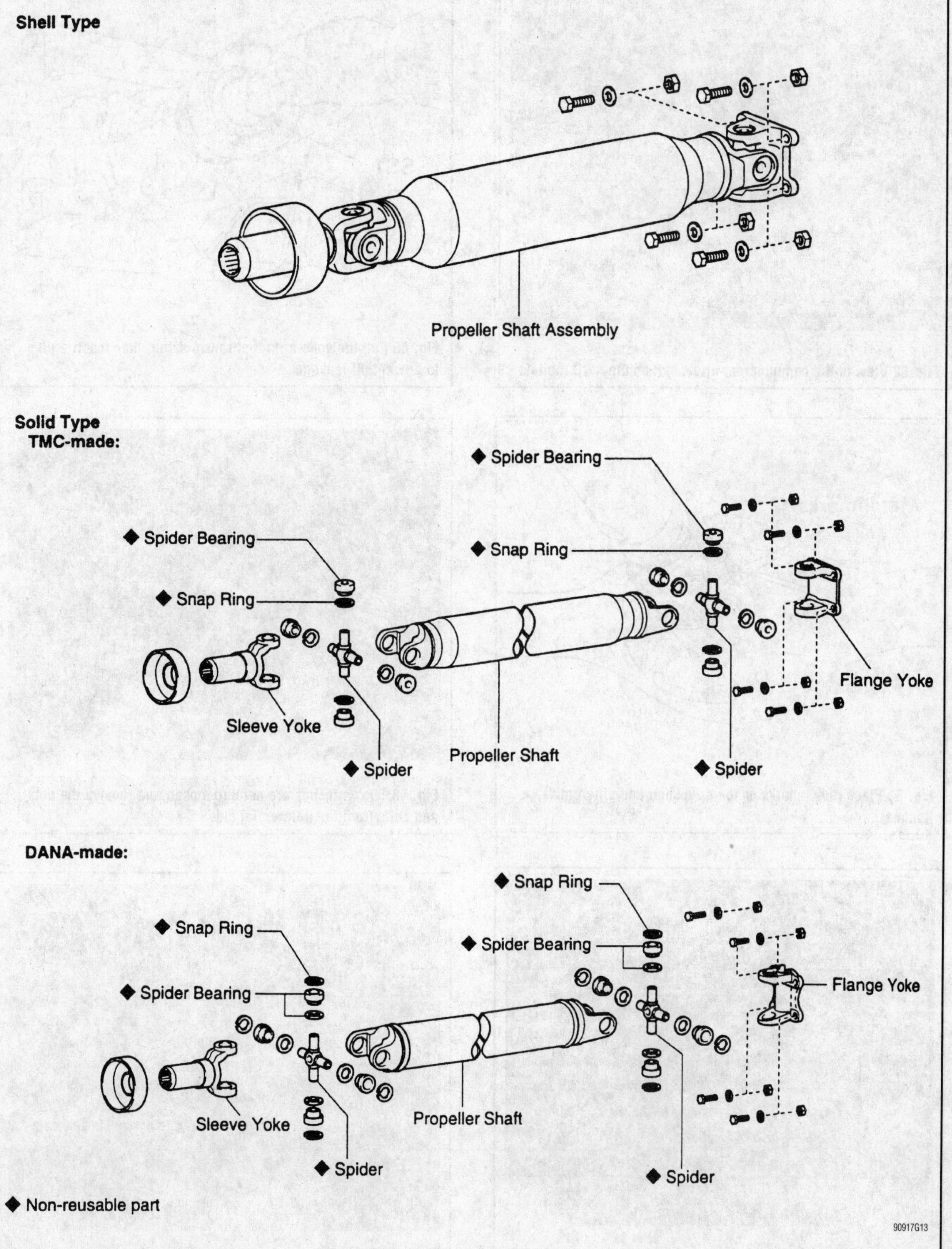

## DRIVE TRAIN 7-25

**Shell Type**

Propeller Shaft Assembly

**Solid Type
TMC-made:**

◆ Spider Bearing
◆ Spider Bearing
◆ Snap Ring
◆ Snap Ring
Flange Yoke
Sleeve Yoke
Propeller Shaft
◆ Spider
◆ Spider

**DANA-made:**

◆ Snap Ring
◆ Snap Ring
◆ Spider Bearing
◆ Spider Bearing
Flange Yoke
Sleeve Yoke
Propeller Shaft
◆ Spider
◆ Spider

◆ Non-reusable part

Fig. 81 Exploded view of the common 2WD driveshaft and U-joints

# 7-26 DRIVE TRAIN

Fig. 82 View of the common rear driveshaft on the 4WD models

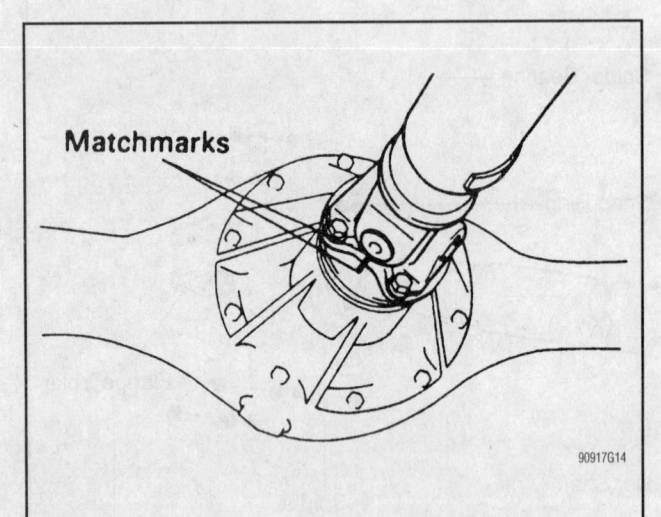

Fig. 83 Place matchmarks on the driveshaft and differential flanges

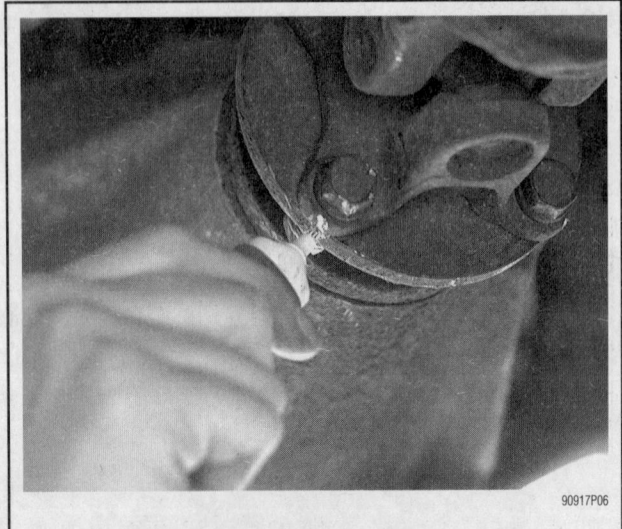

Fig. 84 A whiteout pen works well to make matchmarks

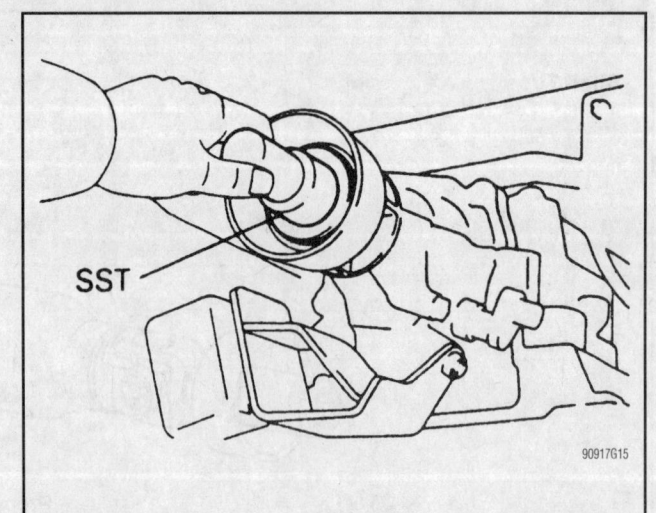

Fig. 85 Pull the yoke from the transmission, then insert a plug to prevent oil leakage

Fig. 86 Two wrenches are need to loosen and remove the nuts and bolts from the differential side

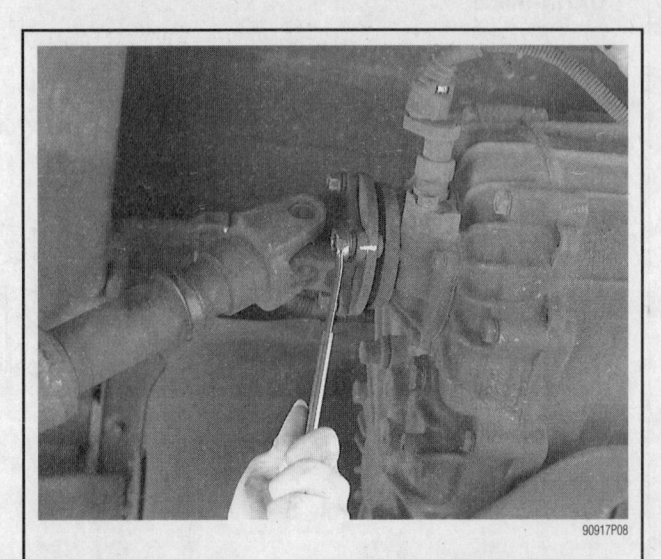

Fig. 87 On the transfer case side, only the bolt need be removed

# DRIVE TRAIN 7-27

Fig. 88 Make sure the matchmarks line up when installing the driveshaft

8. On 4WD, align the matchmarks on the transfer case and driveshaft.
  a. Install the four washers and nuts to hold the driveshaft to the transfer case. Tighten the nuts to 54 ft. lbs. (74 Nm).
  b. Align the matchmarks on the driveshaft and differential flanges.
  c. Install the four washers, bolts and nuts to the driveshaft and differential carrier. Tighten the bolts to 54 ft. lbs. (74 Nm).
9. Lower the vehicle and connect the negative battery cable to the battery.

## U-JOINT REPLACEMENT

Refer to U-Joint Replacement in the Front Driveshaft procedure.

## Center Support Bearing

### REMOVAL & INSTALLATION

▶ See Figures 89, 90, 91 and 92

1. Remove the front driveshaft assembly.
2. Place matchmarks on the flanges of the front driveshaft and intermediate shaft.
3. Remove the 4 bolts and nuts.

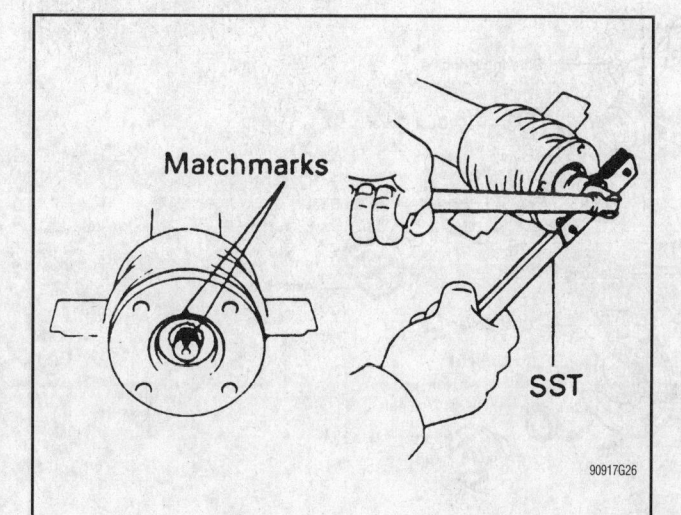

Fig. 89 Stake the nut, then retain the flange and remove the nut

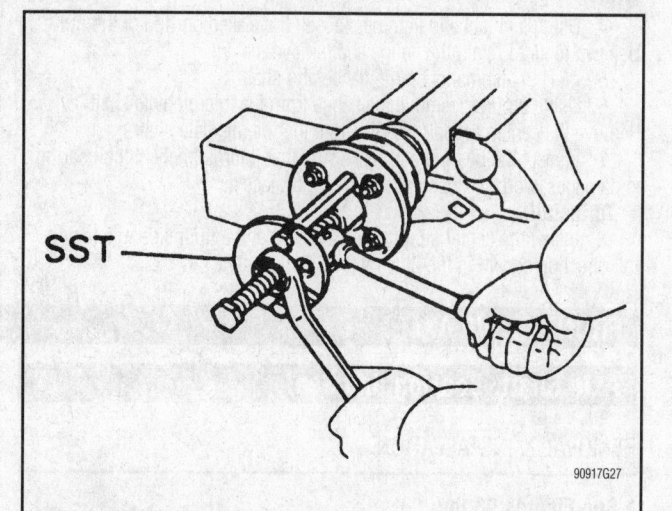

Fig. 90 Remove the flange from the shaft, then separate the center support bearing using a puller

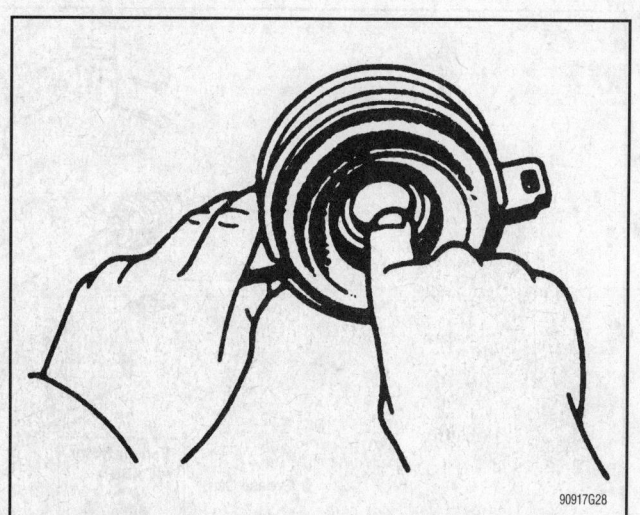

Fig. 91 Check the play of the center bearing, be sure it moves smoothly

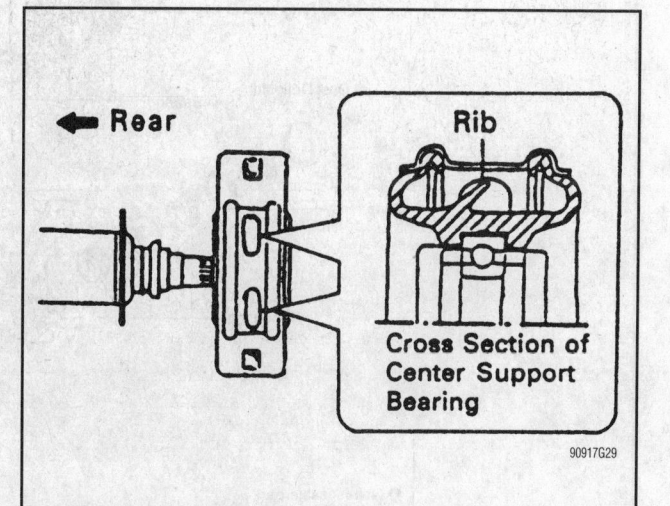

Fig. 92 Install the center bearing so that the rib is placed as shown

## 7-28 DRIVE TRAIN

4. Using a chisel and hammer, loosen the staked portion of the nut. Use two tools to retain the flange and remove the nut.
5. Place matchmarks on the flange and shaft.
6. Using a puller, remove the flange from the intermediate shaft. Remove the center support bearing from the intermediate shaft.
7. Inspect the bearing and make sure that it turns freely. If the bearing is damages, worn or does not turn freely, replace it.

**To install:**

8. Install the center support bearing so that the rib inside it is facing the direction shown in the illustration.

9. Install the flange on the intermediate shaft as follows:
    a. Coat the splines of the intermediate shaft with MP grease. Place the flange on the shaft and align the marks.
    b. Using a retaining tool, press the bearing into position by tightening down a new nut to 134 ft. lbs. (181 Nm).
    c. Loosen the nut.
    d. Tighten the nut again to 51 ft. lbs. (69 Nm).
    e. Using a chisel and hammer, stake the nut.
10. Install the front driveshaft.

## FRONT DRIVE AXLE

### Axle Shaft, Bearing and Seal

REMOVAL & INSTALLATION

▶ See Figures 93 thru 98

1. Raise and safely support the front of the vehicle securely on jackstands.
2. If equipped, remove the speed sensor.
3. Remove the front brake caliper and disc.
4. Place a dial indicator near the center of the axle hub and check the backlash in the bearing shaft direction. maximum is 0.0020 inch (0.05mm). If the specification is greater than the specified amount, replace the hub.
5. Install the brake disc and caliper, the remove the cotter in and lock cap.
6. Have an assistant apply the brakes and remove the nut.

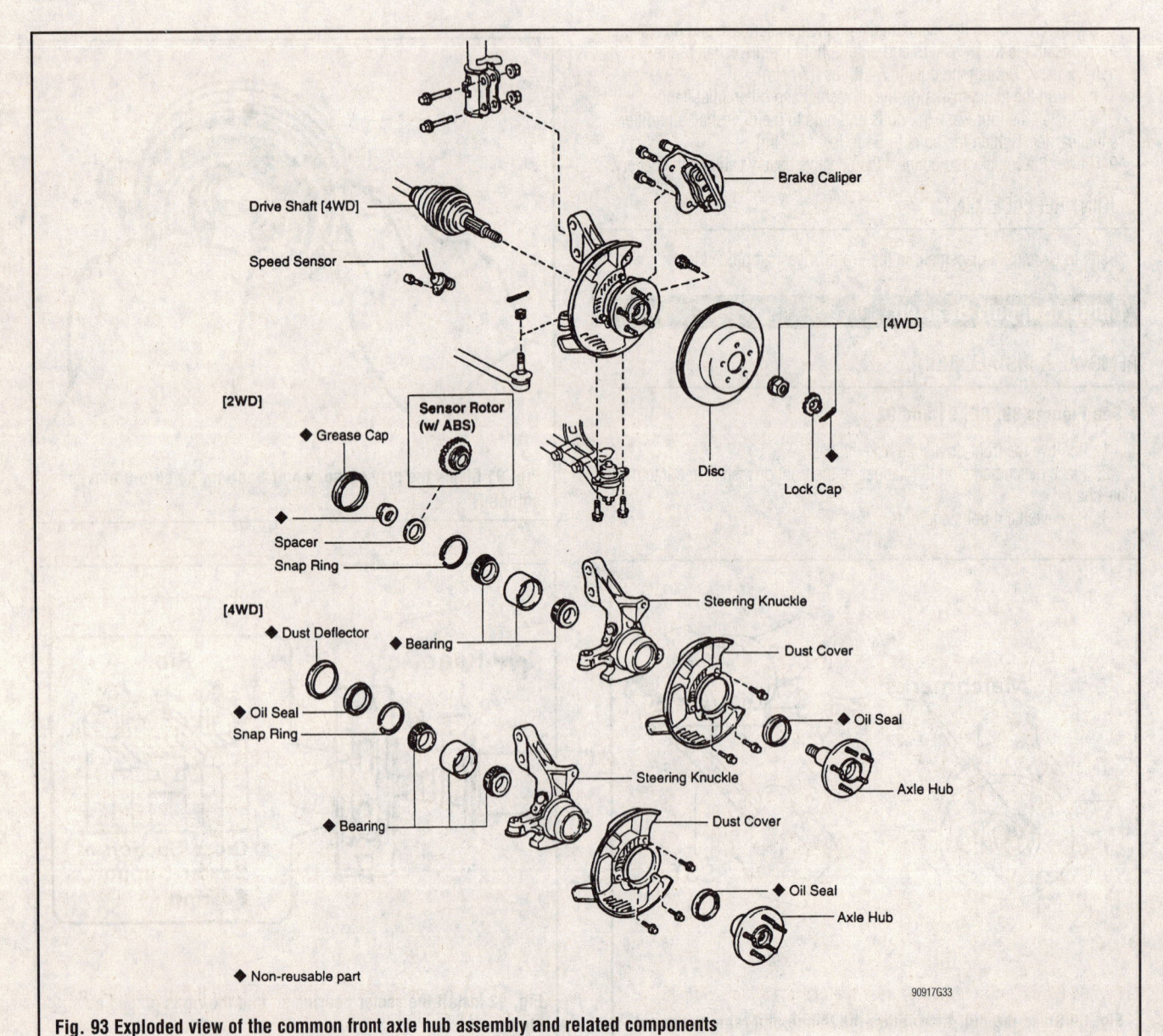

Fig. 93 Exploded view of the common front axle hub assembly and related components

# DRIVE TRAIN  7-29

7. Remove the caliper and disc.
8. Loosen the 2 nuts on the lower side of the shock absorber.

➡ **Do not remove the bolts!**

9. Loosen the bolts for the lower ball joint. Once again, do not remove them.
10. Disconnect the tie rod end from the steering knuckle. Discard the cotter pin.

➡ **A puller will be needed to separate the tie rod end from the knuckle.**

11. Remove the 2 bolts on the lower ball joint and disconnect the steering knuckle.
    a. Remove the 2 nuts and bolts on the lower side of the shock absorber.
    b. Remove the steering knuckle with the axle hub.

➡ **Be careful not to damage the speed sensor rotor (on models with ABS), oil seal and drive shaft boot.**

12. Using a puller, remove the axle hub.
13. With a press, remove the bearing from the axle hub. Remove the oil seal from the axle hub.
14. Remove the 3 bolts and dust cover. Carefully pry the dust deflector out of the knuckle. Next, with a puller, remove the inner oil seal.
15. Using snap ring pliers, remove the snap ring. Place the outer bearing above the outer race on the outer side. Press the bearing out.

**To assemble:**

16. Press the bearing into the steering knuckle. If the inner race comes loose from the bearing outer race, be sure to install them on the same side as before.
    a. Using snap ring pliers, install the snap ring.
17. Place the outer bearing into position, then using a hammer carefully tap the new oil seal until it is flush with the end surface of the steering knuckle.
18. Install the dust cover with 3 bolts.
19. Using the press, install the axle hub.
20. Tap the new outer seal into the steering knuckle.
21. Tap a new dust deflector into position.
22. Position the steering knuckle.

➡ **Be careful not to damage the speed sensor rotor on models with ABS and the oil seal and driveshaft boot.**

   a. Install the 2 bolts and temporarily tighten the nut.
   b. Temporarily install the 2 bolts and connect the steering knuckle and lower ball joint.
23. Attach the tie rod end to the steering knuckle. Be sure to use a new cotter pin. Tighten the tie rod end nut to 36 ft. lbs. (49 Nm).

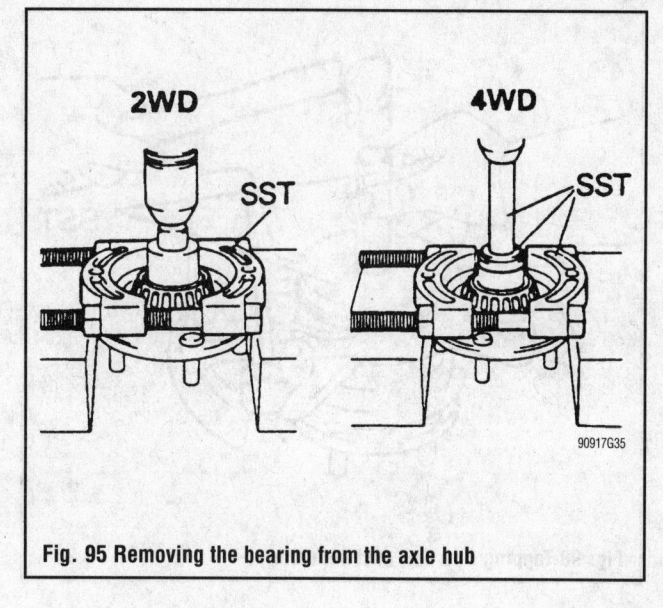

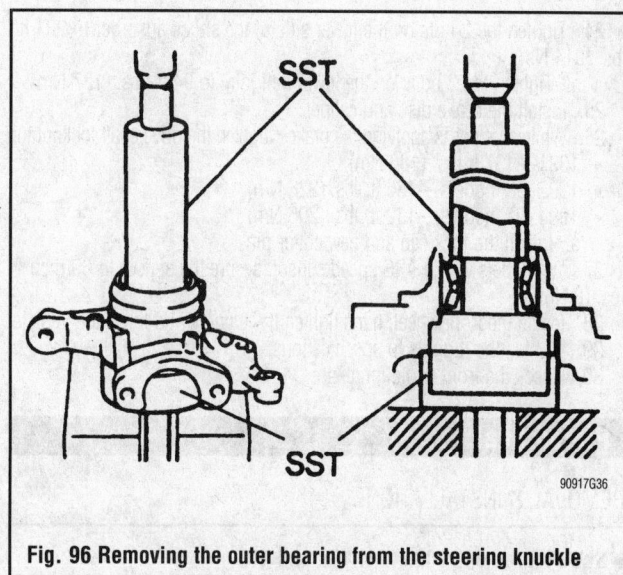

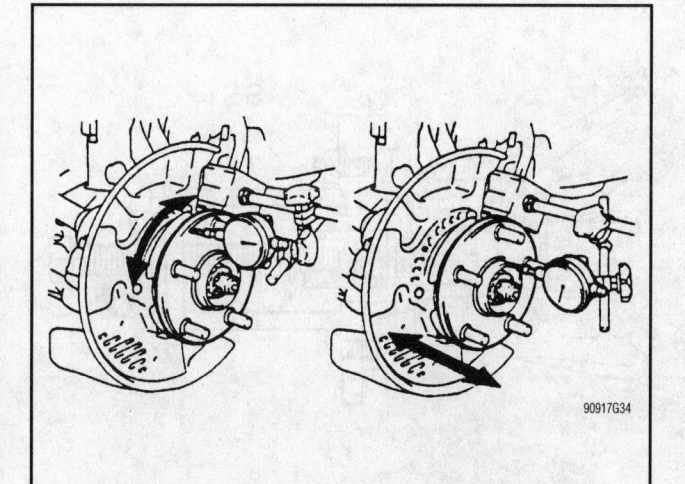

Fig. 94 Place a dial indicator near the center of the axle hub and check the backlash in the bearing shaft direction

Fig. 95 Removing the bearing from the axle hub

Fig. 96 Removing the outer bearing from the steering knuckle

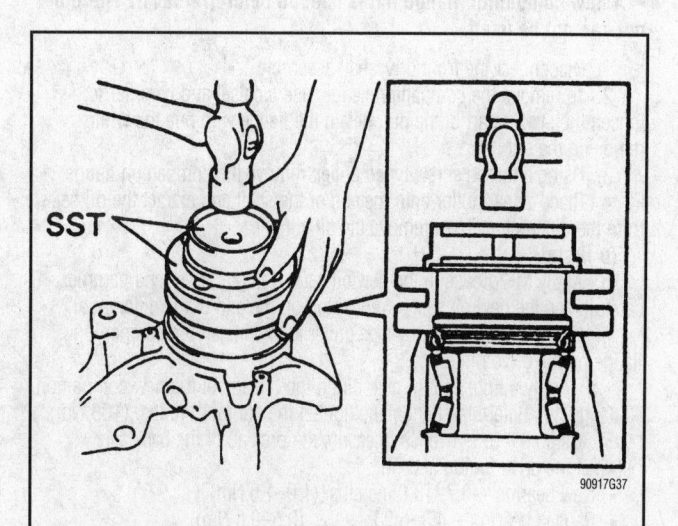

Fig. 97 Tap the outer seal into position until it is flush with the end surface of the knuckle

# 7-30 DRIVE TRAIN

Fig. 98 Tapping in a new dust deflector

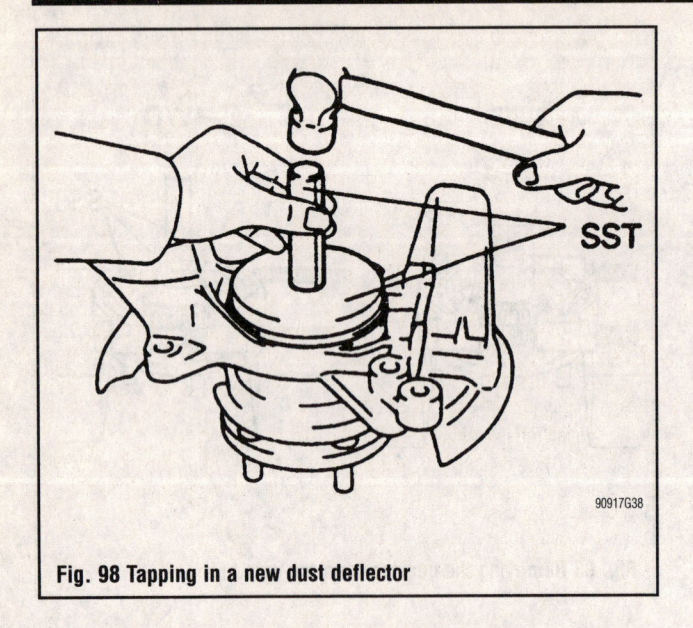

Fig. 99 The front 4WD differential oil seal is located behind the companion flange

24. Tighten the 2 nuts on the lower side of the shock absorber to 231 ft. lbs. (314 Nm).
   a. Tighten the 2 bolts on the lower ball joint to 94 ft. lbs. (127 Nm).
25. Install the brake disc and caliper.
26. While a helper is applying the brakes, tighten the drive shaft locknut to:
- 1991—137 ft lbs. (186 Nm)
- 1992–93 models—166 ft. lbs. (226 Nm)
- 1994–97 models—152 ft. lbs. (206 Nm)

   a. Install the lock cap and new cotter pin.
27. On models with a ABS speed sensor, secure the sensor to 69 inch lbs. (8 Nm).
28. Install the front wheel, hand tighten the lugnuts and lower the vehicle.
29. Tighten the lugnuts to specifications.
30. Check the front end alignment.

## Pinion Seal

### REMOVAL & INSTALLATION

♦ See Figures 99, 100, 101, 102 and 103

➡A new companion flange nut is needed before removal. The old nut can not be used.

1. Disconnect the front driveshaft assembly.
2. To remove the companion flange, use a chisel and hammer to loosen the staked part of the nut. Retain the flange with one too while removing the nut.
3. Using a forced screw typed puller, remove the companion flange.
4. Place a seal puller onto the end of the shaft and extract the oil seal from the differential. Then remove the oil slinger.

**To install:**

5. Apply MP grease to the new oil seal. Using a driver and hammer, carefully tap the new oil seal into position on the end of the differential.
6. Using the forced screw type puller again, install the companion flange on the drive pinion.
   a. Apply a light coat of gear oil on the threads of the new companion flange nut. Retain the flange and tighten the nut to 80 ft. lbs. (108 Nm).
7. Using a torque wrench, measure the preload of the backlash between the drive pinion and ring gear.
- New bearing—8.7–13.9 inch lbs. (1.0–1.6 Nm)
- Reused bearing—4.3–6.9 inch lbs. (0.5–0.8 Nm)
8. If the preload is greater than specification, replace the bearing spacer.
9. If the preload is less than specification, retighten the nut to 9 ft. lbs. (13 Nm) a little at a time until the specified preload is reached.

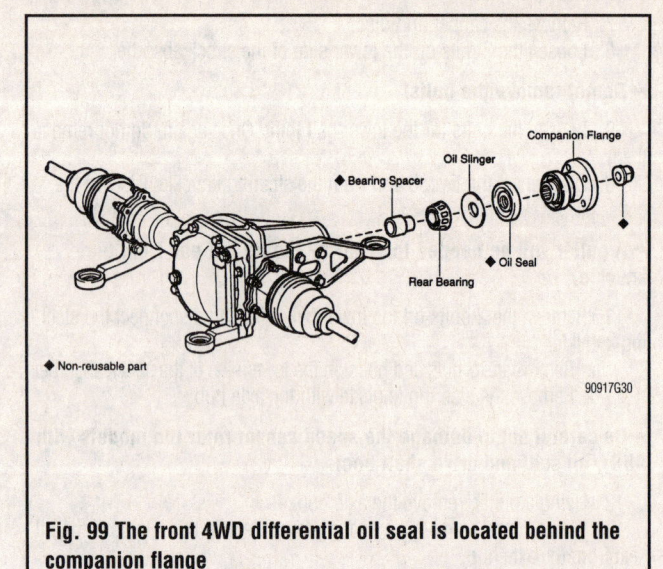

Fig. 100 Use a chisel and hammer to loosen the staked nut

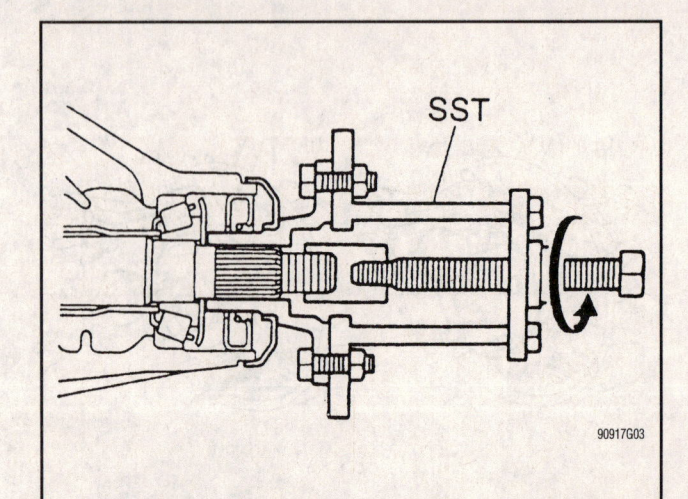

Fig. 101 Use a screw type puller and remove the companion flange . . .

# DRIVE TRAIN    7-31

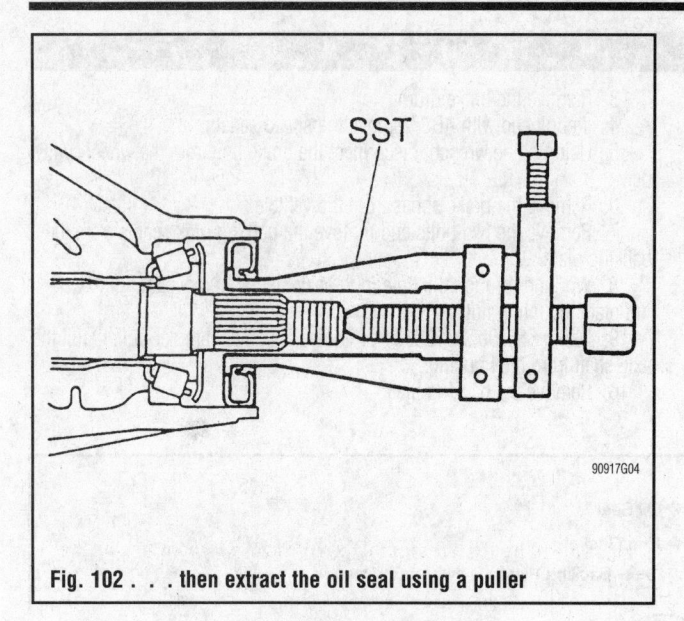

bolts, 6 cushions and collars. Lower the jack and remove the front differential assembly.

7. Remove the bolts and No. 1 differential support. Remove the 2 bolts and No. 2 differential support. Remove the 4 bolts retaining the differential support.

**To install:**

8. Install the differential support with the 4 bolts and tighten them to 116 ft. lbs. (157 Nm).

9. Install the No. 2 differential support with the 21 bolts and tighten to 48 ft. lbs. (65 Nm). Attach the No. 1 differential support and tighten that to 51 ft. lbs. (70 Nm).

10. Jackup the front differential assembly and install the collars, cushions and support bolts to the 3 support. Tighten the 3 bolts to 54 ft. lbs. (73 Nm).

11. Attach the No. 1 and No. 2 differential support protectors and tighten them to 9 ft. lbs. (12 Nm).

12. Install the left and No. 2 engine under covers.

13. Connect the halfshafts to the side gear shafts. Align the matchmarks and connect the halfshaft to the side gears shaft with the 6 bolts and nuts. Tighten them to 51 ft. lbs. (69 Nm).

14. Connect the front driveshaft.

15. Fill the differential with the correct amount of gear oil.

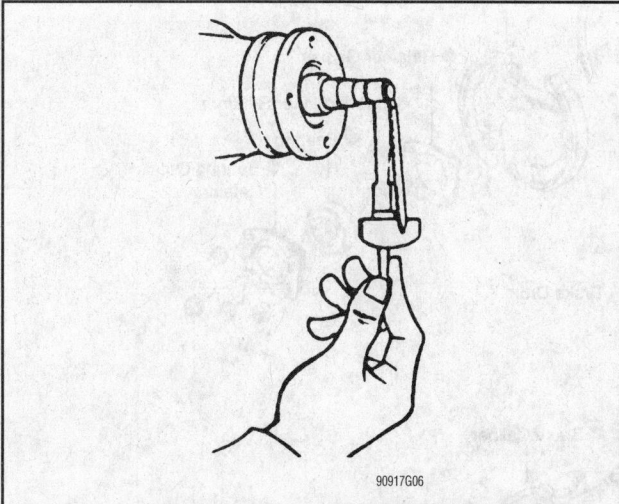

Fig. 102 . . . then extract the oil seal using a puller

Fig. 103 Use a torque meter to measure the preload of the backlash between the drive pinion and ring gear

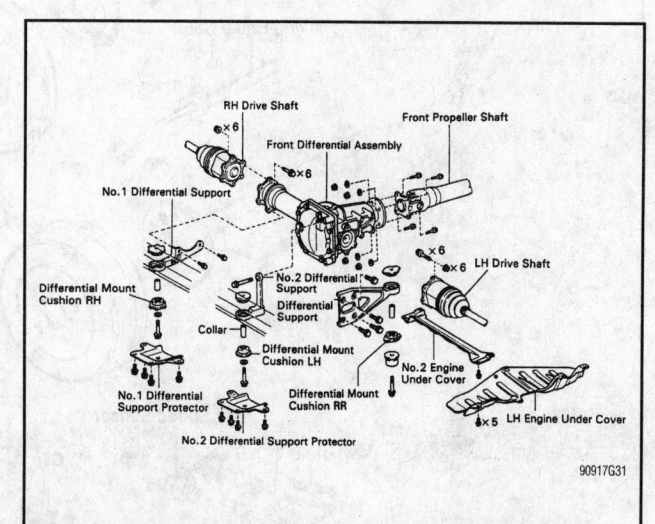

Fig. 104 Exploded view of the common 4WD front differential assembly

10. If the maximum torque is exceeded while retightening the nut, replace the bearing spacer and repeat the preload procedure. Do not back-off the pinion nut to reduce preload. Maximum torque is 174 ft. lbs. (235 Nm).

11. Stake the drive pinion nut.
12. Connect the front driveshaft.
13. Check the differential fluid level.

## Axle Housing Assembly

### REMOVAL & INSTALLATION

▶ See Figures 104 and 105

1. Drain the differential oil.
2. Disconnect the front driveshaft.
3. Detach the front halfshafts from the side gear shafts.
   a. Place matchmarks on the halfshaft and remove the 6 bolts and nuts retaining the shaft and side gear.
   b. Disconnect the halfshafts from the side gear shaft.
4. Remove the No. 2 and left engine under cover.
5. Remove the No. 1 and No. 2 differential support protectors.
6. Support the front differential with a jack. Remove the 3 support

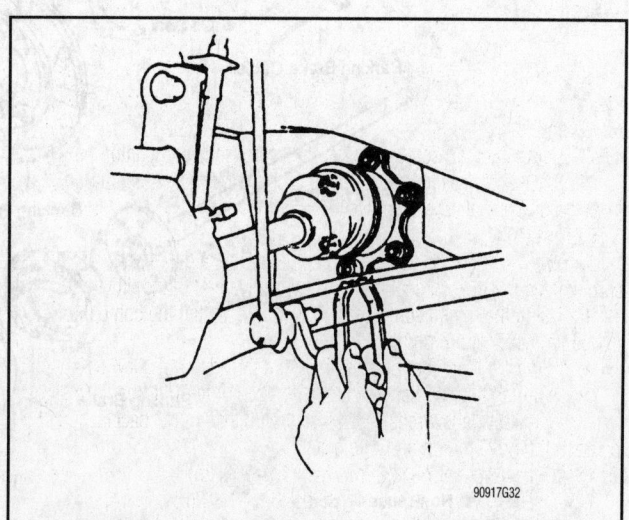

Fig. 105 Remove the 6 bolts retaining the side gear shafts to the differential

# 7-32 DRIVE TRAIN

## REAR AXLE

### Axle Shaft, Bearing and Seal

▶ See Figure 106

REMOVAL & INSTALLATION

**With Drum Brakes**

▶ See Figures 107, 108 and 109

1. Raise and safely support the rear of the vehicle.
2. Remove the wheel and tire assembly.
3. Remove the brake drum.
4. If equipped with ABS, remove the speed sensor.
5. Using a line wrench, disconnect the brake line from the wheel cylinder.
6. Remove the brake shoes from the vehicle.
7. Remove the two bolts and remove the parking brake cable from the backing plate.
8. Working through the hole in the axle flange, remove the four backing plate mounting nuts.
9. Using SST 09520–00031 or equivalent slide hammer puller, pull the axle shaft from the housing.
10. Remove the backing plate.

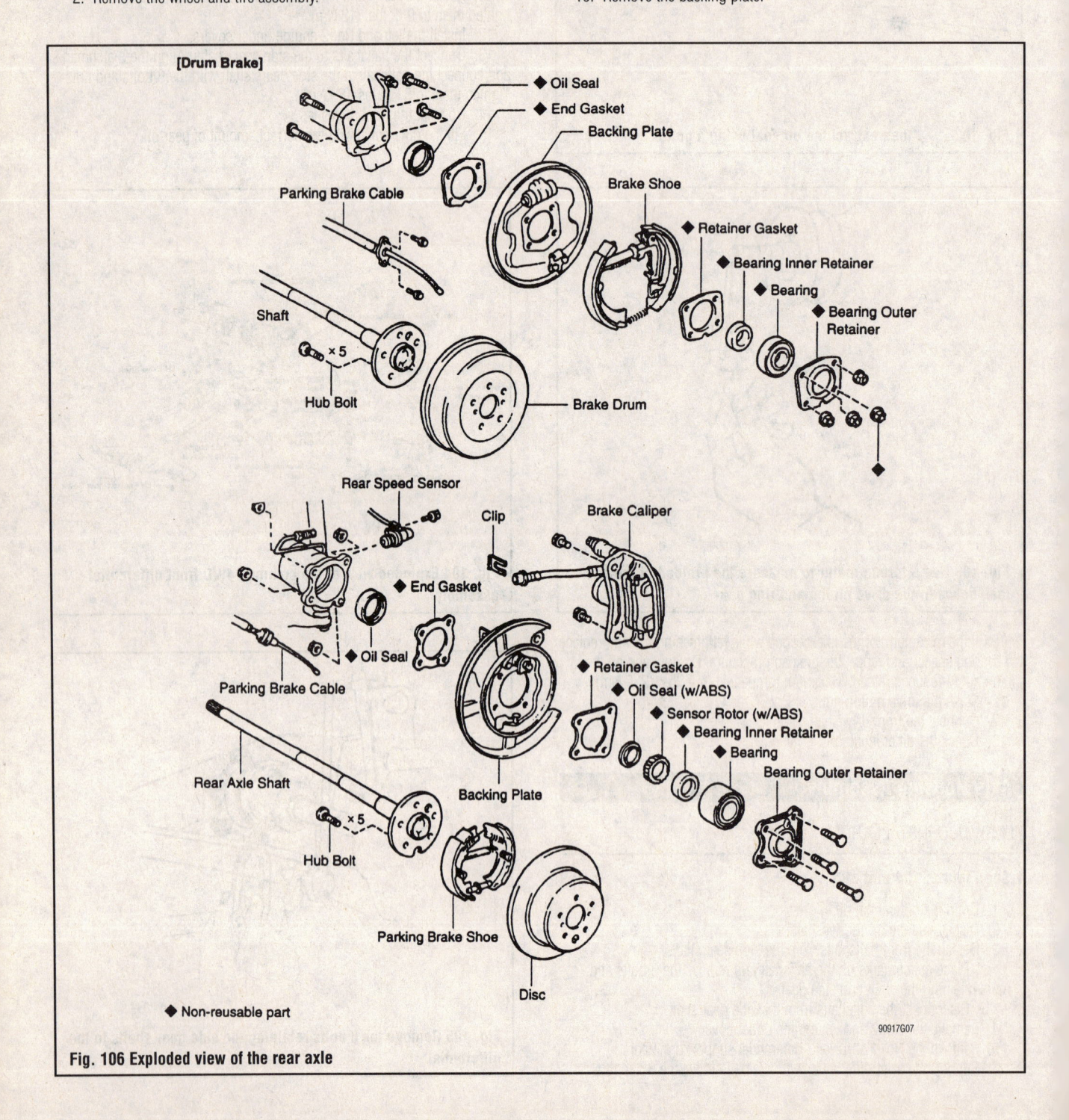

Fig. 106 Exploded view of the rear axle

# DRIVE TRAIN  7-33

11. Remove the end gasket to the axle housing.
12. If equipped with ABS, press the seal and speed sensor rotor from the axle shaft.
13. Using a grinder, grind down the inner bearing retainer on the axle shaft. Using a chisel and a hammer, cut off the retainer and remove it from the shaft.

### ✸✸ WARNING

**When removing the bearing, be careful not to damage the axle shaft.**

14. Using a press, press the bearing from the axle shaft.
15. Remove the bearing outer retainer.
16. Using a seal puller, extract the oil seal from the axle housing.

**To install:**
17. With a driver and hammer, insert the oil seal and drive it in 0.236 inch (6.0mm).
18. Install the bearing outer retainer to the axle shaft.
19. Using a suitable driver (SST 09506–30012) or equivalent and a press, install a new bearing.
20. Heat the new inner retainer to approximately 302°F (150°C) in an oil bath. Using a suitable installer and a press, install the inner retainer to the axle shaft while the retainer is still hot.

➥**Face the non-beveled side of the inner retainer toward the bearing.**

21. If equipped with ABS, carefully install the speed sensor rotor. Using a suitable installer and a press, install the new oil seal.

➥**Only ABS models are equipped with two oil seals!**

22. Apply liquid sealant on a new axle housing gasket and install the end gasket on the rear axle housing.
23. Install the backing plate.
24. Using a suitable tool, install the rear axle shaft.

➥**Be careful not to damage the oil seal and speed sensor rotor (w/ABS).**

25. Install the backing plate mounting nuts. Tighten the nuts to 59 ft. lbs. (80 Nm).
26. Install the parking brake cable, brake shoes, and the drum.
27. Connect the brake line to the wheel cylinder.
28. Bleed the brake system.
29. Install the rear wheel and lower the vehicle.
30. Road test the vehicle for proper operation.

**With Disc Brakes**

▶ See Figures 107, 108, 109 and 110

1. Raise and safely support the rear of the vehicle.
2. Remove the wheel and tire assembly.
3. If equipped with ABS brakes, remove the speed sensor.
4. Using a line wrench, disconnect the brake line from the brake hose.
5. Disconnect the brake hose from the axle bracket by removing the clip.
6. Remove the brake caliper support by removing the two bolts.
7. Remove the disc and parking brake shoes.
8. Remove the parking brake cable.
9. Remove the backing plate by removing the four mounting nuts.
10. Using SST 09520–00031 or equivalent (slide hammer puller), pull the axle shaft from the housing.
11. Remove the axle housing end gasket.
12. Remove the four bolts and disconnect the backing plate from the axle shaft.
13. If equipped with ABS, press the seal and speed sensor rotor from the axle shaft.
14. Using a grinder, grind down the inner bearing retainer on the axle shaft. Using a chisel and a hammer, cut off the retainer and remove it from the shaft.

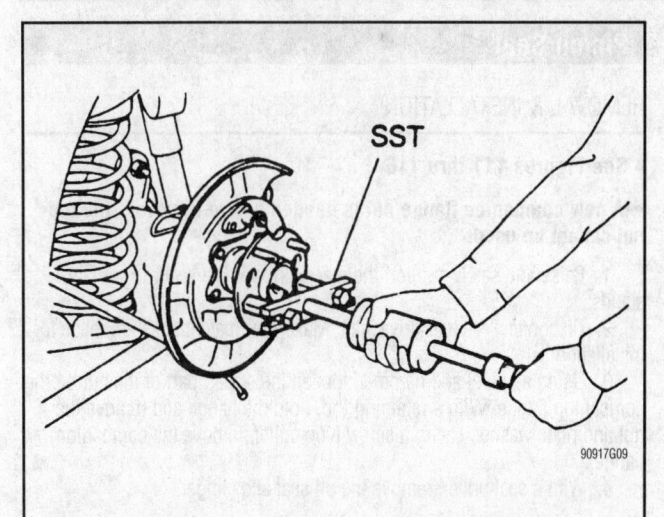

Fig. 107 Use a slide hammer puller to extract the axle shaft from the housing

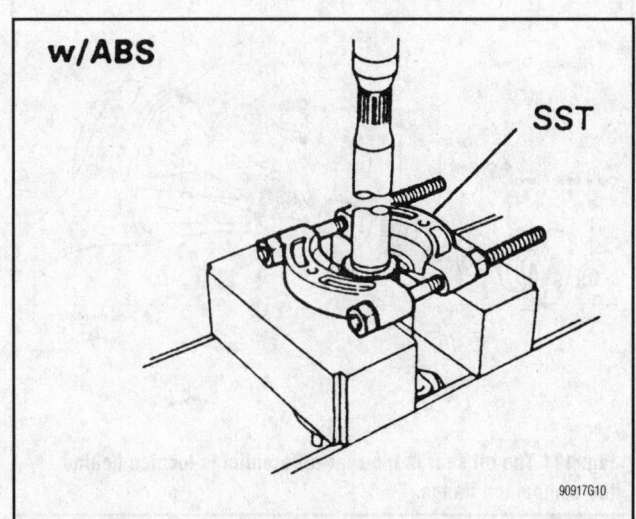

Fig. 108 Press out the ABS sensor rotor very carefully, do not damage the serrated edges

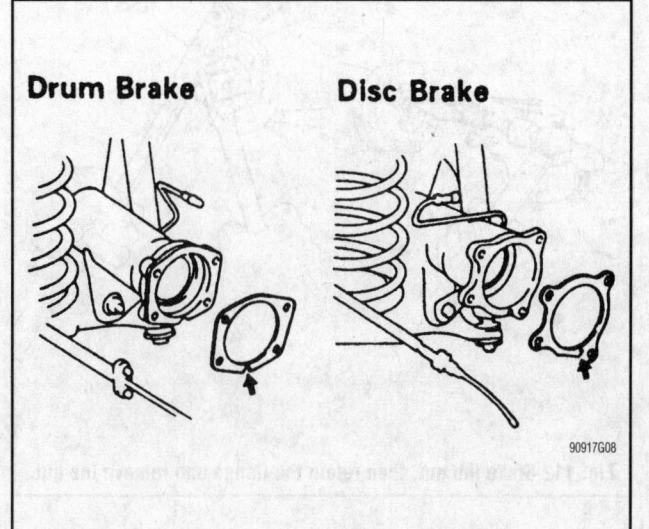

Fig. 109 Apply sealant to the new gasket on both sides

# 7-34 DRIVE TRAIN

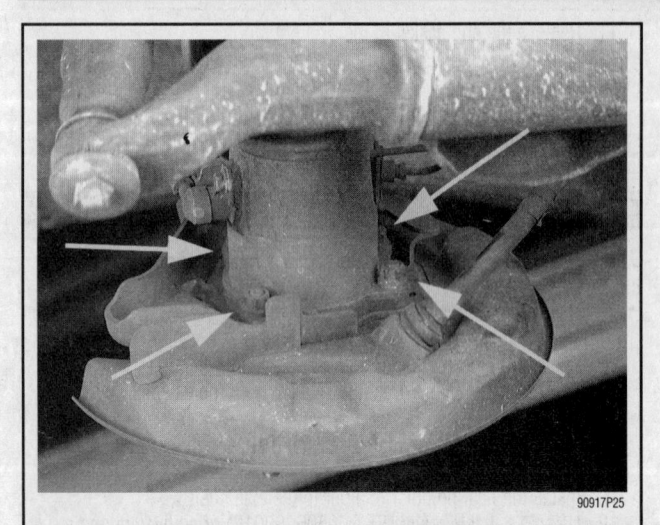

Fig. 110 These four nuts retain the backing plate on the rear axle

### ✼✼ WARNING

**When removing the bearing, be careful not to damage the axle shaft.**

15. Using a press, press the bearing from the axle shaft.
16. Remove the bearing outer retainer.
17. Using a seal puller, extract the oil seal from the axle housing.

**To install:**

18. With a driver and hammer, insert the oil seal and drive it in 0.138 inch (3.5mm).
19. Place a new retainer gasket and bearing on the backing plate. Using a socket wrench and hammer, install the four bolts for the backing plate.
20. Install the backing plate to the axle shaft.
21. Using SST 09506–30012 or equivalent (drive pinion rear bearing cone replace) and a press, install a new bearing.
22. Heat the new inner retainer to approximately 302°F (150°C) in an oil bath. Using a suitable installer and a press, install the inner retainer to the axle shaft while the retainer is still hot.

➥Face the non-beveled side of the inner retainer toward the bearing.

23. If equipped with ABS, carefully install the speed sensor rotor. Using a suitable installer and a press, install the new oil seal.
24. Apply liquid sealant on a new axle housing gasket and install the end gasket on the rear axle housing.
25. Using a suitable tool, install the rear axle shaft.

➥Be careful not to damage the oil seal and speed sensor rotor (w/ABS).

26. Install the backing plate mounting nuts. Tighten the nuts to 59 ft. lbs. (80 Nm).
27. Install the parking brake cable and parking brake shoes.
28. Install the rotor.
29. Install the brake caliper support and secure with the two bolts. Tighten the bolts to 65 ft. lbs. (88 Nm).
30. Install the brake hose to the axle bracket and attach the clip.
31. Connect the brake line to the brake hose.
32. If equipped with ABS brakes, install and secure the speed sensor.
33. Install the wheels to the vehicle.
34. Lower the vehicle.

## Pinion Seal

### REMOVAL & INSTALLATION

▶ See Figures 111 thru 116

➥A new companion flange nut is needed before removal. The old nut cannot be used.

1. Raise and safely support the rear of the vehicle securely on jackstands.
2. Disconnect the rear driveshaft. Make sure matchmarks are made for installation.
3. Using a chisel and hammer, loosen the staked part of the nut on the companion flange. With a retaining too, hold the flange and remove the nut and plate washer. Using a screw type puller, remove the companion flange.
4. With a seal puller, remove the oil seal and slinger.

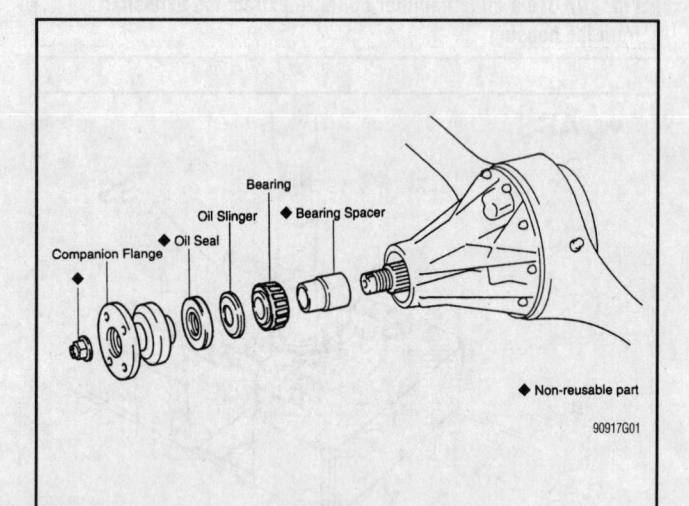

Fig. 111 The oil seal in the rear differential is located behind the companion flange

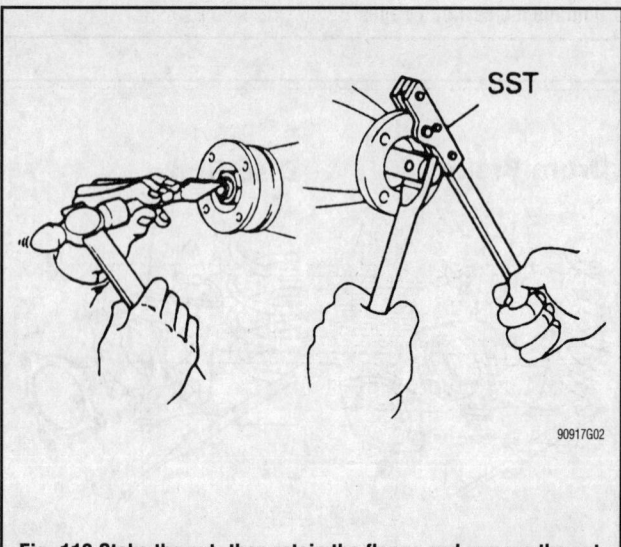

Fig. 112 Stake the nut, then retain the flange and remove the nut

# DRIVE TRAIN    7-35

**Fig. 113 Use a screw type puller and remove the companion flange . . .**

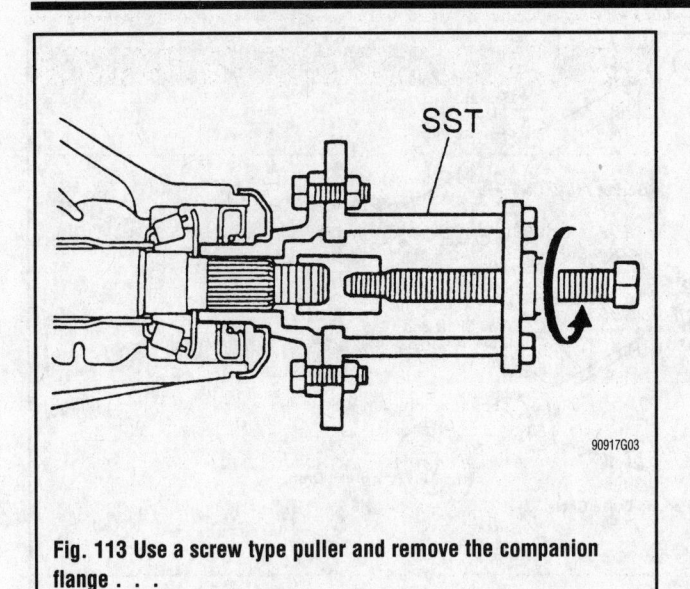

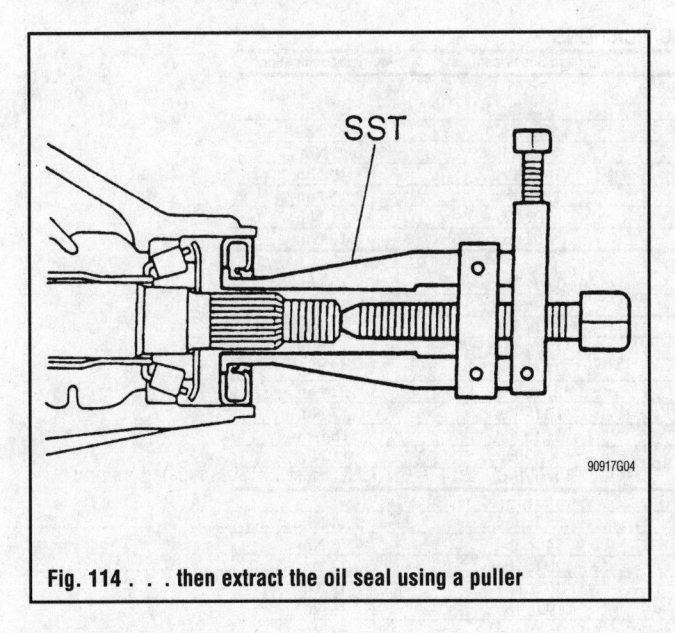

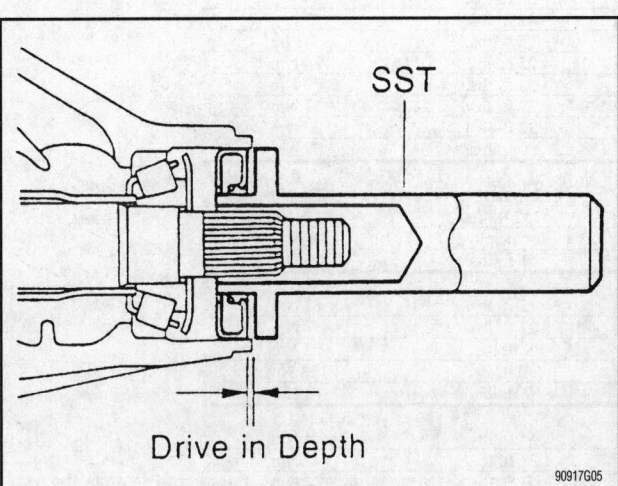

**Fig. 114 . . . then extract the oil seal using a puller**

**Fig. 115 Drive a new oil seal into the differential lubricated with MP grease**

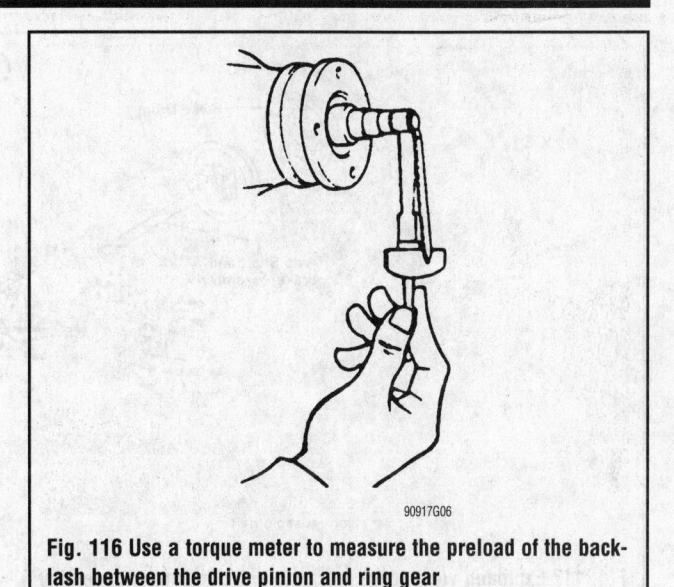

**Fig. 116 Use a torque meter to measure the preload of the backlash between the drive pinion and ring gear**

**To install:**

5. Insert the new oil slinger, then apply MP grease on the new oil seal and drive it into the housing. Drive depth is approximately 0.0059 inches (1.5mm).
6. With the screw type puller, install the companion flange on the drive pinion. Place the plate washer on the companion flange.
    a. Apply a light coat of gear oil on the threads of a new companion flange nut. Retain the flange and tighten the nut to 80 ft. lbs. (108 Nm).
7. Adjust the drive pinion preload as follows:
    a. Using a torque meter, measure the preload of the backlash between the drive pinion and ring gear.
    - New bearing—10.4–16.5 inch lbs. (1.2–1.9 Nm)
    - Reused bearing—5.2–8.7 inch lbs. (0.6–1.0 Nm)
    b. If the preload is greater than specification, replace the bearing spacer.
    c. If the preload is less than specification, retighten the nut to 9 ft. lbs. (13 Nm) a little at a time until the specified preload is reached.
8. If the maximum torque is exceeded while retightening the nut, replace the bearing spacer and repeat the preload procedure. Do not back-off the pinion nut to reduce preload. Maximum torque is 174 ft. lbs. (235 Nm).
9. Stake the drive pinion nut.
10. Connect the rear driveshaft.
11. Check and top-off the differential fluid level.
12. Lower the rear of the vehicle and test drive the vehicle.

## Differential Carrier

### REMOVAL & INSTALLATION

▶ See Figure 117

1. Remove the drain plug and drain all the differential fluid from the carrier.
2. Remove the rear axle shafts.
3. Disconnect the rear driveshaft.
4. Lower the rear differential assembly from the vehicle.

**To install:**

5. Position a new gasket and attach the differential carrier. Tighten the bolts to 18 ft. lbs. (25 Nm).
6. Install the rear driveshaft assembly.
7. Install the rear axle shafts and fill the differential carrier with the correct type and amount of gear oil. The fluid should be just flowing out of the fill plug hole.

# 7-36 DRIVE TRAIN

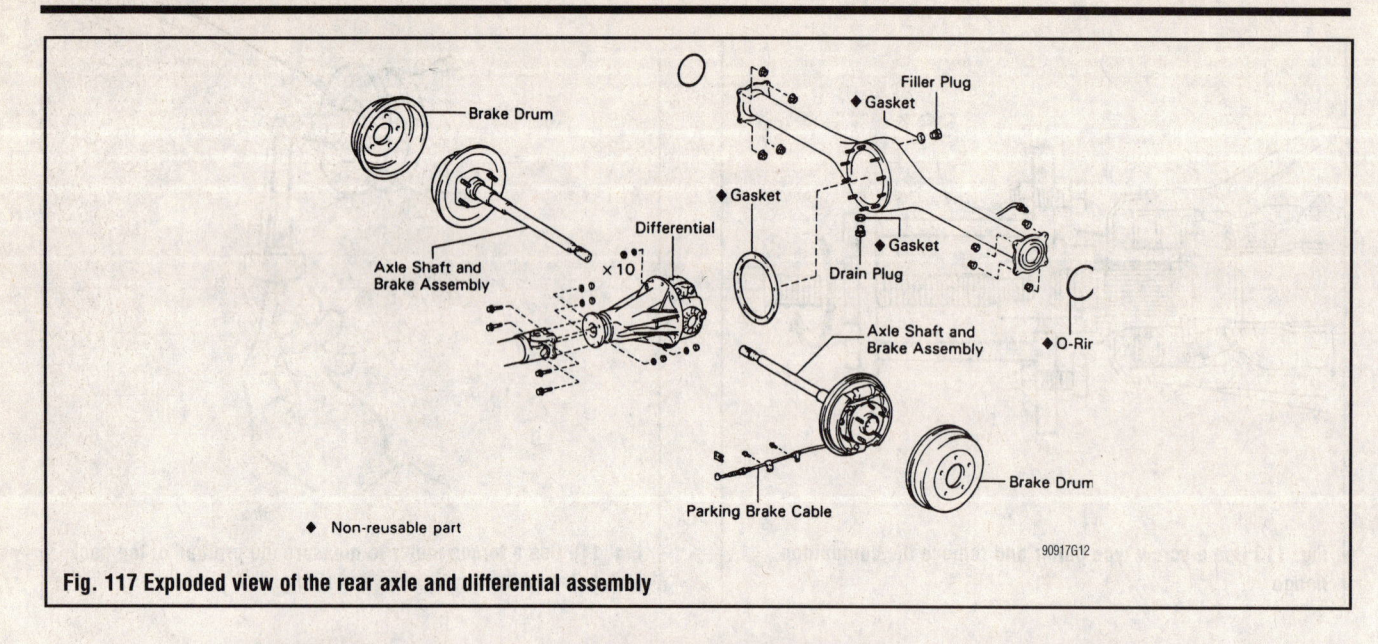

Fig. 117 Exploded view of the rear axle and differential assembly

◆ Non-reusable part

### TORQUE SPECIFICATIONS

| Components | English Specifications | Metric Specifications |
|---|---|---|
| **Clutch** | | |
| Clutch master cylinder-to-mounting bracket | 9 ft. lbs. | 12 Nm |
| Slave (release) cylinder | 9 ft. lbs. | 12 Nm |
| Accumulator bracket-to-housing | 48 inch lbs | 5 Nm |
| Clutch cover-to-flywheel | 14 ft. lbs. | 19 Nm |
| Clutch line union | 11 ft. lbs. | 15 Nm |
| Bleeder plug | 8 ft. lbs. | 11 Nm |
| Accumulator bracket-to-frame | 9 ft. lbs. | 12 Nm |
| **Manual Transmission** | | |
| Straight screw plug | 14 ft. lbs. | 19 Nm |
| Extension housing-to-transmission case (2WD) | 27 ft. lbs. | 37 Nm |
| Transfer adapter-to-transmission case (4WD) | 27 ft. lbs. | 37 Nm |
| Front bearing retainer-to-transmission case | 12 ft. lbs. | 17 Nm |
| Back-up light switch | 27 ft. lbs. | 37 Nm |
| Clutch housing-to-transmission case | 27 ft. lbs. | 37 Nm |
| Shift lever housing-to-transmission case | 12 ft. lbs. | 17 Nm |
| Shift lever retainer-to-extension housing | 13 ft. lbs. | 18 Nm |
| Oil receiver-to-extension housing (2WD) | 8 ft. lbs. | 11 Nm |
| Speedometer drive gear lockplate (2WD) | 8 ft. lbs. | 11 Nm |
| **Automatic Transmission** | | |
| Oil cooler pipe union nut | 25 ft. lbs. | 34 Nm |
| Drive plate-to-crankshaft | 54 ft. lbs. | 76 Nm |
| Torque converter clutch-to-drive plate (1990-91) | 20 ft. lbs. | 27 Nm |
| Torque converter clutch-to-drive plate (1993-97) | 30 ft. lbs. | 41 Nm |
| Center support-to-transmission case | 19 ft. lbs. | 25 Nm |
| Transmission housing-to-case 10mm (1991-92) | 25 ft. lbs. | 34 Nm |
| Transmission housing-to-case 12mm (1991-92) | 42 ft. lbs. | 57 Nm |
| Transmission housing-to-case (2WD) | 25 ft. lbs. | 34 Nm |
| Transmission housing-to-case (4WD) | 25 ft. lbs. | 34 Nm |
| Engine-to-transmission | 53 ft. lbs. | 72 Nm |
| Engine-to-stiffener plate | 27 ft. lbs. | 37 Nm |
| Rear transmission mounting (1991-95) | 22 ft. lbs. | 29 Nm |
| Rear transmission mounting (1996-97) | 50 ft. lbs. | 67 Nm |
| **Halfshaft** | | |
| Drive shaft locknut (1991-93) | 166 ft. lbs. | 226 Nm |
| Drive shaft locknut (1994-97) | 152 ft. lbs. | 206 Nm |
| ABS speed sensor | 69 inch lbs. | 8 Nm |
| Drive shaft-to-differential | 51 ft. lbs. | 69 Nm |
| **Transfer Case** | | |
| Screw plug for the oil pump body | 13 ft. lbs. | 17 Nm |
| Front case-to-rear case | 27 ft. lbs. | 37 Nm |
| Extension housing-to-rear case | 9 ft. lbs. | 12 Nm |
| Companion flange lock nut | 90 ft. lbs. | 123 Nm |
| Speed sensor-to-extension housing | 9 ft. lbs. | 12 Nm |
| **Propeller shaft** | | |
| Propeller shaft-to-differential (2WD) | 54 ft. lbs. | 74 Nm |
| Front propeller shaft-to-front differential (4WD) | 31 ft. lbs. | 42 Nm |
| Rear propeller shaft-to-rear differential (4WD) | 54 ft. lbs. | 74 Nm |
| Rear propeller shaft-to-transfer | 54 ft. lbs. | 74 Nm |
| Intermediate shaft-to-propeller shaft | 31 ft. lbs. | 42 Nm |
| Center support bearing-to-body | 27 ft. lbs. | 36 Nm |

**WHEELS 8-2**
WHEEL ASSEMBLY 8-2
   REMOVAL & INSTALLATION 8-2
   INSPECTION 8-2
WHEEL LUG STUDS 8-2
   REMOVAL & INSTALLATION 8-2
**FRONT SUSPENSION 8-4**
COIL SPRINGS 8-5
   REMOVAL & INSTALLATION 8-5
MACPHERSON STRUTS 8-6
   REMOVAL & INSTALLATION 8-6
   OVERHAUL 8-8
LOWER BALL JOINT 8-8
   INSPECTION 8-8
   REMOVAL & INSTALLATION 8-8
STABILIZER BAR 8-9
   REMOVAL & INSTALLATION 8-9
LOWER CONTROL ARM 8-10
   REMOVAL & INSTALLATION 8-10
   CONTROL ARM BUSHING
    REPLACEMENT 8-12
KNUCKLE AND SPINDLE 8-12
   REMOVAL & INSTALLATION 8-12
FRONT HUB AND BEARING 8-13
   REMOVAL & INSTALLATION 8-13
WHEEL ALIGNMENT 8-15
   CASTER 8-15
   CAMBER 8-16
   TOE 8-16
**REAR SUSPENSION 8-17**
COIL SPRINGS 8-18
   REMOVAL & INSTALLATION 8-18
SHOCK ABSORBERS 8-18
   REMOVAL & INSTALLATION 8-18
   TESTING 8-19
LOWER CONTROL ARM 8-19
   REMOVAL & INSTALLATION 8-19
UPPER CONTROL ARM 8-20
   REMOVAL & INSTALLATION 8-20
LATERAL CONTROL ROD 8-20
   REMOVAL & INSTALLATION 8-20
**STEERING 8-21**
STEERING WHEEL 8-21
   REMOVAL & INSTALLATION 8-21
TURN SIGNAL (COMBINATION)
  SWITCH 8-25
   REMOVAL & INSTALLATION 8-25
IGNITION LOCK CYLINDER 8-26
   REMOVAL & INSTALLATION 8-26
STEERING LINKAGE 8-26
   REMOVAL & INSTALLATION 8-26
POWER STEERING GEAR 8-28
   REMOVAL & INSTALLATION 8-28
POWER STEERING PUMP 8-28
   REMOVAL & INSTALLATION 8-28
   BLEEDING 8-30

**SPECIFICATIONS CHART**
   TORQUE SPECIFICATIONS 8-31
**TROUBLESHOOTING CHART**
   POWER STEERING PUMP 8-32

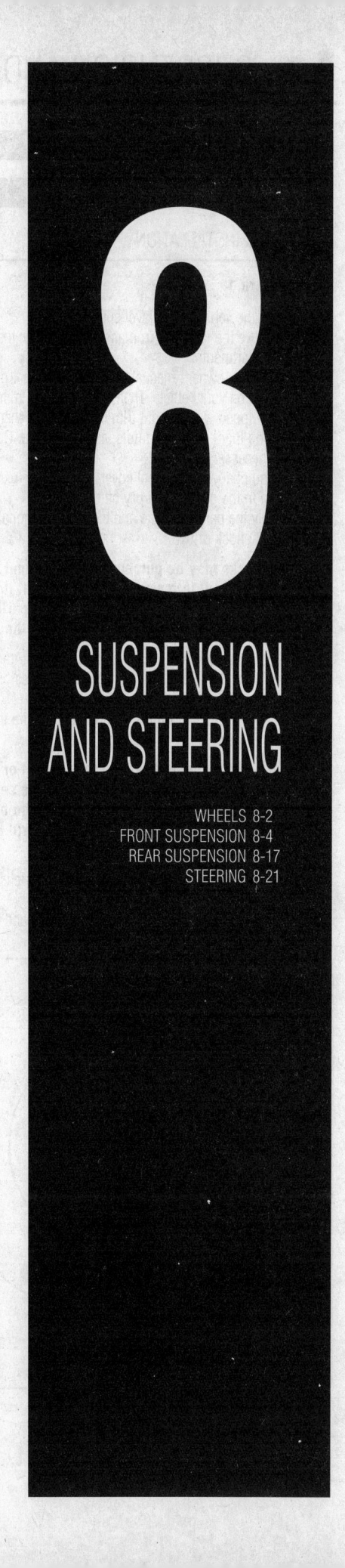

# 8

# SUSPENSION AND STEERING

WHEELS 8-2
FRONT SUSPENSION 8-4
REAR SUSPENSION 8-17
STEERING 8-21

# 8-2 SUSPENSION AND STEERING

## WHEELS

### Wheel Assembly

REMOVAL & INSTALLATION

▶ See Figure 1

1. Park the vehicle on a level surface.
2. Remove the jack, tire iron and, if necessary, the spare tire from their storage compartments.
3. Check the owner's manual or refer to Section 1 of this manual for the jacking points on your vehicle. Then, place the jack in the proper position.
4. If equipped with lug nut trim caps, remove them by either unscrewing or pulling them off the lug nuts, as appropriate. Consult the owner's manual, if necessary.
5. If equipped with a wheel cover or hub cap, insert the tapered end of the tire iron in the groove and pry off the cover.
6. Apply the parking brake and block the diagonally opposite wheel with a wheel chock or two.

➡ Wheel chocks may be purchased at your local auto parts store, or a block of wood cut into wedges may be used. If possible, keep one or two of the chocks in your tire storage compartment, in case any of the tires has to be removed on the side of the road.

7. If equipped with an automatic transmission/transaxle, place the selector lever in **P** or Park; with a manual transmission/transaxle, place the shifter in Reverse.
8. With the tires still on the ground, use the tire iron/wrench to break the lug nuts loose.

➡ **If a nut is stuck, never use heat to loosen it or damage to the wheel and bearings may occur. If the nuts are seized, one or two heavy hammer blows directly on the end of the bolt usually loosens the rust. Be careful, as continued pounding will likely damage the brake drum or rotor.**

9. Using the jack, raise the vehicle until the tire is clear of the ground. Support the vehicle safely using jackstands.
10. Remove the lug nuts, then remove the tire and wheel assembly.

To install:

11. Make sure the wheel and hub mating surfaces, as well as the wheel lug studs, are clean and free of all foreign material. Always remove rust from the wheel mounting surface and the brake rotor or drum. Failure to do so may cause the lug nuts to loosen in service.
12. Install the tire and wheel assembly and hand-tighten the lug nuts.
13. Using the tire wrench, tighten all the lug nuts, in a crisscross pattern, until they are snug.
14. Raise the vehicle and withdraw the jackstand, then lower the vehicle.
15. Using a torque wrench, tighten the lug nuts in a crisscross pattern to 76 ft. lbs. (103 Nm). Check your owner's manual or refer to Section 1 of this manual for the proper tightening sequence.

### ✱✱ WARNING

**Do not overtighten the lug nuts, as this may cause the wheel studs to stretch or the brake disc (rotor) to warp.**

16. If so equipped, install the wheel cover or hub cap. Make sure the valve stem protrudes through the proper opening before tapping the wheel cover into position.
17. If equipped, install the lug nut trim caps by pushing them or screwing them on, as applicable.
18. Remove the jack from under the vehicle, and place the jack and tire iron/wrench in their storage compartments. Remove the wheel chock(s).
19. If you have removed a flat or damaged tire, place it in the storage compartment of the vehicle and take it to your local repair station to have it fixed or replaced as soon as possible.

INSPECTION

Inspect the tires for lacerations, puncture marks, nails and other sharp objects. Repair or replace as necessary. Also check the tires for treadwear and air pressure as outlined in Section 1 of this manual.

Check the wheel assemblies for dents, cracks, rust and metal fatigue. Repair or replace as necessary.

### Wheel Lug Studs

REMOVAL & INSTALLATION

**With Disc Brakes**

▶ See Figures 2 and 3

1. Raise and support the appropriate end of the vehicle safely using jackstands, then remove the wheel.
2. Remove the brake pads and caliper. Support the caliper aside using wire or a coat hanger. For details, please refer to Section 9 of this manual.
3. Remove the outer wheel bearing and lift off the rotor. For details on wheel bearing removal, installation and adjustment, please refer to Section 1 of this manual.
4. Properly support the rotor using press bars, then drive the stud out using an arbor press.

➡ **If a press is not available, CAREFULLY drive the old stud out using a blunt drift. MAKE SURE the rotor is properly and evenly supported or it may be damaged.**

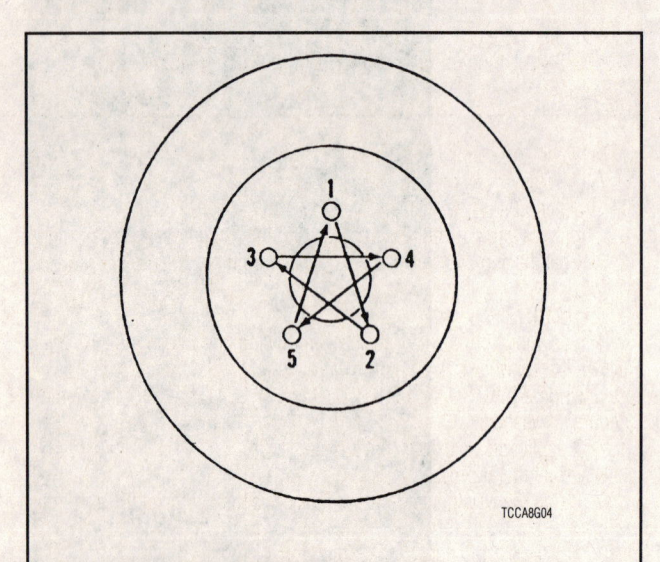

Fig. 1 Typical wheel lug tightening sequence

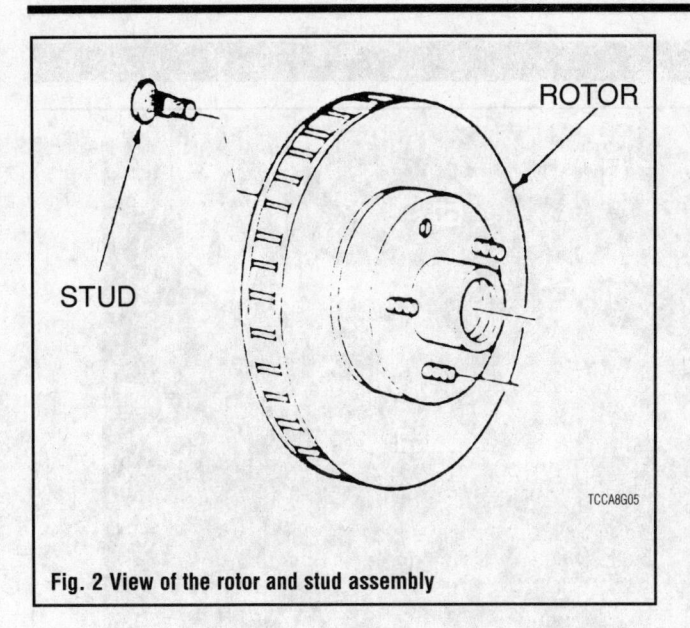

# SUSPENSION AND STEERING  8-3

Fig. 2 View of the rotor and stud assembly

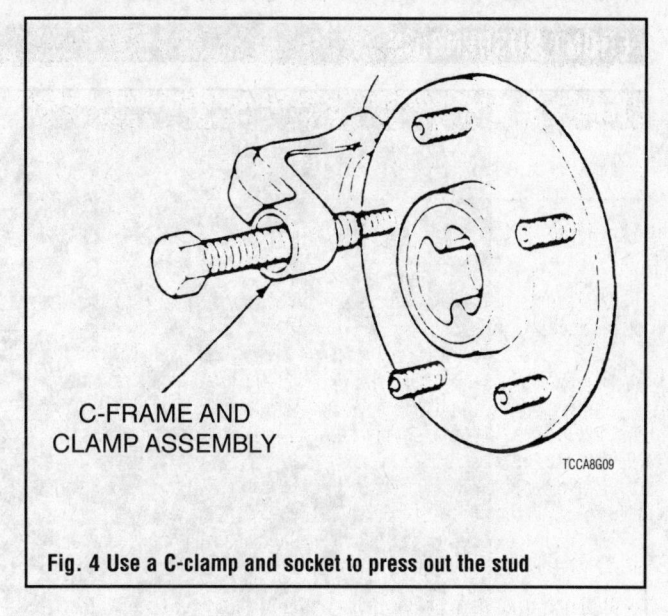

Fig. 4 Use a C-clamp and socket to press out the stud

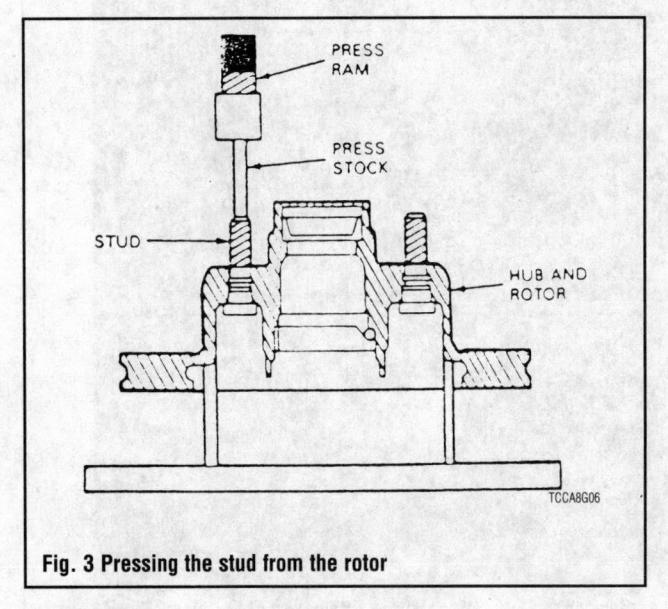

Fig. 3 Pressing the stud from the rotor

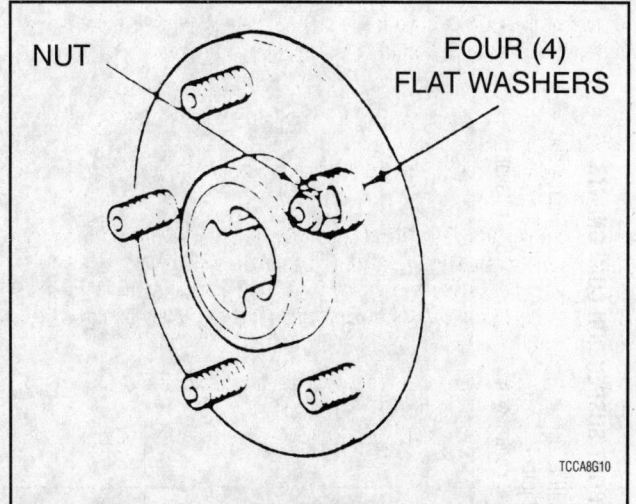

Fig. 5 Force the stud onto the axle flange using washers and a lug nut

**To install:**

5. Clean the stud hole with a wire brush and start the new stud with a hammer and drift pin. Do not use any lubricant or thread sealer.
6. Finish installing the stud by installing the lugnut and tightening it.
7. Install the rotor and adjust the wheel bearings.
8. Install the brake caliper and pads.
9. Install the wheel, then remove the jackstands and carefully lower the vehicle.
10. Tighten the lug nuts to the proper torque.

## With Drum Brakes

▶ See Figures 4 and 5

1. Raise the vehicle and safely support it with jackstands, then remove the wheel.
2. Remove the brake drum.
3. If necessary to provide clearance, remove the brake shoes, as outlined in Section 9 of this manual.
4. Using a large C-clamp and socket, press the stud from the axle flange.
5. Coat the serrated part of the stud with liquid soap and place it into the hole.

**To install:**

6. Position about 4 flat washers over the stud and thread the lug nut. Hold the flange while tightening the lug nut, and the stud should be drawn into position. MAKE SURE THE STUD IS FULLY SEATED, then remove the lug nut and washers.
7. If applicable, install the brake shoes.
8. Install the brake drum.
9. Install the wheel, then remove the jackstands and carefully lower the vehicle.
10. Tighten the lug nuts to the proper torque.

# 8-4 SUSPENSION AND STEERING

## FRONT SUSPENSION

**FRONT SUSPENSION COMPONENTS**

1. Stabilizer bar
2. Ball joint
3. Lower control arm
4. Tie rod end
5. Strut and coil
6. Halfshaft

# SUSPENSION AND STEERING  8-5

## Coil Springs

### REMOVAL & INSTALLATION

▶ See Figures 6, 7, 8, 9 and 10

1. Raise and safely support the front of the vehicle securely on jackstands.
2. Remove the shock and coil spring assembly.
3. Install two nuts and a bolt to the bracket at the lower portion of the shock absorber and secure the assembly in a vise. Using a spring compressor, compress the coil.

### ✱✱ WARNING

**When holding the shock absorber with the coil spring removed, do not hold it by the spring lower seat. Do not knock the spring lower seat. Do not use an impact wrench.**

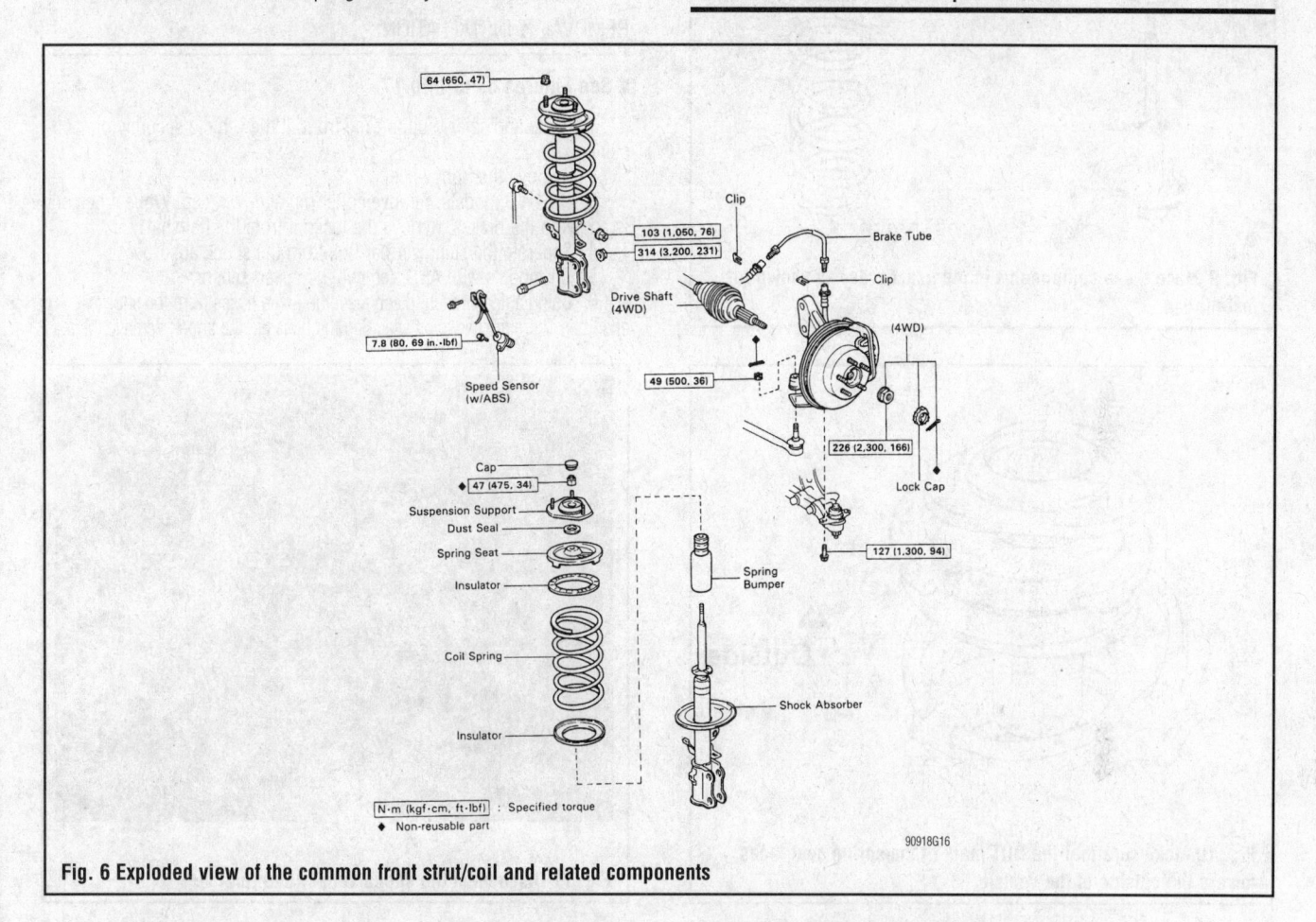

Fig. 6 Exploded view of the common front strut/coil and related components

Fig. 7 This cap covers the top of the strut where the upper bearing retaining nut is located

Fig. 8 Install a spring compressor on the oil/strut assembly

# 8-6 SUSPENSION AND STEERING

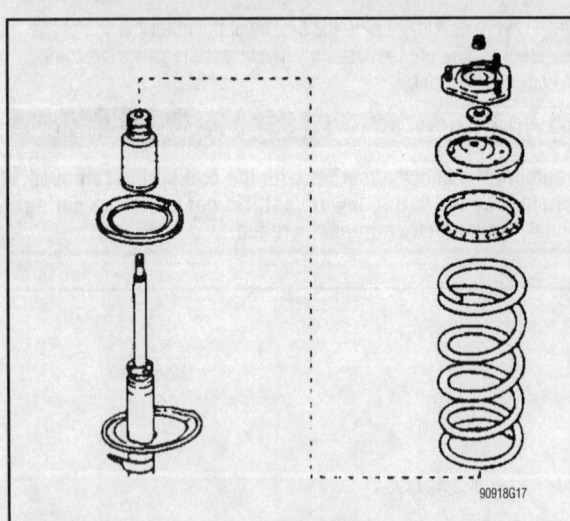

**Fig. 9 Place these components in the exact order as shown for installation**

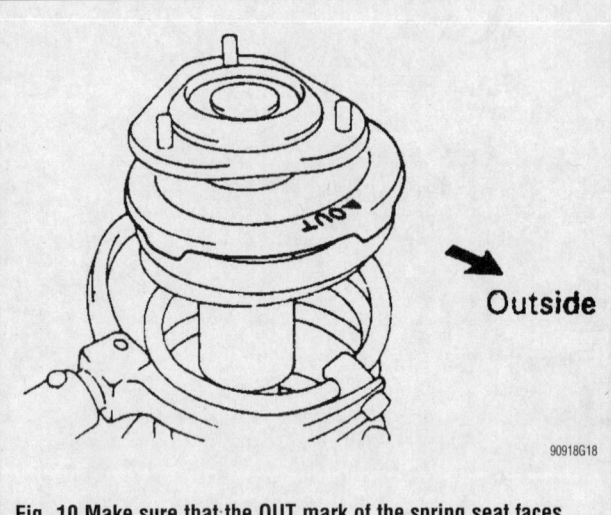

**Fig. 10 Make sure that the OUT mark of the spring seat faces toward the outside of the vehicle.**

4. Using a retaining tool to hold the suspension support, remove the nut.
5. Remove the following components:
- Suspension support
- Dust seal
- Spring seat
- Upper insulator
- Coil spring
- Spring bumper
- Lower insulator

**To assemble:**

6. To attach the coil spring to the suspension support, first start by installing the lower insulator onto the shock.

   a. Install the spring bumper to the shock piston rod.

   b. Using a spring compressor, compress the coil and install onto the shock.

➡ Fit the lower end of the coil spring into the gap of the spring lower seat.

   c. Install the upper insulator and spring seat.

   d. Install the dust seal and suspension support. Using a retaining tool to hold the spring seat, install a new nut and tighten to 34 ft. lbs. (47 Nm).

   e. Rotate the spring seat toward the outside of the vehicle and remove the tool.

➡ There should be a marking (OUT) on the seat.

7. With the jack, install the shock and coil spring assembly into the vehicle and tighten the three upper side nuts to 47 ft. lbs. (64 Nm).
8. Install the wheel, hand tighten the lug nuts.
9. Lower the vehicle and tighten the lugnuts to 76 ft. lbs. (103 Nm).

## MacPherson Struts

### REMOVAL & INSTALLATION

♦ See Figures 6, 11 thru 17

1. Raise and safely support the front of the vehicle securely on jackstands.
2. Remove the front wheel.
3. On 4WD models, remove cotter pin and lock cap. While a helper is applying the brakes, remove the locknut from the halfshaft.
4. Separate the stabilizer bar link from the shock absorber.
5. On models with ABS, remove the speed sensor.
6. Using a line wrench, disconnect the brake hoses from the shock absorber. There are two clips attaching the hoses to the shock, remove them.

**Fig. 11 Disconnect the speed sensor and remove**

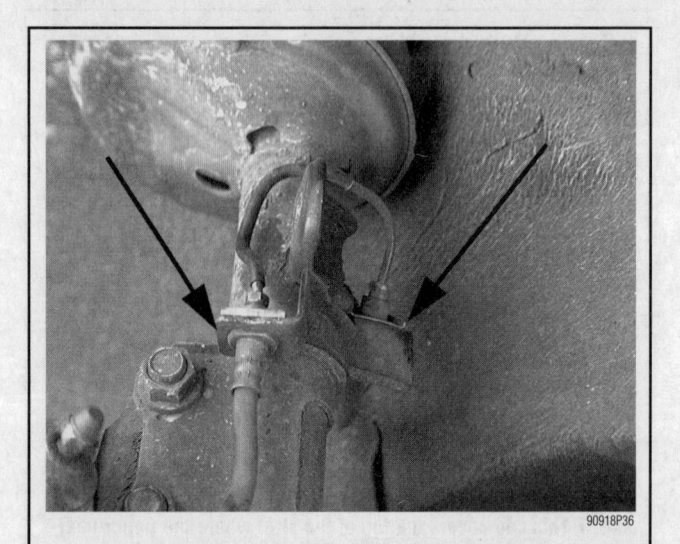

**Fig. 12 Remove these two clips on the strut housing**

## SUSPENSION AND STEERING  8-7

7. Loosen the two nuts on the lower side of the shock absorber. Loosen the two bolts on the lower ball joint. Do not remove the nuts and bolts.
8. Disconnect the tie rod end from the steering knuckle.
9. Remove the steering knuckle.
10. Using a jack, support the shock absorber with coil spring, then remove the upper shock nuts.

    a. If working on the left side, remove the cluster finish lower panel and knee panel.

    b. If working on the right side, remove the glove compartment door.

    c. Remove the three nuts on the upper side of the shock absorber. Theses nuts are located in the vehicle in the footwells, up under the dashboard.
11. Lower the jack and remove the shock and coil spring assembly.

**To assemble:**

12. With the jack, install the shock and coil spring assembly into the vehicle and tighten the three upper side nuts to 47 ft. lbs. (64 Nm).
13. Install the glove compartment door and left side cluster finish panels if removed.
14. Install the steering knuckle and temporarily tighten the nuts. Temporarily install the two bolts and connect the knuckle to the lower ball joint.
15. Connect the tie rod end to the steering knuckle and install the nut. Tighten the nut to 36 ft. lbs. (49 Nm). Be sure to install a new cotter pin.

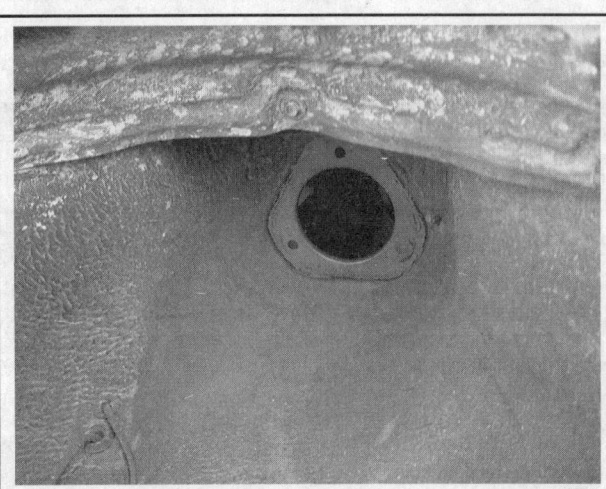

Fig. 13 Remove the pipe attaching to the brake hoses on the strut

Fig. 14 Loosen the two nuts on the lower portion of the strut

Fig. 15 Removing the trim panels will allow access to the upper strut nuts

Fig. 16 Place the spring and strut assembly into this hole on the wheelwell

Fig. 17 Inspect the bolts and nuts for damaged threads prior to installation

## SUSPENSION AND STEERING

16. Tighten the two nuts on the lower portion of the shock absorber to 231 ft. lbs. (314 Nm). Tighten the two bolts on the lower ball joint to 94 ft. lbs. (127 Nm).
17. Attach the brake hose and tube then secure with the 2 clips to the shock absorber.
18. If equipped, install the speed sensor and tighten the retaining bolt to 69 inch lbs. (8 Nm).
19. Attach the stabilizer bar link to the shock absorber and tighten the nut to 76 ft. lbs. (103 Nm).
20. Bleed the brake system.
21. While a helper is applying the brakes, tighten the drive shaft locknut to:
    - 1991—137 ft lbs. (186 Nm)
    - 1992–93 models—166 ft. lbs. (226 Nm)
    - 1994–97 models—152 ft. lbs. (206 Nm)
    a. Install the lock cap and new cotter pin.
22. On models with a ABS speed sensor, secure the sensor to 69 inch lbs. (8 Nm).
23. Install the front wheel, hand tighten the lug nuts and lower the vehicle.
24. tighten the lug nuts to specifications.
25. Check the front end alignment.

### OVERHAUL

The Toyota Previa front struts can not be disassembled or overhauled. For removal of the coil spring, refer to the Coil Spring procedure in this section.

## Lower Ball Joint

### INSPECTION

▶ See Figure 18

1. Remove the ball joint from the lower control arm and place it into a vise.
2. Flip the ball joint stud back and forth 5 times before installing the nut.
3. Using a torque wrench, turn the nut continuously one turn every 2–4 seconds and take the torque reading on the 5th turn. The turning torque should be 13–35 inch lbs. (2–4 Nm).
4. If the ball joint fails the testing, replace it.

### REMOVAL & INSTALLATION

▶ See Figures 19, 20, 21 and 22

1. Raise and support the vehicle.
2. Remove the ball joint bolts connecting it to the steering knuckle.

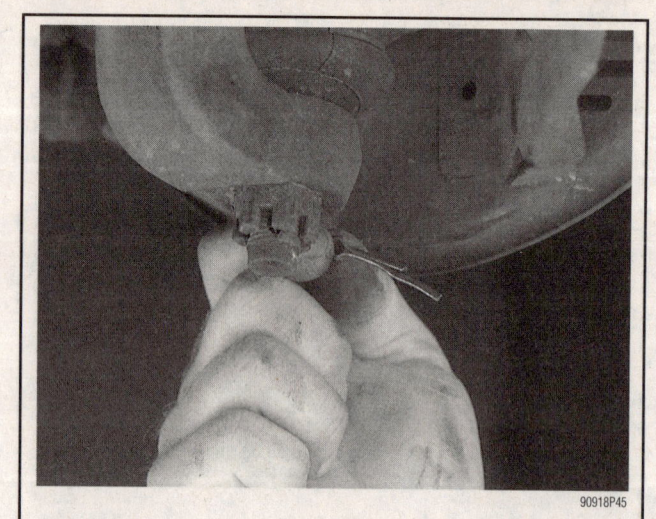

Fig. 19 Remove the cotter pin from the lower part of the ball joint

Fig. 20 Loosen but do not remove the lower nut

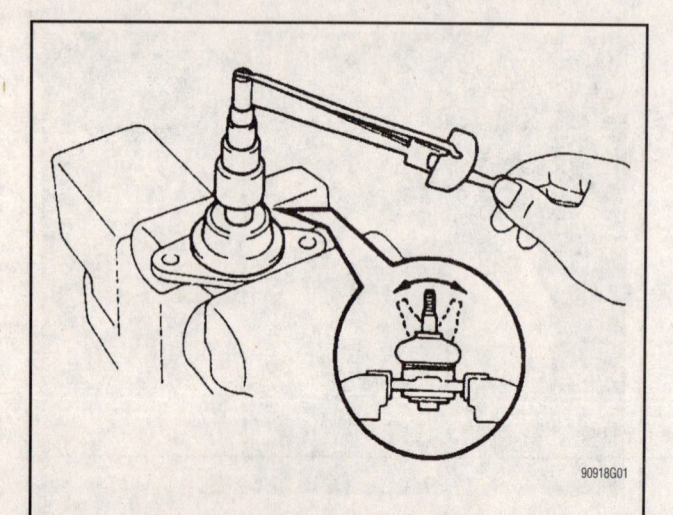

Fig. 18 Using a torque gauge, turn the nut continuously one turn per 2-4 seconds

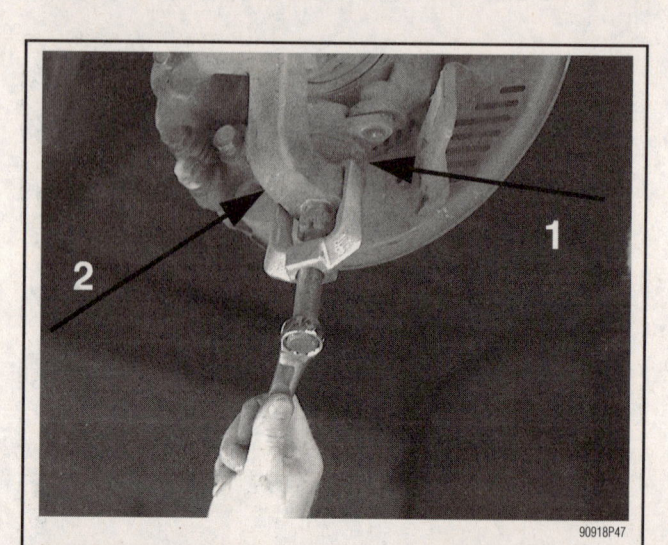

Fig. 21 Place a ball joint remover between the lower control arm (2) and ball joint (1)

## SUSPENSION AND STEERING  8-9

3. Remove the cotter pin.
4. Loosen but do not remove the nut.
5. Using a puller, separate the ball joint from the control arm.

**To install:**

6. Insert the ball joint on the end of the lower control arm. Install a new cotter pin and tighten the nut to 76 ft. lbs. (103 Nm).
7. Attach the ball joint end of the lower control arm to the steering knuckle, tighten the bolts to 94 ft. lbs. (127 Nm).
8. Lower the vehicle and have the front end alignment checked.

### Stabilizer Bar

REMOVAL & INSTALLATION

► See Figures 23, 24, 25, 26 and 27

1. Raise and safely support the front of the vehicle securely on jackstands.
2. Remove both front wheels.
3. Unbolt and remove the engine undercovers.
4. Unbolt and remove the stabilizer bar links from the left and right sides.

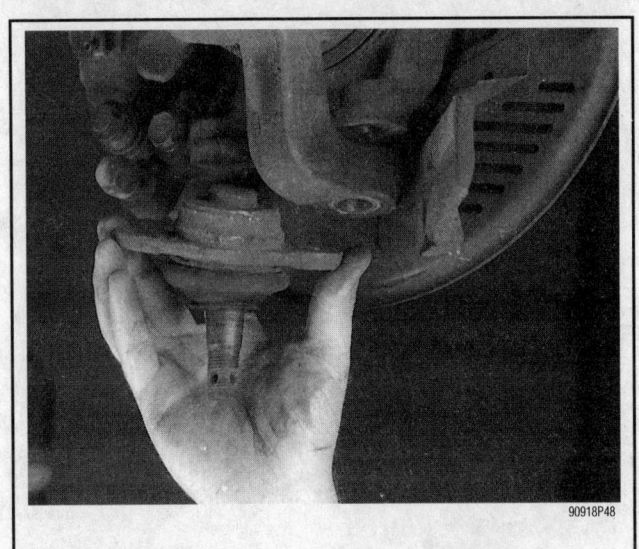

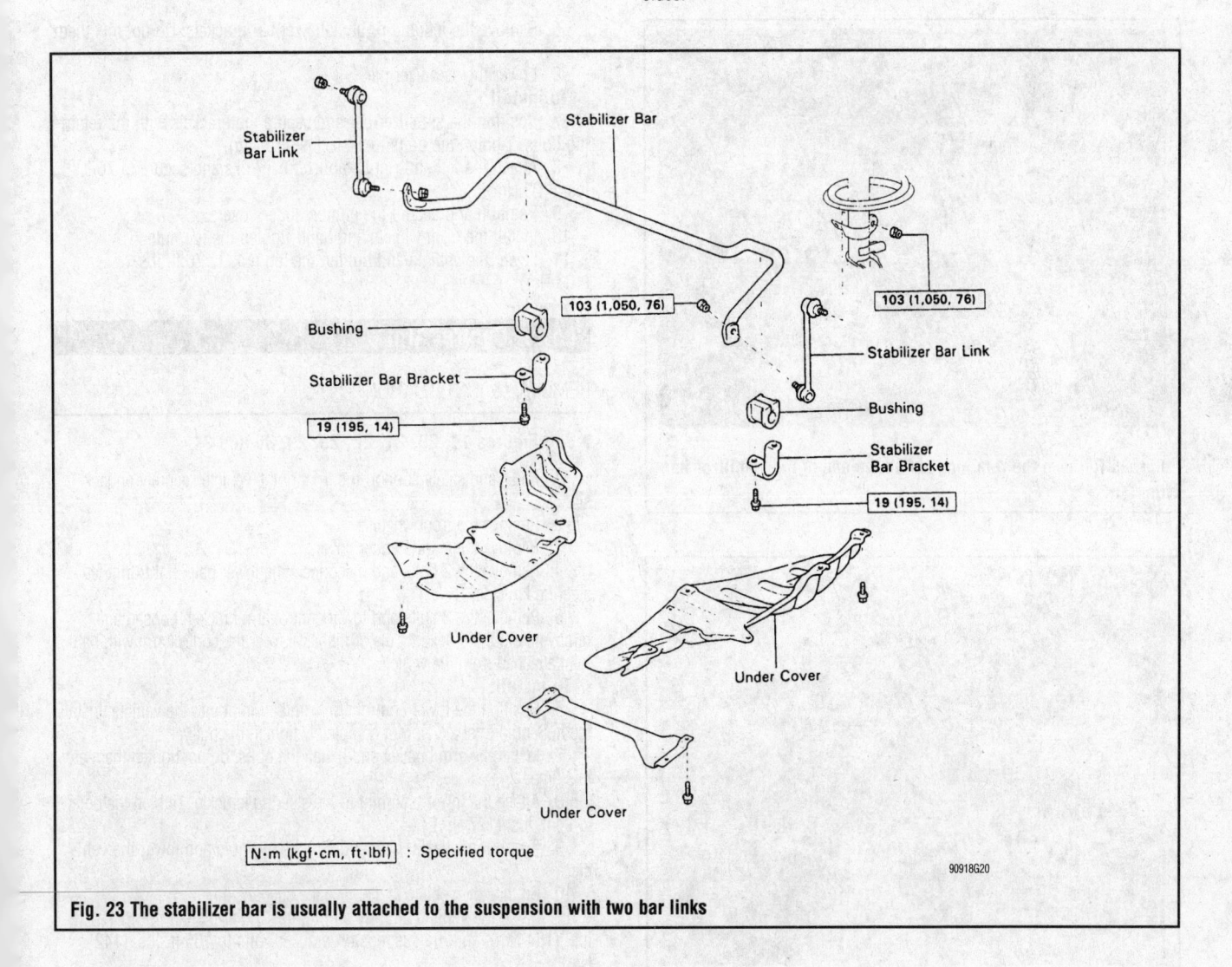

Fig. 22 The ball joint will pop out of the lower control arm

Fig. 23 The stabilizer bar is usually attached to the suspension with two bar links

## 8-10 SUSPENSION AND STEERING

Fig. 24 Remove the front left and right side engine covers

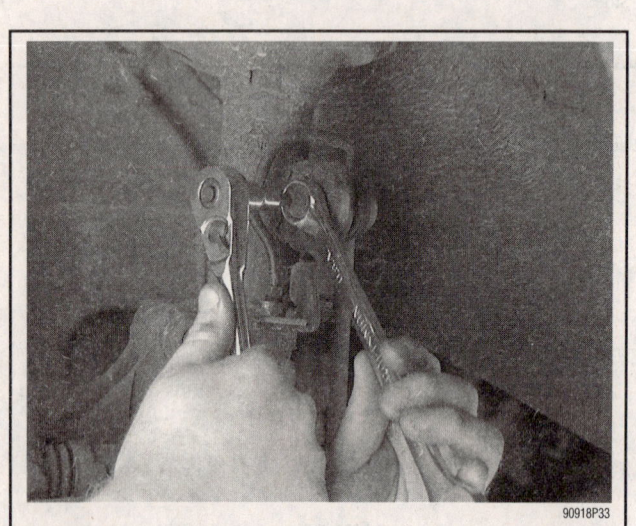

Fig. 25 Remove the retaining nut on the end of the stabilizer bar link

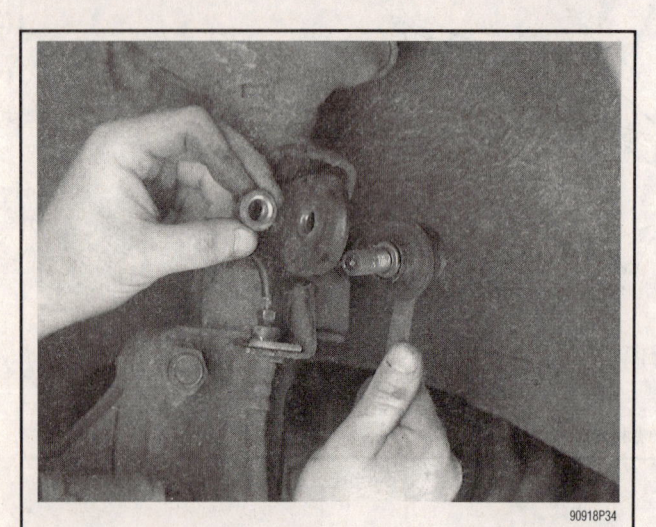

Fig. 26 Inspect the threads of the link and nut prior to installation

Fig. 27 The brackets are held in by two bolts

5. Remove the left and right stabilizer bar brackets. Do not mix them up.
6. Lower the stabilizer bar.

**To install:**

7. Position the stabilizer bar and secure the brackets with the retaining bolts. Tighten the bolts to 14 ft. lbs. (19 Nm).
8. Attach the left and right stabilizer bar links and secure to 76 ft. lbs. (103 Nm).
9. Position and secure the engine under covers.
10. Install the front wheels and hand-tighten the lug nuts.
11. Lower the vehicle and tighten the lug nuts to 76 ft. lbs. (103 Nm).

### Lower Control Arm

REMOVAL & INSTALLATION

▶ See Figures 19, 20, 21, 22, 28, 29, 30 and 31

1. Raise and safely support the front of the vehicle securely on jackstands.
2. Remove the front wheels.
3. Remove the engine under covers.
4. Remove the 2 bolts and disconnect the lower ball joint from the steering knuckle.
5. Remove the 2 bolts and lower control arm bracket. Loosen and remove the nut then extract the arm shaft. Lower the control arm with ball joint attached from the vehicle.

**To install:**

6. Position the lower control arm with ball joint into the vehicle. Install the nut and arm shaft. Do not completely tighten the nut yet.
7. Install the arm bracket and install the bolts. do not tighten them at this time.
8. Attach the lower ball joint to the steering knuckle. Tighten the bolts to 94 ft. lbs. (127 Nm).
9. Install the wheels, hand-tighten the lug nuts and lower the vehicle.
10. Bounce the vehicle to stabilize the suspension.
11. Raise the vehicle slightly and tighten the arm shaft nut to 121 ft. lbs. (164 Nm). and the suspension bracket bolts to 105 ft. lbs. (142 Nm).
12. Lower the vehicle again and tighten the lug nuts to specification.
13. Check the front end alignment.

## SUSPENSION AND STEERING 8-11

Fig. 28 View of the common front suspension lower control arms and related components

Fig. 29 Remove the lower control arm bracket retaining bolts . . .

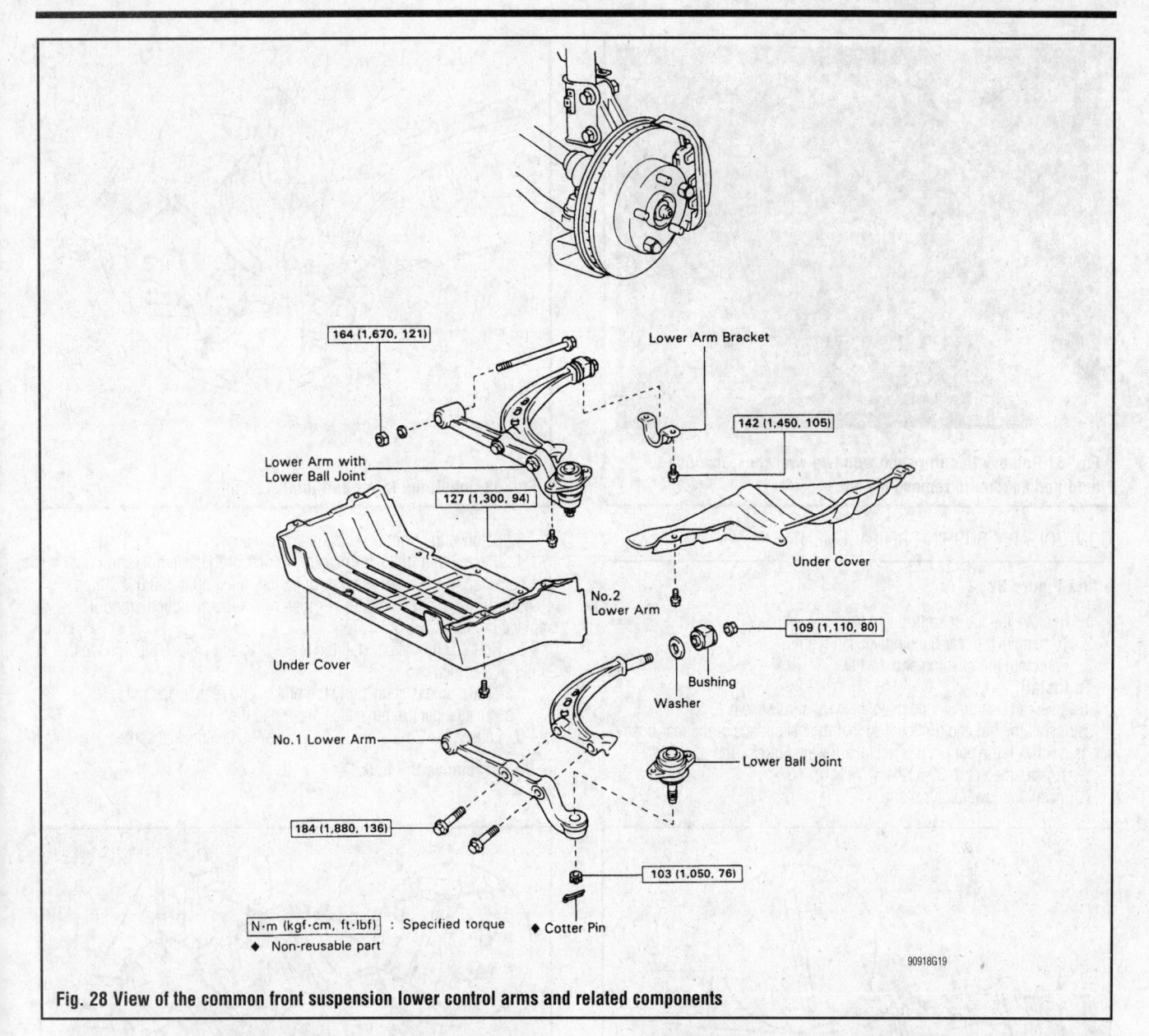

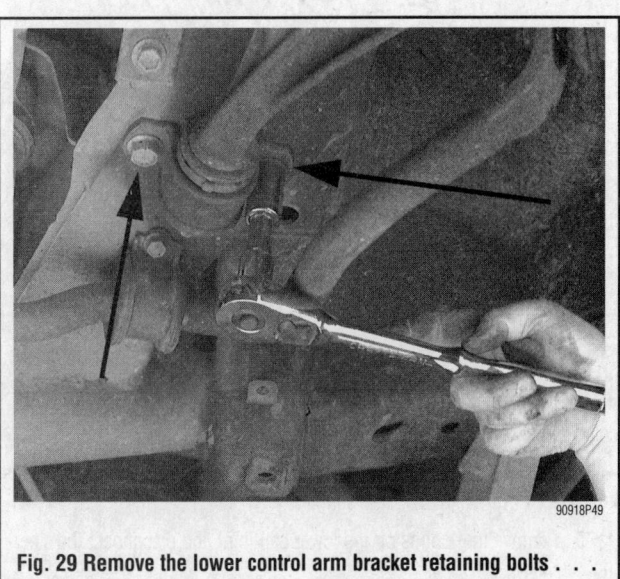

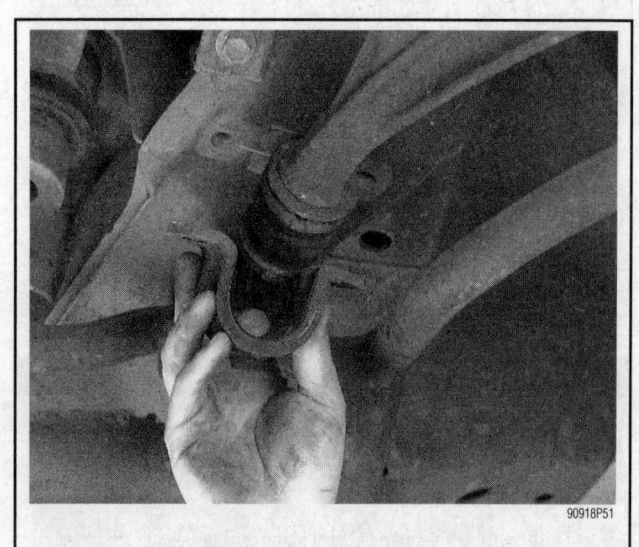

Fig. 30 . . . then remove the bracket from the control arm

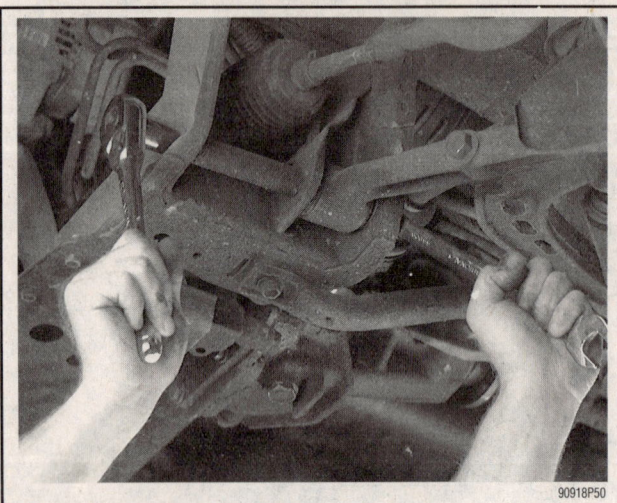

## 8-12 SUSPENSION AND STEERING

Fig. 31 Remove the arm shaft with two wrenches, use one to hold and another to remove the nut

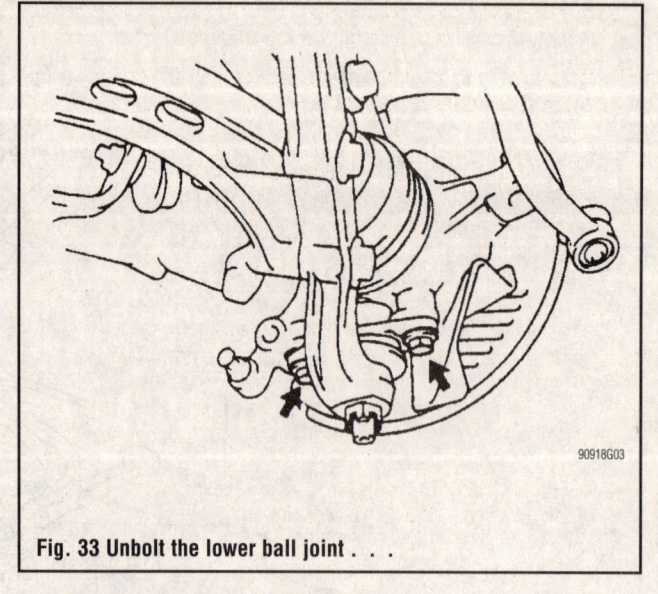

Fig. 33 Unbolt the lower ball joint . . .

### CONTROL ARM BUSHING REPLACEMENT

♦ See Figure 32

1. Remove the lower control arm from the vehicle.
2. To remove the rear bushing, loosen the nut.
3. Force out the bushing and washer.

**To install:**

4. Insert a bushing and position the washer as shown.
5. Install the nut and tighten it so that the flat surface of the rear bushing is level with the upper surface of the lower control arm.
6. Tighten the nut to 80 ft. lbs. (109 Nm).
7. Install the lower control arm.

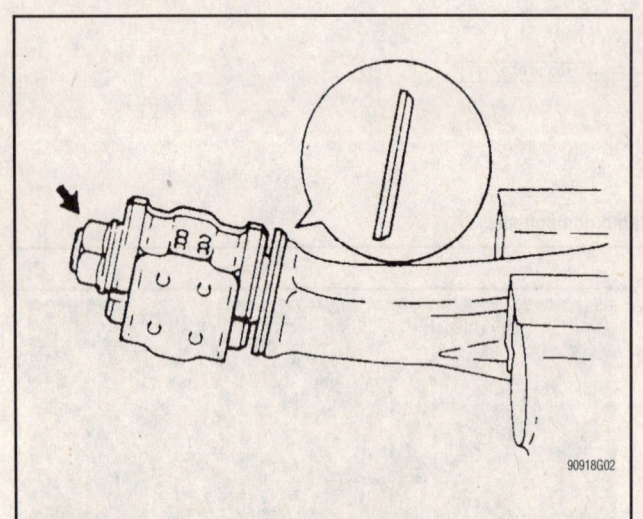

3. Remove the front brake caliper and disc.
4. Place a dial indicator near the center of the axle hub and check the backlash in the bearing shaft direction. maximum is 0.0020 inch (0.05mm). If the specification is greater than the specified amount, replace the hub.
5. On 4WD models, install the brake disc and caliper, the remove the cotter in and lock cap.
   a. Have an assistant apply the brakes and remove the nut.
   b. Once again, remove the caliper and disc.
6. Loosen the 2 nuts on the lower side of the shock absorber.

➡ Do not remove the bolts!

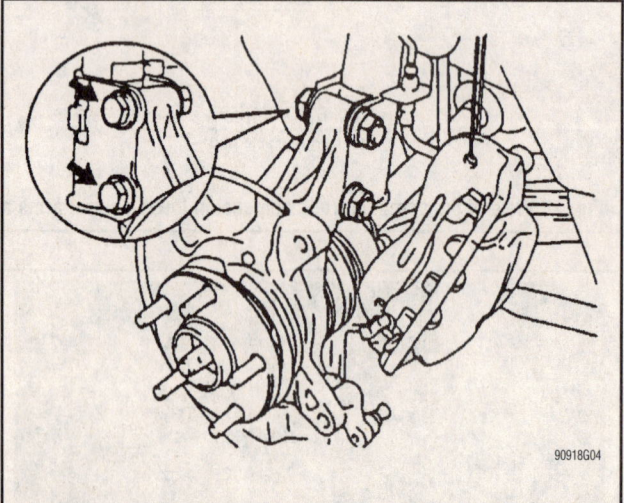

Fig. 32 Place the washer into position and secure the bushing with the nut

Fig. 34 . . . then remove the two nuts and bolts on the lower side of the strut

### Knuckle and Spindle

#### REMOVAL & INSTALLATION

♦ See Figures 33 and 34

1. Raise and safely support the front of the vehicle securely on jackstands.
2. If equipped, remove the speed sensor.

7. Loosen the bolts for the lower ball joint. Once again, do not remove them.
8. Disconnect the tie rod end from the steering knuckle. Discard the cotter pin.

➡ A puller will be needed to separate the tie rod end from the knuckle.

9. Remove the 2 bolts on the lower ball joint and disconnect the steering knuckle.

# SUSPENSION AND STEERING  8-13

a. Remove the 2 nuts and bolts on the lower side of the shock absorber.
b. Remove the steering knuckle with the axle hub.

➡ **Be careful not to damage the speed sensor rotor (on models with ABS), oil seal and drive shaft boot.**

### To install:

10. Position the steering knuckle and axle hub assembly.
    a. Install the 2 bolts and temporarily tighten the nut.
    b. Temporarily install the 2 bolts and connect the steering knuckle and lower ball joint.
11. Attach the tie rod end to the steering knuckle. Be sure to use a new cotter pin. Tighten the tie rod end nut to 36 ft. lbs. (49 Nm).
12. Tighten the 2 nuts on the lower side of the shock absorber to 231 ft. lbs. (314 Nm).
    a. Tighten the 2 bolts on the lower ball joint to 94 ft. lbs. (127 Nm).
13. On 4WD models, install the brake disc and caliper.
    a. While a helper is applying the brakes, tighten the drive shaft locknut to:
    - 1991—137 ft lbs. (186 Nm)
    - 1992–93 models—166 ft. lbs. (226 Nm)
    - 1994–97 models—152 ft. lbs. (206 Nm)
    b. Install the lock cap and new cotter pin.
14. On models with a ABS speed sensor, secure the sensor to 69 inch lbs. (8 Nm).
15. Install the front wheel, hand tighten the lug nuts and lower the vehicle.
16. Tighten the lug nuts to specifications.
17. Check the front end alignment.

## Front Hub and Bearing

### REMOVAL & INSTALLATION

◆ **See Figures 35 thru 44**

1. On 4WD models, remove the steering knuckle and axle hub assembly.
2. On 2WD models, using a flatbladed tool, remove the grease cap.
    a. Using a chisel and hammer, release the nut caulking.
    b. Remove the locknut.
    c. Remove the spacer/ABS speed sensor rotor.

➡ **On models equipped with ABS, take care not to scratch the serration's of the sensor rotor.**

3. Separate the axle hub with a puller.

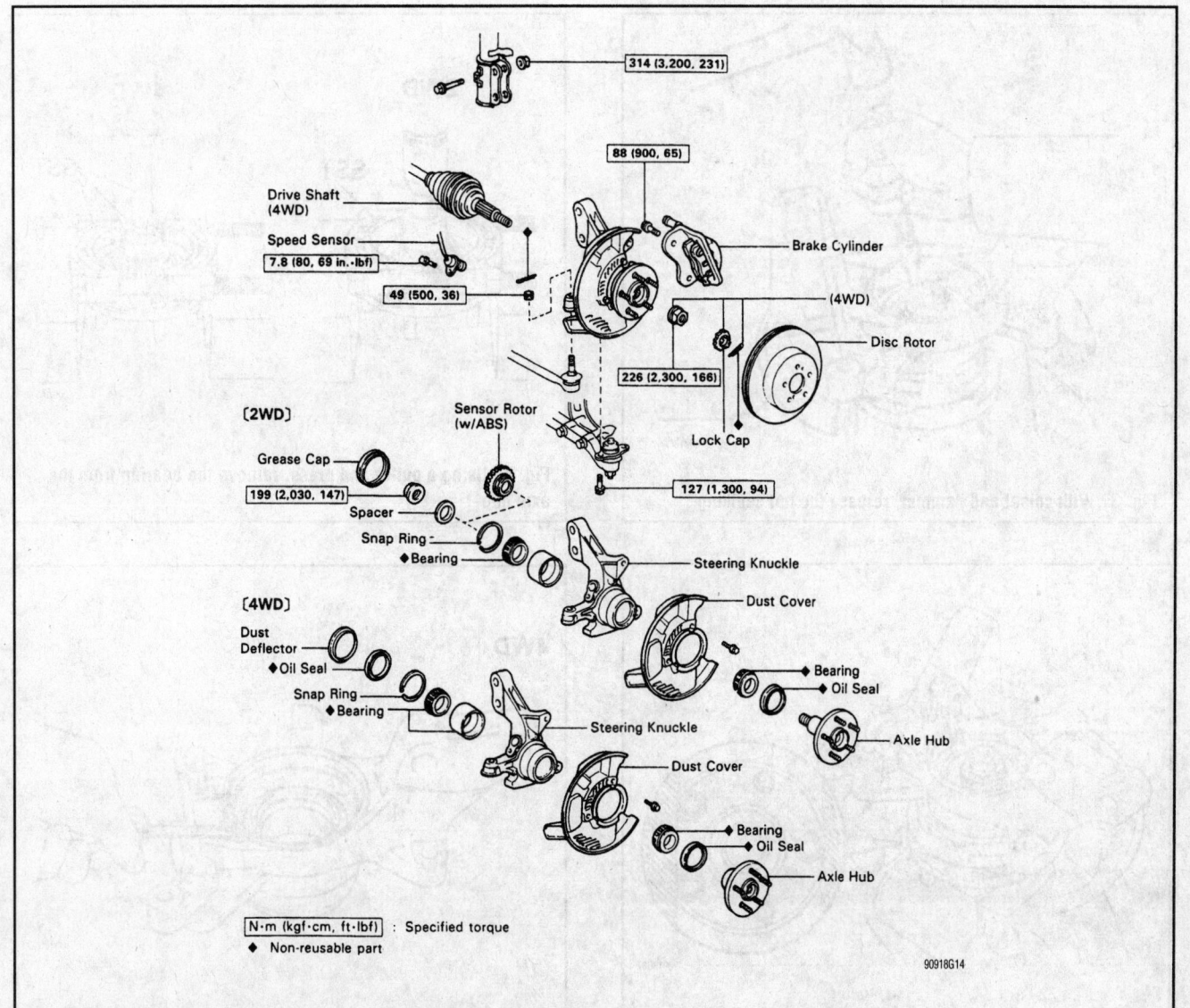

Fig. 35 Exploded view of the common front axle bearing and hub assemblies

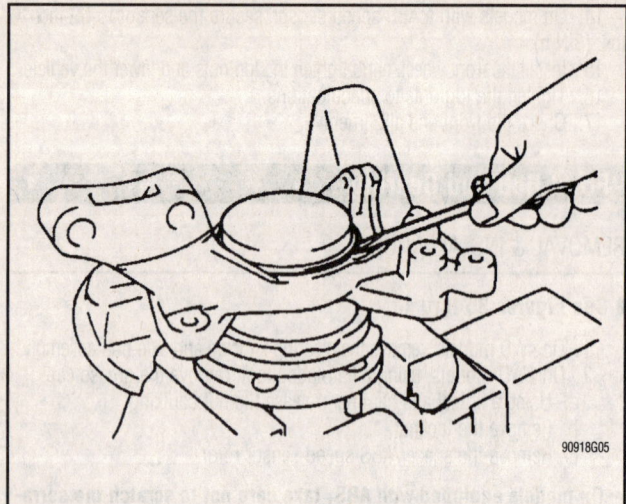

## 8-14 SUSPENSION AND STEERING

Fig. 36 Using a flatbladed tool, pry off the grease cap—2WD models

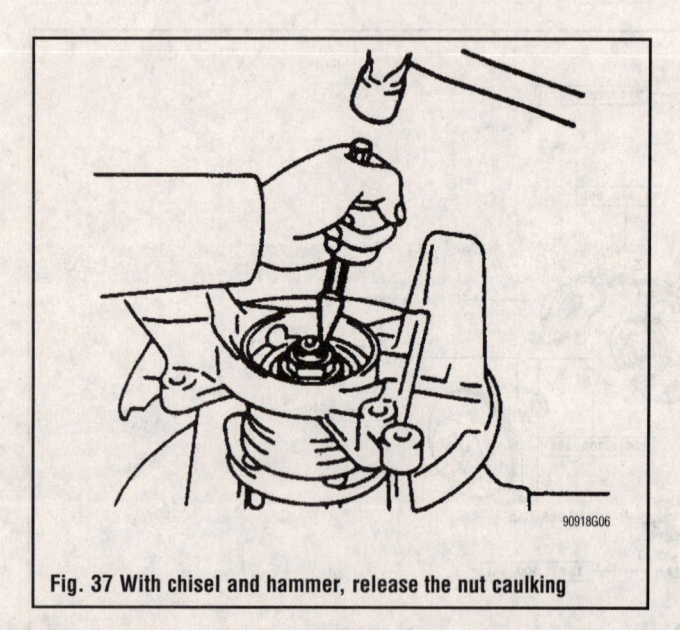

Fig. 37 With chisel and hammer, release the nut caulking

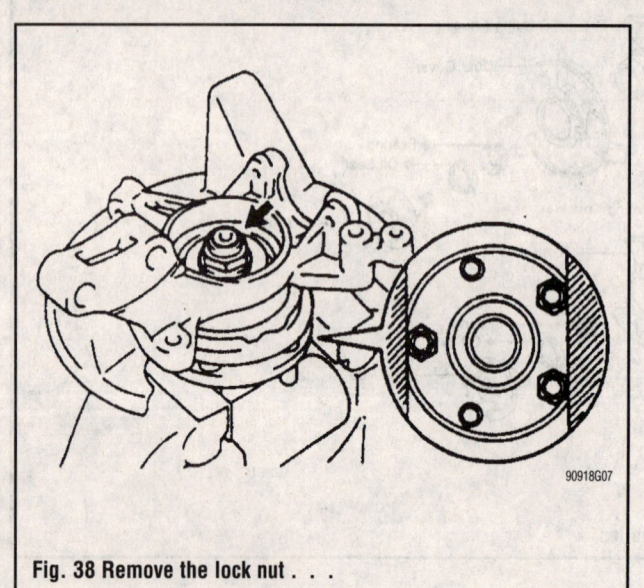

Fig. 38 Remove the lock nut . . .

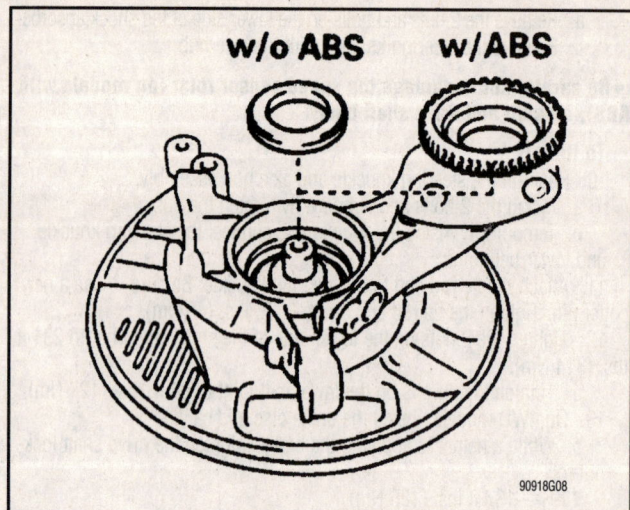

Fig. 39 . . . then remove the spacer or ABS sensor rotor—2WD models

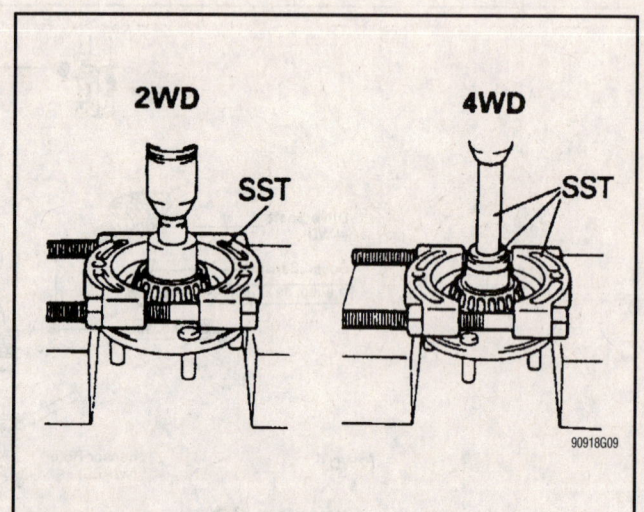

Fig. 40 Using a puller and press, remove the bearing from the axle hub

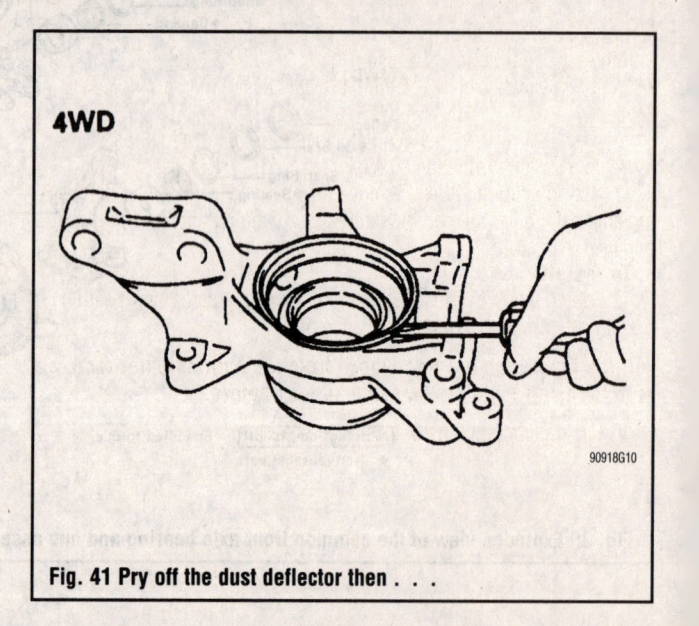

Fig. 41 Pry off the dust deflector then . . .

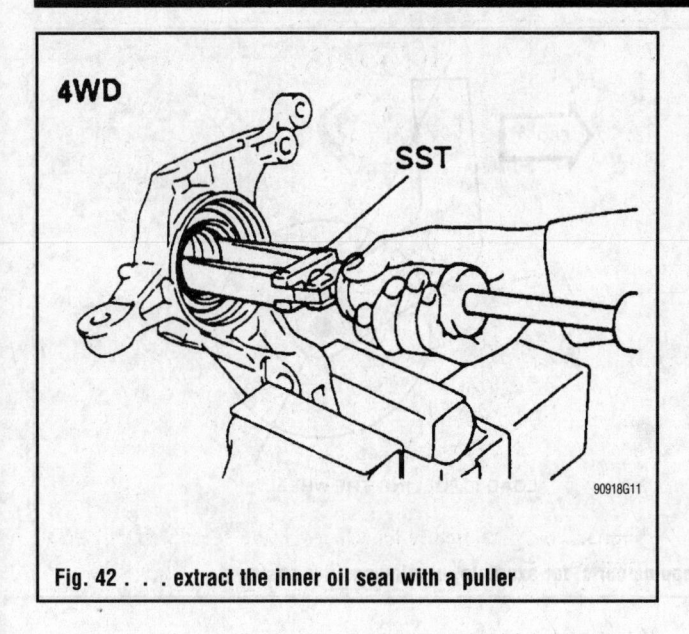

# SUSPENSION AND STEERING  8-15

**Fig. 42 . . . extract the inner oil seal with a puller**

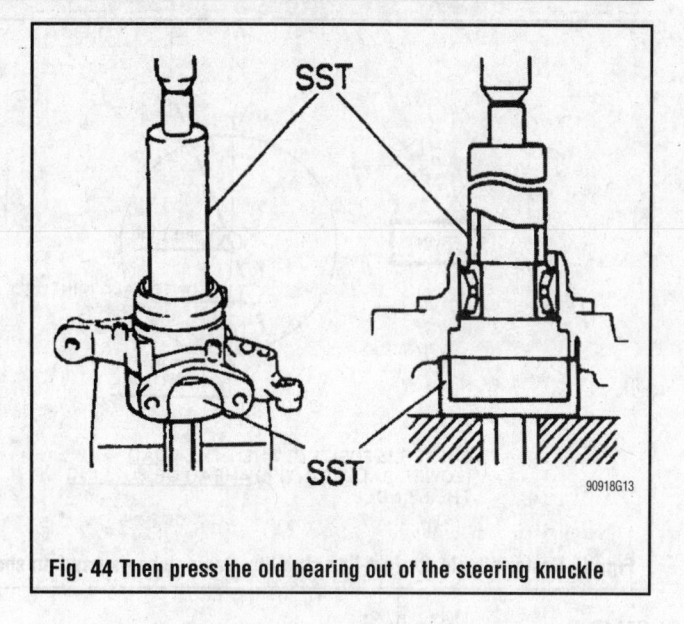

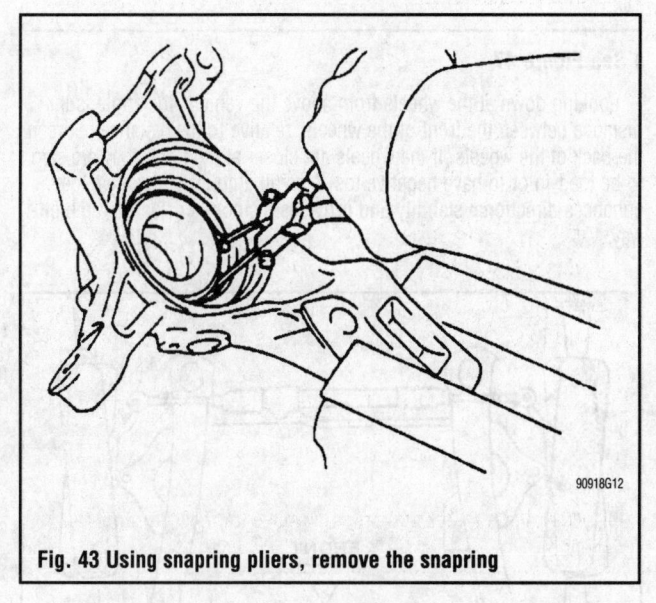

**Fig. 43 Using snapring pliers, remove the snapring**

**Fig. 44 Then press the old bearing out of the steering knuckle**

4. Using a puller and press, remove the bearing from the axle hub. Pull the oil seal from the hub also.
5. Remove the 3 bolts retaining the dust cover, then pull the dust cover off.
6. On 4WD models, using a flatbladed tool, remove the dust deflector. With a puller, extract the oil seal.
7. Using snapring pliers, remove the snapring. Place the outer bearing above the outer race on the outer side. Using a puller and press, remove the bearing.

**To install:**

8. Using a hub bearing installer and a press, insert a new bearing into the steering knuckle.

➡If the inner race becomes loose from the bearing outer race, be sure to install them on the same side as before.

9. Using snapring pliers, install the snapring.
10. Position the outer bearing. Install a new oil seal until it is flush with the end surface of the steering knuckle.
11. Install the dust cover and secure the 3 bolts to 9 ft. lbs. (12 Nm).
12. Using an axle hub installation tool and press, install the axle hub.
13. On the 2WD models, install the spacer ABS speed sensor rotor.

➡Take care not to scratch the serration's of the sensor rotor.

## Wheel Alignment

If the tires are worn unevenly, if the vehicle is not stable on the highway or if the handling seems uneven in spirited driving, the wheel alignment should be checked. If an alignment problem is suspected, first check for improper tire inflation and other possible causes. These can be worn suspension or steering components, accident damage or even unmatched tires. If any worn or damaged components are found, they must be replaced before the wheels can be properly aligned. Wheel alignment requires very expensive equipment and involves minute adjustments which must be accurate; it should only be performed by a trained technician. Take your vehicle to a properly equipped shop.

Following is a description of the alignment angles which are adjustable on most vehicles and how they affect vehicle handling. Although these angles can apply to both the front and rear wheels, usually only the front suspension is adjustable.

### CASTER

▶ See Figure 45

Looking at a vehicle from the side, caster angle describes the steering axis rather than a wheel angle. The steering knuckle is attached to a control arm or strut at the top and a control arm at the bottom. The wheel pivots around the line between these points to steer the vehicle. When the upper point is tilted back, this is described as positive caster. Having a positive caster tends to make the wheels self-centering, increasing directional stability. Excessive positive caster makes the wheels hard to steer, while an uneven caster will cause a pull to one side. Overloading the vehicle or sagging rear springs will affect caster, as will raising the rear of the vehicle. If the rear of the vehicle is lower than normal, the caster becomes more positive.

# 8-16 SUSPENSION AND STEERING

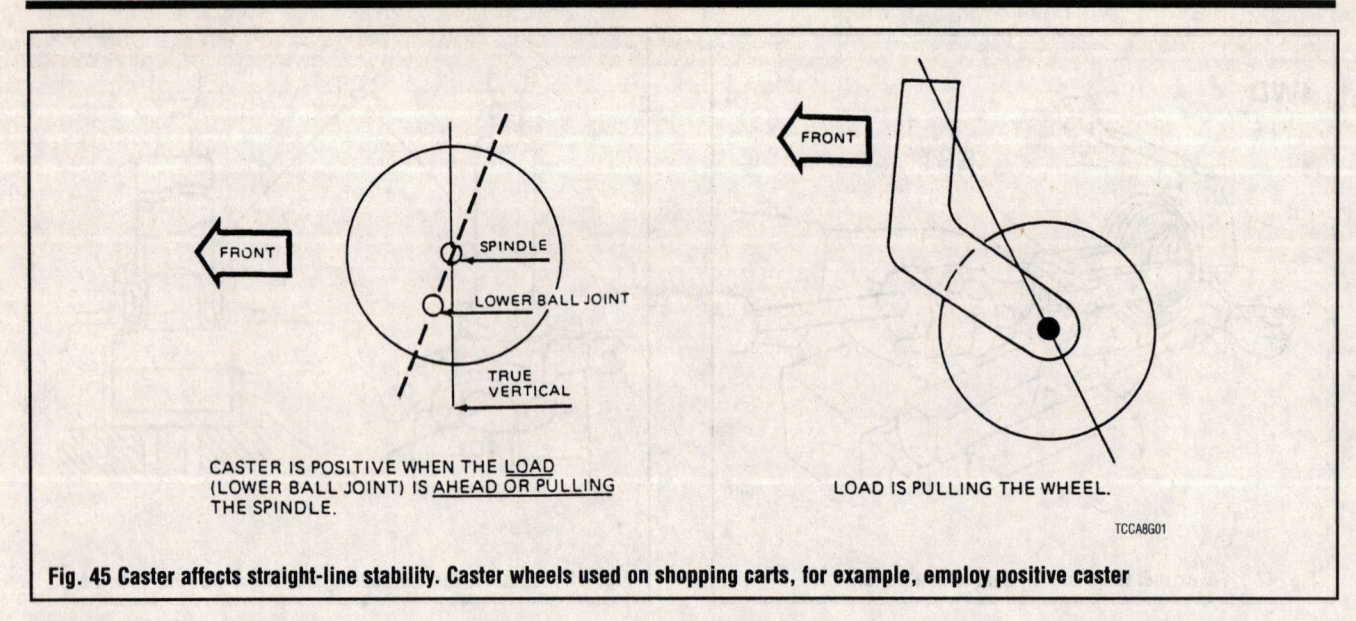

Fig. 45 Caster affects straight-line stability. Caster wheels used on shopping carts, for example, employ positive caster

## CAMBER

▶ See Figure 46

Looking from the front of the vehicle, camber is the inward or outward tilt of the top of wheels. When the tops of the wheels are tilted in, this is negative camber; if they are tilted out, it is positive. In a turn, a slight amount of negative camber helps maximize contact of the tire with the road. However, too much negative camber compromises straight-line stability, increases bump steer and torque steer.

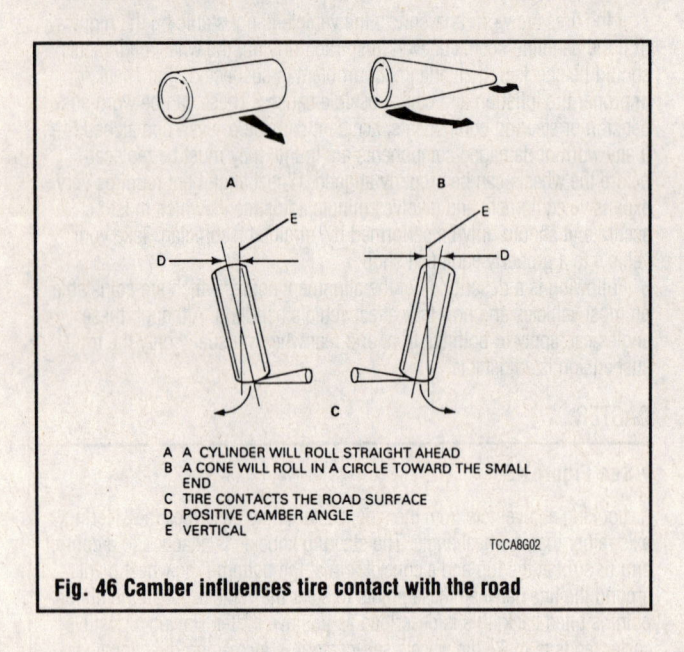

Fig. 46 Camber influences tire contact with the road

## TOE

▶ See Figure 47

Looking down at the wheels from above the vehicle, toe angle is the distance between the front of the wheels, relative to the distance between the back of the wheels. If the wheels are closer at the front, they are said to be toed-in or to have negative toe. A small amount of negative toe enhances directional stability and provides a smoother ride on the highway.

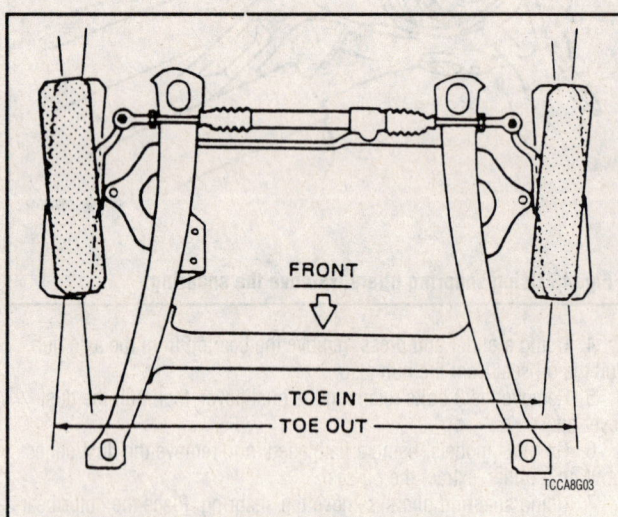

Fig. 47 With toe-in, the distance between the wheels is closer at the front than at the rear

## SUSPENSION AND STEERING 8-17

**REAR SUSPENSION**

**REAR SUSPENSION COMPONENTS**

1. Coil spring
2. Shock absorber
3. Load Sensing Proportioning Valve (LSPV) spring
4. Upper control arm
5. Lower control arm
6. Rear axle housing

## 8-18 SUSPENSION AND STEERING

### Coil Springs

**REMOVAL & INSTALLATION**

1. Raise and support the rear of the vehicle.
2. Remove the rear shock absorber.
3. Push down on the lower control arm enough to allow the coil spring to slide out.
4. Remove the upper and lower coil insulators. inspect and replace them if they are deteriorated.

**To install:**

5. Install the coil spring on the lower control arm with the upper and lower insulators.
   a. Fit the lower end of the coil spring into the gap of the spring seat of the lower control arm.
6. Install the shock absorber.
7. Lower the vehicle.

### Shock Absorbers

**REMOVAL & INSTALLATION**

▶ See Figures 48 thru 53

1. Raise and support the rear of the vehicle.
2. Support the rear axle housing with a jack.
3. Disconnect the shock absorber from the lower control arm.
4. Remove the bushings and washer.
5. Remove the upper shock bolt and slide the absorber off the pin.

**To install:**

6. Position the shock on to the upper pin with the washer on the inside.

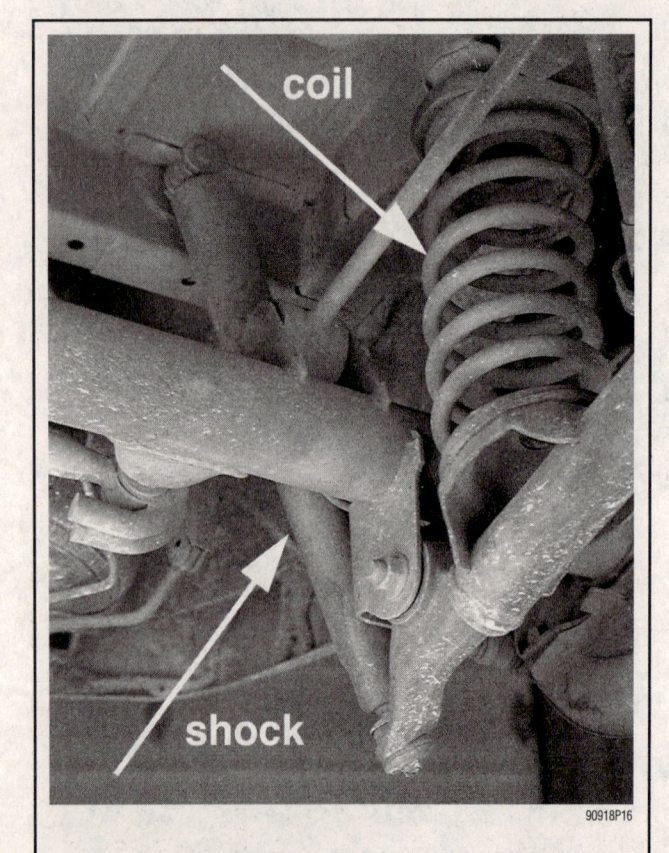

Fig. 48 The rear shocks are located near the coil spring

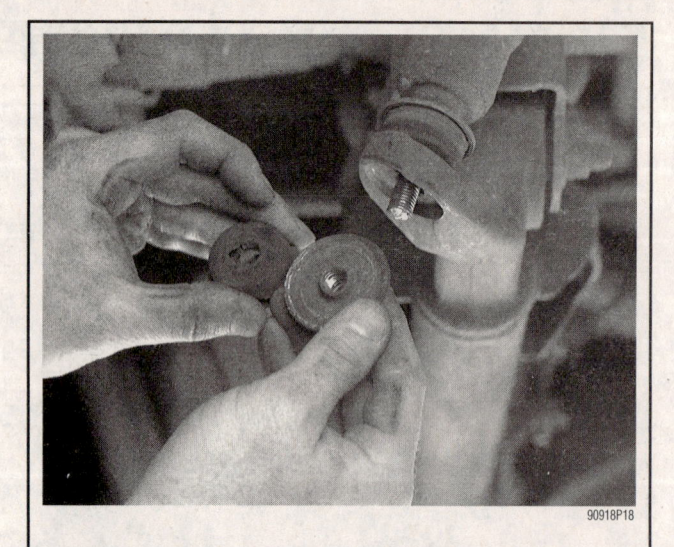

Fig. 49 Remove the lower shock nut and washer with bushing

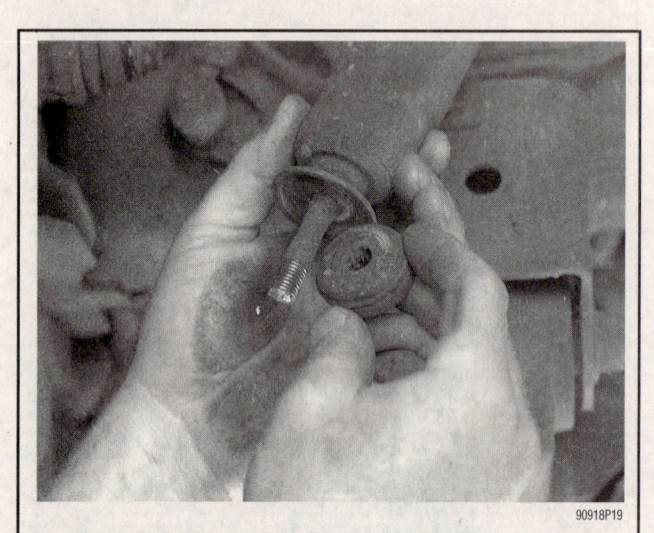

Fig. 50 Lift the shock absorber out of the lower control arm along with the bushing

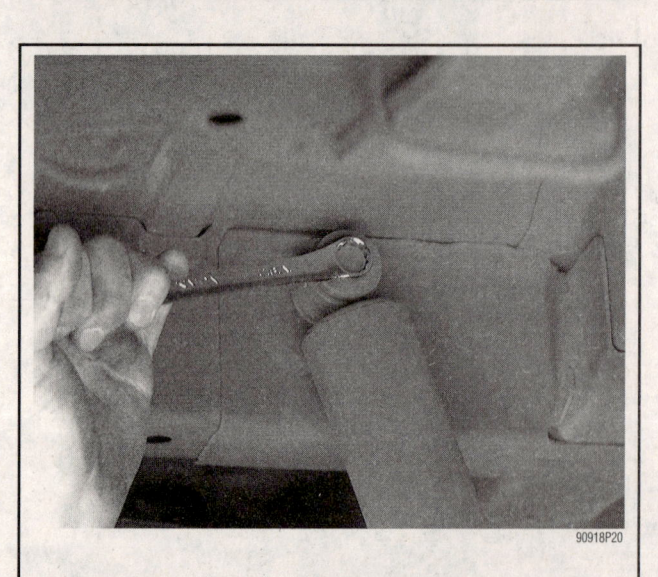

Fig. 51 Remove the upper shock mounting bolt . . .

# SUSPENSION AND STEERING  8-19

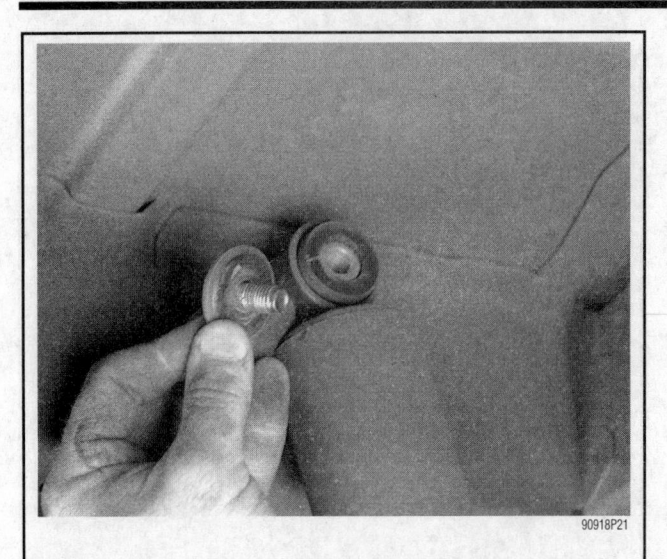

Fig. 52 . . . a washer will come out with the bolt

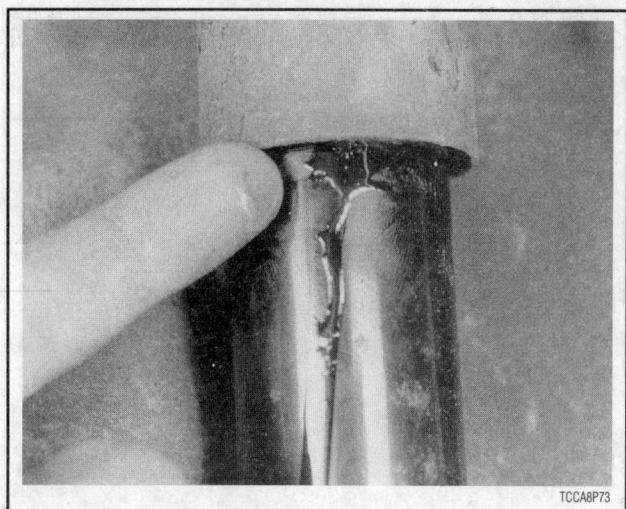

Fig. 54 When fluid is seeping out of the shock absorber, it's time to replace it

Fig. 53 Now you can extract the shock from the vehicle

7. Place the bushings and washer on the bottom of the shock.
8. Place the shock with components onto the lower control arm.
9. Tighten the upper bolt to 27 ft. lbs. (37 Nm).
10. Tighten the lower nut until the bolt protrudes 0.0059 inch (1.5mm).
11. Lower the jack from the axle housing.
12. Lower the vehicle.

## TESTING

♦ See Figure 54

The purpose of the shock absorber is simply to limit the motion of the spring during compression and rebound cycles. If the vehicle is not equipped with these motion dampers, the up and down motion would multiply until the vehicle was alternately trying to leap off the ground and to pound itself into the pavement.

Contrary to popular rumor, the shocks do not affect the ride height of the vehicle. This is controlled by other suspension components such as springs and tires. Worn shock absorbers can affect handling; if the front of the vehicle is rising or falling excessively, the "footprint" of the tires changes on the pavement and steering is affected.

The simplest test of the shock absorber is simply push down on one corner of the unladen vehicle and release it. Observe the motion of the body as it is released. In most cases, it will come up beyond it original rest position, dip back below it and settle quickly to rest. This shows that the damper is controlling the spring action. Any tendency to excessive pitch (up-and-down) motion or failure to return to rest within 2-3 cycles is a sign of poor function within the shock absorber. Oil-filled shocks may have a light film of oil around the seal, resulting from normal breathing and air exchange. This should NOT be taken as a sign of failure, but any sign of thick or running oil definitely indicates failure. Gas filled shocks may also show some film at the shaft; if the gas has leaked out, the shock will have almost no resistance to motion.

While each shock absorber can be replaced individually, it is recommended that they be changed as a pair (both front or both rear) to maintain equal response on both sides of the vehicle. Chances are quite good that if one has failed, its mate is weak also.

## Lower Control Arm

### REMOVAL & INSTALLATION

♦ See Figure 55

1. Jack the vehicle up and support the body with stands.
2. Support the rear axle housing with a jack.
3. Disconnect the brake tube from the brake hose. Remove the clip and disconnect the hose from the body.
4. On models with ABS, remove the ABS warning harness bracket.
5. Disconnect the Load Sensing Proportioning Valve spring from the lower control arm.
6. Disconnect the shock absorber from the lower control arm.
7. To remove the lateral control rod, remove the nut and bolt. Extract the lateral control rod with the bushings.
8. To remove the lower control arm, disconnect the parking brake cable from the lower control arm.

➡The coil spring with insulators should be removed once the lower control arm is.

  a. Lower the rear axle insulator and lower insulator.
  b. Remove the two nuts, tow bolts and the lower control arm.

**To install:**

9. Place the lower control arm and temporarily install the two bolts and nuts.

## 8-20 SUSPENSION AND STEERING

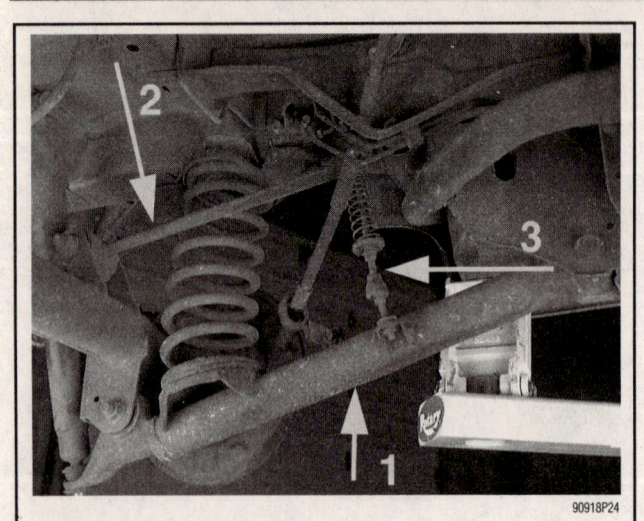

Fig. 55 Lower control arm (1), upper control arm (2) and LSPV spring (3)

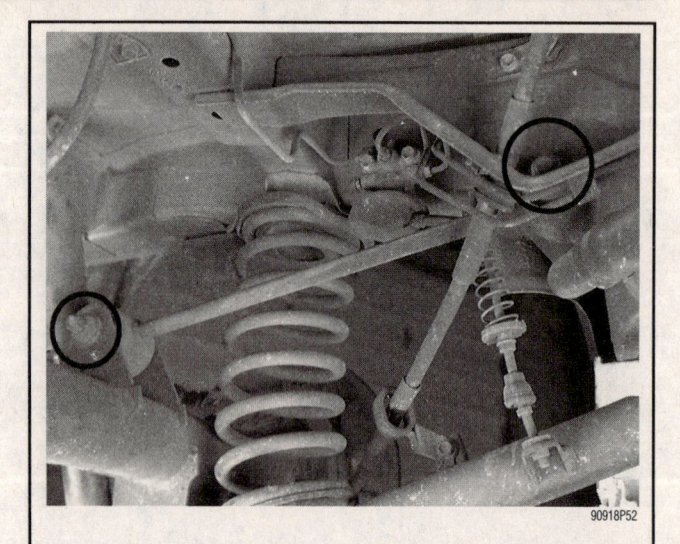

Fig. 56 The upper control arm is secured with these two nuts

10. Install the coil spring on the lower control arm with the upper and lower insulators.
   a. Fit the lower end of the coil spring into the gap of the spring seat of the lower control arm.
   b. Jack up the rear of the axle housing.
11. Connect the parking brake cable to the lower control arm.
12. Install the lateral control rod with bushings. Temporarily install the bolt and two nuts.
13. Connect the shock absorber to the lower control arm and tighten the new until the bolt protrudes 0.059 inch (1.54mm) or more.
14. Connect the LSPV spring to the lower control arm and tighten to 9 ft. lbs. (13 Nm).
15. On models with ABS, install the ABS wiring harness bracket.
16. Connect the brake hose to the body with the clip. attach the brake tube.
17. Lower the vehicle and stabilize the suspension. Bounce the vehicle up and down several times to stabilize the suspension.
18. Jack up the vehicle and support the rear axle housing with stands.
19. Tighten the two nuts of the upper control arm to 156 ft. lbs. (211 Nm). Tighten the two nuts on the lower control arm to, body side—156 ft. lbs. (211 Nm), and axle housing side—181 ft. lbs. (245 Nm).
20. Tighten the nuts of the lateral control rod on the body side to 156 ft. lbs. (211 Nm) and the axle housing side to 43 ft. lbs. (59 Nm).
21. Bleed the brake system.
22. Lower the vehicle.

### Upper Control Arm

REMOVAL & INSTALLATION

▶ See Figure 56

1. Jack the vehicle up and support the body with stands.
2. Support the rear axle housing with a jack.
3. Disconnect the brake tube from the brake hose. Remove the clip and disconnect the hose from the body.
4. On models with ABS, remove the ABS warning harness bracket.
5. Disconnect the Load Sensing Proportioning Valve spring from the lower control arm.
6. Disconnect the shock absorber from the lower control arm.
7. To remove the lateral control rod, remove the nut and bolt. Extract the lateral control rod with the bushings.
8. To remove the lower control arm, disconnect the parking brake cable from the lower control arm.

➡The coil spring with insulators should be removed once the lower control arm is.
   a. Lower the rear axle insulator and lower insulator.
   b. Remove the two nuts, tow bolts and the lower control arm.
9. To remove the upper control arm, loosen the two nuts, bolts and extract the arm.

**To install:**
10. Place the upper control arm and temporarily install the tow bolts and nuts.
11. Place the lower control arm and temporarily install the two bolts and nuts.
12. Install the coil spring on the lower control arm with the upper and lower insulators.
   a. Fit the lower end of the coil spring into the gap of the spring seat of the lower control arm.
   b. Jack up the rear of the axle housing.
13. Connect the parking brake cable to the lower control arm.
14. install the lateral control rod with bushings. Temporarily install the bolt and two nuts.
15. Connect the shock absorber to the lower control arm and tighten the new until the bolt protrudes 0.059 inch (1.54mm) or more.
16. Connect the LSPV spring to the lower control arm and tighten to 9 ft. lbs. (13 Nm).
17. On models with ABS, install the ABS wiring harness bracket.
18. Connect the brake hose to the body with the clip. attach the brake tube.
19. Lower the vehicle and stabilize the suspension. Bounce the vehicle up and down several times to stabilize the suspension.
20. Jack up the vehicle and support the rear axle housing with stands.
21. Tighten the two nuts of the upper control arm to 156 ft. lbs. (211 Nm). Tighten the two nuts on the lower control arm to, body side—156 ft. lbs. (211 Nm), and axle housing side—181 ft. lbs. (245 Nm).
22. Tighten the nuts of the lateral control rod on the body side to 156 ft. lbs. (211 Nm) and the axle housing side to 43 ft. lbs. (59 Nm).
23. Bleed the brake system.
24. Lower the vehicle.

### Lateral Control Rod

REMOVAL & INSTALLATION

1. Jack the vehicle up and support the body with stands.
2. Support the rear axle housing with a jack.
3. If necessary, disconnect the brake tube from the brake hose. Remove the clip and disconnect the hose from the body.

## SUSPENSION AND STEERING  8-21

4. On models with ABS, remove the ABS warning harness bracket.
5. Disconnect the Load Sensing Proportioning Valve spring from the lower control arm.
6. Disconnect the shock absorber from the lower control arm.
7. Remove the nut and bolt retaining the lateral control rod. Extract the lateral control rod with the bushings.

**To install:**

8. Install the lateral control rod with bushings. Temporarily install the bolt and two nuts.
9. Connect the shock absorber to the lower control arm and tighten the new until the bolt protrudes 0.059 inch (1.54mm) or more.
10. Connect the LSPV spring to the lower control arm and tighten to 9 ft. lbs. (13 Nm).
11. On models with ABS, install the ABS wiring harness bracket.
12. If removed, connect the brake hose to the body with the clip. Attach the brake tube.
13. Lower the vehicle and stabilize the suspension. Bounce the vehicle up and down several times to stabilize the suspension.
14. Jack up the vehicle and support the rear axle housing with stands.
15. Tighten the nuts of the lateral control rod on the body side to 156 ft. lbs. (211 Nm) and the axle housing side to 43 ft. lbs. (59 Nm).
16. If the lines were cracked, bleed the brake system.
17. Lower the vehicle.

## STEERING

### Steering Wheel

#### REMOVAL & INSTALLATION

**1991 Models**

♦ See Figure 57

➡ The 1991 models are the only Previa vans that are not equipped with an air bag.

### ※※ WARNING

Do not attempt to remove or install the steering wheel by hammering on it. Damage to the energy-absorbing steering column could result.

1. Disconnect the negative battery cable. Position the front wheels straight ahead.
2. Unfasten the horn and turn signal multi-connector(s) at the base of the steering column shroud.

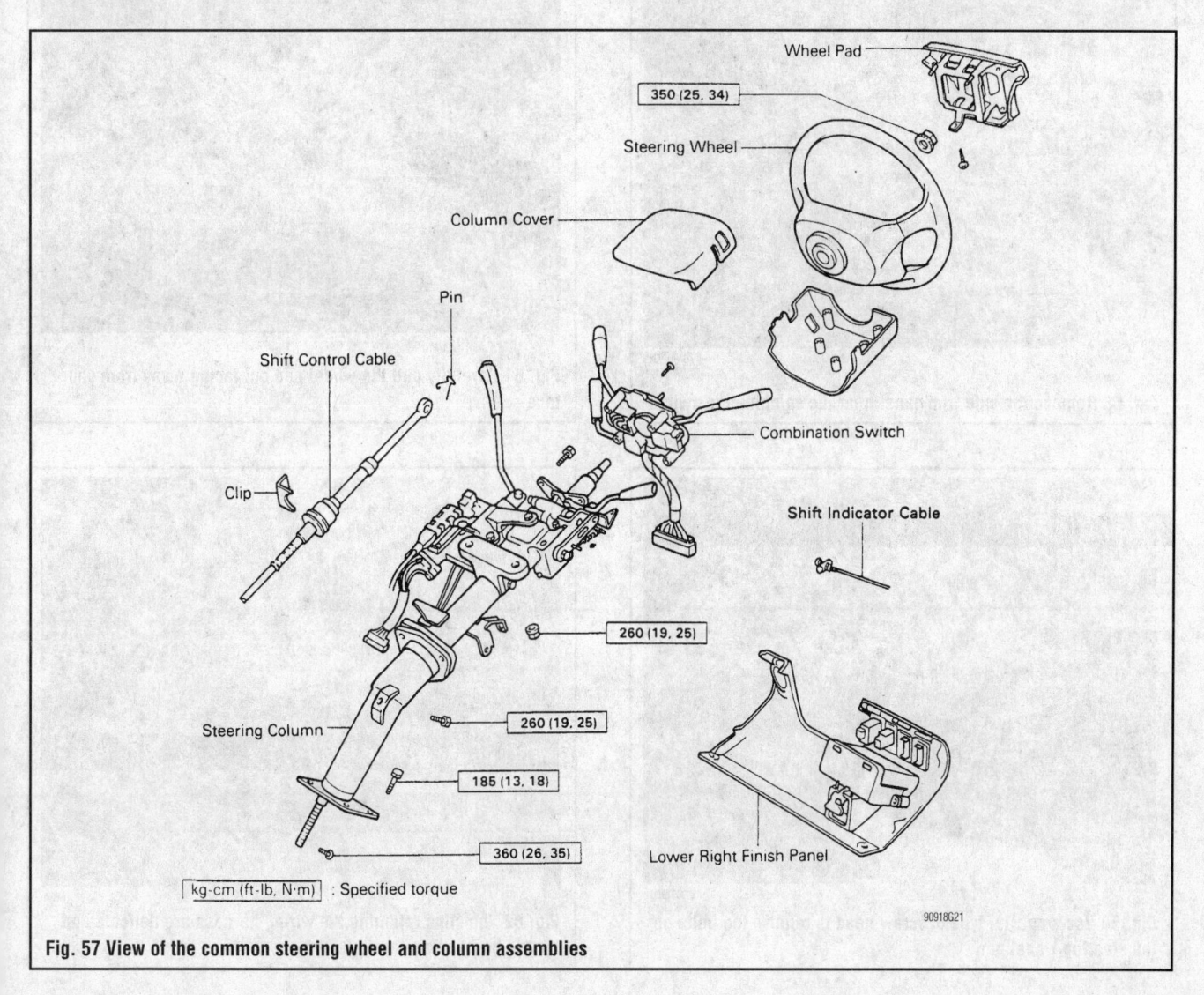

Fig. 57 View of the common steering wheel and column assemblies

## 8-22 SUSPENSION AND STEERING

3. Loosen the trim pad retaining screws from the back side of the steering wheel. Remove the pad by lifting it toward the top of the wheel.
4. Lift the trim pad and horn button assembly from the wheel.
5. Remove the steering wheel hub retaining nut.
6. Scribe matchmarks on the hub and shaft to aid in correct installation.
7. Use a suitable puller to remove the steering wheel.
8. Installation is the reverse of removal. Tighten the wheel retaining nut to 26 ft. lbs. (35 Nm).

### 1992–94 Models

▶ See Figures 58 thru 71

**※※ CAUTION**

To avoid possible unexpected deployment of the air bag (if equipped), work must not be started after approximately 90 seconds or longer from the time the ignition switch is turned OFF and the negative battery cable disconnected.

1. Disconnect the negative battery cable. Wait 90 seconds once the cable is removed before proceeding.

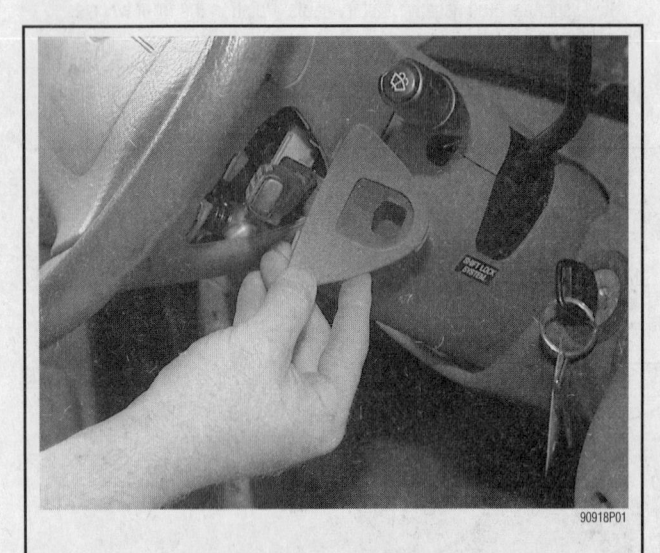

Fig. 60 Torx head screws are used

Fig. 58 Remove the side trim panel near the combination switch

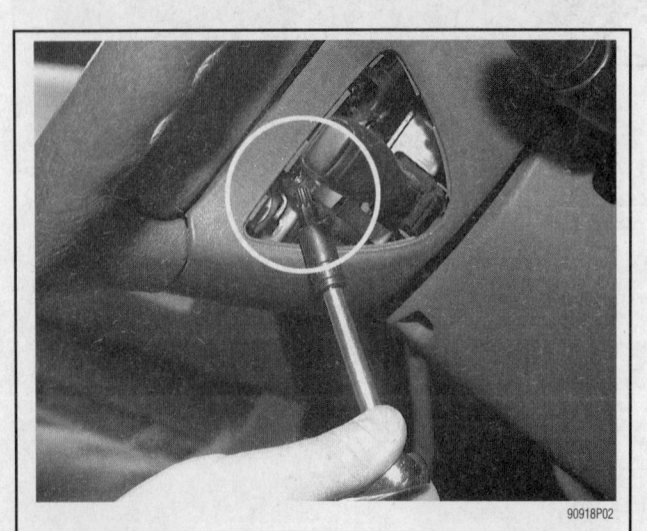

Fig. 59 Use a special type of screw head to remove the bolts on the steering wheel pad

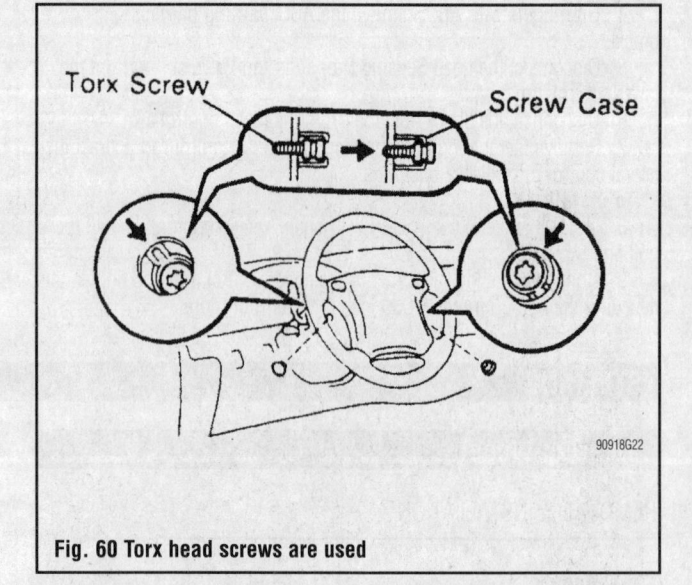

Fig. 61 Carefully pull the wheel pad out facing away from your face

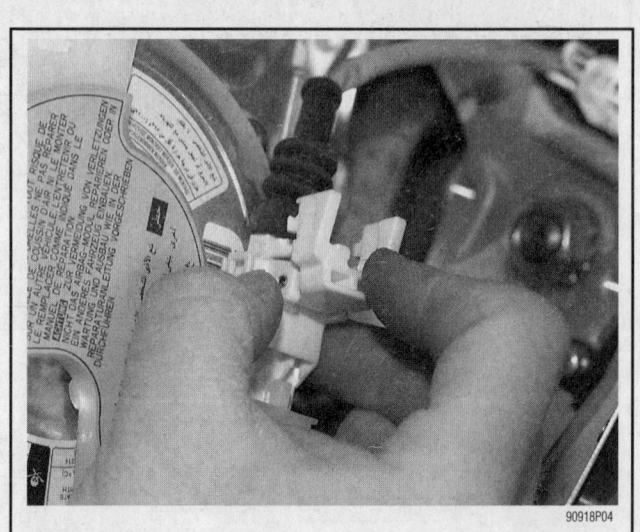

Fig. 62 The clips retaining the wiring harness are delicate and should be handled carefully

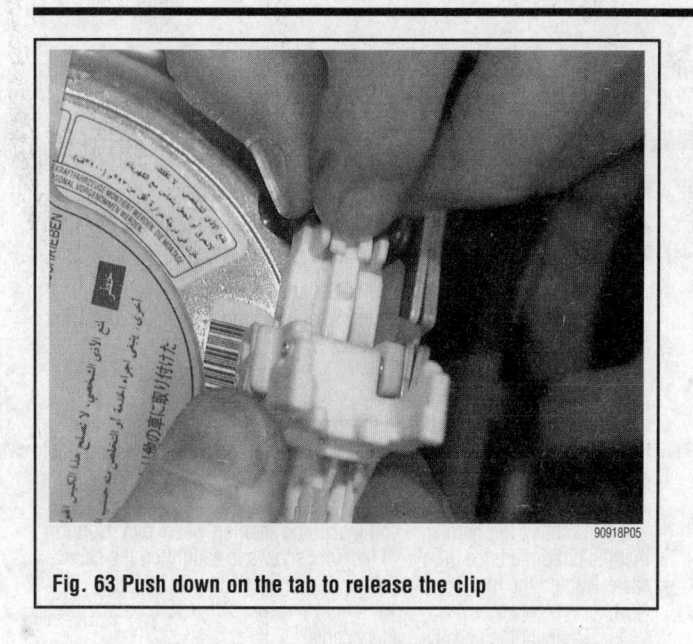

## SUSPENSION AND STEERING 8-23

Fig. 63 Push down on the tab to release the clip

Fig. 64 Depress the wiring harness clamp to the steering common to separate

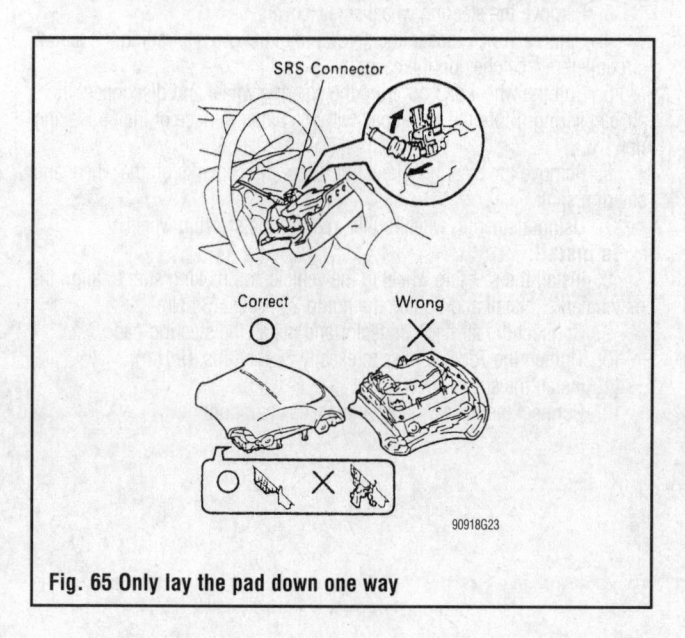

Fig. 65 Only lay the pad down one way

Fig. 66 Remove the nut on the end of the steering shaft . . .

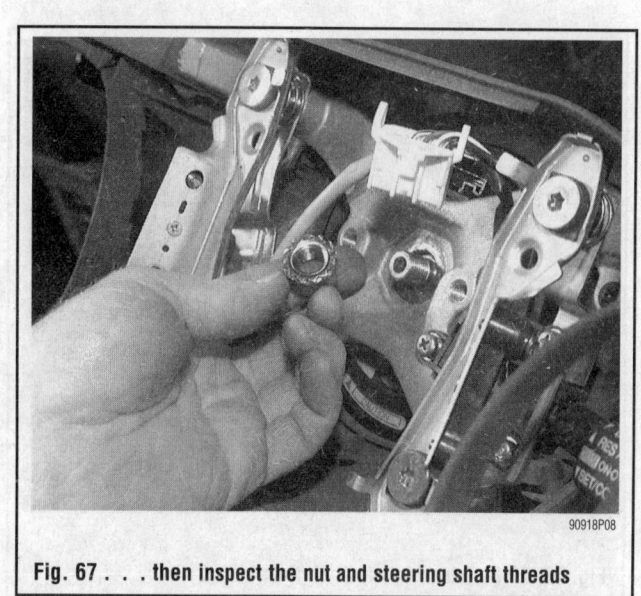

Fig. 67 . . . then inspect the nut and steering shaft threads

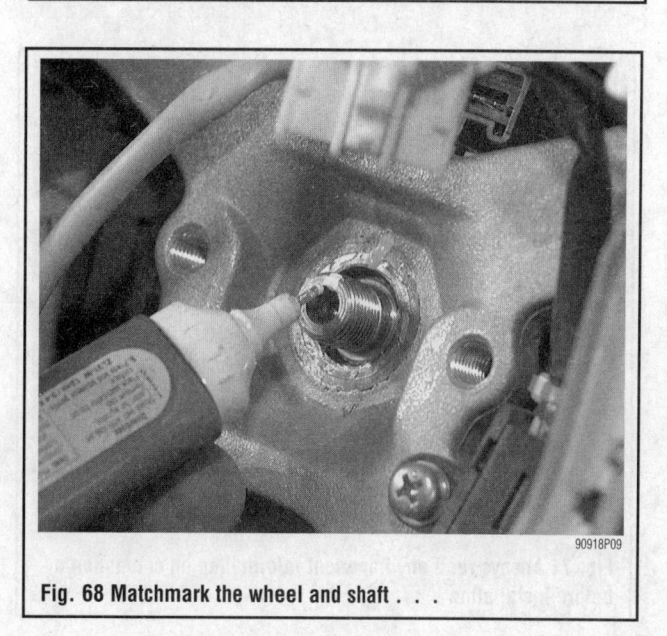

Fig. 68 Matchmark the wheel and shaft . . .

## 8-24 SUSPENSION AND STEERING

Fig. 69 . . . then install a puller

Fig. 70 Lift the steering wheel off the shaft

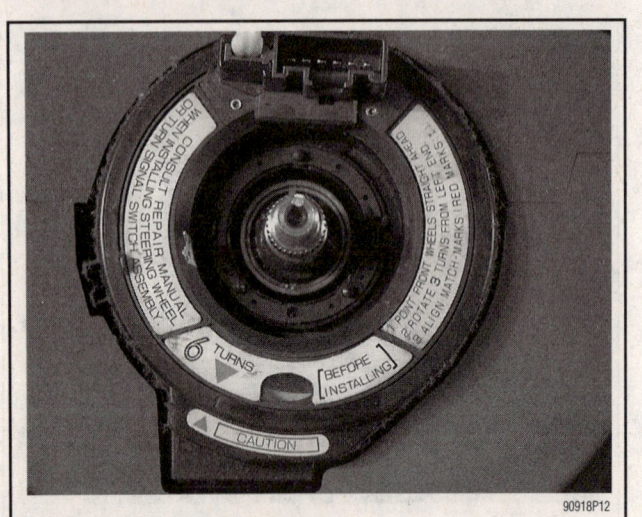

Fig. 71 Always read any important information on components before installation

2. Position the wheels straight ahead.
3. Loosen and remove the steering wheel center cover (pad) retaining screws, if equipped. There will be a trim panel on the side of the steering wheel to be removed to access the pad bolts.
4. Pull the center cover pad from the steering wheel and disconnect the air bag wiring.

➡ When storing the wheel pad (vehicles equipped with air bag), keep the upper surface of the pad facing upward.

5. Disconnect the horn wire. Matchmark the wheel and the shaft.
6. Using an appropriate steering wheel puller tool (09609–20011 or equivalent), remove the steering wheel.

**To install:**

7. Center the spiral cable.
8. Align the matchmarks on the steering wheel and main shaft and install the steering wheel to the shaft. Install and tighten the retaining nut to approximately 25 ft. lbs (34 Nm).
9. If equipped, connector the air bag harness.
10. Connect the horn wire and install the steering wheel pad. Confirm that the circumference groove of the Torx screws is caught on the screw case. Tighten the four Torx screws on the wheel pad to 65 inch lbs. (7 Nm).
11. Connect the negative battery cable.
12. Check the steering wheel center point after installation.

### 1995–97 Models

➡ Do not attempt to remove or install the steering wheel by hammering on it. Damage to the energy-absorbing steering column could result.

**❄❄ CAUTION**

To avoid personal injury when working on air bag equipped vehicles, work must be started after 90 seconds or longer from the time the ignition switch is turned to the LOCK position and the negative battery terminal is disconnected. If the air bag system is disconnected with the ignition switch at the ON or ACC, diagnostic codes will be set. When removing the air bag, take care not to pull the air bag wire harness. When carrying the wheel pad, carry it with the upper surface facing away. When storing it, keep the upper surface of the pad facing upward.

1. Disconnect the negative battery cable.
2. Place the front wheels facing straight ahead.
3. Remove the steering wheel screw covers.
4. Using a Torx®, loosen the screws until the groove trailing the screw circumference catches on the case.
5. Pull the wheel pad out from the steering wheel and disconnect the air bag wiring. Store the wheel pad with the upper surface of the pad facing upward.
6. Remove the steering wheel nut. Place matchmarks on the wheel and steering shaft.
7. Using a steering wheel puller, remove the steering wheel.

**To install:**

8. Install the steering wheel to the vehicle and making sure to align the matchmarks. Install and tighten the nut to 25 ft. lbs. (34 Nm).
9. Connect the air bag connector and install the steering pad.
10. Tighten the Torx® screws to exactly 78 inch lbs. (9 Nm).
11. Install the screw covers.
12. Connect the battery cable and check operation.

# SUSPENSION AND STEERING  8-25

## Turn Signal (Combination) Switch

### REMOVAL & INSTALLATION

▶ See Figure 72

**Without Airbag System**

The turn signal or combination switch is an assembly of different switches combined. Each one can be detached from the switch once the assembly is removed.
1. Disconnect the negative battery cable.
2. Remove the lower dash cover and the air duct.
3. Unscrew and separate the upper and lower steering column covers.
4. Remove the steering wheel. Refer to the necessary service procedure.
5. Unscrew the retaining screws and remove the switch.
6. Disconnect the wiring at the harness.

**To install:**
7. Place the switch in correct position and tighten the bolts.
8. Connect the wiring harness and reinstall the steering wheel.
9. Reinstall the and attach column cover(s).
10. Install the lower dash trim panel.
11. Connect the negative battery cable. Check system for proper operation.

**With Airbag System**

▶ See Figures 73 and 74

1. Disconnect the negative battery cable. Wait at least 90 seconds before working on the vehicle.

### ✷✷ CAUTION

On models with an airbag, wait at least 90 seconds from the time that the ignition switch is turned to the LOCK position and the battery is disconnected before performing any further work.

2. Remove (matchmark before removal) the steering wheel, as outlined in this Section.

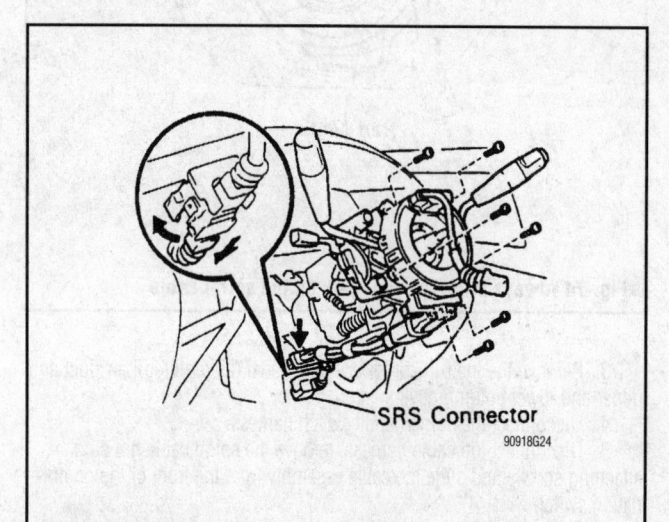

Fig. 73 There are quite a few screws to be removed for the combination switch

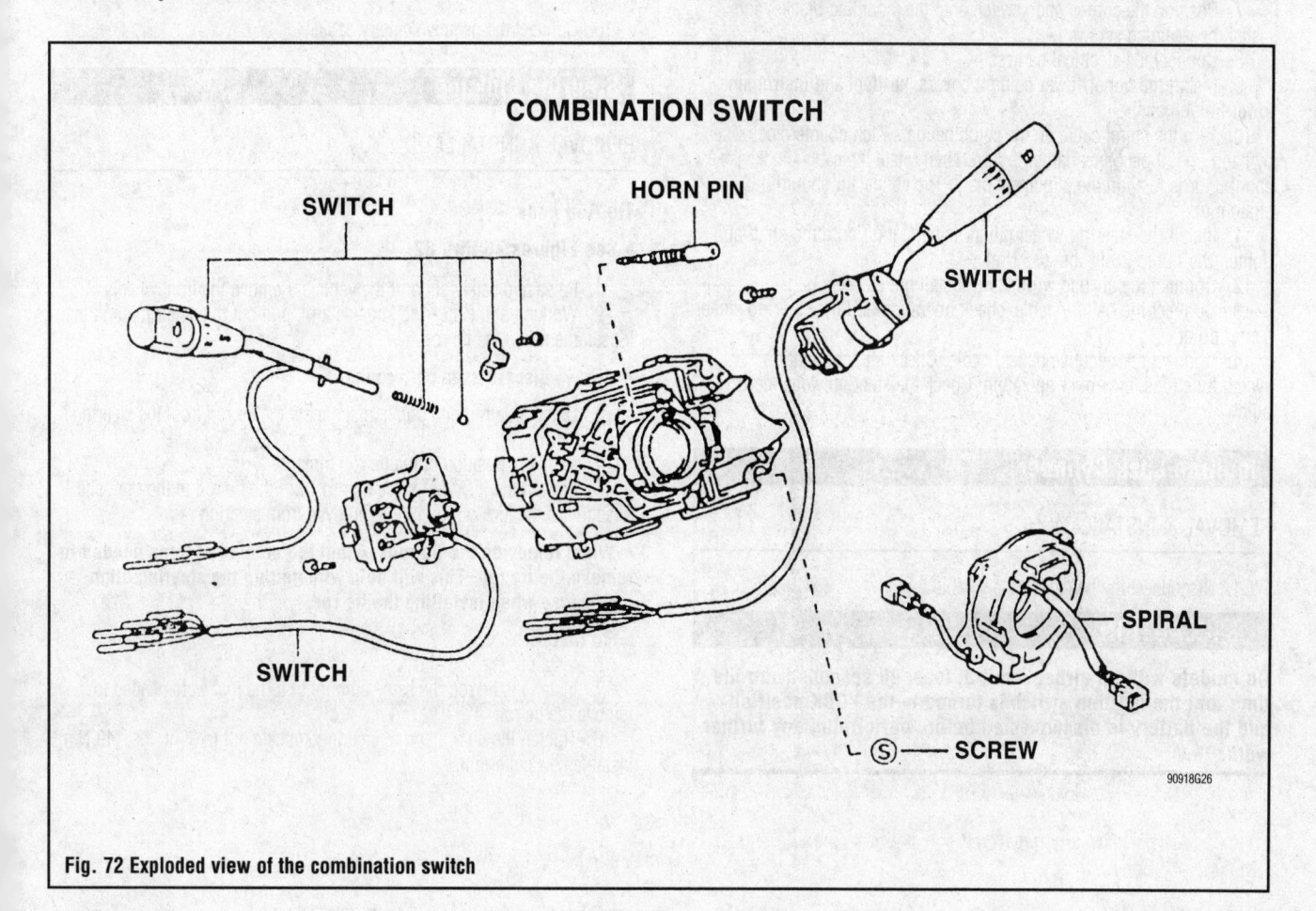

Fig. 72 Exploded view of the combination switch

# 8-26 SUSPENSION AND STEERING

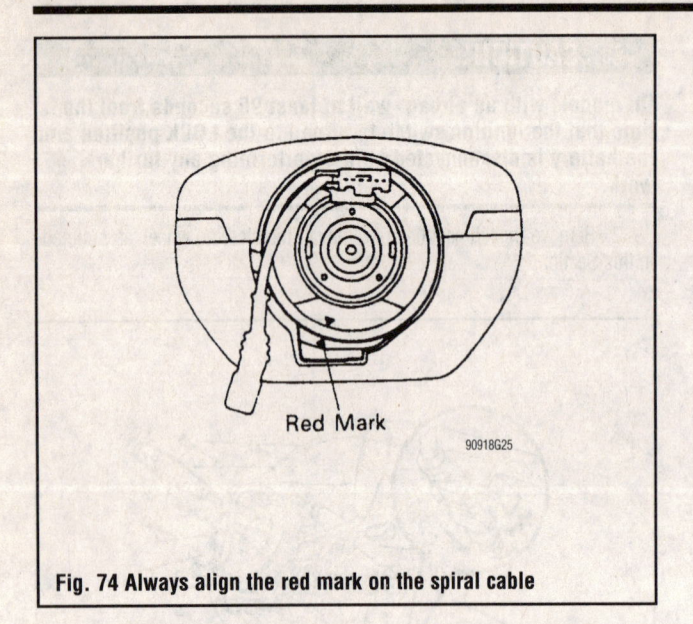

**Fig. 74 Always align the red mark on the spiral cable**

3. Remove the instrument lower finish panel (as required), air duct and upper and lower column covers.
4. Disconnect the combination switch harness.
5. Disconnect the cable harness, remove the spiral cable housing attaching screws and slide the cable assembly from the front of the combination switch.
6. Remove the screws that attach the combination switch to its mounting brackets and remove the combination switch from the vehicle.

**To install:**
7. Position the combination switch onto the mounting bracket and install the retaining screws.
8. Connect the electrical harness.
9. Install the upper/lower column covers, air duct and instrument lower finish panel.
10. Turn the spiral cable on the combination switch counterclockwise by hand until it becomes harder to turn. Then rotate the cable clockwise about 3 turns to align the alignment mark. The connector should be straight up.
11. Install the steering wheel (align matchmarks) onto the shaft and tighten the nut to 26 ft. lbs. (35 Nm).
12. Connect the air bag wiring and install the steering pad.
13. Connect the battery cable, check operation and the steering wheel center point.
14. Connect the negative battery cable. Check all combination switch functions for proper operation. Check the steering wheel center point.

## Ignition Lock Cylinder

### REMOVAL & INSTALLATION

1. Disconnect the negative battery cable.

**✸✸ CAUTION**

On models with an airbag, wait at least 90 seconds from the time that the ignition switch is turned to the LOCK position and the battery is disconnected before performing any further work.

2. Unscrew the retaining screws and remove the upper and lower steering column covers.
3. Remove the 2 retaining screws and remove the steering column trim.
4. Turn the ignition key to the **ACC** position.
5. Push the lock cylinder stop in with a small, round object (cotter pin, punch, etc.) and pull out the ignition key and the lock cylinder.

➡ You may find that removing the steering wheel and the combination switch makes the job easier.

6. Loosen the mounting screw and withdraw the ignition switch from the lock housing.
7. Remove the wiring harness bands or clips. Disconnect the ignition switch harness.

**To install:**
8. Position the ignition switch so that the recess and the bracket tab are properly aligned. Install the retaining screw.
9. Make sure that both the lock cylinder and the column lock are in the **ACC** position. Slide the cylinder into the lock housing until the stop tab engages the hole in the lock.
10. Make certain the stop tab is firmly seated in the slot. Turn the key to each switch position, checking for smoothness of motions and a positive feel. Remove and insert the key a few times, each time turning the key to each switch position.
11. Connect the switch if it was removed from the lock assembly.
12. Connect the wiring harness and check the assembly for proper operation.
13. Reinstall or connect any wiring bands, clips or retainers which were loosened. It is important that the wiring be correctly contained and out of the way of any moving parts.
14. Reinstall the combination switch and the steering wheel if they were removed.
15. Install the steering column trim and the upper and lower column covers.
16. Connect the negative battery cable.

## Steering Linkage

### REMOVAL & INSTALLATION

**Tie Rod Ends**

♦ See Figures 75 thru 82

1. Raise and safely support the vehicle. Remove the front wheels.
2. Working at the steering knuckle arm, pull out the cotter pin and then loosen the nut to the tie rod.

➡ Always discard used cotter pins.

3. Using a tie rod end puller, disconnect the tie rod from the steering knuckle arm.
4. Mark the position of the tie rod threads.
5. Loosen the locknut for the tie rod. Turn the tie rod in the opposite direction of the lock nut until it is removed from steering rack.

➡ When removing the tie rods, count the amount of turns needed to remove the tie rod. This will help with getting the steering alignment close when installing the tie rod.

**To install:**
6. Install the tie rod end.
7. Install the tie rod the same amount of turns that were needed to remove the tie rod.
8. Tighten the tie rod end to steering knuckle nut to 36 ft. lbs. (49 Nm). Install a new cotter pin.

## SUSPENSION AND STEERING 8-27

Fig. 75 Remove the cotter pin and discard it

Fig. 76 Loosen the nut on the tie rod end where the steering knuckle meets

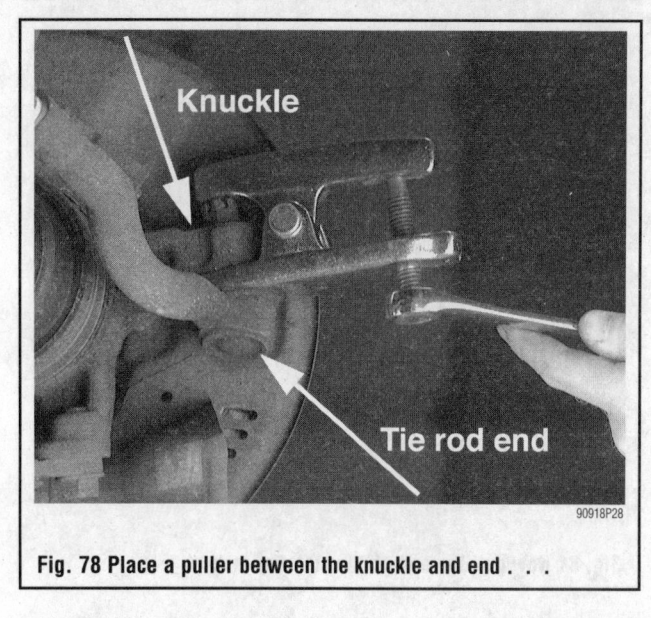

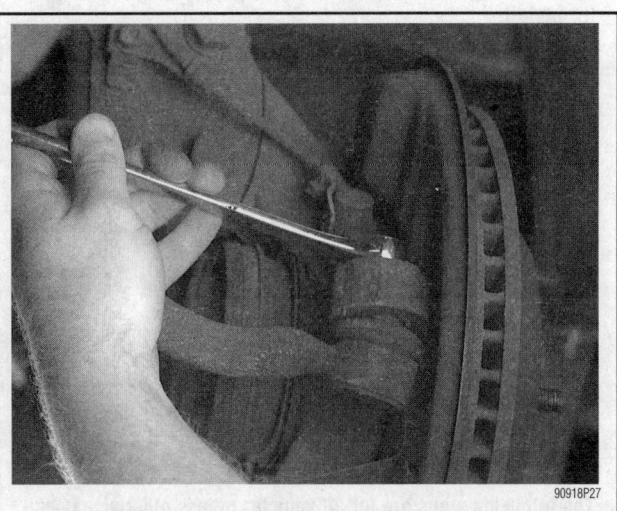

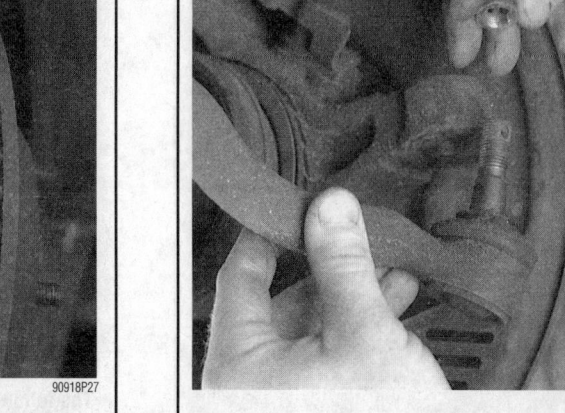

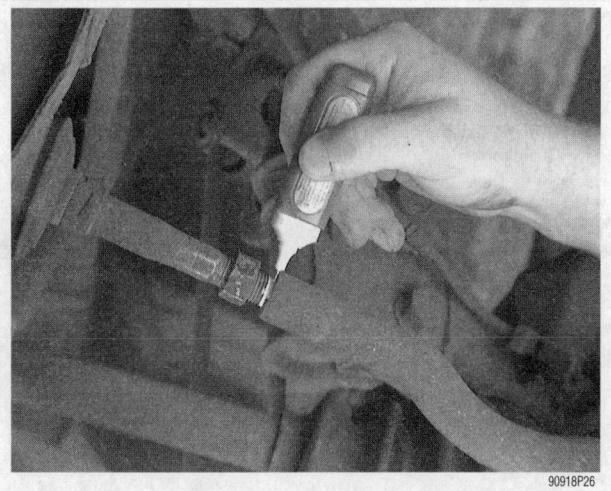

Fig. 77 Always matchmark the tie rod end threads prior to removal

Fig. 78 Place a puller between the knuckle and end . . .

Fig. 79 . . . the end should pop out with ease

Fig. 80 Loosen the locknut from the tie rod

# 8-28 SUSPENSION AND STEERING

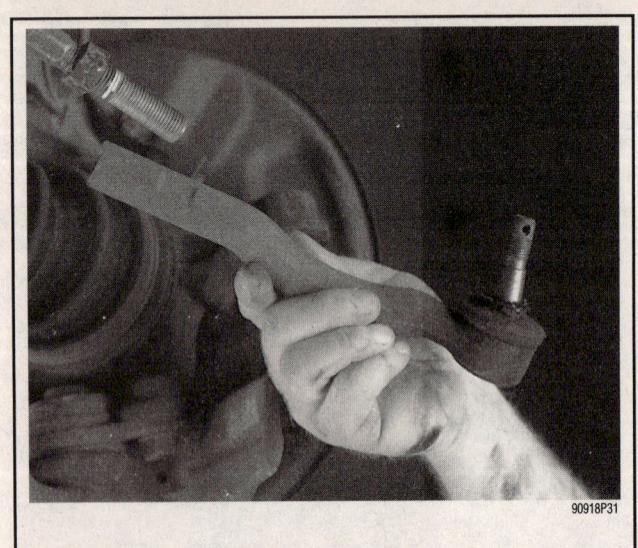

Fig. 81 Now pull the end off the steering rack

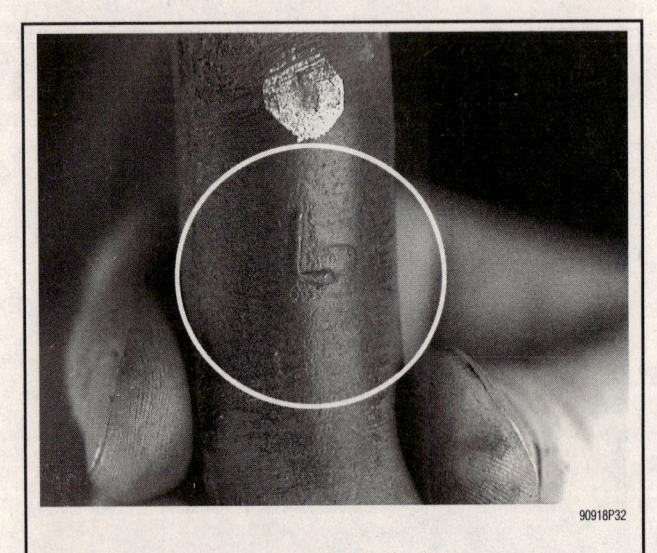

Fig. 82 Each tie rod is marked with an L or R for left and right

➡If the hole on the tie rod does not line up with the nut, always tighten the nut until the hole lines up.

9. Install the front wheels and lower the vehicle. Check the front end alignment.
10. Tighten the tie rod locknut to 67 ft. lb (91 Nm).
11. Check steering wheel center point and front end alignment. Adjust the alignment as needed.

## Power Steering Gear

### REMOVAL & INSTALLATION

◆ See Figure 83

1. Remove the battery from the vehicle.
2. Raise the vehicle and support safely.
3. Remove the front wheels.
4. Remove the engine undercovers.
5. Remove the cotter pins and the nuts to the tie rod ends.
6. Using a separator tool, disconnect the tie rod ends from the steering knuckle.
7. Place matchmarks on the universal joint and steering column shaft.
8. Remove the lower bolt and loosen the upper bolt to the sliding yoke. Slide the yoke upward to disconnect the sliding yoke from the rack and pinion.
9. Disconnect the pressure and return pipes using a line wrench.
10. If equipped with 4WD, remove the front differential assembly.
11. Remove the equipment drive housing No. 2 insulator and equipment drive housing No. 3 stay by removing the two bolts and three nuts.
12. On some vehicles, remove the bracket bolts and grommets. Turn the housing toward the back side and slide the housing to the right side. Put the left tie rod end in the body panel.
13. On 1995–97 vehicles, remove the bolt and disconnect the clamp from the rack housing.
    a. Remove the four bracket bolts and the brackets from the steering rack.
14. Pull the housing out through the opening in the left side of the body.
15. On 1995–97 vehicles, remove the grommets from the steering rack.

**To install:**

16. On 1994 vehicles, install the gear housing and tighten the mounting bolts to 56 ft. lbs. (76 Nm).
    a. On 1994 4WD, install the front differential assembly, equipment driveshaft housing insulator and drive housing stay.
    b. Connect the pressure and return pipes using flarenut wrenches. Tighten the fittings to 33 ft. lbs. (44 Nm).
17. On 1995–97 vehicles, install the grommets to the rack and pinion.
    a. Install the gear housing and tighten the mounting bolts to 70 ft. lbs. (95 Nm).
    b. Connect the power steering lines to the power steering rack and pinion. Tighten the steering lines to 27 ft. lbs. (36 Nm).
    c. Install the bolt to hold the clamp and power steering lines to the steering rack.
    d. Install the equipment drive housing No. 2 insulator and equipment drive housing No. 3 stay by installing the two bolts and three nuts. Tighten the bolts to 13 ft. lbs. (18 Nm) and the nuts to 18 ft. lbs. (25 Nm).

➡The following steps are for all vehicles unless otherwise specified.

18. Install the lower bolt to the sliding yoke. Tighten the upper and lower bolts to 26 ft. lbs. (35 Nm).
19. On 1995–97 vehicles, 4WD only: install the front differential assembly.
20. Connect the tie rod ends to the steering knuckle and tighten the nuts to 36 ft. lbs. (49 Nm). Install a new cotter pin.
21. Install the engine undercovers.
22. Install the battery to the vehicle.
23. Install the front wheels and lower the vehicle.
24. Perform a front end alignment.

## Power Steering Pump

### REMOVAL & INSTALLATION

◆ See Figure 84

1. Disconnect the negative battery cable from the battery.
2. Remove the air duct by removing the six screws.

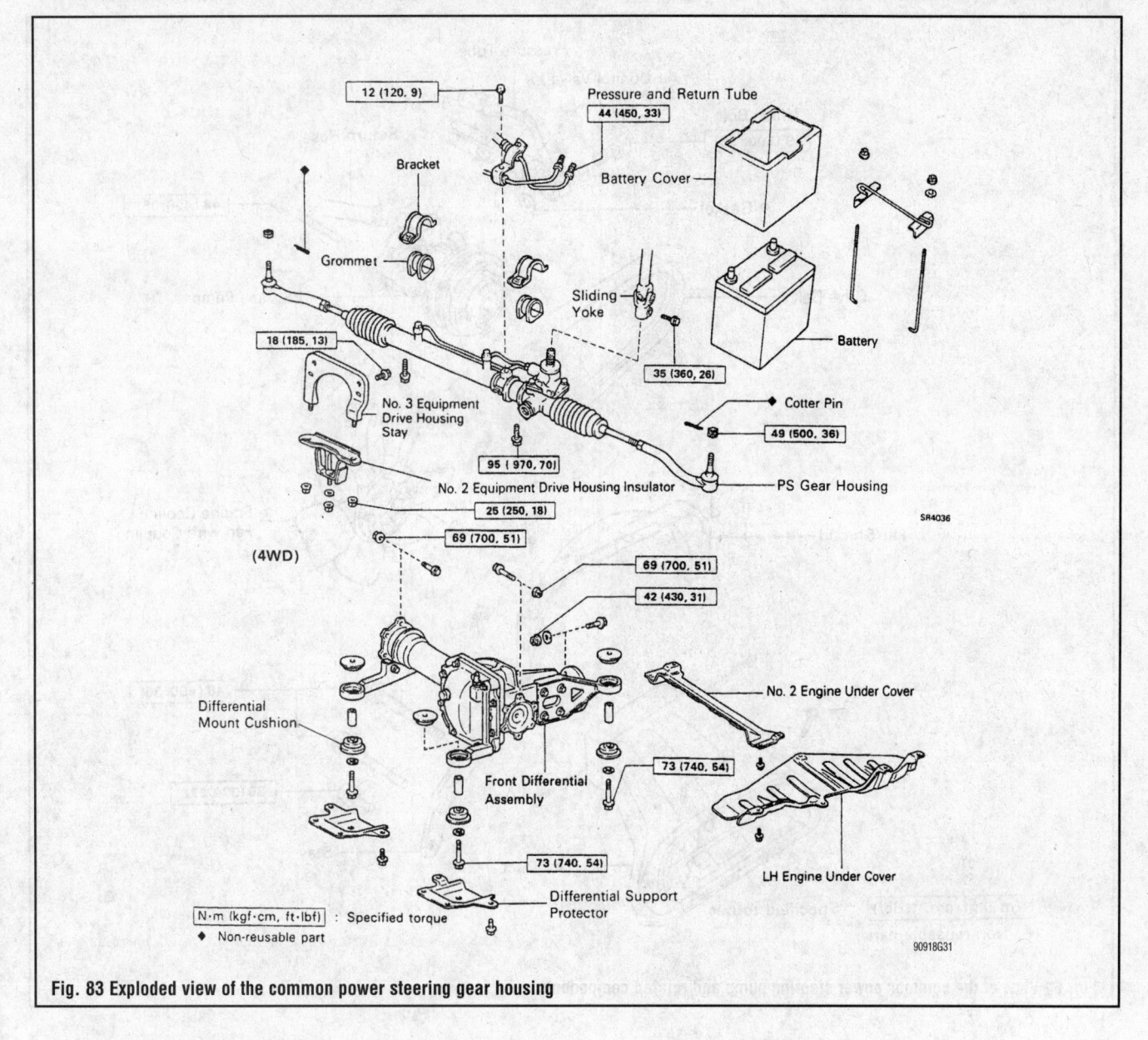

## SUSPENSION AND STEERING 8-29

Fig. 83 Exploded view of the common power steering gear housing

3. Remove the upper fan shroud by removing the four bolts.
4. Remove the engine cooling fan with coupling by removing the four nuts.
5. Place a suitable drain pan into position and disconnect the return hose from the power steering pump. Drain the fluid from the power steering pump.
6. On some non-supercharged engines: loosen the bolt and nut to the alternator and remove the drive belt from the engine.
7. On 1995 supercharged and 1996 engines: disconnect the pressure feed tube bracket by removing the bolt.
8. Disconnect the pressure tube from the power steering pump.
9. On 1995 supercharged and 1996 engines: loosen the adjusting bolt and the No. 1 idler pulley nut and remove the drive belt from the engine.
10. Remove the pump mounting bolts and remove the power steering pump from the vehicle.

**To install:**

11. Install the power steering pump to the engine and install the four bolts. Tighten the bolts as follows:

- Long: 35 ft. lbs. (48 Nm)
- short: 27 ft. lbs. (36 Nm)

12. On 1995 non-supercharged engines: install the drive belt and adjust the tension by pulling back on the alternator. Tighten the bolt for the alternator to 37 ft. lbs. (50 Nm) and the nut to 13 ft. lbs. (18 Nm).
13. On 1995 supercharged and 1996 engines: install the drive belt and tighten the adjusting bolt and No. 1 idler pulley nut.
14. Connect the return hose to the power steering pump.
15. Connect the pressure feed line by installing the two gaskets and union bolt. Tighten the bolt to 36 ft. lbs. (49 Nm).
16. On 1995 supercharged and 1996 engines: connect the pressure feed tube bracket by install the bolt. Tighten the bolt to 10 ft. lbs. (13 Nm).
17. Install the engine cooling fan with coupling by installing the four nuts. Tighten the nuts to 10 ft. lbs. (13 Nm).
18. Install the upper fan shroud with the four bolts.
19. Install the air duct with the four screws.
20. Fill and bleed the power steering system.
21. Connect the negative battery cable to the battery.

## 8-30 SUSPENSION AND STEERING

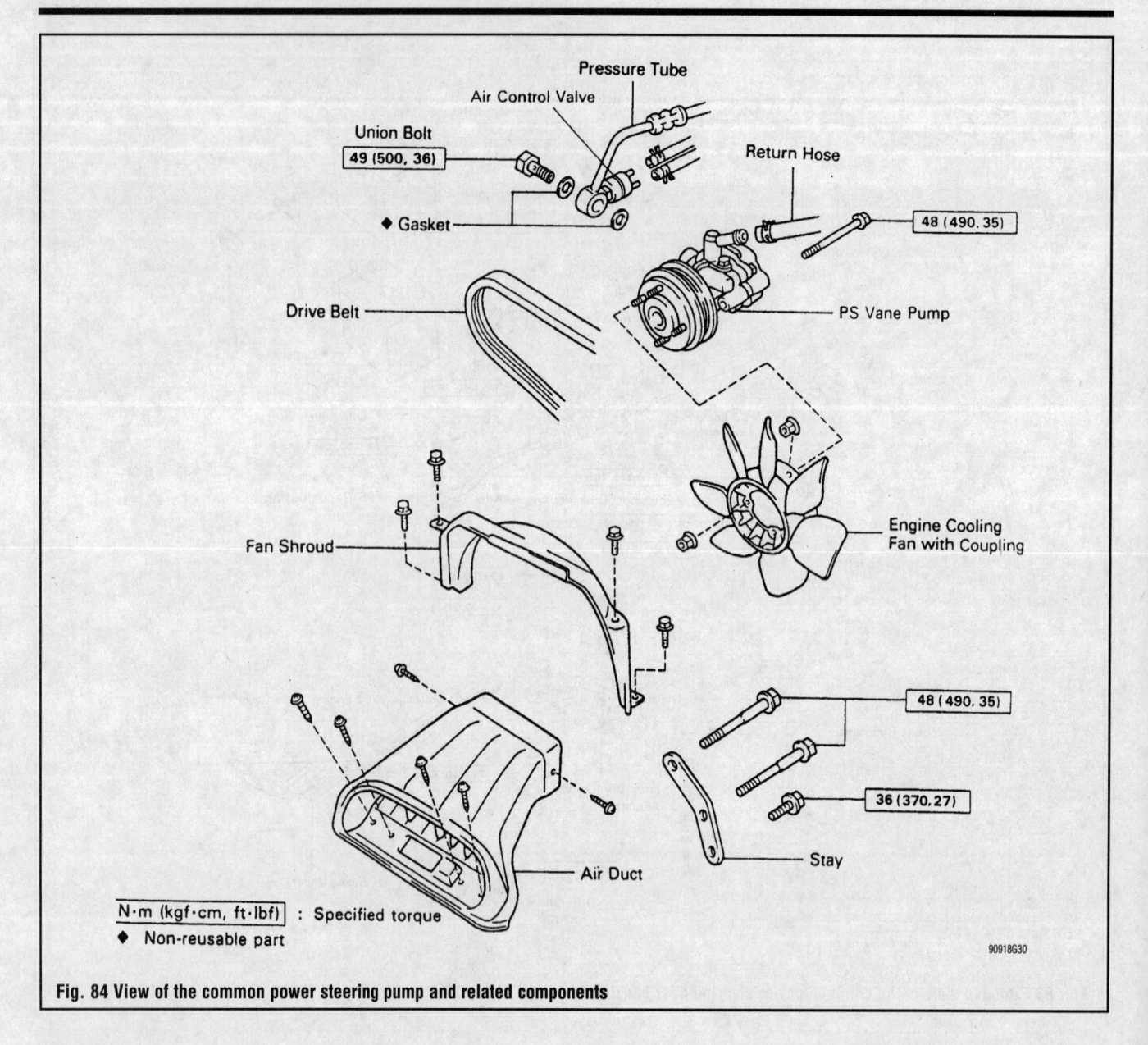

Fig. 84 View of the common power steering pump and related components

### BLEEDING

◆ See Figure 85

1. Raise and safely support the vehicle.
2. Fill the pump reservoir with power steering fluid.
3. With the engine speed below 1000 rpms, rotate the steering wheel from lock-to-lock several times and keep it in full lock for 2–3 seconds. Then turn the wheel to the reverse full lock and keep it in that position for 2–3 seconds.
4. Check that the fluid in the reservoir is not foamy or cloudy and does not rise over maximum when the engine is stopped.

➡Perform the bleeding procedure until all of the air is bled from the system.

5. The fluid level should not have risen more than 0.20 inch (5mm); if it does, check the pump.

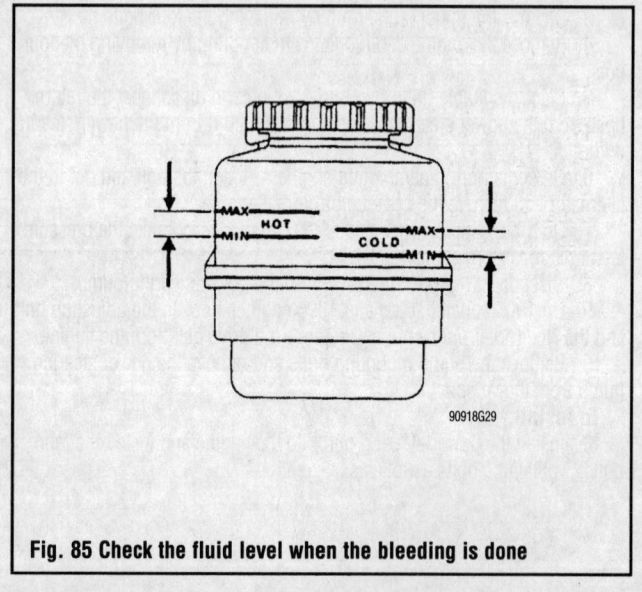

Fig. 85 Check the fluid level when the bleeding is done

# SUSPENSION AND STEERING 8-31

## TORQUE SPECIFICATIONS

| Components | | English Specifications | Metric Specifications |
|---|---|---|---|
| **Front Suspension:** | | | |
| Axle hub bearing lock nut (2WD) | | 147 ft. lbs. | 199 Nm |
| Tie rod end-to-steering knuckle | | 36 ft. lbs. | 49 Nm |
| Steering knuckle-strut | | 231 ft. lbs. | 314 Nm |
| Steering knuckle-to-lower ball joint | | 94 ft. lbs. | 127 Nm |
| Steering knuckle-to-ABS sensor | | 69 inch lbs. | 8 Nm |
| Drive shaft locknut | 1991 | 137 ft. lbs. | 186 Nm |
| | 1992-93 | 166 ft. lbs | 266 Nm |
| | 1994-97 | 152 ft. lbs | 206 Nm |
| Differential carrier cover set bolt | | 34 ft. lbs. | 47 Nm |
| Differential tube-to-carrier | | 65 ft. lbs. | 88 Nm |
| Drive shaft-to-side gear | | 51 ft. lbs. | 69 Nm |
| Front differential bearing cap | | 58 ft. lbs. | 78 Nm |
| Front differential drain plug | | 36 ft. lbs. | 49 Nm |
| Front differential filler plug | | 29 ft. lbs. | 39 Nm |
| Front differential-to-propeller shaft | | 31 ft. lbs. | 42 Nm |
| Hub nut | | 76 ft lbs. | 103 Nm |
| Differential carrier-to-differential support | | | |
| | 1991 | 59 ft. lbs. | 80 Nm |
| | 1992-97 | 116 ft. lbs. | 157 Nm |
| Differential carrier-to-No. 2 support | | 48 ft. lbs. | 65 Nm |
| Differential support bolt | | 54 ft. lbs. | 73 Nm |
| Lower ball joint-to-control arm | | 76 ft. lbs. | 103 Nm |
| No. 1 differential support-to-differential tube | | 51 ft. lbs. | 70 Nm |
| Suspension support-to-strut | | 34 ft. lbs. | 47 Nm |
| Suspension-to-body | | 47 ft. lbs. | 64 Nm |
| No. 1 lower arm-to-No. 2 lower arm | | 136 ft. lbs. | 184 Nm |
| No. 2 lower arm-to-bushing | 1991 | 141 ft. lbs. | 194 Nm |
| | 1992-97 | 109 ft. lbs. | 180 Nm |
| No. 1 lower arm-to-body | | 121 ft. lbs. | 164 Nm |
| Lower arm bracket-to-body | | 105 ft. lbs. | 142 Nm |
| Stabilizer bar link nut | | 76 ft. lbs. | 103 Nm |
| Stabilizer bar bracket | | 14 ft. lbs. | 19 Nm |
| Lugnuts | | 76 ft. lbs. | 103 Nm |
| **Rear Suspension:** | | | |
| Adjusting locknut | | 9 ft. lbs. | 13 Nm |
| Backing plate set nut | | 53 ft. lbs. | 73 Nm |
| Differential bearing cap | | 58 ft. lbs. | 78 Nm |
| Differential carrier-to-axle housing | | 20 ft. lbs. | 27 Nm |
| Differential drain plug | | 36 ft. lbs. | 49 Nm |
| Differential filler plug | | 36 ft. lbs. | 49 Nm |
| Lateral control rod-to-axle housing | | 43 ft. lbs. | 59 Nm |
| Lateral control rod-to-body | | 156 ft. lbs. | 211 Nm |
| Lower control arm-to-LVSP spring | | 9 ft. lbs. | 13 Nm |
| Lower control arm-to-axle housing | | 181 ft. lbs. | 245 Nm |
| Lower control arm-to-body | | 156 ft. lbs. | 211 Nm |
| Propeller shaft-to-differential | | 54 ft. lbs. | 74 Nm |
| Ring gear set bolt | | 71 ft. lbs. | 97 Nm |
| Shock absorber-to-body | | 27 ft. lbs. | 37 Nm |
| Upper control arm-to-axle housing | | 156 ft. lbs. | 211 Nm |
| Upper control arm-to-body | | 156 ft. lbs. | 211 Nm |

90918C01

## SUSPENSION AND STEERING

### Troubleshooting the Power Steering Pump

| Problem | Cause | Solution |
|---|---|---|
| Chirp noise in steering pump | • Loose belt | • Adjust belt tension to specification |
| Belt squeal (particularly noticeable at full wheel travel and stand still parking) | • Loose belt | • Adjust belt tension to specification |
| Growl noise in steering pump | • Excessive back pressure in hoses or steering gear caused by restriction | • Locate restriction and correct. Replace part if necessary. |
| Growl noise in steering pump (particularly noticeable at stand still parking) | • Scored pressure plates, thrust plate or rotor<br>• Extreme wear of cam ring | • Replace parts and flush system<br>• Replace parts |
| Groan noise in steering pump | • Low oil level<br>• Air in the oil. Poor pressure hose connection. | • Fill reservoir to proper level<br>• Tighten connector to specified torque. Bleed system by operating steering from right to left—full turn. |
| Rattle noise in steering pump | • Vanes not installed properly<br>• Vanes sticking in rotor slots | • Install properly<br>• Free up by removing burrs, varnish, or dirt |
| Swish noise in steering pump | • Defective flow control valve | • Replace part |
| Whine noise in steering pump | • Pump shaft bearing scored | • Replace housing and shaft. Flush system. |
| Hard steering or lack of assist | • Loose pump belt<br>• Low oil level in reservoir<br>NOTE: Low oil level will also result in excessive pump noise<br>• Steering gear to column misalignment<br>• Lower coupling flange rubbing against steering gear adjuster plug<br>• Tires not properly inflated | • Adjust belt tension to specification<br>• Fill to proper level. If excessively low, check all lines and joints for evidence of external leakage. Tighten loose connectors.<br>• Align steering column<br>• Loosen pinch bolt and assemble properly<br>• Inflate to recommended pressure |
| Foaming milky power steering fluid, low fluid level and possible low pressure | • Air in the fluid, and loss of fluid due to internal pump leakage causing overflow | • Check for leaks and correct. Bleed system. Extremely cold temperatures will cause system aeration should the oil level be low. If oil level is correct and pump still foams, remove pump from vehicle and separate reservoir from body. Check welsh plug and body for cracks. If plug is loose or body is cracked, replace body. |
| Low pump pressure | • Flow control valve stuck or inoperative<br>• Pressure plate not flat against cam ring | • Remove burrs or dirt or replace. Flush system.<br>• Correct |
| Momentary increase in effort when turning wheel fast to right or left | • Low oil level in pump<br>• Pump belt slipping<br>• High internal leakage | • Add power steering fluid as required<br>• Tighten or replace belt<br>• Check pump pressure. (See pressure test) |
| Steering wheel surges or jerks when turning with engine running especially during parking | • Low oil level<br>• Loose pump belt<br>• Steering linkage hitting engine oil pan at full turn<br>• Insufficient pump pressure | • Fill as required<br>• Adjust tension to specification<br>• Correct clearance<br>• Check pump pressure. (See pressure test). Replace flow control valve if defective. |

**BRAKE OPERATING SYSTEM 9-2**
BASIC OPERATING PRINCIPLES 9-2
    DISC BRAKES 9-2
    DRUM BRAKES 9-2
    POWER BOOSTERS 9-3
BRAKE LIGHT SWITCH 9-3
    REMOVAL & INSTALLATION 9-3
MASTER CYLINDER 9-3
    REMOVAL & INSTALLATION 9-3
POWER BRAKE BOOSTER 9-5
    REMOVAL & INSTALLATION 9-5
PROPORTIONING VALVE 9-6
    REMOVAL & INSTALLATION 9-6
    FLUID PRESSURE ADJUSTMENT 9-7
BRAKE HOSES AND PIPES 9-8
    REMOVAL & INSTALLATION 9-8
BLEEDING THE BRAKE SYSTEM 9-11
    MASTER CYLINDER 9-11
    LINES & WHEEL CIRCUITS 9-12
**DISC BRAKES 9-13**
BRAKE PADS 9-13
    REMOVAL & INSTALLATION 9-13
    INSPECTION 9-17
BRAKE CALIPER 9-17
    REMOVAL & INSTALLATION 9-17
    OVERHAUL 9-18
BRAKE DISC (ROTOR) 9-20
    REMOVAL & INSTALLATION 9-20
    INSPECTION 9-22
**DRUM BRAKES 9-22**
BRAKE DRUMS 9-22
    REMOVAL & INSTALLATION 9-22
    INSPECTION 9-23
BRAKE SHOES 9-23
    INSPECTION 9-23
    REMOVAL & INSTALLATION 9-24
    ADJUSTMENTS 9-26
WHEEL CYLINDERS 9-26
    REMOVAL & INSTALLATION 9-26
    OVERHAUL 9-26
**PARKING BRAKE 9-28**
CABLE(S) 9-28
    REMOVAL & INSTALLATION 9-28
    ADJUSTMENT 9-29
BRAKE SHOES 9-29
    REMOVAL & INSTALLATION 9-29
    ADJUSTMENTS 9-32
**ANTI-LOCK BRAKE SYSTEM 9-33**
GENERAL INFORMATION 9-33
DIAGNOSIS AND TESTING 9-34
    DATA LINK CONNECTORS (DLC) 9-34
    READING CODES 9-34
    CLEARING TROUBLE CODES 9-35
CONTROL RELAYS 9-35
    TESTING 9-35
    REMOVAL & INSTALLATION 9-39
SPEED SENSORS 9-39
    TESTING 9-39
    REMOVAL & INSTALLATION 9-40
ACTUATOR 9-42
    REMOVAL & INSTALLATION 9-42
ABS ECM 9-42
    REMOVAL & INSTALLATION 9-42
DECELERATION SENSOR 9-42
    TESTING 9-42
SENSOR RING (ROTOR) 9-42
    REMOVAL & INSTALLATION 9-42
BLEEDING THE ABS SYSTEM 9-42
**SPECIFICATIONS CHART**
BRAKE SPECIFICATIONS 9-43
**TROUBLESHOOTING CHART**
THE BRAKE SYSTEM OP9-44

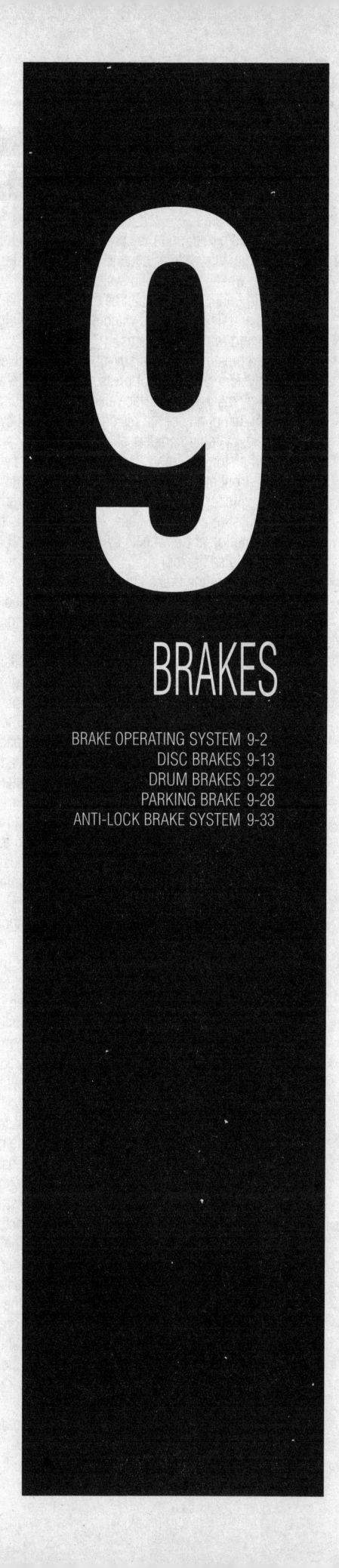

# 9
# BRAKES

BRAKE OPERATING SYSTEM 9-2
DISC BRAKES 9-13
DRUM BRAKES 9-22
PARKING BRAKE 9-28
ANTI-LOCK BRAKE SYSTEM 9-33

# 9-2 BRAKES

## BRAKE OPERATING SYSTEM

### Basic Operating Principles

Hydraulic systems are used to actuate the brakes of all modern automobiles. The system transports the power required to force the frictional surfaces of the braking system together from the pedal to the individual brake units at each wheel. A hydraulic system is used for two reasons.

First, fluid under pressure can be carried to all parts of an automobile by small pipes and flexible hoses without taking up a significant amount of room or posing routing problems.

Second, a great mechanical advantage can be given to the brake pedal end of the system, and the foot pressure required to actuate the brakes can be reduced by making the surface area of the master cylinder pistons smaller than that of any of the pistons in the wheel cylinders or calipers.

The master cylinder consists of a fluid reservoir along with a double cylinder and piston assembly. Double type master cylinders are designed to separate the front and rear braking systems hydraulically in case of a leak. The master cylinder converts mechanical motion from the pedal into hydraulic pressure within the lines. This pressure is translated back into mechanical motion at the wheels by either the wheel cylinder (drum brakes) or the caliper (disc brakes).

Steel lines carry the brake fluid to a point on the vehicle's frame near each of the vehicle's wheels. The fluid is then carried to the calipers and wheel cylinders by flexible tubes in order to allow for suspension and steering movements.

In drum brake systems, each wheel cylinder contains two pistons, one at either end, which push outward in opposite directions and force the brake shoe into contact with the drum.

In disc brake systems, the cylinders are part of the calipers. At least one cylinder in each caliper is used to force the brake pads against the disc.

All pistons employ some type of seal, usually made of rubber, to minimize fluid leakage. A rubber dust boot seals the outer end of the cylinder against dust and dirt. The boot fits around the outer end of the piston on disc brake calipers, and around the brake actuating rod on wheel cylinders.

The hydraulic system operates as follows: When at rest, the entire system, from the piston(s) in the master cylinder to those in the wheel cylinders or calipers, is full of brake fluid. Upon application of the brake pedal, fluid trapped in front of the master cylinder piston(s) is forced through the lines to the wheel cylinders. Here, it forces the pistons outward, in the case of drum brakes, and inward toward the disc, in the case of disc brakes. The motion of the pistons is opposed by return springs mounted outside the cylinders in drum brakes, and by spring seals, in disc brakes.

Upon release of the brake pedal, a spring located inside the master cylinder immediately returns the master cylinder pistons to the normal position. The pistons contain check valves and the master cylinder has compensating ports drilled in it. These are uncovered as the pistons reach their normal position. The piston check valves allow fluid to flow toward the wheel cylinders or calipers as the pistons withdraw. Then, as the return springs force the brake pads or shoes into the released position, the excess fluid reservoir through the compensating ports. It is during the time the pedal is in the released position that any fluid that has leaked out of the system will be replaced through the compensating ports.

Dual circuit master cylinders employ two pistons, located one behind the other, in the same cylinder. The primary piston is actuated directly by mechanical linkage from the brake pedal through the power booster. The secondary piston is actuated by fluid trapped between the two pistons. If a leak develops in front of the secondary piston, it moves forward until it bottoms against the front of the master cylinder, and the fluid trapped between the pistons will operate the rear brakes. If the rear brakes develop a leak, the primary piston will move forward until direct contact with the secondary piston takes place, and it will force the secondary piston to actuate the front brakes. In either case, the brake pedal moves farther when the brakes are applied, and less braking power is available.

All dual circuit systems use a switch to warn the driver when only half of the brake system is operational. This switch is usually located in a valve body which is mounted on the firewall or the frame below the master cylinder. A hydraulic piston receives pressure from both circuits, each circuit's pressure being applied to one end of the piston. When the pressures are in balance, the piston remains stationary. When one circuit has a leak, however, the greater pressure in that circuit during application of the brakes will push the piston to one side, closing the switch and activating the brake warning light.

In disc brake systems, this valve body also contains a metering valve and, in some cases, a proportioning valve. The metering valve keeps pressure from traveling to the disc brakes on the front wheels until the brake shoes on the rear wheels have contacted the drums, ensuring that the front brakes will never be used alone. The proportioning valve controls the pressure to the rear brakes to lessen the chance of rear wheel lock-up during very hard braking.

Warning lights may be tested by depressing the brake pedal and holding it while opening one of the wheel cylinder bleeder screws. If this does not cause the light to go on, substitute a new lamp, make continuity checks, and, finally, replace the switch as necessary.

The hydraulic system may be checked for leaks by applying pressure to the pedal gradually and steadily. If the pedal sinks very slowly to the floor, the system has a leak. This is not to be confused with a springy or spongy feel due to the compression of air within the lines. If the system leaks, there will be a gradual change in the position of the pedal with a constant pressure.

Check for leaks along all lines and at wheel cylinders. If no external leaks are apparent, the problem is inside the master cylinder.

## DISC BRAKES

Instead of the traditional expanding brakes that press outward against a circular drum, disc brake systems utilize a disc (rotor) with brake pads positioned on either side of it. An easily-seen analogy is the hand brake arrangement on a bicycle. The pads squeeze onto the rim of the bike wheel, slowing its motion. Automobile disc brakes use the identical principle but apply the braking effort to a separate disc instead of the wheel.

The disc (rotor) is a casting, usually equipped with cooling fins between the two braking surfaces. This enables air to circulate between the braking surfaces making them less sensitive to heat buildup and more resistant to fade. Dirt and water do not drastically affect braking action since contaminants are thrown off by the centrifugal action of the rotor or scraped off the by the pads. Also, the equal clamping action of the two brake pads tends to ensure uniform, straight line stops. Disc brakes are inherently self-adjusting. There are three general types of disc brake:

1. A fixed caliper.
2. A floating caliper.
3. A sliding caliper.

The fixed caliper design uses two pistons mounted on either side of the rotor (in each side of the caliper). The caliper is mounted rigidly and does not move.

The sliding and floating designs are quite similar. In fact, these two types are often lumped together. In both designs, the pad on the inside of the rotor is moved into contact with the rotor by hydraulic force. The caliper, which is not held in a fixed position, moves slightly, bringing the outside pad into contact with the rotor. There are various methods of attaching floating calipers. Some pivot at the bottom or top, and some slide on mounting bolts. In any event, the end result is the same.

## DRUM BRAKES

Drum brakes employ two brake shoes mounted on a stationary backing plate. These shoes are positioned inside a circular drum which rotates with the wheel assembly. The shoes are held in place by springs. This allows them to slide toward the drums (when they are applied) while keeping the linings and drums in alignment. The shoes are actuated by a wheel cylinder which is mounted at the top of the backing plate. When the brakes are applied, hydraulic pressure forces the wheel cylinder's actuating links outward. Since these links bear directly against the top of the brake shoes, the tops of the shoes are then forced against the inner side of the drum. This action forces the bottoms of the two shoes to contact the brake drum by rotating the entire assembly slightly (known as servo action). When pressure within the wheel cylinder is relaxed, return springs pull the shoes back away from the drum.

Most modern drum brakes are designed to self-adjust themselves during application when the vehicle is moving in reverse. This motion causes both shoes to rotate very slightly with the drum, rocking an adjusting lever, thereby causing rotation of the adjusting screw. Some drum brake systems are designed to self-adjust during application whenever the brakes are applied. This on-board adjustment system reduces the need for maintenance adjustments and keeps both the brake function and pedal feel satisfactory.

## POWER BOOSTERS

Virtually all modern vehicles use a vacuum assisted power brake system to multiply the braking force and reduce pedal effort. Since vacuum is always available when the engine is operating, the system is simple and efficient. A vacuum diaphragm is located on the front of the master cylinder and assists the driver in applying the brakes, reducing both the effort and travel he must put into moving the brake pedal.

The vacuum diaphragm housing is normally connected to the intake manifold by a vacuum hose. A check valve is placed at the point where the hose enters the diaphragm housing, so that during periods of low manifold vacuum brakes assist will not be lost.

Depressing the brake pedal closes off the vacuum source and allows atmospheric pressure to enter on one side of the diaphragm. This causes the master cylinder pistons to move and apply the brakes. When the brake pedal is released, vacuum is applied to both sides of the diaphragm and springs return the diaphragm and master cylinder pistons to the released position.

If the vacuum supply fails, the brake pedal rod will contact the end of the master cylinder actuator rod and the system will apply the brakes without any power assistance. The driver will notice that much higher pedal effort is needed to stop the car and that the pedal feels harder than usual.

### Vacuum Leak Test

1. Operate the engine at idle without touching the brake pedal for at least one minute.
2. Turn off the engine and wait one minute.
3. Test for the presence of assist vacuum by depressing the brake pedal and releasing it several times. If vacuum is present in the system, light application will produce less and less pedal travel. If there is no vacuum, air is leaking into the system.

### System Operation Test

1. With the engine **OFF**, pump the brake pedal until the supply vacuum is entirely gone.
2. Put light, steady pressure on the brake pedal.
3. Start the engine and let it idle. If the system is operating correctly, the brake pedal should fall toward the floor if the constant pressure is maintained.

Power brake systems may be tested for hydraulic leaks just as ordinary systems are tested.

## Brake Light Switch

### REMOVAL & INSTALLATION

♦ See Figure 1

1. Disconnect the wiring from the stop light switch.
2. Loosen the stop light switch lock nut and remove the assembly.

**To install:**

3. Position the switch and secure with the lock nut.
4. Adjust the clearance of the switch. This can be done by turning the switch assembly. Clearance between the switch and the brake pedal stopper should be 0.02–0.09 inch (0.5–2.4mm).

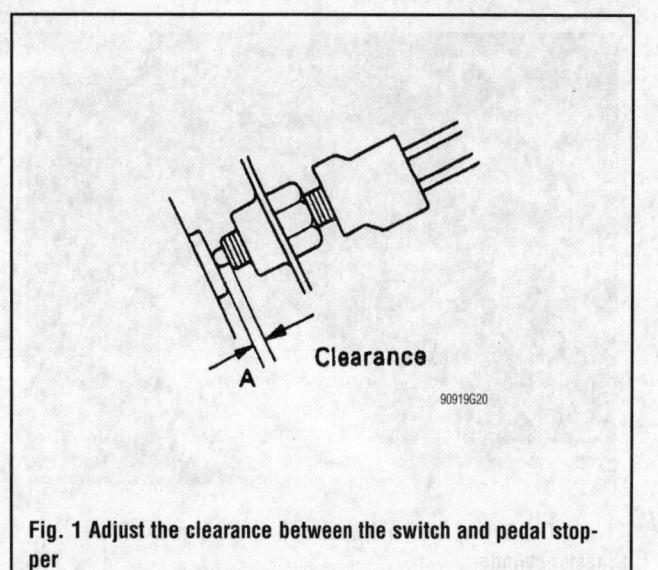

Fig. 1 Adjust the clearance between the switch and pedal stopper

5. Attach the wiring to the switch.
6. Test the system.

## Master Cylinder

### REMOVAL & INSTALLATION

♦ See Figures 2 thru 10

### ✲✲ WARNING

Clean, high quality brake fluid is essential to the safe and proper operation of the brake system. You should always buy the highest quality brake fluid that is available. If the brake fluid becomes contaminated, drain and flush the system, then refill the master cylinder with new fluid. Never reuse any brake fluid. Any brake fluid that is removed from the system should be discarded.

1. Disconnect the negative battery cable from the battery.
2. If equipped, disconnect the level warning switch connector from the master cylinder.
3. A small screen is located inside the reservoir, remove it.

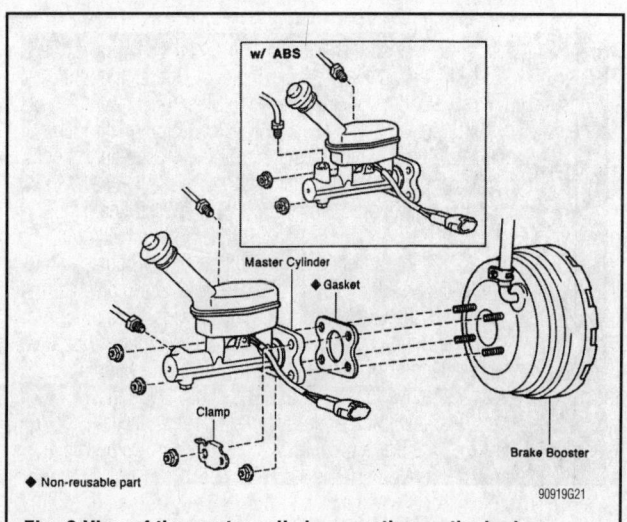

Fig. 2 View of the master cylinder mounting on the brake booster

# 9-4 BRAKES

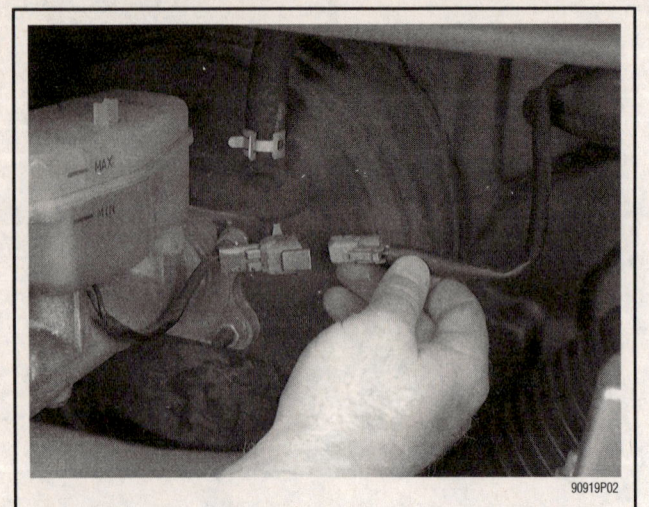

**Fig. 3 Disconnect the level warning harness from the brake master cylinder**

**Fig. 6 Unscrew and carefully remove the brake line from the cylinder**

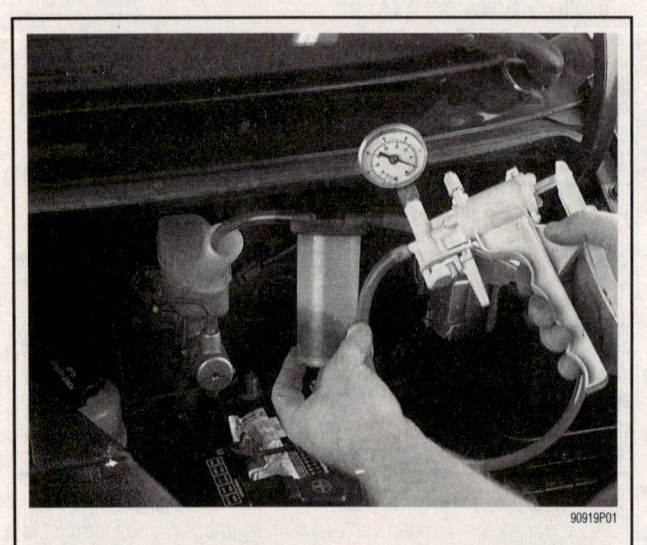

**Fig. 4 Siphon out the old brake fluid from the reservoir**

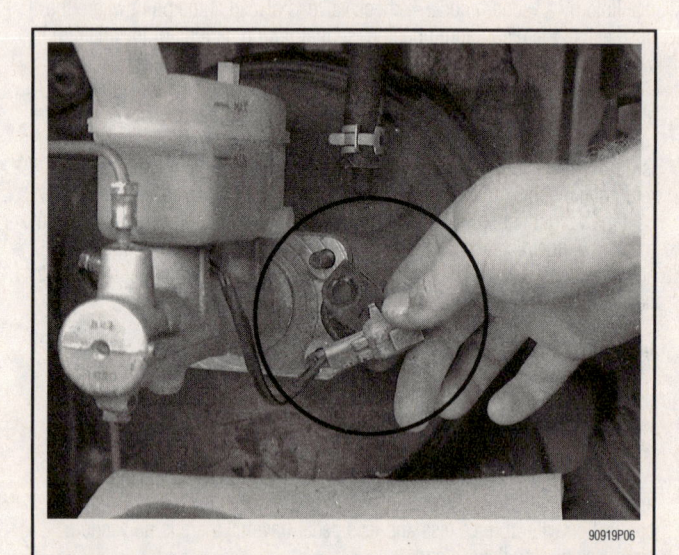

**Fig. 7 The upper left retaining nut has a bracket behind it**

**Fig. 5 Only use a brake line wrench to disconnect the metal tubes**

**Fig. 8 Place a rag under the cylinder to catch any spilt fluid from the cylinder during removal**

# BRAKES 9-5

4. Using a syringe, remove the brake fluid from the master cylinder.
5. Using a line wrench, disconnect the brake lines from the master cylinder.
6. Remove the master cylinder-to-power booster mounting nuts.
7. A bracket is behind one of the retaining nuts, remove this and set aside.
8. Remove the master cylinder assembly and gasket from the power brake unit.
9. It is recommended to discard the old gasket if the unit has never been removed.

**To install:**
10. Adjust the length of the brake booster pushrod as follows:
   a. Install a new gasket on the master cylinder.
   b. Install SST 09737–00010, or equivalent, on the master cylinder gasket and lower the pin until its tip slightly touches the piston.
   c. Turn the tool upside down and position it on the brake booster.
   d. Measure the clearance between the booster pushrod and the pin head on the SST tool.
   e. There should not be any clearance. If not, adjust the booster pushrod length until the pushrod lightly touches the pin head.

➡ **When adjusting the pushrod, depress the brake pedal so that the pushrod sticks out.**

11. Remove the SST tool and install the master cylinder to the brake booster using a new gasket.
12. Install the master cylinder four nuts and torque the nuts to 9 ft. lbs. (13 Nm).
13. Using a line wrench, connect the two brake lines to the master cylinder. Torque the union nuts to 11 ft. lbs. (15 Nm).
14. Connect the level warning switch connector.
15. Place the screen into the reservoir.
16. Fill the brake reservoir with brake fluid and bleed the brake system.
17. Check and adjust brake pedal.
18. Connect the negative battery cable to the battery.

## Power Brake Booster

### REMOVAL & INSTALLATION

♦ See Figures 11, 12, 13 and 14

1. Remove the brake master cylinder.
2. Disconnect the vacuum hose from the brake booster.
3. To disconnect the brake pedal from the booster clevis, first remove the clip. Loosen the lock nut, then remove the clevis pin.

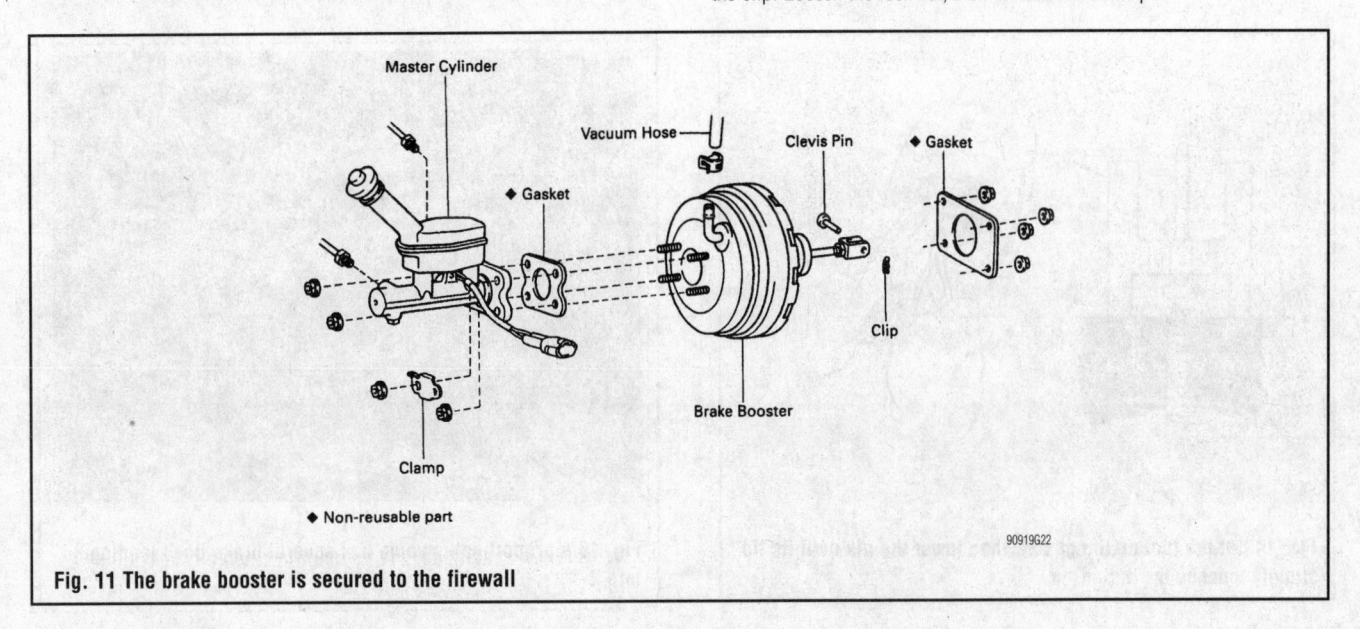

Fig. 9 Extract the master cylinder from the four studs from the brake booster

Fig. 10 Remove and discard the old gasket

Fig. 11 The brake booster is secured to the firewall

# 9-6 BRAKES

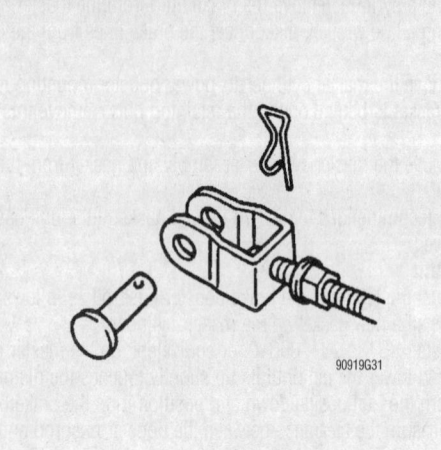

Fig. 12 Remove the clip to slide the clevis pin out of the pedal clevis

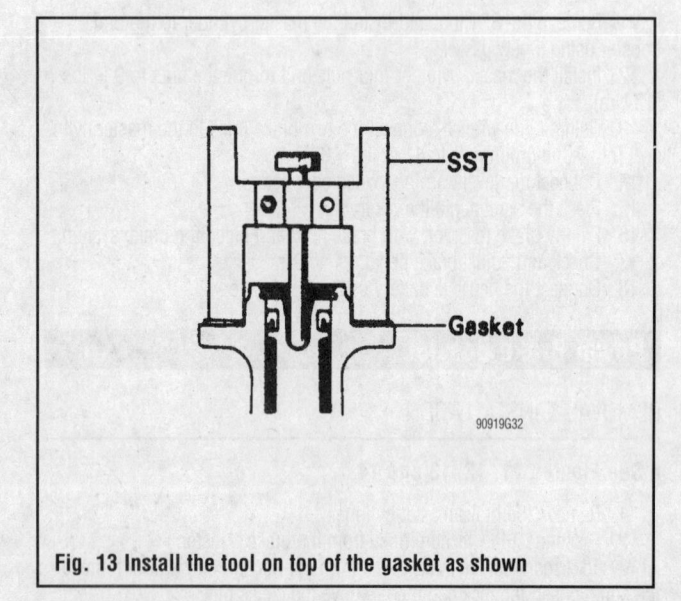

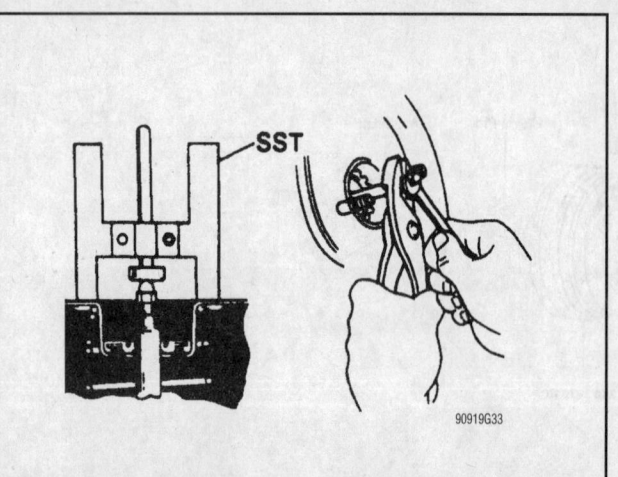

Fig. 13 Install the tool on top of the gasket as shown

Fig. 14 Set the tool on the gasket, then lower the pin until its tip slightly touches the piston

4. Remove the 4 mounting nuts, clevis and extract the booster from the firewall. Discard the gasket.

**To install:**

5. Position a new gasket and install the booster to the firewall, secure the retaining nuts to 9 ft. lbs. (13 Nm).
6. Install the clevis pin to the clevis through the brake pedal and secure the pin with the clip.
7. Adjust the length of the booster pushrod:
   a. Install the gasket for the master cylinder.
   b. Set the push pin SST 09737–00010 or equivalent, on the gasket and lower the pin until its tip slightly touches the piston.
   c. Turn the tool upside down, and position it on the booster.
   d. Measure the clearance between the booster pushrod and pin head of the tool. Clearance should be 0 inch (0mm).
   e. Adjust the booster pushrod length until the pushrod lightly touches the pin head.

➡ **When adjusting the pushrod, depress the brake pedal so that the rod sticks out.**

8. Install the master cylinder.
9. Connect the vacuum hose to the booster.
10. Fill the brake master cylinder reservoir with brake fluid and then bleed the brake system.
11. Check for fluid leakage.
12. Do an operational test.

## Proportioning Valve

### REMOVAL & INSTALLATION

♦ See Figure 15

1. Disconnect the brake lines from the valve body.
2. Remove the locknut and disconnect the spring from the lower control arm.
3. Remove the 2 mounting bolts and extract the LSP and BV assembly.

**To install:**

4. Attach the valve assembly to the vehicle and tighten the bolts to 14 ft. lbs. (19 Nm).
5. Position the spring on the lower control arm and set the length with the adjusting nut. The initial set length should be 1.18 inch (30mm). Tighten the assembly to 9 ft. lbs. (13 Nm).
6. Connect the brake lines and secure each one to 11 ft. lbs. (15 Nm).

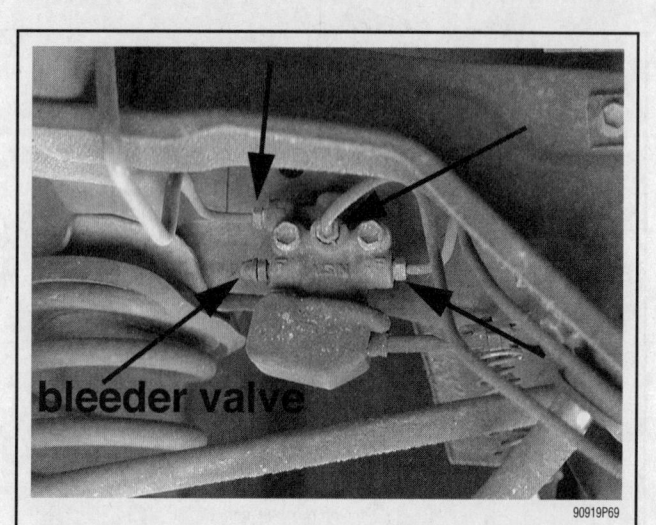

Fig. 15 A proportioning valve has several brake lines leading into it

# Brakes 9-7

7. Fill the brake master cylinder with fresh brake fluid, then bleed the brake system.
8. Check and adjust the fluid pressure.
9. Test driver the vehicle.

## FLUID PRESSURE ADJUSTMENT

▶ See Figures 16 thru 24

1. Set the vehicle unladen.
2. Measure the rear axle load and note the value.
3. Set the rear axle load. Standard load is 2028 lbs. (920 kg).
4. Install a Load Sensing Proportioning gauge (SST 09709–29017) and bleed the air from the system.
5. Raise the front brake pressure to the following specifications and check the pressure of the rear brakes.

➡ The brake pedal should not be depressed twice and returned while setting to the specified pressure.

6. Read the value of the rear pressure 2 seconds after adjusting the specified fluid pressure.

Fig. 18 Place the vehicle without a load and measure the rear axle load

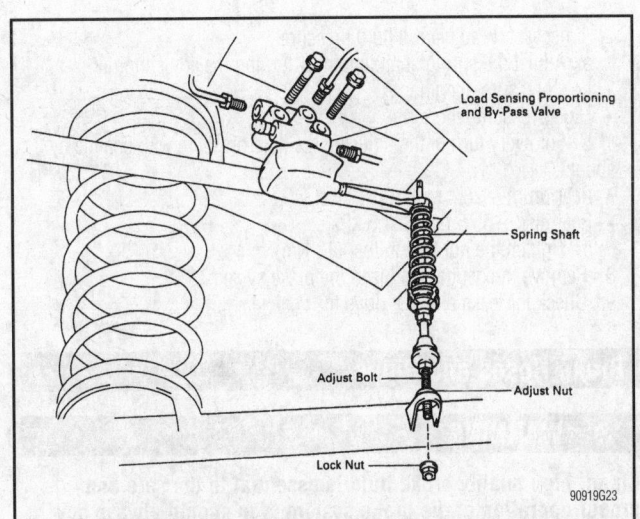

Fig. 16 The Load Sensing Proportioning and By-Pass valve with adjuster is located near the rear axle of the vehicle

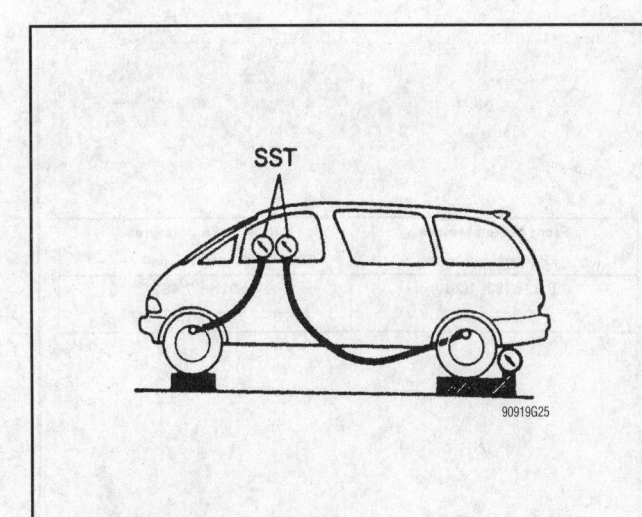

Fig. 19 Attach brake pressure gauges to the front and rear brakes, then bleed the lines

| Front brake pressure kPa (kgf/cm², psi) | Rear brake pressure kPa (kgf/cm², psi) |
|---|---|
| 9,807 (100, 1,422) | 5,728 – 6,708 (58.4 – 68.4, 831 – 971) |

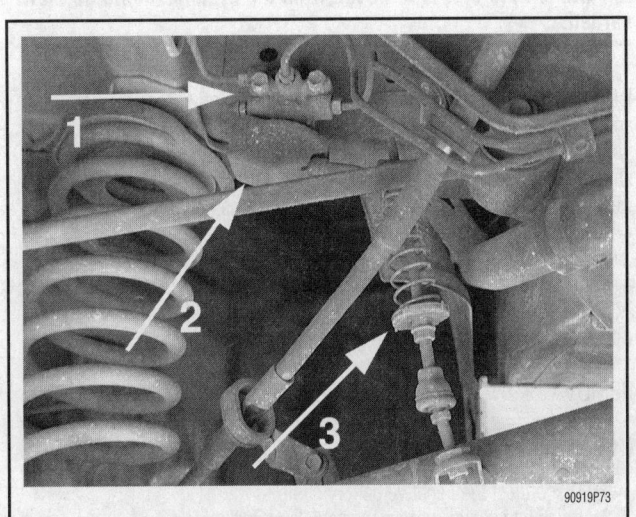

Fig. 17 Load sensing proportioning valve (1), by-pass valve (2) and load sensing spring (3)

Fig. 20 Rear pressure with rear drum brakes

## 9-8 BRAKES

| Front brake pressure<br>kPa (kgf/cm², psi) | Rear brake pressure<br>kPa (kgf/cm², psi) |
|---|---|
| 8,826 (90, 1,280) | 6,659 – 7,639<br>(67.9 – 77.9, 966 – 1,108) |

Fig. 21 Rear pressure with rear disc brakes and without ABS

| Front brake pressure<br>kPa (kgf/cm², psi) | Rear brake pressure<br>kPa (kgf/cm², psi) |
|---|---|
| 8,826 (90, 1,280) | 6,502 – 7,482<br>(66.3 – 76.3, 943 – 1,085) |

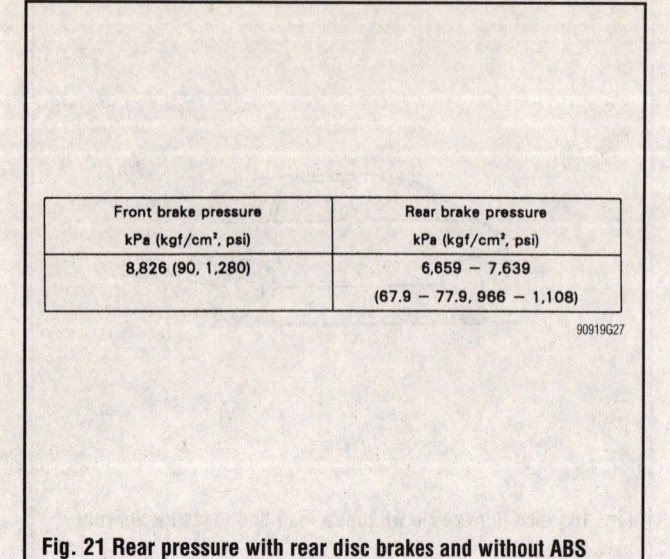

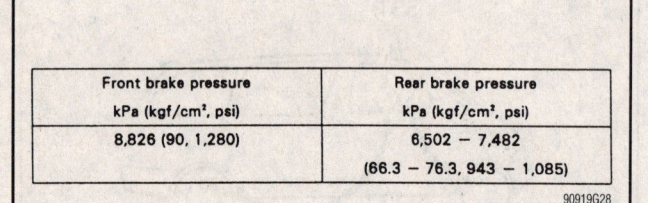

Fig. 22 Rear pressure with rear disc brakes and ABS

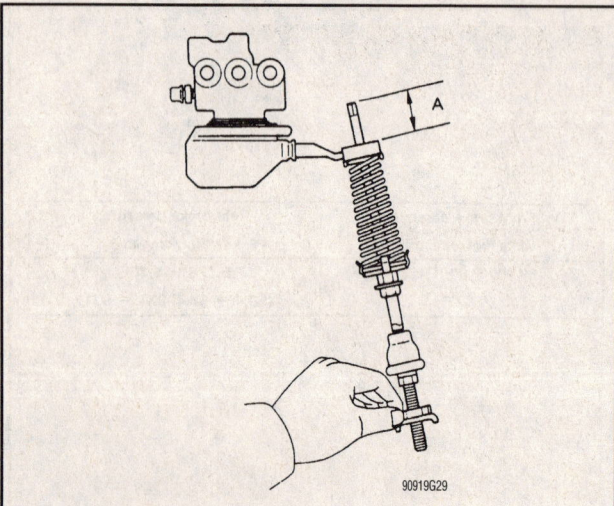

Fig. 23 Turning the adjusting nut to lengthen or shorten the pressure

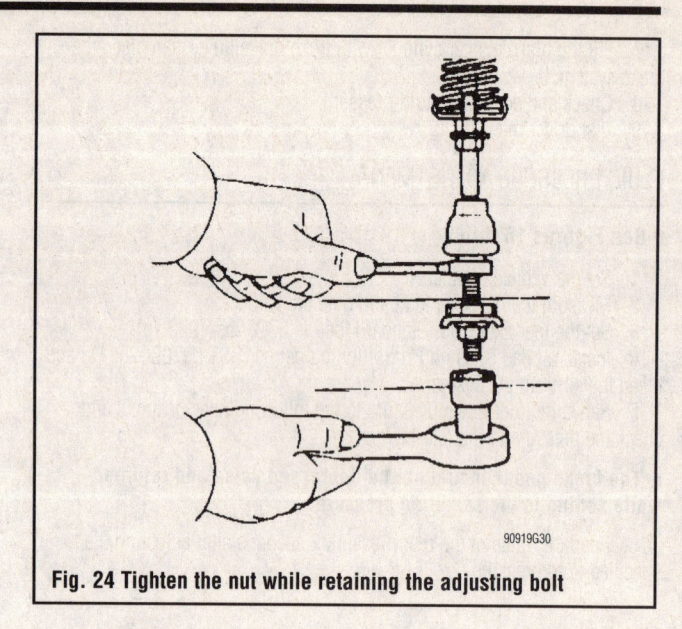

Fig. 24 Tighten the nut while retaining the adjusting bolt

7. If necessary, adjust the fluid pressure:
   a. Adjust the spring shaft length by turning the adjusting nut.
   - Low pressure–lengthen A
   - High pressure–shorten A
   b. For every turn of the adjuster, the fluid pressure with change by about:
   - Rear drum—28.4 psi (196.1 kPa)
   - Rear disc—55.5 psi (381.5 kPa)
   c. Tighten the nut to 9 ft. lbs. (13 Nm).
8. Remove the gauge and bleed the brake system.
9. Check for leaks and test drive the vehicle.

### Brake Hoses and Pipes

**✲✲ WARNING**

**Clean, high quality brake fluid is essential to the safe and proper operation of the brake system. You should always buy the highest quality brake fluid that is available. If the brake fluid becomes contaminated, drain and flush the system, then refill the master cylinder with new fluid. Never reuse any brake fluid. Any brake fluid that is removed from the system should be discarded.**

Metal lines and rubber brake hoses should be checked frequently for leaks and external damage. Metal lines are particularly prone to crushing and kinking under the vehicle. Any such deformation can restrict the proper flow of fluid and therefore impair braking at the wheels. Rubber hoses should be checked for cracking or scraping; such damage can create a weak spot in the hose and it could fail under pressure.

Any time the lines are removed or disconnected, extreme cleanliness must be observed. Clean all joints and connections before disassembly (use a stiff bristle brush and clean brake fluid); be sure to plug the lines and ports as soon as they are opened. New lines and hoses should be flushed clean with brake fluid before installation to remove any contamination.

REMOVAL & INSTALLATION

▶ See Figures 25 thru 36

1. Disconnect the negative battery cable.
2. Raise and safely support the vehicle on jackstands.
3. Remove any wheel and tire assemblies necessary for access to the particular line you are removing.

# BRAKES 9-9

Fig. 25 Use a brush to clean the fittings of any debris

Fig. 26 Remove any clips retaining the hoses

Fig. 27 A good line wrench is necessary for brake line removal

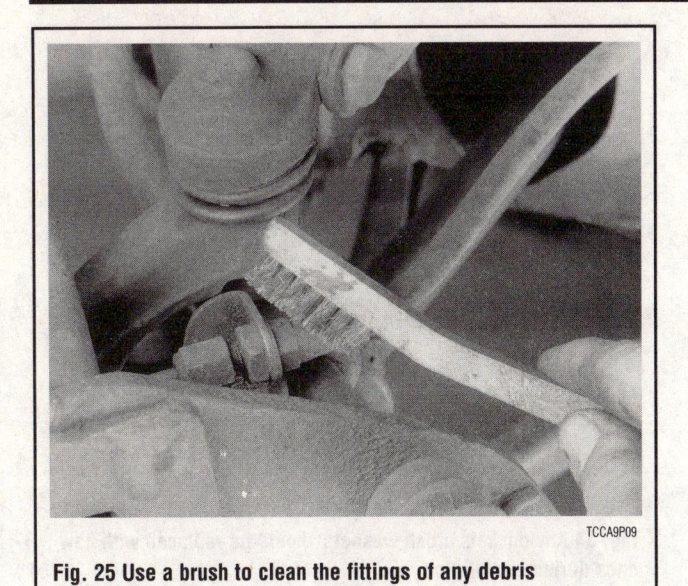

Fig. 28 Inspect the hose threads and pipe ends when they are separated

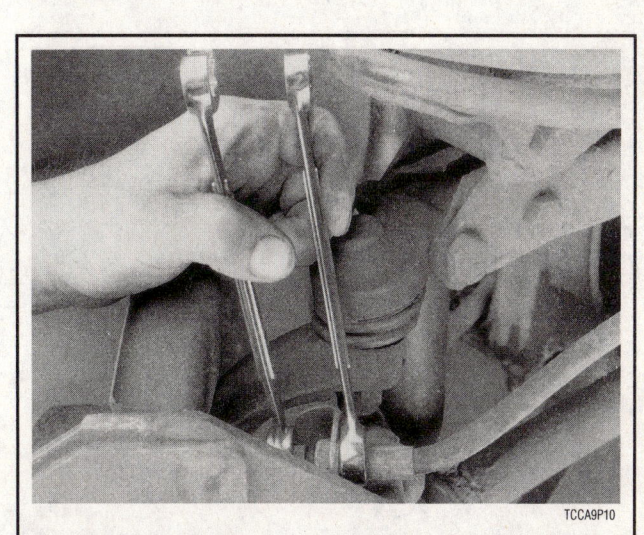

Fig. 29 Use two wrenches to loosen the fitting. If available, use flare nut type wrenches

Fig. 30 A single bolt holds the hose to the caliper

# 9-10 BRAKES

Fig. 31 Remove this bolt . . .

Fig. 32 . . . fluid may spew out of the orifice when loosened . . .

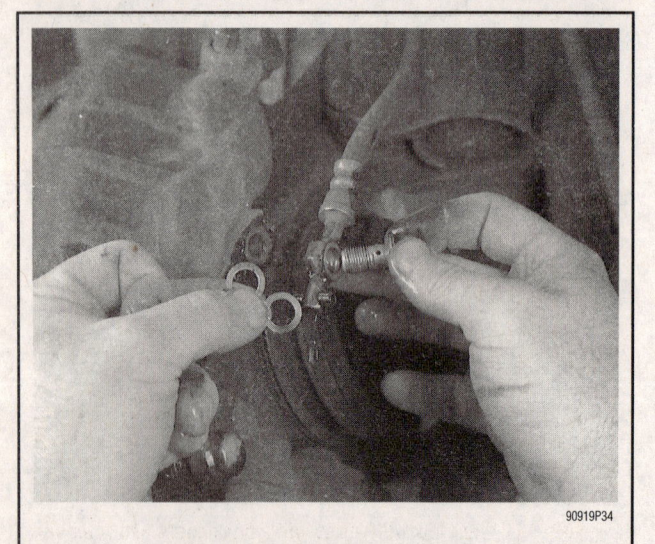

Fig. 33 . . . along with any gaskets and washers

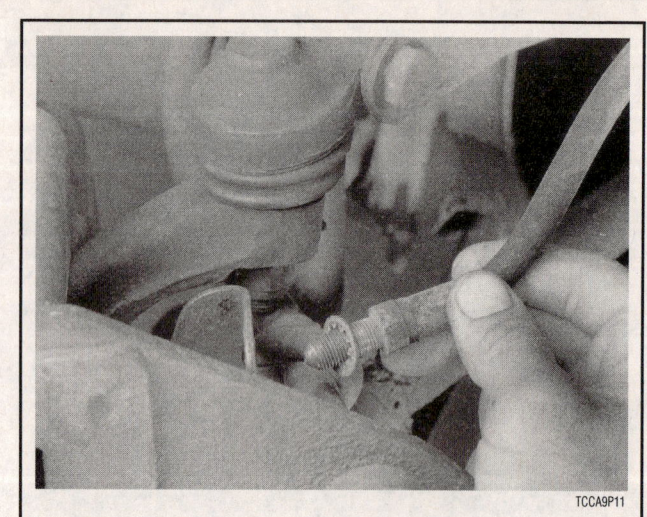

Fig. 34 Any gaskets/crush washers should be replaced with new ones during installation

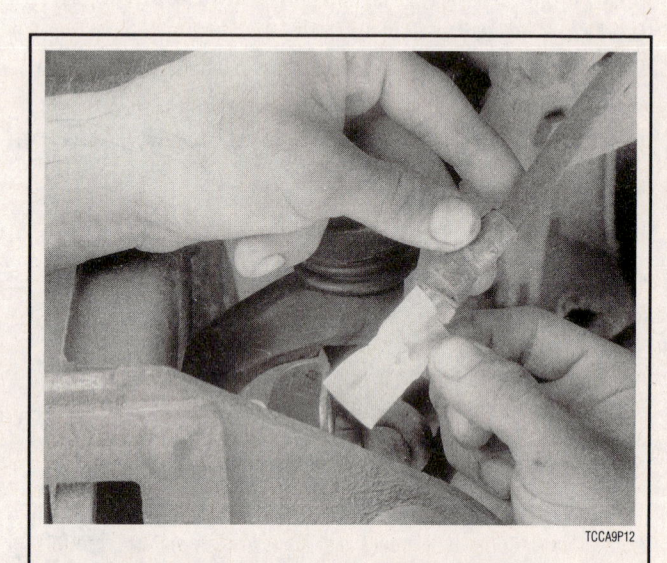

Fig. 35 Tape or plug the line to prevent contamination

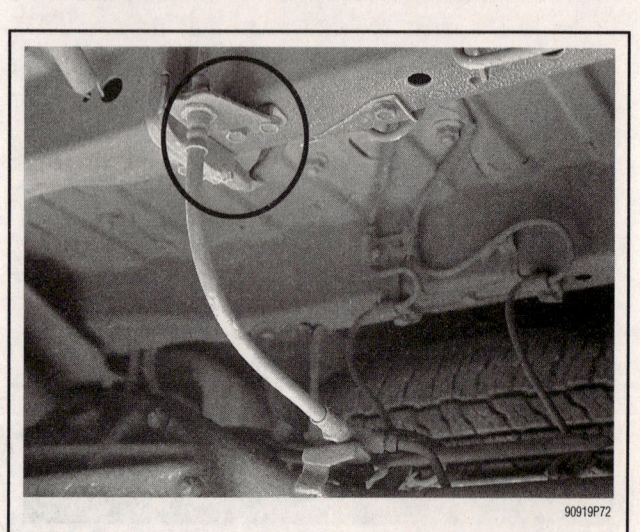

Fig. 36 Be sure all brackets and clips are in place during installation

# BRAKES 9-11

4. Thoroughly clean the surrounding area at the joints to be disconnected.
5. Place a suitable catch pan under the joint to be disconnected.
6. Using two wrenches (one to hold the joint and one to turn the fitting), disconnect the hose or line to be replaced.
7. Disconnect the other end of the line or hose, moving the drain pan if necessary. Always use a back-up wrench to avoid damaging the fitting.
8. Disconnect any retaining clips or brackets holding the line and remove the line from the vehicle.

➡ If the brake system is to remain open for more time than it takes to swap lines, tape or plug each remaining clip and port to keep contaminants out and fluid in.

### To install:
9. Install the new line or hose, starting with the end farthest from the master cylinder. Connect the other end, then confirm that both fittings are correctly threaded and turn smoothly using finger pressure. Make sure the new line will not rub against any other part. Brake lines must be at least 1/2 in. (13mm) from the steering column and other moving parts. Any protective shielding or insulators must be reinstalled in the original location.

### ✱✱ WARNING

Make sure the hose is NOT kinked or touching any part of the frame or suspension after installation. These conditions may cause the hose to fail prematurely.

10. Using two wrenches as before, tighten each fitting.
11. Install any retaining clips or brackets on the lines.
12. If removed, install the wheel and tire assemblies, then carefully lower the vehicle to the ground.
13. Refill the brake master cylinder reservoir with clean, fresh brake fluid, meeting DOT 3 specifications. Properly bleed the brake system.
14. Connect the negative battery cable.

## Bleeding the Brake System

### ✱✱ WARNING

Clean, high quality brake fluid is essential to the safe and proper operation of the brake system. You should always buy the highest quality brake fluid that is available. If the brake fluid becomes contaminated, drain and flush the system, then refill the master cylinder with new fluid. Never reuse any brake fluid. Any brake fluid that is removed from the system should be discarded.

It is necessary to bleed the hydraulic system any time the system has been opened or has trapped air within the fluid lines. It may be necessary to bleed the system at all four brakes if air has been introduced through a low fluid level or by disconnecting brake pipes at the master cylinder.

If a line is disconnected at one wheel only, generally only that brake needs bleeding. If lines are disconnected at any fitting between the master cylinder and the brake, the system served by the disconnected pipe must be bled.

### ✱✱ WARNING

Do not allow brake fluid to splash or spill onto painted surfaces; the paint will be damaged. If spillage occurs, flush the area immediately with clean water.

## MASTER CYLINDER

▸ See Figures 37, 38 and 39

If the master cylinder has been removed, the lines disconnected or the reservoir allowed to run dry, the cylinder must be bled before the lines are bled. To bleed the master cylinder:

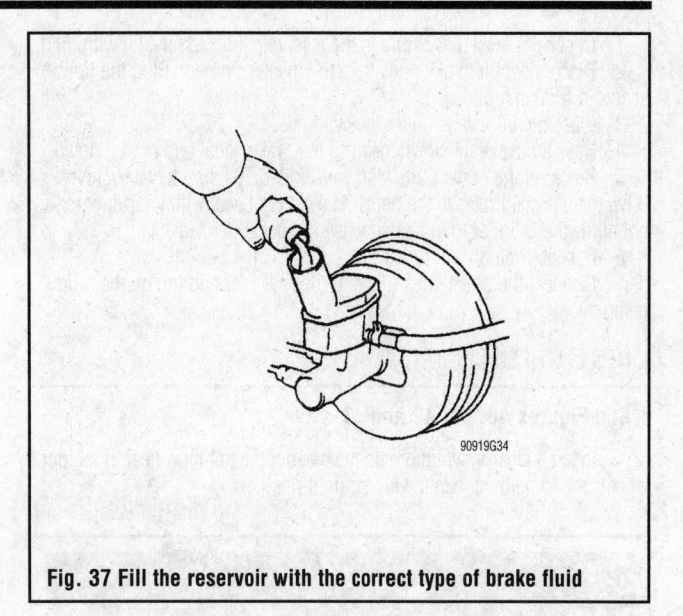

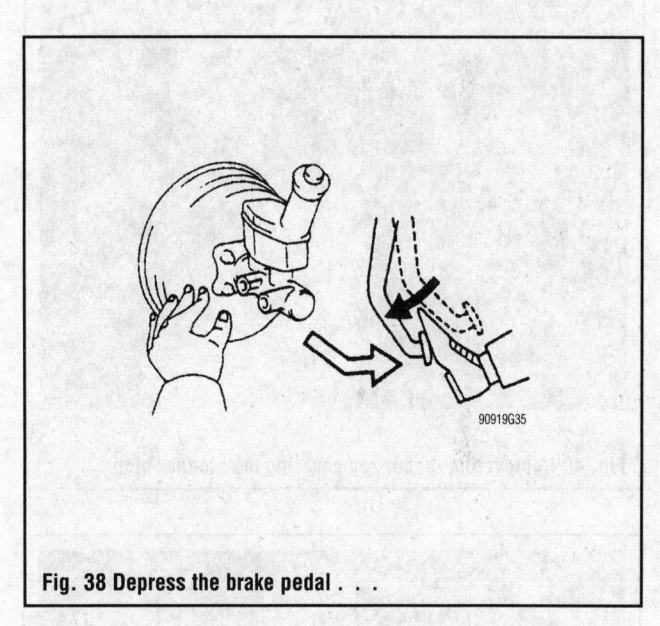

Fig. 37 Fill the reservoir with the correct type of brake fluid

Fig. 38 Depress the brake pedal . . .

Fig. 39 . . . then, block the ports with your fingers and release the pedal

## 9-12  BRAKES

1. Check the level of the fluid in the reservoir. If necessary, fill with fluid.
2. Disconnect the brake lines from the master cylinder. Plug the lines to keep dirt from entering.
3. Place a pan or rags under the cylinder.
4. Have an assistant slowly depress the brake pedal and hold it down.
5. Block off the outlet ports with your fingers. Be sure to wear gloves. Have the assistant release the pedal. Make a tight seal with your fingers; do not allow the cylinder to ingest air when the pedal is released.
6. Repeat three or four times.
7. Connect the brake lines to the master cylinder and top up the fluid reservoir.

### LINES & WHEEL CIRCUITS

▶ See Figures 40, 41, 42 and 43

1. Insert a clear vinyl tube onto the bleeder plug at the wheel. If all four wheels are to be bled, begin with the right rear.

2. Insert the other end of the tube into a jar which is half filled with brake fluid. Make sure the end is submerged in the fluid.
3. Have an assistant slowly pump the brake pedal several times. On the last pump, have the assistant hold the pedal fully depressed. While the pedal is depressed, open the bleeder plug until fluid starts to run out, then close the plug.

➡ If the brake pedal is pumped too fast, small air bubbles will form in the brake fluid which will be very difficult to remove.

4. Repeat this procedure until no air bubbles are visible in the hose. Close the bleeder port.

➡ Constantly replenish the brake fluid in the master cylinder reservoir, so that it does not run out during bleeding.

5. If bleeding the entire system, repeat the procedure at the left rear wheel, the right front wheel and the left front wheel in that order.
6. Bleed the load sensing proportioning and bypass valve.

Fig. 40 Remove the rubber cap covering the bleeder plug

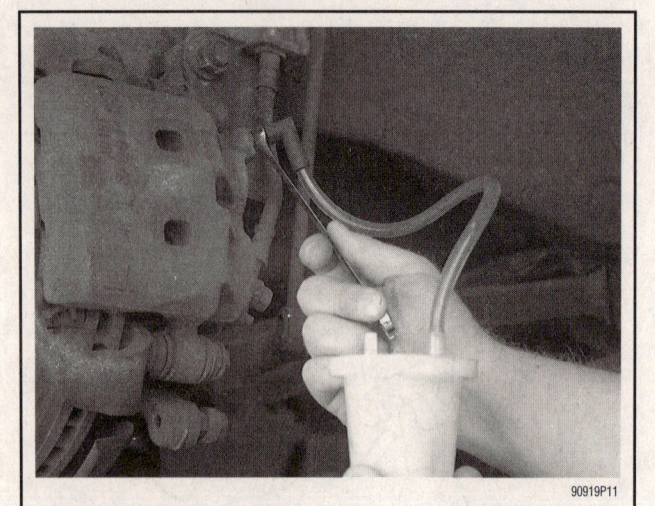

Fig. 41 Place a jar with clear tubing on the plug and begin the bleeding process

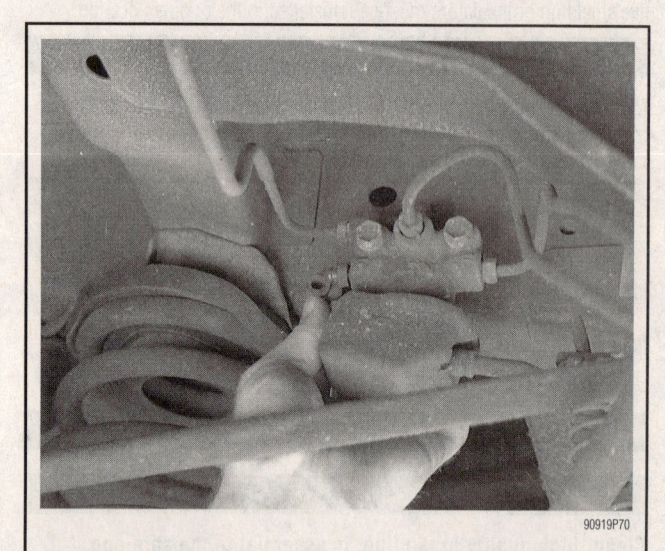

Fig. 42 Remove the bleeder plug on the proportioning valve . . .

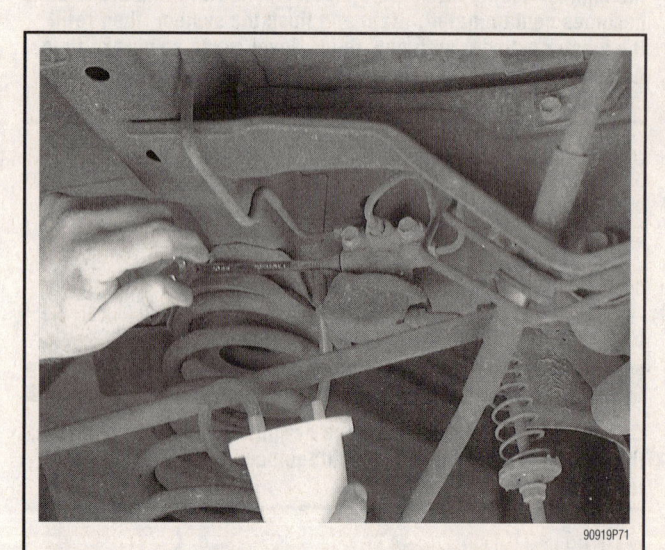

Fig. 43 . . . then bleed the valve

# Brakes  9-13

## DISC BRAKES

### ✽✽ CAUTION

Brake fluid contains polyglycol ethers and polyglycols. Avoid contact with the eyes and wash your hands thoroughly after handling brake fluid. If you do get brake fluid in your eyes, flush your eyes with clean, running water for 15 minutes. If eye irritation persists, or if you have taken brake fluid internally, IMMEDIATELY seek medical assistance.

### Brake Pads

#### REMOVAL & INSTALLATION

**Front**

♦ See Figures 44 thru 55

### ✽✽ CAUTION

Brake pads may contain asbestos, which has been determined to be a cancer causing agent. Never clean the brake surfaces with compressed air! Avoid inhaling any dust from any brake surfaces. When cleaning brake surfaces, use a commercially available brake cleaning fluid.

1. Raise and safely support the front of the vehicle.
2. Remove the front wheels and temporarily fasten the rotor disc with the hub nuts.

➡ Always replace the front disc pads as a set.

3. Hold the sliding pin on the bottom of the caliper and loosen the installation bolt.
4. Remove the lower installation bolt.
5. Lift up the caliper and suspend it securely. Do not remove the upper installation bolt.
6. Remove the following parts:
   a. The 2 anti squeal springs.
   b. The 2 brake pads.
   c. The 4 anti squeal shims.
   d. The 4 pad support plates.

To install:

7. Install the pad support plates.
8. Install a pad wear indicator plate to the pad. Install the anti-squeal shims and support plates to each pad.

➡ It recommended that a suitable anti-squeal compound (available at your local parts house) be applied to both sides of the inner anti-squeal shim.

9. Draw out a small amount of brake fluid from the brake reservoir. Press in the caliper piston with a suitable tool.
10. Press the brake piston in carefully so the boot will not become wedged.
11. Install the two pads so that the wear indicator plate is facing upward. Do not allow oil or grease to get in the rubbing face of the pads.
12. Lower and install the caliper. Tighten the sliding main pin to 27 ft. lbs. (36 Nm).

➡ When installing the sliding main pin, be careful that the plug installed in the torque plate does not come loose.

Fig. 45 . . . and remove it

Fig. 44 Loosen the installation bolt . . .

Fig. 46 Lift the caliper and suspend

# 9-14 BRAKES

Fig. 47 A hanger is a good tool to suspend a caliper out of the way

Fig. 48 Remove the two anti-squeal springs . . .

Fig. 49 Pull the front pad out with the clips and plates attached

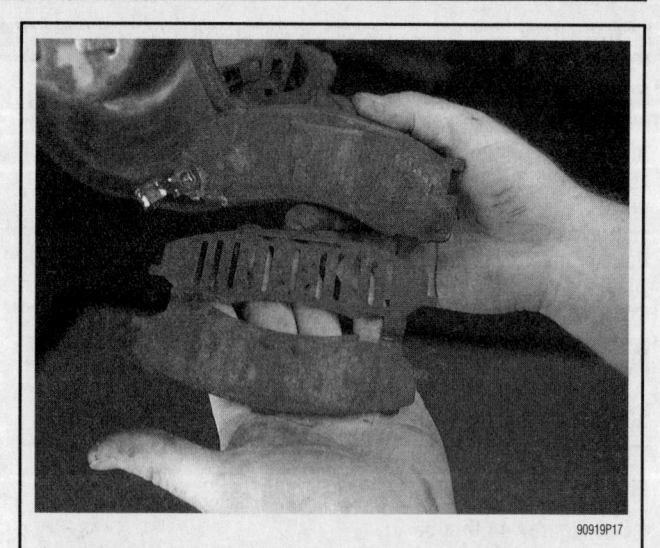

Fig. 50 There should be two plates on each brake pad

Fig. 51 Remove the springs also

Fig. 52 Next remove the rear pad

# BRAKES 9-15

13. Install the front wheels and lower the vehicle.
14. Check the fluid level in the master cylinder and add as necessary. Be sure to pump the brake pedal a few times before road testing the vehicle.

**Rear**

▶ See Figures 56 thru 63

### ❋❋ CAUTION

**Brake pads may contain asbestos, which has been determined to be a cancer causing agent. Never clean the brake surfaces with compressed air! Avoid inhaling any dust from any brake surfaces. When cleaning brake surfaces, use a commercially available brake cleaning fluid.**

1. Raise and safely support the rear of the vehicle.
2. Remove the rear wheels and temporarily fasten the rotor disc with the hub nuts.

➡**Always replace the rear disc pads as a set.**

3. Hold the sliding pin on the bottom of the caliper and loosen the installation bolt.

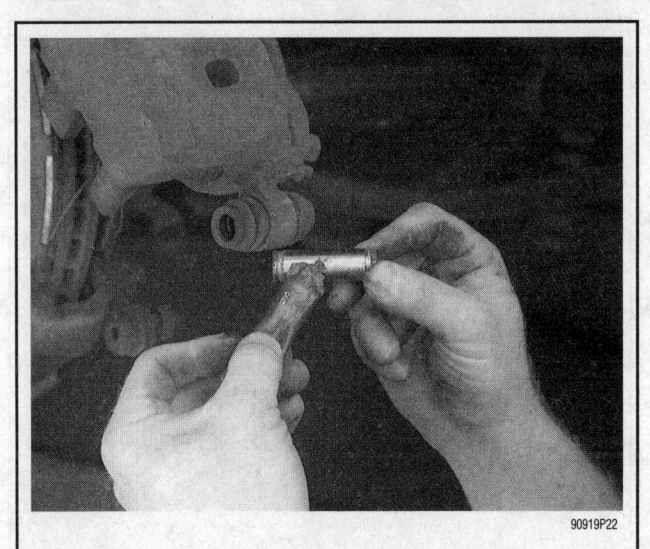

Fig. 53 Lubricate the sliding pin . . .

Fig. 54 . . . and springs as needed for installation of the pads

Fig. 55 Compress the pistons to install the brake pads

Fig. 56 Remove the lower installation bolt on the rear brake caliper

Fig. 57 Lift the caliper and . . .

# 9-16 BRAKES

Fig. 58 . . . support it with a cord or hanger wire

Fig. 61 Compress the piston to install the pads

Fig. 59 Remove the pads with shims . . .

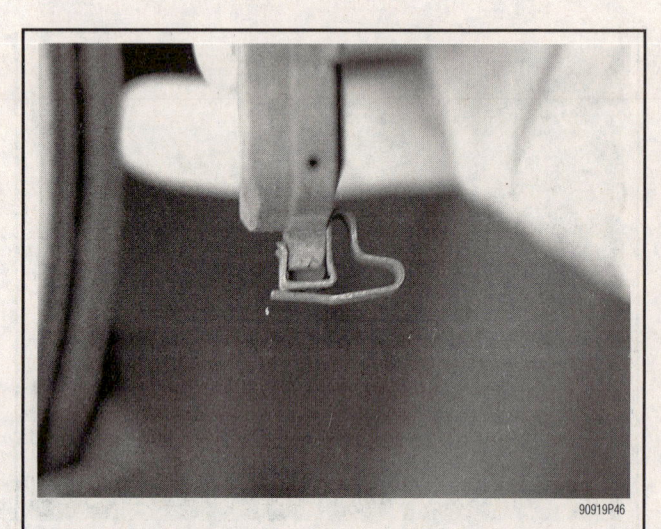

Fig. 62 Be sure the clips are positioned on the new pads correctly

Fig. 60 . . . and clips

Fig. 63 Insert the pads with the correct side facing the rotor surface

# BRAKES  9-17

4. Remove the lower installation bolt.
5. Lift up the caliper and suspend it securely. Do not remove the upper installation bolt.
6. Remove the following parts:
   a. The 2 anti squeal springs.
   b. The 2 brake pads.
   c. The 4 anti squeal shims.
   d. The 4 pad support plates.

**To install:**

7. Install the pad support plates.
8. Install a pad wear indicator plate to the pad. Install the anti-squeal shims and support plates to each pad.

➡ It recommended that a suitable anti-squeal compound (available at your local parts house) be applied to both sides of the inner anti-squeal shim.

9. Draw out a small amount of brake fluid from the brake reservoir. Press in the caliper piston with a suitable tool.
10. Press the brake piston in carefully so the boot will not become wedged.
11. Install the two pads so that the wear indicator plate is facing upward. Do not allow oil or grease to get in the rubbing face of the pads.
12. Lower and install the caliper. Tighten the sliding main pin to 18 ft. lbs. (25 Nm).

➡ When installing the sliding main pin, be careful that the plug installed in the torque plate does not come loose.

13. Install the rear wheels and lower the vehicle.
14. Check the fluid level in the master cylinder and add as necessary. Be sure to pump the brake pedal a few times before road testing the vehicle.

## INSPECTION

▶ See Figure 64

The brake pads may be inspected without removal. With the front or rear end elevated and supported, remove the wheel(s). On front wheels, unlock the steering column lock and turn the wheel so that the brake caliper is out from under the fender.

View the pads, inner and outer, through the cut-out in the center of the caliper. Remember to look at the thickness of the pad friction material (the part that actually presses on the disc) rather than the thickness of the backing plate which does not change with wear.

Keep in mind that you are looking at the profile of the pad, not the whole thing. Brake pads can wear on a taper which may not be visible through the window. It is also not possible to check the contact surface for cracking or scoring from this position. This quick check can be helpful only as a reference; detailed inspection requires pad removal.

## Brake Caliper

### REMOVAL & INSTALLATION

▶ See Figures 65 thru 71

1. Disconnect the negative battery cable from the battery.
2. Raise and support the vehicle safely.
3. Remove the wheels.
4. Disconnect the brake hose from the caliper by removing the union bolt and two gaskets. Plug the end of the hose to prevent loss of fluid.

➡ Have a pan ready to catch any spilt brake fluid.

5. Remove the bolts that attach the caliper to the torque plate.
6. Lift the bottom of the caliper up and remove the caliper assembly.

Fig. 65 Remove the upper caliper mounting bolt . . .

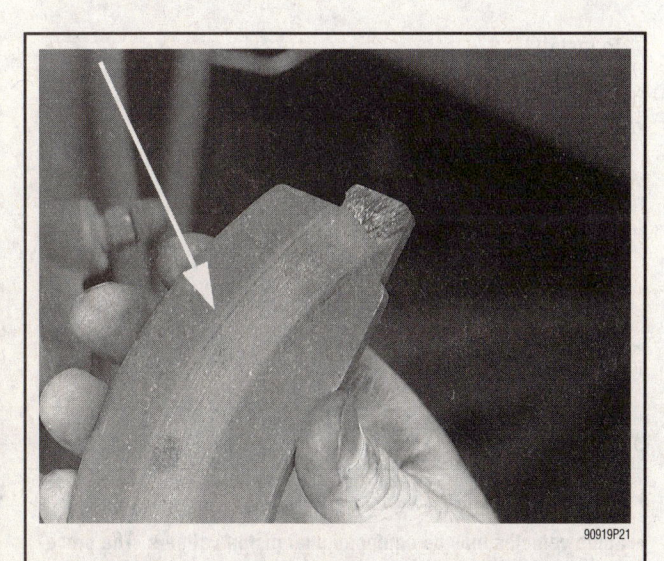

Fig. 64 Inspect the pads for wear when removed

Fig. 66 . . . then remove the bottom bolt

# 9-18 BRAKES

Fig. 67 The lower bolt is larger than the top

Fig. 68 The entire caliper should slide off the disc

Fig. 69 Two bolts hold the rear caliper

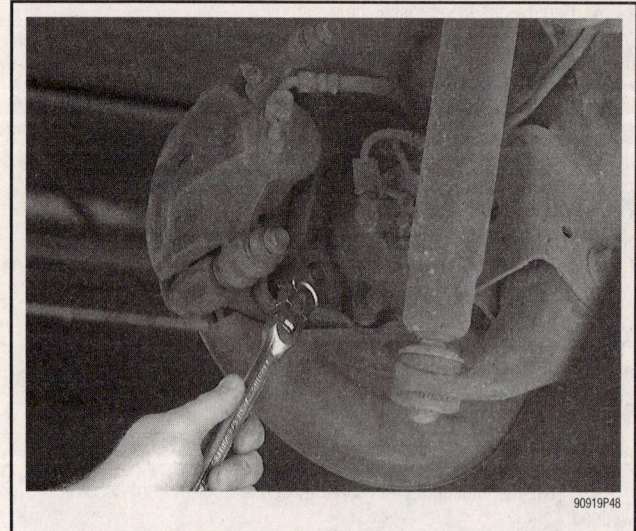

Fig. 70 Remove bolt the bolts . . .

Fig. 71 . . . then lift the rear caliper off the brake disc

To install:

7. Grease the caliper slides and bolts with lithium grease or equivalent. Install the caliper and secure with the bolts. Tighten the front caliper bolts to 27 ft. lbs. (36 Nm) and the rear to 18 ft. lbs. (25 Nm).

8. Reconnect the brake hose to the caliper, using two new washers. Make sure the flexible hose lock is securely in the lock hole of the caliper. Tighten the union bolt to 22 ft. lbs. (30 Nm). Also, verify that the brake hose is not twisted.

9. Fill the brake system to the proper level and bleed the brake system.

10. Install the tire and wheel assembly.

11. Top off the brake fluid level in the master cylinder. Check for leaks and proper brake operation.

12. Connect the negative battery cable to the battery.

## OVERHAUL

▶ See Figures 72 thru 79

➡Some vehicles may be equipped dual piston calipers. The procedure to overhaul the caliper is essentially the same with the exception of multiple pistons, O-rings and dust boots.

# Brakes 9-19

1. Remove the caliper from the vehicle and place on a clean workbench.

> ※ **CAUTION**
>
> NEVER place your fingers in front of the pistons in an attempt to catch or protect the pistons when applying compressed air. This could result in personal injury!

➡Depending upon the vehicle, there are two different ways to remove the piston from the caliper. Refer to the brake pad replacement procedure to make sure you have the correct procedure for your vehicle.

2. The first method is as follows:
   a. Stuff a shop towel or a block of wood into the caliper to catch the piston.
   b. Remove the caliper piston using compressed air applied into the caliper inlet hole. Inspect the piston for scoring, nicks, corrosion and/or worn or damaged chrome plating. The piston must be replaced if any of these conditions are found.
3. For the second method, you must rotate the piston to retract it from the caliper.

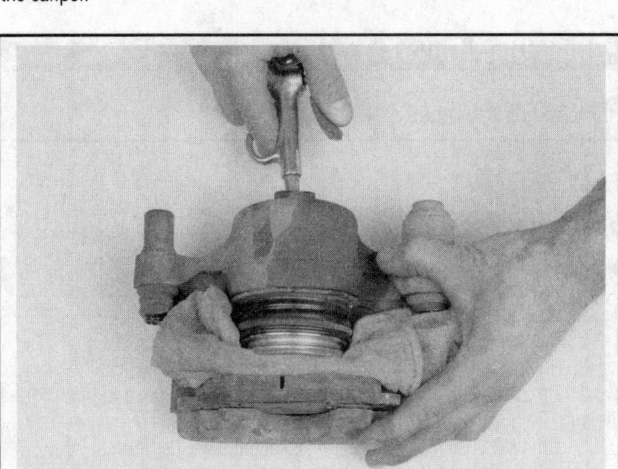

Fig. 72 For some types of calipers, use compressed air to drive the piston out of the caliper, but make sure to keep your fingers clear

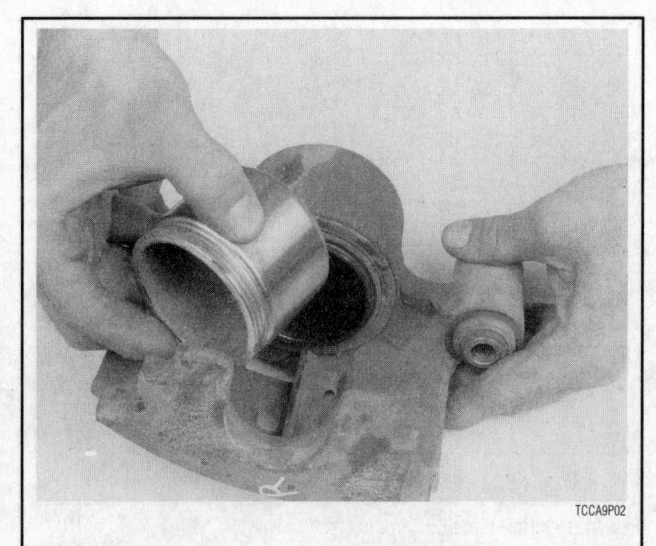

Fig. 73 Withdraw the piston from the caliper bore

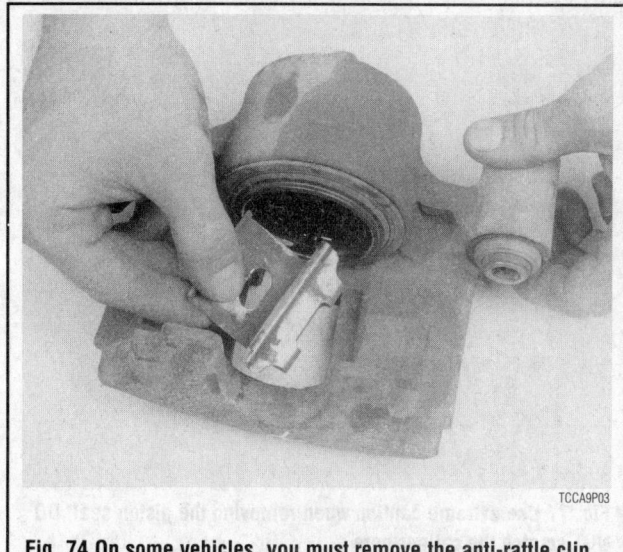

Fig. 74 On some vehicles, you must remove the anti-rattle clip

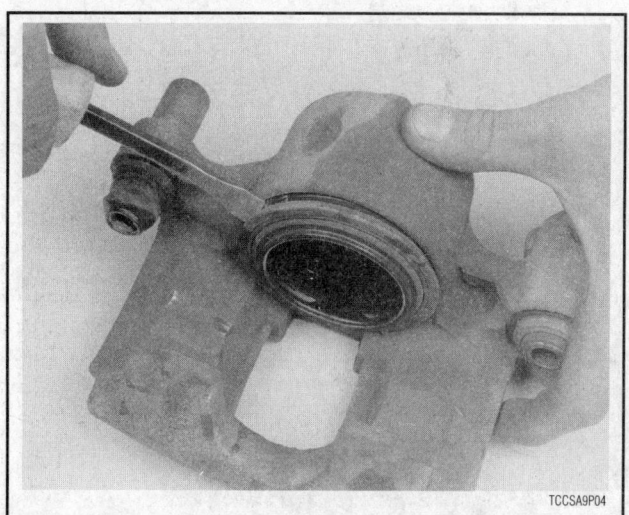

Fig. 75 Use a prytool to carefully pry around the edge of the boot . . .

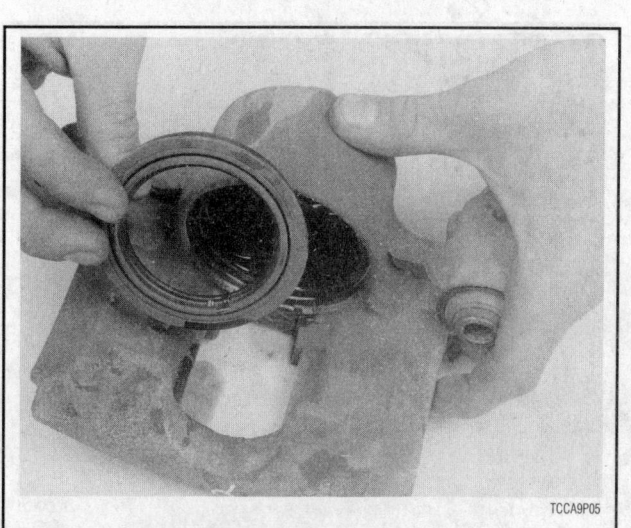

Fig. 76 . . . then remove the boot from the caliper housing, taking care not to score or damage the bore

# 9-20 BRAKES

4. If equipped, remove the anti-rattle clip.
5. Use a prytool to remove the caliper boot, being careful not to scratch the housing bore.
6. Remove the piston seals from the groove in the caliper bore.
7. Carefully loosen the brake bleeder valve cap and valve from the caliper housing.
8. Inspect the caliper bores, pistons and mounting threads for scoring or excessive wear.
9. Use crocus cloth to polish out light corrosion from the piston and bore.
10. Clean all parts with denatured alcohol and dry with compressed air.

**To assemble:**
11. Lubricate and install the bleeder valve and cap.
12. Install the new seals into the caliper bore grooves, making sure they are not twisted.
13. Lubricate the piston bore.
14. Install the pistons and boots into the bores of the calipers and push to the bottom of the bores.
15. Use a suitable driving tool to seat the boots in the housing.
16. Install the caliper in the vehicle.
17. Install the wheel and tire assembly, then carefully lower the vehicle.
18. Properly bleed the brake system.

## Brake Disc (Rotor)

### REMOVAL & INSTALLATION

**Front**

*1991–1994 MODELS*

▶ See Figures 80 and 81

1. Raise the vehicle and support it safely.
2. Remove the wheel and tire assembly.
3. Remove the brake caliper.
4. On 2WD vehicles, remove the grease cap, cotter pin and nut from the hub. Remove the rotor from the vehicle.
5. On 4WD vehicles, remove the locknut and washer from the free wheeling hub. Remove the adjusting nut and thrust washer. Remove the hub with disc together with the outer bearing.

**To install:**
6. Before installing the rotor, thoroughly clean and repack the wheel bearings, using MP grease. Coat inside the hub and cap with MP grease.

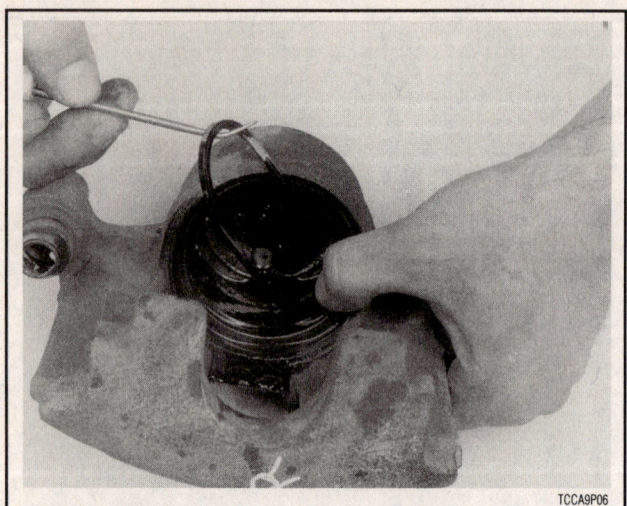

Fig. 77 Use extreme caution when removing the piston seal; DO NOT scratch the caliper bore

Fig. 78 Use the proper size driving tool and a mallet to properly seal the boots in the caliper housing

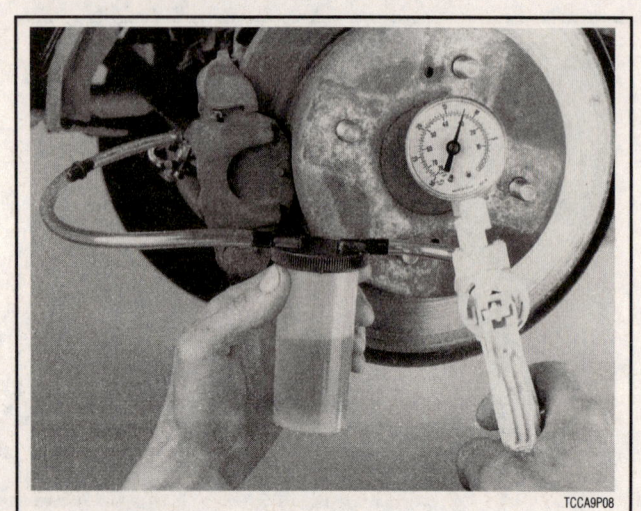

Fig. 79 There are tools, such as this Mighty-Vac, available to assist in proper brake system bleeding

Fig. 80 Remove and support the brake caliper

# BRAKES 9-21

Fig. 81 Pull the front rotor off the hub

7. Install a new bearing seal. Coat the seal lip with Multi Purpose grease.
8. On 2WD vehicles, install the rotor, outer bearing and thrust washer. Adjust the bearing preload.
9. On 4WD vehicles, install the free wheeling hub locknut and washer. Adjust the preload and check that the bearing has no play. Secure the lock nut by bending one of the lock washer teeth inward and the other lock washer teeth outward.
10. On 2WD vehicles, install the locknut, cotter pin and hub grease cap.
11. On 4WD vehicles, install the free wheeling hub or automatic locking hub.
12. Install the brake caliper.
13. Install the wheel and tire assembly.
14. Check and adjust the brake fluid level.
15. Road test the vehicle for proper operation.

### 1995–97 MODELS

1. Disconnect the negative battery cable to the battery.
2. Loosen the wheel lugs slightly, then raise and safely support the vehicle.
3. Remove the wheel(s) and temporarily install two of the wheel lug nuts.
4. Hold the sliding pin on the bottom with a wrench and loosen the installation bolt.
5. Remove the two installation bolts holding the caliper to the torque plate.
6. Remove the caliper from the torque plate and hang the caliper from a piece of wire. Do not disconnect the brake hose.

### ✴✴ WARNING

**Do not allow the caliper to hang freely from the vehicle. Always support the caliper with a wire from the vehicle.**

7. Unbolt and remove the torque plate.
8. Remove the two wheel nuts and pull the disc from the axle hub.

**To install:**

9. Position the new rotor disc onto the hub and reinstall the two wheel nuts temporarily.
10. Install the torque plate onto the vehicle. Tighten the two torque plate bolts to 65 ft. lbs. (88 Nm). Make sure the brake pads are seated correctly within the torque plate.
11. Install the caliper to the torque plate. Tighten the installation bolts to 27 ft. lbs. (36 Nm).
12. Remove the wheel lug nuts and install the wheels. Secure the wheel lugs.
13. Lower the vehicle and tighten the lug nuts. Before moving the vehicle, make sure to pump the brake pedal to seat the brake pads against the rotors.
14. Connect the negative battery cable to the battery.

### Rear

▶ See Figures 82 and 83

1. Loosen the rear lugnuts and raise and support the vehicle.
2. Remove the rear wheel.
3. Raise and support the caliper assembly.
4. If necessary, remove the adjuster rubber cover and adjust the parking brake to create some slack in the line.
5. Slide the rotor off the hub.

**To install:**

6. Position the disc onto the hub.
7. Lower the caliper and secure.
8. Install the rear wheel.
9. Lower the vehicle, install the lugnuts and tighten to 76 ft. lbs. (103 Nm).
10. Adjust the parking brake, if necessary.

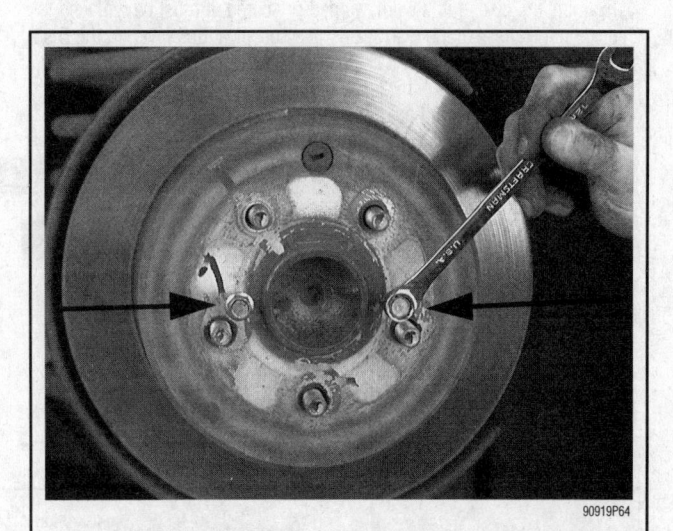

Fig. 82 Use two bolts to draw the bolts of the hub

Fig. 83 Slide the rotor off the rear axle hub

## 9-22 BRAKES

### INSPECTION

#### Front

▶ See Figure 84

Examine the disc. If it is worn, warped or scored, it must be replaced. Check the thickness of the disc against the specifications given in the Disc and Pad Specifications chart. If it is below specifications, replace it. Use a micrometer to measure the thickness.

The disc run-out should be measured before the disc is removed and again, after the disc is installed. Use a dial indicator mounted on a magnet type stand (attached to the shock absorber shaft) to determine runout. Position the dial so the stylus is 0.39 inch (10mm) from the outer edge of the rotor disc. The maximum allowable runout is 0.0028 inch (0.07mm). If runout exceeds the specification, replace the disc.

➡Be sure that the wheel bearing nut is properly tightened. If it is not, an inaccurate run-out reading may be obtained. If different run-out readings are obtained with the same disc, between removal and installation, this is probably the cause.

#### Rear

Examine the disc. If it is worn, warped or scored, it must be replaced. Check the thickness of the disc against the specifications given in the Disc and Pad Specifications chart. If it is below specifications, replace it. Use a micrometer to measure the thickness.

The disc run-out should be measured before the disc is removed and again, after the disc is installed. Use a dial indicator mounted on a magnet type stand (attached to the shock absorber shaft) to determine runout. Position the dial so the stylus is 0.39 inch (10mm) from the outer edge of the rotor disc. The maximum allowable runout 0.0039 inch (0.10mm). If the runout exceeds the specification, replace the disc.

Fig. 84 Check the rotor for scoring

## DRUM BRAKES

### ✱✱ CAUTION

Older brake pads or shoes may contain asbestos, which has been determined to be cancer causing agent. Never clean the brake surfaces with compressed air! Avoid inhaling any dust from any brake surface! When cleaning brake surfaces, use a commercially available brake cleaning fluid.

### Brake Drums

#### REMOVAL & INSTALLATION

▶ See Figures 85 and 86

1. Loosen the rear wheel lug nuts slightly. Release the parking brake.

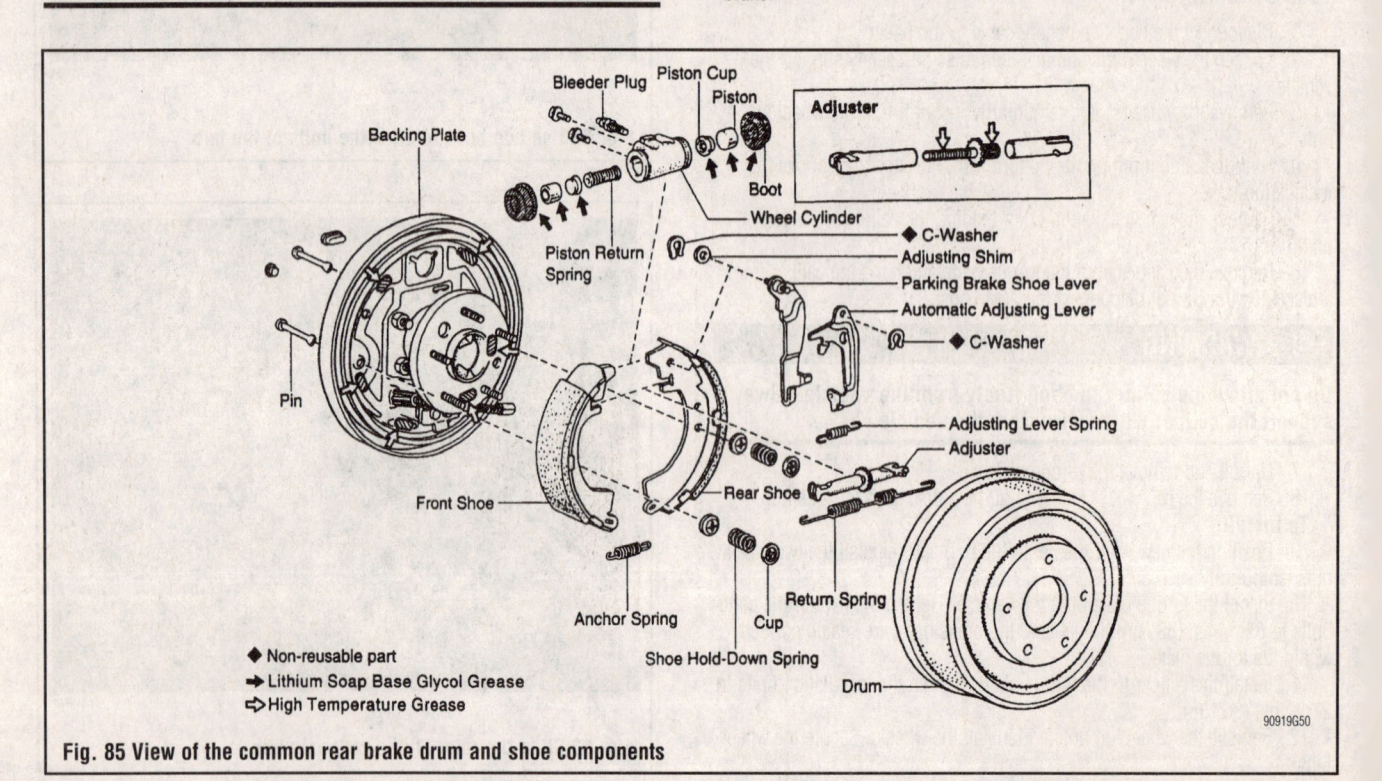

Fig. 85 View of the common rear brake drum and shoe components

# BRAKES 9-23

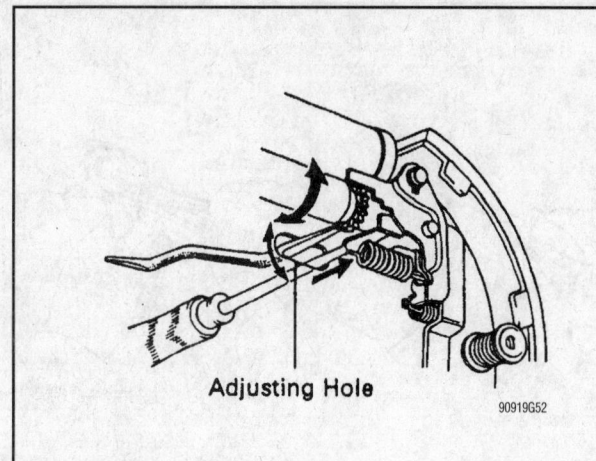

**Fig. 86 Insert a brake tool or screwdriver through the backing plate adjustment hole to reduce the slack of the shoes**

**Fig. 87 Place a caliper inside the drum to measure the diameter**

2. Block the front wheels, raise the rear of the car, and safely support it with jackstands.
3. Remove the lug nuts and the wheel.
4. Tap the drum lightly with a mallet to free the drum if resistance is felt. Sometimes brake drums are stubborn. If the drum is difficult to remove, perform the following:
    a. Remove the adjusting hole plug, then insert the end of a bent wire (a coat hanger will do nicely) through the hole in the brake drum and hold the automatic adjusting lever away from the adjuster.
    b. Reduce the brake shoe adjustment by turning the adjuster bolt with a brake adjuster tool. The drum should now be loose enough to remove without much effort.

**To install:**
5. Clean the drum and inspect it as detailed in this Section.
6. Install the brake drum and pull the parking brake lever all the way up until a clicking sound can no longer be heard.
7. Verify that the rear wheels will not turn. If the rear wheels turn, adjust the parking brake cable as necessary.
8. Release the parking brake and remove the brake drum. Measure the brake drum inside diameter and diameter of the brake shoes. Check that the difference between the diameters is the correct shoe clearance. Clearance is: 0.024 in. (6mm).
9. If the brake shoe clearance is not correct, adjust the brake shoes until the clearance is correct.
10. Reinstall the brake drum, install the wheel(s), and safely lower the vehicle. Retighten the lug nuts and pump the brake pedal before moving the vehicle.
11. Road test the vehicle for proper brake operation.

## INSPECTION

▶ See Figure 87

1. Clean the drum.
2. Inspect the drum for scoring, cracks, grooves and out-of-roundness. Replace the drum or have it "turned" at a machine or brake specialist shop, as required. Light scoring may be removed by dressing the drum with fine emery cloth.
3. Measure the inside diameter of the drum. A tool called a H-gauge caliper is used. See the Brake Specifications chart for your vehicle.

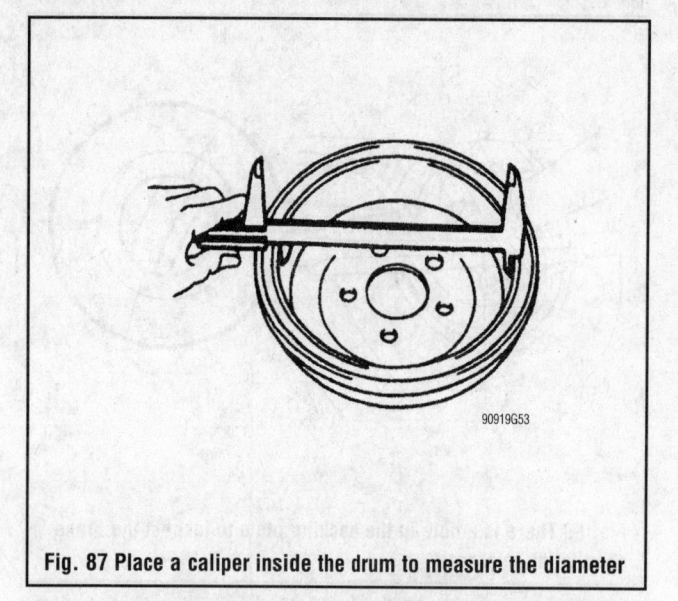

## Brake Shoes

### INSPECTION

▶ See Figures 88, 89, 90, 91 and 92

➡ When servicing drum brakes, only dissemble and assemble one side at a time, leaving the remaining side intact for reference.

1. Inspect all parts for rust and damage.
2. Measure the lining thickness. The minimum allowable thickness is 0.039 inch (1.0mm). If the lining does not meet the minimum specification, replace it.

➡ If one of the brake shoes needs to be replaced, replace all the rear shoes in order to maintain even braking.

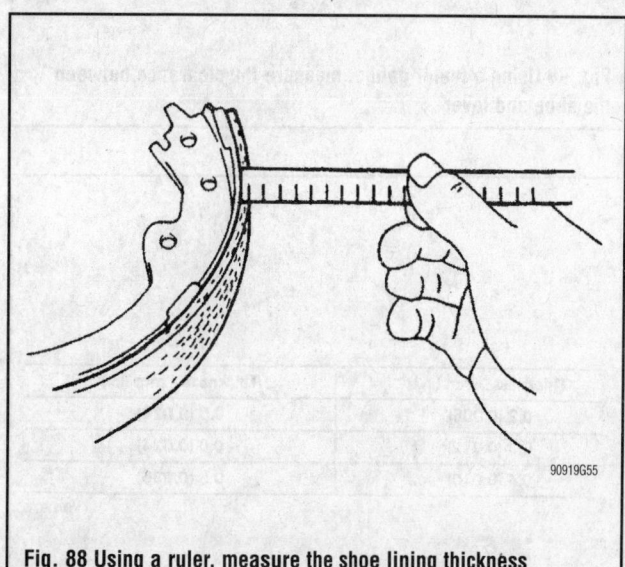

**Fig. 88 Using a ruler, measure the shoe lining thickness**

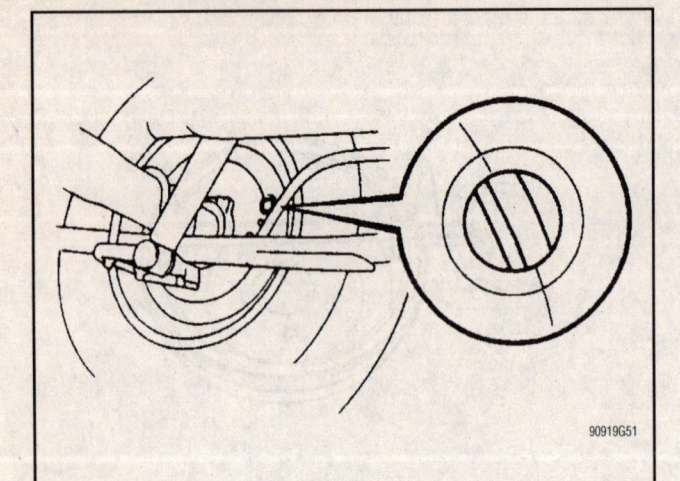

# 9-24 BRAKES

Fig. 89 There is a hole in the backing plate to inspect the brake shoe lining thickness

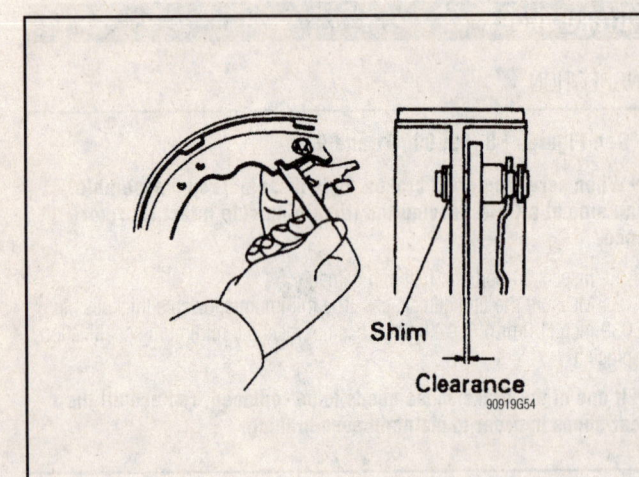

Fig. 90 Using a feeler gauge, measure the clearance between the shoe and lever

| Thickness mm (in.) | Thickness mm (in.) |
|---|---|
| 0.2 (0.008) | 0.5 (0.020) |
| 0.3 (0.012) | 0.6 (0.024) |
| 0.4 (0.016) | 0.9 (0.035) |

Fig. 91 C-washer/shims come in many sizes

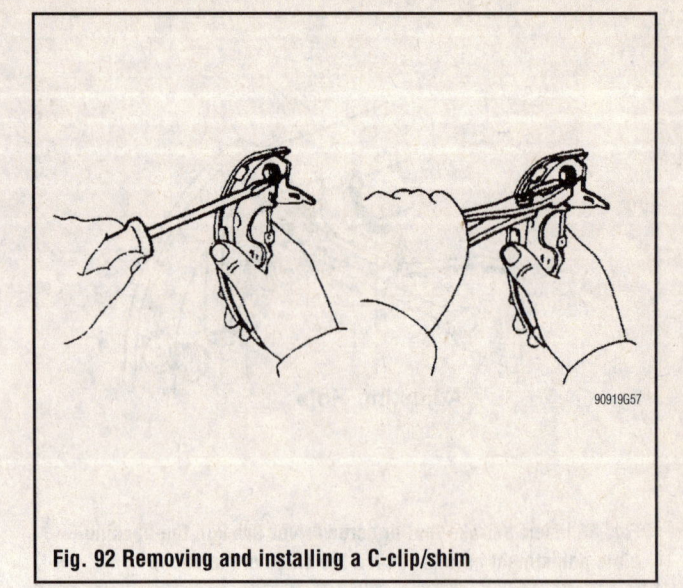

Fig. 92 Removing and installing a C-clip/shim

3. Measure inside diameter of the drum as detailed in this Section.
4. Place the shoe into the drum and check that the lining is in proper contact with the drum's surface. If the contact is improper, repair the lining with a brake shoe grinder or replace the shoe.
5. To measure the clearance between brake shoe and parking brake lever, temporarily install the parking brake and automatic adjusting levers onto the rear shoe, using a new C-washer/shim. Replace the shim with the correct size, check the chart. With a feeler gauge, measure the clearance between the shoe and the lever. The clearance should be 0.013 inch (0.35mm). If the clearance is not as specified, use a shim to adjust it. When the clearance is correct, stake the C-washer with pliers.

## REMOVAL & INSTALLATION

♦ See Figures 93, 94, 95, 96 and 97

➡When servicing drum brakes, only dissemble and assemble one side at a time, leaving the remaining side intact for reference.

1. Loosen the rear wheel lug nuts slightly. Release the parking brake.
2. Block the front wheels, raise the rear of the vehicle, and safely support it with jackstands.

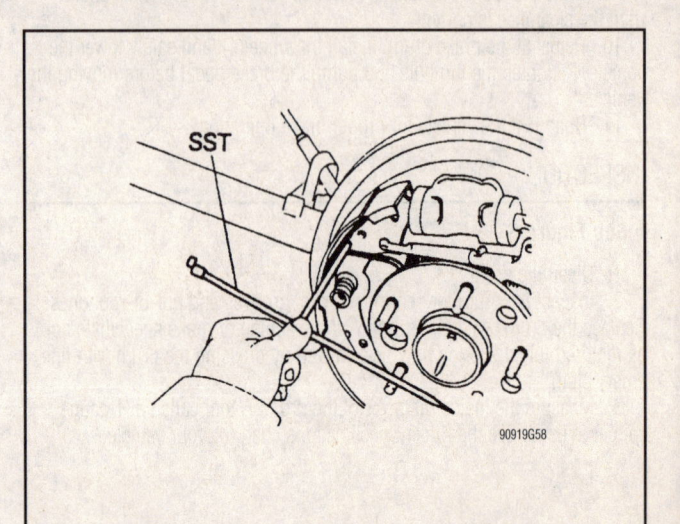

Fig. 93 Using a brake tool, remove the return spring from the front brake shoe

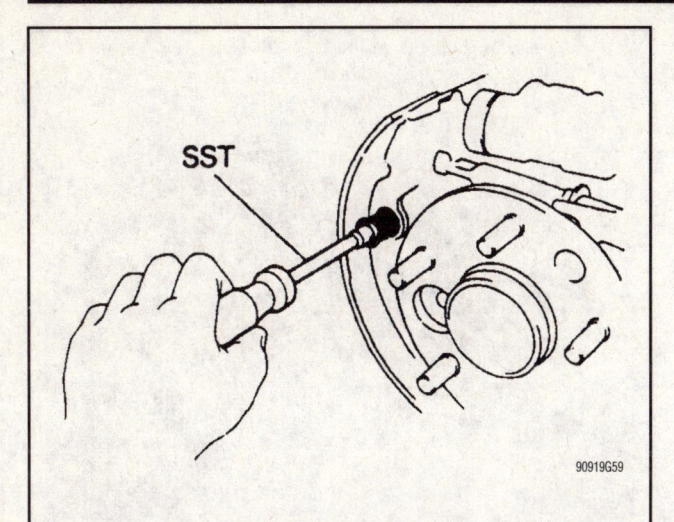

# BRAKES 9-25

**Fig. 94 The hold-down spring, 2 cups and pin are removed with a brake tool also**

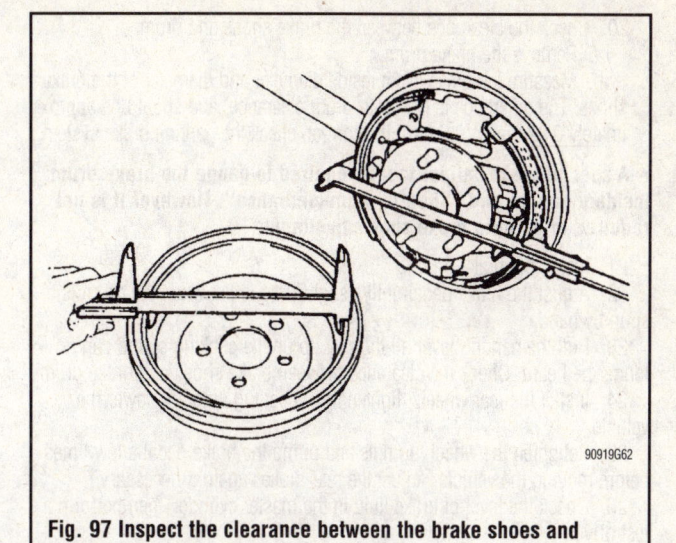

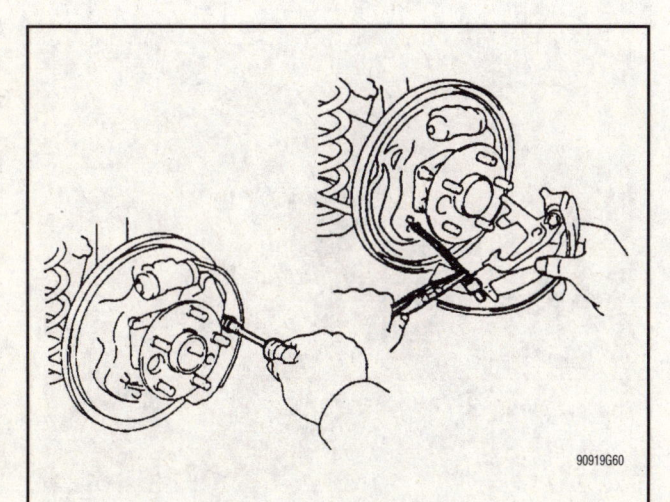

**Fig. 95 When removing the rear shoe, the brake cable will be attached, disconnect it**

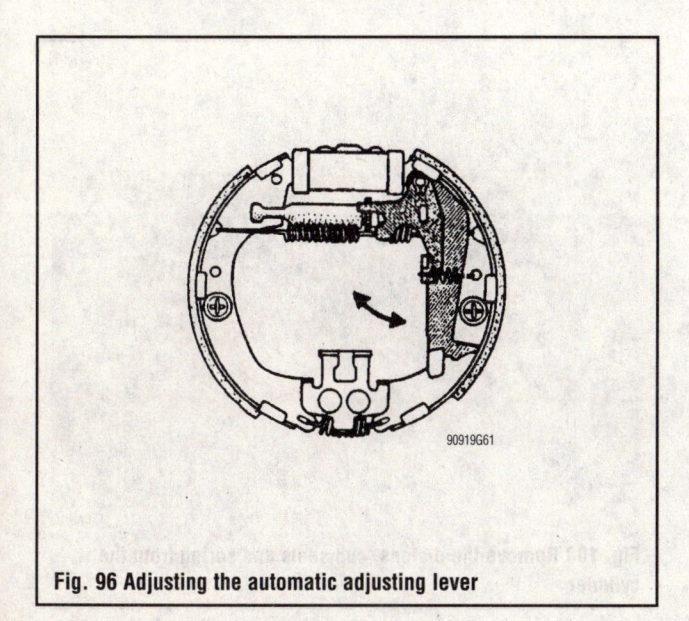

**Fig. 96 Adjusting the automatic adjusting lever**

**Fig. 97 Inspect the clearance between the brake shoes and drum using a caliper tool**

3. Remove the wheel lug nuts and the wheel.
4. Remove the brake drum.

➥**Do not depress the brake pedal once the brake drum has been removed.**

5. Carefully unhook the return spring from the leading (front) brake shoe.
6. Press the hold-down spring retainer in and turn the pin on the front brake shoe.
7. Remove the hold-down spring, retainers and the pin for the front brake shoe.
8. Pull out the brake shoe and unhook the anchor spring from the lower edge.
9. Remove the hold-down spring from the trailing (rear) shoe. Pull the shoe out with the adjuster, automatic adjuster assembly and springs attached. Disconnect the parking brake cable. Remove the tension/return and anchor springs from the rear shoe.
10. Unhook the adjusting lever spring from the rear shoe and then remove the automatic adjuster assembly.

**To install:**
11. Inspect the shoes for signs of unusual wear or scoring.
12. Check the wheel cylinder for any sign of fluid seepage or frozen pistons.
13. Clean and inspect the brake backing plate and all other components. Check that the brake drum inner diameter is within specified limits. Lubricate the backing plate at the positions the brakes come in contact with the backing plate. Also lubricate the anchor plate.
14. Mount the automatic adjuster assembly onto a new rear brake shoe.
15. Connect the parking brake cable to the rear shoe, then install the automatic adjusting lever, spring and E-ring. Position the rear shoe so the lower end rides in the anchor plate and the upper end is against the boot of the wheel cylinder.
16. Install the pin and the hold-down spring. Press the retainer down over the pin and rotate the pin so the crimped edge is held by the retainer.
17. Place the front brake into position and install the anchor spring between the front and rear shoes. Stretch the spring enough so the front shoe will fit as the rear did. Install the hold-down spring, pin and retainer to the front brake shoe.
18. Connect the return spring to the front brake shoe.
19. Check the operation of the automatic adjuster mechanism:
   a. Apply the parking brake lever and verifying the adjusting bolt turns.
   b. Adjust the strut to where it is the shortest possible length.
   c. Install the brake drum.
   d. Apply the parking brake lever until the clicking sound can no longer be heard.

# 9-26 BRAKES

20. Check the clearance between the brake shoes and drum:
    a. Remove the brake drum.
    b. Measure the brake drum inside diameter and diameter of the brake shoes. The difference is "Shoe-to-drum clearance" and should be approximately 0.024 inch (0.6mm). If incorrect, check the parking brake system.

➡A special brake caliper tool is required to gauge the brake drum inside diameter and "Shoe-to-drum clearance". However it is not required to perform brake shoe adjustment.

21. Install the brake drum.
22. Adjust the brake pedal until a slight drag is felt when the drum is spun by hand.
23. Pull the parking lever all the way up until a clicking sound can no longer be heard. Check the clearance between brake shoes and brake drum.
24. Install the rear wheels, tighten the wheel lug nuts and lower the vehicle.
25. Retighten the wheel lug nuts and pump the brake pedal a few times before moving the vehicle. Adjust the rear brakes again if necessary.
26. Check the level of brake fluid in the master cylinder, then perform a test drive.

## ADJUSTMENTS

All models are equipped with self-adjusting rear drum brakes. Under normal conditions, adjustment of the rear brake shoes should not be necessary. However, if an initial adjustment is required insert the blade of a brake adjuster tool or a screw driver into the hole in the brake drum and turn the adjuster slowly. The tension is set correctly if the tire and wheel assembly will rotate approximately 3 times when spun with moderate force. Do not over adjust the brake shoes. Before adjusting the rear drum brake shoes, make sure emergency brake is in the OFF position, and all cables are free.

## Wheel Cylinders

### REMOVAL & INSTALLATION

1. Plug the master cylinder inlet to prevent hydraulic fluid from leaking. Raise and safely support the vehicle.

**✱✱ CAUTION**

Brake fluid contains polyglycol ethers and polyglycols. Avoid contact with the eyes and wash your hands thoroughly after handling brake fluid. If you do get brake fluid in your eyes, flush your eyes with clean, running water for 15 minutes. If eye irritation persists, or if you have taken brake fluid internally, IMMEDIATELY seek medical assistance.

2. Remove the brake drums and shoes.
3. Working from behind the backing plate, disconnect the hydraulic line from the wheel cylinder.
4. Unfasten the screws retaining the wheel cylinder and withdraw the cylinder.

**To install:**

5. Attach the wheel cylinder to the backing plate. Tighten the bolts to 7 ft. lbs. (10 Nm).
6. Connect the hydraulic line to the wheel cylinder and tighten it.
7. Install the brake shoes and drums. Make all the necessary adjustments.
8. Fill the master cylinder to the proper level with clean brake fluid bleed the brake system. Check the brake system for leaks.

### OVERHAUL

▶ See Figures 98 thru 107

Wheel cylinder overhaul kits may be available, but often at little or no savings over a reconditioned wheel cylinder. It often makes sense with

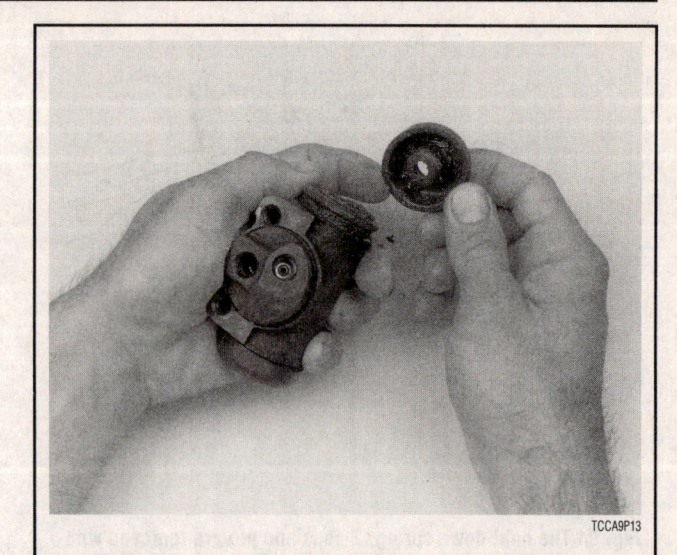

Fig. 98 Remove the outer boots from the wheel cylinder

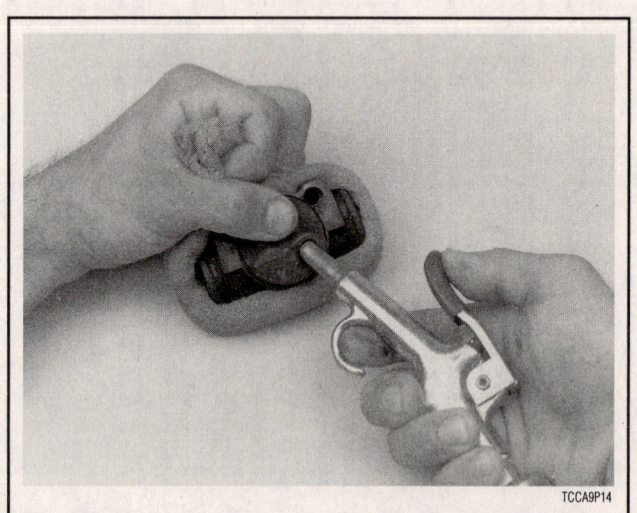

Fig. 99 Compressed air can be used to remove the pistons and seals

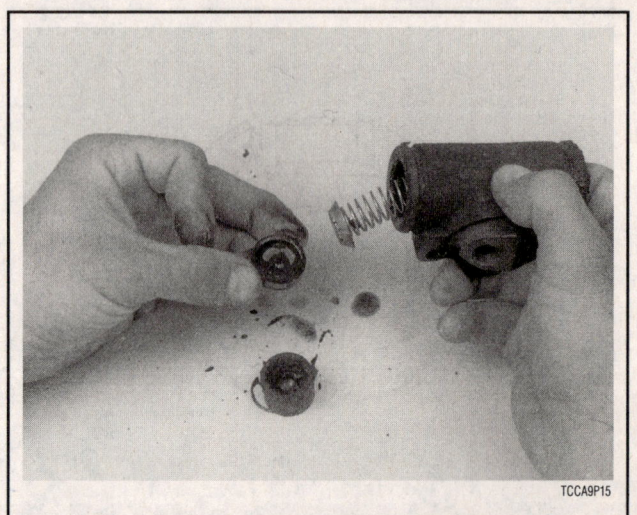

Fig. 100 Remove the pistons, cup seals and spring from the cylinder

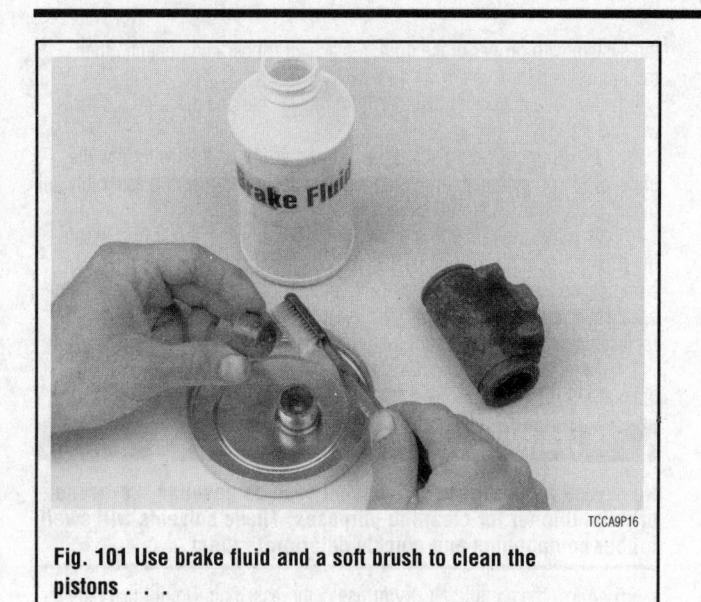

BRAKES **9-27**

Fig. 101 Use brake fluid and a soft brush to clean the pistons . . .

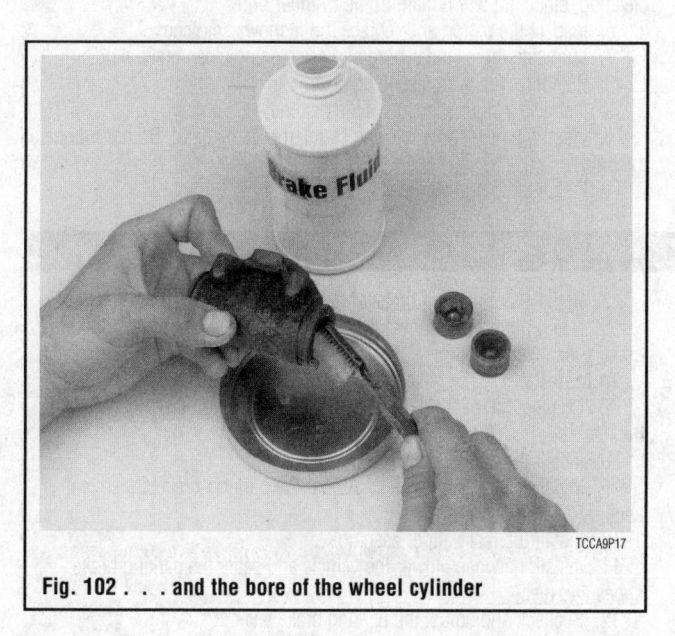

Fig. 102 . . . and the bore of the wheel cylinder

Fig. 103 Once cleaned and inspected, the wheel cylinder is ready for assembly

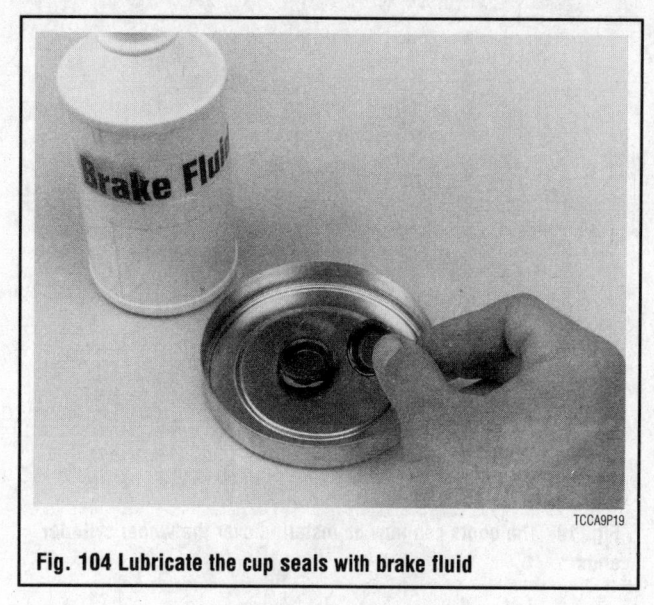

Fig. 104 Lubricate the cup seals with brake fluid

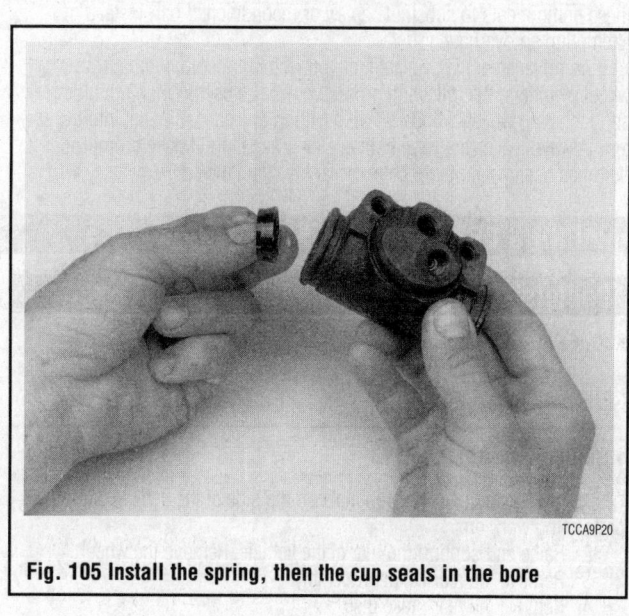

Fig. 105 Install the spring, then the cup seals in the bore

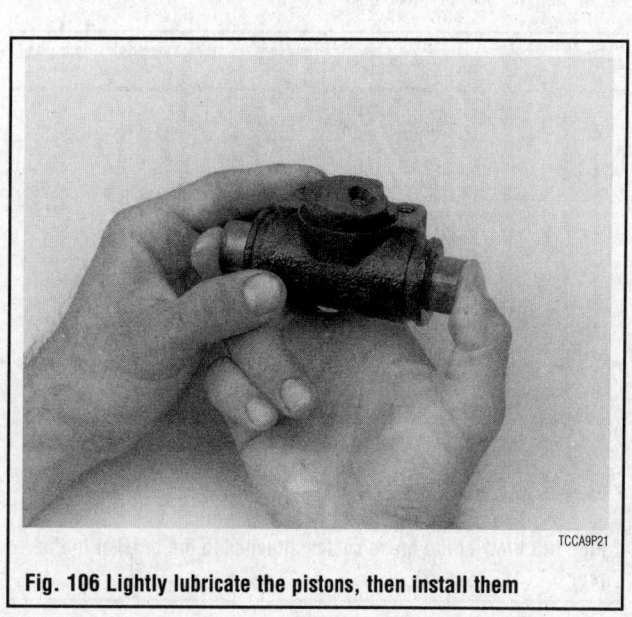

Fig. 106 Lightly lubricate the pistons, then install them

# 9-28 BRAKES

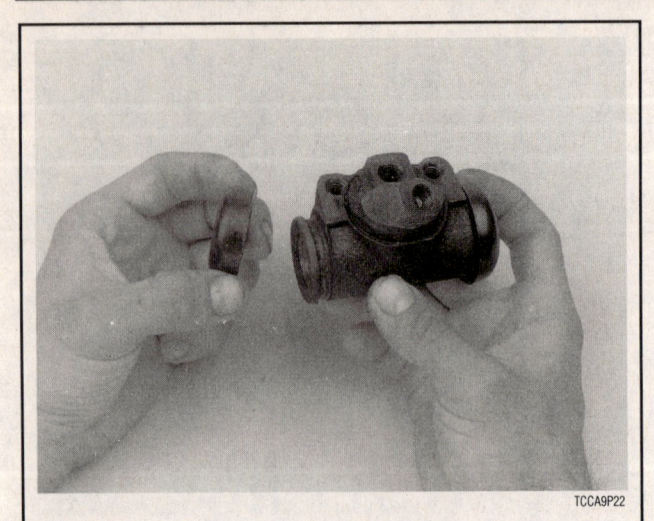

Fig. 107 The boots can now be installed over the wheel cylinder ends

these components to substitute a new or reconditioned part instead of attempting an overhaul.

If no replacement is available, or you would prefer to overhaul your wheel cylinders, the following procedure may be used. When rebuilding and installing wheel cylinders, avoid getting any contaminants into the system. Always use clean, new, high quality brake fluid. If dirty or improper fluid has been used, it will be necessary to drain the entire system, flush the system with proper brake fluid, replace all rubber components, then refill and bleed the system.

1. Remove the wheel cylinder from the vehicle and place on a clean workbench.
2. First remove and discard the old rubber boots, then withdraw the pistons. Piston cylinders are equipped with seals and a spring assembly, all located behind the pistons in the cylinder bore.
3. Remove the remaining inner components, seals and spring assembly. Compressed air may be useful in removing these components. If no compressed air is available, be VERY careful not to score the wheel cylinder bore when removing parts from it. Discard all components for which replacements were supplied in the rebuild kit.
4. Wash the cylinder and metal parts in denatured alcohol or clean brake fluid.

### ✱✱ WARNING

**Never use a mineral-based solvent such as gasoline, kerosene or paint thinner for cleaning purposes. These solvents will swell rubber components and quickly deteriorate them.**

5. Allow the parts to air dry or use compressed air. Do not use rags for cleaning, since lint will remain in the cylinder bore.
6. Inspect the piston and replace it if it shows scratches.
7. Lubricate the cylinder bore and seals using clean brake fluid.
8. Position the spring assembly.
9. Install the inner seals, then the pistons.
10. Insert the new boots into the counterbores by hand. Do not lubricate the boots.
11. Install the wheel cylinder.

## PARKING BRAKE

### Cable(s)

▶ See Figure 108

REMOVAL & INSTALLATION

▶ See Figures 109 and 110

1. Loosen the rear wheel lugnuts on the side of the vehicle you are performing work on.
2. Raise and support the rear of the vehicle. Remove the wheel.
3. Remove the rear caliper assembly.
4. Remove the rear brake disc.
5. Remove the parking brake shoes.
6. Using pliers, disconnect the parking brake cable form the parking brake shoe lever.

**To install:**

7. Connect the parking brake cable to the parking brake shoe lever of the rear shoe.
8. Install the parking brake shoes.
9. Install the rear brake disc. Adjust the parking brake shoe clearance.
10. Install the rear caliper assembly.
11. Install the wheel, lower the vehicle and settle the parking brake shoes and disc.
12. Recheck and adjust the parking brake lever.

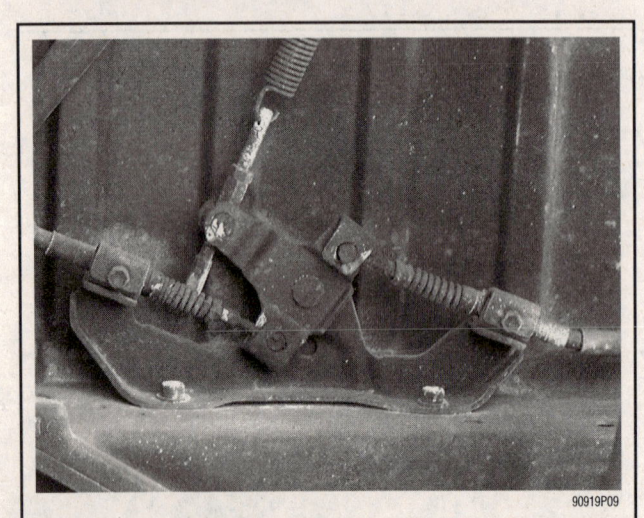

Fig. 108 View of the brake cables attached to the bracket in the rear

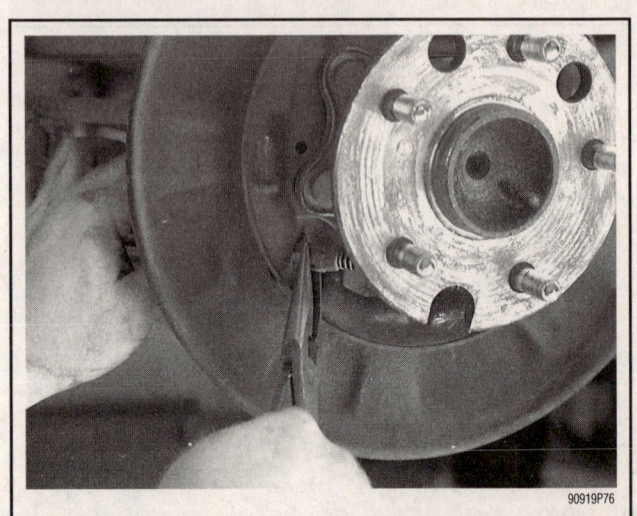

Fig. 109 Use pliers to disconnect the parking brake cable from the lever . . .

# Brakes  9-29

## ADJUSTMENT

1. Pull the parking brake lever all the way up and count the number of clicks. The correct number of clicks should be 4–5.
2. If necessary to adjust the parking brake, make sure that the rear brake shoe has been adjusted before making any adjustment at the parking brake handle.
3. Raise and safely support the vehicle. Loosen the two adjusting nuts and adjust parking brake cable No. 1 until travel is correct.

## Brake Shoes

### REMOVAL & INSTALLATION

▶ See Figures 111 thru 125

➡ Some of the parking brake assembly springs are color coded green, blue, white. The remainder of the springs have no color. Make sure that all springs are installed in their proper locations.

1. Loosen the rear wheel lugs slightly and raise the rear of the vehicle and support it safely. Remove the rear wheels.

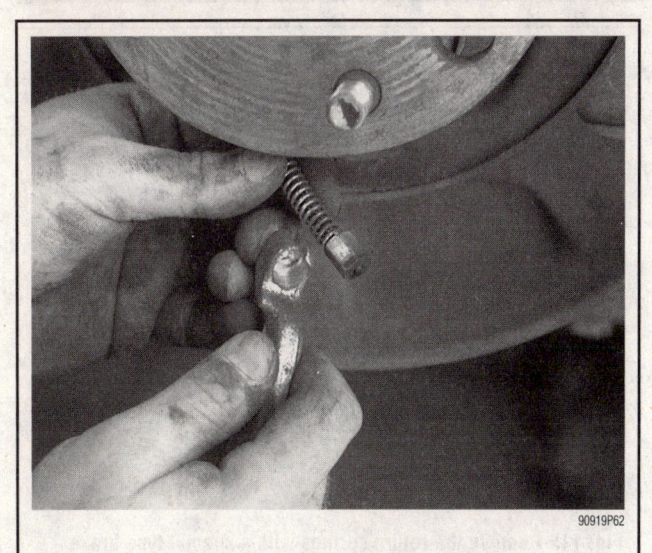

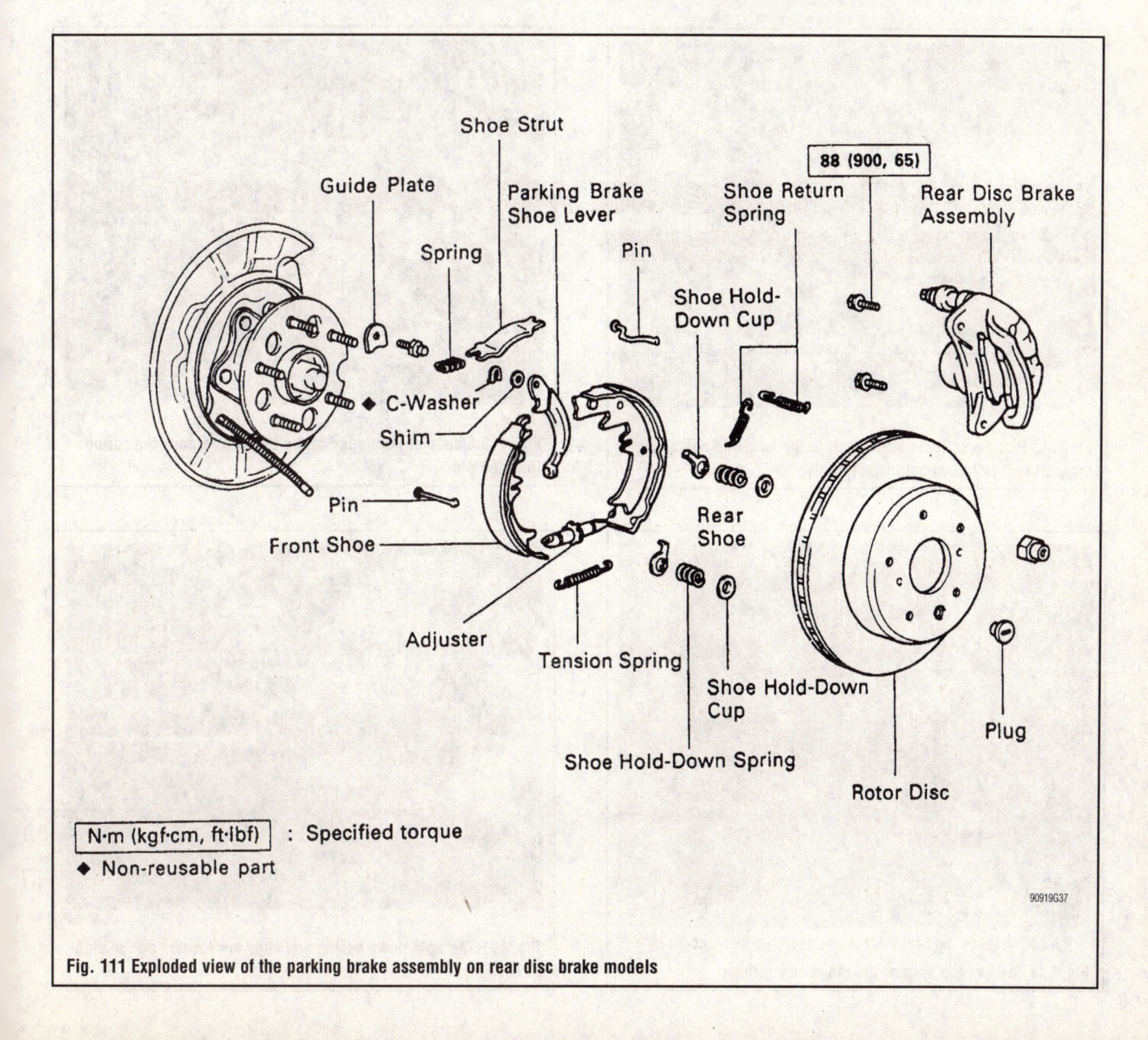

Fig. 110 . . . the lever has a hole to retain the cable

Fig. 111 Exploded view of the parking brake assembly on rear disc brake models

## 9-30 BRAKES

Fig. 112 Remove the rubber plug hiding the adjuster

Fig. 115 Remove the return springs with a special type brake tool

Fig. 113 Place a suitable brake tool, in the hole and adjust the brakes to allow the wheel to spin freely

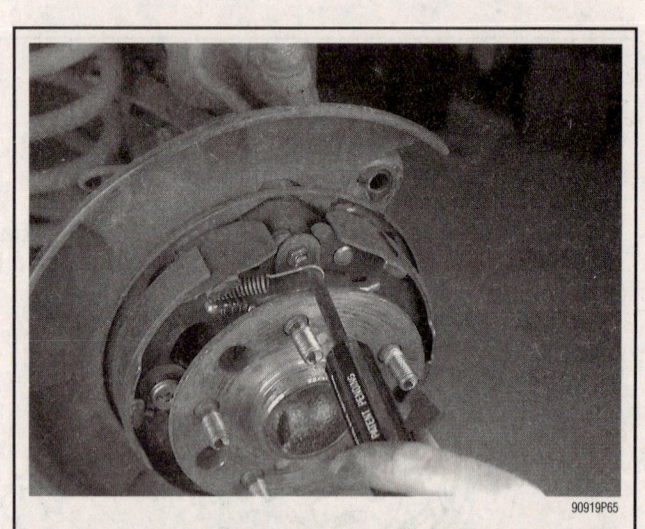

Fig. 116 A special flatbladed brake tool can remove the springs from the pin

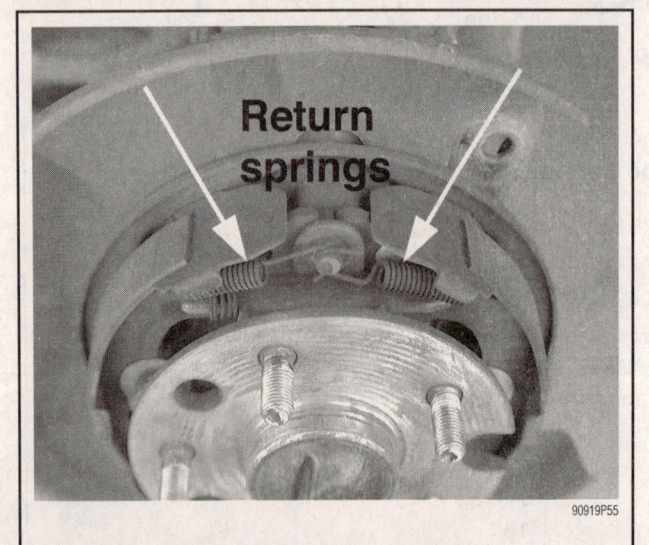

Fig. 114 The two top springs are the return springs

Fig. 117 The hold-down spring and cups are located on the side of each shoe

# Brakes 9-31

Fig. 118 A pair of needle nose pliers are used to remove the pin retaining the hold-down spring and cups

Fig. 119 Remove the brake shoe strut with spring attached, then . . .

Fig. 120 Grab both shoes and extract them out from the bottom

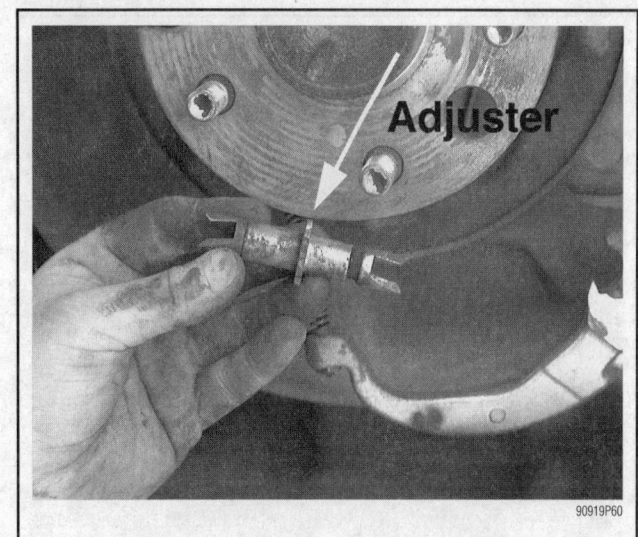

Fig. 121 Slip the adjuster out from between each shoe

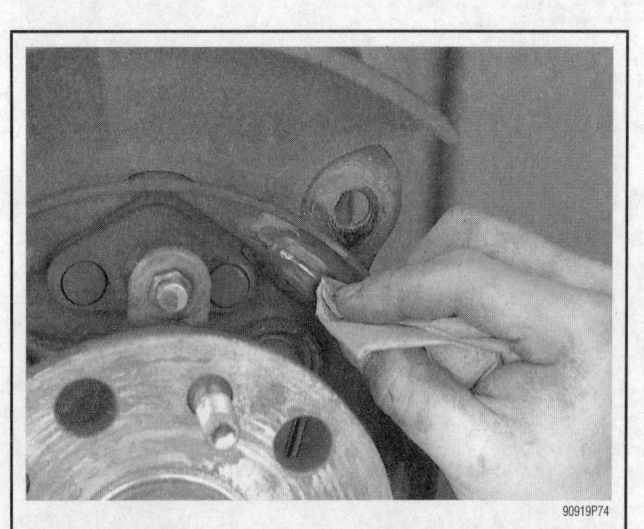

Fig. 122 The tension spring should be attached to the bottom of the shoes, remove it

Fig. 123 Clean the backing plate mating areas where the lubricant is placed

## 9-32 BRAKES

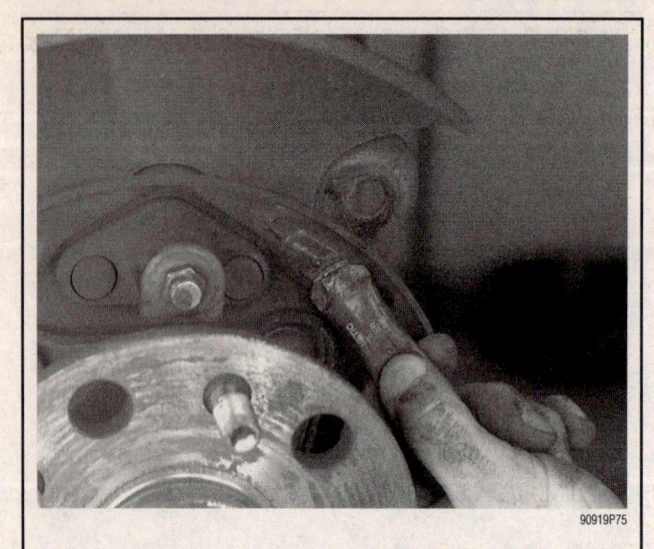

**Fig. 124 Coat the mating areas with Lithium grease**

2. Remove the two mounting bolts and disconnect the rear disc brake assembly. Suspend the disc with wire from the strut spring or a convenient location on the body.
3. Place matchmarks on the axle hub and disc, then pull the disc from the hub. If the disc is stubborn, return the shoe adjuster until the wheel spins freely, and remove the disc.
4. Using a suitable spring tool, remove the return springs.
5. Remove the hold-down spring, cups and pin on each side.
6. Remove the shoe strut with the adjuster spring.
7. Slide the front shoe out and remove the adjuster. Unhook the tension spring and remove the front shoe.
8. Slide the rear shoe out and remove the tension spring. Disconnect the parking brake cable from the lever..

**To install:**

9. Lubricate all shoe sliding surfaces of the backing plate and the threads and head of the adjuster with a high temperature Lithium grease or equivalent.
10. Connect the parking brake cable to the to the rear shoe lever. Install the shoe hold down springs, cups and pins.
11. Slide the rear shoe in between the hold down spring cup and the backing plate.

### ✱✱ CAUTION

Do not allow the brake shoe rubbing surface to come in contact with the grease on the backing plate.

12. Hook the one end of the tension spring to the rear shoe and connect the front shoe to the other end of the spring. Install the adjuster between the front and rear shoes. Slide the front shoe in between the hold down spring cup and the backing plate.
13. Install the strut so that the spring end is forward.
14. Install the front and then the rear return springs using the removal tool.
15. Before installing the disc, lightly polish the disc and shoe surfaces with a fine grit emery cloth. Position the rotor disc onto the axle hub so that the hole on the rear axle shaft is aligned with the service hole on the disc.
16. Adjust the parking brake shoe clearance, then settle the parking brake shoes and disc.
17. Attach the disc brake assembly to the backing plate and tighten the bolt to 34 ft. lbs. (47 Nm).
18. Install the rear wheels and lower the vehicle.

### ADJUSTMENTS

After the brake disc is installed, the parking brake shoe clearance must be adjusted.

1. Temporarily install the lug nuts.
2. Remove the adjuster hole plug.
3. Using a brake tool, turn the adjuster and expand the shoes until the disc locks.
4. Return the adjuster eight notches.
5. Install the hole plug.
6. Install the rear brake caliper assembly, remove the lugnuts.
7. Install the rear wheel.
8. Settle the parking brake shoes and disc as follows:
   a. Drive the vehicle at about 321 mph (50 km) on a safe, level and dry road.
   b. With the parking brake release button pushed in, pull on the lever with 20 lb. (88N) of force.
   c. Drive the vehicle for about ¼ miles (400 meters) in this condition.
   d. Repeat the procedure 2 or 3 times.
9. Recheck and adjust the parking brake lever travel.

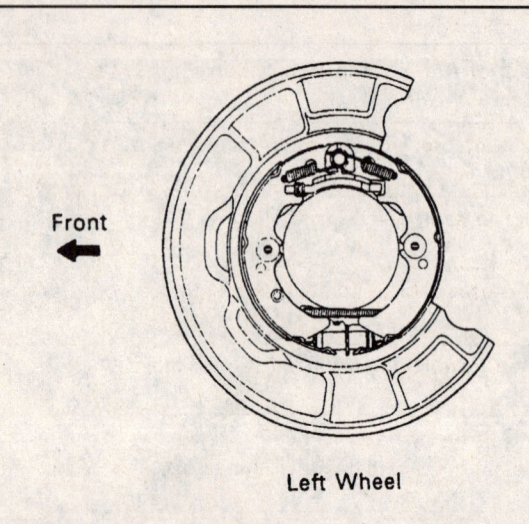

**Fig. 125 Assemble the parking brake components in the correct direction**

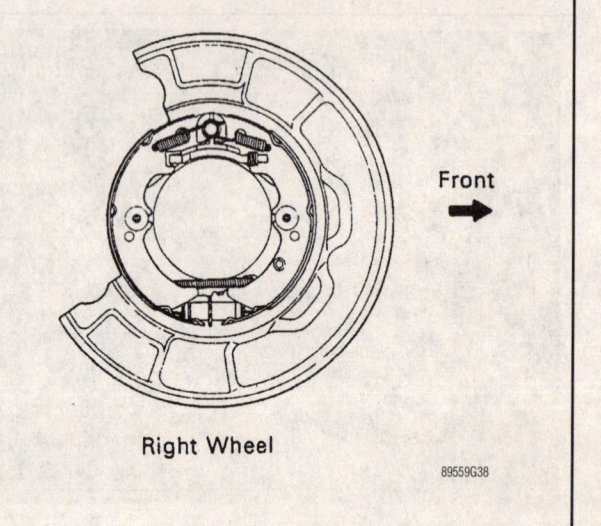

# Brakes 9-33

## ANTI-LOCK BRAKE SYSTEM

### General Information

♦ See Figure 126

The ABS is a brake system which controls the wheel cylinder hydraulic pressure of all four wheels during sudden braking and braking on slippery road surfaces, prevent the wheels from locking. This ABS provides the following benefits:

1. Enables steering round an obstacle with a greater degree of certainty even when panic braking.
2. Enables stopping in a panic brake while keeping effect upon stability and steerability to a minimum, even on curves.

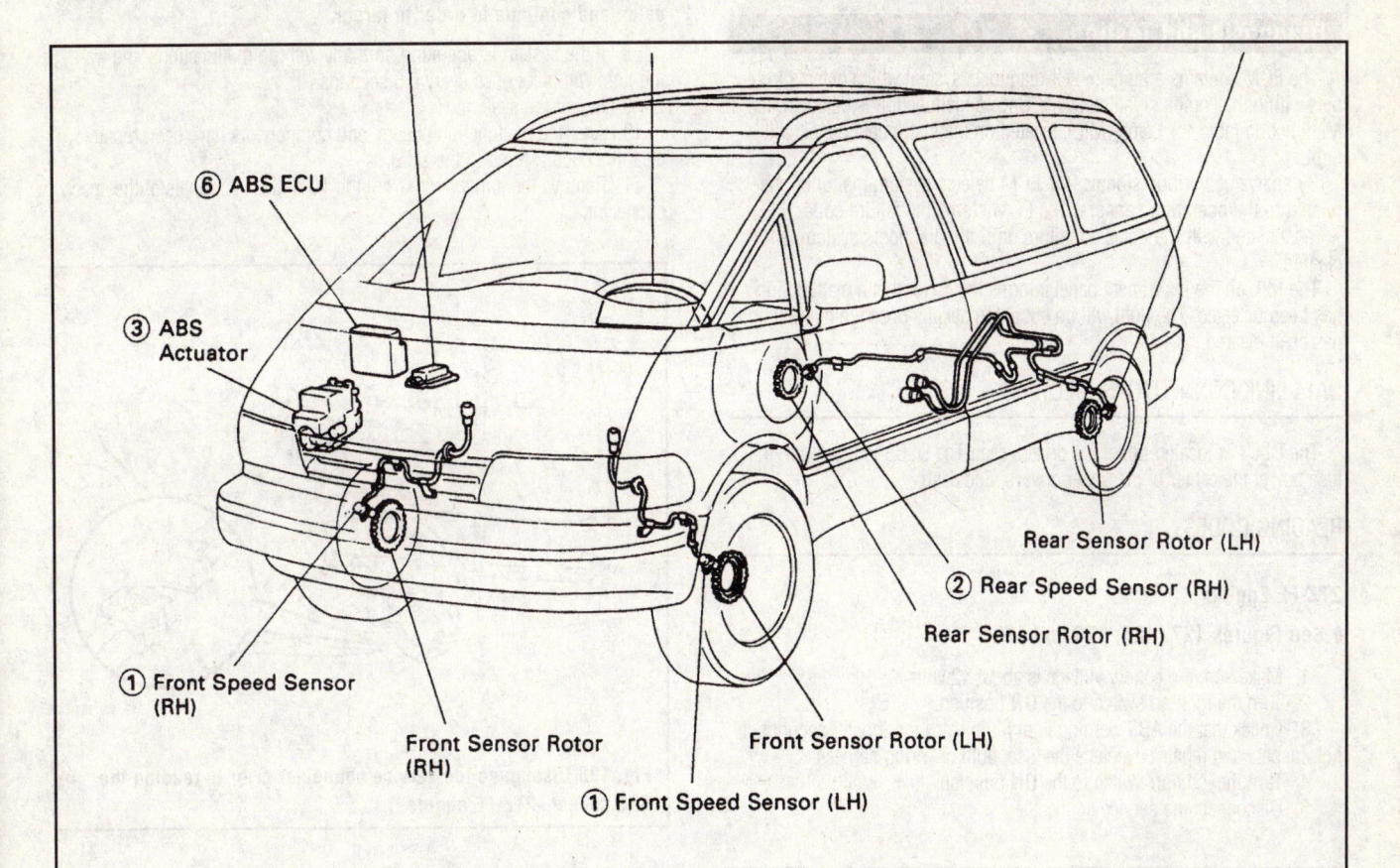

### COMPONENTS FUNCTION

| No. | Components | Function |
| --- | --- | --- |
| 1 | Front Speed Sensor | Detects the wheel speed of each of the left and right front wheels from the rotation of the sensor rotor. |
| 2 | Rear Speed Sensor | Detects the wheel speed of each of the left and right rear wheels from the rotation of the sensor rotor. |
| 3 | ABS Actuator | Controls the brake fluid pressure to each disc brake cylinders through signals from the ECU. |
| 4 | Deceleration Sensor (For 4WD model) | Detects the deceleration speed of the vehicle and sends a signal accordingly to the ABS ECU. |
| 5 | ABS Warning Light | Lights up to alert the driver when trouble has occurred in the Anti-Lock Brake System. |
| 6 | ABS ECU | According the wheel speed signals from the each sensor, it calculates acceleration, deceleration and slip values and sends signals to the actuator to control brake fluid pressure. |

Fig. 126 ABS system component locations and functions

# 9-34 Brakes

The function of the ABS is to help maintain directional stability and vehicle steerabilty on most road surface conditions. However, the system cannot prevent the vehicle from skidding if the cornering speed limit is exceeded.

The ABS has a longitudinal sensor to match braking characteristics to the full-time four wheel drive on 4WD models.

In case a malfunction occurs, a diagnosis function and fail-safe system have been adopted for the ABS to increase serviceability.

## Diagnosis and Testing

The ECM contains a built-in, self-diagnosis system which detects troubles within the engine signal network. Once a malfunction is detected, the Malfunction Indicator Lamp (MIL), located on the instrument panel, will light.

By analyzing various signals, the ECM detects system malfunctions related to the operating sensors. The ECM stores the failure code associated with the detected failure until the diagnosis system is cleared.

The MIL on the instrument panel informs the driver that a malfunction has been detected. The light will go out automatically once the malfunction has been cleared.

### DATA LINK CONNECTORS (DLC)

The DLC1 is located under the drivers seat. The DLC3 is located in the fuse box at the center of the upper driver's side dash.

### READING CODES

**2TZ-FE Engine**

♦ See Figures 127, 128, 129 and 130

1. Make sure the battery voltage is about 12 volts.
2. Turn the ignition switch to the **ON** position.
3. Check that the ABS warning light illuminates for about 3 seconds. If not, inspect and repair or replace the fuse, bulb or wiring harness.
4. Turn the ignition switch to the **ON** position.
5. Disconnect the service connector.
6. Using a jumper wire connect terminals Tc to E1 of the check connector.
7. In the event that there is a malfunction, 4 seconds later the warning light will begin to blink. Read the number of blinks.

➥The first number of blinks will equal the first digit of as two digit code. After a 1.5 second pause, the 2nd number of blinks will equal the 2nd number of the two digit code. If there are more than two or more codes, there will be a 2.5 second pause between codes. The indication will begin after a 4.0 second pause from the smaller value and continue in order to larger.

8. If the system is operating normally with no malfunctions, the warning light will blink once every 0.5 seconds.
9. Repair the system.
10. After the malfunction occurs, and components have been repaired, clear the coeds stored in the ECM.
11. Remove the jumper wire from the TC and E1 terminals of the check connector.

Fig. 127 The ABS warning light is located in the instrument panel

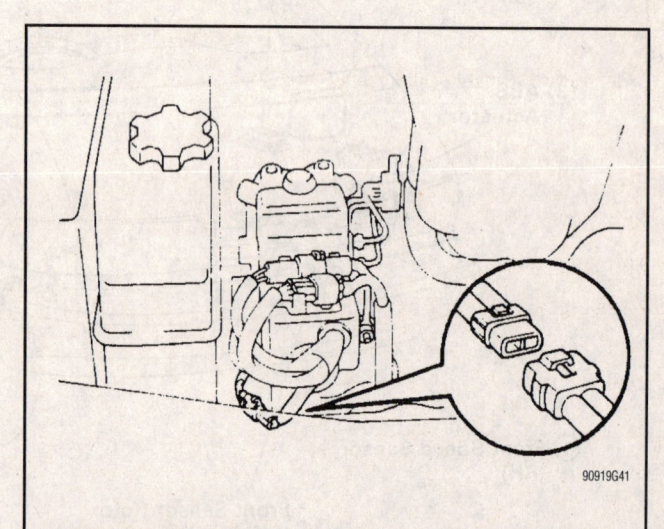

Fig. 128 Disengage the service connector prior to reading the ABS codes—2TZ-FE engine

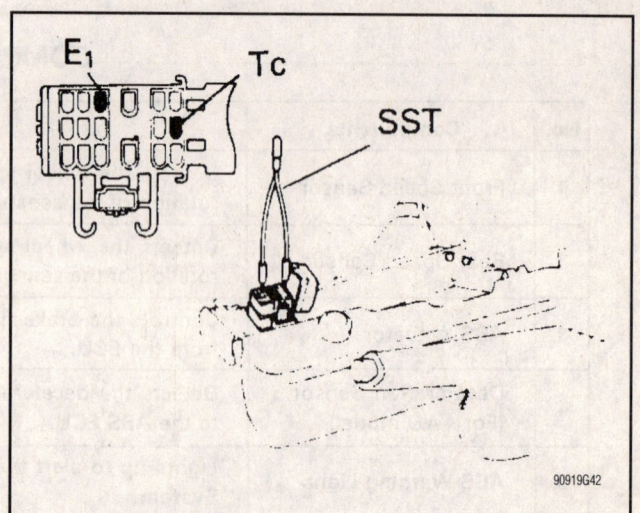

Fig. 129 ABS Tc and E1 terminal locations of the check connector—2TZ-FE engine

# BRAKES 9-35

**Fig. 130 ABS trouble code example—2TZ-FE engine**

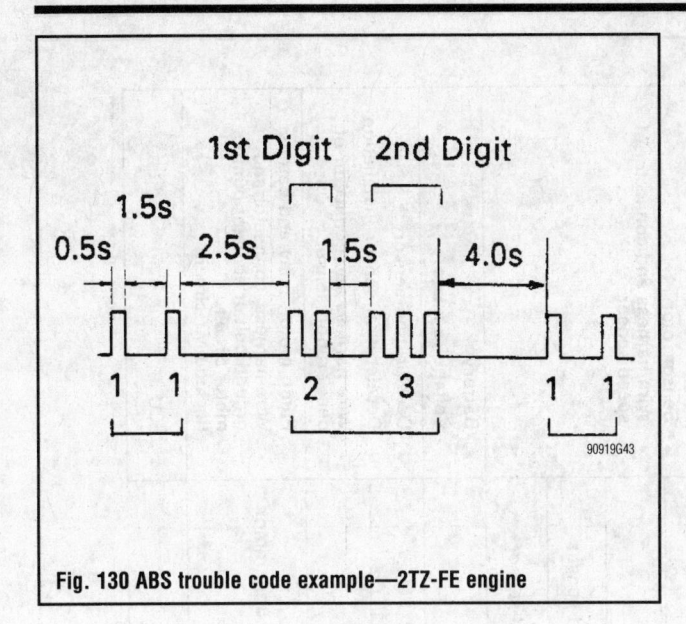

12. Attach the service connector.
13. Turn the ignition switch to the **ON** position and check that the ABS light goes off after the warning light goes on for about 3 seconds.

### 2TZ-FZE Engine

♦ See Figures 131, 132 and 133

1. Make sure the battery voltage is about 12 volts.
2. Turn the ignition switch to the **ON** position.
3. Check that the ABS warning light illuminates for about 3 seconds. If not, inspect and repair or replace the fuse, bulb or wiring harness.
4. Turn the ignition switch to the **ON** position.
5. Using a jumper wire connect terminals TC to E1 of the DLC1.
6. Pull out the short pin.
7. In the event that there is a malfunction, 4 seconds later the warning light will begin to blink. Read the number of blinks.

➡ The first number of blinks will equal the first digit of as two digit code. After a 1.5 second pause, the 2nd number of blinks will equal the 2nd number of the two digit code. If there are more than two or more codes, there will be a 2.5 second pause between codes. The indication will begin after a 4.0 second pause from the smaller value and continue in order to larger.

8. If the system is operating normally with no malfunctions, the warning light will blink once every 0.5 seconds.
9. Repair the system.
10. After the malfunction occurs, and components have been repaired, clear the coeds stored in the ECM.
11. Remove the jumper wire from the TC and E1 terminals of the DLC1.
12. Install the short pin in the DLC1.
13. Turn the ignition switch to the **ON** position and check that the ABS light goes off after the warning light goes on for about 3 seconds.

### CLEARING TROUBLE CODES

1. Turn the ignition switch to the **ON** position.
2. Disconnect the service connector, or pull the short pin, depending on the type your model has.
3. Using a jumper wire, connect terminals Tc and E1 of the DLC1.
4. Depress the brake pedal 8 or more times within 3 seconds.
5. Check that the warning light shows a normal code.
6. Attach the service connector or install the short pin.
7. Remove the jumper wire and double check the warning light is at normal code.

## Control Relays

### TESTING

#### 1991–93 Models

♦ See Figures 134, 135, 136, 137 and 138

1. With the ignition switch **OFF**, remove the 2 control relays from the actuator. For identification, the solenoid relay has 5 terminals; the pump motor relay has 4 terminals.
2. Check the continuity of the pump motor relay. There should be continuity between terminals 1 and 2. There should be no continuity between terminals 3 and 4 or between terminals 1 and 4.
3. Apply battery voltage to terminal 1 and connect terminal 2 to battery ground. There should be continuity between terminals 3 and 4 but no continuity between terminals 1 and 4.
4. Check the continuity of the solenoid relay. There should be continuity between terminals 1 and 3 as well as between terminals 2 and 4. There should be no continuity between terminals 4 and 5.
5. Apply battery voltage to terminal 3 and connect terminal 1 to battery ground. There should be continuity between terminals 4 and 5 but no continuity between terminals 2 and 4.
6. All continuity checks must be met; if any check reveals a fault, the relay must be replaced.

#### 1994–97 Models

♦ See Figures 139, 140, 141, 142 and 143

1. To inspect the motor relay circuit, turn the ignition switch **OFF** and remove the control relay from the actuator.
2. Inspect the continuity of the motor relay circuit. Check that there is continuity between terminals 3 and 4, and no continuity between terminals 1 and 2.
3. If continuity is not as specified above, replace the relay.

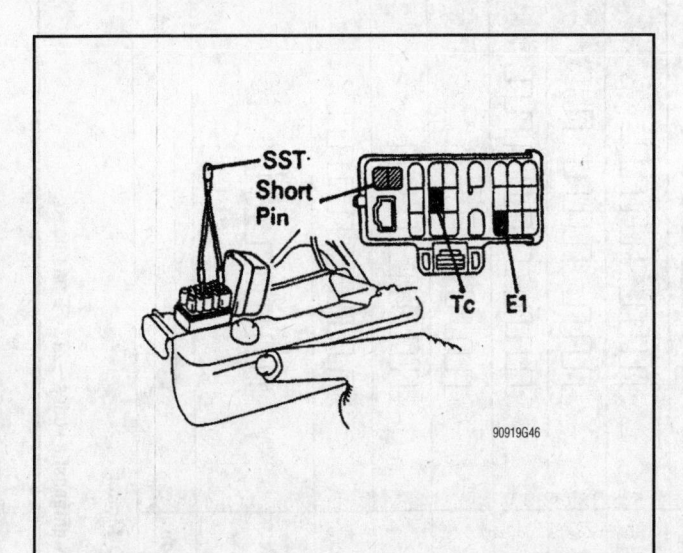

**Fig. 131 The short pin is located in the DLC1—2TZ-FZE engine**

## 9-36 BRAKES

| Code No. | Light Pattern | Diagnosis | Trouble Part |
|---|---|---|---|
| 11 | ON / OFF | Open circuit in solenoid relay circuit | • Actuator inside wire harness<br>• Solenoid relay<br>• Wire harness and connector of solenoid relay circuit (Include AST circuit) |
| 12 | | Short circuit in solenoid relay circuit | |
| 13 | | Open circuit in pump motor relay circuit | • Actuator inside wire harness<br>• Pump motor relay<br>• Wire harness and connector of pump motor relay circuit (include MT circuit) |
| 14 | | Short circuit in pump motor relay circuit | |
| 21 | | Open or short circuit in 3 position solenoid of front right wheel | • Actuator solenoid<br>• Wire harness and connector of actuator solenoid circuit |
| 22 | | Open or short circuit in 3 position solenoid of front left wheel | |
| 23 | | Open or short circuit in 3 position solenoid of rear wheel | |
| 31 | | Front right wheel speed sensor signal malfunction | • Speed sensor<br>• Sensor rotor<br>• Wire harness and connector of speed sensor |
| 32 | | Front left wheel speed sensor signal malfunction | |
| 33 | | Rear right wheel speed sensor signal malfunction | |
| 34 | | Rear left wheel speed sensor signal malfunction | |
| 35 | | Open circuit in front left or rear right wheel speed sensor | |
| 36 | | Open circuit in front right or rear left wheel speed sensor | |
| 41 | | Abnormally high or low battery voltage | • Battery<br>• Voltage regulator |
| *43 | | Malfunction in deceleration sensor | • Deceleration sensor<br>• Deceleration sensor installation |
| *44 | | Open or short circuit in deceleration sensor | • Wire harness and connector of deceleration sensor |
| 51 | | Pump motor of actuator locked or open circuit in pump motor circuit in actuator | • Pump motor, relay and battery<br>• Wire harness, connector and ground bolt or actuator pump motor circuit (Include MT circuit) |
| Always on | | Malfunction in ECU | • ECU |

*: For 4WD Model

Fig. 132 ABS diagnostic codes—2TZ-FE engine

# Brakes 9-37

| DTC No. | Detection Item | Trouble Area |
|---|---|---|
| 11 | Open circuit in ABS solenoid relay circuit | • Actuator inside wire harness<br>• ABS solenoid relay<br>• Wire harness and connector of solenoid relay circuit |
| 12 | Short circuit in ABS solenoid relay circuit | |
| 13 | Open circuit in ABS motor relay circuit | • Actuator inside wire harness<br>• ABS motor relay<br>• Wire harness and connector of motor relay circuit |
| 14 | Short circuit in ABS motor relay circuit | |
| 21 | Open or short circuit in 2 position solenoid of right front wheel | • Actuator solenoid<br>• Wire harness and connector of actuator solenoid circuit |
| 22 | Open or short circuit in 2 position solenoid of left front wheel | |
| 23 | Open or short circuit in 2 position solenoid of rear wheel | |
| 31 | Right front wheel speed sensor signal malfunction | • Speed sensor<br>• Sensor rotor<br>• Wire harness and connector of speed sensor |
| 32 | Left front wheel speed sensor signal malfunction | |
| 33 | Right rear wheel speed sensor signal malfunction | |
| 34 | Left rear wheel speed sensor signal malfunction | |
| 41 | Low battery positive voltage | • Battery<br>• Voltage regulator |
| 49 | Open circuit in stop light circuit | • Wire harness and connector of stop light circuit |
| 51 | Pump motor is locked<br>Open in pump motor ground | • Pump motor, relay and battery<br>• Wire harness, connector and ground bolt or actuator pump motor circuit |
| Always ON | Malfunction in ECU<br>Abnormally high battery positive voltage | • Battery<br>• Voltage regulator<br>• ECU |

Fig. 133 ABS diagnostic codes—2TZ-FZE engine

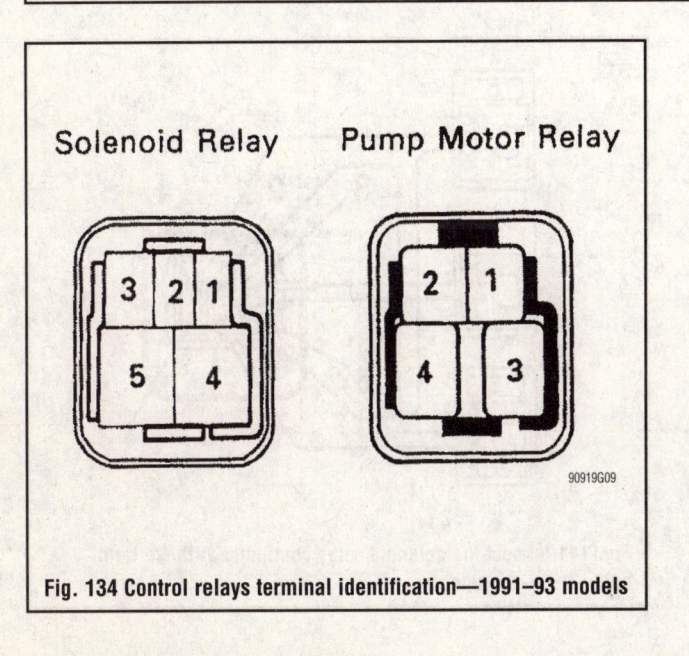

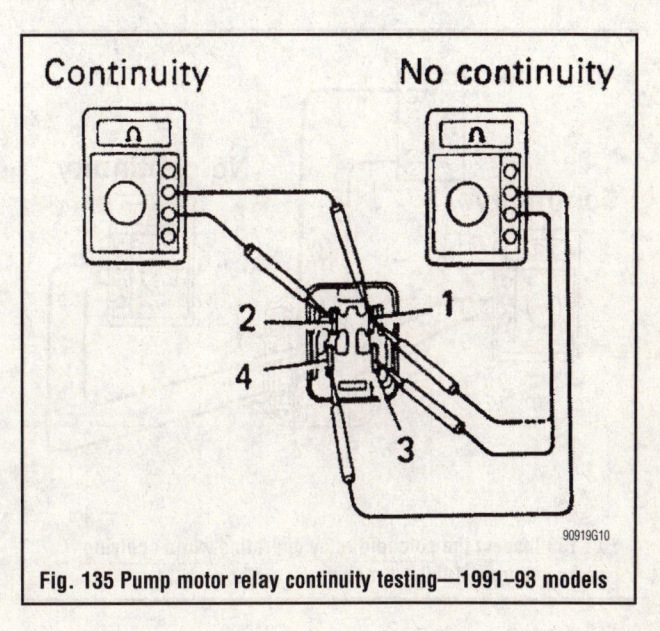

Fig. 134 Control relays terminal identification—1991-93 models

Fig. 135 Pump motor relay continuity testing—1991-93 models

9-38　BRAKES

Fig. 136 Check the continuity with battery voltage for the pump motor relay—1991–93 models

Fig. 137 Inspect the solenoid relay continuity at these terminals—1991–93 models

Fig. 138 Inspect the solenoid relay operation while applying battery voltage—1989–91 models

Fig. 139 Pump motor relay continuity testing—1994–97 models

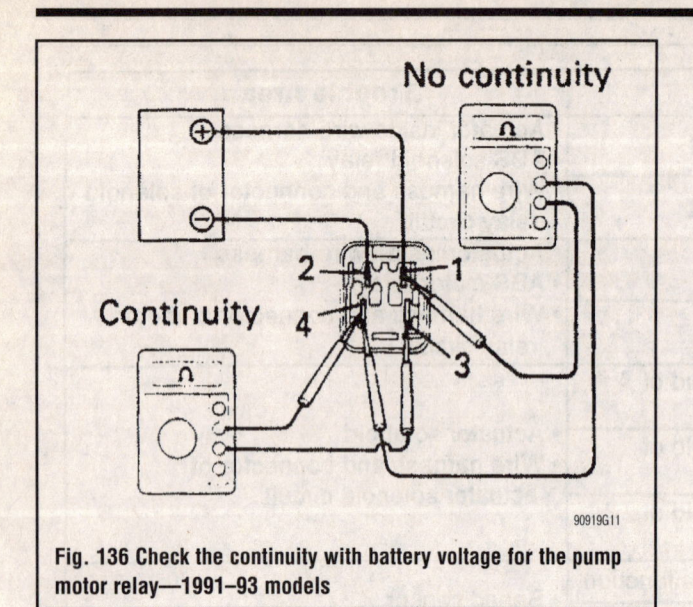

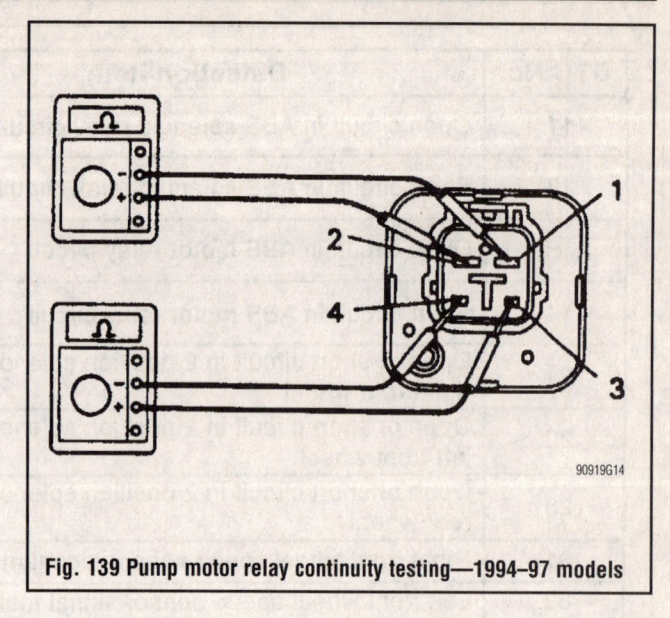

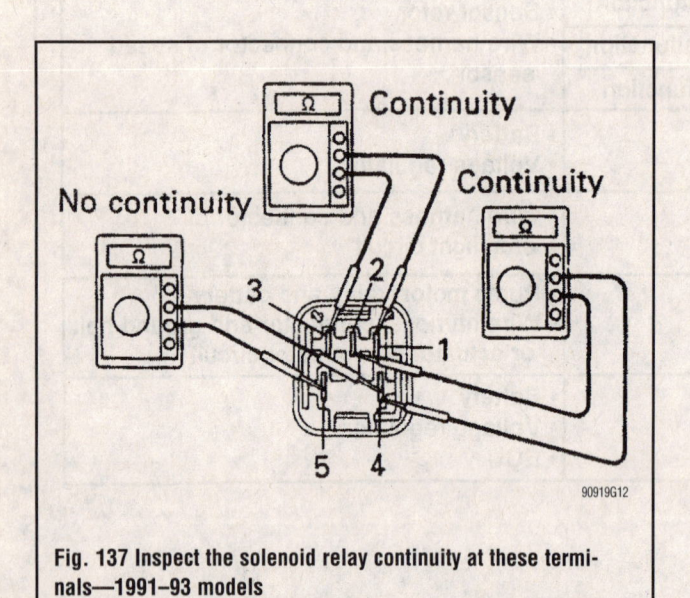

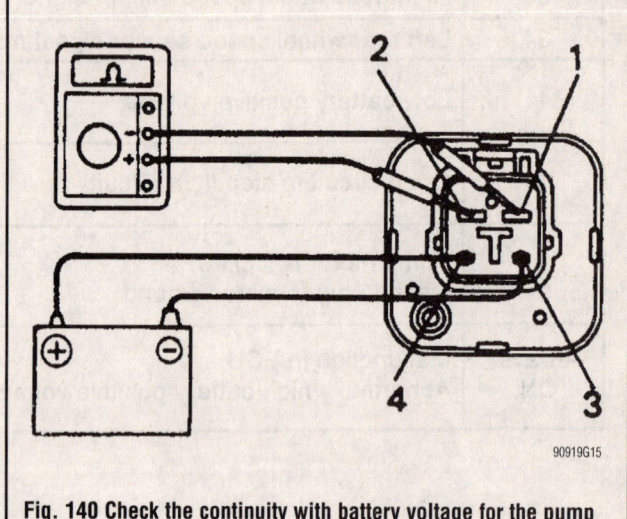

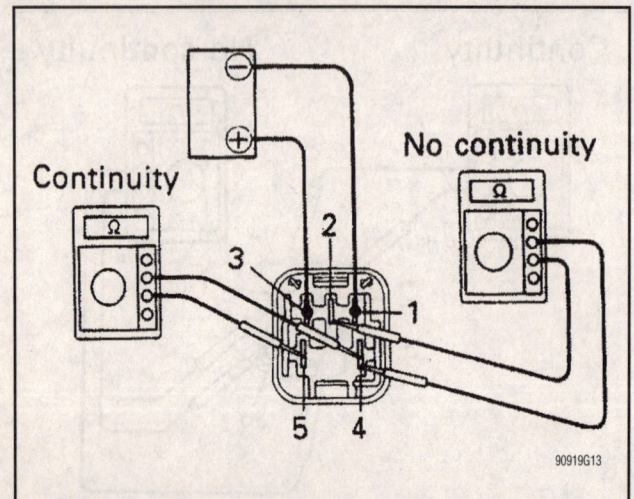

Fig. 140 Check the continuity with battery voltage for the pump motor relay—1994–97 models

Fig. 141 Inspect the solenoid relay continuity at these terminals—1994–97 models

# Brakes 9-39

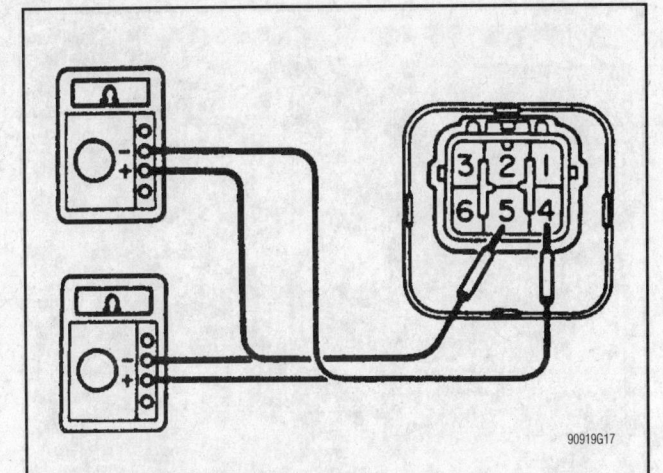

**Fig. 142 Connect the positive lead of the ohmmeter to terminal 5 and the negative to lead 4 of the solenoid relay—1994–97 models**

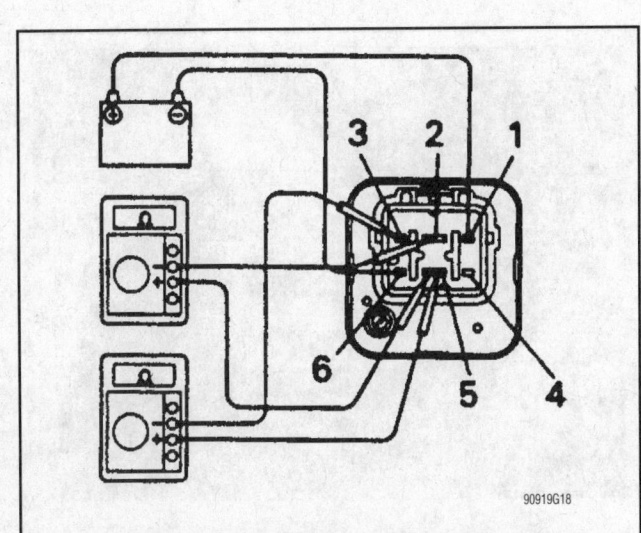

**Fig. 143 Inspect the solenoid relay operation while applying battery voltage—1994–97 models**

4. Connect a jumper wire from the positive battery terminal to terminal 4. Connect a jumper wire from the negative battery terminal to terminal 3 of the relay.
5. Using an ohm meter, check for continuity between terminals 1 and 2 of the relay. Replace the relay if the test results indicate no continuity.
6. To inspect the solenoid relay circuit, with the relay off of the actuator, check for continuity between terminals 1 and 6.
7. Check that there is no continuity between terminals 2 and 5.
8. Check that there is continuity between terminals 3 and 5.
9. Connect the positive lead of an ohmmeter to terminal 5 and the negative lead to terminal 4 of the relay. There should be continuity. Reverse the leads of the ohm meter and observe the readings. There should be no continuity.
10. If continuity readings differ from specified results, replace the relay.

## REMOVAL & INSTALLATION

The control relays are located in the actuator. There is a plastic case surrounding them, remove this case and unplug the relays.

### Speed Sensors

#### TESTING

▶ See Figures 144, 145 and 146

1. Inspect the sensor. Disconnect the speed sensor wiring.
2. Measure the resistance between terminals. Standard resistance is:
   - Front—0.6–1.8 kilometers
   - 1.05–1.45 kilometers
3. If the resistance value is not within specifications, replace the speed sensor.
4. Check that there is no continuity between each terminal and the sensor body.
5. If there is continuity, replace the sensor.
6. Connect the speed sensor wiring.

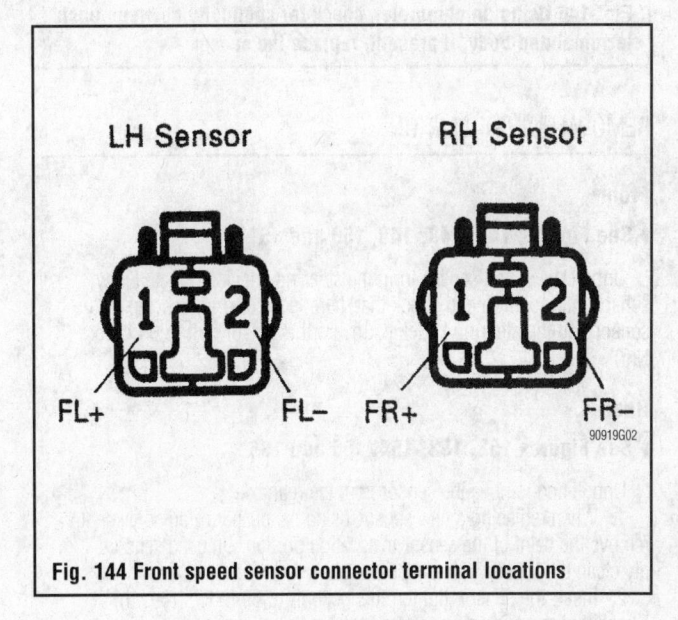

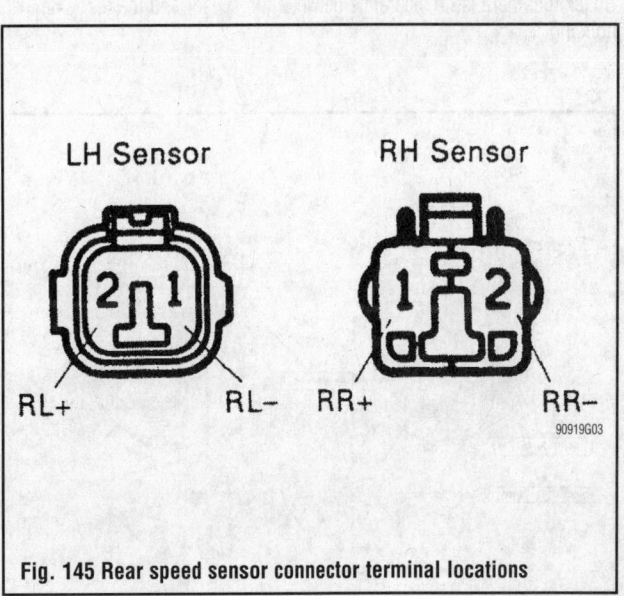

**Fig. 144 Front speed sensor connector terminal locations**

**Fig. 145 Rear speed sensor connector terminal locations**

## 9-40 Brakes

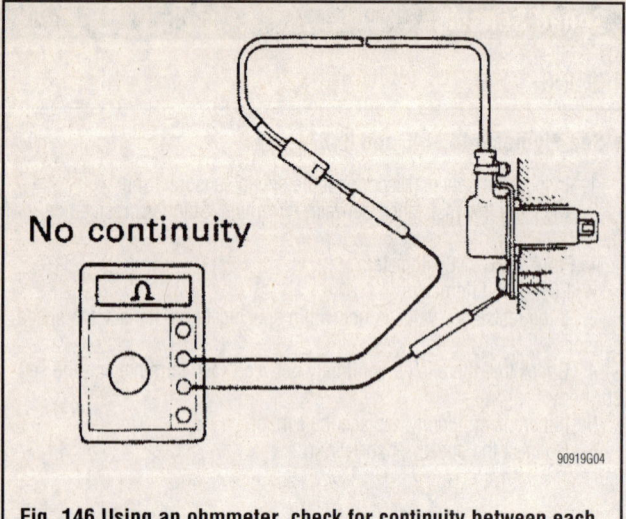

Fig. 146 Using an ohmmeter, check for continuity between each terminal and body, if present, replace the sensor

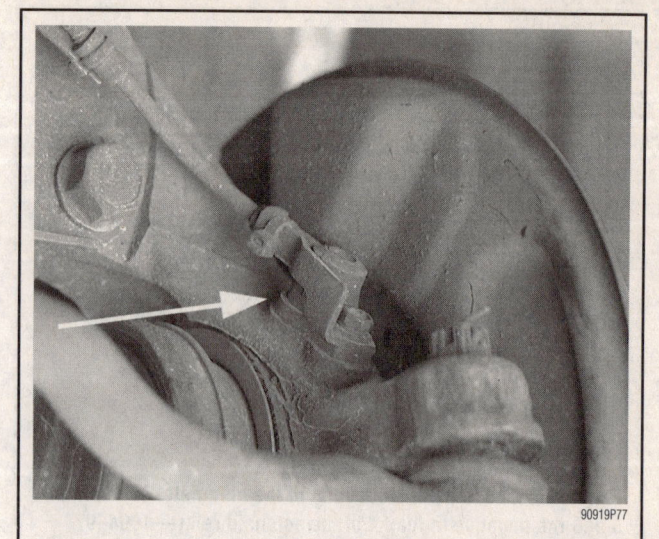

Fig. 148 The speed sensor is bolted into the knuckle

### REMOVAL & INSTALLATION

#### Front
▶ See Figures 147, 148, 149, 150 and 151

Unbolt the speed sensor from the steering knuckle. Place a new sensor into position and check that there is no clearance between the sensor and the steering knuckle. Secure the sensor bolt to 69 ft. lbs. (8 Nm).

#### Rear
▶ See Figures 152, 153, 154, 155 and 156

Unbolt and remove the sensor from the rear axle.
1. When replacing a new sensor, using sandpaper or an equivalent, remove the paint of the sensor installation portion. On used sensors, simply clean the sensor with a paper towel.
2. Insert the sensor, tighten the lockbolt to 69 ft. lbs. (8 Nm). Check that there is no clearance between the sensor and the rear axle housing.

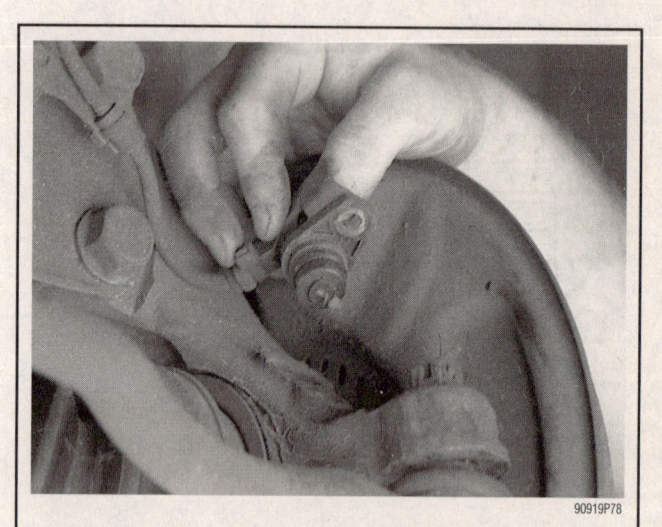

Fig. 149 Remove the one bolt and lift the speed sensor out of the knuckle

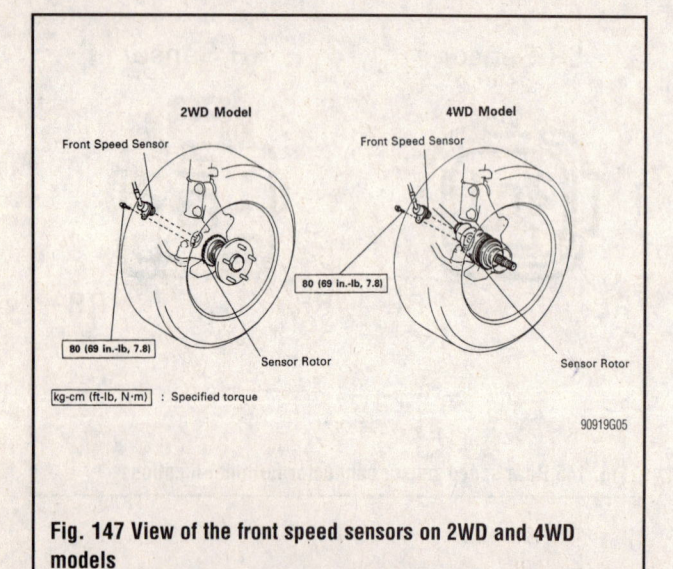

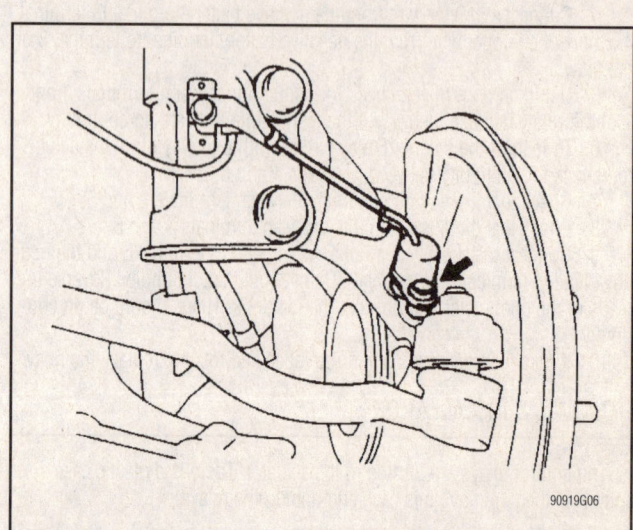

Fig. 147 View of the front speed sensors on 2WD and 4WD models

Fig. 150 Unbolt and remove the front speed sensor from the steering knuckle

## Brakes 9-41

Fig. 151 Clean the sensor prior to installation

Fig. 152 Rear speed sensor location

Fig. 153 Remove the one bolt holding the speed sensor then . . .

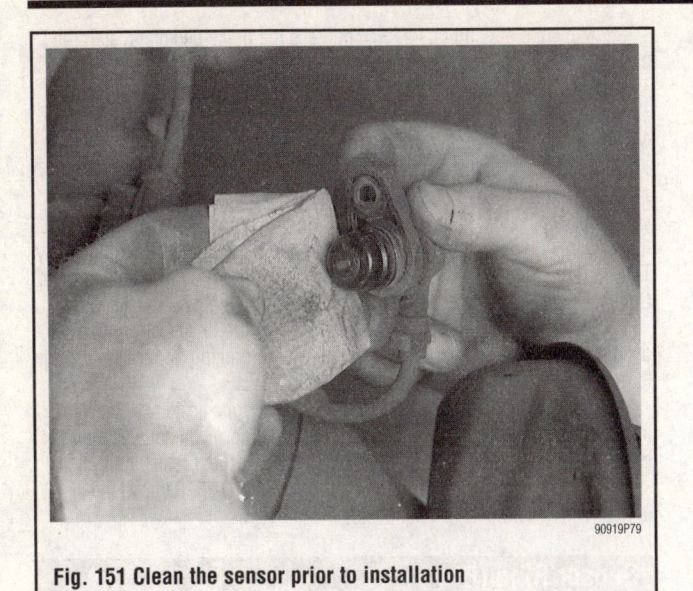

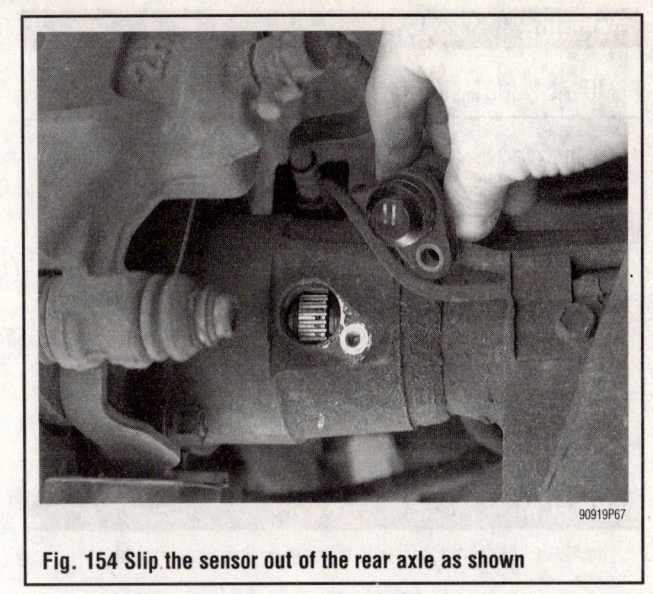

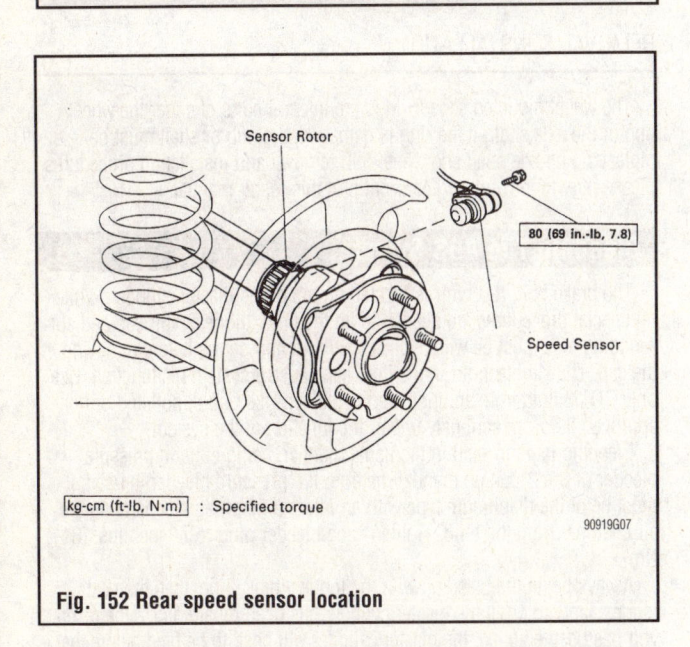

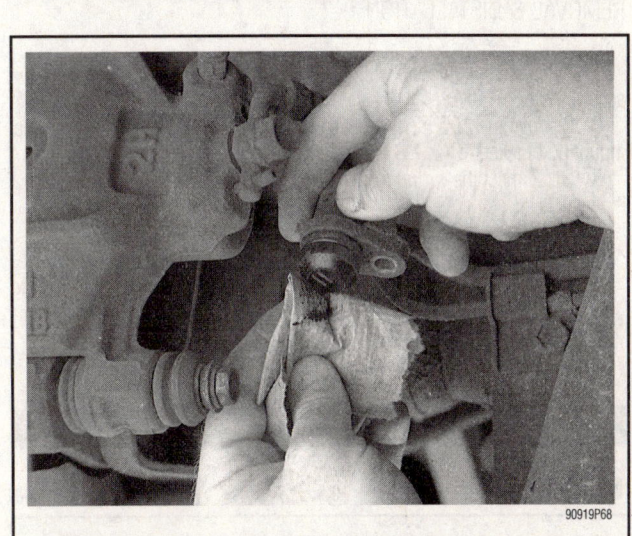

Fig. 154 Slip the sensor out of the rear axle as shown

Fig. 155 When installing the old sensor, clean it before inserting into the axle

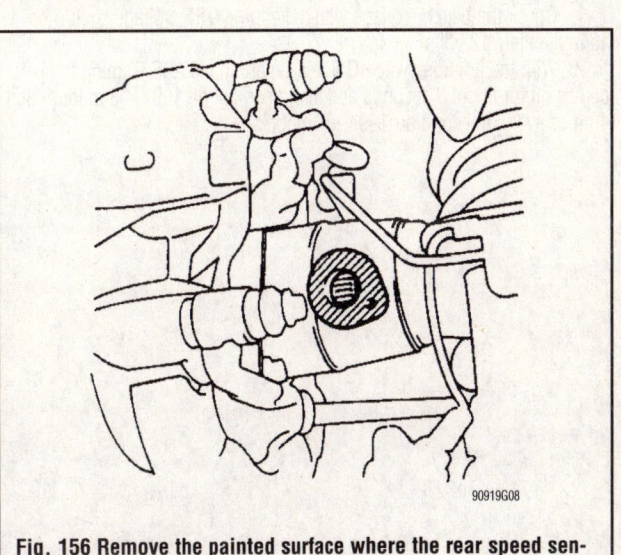

Fig. 156 Remove the painted surface where the rear speed sensor is inserted with sandpaper

# 9-42 BRAKES

## Actuator

### REMOVAL & INSTALLATION

1. Disconnect the brake lines leading to the actuator.
2. Disconnect the electrical wiring attached to the actuator.
3. Remove the bolts and extract the actuator from the vehicle. Remove the nuts retaining the bracket to the unit.

**To install:**

4. Attach the bracket to the actuator, tighten to 48 inch lbs. (5 Nm).
5. Secure the actuator with bracket to the vehicle and tighten the bolts to 14 ft. lbs. (19 Nm).
6. Attach the electrical wiring to the unit.
7. Attach the brake lines and tighten each to 11 ft. lbs. (15 Nm).
8. Fill the brake master cylinder reservoir with new brake fluid. Bleed the system and check for leaks.

## ABS ECM

The ABS ECM can be located in the front engine compartment.

### REMOVAL & INSTALLATION

1. If the van is equipped with a C/D player, remove the amplifier to access the ABS ECM.
2. Remove the ABS ECM cover (if equipped) and the computer from the mounting bracket.
3. Disconnect the wiring from the ECM and remove the computer from the vehicle.

**To install:**

4. Connect the harnesses and insert the wiring harness to the clamp.
5. Position the computer and install it with the 5 screws, tighten them to 48 inch lbs. (5 Nm).
6. Install the computer cover, if equipped.
7. Install the C/D amplifier if equipped.

## Deceleration Sensor

### TESTING

➡ The following procedures require driving the vehicle while it is in the diagnostic mode. The anti-lock system will be disabled; only normal braking function will be available.

1. Check the battery voltage with the engine **OFF**; voltage should be approximately 12 volts.
2. With the ignition switch **ON**, make certain the ABS warning lamp comes on for about 3 seconds and then goes out on 1991–93 model's and 4 times every 1 second on 1994–97 models.
3. Apply the parking brake fully, depress the brake pedal and start the engine.
4. After a short delay, the ABS dashboard warning lamp should flash about once every second. This is slower than the usual system flashing when transmitting a code.
5. Release the parking brake and drive the vehicle straight ahead at 12.4 mph (20 kph) or greater speed. Lightly depress the brake pedal; there should be no change in the flashing dashboard lamp.
6. Continue to drive at the same speed and apply the brakes moderately. The warning lamp should stop flashing and remain on during braking only. Once the brake is released, flashing continues at the previous rate.
7. Continue driving at the same speed; apply the brakes strongly. The dash warning lamp should remain on during the braking period and change to a rapid flash when the brakes are released.
8. If the warning lamp display does not meet specifications, check the installation of the deceleration sensor. It must be correctly and securely installed. If installation is proper, replace the sensor and retest the system.
9. Stop the vehicle and turn the ignition switch **OFF**. Remove the jumper wire from the check connector.

## Sensor Ring (Rotor)

### REMOVAL & INSTALLATION

The wheel mounted sensor rings are integral parts of either the wheel hub or the axle shaft; if the ring is damaged, the hub or shaft must be replaced. For axle shaft and wheel hub removal and installation procedures, please refer to the appropriate section of this repair manual.

## Bleeding The ABS System

The brake fluid reservoir is located on top of the master cylinder. While no special procedures are needed to fill the fluid, the reservoir cap and surrounding area must be wiped clean of all dirt and debris before removing the cap. The slightest dirt in the fluid can cause a system malfunction. Use only DOT 3 fluid from an unopened container. Use of old, polluted or non-approved fluid can seriously impair the function of the system.

Bleeding is performed in the usual manner, using either a pressure bleeder or the 2-person manual method. If a pressure bleeder is used, it must be of the diaphragm type with an internal diaphragm separating the air chamber from the fluid. Tighten each bleeder plug to 74 inch lbs. (8 Nm).

Always begin the bleeding with the longest brake line, then the next longest, and so on. If the master cylinder has been repaired or if the reservoir has been emptied, the master cylinder will need to be bled before the individual lines and calipers. During any bleeding procedure, make certain to maintain the fluid level above the MIN line on the reservoir. When the bleeding procedure is complete, fill the reservoir to the MAX line before reinstalling the cap.

## BRAKE SPECIFICATIONS
All measurements in inches unless noted

| Year | Model | | Master Cylinder Bore | Brake Disc Original Thickness | Brake Disc Minimum Thickness | Maximum Runout | Brake Drum Original Inside Diameter | Brake Drum Max. Wear Limit | Maximum Machine Diameter | Minimum Lining Thickness Front | Minimum Lining Thickness Rear |
|---|---|---|---|---|---|---|---|---|---|---|---|
| 1991 | Previa | | — | 0.866 | 0.827 | 0.0028 | 10.00 | 10.079 | — | 0.039 | 0.004 |
| 1992 | Previa | F | — | — | ① | 0.0028 | — | — | — | 0.039 | — |
| | Previa | R | — | 0.709 | 0.669 | 0.0039 | 10.00 | 10.079 | — | — | 0.039 |
| 1993 | Previa | F | — | — | ① | 0.0028 | — | — | — | 0.039 | — |
| | Previa | R | — | 0.709 | 0.669 | 0.0039 | 10.00 | 10.079 | — | — | 0.039 |
| 1994 | Previa | F | — | ② | ① | 0.0028 | — | — | — | 0.039 | — |
| | Previa | R | — | 0.709 | 0.669 | 0.0039 | 10.00 | 10.18 | — | — | 0.039 |
| 1995 | Previa | F | — | ③ | ④ | 0.0028 | — | — | — | 0.039 | — |
| | Previa | R | — | 0.709 | 0.669 | 0.0039 | 10.00 | 10.18 | — | — | 0.039 |
| 1996 | Previa | F | — | ③ | ④ | 0.0028 | — | — | — | 0.039 | — |
| | Previa | R | — | 0.709 | 0.669 | 0.0039 | 10.00 | 10.18 | — | — | 0.039 |
| 1997 | Previa | F | — | 0.866 | 0.787 | 0.0028 | — | — | — | 0.039 | — |
| | Previa | R | — | 0.709 | 0.650 | 0.0039 | 10.00 | 10.18 | — | — | 0.039 |

① Single piston: with rear disc 0.787 inch
　　with rear drum 0.906 inch
　Dual piston: 0.906 inch
② Single piston: with rear disc 0.886 inch
　　with rear drum 0.984 inch
　Dual piston: 0.984 inch
③ Single piston: 0.886 inch
　Dual piston: 0.984 inch
④ Single piston: 0.787 inch
　Dual piston: 0.906 inch

## Troubleshooting the Brake System

| Problem | Cause | Solution |
|---|---|---|
| Low brake pedal (excessive pedal travel required for braking action.) | • Excessive clearance between rear linings and drums caused by inoperative automatic adjusters | • Make 10 to 15 alternate forward and reverse brake stops to adjust brakes. If brake pedal does not come up, repair or replace adjuster parts as necessary. |
|  | • Worn rear brakelining | • Inspect and replace lining if worn beyond minimum thickness specification |
|  | • Bent, distorted brakeshoes, front or rear | • Replace brakeshoes in axle sets |
|  | • Air in hydraulic system | • Remove air from system. Refer to Brake Bleeding. |
| Low brake pedal (pedal may go to floor with steady pressure applied.) | • Fluid leak in hydraulic system | • Fill master cylinder to fill line; have helper apply brakes and check calipers, wheel cylinders, differential valve tubes, hoses and fittings for leaks. Repair or replace as necessary. |
|  | • Air in hydraulic system | • Remove air from system. Refer to Brake Bleeding. |
|  | • Incorrect or non-recommended brake fluid (fluid evaporates at below normal temp). | • Flush hydraulic system with clean brake fluid. Refill with correct-type fluid. |
|  | • Master cylinder piston seals worn, or master cylinder bore is scored, worn or corroded | • Repair or replace master cylinder |
| Low brake pedal (pedal goes to floor on first application—o.k. on subsequent applications.) | • Disc brake pads sticking on abutment surfaces of anchor plate. Caused by a build-up of dirt, rust, or corrosion on abutment surfaces | • Clean abutment surfaces |
| Fading brake pedal (pedal height decreases with steady pressure applied.) | • Fluid leak in hydraulic system | • Fill master cylinder reservoirs to fill mark, have helper apply brakes, check calipers, wheel cylinders, differential valve, tubes, hoses, and fittings for fluid leaks. Repair or replace parts as necessary. |
|  | • Master cylinder piston seals worn, or master cylinder bore is scored, worn or corroded | • Repair or replace master cylinder |
| Decreasing brake pedal travel (pedal travel required for braking action decreases and may be accompanied by a hard pedal.) | • Caliper or wheel cylinder pistons sticking or seized | • Repair or replace the calipers, or wheel cylinders |
|  | • Master cylinder compensator ports blocked (preventing fluid return to reservoirs) or pistons sticking or seized in master cylinder bore | • Repair or replace the master cylinder |
|  | • Power brake unit binding internally | • Test unit according to the following procedure:<br>(a) Shift transmission into neutral and start engine<br>(b) Increase engine speed to 1500 rpm, close throttle and fully depress brake pedal<br>(c) Slow release brake pedal and stop engine<br>(d) Have helper remove vacuum check valve and hose from power unit. Observe for backward movement of brake pedal.<br>(e) If the pedal moves backward, the power unit has an internal bind—replace power unit |

TCCA9C01

**EXTERIOR 10-2**
DOORS 10-2
   REMOVAL & INSTALLATION 10-2
   ADJUSTMENT 10-5
HOOD 10-7
   REMOVAL & INSTALLATION 10-7
   ALIGNMENT 10-7
TAILGATE 10-8
   REMOVAL & INSTALLATION 10-8
   ALIGNMENT 10-8
GRILLE 10-8
   REMOVAL & INSTALLATION 10-8
OUTSIDE MIRRORS 10-8
   REMOVAL & INSTALLATION 10-8
ANTENNA 10-11
   REPLACEMENT 10-11
FENDERS 10-11
   REMOVAL & INSTALLATION 10-11
POWER SUNROOF 10-12
   REMOVAL & INSTALLATION 10-12
**INTERIOR 10-13**
INSTRUMENT PANEL AND PAD 10-13
   REMOVAL & INSTALLATION 10-13
DOOR PANELS 10-17
   REMOVAL & INSTALLATION 10-17
DOOR LOCKS 10-20
   REMOVAL & INSTALLATION 10-20
TAILGATE LOCK 10-20
   REMOVAL & INSTALLATION 10-20
DOOR GLASS AND REGULATOR 10-20
   REMOVAL & INSTALLATION 10-20
ELECTRIC WINDOW MOTOR 10-22
   REMOVAL & INSTALLATION 10-22
WINDSHIELD AND FIXED GLASS 10-22
   REMOVAL & INSTALLATION 10-22
   WINDSHIELD CHIP REPAIR 10-22
INSIDE REAR VIEW MIRROR 10-26
   REPLACEMENT 10-26
SEATS 10-26
   REMOVAL & INSTALLATION 10-26
**SPECIFICATIONS CHART**
   TORQUE SPECIFICATIONS 10-28

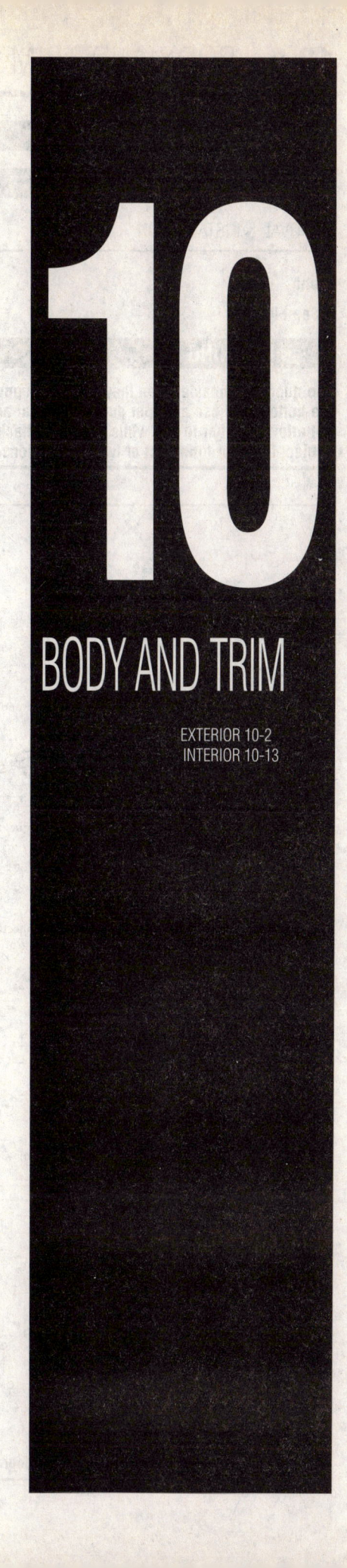

# 10

## BODY AND TRIM

EXTERIOR 10-2
INTERIOR 10-13

## 10-2 BODY AND TRIM

## EXTERIOR

### Doors

REMOVAL & INSTALLATION

**Front**

▶ See Figure 1

**⁂ WARNING**

The doors are heavier than they appear. Support the door from the bottom and use a helper during removal and installation. Do not allow the door to sag while partially attached and do not subject the door to impact or twisting motions.

1. Turn the ignition key to the **OFF** position. Disconnect the negative battery cable. Wait at least 90 seconds from the time the negative battery was disconnected to start work.

**⁂ CAUTION**

Some models covered by this manual may be equipped with a Supplemental Restraint System (SRS), which uses an air bag. Whenever working near any of the SRS components, such as the impact sensors, the air bag module, steering column and instrument panel, disable the SRS, as described in Section 6.

2. If equipped with power door locks, windows or any other power option located on the door, remove the inner door panel and disconnect the electrical component.

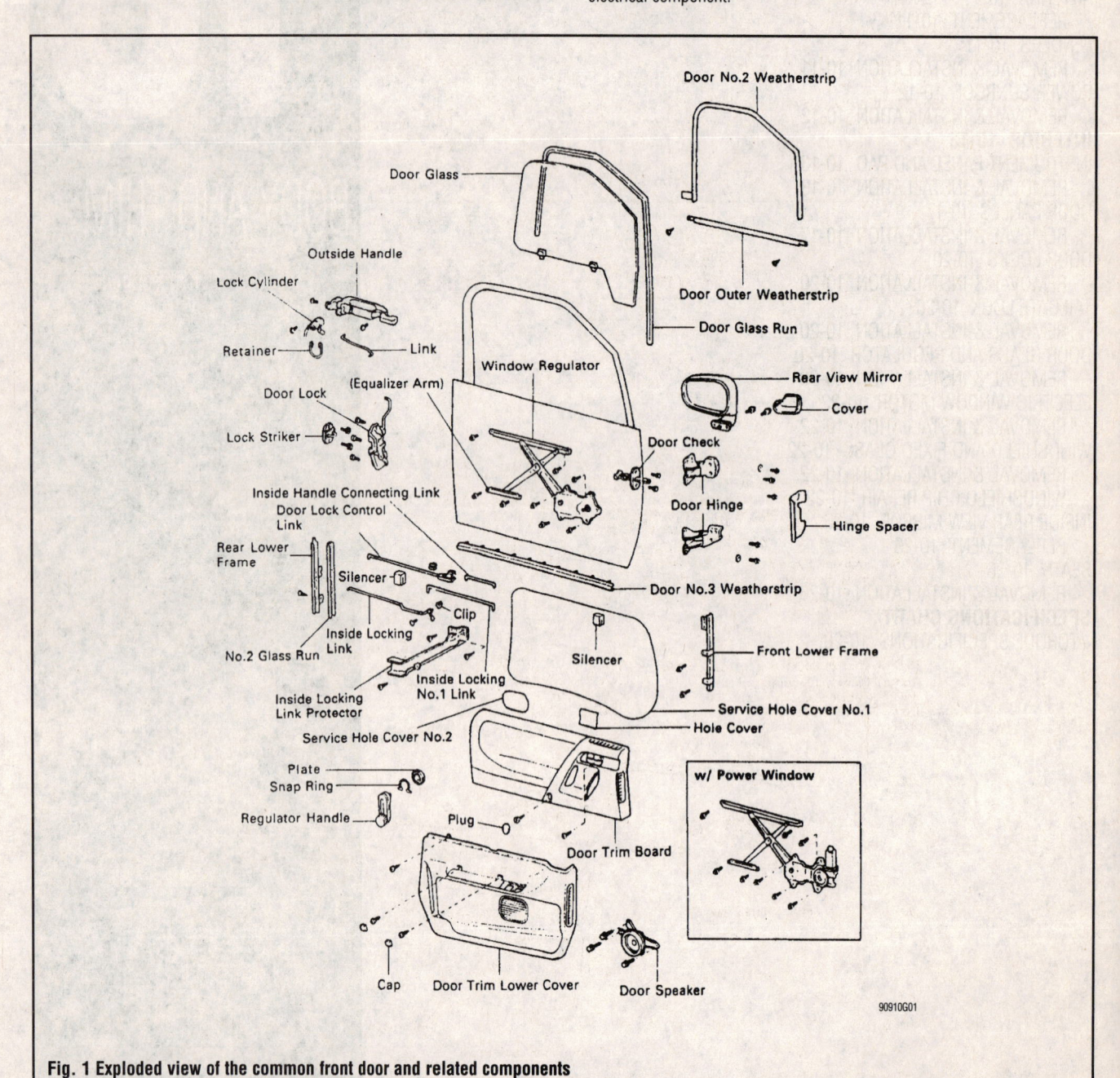

Fig. 1 Exploded view of the common front door and related components

# BODY AND TRIM  10-3

3. Remove the wire harness retainers and extract the harness from the door.

4. Use a floor jack padded with rags or soft lumber to support the door at its lower midpoint. Use a felt tip marker to outline the hinge position on the door.

5. Disconnect the door check rod. To prevent the rod from falling inside the door, install the retainer into the hole in the end of the check rod.

6. Have a helper support the door, keeping it upright at all times. Remove the bolts holding the upper and lower hinges for the door.

7. Using two people, lift the door clear of the van.

8. The door hinge may be removed from the body if necessary.

**To install:**

9. If the door hinge is removed from the body, reinstall it and tighten the bolts securely.

10. Place the door in position and support it. Use the jack to fine tune the position until the bolt holes and matchmark (hinge outline) align.

11. Apply an appropriate amount of multipurpose grease to the lower hinge and cam sliding area. Using engine oil, lubricate between the lower hinge pin and the roller.

12. Install the hinge bolts and nuts. Tighten the bolts securely.

13. If all has gone well, the door should almost be in the original position. Refer to the door adjustment procedures to align the door and body. It may be necessary to loosen the hinge bolts and reposition the door; remember to retighten them each time or the door will shift out of place.

14. Once adjusted, connect the door check lever and install the pin. Install the hinge covers if any were removed.

15. Route the wiring harness(es) into the body and connect them to their leads.

16. Connect the negative battery cable.

17. Test the operation of any electrical components in the door (locks, mirrors, speakers, etc.) and test drive the car, checking the door for air leaks and rattles.

## Sliding

▶ See Figures 2, 3, 4, 5 and 6

1. Using a taped flatbladed tool, remove the end molding from the door.
2. Remove the bolt and catch spring.
3. Remove the door handle with clip. Use a rag or special clip removal tool.
4. Slide the door rearward to disconnect the upper, lower and center rollers from the rails, then remove the sliding door.

**To install:**

5. Slide the door forward to connect the center roller, the lower and upper rollers to the rails. install the sliding door.
6. Install and secure the bolt and catch spring.
7. Inspect the clips on the door molding. Replace any broken clips and attach to the door.

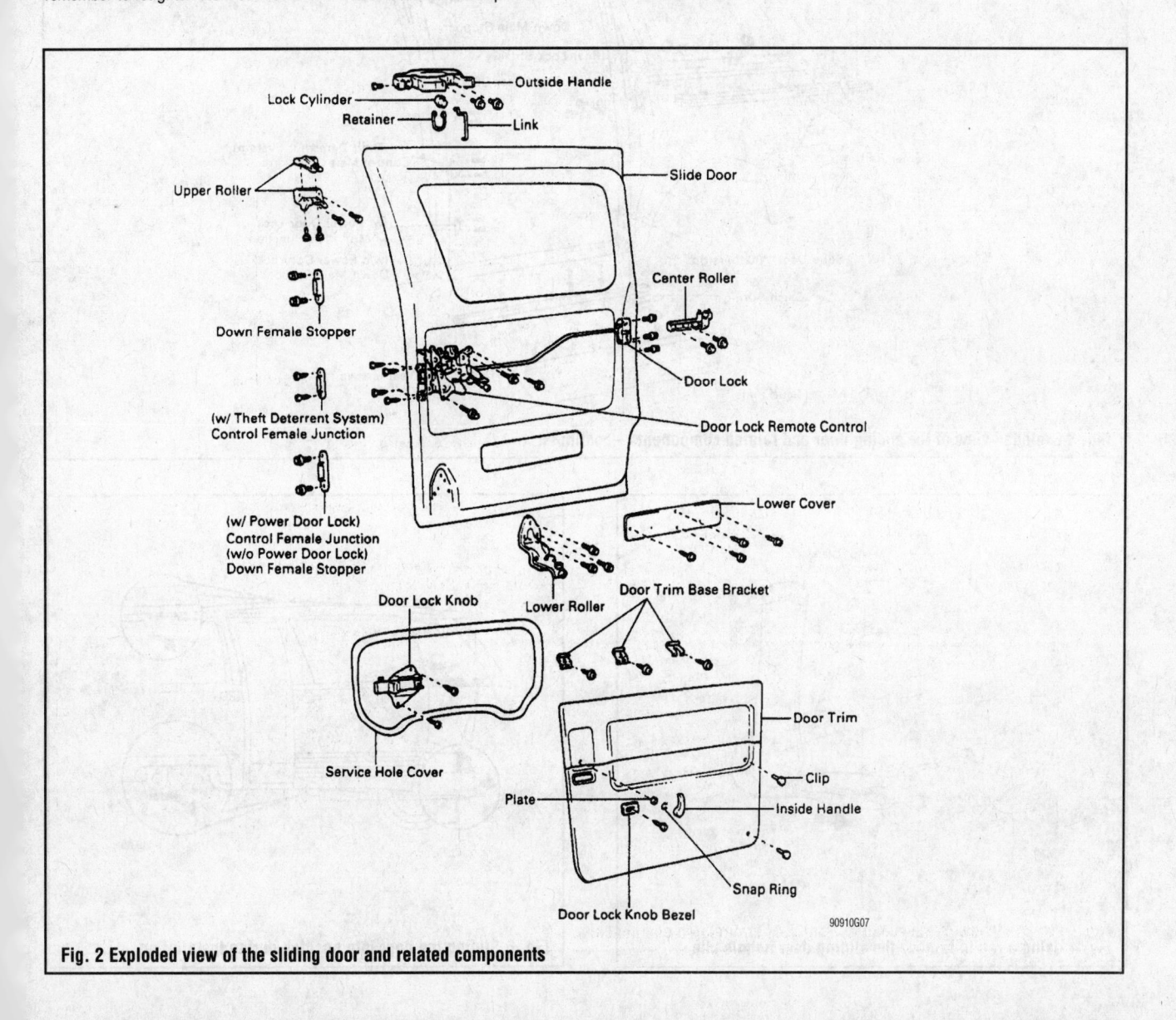

Fig. 2 Exploded view of the sliding door and related components

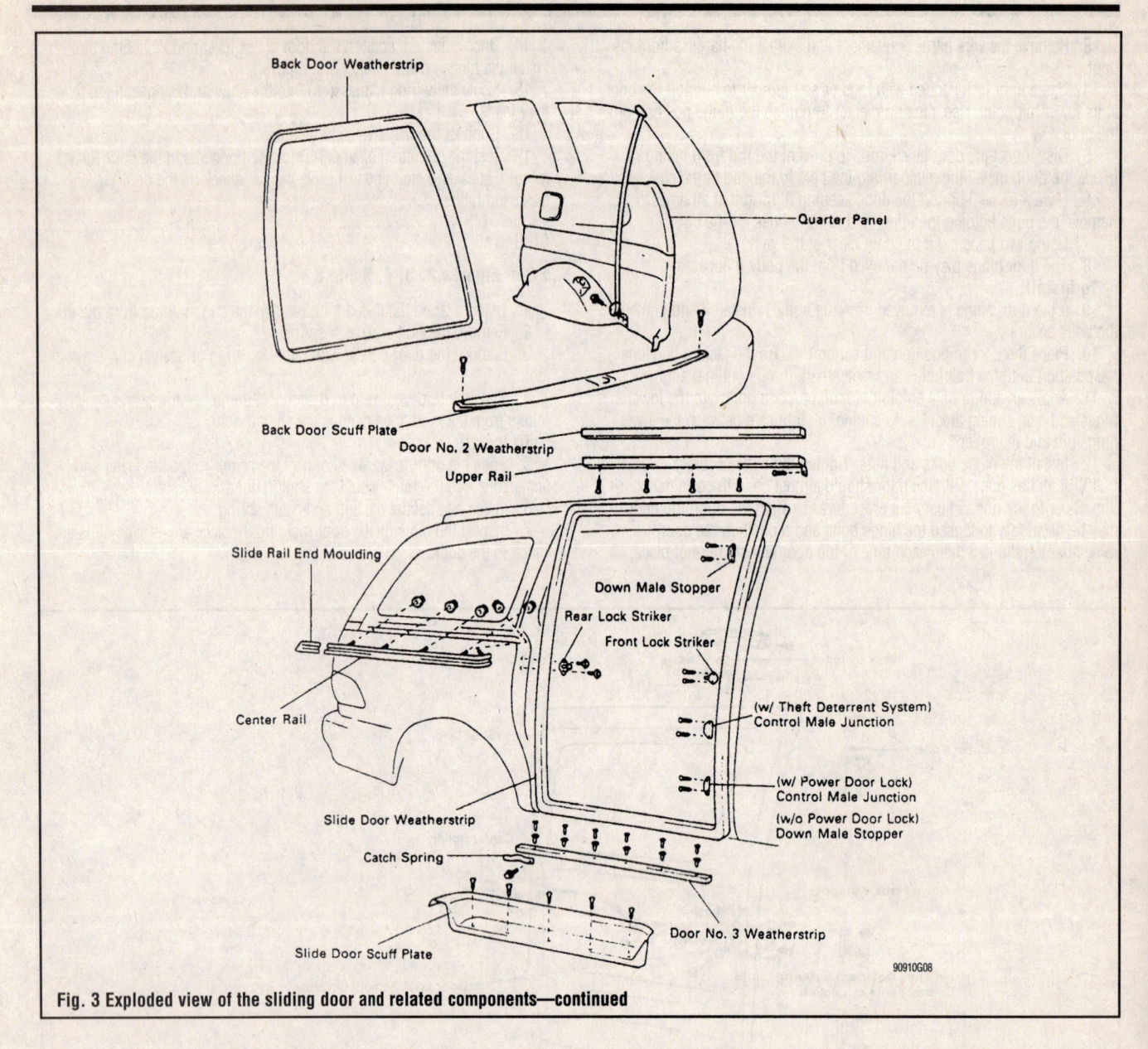

## 10-4 BODY AND TRIM

Fig. 3 Exploded view of the sliding door and related components—continued

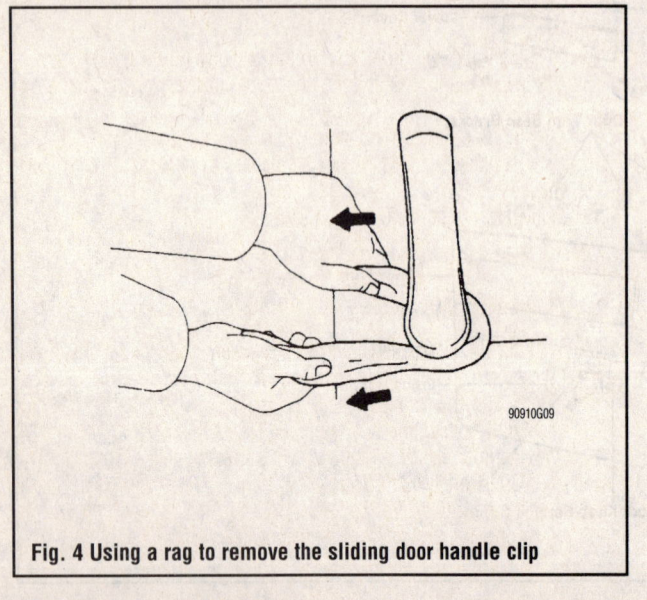

Fig. 4 Using a rag to remove the sliding door handle clip

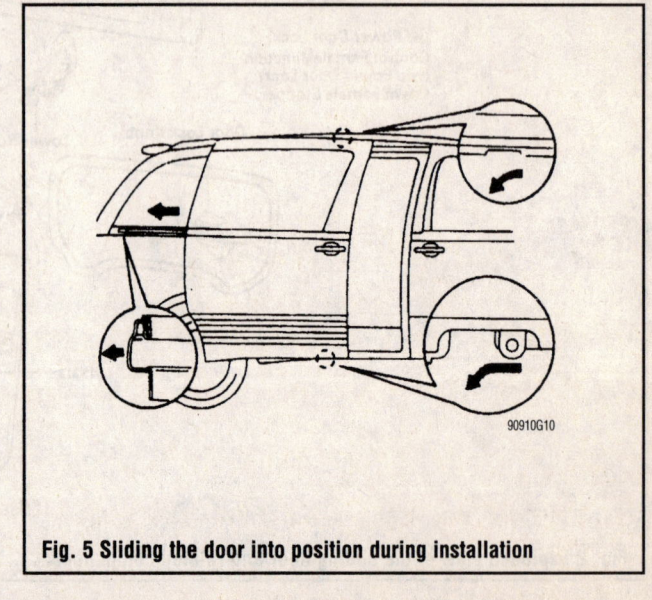

Fig. 5 Sliding the door into position during installation

# BODY AND TRIM  10-5

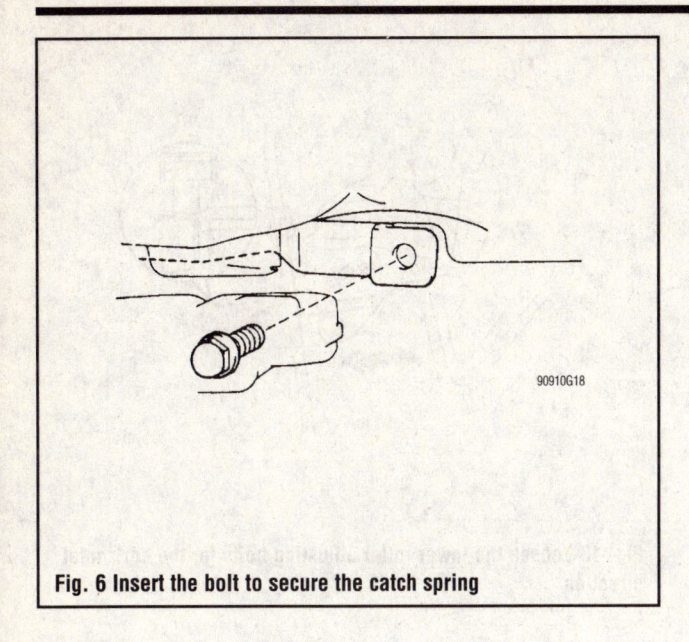

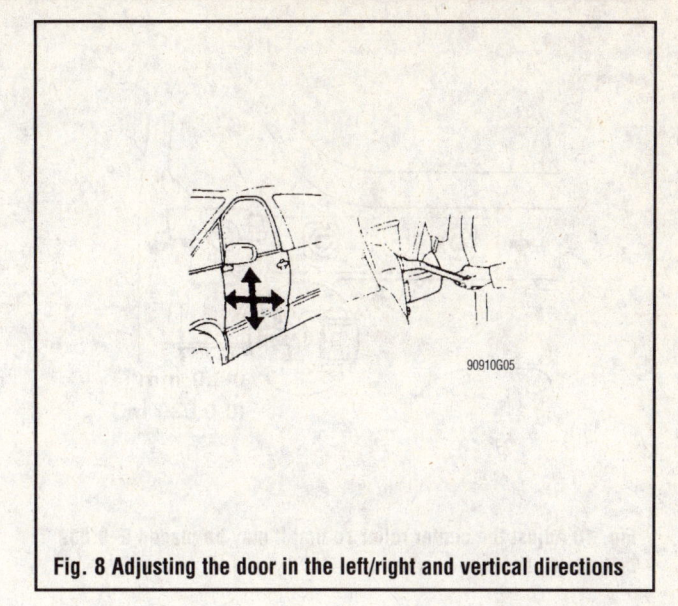

**Fig. 6 Insert the bolt to secure the catch spring**

## ADJUSTMENT

### Front

♦ See Figures 7, 8 and 9

➡ Since the centering bolt is used as the door hinge and lock set bolt, the door and lock can not be adjusted with it on. Substitute the bolt with a washer for the centering bolt.

1. Remove the hinge spacer.

To adjust the door in forward, rearward and vertical directions, perform the following adjustment:

2. Loosen the body side hinge bolts.
3. Adjust the door to the desired position.
4. Secure the body side hinge bolts or nuts and check the door for proper alignment.

To adjust the door in left, right and vertical directions, perform the following adjustments:

5. Loosen the door side hinge bolts slightly.

➡ Substitute the bolt with a washer for the centering bolt.

6. Adjust the door to the desired position.

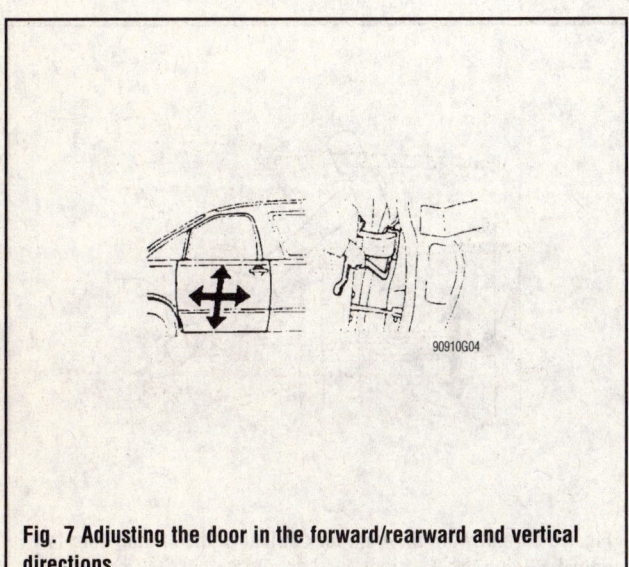

**Fig. 7 Adjusting the door in the forward/rearward and vertical directions**

**Fig. 8 Adjusting the door in the left/right and vertical directions**

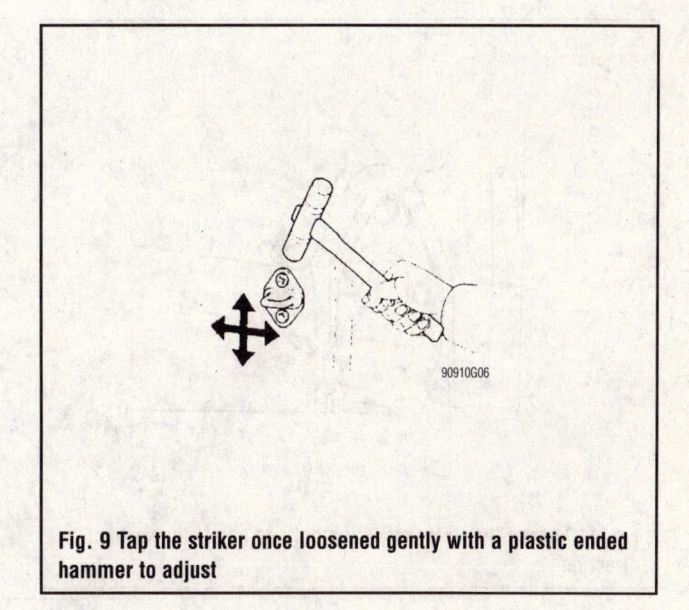

**Fig. 9 Tap the striker once loosened gently with a plastic ended hammer to adjust**

7. Secure the door side hinge bolts and check the door for proper alignment.

To adjust the door lock striker, perform the following procedure:

8. Check that the door fit and the door lock linkages are adjusted properly.
9. Slightly loosen the striker mounting screws to adjust.
10. Using a plastic tipped hammer, tap the striker until the desired position is obtained.
11. Tighten the striker mounting screws.

### Sliding

♦ See Figures 10 thru 16

To adjust the side of the door in forward/rearward and vertical directions:

1. Remove the 2 bolts and the rear lock striker.
2. Remove the door trim.
3. Loosen the center roller mounting bolts to adjust.
4. With the door closed, adjust the center roller so that it may be placed 0–0.039 inch (0–1.0mm) above the race.

To adjust the door in the vertical direction:

5. While opening the door, loosen the lower roller mounting bolts to adjust.

## 10-6 BODY AND TRIM

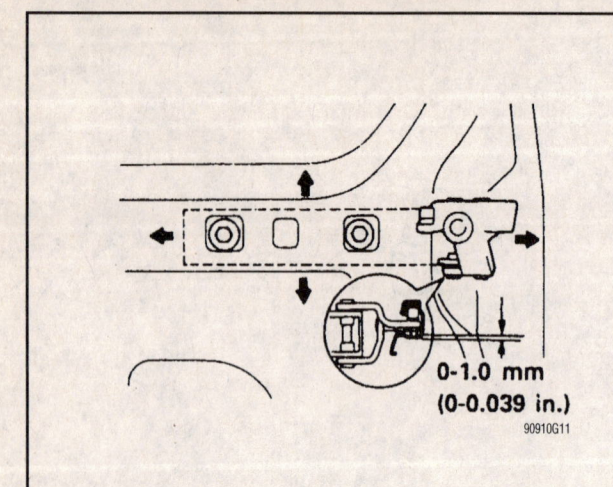

Fig. 10 Adjust the center roller so that it may be placed 0–0.039 inch above the race as shown

Fig. 11 Loosen the roller mounting bolts to adjust the vertical direction

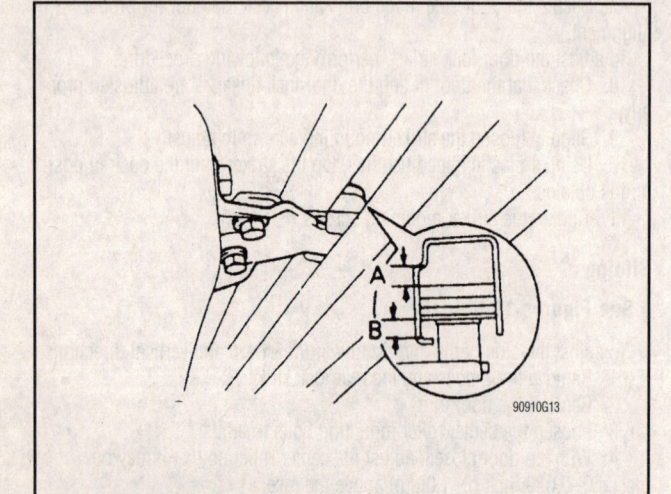

Fig. 12 On the horizontal adjustment, be sure the clearance is between the upper roller and rail is as specified

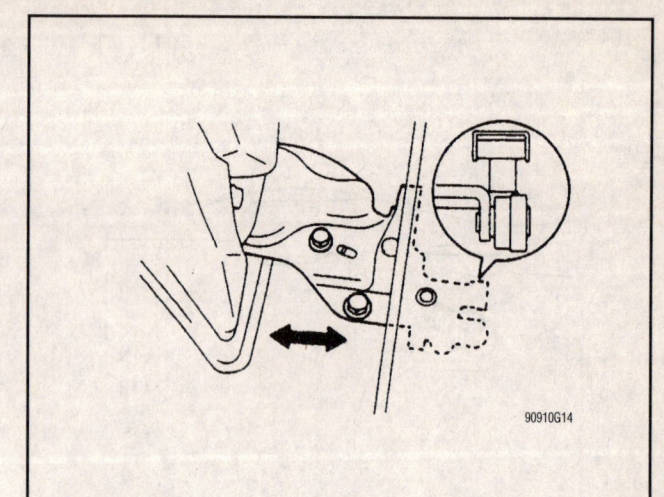

Fig. 13 Loosen the lower roller adjusting bolts for the horizontal direction

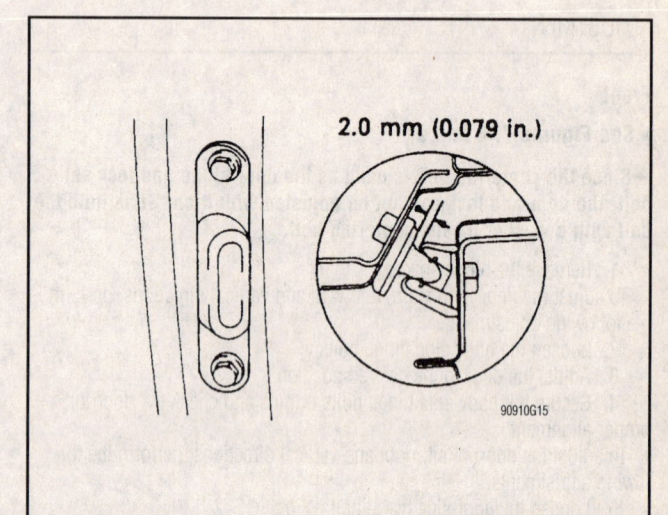

Fig. 14 Adjust the down female stopper so that it may be placed above the race

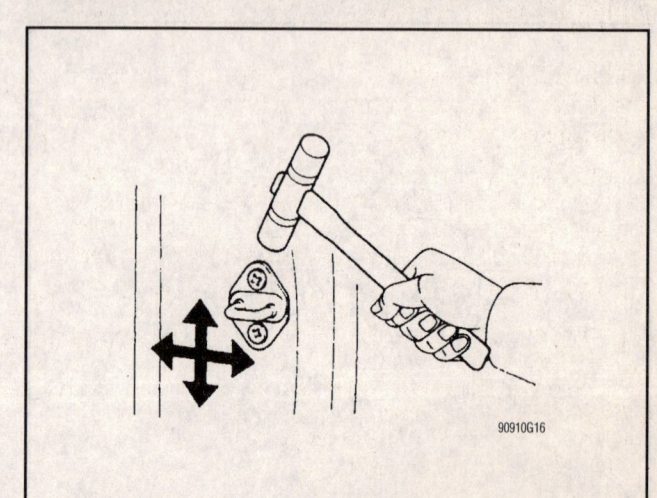

Fig. 15 carefully tap the front lock striker of the sliding door to adjust

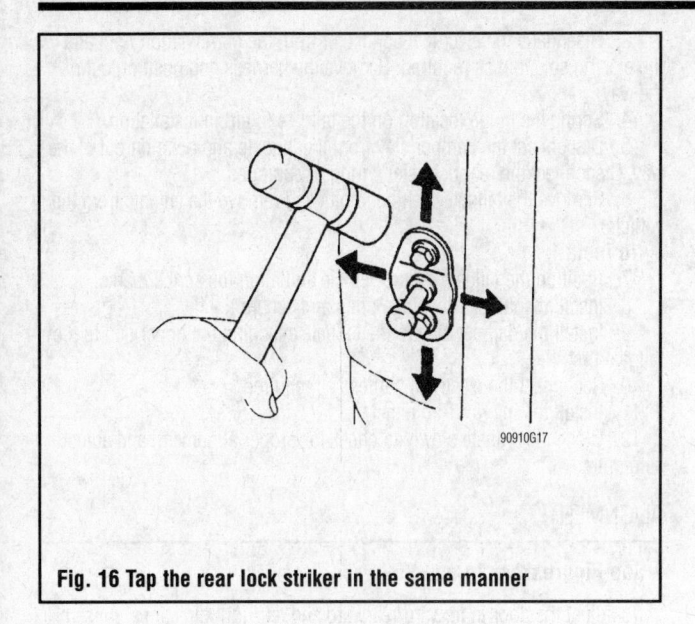

# BODY AND TRIM  10-7

**Fig. 16 Tap the rear lock striker in the same manner**

To adjust the door in the horizontal direction:
6. Loosen upper roller adjusting bolts to adjust.
7. Ensure that the clearance between the upper roller and rail are as shown in the illustration throughout the stroke.
   a. Clearance should be:
   - A—0.177 inch (4.5mm)
   - B—0.173 inch (4.4mm)
8. Loosen the lower roller adjusting bolts to adjust.

To adjust the female stopper:
9. Loosen the door side down female stopper mounting bolts to adjust.
10. With the door closed, adjust the down female stopper so that it may be placed 0.079 inch (2.0mm) above the race.

To adjust the front lock striker:
11. Check that the door fit and door lock linkages are adjusted correctly.
12. Loosen the striker mounting screws to adjust.
13. Using a plastic hammer, tap the striker to adjust it.

To adjust the rear lock striker:
14. Check that the door fit and door linkages are adjusted correctly.
15. Loosen the striker mounting bolts to adjust.
16. Using a plastic headed hammer, tap the striker to adjust.

## Hood

### REMOVAL & INSTALLATION

♦ See Figure 17

1. Open the hood completely.
2. Protect the cowl panel and hood from scratches during this operation. Apply protection tape or cover body surfaces before starting work.
3. Scribe a mark showing the location of each hinge on the hood to aid in alignment during installation.
4. Disconnect any windshield washer hoses.
5. Prop the hood in the upright position. Disconnect the hood prop cylinder(s) from the hood (if equipped).
6. Have an assistant help hold the hood while you remove the hood-to-hinge bolts. Use care not to damage hood or vehicle during hood removal.
7. Lift the hood off of the vehicle.

**To install:**
8. Position he hood on hinges and align with the scribe marks.
9. Install and tighten the mounting bolts with enough torque to hold hood in place.

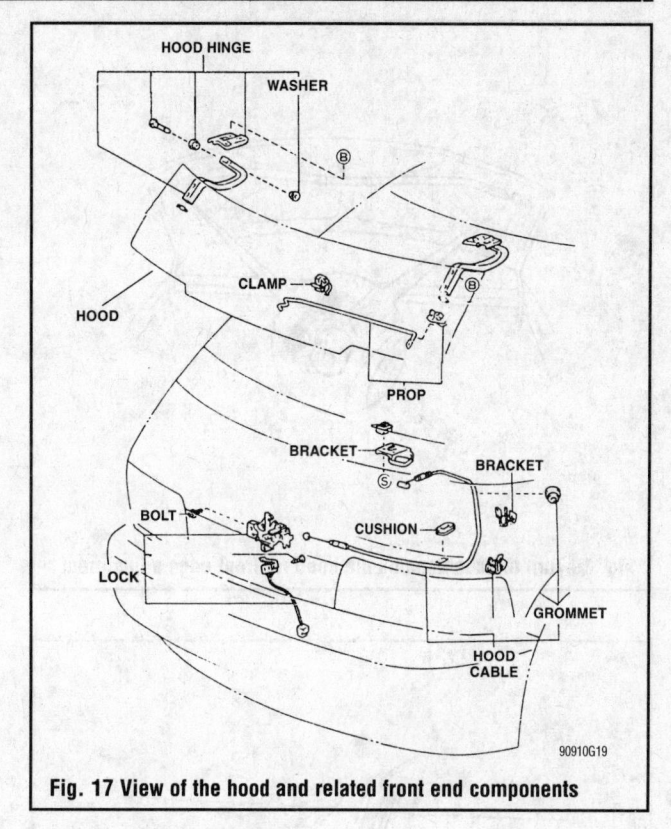

**Fig. 17 View of the hood and related front end components**

10. Install the hood prop cylinders as required.
11. Close the hood slowly to check for proper alignment. Do not slam the hood closed, alignment is normally required.
12. Open the hood and adjust so that all clearances are the same and the hood panel is flush with the body.
13. After all adjustments are complete, tighten hinge mounting bolts to 8–10 ft. lbs. (11–14 Nm).

### ALIGNMENT

♦ See Figures 18, 19 and 20

Since the centering bolt, which has a chamfered shoulder, is used as the hood hinge and the lock set bolt, the hood and lock can't be adjusted with it

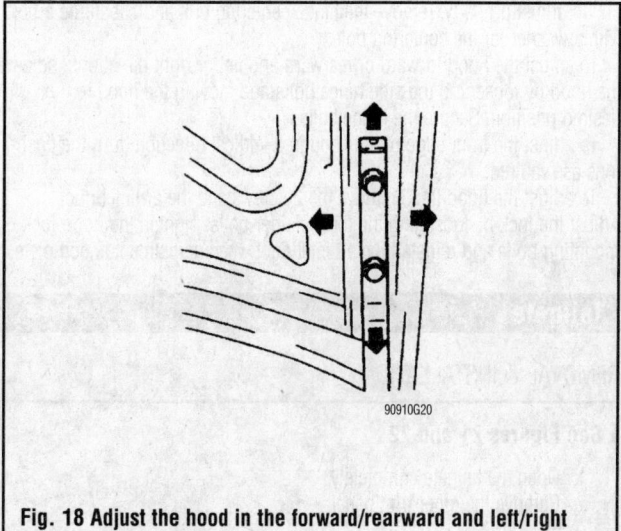

**Fig. 18 Adjust the hood in the forward/rearward and left/right directions by loosening the bolts**

# 10-8 BODY AND TRIM

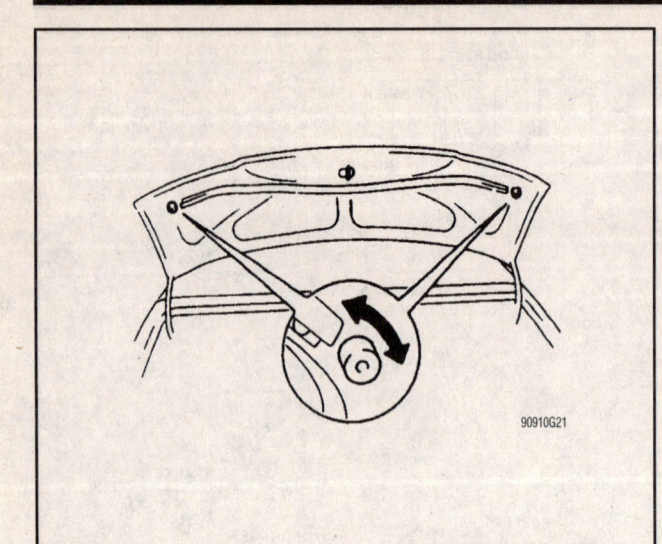

**Fig. 19 Turn the cushions on the hood for front edge adjustment**

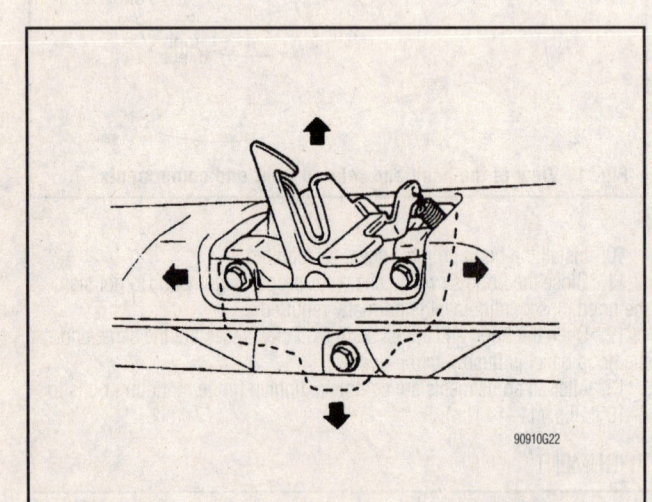

**Fig. 20 Loosen hood lock bolts, then position the lock bolts to adjust. Secure at the desired location**

on. To adjust properly, remove the hinge centering bolt and substitute a bolt with a washer for the centering bolt.

To adjust the hood forward or rearward and left or right directions, adjust the hood by loosening the side hinge bolts and moving the hood to the desired position. Secure the hinge bolts.

To adjust the front edge of the hood in a vertical direction, turn the cushions as required.

To adjust the hood lock, remove the 2 screws and the air inlet duct. Adjust the lock by loosening the lock retainer bolts. Tighten the hood lock mounting bolts and reinstall the air inlet duct when adjustment is complete.

## Tailgate

### REMOVAL & INSTALLATION

▶ See Figures 21 and 22

1. Open the tailgate completely.
2. Remove the inner trim panel.
3. Disengage the electrical connector from the combination light and the electric solenoid as required. Remove the harness and position out of the way.
4. Scribe the hinge location on the tailgate to aid in installation.
5. Disconnect the damper stay from the tailgate and position out of the way. Disconnect the rear defroster wiring, if equipped.
6. Remove the tailgate-to-hinge bolts and remove the tailgate from the vehicle.

**To install:**
7. Position the tailgate on the vehicle and align the scribe marks.
8. Install the tailgate-to-hinge bolts and secure tightly.
9. Install the damper stay to the tailgate attaching the upper end to the tailgate first.
10. Reconnect the electrical harness as required.
11. Install the interior trim panel.
12. Close the tailgate slowly to check for proper alignment, and adjust as required.

### ALIGNMENT

▶ See Figures 23, 24 and 25

To adjust the door in forward/rearward and left/right directions, loosen the hinge bolts and position the tailgate as required and secure.

To adjust the door in forward/rearward and vertical directions, loosen the body side hinge nuts to adjust.

To adjust the side female stopper:
1. Loosen the stopper mounting bolts, then using a plastic tipped hammer, tap the striker to adjust.

To adjust the tailgate lock striker:
2. Remove the 2 screws (on each end) from the back door scuff plate, then carefully pull to release it.

➡ Be careful not to damage the clip during removal.

3. Check that the door fit and linkages are adjusted correctly.
4. Loosen the striker mounting screws to adjust.
5. Using a plastic tipped hammer, tap the striker to adjust. Secure the bolts.

## Grille

### REMOVAL & INSTALLATION

▶ See Figure 26

The grille can be removed without removing any other parts. The grille is held on by a number of fasteners. Raise the hood and look for screws placed vertically in front of the metalwork. Remove the retainer screws and lift the grille from the vehicle.

On installation, make sure that all the retainers are installed in their original locations.

## Outside Mirrors

### REMOVAL & INSTALLATION

#### Power

▶ See Figures 27, 28, 29 and 30

1. Remove the upper door trim panel.
2. From the outside of the vehicle, separate the mirror trim cover.
3. Pull the plastic covering away from the door shell.
4. Locate the wiring harness for the power mirror.
5. Separate the wiring harness.

**BODY AND TRIM** **10-9**

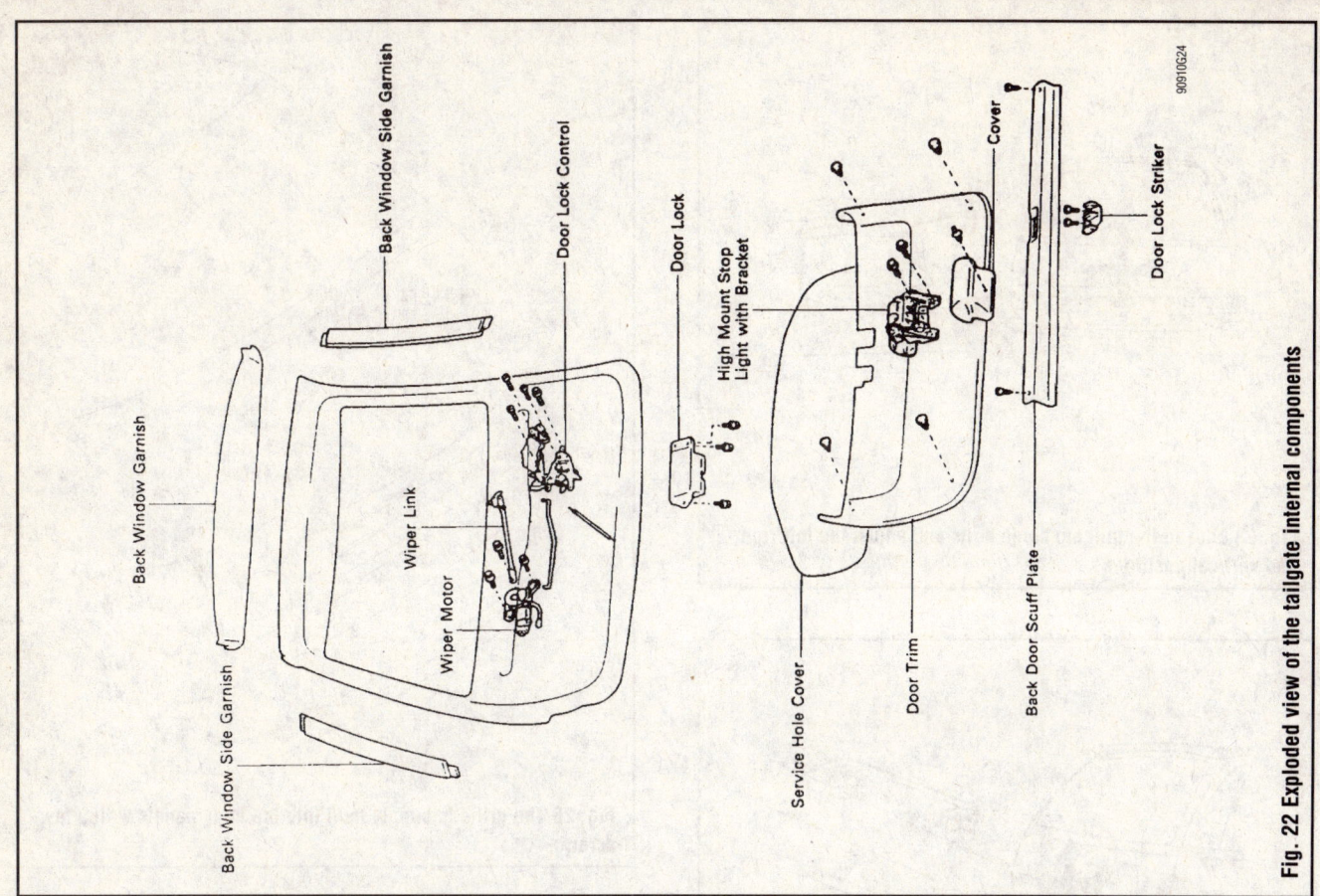

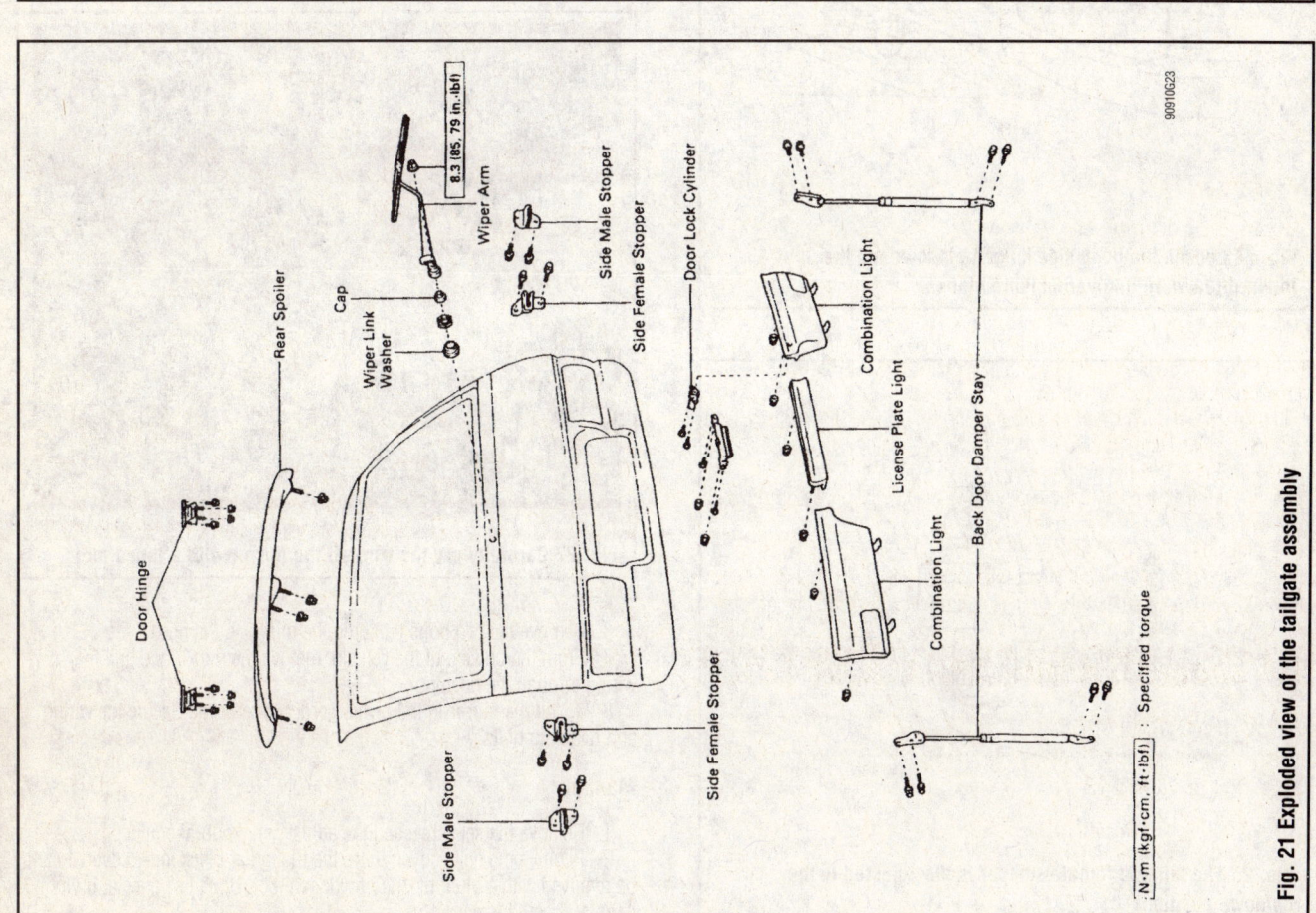

Fig. 22 Exploded view of the tailgate internal components

Fig. 21 Exploded view of the tailgate assembly

## 10-10 BODY AND TRIM

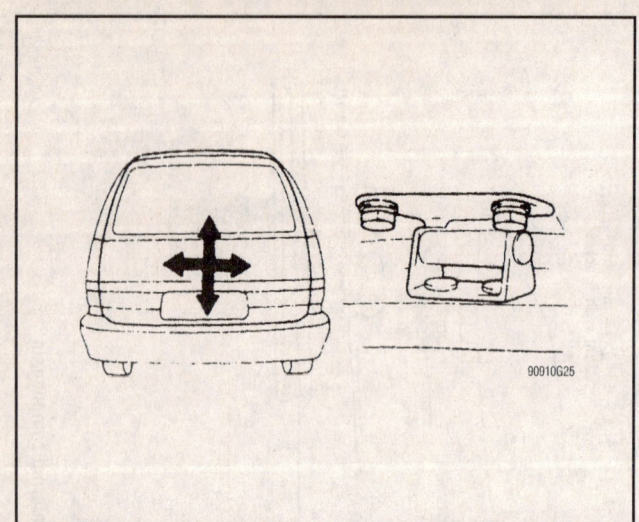

Fig. 23 Loosen the tailgate hinge bolts and adjust the left/right and vertical positions

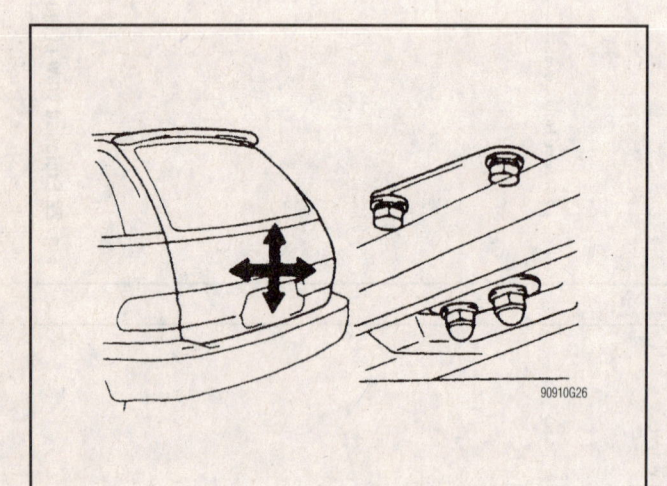

Fig. 24 Loosen the body side hinge nuts to adjust the forward/rearward and vertical directions

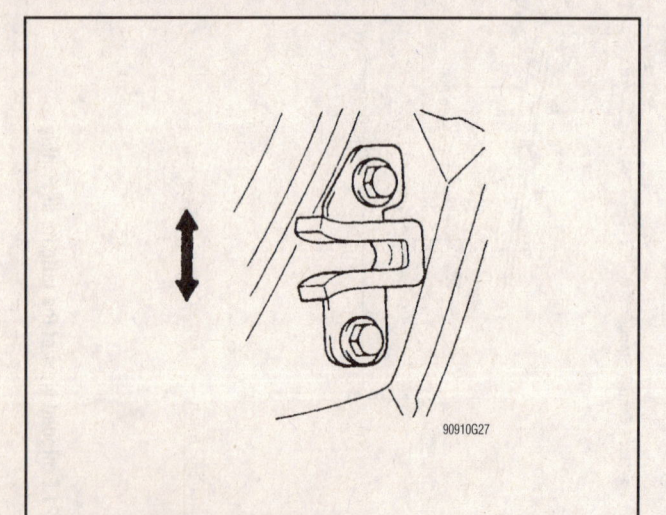

Fig. 25 The tailgate female stopper is the adjusted in the up/down positions

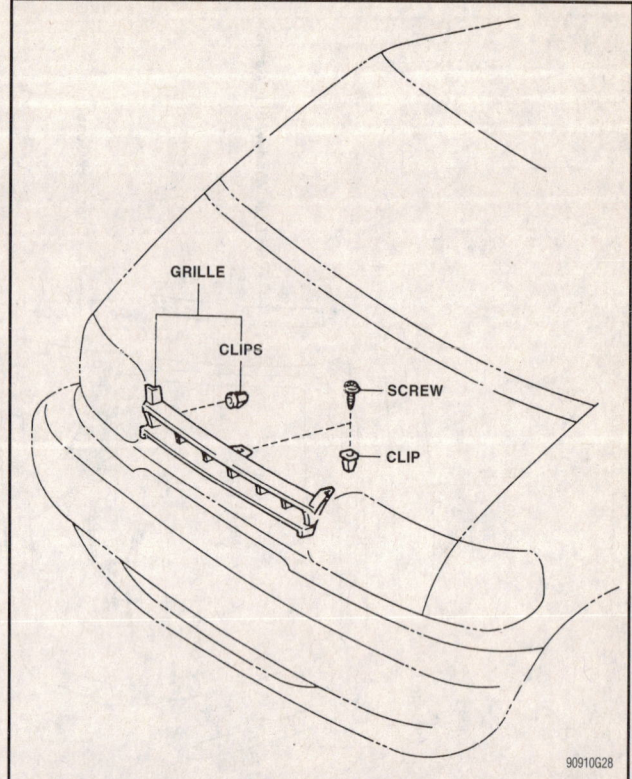

Fig. 26 The grille is simply held into the body panels with a few screws

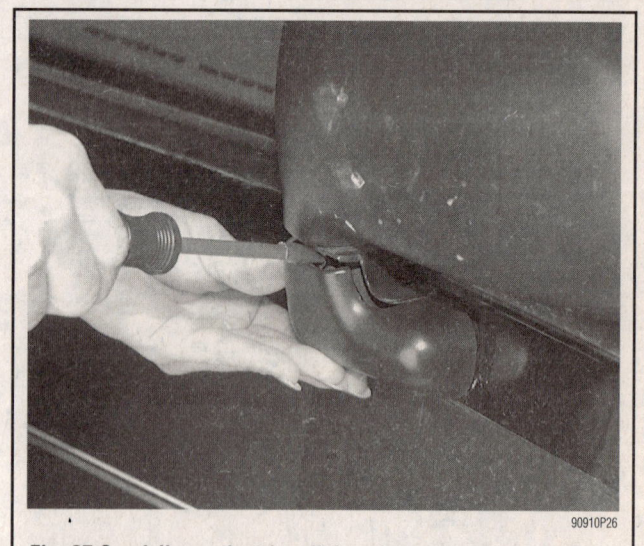

Fig. 27 Carefully pry the trim off the mirror with a taped tool

6. Remove the two bolts retaining the mirror to the door.
7. From the outside of the vehicle, remove the mirror and pull the wiring through the opening.
8. Install the mirror in the reverse order of removal. Secure the wiring and retaining bolts.

**Manual**

1. Remove the set screw and the adjustment knob, if equipped.
2. Remove the delta cover; that's the triangular black inner cover. It can be removed with a blunt plastic or wooden tool. Don't use a metal prytool; the plastic will be marred.

# BODY AND TRIM  10-11

3. Depending on the style of mirror, there may be concealment plugs or other minor parts under the delta cover—remove them.
4. Support the mirror housing from the outside and remove the bolts or nuts holding the mirror to the door.
5. Remove the mirror assembly.

**To install:**
6. Fit the mirror to the door and install the nuts and bolts to hold it. Pay particular attention to the placement and alignment of any gaskets or weatherstrips around the mirror; serious wind noises may result from careless work.
7. Install any concealment plugs, dust boots or seals which were removed.
8. Install the delta cover and install the adjustment knob, if it was removed.
9. Cycle the mirror several times to make sure that it works properly.

## Antenna

### REPLACEMENT

Some antenna masts are attached to the side of the windshield pillar on the drivers side. Simply unscrew the two plastic holders and proceed with cable removal. there will be on some models a rear antenna incorporated in the rear windshield. this can only be replaced with the glass.

Disconnect the antenna cable at the radio by pulling it straight out of the set. Depending on access, this may require loosening the radio and pulling it out of the dash. Working under the instrument panel, disengage the cable from its retainers.

➡ **On some models, it may be necessary to remove the instrument panel pad to get at the cable.**

Outside, unsnap the cap from the antenna base. Remove the screw(s) and lift off the antenna base, pulling the cable with it, carefully. When reinstalling, make certain the antenna mount area is clean and free of rust and dirt. The antenna must make a proper ground contact through its base to work properly. Install the screws and route the cable into the interior. Make certain the cable is retained in the clips, etc. Attach the cable to the radio; reinstall the radio if it was removed.

## Fenders

### REMOVAL & INSTALLATION

▸ See Figure 31

1. Remove the inner liner from the fender to be removed.

### ✷✷ WARNING

**Be careful of the SRS modules located in the wheel wells, these must not be damaged or bumped during removal of the liner or fender.**

2. Remove of disconnect all electrical items attached to the fender.
3. If necessary, remove the front bumper assembly.
4. Remove all bolts attaching the fender and the brace to the firewall and the radiator/grille panel.
5. Remove the rear attaching bolts through the pillar opening and remove the fender from the vehicle.

**To install:**
6. Attach the fender to the vehicle with the mounting bolts and tighten securely. Make sure the fender is aligned correctly with all other panels.
7. If removed, attach the front bumper.
8. Install and connect all electrical components removed.
9. Attach the inner fender liner.

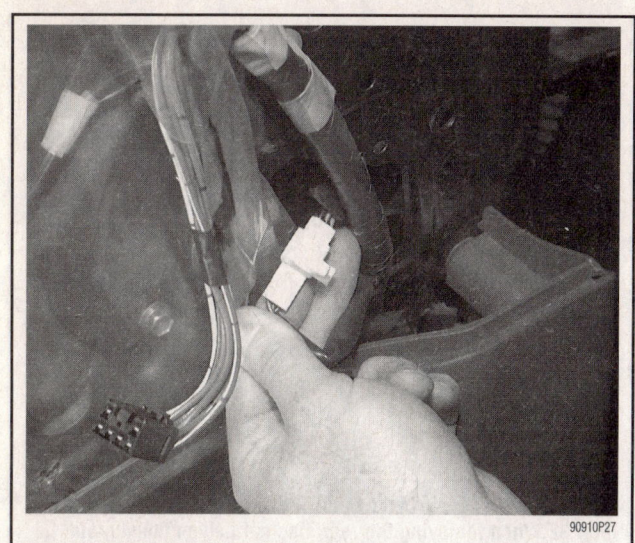

Fig. 28 Locate the wiring harness for the power mirror

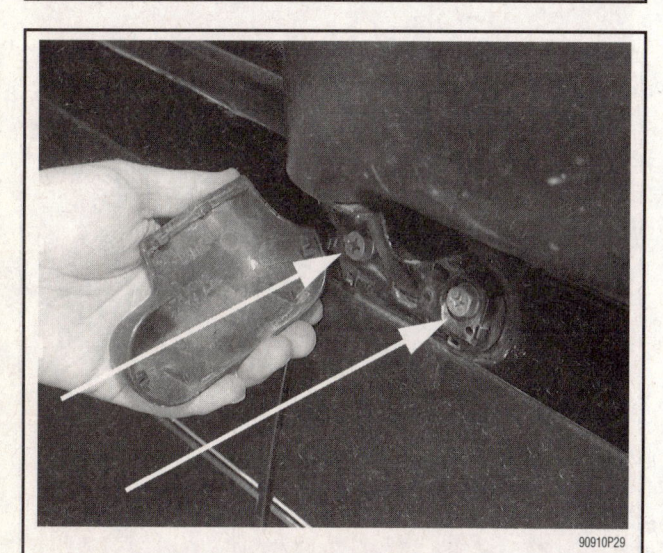

Fig. 29 Remove these two mirror retaining bolts

Fig. 30 Pull the wiring for the mirror through the opening

# 10-12 BODY AND TRIM

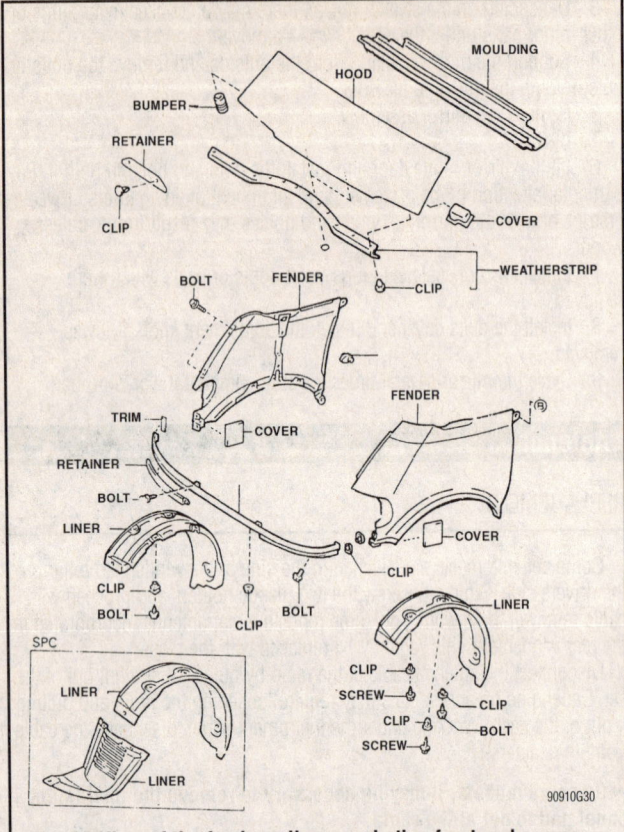

Fig. 31 View of the fenders, liners and other front end components

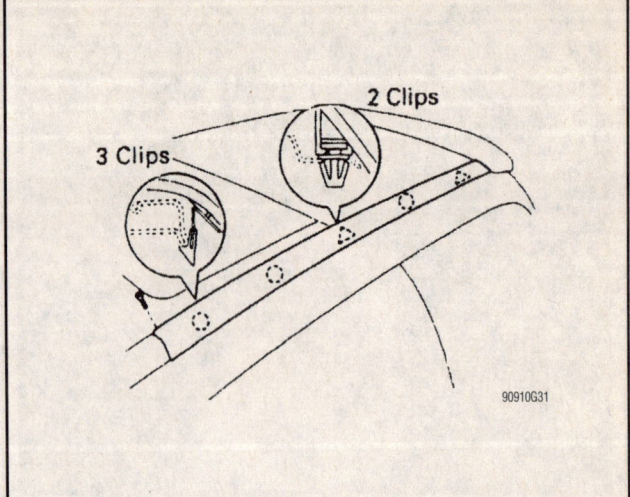

Fig. 32 When removing the rear side garnish on the sunroof, be careful pulling on the clips

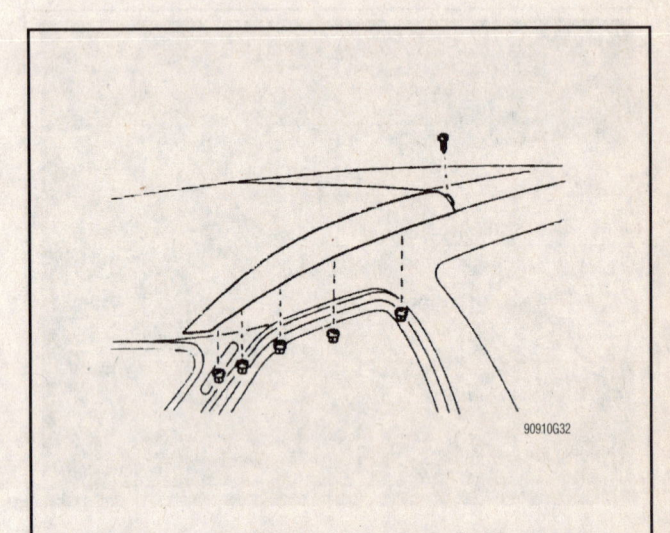

Fig. 33 The front roof side garnish is attached with one screw and five nuts

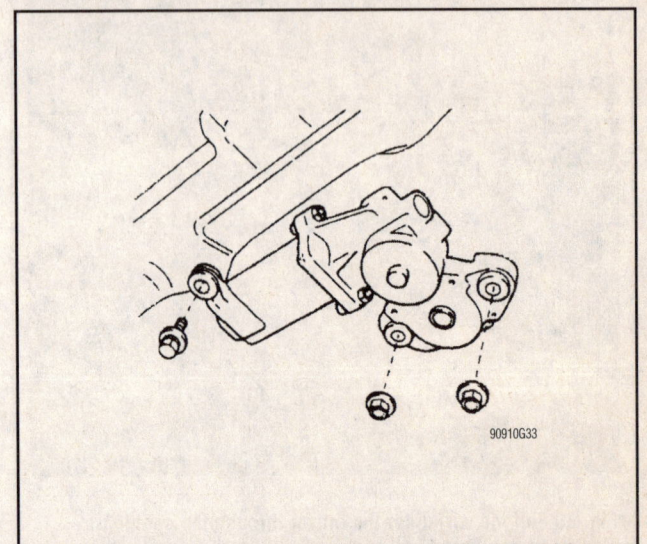

Fig. 34 Remove the sunroof motor, then disconnect the wiring

## Power Sunroof

### REMOVAL & INSTALLATION

▶ See Figures 32, 33, 34 and 35

1. Open the sliding moon roof.
2. Disconnect the negative battery cable. Wait at least 90 seconds before proceeding on models equipped with an air bag.
3. Remove the roof headliner.
4. Unscrew and remove the rear roof side garnish. The trim can be carefully pulled off. Watch for broken clips and replace as needed.
5. Remove the front roof side garnish. There is one screw and 5 nuts.
6. Remove the drive motor retained by two nuts and a bolt. Disconnect the wiring attached to the motor.
7. Detach the sliding moon roof garnish held in place with one screw.
8. Remove the sliding moon roof glass from the cable held in by four nuts.
   a. Slide the glass rearward to remove it.
9. Remove the wind deflector panel, only two nuts retain the panel.
10. Unscrew and separate the slide roof rail. Remove the four nuts and the side roof front rail. Remove the three nuts and slide the rear rail.
11. Remove the roof guide nut and slide the guide off.
12. Remove the eight bolts for the drive cable and extract the cable.
13. Pull the weatherstrip off the roof.

**To install:**

14. Attach the weatherstrip to the opening in the roof.
15. Attach and secure the drive cable with the eight bolts.
16. Install the slide roof rear guide. Position and secure the front guide with the nut.

# BODY AND TRIM  10-13

17. Install the panel with two nuts and secure.
18. Slide the glass forward to insert into the slide roof rail. install the glass to the drive cable. Install the four nuts.
19. Slide the sliding roof rearward to the rear end. Remove the screw and cam plate cover. Loosen the large screw at the back side of the drive shaft, then turn the drive shaft by hand to align the housing and gear point mark as shown in the illustration. Install the cam plate cover with the screw. attach the wiring. Install the motor and secure with the nuts and bolt.
20. Adjust the roof.
21. Install the sliding roof garnish and secure.
22. Install the front roof side garnish and secure with the five nuts and screw.
23. Tap the rear roof side garnish to install and secure with the screw.
24. Doubler check that all garnishes and components are secure, there is nothing worse than installing all the components and having a rattle.
25. Install the headliner.
26. Connect the negative battery cable.

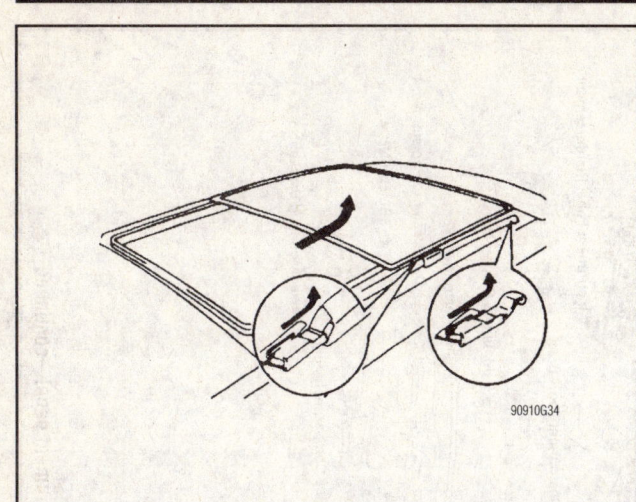

Fig. 35 When removing the glass, slide it rearward to extract

## INTERIOR

### Instrument Panel and Pad

REMOVAL & INSTALLATION

♦ See Figures 38 thru 49

1. Disconnect the negative battery cable. Wait at least 90 seconds on models equipped with an airbag.
2. Remove the assist grips on either door.
3. Carefully remove the garnishes on the door pillars.
4. Pull the rear edge of the side defroster nozzle upward and remove it.
5. Remove the steering wheel.
6. Unscrew and separate the steering column covers.
7. If necessary, remove the door scuff panels.
8. Remove the two screws and extract the side panel.
9. If necessary, remove the hood release lever. Unscrew the lever and pull if forward to remove.
10. On the cluster finish lower panel remove the two small covers and remove the 5 screws retaining the panel.
11. Five bolts retain the knee panel, loosen and remove them.
12. Push up the release lock at the center on the lower side of the cluster finish center upper panel.
13. On the console box, press on the sides of the box while pulling the box outward, then remove the box.
14. On the ash tray and cup holder, remove the four screws and extract the ash tray retainer and cup holder. Disconnect the wiring.

Fig. 36 Common clip removal procedures

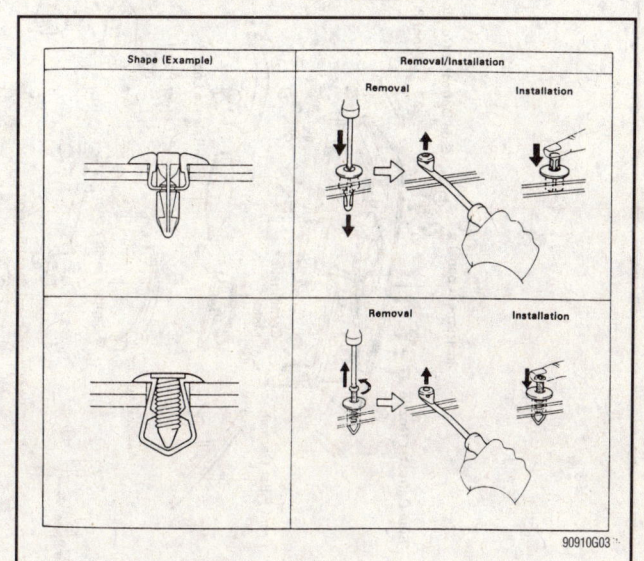

Fig. 37 Common clip removal procedures (continued)

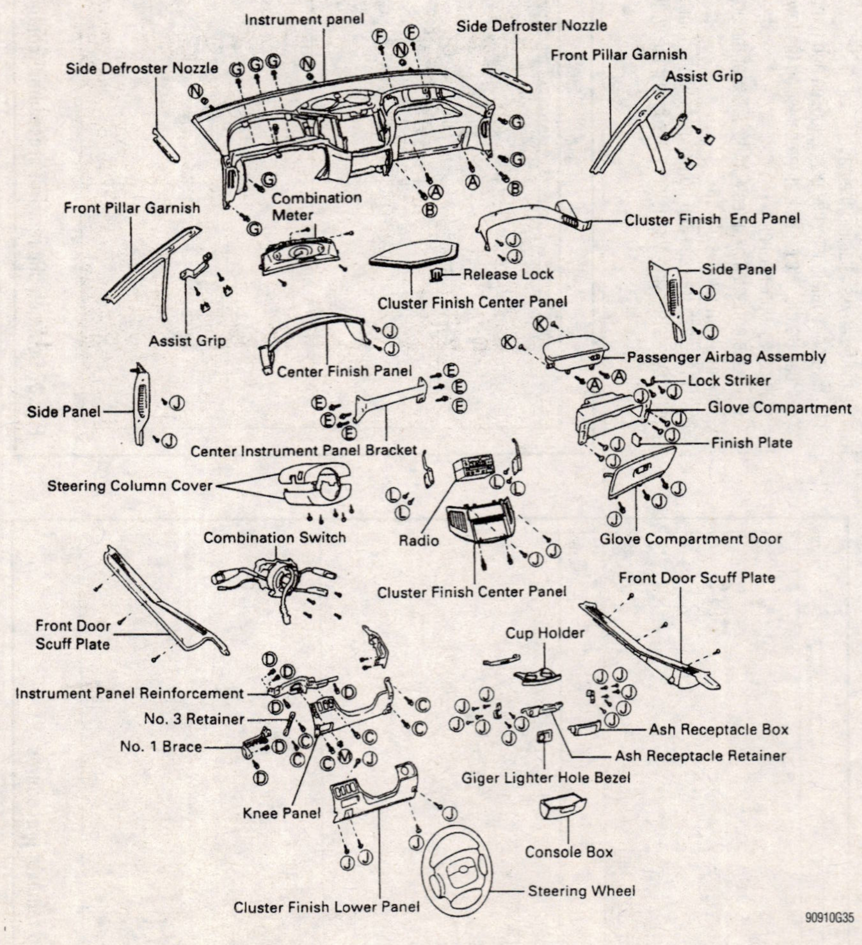

# 10-14 BODY AND TRIM

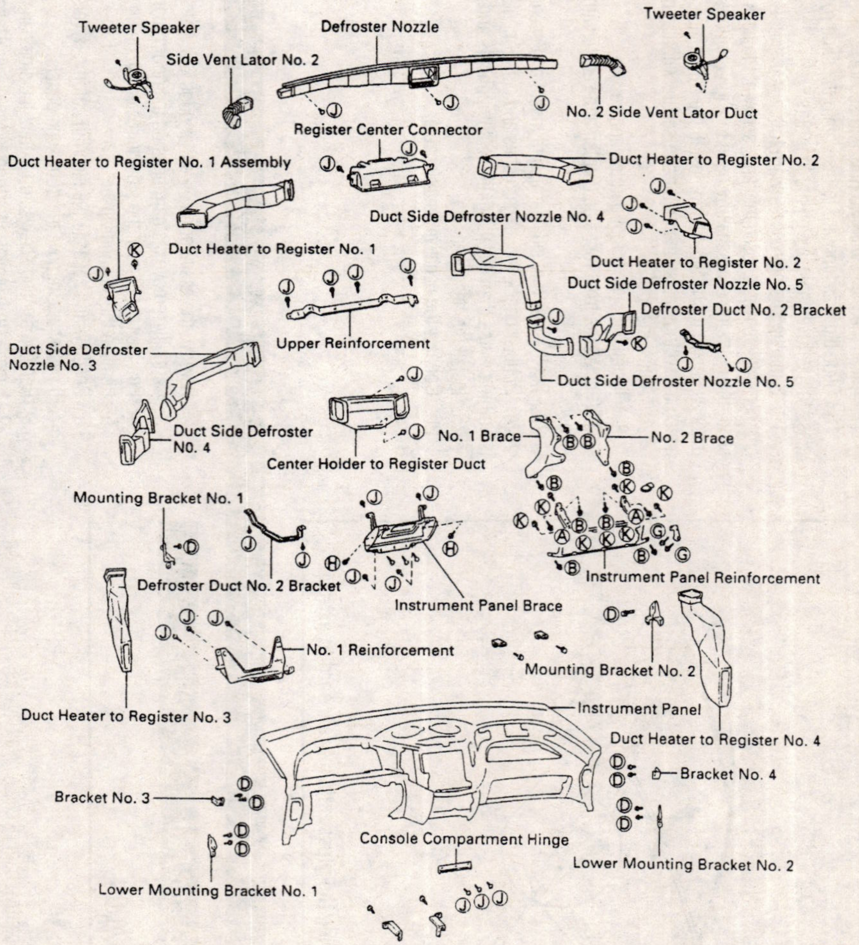

Fig. 39 Exploded view of the common instrument panel—continued

Fig. 38 Exploded view of the common instrument panel

## BODY AND TRIM 10-15

HINT: Screw sizes in the illustration on the previous page are indicated using the code below for removal and installation of instrument panel.

mm (in.)

| Code | Shape | Size | Code | Shape | Size | Code | Shape | Size |
|---|---|---|---|---|---|---|---|---|
| A | | Φ = 8 (0.31)<br>L = 40 (1.57) | B | | Φ = 8 (0.31)<br>L = 20 (0.79) | C | | Φ = 8 (0.31)<br>L = 16 (0.79) |
| D | | Φ = 8 (0.31)<br>L = 12 (0.47) | E | | Φ = 6 (0.24)<br>L = 27 (1.06) | F | | Φ = 6 (0.24)<br>L = 20 (0.79) |
| G | | Φ = 6 (0.24)<br>L = 16 (0.63) | H | | Φ = 5 (0.20)<br>L = 18 (0.71) | I | | Φ = 5 (0.20)<br>L = 12 (0.47) |
| J | | Φ = 5.22 (0.2055)<br>L = 16 (0.63) | K | | Φ = 5.22 (0.2055)<br>L = 12 (0.47) | L | | Φ = 5 (0.20)<br>L = 12 (0.47) |
| M | | — | N | | — | | | |

Fig. 40 Bolt size chart for the instrument panel

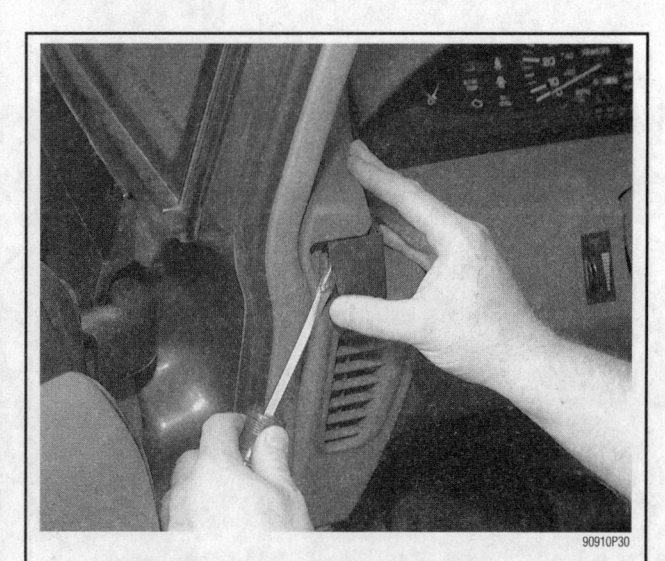

Fig. 41 Pry out the panel on the side of the dash

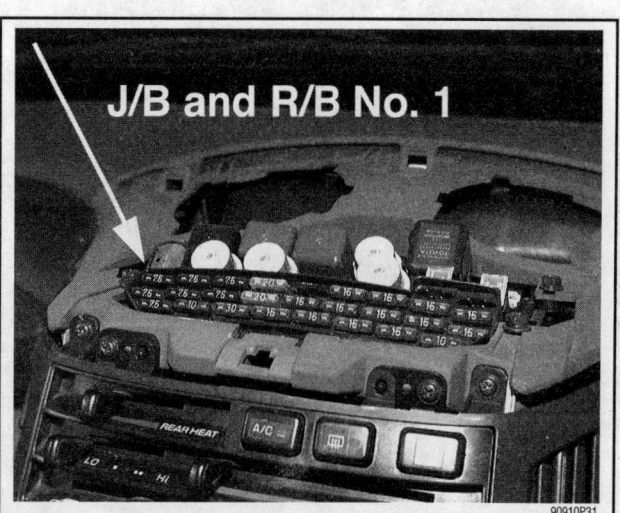

Fig. 42 Lift up the center upper panel to access the J/B and R/B No. 1

## 10-16 BODY AND TRIM

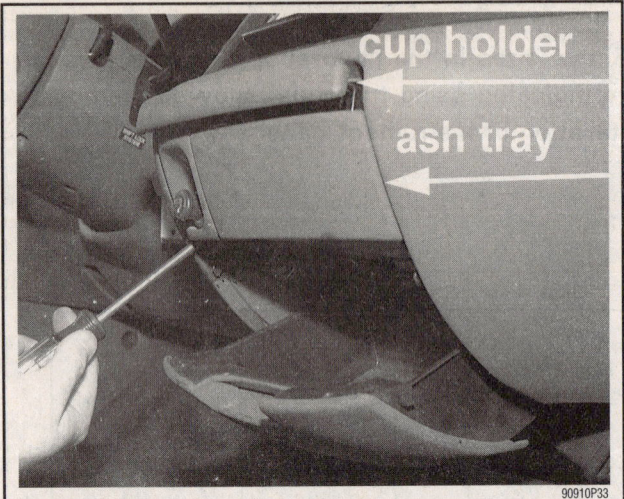

Fig. 43 There are four screws retaining the cup holder and ash tray receptacle . . .

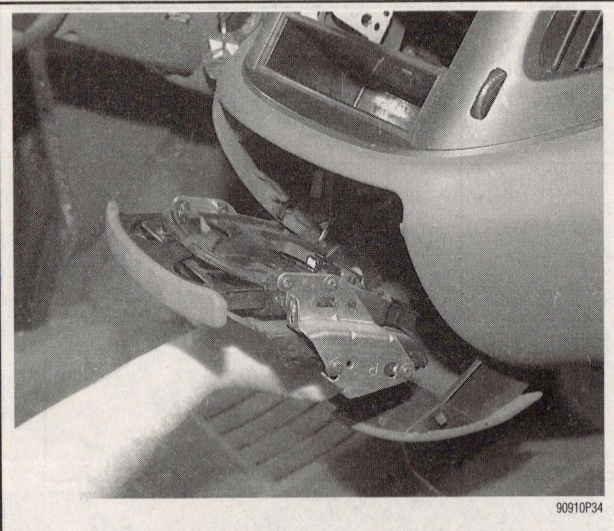

Fig. 44 . . . now lift the assembly out from the dash

Fig. 45 Unscrew the radio cluster finish panel (this vehicle was not equipped with a radio)

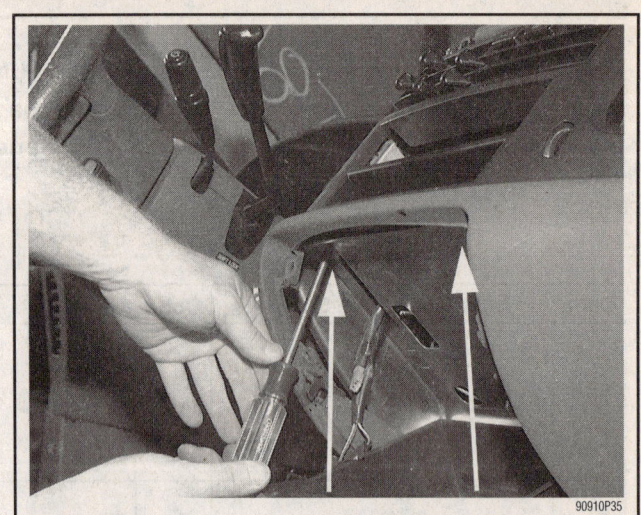

Fig. 46 The radio console has two screws up underneath to access for removal

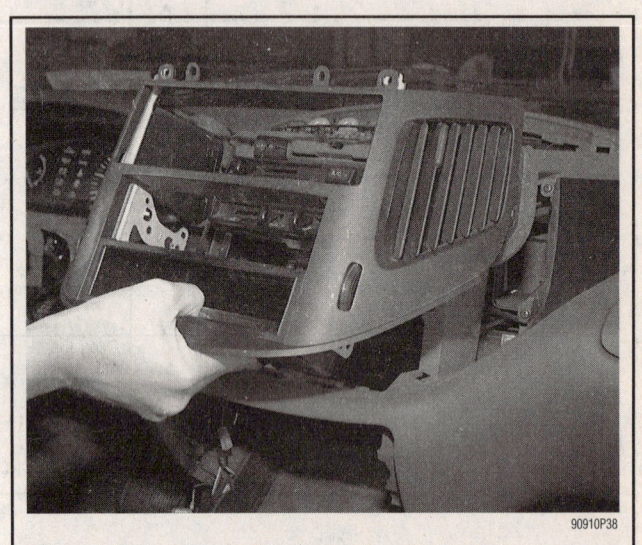

Fig. 47 Slide the finish panel out from the dash

Fig. 48 Unscrew and remove the upper cluster finish panel . . .

# BODY AND TRIM  10-17

**Fig. 49 . . . then remove these screws from the cluster**

15. Remove the cluster finish center panel with radio. There are two screws, two up underneath. Then disconnect the wiring.
16. Unscrew and pry out the cluster finish end panel from the dash.
17. To remove the combination member, extract the four retaining screws. On the A/T transmission, disconnect the cable from the control lever. Be sure the lever is in the **P** position. Remove the cable from the roller, then the meter. disconnect the harnesses from the back of the meter assembly.
18. For the glove box, remove the two screws and the door with hinge.
19. Unbolt the heater control assembly and allow to hang from the dash with the cables connected.
20. Very carefully, unbolt the J/B and R/B No. 1 from the dash.
21. On automatic transmissions, remove the shift lever. Remove the two bolts and the detent plate. Remove the through bolt, nut and shift lever. Disconnect the wiring from the overdrive switch.
22. On the instrument panel, remove the ten bolts, three screws, three nuts and panel.

**To install:**
23. Attach the instrument panel to the dash and secure the bolts and nuts.
24. On A/T models, adjust the shift lock pin. install the shift lever with the through bolt and nut. Position the detent plate and secure with the two bolts. Attach the wiring harness to the overdrive switch.
25. Install the J/B and R/B No. 1 and secure.
26. Attach the heater control assembly and tighten the retaining screws.
27. Install the combination meter, connect all wiring and secure the screws.
28. Position the cluster finish end panel and tap to secure. tighten the two screws on the end of the panel.
29. Install the cluster finish end panel.
30. Attach the cluster finish center panel with radio and connect all wiring.
31. Install the ash tray retainer and cup holder.
32. Install all the remaining components and secure.
33. Connect the negative battery cable. Reset any electrical components such as the radio.

## Door Panels

### REMOVAL & INSTALLATION

**Front**

▶ See Figures 50 thru 61

1. On models without power windows, remove the window regulator handle. A rag may be used to push the handle clip out from behind. Or use a special door handle clip removal tool.
2. On models with power mirrors, insert a tapped pry tool between the door trim and the switch to separate the two.
3. Pop off the upper trim panel round screw cover and remove the screw.

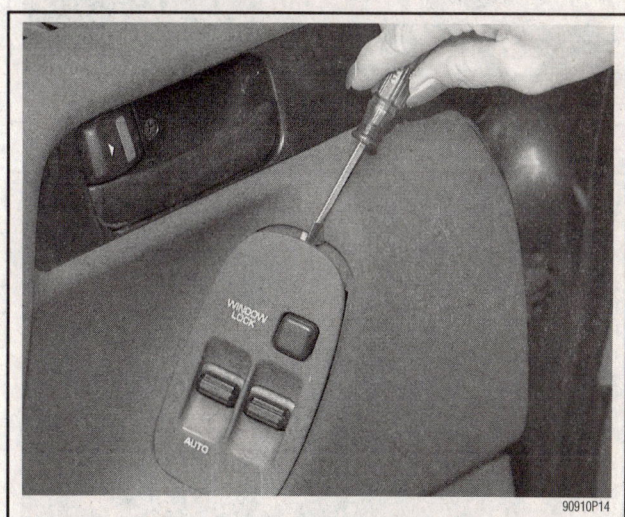

**Fig. 50 Carefully pry the power window switch from the door panel**

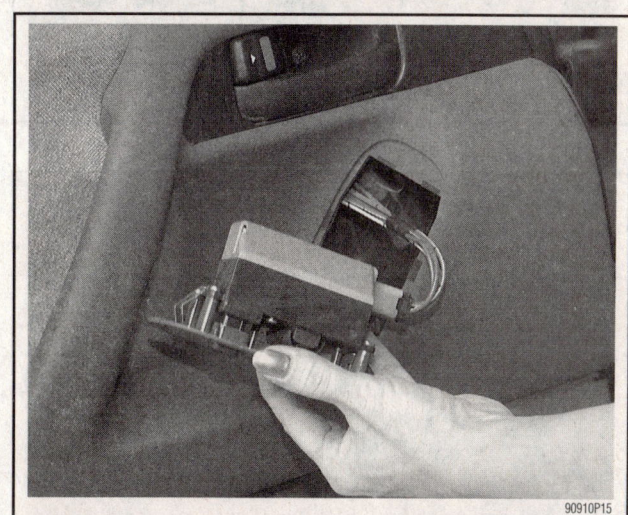

**Fig. 51 When extracting the switch do not pull it out too far because of the wiring**

# 10-18 BODY AND TRIM

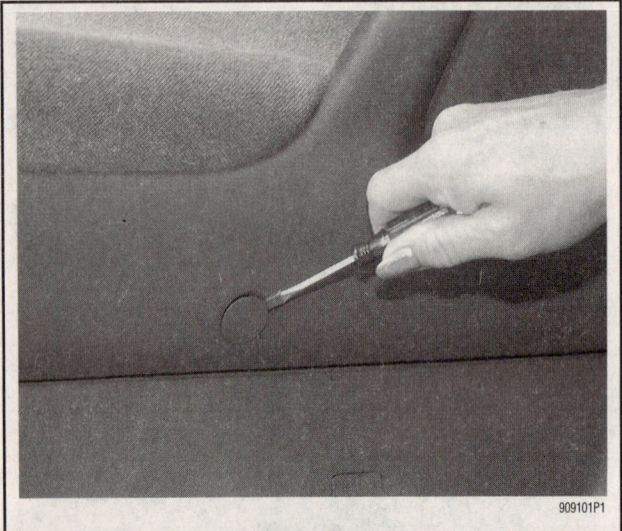

Fig. 52 Separate the wiring harness from the switch assembly

Fig. 53 Carefully pop off the screw trim cover . . .

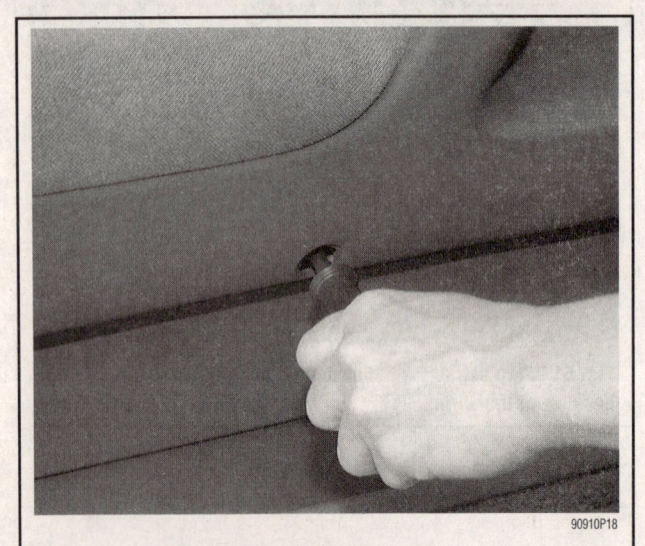

Fig. 54 . . . and remove the hidden screw

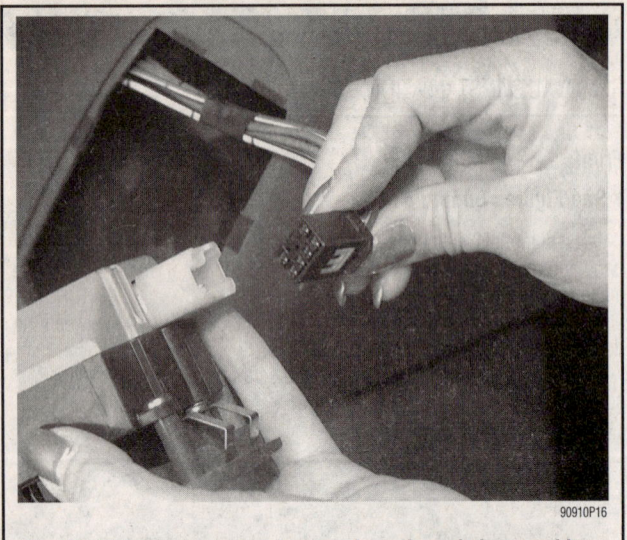

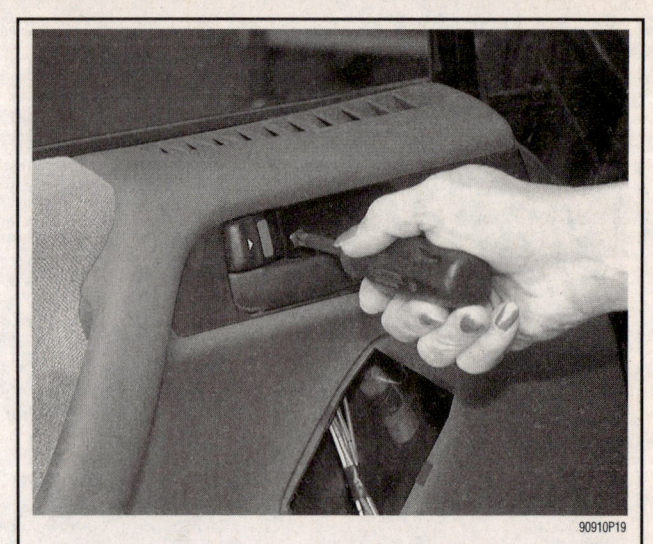

Fig. 55 Remove the screw above the door handle

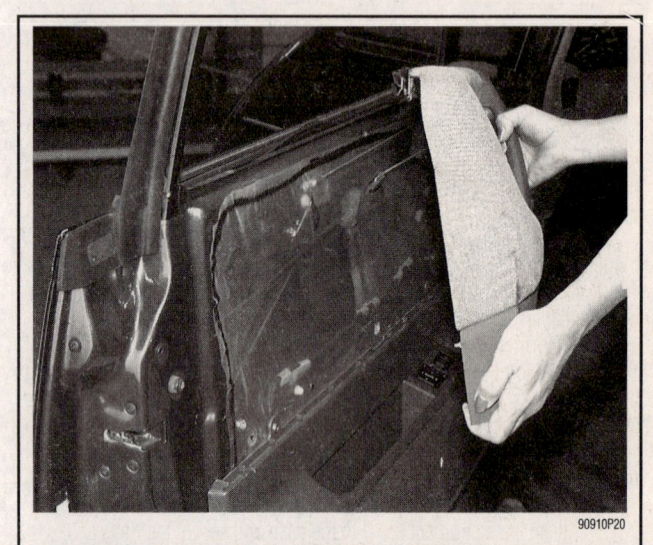

Fig. 56 Lift the upper door trim panel off the shell . . .

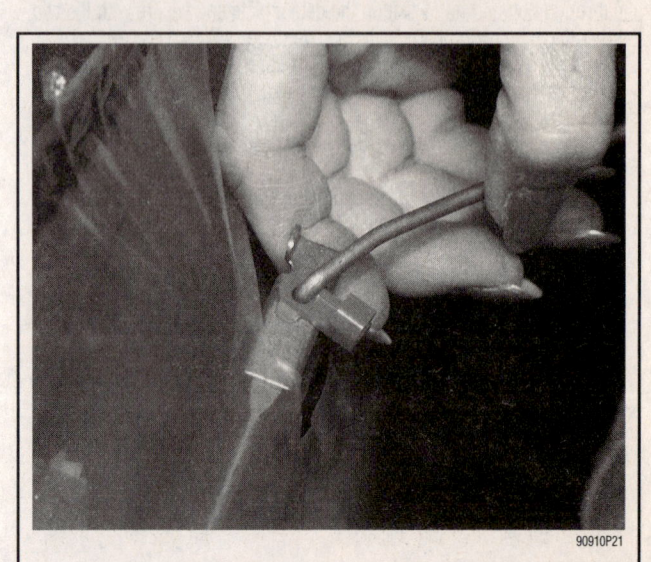

Fig. 57 Disconnect the linkages from the door panel

# BODY AND TRIM 10-19

**Fig. 58 Using a taped tool, pry the cover over the retaining screw off**

**Fig. 59 Pry the lower door panel away from the shell**

**Fig. 60 Disconnect any accessory wiring behind the lower door trim panel**

**Fig. 61 Extracting the lower door trim panel with the accessories disconnected**

4. Remove the screw around the door handle.
5. Once all the screws are removed from the upper trim panel, pry the panel away from the door shell but be careful of the linkages.
6. Disconnect the linkages from the door panel.
7. On the lower door panel, carefully pry the screw cover off and remove the screw.
8. Using some force, pry the lower trim panel from the door.
9. Behind the lower door panel is wiring from the window and other accessories, disconnect them.
10. Install the components in the reverse order of removal. Be sure to secure all wiring connections.

## Tailgate

▶ See Figures 62, 63 and 64

1. Raise the tailgate.
2. Remove the screw type retainers.
3. Once unscrewed, the clips can be pulled out from the trim panel.
4. Pull the screw type clip from the body.
5. Carefully pry too loosen the panel from the tailgate. Pull the trim panel away from the body. Watch out for clips that may be broken and replace any if necessary.

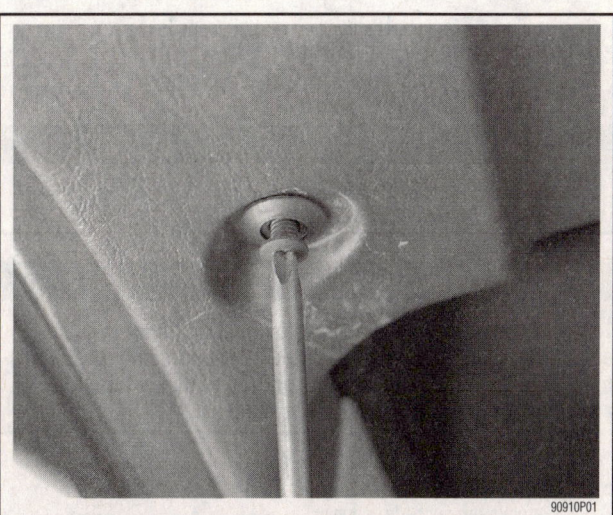

**Fig. 62 Unscrew the screw-type clips from the tailgate trim panel**

## 10-20  BODY AND TRIM

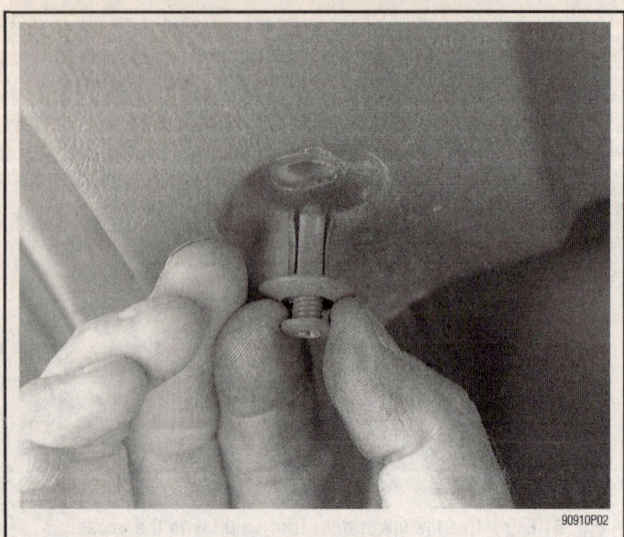

**Fig. 63 Pull the clip from the body trim panel**

**Fig. 64 Pull the trim panel away from the body**

6. Position the trim panel and attach it to the door. Be careful not to damage any of the clips.
7. Secure the panel by installing the screw-type clips.

### Door Locks

#### REMOVAL & INSTALLATION

> **CAUTION**
>
> To avoid possible unexpected deployment of the air bag (if equipped), work must not be started after approximately 90 seconds or longer from the time the ignition switch is turned OFF and the negative battery cable disconnected.

1. Disconnect the negative battery cable. Wait 90 seconds once the cable is removed before proceeding.
2. Remove the door trim panels.
3. Disconnect the inside handle connecting linkage.
4. Disconnect the locking No. 1 link.
5. Remove the service hole cover. Using a clip remover, extract the five screw grommets, then remove the no. 1 and No. 2 hole covers.
6. Disconnect the two links from the door lock.
7. Using a clip removal tool, extract the clips.
8. Remove the two links then the silencer. Turn the clamp, then pull out the door control link and inside locking link.
9. Remove the three screws and the locking link protector.
10. Disconnect the two links from the outside handle and the lock cylinder.
11. On models with power locks, disconnect the wiring.
12. Remove the lock attaching screws, then the out the lock through the service hole.
13. When installing, secure all components and use new sealant on the service hole covers.
14. Install the door panels and trim.

### Tailgate Lock

#### REMOVAL & INSTALLATION

▶ See Figures 65 thru 70

1. Remove the tailgate trim panel.
2. Remove the three screws attaching the locking mechanism to the door housing.
3. Disconnect the linkage from the door lock.
4. On power locks, disconnect the harness form the solenoid.
5. Detach the cable from the latch, then extract the assembly from the vehicle.
6. Attach the cable to the latch.
7. Secure the wiring (if equipped) and linkage to the assembly.
8. Position the assembly into the body of the vehicle and secure with the retaining screws.
9. Install the secure the tailgate trim panel.

### Door Glass and Regulator

#### REMOVAL & INSTALLATION

▶ See Figure 71

1. Disconnect the negative battery cable. Wait at least 90 seconds on models with an airbag.

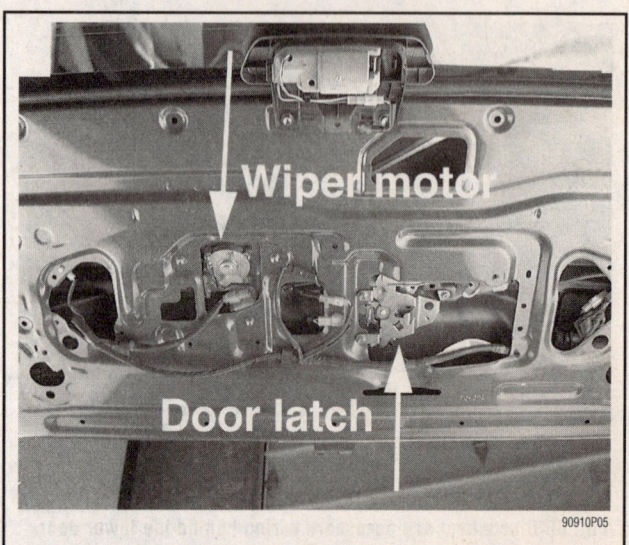

**Fig. 65 Common view of the rear tailgate inside components**

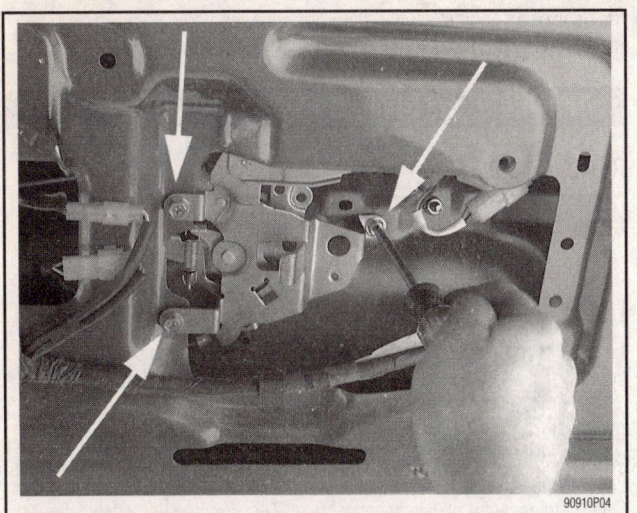

## BODY AND TRIM  10-21

Fig. 66 Remove these three screws for the door locking mechanism

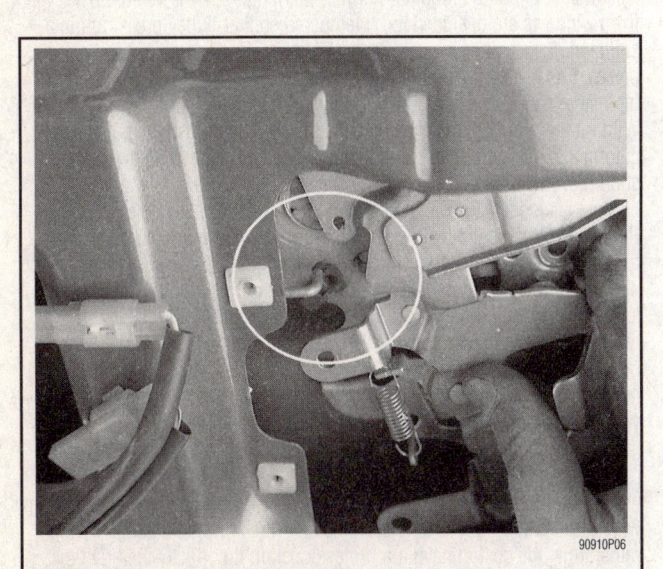

Fig. 67 Disconnect the linkage from the door lock

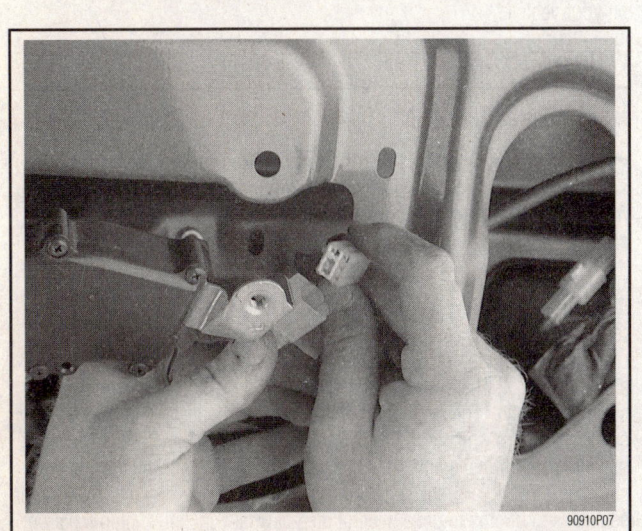

Fig. 68 Detach the wiring from the solenoid on power locking type models

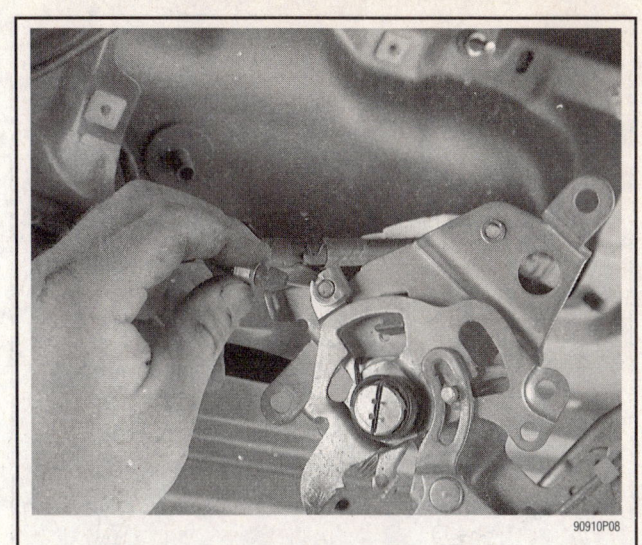

Fig. 69 Separate the cable from the latch . . .

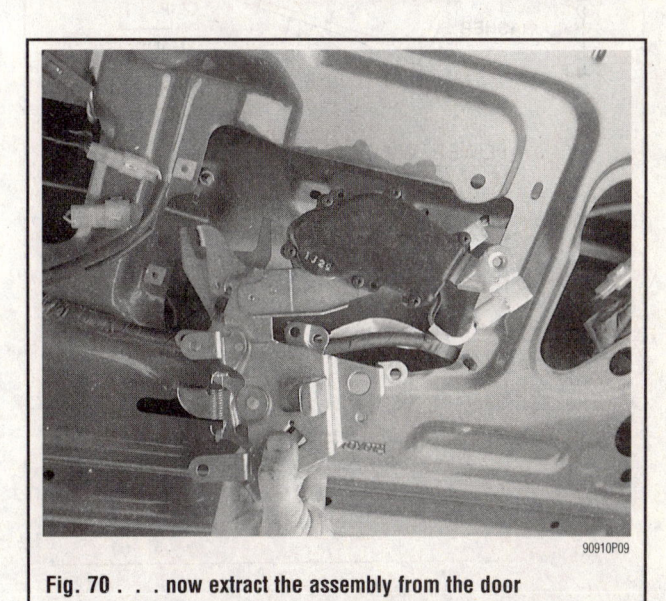

Fig. 70 . . . now extract the assembly from the door

### ✱✱ CAUTION

Some models covered by this manual may be equipped with a **Supplemental Restraint System (SRS)**, which uses an air bag. Whenever working near any of the SRS components, such as the impact sensors, the air bag module, steering column and instrument panel, disable the SRS, as described in Section 6.

2. Remove the front door panel to gain access to the regulator assembly.
3. Remove the service hole cover(s).
4. Lower the regulator until the door glass is in the fully open position.
5. Remove the two glass channel mount bolts.
6. Pull the glass up and out of the door.
7. If equipped, unbolt and remove the inside door panel frame.
8. If equipped with power windows, disconnect the electrical wiring.
9. Remove the equalizer arm bracket mounting bolts.
10. Remove the window regulator mounting bolts and remove the regulator (with the power window motor attached) through the service hole.

**To install:**

11. Coat all the window regulator sliding surfaces with multi-purpose grease.

# 10-22 BODY AND TRIM

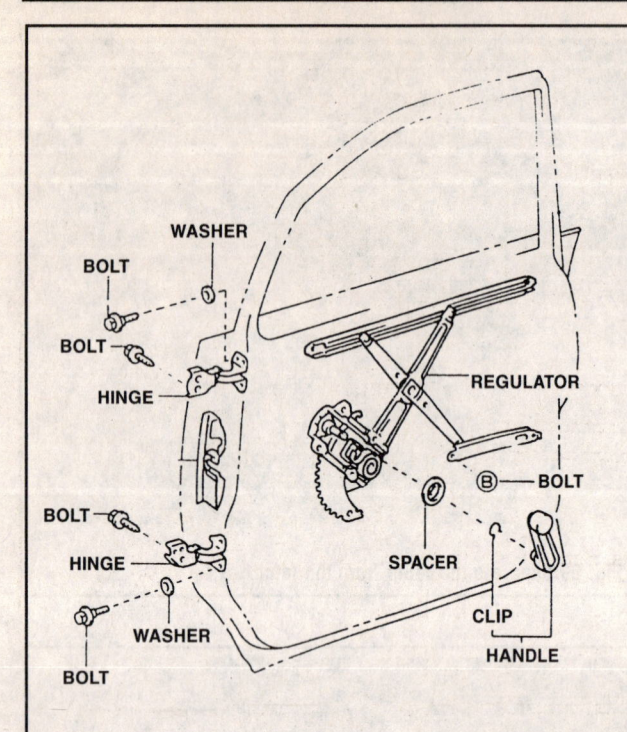

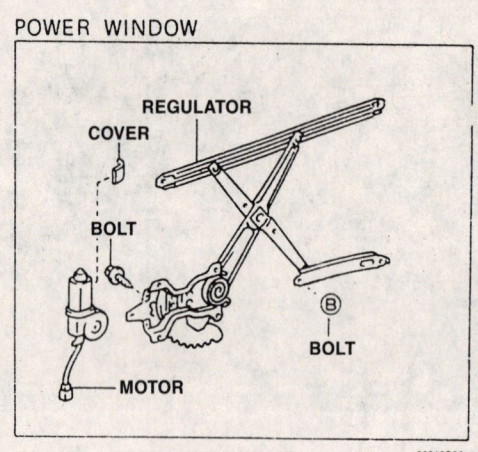

**Fig. 71 View of the window regulator, with and without power windows**

12. Place the regulator (with the power window motor) through the service hole and install the mounting bolts. Connect the power window connector if equipped.
13. Place the door glass into the door cavity.
14. Connect the glass to the regulator with the channel mount bolts.
15. With the equalizer arm, raise the glass to the almost closed position and make sure that the leading and trailing edges of the glass are equidistant from the top of the glass channel. If not, adjust the equalizer arm to achieve an even fit.
16. Install the service hole cover.
17. Install the door panel and reconnect the negative battery cable.

## Electric Window Motor

### REMOVAL & INSTALLATION

The power window motor, if equipped, is attached to the window regulator. If service is required, remove the window regulator from the inside of the door panel and detach the motor from the regulator. Removal and installation of the regulator is described in this Section.

## Windshield and Fixed Glass

### REMOVAL & INSTALLATION

▶ See Figure 72

If your windshield, or other fixed window, is cracked or chipped, you may decide to replace it with a new one yourself. However, there are two main reasons why replacement windshields and other window glass should be installed only by a professional automotive glass technician: safety and cost.

The most important reason a professional should install automotive glass is for safety. The glass in the vehicle, especially the windshield, is designed with safety in mind in case of a collision. The windshield is specially manufactured from two panes of specially-tempered glass with a thin layer of transparent plastic between them. This construction allows the glass to "give" in the event that a part of your body hits the windshield during the collision, and prevents the glass from shattering, which could cause lacerations, blinding and other harm to passengers of the vehicle. The other fixed windows are designed to be tempered so that if they break during a collision, they shatter in such a way that there are no large pointed glass pieces. The professional automotive glass technician knows how to install the glass in a vehicle so that it will function optimally during a collision. Without the proper experience, knowledge and tools, installing a piece of automotive glass yourself could lead to additional harm if an accident should ever occur.

Cost is also a factor when deciding to install automotive glass yourself. Performing this could cost you much more than a professional may charge for the same job. Since the windshield is designed to break under stress, an often life saving characteristic, windshields tend to break VERY easily when an inexperienced person attempts to install one. Do-it-yourselfers buying two, three or even four windshields from a salvage yard because they have broken them during installation are common stories. Also, since the automotive glass is designed to prevent the outside elements from entering your vehicle, improper installation can lead to water and air leaks. Annoying whining noises at highway speeds from air leaks or inside body panel rusting from water leaks can add to your stress level and subtract from your wallet. After buying two or three windshields, installing them and ending up with a leak that produces a noise while driving and water damage during rainstorms, the cost of having a professional do it correctly the first time may be much more alluring. We here at Chilton, therefore, advise that you have a professional automotive glass technician service any broken glass on your vehicle.

### WINDSHIELD CHIP REPAIR

▶ See Figures 73 thru 87

➡ **Check with your state and local authorities on the laws for state safety inspection. Some states or municipalities may not allow chip repair as a viable option for correcting stone damage to your windshield.**

Although severely cracked or damaged windshields must be replaced, there is something that you can do to prolong or even prevent the need for replacement of a chipped windshield. There are many companies which offer windshield chip repair products, such as Loctite's® Bullseye™ windshield repair kit. These kits usually consist of a syringe, pedestal and a sealing adhesive. The syringe is mounted on the pedestal and is used to create a vacuum which pulls the plastic layer against the glass. This helps make the chip transparent. The adhesive is then injected which seals the chip and helps to prevent further stress cracks from developing. Refer to the sequence of photos to get a general idea of what windshield chip repair involves.

➡ **Always follow the specific manufacturer's instructions.**

## BODY AND TRIM   10-23

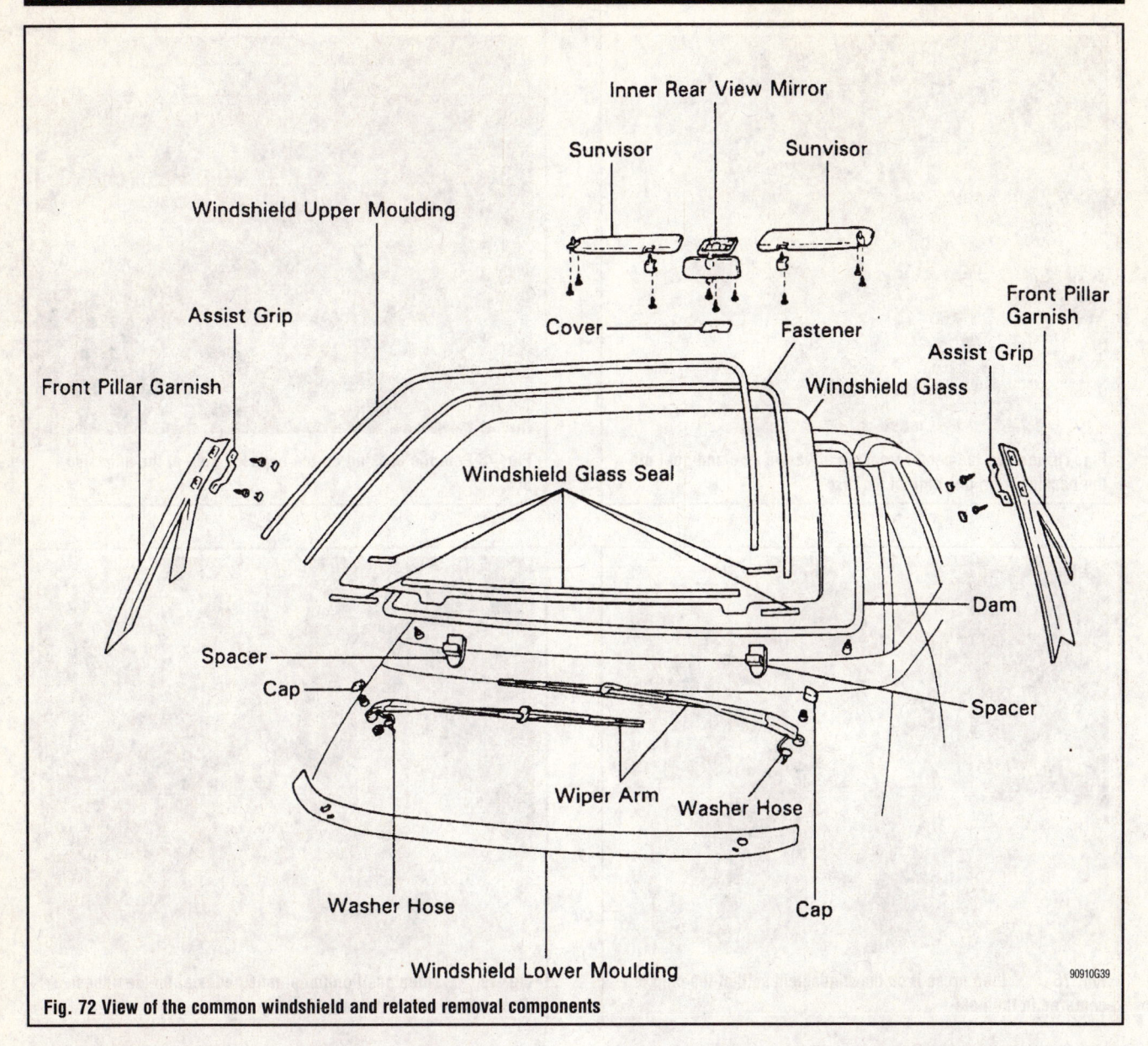

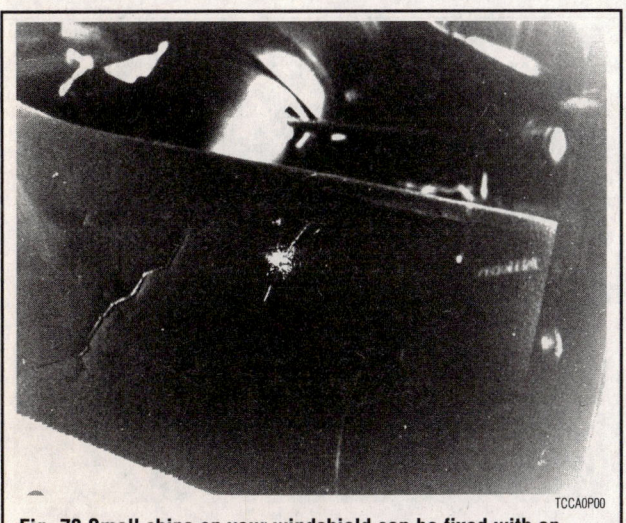

**Fig. 72 View of the common windshield and related removal components**

**Fig. 73 Small chips on your windshield can be fixed with an aftermarket repair kit, such as the one from Loctite®**

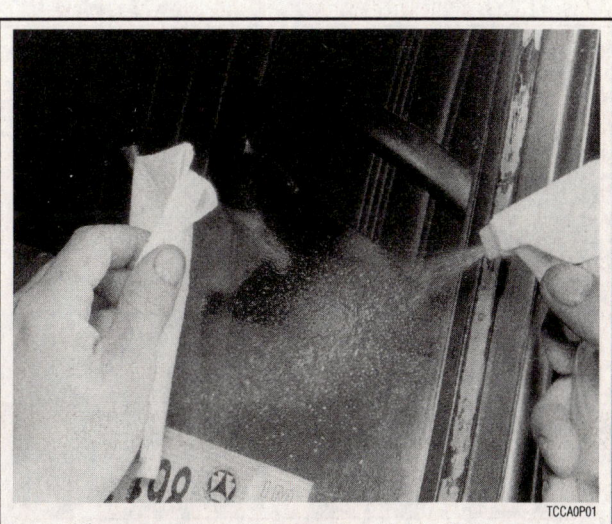

**Fig. 74 To repair a chip, clean the windshield with glass cleaner and dry it completely**

## 10-24 BODY AND TRIM

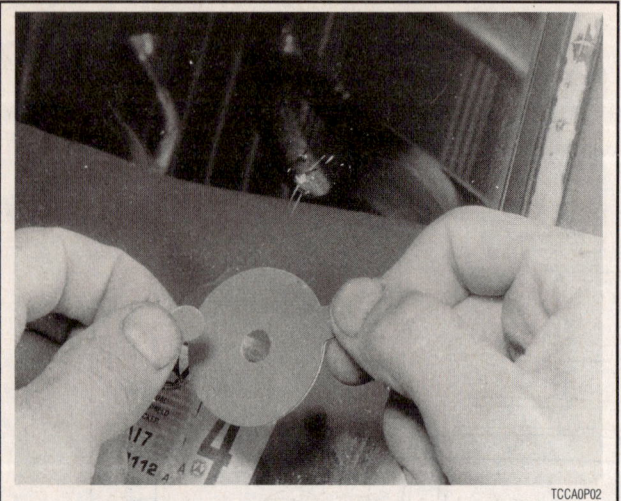

Fig. 75 Remove the center from the adhesive disc and peel off the backing from one side of the disc . . .

Fig. 78 Peel the backing off the exposed side of the adhesive disc . . .

Fig. 76 . . . then press it on the windshield so that the chip is centered in the hole

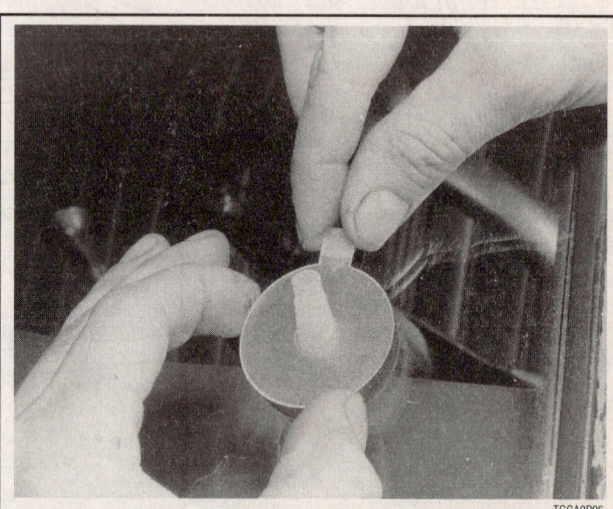

Fig. 79 . . . then position the plastic pedestal on the adhesive disc, ensuring that the tabs are aligned

Fig. 77 Be sure that the tab points upward on the windshield

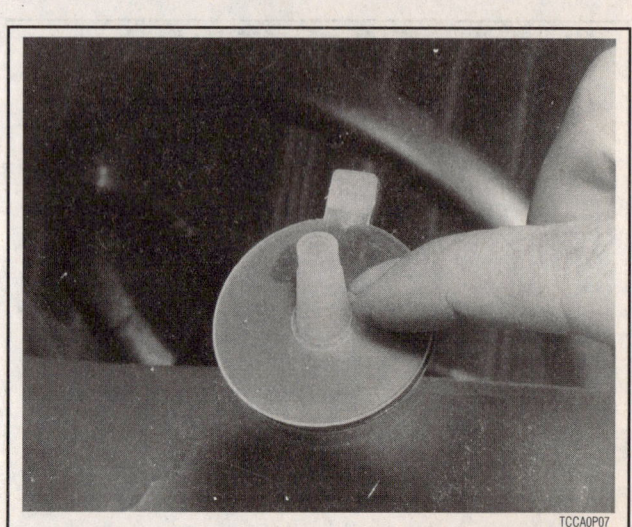

Fig. 80 Press the pedestal firmly on the adhesive disc to create an adequate seal . . .

# BODY AND TRIM 10-25

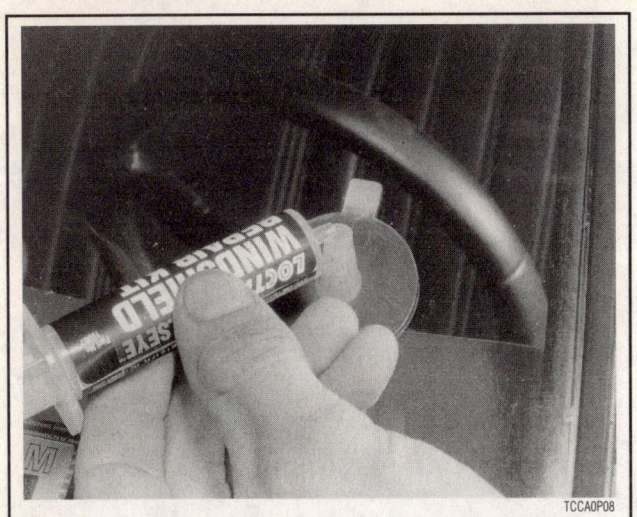

Fig. 81 . . . then install the applicator syringe nipple in the pedestal's hole

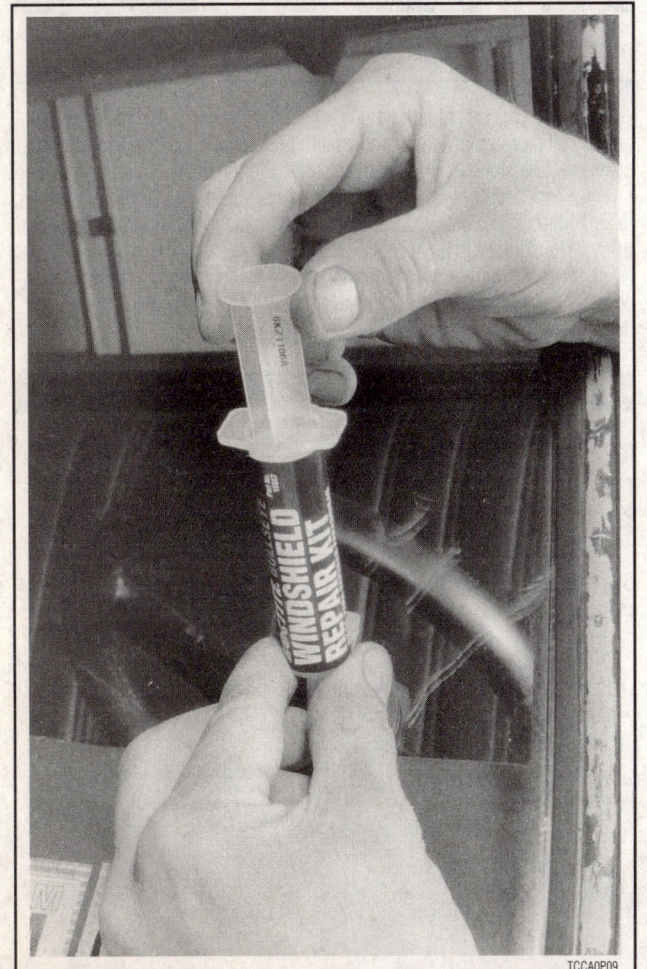

Fig. 82 Hold the syringe with one hand while pulling the plunger back with the other hand

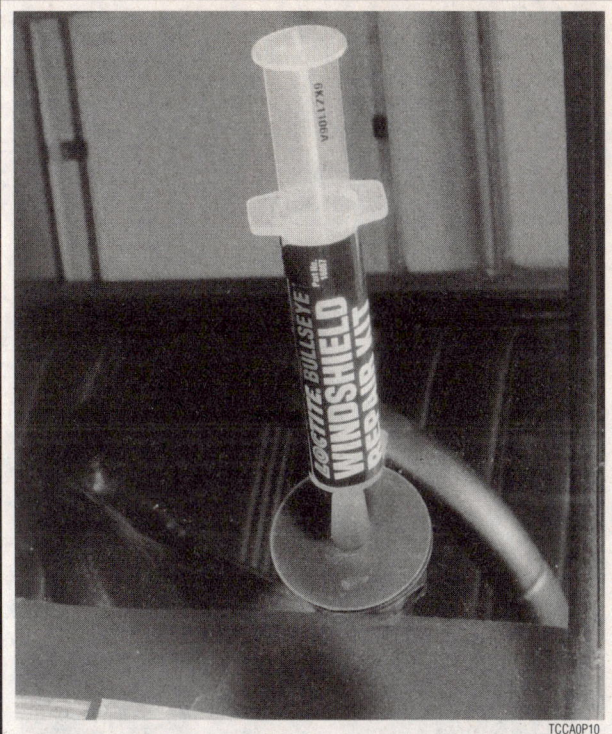

Fig. 83 After applying the solution, allow the entire assembly to sit until it has set completely

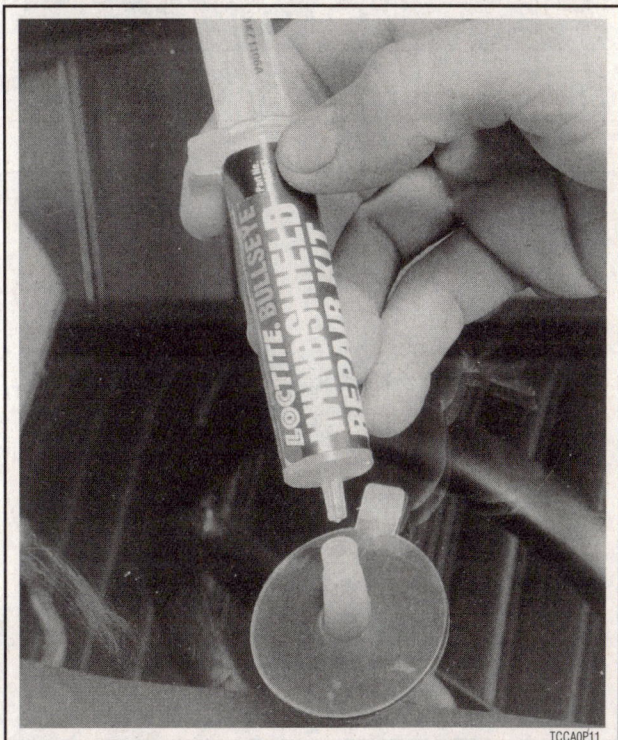

Fig. 84 After the solution has set, remove the syringe from the pedestal . . .

# 10-26 BODY AND TRIM

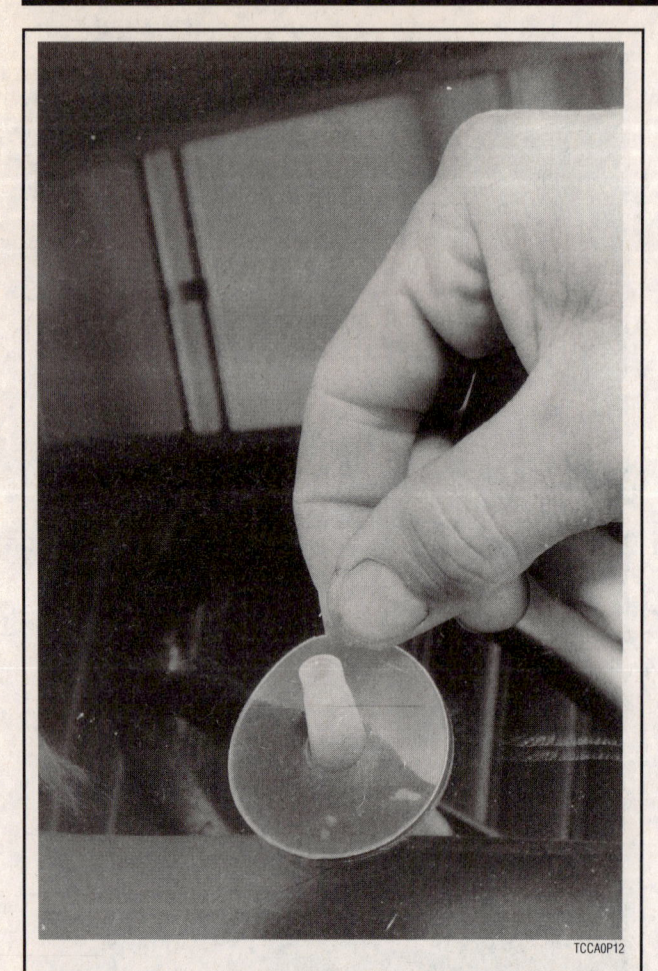

Fig. 85 . . . then peel the pedestal off of the adhesive disc . . .

Fig. 86 . . . and peel the adhesive disc off of the windshield

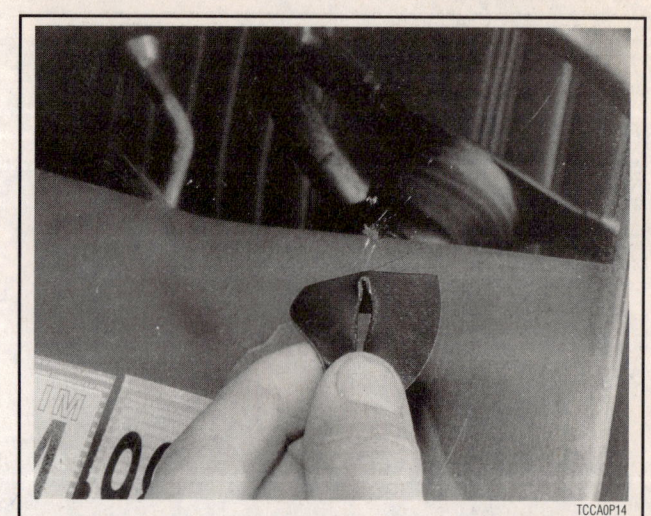

Fig. 87 The chip will still be slightly visible, but it should be filled with the hardened solution

## Inside Rear View Mirror

### REPLACEMENT

The inside mirror is held to its bracket by screws. Usually these are covered by a colored plastic housing which must be removed for access. These covers can be stubborn; take care not to gouge the plastic during removal.

Once exposed, the screws are easily removed. The mirror mounts are designed to break away under impact, thus protecting your head and face from serious injury in an accident.

Reassembly requires only common sense (which means you can do it wrong—pay attention); make sure everything fits without being forced and don't overtighten any screws or bolts.

## Seats

### REMOVAL & INSTALLATION

▶ See Figures 88, 89, 90, 91 and 92

The seat in the Previa van are all removed basically in the same manner. Some seats may have wiring near by that may need to be placed to the side to access the bolts.

1. Locate the seat track retaining bolts. A cover may be hiding them.
2. Remove the bolt covers.
3. Remove the seat track retaining bolts and extract the unit from the vehicle.

**To install:**

4. Position the seat with track onto the floorpan and secure with the retaining bolts.

## BODY AND TRIM 10-27

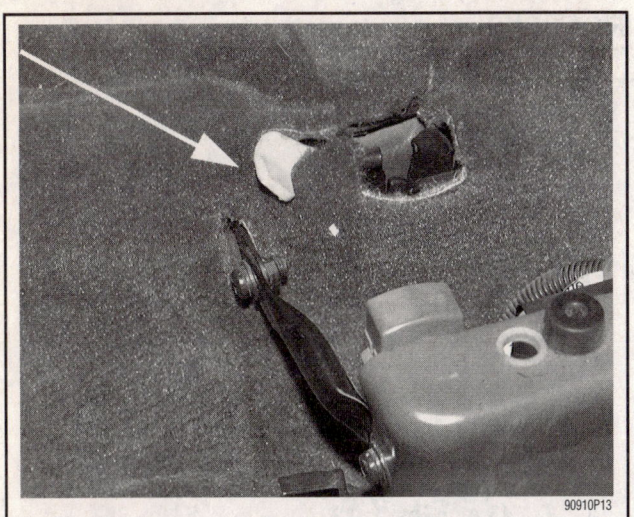

Fig. 88 Pull this lever to lift up the drivers seat to access the engine compartment

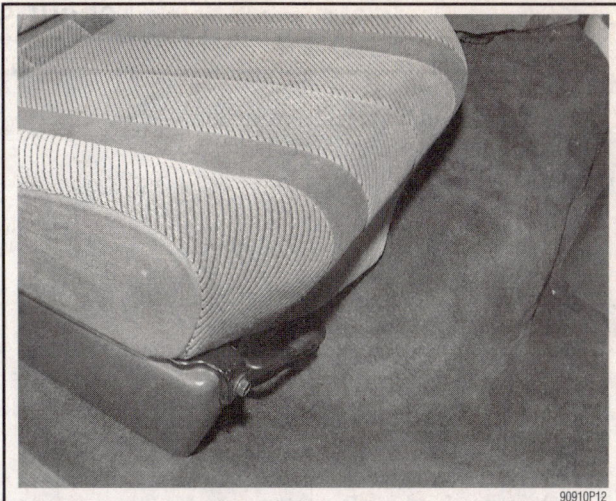

Fig. 91 View of the passengers side seat track front retaining bolts

Fig. 89 Removing the passengers side seat assembly

Fig. 92 Remove the covers on either side of the seat legs

Fig. 90 View of the passengers side seat track rear retaining bolts

## BODY AND TRIM

### TORQUE SPECIFICATIONS

| Components | English Specifications | Metric Specifications |
|---|---|---|
| Hood hinge-to-hood | 8-10 ft. lbs. | 11-14 Nm |
| Front door window regulator set bolt | 43 inch lbs. | 5 Nm |
| Sliding door lock control set bolt | 69 inch lbs. | 8 Nm |
| Back door lock control set bolt | 69 inch lbs. | 8 Nm |
| Front seat-to-leg | 29 ft. lbs. | 39 Nm |
| Front seat leg-to-body | 29 ft. lbs. | 39 Nm |
| Front seat lock-to-body | 29 ft. lbs. | 39 Nm |
| Rear No. 1 seat leg-to-body (separate type) | 29 ft. lbs. | 39 Nm |
| Rear bench seat lock bracket-to-body | 29 ft. lbs. | 39 Nm |
| Rear seat No. 2-to-body | 29 ft. lbs. | 39 Nm |
| Rear seat No. 2 lock striker-to-body | 29 ft. lbs. | 39 Nm |
| Seat belt shoulder anchor-to-body | 31 ft. lbs. | 42 Nm |
| Seat belt anchor-to-body | 31 ft. lbs. | 42 Nm |
| Seat belt anchor plate-to-body | 31 ft. lbs. | 42 Nm |
| Emergancy Locking Retractor-to-body | 43 inch lbs. | 5 Nm |

# GLOSSARY

**AIR/FUEL RATIO:** The ratio of air-to-gasoline by weight in the fuel mixture drawn into the engine.

**AIR INJECTION:** One method of reducing harmful exhaust emissions by injecting air into each of the exhaust ports of an engine. The fresh air entering the hot exhaust manifold causes any remaining fuel to be burned before it can exit the tailpipe.

**ALTERNATOR:** A device used for converting mechanical energy into electrical energy.

**AMMETER:** An instrument, calibrated in amperes, used to measure the flow of an electrical current in a circuit. Ammeters are always connected in series with the circuit being tested.

**AMPERE:** The rate of flow of electrical current present when one volt of electrical pressure is applied against one ohm of electrical resistance.

**ANALOG COMPUTER:** Any microprocessor that uses similar (analogous) electrical signals to make its calculations.

**ARMATURE:** A laminated, soft iron core wrapped by a wire that converts electrical energy to mechanical energy as in a motor or relay. When rotated in a magnetic field, it changes mechanical energy into electrical energy as in a generator.

**ATMOSPHERIC PRESSURE:** The pressure on the Earth's surface caused by the weight of the air in the atmosphere. At sea level, this pressure is 14.7 psi at 32°F (101 kPa at 0°C).

**ATOMIZATION:** The breaking down of a liquid into a fine mist that can be suspended in air.

**AXIAL PLAY:** Movement parallel to a shaft or bearing bore.

**BACKFIRE:** The sudden combustion of gases in the intake or exhaust system that results in a loud explosion.

**BACKLASH:** The clearance or play between two parts, such as meshed gears.

**BACKPRESSURE:** Restrictions in the exhaust system that slow the exit of exhaust gases from the combustion chamber.

**BAKELITE:** A heat resistant, plastic insulator material commonly used in printed circuit boards and transistorized components.

**BALL BEARING:** A bearing made up of hardened inner and outer races between which hardened steel balls roll.

**BALLAST RESISTOR:** A resistor in the primary ignition circuit that lowers voltage after the engine is started to reduce wear on ignition components.

**BEARING:** A friction reducing, supportive device usually located between a stationary part and a moving part.

**BIMETAL TEMPERATURE SENSOR:** Any sensor or switch made of two dissimilar types of metal that bend when heated or cooled due to the different expansion rates of the alloys. These types of sensors usually function as an on/off switch.

**BLOWBY:** Combustion gases, composed of water vapor and unburned fuel, that leak past the piston rings into the crankcase during normal engine operation. These gases are removed by the PCV system to prevent the buildup of harmful acids in the crankcase.

**BRAKE PAD:** A brake shoe and lining assembly used with disc brakes.

**BRAKE SHOE:** The backing for the brake lining. The term is, however, usually applied to the assembly of the brake backing and lining.

**BUSHING:** A liner, usually removable, for a bearing; an anti-friction liner used in place of a bearing.

**CALIPER:** A hydraulically activated device in a disc brake system, which is mounted straddling the brake rotor (disc). The caliper contains at least one piston and two brake pads. Hydraulic pressure on the piston(s) forces the pads against the rotor.

**CAMSHAFT:** A shaft in the engine on which are the lobes (cams) which operate the valves. The camshaft is driven by the crankshaft, via a belt, chain or gears, at one half the crankshaft speed.

**CAPACITOR:** A device which stores an electrical charge.

**CARBON MONOXIDE (CO):** A colorless, odorless gas given off as a normal byproduct of combustion. It is poisonous and extremely dangerous in confined areas, building up slowly to toxic levels without warning if adequate ventilation is not available.

**CARBURETOR:** A device, usually mounted on the intake manifold of an engine, which mixes the air and fuel in the proper proportion to allow even combustion.

**CATALYTIC CONVERTER:** A device installed in the exhaust system, like a muffler, that converts harmful byproducts of combustion into carbon dioxide and water vapor by means of a heat-producing chemical reaction.

**CENTRIFUGAL ADVANCE:** A mechanical method of advancing the spark timing by using flyweights in the distributor that react to centrifugal force generated by the distributor shaft rotation.

**CHECK VALVE:** Any one-way valve installed to permit the flow of air, fuel or vacuum in one direction only.

**CHOKE:** A device, usually a moveable valve, placed in the intake path of a carburetor to restrict the flow of air.

**CIRCUIT:** Any unbroken path through which an electrical current can flow. Also used to describe fuel flow in some instances.

**CIRCUIT BREAKER:** A switch which protects an electrical circuit from overload by opening the circuit when the current flow exceeds a predetermined level. Some circuit breakers must be reset manually, while most reset automatically.

**COIL (IGNITION):** A transformer in the ignition circuit which steps up the voltage provided to the spark plugs.

**COMBINATION MANIFOLD:** An assembly which includes both the intake and exhaust manifolds in one casting.

## GLOSSARY

**COMBINATION VALVE:** A device used in some fuel systems that routes fuel vapors to a charcoal storage canister instead of venting them into the atmosphere. The valve relieves fuel tank pressure and allows fresh air into the tank as the fuel level drops to prevent a vapor lock situation.

**COMPRESSION RATIO:** The comparison of the total volume of the cylinder and combustion chamber with the piston at BDC and the piston at TDC.

**CONDENSER:** 1. An electrical device which acts to store an electrical charge, preventing voltage surges. 2. A radiator-like device in the air conditioning system in which refrigerant gas condenses into a liquid, giving off heat.

**CONDUCTOR:** Any material through which an electrical current can be transmitted easily.

**CONTINUITY:** Continuous or complete circuit. Can be checked with an ohmmeter.

**COUNTERSHAFT:** An intermediate shaft which is rotated by a mainshaft and transmits, in turn, that rotation to a working part.

**CRANKCASE:** The lower part of an engine in which the crankshaft and related parts operate.

**CRANKSHAFT:** The main driving shaft of an engine which receives reciprocating motion from the pistons and converts it to rotary motion.

**CYLINDER:** In an engine, the round hole in the engine block in which the piston(s) ride.

**CYLINDER BLOCK:** The main structural member of an engine in which is found the cylinders, crankshaft and other principal parts.

**CYLINDER HEAD:** The detachable portion of the engine, usually fastened to the top of the cylinder block and containing all or most of the combustion chambers. On overhead valve engines, it contains the valves and their operating parts. On overhead cam engines, it contains the camshaft as well.

**DEAD CENTER:** The extreme top or bottom of the piston stroke.

**DETONATION:** An unwanted explosion of the air/fuel mixture in the combustion chamber caused by excess heat and compression, advanced timing, or an overly lean mixture. Also referred to as "ping".

**DIAPHRAGM:** A thin, flexible wall separating two cavities, such as in a vacuum advance unit.

**DIESELING:** A condition in which hot spots in the combustion chamber cause the engine to run on after the key is turned off.

**DIFFERENTIAL:** A geared assembly which allows the transmission of motion between drive axles, giving one axle the ability to turn faster than the other.

**DIODE:** An electrical device that will allow current to flow in one direction only.

**DISC BRAKE:** A hydraulic braking assembly consisting of a brake disc, or rotor, mounted on an axle, and a caliper assembly containing, usually two brake pads which are activated by hydraulic pressure. The pads are forced against the sides of the disc, creating friction which slows the vehicle.

**DISTRIBUTOR:** A mechanically driven device on an engine which is responsible for electrically firing the spark plug at a predetermined point of the piston stroke.

**DOWEL PIN:** A pin, inserted in mating holes in two different parts allowing those parts to maintain a fixed relationship.

**DRUM BRAKE:** A braking system which consists of two brake shoes and one or two wheel cylinders, mounted on a fixed backing plate, and a brake drum, mounted on an axle, which revolves around the assembly.

**DWELL:** The rate, measured in degrees of shaft rotation, at which an electrical circuit cycles on and off.

**ELECTRONIC CONTROL UNIT (ECU):** Ignition module, module, amplifier or igniter. See Module for definition.

**ELECTRONIC IGNITION:** A system in which the timing and firing of the spark plugs is controlled by an electronic control unit, usually called a module. These systems have no points or condenser.

**END-PLAY:** The measured amount of axial movement in a shaft.

**ENGINE:** A device that converts heat into mechanical energy.

**EXHAUST MANIFOLD:** A set of cast passages or pipes which conduct exhaust gases from the engine.

**FEELER GAUGE:** A blade, usually metal, or precisely predetermined thickness, used to measure the clearance between two parts.

**FIRING ORDER:** The order in which combustion occurs in the cylinders of an engine. Also the order in which spark is distributed to the plugs by the distributor.

**FLOODING:** The presence of too much fuel in the intake manifold and combustion chamber which prevents the air/fuel mixture from firing, thereby causing a no-start situation.

**FLYWHEEL:** A disc shaped part bolted to the rear end of the crankshaft. Around the outer perimeter is affixed the ring gear. The starter drive engages the ring gear, turning the flywheel, which rotates the crankshaft, imparting the initial starting motion to the engine.

**FOOT POUND (ft. lbs. or sometimes, ft.lb.):** The amount of energy or work needed to raise an item weighing one pound, a distance of one foot.

**FUSE:** A protective device in a circuit which prevents circuit overload by breaking the circuit when a specific amperage is present. The device is constructed around a strip or wire of a lower amperage rating than the circuit it is designed to protect. When an amperage higher than that stamped on the fuse is present in the circuit, the strip or wire melts, opening the circuit.

**GEAR RATIO:** The ratio between the number of teeth on meshing gears.

**GENERATOR:** A device which converts mechanical energy into electrical energy.

**HEAT RANGE:** The measure of a spark plug's ability to dissipate heat from its firing end. The higher the heat range, the hotter the plug fires.

# GLOSSARY 10-31

**HUB:** The center part of a wheel or gear.

**HYDROCARBON (HC):** Any chemical compound made up of hydrogen and carbon. A major pollutant formed by the engine as a byproduct of combustion.

**HYDROMETER:** An instrument used to measure the specific gravity of a solution.

**INCH POUND (inch lbs.; sometimes in.lb. or in. lbs.):** One twelfth of a foot pound.

**INDUCTION:** A means of transferring electrical energy in the form of a magnetic field. Principle used in the ignition coil to increase voltage.

**INJECTOR:** A device which receives metered fuel under relatively low pressure and is activated to inject the fuel into the engine under relatively high pressure at a predetermined time.

**INPUT SHAFT:** The shaft to which torque is applied, usually carrying the driving gear or gears.

**INTAKE MANIFOLD:** A casting of passages or pipes used to conduct air or a fuel/air mixture to the cylinders.

**JOURNAL:** The bearing surface within which a shaft operates.

**KEY:** A small block usually fitted in a notch between a shaft and a hub to prevent slippage of the two parts.

**MANIFOLD:** A casting of passages or set of pipes which connect the cylinders to an inlet or outlet source.

**MANIFOLD VACUUM:** Low pressure in an engine intake manifold formed just below the throttle plates. Manifold vacuum is highest at idle and drops under acceleration.

**MASTER CYLINDER:** The primary fluid pressurizing device in a hydraulic system. In automotive use, it is found in brake and hydraulic clutch systems and is pedal activated, either directly or, in a power brake system, through the power booster.

**MODULE:** Electronic control unit, amplifier or igniter of solid state or integrated design which controls the current flow in the ignition primary circuit based on input from the pick-up coil. When the module opens the primary circuit, high secondary voltage is induced in the coil.

**NEEDLE BEARING:** A bearing which consists of a number (usually a large number) of long, thin rollers.

**OHM:** (Ω) The unit used to measure the resistance of conductor-to-electrical flow. One ohm is the amount of resistance that limits current flow to one ampere in a circuit with one volt of pressure.

**OHMMETER:** An instrument used for measuring the resistance, in ohms, in an electrical circuit.

**OUTPUT SHAFT:** The shaft which transmits torque from a device, such as a transmission.

**OVERDRIVE:** A gear assembly which produces more shaft revolutions than that transmitted to it.

**OVERHEAD CAMSHAFT (OHC):** An engine configuration in which the camshaft is mounted on top of the cylinder head and operates the valve either directly or by means of rocker arms.

**OVERHEAD VALVE (OHV):** An engine configuration in which all of the valves are located in the cylinder head and the camshaft is located in the cylinder block. The camshaft operates the valves via lifters and pushrods.

**OXIDES OF NITROGEN (NOx):** Chemical compounds of nitrogen produced as a byproduct of combustion. They combine with hydrocarbons to produce smog.

**OXYGEN SENSOR:** Use with the feedback system to sense the presence of oxygen in the exhaust gas and signal the computer which can reference the voltage signal to an air/fuel ratio.

**PINION:** The smaller of two meshing gears.

**PISTON RING:** An open-ended ring with fits into a groove on the outer diameter of the piston. Its chief function is to form a seal between the piston and cylinder wall. Most automotive pistons have three rings: two for compression sealing; one for oil sealing.

**PRELOAD:** A predetermined load placed on a bearing during assembly or by adjustment.

**PRIMARY CIRCUIT:** the low voltage side of the ignition system which consists of the ignition switch, ballast resistor or resistance wire, bypass, coil, electronic control unit and pick-up coil as well as the connecting wires and harnesses.

**PRESS FIT:** The mating of two parts under pressure, due to the inner diameter of one being smaller than the outer diameter of the other, or vice versa; an interference fit.

**RACE:** The surface on the inner or outer ring of a bearing on which the balls, needles or rollers move.

**REGULATOR:** A device which maintains the amperage and/or voltage levels of a circuit at predetermined values.

**RELAY:** A switch which automatically opens and/or closes a circuit.

**RESISTANCE:** The opposition to the flow of current through a circuit or electrical device, and is measured in ohms. Resistance is equal to the voltage divided by the amperage.

**RESISTOR:** A device, usually made of wire, which offers a preset amount of resistance in an electrical circuit.

**RING GEAR:** The name given to a ring-shaped gear attached to a differential case, or affixed to a flywheel or as part of a planetary gear set.

**ROLLER BEARING:** A bearing made up of hardened inner and outer races between which hardened steel rollers move.

## GLOSSARY

**ROTOR:** 1. The disc-shaped part of a disc brake assembly, upon which the brake pads bear; also called, brake disc. 2. The device mounted atop the distributor shaft, which passes current to the distributor cap tower contacts.

**SECONDARY CIRCUIT:** The high voltage side of the ignition system, usually above 20,000 volts. The secondary includes the ignition coil, coil wire, distributor cap and rotor, spark plug wires and spark plugs.

**SENDING UNIT:** A mechanical, electrical, hydraulic or electro-magnetic device which transmits information to a gauge.

**SENSOR:** Any device designed to measure engine operating conditions or ambient pressures and temperatures. Usually electronic in nature and designed to send a voltage signal to an on-board computer, some sensors may operate as a simple on/off switch or they may provide a variable voltage signal (like a potentiometer) as conditions or measured parameters change.

**SHIM:** Spacers of precise, predetermined thickness used between parts to establish a proper working relationship.

**SLAVE CYLINDER:** In automotive use, a device in the hydraulic clutch system which is activated by hydraulic force, disengaging the clutch.

**SOLENOID:** A coil used to produce a magnetic field, the effect of which is to produce work.

**SPARK PLUG:** A device screwed into the combustion chamber of a spark ignition engine. The basic construction is a conductive core inside of a ceramic insulator, mounted in an outer conductive base. An electrical charge from the spark plug wire travels along the conductive core and jumps a preset air gap to a grounding point or points at the end of the conductive base. The resultant spark ignites the fuel/air mixture in the combustion chamber.

**SPLINES:** Ridges machined or cast onto the outer diameter of a shaft or inner diameter of a bore to enable parts to mate without rotation.

**TACHOMETER:** A device used to measure the rotary speed of an engine, shaft, gear, etc., usually in rotations per minute.

**THERMOSTAT:** A valve, located in the cooling system of an engine, which is closed when cold and opens gradually in response to engine heating, controlling the temperature of the coolant and rate of coolant flow.

**TOP DEAD CENTER (TDC):** The point at which the piston reaches the top of its travel on the compression stroke.

**TORQUE:** The twisting force applied to an object.

**TORQUE CONVERTER:** A turbine used to transmit power from a driving member to a driven member via hydraulic action, providing changes in drive ratio and torque. In automotive use, it links the driveplate at the rear of the engine to the automatic transmission.

**TRANSDUCER:** A device used to change a force into an electrical signal.

**TRANSISTOR:** A semi-conductor component which can be actuated by a small voltage to perform an electrical switching function.

**TUNE-UP:** A regular maintenance function, usually associated with the replacement and adjustment of parts and components in the electrical and fuel systems of a vehicle for the purpose of attaining optimum performance.

**TURBOCHARGER:** An exhaust driven pump which compresses intake air and forces it into the combustion chambers at higher than atmospheric pressures. The increased air pressure allows more fuel to be burned and results in increased horsepower being produced.

**VACUUM ADVANCE:** A device which advances the ignition timing in response to increased engine vacuum.

**VACUUM GAUGE:** An instrument used to measure the presence of vacuum in a chamber.

**VALVE:** A device which control the pressure, direction of flow or rate of flow of a liquid or gas.

**VALVE CLEARANCE:** The measured gap between the end of the valve stem and the rocker arm, cam lobe or follower that activates the valve.

**VISCOSITY:** The rating of a liquid's internal resistance to flow.

**VOLTMETER:** An instrument used for measuring electrical force in units called volts. Voltmeters are always connected parallel with the circuit being tested.

**WHEEL CYLINDER:** Found in the automotive drum brake assembly, it is a device, actuated by hydraulic pressure, which, through internal pistons, pushes the brake shoes outward against the drums.

# MASTER INDEX

ABS ECM 9-42
    REMOVAL & INSTALLATION 9-42
ACTUATOR 9-42
    REMOVAL & INSTALLATION 9-42
**AIR BAG (SUPPLEMENTAL RESTRAINT SYSTEM) 6-9**
AIR CLEANER (ELEMENT) 1-19
    REMOVAL & INSTALLATION 1-19
AIR CONDITIONING COMPONENTS 6-17
    REMOVAL & INSTALLATION 6-17
AIR CONDITIONING SYSTEM 1-42
    PREVENTIVE MAINTENANCE 1-43
    SYSTEM INSPECTION 1-43
    SYSTEM SERVICE & REPAIR 1-42
**AIR POLLUTION 4-2**
ALTERNATOR 2-9
    REMOVAL & INSTALLATION 2-10
    TESTING 2-9
ALTERNATOR PRECAUTIONS 2-9
ANTENNA 10-11
    REPLACEMENT 10-11
**ANTI-LOCK BRAKE SYSTEM 9-33**
**AUTOMATIC TRANSMISSION 7-13**
AUTOMATIC TRANSMISSION (FLUIDS AND LUBRICANTS) 1-56
    DRAIN & REFILL 1-57
    FLUID RECOMMENDATIONS 1-56
    LEVEL CHECK 1-56
    PAN & FILTER SERVICE 1-58
AUTOMATIC TRANSMISSION ASSEMBLY 7-17
    ADJUSTMENTS 7-19
    REMOVAL & INSTALLATION 7-17
**AUTOMOTIVE EMISSIONS 4-3**
AUTOMOTIVE POLLUTANTS 4-2
    HEAT TRANSFER 4-2
    TEMPERATURE INVERSION 4-2
AVOIDING THE MOST COMMON MISTAKES 1-2
AVOIDING TROUBLE 1-2
AXLE HOUSING ASSEMBLY 7-31
    REMOVAL & INSTALLATION 7-31
AXLE SHAFT, BEARING AND SEAL (FRONT DRIVE AXLE) 7-28
    REMOVAL & INSTALLATION 7-28
AXLE SHAFT, BEARING AND SEAL (REAR AXLE) 7-32
    REMOVAL & INSTALLATION 7-32
BACK-UP LIGHT/NEUTRAL SAFETY SWITCH 7-15
    ADJUSTMENT 7-17
    REMOVAL & INSTALLATION 7-15
BACK-UP LIGHT SWITCH 7-2
    REMOVAL & INSTALLATION 7-2
BASIC CHARGING SYSTEM PROBLEMS 2-18
BASIC ELECTRICAL THEORY 6-2
    OHM'S LAW 6-2
    THE WATER ANALOGY 6-2
**BASIC FUEL SYSTEM DIAGNOSIS 5-2**
BASIC OPERATING PRINCIPLES 9-2
    DISC BRAKES 9-2
    DRUM BRAKES 9-2
    POWER BOOSTERS 9-3
BASIC STARTING SYSTEM PROBLEMS 2-17
BATTERY 1-23
    BATTERY FLUID 1-24
    CABLES 1-25
    CHARGING 1-26
    GENERAL MAINTENANCE 1-24
    PRECAUTIONS 1-23
    REPLACEMENT 1-26
**BATTERY CABLES 6-9**
BELTS 1-26
    INSPECTION 1-26
    REMOVAL, INSTALLATION & ADJUSTMENT 1-28
BLEEDING THE ABS SYSTEM 9-42

## 10-34 MASTER INDEX

BLEEDING THE BRAKE SYSTEM 9-11
    LINES & WHEEL CIRCUITS 9-12
    MASTER CYLINDER 9-11
BLOWER MOTOR 6-13
    REMOVAL & INSTALLATION 6-13
BLOWER MOTOR RESISTOR 6-17
    REMOVAL & INSTALLATION 6-17
BODY LUBRICATION AND MAINTENANCE 1-69
    BODY DRAIN HOLES 1-69
    DOOR HINGES & HINGE CHECKS 1-69
    LOCK CYLINDERS 1-69
    TAILGATE 1-59
BOLTS, NUTS AND OTHER THREADED RETAINERS 1-9
BRAKE CALIPER 9-17
    OVERHAUL 9-18
    REMOVAL & INSTALLATION 9-17
BRAKE DISC (ROTOR) 9-20
    INSPECTION 9-22
    REMOVAL & INSTALLATION 9-20
BRAKE DRUMS 9-22
    INSPECTION 9-23
    REMOVAL & INSTALLATION 9-22
BRAKE HOSES AND PIPES 9-8
    REMOVAL & INSTALLATION 9-8
BRAKE LIGHT SWITCH 9-3
    REMOVAL & INSTALLATION 9-3
BRAKE MASTER CYLINDER 1-67
    FLUID RECOMMENDATIONS 1-67
    LEVEL CHECK 1-67
**BRAKE OPERATING SYSTEM 9-2**
BRAKE PADS 9-13
    INSPECTION 9-17
    REMOVAL & INSTALLATION 9-13
BRAKE SHOES (DRUM BRAKES) 9-23
    ADJUSTMENTS 9-26
    INSPECTION 9-23
    REMOVAL & INSTALLATION 9-24
BRAKE SHOES (PARKING BRAKE) 9-29
    ADJUSTMENTS 9-32
    REMOVAL & INSTALLATION 9-29
BRAKE SPECIFICATIONS 9-43
THE BRAKE SYSTEM (TROUBLESHOOTING CHART) 9-44
BUY OR REBUILD? 3-53
CABLE(S) 9-28
    ADJUSTMENT 9-29
    REMOVAL & INSTALLATION 9-28
CAMSHAFT, BEARINGS AND LIFTERS 3-38
    INSPECTION 3-45
    REMOVAL & INSTALLATION 3-38
CAMSHAFT POSITION SENSOR 4-28
    OPERATION 4-28
    REMOVAL & INSTALLATION 4-29
    TESTING 4-29
CAPACITIES 1-77
CENTER SUPPORT BEARING 7-27
    REMOVAL & INSTALLATION 7-27
CHARGE AIR COOLER (CAC) 3-14
    REMOVAL & INSTALLATION 3-14
**CHARGING SYSTEM 2-9**
CHASSIS GREASING 1-69
CIRCUIT BREAKERS 6-38
    REPLACEMENT 6-38
    RESETTING 6-39
**CIRCUIT PROTECTION 6-37**
CLEARING CODES 4-33
    2TZ-FE ENGINE 4-33
    2TZ-FZE ENGINE 4-34

CLOCK 6-29
    REMOVAL & INSTALLATION 6-29
**CLUTCH 7-8**
CLUTCH ACCUMULATOR 7-12
    REMOVAL & INSTALLATION 7-12
CLUTCH MASTER CYLINDER 1-68
    FLUID RECOMMENDATIONS 1-68
    LEVEL CHECK 1-68
COIL SPRINGS (FRONT SUSPENSION) 8-5
    REMOVAL & INSTALLATION 8-5
COIL SPRINGS (REAR SUSPENSION) 8-18
    REMOVAL & INSTALLATION 8-18
COLD START INJECTOR 5-11
    REMOVAL & INSTALLATION 5-11
COMPANION FLANGE SEAL 7-20
    REMOVAL & INSTALLATION 7-20
**COMPONENT LOCATIONS**
    UNDERHOOD MAINTENANCE COMPONENT LOCATIONS 1-17
    UNDERVEHICLE MAINTENANCE COMPONENT LOCATIONS 1-18
**COMPONENT LOCATIONS 4-30**
CONTROL CABLES 6-17
    ADJUSTMENT 6-17
    REMOVAL & INSTALLATION 6-17
CONTROL PANEL 6-19
    REMOVAL & INSTALLATION 6-19
CONTROL RELAYS 9-35
    REMOVAL & INSTALLATION 9-39
    TESTING 9-35
COOLANT TEMPERATURE SENSOR (ELECTRONIC ENGINE CONTROLS) 4-22
    OPERATION 4-22
    REMOVAL & INSTALLATION 4-23
    TESTING 4-22
COOLANT TEMPERATURE SENSOR (SENDING UNITS AND SENSORS) 2-16
    REMOVAL & INSTALLATION 2-16
    TESTING 2-16
COOLING SYSTEM 1-65
    DRAIN & REFILL 1-66
    FLUID RECOMMENDATIONS 1-65
    FLUSHING & CLEANING THE SYSTEM 1-67
    LEVEL CHECK 1-65
CRANKCASE EMISSIONS 4-4
CRANKSHAFT POSITION SENSOR (ELECTRONIC ENGINE CONTROLS) 4-29
    OPERATION 4-29
    REMOVAL & INSTALLATION 4-29
    TESTING 4-29
CRANKSHAFT POSITION (CKP) SENSOR (ELECTRONIC SPARK ADVANCE SYSTEM) 2-8
**CRUISE CONTROL 6-20**
CRUISE CONTROL TROUBLESHOOTING 6-20
CV-BOOTS 1-30
    INSPECTION 1-30
CYLINDER HEAD (ENGINE MECHANICAL) 3-26
    REMOVAL & INSTALLATION 3-26
CYLINDER HEAD (ENGINE RECONDITIONING) 3-57
    ASSEMBLY 3-63
    DISASSEMBLY 3-57
    INSPECTION 3-60
    REFINISHING & REPAIRING 3-62
DASH-MOUNTED SWITCHES 6-28
    REMOVAL & INSTALLATION 6-28
DATA LINK CONNECTOR (DLC) 4-31
DECELERATION SENSOR 9-42
    TESTING 9-42
DETERMINING ENGINE CONDITION 3-52

# MASTER INDEX   10-35

COMPRESSION TEST   3-53
OIL PRESSURE TEST   3-53
DIAGNOSIS AND TESTING (ANTI-LOCK BRAKE SYSTEM)   9-34
   CLEARING TROUBLE CODES   9-35
   DATA LINK CONNECTORS (DLC)   9-34
   READING CODES   9-34
DIAGNOSIS AND TESTING (ELECTRONIC SPARK ADVANCE SYSTEM)   2-2
   NO START TEST   2-2
   SIGNAL GENERATOR AIR GAP INSPECTION   2-3
DIFFERENTIAL CARRIER   7-35
   REMOVAL & INSTALLATION   7-35
**DISC BRAKES   9-13**
DISCONNECTING THE CABLES   6-9
DISTRIBUTOR   2-5
   REMOVAL & INSTALLATION   2-5
DISTRIBUTOR CAP AND ROTOR   1-34
   INSPECTION   1-35
   REMOVAL & INSTALLATION   1-34
DO'S   1-7
DOME LIGHT   6-33
   REMOVAL & INSTALLATION   6-33
DON'TS   1-8
DOOR GLASS AND REGULATOR   10-20
   REMOVAL & INSTALLATION   10-20
DOOR LOCKS   10-20
   REMOVAL & INSTALLATION   10-20
DOOR PANELS   10-17
   REMOVAL & INSTALLATION   10-17
DOORS   10-2
   ADJUSTMENT   10-5
   REMOVAL & INSTALLATION   10-2
DRIVE AXLE   1-63
   DRAIN & REFILL   1-63
   FLUID RECOMMENDATIONS   1-63
   LEVEL CHECK   1-63
**DRIVELINE   7-21**
DRIVEN DISC AND PRESSURE PLATE   7-9
   ADJUSTMENTS   7-11
   REMOVAL & INSTALLATION   7-9
**DRUM BRAKES   9-22**
ELECTRIC WINDOW MOTOR   10-22
   REMOVAL & INSTALLATION   10-22
ELECTRICAL COMPONENTS   6-2
   CONNECTORS   6-4
   GROUND   6-3
   LOAD   6-4
   POWER SOURCE   6-2
   PROTECTIVE DEVICES   6-3
   SWITCHES & RELAYS   6-3
   WIRING & HARNESSES   6-4
**ELECTRONIC ENGINE CONTROLS   4-17**
**ELECTRONIC SPARK ADVANCE SYSTEM   2-2**
**EMISSION CONTROLS   4-5**
ENGINE (ENGINE MECHANICAL)   3-6
   REMOVAL & INSTALLATION   3-6
ENGINE (FLUIDS AND LUBRICANTS)   1-52
   OIL & FILTER CHANGE   1-53
   OIL LEVEL CHECK   1-52
ENGINE (SERIAL NUMBER IDENTIFICATION)   1-14
ENGINE (TRAILER TOWING)   1-70
ENGINE BLOCK   3-64
   ASSEMBLY   3-68
   DISASSEMBLY   3-64
   GENERAL INFORMATION   3-64
   INSPECTION   3-65
   REFINISHING   3-67

ENGINE CONTROL MODULE (ECM)   4-17
   OPERATION   4-17
   PRECAUTIONS   4-17
   REMOVAL & INSTALLATION   4-17
ENGINE FAN   3-17
   REMOVAL & INSTALLATION   3-17
ENGINE IDENTIFICATION   1-16
**ENGINE MECHANICAL   3-2**
ENGINE MECHANICAL SPECIFICATIONS   3-2
ENGINE OVERHAUL TIPS   3-54
   CLEANING   3-54
   OVERHAUL TIPS   3-54
   REPAIRING DAMAGED THREADS   3-55
   TOOLS   3-54
ENGINE PREPARATION   3-56
**ENGINE RECONDITIONING   3-52**
ENGINE START-UP AND BREAK-IN   3-71
   BREAKING IT IN   3-71
   KEEP IT MAINTAINED   3-71
   STARTING THE ENGINE   3-71
**ENTERTAINMENT SYSTEMS   6-21**
EQUIPMENT DRIVE HOUSING   3-25
   REMOVAL & INSTALLATION   3-25
EQUIPMENT DRIVESHAFT   3-19
   PRECAUTIONS   3-19
   REMOVAL & INSTALLATION   3-20
EVAPORATIVE CANISTER (CHARCOAL CANISTER)   1-23
   SERVICING   1-23
EVAPORATIVE EMISSION CONTROLS   4-6
   COMPONENT TESTING   4-6
   OPERATION   4-6
   REMOVAL & INSTALLATION   4-9
EVAPORATIVE EMISSIONS   4-4
EXHAUST GAS RECIRCULATION SYSTEM   4-9
   COMPONENT TESTING   4-10
   OPERATION   4-9
   REMOVAL & INSTALLATION   4-15
EXHAUST GASES   4-3
   CARBON MONOXIDE   4-3
   HYDROCARBONS   4-3
   NITROGEN   4-3
   OXIDES OF SULFUR   4-4
   PARTICULATE MATTER   4-4
EXHAUST MANIFOLD   3-10
   REMOVAL & INSTALLATION   3-10
**EXHAUST SYSTEM   3-49**
EXTENSION HOUSING SEAL (AUTOMATIC TRANSMISSION)   7-17
   REMOVAL & INSTALLATION   7-17
EXTENSION HOUSING SEAL (MANUAL TRANSMISSION)   7-2
   REMOVAL & INSTALLATION   7-2
EXTENSION HOUSING SEAL (TRANSFER CASE)   7-20
   REMOVAL & INSTALLATION   7-20
**EXTERIOR   10-2**
**FASTENERS, MEASUREMENTS AND CONVERSIONS   1-9**
FENDERS   10-11
   REMOVAL & INSTALLATION   10-11
**FIRING ORDERS   2-8**
FLARE NUT TYPE   5-2
FLUID DISPOSAL   1-50
**FLUIDS AND LUBRICANTS   1-50**
FLYWHEEL/FLEXPLATE   3-49
   REMOVAL & INSTALLATION   3-49
FOG/DRIVING LIGHTS   6-34
   REMOVAL & INSTALLATION   6-34
**FRONT DRIVE AXLE   7-28**
FRONT DRIVESHAFT AND U-JOINTS   7-21
   REMOVAL & INSTALLATION   7-21
   U-JOINT REPLACEMENT   7-23

# MASTER INDEX

FRONT HUB AND BEARING  8-13
   REMOVAL & INSTALLATION  8-13
**FRONT SUSPENSION  8-4**
FUEL AND ENGINE OIL RECOMMENDATIONS  1-50
   FUEL  1-51
   OIL  1-50
   OPERATION IN FOREIGN COUNTRIES  1-52
FUEL FILTER  1-19
   REMOVAL & INSTALLATION  1-19
**FUEL INJECTION SYSTEM  5-2**
FUEL INJECTORS  5-4
   REMOVAL & INSTALLATION  5-4
   TESTING  5-8
**FUEL LINES AND FITTINGS  5-2**
FUEL PRESSURE REGULATOR  5-8
   REMOVAL & INSTALLATION  5-8
FUEL PUMP  5-3
   REMOVAL & INSTALLATION  5-3
   TESTING  5-4
**FUEL TANK  5-13**
FUSE APPLICATIONS—1991–92 MODELS  6-39
FUSE APPLICATIONS—1993–97 MODELS  6-40
FUSES  6-37
   REPLACEMENT  6-37
FUSIBLE LINKS  6-38
   REPLACEMENT  6-38
GASOLINE ENGINE TUNE-UP SPECIFICATIONS  1-42
GENERAL ENGINE SPECIFICATIONS  1-16
GENERAL INFORMATION (AIR BAG)  6-9
   ARMING THE SYSTEM  6-12
   DISARMING THE SYSTEM  6-12
   SERVICE PRECAUTIONS  6-11
   SYSTEM COMPONENTS  6-10
   SYSTEM OPERATION  6-9
GENERAL INFORMATION (ANTI-LOCK BRAKE SYSTEM)  9-33
GENERAL INFORMATION (CHARGING SYSTEM)  2-9
GENERAL INFORMATION (ELECTRONIC ENGINE CONTROLS)  4-17
GENERAL INFORMATION (ELECTRONIC SPARK ADVANCE SYSTEM)  2-2
GENERAL INFORMATION (FUEL INJECTION SYSTEM)  5-2
GENERAL INFORMATION (SENDING UNITS AND SENSORS)  2-16
GENERAL INFORMATION (STARTING SYSTEM)  2-12
GENERAL INFORMATION (TROUBLE CODES)  4-31
GENERAL RECOMMENDATIONS  1-70
GRILLE  10-8
   REMOVAL & INSTALLATION  10-8
HALFSHAFT  7-4
   OVERHAUL  7-7
   REMOVAL & INSTALLATION  7-4
HANDLING A TRAILER  1-70
HEADLIGHT SWITCH  6-28
   REMOVAL & INSTALLATION  6-28
HEADLIGHTS  6-29
   AIMING  6-30
   REMOVAL & INSTALLATION  6-29
HEATER WATER CONTROL VALVE  6-17
   REMOVAL & INSTALLATION  6-17
**HEATING AND AIR CONDITIONING  6-12**
HITCH (TONGUE) WEIGHT  1-70
HOOD  10-7
   ALIGNMENT  10-7
   REMOVAL & INSTALLATION  10-7
HORN  6-29
   REMOVAL & INSTALLATION  6-29
HOSES  1-28
   INSPECTION  1-28
   REMOVAL & INSTALLATION  1-29
**HOW TO USE THIS BOOK  1-2**
HYDRAULIC SYSTEM BLEEDING  7-13

ICE BOX MOTOR  6-17
   REMOVAL & INSTALLATION  6-17
IDLE AIR CONTROL (IAC) VALVE  4-20
   OPERATION  4-20
   REMOVAL & INSTALLATION  4-22
   TESTING  4-21
IDLE SPEED AND MIXTURE ADJUSTMENTS  1-42
IGNITER  2-5
   REMOVAL & INSTALLATION  2-5
IGNITION COIL  2-4
   REMOVAL & INSTALLATION  2-4
   TESTING  2-4
IGNITION LOCK CYLINDER  8-26
   REMOVAL & INSTALLATION  8-26
IGNITION TIMING  1-35
   GENERAL INFORMATION  1-35
   INSPECTION & ADJUSTMENT  1-36
INDUSTRIAL POLLUTANTS  4-2
INSIDE REAR VIEW MIRROR  10-26
   REPLACEMENT  10-26
INSPECTION  3-49
   REPLACEMENT  3-51
INSTRUMENT CLUSTER  6-27
   REMOVAL & INSTALLATION  6-27
INSTRUMENT PANEL AND PAD  10-13
   REMOVAL & INSTALLATION  10-13
**INSTRUMENTS AND SWITCHES  6-27**
INTAKE AIR TEMPERATURE (IAT) SENSOR  4-23
   OPERATION  4-23
INTAKE MANIFOLD  3-10
   REMOVAL & INSTALLATION  3-10
**INTERIOR  10-13**
**JACKING  1-72**
JACKING PRECAUTIONS  1-73
**JUMP STARTING A DEAD BATTERY  1-72**
JUMP STARTING PRECAUTIONS  1-72
JUMP STARTING PROCEDURE  1-72
KNOCK SENSOR  4-20
   OPERATION  4-20
   REMOVAL & INSTALLATION  4-20
   TESTING  4-20
KNUCKLE AND SPINDLE  8-12
   REMOVAL & INSTALLATION  8-12
LATERAL CONTROL ROD  8-20
   REMOVAL & INSTALLATION  8-20
LICENSE PLATE LIGHT  6-35
   REMOVAL & INSTALLATION  6-35
LIGHT BULB APPLICATIONS  6-36
**LIGHTING  6-29**
LOWER BALL JOINT  8-8
   INSPECTION  8-8
   REMOVAL & INSTALLATION  8-8
LOWER CONTROL ARM (FRONT SUSPENSION)  8-10
   CONTROL ARM BUSHING REPLACEMENT  8-12
   REMOVAL & INSTALLATION  8-10
LOWER CONTROL ARM (REAR SUSPENSION)  8-19
   REMOVAL & INSTALLATION  8-19
MACPHERSON STRUTS  8-6
   OVERHAUL  8-8
   REMOVAL & INSTALLATION  8-6
MAINTENANCE LIGHTS  1-50
   RESETTING  1-50
MAINTENANCE OR REPAIR?  1-2
**MANUAL TRANSMISSION  7-2**
MANUAL TRANSMISSION (FLUIDS AND LUBRICANTS)  1-55
   DRAIN & REFILL  1-55
   FLUID RECOMMENDATIONS  1-55
   LEVEL CHECK  1-55

# MASTER INDEX  10-37

MANUAL TRANSMISSION ASSEMBLY  7-2
   REMOVAL & INSTALLATION  7-2
MASS AIRFLOW METER (MAF)  4-24
   OPERATION  4-24
   REMOVAL & INSTALLATION  4-25
   TESTING  4-25
MASTER CYLINDER (BRAKE OPERATING SYSTEM)  9-3
   REMOVAL & INSTALLATION  9-3
MASTER CYLINDER (CLUTCH)  7-12
   REMOVAL & INSTALLATION  7-12
MODEL IDENTIFICATION  1-14
NATURAL POLLUTANTS  4-2
OIL PAN  3-31
   REMOVAL & INSTALLATION  3-31
OIL PRESSURE SENSOR  2-16
   REMOVAL & INSTALLATION  2-17
   TESTING  2-16
OIL PUMP  3-32
   REMOVAL & INSTALLATION  3-32
OUTSIDE MIRRORS  10-8
   REMOVAL & INSTALLATION  10-8
OXYGEN SENSOR  4-18
   OPERATION  4-18
   REMOVAL & INSTALLATION  4-19
   TESTING  4-18
**PARKING BRAKE  9-28**
PCV VALVE  1-21
   REMOVAL & INSTALLATION  1-21
PINION SEAL (FRONT DRIVE AXLE)  7-30
   REMOVAL & INSTALLATION  7-30
PINION SEAL (REAR AXLE)  7-34
   REMOVAL & INSTALLATION  7-34
POSITIVE CRANKCASE VENTILATION (PCV) SYSTEM  4-5
   OPERATION  4-5
   REMOVAL & INSTALLATION  4-6
   TESTING  4-5
POWER BRAKE BOOSTER  9-5
   REMOVAL & INSTALLATION  9-5
POWER STEERING GEAR  8-28
   REMOVAL & INSTALLATION  8-28
POWER STEERING PUMP (FLUIDS AND LUBRICANTS)  1-68
   FLUID RECOMMENDATIONS  1-68
   LEVEL CHECK  1-68
POWER STEERING PUMP (STEERING)  8-28
   BLEEDING  8-30
   REMOVAL & INSTALLATION  8-28
POWER STEERING PUMP (TROUBLESHOOTING CHART)  8-32
POWER SUNROOF  10-12
   REMOVAL & INSTALLATION  10-12
PROPORTIONING VALVE  9-6
   FLUID PRESSURE ADJUSTMENT  9-7
   REMOVAL & INSTALLATION  9-6
RADIATOR  3-14
   REMOVAL & INSTALLATION  3-14
RADIO RECEIVER/AMPLIFIER/TAPE PLAYER/CD PLAYER  6-21
   REMOVAL & INSTALLATION  6-21
READING CODES  4-32
   2TZ-FE ENGINE  4-32
   2TZ-FZE ENGINE  4-33
**REAR AXLE  7-32**
REAR DRIVESHAFT AND U-JOINTS  7-24
   REMOVAL & INSTALLATION  7-24
   U-JOINT REPLACEMENT  7-27
REAR MAIN SEAL  3-48
   REMOVAL & INSTALLATION  3-48
**REAR SUSPENSION  8-17**
RECOMMENDED MAINTENANCE INTERVALS  1-74
RELAYS  6-39
   REPLACEMENT  6-39
RELIEVING FUEL SYSTEM PRESSURE  5-2
REVERSE LIGHTS  6-36
   REMOVAL & INSTALLATION  6-36
ROCKER ARM (VALVE) COVER  3-7
   REMOVAL & INSTALLATION  3-7
**ROUTINE MAINTENANCE AND TUNE-UP  1-17**
SEATS  10-26
   REMOVAL & INSTALLATION  10-26
**SENDING UNITS AND SENSORS  2-16**
SENSOR RING (ROTOR)  9-42
   REMOVAL & INSTALLATION  9-42
**SERIAL NUMBER IDENTIFICATION  1-14**
**SERVICING YOUR VEHICLE SAFELY  1-7**
SHOCK ABSORBERS  8-18
   REMOVAL & INSTALLATION  8-18
   TESTING  8-19
SLAVE CYLINDER  7-12
   REMOVAL & INSTALLATION  7-12
SPARK PLUG WIRES  1-34
   TESTING  1-34
SPARK PLUGS  1-30
   INSPECTION & GAPPING  1-33
   REMOVAL & INSTALLATION  1-31
   SPARK PLUG HEAT RANGE  1-31
SPEAKERS  6-22
   REMOVAL & INSTALLATION  6-22
SPECIAL TOOLS  1-7
**SPECIFICATIONS CHARTS**
   BRAKE SPECIFICATIONS  9-43
   CAPACITIES  1-77
   ENGINE IDENTIFICATION  1-16
   ENGINE MECHANICAL SPECIFICATIONS  3-2
   FUSE APPLICATIONS—1991–92 MODELS  6-39
   FUSE APPLICATIONS—1993–97 MODELS  6-40
   GASOLINE ENGINE TUNE-UP SPECIFICATIONS  1-42
   GENERAL ENGINE SPECIFICATIONS  1-16
   LIGHT BULB APPLICATIONS  6-36
   RECOMMENDED MAINTENANCE INTERVALS  1-74
   TORQUE SPECIFICATIONS (BODY AND TRIM)  10-28
   TORQUE SPECIFICATIONS (DRIVE TRAIN)  7-36
   TORQUE SPECIFICATIONS (ENGINE AND ENGINE OVERHAUL)  3-72
   TORQUE SPECIFICATIONS (SUSPENSION AND STEERING)  8-31
   VEHICLE IDENTIFICATION CHART  1-14
SPEED SENSORS  9-39
   REMOVAL & INSTALLATION  9-40
   TESTING  9-39
SPEEDOMETER, TACHOMETER, AND GAUGES  6-28
   REMOVAL & INSTALLATION  6-28
STABILIZER BAR  8-9
   REMOVAL & INSTALLATION  8-9
STANDARD AND METRIC MEASUREMENTS  1-13
START INJECTOR TIME SWITCH  5-12
   REMOVAL & INSTALLATION  5-12
   TESTING  5-12
STARTER  2-12
   RELAY REPLACEMENT  2-15
   REMOVAL & INSTALLATION  2-13
   SOLENOID REPLACEMENT  2-15
   TESTING  2-12
**STARTING SYSTEM  2-12**
**STEERING  8-21**
STEERING LINKAGE  8-26
   REMOVAL & INSTALLATION  8-26
STEERING WHEEL  8-21
   REMOVAL & INSTALLATION  8-21
SUPERCHARGER (ENGINE MECHANICAL)  3-11
   REMOVAL & INSTALLATION  3-11

# MASTER INDEX

SUPERCHARGER (FLUIDS AND LUBRICANTS) 1-65
    DRAIN & REFILL 1-65
    FLUID RECOMMENDATIONS 1-65
    LEVEL CHECK 1-65
SUPERCHARGER BY-PASS (SCB) VALVE 3-13
    REMOVAL & INSTALLATION 3-13
TAIL LIGHTS 6-32
    REMOVAL & INSTALLATION 6-32
TAILGATE 10-8
    ALIGNMENT 10-8
    REMOVAL & INSTALLATION 10-8
TAILGATE LOCK 10-20
    REMOVAL & INSTALLATION 10-20
TANK ASSEMBLY 5-13
    REMOVAL & INSTALLATION 5-13
TEST EQUIPMENT 6-5
    JUMPER WIRES 6-5
    MULTIMETERS 6-6
    TEST LIGHTS 6-5
TESTING 6-6
    OPEN CIRCUITS 6-6
    RESISTANCE 6-8
    SHORT CIRCUITS 6-7
    VOLTAGE 6-7
    VOLTAGE DROP 6-7
THERMOSTAT 3-8
    REMOVAL & INSTALLATION 3-8
THIRD BRAKE LIGHT 6-35
    REMOVAL & INSTALLATION 6-35
THROTTLE BODY 5-4
    REMOVAL & INSTALLATION 5-4
THROTTLE POSITION SENSOR 4-26
    ADJUSTMENT 4-28
    OPERATION 4-26
    REMOVAL & INSTALLATION 4-27
    TESTING 4-26
TIMING CHAIN AND GEARS 3-34
    REMOVAL & INSTALLATION 3-34
TIMING CHAIN COVER AND SEAL 3-33
    REMOVAL & INSTALLATION 3-33
    SEAL REPLACEMENT 3-34
TIRES AND WHEELS 1-46
    CARE OF SPECIAL WHEELS 1-50
    INFLATION & INSPECTION 1-48
    TIRE DESIGN 1-47
    TIRE ROTATION 1-46
    TIRE STORAGE 1-47
**TOOLS AND EQUIPMENT 1-3**
TORQUE 1-10
    TORQUE ANGLE METERS 1-12
    TORQUE WRENCHES 1-10
TORQUE SPECIFICATIONS (BODY AND TRIM) 10-28
TORQUE SPECIFICATIONS (DRIVE TRAIN) 7-36
TORQUE SPECIFICATIONS (ENGINE AND ENGINE OVERHAUL) 3-72
TORQUE SPECIFICATIONS (SUSPENSION AND STEERING) 8-31
**TOWING THE VEHICLE 1-71**
**TRAILER TOWING 1-70**
TRAILER WEIGHT 1-70
**TRAILER WIRING 6-36**
**TRANSFER CASE 7-20**
TRANSFER CASE (FLUIDS AND LUBRICANTS) 1-61
    DRAIN & REFILL 1-61
    FLUID RECOMMENDATIONS 1-61
    LEVEL CHECK 1-61
TRANSFER CASE ASSEMBLY 7-20
    REMOVAL & INSTALLATION 7-20
TRANSMISSION (SERIAL NUMBER IDENTIFICATION) 1-16
TRANSMISSION (TRAILER TOWING) 1-70

**TROUBLE CODES 4-31**
**TROUBLESHOOTING CHARTS**
    BASIC CHARGING SYSTEM PROBLEMS 2-18
    BASIC STARTING SYSTEM PROBLEMS 2-17
    THE BRAKE SYSTEM 9-44
    CRUISE CONTROL TROUBLESHOOTING 6-20
    POWER STEERING PUMP 8-32
TROUBLESHOOTING ELECTRICAL SYSTEMS 6-6
TURN SIGNAL (COMBINATION) SWITCH 8-25
    REMOVAL & INSTALLATION 8-25
TURN SIGNAL/MARKER LIGHT 6-31
    REMOVAL & INSTALLATION 6-31
**UNDERSTANDING AND TROUBLESHOOTING ELECTRICAL SYSTEMS 6-2**
UNDERSTANDING THE AUTOMATIC TRANSMISSION 7-13
    HYDRAULIC CONTROL SYSTEM 7-15
    PLANETARY GEARBOX 7-14
    SERVOS AND ACCUMULATORS 7-15
    TORQUE CONVERTER 7-13
UNDERSTANDING THE CLUTCH 7-8
UNDERSTANDING THE MANUAL TRANSMISSION 7-2
UNDERVEHICLE MAINTENANCE COMPONENT LOCATIONS 1-18
UNION BOLT TYPE 5-2
UPPER CONTROL ARM 8-20
    REMOVAL & INSTALLATION 8-20
**VACUUM DIAGRAMS 4-39**
VALVE LASH 1-38
    ADJUSTMENT 1-38
VEHICLE 1-14
VEHICLE IDENTIFICATION CHART 1-14
VOLUME AIRFLOW METER 4-23
    OPERATION 4-23
    REMOVAL & INSTALLATION 4-24
    TESTING 4-23
WATER PUMP 3-17
    REMOVAL & INSTALLATION 3-17
WHEEL ALIGNMENT 8-15
    CAMBER 8-16
    CASTER 8-15
    TOE 8-16
WHEEL ASSEMBLY 8-2
    INSPECTION 8-2
    REMOVAL & INSTALLATION 8-2
WHEEL BEARINGS 1-69
WHEEL CYLINDERS 9-26
    OVERHAUL 9-26
    REMOVAL & INSTALLATION 9-26
WHEEL LUG STUDS 8-2
    REMOVAL & INSTALLATION 8-2
**WHEELS 8-2**
WHERE TO BEGIN 1-2
WINDSHIELD AND FIXED GLASS 10-22
    REMOVAL & INSTALLATION 10-22
    WINDSHIELD CHIP REPAIR 10-22
WINDSHIELD WASHER MOTOR 6-26
    REMOVAL & INSTALLATION 6-26
WINDSHIELD WIPER BLADE AND ARM 6-23
    REMOVAL & INSTALLATION 6-23
WINDSHIELD WIPER MOTOR 6-25
    REMOVAL & INSTALLATION 6-25
WINDSHIELD WIPER SWITCH 6-28
    REMOVAL & INSTALLATION 6-28
WINDSHIELD WIPERS 1-44
    ELEMENT (REFILL) CARE & REPLACEMENT 1-44
**WINDSHIELD WIPERS AND WASHERS 6-23**
WIRE AND CONNECTOR REPAIR 6-8
**WIRING DIAGRAMS 6-41**